TEACHER'S EDITION

GRADE 12

Program Consultants:
Kylene Beers
Martha Hougen
Elena Izquierdo
Carol Jago
Erik Palmer
Robert E. Probst

Copyright © 2020 by Houghton Mifflin Harcourt Publishing Company

All rights reserved. No part of this work may be reproduced or transmitted in any form or by any means, electronic or mechanical, including photocopying or recording, or by any information storage or retrieval system, without the prior written permission of the copyright owner unless such copying is expressly permitted by federal copyright law. Requests for permission to make copies of any part of the work should be submitted through our Permissions website at https://customercare.hmhco.com/contactus/Permissions.html or mailed to Houghton Mifflin Harcourt Publishing Company, Attn: Intellectual Property Licensing, 9400 Southpark Center Loop, Orlando, Florida 32819-8647.

Front Cover Photo Credits: (outer ring): ©Mike Liu/Shutterstock, (inner ring): ©Nigel Killeen/Moment Open/Getty Images, (c) ©Carrie Garcia/Houghton Mifflin Harcourt, (c overlay): ©Eyewire/Getty Images, (bc overlay): ©elenamiv/Shutterstock

Back Cover Photo Credits: (Units 1-6): ©Print Collector/Hulton Archive/Getty Images; ©Christophel Fine Art/Getty Images; ©A. Dagli Orti/De Agostini Editorial/Getty Images; ©Tonktiti/Shutterstock; ©jgorzynik/iStockphoto/Getty Images; ©Friedemann Vogel/Getty Images

Printed in the U.S.A.

ISBN 978-1-328-47490-2

1 2 3 4 5 6 7 8 9 10 0690 27 26 25 24 23 22 21 20 19 18

4500718811   A B C D E F G

If you have received these materials as examination copies free of charge, Houghton Mifflin Harcourt Publishing Company retains title to the materials and they may not be resold. Resale of examination copies is strictly prohibited.

Possession of this publication in print format does not entitle users to convert this publication, or any portion of it, into electronic format.

Teacher's Edition Table of Contents

Program Consultants	T2
Into Literature Overview	T4
Data-Driven Differentiation and Assessment	T14
Foster a Learning Culture	T18
Build a Culture of Professional Growth	T20
Annotated Student Edition Table of Contents	T22
Into Literature Dashboard	T40
Into Literature Studios	T42
Featured Essays	
Notice & Note	T44
Reading and Writing Across Genres	T58

Unit 1	1
Unit 2	138
Unit 3	360
Unit 4	490
Unit 5	586
Unit 6	690

Student Resources	R1

into Literature
PROGRAM CONSULTANTS

Kylene Beers

Nationally known lecturer and author on reading and literacy; coauthor with Robert Probst of *Disrupting Thinking, Notice & Note: Strategies for Close Reading,* and *Reading Nonfiction*; former president of the National Council of Teachers of English. Dr. Beers is the author of *When Kids Can't Read: What Teachers Can Do* and coeditor of *Adolescent Literacy: Turning Promise into Practice*, as well as articles in the Journal of Adolescent and Adult Literacy. Former editor of *Voices from the Middle,* she is the 2001 recipient of NCTE's Richard W. Halley Award, given for outstanding contributions to middle school literacy. She recently served as Senior Reading Researcher at the Comer School Development Program at Yale University as well as Senior Reading Advisor to Secondary Schools for the Reading and Writing Project at Teachers College.

Martha Hougen

National consultant, presenter, researcher, and author. Areas of expertise include differentiating instruction for students with learning difficulties, including those with learning disabilities and dyslexia; and teacher and leader preparation improvement. Dr. Hougen has taught at the middle school through graduate levels. In addition to peer-reviewed articles, curricular documents, and presentations, Dr. Hougen has published two college textbooks: *The Fundamentals of Literacy Instruction and Assessment Pre-K–6* (2012) and *The Fundamentals of Literacy Instruction and Assessment 6–12* (2014). Dr. Hougen has supported Educator Preparation Program reforms while working at the Meadows Center for Preventing Educational Risk at The University of Texas at Austin and at the CEEDAR Center, University of Florida.

Elena Izquierdo

Nationally recognized teacher educator and advocate for English language learners. Dr. Izquierdo is a linguist by training, with a Ph.D. in Applied Linguistics and Bilingual Education from Georgetown University. She has served on various state and national boards working to close the achievement gaps for bilingual students and English language learners. Dr. Izquierdo is a member of the Hispanic Leadership Council, which supports Hispanic students and educators at both the state and federal levels. She served as Vice President on the Executive Board of the National Association of Bilingual Education and as Publications and Professional Development Chair.

Carol Jago

Teacher of English with 32 years of experience at Santa Monica High School in California; author and nationally known lecturer; former president of the National Council of Teachers of English. Ms. Jago currently serves as Associate Director of the California Reading and Literature Project at UCLA. With expertise in standards assessment and secondary education, Ms. Jago is the author of numerous books on education, including *With Rigor for All* and *Papers, Papers, Papers*, and is active with the California Association of Teachers of English, editing its scholarly journal *California English* since 1996. Ms. Jago also served on the planning committee for the 2009 NAEP Readig Framework and the 2011 NAEP Writing Framework.

Erik Palmer

Veteran teacher and education consultant based in Denver, Colorado. Author of *Well Spoken: Teaching Speaking to All Students* and *Digitally Speaking: How to Improve Student Presentations with Technology*. His areas of focus include improving oral communication, promoting technology in classroom presentations, and updating instruction through the use of digital tools. He holds a bachelor's degree from Oberlin College and a master's degree in curriculum and instruction from the University of Colorado.

Robert E. Probst

Nationally respected authority on the teaching of literature; Professor Emeritus of English Education at Georgia State University. Dr. Probst's publications include numerous articles in *English Journal* and *Voices from the Middle*, as well as professional texts including (as coeditor) *Adolescent Literacy: Turning Promise into Practice* and (as coauthor with Kylene Beers) *Disrupting Thinking, Notice & Note: Strategies for Close Reading,* and *Reading Nonfiction*. He regularly speaks at national and international conventions including those of the International Literacy Association, the National Council of Teachers of English, the Association for Supervision and Curriculum Development, and the National Association of Secondary School Principals. He has served NCTE in various leadership roles, including the Conference on English Leadership Board of Directors, the Commission on Reading, and column editor of the NCTE journal *Voices from the Middle*. He is also the 2007 recipient of the CEL Outstanding Leadership Award.

Program Consultants

Lead and Learn

Students who communicate...

- **Listen** actively
- **Present** effectively
- **Expand** vocabulary
- **Question** appropriately
- **Engage** constructively

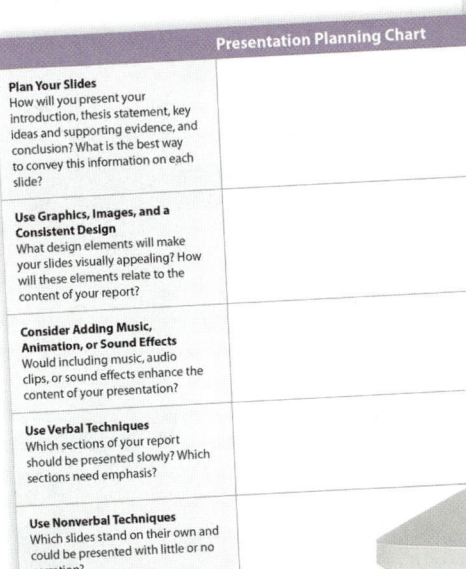
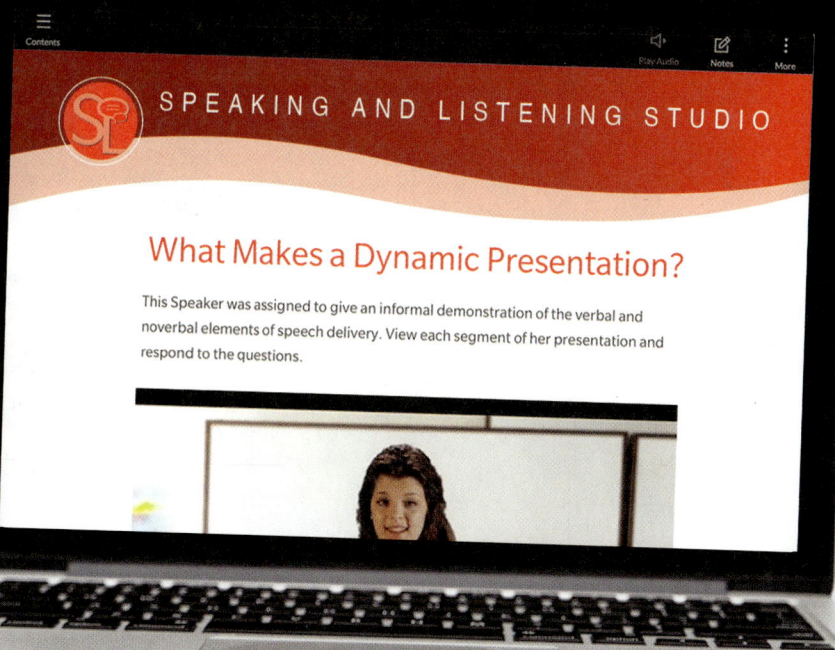

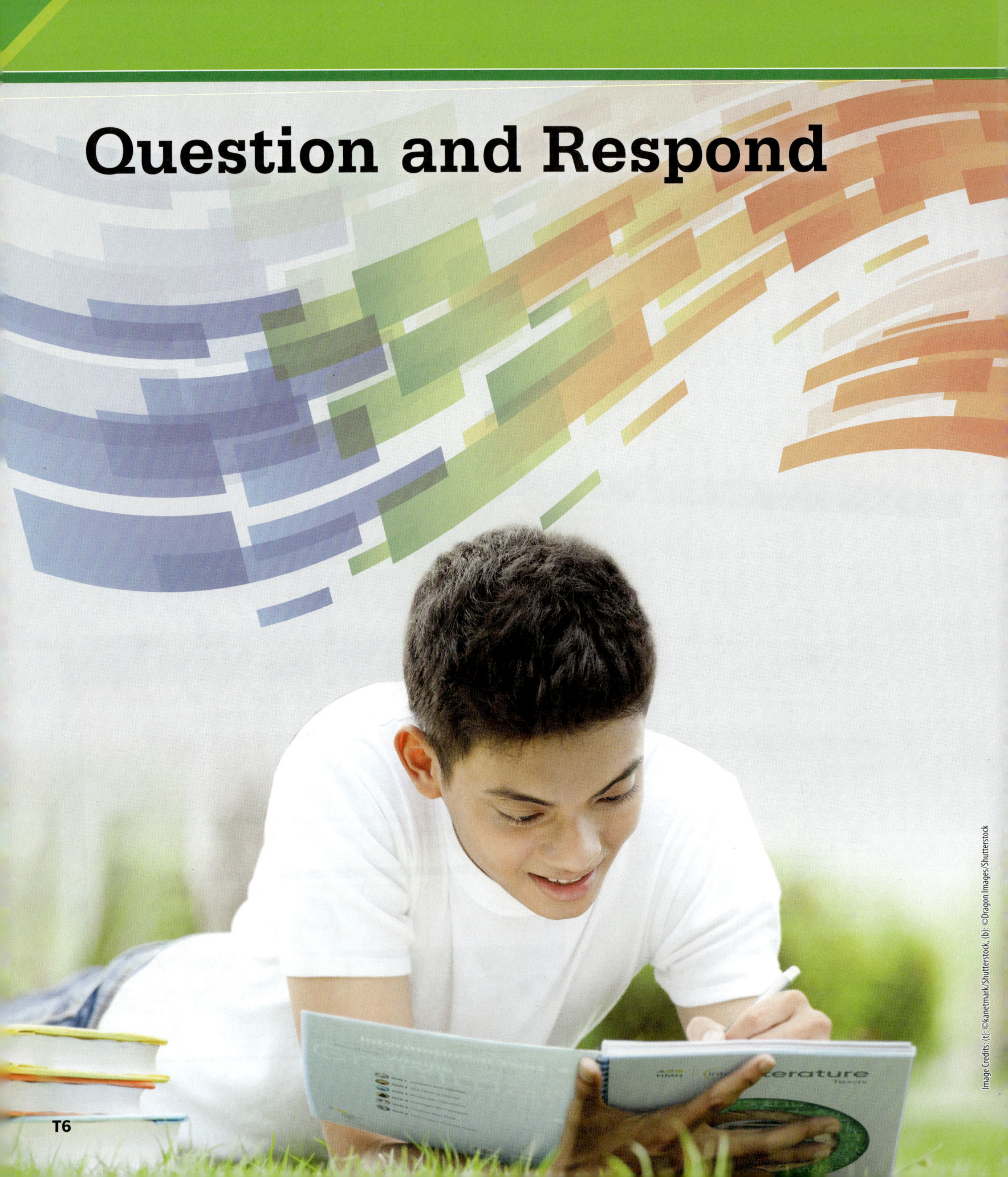

Students who read...

- **Acquire** fluency
- **Choose** independently
- **Monitor** understanding
- **Annotate** and use evidence
- **Write** and discuss within and across texts

Image Credits: (t): ©kanetmark/Shutterstock, (b): ©MSSA/Shutterstock

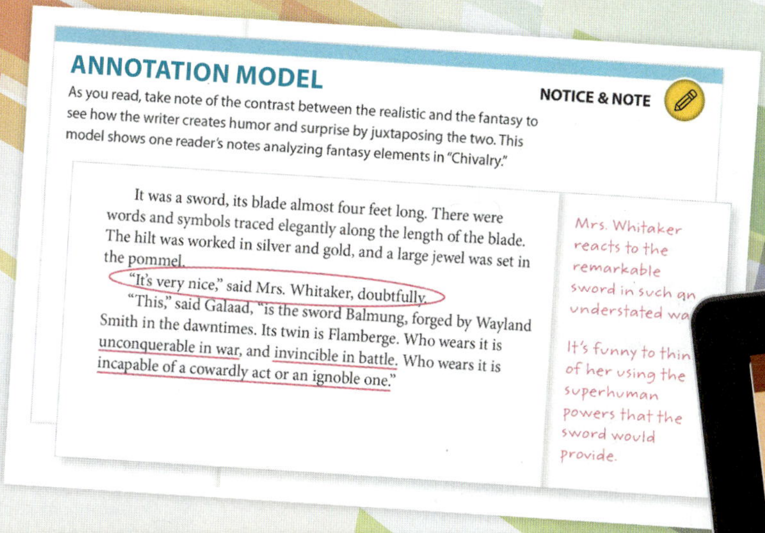

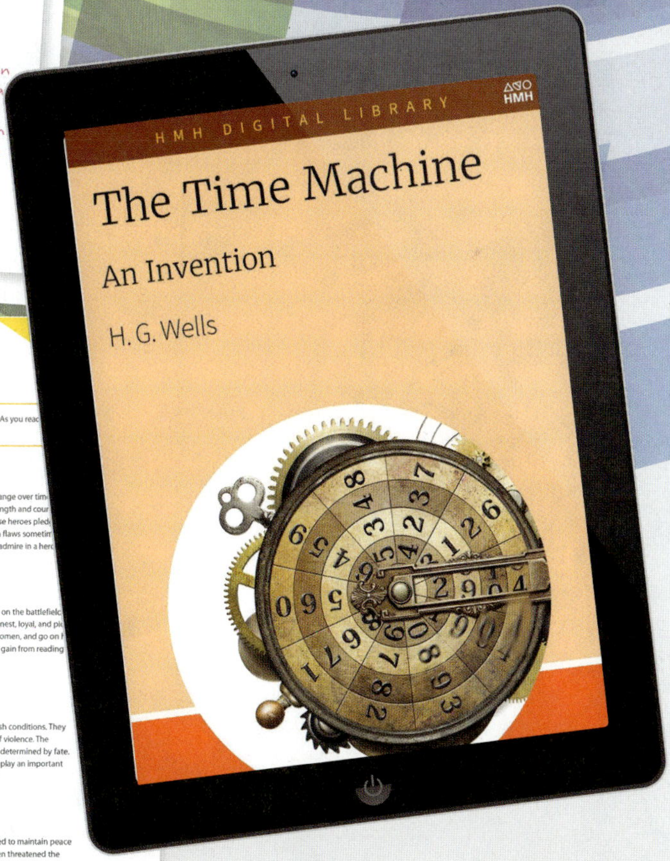

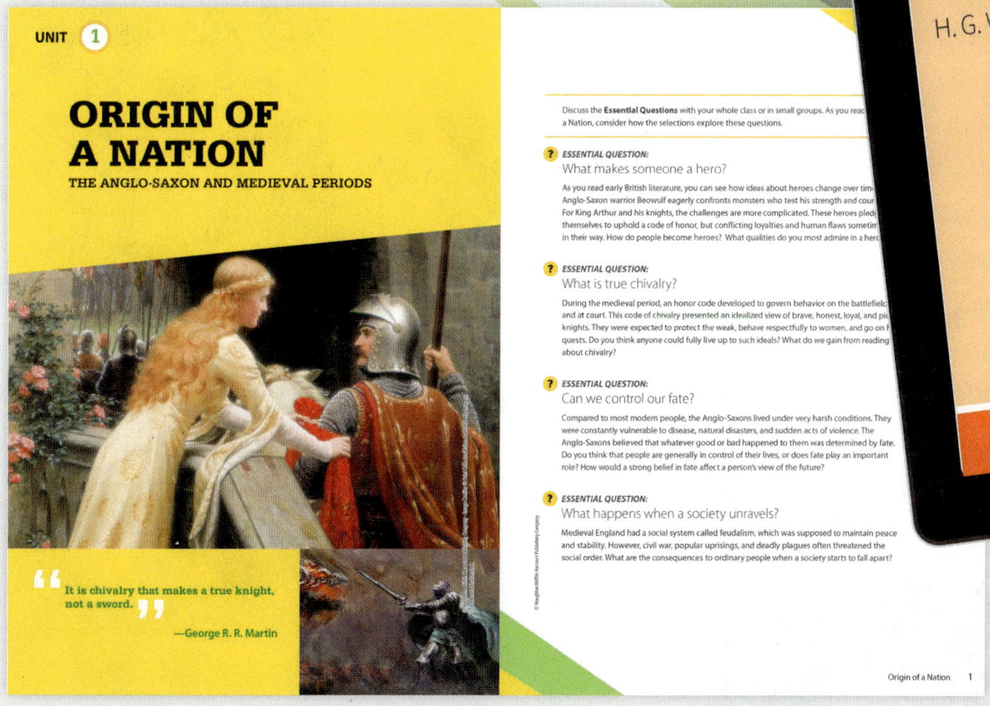

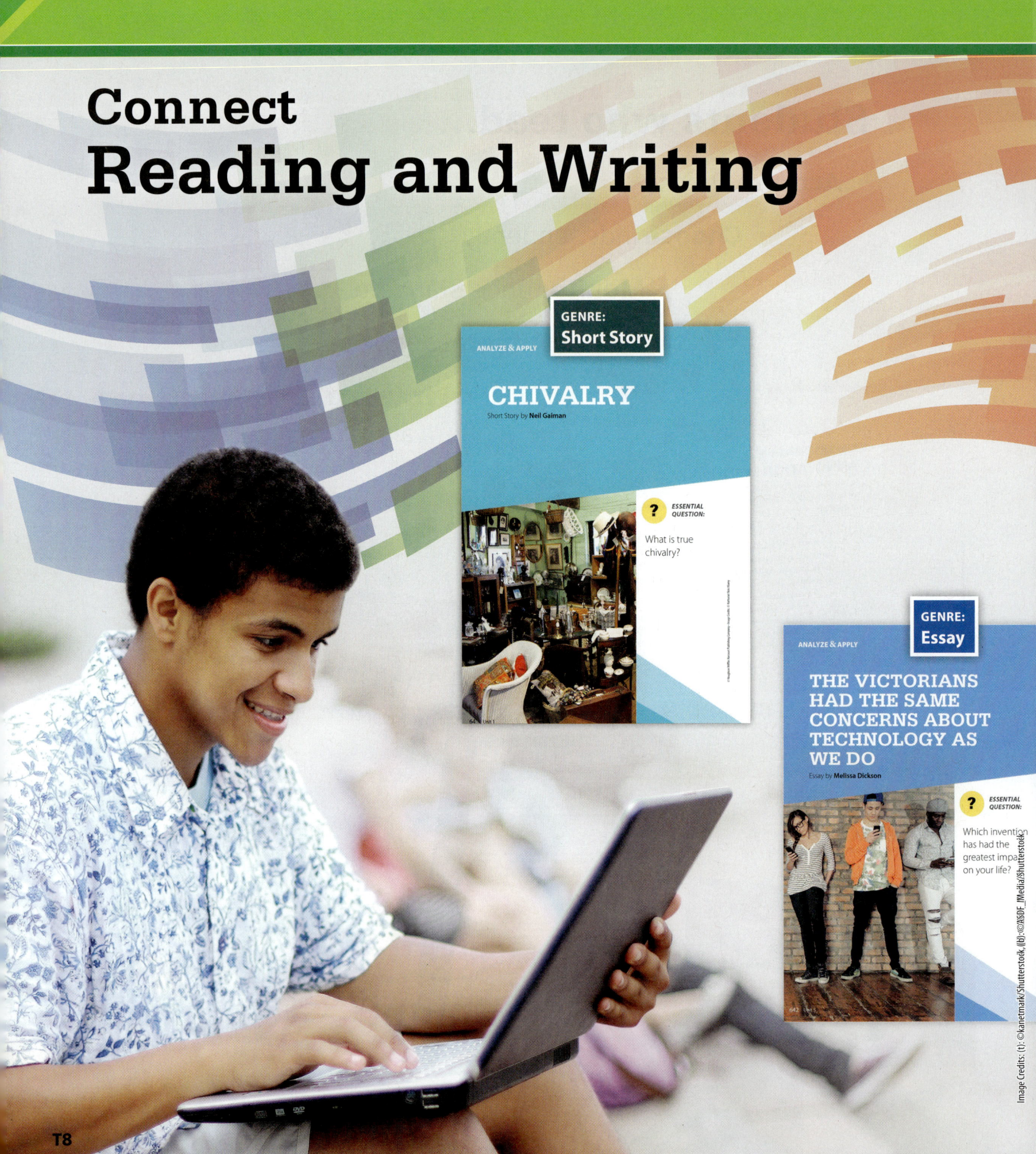

Students who explore genre...

- **Analyze** features
- **Understand** effects of authors' choices
- **Emulate** craft
- **Use** mentor texts
- **Synthesize** ideas

GENRE ELEMENTS: ESSAY

- has an introduction that includes the broader subject as well as a specific topic, hooks the audience, and briefly describes how the topic will be developed
- contains a thesis statement that offers some original insight on the topic
- contains well-developed body paragraphs, each with a main idea related to the writer's thesis statement or position, and tangible evidence that supports those ideas
- has a conclusion that often neatly summarizes the topic and leaves the audience with something to think about

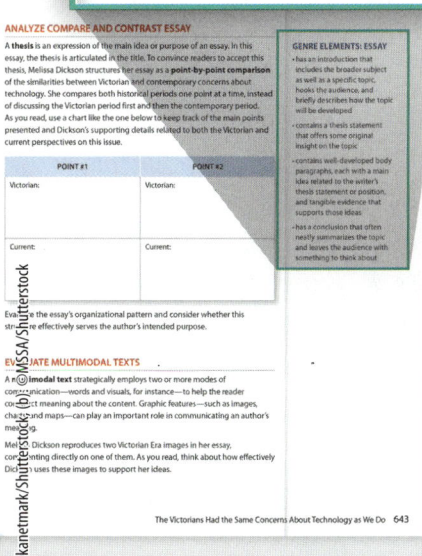

Craft and Communicate

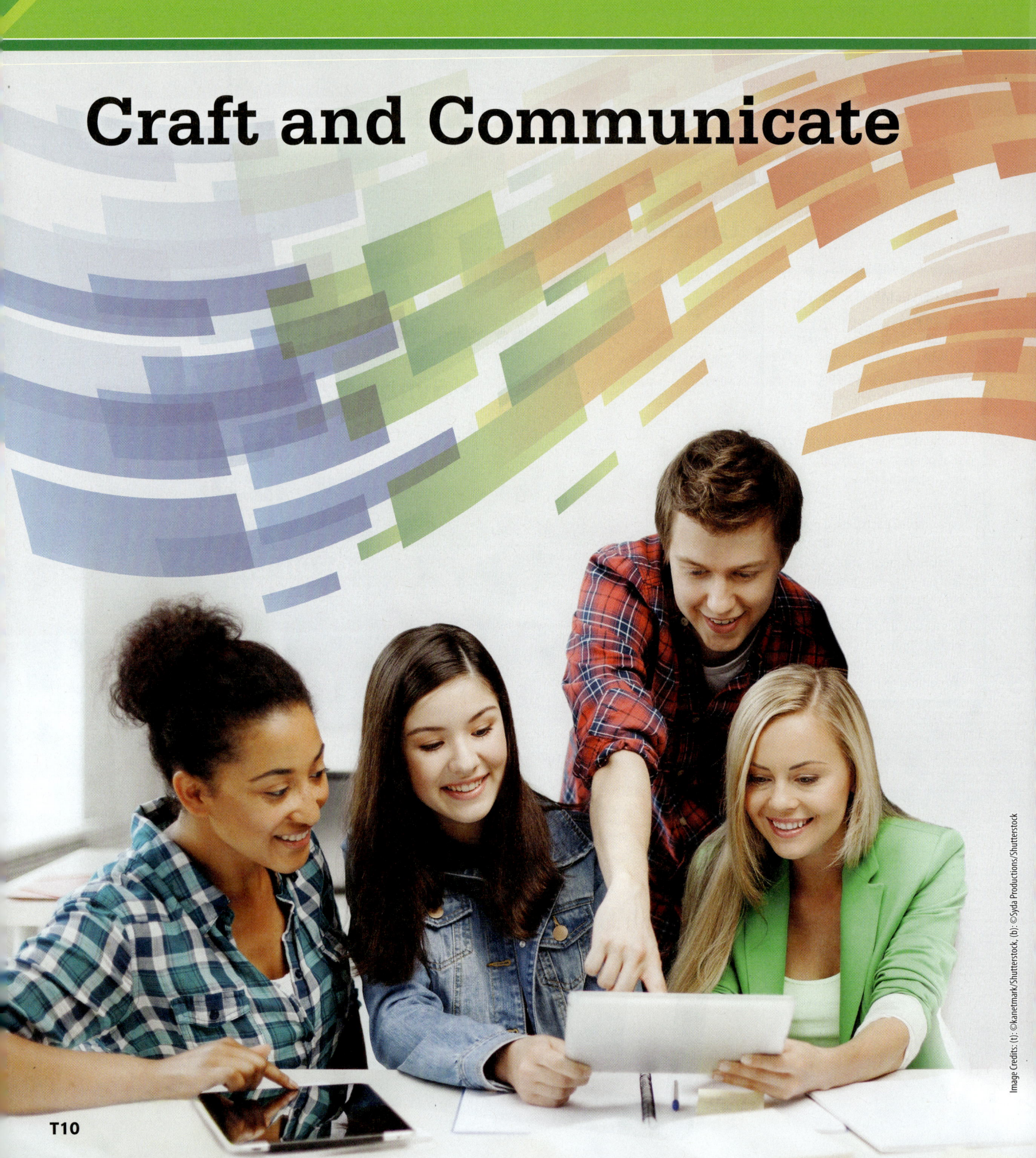

Students who compose...

- **Inform,** argue, and connect
- **Create** in a literary genre
- **Imitate** mentor texts
- **Apply** conventions
- **Use** process and partners

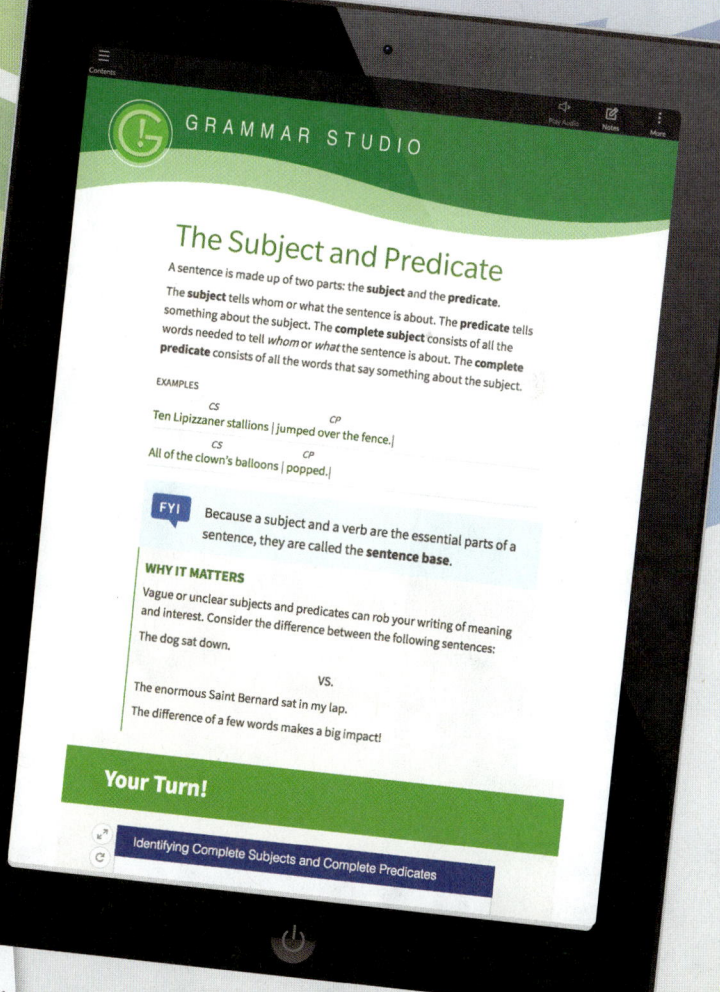

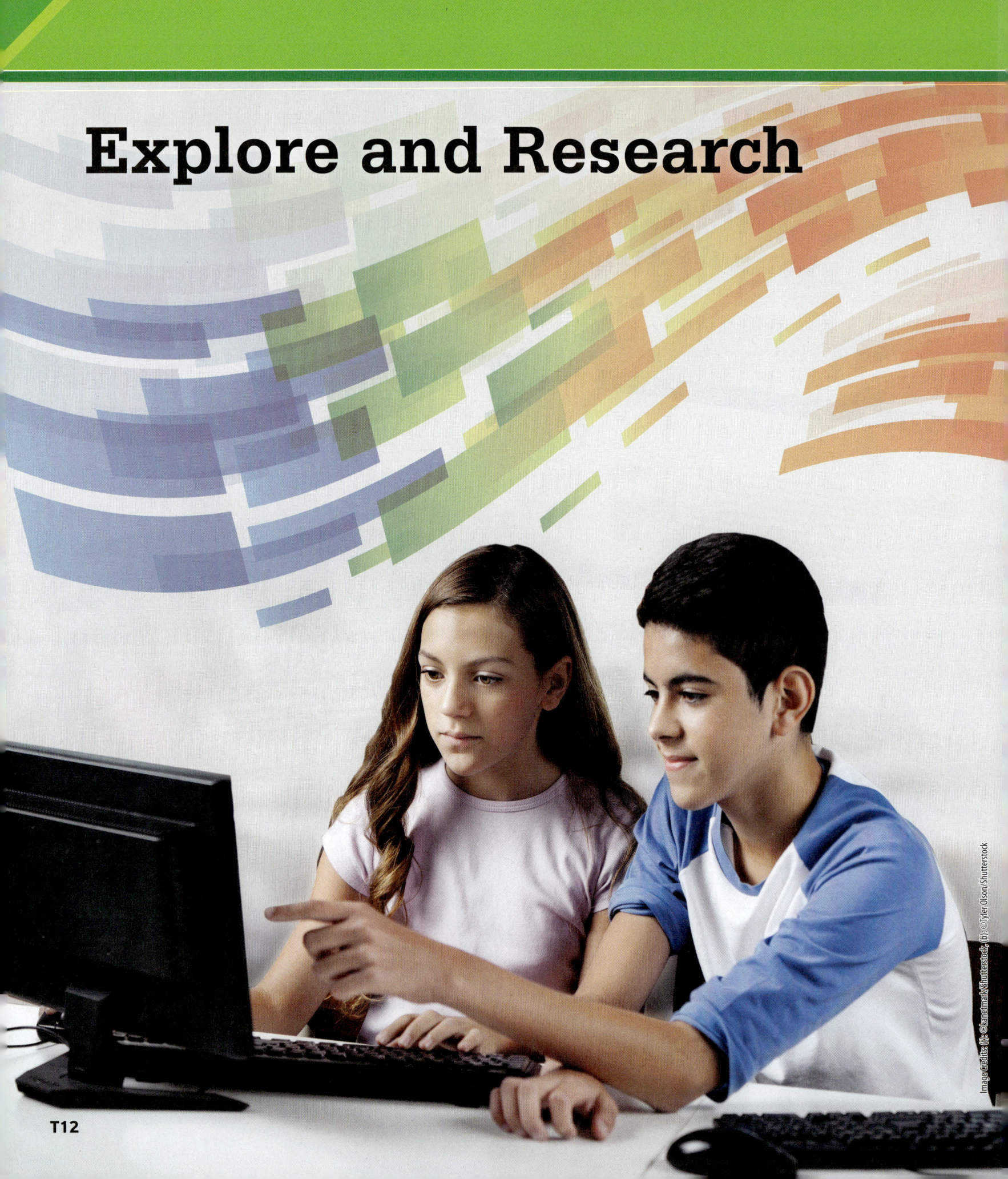

Students who inquire...

- **Generate** questions
- **Plan** and revise
- **Synthesize** information
- **Cite** sources
- **Deliver** results

RESEARCH TIP
When researching, focus on reliable sources. Web addresses that end in *.gov*, *.org*, and *.edu* are mostly reliable and credible websites. Also, try and distinguish between primary and secondary sources and analyze which documents serve as fact-based information versus opinions. Finally, keep an eye out for articles written by historians who have studied this subject in depth.

Maximize Growth through Data-Driven Differentiation and Assessment

Ongoing assessment and data reporting provide critical feedback loops to teachers and students, so that each experience encourages self-assessment and reflection, and drives positive learning outcomes for all students.

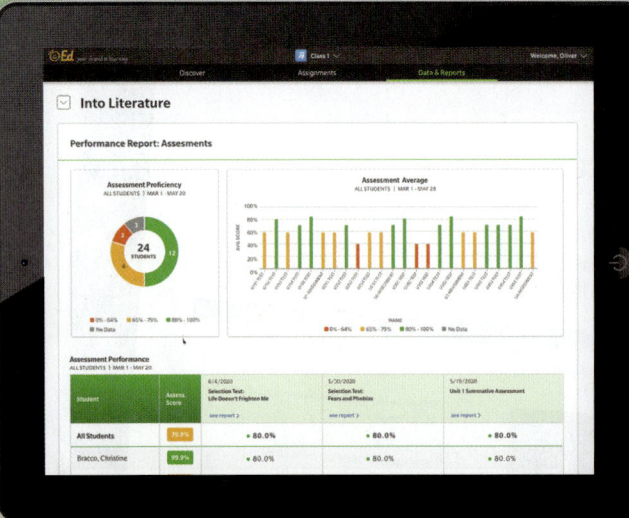

Actionable reports drive grouping and instructional recommendations appropriate for each learner.

Program Assessments

Adaptive Growth Measure

3 times per year

Adaptive Growth Measure allows teachers to gain an understanding of where students are on the learning continuum and identify students in need of intervention or enrichment.

Unit Assessments

6 times per year

Unit Assessments identify mastery of skills covered during the course of the unit across all literacy strands.

Ongoing Feedback from Daily Classroom Activities

Formative Assessment data is collected across a variety of student activities to help you make informed instructional decisions based on data.

- Check Your Understanding
- Selection Tests
- Writing Tasks
- Independent Reading
- Usage Data
- Online Essay Scoring
- Teacher Observations
- Research Projects

Assessments

HMH Into Literature has a comprehensive suite of assessments to help you determine what your students already know and how they are progressing through the program lessons.

Diagnostic Assessment for Reading is an informal, criterion-referenced assessment designed to diagnose the specific reading comprehension skills that need attention.

Skills-based Diagnostic Assessments will help you quickly gauge a student's mastery of common, grade-level appropriate skills.

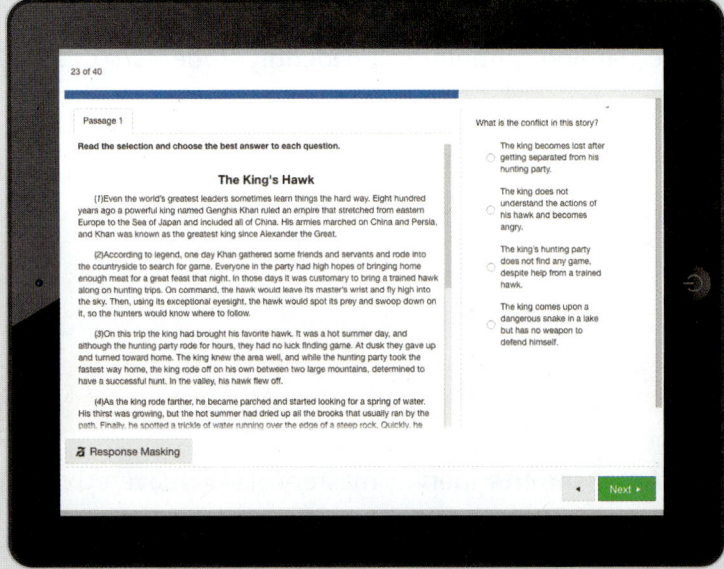

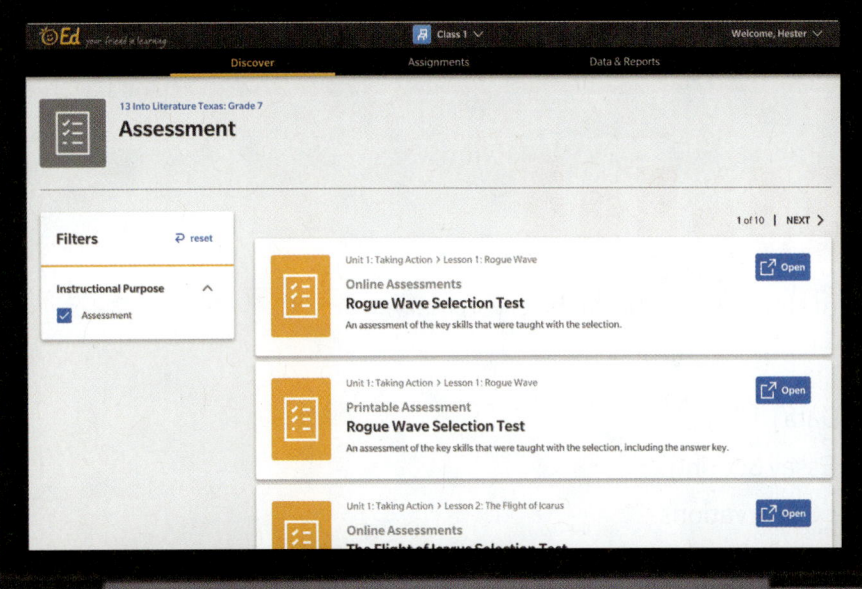

Every selection in the *Into Literature* program has a corresponding **Selection Test,** focusing on the skills taught in each lesson.
- Analyze & Apply
- Collaborate & Compare, and
- Independent Reading

A **Unit Test** assesses mastery of the skills taught in the entire Unit using new readings aligned with the Unit topic.

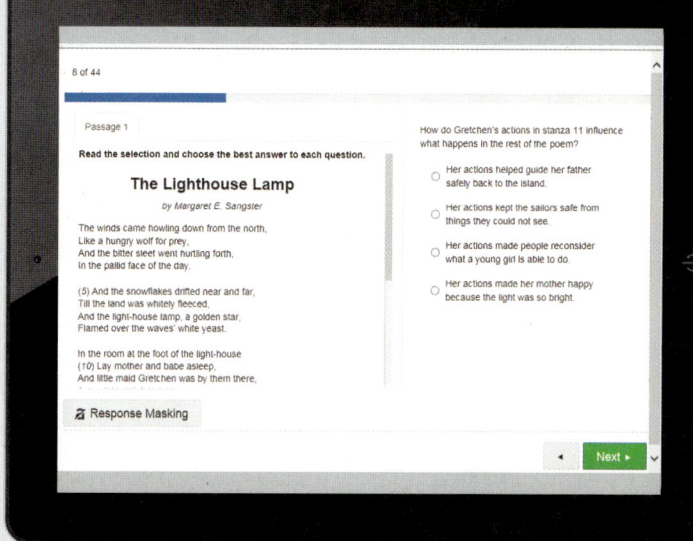

The **Diagnostic Screening Test** for Grammar, Usage, and Mechanics provides an assessment of strengths and weaknesses in the conventions of written English.

Each Module in the Grammar Studio has a **Diagnostic Assessment** and a **Summative Assessment,** for before and after instruction.

Foster a Learning Culture

As you encourage a culture of responsibility and collaboration, essential for students' success in the world of work, you will find learning activities that are social, active, and student owned.

COLLABORATE & COMPARE lessons are designed to support individual accountability as well as team aptitude. These lessons require students to read and annotate texts and compare their response in a collaborative project.

PEER REVIEW is a critical part of students' creative process. Tools like Checklists for writing and listening and speaking tasks and the Revision Guide with questions, tips, and techniques offer practical support for peer interaction.

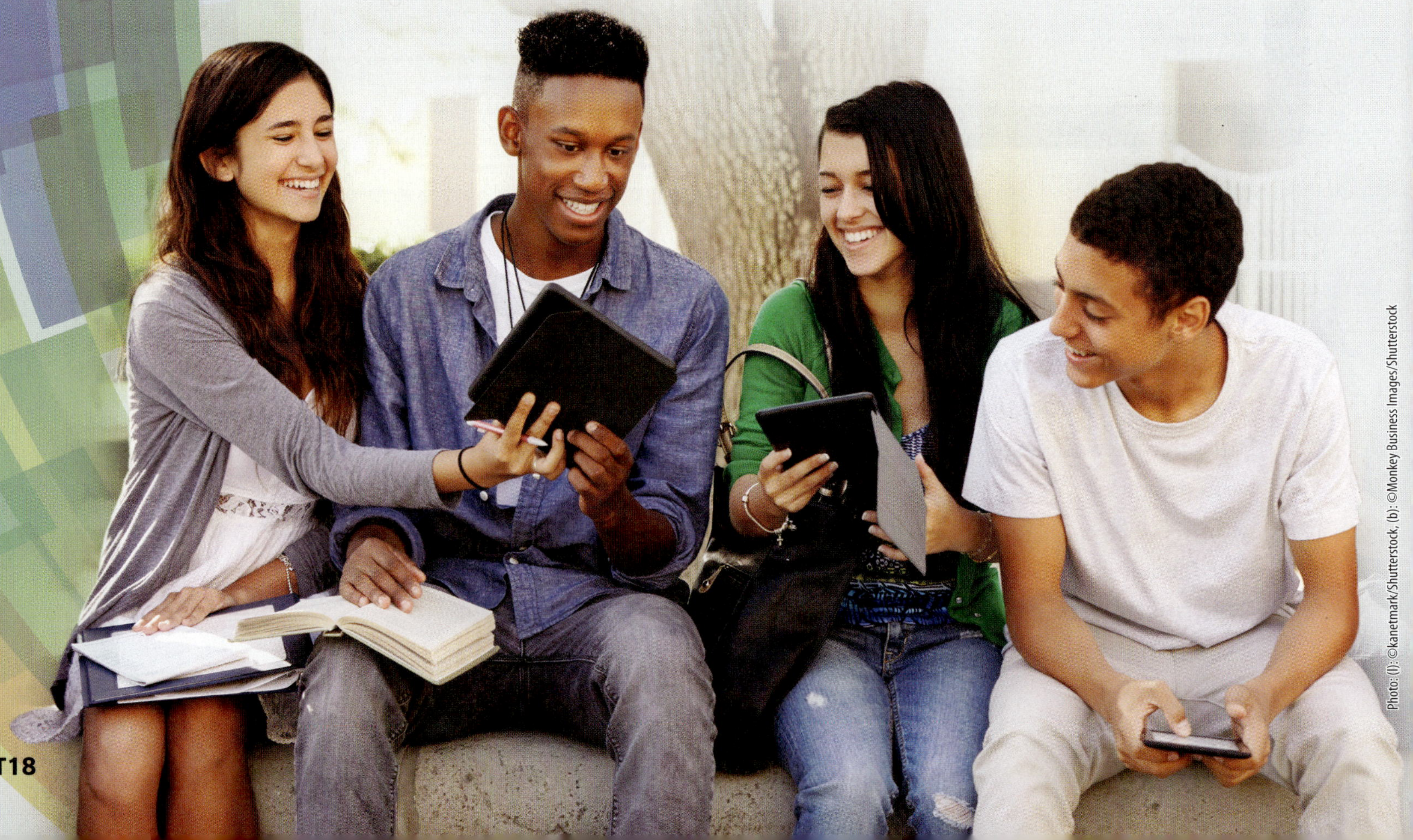

Photo: (l): ©kanetmark/Shutterstock, (b): ©Monkey Business Images/Shutterstock

LEARNING MINDSET notes and strategies in your Teacher's Edition are designed to help students acquire the attitude of perseverance through learning obstacles. Other resources like ongoing formative assessments, peer evaluation, and Reflect on the Unit questions encourage students to monitor their progress and develop metacognitive ability.

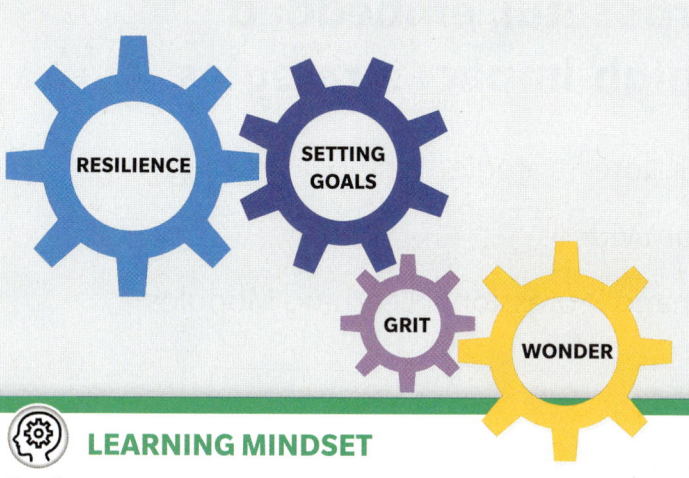

Build a Culture of Professional Growth

Embedded and on-going Professional Learning empowers you to develop high-impact learning experiences that provide all your students with opportunities for reading and writing success.

Build agency with purposeful, embedded teacher support and high-impact strategies

- Notice & Note Strategies for Close Reading
- Classroom Videos
- On-Demand Professional Learning Modules

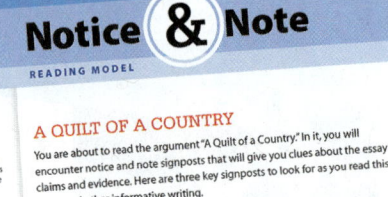

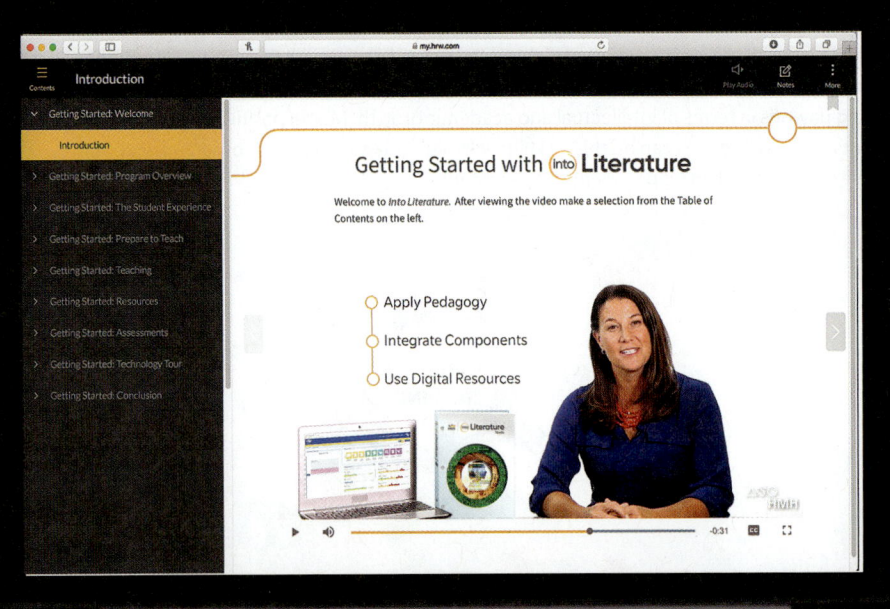

Grow Your Practice with Personalized Blended Professional Learning

- **Getting Started Course and Professional Learning Guide:** Learn the program components, pedagogy, and digital resources to successfully teach with *Into Literature*.

- **Follow-Up:** Choose from relevant instructional topics to create a personalized in-person or online Follow-Up experience to deepen program mastery and enhance teaching practices.

- **Coaching and Modeling:** Experience just-in-time support to ensure continuous professional learning that is student-centered and grounded in data.

- **askHMH:** Get on-demand access to program experts who will answer questions and provide personalized conferencing and digital demonstrations to support implementation.

- **Technical Services:** Plan, prepare, implement, and operate technology with ease.

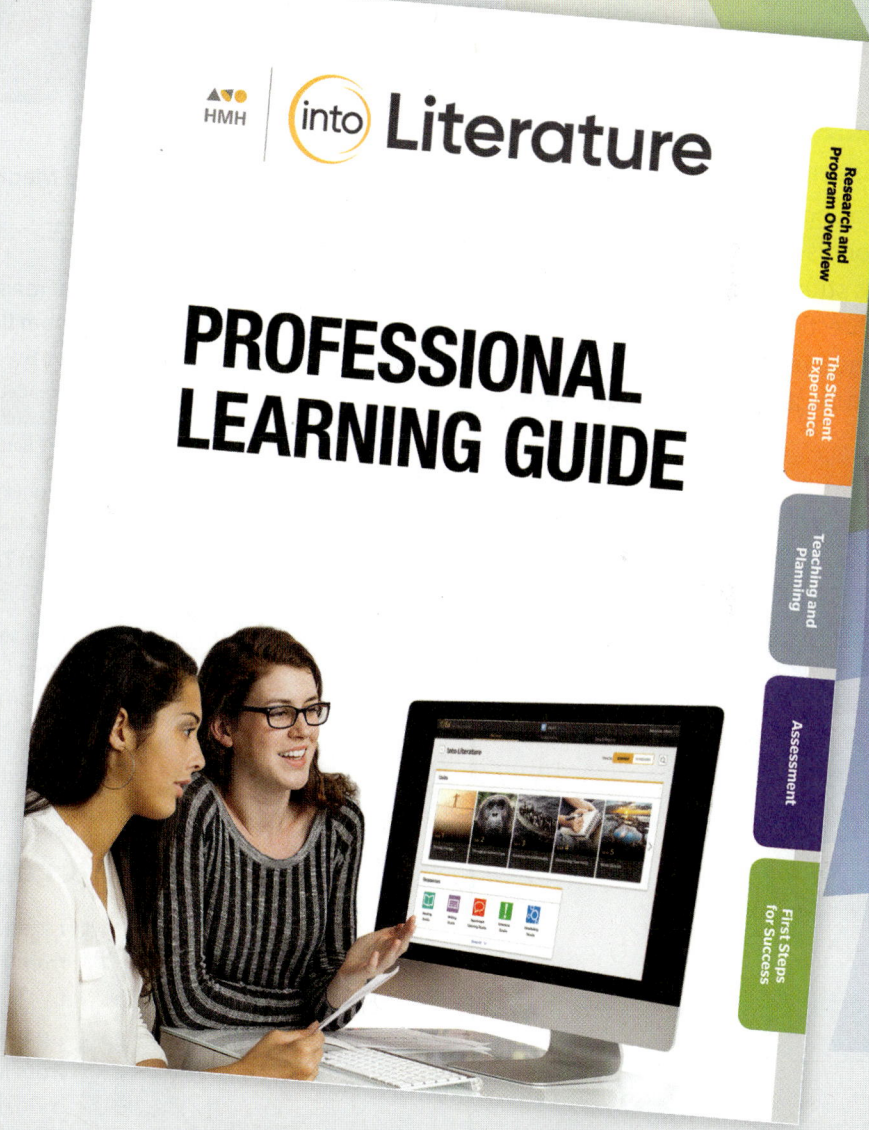

Annotated Student Edition Table of Contents

UNIT **1**

Instructional Overview and Resources 1A

UNIT **1**

ORIGIN OF A NATION
PAGE 1

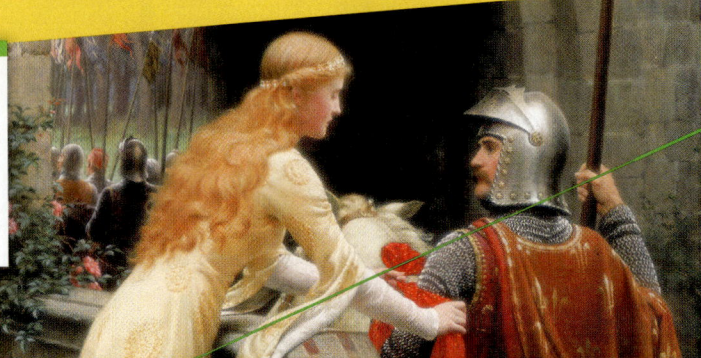

Topical Focus
Each unit reflects a topic linking selections, Essential Questions, a quotation, and unit tasks for analysis, discussion, synthesis, and response.

 ESSENTIAL QUESTIONS
- What makes someone a hero?
- What is true chivalry?
- Can we control our fate?
- What happens when a society unravels?

Essential Questions
Posing thought-provoking ideas for discussion and reflection as students read, the Essential Questions stimulate analysis and synthesis, leading to a richer understanding of the unit's texts.

The Anglo-Saxon and Medieval Periods 2

ANALYZE & APPLY

EPIC POEM
from **Beowulf** 6
by the Beowulf Poet, *translated by* Seamus Heaney
Grendel
Beowulf
The Battle with Grendel

NARRATIVE POEM
The Wife of Bath's Tale
from The Canterbury Tales 24
by Geoffrey Chaucer, *translated by* Nevill Coghill

ROMANCE
from **Le Morte d'Arthur** 44
by Sir Thomas Malory, *retold by* Keith Baines

SHORT STORY   **MENTOR TEXT**
Chivalry 64
by Neil Gaiman

COLLABORATE & COMPARE

LETTERS
from **The Paston Letters** 82
by the Paston Family

COMPARE PRIMARY SOURCES

DIARY
from **My Syrian Diary** 96
by Marah

FM6   Grade 12

UNIT 1

COMPARE THEMES

POEM
The Wanderer 110
by Anonymous, *translated by* Burton Raffel

POEM
Loneliness 118
by Fanny Howe

INDEPENDENT READING 126
These selections can be accessed through the digital edition.

EPIC POEM
from Beowulf
by the Beowulf Poet, *translated by* Burton Raffel

Grendel's Mother	The Death of Beowulf
The Battle with Grendel's Mother	Mourning Beowulf
Beowulf's Last Battle	

ARTICLE
Beowulf Is Back!
by James Parker

BALLAD
Barbara Allan
by Anonymous

ARTICLE
Journeymen Keep the Medieval Past Alive
by Melissa Eddy

Suggested Novel Connection

NOVEL
Grendel
by John Gardner

Key Learning Objectives
In abbreviated form, each unit's main instructional goals are listed for planning and quick reference.

Unit 1 Tasks
- Write a Short Story 128
- Create a Podcast 135

Reflect on the Unit 137

Key Learning Objectives
- Analyze characteristics of an epic poem
- Analyze Old English poetry
- Analyze narrator
- Analyze conflict
- Make predictions
- Analyze characterization
- Make inferences
- Analyze tone

Online Ed Visit the Interactive Student Edition for:
- Unit and Selection Videos
- Media Selections
- Selection Audio Recordings
- Enhanced Digital Instruction

Additional Connections
- **The Canterbury Tales** by Geoffrey Chaucer (narrative poem)
- **A Connecticut Yankee in King Arthur's Court** by Mark Twain (novel)

Contents   FM7

Annotated Student Edition Table of Contents

UNIT

Instructional Overview
and Resources 138A

UNIT
A CELEBRATION OF HUMAN ACHIEVEMENT
PAGE 138

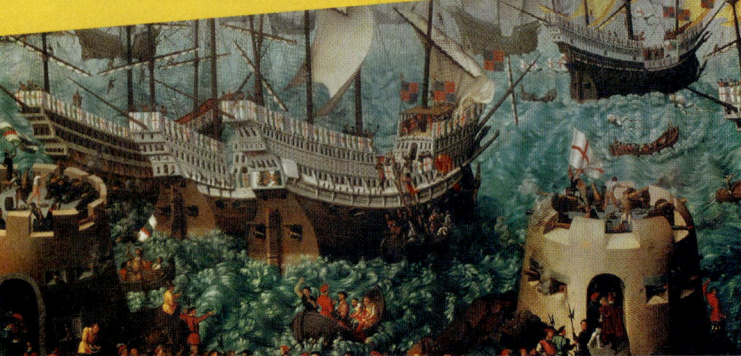

? ESSENTIAL QUESTIONS
- What can drive someone to seek revenge?
- How does time affect our feelings?
- What's the difference between love and passion?
- How do you defy expectations?

The English Renaissance 140

ANALYZE & APPLY

Analyze & Apply
This section of the Table of Contents groups a variety of selections for analysis, annotation, and application of the Notice & Note protocol, as well as standards instruction.

DRAMA
Shakespearean Drama 144
The Tragedy of Hamlet 146
by William Shakespeare

FILM CLIP
from Hamlet 276
by BBC Shakespeare

LITERARY CRITICISM   **MENTOR TEXT**
Hamlet's Dull Revenge 280
by René Girard

POEMS
Sonnet 30 294
Sonnet 75 300
by Edmund Spenser

POEM
A Valediction: Forbidding Mourning 304
by John Donne

FM8   Grade 12

UNIT 2

COLLABORATE & COMPARE

COMPARE THEMES

POEM
To His Coy Mistress 312
by Andrew Marvell

POEM
Twenty-One Love Poems (Poem III) 318
by Adrienne Rich

COMPARE ACROSS GENRES

SPEECH
from Speech Before the Spanish Armada Invasion 324
by Queen Elizabeth I

ARTICLE
For Army Infantry's First Women, Heavy Packs and the Weight of History 334
by Dave Philipps

Collaborate & Compare
This section of the Table of Contents provides a comparative analysis of two selections linked by topic but different in genre, craft, or focus. Standards instruction and annotation are also applied.

Contents   FM9

Annotated Student Edition Table of Contents

UNIT 2

Independent Reading
Interactive digital texts linked to the unit topic and in a wide range of genres and Lexile levels provide additional resources for students' independent reading, expanding student choice and experience.

 **INDEPENDENT READING** 350
These selections can be accessed through the digital edition.

 **POEMS**
Sonnet 18
Sonnet 29
Sonnet 130
by William Shakespeare

 **ARTICLE**
Elizabeth I: The Reality Behind the Mask
by Brenda Ralph Lewis

UNIT 2

POEM
The Passionate Shepherd to His Love
by Christopher Marlowe

POEM
The Nymph's Reply to the Shepherd
by Sir Walter Raleigh

Suggested Novel Connection

NOVEL
Don Quixote
by Miguel de Cervantes Saavedra

Unit 2 Task
- Write a Literary Analysis 352

Reflect on the Unit 359

Additional Connections

- **Dr, Faustus**
  by Christopher Marlowe
  (drama)

- **Selected Poems**
  by John Donne (poetry)

Key Learning Objectives
- Analyze dramatic plot
- Analyze conflict
- Analyze soliloquy
- Analyze arguments
- Analyze key ideas
- Analyze sonnets
- Analyze metaphysical conceits
- Interpret figurative language
- Analyze speaker
- Analyze rhetorical devices
- Analyze text features

 Visit the Interactive Student Edition for:
- Unit and Selection Videos
- Media Selections
- Selection Audio Recordings
- Enhanced Digital Instruction

Contents FM11

Annotated Student Edition Table of Contents

UNIT 3

Instructional Overview and Resources 360A

UNIT 3

TRADITION AND REASON

PAGE 360

 ESSENTIAL QUESTIONS

- How can satire change people's behavior?
- What is your most memorable experience?
- What keeps women from achieving equality with men?
- Why are plagues so horrifying?

The Restoration and the 18th Century 362

ANALYZE & APPLY

POEM
from The Rape of the Lock 366
by Alexander Pope

SATIRE
A Modest Proposal 378
by Jonathan Swift

EDITORIAL
Satire Is Dying Because the Internet Is Killing It 396
by Arwa Mahdawi

DIARY
from The Journal and Letters of Fanny Burney: An Encounter with King George III............................. 406
by Fanny Burney

COLLABORATE & COMPARE

COMPARE ACROSS GENRES

ARGUMENT
from A Vindication of the Rights of Woman 420
by Mary Wollstonecraft

ARTICLE
Education Protects Women from Abuse 434
by Olga Khazan

FM12 Grade 12

UNIT 3

COMPARE ACROSS GENRES

NOVEL
from A Journal of the Plague Year 448
by Daniel Defoe

MEMOIR   MENTOR TEXT
from Inferno: A Doctor's Ebola Story 462
by Steven Hatch, M.D.

> **Mentor Text**
> This selection exemplifies genre characteristics and craft choices that will be used in end-of-unit writing tasks as models for students.

INDEPENDENT READING 478
These selections can be accessed through the digital edition.

POEM
Elegy Written in a Country Churchyard
by Thomas Gray

ARTICLE
Once Below Gas Station, Virginia Cemetery Restored
by Wyatt Andrews

POEM
On Her Loving Two Equally
by Aphra Behn

ARTICLE
King George's Letters Betray Madness, Computer Finds
by Mindy Weisberger

Suggested Novel Connection

NOVEL
Candide
by Voltaire

Unit 3 Tasks
- Write a Personal Narrative 480
- Present a Narrative 487

Reflect on the Unit 489

Additional Connections

- **Gulliver's Travels**
  by Jonathan Swift (novel)

- **Robinson Crusoe**
  by Daniel Defoe (novel)

Key Learning Objectives
- Analyze satire
- Analyze mock epic
- Understand author's purpose
- Analyze tone
- Connect to history
- Evaluate arguments
- Analyze counterarguments
- Analyze graphic features
- Analyze historical setting
- Analyze narrator

 Visit the Interactive Student Edition for:
- Unit and Selection Videos
- Media Selections
- Selection Audio Recordings
- Enhanced Digital Instruction

Contents   FM13

Annotated Student Edition Table of Contents

UNIT 4

Instructional Overview
and Resources.........490A

UNIT 4

EMOTION AND EXPERIMENTATION
PAGE 490

 ESSENTIAL QUESTIONS

- What can nature offer us?
- How do you define beauty?
- How can science go wrong?
- What shapes your outlook on life?

The Flowering of Romanticism...492

ANALYZE & APPLY

 **POEMS**
Lines Composed a Few Miles Above Tintern Abbey 496
Composed upon Westminster Bridge,
September 3, 1802 506
I Wandered Lonely As a Cloud 508
by William Wordsworth

 **POEM**
Ode on a Grecian Urn 512
by John Keats

 **NOVEL**
from Frankenstein 520
by Mary Shelley

 **ESSAY**   **MENTOR TEXT**
Frankenstein: Giving Voice to the Monster 534
by Langdon Winner

COLLABORATE & COMPARE

 **POEM**
Ode to the West Wind 546
by Percy Bysshe Shelley

COMPARE
THEMES

 **POEM**
Song of a Thatched Hut Damaged in Autumn Wind 554
by Du Fu

FM14   Grade 12

Variety of Genres

Each unit is comprised of different kinds of texts or genres. Essential characteristics of each genre are identified and illustrated. Students then apply those characteristics to their own writing.

UNIT 4

COMPARE POEMS

POEMS
from Songs of Innocence 560
    The Lamb 564
    The Chimney Sweeper 566
from Songs of Experience 568
    The Tyger 568
    The Chimney Sweeper 570
by William Blake

INDEPENDENT READING 576
These selections can be accessed through the digital edition.

EXPLANATORY ESSAY
William Blake: Visions and Verses
by Rachel Galvin

POEM
Frost at Midnight
by Samuel Taylor Coleridge

PERSONAL NARRATIVE
Walking with Wordsworth
by Bruce Stutz

EXPLANATORY ESSAY
from A Defense of Poetry
by Percy Bysshe Shelley

POEM
The Skylark
by John Clare

Suggested Novel Connection

NOVEL
Pride and Prejudice
by Jane Austen

> **Suggested Novel Connection**
> One extended text is recommended for its topical and thematic connection to other texts in the unit.

Additional Connections
- **The Count of Monte Cristo**
  by Alexander Dumas (novel)
- **A Tale of Two Cities**
  by Charles Dickens (novel)

 Unit 4 Task
• Write an Explanatory Essay 578

Reflect on the Unit 585

Key Learning Objectives
- Analyze Romantic poetry
- Analyze imagery
- Analyze stanza structure
- Analyze rhyme scheme
- Analyze science fiction
- Analyze motivation
- Evaluate essay
- Analyze form
- Analyze diction
- Analyze symbols

Visit the Interactive Student Edition for:
- Unit and Selection Videos
- Media Selections
- Selection Audio Recordings
- Enhanced Digital Instruction

Contents FM15

Annotated Student Edition Table of Contents

UNIT 5

Instructional Overview and Resources 586A

UNIT 5

AN ERA OF RAPID CHANGE
PAGE 586

? ESSENTIAL QUESTIONS

- What is a true benefactor?
- How do you view the world?
- What brings out cruelty in people?
- Which invention has had the greatest impact on your life?

The Victorians 588

ANALYZE & APPLY

NOVEL
from Jane Eyre 592
by Charlotte Brontë

DOCUMENTARY
Factory Reform 610
by Timelines.tv

NARRATIVE POEM
The Lady of Shalott 614
by Alfred, Lord Tennyson

NOVEL
from Great Expectations 626
by Charles Dickens

ESSAY   **MENTOR TEXT**
The Victorians Had the Same Concerns
About Technology as We Do 642
by Melissa Dickson

COLLABORATE & COMPARE

COMPARE THEMES

POEM
Dover Beach 654
by Matthew Arnold

POEM
The Darkling Thrush 660
by Thomas Hardy

FM16   Grade 12

UNIT 5

COMPARE THEMES

POEM

My Last Duchess 666
by Robert Browning

POEM
Confession 672
by Linh Dinh

 INDEPENDENT READING 678
These selections can be accessed through the digital edition.

POEM

Sonnet 43
by Elizabeth Barrett Browning

POEM

Remembrance
by Emily Brontë

ARTICLE

The Great Exhibition
by Lara Kriegel

SHORT STORY

Christmas Storms and Sunshine
by Elizabeth Cleghorn Gaskell

ESSAY

Evidence of Progress
by Thomas Babington Macaulay

Suggested Drama Connection

DRAMA

A Doll's House
by Henrik Ibsen

Unit 5 Tasks
- Write a Research Report 680
- Give a Multimodal Presentation 687

Reflect on the Unit 689

Tasks
Each unit concludes with one or two culminating tasks that demonstrate essential understandings, synthesizing ideas and text references in oral and written responses.

Key Learning Objectives
- Analyze setting
- Analyze first-person point of view
- Evaluate documentaries
- Analyze allegory
- Analyze mood
- Analyze characterization
- Analyze compare-and-contrast essay
- Analyze sound devices
- Analyze imagery
- Draw conclusions about speakers

 Visit the Interactive Student Edition for:
- Unit and Selection Videos
- Media Selections
- Selection Audio Recordings
- Enhanced Digital Instruction

Additional Connections
- **Jane Eyre**
  by Charlotte Brontë (novel)
- **Tess of the D'Urbervilles**
  by Thomas Hardy (novel)

Annotated Student Edition Table of Contents

UNIT 6

Instructional Overview and Resources 690A

UNIT 6

NEW IDEAS, NEW VOICES

PAGE 690

 ESSENTIAL QUESTIONS

- What makes people feel insecure?
- Why is it hard to resist social pressure?
- What is the power of symbols?
- When should the government interfere in our decisions?

Modern and Contemporary Literature 692

ANALYZE & APPLY

SHORT STORY
A Cup of Tea 696
by Katherine Mansfield

POEM
The Love Song of J. Alfred Prufrock 712
by T. S. Eliot

ESSAY
Shooting an Elephant 722
by George Orwell

SHORT STORY
My Daughter the Racist 738
by Helen Oyeyemi

COLLABORATE & COMPARE

COMPARE THEMES

POEM
The Second Coming 756
by William Butler Yeats

POEM
Symbols? I'm Sick of Symbols 762
by Fernando Pessoa

FM18   Grade 12

Cultural Diversity

Each unit includes a rich array of selections that represent multicultural authors and experiences.

UNIT 6

COMPARE ARGUMENTS

MENTOR TEXTS

SPEECH
Budget 2016: George Osborne's Speech 768
by George Osborne

EDITORIAL
Will the Sugar Tax Stop Childhood Obesity? 778
by Chris Hall

Online Ed

INDEPENDENT READING 790
These selections can be accessed through the digital edition.

SHORT STORY
Araby
by James Joyce

SPEECH
Professions for Women
by Virginia Woolf

POEM
Do Not Go Gentle into That Good Night
by Dylan Thomas

POEM
Digging
by Seamus Heaney

SHORT STORY
Marriage Is a Private Affair
by Chinua Achebe

Suggested Novel Connection

NOVEL
Things Fall Apart
by Chinua Achebe

Unit **Tasks**
- Write an Argument 792
- Debate an Issue 799

Reflect on the Unit 801

Additional Connections

- **The Piano Lesson**
  by August Wilson (drama)

- **A Portrait of the Artist as a Young Man**
  by James Joyce (novel)

Reflection
Students may pause and reflect on their process and understanding of the selections and the themes in each unit.

Key Learning Objectives
- Analyze third-person point of view
- Analyze stream of consciousness
- Analyze reflective essay
- Analyze irony
- Analyze setting
- Understand symbolism
- Analyze rhythmic patterns
- Evaluate persuasive techniques
- Analyze inductive reasoning

 Visit the Interactive Student Edition for:
- Unit and Selection Videos
- Media Selections
- Selection Audio Recordings
- Enhanced Digital Instruction

Contents FM19

SELECTIONS BY GENRE

FICTION

NOVEL

from **Frankenstein**
Mary Shelley 520

from **Great Expectations**
Charles Dickens 626

from **Jane Eyre**
Charlotte Brontë 592

from **A Journal of the Plague Year**
Daniel Defoe 448

from **Le Morte d'Arthur**
Sir Thomas Malory
retold by Keith Baines
ROMANCE 44

SHORT STORY

Araby
James Joyce .... Online

Chivalry
Neil Gaiman 64

Christmas Storms and Sunshine
Elizabeth Cleghorn Gaskell .... Online

A Cup of Tea
Katherine Mansfield 696

Marriage Is a Private Affair
Chinua Achebe .... Online

My Daughter the Racist
Helen Oyeyemi 738

NONFICTION

ARGUMENT

from **A Defense of Poetry**
Percy Bysshe Shelley
EXPLANATORY ESSAY .... Online

Hamlet's Dull Revenge
René Girard
LITERARY CRITICISM 280

A Modest Proposal
Jonathan Swift
SATIRE 378

Satire is Dying Because the Internet Is Killing It
Arwa Mahdawi
EDITORIAL 396

from **A Vindication of the Rights of Woman**
Mary Wollstonecraft 420

Will the Sugar Tax Stop Childhood Obesity?
Chris Hall
EDITORIAL 778

MEMOIR/DIARY

from **The Journal and Letters of Fanny Burney: An Encounter with King George III**
Fanny Burney
DIARY 406

from **Inferno: A Doctor's Ebola Story**
Steven Hatch, M.D.
MEMOIR 462

FM20 Grade 12

from **My Syrian Diary**
Marah
DIARY 96

INFORMATIONAL TEXT

Beowulf Is Back!
James Parker .... Online

Education Protects Women from Abuse
Olga Khazan 434

Elizabeth I: The Reality Behind the Mask
Brenda Ralph Lewis .... Online

Evidence of Progress
Thomas Babington Macaulay
ESSAY .... Online

For Army Infantry's First Women, Heavy Packs and the Weight of History
Dave Philipps 334

Frankenstein: Giving Voice to the Monster
Langdon Winner
ESSAY 534

The Great Exhibition
Lara Kriegel .... Online

Journeymen Keep the Medieval Past Alive
Melissa Eddy .... Online

King George's Letters Betray Madness, Computer Finds
Mindy Weisberger .... Online

Once Below Gas Station, Virginia Cemetery Restored
Wyatt Andrews .... Online

The Victorians Had the Same Concerns about Technology as We Do
Melissa Dickson
ESSAY 642

Walking with Wordsworth
Bruce Stutz
PERSONAL NARRATIVE .... Online

William Blake: Visions and Verses
Rachel Galvin
EXPLANATORY ESSAY .... Online

LETTER

from **The Paston Letters**
The Paston Family 82

NARRATIVE NONFICTION

Shooting an Elephant
George Orwell
ESSAY 722

SPEECH

Budget 2016: George Osborne's Speech
George Osborne
ARGUMENT 768

Professions for Women
Virginia Woolf .... Online

from **Speech Before the Spanish Armada Invasion**
Queen Elizabeth I 324

POETRY

Barbara Allan
Anonymous
BALLAD .... Online

from **Beowulf**
The Beowulf Poet
translated by Seamus Heaney
EPIC POEM 6

from **Beowulf**
The Beowulf Poet
translated by Burton Raffel
EPIC POEM .... Online

Selections by Genre FM21

SELECTIONS BY GENRE

The Chimney Sweeper
from **Songs of Experience**
William Blake 570

The Chimney Sweeper
from **Songs of Innocence**
William Blake 566

Composed upon Westminster Bridge, September 3, 1802
William Wordsworth 506

Confession
Linh Dinh 672

The Darkling Thrush
Thomas Hardy 660

Digging
Seamus Heaney .... Online

Do Not Go Gentle into That Good Night
Dylan Thomas .... Online

Dover Beach
Matthew Arnold 654

Elegy Written in a Country Churchyard
Thomas Gray .... Online

Frost at Midnight
Samuel Taylor Coleridge .... Online

I Wandered Lonely As a Cloud
William Wordsworth 508

The Lady of Shalott
Alfred, Lord Tennyson
NARRATIVE POEM 614

The Lamb
from **Songs of Innocence**
William Blake 564

Lines Composed a Few Miles Above Tintern Abbey
William Wordsworth 496

Loneliness
Fanny Howe 118

The Love Song of J. Alfred Prufrock
T. S. Eliot 712

My Last Duchess
Robert Browning 666

The Nymph's Reply to the Shepherd
Sir Walter Raleigh .... Online

Ode on a Grecian Urn
John Keats 512

Ode to the West Wind
Percy Bysshe Shelley 546

On Her Loving Two Equally
Aphra Behn .... Online

The Passionate Shepherd to His Love
Christopher Marlowe .... Online

from **The Rape of the Lock**
Alexander Pope 366

Remembrance
Emily Brontë .... Online

The Second Coming
William Butler Yeats 756

The Skylark
John Clare .... Online

Song of a Thatched Hut Damaged in Autumn Wind
Du Fu 554

Sonnet 18
William Shakespeare . . . . Online

Sonnet 29
William Shakespeare . . . . Online

Sonnet 30
Edmund Spenser 294

Sonnet 43
Elizabeth Barrett Browning . . . . Online

Sonnet 75
Edmund Spenser 300

Sonnet 130
William Shakespeare . . . . Online

Symbols? I'm Sick of Symbols
Fernando Pessoa 762

To His Coy Mistress
Andrew Marvell 312

Twenty-One Love Poems (Poem III)
Adrienne Rich 318

The Tyger
from Songs of Experience
William Blake 568

A Valediction: Forbidding Mourning
John Donne 304

The Wanderer
Anonymous
translated by Burton Raffel 110

The Wife of Bath's Tale
from The Canterbury Tales
Geoffrey Chaucer
translated by Nevill Coghill
NARRATIVE POEM 24

DRAMA

The Tragedy of Hamlet
William Shakespeare 146

MEDIA STUDY

Factory Reform
by Timelines.tv
DOCUMENTARY 610

***from* Hamlet**
by BBC Shakespeare
FILM CLIP 276

HMH
Into Literature Dashboard

Easy to use and personalized for your learning.

- Monitor your progress in the course.
- Review your assignments and check your progress.
- Quickly access content and search program resources.

Explore Online to Experience the Power of HMH *Into Literature*

All in One Place
Readings and assignments are supported by a variety of resources to bring literature to life and give you the tools you need to succeed.

Supporting 21st-Century Skills
Whether you're working alone or collaborating with others, it takes effort to analyze the complex texts and competing ideas that bombard us in this fast-paced world. What will help you succeed? Staying engaged and organized. The digital tools in this program will help you take charge of your learning.

FM24

Ignite Your Investigation

You learn best when you're engaged. The **Stream to Start** videos at the beginning of every unit are designed to spark your interest before you read. Get curious and start reading!

Learn How to Close Read

Close reading effectively is all about examining the details. See how it's done by watching the **Close Read Screencasts** in your eBook. Hear modeled conversations on targeted passages.

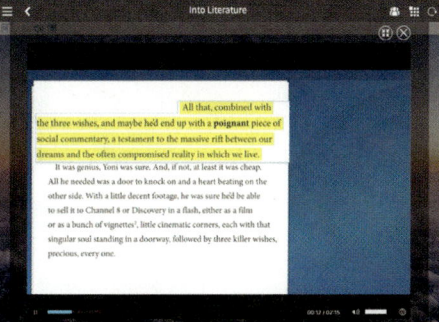

Personalized Annotations

My Notes encourages you to take notes as you read and allows you to mark the text in your own customized way. You can easily access annotations to review later as you prepare for exams.

Interactive Graphic Organizers

Graphic organizers help you process, summarize, and keep track of your learning and prepare for end-of-unit writing tasks. **Word Networks** help you learn academic vocabulary, and **Response Logs** help you explore and deepen your understanding of the **Essential Questions** in each unit.

No Wi-Fi? No problem!

With HMH *Into Literature,* you always have access: download when you're online and access what you need when you're offline. Work offline and then upload when you're back online.

Communicate "Raise a Hand" to ask or answer questions without having to be in the same room as your teacher.

Collaborate Collaborate with your teacher via chat and work with a classmate to improve your writing.

FM25

HMH
Into Literature
STUDIOS

All the help you need to be successful in your literature class is one click away with the Studios. These digital-only lessons are here to tap into the skills that you already use and help you sharpen those skills for the future.

Online Ed — Easy-to-find resources, organized in five separate STUDIOS. On demand and on ED!

Look for links in each lesson to take you to the appropriate Studio.

READING STUDIO
Go beyond the book with the Reading Studio. With over 100 full-length downloadable titles to choose from, find the right story to continue your journey.

WRITING STUDIO
Being able to write clearly and effectively is a skill that will help you throughout life. The Writing Studio will help you become an expert communicator—in print or online.

SPEAKING & LISTENING STUDIO
Communication is more than just writing. The Speaking & Listening Studio will help you become an effective speaker and a focused listener.

GRAMMAR STUDIO
Go beyond traditional worksheets with the Grammar Studio. These engaging, interactive lessons will sharpen your grammar skills.

VOCABULARY STUDIO
Learn the skills you need to expand your vocabulary. The interactive lessons in the Vocabulary Studio will grow your vocabulary to improve your reading.

Essay on Notice & Note

Dr. Kylene Beers and Dr. Robert E. Probst

In reading, as in almost everything else, paying attention is most important.

You wouldn't stand in the batter's box, facing a hard-throwing pitcher, with your mind wandering to what you may have for dinner that evening. The prospect of a fastball coming toward you at 80 miles an hour tends to focus the mind.

And you wouldn't attempt to sing a difficult song in front of a large crowd with your thoughts on what dress you're going to wear to the dance this coming weekend. The need to hit the high note, without cracking, in front of 500 people evokes concentration.

Paying attention is essential.

It's the same with reading. Of course, if you don't concentrate while reading, you won't suffer the pain of being knocked down by the fastball or the embarrassment of failing to hit the notes in front of the crowd, but you'll miss what the text offers. If you don't pay attention, there is barely any purpose in picking up the text at all.

But there is a purpose in reading. And that purpose, that point, is to enable us to change. The change may be slight, or it might be dramatic. We might, at one extreme, simply get a little more information that we need:

- Where is tonight's game?
- What time is band practice?
- What pages do we need to read for homework?

Reading for that sort of information doesn't dramatically change who we are, but it does change us slightly. Or, at least, it *might* change us slightly. Obviously, it is *we*, the readers, who must do the changing. The text doesn't do it for us. When we read that tonight's game is away, instead of at home, we have to change our plans to let us get to the other school. We have to take in the information and do something with it. If we don't, if we show up at the home field despite what we have read, the reading will have been pointless, a waste of time. And the evening will be wasted, as well. We have to pay attention to the book — what's on the page, and to our heads — what we thought before we read and what we now think. And we have to take it to heart — that is to say, we have to act on what we now know and think.

FM 28

Other reading, however, might enable us to change more significantly. We might change our thinking about an important problem, or we might change our attitude about an important issue. We can't tell you which text will do that for you or how you might grow and change as a result of reading it. That's much too individual. It's hard to predict unless you know the reader well and know some of the texts that might matter to him or her:

- Some of us might read about child labor in foreign countries and change our minds about what we will buy and what we will boycott.
- You might read *To Kill a Mockingbird*, and change your thinking about race relations.
- You might read about climate change and wonder what you can do to help preserve the earth.

We can't know exactly what book will be powerful for which reader. But we can safely predict that if you don't notice what the text offers, think about it, and take what matters to you into your head and heart, then the reading probably won't mean much to you.

We're going to urge you to pay attention to three elements as you read:

- **The Book.** Or whatever text you have in your hand, whether it is a book, an article, a poem, or something else. We are going to urge you to listen carefully to what it tells you, and we're going to give you some strategies that we hope will make that easy for you to do.
- **Your Head.** We're going to ask you also to pay attention to your own thoughts. If it's an article you're reading, then keep in mind what you thought about the topic before you began, and then think seriously about how you might have changed your thinking as a result of what you've read. If it's a story or a poem or a movie, then think about what thoughts or feelings it brought to mind and how they might have shaped your reaction to the text.
- **Your Heart.** Finally, we encourage you to ask yourself what you want to carry away from the reading. What matters to you? How might you change your thinking? How might you have shifted your attitudes about something, even if only slightly? What do you take to heart?

It all begins with noticing.

But there's a lot in a book to notice, so it might help to keep in mind just a few things that you will probably see in almost any text (unless it is very short). We call these elements "signposts" because they serve readers just as signposts or street signs serve drivers — they alert them to something significant. The careless driver, who doesn't pay attention and misses a stop sign or a hairpin-curve sign, is likely to end up in trouble. The lazy reader, who doesn't notice the signposts, won't end up in trouble — he just isn't likely to know what's going on in the text.

THE FICTION SIGNPOSTS

We want to share 6 signposts that help you when reading fiction.

▶ CONTRASTS AND CONTRADICTIONS

Without a contrast or a contradiction, everything is just the same, just the usual, just what you would have expected. Boring.

But when some event occurs that contrasts vividly with what you would have expected, then you are likely — if you're paying attention — to notice it.

When a friend's behavior suddenly changes and contrasts with what you would expect, you will notice it and ask yourself why. Similarly, when a character in a story does something drastically different from what he has usually done, you should pause and wonder why. Or, when a writer gives you an idea that contradicts the thoughts you have always held, again you might slow down and ask yourself, "is she right or am I? Should I accept those thoughts or reject them? Is the answer somewhere in between what I have read and what I used to think?" Keep in mind the general question "Why is the character doing or saying that?" and it will lead you to other questions you might ask about the moment of contrast and contradiction, that moment when you bump into something unexpected.

> In Neil Gaiman's "Chivalry," a student has noted a **CONTRAST AND CONTRADICTION** and asked this question: Why would the character act and feel this way?

Then she walked into her parlor and looked at the mantelpiece: at the little china basset hound, and the Holy Grail, and the photograph of her late husband Henry, shirtless, smiling and eating an ice cream in black and white, almost forty years away.

Mrs. Whitaker looks closely at the photograph of her late husband when he was young, as if she's thinking about him.

She went back into the kitchen. The kettle had begun to whistle. She poured a little steaming water into the teapot, swirled it around, and poured it out. Then she added two spoonfuls of tea and one for the pot and poured in the rest of the water. All this she did in silence.

She turned to Galaad then, and she looked at him. "Put that apple away," she told Galaad, firmly. "You shouldn't offer things like that to old ladies. It isn't proper."

Perhaps she refuses to take the apple, which could have restored her youth, because she misses him. Galaad's offer may not be "proper" because Mrs. Whitaker doesn't want to betray the memory of her husband.

AHA MOMENT

Sometimes too many days go by without one of those moments when you suddenly understand something. But when you have such a moment you recognize that it's important and you stop and think about it. One day you might suddenly say to yourself "I'm echoing everything my friends say, but I don't really believe any of it." That's an important moment that may lead to a change in what you do, or at least to some hard thinking about the choices you have made. You've had an insight — an Aha — and you have to ask yourself what it means.

In the same way, the character in the story will almost always come to some insight into his situation, some "Aha" moment in which he realizes, perhaps suddenly, something about himself, his situation, or his life. When you come to such a moment, ask yourself "How will this change things?" Because it almost always will. Aha Moments are usually indicated with phrases such as "I knew," "I understood," "He figured it out," "She slowly realized," or "She nodded, knowing what she had to do . . ."

In Katherine Mansfield's "A Cup of Tea," a student has noted an AHA MOMENT and asked this question: How might this change things?

"<u>Pretty?</u>" <u>Rosemary was so surprised that she blushed</u>. "Do you think so? I—<u>I hadn't thought about it.</u>"

"Good Lord!" Philip struck a match. "<u>She's absolutely lovely. Look again, my child. I was bowled over when I came into your room</u> just now. However . . . I think you're making a ghastly mistake. Sorry, darling, if I'm crude and all that. But <u>let me know if Miss Smith is going to dine with us</u> in time for me to look up *The Milliner's Gazette*."

"<u>You absurd creature!</u>" said Rosemary, and she went out of the library, but not back to her bedroom. She went to her writing-room and sat down at her desk. <u>Pretty! Absolutely lovely! Bowled over! Her heart beat like a heavy bell. Pretty! Lovely!</u>

Rosemary blushes, an Aha Moment, when she realizes that her husband thinks "Miss Smith" is pretty.

Then he says the girl is "absolutely lovely" and wonders if she's going to eat dinner with them.

I'll bet Rosemary's attitude changes. She sounds jealous enough to quit pitying the girl, and she might even try to keep her away from Philip.

TOUGH QUESTIONS

"Do you want pizza or spaghetti for dinner?" really isn't a tough question, even if you can't make up your mind. Your answer isn't going to change much of anything, and tomorrow you probably won't even remember that you made a choice. You aren't going to think about it for very long or very hard, and no one will ever write a book about the choice between pizza and spaghetti. If they do, we won't read it.

A tough question is one we struggle with, one that might change the course of our lives — one, at least, that will have some serious consequences for us. "Should I play football, as the coach wants me to, or should I join the band, as I want to?" "Should I follow the crowd, as everyone is pressing me to do, or should I respect my own thoughts and let the crowd condemn me for it?" These are tough questions, and how we might answer them will shape the days to come.

Often a story, even an entire book, is built around the tough question. If we ask ourselves "What does this make me wonder about?" We will probably be led into exploring the same issue the character or the writer is exploring. The writer probably wanted to see what would happen if his character answered the question in a certain way. If you notice the tough question, and ask yourself about it, you will probably be looking at the main issue of the book.

In Geoffrey Chaucer's "The Wife of Bath's Tale," a student has noted a TOUGH QUESTION and asked this: What does this question make me wonder about?

"You have two choices; which one will you try?
To have me old and ugly till I die,
But still a loyal, true, and humble wife
That never will displease you all her life,
Or would you rather I were young and pretty
And chance your arm what happens in a city
Where friends will visit you because of me,
Yes, and in other places too, maybe.
Which would you have? The choice is all your own."

I wonder how I'd answer the same Tough Question. What leads to lasting happiness in a relationship? How important is appearance? Is it possible to ignore appearance, even if you know you'll be loved and supported forever?

WORDS OF THE WISER

You may think that you have heard too many of these in your own life.

You probably think there is always someone around who wants to offer you advice, teach you how things are, and tell you what to do and how to think. Sometimes these wise words are right, truly wise, and sometimes they are wrong. But they are almost always an effort to guide you, or the character, to teach something about living in the world.

In a story, we usually hear Words of the Wiser in a quiet moment, when two characters are in a serious conversation about a problem or a decision. Usually the one who is — or thinks she is — wiser, will offer a serious lesson about life. The story will be about the character struggling along, unwilling to learn that lesson until the end; or about the character accepting the lesson and following it to whatever adventures it leads; or perhaps, in rare cases, about the words of the wiser not being wise after all.

In any case, when you notice Words of the Wiser in the story you should ask the same question you are likely to ask in your own life — "What is the lesson, and how will it affect the character (or me)?"

> In William Shakespeare's *The Tragedy of Hamlet*, a student has noted **WORDS OF THE WISER** and asked this question: What is the life lesson, and how might this affect the character?

Ophelia. No more but so?
Laertes.　　　　　　Think it no more.
For nature, crescent, does not grow alone
In thews and bulk, but, as this temple waxes,
The inward service of the mind and soul
Grows wide withal. <u>Perhaps he loves you now</u>,
And now no soil nor cautel doth besmirch
The virtue of his will; <u>but you must fear</u>,
<u>His greatness weighed, his will is not his own</u>,
<u>For he himself is subject to his birth</u>.
He may not, as unvalued persons do,
Carve for himself, for <u>on his choice depends</u>
<u>The safety and the health of this whole state</u>.
<u>And therefore must his choice be circumscribed</u>
<u>Unto the voice and yielding of that body</u>
<u>Whereof he is the head</u>.

Laertes is trying to convince Ophelia that she shouldn't love Hamlet, no matter how they currently feel about each other.

His Words of the Wiser suggest that Hamlet will always do what's best for Denmark, even if it means marrying someone else.

Ophelia might reject Hamlet or pretend not to love him, despite her feelings.

FM 33

AGAIN AND AGAIN

One teacher I had always called on the second or third person to raise a hand, or perhaps on some student who was looking out the window — never on the first hand in the sky.

It happened again and again. Until, of course, I got clever and decided to shoot my hand up quickly even though I didn't have the foggiest notion what the answer was. That must have been the day that the teacher recognized the lesson of Again and Again, and realized that he had established a pattern. Or perhaps he had been planning the switch all along. In any case, it was the day I shot my hand up first that he decided to change his routine. At my expense....

Something that happens over and over, again and again, establishes a pattern. If we pay attention, we'll notice that pattern and ask ourselves, "Why does this happen over and over, again and again?" In our lives, the again and again moment probably teaches us something about our friends, or our teachers, or, perhaps, about the way the world works. And sometimes it alerts us to something that is likely to change.

In any case, whenever we notice something happening again and again, we should take note of it, and ask ourselves "Why does this keep happening repeatedly?" Our answer may be that it teaches us some consistent pattern that we can rely on. Or it may be that it is setting up expectations that we can predict will suddenly not be met. It may be leading us into a surprising Contrast and Contradiction. That, after all is what my teacher did to me. If I had thought more carefully about the Again and Again, and asked myself why he was always avoiding the first hand that waved, I might have guessed that he was preparing a trick and that one day he would call on that first hand.

In Sir Thomas Malory's *Le Morte D'Arthur*, a student has noted an instance of AGAIN AND AGAIN and asked this question: Why might the author bring this up again and again?

For three weeks, while Sir Gawain was recovering, the siege was relaxed and both sides skirmished only halfheartedly. But once recovered, Sir Gawain rode up to the castle walls and challenged Sir Launcelot again:
"Sir Launcelot, traitor! Come forth, it is Sir Gawain who challenges you."
"Sir Gawain, why these insults? I have the measure of your strength and you can do me but little harm."
"Come forth, traitor, and this time I shall make good my revenge!" Sir Gawain shouted.
"Sir Gawain, I have once spared your life; should you not beware of meddling with me again?"

Launcelot has been trying to end the conflict with Arthur, but Sir Gawain has resisted Again and Again, insisting that the kingdom's honor is at stake.

Malory might be bringing up Gawain's repeated attacks to show how a sense of lasting dishonor can prevent peace.

▶ MEMORY MOMENT

Sometimes, in a reflective moment, a memory will surprise you. You won't have been trying to remember that day, or that person, or that event. It will just pop up like an almost forgotten old friend who knocks at your door and surprises you.

But something called that memory up at that moment. Something that was happening right now reached into your distant past and pulled that memory into your thoughts. Figuring out why that happened will probably tell you something important. It may explain why you are feeling the way you are feeling. It may even explain why you are acting as you are at the moment.

In a story, the Memory Moment is an author's creation. She has decided to reach back into the past for something that she thinks you, as a reader, need to know. It's easy to skip over these moments. After all, you want to go forwards, not backwards, and the Memory Moment steps back into the past. But it's probably important to ask yourself "Why is this moment important?" Because you can assume that if the writer is any good at all, she thinks you should notice it and take note of it.

> **In the epic poem *Beowulf*, a student has noted a MEMORY MOMENT and asked this question: Why might this memory be important?**

Hrothgar, the helmet of Shieldings, spoke:
"Beowulf, my friend, you have travelled here
to favour us with help and to fight for us.
<u>There was a feud one time, begun by your father.</u>
With his own hands <u>he had killed Heatholaf,</u>
who was a Wulfing; <u>so war was looming
and his people, in fear of it, forced him to leave.</u>
<u>He came away then over rolling waves
to the South-Danes here</u>, the sons of honour.
I was then in the first flush of kingship,
establishing my sway over all the rich strongholds
of this heroic land. Heorogar,
my older brother and the better man,
also a son of Halfdane's, had died.
Finally <u>I healed the feud by paying:</u>
<u>I shipped a treasure-trove to the Wulfings
and Ecgtheow acknowledged me with oaths of allegiance.</u>"

Hrothgar relates the memory of his favor to Ecgtheow, explaining that Ecgtheow had sworn "oaths of allegiance" to him.

This Memory Moment explains why Beowulf feels obliged to assist the Danes in their fight: his family owes Hrothgar a debt for having ended the feud with the Wulfings.

FM 35

NONFICTION SIGNPOSTS

Nonfiction has text clues as well. Just as in fiction, they invite you to stop and think about what's happening. These clues will help you focus on author's purpose — a critical issue to keep in mind when reading nonfiction. More importantly, these signposts will help you as you keep in mind what we call the Three Big Questions. These questions ought to guide all the reading we do, but especially the nonfiction reading. As you read, just keep asking yourself:

- What surprised me?
- What did the author think I already knew?
- What changed, challenged, or confirmed my thinking?

That first one will keep you thinking about the text. Just look for those parts that make you think, "Really!?!" and put an exclamation point there. The second one will be helpful when the language is tough, or the author is writing about something you don't know much about. Mark those points with a question mark and decide if you need more information. That final question, well, that question is why we read. Reading ought to change us. It ought to challenge our thinking. And sometimes it will confirm it. When you find those parts, just put a "C" in the margin. When you review your notes, you will decide if your thinking was changed, challenged, or confirmed.

As you're looking at what surprised you, or thinking about what is challenging you, or perhaps even as you find a part where it seems the author thinks you know something that you don't, you might discover that one of the following signposts appears right at that moment. So, these signposts help you think about the Three Big Questions. We have found five useful signposts for nonfiction.

▶ CONTRASTS AND CONTRADICTIONS

The world is full of contrasts and contradictions — if it weren't, it would be a pretty dull place to live.

This is the same Contrast and Contradiction that you are familiar with from fiction. It's that moment when you encounter something you didn't expect, something that surprises you. It may be a fact that you find startling, a perspective that you had never heard before, or perhaps an argument that is new to you. We should welcome those moments, even though they may be disconcerting. They give us the opportunity to change our minds about things, to sharpen our thinking. The last person we want to become is that reader who reads only to confirm what he has already decided. That reader is committed to not learning, not growing, and standing absolutely still intellectually.

> In Marah's *My Syrian Diary*, a student has noted **CONTRASTS AND CONTRADICTIONS** and asked this question: What is the difference, and why does it matter?

<u>My city was once magnificent.</u> In spring, <u>it bloomed. We used to wake up to the sound of birds chirping</u> and <u>to the fragrant scent of flowers.</u> Today, spring is here again. But what kind of spring is this? <u>We now wake up to the sound of falling bombs.</u>

Every day, <u>we open our eyes to our bleak reality: to the mortar shells that bring fear, death, disease and destruction.</u> It has <u>robbed us of our loved ones, destroyed our special places, hurt our close friends.</u> Take my neighbor's daughter. At just seven years old, she has <u>lost the ability to speak after a rocket landed close to our street.</u>

Marah contrasts the past with current life in the city, which drives the point home: sights, sounds, and scents have been transformed by the conflict.

The beauties of spring and the city's magnificence have been lost.

▶ EXTREME AND ABSOLUTE LANGUAGE

We are all guilty of overstatement all the time.

Well, that's an overstatement. We aren't all guilty, and those of us who are probably aren't guilty all of the time. When we hear "all," or "none," or "always," or "never," we can be absolutely certain — let's make that "almost certain" — that we are hearing absolute language. All it takes is one exception to make the claim false.

But we do tend to exaggerate and occasionally overstate our claims. Absolute language is easy to spot, and it's often harmless over-statement. Extreme language approaches absolute language but usually stops short. Much of the time, it's harmless, too. When you tell your buddy you're starving, you probably aren't. Or when you say you just heard the funniest joke in the world, even though that's probably not true, your comment causes no real harm.

Sometimes, however, an extreme statement is potentially dangerous. If, for example, someone in authority were to say something like, "I am 100% certain that the airline crash was caused by terrorists," and we had not yet even found the black box that would explain the cause of the accident, then gullible listeners might believe and form opinions based on that statement, even though the phrase "100% certain" shows us clearly that it is an extreme statement. After all, no one ever claims to be 100% certain unless he isn't. So the question becomes, "How certain is he?" 80%? 40%? 20%?

When we spot absolute or extreme language, we should ask ourselves "Why did the author say it this way?" Sometimes the answer will be revealing.

In the Paston Family's *The Paston Letters*, a student has noted EXTREME AND ABSOLUTE LANGUAGE and asked this question: Why did the author use this language?

The duke's men <u>ransacked the church</u>, and <u>carried off</u> (all) the goods that <u>were left</u> there, both ours and the tenants, and <u>left little behind</u>; they stood on the <u>high altar and ransacked the images</u>, and <u>took away</u> (everything) <u>they could find</u>. They shut the parson out of the church until they had finished, and <u>ransacked</u> (everyone's) <u>house in the town five or six times. The ringleaders in the thefts</u> were the bailiff of Eye and the bailiff of Stradbroke, Thomas Slyford. And Slyford was the leader in <u>robbing the church</u> and, after the bailiff of Eye, it is he who has most of the proceeds of the robbery. As for the lead, brass, pewter, iron, doors, gates, and other household stuff, men from Costessey and Cawston have got it, and <u>what they could not carry they hacked up in the most spiteful fashion</u>. If possible, <u>I would like some reputable men to be sent for from the king, to see how things are</u> both there and at the lodge, before any snows come, so that they can report the truth....

Throughout her letter, Paston uses both Extreme and Absolute Language.

Not only does her use of language stress the injustice of the attacks, but it also communicates how widespread and serious the attacks have been.

Paston's language emphasizes a distinct message to her husband: you need to come home, and you should bring help from the king when you do.

▶ NUMBERS AND STATS

"If I've told you once, I've told you a million times...."

Those are numbers — 1 (once) and 1,000,000 — though we prefer to see that as Extreme and Absolute Language. Still, it allows us to make the point, which is that numbers are used to make a point. In this case they reveal that the speaker is annoyed at how often he has to repeat himself for you to get the message. You barely have to ask the anchor question "Why did the writer or speaker use those numbers or amounts?"

FM 38

But that's the question you should ask when numbers or stats or amounts appear in something you are reading. Writers include them because they think those numbers, which look like hard, objective, indisputable data, will be persuasive. The questions are, "What are they trying to persuade you to think or believe?" And, "Are the numbers reliable?"

When a writer tells you, for instance, that 97-98% of scientists who have studied the issue think that humans are affecting the environment in damaging ways, we probably want to ask what those figures tell us, both about the situation and the writer's purpose. Our answer will probably be that the writer believes the scientists have reached a consensus that we are endangering the planet. The writer might have said "most of the scientists agree," but "most" is vague. It could mean anything from slightly more than half to almost all. But "97-98%" is much more precise. And it's very close to 100%, so it should be persuasive. Numbers and stats help us visualize what the author is trying to show; it's up to you to decide if there's more you need to know.

> In George Osborne's speech "Budget 2016," a student has noted **NUMBERS AND STATS** and asked this question: Why did the author use these numbers or amounts?

Mr. Deputy Speaker, you cannot have a long term plan for the country unless you have a long term plan for our children's health care. Here are the facts we know.

- Five-year-old children are consuming their body weight in sugar every year.
- Experts predict that within a generation, over half of all boys and 70% of girls could be overweight or obese.

Here's another fact that we all know. Obesity drives disease. It increases the risk of cancer, diabetes and heart disease—and it costs our economy £27 billion a year. . . .

Osborne includes these startling Numbers and Stats because they clearly communicate a significant threat to children's health in the long term.

They also suggest that the extraordinary cost of obesity-related diseases will continue to rise, if children's health care is not addressed.

QUOTED WORDS

American writer Ambrose Bierce said that quotation is "The act of repeating erroneously the words of another." When writers use quotations they are probably doing one of two things. They may be giving you an individual example so that you can see what some person thought or felt about a certain situation, event, or idea. In that case, the writer is probably trying to help you see the human impact of what otherwise might be an abstract idea, difficult to imagine. A writer might, for instance, tell you about the massive damage Hurricane Harvey brought to the coast of Texas. A description of the widespread destruction will give you a picture of what happened; but the quoted words of someone who heard the hundred-mile-an-hour winds for hours when the storm came ashore or whose house was flooded by the rising waters will give you a feel for the impact of the storm on a real person.

Writers also use quoted words to lend authority to a claim they are making. Quoting the authority adds some credibility to the situation. The Houston meteorologist who has studied the data and reports, "Harvey dumped more water in a shorter period of time on Houston than any other storm in Houston's history" ought to be believed more than the guy on the street corner who announces, "This is the worst storm ever."

> In Langdon Winner's "Frankenstein: Giving Voice to the Monster," a student has noted **QUOTED WORDS** and asked this question: Why is this person quoted or cited, and what did this add?

In a BBC interview last year, (Stephen Hawking) warned, "The development of full artificial intelligence could spell the end of the human race. . . . Humans, limited by slow biological evolution, couldn't compete and would be superseded by AI. . . . One can imagine such technology outsmarting financial markets, out-inventing human researchers, out-manipulating human leaders, and developing weapons we cannot even understand. Whereas the short-term impact of AI depends on who controls it, the long-term impact depends on whether it can be controlled at all."

I had no idea that a scientist as famous as the late Stephen Hawking saw danger in the development of artificial intelligence!

Winner includes Hawking's Quoted Words because Hawking is a trusted authority who poses concerns similar to those of Mary Shelley, supporting Winner's purpose.

▶ WORD GAPS

Unless we read such simple texts that we know everything there is to know about the subject, we will almost inevitably stumble into the gap between the writer's vocabulary and ours. Although that's occasionally frustrating, we might see it as an opportunity to sharpen our understanding. We might either learn a new word or learn how a word we already know might be used in a new way.

If we are in a hurry (and reading in a hurry is probably a bad idea because it doesn't give us time to think), then when we encounter a new word our first question might be, "Can I get by without knowing this word?" If you can, maybe you should make what sense you can of the sentence and move on. When we do that we lose the opportunity to learn something, but occasionally we just don't have the time. At the very least, you might jot down the word on the blank pages at the back of the book as a reminder to look it up later, so that the opportunity won't be completely lost.

A better way to approach the problem of the unknown word, however, might be to strategically ask several questions. Obviously the first step is to see if the word is at least partially explained by the context. For instance, if you read "hard, objective, indisputable data," and you don't know what "indisputable" means, you can easily figure out that it is something close to "hard" or "objective." Perhaps it means "definite," "not arguable," or something similar. Close enough. If you can get that far you can probably go on without losing much. You may want to ask someone later what the word "indisputable" means, or look it up in the dictionary, but at the moment you will be able to read on.

If that easy fix doesn't work, however, you might start with "Do I know this word from somewhere else?" If you do, then you have a place to begin. What the word meant in the context with which you are familiar might be a clue to what it means in this new context. For instance, you know what it means when someone says, "I'm depositing my paycheck in the bank." But then you hear your friend say, "You can bank on me." You know your friend isn't becoming a financial lending institution. But, if you'll give yourself a moment to think about what you know about banks, then you might be able to figure out that this means you can count on your friend.

Sometimes, the word is a technical word, a term used primarily by experts in the field, and if you don't know the language of that field, you'll simply need to look it up.

> **In Dr. Steven Hatch's *Inferno: A Doctor's Ebola Story*, a student has noted a WORD GAP and asked this question: Can I find clues in the sentence to help me understand the word?**

But what was he concerned about? <u>He was, after all, cured</u>, possessing <u>Ebola-specific antibodies</u> and (lymphocytes) <u>which now made him immune to a repeat infection</u>. But . . . did he know that? As I spoke with him, I sat there puzzling this over. <u>Surely he knew at some intuitive level that he was not at risk of getting sick again</u> while he spent day after day convalescing, although maybe he had thought a reset button had been pressed when he emerged from the decontamination shower. <u>But how to explain a concept like acquired immunity to someone who probably had no formal education beyond grade school?</u>

"Lymphocytes" is a technical word, but the sentence provides clues to its meaning. The word is related to curing George and to making him "immune to repeat infection."

FM 41

The essay by program consultant Carol Jago is an accessible explanation of **genre** and its importance. Genre has an elevated role in the new standards—both in reading and writing.

Ask students to read the first and second paragraphs and then to write their own definition of genre in the margin of their book.

If your students need an analogy to better understand **genre**, explain that genre refers to different categories or kinds of texts we read. This is similar to vehicles that we use for transportation. Vehicles transport people and goods but may be trucks, vans, sedans or sports cars—different categories for vehicles—different genres for texts.

Ask students to turn to a partner and provide examples of their favorite genre.

READING AND WRITING ACROSS GENRES

by Carol Jago

Reading is a first-class ticket around the world. Not only can you explore other lands and cultures, but you can also travel to the past and future. That journey is sometimes a wild ride. Other books can feel like comfort food, enveloping you in an imaginative landscape full of friends and good times. Making time for reading is making time for life.

Genre

One of the first things readers do when we pick up something to read is notice its genre. You might not think of it exactly in those terms, but consider how you approach a word problem in math class compared to how you read a science fiction story. Readers go to different kinds of text for different purposes. When you need to know how to do or make something, you want a reliable, trusted source of information. When you're in the mood to spend some time in a world of fantasy, you happily suspend your normal disbelief in dragons.

In every unit of *Into Literature,* you'll find a diverse mix of genres all connected by a common theme, allowing you to explore a topic from many different angles.

FM42

Writer's Craft

Learning how writers use genre to inform, to explain, to entertain, or to surprise readers will help you better understand—as well as enjoy—your reading. Imitating how professional writers employ the tools of their craft—descriptive language, repetition, sensory images, sentence structure, and a variety of other features—will give you many ideas for making your own writing more lively.

GENRE ELEMENTS: SHORT STORY
- is a work of short fiction that centers on a single idea and can be read in one sitting
- usually includes one main conflict that involves the characters and keeps moving
- includes the basic elements of fiction—plot, character, setting, and theme
- may be based on real and historical events

GENRE ELEMENTS: INFORMATIONAL TEXT
- provides factual information
- includes evidence to support ideas
- contains text features
- includes many forms, such as news articles and essays

GENRE ELEMENTS: LITERARY NONFICTION
- shares factual information, ideas, or experiences
- develops a key insight about the topic that goes beyond the facts
- uses literary techniques such as figurative language, narration
- reflects a personal involvement in the

GENRE ELEMENTS: POETRY
- may use figurative language, including personification
- often includes imagery that appeals to the five senses
- expresses a theme, or a "big idea" message about life

Into Literature provides you with the tools you need to understand the elements of all the critical genres and advice on how to learn from professional texts to improve your own writing in those genres.

Reading with Independence

Finding a good book can sometimes be a challenge. Like every other reader, you have probably experienced "book desert" when nothing you pick up seems to have what you are looking for (not that it's easy to explain exactly what you are looking for, but whatever it is, "this" isn't it). If you find yourself in this kind of reading funk, bored by everything you pick up, give yourself permission to range more widely, exploring graphic novels, contemporary biographies, books of poetry, historical fiction. And remember that long doesn't necessarily mean boring. My favorite kind of book is one that I never want to end.

Take control over your own reading with *Into Literature's* Reader's Choice selections and the HMH Digital Library. And don't forget: your teacher, librarian, and friends can offer you many more suggestions.

SHORT STORY
Marriage Is a Private Affair
Chinua Achebe
Nnaemeka married for love, offending his father. Can he bridge the rift he created by choosing his own path?

EPIC POEM
from Beowulf
translated by Burton Raffel
Beowulf faces one last challenging enemy—a fiery dragon that threatens the safety of his people.

ARTICLE
Elizabeth I: The Reality Behind the Mask
Brenda Ralph Lewis
Discover the real Queen Elizabeth I, who exercised great skill to disguise her true personality.

FM43

Direct students to read the paragraph under the heading "writer's craft." Ask students to write their own definition of writer's craft in the margin of *Into Literature*. Discuss, asking students to cite examples.

Encourage students to find the Genre Elements chart with each selection in *Into Literature*.

Call students' attention to the **Reader's Choice** selections listed at the end of each unit and show students how to find the **HMH Digital Library** in the **Reading Studio.**

TEACHER'S EDITION

GRADE 12

Program Consultants:
Kylene Beers
Martha Hougen
Elena Izquierdo
Carol Jago
Erik Palmer
Robert E. Probst

UNIT 1

Instructional Overview and Resources

		Instructional Focus	Online Ed Resources
	**Unit Introduction** **Origin of a Nation: The Anglo-Saxon and Medieval Periods**	Unit 1 Essential Question Unit 1 Academic Vocabulary	**Stream to Start:** Origin of a Nation: The Anglo-Saxon and Medieval Periods Unit 1 Response Log

ANALYZE & APPLY

	**from "Beowulf: Grendel, Beowulf, The Battle with Grendel"** Epic poem by the Beowulf Poet, translated by Seamus Heaney **Lexile N/A**	**Reading** • Analyze Characteristics of an Epic Poem • Analyze Old English Poetry **Writing:** Write a Poem **Speaking and Listening:** Present an Epic **Vocabulary:** Homophones **Language Conventions:** Mood	Audio **Close Read Screencast:** Modeled Discussion **Reading Studio:** Notice & Note **Speaking and Listening Studio:** Giving a Presentation **Vocabulary Studio:** Homophones
	from "The Canterbury Tales: The Wife of Bath's Tale" Narrative poem by Geoffrey Chaucer, translated by Nevill Coghill **Lexile N/A**	**Reading** • Analyze Structure • Analyze Narrator **Writing:** Write a Short Story **Speaking and Listening:** Present a Short Story **Vocabulary:** Usage **Language Conventions:** Inverted Sentences	Audio **Reading Studio:** Notice & Note **Writing Studio:** Writing Narratives **Speaking and Listening Studio:** Giving a Presentation **Vocabulary Studio:** Multiple-Meaning Words **Grammar Studio:** Sentence Structure
	**from "Le Morte d'Arthur"** Romance by Sir Thomas Malory, retold by Keith Baines **Lexile 1130L**	**Reading** • Analyze Conflict • Make Predictions **Writing:** Create a Hero **Speaking and Listening:** Direct a Scene **Vocabulary:** Multiple Meaning Words **Language Conventions:** Tone	Audio **Reading Studio:** Notice & Note **Writing Studio:** Writing Narratives **Speaking and Listening Studio:** Giving a Presentation **Vocabulary Studio:** Multiple-Meaning Words **Grammar Studio:** Adjectives

SUGGESTED PACING: 30 DAYS

Unit Introduction	from Beowulf: Grendel, Beowulf, The Battle with Grendel	from The Canterbury Tales: The Wife of Bath's Tale	from Le Morte d'Arthur	Chivalry
1	2 3 4 5 6 7	8 9 10	11 12 13	14 15 16

PLAN

English Learner Support	Differentiated Instruction	Assessment
• Text X-Ray • Understand New Vocabulary • Oral Assessment • Acquire New Vocabulary • Vocabulary Strategy • Language Conventions	**When Students Struggle** • Understand Characterization **To Challenge Students** • Discuss Characterization • Conduct Research	**Selection Test**
• Text X-Ray • Use Sentence Variety • Learning Strategies • Compare and Contrast • Express Feelings, Ideas, and Opinions • Vocabulary Strategy • Implicit and Explicit Language • Demonstrate Comprehension • Oral Assessment • Language Conventions	**When Students Struggle** • Understand Literary Terms • Order of Events **To Challenge Students** • Do the Research	**Selection Test**
• Text X-Ray • Acquire New Vocabulary • Confirm Understanding • Develop Fluency • Understand Idioms • Understand Prefixes • Use Visual and Contextual Support • Oral Assessment • Vocabulary Strategy • Language Conventions	**When Students Struggle** • Identify Plot Points • Summarize • Identify Conflict and Motivation • Reteaching: Analyze Conflict **To Challenge Students** • Compare Characters • Analyze Theme	**Selection Test**

from **The Paston Letters/**
from **My Syrian Diary**
17 › 18 › 19 › 20

The Wanderer/Loneliness
21 › 22 › 23 › 24 › 25

Independent Reading
26 › 27

End of Unit
28 › 29 › 30

Origin of a Nation: The Anglo-Saxon and Medieval Periods

PLAN

UNIT 1 Continued

		Instructional Focus	**Online Ed Resources**
	Mentor Text "Chivalry" Short Story by Neil Gaiman Lexile 810L	**Reading** • Analyze Characterization • Analyze Fantasy **Writing:** Write a Fantasy Scene **Speaking and Listening:** Dramatize a Fantasy Scene **Vocabulary:** Context Clues **Language Conventions:** Appositives and Appositive Phrases	**Audio** **Close Read Screencasts:** Modeled Discussion **Reading Studio:** Notice & Note **Writing Studio:** Writing as a Process **Speaking and Listening Studio:** Giving a Presentation **Vocabulary Studio:** Context Clues **Grammar Studio:** Appositives and Appositive Phrases

COLLABORATE & COMPARE

		Instructional Focus	**Online Ed Resources**
	from "The Paston Letters" Letters by the Paston family Lexile 1250L	**Reading** • Analyze Primary Sources • Make Inferences **Writing:** Write a Short Dramatic Scene **Speaking and Listening:** Enact the Scene **Vocabulary:** Consult a Dictionary **Language Conventions:** Subject-Verb Agreement	**Audio** **Reading Studio:** Notice & Note **Writing Studio:** Writing Narratives **Vocabulary Studio:** Consulting a Dictionary **Grammar Studio:** Subject-Verb Agreement
	from "My Syrian Diary" Diary by Marah Lexile 880L	**Reading** • Evaluate Author's Purpose • Connect **Writing:** Write a Compare and Contrast Essay **Speaking and Listening:** Share and Discuss Connections **Vocabulary:** Latin Roots **Language Conventions:** Formal and Informal Language	**Audio** **Reading Studio:** Notice & Note **Writing Studio:** Writing Informative Texts **Speaking and Listening Studio:** Participating in Collaborative Discussions **Vocabulary Studio:** Latin Roots
	Collaborate & Compare	**Reading:** Compare Primary Sources	
	"The Wanderer" Poem by Anonymous, translated by Burton Raffel "Loneliness" Poem by Fanny Howe	**Reading** • Analyze Tone • Monitor Comprehension **Writing:** Create an Imagery Board **Speaking and Listening:** Discuss the Poems	**Audio** **Close Read Screencast:** Modeled Discussions **Reading Studio:** Notice & Note **Speaking and Listening Studio:** Participating in Collaborative Discussions
	Collaborate & Compare	**Reading:** Compare Themes	

PLAN

English Learner Support	Differentiated Instruction	Online Ed Assessment
• Text X-Ray • Use Visual Support • Practice Appositives • Compare • Use Context • Identify • Retell • Oral Assessment	**When Students Struggle** • Contrast Realistic and Fantastical Elements • Ask Questions • Compare **To Challenge Students** • Research Legends	**Selection Test**
• Text X-Ray • Distinguish Singular and Plural Verbs • Speak Using Basic and Academic Language • Understand Subject-Verb Agreement • Demonstrate Comprehension • Make Inferences • Oral Assessment • Vocabulary Strategy • Language Conventions	**When Students Struggle** • Evaluate Types of Information • Comprehension Support • Reteaching **To Challenge Students** • Hypothesize	**Selection Test**
• Text X-Ray • Internalize Academic Vocabulary • Oral Assessment • Distinguish Formal and Informal Language	**When Students Struggle** • Summarize Details • Reteaching: Evaluate Author's Purpose **To Challenge Students** • Evaluate Author's Use of Detail	**Selection Test**
• Confirm Understanding	**When Students Struggle** • Participate in Group Discussions	
• Text X-Ray • Paraphrase Text • Understand Text Structure • Acquire Vocabulary • Understand Idioms • Oral Assessment • Use Contextural Support	**When Students Struggle** • Visualize Character • Analyze Imagery • Identify Author's Purpose • Reteaching: Analyze Tone **To Challenge Students** • Make Additional Connections	**Selection Test**
• Ask Questions	**When Students Struggle** • Visualize Key Details	

Origin of a Nation: The Anglo-Saxon and Medieval Periods

PLAN

UNIT 1 Continued

Online

INDEPENDENT READING

The Independent Reading selections are only available in the eBook.

Go to the Reading Studio for more information on NOTICE & NOTE.

Instructional Focus

 from "*Beowulf*: Grendel's Mother, The Battle with Grendel's Mother, Beowulf's Last Battle, The Death of Beowulf, Mourning Beowulf" Epic poem translated by Burton Raffel

Online Resources

 "Beowulf Is Back!" Article by James Parker
Lexile 1200L

END OF UNIT

Writing Task: Write a Short Story

Speaking Task: Create a Podcast

Reflect on the Unit

Writing: Write a Short Story
Language Conventions: Use Active and Passive Voice Appropriately
Create a Podcast

Unit 1 Response Log
Mentor Text: "Chivalry"
Writing Studio: Writing Narratives
Speaking and Listening Studio: Using Media in a Presentation
Grammar Studio: Active and Passive Voice

1E Unit 1

PLAN

English Learner Support	Differentiated Instruction	 Assessment
 "Barbara Allen" Ballad by Anonymous	 "Journeymen Keep the Medieval Past Alive" Article by Melissa Eddy **Lexile 1220L**	**Selection Tests**
END OF UNIT • Language X-Ray • Understand Academic Language • Narrate • Use the Mentor Text • Use Passive Voice • Adapt the Podcast	**When Students Struggle** • Draft the Short Story • Use the Passive Voice • Use Intonation **To Challenge Students** • Comparative Analysis	**Unit Test**

TEACH

DISCUSS THE QUOTATION

Tell students that this quotation is from *A Song of Ice and Fire* saga, a popular fantasy series set in a fictional world that was modeled in part after England. The American author George R. R. Martin drew on such parts of English history as the Wars of the Roses as inspiration for some of the events in his novels. Point out that in modern culture, knights are often portrayed as a type of hero. This quotation expresses the thought that there is more to being a hero than simply fighting enemies.

Ask students how they define the concepts of chivalry and knighthood. Have them support their definitions with examples from prior learning or popular culture.

■ English Learner Support

Use Visuals to Understand Draw students' attention to the two images on this page to help explain the concept of chivalry. Point out that the word *sword* in the quote is a metaphor for warrior-like actions. If necessary, provide definitions for the following specialized vocabulary:

- A *knight* was a soldier in the past who was usually of high social rank; defended a specific ruler; and was expected to exemplify chivalry.
- *Chivalry* was a set of ideals for knights, which included showing bravery, loyalty, honor, and courtesy to women. **SUBSTANTIAL/MODERATE**

UNIT 1

ORIGIN OF A NATION

THE ANGLO-SAXON AND MEDIEVAL PERIODS

" It is chivalry that makes a true knight, not a sword. "

—George R. R. Martin

LEARNING MINDSET

Growth Mindset Explain to students that many of the concepts introduced in the quotation and Essential Questions are complex, and they are not expected to have all the answers yet. As they read the selections, they should keep an open mind and integrate what they learn with what they may already know in order to gain a better understanding. For some students, developing a growth mindset may mean admitting that they have more to learn about a specific topic as well as opening their minds to look at questions from new perspectives.

UNIT 1

Discuss the **Essential Questions** with your whole class or in small groups. As you read Origin of a Nation, consider how the selections explore these questions.

? ESSENTIAL QUESTION:
What makes someone a hero?

As you read early British literature, you can see how ideas about heroes change over time. The Anglo-Saxon warrior Beowulf eagerly confronts monsters who test his strength and courage. For King Arthur and his knights, the challenges are more complicated. These heroes pledge themselves to uphold a code of honor, but conflicting loyalties and human flaws sometimes get in their way. How do people become heroes? What qualities do you most admire in a hero?

? ESSENTIAL QUESTION:
What is true chivalry?

During the medieval period, an honor code developed to govern behavior on the battlefield and at court. This code of chivalry presented an idealized view of brave, honest, loyal, and pious knights. They were expected to protect the weak, behave respectfully to women, and go on holy quests. Do you think anyone could fully live up to such ideals? What do we gain from reading about chivalry?

? ESSENTIAL QUESTION:
Can we control our fate?

Compared to most modern people, the Anglo-Saxons lived under very harsh conditions. They were constantly vulnerable to disease, natural disasters, and sudden acts of violence. The Anglo-Saxons believed that whatever good or bad happened to them was determined by fate. Do you think that people are generally in control of their lives, or does fate play an important role? How would a strong belief in fate affect a person's view of the future?

? ESSENTIAL QUESTION:
What happens when a society unravels?

Medieval England had a social system called feudalism, which was supposed to maintain peace and stability. However, civil war, popular uprisings, and deadly plagues often threatened the social order. What are the consequences to ordinary people when a society starts to fall apart?

TEACH

Connect to the
ESSENTIAL QUESTION

Read aloud the Essential Questions and the paragraphs that follow them. Open the discussion of each idea by having students respond to the questions that conclude each paragraph.

? ESSENTIAL QUESTION:
What makes someone a hero?

Extend the discussion to include the idea of the "flawed hero." Why do many readers (and in modern times, viewing audiences) prefer flawed heroes to flawless ones? Which types of flaws are acceptable in a hero, and which are unacceptable?

? ESSENTIAL QUESTION:
What is true chivalry?

Encourage students to think about ways in which the ideals and traditions of chivalry lasted beyond the Middle Ages. What does chivalry mean in the modern world, and how is it viewed?

? ESSENTIAL QUESTION:
Can we control our fate?

Explain to students that in psychology, a person's *locus of control* is their view of how much control they have over their life. A person with an *internal* locus of control believes that they have influence over their own actions and the events of their life. A person with an *external* locus of control believes that factors outside the self like fate and chance are the primary influences on their life. Challenge students to identify personal, social, and cultural factors that might affect whether a person develops an internal or external locus of control.

? ESSENTIAL QUESTION:
What happens when a society unravels?

Help students connect to their own lives by having them identify systems in the modern world that are designed to maintain peace and stability. How might those systems be threatened, and what might be the consequences for the students personally if modern social or governmental systems fell apart?

TEACH

THE ANGLO-SAXON AND MEDIEVAL PERIODS

The following essay provides students with a historical context for the Unit 1 selections. It presents a brief overview of England's early history and how historical events influenced the development of the English language and British literature.

The Anglo-Saxons Tell students that the origins of the King Arthur myths and legends later immortalized by the French and English writers in the 12th–15th centuries likely date back to the very beginning of the Anglo-Saxon period. When the Angles, Saxons, and other Germanic tribes began to invade England, the native Britons, perhaps led by a Celtic chieftain named Arthur, fought a series of battles against the invaders. Eventually, however, the Britons were driven to the west (Cornwall and Wales), the north (Scotland), and across the English Channel to an area of France later known as Brittany. In each of these areas, distinct cultural and linguistic differences arose that still exist.

The Norman Invasion William the Conqueror was not the only notable Norman ruler. His great-grandson, Henry Plantagenet, took the throne as Henry II and became memorable for his reform of the judicial system and his contributions to the development of English common law. Henry's grandson Richard I, known as Richard the Lion-Hearted, spent much of his reign fighting wars abroad. In Richard's absence, his younger brother John plotted against him. John later became the infamous King John, unpopular with his subjects and the villain of the Robin Hood legends.

COLLABORATIVE DISCUSSION

Ask groups to share their reasons with the class. If groups struggle, encourage them to reread the second paragraph under "The Anglo-Saxons."

THE ANGLO-SAXON AND MEDIEVAL PERIODS

When people think of the Middle Ages, they often think of elegant kings and queens in grand castles and shining knights on horseback. In reality, life was harsh, with diseases such as the Black Death taking their toll. The Middle Ages (or medieval period) in England lasted about 1,000 years, from the fall of the Roman Empire to the rise of the Renaissance. This was a time of religious, social, and political upheaval. Despite these challenges, it was also a time of cultural development. By the end of the Middle Ages (around 1485), England had established its own distinct literary tradition.

The Anglo-Saxons The Roman Empire had conquered all of the area now known as England (which they called Britania) by the year 90. By the year 200, though, the Roman Empire was in decline. Areas on the edges of the empire, like Britania, were under constant attack. One group of Germanic invaders, the Anglo-Saxons, began to conquer Britania around 450.

The Anglo-Saxons did not originally have written literature. Instead, they had poems and songs that were passed down from generation to generation orally. These poems and songs were composed in various dialects of Old English. They usually had heroic themes related to important events of the past (such as *Beowulf*) or more recent battles and victories.

In 597 a monk, later known as St. Augustine, was sent to bring Christianity to the Anglo-Saxon rulers of England. Christianity spread, and with it, written literature. Some early texts were translated from Latin into Old English, and Anglo-Saxon poems and songs were written down for the first time. Very few examples of Old English poetry remain, but those that do give evidence of the rich oral tradition that preceded them. They also show the religious shift in Anglo-Saxon culture as Christian themes were incorporated into heroic tales that referenced an older pagan era.

The Norman Invasion In 1066 Normans led by William I "The Conqueror" defeated the Anglo-Saxons at the Battle of Hastings. Soon after, William I was crowned King of England. The Normans came from Northern France, and under William I much of the nobility of England now spoke French. With the introduction of French influence, the English language continued to evolve from its Germanic roots into Early Middle English.

COLLABORATIVE DISCUSSION
In a small group, review the timeline and discuss possible reasons why there are so few literary milestones recorded for the early years in Britain.

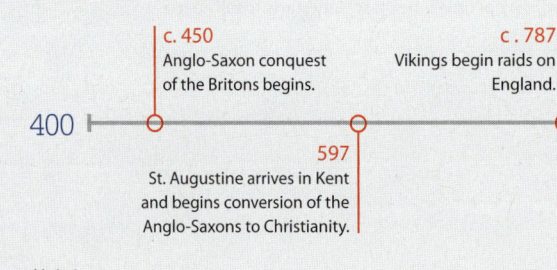

- c. 450 Anglo-Saxon conquest of the Britons begins.
- 597 St. Augustine arrives in Kent and begins conversion of the Anglo-Saxons to Christianity.
- c. 787 Vikings begin raids on England.
- c. 1000 The single surviving manuscript of *Beowulf* is copied.

2 Unit 1

 ENGLISH LEARNER SUPPORT

Build Background Knowledge To aid comprehension of the essay, provide students with the following definitions:

- *upheaval*: disruption, upset, or disturbance
- *decline*: a process of gradual deterioration or failure
- *evolve*: to undergo gradual change or development
- *alliance*: a connection between two groups that benefits both, usually socially or politically
- *pandemic*: a disease affecting a large area of the world and a large portion of the population
- *oppression*: abuse of power
- *discontent*: unhappiness and desire for better circumstances
- *revolutionize*: to bring about radical or extreme change

ALL LEVELS

2   Unit 1

Literature, too, was influenced by the blending of the Briton, Anglo-Saxon, and French cultures that followed the invasion. Nobles in the court of William I and his successors were fascinated by tales of King Arthur. These tales, based on an earlier Briton oral tradition, had been recorded by historian Geoffrey of Monmouth in his Latin work *The History of the Kings of Britain*. French poets of the 12th and 13th centuries expanded on these legends in works called romances that dealt with themes of chivalry and courtly love. Later, in the 15th century, the Arthurian romances written by the French poets were translated into English and used by Sir Thomas Malory as source material for his own versions of the legends, which remain popular to this day.

Turbulent Times Although William I's conquest of England had created ties between England and France, which had been strengthened by marriage alliances of later kings, these ties did not last. In 1337 war broke out as French and English rulers fought over control of lands on the European continent. The struggle continued on and off until roughly 1453, thereby earning the name the Hundred Years' War.

About the same time, a major event occurred that would forever change European society—the Black Death. Between 1347 and 1351, a pandemic broke out that killed an estimated one-third of Europe's total population. The sudden loss of so many lives created social instability. When combined with high taxes for the wars in France and oppression by the church and the nobility, there was widespread discontent in England's lower classes. In 1381 the Peasants' Revolt broke out. Rebels marched on London, killing several royal officials before the rebellion was put down.

RESEARCH
What about this historical period interests you? Choose a topic, event, or person to learn more about. Then add your own entry to the timeline.

Timeline:
- 1066 Norman conquest of England by William I "The Conqueror."
- 1170 Archbishop Thomas Becket is murdered in Canterbury Cathedral.
- c.1136 Geoffrey of Monmouth writes *History of the Kings of Britain* in Latin.
- 1348 The Black Death spreads throughout Europe.
- c. 1387 Geoffrey Chaucer begins work on *The Canterbury Tales*.
- c. 1450 Johannes Gutenberg develops a printing press with movable type.
- 1485 Henry Tudor defeats Richard III and becomes King Henry VII, ending the War of the Roses.
- 1500

Origin of a Nation 3

WHEN STUDENTS STRUGGLE...

Vocabulary Support Students may struggle with advanced vocabulary or subject-specific terms used in the historical background essays that begin each unit. Encourage students to start by skimming the essay to familiarize themselves with its content, marking words that they do not recognize or that are used in an unfamiliar context. Students can then consult a dictionary to clarify the vocabulary, perhaps making notes in the margin where the words are used before rereading the essay for comprehension.

TEACH

Turbulent Times The medieval church, led by the Pope in Rome, had tremendous power. It owned more land than any other entity in Europe and had the power to establish taxes, make its own laws, and run its own courts. The church held a degree of control over kings and nobles by threatening them with *excommunication*, or removal from church membership. At times, however, the church's power led to conflicts with the monarchy. When Henry II's archbishop and friend Thomas Becket began placing the church's interests over those of the crown, four knights loyal to the king murdered him in 1170. Becket was declared a saint in 1173, and his shrine at Canterbury became a popular destination for religious pilgrims like those described in *The Canterbury Tales*. Ask students to consider why the threat of excommunication was enough to keep many people loyal to the medieval church. Discuss how the power of the church and the relationship between the church and the monarchy might have affected nobles and commoners, either similarly or differently.

RESEARCH

To learn more about their chosen topic, encourage students to search for primary sources from this historical period. Have students choose excerpts from a source to present to the class.

Origin of a Nation 3

TEACH

The End of an Era The Wars of the Roses takes its name from the symbols of the two warring families, the Lancastrians and the Yorkists. The symbol of the House of York was a white rose, while the symbol of the House of Lancaster was a red rose. Henry Tudor, who became King Henry VII when he ascended the throne in 1485, was from the House of Lancaster. He united the two families by marrying Elizabeth of York in 1486.

CHECK YOUR UNDERSTANDING

Have students answer the questions independently.

Answers:

1. B
2. H
3. D

If students answer any question incorrectly, have them reread the text to confirm their understanding.

Although the Peasants' Revolt ultimately failed, it was against this backdrop of social unrest that many major works of Middle English literature were written. Chaucer, for instance, was likely living in London and employed by the court of King Richard II at the time. Later that same decade, he would begin writing his best-known works, including *The Canterbury Tales*.

The End of an Era In 1455 a civil war known as The War of the Roses broke out in England, as two branches of the royal family struggled for control. In 1485 Henry VII defeated Richard II to ascend to the throne. Some historians use this event to mark the end of the Middle Ages in England. Over the course of a millennium, English literature had developed from a small collection of Old English poems, based on an earlier oral tradition, to a much larger body of poetry and prose that reflected the political, cultural, and linguistic shifts in English society. As England moved from the Middle Ages into the Renaissance, the introduction of printing presses with movable type promised to revolutionize reading, writing, and literature in ways that could not yet be imagined.

CHECK YOUR UNDERSTANDING

Chose the best answer to each question.

1. Which event most directly affected the rise of written literature in England?
   - A The conquest of the Britons by the Romans
   - B The spread of Christianity
   - C The conquest of the Anglo-Saxons by the Normans
   - D The development of printing with movable type

2. Which was a result of the Norman conquest of England?
   - F Written literature replacing the oral tradition
   - G The death of one-third of the population
   - H Blending of Anglo-Saxon and French cultures and languages
   - J Widespread social unrest and revolt

3. Which factor did **not** contribute to unrest among the lower classes in the late Middle Ages?
   - A Black Death
   - B Hundred Years' War
   - C Oppression by the church
   - D Conquest by invading armies

ACADEMIC VOCABULARY

Academic Vocabulary words are words you use when you discuss and write about texts. In this unit, you will learn the following five words:

- ☑ collapse
- ☐ displace
- ☐ military
- ☐ violate
- ☐ visual

Study the Word Network to learn more about the word **collapse**.

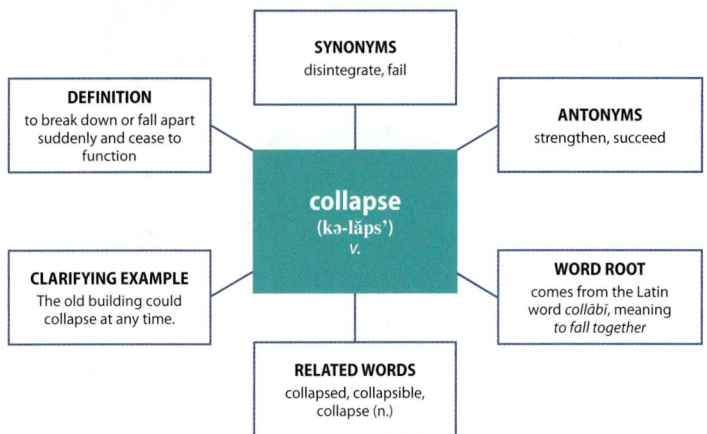

Write and Discuss Discuss the completed Word Network with a partner, making sure to talk through all of the boxes until you both understand the word, its synonyms, antonyms, and related forms. Then, fill out a Word Network for the remaining four words. Use a dictionary or online resource to help you complete the activity.

 Go online to access the Word Networks.

RESPOND TO THE ESSENTIAL QUESTION

In this unit, you will explore four different **Essential Questions** about English literature of the Middle Ages and other related texts. As you read each selection, you will gather your ideas about one of these questions and write about it in a **Response Log**. At the end of the unit, you will have the opportunity to write a **short story** about what makes someone a hero. Filling out the Response Log after you read each text will help you prepare for this writing task.

 You can also go online to access the Response Log.

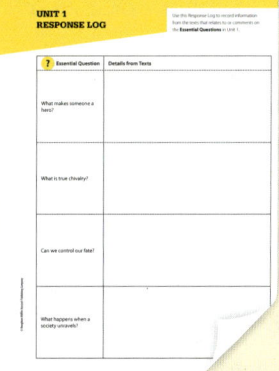

TEACH

ACADEMIC VOCABULARY

Have students complete Word Networks for the remaining four vocabulary words. Encourage them to include all the categories shown in the sample Word Network if possible, but point out that some words do not have clear synonyms or antonyms.

collapse (kə-lăps´) *v.* to break down or fall apart suddenly and cease to function

displace (dĭs-plās´) *v.* to move, shift, or force from the usual place or position (Spanish cognate: *desplazar*)

military (mĭl´ĭ-tĕr´ē) *n.* the armed forces of a nation considered collectively (Spanish cognate: *militar*) *adj.* of, related to, or characteristic of members of the armed forces

violate (vī´ə-lāt´) *tr. v.* to disregard or act in a manner that does not conform to (a law or promise, for example) (Spanish cognate: *violar*)

visual (vĭzh´ōō-əl) *adj.* seen or able to be seen by the eye; visible (Spanish cognate: *visual*)

RESPOND TO THE ESSENTIAL QUESTION

Direct students to the Unit 1 Response Log. Explain that students will use it to record ideas and details from the selections that help answer one of the Essential Questions. When they work on the Writing Task at the end of the unit, their Response Logs will help them think about what they have read and make connections between the texts.

PLAN

BEOWULF
Epic Poem by the Beowulf Poet

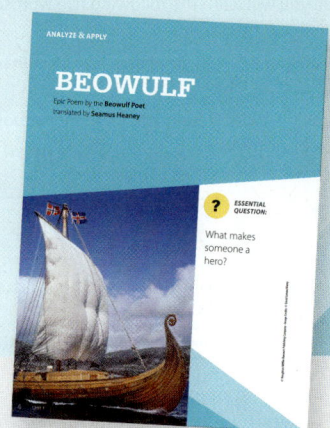

GENRE ELEMENTS
EPIC POETRY

Tell students that the word *epic* lets them know this poem will be a long narrative about grand, heroic events. All **epic poems** are stories, and they often contain similar elements, such as character, setting, plot, tone, conflict, and dialogue. Like most stories, the plots of epic poems often contain rising action, climax, and resolution. Subheads in this epic poem tell which main character or what event each section is about. In this lesson, students will identify and analyze characteristics of an epic poem as well as the techniques of Old English poetry.

LEARNING OBJECTIVES

- Analyze characteristics of epic poems and the techniques of Old English poetry.
- Conduct research about epic poems of various cultures.
- Write a poem about a person with strong ideals and values.
- Present a dramatic passage with appropriate expression.
- Use context to distinguish homophones.
- Identify and apply devices that create mood.
- **Language** Express how words and phrases create specific images and emotions.

TEXT COMPLEXITY

Quantitative Measures	**Beowulf**	Lexile: N/A
Qualitative Measures	**Ideas Presented** Subtle, implied meanings and multiple themes.	
	Structures Used More complex, with support through subheads.	
	Language Used Complex sentence structures with archaic and formal language.	
	Knowledge Required Cultural or historical references and literary techniques may make heavier demands.	

PLAN

RESOURCES

Online

- Unit 1 Response Log
- Selection Audio
- Close Read Screencasts: Modeled Discussions
- Reading Studio: Notice & Note
- Level Up Tutorials: Character Traits
- Speaking and Listening Studio: Giving a Presentation
- Vocabulary Studio: Homophones
- Grammar Studio: Module 8 Lesson 8: Mood
- *Beowulf* Selection Test

SUMMARIES

English

In this excerpt, the warriors of the kingdom of the Danes are in constant, mortal danger from the monster, Grendel. Grendel comes out at night from his lair in the lowland, marshy areas to wreak destruction and ruin. In time, he meets his match in Beowulf, who fights the monster using an unexpected tactic.

Spanish

En este pasaje, los guerreros del reino de Danos estaban en constante y mortal peligro por el monstruo Grendel. Grendel sale de su guarida en las tierras bajas y pantanosas durante la noche para sembrar destrucción y ruina. Con el tiempo, consigue a un contrincante en Beowulf, quien lucha contra el monstruo usando una táctica inesperada.

SMALL-GROUP OPTIONS

Have students work in small groups and pairs to read and discuss the selection.

Activating Academic Vocabulary

- Provide a list of academic vocabulary words and phrases, such as: *character, character development, plot, rising action, conflict, climax, resolution, central idea, dialogue, descriptive language,* and *context.*
- After reading 10–20 lines, model how to use one or more academic vocabulary words and phrases to discuss the text.
- Encourage students to use the academic vocabulary as they discuss and write about the text.

Jigsaw with Experts

- Divide the text into three parts, with each subheading being one part.
- Have students count off, or assign students a numbered section.
- After reading the text, have students form groups with other students who read the same section. Each expert group should discuss its section. Encourage them to use academic vocabulary.
- Then, have students form new groups with a representative from each section. These groups should discuss all the sections and the selection as a whole.

Beowulf 6B

PLAN

Text X-Ray: English Learner Support
for *Beowulf*

Use the Text X-Ray and the supports and scaffolds in the Teacher's Edition to help guide students at different proficiency levels through the selection.

INTRODUCE THE SELECTION
DISCUSS SUPERNATURAL AND REALISTIC ELEMENTS

In this lesson, students will need to be able to distinguish between supernatural and realistic elements. Provide the following explanations:

- A supernatural element is something that is magical and not part of ordinary life.
- A realistic element is anything that can be part of normal life.

Explain to students that because this is an epic poem, it will contain supernatural elements as well as realistic ones.

Ask students to explain why certain elements are supernatural and why others are realistic. Provide sentence frames, such as: _____ *is a supernatural element in the poem because it is impossible to* _____. *I know that* _____ *is realistic because people in real life often* _____.

CULTURAL REFERENCES

The following words or phrases may be unfamiliar to students:

- *Almighty, Creator, Eternal Lord* (lines 7, 21, 23): names that refer to God
- *set out* (line 30): to begin a trip
- *numb with grief* (line 49): so shocked and upset it may not be possible to feel any emotion
- *nowhere to turn* (line 101): there is no way to solve a problem

LISTENING

Identify Mood

Remind students that epic poems often use word choice, alliteration, and imagery to create the mood, or emotions the author wants readers to have. Remind students that alliteration is the repetition of consonant sounds at the beginnings of words, and that imagery creates vivid pictures in readers' minds.

Have students listen as you read lines 45 through 58. Use the following supports with students at varying proficiency levels:

- Have students write separate index cards for the terms *alliteration*, *imagery*, and *word choice*. As you read examples of each, have students hold up the appropriate card. **SUBSTANTIAL**
- As you read the text, pause and repeat examples of alliteration, imagery, and word choice. Then, have students use sentence frames to repeat each example, such as _____ *is an example of alliteration*. (*storied leader sat stricken* and *helpless, humiliated*) **MODERATE**
- After listening to the text, have partners ask and answer questions about the use of alliteration, imagery, and word choice. For example: *How did the word* _____ *make you feel? What picture did you see in your mind when you heard the phrase* _____? **LIGHT**

PLAN

SPEAKING

Analyze Theme

Tell students that the theme in *Beowulf* is universal because it is a life lesson that can be found in the literature of many cultures and time periods. Have students discuss the theme of *Beowulf*.

Use the following supports with students at varying proficiency levels:

- Display and read aloud statements about the poem's theme, such as: *One theme of this poem is about the clash between good and evil. The good Beowulf fights the evil Grendel.* Have students copy the statements and practice saying them aloud to a partner. **SUBSTANTIAL**
- Provide sentence frames for students to use as they discuss the poem's theme or themes. For example: *One theme of this poem is _____. The character _____ represents _____. One event in the poem that shows an example of the theme is _____.* **MODERATE**
- Have partners state the main theme of the poem. Then, have them take turns describing examples from the text that help show this theme. **LIGHT**

READING

Use Context to Define Homophones

Remind students that homophones are words that sound the same but are spelled differently and have different meanings. Have students use context clues to define homophones in the poem.

Use the following supports with students of varying proficiency levels:

- Help students reread lines 1–3. Point out *through* and *hear* and write their homophones on the board (*threw, here*). Define all the homophones, and then ask questions, such as: *Where is the demon prowler going? (through the dark) What does he hear? (a loud banquet)* **SUBSTANTIAL**
- Have pairs reread lines 1–3. Write *threw* and *here* on the board and have them find the corresponding homophones in the text. Then, have students identify and discuss context clues that helped them know the meanings of *through* and *hear*. **MODERATE**
- Provide this word list and have students find the corresponding homophones in lines 1–15: *threw, here, maid, plane, son, sew, four, their, won*. Have partners discuss context clues that help them know the meanings of the homophones in the text. **LIGHT**

WRITING

Write a Poem

Help students understand that a cohesive story in a poem will have a beginning, middle, and end.

Use the following supports with students of varying proficiency levels:

- Help students create a three-row chart labeled *Beginning, Middle,* and *End*. Work with students to add phrases to the chart to help organize their poem. For example: *Beginning: introduce character; state character's values and ideals. Middle: character takes action; why I admire character. End: what happens to character.* Have students add the phrases to their charts. **SUBSTANTIAL**
- Have students create a three-row chart labeled *Beginning, Middle,* and *End*. Tell students to write short phrases in each row describing what will happen in this part of their poem. Have pairs check each other's work for correct spelling. **MODERATE**
- Have students write an outline to show what will be included in the poem's beginning, middle, and end. Guide them to include as many specific details as they can in each section. **LIGHT**

TEACH

? Connect to the ESSENTIAL QUESTION

Discuss the essential question with the class. Have students offer examples of qualities or behaviors that make someone heroic. Compile these items in a list, and then have students look for similarities or differences between the qualities or behaviors they listed. Remind students to look for heroic qualities in the characters in *Beowulf*.

ANALYZE & APPLY

BEOWULF

Epic Poem by the **Beowulf Poet**
translated by **Seamus Heaney**

? ESSENTIAL QUESTION:

What makes someone a hero?

  LEARNING MINDSET

Setting Goals Tell students that setting goals is an important part of developing a learning mindset. Setting goals enables students to plan for success and allows them to track their progress along the way. Discuss setting goals for reading self-selected texts outside of class, such as reading for a certain amount of time or number of pages each day.

GET READY

QUICK START

Think about one of your personal heroes. What characteristics does he or she possess? Write these characteristics in a list that can be shared with your class.

ANALYZE CHARACTERISTICS OF AN EPIC POEM

An **epic poem** is a long narrative poem that celebrates a hero's deeds. Traditional epics, such as *Beowulf*, began as oral poems retold over many generations before they were finally written down. Epic poems share certain characteristics and conventions, which are listed under Genre Elements. Use a chart like this one to help you analyze the characteristics of *Beowulf*.

QUESTIONS	ANSWERS FROM THE POEM
What qualities does the hero display?	*Beowulf displays bravery, strength, and a desire to face a difficult challenge.*
What obstacles must the hero overcome?	*Beowulf must defeat a powerful and evil monster.*
What themes does the epic convey?	*The main themes in the poem are the clash between good and evil and the ultimate triumph of goodness.*
What elements of epic style does the poem include?	*The poem includes a hero who embodies a culture, a supernatural villain, and the universal theme of good vs. evil.*

GENRE ELEMENTS: EPIC POETRY

- written about a hero, who is usually a strong, courageous person of nobility
- usually involves supernatural creatures, great deeds, and perilous journeys
- imbues the hero with traits that reflect the ideals of the larger culture
- conveys universal themes found in the literature of all time periods and cultures, such as good versus evil
- often features long speeches, as well as formal diction and a serious tone

ANALYZE OLD ENGLISH POETRY

Anglo-Saxon poets used techniques that made their verses easier to chant. This chart describes important techniques found in *Beowulf*.

TECHNIQUE	EXAMPLE
Alliteration is the repetition of consonant sounds at the beginning of words. This device helps unify the lines.	In **H**is **s**plendour **H**e **s**et the sun and the moon
The poem's strong **rhythm** is created by four stresses, or beats, in many lines.	´ ´ ´ ´ Sometimes at pagan shrines they vowed
A **caesura** is a pause that divides the line, with each part having two stresses. Usually, at least one stressed syllable in the first part alliterates with a stressed syllable in the second part.	´ ´ ´ ´ When he heard about Grendel // Hygelac's thane ´ ´ ´ ´ Was on home ground // over in Geatland.
Kennings are metaphorical compound words or phrases substituted for simple nouns.	The kenning "Hygelac's trusty retainer" is used in place of the name Beowulf, and "dread of the land" is used in place of the name Grendel.

Beowulf 7

TEACH

QUICK START

Have students name three to five heroic characters. Refer to the list of heroic qualities compiled previously and ask students to match up qualities with the heroes they named. Add any new qualities that may be discussed to the list.

ANALYZE CHARACTERISTICS OF AN EPIC POEM

Review the list of characteristics of an **epic poem** under Genre Elements. Define any terms that are unfamiliar to students, and make sure they understand each item. Ask them to list any stories, movies, television series, or video games that have some epic qualities. Then, explain that *Beowulf* tells the story of a hero who battles two supernatural monsters. As they read the text, have students check their comprehension by discussing, with partners, the elements of the story that are supernatural and those that are realistic. *(Some examples of supernatural elements include Grendel's carrying off and consuming thirty men at once and the way Grendel uses magic to make weapons ineffective against him.)*

ANALYZE OLD ENGLISH POETRY

After reviewing the literary techniques defined in the chart, focus on the following passages:

- Lines 109–116: Ask students to identify who the "he" is in line 109 *(Beowulf)*, as well as the **kenning** that renames him *(Hygelac's thane)*. Ask a volunteer to create a sentence using the **kenning** as the subject.

- Lines 216–224: Ask students to identify examples of **alliteration.** *(fighters/flushed, pledge/protect, wait/whetted, dawn/day, blood-spattered/bench, floor/feasted, slick/slaughter, faithful/following)*

- Lines 390–397: Read this sentence aloud, emphasizing the **rhythm** of four beats per line. Discuss where each pause, or **caesura,** occurs, and have students point out **alliteration.**

Beowulf 7

TEACH

CRITICAL VOCABULARY

Encourage students to read all the sentences before deciding which word best completes each one. Remind them to look for context clues that match the precise meaning of each word.

Answers:

1. unrelenting
2. loathsome
3. aghast
4. wail
5. affliction
6. baleful
7. plight

LANGUAGE CONVENTIONS

To help students understand the impact of language on the **mood** of a text, write this sentence on the board:

The people were happy until an evil beast began to do terrible things.

Then, compare the sentence to the one found in lines 14–16.

ANNOTATION MODEL

Remind students of annotation methods, and explain that they may use their own system for marking up the selection in their write-in text. Their notes in the margin may include questions about ideas that are unclear or topics they want to learn more about. Point out that annotations can be used to identify elements of poetic style, like **caesura** and word choice.

 **GET READY**

CRITICAL VOCABULARY

| aghast | unrelenting | affliction | plight |
| baleful | wail | loathsome | |

To see how many Critical Vocabulary words you already know, use them to complete the sentences.

1. No matter what he tried, he couldn't make the _____ buzzing noise in his head go away.
2. The hero of the story defeated a murderous and _____ monster.
3. He was _____ at the number of casualties that occurred.
4. The village dogs began to _____ in unison at the full moon.
5. The tremors he experienced were side effects of a crippling _____.
6. Her _____ glance was brief, but it made the frightened child retreat.
7. After all of her good fortune in previous years, who could have predicted her unfortunate _____?

LANGUAGE CONVENTIONS

Mood Mood is the feeling or atmosphere that a writer creates for a reader. Poets may use imagery, alliteration, figurative language, descriptions, word order, and word choices to create this atmosphere. The use of these literary elements sets the mood by evoking feelings in the reader.

ANNOTATION MODEL   NOTICE & NOTE

As you read this epic poem out loud, you will recognize many examples of poetic techniques of Old English poetry. This model shows one reader's notes about this excerpt from *Beowulf*.

> Then a powerful demon, a prowler through the dark,
> nursed a hard grievance. It harrowed him
> to hear the din of the loud banquet
> every day in the hall, the harp being struck
> and the clear song of a skilled poet
> telling with mastery of man's beginnings,
> how the Almighty had made the earth

These are examples of caesuras. I pause in the middle of each line, and each part has two stressed syllables.

Word choices create the mood of a crowded, noisy banquet hall.

8   Unit 1

BACKGROUND

In large gathering halls like the one featured in Beowulf, poet-singers provided entertainment to the Anglo-Saxon warriors. They told tales of courage and valor, celebrating great heroes. Sometime between the seventh and ninth centuries, an unknown poet consolidated the oral accounts of Beowulf, the hero who is the subject of this poem. This is the Anglo-Saxon epic that survives today, a testament to the belief that these great warriors would be remembered long after their society disintegrated. Though the poem is translated from Old English, the characteristics of the original poetry remain.

BEOWULF
Epic Poem by the Beowulf Poet
translated by Seamus Heaney

The Angles and the Saxons, as well as other Germanic tribes, came to England from northern Europe starting in the middle of the fifth century. Their culture became the basis for English culture, and their languages fused into Old English, the Anglo-Saxon language. They struggled to survive the challenges presented by nature and were frequently threatened by wars against new invaders. Anglo-Saxons lived communally for protection, loyal to their feudal lords and to their families. They believed in wyrd, or fate, rather than in an afterlife, but they hoped that acquiring fame and treasure through acts of valor would give them a kind of immortality. In this they were aided by the highly valued poets, since their poems passed down the history of the Anglo-Saxon people and taught their values.

By the time the epic Beowulf was written down by a monk in the beginning of the eleventh century, the Anglo-Saxons had converted to Christianity. Thus, in the final version of the poem, Christian references are mingled with the original pagan beliefs.

In this excerpt, the warriors of the kingdom of the Danes are in constant mortal danger from the monster Grendel. Grendel comes out at night from his lair in the lowland, marshy areas to wreak destruction and ruin. In time, he meets his match in Beowulf, who fights the monster using an unexpected tactic.

TEACH

BACKGROUND

Have students read the background on *Beowulf*. Then, explain that, although the poem was composed in England during the Anglo-Saxon age, it is set in sixth-century Scandinavia. Tell students that Beowulf, the hero of the epic, is a Geat, a people who lived in what is now Sweden. He travels to Denmark to help the Danes, who are being terrorized by the monster Grendel. Then, having won fame, he returns home and becomes the king of the Geats, succeeding his uncle.

Explain to students that there is only one historical copy of *Beowulf* in existence. Scholars believe that it dates from the eleventh century. Several individual owners, in turn, had the manuscript in their collections. In 1702, it was given to the nation of Great Britain, but in 1731, a fire broke out where the manuscript was being stored. Thankfully, it escaped relatively unscathed, but time and handling have led to deterioration. To preserve it, it was placed in frames in 1845. The manuscript is now part of the British Library's permanent collection.

TEACH

SETTING A PURPOSE

Direct students to use the Setting a Purpose prompt to focus their reading.

 For **reading** and **speaking support** for students at varying proficiency levels, see the **Text X-Ray** on page 6D.

✏️ ANALYZE CHARACTERISTICS OF AN EPIC POEM

Remind students that universal themes are themes that are easily recognizable because they are repeated across many cultures and contexts. (**Answer:** *These lines describe the universal theme of a struggle between good and evil.*)

 ENGLISH LEARNER SUPPORT

Understand New Vocabulary Help students identify the meanings of words or phrases that they may not be familiar with:

- harrowed (line 2): distressed, or disturbed painfully
- din (line 3): loud noise
- Almighty, Creator, Eternal Lord (lines 7, 21, 23): names that refer to God
- quickened (line 12): gave life to
- set out (line 30): began a trip **SUBSTANTIAL**

✏️ **NOTICE & NOTE**

Notice & Note
Use the side margins to notice and note signposts in the text.

ANALYZE CHARACTERISTICS OF AN EPIC POEM
Annotate: Mark words and phrases in lines 14–29 that give clues about one of this epic poem's universal themes.

Analyze: What is the universal theme described by these lines?

18 marches: borders or boundaries of a country or an area of land.

18 heath: an extensive tract of uncultivated open land covered with herbage and low shrubs; a moor.

19 fens: areas of low wet land having peaty soil.

21 Cain: the eldest son of Adam and Eve. According to the Bible (Genesis 4), he murdered his younger brother, Abel.

SETTING A PURPOSE
As you read, pay attention to the ways the poet uses language and poetic techniques and elements to enhance the telling of Beowulf's heroic deeds.

Grendel

Then a powerful demon, a prowler through the dark,
nursed a hard grievance. It harrowed him
to hear the din of the loud banquet
every day in the hall, the harp being struck
5 and the clear song of a skilled poet
telling with mastery of man's beginnings,
how the Almighty had made the earth
a gleaming plain girdled with waters;
in His splendour He set the sun and the moon
10 to be earth's lamplight, lanterns for men,
and filled the broad lap of the world
with branches and leaves; and quickened life
in every other thing that moved.

So times were pleasant for the people there
15 until finally one, a fiend out of hell,
began to work his evil in the world.
Grendel was the name of this grim demon
haunting the marches, marauding round the heath
and the desolate fens; he had dwelt for a time
20 in misery among the banished monsters,
Cain's clan, whom the Creator had outlawed
and condemned as outcasts. For the killing of Abel
the Eternal Lord had exacted a price:
Cain got no good from committing that murder
25 because the Almighty made him anathema
and out of the curse of his exile there sprang
ogres and elves and evil phantoms
and the giants too who strove with God
time and again until He gave them their reward.

30 So, after nightfall, Grendel set out
for the lofty house, to see how the Ring-Danes
were settling into it after their drink,
and there he came upon them, a company of the best
asleep from their feasting, insensible to pain
35 and human sorrow. Suddenly then
the God-cursed brute was creating havoc:
greedy and grim, he grabbed thirty men
from their resting places and rushed to his lair,

10 Unit 1

CLOSE READ SCREENCAST

Modeled Discussion Have students view the Close Read Screencast in their eBook in which readers discuss and annotate lines 41–51, the aftermath of one of Grendel's attacks.

As a class, view and discuss this video. Then, have students pair up to do an independent close read. Students can record their answers on the Close Read Practice PDF.

 Close Read Practice PDF

NOTICE & NOTE

flushed up and inflamed from the raid,
40 blundering back with the butchered corpses.

Then as dawn brightened and the day broke
Grendel's powers of destruction were plain:
their wassail was over, they wept to heaven
and mourned under morning. Their mighty prince,
45 the storied leader, sat stricken and helpless,
humiliated by the loss of his guard,
bewildered and stunned, staring **aghast**
at the demon's trail, in deep distress.
He was numb with grief, but got no respite
50 for one night later merciless Grendel
struck again with more gruesome murders.
Malignant by nature, he never showed remorse.
It was easy then to meet with a man
shifting himself to a safer distance
55 to bed in the bothies, for who could be blind
to the evidence of his eyes, the obviousness
of that hall-watcher's hate? Whoever escaped
kept a weather-eye open and moved away.

So Grendel ruled in defiance of right,
60 one against all, until the greatest house
in the world stood empty, a deserted wallstead.
For twelve winters, seasons of woe,
the lord of the Shieldings suffered under
his load of sorrow; and so, before long,
65 the news was known over the whole world.
Sad lays were sung about the beset king,
the vicious raids and ravages of Grendel,
his long and **unrelenting** feud,
nothing but war; how he would never
70 parley or make peace with any Dane
nor stop his death-dealing nor pay the death-price.
No counsellor could ever expect
fair reparation from those rabid hands.
All were endangered; young and old
75 were hunted down by that <u>dark death-shadow</u>
who lurked and swooped in the long nights
on the misty moors; nobody knows
where these reavers from hell roam on their errands.

So Grendel waged his lonely war,
80 inflicting constant cruelties on the people,
atrocious hurt. He took over Heorot,

aghast
(ə-găst´) *adj.* struck by shock, terror, or amazement.

ANALYZE OLD ENGLISH POETRY
Annotate: Kennings are often more descriptive than simple nouns. Mark the kenning in line 75.

Interpret: How does kenning help readers visualize Grendel?

unrelenting
(ŭn´rĭ-lĕn´tĭng) *adj.* having or exhibiting uncompromising determination; unyielding.

73 **reparation:** something done to make amends for loss or suffering. In Germanic society, someone who killed another person was generally expected to make a payment to the victim's family as a way of restoring peace.

Beowulf 11

TEACH

✏️ ANALYZE OLD ENGLISH POETRY

Remind students of the definition of **kennings** (metaphorical compound words or phrases substituted for simple nouns). Tell students that **kennings** identify important qualities of, or details about, a character. (**Answer:** *The kenning "dark death-shadow" depicts Grendel as a terrifying dark gray or black figure.*)

 For **listening support** for students at varying proficiency levels, see the **Text X-Ray** on page 6C.

CRITICAL VOCABULARY

aghast: The king of the Danes was aghast, or in shock, after Grendel raided his hall.

ASK STUDENTS what Grendel did that made the king aghast. (*He murdered thirty of the king's men in a single night.*)

unrelenting: Grendel was unrelenting, or unyielding, in his behavior toward the Danes.

ASK STUDENTS which phrases in the poem illustrate ways in which Grendel was unrelenting. (*Phrases that show that Grendel was unrelenting include "nothing but war, would never parley, or make peace with any Dane, nor stop his death-dealing, nor pay the death-price, No counselor could ever expect fair reparation, All were endangered."*)

Beowulf **11**

WHEN STUDENTS STRUGGLE...

Understand Characterization To help students understand the significance of the first two stanzas on this page, draw a two-column chart with the headings "Grendel" and "Heorot." Read aloud lines 1–2 and 15–29. Ask students what they learn about Grendel. Encourage them to use phrases from the text. Write their responses in the appropriate column on the chart. Repeat the process for "Heorot."

 For additional support, go to the **Reading Studio** and assign the following 📶 **Level Up tutorial: Character Traits.**

TEACH

ANALYZE CHARACTERISTICS OF AN EPIC POEM

Tell students to remember that heroic characters embody the cultural values of the author. The *Beowulf* poet came from a culture that admired physical strength, bravery, decisiveness, leadership, and nobility. (**Answer:** *The king needs defenders, or help, and Beowulf is influential and powerful enough to provide it.*)

■ English Learner Support

Acquire New Vocabulary Create a semantic web using the word *high-born* (line 113). Place the word *high-born* in the middle of a circle and have students connect synonyms such as *noble, royal,* or *wealthy* to it. Then, have them write a definition based on their web. (**high-born** – *of noble or royal birth, belonging to an aristocracy*) **MODERATE**

CRITICAL VOCABULARY

affliction: Although the word *affliction* is most commonly associated with a disease or malady, in this poem, it refers to a national crisis that is causing deep pain for the king.

ASK STUDENTS to describe the nature of the affliction that Hrothgar is suffering from. (*Hrothgar is suffering from the loss of his men and from the fear that he will not be able to stop Grendel.*)

NOTICE & NOTE

haunted the glittering hall after dark,
but the throne itself, the treasure-seat,
he was kept from approaching; he was the Lord's outcast.

85 These were hard times, heart-breaking
for the prince of the Shieldings; powerful counsellors,
the highest in the land, would lend advice,
plotting how best the bold defenders
might resist and beat off sudden attacks.
90 Sometimes at pagan shrines they vowed
offerings to idols, swore oaths
that the killer of souls might come to their aid
and save the people. That was their way,
their heathenish hope; deep in their hearts

95 The Almighty Judge: These references to God show the influence of Christianity on the *Beowulf* poet.

95 they remembered hell. The Almighty Judge
of good deeds and bad, the Lord God,
Head of the Heavens and High King of the World,
was unknown to them. Oh, cursed is he
who in time of trouble has to thrust his soul
100 in the fire's embrace, forfeiting help;
he has nowhere to turn. But blessed is he
who after death can approach the Lord
and find friendship in the Father's embrace.

affliction
(ə-flĭk´shən) *n.* something that causes suffering or pain.

So that troubled time continued, woe
105 that never stopped, steady **affliction**
for Halfdane's son, too hard an ordeal.
There was panic after dark, people endured
raids in the night, riven by the terror.

Beowulf

109 Hygelac's thane: a warrior loyal to Hygelac, king of the Geats (and Beowulf's uncle).

ANALYZE CHARACTERISTICS OF AN EPIC POEM
Annotate: Mark words and phrases in lines 109–124 that characterize Beowulf as a hero.

Infer: What is the hero's motivation to go on this quest?

When he heard about Grendel, Hygelac's thane
110 was on home ground, over in Geatland.
There was no one else like him alive.
In his day, he was the mightiest man on earth,
high-born and powerful. He ordered a boat
that would ply the waves. He announced his plan:
115 to sail the swan's road and search out that king,
the famous prince who needed defenders.
Nobody tried to keep him from going,
no elder denied him, dear as he was to them.
Instead, they inspected omens and spurred
120 his ambition to go, whilst he moved about
like the leader he was, enlisting men,
the best he could find; with fourteen others

12 Unit 1

TO CHALLENGE STUDENTS . . .

Discuss Characterization Ask students to address these questions in small groups:

Do you think Beowulf, Hrothgar, and Grendel are "types" in the sense that they are either all good or all bad? Does the poet portray them as characters with more than one dimension? What tone does the poet use to describe each character? What **kennings** and other descriptive words are used to develop an image of each character? What details reveal the traits of each character? What is each character's function in the poem?

Have students share their conclusions with the class.

the warrior boarded the boat as captain,
a canny pilot along coast and currents. . . .

                    At the door of the hall,
125 Wulfgar duly delivered the message:
"My lord, the conquering king of the Danes,
bids me announce that he knows your ancestry;
also that he welcomes you here to Heorot
and salutes your arrival from across the sea.
130 You are free now to move forward
to meet Hrothgar, in helmets and armour,
but shields must stay here and spears be stacked
until the outcome of the audience is clear."

The hero arose, surrounded closely
135 by his powerful thanes. A party remained
under orders to keep watch on the arms;
the rest proceeded, led by their prince
under Heorot's roof. And standing on the hearth
in webbed links that the smith had woven,
140 the fine-forged mesh of his gleaming mail-shirt,
resolute in his helmet, Beowulf spoke:
"Greetings to Hrothgar. I am Hygelac's kinsman,
one of his hall-troop. When I was younger,
I had great triumphs. Then news of Grendel,
145 hard to ignore, reached me at home:
sailors brought stories of the **plight** you suffer
in this legendary hall, how it lies deserted,
empty and useless once the evening light
hides itself under heaven's dome.
150 So every elder and experienced councilman
among my people supported my resolve
to come here to you, King Hrothgar,
because all knew of my awesome strength.
They had seen me boltered in the blood of enemies
155 when I battled and bound five beasts,
raided a troll-nest and in the night-sea
slaughtered sea-brutes. I have suffered extremes
and avenged the Geats (their enemies brought it
upon themselves, I devastated them).
160 Now I mean to be a match for Grendel,
settle the outcome in single combat.
And so, my request, O king of Bright-Danes,
dear prince of the Shieldings, friend of the people
and their ring of defence, my one request
165 is that you won't refuse me, who have come this far,

NOTICE & NOTE

LANGUAGE CONVENTIONS
Annotate: Mark the words or phrases in lines 134–141 describing Beowulf.
Analyze: What mood is created by the poet's word choice?

140 mail-shirt: flexible body armor made of metal links or overlapping metal scales.

plight
(plīt) *n.* a situation, especially a bad or unfortunate one.

Beowulf 13

TEACH

LANGUAGE CONVENTIONS

Suggest to students that there are many words the poet could have chosen instead of the ones he did. Suggest that by using different words, the poet could have changed the **mood.** Tell them to consider what impression is created by the words describing Beowulf. (**Answer:** *The mood the author sets is one of significance and hopefulness.*)

IMPROVE READING FLUENCY

Targeted Passage Have students work with partners to read lines 134–149. First, use lines 125–133 to model how to read using the correct **rhythm,** intonation, and emphasis. Have students follow along in their books as you read. Then, have partners take turns reading lines 134–141 and then lines 142–149 to each other. Encourage students to provide feedback and support for pronunciation and meter. Remind students that when they are reading aloud for an audience, they should pace their reading so the audience has time to understand difficult concepts.

 Go to the **Reading Studio** for additional support in developing fluency.

CRITICAL VOCABULARY

plight: Beowulf came to help King Hrothgar in his plight, or unfortunate situation.

ASK STUDENTS to describe the plight that Hrothgar was facing. (*Due to Grendel's raids, Hrothgar's hall was deserted, empty, and useless every night.*)

Beowulf 13

TEACH

MEMORY MOMENT

Help students use context clues to determine that Ecgtheow (line 207) is the name of Beowulf's father. (**Answer:** *Hrothgar is glad to welcome Beowulf to his lands, in part because he had known Beowulf's father.*)

ENGLISH LEARNER SUPPORT

Acquire New Vocabulary Remind students that many English words have multiple meanings, depending upon the context in which they appear. Ask students to work in pairs to look up each of the following words in a dictionary to determine the meaning that best fits the context of the poem:

heighten (line 170)

just (line 176)

flush (line 200)

sway (line 201)

Ask volunteers to define each word for the class.

MODERATE

 **NOTICE & NOTE**

the privilege of purifying Heorot,
with my own men to help me, and nobody else.
I have heard moreover that the monster scorns
in his reckless way to use weapons;
170 therefore, to heighten Hygelac's fame
and gladden his heart, I hereby renounce
sword and the shelter of the broad shield,
the heavy war-board: hand-to-hand
is how it will be, a life-and-death
175 fight with the fiend. Whichever one death fells
must deem it a just judgement by God.
If Grendel wins, it will be a gruesome day;
he will glut himself on the Geats in the war-hall,
swoop without fear on that flower of manhood
180 as on others before. Then my face won't be there
to be covered in death: he will carry me away
as he goes to ground, gorged and bloodied;
he will run gloating with my raw corpse
and feed on it alone, in a cruel frenzy,
185 fouling his moor-nest. No need then
to lament for long or lay out my body:
if the battle takes me, send back my mail-shirt,
this breast-webbing that Weland fashioned
and Hrethel gave me, to Lord Hygelac.
190 Fate goes ever as fate must."

188 Weland: a famous blacksmith and magician.

189 Hrethel (hrĕth´əl): a former king of the Geats—Hygelac's father and Beowulf's grandfather.

MEMORY MOMENT

Notice & Note: Mark the words or phrases in lines 191–207 highlighting the history between Hrothgar and Beowulf.

Infer: What can you infer from Hrothgar sharing this story of the relationship between himself and the poem's hero?

196 Wulfing: a member of another Germanic tribe.

Hrothgar, the helmet of Shieldings, spoke:
"Beowulf, my friend, you have travelled here
to favour us with help and to fight for us.
There was a feud one time, begun by your father.
195 With his own hands he had killed Heatholaf,
who was a Wulfing; so war was looming
and his people, in fear of it, forced him to leave.
He came away then over rolling waves
to the South-Danes here, the sons of honour.
200 I was then in the first flush of kingship,
establishing my sway over all the rich strongholds
of this heroic land. Heorogar,
my older brother and the better man,
also a son of Halfdane's, had died.
205 Finally I healed the feud by paying:
I shipped a treasure-trove to the Wulfings
and Ecgtheow acknowledged me with oaths of allegiance.

"It bothers me to have to burden anyone
with all the grief Grendel has caused

APPLYING ACADEMIC VOCABULARY

☐ collapse    displace    military   ☐ violate   ☐ visual

Write and Discuss Have students turn to a partner to discuss the following questions. Guide students to include the academic vocabulary words *military* and *displace* in their responses. Ask volunteers to share their responses with the class.

- What **military** terms are found in lines 168-190?
- Why was Beowulf's father **displaced**?

210 and the havoc he has wreaked upon us in Heorot,
our humiliations. My household-guard
are on the wane, fate sweeps them away
into Grendel's clutches—
  but God can easily
halt these raids and harrowing attacks!

215 "Time and again, when the goblets passed
and seasoned fighters got flushed with beer
they would pledge themselves to protect Heorot
and wait for Grendel with whetted swords.
But when dawn broke and day crept in
220 over each empty, blood-spattered bench,
the floor of the mead-hall where they had feasted
would be slick with slaughter. And so they died,
faithful retainers, and my following dwindled.

"Now take your place at the table, relish
225 the triumph of heroes to your heart's content."

Then a bench was cleared in that banquet hall
so the Geats could have room to be together
and the party sat, proud in their bearing,
strong and stalwart. An attendant stood by
230 with a decorated pitcher, pouring bright
helpings of mead. And the minstrel sang,
filling Heorot with his head-clearing voice,
gladdening that great rally of Geats and Danes. . . .

The Battle with Grendel

In off the moors, down through the mist bands
235 God-cursed Grendel came greedily loping.
The bane of the race of men roamed forth,
hunting for a prey in the high hall.
Under the cloud-murk he moved towards it
until it shone above him, a sheer keep
240 of fortified gold. Nor was that the first time
he had scouted the grounds of Hrothgar's dwelling—
although never in his life, before or since,
did he find harder fortune or hall-defenders.
Spurned and joyless, he journeyed on ahead
245 and arrived at the bawn. The iron-braced door
turned on its hinge when his hands touched it.
Then his rage boiled over, he ripped open
the mouth of the building, maddening for blood,

ANALYZE CHARACTERISTICS OF AN EPIC POEM

Annotate: Mark the words or phrases in lines 245–251 that illustrate Grendel's power.

Compare: How does Grendel's power compare to what you've read about Beowulf's abilities?

TEACH

ANALYZE CHARACTERISTICS OF AN EPIC POEM

Help students to understand that the term "iron braced" means that the door was reinforced with iron bars. Also make sure that they understand that "mouth of the building" refers to the door. (**Answer:** *Beowulf is described as the strongest man alive, but Grendel possesses supernatural strength.*)

TO CHALLENGE STUDENTS . . .

Conduct Research Explain to students that for years, scholars remained skeptical about the description of the hall and the beautifully crafted treasures mentioned in *Beowulf*, believing that they were the product of an overactive poetic imagination. Tell students that the 1939 discovery of an Anglo-Saxon burial site changed scholarly opinion. Have students work in small groups to research the Sutton Hoo excavations. Suggest that each group explore a different facet of the topic: the discovery, the treasures unearthed, the historical information learned from the site, and the current status of the site. Have groups share their information in the form of an oral report or a media presentation.

TEACH

✏️ ANALYZE OLD ENGLISH POETRY

Remind students that a **caesura** is a pause that divides the line, with each part having two stresses. Point out that this poem was an important part of an oral tradition before it was written down. The pauses and the stress placed on certain words helped to convey dramatic moments to listeners. (**Answer:** Bursting *and* back-tracking *are the stressed, alliterative words. The caesuras help to make the pace of the poem sound more dramatic.*)

 ENGLISH LEARNER SUPPORT

Understand New Vocabulary Help students identify the meanings of words or phrases that they may not be familiar with:

- quartered (line 254): lodging together
- glee (line 254): open delight
- mayhem (line 255): violence or damage
- ravening (line 258): eating greedily
- mauled (line 264): injured **SUBSTANTIAL**

 **NOTICE & NOTE**

baleful
(bāl′fəl) *adj.* harmful or malignant in intent or effect.

ANALYZE OLD ENGLISH POETRY
Annotate: Poets often use a caesura to create a dramatic pause. Mark the caesuras in lines 283–284.

Analyze: Which alliterative words carry the stresses in these two lines? How does the poet use caesuras in these lines to enhance the story?

---

pacing the length of the patterned floor
250　with his loathsome tread, while a **baleful** light,
　　flame more than light, flared from his eyes.
　　He saw many men in the mansion, sleeping,
　　a ranked company of kinsmen and warriors
　　quartered together. And his glee was demonic,
255　picturing the mayhem: before morning
　　he would rip life from limb and devour them,
　　feed on their flesh; but his fate that night
　　was due to change, his days of ravening
　　had come to an end.

　　　　　　　　　　　　Mighty and canny,
260　Hygelac's kinsman was keenly watching
　　for the first move the monster would make.
　　Nor did the creature keep him waiting
　　but struck suddenly and started in;
　　he grabbed and mauled a man on his bench,
265　bit into his bone-lappings, bolted down his blood
　　and gorged on him in lumps, leaving the body
　　utterly lifeless, eaten up
　　hand and foot. Venturing closer,
　　his talon was raised to attack Beowulf
270　where he lay on the bed; he was bearing in
　　with open claw when the alert hero's
　　comeback and armlock forestalled him utterly.
　　The captain of evil discovered himself
　　in a handgrip harder than anything
275　he had ever encountered in any man
　　on the face of the earth. Every bone in his body
　　quailed and recoiled, but he could not escape.
　　He was desperate to flee to his den and hide
　　with the devil's litter, for in all his days
280　he had never been clamped or cornered like this.
　　Then Hygelac's trusty retainer recalled
　　his bedtime speech, sprang to his feet
　　and got a firm hold // fingers were bursting, //
　　the monster back-tracking // the man overpowering. //
285　The dread of the land was desperate to escape,
　　to take a roundabout road and flee
　　to his lair in the fens. The latching power
　　in his fingers weakened; it was the worst trip
　　the terror-monger had taken to Heorot.
290　And now the timbers trembled and sang,
　　a hall-session that harrowed every Dane
　　inside the stockade: stumbling in fury,

the two contenders crashed through the building.
The hall clattered and hammered, but somehow
295 survived the onslaught and kept standing:
it was handsomely structured, a sturdy frame
braced with the best of blacksmith's work
inside and out. The story goes
that as the pair struggled, mead-benches were smashed
300 and sprung off the floor, gold fittings and all.
Before then, no Shielding elder would believe
there was any power or person upon earth
capable of wrecking their horn-rigged hall
unless the burning embrace of a fire
305 engulf it in flame. Then an extraordinary
wail arose, and bewildering fear
came over the Danes. Everyone felt it
who heard that cry as it echoed off the wall,
a God-cursed scream and strain of catastrophe,
310 the howl of the loser, the lament of the hell-serf
keening his wound. He was overwhelmed,
manacled tight by the man who of all men
was foremost and strongest in the days of this life.

But the earl-troop's leader was not inclined
315 to allow his caller to depart alive:
he did not consider that life of much account
to anyone anywhere. Time and again,
Beowulf's warriors worked to defend
their lord's life, laying about them
320 as best they could with their ancestral blades.
Stalwart in action, they kept striking out
on every side, seeking to cut
straight to the soul. When they joined the struggle
there was something they could not have known at the
     time,
325 that no blade on earth, no blacksmith's art
could ever damage their demon opponent.
He had conjured the harm from the cutting edge
of every weapon. But his going away
out of this world and the days of his life
330 would be agony to him, and his alien spirit
would travel far into fiends' keeping.

Then he who had harrowed the hearts of men
with pain and affliction in former times
and had given offence also to God
335 found that his bodily powers failed him.

NOTICE & NOTE

wail
(wāl) *v.* to make a long, loud, high-pitched cry, as in grief, sorrow, or fear.

ANALYZE CHARACTERISTICS OF AN EPIC POEM
Annotate: Mark words and phrases in lines 318–331 that tell why Beowulf's companion warriors could not defeat Grendel.

Analyze: What characteristic of an epic poem does this typify?

Beowulf   17

TEACH

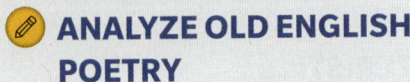 **ANALYZE OLD ENGLISH POETRY**

Remind students that **alliteration** is the repetition of consonant sounds at the beginning of words. Explain to students that the repetition of sounds can enhance the meaning of words when they are read orally. (**Answer:** The use of alliteration in the phrases "sinews split" and "bone-lappings burst" conveys the trauma of Grendel's wounds because of the harsh, repeated sounds.)

CRITICAL VOCABULARY

loathsome: No one watched Grendel's loathsome, or abhorrent, behavior as he died.

ASK STUDENTS what behavior of the Danes Grendel found loathsome. (*Grendel considered the noise that came from Heorot, including the sound of the harp and singing, to be loathsome.*)

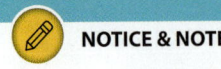 **NOTICE & NOTE**

340 Sinews: the tendons that connect muscles to bones.

ANALYZE OLD ENGLISH POETRY
Annotate: Poets often use alliteration to create rhythm, emphasis, and mood. Mark the alliteration in line 340–345.

Infer: How does the poet's use of alliteration enhance the description of Grendel's wounds?

Hygelac's kinsman kept him helplessly
locked in a handgrip. As long as either lived,
he was hateful to the other. The monster's whole
body was in pain, a tremendous wound
340 appeared on his shoulder. Sinews split
and the bone-lappings burst. Beowulf was granted
the glory of winning; Grendel was driven
under the fen-banks, fatally hurt,
to his desolate lair. His days were numbered,
345 the end of his life was coming over him,
he knew it for certain; and one bloody clash
had fulfilled the dearest wishes of the Danes.
The man who had lately landed among them,
proud and sure, had purged the hall,
350 kept it from harm; he was happy with his nightwork
and the courage he had shown. The Geat captain
had boldly fulfilled his boast to the Danes:
he had healed and relieved a huge distress,
unremitting humiliations,
355 the hard fate they'd been forced to undergo,
no small affliction. Clear proof of this
could be seen in the hand the hero displayed
high up near the roof: the whole of Grendel's
shoulder and arm, his awesome grasp.

360 Then morning came and many a warrior
gathered, as I've heard, around the gift-hall,
clan-chiefs flocking from far and near
down wide-ranging roads, wondering greatly
at the monster's footprints. His fatal departure
365 was regretted by no-one who witnessed his trail,
the ignominious marks of his flight
where he'd skulked away, exhausted in spirit
and beaten in battle, bloodying the path,
hauling his doom to the demons' mere.
370 The bloodshot water wallowed and surged,
there were **loathsome** upthrows and overturnings
of waves and gore and wound-slurry.
With his death upon him, he had dived deep
into his marsh-den, drowned out his life
375 and his heathen soul: hell claimed him there.

Then away they rode, the old retainers
with many a young man following after,
a troop on horseback, in high spirits
on their bay steeds. Beowulf's doings
380 were praised over and over again.

loathsome
(lōth´səm) *adj.* causing loathing; abhorrent.

Nowhere, they said, north or south
between the two seas or under the tall sky
on the broad earth was there anyone better
to raise a shield or to rule a kingdom.
385 Yet there was no laying of blame on their lord,
the noble Hrothgar; he was a good king.

At times the war-band broke into a gallop,
letting their chestnut horses race
wherever they found the going good
390 on those well-known tracks. Meanwhile, a thane
of the king's household, a carrier of tales,
a traditional singer deeply schooled
in the lore of the past, linked a new theme
to a strict metre. The man started
395 to recite with skill, rehearsing Beowulf's
triumphs and feats in well-fashioned lines,
entwining his words.

NOTICE & NOTE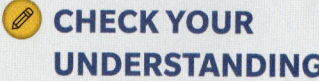

CHECK YOUR UNDERSTANDING

Answer these questions before moving on to the **Analyze the Text** section on the following page.

1 Why does Grendel hate humanity?

   A He is an outcast member of the nobility.

   B He is cursed and envious of the Danes' celebrations.

   C The Danes had persecuted and exiled him.

   D His home had been destroyed to make way for people.

2 Where does the final battle take place?

   F Hrothgar's mead hall

   G Grendel's cave lair

   H Beowulf's castle

   J Wulfgar's beach

3 Beowulf defeats Grendel by —

   A using a magic sword

   B setting fire to his lair

   C chasing him out to sea

   D fighting without weapons

Beowulf   19

TEACH

CHECK YOUR UNDERSTANDING

Have students answer the questions independently.

Answers:

1. B

2. F

3. D

If they answer any questions incorrectly, have them reread the text to confirm their understanding. Then, they may proceed to ANALYZE THE TEXT on page 20.

ENGLISH LEARNER SUPPORT

Oral Assessment Use the following questions to assess students' comprehension and speaking skills.

1. Why did Grendel hate people so much? *(Grendel hated people because he was cursed by God.)*

2. Where does the fight between Beowulf and Grendel happen? *(The final battle happens in Hrothgar's mead hall.)*

3. How does Beowulf beat Grendel? *(Beowulf beats Grendel by using his bare hands.)* **SUBSTANTIAL/MODERATE**

Beowulf   **19**

APPLY

ANALYZE THE TEXT

Possible answers:

1. **DOK 4:** *Two kennings that refer to Grendel are "prowler through the dark," and "God-cursed beast." The author is clear that Grendel is a symbol of ultimate evil, and is without honor.*

2. **DOK 3:** *Christian mythos is ever-present in the tale; Christian ideas are fully integrated because they are embodied in different ways in all of the characters.*

3. **DOK 4:** *The use of alliteration and of caesuras would allow a performer to better emphasize the most dramatic elements of the poem, especially the battle between Beowulf and Grendel.*

4. **DOK 4:** *The universal theme of a struggle between good and evil, as well as the ultimate and inevitable victory of good, are encapsulated in the struggle between the two main characters.*

5. **DOK 4:** *Hrothgar values loyalty. He generously paid a substantial debt for Beowulf's father, who subsequently pledged his loyalty to the king. Hrothgar also speaks with regret about the men who were loyal to him who died in his service.*

RESEARCH

Remind students that they should confirm any information they find by checking multiple sources and assessing the credibility of each one.

Connect As students discuss with partners, encourage them to identify the specific values and beliefs they feel are reflected in their selections. Suggest that they print or write out the lyrics to each song or statement in each book/movie/show and circle words or phrases that suggest these values. *(Student answers will vary.)*

 **RESPOND**

ANALYZE THE TEXT

Support your responses with evidence from the text. 📓 **NOTEBOOK**

1. **Analyze** Identify two kennings associated with Grendel. How do these phrases convey the poet's attitude toward the character?

2. **Draw Conclusions** Reread lines 85–103, which describe how Hrothgar's followers prayed for protection from Grendel's attacks. Are these Christian ideas fully integrated into the epic? Explain why or why not.

3. **Evaluate** Reread lines 268–313. The poet uses various techniques—alliteration, caesura, kennings—in the description of the battle between Grendel and Beowulf. How might these techniques have helped Anglo-Saxon poets chant or sing the poem and convey its meaning?

4. **Analyze** Identify and explain a universal theme conveyed by the description of the battle between Beowulf and Grendel.

5. **Notice & Note** Reread Hrothgar's speech in lines 191–225. What values are reflected in his recollection of his relationship with Beowulf's father and of the efforts of his followers to stop Grendel?

RESEARCH TIP
When you research online, use reliable websites. Often these have .org or .edu web addresses. Be wary of information from publicly sourced sites; information that can be changed, supplemented, and otherwise edited by the general public is not always accurate.

RESEARCH

Traditional epic poems reflect the values and beliefs of the prevailing culture, as *Beowulf* reflects values of Anglo-Saxon society. Many cultures have produced epic poetry. Briefly research other epic poems and use a chart like the one below to pose and answer research questions about the epics.

QUESTION	ANSWER
What culture is represented in the *Iliad*, and who is its author?	Greek, Homer
In what language was *Emperor Shaka the Great* originally compiled?	Zulu
Paradise Lost, by John Milton, is based on what famous story?	The Bible

Connect Consider which kinds of stories in today's society might be seen as epics. Make a list of several books, movies, TV shows, songs, or other kinds of stories that feature heroes and reflect the values and beliefs of our culture. Share your list with a partner and discuss what makes a story an epic.

 LEARNING MINDSET

Belonging Encourage students to share their reflections on *Beowulf* with their classmates. Emphasize that each one of them has a unique perspective and will likely understand the text in a way that is different from any of their classmates. Tell students that they can help each other better understand texts by sharing their perspectives with their classmates.

CREATE AND PRESENT

Write a Poem Write a poem about someone whose ideals and values you admire. Review your notes on the Quick Start activity before you begin.

❑ Employ at least one technique that you have learned about in this lesson, such as alliteration or kennings.

❑ Think about the form and tone that will best suit your message.

❑ Use a strong rhythm to help make your poem memorable.

❑ Have a partner read your poem and give you feedback. Make revisions, if necessary.

Present an Epic *Beowulf* is full of action and drama and is best appreciated when read aloud. With a partner, present a passage from the epic poem.

❑ Select a passage that features exciting action, rich poetic language, or dialogue between two characters.

❑ With your partner, decide how you will divide the passage and who will read each part.

❑ Practice reading with expression, gestures, and appropriate volume.

❑ Present your reading of the epic to your classmates.

RESPOND TO THE ESSENTIAL QUESTION

 What makes someone a hero?

Gather Information Review your annotations and notes on *Beowulf*. Then, add relevant information to your Response Log. As you determine which information to include, think about:

- the motivation of a hero
- the importance of cultural values
- how the actions of one person can benefit the community

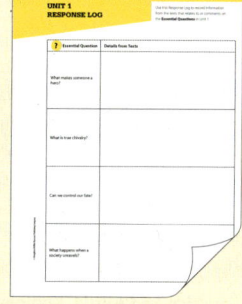

RESPOND

Go to the **Speaking and Listening Studio** for more on giving a presentation.

ACADEMIC VOCABULARY

As you write and discuss what you learned from the poem, be sure to use the Academic Vocabulary words. Check off each of the words that you use.

❑ collapse
❑ displace
❑ military
❑ violate
❑ visual

APPLY

CREATE AND PRESENT

Write a Poem Encourage students to think about which elements of poetry, including meter, diction, and literary devices, that they want to use before they begin to write. Emphasize that the poem should tell a cohesive story—with a beginning, middle, and end—about the person who is the subject of the poem.

 For **writing support** for students at varying proficiency levels, see the **Text X-Ray** on page 6D.

Present an Epic Remind students that for most of human history, stories were passed down through cultures via an oral tradition. Encourage students to focus on expressiveness, intonation, and **rhythm** as they read their chosen passage.

RESPOND TO THE ESSENTIAL QUESTION

Allow time for students to add details from *Beowulf* to their Unit 1 Response Logs.

APPLY

CRITICAL VOCABULARY

Answers:

1. a
2. b
3. b
4. a
5. b
6. b
7. b

VOCABULARY STRATEGY:
Homophones

Answers:

1. *their*—the possessive form of *they*
2. *plain*—obvious to the perception or mind, evident; *see*—to take note of, recognize
3. *morning*—the first part of the day
4. *heard*—to learn by hearing; be told by others
5. *sail*—to travel by water in a vessel

 **RESPOND**

WORD BANK
aghast
unrelenting
affliction
plight
baleful
wail
loathsome

CRITICAL VOCABULARY

Practice and Apply Choose the letter of the best answer to each question. Explain your answer.

1. Which is an example of a **baleful** action?
   a. throwing a rock intentionally b. dropping a rock accidentally

2. Which is more likely to sound like a **wail**?
   a. a child shouting for joy b. a child having a tantrum

3. Which can be described as an **affliction**?
   a. a case of hiccups b. a case of chickenpox

4. Which is likely to be **unrelenting**?
   a. a persistent suitor b. a casual acquaintance

5. Which is more likely to leave you **aghast**?
   a. finding a scratch on your car b. witnessing a car accident

6. Which is more likely to be considered a **plight**?
   a. finding a wallet at a store b. leaving your wallet at a store

7. Which would make you feel **loathsome**?
   a. doing a mud run b. wading through a sewer

VOCABULARY STRATEGY:
Homophones

 Go to the **Vocabulary Studio** for more on homophones.

When listening to poetry read aloud, the audience has to be able to recognize **homophones.** These are words that have the same pronunciation but different spellings and meanings. Listeners use context clues to figure out which word is intended. For instance, the critical vocabulary word *wail* is a homophone found in line 306: "Then an extraordinary / wail arose . . . " *Wail* is pronounced the same as the word for a large sea mammal, but the context helps the listener understand that this word means "to make a long, loud, high-pitched cry, as in grief, sorrow, or fear."

Practice and Apply Complete each sentence with the correct choice from the homophones in parentheses. Define the word you choose.

1. At one point, Grendel grabbed 30 men from (their, there) resting places and took them to his lair.
2. Grendel's powers of destruction were (plane, plain) to (sea, see).
3. He always struck at nighttime, and his mayhem was complete before (morning, mourning) came.
4. When Beowulf (herd, heard) about Grendel, he was at home in Geatland.
5. His plan was to (sail, sale) the swan's road and offer to defend the king.

22 Unit 1

ENGLISH LEARNER SUPPORT

Vocabulary Strategy Give students additional practice in distinguishing between homophones. Write the following sentences from page 18 on the board.

The monster's _____ (whole/hole) body was in _____ (pane/pain), a tremendous wound appeared on his shoulder.

Then, away they _____ (road/rode), the old retainers with many a young man following after, a troop on horseback.

Ask students to determine the correct choice based on context clues. **MODERATE**

LANGUAGE CONVENTIONS:
Mood

Mood is the feeling or atmosphere that a writer creates for the reader. Poets may use imagery, figurative language, alliteration or other sound devices, and word choices to create mood.

In lines 41–52, the Beowulf poet describes the scene at the banquet hall. Read this passage from the poem:

> Then as dawn brightened and the day broke
> Grendel's powers of destruction were plain:
> their wassail was over, they wept to heaven
> and mourned under morning. Their mighty prince,
> the storied leader, sat stricken and helpless,
> humiliated by the loss of his guard,
> bewildered and stunned, staring aghast
> at the demon's trail, in deep distress.
> He was numb with grief, but got no respite
> for one night later merciless Grendel
> struck again with more gruesome murders.
> Malignant by nature, he never showed remorse.

The chart gives examples of literary devices used in these lines:

LITERARY DEVICE	EXAMPLES
Imagery	wept to heaven, numb with grief
Alliteration	and mourned under morning. Their mighty prince
Word Choice	mourned, helpless, humiliated, distress, grief

These devices create a mood of sadness and despair. This mood helps underscore the difficult situation facing King Hrothgar. It also helps to establish Grendel as a vicious, uncaring beast, imbued with supernatural powers. The mood also builds suspense as readers wonder how Beowulf will conquer such an evil, dangerous opponent.

Practice and Apply Complete these activities independently.

1. Choose a passage from the poem that conveys a distinct mood—for example, lines 14–40 or 234–268. Identify the mood of the passage you've chosen and the literary devices that help to create this mood.

2. With the passage from *Beowulf* as a guide, use what you learned about literary devices to write an original passage that creates a similar mood.

3. Read your passage aloud to a partner. Have your partner identify the mood and evaluate your success in conveying it.

RESPOND

APPLY

LANGUAGE CONVENTIONS:
Mood

To help students understand the impact of language on the **mood** of a text, write these sentences on the board:

When their party ended, they cried out with sadness.

The trusted leader sat motionless, not knowing what to do.

The monster didn't seem to care about their pain.

As a class, compare the **mood** that the sentences on the board create with the **mood** conveyed by the original text of the poem.

Practice and Apply Encourage partners to give feedback to each other about how effectively their passage created the desired **mood** and suggest any other literary devices that might have helped create the **mood**. *(Students' passages will vary.)*

ENGLISH LEARNER SUPPORT

Language Conventions Understanding **mood** requires a knowledge of literary devices, including **alliteration**. Use the following supports with students at varying proficiency levels:

- Have students review the definition of **alliteration**. Then guide them in finding examples in lines 14–16. *(finally/fiend; work/world)* **SUBSTANTIAL**

- Ask students to find examples of **alliteration** in lines 17–20. *(Grendel/grim; haunting/heath; marches/marauding; desolate/dwelt; misery/monsters)* **MODERATE**

- Have students write a sentence of their own that contains two examples of **alliteration**. Ask them to switch with a partner. Have partners circle and identify the examples.
  LIGHT

PLAN

from THE CANTERBURY TALES: THE WIFE OF BATH'S TALE

Narrative Poem by Geoffrey Chaucer

GENRE ELEMENTS
NARRATIVE POEM

Tell students that a **narrative poem** is like a short story written in verse using techniques such as rhyme, meter, and figurative language. It also relies on elements of prose fiction such as character, setting, plot, narrator and theme to tell a story. Narrative poems include epic poems and ballads.

LEARNING OBJECTIVES

- Analyze structure and narrator.
- Research laws concerning women's roles in England during the Middle Ages.
- Write a short story.
- Present a short story with expression.
- Compare usage of words.
- Understand inverted sentences.
- **Language** Ask a partner questions about characters in a narrative poem.

TEXT COMPLEXITY

Quantitative Measures	The Wife of Bath's Tale	Lexile: N/A
Qualitative Measures	**Ideas Presented** Subtle, implied meanings and multiple themes. Use of irony.	
	Structures Used More complex with parallel plot lines. Some support through subheads.	
	Language Used Complex sentence structures, such as inverted sentences, with use of archaic and formal language.	
	Knowledge Required Complex ideas. Cultural and literary knowledge may make heavier demands.	

24A Unit 1

PLAN

RESOURCES

Online

- Unit 1 Response Log
- Selection Audio
- Reading Studio: Notice & Note
- Writing Studio: Writing Narratives
- Speaking and Listening Studio: Giving a Presentation
- Vocabulary Studio: Multiple-Meaning Words
- Grammar Studio: Module 1 Lesson 4: Finding the Subject of a Sentence
- "The Wife of Bath's Tale" Selection Test

SUMMARIES

English

In *The Canterbury Tales*, 30 pilgrims on their way to the shrine of Canterbury agree to go together and tell tales along the way. The pilgrims are a very diverse group of people that show the wide range of class, attitudes, and jobs in the Middle Ages. In *The Wife of Bath's Tale*, the narrator is a woman who shocks her traveling companions with her modern beliefs about marriage and female power. She tells a tale about a knight who must marry an ugly old woman, with some surprising results.

Spanish

En "Los cuentos de Canterbury", 30 peregrinos en camino al altar de Canterbury deciden ir juntos y contar cuentos durante el camino. Los peregrinos son un grupo diverso, quienes muestran una gran gama de clases, actitudes y trabajos durante la Edad Media. En el "Cuento de la esposa de Bath", la voz narrativa es una mujer quien asombra a sus compañeros de viaje con sus creencias modernas acerca del matrimonio y el poder femenino. Cuenta la historia de un caballero obligado a casarse con una mujer vieja y fea, con un resultado sorprendente.

SMALL-GROUP OPTIONS

Have students work in small groups and pairs to read and discuss the selection.

Double-Entry Journal

- Have students use a notebook for recording their double entry notes.
- Show students how to create a two-column format by drawing a line from top to bottom on a piece of loose-leaf paper. Name the left head *Quotes from the Text* and the right head *My Notes*.
- Encourage students to copy important or confusing text passages in the left column.
- Then, have students write their own questions, restatements, or interpretations in the right column next to the quoted material.

Silent Sustained Reading

- Tell students that they will read silently for 30 minutes.
- Provide a chart for students to record the title, date, and number of lines or pages of the narrative poem they read.
- Direct students to record unfamiliar vocabulary words or phrases as they read.
- After reading, ask individual students to provide an oral summary of what they read. Help students use context to define unfamiliar words and phrases.

The Wife of Bath's Tale

PLAN

Text X-Ray: English Learner Support
for "The Wife of Bath's Tale"

Use the Text X-Ray and the supports and scaffolds in the Teacher's Edition to help guide students at different proficiency levels through the selection.

INTRODUCE THE SELECTION
DISCUSS AUTHOR'S CHOICES

In this lesson, students will need to be able to discuss why Chaucer chose the device of having a character narrate a story to other characters in the story.

Remind students that authors make choices about how they will tell their stories. Chaucer has cleverly chosen to have a character tell an exemplum, which is a story told to illustrate an intellectual idea. In this way, Chaucer can subtly comment on the idea through the opinions of his characters.

Ask students to discuss why an author might choose to have a character tell a story. Provide sentence frames, such as: *A character's attitude toward the story she/he tells gives us information about ____. It is not effective for an author to directly state his/her opinion in a narrative poem because ____.*

CULTURAL REFERENCES

The following words or phrases may be unfamiliar to students:

- *as good as dead* (lines 66): sure to die
- *took his leave* (line 92): departed or left
- *all the same* (line 96): still, despite his efforts
- *dance attendance* (line 107): to wait on someone and obey their every wish

LISTENING

Understand Content

Read aloud 5–10 lines of the poem and have students chorally repeat each line after you. Work with students to correctly pronounce the rhyming words at the ends of the lines.

Use the following supports with students at varying proficiency levels:

- Repeat certain lines and ask either/or questions about them. For example: *Did the Wife of Bath say it or did the Friar say it? Who wanted the Wife of Bath to tell her tale, the Host or the Friar?* **SUBSTANTIAL**
- After reading, ask general content questions to assess listening comprehension. For example: *What does the Friar say? Who does he say it to?* Have students respond in simple sentences. **MODERATE**
- After listening to short chunks of the text, have partners ask and answer questions about what they heard. For example: *What is the Friar like? Do you think he is being nice to the wife of Bath? Why or why not?* **LIGHT**

PLAN

SPEAKING

Analyze Character

Tell students that Chaucer chose to include a variety of character types to make shrewd insights about human nature and to give readers a good picture of life in the Middle Ages.

Use the following supports with students at varying proficiency levels:

- Help students write the names of the characters in the poem on separate index cards. Then, as you say short sentences about each character, have students repeat each sentence and hold up the appropriate character card. For example: *This character is rude to the Wife of Bath. (Friar)* **SUBSTANTIAL**
- Have partners write a list of the characters in the poem. Then, have them take turns asking and answering simple questions about each character. Provide question starters, such as, *Why do you think that ____? How did you feel when (character) ____?* **MODERATE**
- Ask one half of a pair to role play a character from the poem. Direct their partners to interview that character about the role of women in the Middle Ages. Provide model questions, such as: *Do you think all women should get married? Why or why not?* **LIGHT**

READING

Think Aloud to Improve Comprehension

Remind students that it's a good idea to pause as they read to ask themselves questions about what they read. Model how to use Think Alouds as you read.

Use the following supports with students of varying proficiency levels as they silently read lines 29–44 while you read them aloud:

- After reading, point to the text and model a Think Aloud: *I will look for periods so I can break the text into sentences. The first three lines are one sentence. The main idea is that there used to be a land full of fairies. Then, I read the next two sentences and see the word "but." This tells me about a problem: there are no more fairies. I wonder why? I will keep reading to see if I can find out.* Ask yes/no questions to assess students' comprehension of the Think Aloud. **SUBSTANTIAL**
- Have small groups continue to read the text under the second subhead and take turns using the strategy to recite their own brief Think Aloud. Supply sentence frames, such as: *I think the main idea of this sentence is ____. I will keep reading to find out ____.* **MODERATE**
- Have partners start from the beginning of the text to read chunks of about 10 lines. Have them take turns pausing to recite their own Think Aloud. **LIGHT**

WRITING

Write a Short Story

Tell students they need to fully understand each character before they can write a character's dialogue, thoughts, or actions.

Use the following supports with students of varying proficiency levels:

- Support students as they sketch or draw the Friar, Summoner, Host, and Wife, labeling their sketches with descriptive words. Provide and discuss a word bank for students to use. **SUBSTANTIAL**
- Have students create word webs for each of the four characters that will be in their story, with character names and descriptions in the outer circles. **MODERATE**
- Set a timer for 3–5 minutes and have students do an automatic writing exercise answering this question about each of the four characters in their story: *What do I want?* **LIGHT**

TEACH

? Connect to the ESSENTIAL QUESTION

The concept of chivalry, that is, a sense of courteous and honorable behavior expected of a knight, peaked between the 12th and 13th centuries during the Middle Ages. Today, we often hear the phrase, "chivalry is dead," which speaks to the lack of courteous display towards women. Have students consider whether they think chivalry is, in fact, dead, and what has contributed to this shift in values.

ANALYZE & APPLY

THE WIFE OF BATH'S TALE
from THE CANTERBURY TALES

Narrative Poem by **Geoffrey Chaucer**
translated by **Nevill Coghill**

? ESSENTIAL QUESTION:

What is true chivalry?

LEARNING MINDSET

Growth Mindset Remind students that having a growth mindset involves practicing with a goal of improvement. Encourage students to create personal study plans using a variety of strategies. As students review the selections, have them create their own strategies for learning. Students should identify the strategies and skills that complement each other. Finally, have students share their notes together and discuss what works best for them.

QUICK START

What do you think is most important for a successful romantic relationship? Write a paragraph in response to this question. Then discuss your thoughts with a partner.

ANALYZE STRUCTURE

The Canterbury Tales has a complex structure that features a **frame story**—a story that surrounds and binds together one or more different narratives in a single work. The frame story in *The Canterbury Tales* begins with a General Prologue, in which the characters, setting, and storytelling premise are introduced. It also includes interactions among characters in the breaks between tales, when they often interrupt and argue with one another.

In addition to unifying the tales told by the pilgrims, the frame story provides a vivid portrait of each pilgrim. Through the initial descriptions as well as the later interactions among the pilgrims, readers learn about the positions they occupy in medieval society. These interactions enable Chaucer to present insights about practices and institutions in this time period; for example, his portrayals of clergy and church officials reveal corruption in the church.

Chaucer also uses the frame story to explore relationships between pilgrims. In "The Wife of Bath's Prologue," the Friar interrupts the Wife of Bath's long account of her five husbands, which prefaces her actual story: "Well, Ma'am . . . as God may send me bliss, / This is a long preamble to a tale!" She finds an opportunity to get back at him as she starts to tell her tale.

ANALYZE NARRATOR

The **narrator** of a story is the character or voice that tells the story's events to the reader. Chaucer used multiple narrators for *The Canterbury Tales*. The narrator of the frame story describes the pilgrims and records their exchanges with one another. The pilgrims, in turn, narrate their own tales. You can gain insight into the Wife of Bath by examining the following elements in her narration:

SUBJECT AND THEME	DIRECT STATEMENTS	TONE
When narrators are also characters in a story, they usually choose subjects and themes relevant to their own experiences. For example, the Wife of Bath, who has been married five times, tells a tale about relationships between men and women.	Narrators sometimes comment directly on characters and events. The Wife of Bath makes statements on several topics, such as the type of husband she values and the ability of women to keep secrets.	A narrator's tone, or attitude toward a subject, provides clues about the narrator's personality. Usually tone is communicated through word choice and details. Notice the words that the Wife of Bath uses to describe the knight's plight. What kind of person comes across through this tone?

GENRE ELEMENTS: NARRATIVE POETRY

- tells a story using elements of prose fiction such as character, setting, plot, narrator, and theme
- written in verse, with techniques such as rhyme, meter, and figurative language
- includes epic poems and ballads

TEACH

CRITICAL VOCABULARY

Encourage students to read all the sentences before deciding which word best completes each one. Remind them to look for context clues that match the precise meaning of each word.

Answers:

1. *bequeath*
2. *virtue*
3. *sovereignty*
4. *preamble*
5. *rebuke*

■ English Learner Support

Use Cognates Tell students that some of the Critical Vocabulary words have Spanish cognates: *virtue/virtud, preamble/preámbulo, sovereignty/soberanía.*
ALL LEVELS

LANGUAGE CONVENTIONS

Review the information about inverted sentences and ask students to explain this in their own words. Then, read aloud the sample sentence, with emphasis on the clauses that are inverted. Ask students to rewrite the sentence, but this time, with the clauses where they traditionally appear (subject followed by a verb).

Discuss the effect that inverting the subject and verb has on the sentence. *(The inversion of the subject and the verb adds emphasis on certain words or phrases.)* Ask students why they think this might be useful.

ANNOTATION MODEL

Remind students to review the definition of **frame story** on page 25 before they begin annotating. Tell students that they may underline important details that describe the Wife of Bath's personality, circle key words, or even highlight sections that provide clues about the different characters and the relationships between them. Point out that they may follow this suggestion or use their own system for marking up the selection in their write-in text. They may want to color-code their annotations by using highlighters. Their notes in the margin may include questions about ideas that are unclear or topics they want to learn more about.

26   Unit 1

 **GET READY**

CRITICAL VOCABULARY

preamble   virtue   sovereignty   bequeath   rebuke

To see how many Critical Vocabulary words you already know, use them to complete the sentences.

1. The Wife of Bath chose some of her husbands based on what they could _____ to her.
2. Nuns' habits are designed to protect the _____ of the wearer.
3. Since the Wife of Bath has _____ over her financial affairs, she can spend her money on whatever she likes.
4. The Friar objected to the lengthy _____ to the Wife of Bath's tale.
5. The Summoner responded to the Friar's comments with a _____.

LANGUAGE CONVENTIONS

Inverted Sentences In this lesson you will learn about inverted sentences, where the normal order of a subject followed by a verb is reversed. Notice how Chaucer uses inversion in this line:

> But truly poor are they who whine and fret.

Notice that the verb *are* precedes the subject *they*. As you read "The Wife of Bath's Tale," note other examples of inverted sentences.

ANNOTATION MODEL   NOTICE & NOTE

As you read, note clues about the personality of the Wife of Bath and also about the frame story that surrounds her tale. This model shows one reader's notes about the prologue to the tale.

> The Friar laughed when he had heard all this.
> "Well, Ma'am," he said, "as God may send me bliss,
> This is a long preamble to a tale!"
> But when the Summoner heard the Friar rail,
> "Just look!" he cried, "by the two arms of God!
> These meddling friars are always on the prod!
> Don't we all know a friar and a fly
> Go prod and buzz in every dish and pie!"

This suggests that the Wife of Bath is long-winded.

Seems like the Summoner doesn't like the Friar. Maybe they quarreled earlier.

26   Unit 1

BACKGROUND

Geoffrey Chaucer (1342?–1400) came from a prosperous, though not noble, family. His father was a wine merchant who could afford to give him a good education. Chaucer grew up in London at a time when the city was growing due to expansion of commerce. In 1357 he became an attendant in an aristocrat's court, which put him in contact with influential people such as John of Gaunt, who became his lifelong patron. Two years later he went to France to fight in the Hundred Years' War. When he was captured, his family's connections to King Edward III helped secure his safe return.

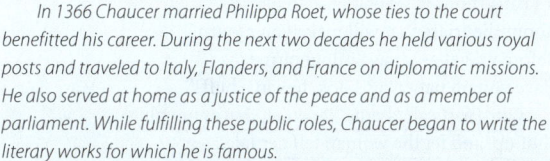

THE WIFE OF BATH'S TALE

Narrative Poem by Geoffrey Chaucer
translated by Nevill Coghill

In 1366 Chaucer married Philippa Roet, whose ties to the court benefitted his career. During the next two decades he held various royal posts and traveled to Italy, Flanders, and France on diplomatic missions. He also served at home as a justice of the peace and as a member of parliament. While fulfilling these public roles, Chaucer began to write the literary works for which he is famous.

Chaucer is widely considered to be the first great English author. He wrote in Middle English, which was starting to replace French and Latin as England's main literary language. Chaucer's best-known work, *The Canterbury Tales*, is a collection of mostly verse tales in a variety of genres. The book is distinguished by its realism, earthy humor, and shrewd insights into human nature. Chaucer depicts a group of pilgrims traveling to the shrine of St. Thomas à Becket in Canterbury. At the beginning of their journey, the host of a tavern where they stop to rest proposes a storytelling contest, with the winner to receive a free dinner. Chaucer's pilgrims represent a cross-section of medieval society, allowing him to satirize institutions of his time. Each tale is preceded by a prologue in which the characters exchange commentary.

In addition to *The Canterbury Tales*, Chaucer wrote other notable works including the tragic verse romance *Troilus and Criseyde*. Upon his death, he was buried in Westminster Abbey, an honor rarely given to a commoner.

TEACH

BACKGROUND

After students read the background note, explain that many great authors have used their work as a means to offer social commentary on different institutions, practices, beliefs, and even on leaders. Similarly, in *The Canterbury Tales*, Chaucer addresses some of the practices in England's medieval society. Ask students to pay close attention to the different aspects of English society Chaucer addresses in "The Wife of Bath's Tale" and what strategies he uses to execute this commentary effectively.

ENGLISH LEARNER SUPPORT

Use Sentence Variety Ask students to pair up and practice using a variety of grammatical structures, sentence lengths, and sentence types to discuss Chaucer's life. Provide students with a list of sentence starters and language frames in a variety of sentence lengths and types that include connecting words for compound and complex sentences, such as these:

- Before I read the background on Chaucer, I believed _____.
- Chaucer was a _____, but he _____.
- I believe that "The Wife of Bath's Tale is about _____. **ALL LEVELS**

WHEN STUDENTS STRUGGLE...

Understand Literary Terms Have students work in pairs or groups to define *realism* and *satirize*, both of which appear in the Background on page 27, to better contextualize Chaucer's work. Encourage students to use context clues to determine word meanings before consulting a dictionary.

 For additional support, go to the **Reading Studio** and assign the following Level Up tutorial: **Using Context Clues.**

TEACH

SETTING A PURPOSE

Direct students to use the Setting a Purpose prompt to focus their reading.

 ANALYZE STRUCTURE

Remind students that the **frame story** provides details about the characters and sheds light on the relationships between them. (**Answer:** *The relationship between the Friar and the Summoner is tumultuous; they appear to have conflict from the past. The relationship between the Friar and the Wife of Bath is also tense – the Wife of Bath follows her own rules, which likely offends the Friar.*)

CRITICAL VOCABULARY

preamble: The author uses preamble to describe the introduction to the Wife of Bath's account of her experiences.

ASK STUDENTS if they have ever heard the term preamble and in what contexts. Tell them that important historical documents, such as the US Constitution, have a preamble at the beginning. Have them consider why these documents might have a preamble. (*The preamble briefly explains what is in the Constitution and why those details are included.*)

 **NOTICE & NOTE**

Notice & Note
Use the side margins to notice and note signposts in the text.

ANALYZE STRUCTURE
Annotate: Mark phrases in lines 1–28 that show how the frame story provides details about relationships between pilgrims.

Draw Conclusions: What is the relationship between the Friar and the Summoner? the Friar and the Wife of Bath?

preamble
(prĕam´bəl, prē-ăm´-) *n.* a preliminary statement.

33 mead: meadow.

SETTING A PURPOSE

As you read, pay attention to details that reveal the personality of the Wife of Bath and her opinions about men and women.

The Wife of Bath's Prologue

The Friar laughed when he had heard all this.
"Well, Ma'am," he said, "as God may send me bliss,
This is a long **preamble** to a tale!"
But when the Summoner heard the Friar rail,
5 "Just look!" he cried, "by the two arms of God!
These meddling friars are always on the prod!
Don't we all know a friar and a fly
Go prod and buzz in every dish and pie!
What do you mean with your 'preambulation'?
10 Amble yourself, trot, do a meditation!
You're spoiling all our fun with your commotion."
The Friar smiled and said, "Is that your motion?
I promise on my word before I go
To find occasion for a tale or so
15 About a summoner that will make us laugh."
"Well, damn your eyes, and on my own behalf,"
The Summoner answered, "mine be damned as well
If I can't think of several tales to tell
About the friars that will make you mourn
20 Before we get as far as Sittingbourne.
Have you no patience? Look, he's in a huff!"
   Our Host called out, "Be quiet, that's enough!
Shut up, and let the woman tell her tale.
You must be drunk, you've taken too much ale.
25 Now, Ma'am, you go ahead and no demur."
"All right," she said, "it's just as you prefer,
If I have licence from this worthy friar."
"Nothing," said he, "that I should more desire."

The Wife of Bath's Tale

When good King Arthur ruled in ancient days
30 (A king that every Briton loves to praise)
This was a land brim-full of fairy folk.
The Elf-Queen and her courtiers joined and broke
Their elfin dance on many a green mead,
Or so was the opinion once, I read,
35 Hundreds of years ago, in days of yore.
But no one now sees fairies any more.
For now the saintly charity and prayer

 ENGLISH LEARNER SUPPORT

Learning Strategies Provide students with a graphic organizer they can use to record the names of the main characters in "The Wife of Bath's Prologue" and observations they make about each one. Have students pay close attention to the type of language that the characters use. What can be inferred about their personalities or behaviors based on the language they use? Explain to students that they will be using inductive reasoning when drawing conclusions about a character based on a set of observations. Once they complete the organizer, have them form small groups and compare their ideas. They may repeat this process for other sections of the selection. **LIGHT**

Of holy friars seem to have purged the air;
They search the countryside through field and stream
40 As thick as motes that speckle a sun-beam,
Blessing the halls, the chambers, kitchens, bowers,
Cities and boroughs, castles, courts and towers,
Thorpes, barns and stables, outhouses and dairies,
And that's the reason why there are no fairies.
45 Wherever there was wont to walk an elf
Today there walks the holy friar himself
As evening falls or when the daylight springs,
Saying his matins and his holy things,
Walking his limit round from town to town.
50 Women can now go safely up and down
By every bush or under every tree;
There is no other incubus but he,
So there is really no one else to hurt you
And he will do no more than take your **virtue**.

55   Now it so happened, I began to say,
Long, long ago in good King Arthur's day,
There was a knight who was a lusty liver.
One day as he came riding from the river
He saw a maiden walking all forlorn
60 Ahead of him, alone as she was born.
And of that maiden, spite of all she said,
By very force he took her maidenhead.
   This act of violence made such a stir,
So much petitioning to the king for her,
65 That he condemned the knight to lose his head
By course of law. He was as good as dead
(It seems that then the statutes took that view)
But that the queen, and other ladies too,
Implored the king to exercise his grace
70 So ceaselessly, he gave the queen the case
And granted her his life, and she could choose
Whether to show him mercy or refuse.

   The queen returned him thanks with all her might,
And then she sent a summons to the knight
75 At her convenience, and expressed her will:
"You stand, for such is the position still,
In no way certain of your life," said she,
"Yet you shall live if you can answer me:
What is the thing that women most desire?
80 Beware the axe and say as I require.

NOTICE & NOTE

40 **motes:** specks of dust.
41 **bowers:** bedrooms.
43 **thorpes:** villages; **outhouses:** sheds.
45 **wherever . . . elf:** wherever an elf was accustomed to walk.
49 **limit:** the area to which a friar was restricted in his begging for donations.
52 **incubus** (ĭnˈkyə-bəs): an evil spirit believed to descend on women.

virtue
(vûrˈchoo) *n. Archaic* chastity, especially in a woman.

61 **of that maiden . . . maidenhead:** in spite of the maiden's protests, he robbed her of her virginity.

CONTRASTS AND CONTRADICTIONS

Notice & Note: In lines 66–72, mark the words or phrases indicating behavior that would not be consistent with the behavior of a traditional medieval king.

Infer: What does this contradiction demonstrate about the Wife of Bath's views on the relationship between men and women?

The Wife of Bath's Tale 29

TEACH

CONTRASTS AND CONTRADICTIONS

Explain to students that contrasts and contradictions can help students understand similarities and differences between two or more ideas, characters, themes, etc. Have students identify the details in lines 66–72 that contrast the behavior of the king with other medieval kings. Then, have students answer the question to determine how the Wife of Bath feels about the relationship between men and women. (**Answer:** *The Wife of Bath seems to believe that men are at the mercy of women – women hold the power in relationships.*)

■ English Learner Support

Compare and Contrast Guide students to understand that when comparing, you identify ideas that are the same; when you contrast, you identify ideas that are different. Ask students to draw a Venn diagram that allows them to compare and contrast the behavior of the king in "The Wife of Bath's Tale" with that of a traditional medieval king. The labels of the Venn diagram should be "Bath's Tale King" and "Medieval Kings." Remind students to draw on prior knowledge – what have they heard, seen, or read about traditional kings. Allow students to work in small groups to discuss their ideas and to complete their Venn diagrams.

WHEN STUDENTS STRUGGLE . . .

Order of Events Have students work individually or in pairs to put the events described on page 29 in the order in which they occurred. Write these sentences on the board in mixed order: the knight saw the maiden (*first*), the maiden walked alone (*next*), the queen asked the knight a question (*last*).

 For additional support, go to the **Reading Studio** and assign the following Level Up tutorial: **Main Ideas and Supporting Details.**

CRITICAL VOCABULARY

virtue: Chastity, especially in women, was a quality that was valued and made them more eligible for a husband.

ASK STUDENTS why they think it was important for a woman to have virtue. Was it necessary for a man to also be virtuous? How has this changed in the 21st century? (*Sometimes, women and men are judged according to different standards. In a society where women depended so heavily on their husbands for their livelihood, it makes sense that women were willing to follow the rules even if they found them to be unjust.*)

The Wife of Bath's Tale 29

TEACH

ANALYZE NARRATOR

Remind students that the **narrator** in the story is the character or voice that recounts the events of the story. In this case, the Wife of Bath is the narrator. Direct students to identify the third person point of view from which the Wife of Bath speaks in lines 99-108, as well as her pleased tone. (**Answer:** The Wife of Bath seems pleased and eager to give the knight an answer as he is interested in a woman's opinion. She says, "A man can win us best with flattery. To dance attendance on us, make a fuss, Ensnares us all, the best and worst of us.)

ENGLISH LEARNER SUPPORT

Express Feelings, Ideas, and Opinions Remind students that the knight was sent on a journey to find out what women want. Instruct students to reread lines 92–123 and ask them to find answers to this big question, "What do women want?"

- Display the big question, "What do women want?" Ask students to use drawings to answer the question and draw evidence from their own experiences or other texts they have read to support their ideas. You may provide students with sentence stems such as: I drew _____ because I believe that women want _____. **SUBSTANTIAL**

- Display the big question, "What do women want?" In groups of four, ask students to find answers to this question, drawing evidence from the selection. **MODERATE**

- Display the big question, "What do women want?" Tell students to identify pieces of evidence and details to support their ideas. Then, in pairs, ask them to discuss their findings, making sure to support their answers with evidence from the selection or other texts they have read. **LIGHT**

NOTICE & NOTE

"If you can't answer on the moment, though,
I will concede you this: you are to go
A twelvemonth and a day to seek and learn
Sufficient answer, then you shall return.
85 I shall take gages from you to extort
Surrender of your body to the court."

    Sad was the knight and sorrowfully sighed,
But there! All other choices were denied,
And in the end he chose to go away
90 And to return after a year and day
Armed with such answer as there might be sent
To him by God. He took his leave and went.

    He knocked at every house, searched every place,
Yes, anywhere that offered hope of grace.
95 What could it be that women wanted most?
But all the same he never touched a coast,
Country or town in which there seemed to be
Any two people willing to agree.

    Some said that women wanted wealth and treasure,
100 "Honor," said some, some "Jollity and pleasure,"
Some "Gorgeous clothes" and others "Fun in bed,"
"To be oft widowed and remarried," said
Others again, and some that what most mattered
Was that we should be cosseted and flattered.
105 That's very near the truth, it seems to me;
A man can win us best with flattery.
To dance attendance on us, make a fuss,
Ensnares us all, the best and worst of us.

    Some say the things we most desire are these:
110 Freedom to do exactly as we please,
With no one to reprove our faults and lies,
Rather to have one call us good and wise.
Truly there's not a woman in ten score
Who has a fault, and someone rubs the sore,
115 But she will kick if what he says is true;
You try it out and you will find so too.
However vicious we may be within
We like to be thought wise and void of sin.
Others assert we women find it sweet
120 When we are thought dependable, discreet
And secret, firm of purpose and controlled,
Never betraying things that we are told.
But that's not worth the handle of a rake;

85 gages: pledges.

104 cosseted (kŏs´ĭ-tĭd): pampered.

ANALYZE NARRATOR
Annotate: Mark words or phrases in lines 99–108 that convey the Wife of Bath's tone.
Infer: What is her attitude toward the knight's quest for an answer?

113 ten score: 200.

115 but she will: who will not.

118 void of sin: sinless.

30 Unit 1

APPLYING ACADEMIC VOCABULARY

☐ collapse ☑ displace ☐ military ☐ violate ☑ visual

Write and Discuss Have students turn to a partner to discuss the following questions. Guide students to include the academic vocabulary words *displace* and *visual* in their responses. Ask volunteers to share their responses with the class.

- What would happen if a civilian or commoner tried to **displace** a member of the royal family?
- Which details in "The Wife of Bath's Tale" have painted the best **visual** for you so far?

Women conceal a thing? For Heaven's sake!
125 Remember Midas? Will you hear the tale?

Among some other little things, now stale,
Ovid relates that under his long hair
The unhappy Midas grew a splendid pair
Of ass's ears; as subtly as he might,
130 He kept his foul deformity from sight;
Save for his wife, there was not one that knew.
He loved her best, and trusted in her too.
He begged her not to tell a living creature
That he possessed so horrible a feature.
135 And she—she swore, were all the world to win,
She would not do such villainy and sin
As saddle her husband with so foul a name;
Besides to speak would be to share the shame.
Nevertheless she thought she would have died
140 Keeping this secret bottled up inside;
It seemed to swell her heart and she, no doubt,
Thought it was on the point of bursting out.

Fearing to speak of it to woman or man,
Down to a reedy marsh she quickly ran
145 And reached the sedge. Her heart was all on fire
And, as a bittern bumbles in the mire,
She whispered to the water, near the ground,
"Betray me not, O water, with thy sound!
To thee alone I tell it: it appears
150 My husband has a pair of ass's ears!
Ah! My heart's well again, the secret's out!
I could no longer keep it, not a doubt."
And so you see, although we may hold fast
A little while, it must come out at last,
155 We can't keep secrets; as for Midas, well,
Read Ovid for his story; he will tell.

This knight that I am telling you about
Perceived at last he never would find out
What it could be that women loved the best.
160 Faint was the soul within his sorrowful breast,
As home he went, he dared no longer stay;
His year was up and now it was the day.

As he rode home in a dejected mood
Suddenly, at the margin of a wood,
165 He saw a dance upon the leafy floor

NOTICE & NOTE

125 Midas: a legendary king of Phrygia, in Asia Minor.

127 Ovid (ŏv´ĭd): an ancient Roman poet whose *Metamorphoses* is a storehouse of Greek and Roman legends.

131 save: except.

ANALYZE NARRATOR
Annotate: Reread lines 143–156. Mark the Wife of Bath's hint that Midas's secret will not be safe after his wife whispers it to the water.

Draw Conclusions: Why might Chaucer have chosen to include this long digression in the narrator's story?

145 sedge: marsh grasses.

146 bumbles in the mire: booms in the swamp. (The bittern, a wading bird, is famous for its loud call.)

The Wife of Bath's Tale 31

TEACH

ANALYZE NARRATOR

Remind students that the **narrator** in the story often has information that other characters or the reader does not have. The narrator can shed light on or contextualize the events in the story and help the reader make sense of it all. Direct students to consider language that hints that Midas's secret will not be safe. (**Answer:** *"To thee alone I tell it; it appears;"* this suggests that someone or something may be listening. Chaucer might have included this digression to convey how long-winded the Wife of Bath is – she is also full of contradictions, and while she is a defender of women's rights and touts how noble they are, this digression also suggests that women cannot keep secrets, or can't be trusted.)

TO CHALLENGE STUDENTS . . .

Do the Research On page 31, Chaucer references the story of King Midas, written by Ovid, an ancient Roman poet. Encourage students to research Ovid's story of King Midas and draw connections between that story and the Wife of Bath's Tale retelling of the story. In groups, ask students to discuss why they think Chaucer includes the story of Midas in this selection.

The Wife of Bath's Tale

TEACH

ENGLISH LEARNER SUPPORT

Vocabulary Strategy Remind students that this is an old text, and as a result, some of the words are obsolete (they are no longer used in the English language), or some of the meanings of words may be unusual. Point out the words in the margins on page 32 and ask students to review their meanings. Tell students to substitute the meanings of the words into the sentences as they read and determine whether the sentence makes sense. **MODERATE**

 **NOTICE & NOTE**

> Of four and twenty ladies, nay, and more.
> Eagerly he approached, in hope to learn
> Some words of wisdom ere he should return;
> But lo! Before he came to where they were,
> 170 Dancers and dance all vanished into air!
> There wasn't a living creature to be seen
> Save one old woman crouched upon the green.
> A fouler-looking creature I suppose
> Could scarcely be imagined. She arose
> 175 And said, "Sir knight, there's no way on from here.
> Tell me what you are looking for, my dear,
> For peradventure that were best for you;
> We old, old women know a thing or two."
>
> "Dear Mother," said the knight, "alack the day!
> 180 I am as good as dead if I can't say
> What thing it is that women most desire;
> If you could tell me I would pay your hire."
> "Give me your hand," she said, "and swear to do
> Whatever I shall next require of you
> 185 —If so to do should lie within your might—
> And you shall know the answer before night."
> "Upon my honor," he answered, "I agree."
> "Then," said the crone, "I dare to guarantee
> Your life is safe; I shall make good my claim.
> 190 Upon my life the queen will say the same.
> Show me the very proudest of them all
> In costly coverchief or jewelled caul
> That dare say no to what I have to teach.
> Let us go forward without further speech."
> 195 And then she crooned her gospel in his ear
> And told him to be glad and not to fear.
>
> They came to court. This knight, in full array,
> Stood forth and said, "O Queen, I've kept my day
> And kept my word and have my answer ready."
>
> 200 There sat the noble matrons and the heady
> Young girls, and widows too, that have the grace
> Of wisdom, all assembled in that place,
> And there the queen herself was throned to hear
> And judge his answer. Then the knight drew near
> 205 And silence was commanded through the hall.
>
> The queen gave order he should tell them all
> What thing it was that women wanted most.

177 peradventure: maybe; possibly.

179 alack the day: an exclamation of sorrow, roughly equivalent to "Woe is me!"

192 coverchief: kerchief; **caul** (kaul): an ornamental hairnet.

195 gospel: message.

197 in full array: in all his finery.

200 heady: giddy; impetuous.
201 grace: gift.

IMPROVE READING FLUENCY

Targeted Passage Have students work with partners to read page 32 in their books. First, use lines 166-178 to model how to read the lines of the poem. Have students follow along in their books as you read the text with appropriate phrasing, emphasis, and pausing where punctuation is used. Then, have partners take turns reading aloud each stanza on this page. Encourage students to provide feedback and support when pronouncing unfamiliar words. Remind students that when they are reading aloud for an audience, they should pace their reading so the audience has time to understand difficult concepts.

 Go to the **Reading Studio** for additional support in developing fluency.

He stood not silent like a beast or post,
But gave his answer with the ringing word
210 Of a man's voice and the assembly heard:

"My liege and lady, in general," said he,
"A woman wants the self-same **sovereignty**
Over her husband as over her lover,
And master him; he must not be above her.
215 That is your greatest wish, whether you kill
Or spare me; please yourself. I wait your will."

In all the court not one that shook her head
Or contradicted what the knight had said;
Maid, wife and widow cried, "He's saved his life!"

220 And on the word up started the old wife,
The one the knight saw sitting on the green,
And cried, "Your mercy, sovereign lady queen!
Before the court disperses, do me right!
'Twas I who taught this answer to the knight,
225 For which he swore, and pledged his honor to it,
That the first thing I asked of him he'd do it,

211 liege (lēj): lord.

sovereignty
(sŏv´ər-ĭn-tē, sŏv´rĭn-tē) *n.*
complete independence and
self-government.

LANGUAGE CONVENTIONS
Annotate: Mark the inverted phrase in lines 217–222.

Analyze: How does this inversion help maintain the pattern of the verse?

The Wife of Bath's Tale 33

TEACH

✏️ ANALYZE NARRATOR

Remind students that the narrator has the power to shape how the reader interacts with the characters and events in the story. The narrator's tone, or his or her attitude toward the events and characters in a story, can impact the ways in which the reader perceives how the story unfolds. Direct students to lines 247–256 and ask them to identify words or phrases that hint at the narrator's tone. (**Answer:** *"I say there was no joy or feast at all, Nothing but heaviness of heart and sorrow."* Based on the way that the Wife of Bath describes the wedding night, the reader comes to perceive it as a lackluster event – no celebration at all; this is in contrast to what we generally feel when we think about weddings.)

■ English Learner Support

Implicit and Explicit Language When discussing lines 232–256, help students understand the difference between implicit and explicit ideas.

- Read aloud line 235 and guide students to understand its meaning. Explain that when the young man says "leave my body free," he is asking the woman not to make him marry her. Ask what he means by "take all my goods." Help students use details, such as "gold," to understand that "all my goods" refers to the man's riches or what he owns. **SUBSTANTIAL**

- Draw students' attention to the phrase "I neglect to tell of the rejoicing and display made at the feast." Ask why the narrator did not describe a joyful celebration at the wedding. Help students use evidence from the text to respond. Guide them to identify that there was no feast or celebration, since the wedding was not a happy occasion for the young man. **MODERATE**

- In pairs, ask students to take turns explaining the differences between implicit and explicit ideas. Direct students to find examples of each from the selection and explain how they contribute to the author's overall tone and message. **LIGHT**

✏️ NOTICE & NOTE

So far as it should lie within his might.
Before this court I ask you then, sir knight,
To keep your word and take me for your wife;
230 For well you know that I have saved your life.
If this be false, deny it on your sword!"

"Alas!" he said, "Old lady, by the Lord
I know indeed that such was my behest,
But for God's love think of a new request,
235 Take all my goods, but leave my body free."
"A curse on us," she said, "if I agree!
I may be foul, I may be poor and old,
Yet will not choose to be, for all the gold
That's bedded in the earth or lies above,
240 Less than your wife, nay, than your very love!"

"My love?" said he. "By heaven, my damnation!
Alas that any of my race and station
Should ever make so foul a misalliance!"
Yet in the end his pleading and defiance
245 All went for nothing, he was forced to wed.
He takes his ancient wife and goes to bed.

Now peradventure some may well suspect
A lack of care in me since I neglect
To tell of the rejoicing and display
250 Made at the feast upon their wedding-day.
I have but a short answer to let fall;
I say there was no joy or feast at all,

Nothing but heaviness of heart and sorrow.
He married her in private on the morrow
255 And all day long stayed hidden like an owl,
It was such torture that his wife looked foul.

Great was the anguish churning in his head
When he and she were piloted to bed;
He wallowed back and forth in desperate style.
260 His ancient wife lay smiling all the while;
At last she said, "Bless us! Is this, my dear,
How knights and wives get on together here?
Are these the laws of good King Arthur's house?
Are knights of his all so contemptuous?
265 I am your own beloved and your wife,
And I am she, indeed, that saved your life;

233 behest (bĭ-hĕst´): promise.

242 race and station: family and rank.

243 misalliance (mĭs´ə-lī´əns): an unsuitable marriage.

ANALYZE NARRATOR
Annotate: Mark words and phrases in lines 247–256 that convey the Wife of Bath's tone.
Draw Conclusions: How does her tone influence readers' views of their wedding night?

258 piloted: led. (In the Middle Ages, the wedding party typically escorted the bride and groom to their bedchamber.)

259 wallowed: (wŏl´ōd) rolled around; thrashed about.

34 Unit 1

And certainly I never did you wrong.
Then why, this first of nights, so sad a song?
You're carrying on as if you were half-witted.
270 Say, for God's love, what sin have I committed?
I'll put things right if you will tell me how."

"Put right?" he cried. "That never can be now!
Nothing can ever be put right again!
You're old, and so abominably plain,
275 So poor to start with, so low-bred to follow;
It's little wonder if I twist and wallow!
God, that my heart would burst within my breast!"

"Is that," said she, "the cause of your unrest?"

"Yes, certainly," he said, "and can you wonder?"

280 "I could set right what you suppose a blunder,
That's if I cared to, in a day or two,
If I were shown more courtesy by you.
Just now," she said, "you spoke of gentle birth,
Such as descends from ancient wealth and worth.
285 If that's the claim you make for gentlemen
Such arrogance is hardly worth a hen.
Whoever loves to work for virtuous ends,
Public and private, and who most intends
To do what deeds of gentleness he can,
290 Take him to be the greatest gentleman.
Christ wills we take our gentleness from Him,
Not from a wealth of ancestry long dim,
Though they **bequeath** their whole establishment
By which we claim to be of high descent.
295 Our fathers cannot make us a bequest
Of all those virtues that became them best
And earned for them the name of gentlemen,
But bade us follow them as best we can.

"Thus the wise poet of the Florentines,
300 Dante by name, has written in these lines,
For such is the opinion Dante launches:
'Seldom arises by these slender branches
Prowess of men, for it is God, no less,
Wills us to claim of Him our gentleness.'
305 For of our parents nothing can we claim
Save temporal things, and these may hurt and maim.

ANALYZE NARRATOR
Annotate: Reread lines 272–286. Mark phrases that suggest the old woman doesn't take the knight's rejection seriously.
Compare: What does the old woman have in common with the Wife of Bath?

bequeath
(bĭ-kwēth´, -kwēth´) *tr.v.*
to pass (something) on to another; hand down.

299 Florentines: the people of Florence, Italy.

300 Dante (dän´tā): a famous medieval Italian poet. Lines 302–304 refer to a passage in Dante's most famous work, *The Divine Comedy*.

306 temporal: worldly, rather than spiritual.

The Wife of Bath's Tale 35

APPLYING ACADEMIC VOCABULARY

 collapse   ☐ displace    military    violate   ☐ visual

Write and Discuss Have students turn to a partner to discuss the following questions. Guide students to include the academic vocabulary words *collapse, military,* and *violate* in their responses. Ask volunteers to share their responses with the class.

- What factors would cause the institution of marriage to **collapse**?
- What do you think it would be like to live a **military** life?
- How would you react if someone were to **violate** your trust?

TEACH

ENGLISH LEARNER SUPPORT

Demonstrate Comprehension Direct students' attention to lines 336–338:

*Gentility must come from God alone.
That we are gentle comes to us by grace
And by no means is it bequeathed with place.*

- Read lines 336-338 for the whole class, modeling how to read a poem, with appropriate emphasis, pauses, and enunciation. After the first read, ask students to brainstorm some ideas about what they think these lines mean. Then, ask students to engage in a shared reading in small groups. After reading the lines a few times in their small groups, ask students to underline familiar words and discuss what those words mean. Then, ask them to circle new or challenging words, and use a reference book to define those terms. Have students work with English-speaking partners to illustrate the new or challenging words and have them record the words in their notebooks. Give students an opportunity to explain what they think lines 336-338 mean based on what they have learned. Encourage them to use the word *bequeath* in their answers. Provide students with sentence frames such as the following to guide their comprehension of lines 336-338:

- *Bequeath* means to _____.
- *We* in line 337 refers to _____.
- *It* in line 338 refers to _____.
- This means that _____ bequeaths humans with _____. **ALL LEVELS**

 **NOTICE & NOTE**

308 gentility (jĕn-tĭl´ĭ-tē): the quality possessed by a gentle, or noble, person.

314 Caucasus (kô´kə-səs): a region of western Asia between the Black and Caspian seas.

321 possessions: beliefs; ideals

325 lording: lord; nobleman.

332 churl (chûrl)**:** low-class person; boor.

339 Valerius (və-lîr´ē-əs): Valerius Maximus, a Roman writer who compiled a collection of historical anecdotes.

340 Tullius (tŭl´ē-əs) **surnamed Hostilius** (hŏ-stĭl´ē-əs): the third king of the Romans.

342 Boethius (bō-ē´thē-əs): a Christian philosopher of the Dark Ages; **Seneca** (sĕn´ĭ-kə): an ancient Roman philosopher, writer, teacher, and politician.

"But everyone knows this as well as I;
For if gentility were implanted by
The natural course of lineage down the line,
310   Public or private, could it cease to shine
In doing the fair work of gentle deed?
No vice or villainy could then bear seed.

"Take fire and carry it to the darkest house
Between this kingdom and the Caucasus,
315   And shut the doors on it and leave it there,
It will burn on, and it will burn as fair
As if ten thousand men were there to see,
For fire will keep its nature and degree,
I can assure you, sir, until it dies.

320   "But gentleness, as you will recognize,
Is not annexed in nature to possessions.
Men fail in living up to their professions;
But fire never ceases to be fire.
God knows you'll often find, if you enquire,
325   Some lording full of villainy and shame.
If you would be esteemed for the mere name
Of having been by birth a gentleman
And stemming from some virtuous, noble clan,
And do not live yourself by gentle deed
330   Or take your father's noble code and creed,
You are no gentleman, though duke or earl.
Vice and bad manners are what make a churl.

"Gentility is only the renown
For bounty that your fathers handed down,
335   Quite foreign to your person, not your own;
Gentility must come from God alone.
That we are gentle comes to us by grace
And by no means is it bequeathed with place.

"Reflect how noble (says Valerius)
340   Was Tullius surnamed Hostilius,
Who rose from poverty to nobleness.
And read Boethius, Seneca no less,
Thus they express themselves and are agreed:
'Gentle is he that does a gentle deed.'
345   And therefore, my dear husband, I conclude
That even if my ancestors were rude,
Yet God on high—and so I hope He will—
Can grant me grace to live in virtue still,

A gentlewoman only when beginning
350 To live in virtue and to shrink from sinning.

"As for my poverty which you reprove,
Almighty God Himself in whom we move,
Believe and have our being, chose a life
Of poverty, and every man or wife,
355 Nay, every child can see our Heavenly King
Would never stoop to choose a shameful thing.
No shame in poverty if the heart is gay,
As Seneca and all the learned say.
He who accepts his poverty unhurt
360 I'd say is rich although he lacked a shirt.
But truly poor are they who whine and fret
And covet what they cannot hope to get.
And he that, having nothing, covets not,
Is rich, though you may think he is a sot.

365 "True poverty can find a song to sing.
Juvenal says a pleasant little thing:
'The poor can dance and sing in the relief
Of having nothing that will tempt a thief.'
Though it be hateful, poverty is good,
370 A great incentive to a livelihood,
And a great help to our capacity
For wisdom, if accepted patiently.
Poverty is, though wanting in estate,
A kind of wealth that none calumniate.
375 Poverty often, when the heart is lowly,
Brings one to God and teaches what is holy,
Gives knowledge of oneself and even lends
A glass by which to see one's truest friends.
And since it's no offense, let me be plain;
380 Do not **rebuke** my poverty again.

"Lastly you taxed me, sir, with being old.
Yet even if you never had been told
By ancient books, you gentlemen engage,
Yourselves in honor to respect old age.
385 To call an old man 'father' shows good breeding,
And this could be supported from my reading.

"You say I'm old and fouler than a fen.
You need not fear to be a cuckold, then.
Filth and old age, I'm sure you will agree,

364 sot: fool.

366 Juvenal (jōō'və-nəl): an ancient Roman satirist.

373 wanting in estate: lacking in grandeur.

374 calumniate (kə-lŭm'nē-āt'): criticize with false statements; slander.

380 rebuke (rĭ-byōōk') v. to criticize sharply or reprimand.

387 fen: marsh.

388 cuckold (kŭk'əld): a husband whose wife is unfaithful.

TEACH

TOUGH QUESTIONS

Explain to students that this signpost is often used to draw students' attention to tough questions or lessons in a piece of fictional work. Direct students to identify the question in lines 393–401 and discuss why this is important. Ask students to consider why it is necessary for the knight to think about this question at this point. (**Answer:** *The question in lines 393–401 is "You have two choices; which one will you try?" To answer this question, the knight must take personal responsibility for his actions and come to terms with his humility. He must also decide what's more important to him – youth and beauty, or wisdom and loyalty. This teaches us, the readers, that as we get older, we must make difficult choices – we must not leave it to others.*)

 ANALYZE NARRATOR

Remind students a narrator's tone might stay the same, or it might change throughout the story. In lines 424–430, the narrator's attitude toward the knight shifts. Ask students to identify shifts in the narrator's tone and language. How does the narrator's tone affect the way the reader perceives the knight at this point in the poem? (**Answer:** *Even though the Wife of Bath uses flowery language to describe the knight's feelings, she likely does not want the reader to sympathize with the knight because his feelings for the old woman change only after her transformation. He basically gets rewarded for behaving badly, and that is not noble.*)

 **NOTICE & NOTE**

TOUGH QUESTIONS

Notice & Note: Mark the tough question in lines 393–401.

Analyze: What internal conflict must the knight resolve to answer this question?

398 chance your arm: take your chance on.

ANALYZE NARRATOR

Annotate: Reread lines 424–430. Mark words and phrases that describe the knight's feelings.

Draw Conclusions: Do you think the Wife of Bath wants readers to sympathize with the knight at this point in the story? Why or why not?

---

390 Are powerful wardens over chastity.
Nevertheless, well knowing your delights,
I shall fulfil your worldly appetites.

"You have two choices; which one will you try?
To have me old and ugly till I die,
395 But still a loyal, true, and humble wife
That never will displease you all her life,
Or would you rather I were young and pretty
And chance your arm what happens in a city
Where friends will visit you because of me,
400 Yes, and in other places too, maybe.
Which would you have? The choice is all your own."

The knight thought long, and with a piteous groan
At last he said, with all the care in life,
"My lady and my love, my dearest wife,
405 I leave the matter to your wise decision.
You make the choice yourself, for the provision
Of what may be agreeable and rich
In honor to us both, I don't care which;
Whatever pleases you suffices me."

410 "And have I won the mastery?" said she,
"Since I'm to choose and rule as I think fit?"
"Certainly, wife," he answered her, "that's it."
"Kiss me," she cried. "No quarrels! On my oath
And word of honor, you shall find me both,
415 That is, both fair and faithful as a wife;
May I go howling mad and take my life
Unless I prove to be as good and true
As ever wife was since the world was new!
And if tomorrow when the sun's above
420 I seem less fair than any lady-love,
Than any queen or empress east or west,
Do with my life and death as you think best.
Cast up the curtain, husband. Look at me!"

And when indeed the knight had looked to see,
425 Lo, she was young and lovely, rich in charms.
In ecstasy he caught her in his arms,
His heart went bathing in a bath of blisses
And melted in a hundred thousand kisses,

And she responded in the fullest measure
430 With all that could delight or give him pleasure.

So they lived ever after to the end
In perfect bliss; and may Christ Jesus send
Us husbands meek and young and fresh in bed,
And grace to overbid them when we wed.
435 And—Jesu hear my prayer!—cut short the lives
Of those who won't be governed by their wives;
And all old, angry niggards of their pence,
God send them soon a very pestilence!

NOTICE & NOTE

ANALYZE STRUCTURE

Annotate: Mark the phrases in lines 432–438 that express the Wife of Bath's thoughts about husbands.

Analyze: In the frame story we learn that the Wife of Bath had five husbands. How does this conclusion relate to her background?

CHECK YOUR UNDERSTANDING

Answer these questions before moving on to the **Analyze the Text** section on the following page.

1. What action leads to the knight's death sentence?

   A He insults the queen.

   B He assaults a maiden.

   C He is unable to answer the queen's question.

   D He assaults the old woman.

2. How does the old woman get the knight to marry her?

   F She gives him money that she received from her father.

   G She magically becomes a beautiful elf like he wants.

   H She makes him pledge to honor her first request.

   J She tricks the Queen into making him marry her.

3. According to the old woman, why should the knight trust that she will be a faithful wife?

   A She is too poor to attract other men.

   B She has vowed to be faithful.

   C She will always be at his side.

   D She looks old and ugly.

The Wife of Bath's Tale 39

APPLY

ANALYZE THE TEXT
Possible answers:

1. **DOK 1:** *The frame of the story establishes the hostility between the Friar and the Wife. Therefore, readers understand the Wife is insulting the Friar through her ironic commentary on the behavior of friars. She ends by accusing friars of taking advantage of maidens in line 54, "And he will do no more than take your virtue," just as the knight does, thus providing a fitting transition into her tale by equating friars and the knight.*

2. **DOK 2:** *The answers to the knight's question show that the Wife enjoys being flattered and made a fuss (lines 105–108); that she doesn't have to have her faults pointed out (lines 111–116); and that she doesn't believe women can keep a secret (lines 120–125).*

3. **DOK 3:** *By the end of the story, the knight has a better understanding of women. He transforms from someone who values youth and good looks to someone who is able to appreciate what a woman has to offer, not just her looks. He also begins to understand that what women want is to have sovereignty over their husbands, and allows the old woman to choose him. This shows maturity and growth.*

4. **DOK 3:** *The Wife of Bath is a consummate storyteller. She builds suspense through strategic digression; she balances the serious parts of the story with humor; and she develops significant themes.*

5. **DOK 4:** *The knight and the old lady "lived ever after to the end In perfect bliss." Essentially, the knight is rewarded for a serious crime. Yet, the happy ending may be seen as necessary to show his change and convey a message about humility and respect.*

RESEARCH

Remind students to use specific search terms or phrases when conducting research. Consider asking students to pair up and brainstorm some search terms they can use before they begin their research.

Extend Students may find poems written at various points over the course of history, which means the views shared in those poems may or may not differ from their own ideas, beliefs, and values. Engage students in a discussion about the poems they have identified and how they can learn from them.

 **RESPOND**

ANALYZE THE TEXT
Support your responses with evidence from the text. NOTEBOOK

1. **Identify** Chaucer's frame story includes the interaction between the Wife of Bath and the Friar in "The Wife of Bath's Prologue." How is their relationship reflected in the tale itself?

2. **Infer** As a narrator, the Wife of Bath comments extensively about the various answers to the knight's question. What do her comments reveal about her own values and ideas? Use evidence from the poem to support the analysis.

3. **Draw Conclusions** Does the knight gain a better understanding of women over the course of the story, or is he basically the same as he was at the beginning? Explain your response.

4. **Critique** In the "Wife of Bath's Prologue," the Friar complains about the Wife of Bath's long, rambling preamble. How effective is she at narrating her tale about the knight? Explain your response.

5. **Notice & Note** In the last four stanzas, the knight's response to the old woman's question resolves the conflict between them. Do you find this conclusion satisfying? Explain why or why not.

RESEARCH

Chaucer's tale reflects the period in which he lived. During the Middle Ages, England's legal system was not nearly as developed as it is today, and women's roles were limited. Do some research on the following questions to find out more about the background to the story.

QUESTION	ANSWER
What rights did women have in medieval Europe?	Women had little or no role to play within the country at large. Their primary roles were to support their husbands.
What opportunities did women have outside of marriage?	Some women were involved in farm work.
What kind of legal system existed in this period?	Early Medieval Justice and Law was dominated by the principles of the Feudal system, which meant the feudal lord presided over most cases.

RESEARCH TIP
When you conduct online research, use specific search terms. If you just type "women's roles," your search might return some relevant information, but most of it won't relate to your topic. However, if you search "women's roles in the Middle Ages," you're more likely to find useful information.

Extend Find another narrative poem with a female speaker. Discuss with a partner what elements of the poem, including vocabulary and imagery, are similar to or different from "The Wife of Bath's Tale." Then, determine which poem speaks more to your own beliefs and discuss this with your partner.

LEARNING MINDSET

Belonging Students who experience a sense of belonging have fewer behavior problems, are more open to critique, take responsible risks, and tend to have more positive attitudes towards their work, their teachers, and their peers. To build a sense of belonging, remind students that they are valued members of your classroom and encourage them to share their ideas even if they don't have all of the right answers.

CREATE AND PRESENT

Write a Short Story Write a short story in which the pilgrims who appear in the "Wife of Bath's Prologue" resume their conversation after she finishes her tale. Reread the prologue before you begin.

❑ Think about how the Friar, the Summoner, and the Host might react to the tale.

❑ Introduce and develop the characters in a way that is consistent with the prologue.

❑ Use dialogue and descriptive details.

❑ Provide a conclusion that resolves the conflict in the story.

Present a Short Story Read your story aloud to a small group.

❑ Practice reading the story so you can present it smoothly.

❑ When reading dialogue, adjust the tone of your voice to reflect how each character would speak.

❑ Use facial expressions and gestures to convey the emotions of the characters.

RESPOND TO THE ESSENTIAL QUESTION

 What is true chivalry?

Gather Information Review your annotations and notes on "The Wife of Bath's Tale." Then, add relevant information to your Response Log. As you determine which information to include, think about:

- the crime that got the knight into trouble
- the knight's reaction when the old woman insists that he marry her
- the lessons that the old woman teaches the knight about true gentility
- the conclusion of the tale

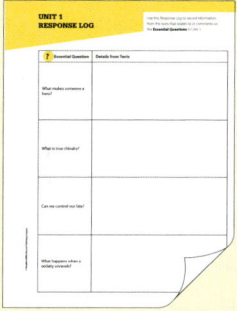

RESPOND

Go to the **Writing Studio** for more on writing a narrative.

Go to the **Speaking and Listening Studio** for more on giving a presentation.

ACADEMIC VOCABULARY

As you write and discuss what you learned from the "The Wife of Bath's Tale," be sure to use the Academic Vocabulary words. Check off each of the words that you use.

❑ collapse
❑ displace
❑ military
❑ violate
❑ visual

The Wife of Bath's Tale   41

APPLY

CREATE AND PRESENT

Write a Short Story Point out that the list on page 41 can serve as a guideline for students' stories. Tell students that before they write their stories, they can brainstorm some ideas using the list to guide their process. Once they have used the list to come up with original ideas, they can draft their stories.

Present a Short Story Remind students to review the list and practice the items that are listed before presenting their short stories. Encourage them to ask each other for advice if they need help with effectively conveying a specific tone or capturing a specific character in their story.

RESPOND TO THE ESSENTIAL QUESTION

Allow time for students to add details from "The Wife of Bath's Tale" to their Unit 1 Response Logs.

APPLY

CRITICAL VOCABULARY

Answers:

1. *a. a monarch's authority*
2. *b. running a free food bank*
3. *b. refusing to do household chores*
4. *a. a last will and testament*
5. *a. an introduction*

VOCABULARY STRATEGY:
Usage

1. *Gentle—kind or soft; rude—impolite or badly behaved; fair—just or honorable; pale*
2. *Sentences will vary.*
3. *Responses will vary.*

 **RESPOND**

WORD BANK
preamble
virtue
sovereignty
bequeath
rebuke

CRITICAL VOCABULARY

Practice and Apply Circle the letter of the best answer to each question. Explain your answer.

1. Which is an example of **sovereignty**?
   a. a monarch's authority
   b. a subject's loyalty

2. Which is likely to involve **virtue**?
   a. running a fast food restaurant
   b. running a free food bank

3. Which is likely to prompt a **rebuke**?
   a. doing household chores quickly
   b. refusing to do household chores

4. Which is used to **bequeath** a gift?
   a. a last will and testament
   b. an invoice

5. Which is involved in a **preamble**?
   a. an introduction
   b. a conclusion

 Go to the **Vocabulary Studio** for more on words with multiple meanings.

VOCABULARY STRATEGY:
Usage

Language is dynamic—new words are continually added, other words are dropped, and still others are used in different ways than they were originally intended. When Geoffrey Chaucer uses the word *virtue* in the line, "And he will do no more than take your virtue," the word *virtue* means "chastity" or "purity." To most readers today, though, *virtue* means "goodness" or "a beneficial quality." Here are other words found in "The Wife of Bath's Tale" that have a different meaning, or usage, today:

WORD IN THE POEM	WHAT IT MEANT IN THE 14TH CENTURY
gentle: "Gentle is he that does a gentle deed."	noble
rude: "even if my ancestors were rude"	of low birth
fair: "And if tomorrow when the sun's above I seem less fair than any lady-love"	beautiful

Practice and Apply Complete the following steps:

1. Write the current definition of each word in the chart.
2. Use each word in a sentence.
3. Form a small group to identify other words in the poem that have changed their meanings over the years. Share the words and their old and new usages with the class.

42 Unit 1

EL ENGLISH LEARNER SUPPORT

Vocabulary Strategy Give students additional practice in determining the meanings of familiar words that have a different usage in "The Wife of Bath's Tale." Write the following words on the board: *pleasure, meek, fresh, pestilence*. Have students work in pairs, copy the words, and determine their usage using context clues. Tell them to look up each word in the dictionary. Then, provide students with fill-in-the-blank questions, and ask them to determine which word completes each sentence. Ask students to discuss other ways they can use the words.

LANGUAGE CONVENTIONS:
Inverted Sentences

An inverted sentence is one in which the normal order of a subject followed by a verb is reversed. Notice how Chaucer uses inversion in these lines from the poem:

> This knight that I am telling you about
> Perceived at last he never would find out
> What it could be that women loved the best.
> Faint was the soul within his sorrowful breast,
> As home he went, he dared no longer stay;
> His year was up and now it was the day.

If Chaucer had chosen not to use inversion, his lines might have appeared this way:

> This knight that I am telling you about
> At last perceived he never would find out
> What it could be that women loved the best.
> His soul within his sorrowful breast was faint,
> As he went home, he dared stay no longer;
> His year was up and now it was the day.

By inverting the sentence in the fourth line, Chaucer preserves the rhyming couplet. Just as importantly, he maintains the effective rhythm of the poem. In the second version of the lines with the subject placed before the verb, the rhythm is lost. In addition the rhythm of the line is stilted and awkward and takes away from the effectiveness of the whole stanza.

Prose writers also use inversion. Varying sentence structure enables writers to refocus the readers' attention. In addition, inverted sentences build up suspense with words and phrases before arriving at the verb and subject. Make sure that your subject and verb agree when writing inverted sentences.

REGULAR ORDER	INVERTED ORDER
"A promise is a promise," the old woman declared.	"A promise is a promise," declared the old woman.
The groom stepped mournfully into the bedroom.	Mournfully into the bedroom stepped the groom.

Practice and Apply Write three inverted sentences about events in "The Wife of Bath's Tale."

RESPOND

Go to the **Grammar Studio** for more on Finding the Subject of a Sentence.

APPLY

LANGUAGE CONVENTIONS:
Inverted Sentences

Remind students that an **inverted sentence** is one in which the order in which the subject and verb appear are reversed. Ask students to provide some examples of inverted sentences they have heard or come up with their own.

Then, ask them to review the example from the selection. Ask a student to read it aloud while others follow. Discuss the impact of Chaucer's words with students, pointing to how the way the lines are structured affect not only delivery, but also the effect the sentence has. Then, ask another student to read the lines had they not been inverted. Ask students to compare and contrast the two examples.

Tell students that varying sentence structure enables writers to refocus the readers' attention. In addition, inverted sentences build up suspense with words and phrases before arriving at the verb and subject. Remind students to make sure that your subject and verb agree when writing inverted sentences.

Practice and Apply Students should demonstrate that they know how to write inverted sentences and can make sense of what the sentence says. Once students have written their inverted sentences, have them share with a partner.

ENGLISH LEARNER SUPPORT

Language Conventions Use the following supports for varying proficiency levels:

- Have students find other inverted sentences in the selection and copy them in their notebooks. **SUBSTANTIAL**
- Have students work with partners to write original inverted sentences. Then, have them meet with another pair to compare their sentences. **MODERATE**
- Ask students to write original sentences related to what they learned from the selection, then transform them into inverted sentences. Ask students to pair up and discuss how their inversions impacted their meaning. **LIGHT**

PLAN

LE MORTE D'ARTHUR
Romance by Sir Thomas Malory

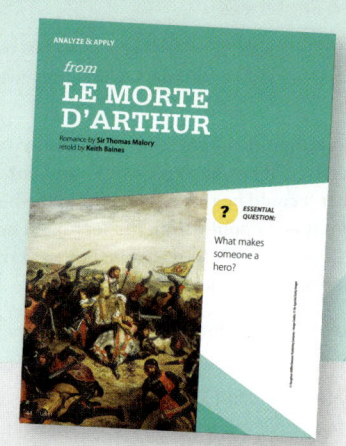

GENRE ELEMENTS
ROMANCE

Tell students that a **romance** may seem complicated, but the plots of romances are generally simple, predictable, and inevitable. Romances portray larger-than-life characters who perform daring deeds. **Chivalry** is one of the most important ideas in a romance. The basic qualities of a chivalrous person are honesty, loyalty, respectfulness, courage, and selflessness. Students will analyze the internal and external conflicts of a chivalrous character and make predictions about what will happen to him.

LEARNING OBJECTIVES
- Analyze conflict and make predictions.
- Conduct research about King Arthur.
- Write a character sketch.
- Direct a scene.
- Use context to define multiple-meaning words.
- Identify tone.
- **Language** Rephrase dialogue, narration, and plot events in simpler, more modern language.

TEXT COMPLEXITY

Quantitative Measures	Le Morte d'Arthur	Lexile: 1130L
Qualitative Measures	**Ideas Presented** Subtle, implied meanings and multiple themes.	
	Structures Used More complex. Some support through subheads.	
	Language Used Complex sentence structures with use of archaic and formal language.	
	Knowledge Required Complex ideas. Cultural and literary knowledge may make heavier demands.	

PLAN

RESOURCES

- Unit 1 Response Log
- Selection Audio
- Reading Studio: Notice & Note
- Writing Studio: Writing Narratives
- Vocabulary Studio: Multiple-Meaning Words
- Grammar Studio: Module 2: Lesson 3: Adjectives
- *Le Morte d'Arthur* Selection Test

SUMMARIES

English
At Sir Gawain's insistence, King Arthur and his army besiege Sir Launcelot at Benwick. Launcelot mortally wounds Sir Gawain in battle as they attack the shore; dying, he writes to Launcelot to forgive him for killing his (Gawain's) brothers and urges him to aid Arthur. As an apparition, Gawain warns Arthur that he will be killed if he attacks before Launcelot arrives. Arthur attempts a truce, but fighting erupts because of a mistake at the signing ceremony. Arthur is mortally wounded; a barge takes the dying Arthur away to Avalon.

Spanish
Por la insistencia de Sir Gawain, el rey Arturo y su ejército asedian a Sir Launcelot en Benwick. Launcelot hiere mortalmente a Sir Gawain en batalla, mientras atacan la costa; moribundo, le escribe a Launcelot que lo perdone por haber matado a sus hermanos y le insta a ayudar a Arturo. Como una aparición, Gawain le advierte a Arturo que será asesinado si ataca antes de que Launcelot llegue. Arturo intenta llegar a una tregua, pero la lucha estalla debido a un error en la ceremonia de la firma. Arturo es herido de muerte; una barcaza lleva al moribundo Arturo a Avalon.

SMALL-GROUP OPTIONS

Have students work in small groups to read and discuss the selection.

Think-Pair-Share
- After students have read the summary of the selection, pose this question to the class: *Why might a dying man forgive someone for killing his brothers?*
- Have students think about the question individually and take notes.
- Invite pairs to discuss their ideas about the question.
- Ask pairs to share their responses with the class.

Send a Problem
- After reading the first 16 paragraphs, ask a student a question about the text.
- Wait 11 seconds for the student to respond.
- If the student has no response, she/he must repeat the question and call on another student to provide the answer.
- Monitor responses and ask another question as needed.

Le Morte d'Arthur 44B

PLAN

Text X-Ray: English Learner Support
for Le Morte d'Arthur

Use the Text X-Ray and the supports and scaffolds in the Teacher's Edition to help guide students at different proficiency levels through the selection.

INTRODUCE THE SELECTION
DISCUSS ROMANCE AND REALISM

In this lesson, students will need to be able to identify and discuss the difference between romance and realism.

Remind students that a romance deals with larger-than-life, idealized characters, exotic settings, the supernatural, hidden or mistaken identity, and heroes who are motivated by faith, love, honor, or adventure. Realism shows people and situations more as they are in real life.

Ask students to compare and contrast romantic and realistic story elements using sentence frames, such as: *One element in the story that shows realism is _____. An example of a romantic element in this story is _____.*

CULTURAL REFERENCES

The following words or phrases may be unfamiliar to students:

- *was brought before* (paragraph 14): was made to appear before someone, usually an authority
- *laughingstock* (paragraph 15): someone made fun of
- *a heavy heart* (paragraph 31): great sadness
- *at my mercy* (paragraph 53): under the control of the speaker, without the ability to get free

LISTENING

Seek Clarification

As students listen to the dramatizations of other groups from p. 61, guide them to ask for clarification as needed.

Use the following supports with students at varying proficiency levels:

- Provide students with a large question mark printed on an index card. Have students hold up the card if they need clarification or to have something repeated. Provide a question bank for students to refer to as they ask their question, such as: *Can you repeat that? What did you mean?* **SUBSTANTIAL**
- Have students write down any questions they have as the dramatizations are being presented. Have them ask questions after the presentation is complete. Provide sentence starters, such as: *Why did you say _____? I don't understand what you mean by _____.* **MODERATE**
- As students watch each dramatization, have them take notes about things that did not sound clear. Then, have them restate their notes as questions they can pose to each group. **LIGHT**

SPEAKING

Rephrase Story Elements

Help students use simpler, more modern language to rephrase dialogue, narration, and plot events.

Use the following supports with students at varying proficiency levels:

- Read aloud the first sentence of the text. Model how to break down the sentence to better understand its meaning, then rephrase each chunk. Have students read aloud the original chunk, then read aloud your rephrasing of each chunk. For example: *When Sir Launcelot ruled France, he settled with his army in the city of Benwick, where his father used to rule.* **SUBSTANTIAL**
- Model how to rephrase the first sentence in simpler, more modern language. Then, have partners chunk the next sentence, defining each chunk. Direct partners to use their definitions and work together to orally rephrase the whole sentence more simply. Allow students to use dictionaries as needed. **MODERATE**
- Model how to rephrase the first sentence in simpler, more modern language. Then, ask partners to work together to orally rephrase the text through paragraph 3. **LIGHT**

READING

Use Punctuation

Remind students to pay close attention to punctuation as they read to understand the full meaning of the text.

Use the following supports with students of varying proficiency levels:

- Explain the punctuation marks in paragraph 40 and have students repeat their names. Have students read paragraph 40 and ask: *What punctuation mark shows emotion?* (exclamation) **SUBSTANTIAL**
- Have students work together to write a list of all the punctuation marks they see in paragraph 40. Then, have partners discuss how each mark helps them know how to read the text. Provide sentence starters, such as: *When I see a comma, I _____.* **MODERATE**
- Have partners take turns reading paragraphs 1–13 aloud to each other, paying close attention to punctuation marks. Have students reread any difficult passages or words more slowly until they can read with greater fluency. **LIGHT**

WRITING

Write a Character Sketch

Tell students they can use a real-life person or fictional character as a starting point, and then add new details to create an original character.

Use the following supports with students of varying proficiency levels:

- Work with students to create a word bank they can use to describe the heroes and their actions. Have students copy the words in their notebooks. **SUBSTANTIAL**
- Have small groups work together to write a list of traits, phrases, or actions that describe heroes. **MODERATE**
- Have partners conduct short interviews about heroes they know or have heard about. Guide them to write up a list of questions to ask before they begin their interviews. Suggest that they form *who, what, where, when, why,* and *how* questions. Then, have each interviewer record each interviewee's responses. **LIGHT**

TEACH

? **Connect to the ESSENTIAL QUESTION**

This excerpt from *Le Morte d'Arthur* tells of the adventures of Sir Launcelot, King Arthur, and the love of both their lives, Gwynevere. Launcelot must defend himself and his actions from Sir Gawain, and prove himself a worthy and chivalrous hero.

ANALYZE & APPLY

from

LE MORTE D'ARTHUR

Romance by **Sir Thomas Malory**
retold by **Keith Baines**

? **ESSENTIAL QUESTION:**

What makes someone a hero?

QUICK START

According to the code of chivalry, knights must always be loyal to their king and country. Write a paragraph about your loyalty to a person or group. Discuss how this sense of loyalty affects your behavior and whether you sometimes struggle to remain loyal.

ANALYZE CONFLICT

Medieval romances typically have exciting plots driven by conflict, a struggle between opposing forces. **External conflict** occurs between a character and an outside force. **Internal conflict** is a struggle within the mind of a character. Both types of conflict can play an important role in the same event. For example, as a knight enters into battle with an enemy, he may struggle internally with doubts about his courage. Often an internal conflict results when a character faces a moral dilemma—a problem in which the character must decide what is morally right. In medieval romances, many characters face moral dilemmas related to their efforts to live up to the code of chivalry. As you read *Le Morte d'Arthur*, look for examples of both external and internal conflict. Analyze how the behavior and underlying motivations of King Arthur, Sir Launcelot, and other knights help create moral dilemmas that influence the plot and theme of the romance.

MAKE PREDICTIONS

When you **make predictions**, you use text clues and prior knowledge to guess what will happen in a story. These predictions may be influenced by your knowledge of the story's genre. For example, if you are reading a romance, you can expect the heroes to act bravely and to make great sacrifices for their ideals. As you read *Le Morte d'Arthur*, use a chart like this one to record your predictions. When you finish reading the text, decide whether you guessed correctly or if you need to correct some predictions.

GENRE ELEMENTS: ROMANCE

- portrays idealized or larger-than-life characters who perform daring deeds
- involves a love relationship
- includes mysterious or supernatural events
- expresses themes related to the code of chivalry

PREDICTION	REASON FOR PREDICTION	OUTCOME
This selection is likely about a knight fighting for justice.	*The cover art, images, and background information indicate this is true.*	*My prediction was correct; the story is about many knights fighting for justice.*
King Arthur will die.	*The title of the story means "The Death of Arthur".*	*My prediction was correct; the king dies at the end of the story.*

TEACH

QUICK START

Have students read the Quick Start question, and invite them to share their paragraphs about their own loyalties. Ask them to discuss times when they struggled to remain loyal and how that turmoil might have led to changes in their behaviors. Then, have the class brainstorm a list of the qualities that make someone heroic, starting with the quality of loyalty.

ANALYZE CONFLICT

Help students understand the difference between external and internal conflicts. Discuss conflicts that some people face and how each type of conflict affects the person's attitudes and behaviors. Then, relate this to the moral dilemmas faced by characters in medieval romances. Point out that these internal struggles and external conflicts affect the characters' choices and actions and reveal the characters' motivations. Explain that conflicts affect the plot of these romances.

MAKE PREDICTIONS

Explain to students that both their own prior knowledge and clues within the text will help them predict what might happen next in a story they are reading. Making predictions is important because it helps readers understand the story and stay interested in it. Discuss how understanding a story's genre can help them know what to expect from the characters and the overall story itself. Ask students for an example of another genre and how understanding that genre helps them predict what characters might do or the conflicts they might face. For example, in an science fiction story, the characters might have to battle aliens or deal with harsh environments and new technology. Link this understanding to the way heroes act in romances. Then, review the chart. Explain how making prediction charts like the one shown on page 45 can be helpful in determining whether or not their predictions were correct.

TEACH

CRITICAL VOCABULARY

Encourage students to read all the sentences before deciding which word best completes each one. Remind them to look for context clues to that match the precise meaning of each word.

Answers:

1. *incumbent*
2. *guile*
3. *usurp*
4. *dominion*
5. *redress*

■ English Learner Support

Use Cognates Tell students that one of the Critical Vocabulary words has a Spanish cognate: *dominion / dominio*. **ALL LEVELS**

LANGUAGE CONVENTIONS

Review the information about tone. Explain that the **tone** of a work expresses the writer's or narrator's feelings about the subject. Remind students that tone is different from the mood of a story, which denotes the feelings elicited from the reader only. Explain how determining the writer's or speaker's tone of a work can lead to a deeper understanding of the meaning of the work.

ANNOTATION MODEL

Remind students of the annotation ideas in Make Predictions on page 45, which offer a method for inferring what will happen next in the story based on what the has already been read. Explain how identifying the external and internal dilemmas of the characters will help them determine the moral dilemmas faced by the characters. Point out that they may follow the suggested annotation model or use their own system for marking up the selection. They may want to color-code their annotations by using highlighters. Their notes in the margin may include notes on the conflicts as well as questions about the moral dilemmas faced by the characters.

46 Unit 1

 **GET READY**

CRITICAL VOCABULARY

| dominion | incumbent | redress | usurp | guile |

To see how many Critical Vocabulary words you already know, use them to complete the sentences.

1. It is _____ upon each individual to complete his or her assigned section for the group project.
2. Beware of those who might lead you astray with words of _____.
3. His violent attempts to _____ the president's power failed.
4. After the war, the people found themselves under the _____ of a new ruler.
5. The employees demanded _____ for poor working conditions.

LANGUAGE CONVENTIONS

Tone In this lesson you will learn to identify tone, or the writer's or narrator's attitude toward the subject. This is communicated through devices such as word choice, detail, and sentence structure, as well as direct statements. While mood refers to the feelings evoked in the reader, tone refers to the attitude and feelings of the speaker, which may not be the same.

ANNOTATION MODEL   NOTICE & NOTE

As you read the selection, identify internal and external conflicts to find evidence of possible moral dilemmas faced by the characters. Mark supporting details you find in the text. In the model, you can see one reader's notes and evaluations.

> Then Sir Galyhud: "Sir, you command knights of royal blood; you cannot expect them to remain meekly within the city walls. I pray you, <u>let us encounter the enemy on the open field</u>, and they will soon repent of their expedition."
>
> And to <u>this the seven knights of West Britain all muttered their assent</u>. Then Sir Launcelot spoke:
>
> "My lords, <u>I am reluctant to shed Christian blood in a war against my own liege</u>; and yet I do know that these lands have already suffered depredation in the wars between King Claudas and my father and uncle, King Ban and King Bors. Therefore <u>I will next send a messenger to King Arthur and sue for peace</u>, for peace is always preferable to war."

Launcelot wishes to support his knights and protect his lands, but he is conflicted because he doesn't want to fight his lord, King Arthur.

46 Unit 1

BACKGROUND

As a young man, Sir Thomas Malory fought in the Hundred Years' War and was knighted in about 1442. Between 1451 and 1469, he collected all of the legends of King Arthur and his knights into one work, Le Morte d'Arthur (The Death of Arthur), which was published in 1485. However, the legends themselves date back much earlier, to the sixth century, having been passed down orally through many generations. Some historians believe that the fictional Arthur was modeled on a real Celtic military leader, although the historical Arthur was undoubtedly very different from Malory's Arthur, who ruled an idealized world of romance, chivalry, and magic.

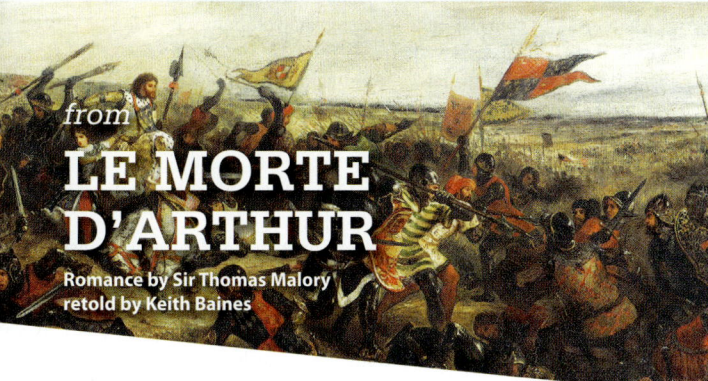

from LE MORTE D'ARTHUR

Romance by Sir Thomas Malory
retold by Keith Baines

SETTING A PURPOSE

As you read, pay attention to the conflicts that each character experiences. Think about whether these conflicts reveal heroic qualities.

King Arthur's favorite knight, Sir Launcelot, has fallen in love with the king's wife, Queen Gwynevere. The secret love affair is exposed by Sir Modred, Arthur's son by another woman, and Gwynevere is sentenced to burn at the stake. While rescuing the imprisoned Gwynevere, Launcelot slays two knights who, unknown to him at the time, are the brothers of Sir Gawain, a favorite nephew of Arthur's. After a reconciliation, Launcelot returns Gwynevere to Arthur to be reinstated as queen. At the urging of Gawain, who still wants revenge on Launcelot, the king banishes Launcelot to France, where the following excerpt begins.

~ THE SIEGE OF BENWICK ~

1   When Sir Launcelot had established **dominion** over France, he garrisoned the towns and settled with his army in the fortified city of Benwick, where his father King Ban had held court.

2   King Arthur, after appointing Sir Modred ruler in his absence, and instructing Queen Gwynevere to obey him, sailed to

NOTICE & NOTE

Notice & Note

Use the side margins to notice and note signposts in the text.

dominion
(də-mĭn´yən) *n.* rule or power to rule; mastery.

Le Morte d'Arthur   47

TEACH

BACKGROUND

After students read the Background note, explain that, before stories were written down, they were told or sung aloud for entertainment. As the stories moved through the generations, they were changed or embellished by the storytellers, so many versions of each story could be found. This excerpt represents only one author's version of these oral tales, and thus may differ from others the students might have encountered.

Explain that scholars still debate whether the King Arthur legends originated with a real person. Only scraps of evidence exist. An early history of Britain lists 12 battles fought by Arthur, mostly in the north of Britain. An appendix in the same history records Arthur's death in battle in the year A.D. 537. Welsh poems describe Arthur in legendary terms as early as the eighth century, allowing the inference that he lived earlier. Archeologists have look for Arthurian sites. One promising site, South Cadbury, was a well-fortified hill fort from about A.D. 500. Some people believe that it may have been the original Camelot.

SETTING A PURPOSE

Direct students to use the Setting a Purpose prompt to focus their reading.

WHEN STUDENTS STRUGGLE . . .

Identify Plot Events To help students engage with the text and keep track of events, invite them to record in words or sketch key scenes as they read. Provide students with a graphic organizer, such as a sequence chart, that they can complete as they read. Remind students to complete the graphic organizer as they read.

  For additional support, go to the **Reading Studio** and assign the following **Level Up tutorial: Plot: Sequence of Events.**

CRITICAL VOCABULARY

dominion: Kings, queens, and presidents are examples of individuals with dominion, or power to rule, over a geographic area.

ASK STUDENTS where Sir Launcelot held dominion. *(France)*

Le Morte d'Arthur   47

TEACH

✏️ ANALYZE CONFLICT

Remind students that an internal conflict is one experienced in a character's own mind and often is related to a moral dilemma faced by the character. Internal conflicts can reveal motivations and character traits. (**Answer:** *Arthur rejects Launcelot's offer not because Sir Gawain convinced him, but because he was torn between doing right by his friend and maintaining his status as a supreme ruler over his dominion, and understood that honor demanded he follow Gawain's recommendations.*)

✏️ NOTICE & NOTE

France with an army of sixty thousand men, and, on the advice of Sir Gawain, started laying waste[1] all before him.

3   News of the invasion reached Sir Launcelot, and his counselors advised him. Sir Bors[2] spoke first:

4   "My lord Sir Launcelot, is it wise to allow King Arthur to lay your lands waste when sooner or later he will oblige you to offer him battle?"

5   Sir Lyonel[3] spoke next: "My lord, I would recommend that we remain within the walls of our city until the invaders are weakened by cold and hunger, and then let us sally forth[4] and destroy them."

6   Next, King Bagdemagus: "Sir Launcelot, I understand that it is out of courtesy that you permit the king to ravage your lands, but where will this courtesy end? If you remain within the city, soon everything will be destroyed."

7   Then Sir Galyhud: "Sir, you command knights of royal blood; you cannot expect them to remain meekly within the city walls. I pray you, let us encounter the enemy on the open field, and they will soon repent of their expedition."

8   And to this the seven knights of West Britain all muttered their assent. Then Sir Launcelot spoke:

9   "My lords, I am reluctant to shed Christian blood in a war against my own liege;[5] and yet I do know that these lands have already suffered depredation[6] in the wars between King Claudas and my father and uncle, King Ban and King Bors. Therefore I will next send a messenger to King Arthur and sue[7] for peace, for peace is always preferable to war."

10 Accordingly a young noblewoman accompanied by a dwarf was sent to King Arthur. They were received by the gentle knight Sir Lucas the Butler.

11 "My lady, you bring a message from Sir Launcelot?" he asked.

12 "My lord, I do. It is for the king."

13 "Alas! King Arthur would readily be reconciled to Sir Launcelot, but Sir Gawain forbids it; and it is a shame, because Sir Launcelot is certainly the greatest knight living."

ANALYZE CONFLICT

Annotate: Mark details and statements in paragraphs 14–16 that reveal King Arthur's internal conflict.

Draw Conclusions: Does Arthur reject Launcelot's offer because he is convinced by Gawain's argument? Explain why or why not.

14 The young noblewoman was brought before the king, and <u>when he had heard Sir Launcelot's entreaties for peace he wept, and would readily have accepted them had not Sir Gawain spoken up:</u>

15 "My liege, if we retreat now we will become a laughingstock, in this land and in our own. Surely our honor demands that we pursue this war to its proper conclusion."

16 "Sir Gawain, <u>I will do as you advise, although reluctantly,</u> for Sir Launcelot's terms <u>are generous and he is still dear to me.</u> I beg you make a reply to him on my behalf."

---

[1] **laying waste:** destroying.
[2] **Sir Bors:** Sir Bors de Ganis, Launcelot's cousin and the son of King Bors.
[3] **Sir Lyonel** (līən-əl): another of Launcelot's cousins.
[4] **sally forth:** rush out suddenly in an attack.
[5] **liege** (lēj): a lord or ruler to whom one owes loyalty and service.
[6] **depredation** (dĕp´rĭ-dā´shən): destruction caused by robbery or looting.
[7] **sue:** appeal; beg.

48 Unit 1

🌐 ENGLISH LEARNER SUPPORT

Acquire New Vocabulary Help students improve their comprehension by teaching the meaning of the following words: *dreary* (paragraph 1, meaning "dismal, bleak"), *glimmer* (paragraph 1, meaning "a faint indication"), *livid* (paragraph 3, meaning "discolored, ashen"), *contempt* (paragraph 7, meaning "state of being despised or dishonored"), *abhorred* (paragraph 10, meaning "to regard with horror or loathing"), and *recompense* (paragraph 14, meaning "amends made for damage or loss"). **ALL LEVELS**

17 Sir Gawain addressed the young noblewoman:

18 "Tell Sir Launcelot that we will not bandy words with him, and it is too late now to sue for peace. Further that I, Sir Gawain, shall not cease to strive against him until one of us is killed."

19 The young noblewoman was escorted back to Sir Launcelot, and when she had delivered Sir Gawain's message they both wept. Then Sir Bors spoke:

20 "My lord, we beseech you, do not look so dismayed! You have many trustworthy knights behind you; lead us onto the field and we will put an end to this quarrel."

21 "My lords, I do not doubt you, but I pray you, be ruled by me: I will not lead you against our liege until we ourselves are endangered; only then can we honorably sally forth and defeat him."

22 Sir Launcelot's nobles submitted; but the next day it was seen that King Arthur had laid siege to the city of Benwick. Then Sir Gawain rode before the city walls and shouted a challenge:

23 "My lord Sir Launcelot: have you no knight who will dare to ride forth and break spears with me? It is I, Sir Gawain."

24 Sir Bors accepted the challenge. He rode out of the castle gate, they encountered, and he was wounded and flung from his horse. His comrades helped him back to the castle, and then Sir Lyonel offered to joust. He too was overthrown and helped back to the castle.

25 Thereafter, every day for six months Sir Gawain rode before the city and overthrew whoever accepted his challenge. Meanwhile, as a result of skirmishes, numbers on both sides were beginning to dwindle. Then one day Sir Gawain challenged Sir Launcelot:

26 "My lord Sir Launcelot: traitor to the king and to me, come forth if you dare and meet your mortal foe, instead of lurking like a coward in your castle!"

27 Sir Launcelot heard the challenge, and one of his kinsmen spoke to him:

28 "My lord, you must accept the challenge, or be shamed forever."

29 "Alas, that I should have to fight Sir Gawain!" said Sir Launcelot. "But now I am obliged to."

30 Sir Launcelot gave orders for his most powerful courser[8] to be harnessed, and when he had armed, rode to the tower and addressed King Arthur:

31 "My lord King Arthur, it is with a heavy heart that I set forth to do battle with one of your own blood; but now it is **incumbent** upon my honor to do so. For six months I have suffered your majesty to lay my lands waste and to besiege me in my own city. My courtesy is repaid with insults, so deadly and shameful that now I must by force of arms seek **redress**."

32 "Have done, Sir Launcelot, and let us to battle!" shouted Sir Gawain.

---
[8] **courser:** a horse trained for battle.

NOTICE & NOTE

ANALYZE CONFLICT
Annotate: Reread paragraphs 20–21. Mark the reason Launcelot gives for delaying the battle.

Analyze: How do the rules of chivalry complicate Launcelot's situation?

incumbent
(ĭn-kŭm′bənt) *adj.* required as a duty or an obligation.

redress
(rĭ-drĕs′) *n.* repayment for a wrong or an injury.

Le Morte d'Arthur 49

TEACH

AHA MOMENT

Explain to students that a character's realization of something that shifts his actions or understanding of himself, others, or the world around him helps readers recognize the character's internal conflict. Discovering a foe's weakness can lead to revelations in how to defeat that enemy, as in this case. (**Answer:** *Launcelot has fought long and hard against Sir Gawain, and with this new understanding, will have an easier time defeating him. He will likely use it to his advantage against this enemy.*)

NOTICE & NOTE

33   Sir Launcelot rode from the city at the head of his entire army. King Arthur was astonished at his strength and realized that Sir Launcelot had not been boasting when he claimed to have acted with forbearance.[9] "Alas, that I should ever have come to war with him!" he said to himself.

34   It was agreed that the two combatants should fight to the death, with interference from none. Sir Launcelot and Sir Gawain then drew apart and galloped furiously together, and so great was their strength that their horses crashed to the ground and both riders were overthrown.

35   A terrible sword fight commenced, and each felt the might of the other as fresh wounds were inflicted with every blow. For three hours they fought with scarcely a pause, and the blood seeped out from their armor and trickled to the ground. Sir Launcelot found to his dismay that Sir Gawain, instead of weakening, seemed to increase in strength as they proceeded, and he began to fear that he was battling not with a knight but with a fiend incarnate.[10] He decided to fight defensively and to conserve his strength.

AHA MOMENT

Notice & Note: Mark the sentence in paragraphs 36–38 that indicates when Launcelot discovers Gawain's secret.

Predict: What do you think Launcelot will do with this newly discovered knowledge?

36   It was a secret known only to King Arthur and to Sir Gawain himself that his strength increased for three hours in the morning, reaching its zenith[11] at noon, and waning again. This was due to an enchantment that had been cast over him by a hermit[12] when he was still a youth. Often in the past, as now, he had taken advantage of this.

37   Thus when the hour of noon had passed, Sir Launcelot felt Sir Gawain's strength return to normal, and knew that he could defeat him.

---

[9] **forbearance** (fôr-bâr´əns): self-control; patient restraint.
[10] **fiend incarnate:** devil in human form.
[11] **zenith:** highest point; peak.
[12] **hermit:** a person living in solitude for religious reasons.

50   Unit 1

APPLYING ACADEMIC VOCABULARY

☐ collapse   ☐ displace   ☑ military   ☐ visual   ☑ violate

Write and Discuss Have students turn to a partner to discuss the following questions. Guide students to include the academic vocabulary words *military* and *violate* in their responses. Ask volunteers to share their responses with the class.

- In what ways might Launcelot's armies differ from today's **military** service?
- What might happen when a knight **violates** the code of chivalry?

38   "Sir Gawain, I have endured many hard blows from you these last three hours, but now beware, for I see that you have weakened, and it is I who am the stronger."

39   Thereupon Sir Launcelot redoubled his blows, and with one, catching Sir Gawain sidelong on the helmet, sent him reeling to the ground. Then he courteously stood back.

40   "Sir Launcelot, I still defy you!" said Sir Gawain from the ground. "Why do you not kill me now? for I warn you that if ever I recover I shall challenge you again."

41   "Sir Gawain, by the grace of God I shall endure you again," Sir Launcelot replied, and then turned to the king:

42   "My liege, your expedition can find no honorable conclusion at these walls, so I pray you withdraw and spare your noble knights. Remember me with kindness and be guided, as ever, by the love of God."

43   "Alas!" said the king, "Sir Launcelot scruples[13] to fight against me or those of my blood, and once more I am beholden to him."

44   Sir Launcelot withdrew to the city and Sir Gawain was taken to his pavilion, where his wounds were dressed. King Arthur was doubly grieved, by his quarrel with Sir Launcelot and by the seriousness of Sir Gawain's wounds.

45   For three weeks, while Sir Gawain was recovering, the siege was relaxed and both sides skirmished only halfheartedly. But once recovered, Sir Gawain rode up to the castle walls and challenged Sir Launcelot again:

46   "Sir Launcelot, traitor! Come forth, it is Sir Gawain who challenges you."

47   "Sir Gawain, why these insults? I have the measure of your strength and you can do me but little harm."

48   "Come forth, traitor, and this time I shall make good my revenge!" Sir Gawain shouted.

49   "Sir Gawain, I have once spared your life; should you not beware of meddling with me again?"

50   Sir Launcelot armed and rode out to meet him. They jousted and Sir Gawain broke his spear and was flung from his horse. He leaped up immediately, and putting his shield before him, called on Sir Launcelot to fight on foot.

51   "The issue[14] of a mare has failed me; but I am the issue of a king and a queen and I shall not fail!" he exclaimed.

52   As before, Sir Launcelot felt Sir Gawain's strength increase until noon, during which period he defended himself, and then weaken again.

53   "Sir Gawain, you are a proved knight, and with the increase of your strength until noon you must have overcome many of your opponents, but now your strength has gone, and once more you are at my mercy."

---

[13] **scruples:** hesitates for reasons of principle.
[14] **issue:** offspring.

NOTICE & NOTE

ANALYZE CONFLICT
Annotate: Mark words and phrases in paragraphs 42–44 that indicate Arthur's feelings toward Launcelot.

Evaluate: What is your opinion of Arthur's handling of this conflict?

Le Morte d'Arthur   51

TEACH

ANALYZE CONFLICT

Using words like *scruples* and phrases like "beholden to him" about Launcelot indicate that King Arthur respects Launcelot, even after all they have endured. (**Answer:** Answers will vary. Example: Arthur was right to allow Launcelot to live considering the knight allowed Gawain to live, even though they were in a battle to the death. It showed that the king was honorable.)

■ **English Learner Support**

Confirm Understanding   Do a Think Aloud to help students mark words that indicate Arthur's feelings. Say: *I see the phrase "beholden to him." Arthur is saying that he is still loyal to Launcelot even though they have been through a lot. I also see that Arthur was "doubly grieved by his quarrel with Sir Launcelot." This also tells me that Arthur cares about Launcelot. Using these clues, I think that Arthur is honorable, and I think he handled the situation well.* Ask students to form an opinion about Sir Gawain or Sir Launcelot. They should look for clues in the text to form their opinions. **LIGHT**

IMPROVE READING FLUENCY

Targeted Passage   Have students work in quads to read aloud paragraphs 38–53, with separate students reading the parts of King Arthur, Lancelot, Sir Gawain, and the narrator. After the first reading, have students exchange parts and read the paragraphs aloud again. Encourage students to provide feedback and support for pronouncing difficult words. Remind students that when they are reading aloud for an audience, they should pace their reading so the audience has time to understand difficult concepts.

 Go to the **Reading Studio** for additional support in developing fluency.

TEACH

✏️ ANALYZE CONFLICT

Remind students that a character's actions can reveal internal or external conflicts. Have students consider whether Modred lived by the code of chivalry, and whether or not his actions were just. (**Answer:** *Launcelot shows respect for the king, even during battles, while Modred shows utter contempt for the king, the queen, and the church with each of his actions.*)

CRITICAL VOCABULARY

usurp: This term is used to describe Modred's taking, or usurping, power from King Arthur.

ASK STUDENTS what might happen if someone attempted to usurp the U.S. president's power. (*This would likely lead to a war between America's armed forces and the usurper's military, and would cause significant unrest within the country.*)

guile: Modred tries to scam the queen into marrying him with guile and trickery.

ASK STUDENTS to identify several types of guile Modred might have used to deceive the queen. (*Since Modred had already had fraudulent letters written about Arthur, he may have tried a similar ploy with Gwynevere. He also might have tried to convince her that Launcelot no longer wanted her.*)

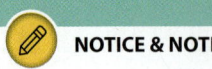
NOTICE & NOTE

54 Sir Launcelot struck out lustily and by chance reopened the wound he had made before. Sir Gawain fell to the ground in a faint, but when he came to he said weakly:

55 "Sir Launcelot, I still defy you. Make an end of me, or I shall fight you again!"

56 "Sir Gawain, while you stand on your two feet I will not gainsay[15] you; but I will never strike a knight who has fallen. God defend me from such dishonor!"

57 Sir Launcelot walked away and Sir Gawain continued to call after him: "Traitor! Until one of us is dead I shall never give in!"

58 For a month Sir Gawain lay recovering from his wounds, and the siege remained; but then, as Sir Gawain was preparing to fight Sir Launcelot once more, King Arthur received news which caused him to strike camp and lead his army on a forced march to the coast, and thence to embark for Britain.

～ THE DAY OF DESTINY ～

59 During the absence of King Arthur from Britain, Sir Modred, already vested with sovereign powers,[16] had decided to usurp the throne. Accordingly, he had false letters written—announcing the death of King Arthur in battle—and delivered to himself. Then, calling a parliament, he ordered the letters to be read and persuaded the nobility to elect him king. The coronation took place at Canterbury and was celebrated with a fifteen-day feast.

60 Sir Modred then settled in Camelot and made overtures to Queen Gwynevere to marry him. The queen seemingly acquiesced, but as soon as she had won his confidence, begged leave to make a journey to London in order to prepare her trousseau.[17] Sir Modred consented, and the queen rode straight to the Tower which, with the aid of her loyal nobles, she manned and provisioned for her defense.

61 Sir Modred, outraged, at once marched against her, and laid siege to the Tower, but despite his large army, siege engines, and guns, was unable to effect a breach. He then tried to entice the queen from the Tower, first by guile and then by threats, but she would listen to neither. Finally the Archbishop of Canterbury came forward to protest:

62 "Sir Modred, do you not fear God's displeasure? First you have falsely made yourself king; now you, who were begotten by King Arthur on his aunt,[18] try to marry your father's wife! If you do not revoke your evil deeds I shall curse you with bell, book, and candle."[19]

usurp
(yo͞o-sûrp′) *v.* to seize unlawfully by force.

ANALYZE CONFLICT
Annotate: Mark the details of Modred's actions in paragraphs 59–61.

Compare: How does Modred differ from Launcelot as an opponent of King Arthur?

guile
(gīl) *n.* clever trickery; deceit.

---

[15] **gainsay:** deny.
[16] **vested with sovereign powers:** given the authority of a king.
[17] **trousseau** (tro͞o′sō): clothes and linens that a bride brings to her marriage.
[18] **begotten . . . aunt:** Modred is the son of Arthur and Queen Margawse, the sister of Arthur's mother, Queen Igraine.
[19] **I shall curse you with bell, book, and candle:** The archbishop is threatening to excommunicate Modred—that is, to deny him participation in the rites of the church. In the medieval ritual of excommunication, a bell was rung, a book was shut, and a candle was extinguished.

52 Unit 1

ENGLISH LEARNER SUPPORT

Develop Fluency Direct students' attention to the clause *Sir Launcelot struck out* in paragraph 54. Point out that *struck out* is a term in baseball. Emphasize that *struck out* is not used in that sense here; in this case, it means "struck or hit with his sword." **ALL LEVELS**

63 "Fie on you! Do your worst!" Sir Modred replied.

64 "Sir Modred, I warn you take heed! or the wrath of the Lord will descend upon you."

65 "Away, false priest, or I shall behead you!"

66 The Archbishop withdrew, and after excommunicating Sir Modred, abandoned his office and fled to Glastonbury. There he took up his abode as a simple hermit, and by fasting and prayer sought divine intercession[20] in the troubled affairs of his country.

67 Sir Modred tried to assassinate the Archbishop, but was too late. He continued to assail the queen with entreaties and threats, both of which failed, and then the news reached him that King Arthur was returning with his army from France in order to seek revenge.

68 Sir Modred now appealed to the barony to support him, and it has to be told that they came forward in large numbers to do so. Why? it will be asked. Was not King Arthur, the noblest sovereign Christendom had seen, now leading his armies in a righteous cause? The answer lies in the people of Britain, who, then as now, were fickle. Those who so readily transferred their allegiance to Sir Modred did so with the excuse that whereas King Arthur's reign had led them into war and strife, Sir Modred promised them peace and festivity.

69 Hence it was with an army of a hundred thousand that Sir Modred marched to Dover to battle against his own father, and to withhold from him his rightful crown.

70 As King Arthur with his fleet drew into the harbor, Sir Modred and his army launched forth in every available craft, and a bloody battle ensued in the ships and on the beach. If King Arthur's army were the smaller, their courage was the higher, confident as they were of the righteousness of their cause. Without stint[21] they battled through the burning ships, the screaming wounded, and the corpses floating on the bloodstained waters. Once ashore they put Sir Modred's entire army to flight.

71 The battle over, King Arthur began a search for his casualties, and on peering into one of the ships found Sir Gawain, mortally wounded. Sir Gawain fainted when King Arthur lifted him in his arms; and when he came to, the king spoke:

72 "Alas! dear nephew, that you lie here thus, mortally wounded! What joy is now left to me on this earth? You must know it was you and Sir Launcelot I loved above all others, and it seems that I have lost you both."

73 "My good uncle, it was my pride and my stubbornness that brought all this about, for had I not urged you to war with Sir Launcelot your subjects would not now be in revolt. Alas, that Sir Launcelot is not here, for he would soon drive them out! And it is at Sir Launcelot's hands that I suffer my own death: the wound which he

MAKE PREDICTIONS

Annotate: Mark the explanation in paragraph 68 for the support Modred receives.

Predict: Do you think Modred will keep this support for long? Why or why not?

---

[20] **divine intercession:** assistance from God.
[21] **stint:** holding back.

Le Morte d'Arthur 53

TEACH

ENGLISH LEARNER SUPPORT

Understand Idioms Help students use context clues to determine the meanings of these idioms in the story:

- *give in* (paragraph 57), "to surrender"
- *put . . . to flight* (paragraph 70), "caused the opposing forces to retreat"
- *came to* (paragraph 71), "returned to consciousness"
- *brought . . . about* (paragraph 73), "made this happen"
- *give up the ghost* (paragraph 80), "die"
- *won the day* (paragraph 80), "triumphed"
- *give battle to* (paragraph 88), "to fight against"

LIGHT

 **NOTICE & NOTE**

dealt me has reopened. I would not wish it otherwise, because is he not the greatest and gentlest of knights?

74 "I know that by noon I shall be dead, and I repent bitterly that I may not be reconciled to Sir Launcelot; therefore I pray you, good uncle, give me pen, paper, and ink so that I may write to him."

75 A priest was summoned and Sir Gawain confessed; then a clerk brought ink, pen, and paper, and Sir Gawain wrote to Sir Launcelot as follows:

76 "Sir Launcelot, flower of the knighthood: I, Sir Gawain, son of King Lot of Orkney and of King Arthur's sister, send you my greetings!

77 "I am about to die; the cause of my death is the wound I received from you outside the city of Benwick; and I would make it known that my death was of my own seeking, that I was moved by the spirit of revenge and spite to provoke you to battle.

78 "Therefore, Sir Launcelot, I beseech you to visit my tomb and offer what prayers you will on my behalf; and for myself, I am content to die at the hands of the noblest knight living.

79 "One more request: that you hasten with your armies across the sea and give succor[22] to our noble king. Sir Modred, his bastard son, has usurped the throne and now holds against him with an army of a hundred thousand. He would have won the queen, too, but she fled to the Tower of London and there charged her loyal supporters with her defense.

80 "Today is the tenth of May, and at noon I shall give up the ghost; this letter is written partly with my blood. This morning we fought our way ashore, against the armies of Sir Modred, and that is how my wound came to be reopened. We won the day, but my lord King Arthur needs you, and I too, that on my tomb you may bestow your blessing."

81 Sir Gawain fainted when he had finished, and the king wept. When he came to he was given extreme unction,[23] and died, as he had anticipated, at the hour of noon. The king buried him in the chapel at Dover Castle, and there many came to see him, and all noticed the wound on his head which he had received from Sir Launcelot.

82 Then the news reached Arthur that Sir Modred offered him battle on the field at Baron Down. Arthur hastened there with his army, they fought, and Sir Modred fled once more, this time to Canterbury.

83 When King Arthur had begun the search for his wounded and dead, many volunteers from all parts of the country came to fight under his flag, convinced now of the rightness of his cause. Arthur marched westward, and Sir Modred once more offered him battle. It was assigned for the Monday following Trinity Sunday, on Salisbury Down.

84 Sir Modred levied fresh troops from East Anglia and the places about London, and fresh volunteers came forward to help Arthur.

---

[22] **succor** (sŭk´ər): *n.* aid in a time of need; relief.
[23] **extreme unction:** a ritual in which a priest anoints and prays for a dying person.

54   Unit 1

APPLYING ACADEMIC VOCABULARY

☑ collapse   ☐ displace   ☐ military   ☐ violate   ☐ visual

Write and Discuss Have students turn to a partner to discuss the following questions. Guide students to include the academic vocabulary word *collapse* in their responses. Ask volunteers to share their responses with the class.

- What caused Sir Gawain and Sir Launcelot's relationship to **collapse**?

Then, on the night of Trinity Sunday, Arthur was vouchsafed[24] a strange dream:

85 He was appareled in gold cloth and seated in a chair which stood on a pivoted scaffold. Below him, many fathoms deep, was a dark well, and in the water swam serpents, dragons, and wild beasts. Suddenly the scaffold tilted and Arthur was flung into the water, where all the creatures struggled toward him and began tearing him limb from limb.

86 Arthur cried out in his sleep and his squires hastened to waken him. Later, as he lay between waking and sleeping, he thought he saw Sir Gawain, and with him a host of beautiful noblewomen. Arthur spoke:

87 "My sister's son! I thought you had died; but now I see you live, and I thank the lord Jesu! I pray you, tell me, who are these ladies?"

88 "My lord, these are the ladies I championed[25] in righteous quarrels when I was on earth. Our lord God has vouchsafed that we visit you and plead with you not to give battle to Sir Modred tomorrow, for if you do, not only will you yourself be killed, but all your noble followers too. We beg you to be warned, and to make a treaty with Sir Modred, calling a truce for a month, and granting him whatever terms he may demand. In a month Sir Launcelot will be here, and he will defeat Sir Modred."

89 Thereupon Sir Gawain and the ladies vanished, and King Arthur once more summoned his squires and his counselors and told them his vision. Sir Lucas and Sir Bedivere were commissioned to make a treaty with Sir Modred. They were to be accompanied by two bishops and to grant, within reason, whatever terms he demanded.

90 The ambassadors found Sir Modred in command of an army of a hundred thousand and unwilling to listen to overtures of peace.

[24] **vouchsafed:** granted.
[25] **championed:** defended or fought for.

MAKE PREDICTIONS
Annotate: Reread paragraphs 86–88. Mark Gawain's warning to Arthur.

Predict: Romance plots often involve supernatural events. How do you think Arthur will respond to this vision? What may be the outcome of his response?

Le Morte d'Arthur 55

TEACH

✏️ MAKE PREDICTIONS

Many people during this time were superstitious and believed that answers came through dreams. Readers can use details from a dream to make predictions about the character or upcoming events. (**Answer:** *Arthur is likely to heed the dream and work toward a truce with Modred, as he does not wish to die nor does he wish for his supporters to be killed. The outcome might be that Modred kills him anyway, just to keep him from ever fully regaining the throne.*)

WHEN STUDENTS STRUGGLE . . .

Summarize Students may find this scene difficult to follow. Help students find the most important points in Arthur's dream by asking the following questions: Whom does Arthur see in his dream? What does this person say about the events of the next day? What advice does this person give? After students have answered the questions, have them write a summary of the scene. Pair students and have them share their summaries and revise if necessary.

 For additional support, go to the **Reading Studio** and assign the following Level Up tutorial: Summarizing.

Le Morte d'Arthur 55

TEACH

ANALYZE CONFLICT

Loyalty is central to the chivalrous code, and sometimes that means doing what needs is necessary to ensure that justice is done for fallen compatriots. (**Answer:** *A theme of loyalty to others is demonstrated by Arthur as he disregards Gawain's warning. It is more important to the king to avenge his knights and do what's right by his kingdom than to worry about his own life.*)

NOTICE & NOTE

However, the ambassadors eventually prevailed on him, and in return for the truce granted him suzerainty[26] of Cornwall and Kent, and succession to the British throne when King Arthur died. The treaty was to be signed by King Arthur and Sir Modred the next day. They were to meet between the two armies, and each was to be accompanied by no more than fourteen knights.

91   Both King Arthur and Sir Modred suspected the other of treachery, and gave orders for their armies to attack at the sight of a naked sword. When they met at the appointed place the treaty was signed and both drank a glass of wine.

92   Then, by chance, one of the soldiers was bitten in the foot by an adder[27] which had lain concealed in the brush. The soldier unthinkingly drew his sword to kill it, and at once, as the sword flashed in the light, the alarums[28] were given, trumpets sounded, and both armies galloped into the attack.

93   "Alas for this fateful day!" exclaimed King Arthur, as both he and Sir Modred hastily mounted and galloped back to their armies. There followed one of those rare and heartless battles in which both armies fought until they were destroyed. King Arthur, with his customary valor, led squadron after squadron of cavalry into the attack, and Sir Modred encountered him unflinchingly. As the number of dead and wounded mounted on both sides, the active combatants continued dauntless until nightfall, when four men alone survived.

94   King Arthur wept with dismay to see his beloved followers fallen; then, struggling toward him, unhorsed and badly wounded, he saw Sir Lucas the Butler and his brother, Sir Bedivere.[29]

95   "Alas!" said the king, "that the day should come when I see all my noble knights destroyed! I would prefer that I myself had fallen. But what has become of the traitor Sir Modred, whose evil ambition was responsible for this carnage?"

ANALYZE CONFLICT
Annotate: Reread paragraphs 96–99. Mark Arthur's explanation for why he must confront Modred now.

Interpret: What theme about chivalry is suggested by Arthur's decision to ignore Gawain's warning?

96   Looking about him King Arthur then noticed Sir Modred leaning with his sword on a heap of the dead.

97   "Sir Lucas, I pray you give me my spear, for I have seen Sir Modred."

98   "Sire, I entreat you, remember your vision—how Sir Gawain appeared with a heaven-sent message to dissuade you from fighting Sir Modred. Allow this fateful day to pass; it is ours, for we three hold the field, while the enemy is broken."

99   "My lords, I care nothing for my life now! <u>And while Sir Modred is at large I must kill him: there may not be another chance.</u>"

100   "God speed you, then!" said Sir Bedivere.

101   When Sir Modred saw King Arthur advance with his spear, he rushed to meet him with drawn sword. Arthur caught Sir Modred below the shield and drove his spear through his body; Sir Modred, knowing that the wound was mortal, thrust himself up to the handle

---

[26] **suzerainty** (sōō´zər-ən-tē): the position of feudal lord.
[27] **adder:** a poisonous snake.
[28] **alarums:** calls to arms.
[29] **Sir Lucas . . . Bedivere:** brothers who are members of King Arthur's court.

ENGLISH LEARNER SUPPORT

Understand Prefixes   Point out these words with the common prefix *un-*: *unwilling* (paragraph 90), *unthinkingly* (paragraph 92), *unflinchingly* (paragraph 93), *unhorsed* (paragraph 94). Have pairs find definitions in a print or online dictionary. Discuss how the repeated use of the prefix reinforces the gloomy tone of this battle scene.   **ALL LEVELS**

of the spear, and then, brandishing his sword in both hands, struck Arthur on the side of the helmet, cutting through it and into the skull beneath; then he crashed to the ground, gruesome and dead.

102   King Arthur fainted many times as Sir Lucas and Sir Bedivere struggled with him to a small chapel nearby, where they managed to ease his wounds a little. When Arthur came to, he thought he heard cries coming from the battlefield.

103   "Sir Lucas, I pray you, find out who cries on the battlefield," he said.

104   Wounded as he was, Sir Lucas hobbled painfully to the field, and there in the moonlight saw the camp followers stealing gold and jewels from the dead, and murdering the wounded. He returned to the king and reported to him what he had seen, and then added:

105   "My lord, it surely would be better to move you to the nearest town?"

106   "My wounds forbid it. But alas for the good Sir Launcelot! How sadly I have missed him today! And now I must die—as Sir Gawain warned me I would—repenting our quarrel with my last breath."

107   Sir Lucas and Sir Bedivere made one further attempt to lift the king. He fainted as they did so. Then Sir Lucas fainted as part of his intestines broke through a wound in the stomach. When the king came to, he saw Sir Lucas lying dead with foam at his mouth.

108   "Sweet Jesu, give him succor!" he said. "This noble knight has died trying to save my life—alas that this was so!"

109   Sir Bedivere wept for his brother.

110   "Sir Bedivere, weep no more," said King Arthur, "for you can save neither your brother nor me; and I would ask you to take my sword Excalibur[30] to the shore of the lake and throw it in the water. Then return to me and tell me what you have seen."

111   "My lord, as you command, it shall be done."

112   Sir Bedivere took the sword, but when he came to the water's edge, it appeared so beautiful that he could not bring himself to throw it in, so instead he hid it by a tree, and then returned to the king.

113   "Sir Bedivere, what did you see?"

114   "My lord, I saw nothing but the wind upon the waves."

115   "Then you did not obey me; I pray you, go swiftly again, and this time fulfill my command."

116   Sir Bedivere went and returned again, but this time too he had failed to fulfill the king's command.

117   "Sir Bedivere, what did you see?"

118   "My lord, nothing but the lapping of the waves."

119   "Sir Bedivere, twice you have betrayed me! And for the sake only of my sword: it is unworthy of you! Now I pray you, do as I command, for I have not long to live."

---

[30] **Excalibur** (ĕk-skăl´ə-bər): Arthur's remarkable sword, which originally came from the Lady of the Lake.

TEACH

ANALYZE CONFLICT

Explain that the legend of the Excalibur sword was long-associated with the legends of the Knights of the Round Table. Excalibur is a special sword and has great significance to Arthur. (**Answer:** *The Lady of the Lake had gifted Arthur with Excalibur, and therefore, wished it returned to her upon his death. When he reported back to Arthur the first time, it was clear that he had not returned the sword, which was what angered Arthur.*)

EL ENGLISH LEARNER SUPPORT

Use Visual and Contextual Support Help students understand the scene by showing images of a barge on the water. Then, ask students why they think Bedivere is crying as the barge moves down the lake. Help students understand that both Bedivere and Arthur know that Arthur will die. This is the last time Bedivere will see his king alive. Make connections with students by asking how they would feel seeing someone they loved or respected for the last time.

 **NOTICE & NOTE**

ANALYZE CONFLICT

Annotate: In paragraph 120, mark the description of what happens to Excalibur.

Infer: How does this description help us understand why Arthur was so upset at Bedivere?

120   This time Sir Bedivere wrapped the girdle around the sheath and hurled it as far as he could into the water. A hand appeared from below the surface, took the sword, waved it thrice, and disappeared again. Sir Bedivere returned to the king and told him what he had seen.

121   "Sir Bedivere, I pray you now help me hence, or I fear it will be too late."

122   Sir Bedivere carried the king to the water's edge, and there found a barge in which sat many beautiful ladies with their queen. All were wearing black hoods, and when they saw the king, they raised their voices in a piteous lament.

123   "I pray you, set me in the barge," said the king.

124   Sir Bedivere did so, and one of the ladies laid the king's head in her lap; then the queen spoke to him:

125   "My dear brother, you have stayed too long: I fear that the wound on your head is already cold."

126   Thereupon they rowed away from the land and Sir Bedivere wept to see them go.

127   "My lord King Arthur, you have deserted me! I am alone now, and among enemies."

128   "Sir Bedivere, take what comfort you may, for my time is passed, and now I must be taken to Avalon[31] for my wound to be healed. If you hear of me no more, I beg you pray for my soul."

129   The barge slowly crossed the water and out of sight while the ladies wept. Sir Bedivere walked alone into the forest and there remained for the night.

130   In the morning he saw beyond the trees of a copse[32] a small hermitage. He entered and found a hermit kneeling down by a fresh tomb. The hermit was weeping as he prayed, and then Sir Bedivere recognized him as the Archbishop of Canterbury, who had been banished by Sir Modred.

131   "Father, I pray you, tell me, whose tomb is this?"

132   "My son, I do not know. At midnight the body was brought here by a company of ladies. We buried it, they lit a hundred candles for the service, and rewarded me with a thousand bezants."[33]

133   "Father, King Arthur lies buried in this tomb."

134   Sir Bedivere fainted when he had spoken, and when he came to he begged the Archbishop to allow him to remain at the hermitage and end his days in fasting and prayer.

135   "Father, I wish only to be near to my true liege."

136   "My son, you are welcome; and do I not recognize you as Sir Bedivere the Bold, brother to Sir Lucas the Butler?"

137   Thus the Archbishop and Sir Bedivere remained at the hermitage, wearing the habits of hermits and devoting themselves to the tomb with fasting and prayers of contrition.[34]

---

[31] **Avalon:** an island paradise of Celtic legend, where heroes are taken after death.
[32] **copse** (kŏps): a grove of small trees.
[33] **bezants** (bĕz´ənts): gold coins.
[34] **contrition** (kən-trĭsh´ən): sincere regret for wrongdoing.

TO CHALLENGE STUDENTS...

Analyze Theme Invite groups of students to discuss the themes that they find in the final battle. Ask groups to create statements about what the story suggests about the nature of war. Point out these details: The war is all but over when it is reignited by accident; although grieved by the carnage, Arthur spurs himself to further violence at the sight of his enemy; Arthur loses his life by ignoring sound advice; the leaders of the two armies kill each other in an act of mutual destruction; and Arthur's mortal enemy is his own child whom he did not raise. Have groups exchange thematic statements and discuss the statements that they receive.

138   Such was the death of King Arthur as written down by Sir Bedivere. By some it is told that there were three queens on the barge: Queen Morgan le Fay, the Queen of North Galys, and the Queen of the Waste Lands; and others include the name of Nyneve, the Lady of the Lake who had served King Arthur well in the past, and had married the good knight Sir Pelleas.

139   In many parts of Britain it is believed that King Arthur did not die and that he will return to us and win fresh glory and the Holy Cross of our Lord Jesu Christ; but for myself I do not believe this, and would leave him buried peacefully in his tomb at Glastonbury, where the Archbishop of Canterbury and Sir Bedivere humbled themselves, and with prayers and fasting honored his memory. And inscribed on his tomb, men say, is this legend:

HIC IACET ARTHURUS,
REX QUONDAM REXQUE FUTURUS.[35]

[35] *Hic iacet Arthurus, rex quondam rexque futurus* (hĭk yä´kĕt är-to͞o´ro͞os rāks kwôn´däm rāk´skwē fo͞o-to͞o´ro͞os) *Latin*: Here lies Arthur, the once and future king.

NOTICE & NOTE

LANGUAGE CONVENTIONS
Annotate: In paragraph 139, mark the direct statement the author makes about Arthur.

Identify: Which word in this statement most directly conveys the narrator's tone in this paragraph?

CHECK YOUR UNDERSTANDING

Answer these questions before moving on to the **Analyze the Text** section.

1 After besieging Sir Launcelot at Benwick, what news compels Arthur to return to Britain?
   A Gwynevere has married Modred.
   B Gwynevere has died.
   C Modred has usurped the throne.
   D Modred has beheaded the Archbishop.

2 How is the conflict between Gawain and Launcelot resolved?
   F Launcelot strikes down Gawain and Gawain surrenders.
   G As Gawain is dying from a wound, he writes a letter to Launcelot asking for his forgiveness.
   H They resolve their problems before Gawain leaves for Britain.
   J After the battle at Dover, Launcelot finds Gawain, and they are able to reconcile their differences.

3 What happens to Arthur at the end of the story?
   A He is killed in a fight with Bedivere after an argument over his sword.
   B He drowns in the lake on his way to Avalon.
   C He is later found living at the hermitage in disguise.
   D Modred mortally wounds him in battle.

Le Morte d'Arthur   59

TEACH

LANGUAGE CONVENTIONS

Remind students that tone is the narrator's attitude toward the subject. An author's word choice often reveals tone. The narrator directly addresses the reader in this statement, using active voice to announce his beliefs and reveal his feelings about the king. (**Answer:** *The narrator's tone is directly conveyed by his use of the word* honored. *It is clear that he believes the king was honorable and deserving of the highest respect.*)

CHECK YOUR UNDERSTANDING

Have students answer the questions independently.

Answers:
1. C
2. G
3. D

If they answer any questions incorrectly, have them reread the text to confirm their understanding. Then, they may proceed to ANALYZE THE TEXT on page 60.

ENGLISH LEARNER SUPPORT

Oral Assessment Use the following questions to assess students' comprehension and speaking skills.

1. Why did Arthur go back to Britain? *(He heard that Modred had taken the throne.)*
2. How does Gawain make peace with Launcelot? *(Gawain writes Launcelot a letter asking for forgiveness).*
3. How does Arthur die? *(Modred hurts him enough in the last battle to kill him.)*

MODERATE/LIGHT

Le Morte d'Arthur   59

APPLY

ANALYZE THE TEXT
Possible answers:

1. **DOK 4:** As a loyal and favorite knight of King Arthur, Launcelot faced internal struggles over falling in love with the king's wife, Gwynevere. His continued loyalty to Arthur is evidenced in hesitation to oppose the king in battle. The guilt he felt over wronging Arthur in this way is possibly what drove him to seek peace and to provide his continued loyalty to the king.

2. **DOK 4:** Gawain is loyal to the king to a fault and seeks revenge on what he sees as Launcelot's betrayals. In his quest for revenge, his commitment to the code of chivalry is reduced. Although Launcelot knew he was wrong in falling in love with the king's wife, throughout the story, he displays loyalty, compassion, and honor in all his words and deeds, thereby making him the greater model of chivalry.

3. **DOK 2:** Malory uses adequate foreshadowing to predict the death of Arthur, including the dream in which Gawain warned him not to engage with Modred the night before the battle. Additionally, the title of the piece alerts the reader to the king's impending doom.

4. **DOK 3:** Malory may have chosen to mention these rumors to put to rest any unsettled beliefs that the king still lived. Sharing the tomb's inscription added further proof that the king was dead and buried.

5. **DOK 4:** Gawain realized that had he not started the war with Launcelot, the kingdom would not have been besieged by war, and the king would not have been put in peril. He admits that his pride and stubbornness got in the way of good sense, and had he behaved more chivalrously, many soldiers who died in battle would still be living.

RESEARCH

Remind students that they should confirm any information they find by checking multiple websites and assessing the credibility of each one.

Connect The legends of King Arthur and the knights of the Round Table have endured because they remind us that we cannot control whom we love, but if we continue forward meeting each challenge with grace, dignity, and consideration for all involved, the ending to the story is likely to be a happier one. They make compelling heroes because of the internal struggles they face; it serves to make them more human, and show that even the best of us can become embroiled in tough situations. Heroes give people someone to respect and admire, helping people to see that anyone can become a hero under the right circumstances.

RESPOND

ANALYZE THE TEXT
Support your responses with evidence from the text. 📓 NOTEBOOK

1. **Analyze** Reread the headnote that explains what has occurred earlier in the romance. How does Launcelot's past behavior lead to the conflict and the moral dilemma he faces in the siege of Benwick?

2. **Evaluate** Compare the actions and motivation of Gawain and Launcelot. Which knight is a greater model of chivalry? Explain.

3. **Predict** A writer's use of hints or clues to indicate events that will occur later in a story is called **foreshadowing.** Does Malory provide enough clues for you to have predicted that Modred will kill Arthur, or does Arthur's death surprise you? Explain.

4. **Draw Conclusions** Reread paragraph 139. Why might Malory have chosen to mention these rumors about Arthur and to share the legend inscribed on Arthur's tomb?

5. **Notice and Note** Reread paragraphs 71–74. What realization does Gawain have about his role in the conflict with Launcelot? Do you agree with the blame he places on himself? Why or why not?

RESEARCH

RESEARCH TIP
When looking for history-related information, focus on more reliable sites, such as history.com, rather than less credible sources. Also, look for articles written by professors and other scholars found in magazines and journals such as *Archaeology Magazine*, which will offer up-to-date findings.

Was Arthur a real historical figure? Historians disagree. Conduct an Internet search to find evidence for both sides of the argument. Use the chart below to record your findings.

EVIDENCE FOR A REAL ARTHUR	EVIDENCE AGAINST A REAL ARTHUR
His legend began before the written word.	*Historians are unable to confirm his existence.*
The legends have been repeated and embellished by a variety of writers throughout history.	*It would have been impossible for him to have been at all the battles attributed to him.*

Connect In spite of the uncertainty of King Arthur's actual existence, his legend has endured for generations. In small groups, discuss the following: Why do you think Arthur and his knights make such compelling heroes? Do you think their struggles with moral dilemmas make them more appealing? If so, why? Discuss the importance of heroes in literature and in real life.

WHEN STUDENTS STRUGGLE . . .

Reteaching: Analyze Conflict Remind students of the two types of conflicts—internal and external—and how they can reveal a character's traits and motivations. Divide the class into small groups and assign each group one or two characters. Have students identify the conflict(s) each character faces, what the conflict reveals about the character, and how the character solves the conflict. Ask a representative of each group to share their ideas. Discuss the ideas with the class and have students take notes on each character.

CREATE AND PRESENT

Create a Hero Write a character sketch of a modern-day hero—real or imaginary. Before you begin, think about the traits of heroes in *Le Morte d'Arthur*. However, keep in mind your hero doesn't need to show physical courage; consider other equally important kinds of heroism.

- ❏ Describe your hero in terms of both personal traits and behavior. How does he or she exhibit heroic qualities through words and actions?
- ❏ How do others view him or her?
- ❏ Relate an incident in which your hero faces a conflict, internal or external, which creates a moral dilemma. How is the conflict resolved?

Direct a Scene Work in small groups to prepare a dramatic scene of a heroic incident. With your group, work out subject matter, mood, and staging of your scene, with one of you serving as the director.

- ❏ As a group, select one incident to dramatize and choose a director.
- ❏ Decide how you will present the scene. As a traditional skit? An impromptu presentation? A dramatic reading? Experiment and clarify questions as you work out the most effective way to present it.
- ❏ Practice and present to the whole class. Request feedback for how well your group conveyed ideas about the qualities of heroism.

RESPOND TO THE ESSENTIAL QUESTION

? What makes someone a hero?

Gather Information Review your annotations and notes on *Le Morte d'Arthur*. Then, add relevant information to your Response Log. As you determine which information to include, think about:

- the definition of a hero and some qualities a hero might possess
- how a hero might face conflicts and moral dilemmas
- the importance of heroes in real life

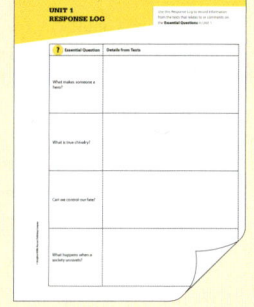

RESPOND

 Go to **Writing Narratives** in the **Writing Studio** to find out more.

 Go to **Giving a Presentation** in the **Speaking and Listening Studio** for help.

ACADEMIC VOCABULARY

As you write and discuss what you learned from the novel excerpt, be sure to use the Academic Vocabulary words. Check off each of the words that you use.

- ❏ collapse
- ❏ displace
- ❏ military
- ❏ violate
- ❏ visual

APPLY

CREATE AND PRESENT

Create a Hero Brainstorm with students the different qualities that a hero might possess. Have them consider different scenarios that might provide an opportunity for someone to act heroically.

 For **writing support** for students at varying proficiency levels, see the Text X-Ray on page 44D.

Direct a Scene Remind students that when they are creating a dramatic incident, the setting, characters, and background need to be introduced first, so the audience understands the context.

RESPOND TO THE ESSENTIAL QUESTION

Allow time for students to add details from *Le Morte d'Arthur* to their Unit 1 Response Logs.

APPLY

CRITICAL VOCABULARY

Answers:

1. guile
2. dominion
3. redress
4. incumbent
5. usurp

VOCABULARY STRATEGY:
Multiple Meaning Words

Answers:

1. adopt: Meaning: take as their own; Context Clues: "later writers . . . essential elements"
2. elements: Meaning : pieces / parts; Context Clues: "Merlin, Excalibur, and Arthur's final repose at Avalon"
3. repose: Meaning: resting place; Context Clues: "Arthur's final repose at Avalon"
4. body: Meaning: collection; Context Clues: "growing body of Arthurian literature"
5. ultimate: Meaning: top / best; Context Clues: "would eventually become . . . literature"

 RESPOND

WORD BANK
dominion
incumbent
redress
usurp
guile

 Go to the **Vocabulary Studio** for more on multiple-meaning words.

CRITICAL VOCABULARY

Practice and Apply Choose the vocabulary word that best completes each sentence. Use the context clues in the sentence to help you decide.

1. _____ might be observed in the actions of an unscrupulous salesman.
2. A kingdom or nation has _____ over its lands.
3. A wronged person might seek _____.
4. It is _____ upon children to do their chores.
5. The cat tried to _____ control of the dog's bed.

VOCABULARY STRATEGY:
Multiple Meaning Words

Incumbent has more than one possible meaning. To determine which meaning applies in a particular instance, readers must consider the **context,** or clues in the surrounding words, sentences, or paragraphs. For example, in the sentence *It is incumbent on my honor to do so,* the context suggests that *incumbent* means "required as a duty or obligation."

Practice and Apply In the passage below, use context to determine the likely meaning of each boldfaced word. Then explain which context clues in the paragraph helped you determine the word's correct meaning.

> The legend of Arthur has captured the imagination of writers since at least 1136, with the appearance of Geoffrey of Monmouth's History of the Kings of Britain. From this text, later writers would **adopt** some of the essential **elements** of Arthurian lore: Merlin, Excalibur, and Arthur's final **repose** at Avalon. A few decades later, the French poet Chrétien de Troyes introduced the character of Launcelot to the growing **body** of Arthurian literature. *Le Morte d'Arthur* (1469), one of the earliest books printed in English, would eventually become the **ultimate** source for writers of Arthurian literature.

ENGLISH LEARNER SUPPORT

Vocabulary Strategy Give students additional practice in determining the meaning of multiple-mean words. Write the following sentences on the board:

- I agree with the **point** you made at the meeting. That pencil has a sharp **point**.
- I will **rock** the baby to sleep. I tripped over a **rock** and hurt my knee.
- Leslie's mom will **drive** us to school today. Please park in the **drive**.

Work with students to find the meanings of each word and then determine how it is used in the sentence. Underline or circle context clues to help students understand how to use the context of a sentence to determine which meaning is used. **ALL LEVELS**

LANGUAGE CONVENTIONS:
Tone

The **tone** of a text is the writer's attitude toward the subject. One way to identify the tone in a narrative work is to look for the **connotations** or emotions that are evoked by the words. Think carefully about the writer's **diction**, or word choices, and what deliberate responses such choices are meant to evoke. Such words might be positive, negative, or neutral.

The tone of the narrator in *Le Morte D'Arthur* is moralizing, expressing judgment about the events and the actions of the characters. Read these examples of the narration to detect the tone:

> A terrible sword fight commenced, and each felt the might of the other as fresh wounds were inflicted with every blow.

> Hence it was with an army of a hundred thousand that Sir Modred marched to Dover to battle against his own father, and to withhold from him his rightful crown.

In the first sentence, the word *terrible* expresses the narrator's negative feelings about the fight that occurred. In the second example, the phrase *withhold from him his rightful crown* shows that the narrator believes Sir Modred's actions are wrong.

Look at the two examples above and think about how the words might change if the narrator had a different attitude toward the subjects and the action. For instance, consider how the second sentence might change if the narrator approved of Sir Modred's action in making himself king and battling his father.

Practice and Apply Write a short narrative using two different tones.

First, write a short narrative of a recent personal experience that you have strong feelings about. For example, you might write about a big mistake that you regret or something new that you did that turned out to be really fun. Be sure to use descriptive and precise language.

Now, imagine that you have a completely different attitude about the event and rewrite your narrative to reflect those different feelings. For example, you might imagine that the really fun thing you did was not fun at all and you regret deciding to do it.

Finally, exchange your work with a partner. Describe your partner's tone in each narrative. Talk about how the words your partner used changed when he or she wrote with a different tone.

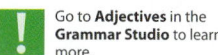

RESPOND

Go to **Adjectives** in the **Grammar Studio** to learn more.

APPLY

LANGUAGE CONVENTIONS:
Tone

Review the information on tone with students. Explain that the tone of a story is the attitude the writer, character, or narrator conveys to the reader on the subject. Explain that word choice conveys different tones, and as such, choosing the right word is essential to conveying the intended tone.

Read the first example sentence. Then, change the word *terrible* to *impressive* and read the sentence aloud again. Ask students to consider how their feelings about the sword fight might change with based on the new word.

Read the second example sentence. Then, change the phrase "withhold from him his rightful crown" to "claim the crown that was rightfully his by birthright" and read the sentence aloud. Ask students to once again consider how this wording change would affect the tone of the story.

Practice and Apply Have several students share their personal narratives with a group. Direct listeners to identify the tone of each work and point out words or phrases that support their assertions. *(Students' narratives will vary.)*

 ENGLISH LEARNER SUPPORT

Language Conventions Use the following supports with students at varying proficiency levels.

Help students understand what tone means and how it affects a piece of literature. Display this sentence: *The terrible battle raged on all night even though the knights were exhausted.*

- Ask students to identify words that might lead to understanding tone. Circle *terrible* and *exhausted*. **SUBSTANTIAL**
- Ask students to replace the words *terrible* and *exhausted* with synonyms that keep the tone of the sentence the same. *(wretched, drained)* **MODERATE**
- Ask students to write a sentence that follows the original sentence and maintains the same tone. **LIGHT**

PLAN

MENTOR TEXT
CHIVALRY
Short Story by Neil Gaiman

This short story serves as a mentor text, a model for students to follow when they come to the Unit 1 Writing Task: Write a Short Story.

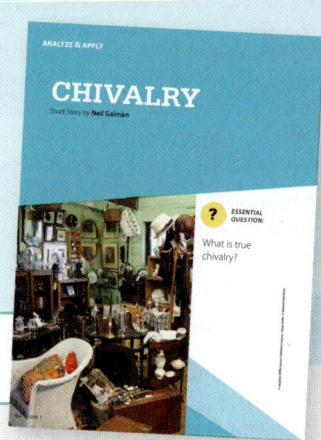

GENRE ELEMENTS
SHORT STORY

Tell students that a **short story** is usually less complex than a novel. Short stories tend to have a small number of characters engaged in a single plot focusing on one incident, often containing elements of fantasy. Generally, short stories cover a short period of time. Many short stories focus on apparently trivial aspects of life in order to reveal perceptive truths about human behavior. In this story, students will analyze the author's characterization of two characters who meet each other in unusual circumstances.

LEARNING OBJECTIVES

- Analyze characterization and fantasy.
- Conduct research about Sir Galahad.
- Write a fantasy scene.
- Dramatize a fantasy scene.
- Use context clues to determine the meaning of words and phrases.
- Identify appositives and appositive phrases.
- **Language** Use connecting words to make writing sound smoother and more natural.

TEXT COMPLEXITY

Quantitative Measures	Chivalry	Lexile: 810L
Qualitative Measures	**Ideas Presented** Much is explicit, but requires some inferential reasoning. Use of irony.	
	Structures Used Clear, chronological, largely conventional.	
	Language Used Mostly explicit, some figurative language, dialect, and archaic language.	
	Knowledge Required Situations and subjects mostly familiar. Some historical and literary references, mostly explained in text.	

64A Unit 1

PLAN

RESOURCES

- Unit 1 Response Log
- 🔊 Selection Audio
- 📖 Reading Studio: Notice & Note
- Level Up Tutorial: Historical and Cultural Context; Character Traits; Methods of Characterization
- Writing Studio: Writing as a Process
- 💬 Speaking and Listening Studio: Giving a Presentation
- Vocabulary Studio: Context Clues
- ❗ Grammar Studio: Module 3 Lesson 6: Appositives and Appositive Phrases
- ✅ "Chivalry" Selection Test

SUMMARIES

English

Mrs. Whitaker, an elderly woman living in modern England, purchases the Holy Grail, an ancient silver chalice purported to have been used by Jesus, at a secondhand shop. Soon after, Sir Galaad, a knight from the Middle Ages, gallops up to her home on horseback on a quest to obtain the Grail. The two characters—one ordinary and one fantastic—get to know each other as they negotiate ownership of the legendary cup.

Spanish

La Sra. Whitaker, una mujer mayor que vive en la Inglaterra moderna, compra el Santo Grial en una tienda de cosas usadas. Es un cáliz de plata antiguo que, según se afirma, fue usado por Jesucristo. Poco después, Sir Galaad, un caballero de la Edad Media, galopa hacia su casa en búsqueda del Santo Grial. Los dos personajes (uno común y el otro fantástico) se conocen y negocian la propiedad de la copa legendaria.

SMALL-GROUP OPTIONS

Have students work in small groups and pairs to read and discuss the selection.

Numbered Heads Together

- After students have read the summary of the story, pose this question to the class: Why might an author want two characters from different backgrounds and time periods to meet?
- Have students form groups of four and number off 1-2-3-4 within the group.
- Have students discuss their responses to the question in their groups.
- Then, call a number from 1–4. The student with that number will then respond for the group.

Three-Minute Review

- After students have read the story, set a timer for three minutes.
- Have students work independently to skim through the story and write clarifying questions about what they read.
- After three minutes, ask volunteers to share their questions.
- Briefly discuss answers to each question.

Chivalry

PLAN

Text X-Ray: English Learner Support
for "Chivalry"

Use the Text X-Ray and the supports and scaffolds in the Teacher's Edition to help guide students at different proficiency levels through the selection.

INTRODUCE THE SELECTION
DISCUSS FANTASY AND REALISM

In this lesson, students will need to be able to identify and discuss the difference between fantasy and realism.

Remind students that fantasy portrays unrealistic, supernatural, or fantastic characters, settings, and events. Realism shows people and situations as they are in ordinary life.

Ask students to compare and contrast fantastic and realistic story elements using sentence frames, such as: *One element in the story that shows this is fantasy is ____. An example of a realistic element in this story is ____. The character ____ is fantastic/ordinary because ____.*

CULTURAL REFERENCES

The following words or phrases may be unfamiliar to students:

- *were no longer what they were* (paragraph 2): had gotten worse or older
- *bits and bobs* (paragraph 3): a random assortment of small things
- *late* (paragraph 18): dead
- *had an early night* (paragraph 97): went to bed early
- *a spot of* (paragraph 98): a little bit of
- *would come with time* (paragraph 105): would eventually be able to be done
- *could of* (paragraph 109): could have
- *gone for* (paragraph 109): fallen in love with
- *to boot* (paragraph 121): also

LISTENING

Identify Irony

As students listen to a rereading of the text, have them identify examples of irony. Tell students to look for ways that the author makes it seem as if nothing fantastic is happening, even when it is.

Use the following supports with students at varying proficiency levels:

- Read aloud paragraphs 10–14. Ask either/or questions to assess students' comprehension of the irony in the section. Explain that irony is the opposite of what is actually the case. For example: *Is the Holy Grail an ordinary cup or a fantastic cup?* **SUBSTANTIAL**
- Have partners take turns reading passages of the story to each other. Direct one student to read aloud paragraphs 10–14. Direct the other student to tell what is ironic about the passage. Provide sentence frames, such as: *Mrs. Whitaker's dialogue is ironic because ____.* Have students switch roles and repeat the process with paragraphs 21–26. **MODERATE**
- Have partners take turns reading passages of the story to each other. Direct one student to read aloud paragraphs 10–14. Direct the other student to tell what is ironic about the passage. Have students switch roles and read paragraphs 21–26. **LIGHT**

PLAN

SPEAKING

Retell the Story

Have students retell the plot of the story using illustrations, such as simple drawings or selected images from print sources.

Use the following supports with students at varying proficiency levels:

- Have students choose one scene from the story to illustrate with simple drawings or selected images from print sources. Work with students to create a word bank of nouns and verbs that describe their images. Help them use the word bank to retell a plot event using simple phrases. **SUBSTANTIAL**
- Have students choose one scene from the story to illustrate. Ask partners to use the visuals to retell the plot events in their chosen scene to each other. Provide sentence starters, such as: *This scene takes place in ____. The characters in this scene are ____.* **MODERATE**
- Have students choose several scenes from the story to illustrate. Ask partners to use the visuals to retell the plot events and discuss the setting and characters in their scenes. **LIGHT**

READING

Compare and Contrast Characters

Remind students to pay close attention to what characters say, think, and do, in addition to how they look, as they compare and contrast Mrs. Whitaker and Sir Galaad.

Use the following supports with students at varying proficiency levels:

- Read aloud paragraphs 30–46 and have students follow along in their text. Create a two-column chart labeled *Mrs. Whitaker* and *Sir Galaad*. List details from the text about each character and read them aloud. Have students repeat them. Have students use a sentence frame to compare and contrast details about the characters. For example: *(Character's name) is ____, but (character's name) is ____.* **SUBSTANTIAL**
- Have partners reread paragraphs 30–46. Direct them to create a two-column chart labeled *Mrs. Whitaker* and *Sir Galaad*. Have students list details from the text about each character. Then, have students use the details to compare and contrast the characters. Provide a sentence frame: *(Character's name) is ____, but (character's name) is ____.* **MODERATE**
- Have partners read aloud paragraphs 30–61, taking turns after every ten lines. Direct them to create a two-column chart labeled *Mrs. Whitaker* and *Sir Galaad* and list details from the text about each character. Have students use the details to compare and contrast the characters. **LIGHT**

WRITING

Use Connecting Words

Tell students that the use of connecting words will make their writing sound smoother and more like natural speech.

Use the following supports with students at varying proficiency levels:

- Provide a list of connecting words and phrases, and have students copy it. Use each word or phrase in a short example sentence. Have students copy it and underline the word or phrase. **SUBSTANTIAL**
- Provide a list of connecting words and phrases, and have students copy it. Provide sentence frames and have students use words from the list to complete them. For example: *Ed ____ Kim went on a trip, __ Ed came back early.* **MODERATE**
- Have small groups list connecting words and phrases. After students write their fantasy scene, have peers suggest connecting words to make the writing flow more smoothly. **LIGHT**

TEACH

ANALYZE & APPLY

 Connect to the ESSENTIAL QUESTION

The story is based on the legends of King Arthur of Camelot and the Knights of the Round Table, who lived by the code of chivalry – faith, personal courage, kindness, and respect for all. Sir Galahad, the knight with the purest heart, was chosen to find the Holy Grail, purported to be the cup that Jesus used at the Last Supper before his crucifixion. The author takes Galahad and the Grail and places them in the ordinary world of modern London. He presents the reader with an imaginary and humorous "culture clash."

MENTOR TEXT

At the end of the unit, students will be asked to write a short story. "Chivalry" provides a model of how a writer can create an effective story by contrasting character and setting.

CHIVALRY

Short Story by **Neil Gaiman**

ESSENTIAL QUESTION:

What is true chivalry?

64 Unit 1

QUICK START

Imagine that a person from the Middle Ages traveled through time to meet you. What would you ask this person? What do you think this person would want to ask you? Make a list of questions for yourself and the time traveler.

ANALYZE CHARACTERIZATION

A writer's method of revealing characters' personalities is called **characterization**. Writers use four basic methods to develop their characters:

- describing a character's physical appearance
- presenting a character's actions, thoughts, and speech
- revealing other characters' reactions to a character
- directly commenting on a character

Characterization is related to other elements of fiction. For example, a writer may place a character in a setting where he or she stands out in some way, which could affect how others view the character. As you read "Chivalry," notice the methods Neil Gaiman uses to develop the two main characters. In addition, pay attention to how the story's setting influences our perception of the characters.

ANALYZE FANTASY

Fantasy is a type of fiction that intentionally portrays unrealistic events, settings, or characters. For example, a story may be set in a nonexistent world, or the characters might have supernatural powers. Although fantasies are often written mainly for entertainment, they can express serious themes about life or society. Neil Gaiman is known for his highly imaginative fantasy writing. In "Chivalry" he mixes elements of the Arthurian legends into the story of an elderly woman living in a dull English town. Use a chart like the one shown to note down realistic and fantasy details in the story.

REALISTIC DETAILS	FANTASY DETAILS
Mrs. Whitaker stops in at a secondhand shop every week on her way home from the post office.	She finds the Holy Grail for sale in the shop.

As you read "Chivalry," keep an eye out for other elements of fantasy and think about how these elements help to move the plot forward.

GET READY

GENRE ELEMENTS: SHORT STORY

- includes the basic elements of fiction—setting, characters, plot, conflict, and theme
- centers on a particular moment or event or follows the life of one character
- can be read in one sitting
- may include elements of fantasy, such as supernatural events

Chivalry 65

TEACH

QUICK START

Have students read the Quick Start prompt. Have pairs of students write two questions they would ask the person from the Middle Ages and two that they think the person would ask them. Then, have each pair join another and ask each other the questions.

ANALYZE CHARACTERIZATION

Refer to the four methods of character development listed in the text and discuss them with the class. For each one, ask students for an example, such as: What descriptive detail about appearance could an author write that would reveal character? *(dirty or outlandish clothes, a careworn face)* When you have an example for each one, remind students that these are the kind of details they should notice in the author's presentation of the characters.

ANALYZE FANTASY

Tell students that the contrast between fantasy and reality is a very important part of the story. Point out the T-chart in the text and have students put the chart in their notes to keep track of these contrasts. It may help students to understand the elements they are to note if they look for specific categories of fantasy elements, including characters, events, and objects. (The modern, realistic setting stays the same throughout the story, but magical objects vary.)

Chivalry **65**

TEACH

CRITICAL VOCABULARY

Give students time to complete the fill-in-the-blank vocabulary exercise. When they have finished, go over the questions verbally, noting which students are having comprehension problems. Ask the class to make up more sentences verbally. You might call on students to make up a story one sentence at a time, each person building on the previous sentences.

Answers:

1. *flotsam*
2. *forge*
3. *pension*
4. *bereft*
5. *ignoble*
6. *appraise*

■ English Learner Support

Use Cognates Tell students that several of the Critical Vocabulary words have Spanish cognates: *pension/pension, forge/fragua, ignoble/innoble*. Ask questions about what these words mean in the story. For example, "Mrs. Whitaker receives a pension. What does that tell us about her?" (*She is elderly.*) **ALL PROFICIENCIES**

LANGUAGE CONVENTIONS

Remind students that an **appositive** is a noun or noun phrase that clarifies something already named. Make sure that students understand how to recognize an appositive in a sentence by comparing descriptive phrases from the text that do not rename a noun with those that do. For example, "It [the stuffed cobra] had been there for six months now, gathering dust, glass eyes gazing balefully at the clothes racks. . . ." The descriptive phrase does not contain a noun that renames what it is describing (the stuffed cobra).

ANNOTATION MODEL

Remind students of the annotation ideas in Analyze Fantasy on page 65, which suggest noting realistic and fantastic details in the short story. Point out that they may follow the suggestion shown here or use their own system for marking up the selection in their write-in text. They may want to color-code their annotations by using highlighters. Their notes in the margin may include questions about ideas that are unclear or topics they want to learn more about.

66 Unit 1

 **GET READY**

CRITICAL VOCABULARY

pension   flotsam   appraise   forge   ignoble   bereft

To see how many Critical Vocabulary words you already know, use them to complete the sentences.

1. After the storm, heaps of _____ washed up on the shore.
2. The metal for the sword was fired in a crude _____.
3. The _____ from her job at the shipbuilding company helped pay her rent and other living expenses.
4. When his grandmother died, he felt _____ for the first time.
5. Some of the crudest, most _____ people have succeeded in politics.
6. I will have an expert _____ the house before I bid on it.

LANGUAGE CONVENTIONS

Appositives and Appositive Phrases In this lesson, you will learn to identify and use appositives and appositive phrases. An appositive is a noun or pronoun that identifies, or renames, another noun or pronoun right beside it. An appositive phrase includes an appositive and its modifiers. Here is an example of an appositive phrase that renames *Arthur*:

> It was signed by Arthur, King of all Britons.

As you read "Chivalry," look out for appositives and appositive phrases.

ANNOTATION MODEL NOTICE & NOTE

As you read, take note of the contrast between the realistic and the fantasy to see how the writer creates humor and surprise by juxtaposing the two. This model shows one reader's notes analyzing fantasy elements in "Chivalry."

> It was a sword, its blade almost four feet long. There were words and symbols traced elegantly along the length of the blade. The hilt was worked in silver and gold, and a large jewel was set in the pommel.
> "It's very nice," said Mrs. Whitaker, doubtfully.
> "This," said Galaad, "is the sword Balmung, forged by Wayland Smith in the dawntimes. Its twin is Flamberge. Who wears it is unconquerable in war, and invincible in battle. Who wears it is incapable of a cowardly act or an ignoble one."

Mrs. Whitaker reacts to the remarkable sword in such an understated way.

It's funny to think of her using the superhuman powers that the sword would provide.

66   Unit 1

BACKGROUND

Neil Gaiman *(b. 1960) is a popular and prolific author who has written novels, comic books, graphic novels, and film and television scripts. He was born and raised in England. As a child, his favorite authors included C. S. Lewis, J. R. R. Tolkien, Ursula K. Le Guin, and other fantasy writers. Gaiman's own writing often features fantasy elements, such as the character Galaad in "Chivalry," who is based on Sir Galahad of the Arthurian legends. The purest of King Arthur's knights, Galahad led the quest to find the Holy Grail, a vessel associated with Christ that was said to have miraculous powers.*

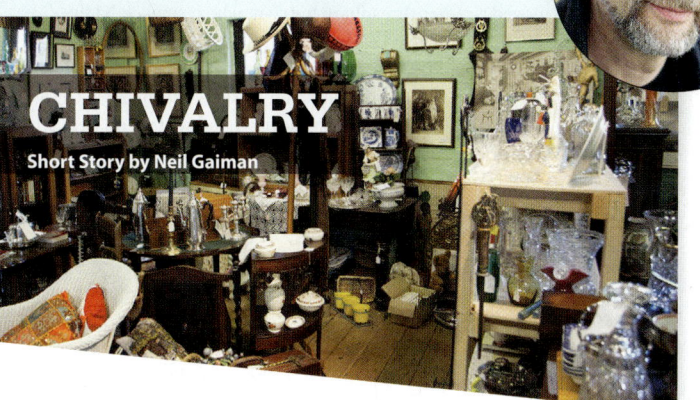

CHIVALRY
Short Story by Neil Gaiman

SETTING A PURPOSE

As you read, pay attention to how Mrs. Whitaker reacts to Galaad and the fantastic objects she comes across in the story.

1 Mrs. Whitaker found the Holy Grail; it was under a fur coat.

2 Every Thursday afternoon Mrs. Whitaker walked down to the post office to collect her **pension**, even though her legs were no longer what they were, and on the way back home she would stop in at the Oxfam Shop and buy herself a little something.

3 The Oxfam Shop sold old clothes, knickknacks, oddments, bits and bobs, and large quantities of old paperbacks, all of them donations: secondhand **flotsam**, often the house clearances of the dead. All the profits went to charity.

4 The shop was staffed by volunteers. The volunteer on duty this afternoon was Marie, seventeen, slightly overweight, and dressed in a baggy mauve jumper that looked like she had bought it from the shop.

5 Marie sat by the till with a copy of *Modern Woman* magazine, filling out a "Reveal Your Hidden Personality" questionnaire. Every now and then, she'd flip to the back of the magazine and check the relative points assigned to an A), B), or C) answer before making up her mind how she'd respond to the question.

NOTICE & NOTE

Notice & Note

Use the side margins to notice and note signposts in the text.

pension
(pĕn′shən) *n.* a sum of money paid regularly as a retirement benefit.

ANALYZE CHARACTERIZATION

Annotate: Mark the details used to characterize Mrs. Whitaker in paragraph 2.

Infer: What can you tell about her from these details?

flotsam
(flŏt′səm) *n.* discarded or unimportant things.

Chivalry 67

TEACH

✏️ ANALYZE FANTASY

Have students note what the text says about the Holy Grail. (**Answer:** *Every other detail is exactly what you would expect to see in the shop. The presence of a valued relic like the Holy Grail here catches the reader off guard.*)

■ English Learner Support

Use Visual Support Help students understand what kind of object the Holy Grail is by reading its description in the text aloud (demonstrating with gestures). Have students draw their version of the Holy Grail. Explain that it is a mythical object with deep religious meaning. **SUBSTANTIAL**

CRITICAL VOCABULARY

appraise: When Mrs. Whitaker appraised the Holy Grail, she was trying to decide whether it was worth buying.

ASK STUDENTS to name qualities other than cost that might be considered in an appraisal. (*beauty, usefulness, personal meaning*)

✏️ **NOTICE & NOTE**

ANALYZE FANTASY
Annotate: Mark the element of fantasy in paragraph 10.
Interpret: Why is this detail humorous in the context of the paragraph?

appraise
(ə-prāz´) *tr.v.* to estimate the price or value of.

6 Mrs. Whitaker puttered around the shop.

7 They still hadn't sold the stuffed cobra, she noted. It had been there for six months now, gathering dust, glass eyes gazing balefully at the clothes racks and the cabinet filled with chipped porcelain and chewed toys.

8 Mrs. Whitaker patted its head as she went past.

9 She picked out a couple of Mills & Boon novels from a bookshelf—*Her Thundering Soul* and *Her Turbulent Heart*, a shilling each—and gave careful consideration to the empty bottle of Mateus Rosé with a decorative lampshade on it before deciding she really didn't have anywhere to put it.

10 She moved a rather threadbare fur coat, which smelled badly of mothballs. Underneath it was a walking stick and a water stained copy of *Romance and Legend of Chivalry* by A. R. Hope Moncrieff, priced at five pence. Next to the book, on its side, was the Holy Grail. It had a little round paper sticker on the base, and written on it, in felt pen, was the price: 30p.

11 Mrs. Whitaker picked up the dusty silver goblet and **appraised** it through her thick spectacles.

12 "This is nice," she called to Marie.

13 Marie shrugged.

14 "It'd look nice on the mantelpiece."

15 Marie shrugged again.

16 Mrs. Whitaker gave fifty pence to Marie, who gave her ten pence change and a brown paper bag to put the books and the Holy Grail in. Then she went next door to the butcher's and bought herself a nice piece of liver. Then she went home.

17 The inside of the goblet was thickly coated with a brownish-red dust. Mrs. Whitaker washed it out with great care, then left it to soak for an hour in warm water with a dash of vinegar added.

18 Then she polished it with metal polish until it gleamed, and she put it on the mantelpiece in her parlor, where it sat between a small soulful china basset hound and a photograph of her late husband, Henry, on the beach at Frinton in 1953.

19 She had been right: It did look nice.

20 For dinner that evening she had the liver fried in breadcrumbs with onions. It was very nice.

21 The next morning was Friday; on alternate Fridays Mrs. Whitaker and Mrs. Greenberg would visit each other. Today it was Mrs. Greenberg's turn to visit Mrs. Whitaker. They sat in the parlor and ate macaroons and drank tea. Mrs. Whitaker took one sugar in her tea, but Mrs. Greenberg took sweetener, which she always carried in her handbag in a small plastic container.

22 "That's nice," said Mrs. Greenberg, pointing to the Grail. "What is it?"

23 "It's the Holy Grail," said Mrs. Whitaker. "It's the cup that Jesus drunk out of at the Last Supper. Later, at the Crucifixion, it caught His precious blood when the centurion's spear pierced His side."

68   Unit 1

🆔 **ENGLISH LEARNER SUPPORT**

Vocabulary Have students make a 2-column chart without headings. Instruct students to sort a list of words into two categories, but do not provide the categories. Provide this list of words for the students to sort: balefully, chipped, decorative, dusty, thickly, soulful, precious. Instruct students to categorize the words by sorting them into two groups. Have students add headings to the two columns to name their groups. Students should recognize that the words in the list can be sorted into adjectives and adverbs. **MODERATE**

24   Mrs. Greenberg sniffed. She was small and Jewish and didn't hold with unsanitary things. "I wouldn't know about that," she said, "but it's very nice. Our Myron got one just like that when he won the swimming tournament, only it's got his name on the side."

25   "Is he still with that nice girl? The hairdresser?"

26   "Bernice? Oh yes. They're thinking of getting engaged," said Mrs. Greenberg.

27   "That's nice," said Mrs. Whitaker. She took another macaroon.

28   Mrs. Greenberg baked her own macaroons and brought them over every alternate Friday: small sweet light brown biscuits with almonds on top.

29   They talked about Myron and Bernice, and Mrs. Whitaker's nephew Ronald (she had had no children), and about their friend Mrs. Perkins who was in hospital with her hip, poor dear.

30   At midday Mrs. Greenberg went home, and Mrs. Whitaker made herself cheese on toast for lunch, and after lunch Mrs. Whitaker took her pills; the white and the red and two little orange ones.

31   The doorbell rang.

32   Mrs. Whitaker answered the door. It was a young man with shoulder-length hair so fair it was almost white, wearing gleaming silver armor, with a white surcoat.

33   "Hello," he said.

34   "Hello," said Mrs. Whitaker.

35   "I'm on a quest," he said.

36   "That's nice," said Mrs. Whitaker, noncommittally.

37   "Can I come in?" he asked.

38   Mrs. Whitaker shook her head. "I'm sorry, I don't think so," she said.

39   "I'm on a quest for the Holy Grail," the young man said. "Is it here?"

40   "Have you got any identification?" Mrs. Whitaker asked. She knew that it was unwise to let unidentified strangers into your home when you were elderly and living on your own. Handbags get emptied, and worse than that.

41   The young man went back down the garden path. His horse, a huge gray charger, big as a shire-horse, its head high and its eyes intelligent, was tethered to Mrs. Whitaker's garden gate. The knight fumbled in the saddlebag and returned with a scroll.

42   It was signed by Arthur, King of All Britons, and charged all persons of whatever rank or station to know that here was Galaad, Knight of the Table Round, and that he was on a Right High and Noble Quest. There was a drawing of the young man below that. It wasn't a bad likeness.

43   Mrs. Whitaker nodded. She had been expecting a little card with a photograph on it, but this was far more impressive.

44   "I suppose you had better come in," she said.

45   They went into her kitchen. She made Galaad a cup of tea, then she took him into the parlor.

LANGUAGE CONVENTIONS

Annotate: Mark all the appositives in paragraph 29.

Analyze: How do they clarify the meaning of the nouns that precede them?

Chivalry   69

TEACH

LANGUAGE CONVENTIONS

Review what an **appositive** is—a noun or noun phrase that clarifies another noun or pronoun. Have students locate the appositives in paragraph 29 and read them aloud. (**Answer:** The appositives answer the question Which? Which nephew? Ronald. Which friend? Mrs. Perkins [poor dear].)

■ English Learner Support

Practice Appositives Write several simple appositives on the board, e.g., "Bob, the official baker, and his wife Selene, the spokeswoman." Point out that "Bob" and "the official baker" refer to the same person as do "the spokeswoman" and "Selene." Repeat, this time asking students to pick out the words that mean the same person. Read aloud the sentence in paragraph 29 and have students pick out the words that name the same person. **MODERATE**

WHEN STUDENTS STRUGGLE...

Contrast Realistic and Fantastic Elements Help students contrast the realistic and fantastical elements in paragraph 42 by using the chart below.

Fantasy Phrases	Realistic Phrases
Signed by Arthur, King of All Britons	There was a drawing of the young man

 For additional support, go to the **Reading Studio** and assign the following **Level Up tutorial: Historical and Cultural Context.**

Chivalry   69

TEACH

ANALYZE CHARACTERIZATION

Have students point out the words in Galaad's speech in paragraph 49 that sound strange to the modern ear. **(Answer:** He speaks very formally and politely ("Gracious Lady") and uses archaic language ("geas"). He also uses religious language ("Holy of Holies," "Blessed Chalice").

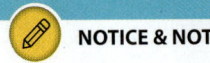 **NOTICE & NOTE**

ANALYZE CHARACTERIZATION
Annotate: Reread paragraphs 47–56. Mark details in Galaad's dialogue that help develop his character.

Analyze: How does Galaad's speech reflect the time period of the Arthurian legends?

46   Galaad saw the Grail on her mantelpiece, and dropped to one knee. He put down the teacup carefully on the russet carpet. A shaft of light came through the net curtains and painted his awed face with golden sunlight and turned his hair into a silver halo.

47   "It is truly the Sangrail[1]," he said, very quietly. He blinked his pale blue eyes three times, very fast, as if he were blinking back tears.

48   He lowered his head as if in silent prayer.

49   Galaad stood up again and turned to Mrs. Whitaker. "Gracious lady, keeper of the Holy of Holies, let me now depart this place with the Blessed Chalice, that my journeyings may be ended and my geas[2] fulfilled."

50   "Sorry?" said Mrs. Whitaker.

51   Galaad walked over to her and took her old hands in his. "My quest is over," he told her. "The Sangrail is finally within my reach."

52   Mrs. Whitaker pursed her lips. "Can you pick your teacup and saucer up, please?" she said.

53   Galaad picked up his teacup apologetically.

54   "No. I don't think so," said Mrs. Whitaker. "I rather like it there. It's just right, between the dog and the photograph of my Henry."

55   "Is it gold you need? Is that it? Lady, I can bring you gold . . ."

56   "No," said Mrs. Whitaker. "I don't want any gold thank *you*. I'm simply not interested."

57   She ushered Galaad to the front door. "Nice to meet you," she said.

58   His horse was leaning its head over her garden fence, nibbling her gladioli. Several of the neighborhood children were standing on the pavement, watching it.

59   Galaad took some sugar lumps from the saddlebag and showed the braver of the children how to feed the horse, their hands held flat. The children giggled. One of the older girls stroked the horse's nose.

60   Galaad swung himself up onto the horse in one fluid movement. Then the horse and the knight trotted off down Hawthorne Crescent.

61   Mrs. Whitaker watched them until they were out of sight, then sighed and went back inside.

62   The weekend was quiet.

63   On Saturday Mrs. Whitaker took the bus into Maresfield to visit her nephew Ronald, his wife Euphonia, and their daughters, Clarissa and Dillian. She took them a currant cake she had baked herself.

64   On Sunday morning Mrs. Whitaker went to church. Her local church was St. James the Less, which was a little more "Don't think of this as a church, think of it as a place where like-minded friends hang out and are joyful" than Mrs. Whitaker felt entirely comfortable with, but she liked the vicar, the Reverend Bartholomew, when he wasn't actually playing the guitar.

---

[1] **Sangrail:** another name for the Holy Grail.
[2] **geas:** an obligation magically imposed on a person.

APPLYING ACADEMIC VOCABULARY

❏ collapse   ❏ displace   ❏ military   ☑ violate   ☑ visual

Write and Discuss Have students turn to a partner to discuss the following questions. Guide students to include the academic vocabulary words *violate* and *visual* in their responses. How does Mrs. Whitaker respond to Galaad's appearance at her door? *(Mrs. Whitaker violates expectations when she calmly welcomes in the medieval knight.)*

- In what ways does Sir Galaad seem out of place in the story's setting? *(Galaad is out of place in both visual and behavioral ways.)*

65 After the service, she thought about mentioning to him that she had the Holy Grail in her front parlor, but decided against it.

66 On Monday morning Mrs. Whitaker was working in the back garden. She had a small herb garden she was extremely proud of: dill, vervain, mint, rosemary, thyme, and a wild expanse of parsley. She was down on her knees, wearing thick green gardening gloves, weeding, and picking out slugs and putting them in a plastic bag.

67 Mrs. Whitaker was very tenderhearted when it came to slugs. She would take them down to the back of her garden, which bordered on the railway line, and throw them over the fence.

68 She cut some parsley for the salad. There was a cough behind her. Galaad stood there, tall and beautiful, his armor glinting in the morning sun. In his arms he held a long package, wrapped in oiled leather.

69 "I'm back," he said.

70 "Hello," said Mrs. Whitaker. She stood up, rather slowly, and took off her gardening gloves. "Well," she said, "now you're here, you might as well make yourself useful."

71 She gave him the plastic bag full of slugs and told him to tip the slugs out over the back of the fence.

72 He did.

73 Then they went into the kitchen.

74 "Tea? Or lemonade?" she asked.

75 "Whatever you're having," Galaad said.

76 Mrs. Whitaker took a jug of her homemade lemonade from the fridge and sent Galaad outside to pick a sprig of mint. She selected two tall glasses. She washed the mint carefully and put a few leaves in each glass, then poured the lemonade.

77 "Is your horse outside?" she asked.

78 "Oh yes. His name is Grizzel."

79 "And you've come a long way, I suppose."

80 "A very long way."

81 "I see," said Mrs. Whitaker. She took a blue plastic basin from under the sink and half-filled it with water. Galaad took it out to Grizzel. He waited while the horse drank and brought the empty basin back to Mrs. Whitaker.

82 "Now," she said, "I suppose you're still after the Grail."

83 "Aye, still do I seek the Sangrail," he said. He picked up the leather package from the floor, put it down on her tablecloth and unwrapped it. "For it, I offer you this."

84 It was a sword, its blade almost four feet long. There were words and symbols traced elegantly along the length of the blade. The hilt was worked in silver and gold, and a large jewel was set in the pommel.

85 "It's very nice," said Mrs. Whitaker, doubtfully.

86 "This," said Galaad, "is the sword Balmung, **forged** by Wayland Smith in the dawn times. Its twin is Flamberge. Who wears it is unconquerable in war, and invincible in battle. Who wears it is incapable of a cowardly act or an **ignoble** one. Set in its pommel is

NOTICE & NOTE

ANALYZE CHARACTERIZATION

Annotate: Reread paragraphs 68–70. Mark details used to describe Galaad.

Analyze: What does Mrs. Whitaker's reaction to Galaad reveal about her character?

forge
(fôrj) *v.* to form (metal, for example) by heating in a forge and beating or hammering into shape.

ignoble
(ĭg-nōʹbəl) *adj.* not noble in quality, character, or purpose; base or dishonorable.

Chivalry   71

TO CHALLENGE STUDENTS

Research Legends In Beowulf, the poet makes reference to armor that was crafted by a smith named Weland. In paragraph 86, Galaad presents Mrs. Whitaker with a sword "forged by Wayland the Smith in the dawn times." Have students research to see if there is a connection between these references. Direct them to online resources for information. Ask students to find other famous stories or legends in which Wayland the Smith appears.

TEACH

ANALYZE CHARACTERIZATION

Direct students' attention to paragraph 68. Discuss how Galaad is described as tall and beautiful. What reaction might you expect from the average person on seeing a tall, beautiful knight in full armor in their garden? Then have students describe how Mrs. Whitaker reacted. (**Answer:** *She is very practical and not interested in investigating anything unfamiliar. Limited by her small, well-ordered world, she is not awed by Galaad's beauty, she only thinks of how he can help her.*)

■ English Learner Support

Compare Direct students' attention to paragraphs 68–70. Read them aloud or have students read them silently, depending on proficiency. Ask students to describe in their own words or act out what the characters are doing. Point out to students that the words *behind* and *stood* indicate where they stood in relation to each other.
SUBSTANTIAL/MODERATE

CRITICAL VOCABULARY

forge: Help students understand that *forge* can be used either as a noun or as a verb.

ASK STUDENTS why a forge would be important to King Arthur's knights. *(to make weapons and armor)*

ignoble: Help students recognize that the prefix *ig-* negates the word *noble*.

ASK STUDENTS for examples of a noble act (*feeding the homeless, saving someone from drowning*) Then ask them for examples of an ignoble act. (*cheating, stealing from a friend*)

Chivalry   71

TEACH

ENGLISH LEARNER SUPPORT

Use Context Help students understand the meaning of *disconsolate (without happiness or comfort)* in paragraph 93. Provide simple sentences that restate the context: "Galaad offered Mrs. Whitaker a magical sword. Mrs. Whitaker was not interested." Ask students how Galaad must have felt, and help them connect this to the meaning of the word. **MODERATE**

NOTICE & NOTE

the sardonynx[3] Bircone, which protects its possessor from poison slipped into wine or ale, and from the treachery of friends."

87 Mrs. Whitaker peered at the sword. "It must be very sharp," she said, after a while.

88 "It can slice a falling hair in twain. Nay, it could slice a sunbeam," said Galaad proudly.

89 "Well, then, maybe you ought to put it away," said Mrs. Whitaker.

90 "Don't you want it?" Galaad seemed disappointed.

91 "No, thank you," said Mrs. Whitaker. It occurred to her that her late husband, Henry, would have quite liked it. He would have hung it on the wall in his study next to the stuffed carp he had caught in Scotland, and pointed it out to visitors.

92 Galaad rewrapped the oiled leather around the sword Balmung and tied it up with white cord.

93 He sat there, disconsolate.

94 Mrs. Whitaker made him some cream cheese and cucumber sandwiches for the journey back and wrapped them in greaseproof paper. She gave him an apple for Grizzel. He seemed very pleased with both gifts.

95 She waved them both good-bye.

96 That afternoon she took the bus down to the hospital to see Mrs. Perkins, who was still in with her hip, poor love. Mrs. Whitaker took her some homemade fruitcake, although she had left out the walnuts from the recipe, because Mrs. Perkins's teeth weren't what they used to be.

97 She watched a little television that evening, and had an early night.

98 On Tuesday the postman called. Mrs. Whitaker was up in the boxroom at the top of the house, doing a spot of tidying, and, taking each step slowly and carefully, she didn't make it downstairs in time. The postman had left her a message which said that he'd tried to deliver a packet, but no one was home.

99 Mrs. Whitaker sighed.

100 She put the message into her handbag and went down to the post office.

101 The package was from her niece Shirelle in Sydney, Australia. It contained photographs of her husband, Wallace, and her two daughters, Dixie and Violet, and a conch shell packed in cotton wool.

102 Mrs. Whitaker had a number of ornamental shells in her bedroom. Her favorite had a view of the Bahamas done on it in enamel. It had been a gift from her sister, Ethel, who had died in 1983.

103 She put the shell and the photographs in her shopping bag. Then, seeing that she was in the area, she stopped in at the Oxfam Shop on her way home.

104 "Hullo, Mrs. W.," said Marie.

---

[3] **sardonynx:** a type of stone.

72 Unit 1

IMPROVE READING FLUENCY

Targeted Passage Use paragraph 75 to model how to read a short story. Have students follow along in their books as you read the text with appropriate phrasing and emphasis. Then, have partners take turns reading aloud each paragraph in the section. Encourage students to provide feedback and support for pronouncing multisyllabic words. Remind students that when they are reading aloud for an audience they should pace their reading so the audience has time to understand difficult concepts. Then have students work with partners to read paragraphs 74–83.

 Go to the **Reading Studio** for additional support in developing fluency.

105 Mrs. Whitaker stared at her. Marie was wearing lipstick (possibly not the best shade for her, nor particularly expertly applied, but, thought Mrs. Whitaker, that would come with time) and a rather smart skirt. It was a great improvement.

106 "Oh. Hello, dear," said Mrs. Whitaker.

107 "There was a man in here last week, asking about that thing you bought. The little metal cup thing. I told him where to find you. You don't mind, do you?"

108 "No, dear," said Mrs. Whitaker. "He found me."

109 "He was really dreamy. Really, really dreamy," sighed Marie wistfully. "I could of gone for him.

110 "And he had a big white horse and all," Marie concluded. She was standing up straighter as well, Mrs. Whitaker noted approvingly.

111 On the bookshelf Mrs. Whitaker found a new Mills & Boon novel—*Her Majestic Passion*—although she hadn't yet finished the two she had bought on her last visit.

112 She picked up the copy of *Romance and Legend of Chivalry* and opened it. It smelled musty. *EX LIBRIS FISHER* was neatly handwritten at the top of the first page in red ink.

113 She put it down where she had found it.

114 When she got home, Galaad was waiting for her. He was giving the neighborhood children rides on Grizzel's back, up and down the street.

115 "I'm glad you're here," she said. "I've got some cases that need moving."

116 She showed him up to the boxroom in the top of the house. He moved all the old suitcases for her, so she could get to the cupboard at the back.

117 It was very dusty up there.

118 She kept him up there most of the afternoon, moving things around while she dusted.

119 Galaad had a cut on his cheek, and he held one arm a little stiffly.

120 They talked a little while she dusted and tidied. Mrs. Whitaker told him about her late husband, Henry; and how the life insurance had paid the house off; and how she had all these things, but no one really to leave them to, no one but Ronald really and his wife only liked modern things. She told him how she had met Henry during the war, when he was in the ARP and she hadn't closed the kitchen blackout curtains all the way; and about the sixpenny dances they went to in the town; and how they'd gone to London when the war had ended, and she'd had her first drink of wine.

121 Galaad told Mrs. Whitaker about his mother Elaine, who was flighty and no better than she should have been and something of a witch to boot; and his grandfather, King Pelles, who was well-meaning although at best a little vague; and of his youth in the Castle of Bliant on the Joyous Isle; and his father, whom he knew as "Le Chevalier Mal Fet," who was more or less completely mad, and was in reality Lancelot du Lac, greatest of knights, in disguise and bereft of his wits; and of Galaad's days as a young squire in Camelot.

ANALYZE FANTASY

Annotate: Reread paragraphs 120–121. Mark examples of fantasy details.

Analyze: What effect does Gaiman create by offering these parallel descriptions of the two characters sharing stories of their backgrounds?

bereft
(bĭ-rĕft´) *adj.* deprived of something.

Chivalry 73

TEACH

ANALYZE FANTASY

Talk about how this passage builds on our knowledge of both Mrs. Whitaker and Galaad. As Galaad offers her more and more valuable gifts in his desire for the Grail, she becomes more and more remarkable in her refusal of the magical objects. (**Answer:** *All these items come from legends and mythology. She does realize the significance but decides to reject the magic.*)

■ English Learner Support

Identify On the board list the three magical objects that Galaad offers Mrs. Whitaker. Have students draw a picture of what they think one of the objects might look like. Ask individual students to describe one of the pictures at their own proficiency level. **SUBSTANTIAL/MODERATE**

 **NOTICE & NOTE**

ANALYZE FANTASY

Annotate: Reread paragraphs 126–139. Mark the descriptions of the items Galaad offers to Mrs. Whitaker in exchange for the Holy Grail.

Evaluate: Identify the significance of the stone, the egg, and the apple. Does Mrs. Whitaker seem to realize the significance of these items? Explain.

122 At five o'clock Mrs. Whitaker surveyed the boxroom and decided that it met with her approval; then she opened the window so the room could air, and they went downstairs to the kitchen, where she put on the kettle.

123 Galaad sat down at the kitchen table.

124 He opened the leather purse at his waist and took out a round white stone. It was about the size of a cricket ball.

125 "My lady," he said, "This is for you, an you give me the Sangrail."

126 Mrs. Whitaker picked up the stone, which was heavier than it looked, and held it up to the light. It was milkily translucent, and deep inside it flecks of silver glittered and glinted in the late-afternoon sunlight. It was warm to the touch.

127 Then, as she held it, a strange feeling crept over her: Deep inside she felt stillness and a sort of peace. *Serenity*, that was the word for it; she felt serene.

128 Reluctantly she put the stone back on the table.

129 "It's very nice," she said.

130 "That is the Philosopher's Stone, which our forefather Noah hung in the Ark to give light when there was no light; it can transform base metals into gold; and it has certain other properties," Galaad told her proudly. "And that isn't all. There's more. Here." From the leather bag he took an egg and handed it to her.

131 It was the size of a goose egg and was a shiny black color, mottled with scarlet and white. When Mrs. Whitaker touched it, the hairs on the back of her neck prickled. Her immediate impression was one of incredible heat and freedom. She heard the crackling of distant fires, and for a fraction of a second she seemed to feel herself far above the world, swooping and diving on wings of flame.

132 She put the egg down on the table, next to the Philosopher's Stone.

133 "That is the Egg of the Phoenix," said Galaad. "From far Araby it comes. One day it will hatch out into the Phoenix Bird itself; and when its time comes, the bird will build a nest of flame, lay its egg, and die, to be reborn in flame in a later age of the world."

134 "I thought that was what it was," said Mrs. Whitaker.

135 "And, last of all, lady," said Galaad, "I have brought you this."

136 He drew it from his pouch, and gave it to her. It was an apple, apparently carved from a single ruby, on an amber stem.

137 A little nervously, she picked it up. It was soft to the touch—deceptively so: Her fingers bruised it, and ruby-colored juice from the apple ran down Mrs. Whitaker's hand.

138 The kitchen filled—almost imperceptibly, magically—with the smell of summer fruit, of raspberries and peaches and strawberries and red currants. As if from a great way away she heard distant voices raised in song and far music on the air.

139 "It is one of the apples of the Hesperides," said Galaad, quietly. "One bite from it will heal any illness or wound, no matter how deep; a second bite restores youth and beauty; and a third bite is said to grant eternal life."

74 Unit 1

 ENGLISH LEARNER SUPPORT

Identify Ask students for single words that name or describe an element of the fantasy genre, for example "magic" or "superpowers." Write the words on the board. Ask students to draw a picture representing one of the words. Beginning students may use the home language to express concepts. **SUBSTANTIAL/MODERATE**

140   Mrs. Whitaker licked the sticky juice from her hand. It tasted like fine wine.

141   There was a moment, then, when it all came back to her—how it was to be young: to have a firm, slim body that would do whatever she wanted it to do; to run down a country lane for the simple unladylike joy of running; to have men smile at her just because she was herself and happy about it.

142   Mrs. Whitaker looked at Sir Galaad, most comely of all knights, sitting fair and noble in her small kitchen.

143   She caught her breath.

144   "And that's all I have brought for you," said Galaad. "They weren't easy to get, either."

145   Mrs. Whitaker put the ruby fruit down on her kitchen table. She looked at the Philosopher's Stone, and the Egg of the Phoenix, and the Apple of Life.

146   Then she walked into her parlor and looked at the mantelpiece: at the little china basset hound, and the Holy Grail, and the photograph of her late husband Henry, shirtless, smiling and eating an ice cream in black and white, almost forty years away.

147   She went back into the kitchen. The kettle had begun to whistle. She poured a little steaming water into the teapot, swirled it around, and poured it out. Then she added two spoonfuls of tea and one for the pot and poured in the rest of the water. All this she did in silence.

148   She turned to Galaad then, and she looked at him.

149   "Put that apple away," she told Galaad, firmly. "You shouldn't offer things like that to old ladies. It isn't proper."

150   She paused, then. "But I'll take the other two," she continued, after a moment's thought. "They'll look nice on the mantelpiece. And two for one's fair, or I don't know what is."

151   Galaad beamed. He put the ruby apple into his leather pouch. Then he went down on one knee, and kissed Mrs. Whitaker's hand.

152   "Stop that," said Mrs. Whitaker. She poured them both cups of tea, after getting out the very best china, which was only for special occasions.

NOTICE & NOTE

CONTRASTS AND CONTRADICTIONS

Notice & Note: Mark words and phrases in paragraphs 141–143 that sharply contrast with the portrayal of Mrs. Whitaker elsewhere in the story.

Interpret: What do you make of the way she looks at Galaad in paragraph 143?

Chivalry   75

TEACH

CONTRASTS AND CONTRADICTIONS

Direct students' attention to paragraphs 141–143. Discuss how Mrs. Whitaker's reaction to the apple is different from her reaction to the other gifts. (**Possible answer:** *Up to now, she has had no reaction to Galaad's striking beauty. It may be that being transported briefly back to her youth has caused her to react like a young girl to his handsome looks.*)

■ **English Learner Support**

Compare   Read or have a proficient student read aloud paragraphs 140–141, which describe the effect of the apple on Mrs. Whitaker. Help students to create analogies to this experience using this sentence frame: Mrs. Whitaker's experience of the apple is like ____." **LIGHT**

WHEN STUDENTS STRUGGLE . . .

Compare   To reinforce the Analyze Characterization skill, have students go back and reread paragraphs 84–85 (Mrs. Whitaker's reaction to Galaad's gift of the magic sword). Note the word that describes her reaction ("doubtfully"). Then, have students return to paragraph 141. Have them pick out words that show how this reaction is different.

 For additional support, go to the **Reading Studio** and assign the following **Level Up tutorial: Methods of Characterization.**

Chivalry   75

TEACH

✏️ ANALYZE CHARACTERIZATION

Have students go back to descriptions of how Mrs. Whitaker relates to Galaad (paragraphs 74–81, 94, and 159–161). Discuss why she might behave in this way toward him. (**Possible answer:** We know that she has no children. It may be that she has come to look upon him almost as a son and will miss him.)

 **NOTICE & NOTE**

153   They sat in silence, drinking their tea.
154   When they had finished their tea they went into the parlor.
155   Galaad crossed himself, and picked up the Grail.
156   Mrs. Whitaker arranged the Egg and the Stone where the Grail had been. The Egg kept tipping on one side, and she propped it up against the little china dog.
157   "They do look very nice," said Mrs. Whitaker.
158   "Yes," agreed Galaad. "They look very nice."
159   "Can I give you anything to eat before you go back?" she asked.
160   He shook his head.
161   "Some fruitcake," she said. "You may not think you want any now, but you'll be glad of it in a few hours' time. And you should probably use the facilities. Now, give me that, and I'll wrap it up for you."
162   She directed him to the small toilet at the end of the hall, and went into the kitchen, holding the Grail. She had some old Christmas wrapping paper in the pantry, and she wrapped the Grail in it, and tied the package with twine. Then she cut a large slice of fruitcake and put it in a brown paper bag, along with a banana and a slice of processed cheese in silver foil.
163   Galaad came back from the toilet. She gave him the paper bag, and the Holy Grail. Then she went up on tiptoes and kissed him on the cheek.
164   "You're a nice boy," she said. "You take care of yourself."
165   He hugged her, and she shooed him out of the kitchen, and out of the back door, and she shut the door behind him. She poured herself another cup of tea, and cried quietly into a Kleenex, while the sound of hoof-beats echoed down Hawthorne Crescent.
166   On Wednesday Mrs. Whitaker stayed in all day.
167   On Thursday she went down to the post office to collect her pension. Then she stopped in at the Oxfam Shop.
168   The woman on the till was new to her. "Where's Marie?" asked Mrs. Whitaker.
169   The woman on the till, who had blue-rinsed gray hair and blue spectacles that went up into diamante points, shook her head and shrugged her shoulders. "She went off with a young man," she said. "On a horse. Tch. I ask you. I'm meant to be down in the Heathfield shop this afternoon. I had to get my Johnny to run me up here, while we find someone else."
170   "Oh," said Mrs. Whitaker. "Well, it's nice that she's found herself a young man."
171   "Nice for her, maybe," said the lady on the till, "But some of us were meant to be in Heathfield this afternoon."
172   On a shelf near the back of the shop Mrs. Whitaker found a tarnished old silver container with a long spout. It had been priced at sixty pence, according to the little paper label stuck to the side. It looked a little like a flattened, elongated teapot.
173   She picked out a Mills & Boon novel she hadn't read before. It was called *Her Singular Love*. She took the book and the silver container up to the woman on the till.

ANALYZE CHARACTERIZATION

Annotate: Mark the detail in paragraph 165 that conveys Mrs. Whitaker's emotional reaction after Galaad leaves.

Infer: Why do you think she reacts this way?

 ENGLISH LEARNER SUPPORT

Retell Read paragraphs 162–165 aloud to students. Call on students to retell the story in their own words. Assist students with comprehension, but do not correct grammar or pronunciation. If student understanding is high, discuss the passage. What did Mrs. Whitaker do for Galaad before he left? Why do you think she did those things?

174 "Sixty-five pee[4], dear," said the woman, picking up the silver object, staring at it. "Funny old thing, isn't it? Came in this morning." It had writing carved along the side in blocky old Chinese characters and an elegant arching handle. "Some kind of oil can, I suppose."

175 "No, it's not an oil can," said Mrs. Whitaker, who knew exactly what it was. "It's a lamp."

176 There was a small metal finger ring, unornamented, tied to the handle of the lamp with brown twine.

177 "Actually," said Mrs. Whitaker, "on second thoughts, I think I'll just have the book."

178 She paid her five pence for the novel, and put the lamp back where she had found it, in the back of the shop. After all, Mrs. Whitaker reflected, as she walked home, it wasn't as if she had anywhere to put it.

[4] **pee:** slang for pence.

NOTICE & NOTE

ANALYZE FANTASY

Annotate: Reread paragraph 174–178. Mark the details that describe the lamp.

Draw Conclusions: What might be special about this lamp? Does Mrs. Whitaker really leave it behind because she has no room for it, or might she have some other reason?

CHECK YOUR UNDERSTANDING

Answer these questions before moving on to the **Analyze the Text** section on the following page.

1 Who has sent Galaad to get the Holy Grail from Mrs. Whitaker?

   A Marie

   B Mrs. Greenberg

   C Sir Lancelot

   D King Arthur

2 What does Mrs. Whitaker have Galaad do for her?

   F Play a song on his lute

   G Make a roast mutton and salad

   H Help her in the garden and move some boxes

   J Teach her how to saddle a horse

3 In exchange for the Holy Grail, Mrs. Whitaker accepts —

   A a beautiful sword

   B a stone and an egg

   C the gift of eternal youth

   D a silver lamp

Chivalry 77

TEACH

ANALYZE FANTASY

Direct students' attention to paragraphs 172, 174, and 175. Talk about where the metal object might have come from and how Mrs. Whitaker knows that it is a lamp. (**Answer:** *It is probably Aladdin's lamp. She may recognize it, as she did the Grail, and so decides that she doesn't want any more fantasy characters interfering in her life.*)

CHECK YOUR UNDERSTANDING

Have students answer the questions independently.

Answers:

1. D
2. H
3. B

If they answer any questions incorrectly, have them reread the text to confirm their understanding. Then they may proceed to ANALYZE THE TEXT on page 78.

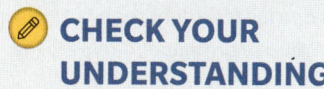

ENGLISH LEARNER SUPPORT

Oral Assessment Use the following questions to assess students' comprehension and speaking skills.

1. Who sent Galaad on his quest for the Holy Grail? (*King Arthur sent Galaad on his quest.*)

2. How does Galaad help Mrs. Whitaker? (*Galaad helps Mrs. Whitaker by doing chores, such as moving boxes and getting rid of snails.*)

3. What does Galaad trade to Mrs. Whitaker for the Holy Grail? (*Galaad gives Mrs. Whitaker a Phoenix egg and the Philosopher's Stone in exchange for the Grail.*) **MODERATE/LIGHT**

APPLY

ANALYZE THE TEXT

Possible answers:

1. **DOK 3:** *Mrs. Whitaker lives life according to plan. She relies on a schedule and does not veer too far off from the expected.*

2. **DOK 4:** *The modern setting along with the usual activities that modern people do serves to make the fantasy elements even more unusual, unexpected, and humorous. Mrs. Whitaker's activities and the tasks that she has Galaad help her with seem even more mundane next to the description of Galaad, his family, and his adventures.*

3. **DOK 2:** *When Mrs. Whitaker held the apple and tasted its juice (like wine), she remembered being young and vibrant, and she may have remembered the first time she tasted wine. But when she looked at the photograph of her late husband, she apparently decided that she would rather grow old than be young or live forever without him.*

4. **DOK 3:** *With the first visit, the characters are introduced. In the second visit, Mrs. Whitaker and Galaad reveal more about themselves and the dialogue is more friendly. In the last visit, they tell each other about their families, there is more emotion, and the conflict and quest of the story is resolved.*

5. **DOK 4:** *Her life was interrupted by the visits of Galaad, but in the end, her life didn't change too much. We don't know if she used the Philosopher's Stone or the Egg of the Phoenix, but her routine after Galaad left went back to normal. She also decided not to buy the lamp—probably so she wouldn't have to worry about another encounter with an object that could affect the direction of her life.*

RESEARCH

Students might also ask questions such as, Where did Galahad look for the Holy Grail? Did he find it? What finally happened to Galahad?

Extend Suggest that students include Sir Percival and Sir Bors in their research. These two knights of the Round Table also searched for the Holy Grail. Look for mentions of the gifts that Galaad brought to Mrs. Whitaker.

78 Unit 1

RESPOND

ANALYZE THE TEXT

Support your responses with evidence from the text. 📓 NOTEBOOK

1. **Draw Conclusions** Consider how Mrs. Whitaker is characterized in the story. What conclusions can you make about how she lives her life?

2. **Analyze** How does Gaiman use the setting of a modern English town to help develop the story's fantastic plot?

3. **Infer** Why does Mrs. Whitaker reject Galaad's offer of the apple of the Hesperides while accepting his other two gifts?

4. **Evaluate** Legends and fairy tales are often structured in patterns of three. In "Chivalry," Galaad visits Mrs. Whitaker three times. How effectively does Gaiman use these visits to develop the relationship between these characters? Explain.

5. **Notice & Note** Does Mrs. Whitaker's behavior at the end of the story suggest that she has been changed by her experience with Galaad and the Holy Grail? Why or why not?

RESEARCH

RESEARCH TIP
When researching, focus on reliable sources. Web addresses that end in *.gov*, *.org*, and *.edu* are mostly reliable and credible websites. Also, try and distinguish between primary and secondary sources and analyze which documents serve as fact-based information versus opinions. Finally, keep an eye out for articles written by historians who have studied this subject in depth.

Sir Galahad was considered one of the greatest knights at King Arthur's court. With a partner, conduct an Internet search to discover more about Sir Galahad. Use the chart below to record your findings.

QUESTION	ANSWER
What were the circumstances of Galahad's birth?	*Sir Galahad was born out of wedlock to Lancelot and Elaine, daughter of King Pelles.*
How did Galahad become one of the Knights of the Round Table?	*His father knights him, and then he sits in a chair meant only for the person who will find the Holy Grail and survives.*
What happened on Galahad's quest to find the Holy Grail?	*Galahad eventually finds the Holy Grail when an angel reveals it to him.*

Extend Find another modern story, novel, or film in which Sir Galahad makes an appearance. Discuss with your partner how the presence of Galahad in this work compares with Gaiman's portrayal of him in "Chivalry."

78 Unit 1

WHEN STUDENTS STRUGGLE . . .

Reteaching: Analyze Character Have students write a description of the two main characters using everything they can remember from the text. Then help them to go back to the text to see how much they remembered and to correct any misconceptions.

 For additional support, go to the **Reading Studio** and assign the following Level Up tutorial: **Character Traits**.

RESPOND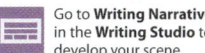

CREATE AND DRAMATIZE

Write a Fantasy Scene Collaborate with a partner to write a short scene involving the mingling of a legendary or historical character with a present-day character. Review your list of questions from the Quick Start activity. Also, think about any fantasy elements from "Chivalry" that would translate well to your scene.

- ❏ Decide where your scene will take place, and think about how the characters might react to this setting.
- ❏ Determine the nature of the interaction between the two characters (for example, it may be humorous or confrontational). Make sure an audience can readily grasp each character's traits and motivations.
- ❏ Convey a message about the past or about contemporary life.

Present the Scene With your partner, prepare a dramatic presentation based on your fantasy scene.

- ❏ Discuss elements of presentation needed to act it out for the rest of the class. Is it part of a traditional play or an impromptu skit? Plan how to stage the scene and figure out what simple props you can use.
- ❏ Determine the emotions you want to stir with the fantasy scene. Are the fantasy elements meant to be humorous, inspiring, or touching? Think of ways to capture and keep your audience's attention.
- ❏ Practice the scene and present it to the class. Ask for feedback.

 Go to **Writing Narratives** in the **Writing Studio** to develop your scene.

Go to **Giving a Presentation** in the **Speaking and Listening Studio** to learn more.

RESPOND TO THE ESSENTIAL QUESTION

 What is true chivalry?

Gather Information Review your annotations and notes on "Chivalry." Then add relevant information to your Response Log. As you determine which information to include, think about:

- the definition and key qualities of chivalry
- Galaad's interactions with others throughout the story
- the importance of chivalry in real life

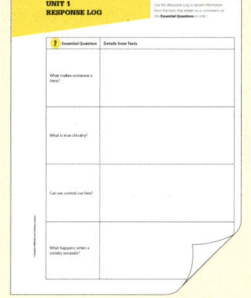

ACADEMIC VOCABULARY

As you write and discuss what you learned from the short story, be sure to use the Academic Vocabulary words. Check off each of the words that you use.

- ❏ collapse
- ❏ displace
- ❏ military
- ❏ violate
- ❏ visual

Chivalry 79

APPLY

CREATE AND DRAMATIZE

Write a Fantasy Scene Remind students of how drama is written [Character name: Speech, *(stage directions)*]. Review the elements of characterization: physical details (posture, movement, voice) and dialogue that conveys personality traits and the character's time and place, and reactions to the setting. The play's theme should be the essential question.

Present the Scene Have students from peer groups critique each other's dramatic scenes before presenting them to the class.

- Students should give concrete, specific ideas for how their peers might improve their scenes.
- Pairs should review the suggestions and decide which ones to incorporate into their scenes.

RESPOND TO THE ESSENTIAL QUESTION

Allow time for students to add details from "Chivalry" to their Unit 1 Response Logs.

 ENGLISH LEARNER SUPPORT

Reteach Character Analysis The teacher and/or capable students will lead a game, Guess the Character. Through actions or a few words, leaders will demonstrate various character traits and have students guess which character they are. For example, a person who stands very straight and brandishes a sword would be Galaad. A person who is expressionless and says, "That's nice," would be Mrs. Whitaker. More advanced students may represent changes in characters and actions as they occurred in the story. The teacher may begin and then call on students as they get the idea. **MODERATE/LIGHT**

Chivalry 79

APPLY

CRITICAL VOCABULARY

Answers:

1. *appraise*
2. *forge*
3. *ignoble*
4. *pension*
5. *bereft*
6. *flotsam*

VOCABULARY STRATEGY:
Context Clues

Answers:

1. Macaroons are probably a type of cookie, since the women are eating them while drinking tea in the parlor, similar to a living room.

2. If the stone is like milk and you can see the inside of it, translucent probably describes something that is white, but you can still see through it.

3. If the egg was mostly black, then the scarlet and white must cover small areas, so mottled probably means spotted or streaked.

RESPOND

WORD BANK
- pension
- flotsam
- appraise
- forge
- ignoble
- bereft

Go to the **Vocabulary Studio** for more on context clues.

CRITICAL VOCABULARY

Practice and Apply Read each scenario. Then select the correct vocabulary word from the word bank to match the scenario.

1. Jennifer took her ring to a jeweler to find out how much it's worth.	
2. By combining the two metals, the jeweler was able to create an object that was as durable as it was beautiful.	
3. The CEO of the company was forced to resign for embezzling from company accounts.	
4. Mrs. Donaldson, after retiring from 30 years as a teacher, will receive sizable monthly payments.	
5. James went hungry at lunchtime because he left his sandwich on the counter.	
6. The Harrison family had a yard sale because they had many items they regarded as "junk" in their garage.	

VOCABULARY STRATEGY:
Context Clues

When reading a text, there are times you'll have to use **context clues** in order to determine the meaning of a word or phrase. Context clues include the other words or descriptions surrounding the unknown term. Understanding the context of a sentence or paragraph can help you to better determine the meaning of unknown words or phrases.

Practice and Apply Follow the instructions to complete the activity:

1. Look at the underlined word in each sentence in the chart.
2. Circle, or highlight, the context clues in the sentence that help the reader to understand the underlined term.
3. Based on the context clues, define the meaning of the underlined word or phrase. Explain how the context clues helped you to determine the meaning.

SENTENCE WITH UNKNOWN TERM	MEANING
1. They sat in the parlor and ate macaroons and drank tea.	
2. It was milky and translucent, and deep inside it flecks of silver glittered in the late-afternoon sunlight.	
3. It was the size of a goose egg and was a shiny black color, mottled with scarlet and white.	

ENGLISH LEARNER SUPPORT

Reteach Review Critical Vocabulary words by modeling sentences that express the word meanings, then asking students to do the same. Beginning students may simply repeat the words ask for clarification in their home language. **ALL LEVELS**

LANGUAGE CONVENTIONS:
Appositives and Appositive Phrases

An **appositive** is a noun or pronoun that identifies, or renames, another noun or pronoun. An **appositive phrase** is made up of an appositive plus its modifiers. Writers use appositives and appositive phrases to add important details without being wordy. Appositives can be either restrictive or nonrestrictive. **Restrictive appositives** provide information necessary for identifying the noun or pronoun that precedes it. In the following sentence, the appositive *Balmung* is needed to identify the preceding noun:

> "This," said Galaad, "is the sword Balmung."

Nonrestrictive appositives only provide additional, or nonessential, information about a noun or pronoun whose meaning is already clear. In this sentence, the appositive phrase *the Reverend Bartholomew* adds extra information that is not needed to understand the basic meaning of the sentence.

> . . . she liked the vicar, the Reverend Bartholomew, when he wasn't actually playing the guitar."

Nonrestrictive appositives and appositive phrases are set off with commas.

Practice and Apply Each sentence below contains an appositive or an appositive phrase. Use a dotted line to mark the appositive or appositive phrase. Then underline the noun or pronoun it identifies or renames.

1. The newspaper *The New York Times* included a famous article about the historical significance of the Holy Grail.
2. Sir Galaad, son of Sir Lancelot, was destined to lead the quest for the Holy Grail.
3. Award-winning author Neil Gaiman enjoys including themes of love in many of his fantasy writings.

Now write a short, detailed paragraph describing a personal possession that is of great importance to you. Use as many appositives and appositive phrases as possible. Exchange paragraphs with a partner, and circle the appositives and appositive phrases in your partner's paragraph.

RESPOND

! Go to **Appositives and Appositive Phrases** in the **Grammar Studio** to learn more.

Chivalry 81

APPLY

LANGUAGE CONVENTIONS:
Appositives and Appositive Phrases

Review the information about appositives and appositive phrases with students. Explain that using appositives helps to give more depth to descriptions of characters, and to clarify exactly who is being mentioned.

Practice and Apply Have partners discuss whether appositives and appositive phrases are used correctly and effectively in their paragraphs. *(Students' paragraphs will vary.)*

Chivalry **81**

PLAN

from THE PASTON LETTERS
Letters by the Paston Family

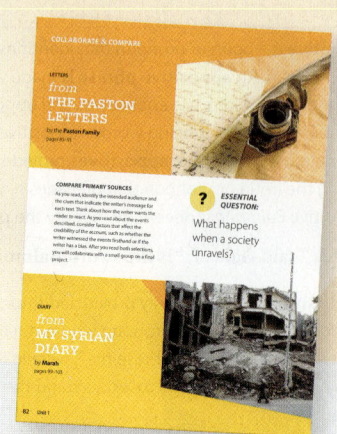

GENRE ELEMENTS
LETTERS

Remind students that **primary sources** are materials written or created by people who were present at events, either as participants or as observers. **Letters** are one example of a primary source. Letters are private correspondence between two people and are intended to be kept private. Some letters, however, have been published because of their literary or historical importance. In this lesson, students will analyze the historical information in letters and use what they know to make inferences about the people and events discussed in the letters.

LEARNING OBJECTIVES

- Analyze primary sources and make inferences.
- Conduct research about the Wars of the Roses.
- Write a short dramatic scene with dialogue.
- Enact a short scene with dialogue.
- Consult a dictionary.
- Identify subject-verb agreement.
- **Language** React to classmates' presentations using a mix of academic and informal language.

TEXT COMPLEXITY

Quantitative Measures	The Paston Letters	Lexile: 1250L
Qualitative Measures	**Ideas Presented** Much is explicit, but moves to more implied meaning. Greater demand for inference.	
	Structures Used Clear, chronological, with support through subheads.	
	Language Used Complex sentence structures with use of archaic and formal language.	
	Knowledge Required Cultural and historical references may make heavier demands.	

PLAN

Online Ed

RESOURCES

- Unit 1 Response Log
- 🔊 Selection Audio
- 📖 Reading Studio: Notice & Note
- Writing Studio: Writing Narratives
- Vocabulary Studio: Consulting a Dictionary
- ❗ Grammar Studio: Module 5 Lesson 1: Subject-Verb Agreement
- ✓ "The Paston Letters" Selection Test

SUMMARIES

English
The Pastons, a wealthy family living in England circa 1420–1500, exchanged many letters. In the first letter, Margaret Paston tells her husband, John, that she has fled their estate for fear of attack. In the next two letters, she describes to her husband events at another Paston estate. The last three letters—between Margaret, her husband, and her son—discuss financial problems, an injury, and the plague.

Spanish
Los Pastons, una familia que vivía en Inglaterra alrededor de 1420-1500, intercambiaban muchas cartas. En su primera carta, Margaret Paston le dice a su esposo que ha huido de su propiedad por miedo a un ataque. En las siguientes dos cartas, describe a su esposo los sucesos en otra de sus propiedades. Las últimas tres cartas entre Margaret, su esposo y su hijo, discuten problemas financieros, una herida y la peste.

SMALL-GROUP OPTIONS

Have students work in small groups and pairs to read and discuss the selection.

Reciprocal Teaching
- Have students read the first letter from Margaret to her husband.
- After reading, ask students to write three to five questions about the section, using these stems: *Why does Margaret say ____? Why did the ____? What happened after ____? How did the ____? Why was the ____?*
- Form teams of three students.
- Have each student offer two questions for group discussion.
- Have each group reach a consensus on the answers and find supporting text evidence.

Think-Pair-Share
- After reading the first and second letters from Margaret to her husband, pose this question: *What words show Margaret's feelings and attitude toward the events she describes?*
- Have students think about the question individually and take notes.
- Then, have students form pairs and listen, discuss, and formulate shared responses to the question.
- Finally, have pairs share their responses with the class.

The Paston Letters 82B

PLAN

Text X-Ray: English Learner Support
for *The Paston Letters*

Use the Text X-Ray and the supports and scaffolds in the Teacher's Edition to help guide students at different proficiency levels through the selection.

INTRODUCE THE SELECTION
DISCUSS PROPERTY DISPUTES

In this lesson, students will need to be able to discuss the details of property disputes. Provide the following explanation:

- A property dispute is a disagreement over who owns a piece of land and the buildings on it.

Explain to students that because the events in the letters took place hundreds of years ago, laws about property ownership were different from laws today.

Ask students to discuss the property dispute described in the letters. Provide sentence frames such as: *There was a property dispute between ____ and ____. Because of the dispute, Margaret Paston had to ____. The men who claimed the right to the Pastons' estate took ____.*

Help students understand that there were property disputes at this time due to the upheaval in England during the Wars of the Roses and the battle for power.

CULTURAL REFERENCES

The following words or phrases may be unfamiliar to students:

- *with all my heart* (paragraph 1): sincerely and completely
- *on my word* (paragraph 1): on my honor; true
- *set up house* (paragraph 2): to start to live in a house
- *set against* (paragraph 6): to cause someone to become enemies
- *a great deal of talk* (paragraph 16): gossip

LISTENING

Use Text Features

Read aloud the italicized summary of the first letter, as well as the first letter itself. Explain that it's important to read the summary before reading the letter to understand the context and to find out who is involved in the correspondence.

Use the following supports with students at varying proficiency levels:

- Ask students some either/or questions about the main idea of the summary and the letter. Provide further support as needed so they understand the questions. For example: *Which tells you only the main points of the letter, the summary or the letter? (summary) Which gives more details about Margaret's situation, the summary or the letter? (letter)* **SUBSTANTIAL**
- Have students describe the purpose of the summary and name two general things they learned from it. Then, have students describe the purpose of the letter and name two specific things they learned from it. Accept phrases and simple sentences as responses. **MODERATE**
- Have students compare and contrast the summary and the letter. Guide them to name three ways the summary and the letter are alike and three ways they are different. **LIGHT**

82C   Unit 1

PLAN

SPEAKING

Respond to Presentations

Review words and phrases students can use to respond to classmates' scenes. For example: academic vocabulary: *scene, dialogue, action, motivation, narrator*; informal vocabulary: *exciting, moving, intense, emotional, like real life.*

Use the following supports with students at varying proficiency levels:
- Model how to use the words in the list in a response. Have students repeat what you say, then practice saying it aloud to a partner. For example: *I thought the dialogue was very moving. Your scene was intense. The character's motivation seemed real.* **SUBSTANTIAL**
- Provide sentence frames with words from the list for students to use to respond to the enactments. For example: *I thought the dialogue was ____. I enjoyed the scene because ____. Your character's motivation seemed ____.* **MODERATE**
- Have students ask and answer questions about the enactments using terms from the list. For example: *What was your character's motivation? Why did you use a narrator?* **LIGHT**

READING

Distinguish Main Idea and Supporting Details

Tell students that the main idea is the most important point the author makes. Supporting details help readers understand the main idea better.

Reread the third letter with students. Use the following supports with those at varying proficiency levels:
- Explain that the main idea of this letter is that the Pastons' property was destroyed and Margaret wants her husband to act quickly to end their troubles. Ask: *What is one supporting detail for this main idea?* Accept single words or phrases. **SUBSTANTIAL**
- After reading, have pairs work to identify the main idea of the letter and two supporting details. Provide language support as needed. **MODERATE**
- After reading, have students write the main idea of the letter. Then, have them list as many supporting details as they can. Have pairs exchange papers and check each other's work. **LIGHT**

WRITING

Write a Dramatic Scene

Work with students to understand the different items in the checklist on page 93 of the Student Edition.

Use the following supports with students at varying proficiency levels:
- Help small groups create the conflict between their characters. Then, have them make a two-column chart with the heads: *Character 1* and *Character 2*. Have students look for nouns, adjectives, and verbs in the text to write dialogue. Help students list words in their chart describing what each character wants or feels. Use the chart to write a brief dialogue on the board. **SUBSTANTIAL**
- Provide sentence frames to help students write dialogue in their scenes. For example: *I never want to _____. If you try to ____, I will ____.* **MODERATE**
- Have students look for places in their dialogue where they can use connecting words and clauses to describe and explain with more specificity. **LIGHT**

The Paston Letters

TEACH

Connect to the ESSENTIAL QUESTION

The Paston letters were written in 15th century England, when conflict among the aristocracy caused social instability and lawlessness. Additionally, the outbreak of the plague resulted in added chaos. These letters illustrate what can happen in people's daily lives when the regular social order unravels due to political upheavals or natural disasters.

COMPARE ACROSS GENRES

Point out that the Paston letters were written to convey important information in private from one family member to another. Knowing that some letters might fall into the wrong hands, the writer did not always include details that the intended reader would know but might not be known to others. The author of *My Syrian Diary,* however, knew she was writing to inform readers who did not understand her experience, so she included as much detail as possible. Ask students to think of situations in which they were communicating to someone who was unfamiliar with a subject. Then ask them to think of situations in which they were communicating with someone very much aware of the subject. How did their language differ in communicating with these different audiences?

COLLABORATE & COMPARE

LETTERS

from THE PASTON LETTERS

by the **Paston Family**
pages 85–91

COMPARE PRIMARY SOURCES

As you read, identify the intended audience and the clues that indicate the writer's message for each text. Think about how the writer wants the reader to react. As you read about the events described, consider factors that affect the credibility of the account, such as whether the writer witnessed the events firsthand or if the writer has a bias. After you read both selections, you will collaborate with a small group on a final project.

ESSENTIAL QUESTION:

What happens when a society unravels?

DIARY

from MY SYRIAN DIARY

by **Marah**
pages 99–103

The Paston Letters

QUICK START

When we have a problem or conflict in our lives, we often reach out to friends or family members for support. Think about a situation in your life for which you would like support from a friend or family member, and write a quick message to the person you choose explaining the situation.

ANALYZE PRIMARY SOURCES

Primary sources such as diaries and letters are materials created by people who took part in or witnessed the events portrayed. These documents can help you learn about the people who wrote them and the period in which they lived. For example, this letter written by a member of the Paston family reveals that the English suffered from terrible plagues in the 1400s.

> Please send me word if any of our friends or well-wishers are dead, for I fear that there is great mortality in Norwich and in other boroughs and towns in Norfolk: I assure you that it is the most widespread plague I ever knew of in England, for by my faith I cannot hear of pilgrims going through the country nor of any other man who rides or goes anywhere, that any town or borough in England is free from the sickness.

As you read these letters, analyze them to see if they are credible sources. Consider whether the writer witnessed the events firsthand or is relying on someone else's account. Also, look for bias in the writer's description of events.

MAKE INFERENCES

When you make **inferences**, you are making logical guesses about a text or character based on your own experiences and the evidences or clues you find in the text. Making inferences is sometimes called "reading between the lines" because you come to understand something in the text that the author has not stated explicitly. For example, when Margaret urges her husband to "take care when you eat or drink in any other men's company, for no one can be trusted," you can infer that she fears his enemies will try to poison him.

As you read the letters from the Paston family, pay close attention to their descriptions of events and people. Record your inferences in a chart like the one shown.

DETAILS FROM THE TEXT	INFERENCES
I am very surprised that you do not send me more news than you have done.	She is afraid that her husband may be in trouble.

GENRE ELEMENTS: LETTERS

- correspondence exchanged between relatives, friends, or acquaintances
- intended to be private rather than for publication
- sometimes published for a wider audience because of the literary or historical importance

GET READY

TEACH

QUICK START

Have students read the Quick Start prompt. To get students started, they may need to do a quick pair-discussion about a problem or conflict they have and who might be able to help. Students can compose their messages in a format they are familiar with, such as a text message or email. Remind students that they are addressing a private message to a specific person.

ANALYZE PRIMARY SOURCES

Explain to students that **primary sources** are different from **secondary sources**, which include nonfiction books and articles, and that secondary sources are usually written based on primary sources. Generate a list of examples of primary sources and ask students to think about who would write them, who the intended audience would be, and what the purpose would be. Explain that some primary sources include bias, or the writer's inclination toward a particular judgment on a topic or issue. Elicit examples of why a writer might have bias or other reasons the information in a primary source may not be credible or accurate.

MAKE INFERENCES

Explain to students that an **inference** is an educated guess based on details in the text and prior knowledge. Tell students that when they read, it is important to pay attention to details and think about what is unstated or implied. Review the example and help students understand the details in the text that led to the inference (when someone is surprised to not hear news, he or she might think the worst). As students read, have them use the chart to note details from the text and their inferences.

TEACH

CRITICAL VOCABULARY

Explain to students that while some of these words will be familiar to them, their meaning in the text will probably be unfamiliar because they are obscure or **archaic**. Tell students to try to guess which words complete the sentences based on a meaning that is related to or near the one they are familiar with.

Answers:

1. *writ*
2. *bailiff*
3. *commend*
4. *quell*
5. *ransack*
6. *affairs*

LANGUAGE CONVENTIONS

Explain to students that **subject-verb agreement** applies to verbs in the present simple and to auxiliary (helping) verbs. Help students understand that the subject and the verb may not be next to each other, and that the verb must agree with the subject rather than other nouns that are part of modifying phrases in the subject.

■ English Learner Support

Distinguish Between Singular and Plural Verbs Remind students that to form the present tense of a regular verb, you add an *-s* or *-es* at the end when their subject is **singular**. Explain that the verbs *to be* and *to have* are **irregular**. Work with students to complete the graphic organizer.

	To have	To be
singular		
plural		

SUBSTANTIAL

ANNOTATION MODEL

Explain to students that one way to annotate text to make inferences is to underline important details. Point out that they may follow this suggestion, or use their own system for marking up the selection in their write-in text. They may want to color-code their annotations by using highlighters. Their notes in the margin may include questions about ideas that are unclear, or topics they want to learn more about.

84 Unit 1

GET READY

CRITICAL VOCABULARY

commend   quell   affairs   bailiff   writ   ransack

Complete the sentences using the Critical Vocabulary words.

1. After hearing both sides of the case, the judge issued a _____ concerning the lord's ownership of the disputed property.
2. The _____ of the estate informed the tenants of the rent increase.
3. While they are out of the country on business, they will _____ the care of their children to their aunt and uncle.
4. We have asked the king to send soldiers to _____ the riot.
5. The villagers feared that the invaders would _____ their homes.
6. My grandfather is very sick and has asked my father to look after his _____ until he can recover.

LANGUAGE CONVENTIONS

Subject-Verb Agreement The subject and verb in a clause must agree in number. The present simple form of a verb will be either **singular** or **plural**, depending on whether the subject of the clause is singular or plural.

Verbs that have compound subjects with *and* are plural. Compound subjects with *or* and *nor* may take either a plural or singular verb, depending on the implied meaning. For pronouns, agreement with the verb will depend on the pronoun's antecedent.

ANNOTATION MODEL   NOTICE & NOTE

As you read, you can make inferences about the author's purpose. In the model, you can see one reader's notes about Margaret's letter to John I.

> *Right worshipful husband*, I commend myself to you, . . . begging that you will not be angry at my leaving the place where you left me. On my word, such news was brought to me by various people who are sympathetic to you and me that I did not dare stay there any longer. I will tell you who the people were when you come home. They let me know that various of Lord Moleyns' men said that if they could get their hands on me they would carry me off and keep me in the castle.

The writer asks that her husband not be angry with her for leaving.

She was afraid to stay and then explains why she was afraid.

I can infer that the writer is afraid and wants her husband to know she is in danger.

84 Unit 1

BACKGROUND

The Paston Family (c. 1421–1500) exchanged many letters that offer valuable insight into a period of war and plague in England. With two noble families battling for the kingdom, landowners often attacked neighbors' estates. The Pastons were prosperous landowners, and their wealth attracted enemies. John I inherited property from his father and acquired more through his marriage to Margaret. Other families challenged the Pastons' claims; John I, who was a lawyer, spent much time in London on these disputes, leaving Margaret to manage their estates alone. The letters you will read are from members of the Paston family to one another.

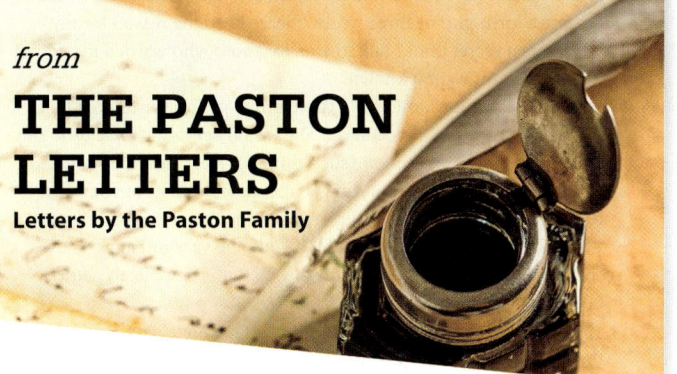

from
THE PASTON LETTERS
Letters by the Paston Family

PREPARE TO COMPARE

As you read, use the details given in the text to make inferences about what life was like in 15th-century England and what kinds of challenges people faced. This will help you to compare this primary source with the diary entry from "My Syrian Diary" that follows.

Margaret Paston was able to deal equally well with small housekeeping problems and with family disasters that included attacks against the Paston manors in the absence of her husband, John I. While she was living at the Paston estate of Gresham, it was attacked by a Lord Moleyns, who claimed rights to the property and ejected Margaret from her home. Margaret first escaped to a friend's house about a mile away; but later, fearing that Moleyns's band of men might kidnap her, she fled to the city of Norwich, where she wrote the following letter to her husband.

Margaret to John I
28 February 1449

1   *Right worshipful husband*, I **commend** myself to you, wishing with all my heart to hear that you are well, and begging that you will not be angry at my leaving the place where you left me. On

NOTICE & NOTE

Notice & Note

Use the side margins to notice and note signposts in the text.

commend
(kə-měnd´) *tr. v.* to commit to the care of another; entrust.

The Paston Letters 85

ENGLISH LEARNER SUPPORT

Speak Using Basic and Academic Language Have students practice speaking about inferences they can make using these sentences frames: *The writer says that ___(fact from text)___. I can infer that ___(my idea)___.* Model the language with an example from the text. Provide them with this graphic organizer to use as they read:

Fact from text:	My idea:

SUBSTANTIAL/MODERATE

TEACH

BACKGROUND

The 15th century was a period of great social unrest and political upheaval in England. Two royal families battled for control of the kingdom in a conflict called the Wars of the Roses. This series of civil wars raged from 1455 to 1485. At the same time, families were devastated by repeated outbreaks of the plague.

Explain that the exchange of letters was an important means of communication at that time, but sending them could be difficult. They were delivered by hand by a servant or perhaps a total stranger—which could take weeks—and the letter might not arrive at all. There was also a danger that the letters could fall into the hands of enemies, which meant writers had to be careful about what they wrote and how they sealed letters. Typically, letters from affluent or noble writers would be folded, fastened by a paper strap, wrapped with silk thread or string, and finally sealed with wax. Prominent families stamped their wax seals with custom-made designs identifying their family. The Paston family exchanged hundreds of letters during this time. They are now a rich source of information and insight into the social and political conditions of this place and time.

PREPARE TO COMPARE

Direct students to use the Prepare to Compare prompt to focus their reading.

CRITICAL VOCABULARY

commend: Margaret trusts her husband and so she commends herself to the protection of her husband.

ASK STUDENTS why Margaret needs safety. *(She has been under attack by neighbors and has had to flee her home.)*

The Paston Letters **85**

TEACH

✏️ ANALYZE PRIMARY SOURCES

Remind students that while writers of primary sources may relate events they personally witnessed, they may also report secondhand information or speculate about what they believe has happened or will happen. Have students look for text clues in paragraph 3 that the writer is reporting secondhand information or speculating. (**Answer**: *Margaret is mainly describing events she was told about and is speculating about the nature of Lord Moleyns's documents. The phrase* He told me that *signals reported information, and the words* supposed *and* expected *show she is speculating.*)

CRITICAL VOCABULARY

quell: Barow wants to meet with John in London to make peace and quell the conflict and anger between them.

ASK STUDENTS to discuss how two people can resolve conflict and quell anger between them. *(Two people trying to quell anger have to listen to each other and compromise.)*

affairs: Margaret wants to know how John's business is in London, so she asks about his personal business.

ASK STUDENTS how they might ask a friend or a family member about their affairs. *(They might ask something like "How's school going?" or "How's your new job?")*

86 Unit 1

 **NOTICE & NOTE**

my word, such news was brought to me by various people who are sympathetic to you and me that I did not dare stay there any longer. I will tell you who the people were when you come home. They let me know that various of Lord Moleyns' men said that if they could get their hands on me they would carry me off and keep me in the castle. They wanted you to get me out again, and said that it would not cause you much heart-ache. After I heard this news, I could not rest easy until I was here, and I did not dare go out of the place where I was until I was ready to ride away. Nobody in the place knew that I was leaving except the lady of the house, until an hour before I went. And I told her that I would come here to have clothes made for myself and the children, which I wanted made, and said I thought I would be here a fortnight[1] or three weeks. Please keep the reason for my departure a secret until I talk to you, for those who warned me do not on any account want it known.

2   I spoke to your mother as I came this way, and she offered to let me stay in this town, if you agree. She would very much like us to stay at her place, and will send me such things as she can spare so that I can set up house until you can get a place and things of your own to set up a household. Please let me know by the man who brings this what you would like me to do. I would be very unhappy to live so close to Gresham as I was until this matter is completely settled between you and Lord Moleyns.

3   Barow[2] told me that there was no better evidence in England than that Lord Moleyns has for [his title to] the manor of Gresham. I told him that I supposed the evidence was of the kind that William Hasard said yours was, and that the seals were not yet cold.[3] That, I said, was what I expected his lord's evidence to be like. I said I knew that your evidence was such that no one could have better evidence, and the seals on it were two hundred years older than he was. Then Barow said to me that if he came to London while you were there he would have a drink with you, to **quell** any anger there was between you. He said that he only acted as a servant, and as he was ordered to do. Purry[4] will tell you about the conversation between Barow and me when I came from Walsingham.[5] I beg you with all my heart, for reverence of God, beware of Lord Moleyns and his men, however pleasantly they speak to you, and do not eat or drink with them; for they are so false that they cannot be trusted. And please take care when you eat or drink in any other men's company, for no one can be trusted.

4   I beg you with all my heart that you will be kind enough to send me word how you are, and how your **affairs** are going, by the man who brings this. I am very surprised that you do not send me more news than you have done....

ANALYZE PRIMARY SOURCES

Annotate: Reread paragraph 3. Mark Margaret Paston's reply to Barow about Lord Moleyns's claims.

Cite Evidence: Was Margaret a participant in the events described in this paragraph? Cite evidence from the text in your response.

quell
(kwĕl) *tr. v.* to pacify; quiet.

affairs
(ə-fârz´) *n.* personal business.

---

[1] **fortnight:** 14 nights, or two weeks.
[2] **Barow:** one of Lord Moleyns's men.
[3] **the seals . . . cold:** A seal, often made by impressing a family emblem on hot wax, was placed on a document to show its authenticity. Margaret is suggesting that Lord Moleyns's documents are recent forgeries.
[4] **Purry:** perhaps a servant or tenant of the Pastons's.
[5] **Walsingham** (wôl´sĭng-əm): a town near Lynn in the English county of Norfolk.

86 Unit 1

WHEN STUDENTS STRUGGLE...

Evaluate Types of Information Help students evaluate the types of information found in a primary source by reading paragraph 3 and sorting the information into the graphic organizer.

Someone told Margaret	
Margaret knows	
Margaret suspects	
Margaret did/said	

In 1465, in still another property dispute, the Paston estate of Hellesdon was attacked by the Duke of Suffolk, who had gained the support of several local officials. Although Margaret and John were not living at Hellesdon at the time, many of their servants and tenants suffered from the extensive damage. In the following two letters, Margaret tells her husband about the devastation.

Margaret to John I
17 October 1465

5   . . . On Tuesday morning John Botillere, also John Palmer, Darcy Arnald your cook and William Malthouse of Aylsham were seized at Hellesdon by the **bailiff** of Eye,[6] called Bottisforth, and taken to Costessey,[7] and they are being kept there still without any warrant or authority from a justice of the peace; and they say they will carry them off to Eye prison and as many others of your men and tenants as they can get who are friendly towards you or have supported you, and they threaten to kill or imprison them.

6   The duke came to Norwich at 10 o'clock on Tuesday with five hundred men and he sent for the mayor, aldermen and sheriffs, asking them in the king's name that they should inquire of the constables of every ward within the city which men had been on your side or had helped or supported your men at the time of any of these gatherings and if they could find any they should take them and arrest them and punish them; which the mayor did, and will do anything he can for him and his men. At this the mayor has arrested a man who was with me, called Robert Lovegold, a brazier,[8] and threatened him that he shall be hanged by the neck. So I would be glad if you could get a **writ** sent down for his release, if you think it can be done. He was only with me when Harlesdon and others attacked me at Lammas.[9] He is very true and faithful to you, so I would like him to be helped. I have no one attending me who dares to be known, except Little John. William Naunton is here with me, but he dares not be known because he is much threatened. I am told that the old lady and the duke have been frequently set against us by what Harlesdon, the bailiff of Costessey, Andrews and Doget the bailiff's son and other false villains have told them, who want this affair pursued for their own pleasure; there are evil rumors about it in this part of the world and other places.

7   As for Sir John Heveningham, Sir John Wyndefeld and other respectable men, they have been made into their catspaws,[10] which will not do their reputation any good after this, I think. . . .

---

[6] **bailiff of Eye:** an administrative official of Eye, a town in the English county of Suffolk.
[7] **Costessey:** an estate owned by the duke of Suffolk.
[8] **brazier** (brā′zhər): a person who makes articles of brass.
[9] **when Harlesdon . . . Lammas** (lăm′əs): when Harlesdon and others of the duke of Suffolk's men attacked on Lammas, a religious feast celebrated on August 1.
[10] **catspaws:** people who are deceived and used as tools by others; dupes.

NOTICE & NOTE

bailiff
(bā′lĭf) *n.* an overseer of an estate; a steward.

LANGUAGE CONVENTIONS
Annotate: In paragraph 5, underline the relative clause *who are friendly towards you or have supported you.* Circle the two verbs.

Subject-Verb Agreement: Are the two verbs singular or plural? Why?

writ
(rĭt) *n.* a written order issued by a court, commanding the party to whom it is addressed to perform or cease performing a specified act.

The Paston Letters   87

IMPROVE READING FLUENCY

Targeted Passage   Have students listen carefully and follow the text as you read the first sentence of paragraph 6 aloud, demonstrating appropriate rate, phrasing, and emphasis. Then, read the sentence again, and have students echo each segment. Have students mark the emphasis and natural pauses as they read. Focus on the pronunciation of the words *constables* and *alderman*. Do several rounds of echo reading before releasing students to pairs to practice reading aloud to each other.

 Go to the **Reading Studio** for additional support in developing fluency.

TEACH

LANGUAGE CONVENTIONS

In the last sentence of paragraph 5, have students focus on the clause they have underlined. A **clause** has a subject and a verb, but does not express a complete thought. Explain that the pronoun *who* is the subject of the clause and has a compound predicate, meaning it has two verbs. Students should identify that *have* and *are* are the plural form. Ask students to identify the **antecedent** of *who: your men and tenants.* (**Answer:** *The two verbs are plural because they agree with the pronoun* who, *which has a plural antecedent.*)

English Learner Support

Understand Subject-Verb Agreement   There is no subject-verb agreement in Cantonese, Haitian, Creole, Hmong, Khmer, Korean, Tagalog, and Vietnamese. So students may omit the -s in third person agreement: *She walk to school.* Help students understand that verbs change form based on the subject's noun. Write a simple sentence on the board, such as *The girl walks to the store.* Underline the s and explain how this is verb agrees with the singular subject. Write another sentence on the board, but omit the s. Have students underline the subject and verb and then correct the sentence so the subject and verb agree. **SUBSTANTIAL**

CRITICAL VOCABULARY

bailiff: Some of the Pastons' servants and friends were taken to prison by the overseer, or bailiff, of an estate.

ASK STUDENTS why a bailiff would be able to make an arrest. (*There was not an official police force at the time. The bailiff had the authority to arrest people suspected of crime.*)

writ: Margaret is asking her husband to get an official legal document, or writ, to get one of their friends released.

ASK STUDENTS who might be able to give a writ to help the friends. (*A judge can order a writ or the ruler could order a writ.*)

The Paston Letters   87

TEACH

EXTREME OR ABSOLUTE LANGUAGE

Explain to students that looking for extreme or absolute language in a primary source can help a reader make inferences about the writer's emotions and purpose for writing. Point out that a writer's emotions in a primary source may create bias or otherwise influence how they report events. Then, have students answer the question by inferring how Margaret feels about the events and what she might want from John. (**Answer:** *The writer is very upset and angry. She wants the recipient to be upset and angry enough to do something about it.*)

CRITICAL VOCABULARY

ransack: The men who came to Hellesdon took things out of the church in a way that was destructive and messy. They ransacked it.

ASK STUDENTS what someone's house might look like after it has been ransacked. (*The house would be a mess, with things all over the floor and furniture out of place or turned over, cabinet doors and drawers left open, etc.*)

 **NOTICE & NOTE**

8   The lodge and remainder of your place was demolished on Tuesday and Wednesday, and the duke rode on Wednesday to Drayton and then to Costessey while the lodge at Hellesdon was being demolished. Last night at midnight Thomas Slyford, Green, Porter and John Bottisforth the bailiff of Eye and others got a cart and took away the featherbeds and all the stuff of ours that was left at the parson's and Thomas Water's house for safe-keeping. I will send you lists later, as accurately as I can, of the things we have lost. Please let me know what you want me to do, whether you want me to stay at Caister[11] or come to you in London.

9   I have no time to write any more. God have you in his keeping. Written at Norwich on St. Luke's eve.[12]

                                                                                         M.P.

Margaret to John I
27 October 1465

10 . . . I was at Hellesdon last Thursday and saw the place there, and indeed no one can imagine what a <u>horrible</u> mess it is unless they see it. Many people come out each <u>day</u>, both from Norwich and elsewhere, to look at it, and they talk of it as a great <u>shame</u>. The duke would have done better to lose £1000[13] than to have caused this to be done, and you have all the more goodwill from people because it has been done so <u>foully</u>. And they made your tenants at Hellesdon and Drayton, and others, help them to break down the walls of both the house and the lodge: God knows, it was against their will, but they did not dare do otherwise for fear. I have spoken with your tenants both at Hellesdon and Drayton, and encouraged them as best I can.

11 The duke's men **ransacked** the church, and carried off all the goods that were left there, both ours and the tenants, and left little behind; they stood on the high altar and ransacked the images, and took away everything they could find. They shut the parson out of the church until they had finished, and ransacked everyone's house in the town five or six times. The ringleaders in the thefts were the bailiff of Eye and the bailiff of Stradbroke, Thomas Slyford. And Slyford was the leader in robbing the church and, after the bailiff of Eye, it is he who has most of the proceeds of the robbery. As for the lead, brass, pewter, iron, doors, gates, and other household stuff, men from Costessey and Cawston have got it, and what they could not carry they hacked up in the most <u>spiteful</u> fashion. If possible, I would like some reputable men to be sent for from the king, to see how things are both there and at the lodge, before any snows come, so that they can report the truth, because otherwise it will not be so plain as it is

ransack
(răn´săk´) *tr. v.* to go through (a place) stealing valuables and causing disarray.

EXTREME OR ABSOLUTE LANGUAGE

Notice & Note: In paragraphs 10 and 11, which strong negative words and phrases does the writer use to describe the situation and actions of Lord Suffolk's men? Mark them.

Infer: How does the writer feel about the events she is recounting? What reaction does the writer of this letter want from the recipient?

---

[11] **Caister:** one of the Paston estates.
[12] **St. Luke's eve:** the eve of St. Luke's Day, October 18. The feasts of major saints were celebrated on specific days throughout the year, and writers often dated letters with the name of a saint's day or eve instead of using days and months.
[13] **£1000:** a thousand pounds (British money).

WHEN STUDENTS STRUGGLE . . .

Comprehension Support Help students break long, complex sentences into short, simple ones, such as the sentence beginning "For reverence of God, . . ." in paragraph 11 on page 89. Model these strategies:

- Replace all semicolons with periods.
- Change commas to periods when the commas separate independent clauses, such as "each day is horrible, and it will be like this" (paragraph 11, page 89)
- Delete coordinating conjunctions, such as *and* and *for*, that the punctuation changes make unnecessary.

Have students read the revised paragraph 11 aloud and summarize its meaning.

now. For reverence of God, finish your business now, for the expense and trouble we have each day is horrible, and it will be like this until you have finished; and your men dare not go around collecting your rents, while we keep here every day more than twenty people to save ourselves and the place; for indeed, if the place had not been strongly defended, the duke would have come here. . . .

12   For the reverence of God, if any respectable and profitable method can be used to settle your business, do not neglect it, so that we can get out of these troubles and the great costs and expenses we have and may have in future. It is thought here that if my lord of Norfolk would act on your behalf, and got a commission to inquire into the riots and robberies committed on you and others in this part of the world, then the whole county will wait on him and do as you wish, for people love and respect him more than any other lord, except the king and my lord of Warwick.[14] . . .

13   Please do let me know quickly how you are and how your affairs are going, and let me know how your sons are. I came home late last night, and will be here until I hear from you again. Wykes came home on Saturday, but he did not meet your sons.

14   God have you in his keeping and send us good news from you. Written in haste on the eve of St. Simon and St. Jude.

By yours, M.P.

---

[14] **the king . . . Warwick** (wôr′ĭk): King Edward IV and the earl of Warwick, a figure so influential that he was known as Warwick the Kingmaker. Warwick put his friend, the Yorkist King Edward IV, on the throne but later turned against him and fought with the Lancastrian faction, who opposed the Yorkists in the War of the Roses.

The Paston Letters   89

APPLYING ACADEMIC VOCABULARY

❏ collapse   ☑ displace   ❏ military   ☑ violate   ❏ visual

Write and Discuss Have students turn to a partner to discuss the following questions. Guide students to include the academic vocabulary words *displace* and *violate* in their responses. Ask volunteers to share their responses with the class.

- In what way did the Duke of Suffolk **violate** the rights of the Pastons and their servants and tenants?
- How were Margaret and the Pastons' tenants **displaced** by the conflict?

TEACH

🗨 ENGLISH LEARNER SUPPORT

Demonstrate Comprehension Direct students' attention to the last two lines of paragraph 11: *if the place had not been strongly defended, the duke would have come here. . .*

- Display this sentence: *If it had not rained, we would have gone to the beach.* Use simple drawings to explain that this means it rained, so we did not go to the beach. Display the following sentences: *The place was strongly defended. The duke came here.* Ask students to answer yes or no to each statement. **SUBSTANTIAL**

- Display the sentences: *The place was strongly defended. The duke came here.* Have students orally rephrase the sentence from the text with the frame *The place _____, so the duke _____.* **MODERATE**

- Have students orally answer the questions: *Did the duke come? Why or why not?* Then, have students explain their answers in complete sentences. **LIGHT**

The Paston Letters   89

TEACH

✏️ MAKE INFERENCES

Remind students that inferences are based on details in the text and prior knowledge. Direct students to identify what Margaret is telling her son to do or not do in paragraphs 15 and 16. Then, ask them to think about what he is doing that causes her to give him these warnings. Remind students of the background information and discuss what a young man in a big city far from home might be doing. What does this tell us about her son's character? (**Answer:** *The writer's son is being very careless with money, is spending way too much, and is being careless even though he might be in danger. He is young, so he is probably having a good time entertaining himself and his friends and indulging in luxuries.*)

■ English Learner Support

Make Inferences Help students find the phrases *pay attention* and *be careful* that signal warnings. Then, ask them to identify the words and phrases that say what the warnings are about. Guide students to the words *danger, expenses,* and *impoverish,* and clarify their meanings, including the relationship between *impoverish* and the Spanish *pobreza* (poverty). Then, have students work in pairs to talk about what Margaret's son is doing and what the reader can understand about him from his behavior. If necessary, allow students to describe his character in their native languages.

NOTICE & NOTE

MAKE INFERENCES
Annotate: Mark the warnings that the writer gives to her son in paragraphs 15 and 16.

Infer: What can you assume about the writer's son's behavior from the warnings she gives him? What kind of person is her son?

Although the Pastons were considered wealthy, they faced continual struggles. They even experienced occasional financial difficulties, particularly after the death of John I in 1466. Margaret's son John II, though frequently in London to deal with family legal matters, seems at times to have paid more attention to his own interests. The Pastons were also affected by the ravages of warfare and disease. The following three letters deal with some of their hardships.

Margaret to her oldest son, John II
28 October 1470

15   . . . Unless you pay more attention to your expenses, you will bring great shame on yourself and your friends, and impoverish them so that none of us will be able to help each other, to the great encouragement of our enemies.

16   Those who claim to be your friends in this part of the world realize in what great danger and need you stand, both from various of your friends and from your enemies. It is rumored that I have parted with so much to you that I cannot help either you or any of my friends, which is no honor to us and causes people to esteem us less. At the moment it means that I must disperse my household and lodge somewhere, which I would be very loath to do if I were free to choose. It has caused a great deal of talk in this town and I would not have needed to do it if I had held back when I could. So for God's sake pay attention and be careful from now on, for I have handed over to you both my own property and your father's, and have held nothing back, either for myself or for his sake. . . .

John II to Margaret
April 1471

17   *Mother*, I commend myself to you and let you know, blessed be God, my brother John is alive and well, and in no danger of dying. Nevertheless he is badly hurt by an arrow in his right arm below the elbow, and I have sent a surgeon to him, who has dressed the wound; and he tells me that he hopes he will be healed within a very short time. John Mylsent is dead. God have mercy on his soul; William Mylsent is alive and all his other servants seem to have escaped.[15] . . .

John II to John III
15 September 1471

18   . . . Please send me word if any of our friends or well-wishers are dead, for I fear that there is great mortality in Norwich and in

---
[15] **my brother John . . . escaped:** John II is describing the battle of Barnet in the Wars of the Roses. The Pastons fought on the Lancastrian side, which King Edward IV's Yorkist forces defeated.

TO CHALLENGE STUDENTS . . .

Hypothesize Point out that editors were responsible for choosing the letters that appear in this grouping. Have students discuss what they think are the organizing principles for the grouping. Ask them to identify similarities and differences from letter to letter. Also have them suggest the overall view of the Paston family and of the Middle Ages that the grouping as a whole conveys.

other boroughs and towns in Norfolk: I assure you that it is the most widespread plague I ever knew of in England, for by my faith I cannot hear of pilgrims going through the country nor of any other man who rides or goes anywhere, that any town or borough in England is free from the sickness. May God put an end to it, when it please him. So, for God's sake, get my mother to take care of my younger brothers and see that they are not anywhere where the sickness is prevalent, and that they do not amuse themselves with other young people who go where the sickness is. If anyone has died of the sickness, or is infected with it in Norwich, for God's sake let her send them to some friend of hers in the country; I would advise you to do the same. I would rather my mother moved her household into the country. . . .

> **NOTICE & NOTE**
>
> **ANALYZE PRIMARY SOURCES**
>
> **Annotate:** John II makes requests of and gives warnings to his brother. Mark them.
>
> **Infer:** Based on this letter, how well did people in the 15th century understand how the plague spread?

CHECK YOUR UNDERSTANDING

Answer these questions before moving on to the **Analyze the Text** section on the following page.

1. Which event does Margaret experience or see firsthand?
   - **A** The execution of Robert Lovegold
   - **B** The aftermath of the ransacking of Hellesdon
   - **C** The excessive spending of John II
   - **D** The battle of Barnet

2. Which sentence from paragraphs 6 and 7 suggests that the Pastons may be able to appeal for recourse to a higher authority than the mayor?
   - **F** *The duke came to Norwich . . . asking them in the king's name that they should inquire of the constables . . . which men had been on your side . . .*
   - **G** *[T]hey have been made into their catspaws . . .*
   - **H** *So I would be glad if you could get a writ sent down for his release, . . .*
   - **J** *I am told that the old lady and the duke have been frequently set against us by what Harlesdon, . . . and other false villains have told them, . . .*

3. The last line of paragraph 14 starts with the phrase "written in haste." What can the reader infer about Margaret Paston from this phrase?
   - **A** She is an impatient and unsympathetic person.
   - **B** She is in a rush to get her letter to a messenger.
   - **C** She is concerned about getting the plague.
   - **D** She is distressed and feels in constant danger.

The Paston Letters 91

TEACH

ANALYZE PRIMARY SOURCES

Direct students to pay attention to what John II is telling John III to do and not to do in paragraph 18. Explain that they can draw conclusions from these requests and warnings about people's understanding of the plague and how it is spread. (**Answer:** *People understood that you could get the plague from being around other people who had it or had been exposed to it.*)

CHECK YOUR UNDERSTANDING

Have students answer the questions independently.

Answers:

1. C
2. H
3. D

If they answer any questions incorrectly, have them reread the text to confirm their understanding. Then they may proceed to ANALYZE THE TEXT on page 92.

ENGLISH LEARNER SUPPORT

Oral Assessment Use the following questions to assess students' comprehension and speaking skills.

1. What did Margaret see at Hellesdon? *(She saw the destroyed buildings.)*
2. What does Margaret ask her husband to do for Robert Lovegold? *(She asks him to get a writ for Robert Lovegold's release.)*
3. Margaret said she wrote a letter in haste, or quickly. Why do you think she had to write a letter quickly? *(She was in fear for her safety.)*

The Paston Letters 91

APPLY

ANALYZE THE TEXT

Possible answers:

1. **DOK 2:** *Margaret does not trust Barow and believes he is dishonest. She says she thinks the documents he cites as evidence to Lord Moleyns's claim are forgeries. She also warns him to be careful not to eat or drink with Lord Moleyns's men after telling him Barow has offered to have a drink with him in London. She might have a bias against Barow because he is a servant of Lord Moleyns.*

2. **DOK 2:** *Many authority figures, including the local representatives of the law, have sided with the Duke of Suffolk, and many other people have been swayed to side against them. Therefore, Margaret would be uncertain about her husband's influence on other authorities.*

3. **DOK 2:** *The Paston family is vulnerable to attacks because many of the local officials have sided against them. In paragraphs 5 and 6, Margaret describes how the bailiff of Eye and the mayor arrested several of their servants.*

4. **DOK 3:** *Women were expected to manage the affairs of the household, but were still expected to consult their husbands on major decisions. Margaret asks her husband not to be angry with her for changing her location and asks permission to set up household at his mother's place in another town. In another letter, she asks if he wants her to stay where she is in Caister or to go to London.*

5. **DOK 4:** *It is possible Margaret is exaggerating about the direness of the situation to convince her son to stop spending money.*

RESEARCH

To help students generate questions, have them review what they already know about this conflict and time period and about wars in general. Encourage them to speculate or make guesses to confirm with their research.

Extend Students may note that in the 15th century, battles were fought hand to hand with various weapons on battlefields, whereas today wars are fought with guns, bombs, boats, and airplanes.

 **RESPOND**

ANALYZE THE TEXT

Support your responses with evidence from the text. 📓 NOTEBOOK

1. **Infer** In the first letter from Margaret to her husband, she explains her conversation with Barow, one of Lord Moleyns's men. What do you think is Margaret's opinion of Barow? Why might she have a bias against him?

2. **Interpret** In paragraph 6, Margaret writes, "So I would be glad if you could get a writ sent down for his release, if you think it can be done." Why is Margaret uncertain as to whether her husband can obtain the writ?

3. **Cause/Effect** What made the Paston family vulnerable to attacks?

4. **Draw Conclusions** What can you determine about women's roles in 15th-century English society from reading these primary sources?

5. **Notice & Note** In her letter to her son John II, Margaret uses strong negative language: *great shame, great encouragement of our enemies, great danger, great deal of talk*. Do you think that Margaret's account is credible? Why might she exaggerate?

RESEARCH TIP
It's always easier to begin a research project by creating a research plan. First, identify exactly what you want to learn. Then make a step-by-step plan to guide your research.

RESEARCH

All these letters except for the first one were written during the Wars of the Roses, a period of great political instability in England. With a partner, research the history of this long conflict. Develop research questions, locate answers in the sources you find, and record the results of your research in a chart like the one below.

QUESTIONS	ANSWERS
Why is it called Wars of the Roses?	They were named after the badges for the two families: the white rose of York and the red Rose of Lancaster.
What were they fighting about?	They were fighting over who should be the king of England.
How did the wars end?	Henry the VII, of Lancaster, defeated Richard III, of York, and then married Elizabeth of York.

Extend How did warfare in medieval England differ from the way wars are fought today? Discuss with your partner.

WHEN STUDENTS STRUGGLE . . .

Reteaching Remind students that an **inference** is a logical guess about the people or events in a text. Students can make inferences using what is stated in the text and their own knowledge and experience. One kind of inference a reader can make is about a writer's emotions. Have students look back at paragraph 18 and look for the statements John II makes, as well as his requests and warnings. Ask students to state what they believe he is feeling. Then, ask them to identify the details from the text and ideas from their own experience.

 For additional support, go to the **Reading Studio** and assign the following 🎬 Level Up tutorial: Making Inferences.

CREATE AND PRESENT

Write a Short Dramatic Scene The letters contain reports of arguments and conflicts. In pairs or in a small group, write a short dramatic scene with at least two characters to recreate one of these scenes through dialogue. You can also imagine that John Paston meets Barow in London for a drink, as Barow proposes, and write that scene.

- Think about the conflict between the characters and what each character wants or believes they are entitled to.
- Make sure that the dialogue goes back and forth with the characters responding to each other, rather than each character presenting their case alone.
- Use language to show the emotions of each character. Remember that people often use strong language when they are upset.
- People are not always truthful when they are arguing about something. Consider having one or more of your characters lie or exaggerate.

Enact the Scene With your partner or group, present your dramatic scene by acting it out in front of the class.

- Use a narrator to set the scene and provide some context before the dialogue begins.
- When you read your part, think about how that person feels at that moment; try to convey that feeling in the way you talk and in your movements and facial expressions.
- After you present your scene, ask your classmates to summarize what happened.

RESPOND TO THE ESSENTIAL QUESTION

 What happens when a society unravels?

Gather Information Review your annotations and notes on *The Paston Letters*. Then add relevant details to your Response Log. As you determine which information to include, think about:

- the challenges Margaret Paston faces
- which strategies the Pastons use to survive and defend themselves
- how the usual rules of society change in wartime

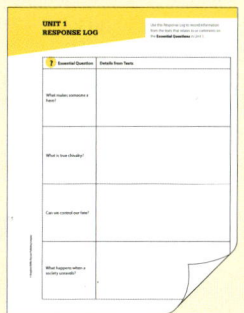

RESPOND

Go to **Writing Narratives** in the **Writing Studio** for more help with writing a dramatic scene.

ACADEMIC VOCABULARY

As you write and discuss what you learned from the *The Paston Letters*, be sure to use the Academic Vocabulary words. Check off each of the words that you use.

- ❏ collapse
- ❏ displace
- ❏ military
- ❏ violate
- ❏ visual

APPLY

CREATE AND PRESENT

Write a Short Dramatic Scene Direct student groups to look back at the text for a conversation or conflict that is described in a letter. Have them identify who was involved, what happened, and what was said. Tell them they will use their imaginations to dramatize the scene.

 For **writing support** for students at varying proficiency levels, see Text X-Ray on page 82D.

Enact the Scene Each student should take on at least one role. One student might be both the narrator and a character. If the scenes have more characters than actors, students may play more than one role or invite students from other groups to read parts. Encourage students to "get into" their characters and use emotion and physical movement to express how the characters are feeling.

RESPOND TO THE ESSENTIAL QUESTION

Allow time for students to add details from *The Paston Letters* to their Unit 1 Response Logs.

APPLY

CRITICAL VOCABULARY

Answers:

1. affairs
2. quell
3. ransack
4. writ
5. bailiff
6. commend

VOCABULARY STRATEGY:
Consult a Dictionary

Answers:

1. to praise; to entrust
2. to put down forcibly; to pacify, quiet
3. something done or experienced; personal business
4. a court attendant entrusted with duties such as the maintenance of order in a courtroom during a trial; an overseer of an estate; a steward.
5. a written order issued by a court, commanding the party to whom it is addressed to perform or cease performing a specified act
6. to search through (something) thoroughly and often roughly/ To go through (a place) stealing valuables and causing disarray

---

 **RESPOND**

WORD BANK
commend
quell
affairs
bailiff
writ
ransack

CRITICAL VOCABULARY

Practice and Apply Write the Critical Vocabulary word that has the same or similar meaning as the given word or phrase.

1. Which vocabulary word has a meaning similar to *business*?
2. Which vocabulary word has a meaning similar to *bring to an end*?
3. Which vocabulary word has a meaning similar to *rob and destroy*?
4. Which vocabulary word has a meaning similar to *court order*?
5. Which vocabulary word has a meaning similar to *steward*?
6. Which vocabulary word has a meaning similar to *entrust*?

VOCABULARY STRATEGY:
Consult a Dictionary

At times you may come across a word that looks familiar, but the meaning you know for that word might not make sense in the way it is being used, making it difficult to understand a sentence. Be aware when reading older texts that the meanings and usage of words change over time, so that an author may use a word in a way that was very common in his or her time, but is now uncommon. An example of this can be found in the first letter you read with Margaret's use of the word *commend*.

It is useful to consult a dictionary to see all the meanings and senses of a word. **Senses** are slightly different usages of the same meaning of a word. The dictionary will list meanings and senses of a word in order from most common to least common. The most common meaning of *commend* is "to praise." However, that meaning doesn't make sense in the context of the letter. A different meaning of *commend* best fits its use in the context: "to entrust."

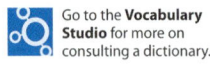 Go to the **Vocabulary Studio** for more on consulting a dictionary.

Practice and Apply Look up each Critical Vocabulary word in the dictionary, and write its most common meaning in the chart. When necessary, write a less common meaning to reflect the word's meaning in *The Paston Letters*.

CRITICAL VOCABULARY WORD	MOST COMMON MEANING	MEANING IN THE PASTON LETTERS
commend	to praise	to entrust
quell		
affairs		
bailiff		
writ		
ransack		

94 Unit 1

 ENGLISH LEARNER SUPPORT

Vocabulary Strategy Remind students that this is an old text, so the meanings of the words may be unusual. Point out that the Critical Vocabulary questions include the cognates *quiet/quieto*, *destroy/destruir*, *court/corte*, and *order/orden*. Have students use these cognates to connect the Critical Vocabulary questions with the Vocabulary Strategy table
ALL LEVELS

94 Unit 1

LANGUAGE CONVENTIONS: Subject-Verb Agreement

Subject–verb agreement means that if the subject is singular, the verb is also singular, and if the subject is plural, the verb is also plural. Verbs in the present simple form, including auxiliary verbs, are plural or singular depending on their subject.

- Nouns in modifying phrases that come between the verb and the subject do not change whether the verb is singular or plural.
- Verbs with compound subjects might be singular or plural depending on the conjunction in the compound subject and the noun closest to the verb.
- Some pronouns always take a singular or plural verb, while for some it will depend on the **antecedent**.

Look at these examples:

The people dying of the plague **are** mostly in the towns.

The verb *are* is plural because the subject is *people*, which is plural. The underlined phrase modifies *people*.

We still have not heard from your sisters, who **have** been away for a month.

We have heard from the husband of one of them, who **has** gotten word that neither has become ill.

In the underlined clauses, the verb is either singular or plural depending on the antecedent of the pronoun *who*. The pronoun *neither* is always singular.

People have tried many ways to avoid getting the plague, but none is certain to work.

Half the people in the town are dead from the plague and none are yet buried.

In the underlined clauses, *none* is either singular or plural depending on its meaning. In the first sentence, *none* means "not one." In the second sentence, *none* means "not any."

A few people have stayed in the town, but most **have** left for the country to try to avoid the plague.

There is very little food left, as most **has** been eaten or destroyed by invading soldiers.

Some pronouns take a singular or plural verb depending on whether they are referring to a count or noncount noun. *People* is a count noun, so it takes the plural verb *have*. *Food* is a noncount noun, so it takes the singular verb *has*.

Practice and Apply Write four pairs of sentences, two using pronouns that always take a singular verb and two using pronouns that can take a singular or plural verb. The first sentence should contain the pronoun's antecedent.

RESPOND

! Go to **Agreement** in the **Grammar Studio** for more on subject-verb agreement.

The Paston Letters 95

APPLY

LANGUAGE CONVENTIONS: Subject-Verb Agreement

Remind students that when a clause or phrase uses a present simple verb form, the verb of the predicate must agree with the verb of the subject. Explain that the main noun may not be next to the verb. In the example, the noun *plague* is part of a phrase that modifies *people*.

Explain that sometimes a clause will be a relative clause that modifies a noun. A relative clause has a relative pronoun as a subject. The relative pronoun might be singular or plural depending on its antecedent. Point out that in the second example sentence, *sisters* is the antecedent for *who*, and in the third example sentence, *husbands* is the antecedent for *who*. Display these sentences:

Your sisters have been away for a month.
The husband has gotten word.

Explain that some pronouns, such as *none* and *most*, might be singular or plural, and that compound subjects might take a singular or plural verb.

Practice and Apply Students should demonstrate that they understand the relationship between pronouns and subject-verb agreement by writing pairs of sentences in which the second sentence contains a pronoun and the first contains its antecedent. Example:

1. My brother came to visit today. He lives in another state. (*He* is the pronoun and *brother* is the antecedent.)

2. Many people were waiting this morning. They have left now. (*They* is the pronoun and *people* is the antecedent.)

ENGLISH LEARNER SUPPORT

Language Conventions Help students understand subject-verb agreement with pronouns and relative clauses. Display this sentence: *The soldiers who want to destroy the village _____ coming.*

- Ask students to identify the nouns. Circle *soldiers* and point out it is the subject. Ask students to complete the sentence with *is* or *are*. **SUBSTANTIAL**
- Ask students to identify the words that say which people (*who want to destroy the village*) and underline them. Circle *soldiers* and point out that it is the subject. Ask students to complete the sentence with *is* or *are* and explain their answer. **LIGHT**
- Display the sentence with the options *want/wants* and *is/are*. Ask students to decide which verbs are correct and to explain their answer. **LIGHT**

The Paston Letters 95

PLAN

MY SYRIAN DIARY
Diary by Marah

GENRE ELEMENTS
DIARY

Remind students that **diaries** are personal accounts of day-to-day events that are narrated from a first-person perspective. Diaries are usually meant as private records, but if authors intend to make the diaries public, they need to include enough context and background information for the entries to make sense to readers. Often, diaries are used as **primary sources** when researching a historical event or time period. In this lesson, students will identify the author's purpose for writing, and will think about how they can connect their own experiences to the text.

LEARNING OBJECTIVES

- Evaluate author's purpose and connect to text.
- Conduct research about Arab Spring protests.
- Write a compare and contrast essay.
- Review connections to diaries.
- Use Latin roots to determine meaning.
- Distinguish between formal and informal language.
- **Language** Discuss the daily life of Syrians using details from a photograph.

TEXT COMPLEXITY

Quantitative Measures	My Syrian Diary	Lexile: 880L
Qualitative Measures	**Ideas Presented** Simple, single meaning. Literal, explicit, and direct. Purpose and stance clear.	
	Structures Used Clear, chronological, conventional.	
	Language Used Explicit, literal, contemporary, familiar language.	
	Knowledge Required Subjects mostly familiar with some references to historical events.	

PLAN

RESOURCES
Online Ed

- Unit 1 Response Log
- 🔊 Selection Audio
- 📖 Reading Studio:
  Notice & Note
- 📝 Writing Studio:
  Writing Informative Texts
- 💬 Speaking and Listening Studio:
  Participating in Collaborative Discussions
- 🔵 Vocabulary Studio:
  Latin Roots
- ✓ "My Syrian Diary" Selection Test

SUMMARIES

English

In 2011 a 15-year-old Syrian girl named Marah wrote an online diary to record her feelings about the events during the Syrian civil war. In these entries, Marah describes how her once beautiful, lively city has been turned into a ruin where injured people roam the streets and children are starving, crying out for a piece of fruit. Marah describes her love of education and her worry for the future, and asks her readers to help share her message and bring the bloody war to an end.

Spanish

En el 2011, una niña siria de 15 años llamada Marah, escribe un diario en línea para documentar sus sentimientos con respecto a los sucesos de la guerra civil siria. En estas entradas, Marah describe cómo su ciudad, una vez bella y alegre, se convirtió en una ruina donde los heridos vagan por las calles y los niños se mueren de hambre, pidiendo un pedazo de fruta. Marah describe su amor por la educación y su preocupación por el futuro y pide la ayuda de sus lectores para compartir su mensaje y llevar la sangrienta guerra a su final.

SMALL-GROUP OPTIONS

Have students work in small groups and pairs to read and discuss the selection.

Three-Minute Review

- As you read the text, pause after every two to three paragraphs.
- Direct students to reread the paragraphs and write clarifying questions. Set a timer for three minutes.
- After three minutes, ask: *What did you notice as you reread the text?*
- Invite volunteers to share clarifying questions.
- Guide small groups to discuss and answer the questions.

Send a Problem

- After reading paragraphs 6–10, pose this question: *How did Marah's feelings about food change?*
- Call on a student to respond. Wait up to 11 seconds.
- If the student has no response, s/he must call on another student by name to answer the same question.
- Have students continue asking each other for assistance as needed. Monitor responses and ask more questions as appropriate.

My Syrian Diary

PLAN

Text X-Ray: English Learner Support
for *My Syrian Diary*

Use the Text X-Ray and the supports and scaffolds in the Teacher's Edition to help guide students at different proficiency levels through the selection.

INTRODUCE THE SELECTION
DISCUSS RIGHTS AND DEPRIVATIONS

In this lesson, students will need to be able to discuss how Syrians suffered many deprivations because they were stripped of their rights.

Provide the following explanations:
- A right is an entitlement or freedom.
- A deprivation is a lack, because something has been taken away.

Guide students to reference rights and deprivations mentioned in the diary as they discuss how life in Syria changed during the civil war.

Provide sentence frames, such as: *One right the Syrians had before the war was _____. One deprivation the Syrians suffered during the war was _____.*

CULTURAL REFERENCES

The following words or phrases may be unfamiliar to students:
- *take my* (paragraph 2): use as an example
- *familiar face* (paragraph 3): the way something usually looks
- *ghost town* (paragraph 4): a deserted or empty place with few or no inhabitants
- *checkpoints* (paragraph 22): guarded places where identification is checked
- *turned upside down* (paragraph 32): changed completely to make no sense

---

LISTENING

Identify Claims and Supporting Evidence

Review with students that a claim is an opinion and supporting evidence are facts. Remind students that authors of diaries may make claims that tell their opinion based on factual evidence. As students listen to the text, have them think about each idea they hear, and whether it is an objective fact that can be proved true or whether it is a subjective opinion or claim.

Have students listen as you reread paragraphs 1–10. Help students identify the claims Marah makes about Syria, and the evidence she uses to support them. Use the following supports with students at varying proficiency levels:

- Say the following two statements from paragraph 2 and have students repeat each, naming the one that tells Marah's claim and the one that gives supporting evidence. Provide language support as needed. *Every day we open our eyes to our bleak reality (claim). At just seven years old, she has lost the ability to speak after a rocket landed close to our street. (evidence)* **SUBSTANTIAL**
- After listening to paragraphs 1–10, have students repeat one of Marah's claims, and read aloud one phrase or sentence that gives evidence to support the claim. **MODERATE**
- After listening to paragraphs 1–10, have students restate two to three of Marah's claims and the related supporting evidence in their own words. **LIGHT**

96C   Unit 1

PLAN

SPEAKING

Use Photographs

Review the photograph that accompanies the text. Help students work together to create a vocabulary word bank—with words such as *fear*, *rubble*, or *debris*—based on the image to use in a discussion of Syria during its civil war.

Use the following supports with students at varying proficiency levels:

- Have students repeat the words from the word bank and point to related items in the photograph. Use the words in simple sentences related to the daily life of Syrians and have students repeat them. **SUBSTANTIAL**
- Have partners use the words from the word bank in simple sentences related to the daily life of Syrians. Provide a sentence starter, such as: *The photograph shows how ____.* **MODERATE**
- Have partners ask each other questions about the daily life of Syrians using the word bank and the photograph. For example: *How did Syrians feel about their city during the war? (The destruction of their city made them feel depressed.)* **LIGHT**

READING

Understand Author's Purpose

Tell students that an author's purpose for writing may or may not be stated directly, and there might be more than one purpose for writing. Help students find words that show Marah's attitude and tone toward her subject. Students should find words that appeal to readers' sense of touch, sight, smell, and sound.

Use the following supports with students at varying proficiency levels:

- Point to paragraph 1 and ask questions to help students identify tone and the purpose of imagery. Discuss with students the difference between negative and positive tones and images. For example: *Is "the sound of falling bombs" a positive or negative sound? (negative)* Point to paragraph 4 and ask: *Is a limping dog a positive or negative image? (negative)* **SUBSTANTIAL**
- Have pairs work together to identify words and phrases that show tone and imagery. Guide them to use sentence frames, such as: *The phrase ____ shows a ____ tone. The image of ____ appeals to my sense of ____.* **MODERATE**
- Have partners ask each other *"Have you ever?"* questions about the imagery in the text. For example: *Have you ever seen decrepit buildings and charred trees? What did they look like? How did they make you feel?* **LIGHT**

WRITING

Write a Compare and Contrast Essay

Remind students that using graphic organizers and taking notes will help them more easily recall and organize similarities and differences when writing their essays.

Use the following supports with students at varying proficiency levels:

- Help students take one to two notes about each essay, using sentence frames, such as: *The purpose of this essay is ____.* Then help students use their notes in a Venn diagram with the titles of the two essays as headings for the outer circles. Model how to record one difference and one similarity. **SUBSTANTIAL**
- Direct students to take notes about each essay, using sentence frames, such as: *The purpose of this essay is to ____.* Then guide students use their notes in a Venn diagram. **MODERATE**
- Have students do the Intermediate activity, then have them explain the information in their Venn diagrams to a partner. **LIGHT**

My Syrian Diary **96D**

TEACH

 Connect to the ESSENTIAL QUESTION

Ask a volunteer to read the Essential Question aloud. Have students look at the image and tell them they will be reading about how civil war changed everyday life for people living in modern Syria.

COMPARE PRIMARY SOURCES

Point out that *My Syrian Diary* is a collection of diary entries, while selections from *The Paston Letters* are letters. Both are primary sources, and both relate to times of social unrest. Ask students whether they have ever kept a diary or written letters to friends or family members and what they included in those entries or letters. Have students keep their experiences in mind as they read *My Syrian Diary*, and think about how the ideas relate to the *The Paston Letters*.

COLLABORATE & COMPARE

DIARY

from
MY SYRIAN DIARY

by **Marah**
pages 99–103

COMPARE PRIMARY SOURCES

Now that you've read selections from *The Paston Letters*, read selections from *My Syrian Diary* and explore how Marah's experiences in 21st-century Syria connect to the experiences of the Paston family in 15th-century England. As you read, think about how *My Syrian Diary* relates to your own experiences, the experiences of other teens, and events that you have seen or heard about in the news. After you are finished, you will complete a final project that involves comparing and contrasting both texts.

 ESSENTIAL QUESTION:

What happens when a society unravels?

LETTERS

from
THE PASTON LETTERS

by the **Paston Family**
pages 85–91

96 Unit 1

My Syrian Diary

QUICK START

Imagine that your society has completely broken down. Schools are closed, and your parents are afraid to let you go outside to see friends. How would you spend your time? What would you do to make your voice heard? Discuss your responses with a classmate.

EVALUATE AUTHOR'S PURPOSE

Authors write for one or more **purposes**: to inform, to entertain, to persuade, to express opinions and feelings, or to provoke emotions in readers. As you read the excerpt from *My Syrian Diary*, make inferences about Marah's purpose or purposes for writing. Try also to determine her **message**, or the main idea she wants to convey.

Authors often use text structure to help them achieve their purposes. The diary excerpt you're about to read combines organizational patterns of chronological order, compare and contrast, and cause and effect. Consider how these structures contribute to the purpose and message of the text.

Another important aspect to keep in mind with relation to the author's purpose is the intended **audience**, or the people the author hopes will read the piece of writing.

As you read, evaluate how well Marah accomplishes her purposes, as well as how effectively she gets her message across and how well she reaches her intended audience.

CONNECT

When readers **connect** to a text, they relate the content to their own knowledge and experience. Published diaries allow readers to gain direct insight into a person's thoughts and feelings about events. As you read excerpts from *My Syrian Diary*, use these questions to help you make connections to the text:

QUESTIONS	ANSWERS
Does the author remind me of myself or of someone I know?	
What do I know about the time, place, events, or situations described in the text?	
How is the text similar to other works I have read?	

GENRE ELEMENTS: DIARY

- personal accounts of day-to-day events
- written from the first-person point of view
- usually kept private
- occasionally published for writing quality or historical significance

---

GET READY

QUICK START

This scenario may be difficult for students to imagine. Have them think about a time, such as during a weather event, that everyone had to stay indoors, and services such as roads, utilities, and communications were affected, and how that changed their normal routines and lives. Ask them what they think would happen if those conditions went on for months or even years.

EVALUATE AUTHOR'S PURPOSE

Explain to students that when writers create texts, they have some kind of reason for doing so, and that the reader can often **infer** or make a guess about, the writer's **purpose** by looking carefully at what the writer chooses to say and how he or she says it. A writer may have multiple purposes, such as to inform and persuade. In the case of a diary, the writer's purpose is often to express and record his or her experiences, thoughts, and emotions. In the case of an online diary such as this one, the writer may want to feel heard by and connected to the rest of the world as a means of managing distress.

CONNECT

Tell students they can gain a deeper understanding of a text by connecting what they read to their own prior knowledge and experiences and imagining themselves in the place of the writer. By doing this, a reader can broaden his or her understanding of the world and the experiences of others, even when they are from very different cultures in other parts of the world. Remind students to use the questions to help them make connections to the text.

TEACH

CRITICAL VOCABULARY

Have students read the Critical Vocabulary words and think about where they may have heard or seen them before. Then have them read each sentence and decide which of the words seems to best complete it. Explain that they will learn more about these words from reading the selection.

Answers:

1. *exorbitant*
2. *mandatory*
3. *deprivation; sustenance*
4. *extract; superficial*

■ **English Learner Support**

Use Cognates Tell students that the Critical Vocabulary words contain two Spanish cognates: *extract/extraer* and *superficial/superficial*.

LANGUAGE CONVENTIONS

Explain to students that the way people use English changes according to the author's purpose and his or her audience. One thing that might change is whether the language is formal or informal. Tell students to think about the difference between **formal** and **informal** clothing, and that *informal* also means *casual*. Elicit examples of situations that are formal and informal and ask students who what they wear and how they talk might change between a formal and informal situation.

 ANNOTATION MODEL

Explain that one way to annotate a model to make inferences about an author's purpose is to underline important details. Point out that students may follow this suggestion or use their own system for marking up the selection in the write-in text. They may want to color-code their annotations by using highlighters. Their notes in the margin may include questions about ideas that are unclear or topics they want to learn more about.

98 Unit 1

 **GET READY**

CRITICAL VOCABULARY

| extract | sustenance | exorbitant | deprivation |
| superficial | mandatory | | |

Complete each sentence using one of the Critical Vocabulary words. Use what you know about word meanings, word parts, and context clues.

1. The _____ prices of the food on display discouraged hungry shoppers from entering the store.

2. After the hurricane, the governor ordered a _____ 9:00 p.m. curfew.

3. Having suffered through the _____ of war, the refugees were overwhelmed by the abundance of _____ they saw in other countries.

4. I could not _____ the splinter from the dog's paw even though the injury appeared to be _____.

LANGUAGE CONVENTIONS

Formal and Informal Language Writing may be divided into two categories: formal language and informal language. **Formal language** follows all rules of grammar and punctuation. It does not include such elements of "everyday" spoken English as slang words and contractions. **Informal language** may not always follow language rules and may include elements taken from spoken language. Pieces written in the first person often use informal language. As you read *My Syrian Diary*, watch for examples of informal language.

ANNOTATION MODEL  NOTICE & NOTE

As you read, mark up details that allow you to make inferences about the author's purpose. Note connections to your own experiences and ideas. In the model, you can see one reader's notes about the selection.

> Every day, we open our eyes to our bleak reality: to the mortar shells that bring fear, death, disease and destruction. It has robbed us of our loved ones, destroyed our special places, hurt our close friends. Take my neighbor's daughter. At just seven years old, she has lost the ability to speak after a rocket landed close to our street.

The language of this passage sounds like it is addressed to people outside of Syria.

If my younger sister couldn't speak due to shock, I would be heartbroken and angry.

98 Unit 1

 ENGLISH LEARNER SUPPORT

Understand English Usage Help students understand that writers of informal texts, such as diaries, may use sentence fragments, slang, idioms, and contractions. Point out the sentence "Take my neighbor's daughter" in paragraph 2. Explain that this is more informal because the subject "you" is understood. In formal English, a subject is typically used. Discuss other usage problems that students might encounter, such as double negatives or word order. In Spanish, double negatives are required in many sentence structures. In English, however, double negatives are not used. Students might also struggle with the placement of modifiers. In Korean and Spanish, for example, word order—such as the placement of adverbials—is freer than it is in English.

BACKGROUND

The Syrian civil war began in 2011 with clashes between the government and antigovernment demonstrators, who protested the lack of freedom under Syrian leader Bashar al-Assad. Rebel factions within the country fought Assad's regime and one another for control of the country. Assad's actions sparked worldwide outrage, prompting many countries to provide funding for the rebels, which escalated the conflict. By 2017, over 400,000 Syrians had died and 11 million were either displaced or had fled abroad. The author of this diary, who was 15 years old in 2011, lived in a besieged neighborhood until she fled Syria for Europe in 2016. She used the pen name Marah to protect her identity.

from MY SYRIAN DIARY
Diary by Marah

PREPARE TO COMPARE

As you read, pay attention to Marah's descriptions of life under siege and how her experiences changed her. Note details that help identify Marah's message and motives for writing.

April 15, 2014

1 My city was once magnificent. In spring, it bloomed. We used to wake up to the sound of birds chirping and to the fragrant scent of flowers. Today, spring is here again. But what kind of spring is this? We now wake up to the sound of falling bombs.

2 Every day, we open our eyes to our bleak reality: to the mortar shells that bring fear, death, disease and destruction. It has robbed us of our loved ones, destroyed our special places, hurt our close friends. Take my neighbor's daughter. At just seven years old, she has lost the ability to speak after a rocket landed close to our street.

3 Today, my city's familiar face has been replaced by the suffering of its residents: the young boy who has been exposed to chemical weapons and is unable to receive treatment. An old man feels powerless after he lost his legs. A young man wears black sunglasses as if to hide a severely scarred face that frightens

NOTICE & NOTE

Notice & Note
Use the side margins to notice and note signposts in the text.

CONTRASTS AND CONTRADICTIONS

Notice & Note: What contrasts does Marah describe in the opening paragraphs?

Analyze: Why does Marah choose to start her diary by describing such striking contrasts?

TEACH

✏️ EVALUATE AUTHOR'S PURPOSE

Explain to students that writers use **rhetorical questions** because they want the reader to think about something or emphasize an idea. Writers do not answer rhetorical questions. (**Answer:** *The questions cause the reader to think about what it would be like to live in a world where fruit is so scarce.*)

CRITICAL VOCABULARY

extract: A woman went blind because she got shrapnel in her eye and the doctors could not extract it.

ASK STUDENTS what they would use to extract a splinter or piece of glass. *(tweezers or a needle)*

sustenance: There was very little food in Marah's city, so they had to eat anything they could find for sustenance to sustain their health.

ASK STUDENTS what someone lost in the woods might find for sustenance. *(edible berries and roots)*

exorbitant: No one had enough money to buy the fruit and candy because the prices were so exorbitant, or costly.

ASK STUDENTS to name something they would never buy because the price is exorbitant. *(possibly designer clothing or luxury cars)*

deprivation: Marah's younger brother does not have enough food or other basic necessities, and he feels that deprivation, or loss, all the time.

ASK STUDENTS what kind of emotions they would feel if they experienced deprivation for a long time. *(sadness, anger, frustration)*

✏️ NOTICE & NOTE

extract
(ĭk-străkt´) *v.* to draw or pull out, often with great force or effort.

sustenance
(sŭs´tə-nəns) *n.* something, especially food, that sustains life or health.

exorbitant
(ĭg-zôr´bĭ-tənt) *adj.* beyond what is reasonable or customary, especially in cost or price.

EVALUATE AUTHOR'S PURPOSE

Annotate: A rhetorical question is a question that does not require a reply. Authors often use rhetorical questions to emphasize a point. Mark the rhetorical questions in paragraph 10.

Evaluate: How does the author's use of rhetorical questions help evoke a response from the reader?

deprivation
(dĕp´rə-vā´shən) *n.* the condition of being deprived; lacking the basic necessities or comforts of life.

---

children. A young woman is now blind after doctors couldn't **extract** the shrapnel from her eyes because they lacked the proper medical equipment and medication.

4   The shelling has turned my city into a ghost town of decrepit buildings and charred trees. Even our animals weren't spared. You often see a limping dog, a dead cat or a bird mourning its destroyed nest.

5   The bombings have not only altered my city's face, but also fundamentally changed its people.

6   During the hardest times, when bombs fell from the sky, we dreamed of bread. We rationed our food intake to one meal a day, depending on whatever greens we could find for **sustenance**.

7   I remember well the day cattle food, or fodder, was smuggled into the city. We milled the animal feed to make dough. It didn't take us long to get used to the bad taste and weird texture of our new "bread." It brought us a semblance of happiness with the little olives, juice or yogurt—Syrian food staples—that we had. Our only concern was to eat. One can never get used to sleeping on an empty stomach.

8   Our collective will to eat meant we started getting creative with the cattle feed. We cooked it as if we were cooking rice or wheat. We became so accustomed to it that we almost forgot what chicken, meat and fruit looked like.

9   One of the hardest days was when we heard that a car carrying fruit and candy had entered the city. At first, we were beyond thrilled, but our happiness was fleeting. The **exorbitant** prices for the items on display meant no one could actually afford them.

10   That day, a young boy with holes in his shoes squeezed his mother's hand as they passed by the fruit car. He begged her for an apple. Holding back her tears, she promised to make him "fodder cake" when they got home. Similarly, a father ignored the car carrying the goods and picked up the pace as he dragged his daughter, who was demanding a banana or an orange. Who would believe that the availability of fruit would be worse than the lack of it? Is it not a child's right to have an apple, a banana or a small piece of candy?

11   In this world, we have been stripped of our rights, starting with food. We try to entertain ourselves to forget our hunger, but there is no power and it is difficult to be without electricity after our lives once depended on it. I feel as if I'm living in the Stone Age. We wash our laundry by hand and burn wood to keep warm. In this new world, everything we know is gone. We miss the things we took for granted, like TVs and laptops.

12   Nowadays, the children refuse to stay indoors. My younger brother gets bored quickly, so my mother keeps him busy by delegating him the task of breaking firewood. His small hands have become thick and calloused. He executes his chore with anger and an air of rebellion. He now lives with a prevailing sense of **deprivation**. His feelings, along with mine, have altered without our knowledge or will.

13   I find myself forming a grudge against people who live outside my city. I wonder, why did this happen to us? What fault have we committed to live this bitter reality? Why were our childhoods stolen?

April 23, 2014

14   I begin my article by asking for help. I feel like I am lost in the middle of a rough sea. I don't know where these crushing waves might take me—to a safe place or to forgetfulness and loss?

15   I am very concerned about my education. It's my greatest priority. I grew up in a family that appreciated education. They enrolled me in a kindergarten that I will never forget. It was expensive, but my parents did not mind because all they cared about was to provide us with the best education from the very beginning.

16   I excelled in that kindergarten and went straight to second grade. My parents and grandparents were proud of me and reinforced my self-confidence. Middle school was fantastic. I drifted with my friends, and thanks to my always-conscious mom, who was my savior during that critical preteen stage, I was able to obtain my middle school diploma.

17   I loved my school immensely and I loved my teachers—especially my Arabic teacher. I adored the subject. School, for me, was like a playground or a picnic that I enjoyed with my friends. My parents never hesitated to provide for my school; their goal was that I obtain the best education, refine my personality and arm myself with a degree that would protect me from misfortune.

18   Then high school took me from childhood to the beginning of maturity and awareness. As the years went by, my fondness for my friends and my teachers had grown. I would see my friends during vacations and share all my secrets with them. My friend Rahaf was the closest to me. After she lost her mother, I watched her way of thinking change. She became like a mother to her little siblings.

19   One year after the beginning of the revolution, the conditions in my city worsened and the missiles intensified. My father decided that we should move out to a safer place. His only concern was to protect his family. We moved to a completely new area and I enrolled in the local school, which was a bad fit. But we had no other option. I formed some **superficial** friendships, and during one semester, I did not even manage to open a book. I thought constantly about my old friends and teachers, but staying in this new area was **mandatory**.

20   Finally, the condition deteriorated in the area where we resettled, which made my dad decide to return to our old city again. My sister and I were very happy that we were going home. But when we returned to our city, we were shocked by the amount of destruction. The schools were all destroyed, and after a while they turned basements into classrooms so we would be protected from the missiles.

21   These new schools were dark with dim lights similar to candles, and were smelly and had very poor ventilation. They were hardly real

NOTICE & NOTE

CONNECT

Annotate: In paragraphs 15–17, circle details that show how the education system in Syria before the war was different from your own experience. Underline details that show how it was the same.

Infer: Why might the author describe her education as her "greatest priority" despite the violence all around her?

superficial
(sōō´pər-fĭsh´əl) *adj.* apparent rather than actual or substantial; shallow.

mandatory
(măn´də-tôr´ē) *adj.* required or commanded by authority; obligatory.

My Syrian Diary   101

WHEN STUDENTS STRUGGLE . . .

Summarize Details Help students make inferences about why education is her "greatest priority" by summarizing the details she provides about her and her family's attitudes and feelings about school. Have them reread paragraphs 15–17 carefully and look for sentences to answer these questions with short written notes: *What does Marah think, feel, and do about her education? What does she think her parents feel about education?* Then, have students use their notes to summarize what Marah says about her and her family's attitude about education.

  For additional support, go to the **Reading Studio** and assign the following **Level Up tutorial: Summarizing.**

TEACH

 CONNECT

Remind students that making connections with the text can help them better understand the author's purpose and ideas. To make connections, they should think about their own experiences and prior knowledge. Ask students to think about what seems strange and what seems familiar to them about Marah's experience with school. (**Answer:** *Education was always a source of positivity and hope, and her parents taught her that a degree would protect her from misfortune.*)

ENGLISH LEARNER SUPPORT

Internalize Academic Vocabulary Check that students understand the following words from paragraphs 15–17 and provide meaning:

- *kindergarten:* class for four- to six-year-old children that is an introduction to school
- *grade:* year in school
- *middle school:* grades 6 through 8
- *enroll:* enter or register for school
- *diploma:* certificate showing that a student has graduated from an educational institution
- *degree:* an academic title given by a high school or college
- *subject:* area of study in school

Practice pronunciation of each of these words. Have students use these words to compare the education systems of their origin countries with American and Syrian education systems.
SUBSTANTIAL

CRITICAL VOCABULARY

superficial: Marah made friends at her new school, but they were not close friendships. They were superficial.

ASK STUDENTS if they prefer superficial or close friendships. (*Students may say they prefer close friendships.*)

mandatory: Marah and her family stayed in the new area because they did not have a choice. It was mandatory.

ASK STUDENTS to talk about something mandatory in their lives that they don't like. (*Students may say, for example, that they don't like following the rules at home.*)

My Syrian Diary   **101**

TEACH

EVALUATE AUTHOR'S PURPOSE

Remind students that authors can have more than one **purpose** and that their purpose may be revealed by **word choice** and **syntax** (the way words and sentences are arranged) and what the writer is asking the reader to do or think. Word choice and syntax may also be chosen to have a specific effect on readers. Have students look for sentences in which Marah is addressing the reader to ask a question or make a request. Have them look for the word *you*. (**Answer:** *The writer wants the reader to pay attention and listen to her story and try to do something to help.*)

NOTICE & NOTE

EVALUATE AUTHOR'S PURPOSE

Annotate: In paragraphs 23–25, mark places where the author directly addresses the reader.

Cause/Effect: What effect does the author hope to have on her readers?

"schools." They felt more like ponds full of diseases. My father refused to send us to such dungeons, but my mom insisted that we should go. A new phase of concern started for them, right there. Do we invest time in such schools that don't even have accreditation?

22 Now I am trying to prepare for Syria's standardized high school tests, but I don't know whether I will pass or whether my score will be officially recognized. Will I take the tests in my city or somewhere else? Will my mom agree to let me go? So many questions stop me from focusing on my studies. My mom refuses to send me out to any other neighborhood because she fears checkpoints and the risks that a young lady like me might face. I've come to hate the fact that I am a girl.

23 Can you imagine that my mom, the one who always believed in the importance of education and planted that belief in me, has suddenly changed? Her excuse comes down to one sentence: "I worry for you." I will never understand that fear or accept what she says. My dream had been to enroll in university, choose a major I like and then start my career. Can I still do that? I don't know.

24 What happened? My mom used to push me forward. I want to study. I desire to live. I desire what's beautiful. I miss my teachers and my friends. They have all left the city. I miss seeing the handsome boys gathering in front of my school. When I was little I liked dreaming big, but now my dreams are fading away. My dreams are limited by the checkpoints. Isn't there someone to help my voice be heard?

25 Everyone is busy with the war, and it seems like no one cares. We don't know how this will end or how it will affect us. I want life, but not this troubled and confusing life that I live now. I want to complete my studies. I don't want to be a neglected period on the margin. I do not want to lose my dreams. Help!

May 1, 2014

26 In my city, guys and girls have undergone a radical change. Everything has changed: their opinions, their aspirations, the way they talk, their expressions and even the way they look.

27 Before, we used to have great conversations. We loved music from the West as well as local music, and we would race to listen to the newest albums. We loved movies of all kinds and in all languages, especially the comedies. We were interested in fashion and design.

28 We were attracted to anything that was new. We lived a wonderful life. We made adolescent mistakes.

29 Now we have turned into old women. Our conversations are all about our daily suffering. Our conversations are now about food, electricity, water and firewood. There is no cell phone coverage and no television. We are deprived of our teenage pastimes.

30 Shopping was one of my favorite activities. We used to go window shopping after school. We used to get excited about a colorful purse

102 Unit 1

APPLYING ACADEMIC VOCABULARY

☐ collapse   ☐ displace   ☑ military   ☐ violate   ☑ visual

Write and Discuss Have students turn to a partner to discuss the following questions. Guide students to include the academic vocabulary words *visual* and *military* in their responses. Ask volunteers to share their responses with the class.

- What kinds of **visual** details does Marah use to give the reader a picture of how her world has change since the start of the war?
- What has happened to **military** boys that causes Marah distress?

or shiny shoes. Now we get that excited about a rare treat, a dessert—even just fruit. Can you believe it?! We never expected this to happen!

31   Even the boys have changed. We used to see them around school, carrying flowers and wrapped presents, wearing their nicest clothes. Their eyes were filled with love, happiness and hope. But now, the street around the school is empty because all the guys are out fighting on the front lines. When we happen to see them, they usually have shaggy hair and dusty shoes, carrying rifles instead of roses. If you look at their faces, all you see is worry and frustration. Because of our horrible reality, they have lost their hope for the future.

32   We have been deprived of fully living this period of our lives. Everything has turned upside down. Everyone is depressed. Sometimes we laugh and cry at the same moment. How did this damned war do this to us?

33   I feel sorry for myself and for all my fellow Syrian youth. I hope that the current situation changes so that our souls and dreams might awaken. I'm afraid we will regret living this period without our rites of passage, not living youth as it is meant to be lived. Will the war impact us for the rest of our lives? How will we make up for what we've lost? Everything is unknown.

NOTICE & NOTE

LANGUAGE CONVENTIONS
Annotate: Mark examples of informal writing in paragraphs 30–33.

Interpret: Why do you think Marah uses an informal writing style?

CHECK YOUR UNDERSTANDING

Answer these questions before moving on to the **Analyze the Text** section on the following page.

1   Which of the following is true?
   A   Marah's mother loses faith in education as a result of the war.
   B   Marah resents the war because it has forced her to grow up quickly.
   C   Marah's life improves after her father moves the family back to their old neighborhood.
   D   Marah hates being a girl because girls cannot fight in the war.

2   Which question best expresses Marah's uncertainty about the future?
   F   Why were our childhoods stolen?
   G   Isn't there someone to help my voice be heard?
   H   How did this damned war do this to us?
   J   How will we make up for what we've lost?

3   Why does Marah's mother say, *I worry for you*?
   A   She knows that the quality of Marah's education is suffering.
   B   She wishes that Marah could have a normal teenage life.
   C   She is concerned about Marah's physical safety in the city.
   D   She is afraid that Marah will give up her hopes and dreams.

My Syrian Diary   103

ENGLISH LEARNER SUPPORT

Oral Assessment

1. How has the war changed life for Marah and her friends? *(They can't enjoy the fun things they did before and can't have the normal experiences of growing up. They are always worried and serious now.)*

2. What does Marah think about the future? *(She doesn't know what will happen.)*

3. Why is Marah's mother worried about her? *(She is worried that Marah will not be safe.)*

TEACH

LANGUAGE CONVENTIONS

Remind students that the way we use language changes according to the situation. Writers may use either formal or informal language, or a mixture of both. Point out that Marah often uses informal language. Ask students to look for examples in paragraphs 30–33 for language they would not expect to see in a formal letter or academic essay. Ask students what effect Marah's use of informal language has on the reader and how the text might be different if she used only formal language. (**Answer:** *Marah uses an informal writing style because she is trying to connect to the reader on a personal level.*)

■ English Learner Support

Distinguish Formal and Informal Language   Point out to students instances of informal language in paragraphs 30–33. Explain that this is language normally used in personal communications or casual conversation.

- Provide students with sentences in which the informal language is rewritten to be formal. For example, this damned war (this awful war) or all the guys (the young men). Have them work in pairs to match the informal language sentence to a revision.   **MODERATE**

- Ask students to explain why this language is informal and how they might rewrite it to be formal.   **LIGHT**

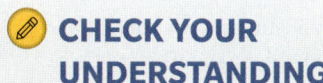

CHECK YOUR UNDERSTANDING

Have students answer the questions independently.

Answers:

1. *B*
2. *J*
3. *C*

If they answer any questions incorrectly, have them reread the text to confirm their understanding. Then they may proceed to ANALYZE THE TEXT on page 104.

My Syrian Diary   103

APPLY

ANALYZE THE TEXT
Possible answers:

1. **DOK 4:** Life in Syrian cities before the war was full of modern conveniences such as electricity, household appliances, and personal electronic devices. Like the author did before the war, I also take these things for granted. I would probably feel lost without them and angry that the war took them away.

2. **DOK 2:** Marah's parents used to be very concerned with her education. Now they are more concerned with keeping their family safe. She may now fight with her parents where she did not before.

3. **DOK 3:** Marah describes women as conversing about the hardships of everyday life and being concerned with household tasks. Her male classmates are now fighting in the war and are angry and serious. If Marah was a boy she would most likely be fighting in the war.

4. **DOK 4:** Marah may have chosen not to discuss politics because it could put her and her family in danger if someone identified her as the writer. Marah is not writing to convince her readers not to support in the war but to inform people about the universal horror of war.

5. **DOK 4:** Marah uses contrast heavily throughout the diary. She discusses almost every topic, including education, food and the activities of everyday life, and her social life, in terms of how much the war has changed everything. This use of contrast helps structure the diary while also engaging the reader's emotions. It moves readers to think about the full impact of war and how they might feel and react if they faced similar drastic changes in their own lives.

RESEARCH

Help students locate a few mainstream news sources and support them in evaluating whether a source is credible. If students find sources that seem to give very different information about the same events, ask them to evaluate the reasons different publications might have for construing events differently or even for giving false information.

Extend Guide students to understand how large, powerful countries participate in and have an interest in conflicts in smaller, less-powerful countries. Give examples of other similar conflicts such as the Vietnam War and Korean War.

104   Unit 1

RESPOND

ANALYZE THE TEXT
Support your responses with evidence from the text. NOTEBOOK

1. **Connect** Review paragraph 11. How was life in Syria before the war similar to or different from your own life? If your own life changed like the author's life did, how do you think you would feel and react?

2. **Infer** How did the priorities of Marah's parents change as a result of the war? How might Marah's relationships with her parents have been affected by these changes?

3. **Evaluate** Review paragraphs 4–8. What organizational pattern or text structure does Marah use in this part of the diary? Is this text structure used effectively to achieve the author's purpose? Why or why not?

4. **Analyze** Marah is living in the middle of a civil war, but she does not discuss politics or take a side in her diary entries. Why might she have chosen to omit political references? What does this decision tell you about her purpose for writing?

5. **Notice & Note** Marah begins her diary by giving contrasting descriptions of her city before and after the start of the war. How is contrast used throughout the rest of the diary? What does Marah achieve through the use of contrast?

RESEARCH TIP
When you research current or recent events, you are likely to find large quantities of information provided by news media. Evaluate news sources critically and remember to check the publication date. Ask yourself: Is this a well-known and credible news source? Is the information presented obviously biased? Is this the most up-to-date information, or is it possible that other important developments have occurred since it was published?

RESEARCH
The Syrian civil war grew out of a wider movement of pro-democracy protests known as the Arab Spring that affected many countries in North Africa and the Middle East. Conduct research to explore the outcomes of the Arab Spring protests in countries other than Syria.

COUNTRY	KEY RESULTS OF ARAB SPRING MOVEMENT

Extend The Arab Spring protests and revolutions were covered heavily in the news and drew significant international attention. Explain why other nations were so interested in the events and outcomes of the Arab Spring. What does their interest tell you about the nature of international politics?

104   Unit 1

WHEN STUDENTS STRUGGLE . . .

Reteaching: Evaluate Author's Purpose Remind students that part of understanding an author's purpose is thinking about whom the intended audience is and what the author wants from them. For example, authors may wish to change the reader's opinion, evoke an emotional reaction, or convince the reader to act. Ask students to look back at the text and think about who Marah expects to read this text and what she wants them to think or do. Then, look for how she tries to get that reaction.

For additional support, go to the **Reading Studio** and assign the following **Level Up tutorial: Author's Purpose.**

RESPOND

CREATE AND DISCUSS

Write a Compare-and-Contrast Essay Write a three- or four-paragraph essay in which you compare and contrast *My Syrian Diary* with another diary you have read. If you have not read another diary, select another nonfiction personal narrative. Consider reviewing your notes and annotations in the text before you begin.

- Introduce the topic of your essay by giving a brief summary or background of *My Syrian Diary* and the other diary.
- Then, explain similarities and differences between the two diaries. Include details about the author's purpose(s) and the diaries' main messages to support your ideas.
- In your final paragraph, state your conclusion about the two diaries.

Share and Discuss Connections In a small group, discuss your conclusions about the diaries you analyzed. Consider how writing in the diary form affects the way authors achieve their purposes, convey their messages, and reach their audiences.

- Review the author's purpose(s) for writing and the message of *My Syrian Diary*.
- Discuss the other diaries that group members chose to compare. Make sure all group members have time to briefly describe the other diaries they chose and the main conclusions they reached in their analyses.
- Finally, end your discussion by identifying conclusions that group members had in common and summarizing the group's findings.

Go to **Writing Informative Texts** in the **Writing Studio** for help with organizing ideas.

Go to **Participating in Collaborative Discussions** in the **Speaking and Listening Studio** for help with group discussion.

RESPOND TO THE ESSENTIAL QUESTION

What happens when a society unravels?

Gather Information Review your annotations and notes on *My Syrian Diary*. Then add relevant details to your Response Log. As you decide which information to include, think about:

- how the writer contrasts past and present
- which parts of society the writer chooses to describe
- the way the writer uses small details to provide evidence for a broader message

ACADEMIC VOCABULARY

As you write and discuss what you learned about *My Syrian Diary*, be sure to use the Academic Vocabulary words. Check off each of the words that you use.

- ❏ collapse
- ❏ displace
- ❏ military
- ❏ violate
- ❏ visual

APPLY

CREATE AND DISCUSS

Write a Compare-and-Contrast Essay Tell students they will be writing an essay using another diary or personal narrative they have read, and discussing the similarities and differences between that diary or narrative and this one. They can write about something they have read for school, a published book, an online diary, or even a v-log. Encourage them to think about the subject, audience, and purpose of the other text. Their conclusions should include what they have learned about the purpose and effects of the two texts by comparing them.

For **writing support** for students at varying proficiency levels, see the **Text X-Ray** on page 96D.

Share and Discuss Connections Remind students to listen to and think about the ideas of everyone in their group and to ask questions if they don't understand something. Encourage students to discuss their own ideas with the goal of generating new ideas as a group.

RESPOND TO THE ESSENTIAL QUESTION

Allow time for students to add details from *My Syrian Diary* to their Unit 1 Response Logs.

APPLY

CRITICAL VOCABULARY

Answers:

1. sustenance; Children rely on their parents for sustenance.
2. superficial; The issue is complex and my understanding is superficial.
3. exorbitant; I don't go to concerts because the ticket prices are exorbitant.
4. extract; It can be hard to extract information from some people.
5. mandatory; Uniforms are mandatory at our school.
6. deprivation; I'm grateful that my family has never really experienced deprivation.

VOCABULARY STRATEGY:
Latin Roots

Answers:

Row 1: ex-, orbit, -ant; the condition of being off-track; beyond what is reasonable or customary

Row 2: deprivation; The state of being deprived; the state of lacking the basic necessities or comforts of life

Row 3: super-, -ial/characterized by being above; apparent rather than actual or substantial, shallow

Row 4: mandatory; characterized by a mandate; required or commanded by authority

---

RESPOND

WORD BANK
extract
sustenance
exorbitant
deprivation
superficial
mandatory

Go to the **Vocabulary Studio** for more on Latin roots.

CRITICAL VOCABULARY

Practice and Apply Determine which vocabulary word best relates to each group of words. Then write a sentence using each vocabulary word.

1. food, comfort, life
2. surface, shallow, insubstantial
3. unreasonable, expensive, high
4. remove, tug, pry
5. required, important, necessary
6. needy, without, underprivileged

VOCABULARY STRATEGY:
Latin Roots

While the English language includes words and word parts that come from many different languages, one of the root languages you will encounter most often in English is Latin. Knowing the meanings of common Latin prefixes, roots, and suffixes can help you determine the definitions of unfamiliar words.

For example, consider the word *extract*. The word *extract* can be broken down into two main parts, the prefix *ex-* and the root *tract*. Both come from Latin. *Ex-* means "out of" or "away from." *Tract* means "to draw" or "pull." When they are put together, you get the word *extract*, which means "to draw or pull out."

Practice and Apply Examine the list of Latin word parts provided below. Use the list to fill out the chart. Then discuss with a partner how the combined definition you get from using word parts is related to the dictionary definition.

super-: above or on top of
orbit: path or track
-ant: action or condition
-ation: condition or state
-ial: related to or characterized by
-ory: related to or characterized by

WORD	PREFIXES, ROOTS, AND SUFFIXES	COMBINED DEFINITION	DICTIONARY DEFINITION
exorbitant			
	deprive, -ation		
superficial			
	mandate, -ory		

ENGLISH LEARNER SUPPORT

Latin Roots Explain to students that the Latin roots and affixes that make up many English words often have cognates with Spanish and other Romance languages (French, Portuguese, and Italian) because of their shared origins in Latin. Students can look for these cognates to help them recognize and decode words in English. For example, the prefix *ex-*, meaning "out of" or "away from," is related to the Spanish word *exito*, which means "to exit." Have students identify the Latin roots in the cognates *extract/extraer* and *superficial/superficial*.

RESPOND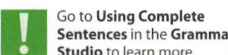

LANGUAGE CONVENTIONS:
Formal and Informal Language

Writing that uses **formal language,** also known as Standard English, follows all of the accepted rules of grammar and punctuation of the English language. Formal language is usually appropriate for academic or professional writing. Essays, news reports, and textbooks are examples of texts that tend to use formal language. Many—but not all—formal writing pieces are written from a third-person perspective.

Writing that uses **informal language** may not always follow language rules and has a more relaxed and conversational tone. Local expressions, slang words, contractions, and sentence fragments that most people use in everyday speech are common in informal writing. Because informal language includes so many elements of spoken English, it is common for pieces written from the first-person perspective to use informal language. Many types of narratives, such as novels, diaries, and personal narratives, use informal language. Informal language is also commonly used for such written communication between individuals as letters and personal (nonprofessional) emails and text messages.

This sentence from *My Syrian Diary* uses informal language:

> In my city, guys and girls have undergone a radical change.

Marah writes the sentence the way she would say it if she were having a conversation. She uses the slang term "guys" to refer to her male peers.

If Marah had used more formal language to write her diary, the sentence might look like this:

> In my city, the young men and women have undergone a radical change.

If the information had been included in an official report instead of a personal diary, it might sound even more formal:

> Young Syrian men and women have undergone radical changes as a result of the ongoing war.

Practice and Apply Select a paragraph or paragraphs from *My Syrian Diary* in which Marah describes her city or an event that took place in her city using informal language. Rewrite the passage using Standard English in the formal style of a news report.

Go to **Using Complete Sentences** in the **Grammar Studio** to learn more.

APPLY

LANGUAGE CONVENTIONS:
Formal and Informal Language

Help students understand the difference between formal and informal language by generating examples of when a writer might want to use each. Generate a list of types of texts and writing situations and have students rank them from most formal to least formal. For example:

1. application letter for a school or job
2. email to a school official
3. office memo
4. note from a teacher to a parent
5. personal blog
6. text message to a friend

Students may not agree on the order of the list. Have them give their reasons for why something should be more formal or informal.

Practice and Apply Have students work in pairs or groups to identify a paragraph from *My Syrian Diary* where the writer uses language that sounds casual and conversational. Explain to them that they will keep the same information but change the language so it fits a news report. Explain that the report will use only the third person rather than *I, we*, and *you*. Provide students with a model news report to follow.

 ENGLISH LEARNER SUPPORT

Language Conventions Select a paragraph from *My Syrian Diary* in which the writer uses informal language. Use the following supports with students at varying proficiency levels:

- Point out the informal language, such as word choice and use of pronouns *I* and *you*. Provide students with formal vocabulary to match the informal word choice and have them rewrite first- and second-person sentences to third person. **SUBSTANTIAL**

- Have students identify words that are informal and the use of first and second person. Then, have students change the informal words to formal ones and rewrite first- and second-person sentences to third person. **MODERATE**

- Have students compare the chosen paragraph to one from a news report. Ask them to explain what is different and to mark the informal language in the chosen paragraph. **LIGHT**

APPLY

COMPARE PRIMARY SOURCES

Remind students what the term **primary source** means and review examples of primary sources, who they might be written by, and who the audience and purpose might be. Ask students to explain what the purpose of a personal letter might be and what the purpose of an online diary might be. Review the contexts that *The Paston Letters* and *My Syrian Diary* were written in and discuss how the contexts, audience, and content are similar.

ANALYZE THE TEXTS

Possible answers:

1. **DOK 3:** Although the Paston letters were produced in 15th century England and Marah's diary was produced in modern-day Syria, both texts were produced by individuals living in violent times of conflict.

2. **DOK 4:** The authors of the Paston letters were writing to family members and did not expect their letters to be published. However, they knew their letters could be intercepted and read by their enemies. Therefore, they left out key details they wanted to disclose only in person. Marah wrote My Syrian Diary knowing that it would be published online, so she left out personal details and focused more on informing her audience about the effects of war.

3. **DOK 4:** Because the purpose of the Pastons' writing was direct communication with family, letters were the most effective form. Marah's purpose was to inform readers outside of her world about the conditions and ongoing events in Syria. The use of a published diary enabled her to do this.

4. **DOK 4:** The authors of the Paston letters could not have used a more effective writing style. In the 15th century, their options for communication would have been limited, and letter writing was one of the most important ways information was transmitted. The author of My Syrian Diary could have chosen several other writing structures. She could have chosen to tell her story in letters, in a memoir or autobiography, or even in a fictionalized account of her own life. Any of these structures could have accomplished her purpose, but they likely would not have been more effective.

108   Unit 1

 **RESPOND**

Collaborate & Compare

COMPARE PRIMARY SOURCES

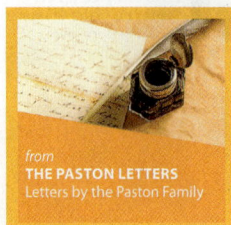

from
THE PASTON LETTERS
Letters by the Paston Family

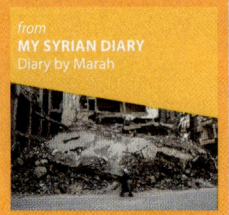

from
MY SYRIAN DIARY
Diary by Marah

Both *The Paston Letters* and *My Syrian Diary* are primary sources that provide firsthand accounts of the authors' experiences. However, they were not written for the same reason. An **author's purpose** is his or her reason for writing. The author may or may not state the purpose directly, depending on the type of document or writing style. If the author does not state his or her purpose, then you must infer it based on details in the text.

As you review the primary sources for hints about the author's purpose, consider the following:

- **Context:** Where, when, and under what circumstances was the text produced?
- **Audience:** Who did the author intend for his or her readers to be?
- **Content:** What main ideas, themes, and messages does the author convey?

In a small group, complete the chart with details from both primary sources.

	THE PASTON LETTERS	MY SYRIAN DIARY
Context		
Audience		
Content		

ANALYZE THE TEXTS

Discuss these questions in your group.

1. **Compare** With your group, review the contexts you cited in your chart. In what ways are the contexts of the sources similar? In what ways are they different?

2. **Analyze** The two sources have very different audiences. Discuss how the audience of each source affects the type of content the author included. Cite textual evidence in your discussion.

3. **Evaluate** The authors of the sources address their audiences using text structures that are related but not identical: letters and diary entries. Discuss the effectiveness of the authors' choices. Is one structure more effective than the other? Explain your reasoning.

4. **Critique** Could either the authors of *The Paston Letters* or the author of *My Syrian Diary* have used a different or more effective writing structure to convey their content and accomplish their purpose? Explain why or why not.

108   Unit 1

 ENGLISH LEARNER SUPPORT

Confirm Understanding Use the following questions to help students compare the two primary sources.

1. Who do the Pastons want to read their letters? Who does Marah want to read her diary?

2. What do the Pastons and Marah tell their readers about?

3. What reactions do the Pastons and Marah want from their readers?

RESPOND

COLLABORATE AND PRESENT

Now your group can continue exploring the ideas in these texts by identifying and comparing the authors' purpose. Follow these steps:

1. **Decide on the most important details** With your group, review your chart to identify the details that tell you the most about the authors' purposes.

2. **Determine the authors' purposes** Determine the author's purpose for each primary source. Remember, an author may have multiple reasons for writing. Those reasons may all contribute to one unified purpose, or the author may have multiple purposes. As a group, create at least one statement of purpose for each source.

3. **Compare Author's Purpose** With your group, discuss whether the authors' purposes are similar or different, and the reasons why these similarities and/or differences might exist or not exist. Use a chart to keep track of the ideas your group generates.

	SIMILAR	DIFFERENT
How?		
Why?		

4. **Present to the Class** As a group, prepare a presentation of your ideas. Be sure to include clear statements of the author's purpose for each source and discuss how the context, audience, and content evidence support your conclusions. You may choose to use charts or other visuals to present your ideas to the class.

Go to **Participating in Collaborative Discussions** in the **Speaking and Listening Studio** for more help.

Collaborate & Compare 109

APPLY

COLLABORATE AND PRESENT

Explain the importance of sharing ideas, asking questions, and listening politely during a group discussion.

1. **Decide on the Most Important Details** Direct students to look at their notes and mark the details they recorded that they think are the most important clues to the author's purpose.

2. **Determine the Authors' Purposes** Direct students to formulate sentences that specifically answer the question of why the writers created the texts and what responses from the readers they had in mind when writing. Remind students that authors may have more than one purpose for writing.

3. **Compare Author's Purpose** Have students contribute all of their ideas to completing the chart. Remind them to think about what is similar and what is different about the writers' circumstances.

4. **Present to the Class** Remind students when they prepare their presentations to think about their audience, to make sure they include all the necessary information, and to present their points clearly.

WHEN STUDENTS STRUGGLE...

Participate in Group Discussions Students may find it difficult to form their thoughts and share with the group. Before the discussion, have them write answers to questions to use in the discussion: *Who wrote it? Who did he or she want to read it? What does the writer want readers to know, feel, or do?* Provide sentence frames to help students convey their ideas. For example: (*The writer*) wrote (*the text*) to (*intended reader*) because he/she needed him/her to _____.

 For additional support, go to the **Reading Studio** and assign the following **Level Up tutorial: Taking Notes and Outlining**.

Collaborate & Compare 109

PLAN

THE WANDERER
Poem by Anonymous

LONELINESS
Poem by Fanny Howe

GENRE ELEMENTS
LYRIC POEM
Remind students that a **lyric poem** is different from a narrative poem because it doesn't focus on traditional story elements like character, setting, and plot. Lyric poems tend to have a musical quality, like the words or lyrics in a song. In this lesson, students will analyze and compare the tones of two poems and how authors use imagery to create tone.

LEARNING OBJECTIVES
- Analyze tone.
- Conduct research about grief.
- Create an imagery board.
- Discuss poetry.
- **Language** Respond to poet's word choice and use of imagery to create tone.

TEXT COMPLEXITY

	The Wanderer/Loneliness	Lexile: NA
Quantitative Measures		
Qualitative Measures	**Ideas Presented** Multiple levels, use of symbolism. Greater demand for inference.	
	Structures Used More complex, lyrical and poetic.	
	Language Used Implied meanings, allusive, figurative, and formal language. Complex sentence structures.	
	Knowledge Required Mostly familiar themes. Historical references may make heavier demands.	

PLAN

Online

RESOURCES

- Unit 1 Response Log
- 🔊 Selection Audio
- Close Read Screencasts: Modeled Discussions
- 📖 Reading Studio: Notice & Note
- 💬 Speaking and Listening Studio: Participating in Collaborative Discussions
- ✅ "The Wanderer" and "Loneliness" Selection Test

SUMMARIES

English

In "The Wanderer," the speaker wanders alone in the cold, remembering past days of serving his lord and feasting with friends. But now that he has lost his lord and friends, he thinks about why he must suffer such hardships and what it means to be alive when there is so much uncertainty. In "Loneliness," the speaker compares loneliness to an uninvited companion who accompanies you wherever you go, even when you are among other people.

Spanish

En "El trotamundos", la voz narrativa deambula sola en el frío, recordando los días en que servía a su señor y tenía banquetes con sus amigos. Pero ahora que perdió a su señor y a sus amigos piensa sobre por qué debe sufrir tales dificultades y qué significa estar vivo entre tantas incertidumbres. En "Soledad", la voz narrativa compara la soledad con un compañero no invitado quien te acompaña a todas partes, incluso cuando estás alrededor de otra gente.

SMALL-GROUP OPTIONS

Have students work in small groups to read and discuss the selections.

Activating Academic Vocabulary

- Provide a list of academic vocabulary words and phrases, such as: *speaker*, *personification*, *tone*, *word choice*, *imagery*, *detail*, *convey*, *lyrical*, *compare*, and *stanza*.
- After reading 10 lines, model how to use one or more academic vocabulary words and phrases to discuss the poems.
- Encourage students to use the academic vocabulary as they discuss and write about the poems.

Send a Problem

- Have students use a notebook for recording their double entry notes.
- Show students how to create a two-column format by drawing a line from top to bottom on each page. The left head is *Quotes from the Poem* and the right head is *My Notes*.
- Encourage students to copy important or confusing verses or stanzas in the left column.
- Students then write their own questions, restatements, or interpretations in the right column next to the quoted material.

The Wanderer / Loneliness **110B**

PLAN

 **Text X-Ray: English Learner Support**
for "The Wanderer" and "Loneliness"

Use the Text X-Ray and the supports and scaffolds in the Teacher's Edition to help guide students at different proficiency levels through the selections.

INTRODUCE THE SELECTION
DISCUSS SOUND DEVICES AND PERSONIFICATION

In this lesson, students will need to be able to discuss how poets use sound devices and personification to create specific emotional responses.

Provide the following explanations:
- Sound devices are used to convey and reinforce meaning through skillful use of sound.
- Personification is the representation of an abstract quality or idea as a human.

Guide students to examples of sound devices and personification as they discuss the tone of each poem.

Provide sentence frames, such as: *One example of a sound device in the poem _____ is _____. The use of this sound device creates a _____ tone because _____. The author of the poem _____ has used personification because _____. The personification of _____ is effective because _____.*

CULTURAL REFERENCES

The following words or phrases may be unfamiliar to students:
- *drunk* (Wanderer, line 8): experienced
- *find your grace in God* (Wanderer, lines 112 and 113): to trust that God will bring you favor
- *character flaws* (Loneliness, line 13): limitations or imperfections in one's personality

LISTENING

Analyze Word Choice and Imagery

Review with students that poets spend a lot of time choosing the right words and creating specific images to achieve the desired tone. As students listen to the poems, have them focus on how words sound and on the pictures that form in their minds.

Use the following supports with students at varying proficiency levels:
- Have students listen as you reread lines 1–5 of "The Wanderer." Write the quote *"frost-cold foam he cuts in the sea, sailing endlessly, aimlessly, in exile"* on the board. Provide language support as needed and ask students to sketch an image and label it with the quote. Then, have students say words that describe the sketches, such as *cold, dark, lonely, sad*. Write students' responses on the board. **SUBSTANTIAL**
- Have students listen as you reread lines 1–5 of "The Wanderer." Write the quote *"frost-cold foam he cuts in the sea, sailing endlessly, aimlessly, in exile"* on the board. Ask students to sketch an image and label it with the quote. Then, have students respond to the text and images with simple sentences. Provide sentence frames: *The image makes me feel _____. The tone of this image is _____. The words "frost-cold foam" make me feel _____.* **MODERATE**
- Have one student read lines 1–5 of "The Wanderer" to a partner. Then have partners discuss the word choices and imagery. Guide them to ask questions, such as: *What did you see in your mind when you heard the phrase "frost-cold foam he cuts in the sea"?* **LIGHT**

110C Unit 1

PLAN

SPEAKING

Compare and Contrast

Review that comparing and contrasting theme and styles of poetry can help us see how life has changed and stayed the same over time.

Use the following supports with students at varying proficiency levels:

- Provide sentence frames to help students compare and contrast the two poems. For example: "The Wanderer" and "Loneliness" are both poems about ____. "The Wanderer" is written in a ____ style, but "Loneliness" is written in ____ style. **SUBSTANTIAL**
- Help partners generate a word bank of academic terms associated with comparison and contrast, such as: similarity, difference, in contrast, both, but, however, also, as well as, the same as. Direct partners to use the word bank as they discuss how the two poems are similar and different. **MODERATE**
- Have partners use the word bank from the Intermediate activity to discuss the theme and style of each poem. Have them use this information to share ideas about how people's lives and feelings have changed and stayed the same over time. **LIGHT**

READING

Use Punctuation

Remind students that lines of poetry are written differently than lines of prose. Review that students need to pay close attention to the punctuation of a poem in order to understand when an idea begins and ends.

Use the following supports with students of varying proficiency levels:

- Help small groups reread lines 1–5 of "The Wanderer" ending with the word "exile." Point out the punctuation marks and ask questions. For example: *Should I pause or stop at the comma after "grace" in line 1? (pause) Is the first line one sentence or does the sentence continue to the next line? (continues to the next line) What punctuation mark shows the end of the first idea in the poem? (semi-colon)* **SUBSTANTIAL**
- Have pairs work together to discuss how to use the punctuation to understand the first 15 lines of *The Wanderer*. Guide them to use sentence frames, such as: *The comma in line 1 tells me that ____. The semi-colon lets me know that ____.* **MODERATE**
- Have partners discuss how to use the punctuation to understand the main ideas of "The Wanderer." Guide them to use specific examples of how different punctuation is used in the poem. **LIGHT**

WRITING

Use Sound Devices

Remind students that alliteration is a sound device in which the sounds of initial consonants in words are the same. Review that poets use alliteration to create a certain tone and mood.

Use the following supports with students of varying proficiency levels:

- Provide a selection of images and have students choose one. Help students name a noun they see in the image. Then provide lists of adjectives that begin with the same initial consonant. Help students put adjectives and nouns together in a descriptive alliterative phrase about the image. **SUBSTANTIAL**
- Provide a selection of images and have students choose one. Have students name a noun they see in the image. Then have them write a short phrase using alliteration to describe it. **MODERATE**
- Have students choose an image and write several phrases or sentences using alliteration to describe it. **LIGHT**

TEACH

 Connect to the
ESSENTIAL QUESTION

Both poems revolve around the idea of fate in daily life. Point out that people are sometimes referred to as being naturally lucky or unlucky. Each poem attempts to answer if we control our own fate.

COMPARE THEMES

The theme in both poems centers around loneliness. Ask students to share their ideas of loneliness. Then, tell students to think about the theme of each poem and be ready to compare them.

COLLABORATE & COMPARE

POEM
THE WANDERER
by **Anonymous**
translated by **Burton Raffel**
pages 113–117

COMPARE THEMES

As you read, notice the key details and memorable images that express each poem's theme or message about loneliness. Then think about how the themes relate to each other. After you read both poems, you will collaborate with a small group on a final project.

 ESSENTIAL QUESTION:

Can we control our fate?

POEM
LONELINESS
by **Fanny Howe**
pages 118–121

QUICK START

How do you cope when you feel lonely? On the chart below, write two or three things that you can depend on to get you through an emotional slump. Explain how these things help you.

WHAT HELPS	HOW IT HELPS
talking to my mom	My mom can calm me down and (sometimes) give me good advice.
playing video games	Video games help me pass the time and make me feel like I'm in control
hanging with my friends	My friends can keep me company and make me laugh.

ANALYZE TONE

Tone is the attitude that the writer shows toward his subject or audience. You can detect the poet's attitude just as you would interpret the attitude of someone speaking to you. The tone of a poem does not necessarily stay the same throughout the work—the author can change it at any time. You can describe the poet's tone using any adjectives that accurately convey attitude.

Some elements in a poem that help identify tone are:
- imagery
- sound devices
- the poet's word choices
- the speaker's feelings or thoughts

Mark up the selection with notes about tone or use a chart like this one:

	"THE WANDERER"	"LONELINESS"
Imagery	"frost-cold foam" and "frozen waves" help develop a gloomy tone.	
Sound devices		
Word choices		
Speaker's feelings and thoughts		

As you analyze "The Wanderer" and "Loneliness," think about how the authors use the elements of lyric poetry to convey tone in their works.

GET READY

GENRE ELEMENTS: LYRIC POEM
- expresses strong feelings or thoughts
- has a musical quality
- deals with intense emotions surrounding events like death, love, or loss
- includes such forms as ode, elegy, and sonnet

TEACH

QUICK START

Have students share with a partner a time when they felt lonely. What did they do to deal with their feelings of loneliness? Which actions helped them feel better? Then, ask students to read the Quick Start, fill in the chart, and share with their partner.

ANALYZE TONE

Have students read the definition of **tone** and help them understand it is important to recognize a poet's tone to better understand the ideas and message the poet is sharing. Review the elements in a poem that help reveal the tone. Explain that **imagery** refers to the words and phrases that create vivid sensory experiences for the reader. **Sound devices** include **alliteration, assonance, consonance, meter, repetition, rhyme, rhyme scheme,** and **rhythm.** Sound devices can be used to emphasize ideas and experiences. Explain that poets carefully choose their words to express their ideas and to appeal to the readers' emotions or senses. Words can have negative or positive **connotations,** so it's important to pay attention to the words a poet chooses. Refer students to the list of elements of **lyric poetry.** As students read both "The Wanderer" and "Loneliness," have them look for elements of lyric poetry, such as words that evoke emotion or those that have rhythm or a musical quality.

TEACH

MONITOR COMPREHENSION

Explain the importance of pausing to monitor comprehension. Review the techniques and strategies. Demonstrate for students how to create pictures in your mind based on the poet's **word choice.** Read these lines from "The Wanderer" aloud:

> Weep nor sigh nor listen to the sickness
> In their souls. So I, lost and homeless,
> Forced to flee the darkness that fell
> On the earth and my lord.

Point out words that help you visualize the wanderer (*lost, homeless, flee the darkness*). Invite students to share what they visualize.

■ English Learner Support

Paraphrase Text Read lines 1–11 of "The Wanderer" aloud and model how to paraphrase the text in simpler language. Explain that the grief-stricken speaker sails about aimlessly, mourning the loss of his dead friends. Then, have students work with partners to read lines 12–20 aloud and practice restating the text in their own words. Ask partners to give each other feedback: How well did the student restate the text in a simpler way with the same meaning?
MODERATE

ANNOTATION MODEL

Explain that one way to annotate a model to find imagery that reveals the tone is to underline important details. Point out that students may follow this suggestion or use their own system for marking up the selection in their write-in text. They may want to color-code their annotations by using highlighters. Their notes in the margin may include questions about ideas that are unclear or themes the poet might be exploring.

112   Unit 1

 **GET READY**

MONITOR COMPREHENSION

Monitoring comprehension involves determining whether you understand what you are reading. If you have difficulty understanding these poems, you can use different techniques to enhance your comprehension. Here are some helpful strategies:

- **Visualize** Read the text aloud and create pictures in your mind based on images in the text.
- **Generate questions** Ask yourself factual questions that can be answered simply and directly from the text (such as *who, what, when, where, why,* or *how*), as well as questions whose answers require gathering information from different parts of the text to make inferences or evaluations.
- **Reread confusing passages** Slow your pace as you read confusing passages a second time. You might also try reading the passages aloud if you won't disturb those around you. If there are words you don't understand, use a dictionary to find synonyms that may fit.
- **Annotate** Mark sections of the text that are meaningful and make notes in the margins in your own words.
- **Paraphrase** Restate the text in your own words. Simplify the text and be sure to maintain the order and meaning of the original.

ANNOTATION MODEL

 NOTICE & NOTE

As you read, identify the author's tone and note whether it changes from passage to passage or stays consistent throughout the work. Use the techniques discussed to monitor your comprehension of the poetry. In the model, you can see one reader's notes about lines 1–11 of "The Wanderer."

> This lonely traveler longs for grace,
> for the mercy of God; grief hangs on
> His heart and follows the frost-cold foam
> He cuts in the sea, sailing endlessly,
> Aimlessly, in exile. Fate has opened
> A single port: memory. He sees
> His kinsmen slaughtered again, and cries:
>   "I've drunk too many lonely dawns,
> Grey with mourning. Once there were men
> To whom my heart could hurry, hot
> With open longing. They're long since dead.

The alliteration emphasizes words that express a grim attitude.

I am picturing a ship adrift in a frozen sea: what a sad image!

112   Unit 1

BACKGROUND

"The Wanderer" is an Old English poem found in The Exeter Book, the largest manuscript collection of Old English poetry that has survived. Before being transcribed sometime in the tenth century, the poem was probably passed down orally. Nothing is known about the poem's author. Like other poems in The Exeter Book, "The Wanderer" reflects the hardship and uncertainty of life in Anglo-Saxon times. Most of the poem is spoken by an Anglo-Saxon warrior who wanders as an exile after losing his lord and companions in battle.

THE WANDERER

Poem by Anonymous
translated by Burton Raffel

PREPARE TO COMPARE

As you read, think about how the speaker is feeling and how the tone is conveyed by the sound devices used. Try to understand and verbalize the main ideas in the poem.

    This lonely traveler longs for grace,
For the mercy of God; grief hangs on
His heart and follows the frost-cold foam
He cuts in the sea, sailing endlessly,
5 Aimlessly, in exile. Fate has opened
A single port: memory. He sees
His kinsmen slaughtered again, and cries:
    "I've drunk too many lonely dawns,
Grey with mourning. Once there were men
10 To whom my heart could hurry, hot
With open longing. They're long since dead.
My heart has closed on itself, quietly
Learning that silence is noble and sorrow
Nothing that speech can cure. Sadness

NOTICE & NOTE

Notice & Note

Use the side margins to notice and note signposts in the text.

ANALYZE TONE

Annotate: Mark words that give clues about the speaker's feelings in lines 8–14.

Analyze: What do the author's word choices make you think about?

The Wanderer / Loneliness 113

TEACH

BACKGROUND

After reading the Background, tell students that Old English poetry is characterized by specific themes and features. The themes often center around battles and heroes, often taking the form of an epic poem. Explain to students that this poem is an **elegy**—a poem in which the speaker mourns for someone (such as a friend or spouse) or something (such as a way of life) that has passed away.

PREPARE TO COMPARE

Direct students to use the Prepare to Compare prompt to focus their reading.

✏️ ANALYZE TONE

Remind students that poets choose their words carefully to reveal their **tone** and emphasize ideas or emotions. Elicit ideas from the students about how the speaker might be feeling. Ask students to cite lines from the poem that make them think this way. (**Possible answer:** *He chooses words that set a sad and melancholy tone. It makes me wonder if the whole poem will be depressing and sad.*)

🗨️ ENGLISH LEARNER SUPPORT

Understand Text Structure Point out the long passages within quotation marks: lines 8–85 and 90–108. Make sure students understand that these sections (most of the poem) are the words of the wanderer. Elicit or explain that the lines that frame the quoted sections are the words of another speaker—perhaps the poet. **ALL LEVELS**

The Wanderer / Loneliness **113**

TEACH

MONITOR COMPREHENSION

Point out to students that this section of the poem is part of a long quotation, which means it's the wanderer's words. The wanderer is telling the reader what happened. Students can use these words to **infer,** or make an educated guess based on their prior knowledge and details in the text, what has happened. (**Answer:** *His place [home] has been lost, his people [relatives] have been killed, and his lord [leader] has been killed.*)

 **NOTICE & NOTE**

MONITOR COMPREHENSION
Annotate: Mark the phrases in lines 22–28 that answer the question: What has the speaker lost?
Infer: What can you infer has happened to the speaker? What questions do you have about him?

31 telling: counting.

43 thanes (thānz): followers of a lord.

15 Has never driven sadness off;
    Fate blows hardest on a bleeding heart.
    So those who thirst for glory smother
    Secret weakness and longing, neither
    Weep nor sigh nor listen to the sickness
20 In their souls. So I, lost and homeless,
    Forced to flee the darkness that fell
    On the earth and my lord.
                            Leaving everything,
    Weary with winter I wandered out
    On the frozen waves, hoping to find
25 A place, a people, a lord to replace
    My lost ones. No one knew me, now,
    No one offered comfort, allowed
    Me feasting or joy. How cruel a journey
    I've traveled, sharing my bread with sorrow
30 Alone, an exile in every land,
    Could only be told by telling my footsteps.
    For who can hear: "friendless and poor,"
    And know what I've known since the long cheerful nights
    When, young and yearning, with my lord I yet feasted
35 Most welcome of all. That warmth is dead.
    He only knows who needs his lord
    As I do, eager for long-missing aid;
    He only knows who never sleeps
    Without the deepest dreams of longing.
40 Sometimes it seems I see my lord,
    Kiss and embrace him, bend my hands
    And head to his knee, kneeling as though
    He still sat enthroned, ruling his thanes.
    And I open my eyes, embracing the air,
45 And see the brown sea-billows heave,
    See the sea-birds bathe, spreading
    Their white-feathered wings, watch the frost
    And the hail and the snow. And heavy in heart
    I long for my lord, alone and unloved.
50 Sometimes it seems I see my kin
    And greet them gladly, give them welcome,

114   Unit 1

WHEN STUDENTS STRUGGLE...

Visualize Character Help students develop a mental picture of the wanderer's character by having them fill out a graphic organizer, such as a web diagram, with words and phrases that describe the wanderer (i.e., grieving over the past, losses, lonely, unhappy, and emotionally weary). Instruct students to visualize him as if he were a person they know and to infer his traits and feelings from what he says about life.

 For additional support, go to the **Reading Studio** and assign the following **Level Up tutorial: Character Traits.**

114   Unit 1

The best of friends. They fade away,
Swimming soundlessly out of sight,
Leaving nothing.
               How loathsome become
55 The frozen waves to a weary heart.
     In this brief world I cannot wonder
   That my mind is set on melancholy,
   Because I never forget the fate
   Of men, robbed of their riches, suddenly
60 Looted by death—the doom of earth,
   Sent to us all by every rising
   Sun. Wisdom is slow, and comes
   But late. He who has it is patient;
   He cannot be hasty to hate or speak,
65 He must be bold and yet not blind,
   Nor ever too craven, complacent, or covetous,
   Nor ready to gloat before he wins glory.
   The man's a fool who flings his boasts
   Hotly to the heavens, heeding his spleen
70 And not the better boldness of knowledge.
   What knowing man knows not the ghostly,
   Waste-like end of worldly wealth:
   See, already the wreckage is there,
   The wind-swept walls stand far and wide,
75 The storm-beaten blocks besmeared with frost,
   The mead-halls crumbled, the monarchs thrown down
   And stripped of their pleasures. The proudest of warriors
   Now lie by the wall: some of them war
   Destroyed; some the monstrous sea-bird
80 Bore over the ocean; to some the old wolf
   Dealt out death; and for some dejected
   Followers fashioned an earth-cave coffin.
   Thus the Maker of men lays waste
   This earth, crushing our callow mirth.
85 And the work of old giants stands withered and still."

NOTICE & NOTE

MONITOR COMPREHENSION

Annotate: Mark unfamiliar words in lines 62–67 where the actions of a wise person are described. Look up the words in a dictionary.

Paraphrase: Restate lines 62–67 in your own words.

69 spleen: bad temper. The spleen is a body organ that was formerly thought to be the seat of strong emotions.

The Wanderer / Loneliness   115

WHEN STUDENTS STRUGGLE...

Analyze Imagery To model an understanding of imagery, read lines 74–75 from "The Wanderer." Point out to students the sense or senses to which the images appeal and the ideas and feelings the images evoke. Explain that the images appeal to sight, touch, and possibly sound. They evoke the idea of barrenness and feelings of cold, grief, and isolation. Ask students to describe an image that a modern poet might present to capture isolation.

 For additional support, go to the **Reading Studio** and assign the following Level Up tutorial: Imagery.

TEACH

MONITOR COMPREHENSION

Explain that **paraphrasing**, or restating ideas in your own words, is an important tool to ensure comprehension. Encourage students to use a dictionary or thesaurus to replace the unfamiliar words in the text with synonyms. This will assist them in paraphrasing challenging text. (**Possible answer:** *It takes time to become a wise person; you have to wait for it. You can't be quick to judge or speak without thinking. A wise person is brave but he doesn't take unnecessary risks. No, he is not cowardly [definition of "craven"], conceited [definition of "complacent"], or envious of what others possess.*)

EL ENGLISH LEARNER SUPPORT

Acquire Vocabulary Explain to students that this poem was written long ago, and that many of the words will be unfamiliar to modern-day readers. Review the meaning of words to help students understand lines 65–85:

- *craven* (line 66): cowardly
- *complacent* (line 66): satisfied with the current situation
- *covetous* (line 66): feeling, expressing, or characterized by a strong or immoderate desire for the possessions of another
- *flings* (line 68): calls out
- *heeding* (line 69): listening to or considering
- *besmeared* (line 75): smeared; spread on a surface
- *dejected* (line 81): being in low spirits; depressed
- *callow* (line 84): immature
- *mirth* (line 84): gladness or merriment
- *withered* (line 85): shriveled, shrunken, or faded

Help students look up the words in the dictionary and find synonyms for each word. Then replace the unfamiliar words with synonyms and reread the lines. Have students work with a partner to summarize the lines. **LIGHT**

The Wanderer / Loneliness   **115**

TEACH

ANALYZE TONE

Explain that **alliteration** was one device used by Old English poets to create a memorable rhythm and musical quality so that storytellers could recite the poem in the oral tradition. Remind students that alliteration is the repetition of consonant sounds at the beginning of words. Then, ask volunteers to describe at least one example of a poem, tongue twister, or chant they know that contains alliteration and note what made it memorable. (**Possible answer:** *The alliteration sounds powerful, almost like a drum beat. It changes the tone from despondent and helpless to uplifting and triumphant.*)

 **NOTICE & NOTE**

He who these ruins rightly sees,
And deeply considers this dark twisted life,
Who sagely remembers the endless slaughters
Of a bloody past, is bound to proclaim:
90   "Where is the war-steed? Where is the warrior?
        Where is his war-lord?
Where now the feasting-places? Where now the mead-hall
    pleasures?
Alas, bright cup! Alas, brave knight!
Alas, you glorious princes! All gone,
Lost in the night, as you never had lived.
95 And all that survives you a serpentine wall,
Wondrously high, worked in strange ways.
Mighty spears have slain these men,
Greedy weapons have framed their fate.
    These rocky slopes are beaten by storms,
100 This earth pinned down by driving snow,
By the horror of winter, smothering warmth
In the shadows of night. And the north angrily
Hurls its hailstorms at our helpless heads.
Everything earthly is evilly born,
105 Firmly clutched by a fickle Fate.
Fortune vanishes, friendship vanishes,
Man is fleeting, woman is fleeting,
And all this earth rolls into emptiness."

    So says the sage in his heart, sitting alone with His
        thought.
110 It's good to guard your faith, nor let your grief come forth
Until it cannot call for help, nor help but heed
The path you've placed before it. It's good to find your grace
In God, the heavenly rock where rests our every hope.

95 serpentine: (sûr´pən-tēn´) winding or twisting, like a snake.

ANALYZE TONE
Annotate: Mark the alliterative words in lines 110–113.

Analyze: How does this phrasing affect the tone of the poem?

116   Unit 1

CHECK YOUR UNDERSTANDING

Answer these questions about "The Wanderer" before moving on to the next selection.

1. The imagery in the poem suggests the setting is —
   A warm and sandy
   B dry and parched
   C cold and wet
   D hot and lush

2. Which of the following images from the poem sets a hopeful tone?
   F *No one knew me, now, / No one offered comfort,*
   G *It's good to find your grace/ In God, the heavenly rock*
   H *Weary with winter I wandered out/ On the frozen waves,*
   J *Alas, you glorious princes! All gone,/ Lost in the night,*

3. One important theme in this poem is —
   A sea journeys cause grief
   B you can't gain wisdom unless you suffer
   C the wise course is to avoid war
   D grief isolates people emotionally

The Wanderer / Loneliness 117

TEACH

CHECK YOUR UNDERSTANDING

Have students answer the questions independently.

Answers:
1. C
2. G
3. D

If they answer any questions incorrectly, have them reread the text to confirm their understanding. Then they may proceed to the next selection.

ENGLISH LEARNER SUPPORT

Oral Assessment Use the following questions to assess students' comprehension and speaking skills.

1. What is the setting of the poem? *(a cold and wet place)*
2. Which line sets a hopeful tone? *(It's good to find your grace / In God, the heavenly rock)*
3. What theme does the author reveal about grief in the poem? *(The idea that grief can be isolating and make one feel alone.)* **SUBSTANTIAL**

The Wanderer / Loneliness 117

TEACH

BACKGROUND

Have students read the Background about author Fanny Howe, and discuss how they think her upbringing might influence her work. Then, read this Fanny Howe quote to the students:

> "I was an arrested adolescent. I still have in me a person who likes telling stories for young readers. . . . Teenagers can say directly what they think of the world, without metaphor or tactics of concealment. This is very liberating as a tool for resistance."

Discuss the meaning of her words and whether students believe it to be true or not. Ask students to share an example of when this has been true in their lives.

PREPARE TO COMPARE

Direct students to use the Prepare to Compare prompt to focus their reading.

MONITOR COMPREHENSION

Discuss why poets might use **personification**. Have students share with a partner an instance of personification in everyday life. For example: The breeze whispers to me. (**Answer:** *Loneliness does the following things: slips in beside you; takes your hand and walks with you; lies down with you; sits beside you; swims with you; swings around on stools; boards the ferry; leans on the motel desk.*)

NOTICE & NOTE

BACKGROUND

Fanny Howe (1940–) *grew up in Cambridge, Massachusetts, part of an artistic and intellectual family. As a girl, she was very close to her father, who taught at Harvard Law School; his influence can be seen in her political and social activism. Howe is an award-winning author of more than 20 books of poetry, fiction, essays, and children's literature. Her poetry is known for its formal experimentation and exploration of religious ideas. Howe has taught literature and fiction writing at various institutions, including Tufts University, Yale University, and the Lannan Center for Poetics and Social Practice at Georgetown University. She now lives back in Cambridge.*

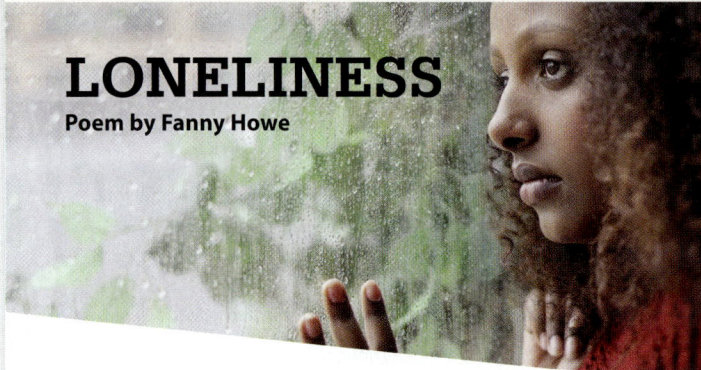

LONELINESS
Poem by Fanny Howe

Notice & Note
Use the side margins to notice and note signposts in the text.

PREPARE TO COMPARE

As you read, look for details that show the author's tone and how this poem approaches the subject of loneliness.

MONITOR COMPREHENSION
Annotate: Personification is the attribution of human qualities to an object, animal, or idea. Mark words and phrases in lines 1–11 that exemplify personification.

Analyze: What are some of the comparisons the author makes?

Loneliness is not an accident or a choice.
It's an uninvited and uncreated companion.
It slips in beside you when you are not aware that a
choice you are making will have consequences.
5   It does you no good even though it's like one of the
elements in the world that you cannot exist without.
It takes your hand and walks with you. It lies down
with you. It sits beside you. It's as dark as a shadow
but it has substance that is familiar.
10 It swims with you and swings around on stools.
It boards the ferry and leans on the motel desk.

Nothing great happens as a result of loneliness.
Your character flaws remain in place. You still stop in
with friends and have wonderful hours among them,
15 but you must run as soon as you hear it calling.

118   Unit 1

WHEN STUDENTS STRUGGLE . . .

Identify Author's Purpose Remind students that authors have a purpose, or a reason for writing. Work with students to generate a list of words and phrases from the poem they believe causes the reader to think, feel, or act a certain way. Next to each word or phrase, have students describe the intended result.

Then, have students answer these questions about the text: *What does the poet want the reader to know, think, feel, or do? What words or phrases help reflect the purpose?*

 For additional support, go to the **Reading Studio** and assign the following **Level Up tutorial: Author's Purpose.**

It does call. And you climb the stairs obediently,
pushing aside books and notes to let it know that you
have returned to it, all is well.
If you don't answer its call, you sense that it will sink
20 towards a deep gravity and adopt a limp.

From loneliness you learn very little. It pulls you
back, it pulls you down.

It's the manifestation of a vow never made but kept:
I will go home now and forever in solitude.

25 And after that loneliness will accompany you to
every airport, train station, bus depot, café, cinema,
and onto airplanes and into cars, strange rooms and
offices, classrooms and libraries, and it will hang near
your hand like a habit.
30 But it isn't a habit and no one can see it.

NOTICE & NOTE

ANALYZE TONE
Annotate: Mark words in lines 21-24 that help set the poem's tone.
Analyze: Is the speaker hopeful about ending her loneliness? Explain.

TEACH

ANALYZE TONE

Remind students that a poet's word choice helps reveal his or her **tone,** or attitude toward the subject. Have students look for descriptive words and phrases that indicate the author's feelings or attitude about loneliness. (**Answer:** *The author is not hopeful about ending her loneliness. She believes she will be "forever in solitude." Key words and phrases help set the tone as being down or melancholy, such as "pulls you down." The phrase "a vow never made but kept" speaks to the inevitability of loneliness—that it arrives and stays without ever having been invited; a promise never made because no one expects to feel lonely.*)

ENGLISH LEARNER SUPPORT

Understand Idioms Explain the figurative meaning of the phrase in line 22, "pulls you down" by first having students demonstrate its literal meaning. Then, have them read the phrase in context. What is the author trying to express to the reader about loneliness? (*Answer: Loneliness makes you feel sad, low, down rather than up or happy.*) **SUBSTANTIAL**

TEACH

✏️ MONITOR COMPREHENSION

Discuss the meanings of *loneliness* and *shame*. (*Loneliness* is not having anybody in one's life and feeling isolated, and *shame* is feeling unworthy of affection.) How do these relate to one another? Why does the author say that they're almost one?

(**Sample answer:** *A person may feel ashamed about being lonely, and shame may inhibit someone from making friendships; these connections help explain the statement that "shame and loneliness are almost one."*)

 **NOTICE & NOTE**

MONITOR COMPREHENSION

Annotate: Reread lines 38–46. Mark any ideas or details that you find confusing.

Draw Conclusions: What connections do you see between loneliness and shame? How do these connections help you understand this passage?

It's your obligation, and your companion warms itself against you.
You are faithful to it because it was the only vow you made finally, when it was unnecessary.

35 If you figured out why you chose it, years later, would you ask it to go?
How would you replace it?

No, saying good-bye would be too embarrassing.
Why?
40 First you might cry.
Because shame and loneliness are almost one.
Shame at existing in the first place. Shame at being visible, taking up space, breathing some of the sky, sleeping in a whole bed, asking for a share.

45 Loneliness feels so much like shame, it always seems to need a little more time on its own.

 ENGLISH LEARNER SUPPORT

Use Contextual Support Read lines 40–46 aloud. Invite students to ask for clarification of any words that are unfamiliar. Then, have students underline the word *shame,* and help students understand that the poet repeats this word to emphasize her feelings. Work with students to find context clues that help students understand the meaning of *shame*. Then confirm with a dictionary definition. **MODERATE**

NOTICE & NOTE

CHECK YOUR UNDERSTANDING

Answer these questions about "Loneliness" before moving on to the **Analyze the Text** section on the following page.

1. The words *You will stop in / with friends and have wonderful hours among them* emphasizes that —
   A you don't have to be alone to be lonely
   B loneliness can be a good friend
   C if you have friends, you won't be lonely
   D you can spend quality time alone

2. In "Loneliness," the feeling named in the title is likened to a —
   F habit
   G choice
   H accident
   J companion

3. The speaker feels like loneliness is —
   A unavoidable in life
   B something to be ashamed of
   C a result of the decisions we make
   D an inherited emotional disability

The Wanderer / Loneliness 121

TEACH

CHECK YOUR UNDERSTANDING

Have students answer the questions independently.

Answers:

1. A
2. J
3. C

If they answer any questions incorrectly, have them reread the text to confirm their understanding. Then they may proceed to ANALYZE THE TEXT on page 122.

 ENGLISH LEARNER SUPPORT

Oral Assessment Use the following questions to assess students' comprehension and speaking skills.

1. What does the speaker mean when she says *You will stop in / with friends and have wonderful hours among them / but you must run as soon as you hear it calling?* (Loneliness is always with you even if you are not alone.)

2. What is the feeling of loneliness compared to? (Loneliness is compared to a companion.)

3. Why does the speaker believe loneliness stays with us? (The speaker believes we make decisions that keep loneliness around.) **MODERATE**

The Wanderer / Loneliness **121**

APPLY

ANALYZE THE TEXT
Possible answers:

1. **DOK 4:** *Anglo-Saxon groups were not welcoming to outsiders, and a person would suffer without protection from a lord. Possible questions: How were Anglo-Saxon groups organized? How did a warrior become a lord?].*

2. **DOK 4:** *The family and the lord were killed in some type of battle. The author uses the phrases "endless slaughters" and "bloody past," but also speaks directly of war-steeds (horses), warriors (soldiers) and war-lord (commander or ruler), now all gone, lost in the night. After the defeat, he had no home or family to return to and so set out on his sea journey.*

3. **DOK 2:** *By this point, the author's tone has changed to one of anger. He is angry at the horrors of war, portraying the weapons as greedy (unable to be satisfied), and railing against nature, which seemed to conspire against him by smothering warmth and angrily hurls its hailstorms at our helpless heads.*

4. **DOK 2:** *Resigned, dutiful, accepting. She uses the words obligation, faithful, and vow, which make me think of marriage vows, and how many people remain in situations because they feel they have no other options: How would you replace it?*

5. **DOK 4:** *I visualize a weight that is sinking and dragging me under with it, pulling against gravity. I interpret these lines to mean that loneliness can, at best, hold you back from doing positive things and, at worst, be debilitating.*

RESEARCH

To help students generate strategies, have them review what they already know about coping with grief. Encourage them to speculate or make guesses to confirm with their research.

Extend If students do not have access to a family physician or if the physician does not have literature on grief or loss, they may conduct an interview with a friend or family member who has experienced grief and record anecdotes to find out what others found to be helpful coping strategies.

 **RESPOND**

ANALYZE THE TEXTS
Support your responses with evidence from the text. 📓 **NOTEBOOK**

1. **Infer** What can you infer about Anglo-Saxon society from reading lines 22–39 of "The Wanderer"? What questions do you have about the Anglo-Saxons?

2. **Interpret** Reread lines 86–94 of "The Wanderer." How did the speaker incur his loss and become a lonely wanderer?

3. **Analyze** Reread lines 97–103 of "The Wanderer." How does the use of personification help develop the tone in this part of the poem?

4. **Analyze** Reread lines 31–37 of "Loneliness." What is the author's tone in this passage, and how do her word choices convey this tone?

5. **Interpret** Reread lines 19–22 of "Loneliness." How do you visualize and interpret these lines?

RESEARCH TIP
It is especially important to use verifiable and reliable sources when researching online for help with sensitive issues. For guidance on mental and emotional health issues, sources with the extensions .org and .edu are preferable.

RESEARCH
People can feel emotionally isolated for many reasons, including major illness or the loss of a loved one. Do an online search to complete the chart below. Look for details about practical ways to help cope with sadness and maintain a measure of control over one's own fate. Expand the chart if you find other helpful measures in your research.

WHAT CAN YOU DO ABOUT GRIEF?	HOW DOES THIS APPROACH HELP?
Start a grief support group.	*Teens share their feelings and find out they are not alone when they are struggling with big problems. Even if their lives are shattered, they have the support of others whose lives are also shattered and are trying to rebuild them.*
Express your feelings in writing or artwork.	*Some teens find it hard to open up and talk. This is one way they can express their feelings so they can be acknowledged and dealt with.*
Seek professional help.	*Some teens need more, especially if you notice: dramatic behavior changes; isolation; depression; extreme anger; guilt; substance abuse; promiscuity*

Extend Your family physician or health-care professional is a good resource for information about dealing with loss and grief. You may be able to visit his or her office and request brochures on this and related subjects.

WHEN STUDENTS STRUGGLE . . .

Reteaching: Analyze Tone Have individuals or partners use a chart to compare the way the tone is established in "The Wanderer" and "Loneliness." Students should look for words or phrases that help them understand the tone and how the speakers feel.

	The Wanderer	Loneliness
Tone		

 For additional support, go to the **Reading Studio** and assign the following 📖 **Level Up tutorial: Tone**.

RESPOND

CREATE AND DISCUSS

Create an Imagery Board With a group, create an imagery board to explore your interpretation of key passages in the poems.

- With the group, choose three passages from the poems that can be visualized and make a statement about a main idea of the poem.
- Create a collage from magazine clippings, photos, or your own drawings to represent each passage.
- Display your collages on a poster board. Under each collage, add the text of the passage it represents.
- Explain to the class how the images you chose help illustrate the tone of the passages you selected.

Discuss the Poems Have a group discussion on how thoughts and feelings are expressed in medieval literature and in contemporary literature.

- Think about the differences and similarities in the authors' situations that affect how each presents his or her views.
- Share your ideas with the group. Support your ideas with details from the poems.
- As a group, draw a conclusion on how each writer feels about loneliness.

RESPOND TO THE ESSENTIAL QUESTION

 Can we control our fate?

Gather Information Review your annotations and notes on "The Wanderer" and "Loneliness." Then add relevant details to your Response Log. As you decide which information to include, think about:

- whether being lonely is an unavoidable part of life
- the effectiveness of literary devices to express the authors' thoughts
- how each speaker responds to his or her loneliness

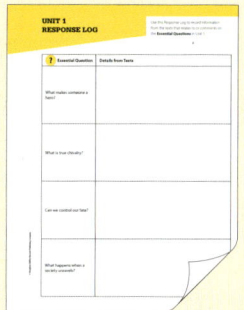

 Go to the **Speaking and Listening Studio** for help with participating in collaborative discussions.

ACADEMIC VOCABULARY
As you write and discuss what you learned from the poems, be sure to use the Academic Vocabulary words. Check off each of the words that you use.

- collapse
- displace
- military
- violate
- visual

The Wanderer / Loneliness 123

APPLY

CREATE AND DISCUSS

Create an Imagery Board Have students form peer groups to provide feedback on each other's imagery boards before presenting them to the class.

- Students should give concrete, specific ideas for how their peers might improve their imagery boards.
- Groups should review the suggestions and decide which ones to incorporate into their imagery boards.
- Groups may then edit or recreate their imagery boards.

Discuss the Poems Review the thoughts and feelings expressed in "The Wanderer" and "Loneliness." Have students note some differences and share why they think a 20th or 21st century author might express thoughts and feelings differently than a medieval author. Guide students to use the information in both Background sections to help them answer the question.

For **writing support** for students at varying proficiency levels, see the **Text X-Ray** on page 110D.

RESPOND TO THE ESSENTIAL QUESTION

Allow time for students to add details from "The Wanderer" and "Loneliness" to their Unit 1 Response Logs.

TO CHALLENGE STUDENTS . . .

Make Additional Connections Have students choose either "The Wanderer" or "Loneliness" and think of other poems they have read with a similar style or a similar theme. Have students compare the poems based on their similarities and then write an original poem in the same manner. Have students recite their poems before the group.

The Wanderer / Loneliness 123

APPLY

COMPARE THEMES

Discuss with students the elements they will have to examine in order to determine the **theme** in each poem. Remind students that themes are not usually directly stated. They must be inferred based on the details in the text. Key statements, events, and images will help them determine each poem's theme, or message, about loneliness.

ANALYZE THE TEXTS

Possible answers:

1. **DOK 2:** *Each is a picture of what appears to be a never-ending journey. One journey is both physical and emotional. The other journey is purely emotional, because the speaker is surrounded by people every day.*

2. **DOK 2:** *We know the wanderer will eventually come to a land mass and his physical journey will end. The author thinks he will be helped through his emotional pain with the help of a higher power, and so that is a hopeful prospect. The speaker in "Loneliness" has already come to her "land mass" physically, but her pain persists. Both speakers appear to be at different stages of grief, but the speaker in "Loneliness" is not presenting a hopeful outlook for her future. This may indicate the author's relatively modern view on the limited benefit of spirituality.*

3. **DOK 3:** *Writers of old seemed really dramatic even when talking about everyday occurrences. In "The Wanderer" the drama is really heightened when talking about the situation, which is very effective for this kind of story. The effectiveness of writing in modern language comes from the fact that it's more relatable since this is the informal way we are accustomed to speaking and receiving information. It is effective for communicating the modern ideas expressed in the Howe poem, but probably not so much if "The Wanderer" was interpreted to read the way we speak now.*

4. **DOK 2:** *The wanderer could be anyone experiencing a dramatically traumatic situation—think war-torn countries and those affected by natural disasters. But none of us are immune to physically and emotionally disruptive circumstances such as divorce as the speaker in "Loneliness" shows. But loneliness can be a state of mind and, as such, we may very well be able to get control of it.*

RESPOND

Collaborate & Compare

THE WANDERER
Poem by Anonymous

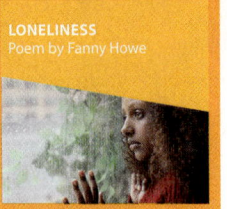

LONELINESS
Poem by Fanny Howe

COMPARE THEMES

Both "The Wanderer" and "Loneliness" express strong thoughts and feelings about loneliness. Even though the poems are about a similar topic, they may express a different theme. A poem's theme is the message about life that it expresses. When you ask yourself, "What significant idea is the poem expressing?" you are asking about the theme.

Often the reader has to infer the theme based on the details presented in the poem. As you review the poems for details that give clues to the theme, consider:

- ❏ **Key statements** made by the speaker or characters
- ❏ **Significant events** that occur in the poem
- ❏ **Memorable images** that describe people or the setting

With your group, complete this chart with details from both poems.

	"THE WANDERER"	"LONELINESS"
Key Statements	"So I, lost and homeless, forced to flee"; physically and emotionally alone	"You will stop in with friends and have wonderful hours" -- emotionally isolated but not physically alone
Significant Events	"He sees his kinsmen slaughtered"; his family is killed by someone else; it is not of his doing	"Loneliness . . . slips in beside you when . . . will have consequences"; the speaker's decision results in loneliness
Memorable Images	"I wandered out on the frozen waves, . . . to replace my lost ones"; desolation and despair, the last man on earth	"Loneliness will accompany you to, . . . classrooms and libraries"; loneliness as a constant presence

ANALYZE THE TEXTS

Discuss these questions in your group.

1. **Compare** With your group, review the images that you cited in your chart. In what ways are the images similar? In what ways are they different? Explain.

2. **Interpret** Both poems describe the way people have dealt with situations that result in loneliness. Discuss each author's view.

3. **Evaluate** "The Wanderer" is translated from Old English; "Loneliness" is a modern-day poem. What do you find effective about each style of writing? What do you find ineffective?

4. **Interpret** What have you learned about loneliness from these poems?

ENGLISH LEARNER SUPPORT

Ask Questions Use the following questions to help students compare the selections.

1. How is the wanderer different from the speaker in "Loneliness"? *(The wanderer is physically alone, but we know his journey will come to an end. The speaker in "Loneliness" is not physically alone, but her pain persists.)*

2. What did the two selections help you understand about loneliness? *(Anyone can be lonely, but we are lonely for different reasons. Some loneliness is physical, while other types of loneliness are internal.)* **MODERATE/LIGHT**

RESPOND

COLLABORATE AND PRESENT

Your group can continue exploring the ideas in these texts by identifying and comparing their themes. Follow these steps:

1. **Decide on the most important details** With your group, review your chart to identify the most important details from each poem. Identify points you agree on and resolve disagreements through discussion based on evidence from the texts.

2. **Create theme statements** Determine a theme statement for each poem. Remember, it is up to you and your group to infer the theme based on details. You can use a chart like the one below to determine the theme each writer expresses.

"THE WANDERER"

DETAIL	DETAIL	DETAIL
He is grieving for his family and friends.	He has lost his home.	He may be looking for relief and comfort from a higher power, though not on this earth.

THEME

Faith and hope may be remedies for loneliness and grief.

"LONELINESS"

DETAIL	DETAIL	DETAIL
She is grieving a loss, perhaps of a marriage.	She has many friends but is still lonely.	She has many mundane things to fill her time but is still lonely.

THEME

Be prepared to pay the price for the life choices we make.

3. **Compare themes** With your group, discuss whether the themes of the poems are similar or different. Listen actively to the members of your group and ask them to clarify any points you do not understand.

4. **Present to the class** Now it is time to present your ideas. Be sure to include clear statements on the theme of each poem. Discuss whether the themes are similar or different. You may adapt the charts or other visuals you created to help convey information to the class.

Go to the **Speaking and Listening Studio** for more on giving a presentation.

Collaborate & Compare 125

APPLY

COLLABORATE AND PRESENT

Explain the importance of sharing ideas, asking questions, and listening politely during a group discussion. Then, direct students to fill out the chart to compare the themes in the two poems.

1. **Decide on the most important details** Direct students to look at their notes and mark the details they think are the most important clues to the author's theme. Remind students to discuss everyone's ideas and then come to a consensus.

2. **Create theme statements** Direct students to formulate complete sentences that specifically express the poet's message about life or human nature. Remind students that the theme of each poem revolves around the idea of loss and loneliness.

3. **Compare themes** Have students contribute all of their ideas to completing the group's chart. Remind them to think about what is similar and what is different about the themes.

4. **Present to the class** Remind students to make sure they include all the necessary information and present their points in a clear and concise way. Review the characteristics of a good presentation, such as eye contact and appropriate volume. Encourage students to create visuals.

WHEN STUDENTS STRUGGLE . . .

Visualize Key Details Explain that visualizing is an important strategy for understanding key ideas in a text and determining the text's theme. Have students use a graphic organizer to visualize what is happening in a text. Have them choose a passage they find difficult and reread it, marking words or phrases they find confusing, and words and phrases that help tell the overall message. Then, tell students to sketch what they visualize. Have pairs consider how their sketches help them better understand the passage.

 For additional support, go to the **Reading Studio** and assign the following **Level Up tutorial: Imagery.**

Collaborate & Compare **125**

INDEPENDENT READING

READER'S CHOICE

Select and Preview Have students review their Unit 1 Response Log and think about what they've already learned about what makes a person a hero. As they choose their Independent Reading selections, encourage them to consider what more they want to know.

NOTICE & NOTE

Explain that some selections may contain multiple signposts; others may contain only one. Moreover, the same type of signpost can occur many times in the same text.

LEARNING MINDSET

Setting Goals Tell students that setting goals is an important part of a learning mindset. Encourage students to set a goal for reading self-selected texts outside class; for example, reading for a set time or number of pages per day. Consider setting up a class progress report for students to track their goals.

INDEPENDENT READING

Reader's Choice

Select and Preview Select one or more of these options from your eBook to continue your exploration of the Essential Questions.
- Read the descriptions to see which text grabs your interest.
- Think about which genres you enjoy reading.

Notice Note

In this unit, you practiced noticing and noting the signposts and asking big questions about nonfiction. As you read independently, these signposts and others will aid your understanding. Below are the key questions to ask when you read literature and nonfiction.

ESSENTIAL QUESTIONS Review the four Essential Questions for this unit on page 1.

Reading Literature: Stories, Poems, and Plays	
Signpost	Key Question
Contrasts and Contradictions	Why did the character act that way?
Aha Moment	How might this change things?
Tough Questions	What does this make me wonder about?
Words of the Wiser	What's the lesson for the character?
Again and Again	Why might the author keep bringing this up?
Memory Moment	Why is this memory important?

Reading Nonfiction: Essays, Articles, and Arguments	
Signpost	Key Question(s)
Big Questions	What surprised me? What did the author think I already knew? What challenged, changed, or confirmed what I already knew?
Contrasts and Contradictions	What is the difference, and why does it matter?
Extreme or Absolute Language	Why did the author use this language?
Numbers and Stats	Why did the author use these numbers or amounts?
Quoted Words	Why was this person quoted or cited, and what did this add?
Word Gaps	Do I know this word from someplace else? Does it seem like technical talk for this topic? Do clues in the sentence help me understand the word?

ENGLISH LEARNER SUPPORT

Develop Fluency Select a passage from the text that matches students' reading abilities. Read the passage aloud while students follow silently.

- Read the passage aloud, then have students read it back in unison. **SUBSTANTIAL**
- Have students read the passage silently multiple times. Ask students to time their reading each time to track their improvement. Then, ask students simple questions and use Think Alouds to provide answers, to help students understand the process, and how to phrase answers. **MODERATE**
- Have students read the passage silently for a set time (for example, 30 minutes) and then identify a word or phrase in the passage that they think best summarizes the main thought. Next, have students work in groups of four for a 4-to-1 routine in which they share their ideas and decide on a word or phrase that summarizes the main thought. Then, have the groups report to the class and explain their choices. **LIGHT**

INDEPENDENT READING

You can preview these texts in Unit 1 of your eBook.
Then, check off the text or texts that you select to read on your own.

☐
EPIC POEM
from **Beowulf**
translated by Burton Raffel

Beowulf faces one last challenging enemy—a fiery dragon that threatens the safety of his people.

☐
ARTICLE
Beowulf Is Back!
James Parker

Can a medieval poem have value in the modern age? Examine Beowulf's timeless appeal to the imagination.

☐
BALLAD
Barbara Allen
Anonymous

A young man lies dying and calls for the woman he loves. She comes—but cannot forgive him.

☐
ARTICLE
Journeymen Keep the Medieval Past Alive
Melissa Eddy

Young adults continue a medieval tradition of hitting the road to gain valuable on-the-job work experience.

Collaborate and Share With a partner, discuss what you learned from at least one of your independent readings.

- Give a brief synopsis or summary of the text.
- Describe any signposts that you noticed in the text and explain what they revealed to you.
- Describe what you most enjoyed or found most challenging about the text. Give specific examples.
- Decide if you would recommend the text to others. Why or why not?

Go to the **Reading Studio** for more resources on **Notice & Note**.

INDEPENDENT READING

MATCHING STUDENTS TO TEXTS

Use the following information to guide students in choosing their texts.

from **Beowulf**
 Genre: epic poem
 Overall Rating: Challenging

Beowulf Is Back   Lexile: 1200L
 Genre: article
 Overall Rating: Challenging

Barbara Allen
 Genre: ballad
 Overall Rating: Challenging

Journeymen Keep the Medieval Past Alive   Lexile: 1220L
 Genre: article
 Overall Rating: Challenging

Collaborate and Share To assess how well students read the selections, walk around the room and listen to their conversations. Encourage students to focus and be specific in their comments.

for Assessment

- Independent Reading Selection Tests

Encourage students to visit the **Reading Studio** to download a handy bookmark of **NOTICE & NOTE** signposts.

WHEN STUDENTS STRUGGLE . . .

Keep a Reading Log As students read their selected texts, have them keep a reading log for each selection to note signposts and their thoughts about them. Use their logs to assess how well they notice and reflect on elements of their texts.

Reading Log for (title)		
Location	Signpost I Noticed	My Notes about it

PLAN

UNIT 1 Tasks

- **WRITE A SHORT STORY**
- **CREATE A PODCAST**

MENTOR TEXT
CHIVALRY
Short Story by Neil Gaiman

LEARNING OBJECTIVES

Writing Task
- Write a short story about a hero.
- Use strategies and graphic organizers to plan a narrative.
- Use the Mentor Text as a model.
- Identify the central conflict.
- Map the rising action, climax, and falling action.
- Decide how setting, characters, conflict, and story events reflect the theme of heroes.
- Use genre characteristics to write a first draft.
- Use a Revision Guide and peer review to revise a draft.
- Edit draft to use active and passive voice correctly.
- Use a rubric to evaluate writing.
- Publish writing to share with an audience.
- **Language** Write with increasing specificity and detail.

Speaking Task
- Adapt a short story as a podcast.
- Choose readers and practice characters; create sound effects.
- Provide and consider advice for improvement.
- **Language** Ask for clarification using the sentence stem: *Why did you _____?*

Assign the Writing Task in *Ed*.

RESOURCES

- Unit 1 Response Log
- Writing Studio: Writing as a Process
- Listening and Speaking Studio: Using Media in a Presentation
- Grammar Studio: Module 8 Lesson 7: Active Voice and Passive Voice

128A Unit 1

PLAN

 # Language X-Ray: English Learner Support

Use the instructions below and the supports and scaffolds in the Teacher's Edition to help you guide students of different proficiency levels.

INTRODUCE THE WRITING TASK

Explain that short stories vary widely in tone. For example, tones can be humorous, frightening, suspenseful, bleak, exciting, or somber. A short story's tone reflects the response authors want readers to have. There are many ways authors can create tone, including word choice, imagery, dialogue, and even punctuation.

Remind students that they must consider their purpose and audience as well as their subject when choosing a tone. Provide a sentence frame to help students articulate their ideas. For example: *My audience will be ____, so a ____ tone is appropriate.*

Brainstorm a list of words and phrases related to audience, purpose, subject, and tone using word webs. Write students' ideas on the board. Then have students use their completed sentence frames and the words from the webs to write a clear statement about the tone of their short story.

WRITING

Analyzing Genre Characteristics

Tell students that one way they can increase specificity and detail in their writing is to pay attention to how authors use genre characteristics.

Use the following supports with students at varying proficiency levels:

- Reread paragraphs 1–4 of *Chivalry*. Explain the meaning of *genre* and *genre characteristics* to students. Then, ask the students questions about genre characteristics in *Chivalry* and help students identify and copy the characteristics they find in the text. **SUBSTANTIAL**
- Work with small groups to develop a list of questions they can ask about genre characteristics. For example: *What details does the author give about Mrs. Whitaker's looks in paragraphs 1–4?* Then have individual students write answers. Accept simple sentences as responses. **MODERATE**
- Provide a list of such genre characteristics as: *description, setting, character, plot, conflict, imagery, tone, word choice*. Have partners write down questions they can ask each other about how Neil Gaiman uses genre characteristics in *Chivalry*. Then have partners write down answers to each other's questions. **LIGHT**

SPEAKING

Asking for Clarification

Provide a sentence frame for students to use as they ask their peers for clarification after a review of each other's scripts. For example: *Why did you ____?*

Use the following supports with students at varying proficiency levels:

- Provide a word bank of terms and phrases students can use as they seek clarification such as: *character, narration, event, setting*. For example: *Why did you include this event? Why did you use narration here?* Have students repeat the questions after you. **SUBSTANTIAL**
- Have partners review each other's scripts, and then write a list of words and phrases they can use when asking for clarification. Have them use their list to ask a few questions about each other's scripts. Provide the sentence frame: *Why did you ____?* **MODERATE**
- Have partners review each other's scripts and then ask for clarification about the characters, narration, setting, conflict, imagery, and resolution. **LIGHT**

Unit 1 Tasks **128B**

WRITING

WRITE A SHORT STORY

Introduce students to the Writing Task by reading the introductory paragraph with them. Remind students to refer to the notes they recorded in the Unit 1 Response Log as they plan and draft their short stories. The Response Log should contain ideas about national heroes from a variety of perspectives, including heroes from the past and the students' own world. Drawing on these different perspectives will make their own writing more interesting and well informed.

 For **writing support** for students at varying proficiency levels, see the **Language X-Ray** on page 128B.

USE THE MENTOR TEXT

Students should use the mentor text, the short story "Chivalry," as a model. Point out that while their stories may be similar in style, topic, or length to the mentor story, they will write an original story using their own ideas about a hero from the past or their own world.

WRITING PROMPT

Review the prompt with students. Encourage them to ask questions about any part of the assignment that is unclear. Make sure they understand that the purpose of their task is to answer the question by writing a short story about a hero from the past or their own world.

 **WRITING TASK**

Write a Short Story

 Go to the **Writing Studio** for help writing narratives.

This unit focuses on literature from the Anglo-Saxon and medieval periods, when England began to develop as a nation. Many works of these periods portrayed national heroes such as Beowulf and King Arthur. For this writing task, you will write a short story about a hero from the past or from your own world. For an example of well-written fiction, you can review, and use as a mentor text, the short story "Chivalry" by Neil Gaiman.

As you write your short story, you can use the notes from your Response Log, which you filled out after reading texts in this unit.

Writing Prompt

Read the information in the box below.

This is the topic or context for your short story.

> Heroes have appeared in literary works throughout history, though ideas about heroes have changed over time.

How might this Essential Question be reflected in a short story?

Think carefully about the following question.

> What makes someone a hero?

Now mark the word or words that suggest what kind of short story you will write.

Write a short story about a hero from the past or in your own world.

Be sure to—

Review these points as you write and again when you finish. Make any needed changes.

- ❑ introduce a setting and main character and establish a clear point of view
- ❑ engage readers by presenting a conflict, situation, or observation that sets the short story in motion
- ❑ develop a plot with a clear and logical sequence of events
- ❑ use a variety of narrative techniques to develop characters, plot, theme, and suspense
- ❑ reveal a significant theme related to the Essential Question
- ❑ conclude by resolving the conflict or by conveying your reflection on the experiences described in the short story

128 Unit 1

 LEARNING MINDSET

Belonging Remind students that they are all valuable members of the class and should support one another as learners. Encourage students to ask for help from a friend or teacher if they need ideas or are struggling with the planning or drafting of their stories.

1 Plan

Before you start writing, you need to plan your short story. When you plan a draft, you often start by selecting a genre that is appropriate for a particular topic, purpose, and audience. For this writing task, you already know that the topic is related to heroes, and you know that the genre will be a short story. Next, you should consider your purpose and audience. Also, it can be helpful to use a range of strategies as part of your planning process. These might include discussing the topic with your classmates, reading about heroes from the past, or thinking about people you've met whom you consider to be heroes.

Short Story Planning Table	
Genre	Short Story
Topic	What makes someone a hero?
Purpose	To entertain readers and to lead them to consider the nature of a true hero
Audience	Classmates; online readers who enjoy stories of adventure and heroism
Ideas from discussion with classmates	Find examples of heroic acts from history; check the news for recent stories of heroism; consider films like the movie "Sully"— heroic airplane pilot; everyday heroes— firefighters, EMTs, doctors …
Ideas from background reading	Stories from 9/11 terrorist attacks— specific heroic acts; novel, Red Badge of Courage; news story— "Grandmother shielded grandson during church shooting"
Personal interests related to topic	My father heroically kept us calm and got us to safety during a flood

Background Reading Review the notes you have taken in your Response Log that relate to the question, "What makes someone a hero?" Texts in this unit provide background reading that will help you formulate the theme and plot of your story.

WRITING TASK

Go to the **Writing Studio** for help with writing as a process.

Notice & Note
From Reading to Writing

As you plan your short story, apply what you've learned about signposts to your own writing. Remember that writers use common features, called signposts, to help convey their message to readers.

Think about how you can incorporate **Tough Questions** into your short story.

 Go to the **Reading Studio** for more resources on **Notice & Note**.

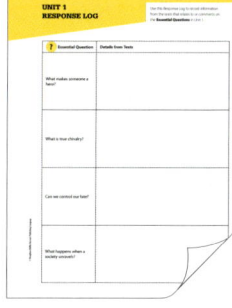

Use the notes from your Response Log as you plan your short story.

Write a Short Story 129

WRITING

1 PLAN

Allow time for students to discuss the topic with partners or in small groups and then to complete the planning table independently.

■ **English Learner Support**

Understand Academic Language Make sure students understand words and phrases used in the table, such as *genre*, *topic*, *purpose*, and *audience*. Use examples as needed. Work with students to fill in the blank sections of the planning table with their own ideas. **SUBSTANTIAL**

NOTICE & NOTE

From Reading to Writing Remind students to incorporate **Tough Questions** into their stories. These questions give their writing purpose and meaning while also making their stories thought-provoking to their readers. Emphasize that Tough Questions should be related to the message of the story.

Background Reading As students plan their stories, remind them to refer to the notes they took in their Response Logs. They may also review the selections to gather ideas for the theme and plot of their stories.

TO CHALLENGE STUDENTS . . .

Comparative Analysis Challenge students to incorporate plot or character elements from a real-life news story about a heroic individual. Students might consider news stories they have read online or in a newspaper or magazine article from the library. They should analyze how the featured person became a hero, what qualities they exhibited, and how others responded to their actions. Encourage students to add notes from the news story to their Response Logs and to think about how they might incorporate details from the news story into their original stories to make their stories more realistic.

Write a Short Story 129

WRITING

Organize Your Ideas Tell students that they should fill the chart completely with details they plan to include in their story. Point out that the story should have a setting, characters, a central conflict, a plot with a climax, and an ending with conflict resolution. The events in the story should also clearly reflect the theme of heroes. Tell students that by thinking about these questions before drafting the story, they can better organize their story and make sure to include all the essential elements.

DEVELOP A DRAFT

Remind students to use the chart as they draft their stories. Point out that they can still make minor adjustments to the elements, such as characters and plot events, as they write their draft. For example, they may decide that a character or a plot event does not support the theme being developed. They can make changes or even remove a character or plot event.

 ENGLISH LEARNER SUPPORT

Narrate Help students begin the writing task by having them work together in pairs to tell their stories orally. Beginning ELLs will need additional language support to complete their narrations. Have students describe each element of their story; then have them write sentences about each element.
SUBSTANTIAL/MODERATE

 **WRITING TASK**

 Go to **Writing Narratives: Narrative Structure** for more help.

Organize Your Ideas After you have gathered ideas from your planning activities, you need to organize them in a way that will help you draft your short story. You can use the chart below to decide on the elements of your story. You can also use the chart to outline the plot of your story.

Story About a Hero	
How does the story begin? What can I do to engage readers and make them want to keep reading?	Story begins with lots of action; crisis during flood. Introduces reader to the main character—older brother
What is the central conflict? Are there any other conflicts related to the central one?	Central conflict: Teenager vs. natural elements— rain/flooding. He's trying to get back home where his younger siblings are home alone in the midst of rising waters. Internal conflict: The young man is dealing with fear of water and drowning.
What is the story's plot? Map out the rising action, climax, and falling action.	Rising action: worsening weather reports; increasing tension between siblings; older brother leaves the house; when he becomes aware of danger he begins to make his way back; several incidents impede his progress each one worse the the one before. Climax: He reaches the house, calms everyone, formulates plan for safety. Falling action: Implements plan for safety.
How do the setting, characters, conflict, and story events reveal a theme about heroes?	Hostile setting, characters with strong ties, external and internal conflict—reveal theme: the ordinary person/anyone can become a hero by making the decision to put the needs of others first.
How does the story end? Is the conflict resolved? How?	Everyone reaches safety (external conflict resolved); the young man has faced his fear in order to save his siblings (internal conflict resolved).

 You might prefer to draft your essay online.

 Develop a Draft

After planning and organizing, you will be ready to begin drafting your short story. Refer to your planning table and your chart of story elements, as well as any notes you took as you studied the texts in this unit. These will provide a kind of map for you to follow as you write. Using a word processor or online writing application makes it easier to revise your first draft.

WHEN STUDENTS STRUGGLE . . .

Draft the Short Story Even with the chart to organize their ideas and story elements, students may struggle to get started on their drafts. Remind students that they don't have to start with the beginning of the story. Encourage them to start by developing a part of the story that they feel most confident about, such as a scene that describes a main event in the story. Once they have this part written, they may feel more confident in taking on the rest of the story. Remind students that they don't have to write everything perfectly in the first draft because they will revise and edit their writing later.

WRITING

Use the Mentor Text

WRITING TASK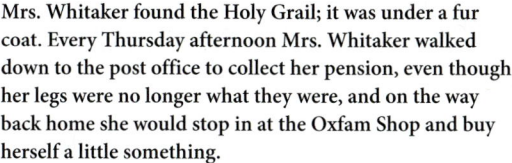

Author's Craft
Your exposition is your first chance to capture the reader's attention. In addition to introducing the main character and the setting, the opening paragraphs should include something that will draw readers into your story. Notice how Neil Gaiman captures the reader's attention in the opening of "Chivalry."

> Mrs. Whitaker found the Holy Grail; it was under a fur coat. Every Thursday afternoon Mrs. Whitaker walked down to the post office to collect her pension, even though her legs were no longer what they were, and on the way back home she would stop in at the Oxfam Shop and buy herself a little something.

The writer starts off with a surprising detail that contrasts with the description of an ordinary setting.

Apply What You've Learned To capture your reader's attention, you might start off with a surprising detail or interesting dialogue.

Genre Characteristics
Sensory details are words, phrases, or sentences that appeal to the reader's senses of sight, hearing, touch, taste, and smell. Notice how the author of "Chivalry" uses sensory details in the following example.

> She moved a rather threadbare fur coat, which smelled badly of mothballs. Underneath it was a walking stick and a water-stained copy of *Romance and Legend of Chivalry* by A. R. Hope Moncrieff, priced at five pence. Next to the book, on its side, was the Holy Grail.

The author provides details that allow you to imagine the smell of the thrift shop and the appearance and position of items that the main character finds there.

Apply What You've Learned The details you include in your own short story should help readers imagine the characters and setting and should draw them into the story. Try to include details that appeal to a variety of senses.

WHY THIS MENTOR TEXT?
"Chivalry" provides a good example of a short story. Use the instruction below to help students use the mentor text as a model for writing an original short story that clearly develops a theme with a conflict and a resolution.

USE THE MENTOR TEXT

Author's Craft Ask a volunteer to read aloud the opening exposition from "Chivalry" (starting from paragraph 1). Discuss how the writer's word choice and specific details capture the reader's attention and draw them into the story. Discuss strategies students might use to come up with an interesting opening exposition for their own stories, such as an experience taken from their lives or one they may have read about.

Genre Characteristics To help students understand how sensory details are used in "Chivalry," have them close their eyes while you read a descriptive passage from the story, such as paragraph 3 or paragraph 10. Tell students to imagine themselves as the character in the scene being described. Have them think about the surroundings of the thrift shop. What else do they imagine they might see, hear, feel, or smell based on the description already given in the story? For example, how would the old fur coat feel when they move it? Discuss how appealing to the senses draws readers into the story and allows them to imagine other details that aren't specifically mentioned.

 ENGLISH LEARNER SUPPORT

Use the Mentor Text Use the following supports with students of varying proficiency levels.

- Read the exposition paragraph aloud. Ask students to list as many specific words and details in the paragraph as they can recall. **SUBSTANTIAL**
- Read the exposition paragraph aloud; invite students to ask about any words or phrases that are unclear. Encourage students to be specific about any details they do not understand. **MODERATE**
- Have students read the exposition paragraph and identify words that make them want to read more. Have them brainstorm how they might use specific words and details in their own stories. **LIGHT**

WRITING

3 REVISE

On Your Own Have students answer each question in the chart to determine how they can use the revision tips and techniques to improve their drafts. Invite volunteers to model their use of revision techniques.

With a Partner Have students ask peer reviewers to evaluate their story by answering the following questions:
- Does my story's beginning capture your attention?
- Is there anything about the sequence of events or the characters in my story that is unclear? Why?
- What questions do you have about my story?

Students should use the reviewer's feedback to make their story's opening more engaging; to clarify events and characters in their story; and to further develop their story's theme.

WRITING TASK

Go to **Writing as a Process: Revising and Editing** for more help.

3 Revise

On Your Own Once you have written your draft, you'll want to go back and look for ways to improve your short story. As you reread and revise, think about whether you have achieved your purpose. The Revision Guide will help you focus on specific elements to make your writing stronger.

Revision Guide

Ask Yourself	Tips	Revision Techniques
1. Does the story have an engaging beginning?	**Mark** the exposition.	**Add** interesting or surprising details about the character or situation.
2. Is there anything confusing about the sequence of events?	**Number** each event in the story.	**Reorder** events if necessary so that they have a logical sequence. **Add** appropriate transitions to clarify the sequence of events.
3. Are the characters fully developed?	**Mark** descriptions of the characters' appearance, thoughts, and actions.	**Add** details that provide insight into the characters' feelings and motivation.
4. Does the dialogue sound natural?	**Mark** important dialogue in the story.	**Add** words and phrases to give each character's dialogue a distinctive style. **Include** contractions and incomplete sentences to make dialogue more informal, or natural.
5. Is the conflict resolved in a logical way?	**Mark** the resolution.	**Add** details to make the resolution more satisfying, and tie up loose ends.

ACADEMIC VOCABULARY

As you conduct your **peer review**, be sure to use these words.

- ☐ collapse
- ☐ displace
- ☐ military
- ☐ violate
- ☐ visual

With a Partner Once you and your partner have worked through the Revision Guide on your own, exchange stories and evaluate each other's draft in a **peer review**. Focus on providing revision suggestions for at least three of the items mentioned in the chart. Explain why you think your partner's draft should be revised and what your specific suggestions are.

When receiving feedback from your partner, listen attentively and ask questions to make sure you fully understand the revision suggestions.

4 Edit

Once you have addressed the plot and other narrative elements in your short story, you can look to improve the finer points of your draft. Edit for proper use of standard English conventions, except in dialogue that you want to be informal. Make sure to correct any misspellings or grammatical errors.

WRITING TASK

> Go to the **Grammar Studio** to learn more about active voice and passive voice.

Language Conventions

Use Active and Passive Voice Appropriately The voice of a verb tells whether its subject performs or receives the action expressed by the verb.

- A verb is in the **active voice** when the subject performs the action.
- A verb is in the **passive voice** when the subject is the receiver of the action.

Usually you should use the active voice to make your writing more concise and direct. However, sometimes you may want to use the passive voice to emphasize the receiver or because the doer of the action is unknown or unimportant. The chart contains examples of active and passive voice from "Chivalry."

Voice	Example
Active Voice	Mrs. Whitaker picked up the dusty silver goblet and appraised it through her thick spectacles.
Passive Voice	The inside of the goblet was thickly coated with a brownish-red dust.

5 Publish

Finalize your short story and choose a way to share it with your audience. Consider these options:

- Read your short story aloud to a small group.
- Publish your story in a zine with other stories by classmates.

Write a Short Story 133

WRITING

4 EDIT

Suggest that students read their drafts aloud to assess how clearly and smoothly their story flows. Have students evaluate whether they have used the active or passive voice appropriately when describing events in their story.

LANGUAGE CONVENTIONS

Use Active and Passive Voice Appropriately Review the information about when it is appropriate to use **active voice** and **passive voice** in a narrative. Then discuss the two sample sentences in the chart, asking students to identify why each example is either active or passive. To show the difference between active and passive voice, change the following sentence to active voice and discuss the difference:

- **Passive voice:** The empty plate was taken from the table by the waiter. (*This sentence is not very concise.*)
- **Active voice:** The waiter took the empty plate from the table. (*This sentence conveys the point in a more direct way.*)

■ English Learner Support

Use Passive Voice Discuss with students how English constructs the passive voice differently from some other languages and requires the verb "to be." Provide sentence stems and frames for students to complete to demonstrate the passive voice, and highlight the use of the verb "to be." (For example: Bicycles <u>are</u> ridden by. . . The letter <u>was</u> written by. . . The game <u>is</u> won by. . .) Then have students create their own sentences using the passive voice.
MODERATE/LIGHT

5 PUBLISH

Students can present their stories as blog posts on a school website. Encourage others to read the stories and write comments about them. The authors can then respond to the comments.

WHEN STUDENTS STRUGGLE . . .

Use the Passive Voice Some students may have difficulty understanding how to use the passive voice appropriately when writing a story. Ask them to identify the subject in the example of passive voice in the chart on this page, and then point out that the subject is the recipient of an action. Remind them that the subject is always the recipient of the action in a sentence in the passive voice. Clarify that while it is generally preferable to use the active voice, sometimes the passive voice should be used to add variety and interest to writing.

Write a Short Story 133

WRITING

USE THE SCORING GUIDE

Allow students time to read the scoring guide and to ask questions about any words, phrases, or concepts that are unclear. Then, have partners exchange the final drafts of their short stories. Ask them to score their partner's story using the scoring guide. Each student should write a paragraph explaining the reasons for the score he or she awarded in each category.

 **WRITING TASK**

Use the scoring guide to evaluate your short story.

Writing Task Scoring Guide: Heroic Short Story

	Organization/Plot Development	Development of Theme	Use of Language Conventions and Dialogue
4	• Exposition captures reader's attention and effectively introduces main character and setting. • Scenes are placed in a logical progression toward a definite climax. • Characters and situations develop clear conflict, which is resolved in the end.	• The story expresses a clear and meaningful theme or message. • Many specific, sensory details are used to add meaning.	• Word choice is appropriate for narration and for character dialogue. • Dialogue helps create strong, vivid characters. • Language elements, such as active and passive voice, are used effectively.
3	• Exposition adequately introduces main character and setting. • Most scenes are placed in a logical progression toward a definite climax. • Characters and situations develop conflict, which is resolved in the end.	• The story expresses a message or theme. • Sufficient, specific sensory details are used to add meaning.	• For the most part, word choice is appropriate for narration and for character dialogue. • Dialogue helps develop characters. • Language elements, such as active and passive voice, are used adequately.
2	• Exposition attempts to introduce main character and setting. • Scenes lack order; weak climax. • Minimal conflict development; no clear resolution.	• Theme is present but poorly developed. • Attempt to use some sensory details is made, but details are general or scarce.	• Basic awareness of proper word choice is clear, but choices often seem awkward or confusing. • Dialogue seems unnatural and not specific to each character. • Weak style and use of language; too many passive voice verbs.
1	• Weak exposition fails to grab reader's attention; main character and setting not adequately introduced. • Scenes are out of order; no definite climax observed. • Little or no obvious conflict.	• Confusing or contradictory themes, or no theme is evident. • Poor use of details.	• Weak word choice. • Minimal dialogue and character development. • Language conventions seem to be ignored.

Creating a Podcast

SPEAKING AND LISTENING TASK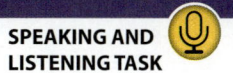

Now that you've written a short story, why not share it with others who enjoy reading tales of heroic adventure? Transform your short story into a podcast—a digital audio file that others can download from the web and listen to.

Go to the **Listening and Speaking Studio** for help using media in a presentation.

A strong podcast…

- contains sound features such as voice-over narration.
- conveys a distinctive tone and point of view.
- appeals to a specific audience.

❶ Adapt Your Story to Create a Podcast

You will need to first format your story into a script to record your podcast.

Planning the Podcast

You will need to adapt your short story to make it easy for a listening audience to understand. One way is to consider turning your story into a dramatic reading, similar to a radio drama or reader's theater. Follow these suggestions to transform your story into an effective podcast.

- ❏ **Decide on the Details** Review your story and identify the characters' dialogue and the essential narration. Think about how strategic use of digital media can enhance your ideas.
- ❏ **Craft Your Script** Your script should indicate the exact words that your story's narrator and characters will say in a recorded audio track. Start by writing your voice-over narration and the dialogue between the characters. Describe which words can be expressed by the characters' manner of speaking rather than with words. For example, the narrator would not need to tell the audience that a character sighed; the audience will hear the sigh in the character's voice. Similarly, omit unnecessary words of attribution, such as *he said* or *she exclaimed*. Then, using the table below, describe the music and sound effects that will match your voice-over narration and dialogue to help convey the tone.
- ❏ **Choose Your Readers** Gather friends and classmates who will read the various characters in your script, and help create various sound effects.

Voice-over narration and dialogue	Music and sound effects
Harold trudged through the mud, the pouring rain drenching his clothes. He didn't care. All he could think about was getting back to the house where the children were.	*Dramatic background music; sounds of pouring rain*

Creating a Podcast 135

SPEAKING AND LISTENING

CREATING A PODCAST

Introduce students to the Speaking and Listening Task by discussing how hearing someone tell a story is different from reading the same story. Point out that people read at different rates, and a reader can also stop and reread a passage to better understand it. Have students consider ways in which a speaker can share a story so that listeners can follow and enjoy it. Remind students that the intonation and emphasis they use as they relate events can make the story more interesting and engaging.

❶ ADAPT YOUR STORY TO CREATE A PODCAST

Have students read the bulleted suggestions about transforming their stories into effective podcasts. Then, discuss with the class some ways to implement these suggestions. For example, discuss how the description of a setting or scene in a story could be given by a narrator in the script. Highlight the importance of choosing readers who will sound like the characters they are portraying. Point out that well-chosen music and sound effects can be used to enhance the story without overshadowing it.

 For **speaking support** for students of varying proficiency levels, see the **Language X-Ray** on page 128B.

🅔🅛 ENGLISH LEARNER SUPPORT

Adapt the Podcast Use the following supports with students of varying proficiency levels:

- Have students identify such key elements in their story as characters, setting, and plot events. Then, help them write sentences that incorporate these elements into narration and dialogue. **SUBSTANTIAL**
- Have students work in small groups to retell their stories, using narration and dialogue and focusing on key elements of the plot. **MODERATE**
- Have students pair with a partner to discuss how best to adapt their stories into a script with dialogue. Then, have the students prepare their podcasts independently. **LIGHT**

Creating a Podcast **135**

SPEAKING AND LISTENING

② CREATE AND UPLOAD YOUR PODCAST

Review the tips with the class, ensuring that all the terms and ideas are clear. Suggest that students practice their podcast before recording it to allow them to gain useful feedback from their peers. Emphasize that speaking before a group makes most people feel nervous, so everyone should be as supportive and helpful as possible.

SPEAKING AND LISTENING TASK

As you work to develop and improve your podcast, be sure to work with your classmates respectfully:

- ❏ listen closely to each other's ideas
- ❏ don't interrupt
- ❏ cooperate as you practice reading your scripts
- ❏ offer helpful suggestions to each other for better dramatic presentation

② Create and Upload Your Podcast

Use sound, dialogue, and narration to share your short story and to appeal to your specific audience.

- ❏ **Produce the Segment** Using podcasting software, record your short story. (Check with your school's media specialist to make sure you have the equipment you need.) With your script as a guide, record your narration and dialogue. Experiment with sounds to present your story clearly and effectively.
- ❏ **Respect Copyright** Use only audio elements for which you have permission. To add music to your track, you can search the Internet for royalty-free audio clips, or you can make your own.
- ❏ **Use Your Voice** The narrator and characters should speak slowly and enunciate words so the audience can understand the events as they unfold. All readers should use intonation in their voices to add emotion and appropriate volume in order to maintain the proper tone.
- ❏ **Add an Extra Voice** Add depth to your podcast by asking a classmate to introduce your story. Or ask someone to lend a brief commentary at the end of your story.
- ❏ **Edit Your Work** Did you make a mistake in your recording? Do you need to include more audio elements to appeal to your audience? Add the finishing touches to your track.
- ❏ **Upload the Final Product** With access to a free podcasting subscription service, you can share your short story with a worldwide audience! Consult available resources for ideas, tips, and additional help, such as knowledgeable peers or a computer or audio/visual teacher. Listen carefully to any instructions you get that will help you produce an engaging podcast and solve potential problems. Then, create and post your podcast for your audience.

WHEN STUDENTS STRUGGLE . . .

Use Intonation If students seem to have difficulty understanding how to add emotion to their reading for the podcast, guide them in deciding where to add intonation. Have students look at their script and underline words that are important to emphasize. Have them note areas where they should change their pace or volume. Remind students to pause appropriately for punctuation. Encourage students to practice reading their script with other students as their test audience. Ask the other students to provide constructive feedback about intonation, pace, and volume. Remind students that the more they practice, the better their podcast will be.

Reflect on the Unit

By completing your short story, you have created a writing product that is enriched by your thoughts about the reading selections. Now is a good time to reflect on what you learned.

Reflect on the Essential Questions

- Review the four Essential Questions on page 1. How have your answers to these questions changed in response to the texts you read in this unit?

- How did the heroes you read about in this unit affect other characters?

- Which characters were expected to uphold the code of chivalry? What do you admire or not admire about their behavior?

- Which characters seem to believe that an outside force governs their lives?

- Think about texts in the unit that show a society that is coming apart. How does this social disorder affect people?

Reflect on Your Reading

- Which selections were the most interesting or surprising to you?

- What conclusions can you draw about the period in which most of these texts were written?

Reflect on the Writing Task

- Which parts of the story were the easiest to write? The hardest to write? Why?

- What improvements did you make to your story as you were revising?

UNIT 1 READING SELECTIONS
- *Beowulf*
- "The Wife of Bath's Tale," from *The Canterbury Tales*
- *Le Morte d'Arthur*
- "Chivalry"
- *The Paston Letters*
- *My Syrian Diary*
- "The Wanderer"
- "Loneliness"

LEARNING MINDSET

Self-Reflection Explain to students that an important part of developing a learning mindset and growing mentally is the ability to recognize strengths and weaknesses. As students reflect on the unit, encourage them to ask themselves the following questions: What did I learn about my writing ability? Did I ask for help if I felt weak in a certain area? How did I handle errors? Am I proud of the work I turned in?

REFLECT ON THE UNIT

Have students reflect on the questions independently and write some notes in response to each one. Then, have students meet with partners or in small groups to discuss their reflections. Circulate during these discussions to identify the questions that are generating the liveliest conversations. Wrap up with a whole-class discussion focused on these questions.

UNIT 2

Instructional Overview and Resources

		Instructional Focus	Online Ed Resources
	**Unit Introduction** **A Celebration of Human Achievement: The English Renaissance (1485–1660)**	Unit 2 Essential Questions Unit 2 Academic Vocabulary	**Stream to Start:** A Celebration of Human Achievement: The English Renaissance (1485–1660) **Unit 2 Response Log**

ANALYZE & APPLY

	"The Tragedy of Hamlet" Drama by William Shakespeare **Lexile N/A**	**Reading** • Analyze Dramatic Plot • Analyze Conflict • Analyze Soliloquy **Writing:** Write a Eulogy **Speaking and Listening:** Discuss the Script **Vocabulary:** Classical Allusion **Language Conventions:** Paradox	🔊 **Audio** **Close Read Screencast:** Modeled Discussion **Reading Studio:** Notice & Note **Writing Studio:** Writing Narratives **Speaking and Listening Studio:** Participating in Collaborative Discussions **Vocabulary Studio:** Classical Allusions **Grammar Studio:** Paradox
	**from "Hamlet"** Film Clip by BBC Shakespeare	**Media:** Analyze Interpretations of Drama **Writing:** Write a Narrative **Speaking and Listening:** Produce a Movie Trailer	**Writing Studio:** Writing Narratives **Speaking and Listening Studio:** Using Media in a Presentation

SUGGESTED PACING: 30 DAYS

Unit Introduction — 1
The Tragedy of Hamlet — 2 3 4 5 6 7
from Hamlet — 8 9 10
Hamlet's Dull Revenge — 11 12
Sonnet 30 / Sonnet 75 — 13 14 15

PLAN

English Learner Support	Differentiated Instruction	Assessment
• Understand Language Structures • Build Background Knowledge	**When Students Struggle** • Take Notes	

English Learner Support		Differentiated Instruction		Assessment
• Text X-Ray • Demonstrate Comprehension • Develop Vocabulary • Use Accessible Language • Share Information • Recognize Verb Forms • Express Ideas • Demonstrate Comprehension • Speak Using Connecting Words • Develop Learning Strategies • Use Accessible Language • Use Context • Take Notes and Analyze • Analyze Sayings and Expression • Take Notes and Collaborate • Take Notes and Summarize	• Write to Narrate • Narrate and Explain • Practice Pronunciation • Draw Inferences • Express Ideas • Look for Language Patterns • Describe and Retell • Understand Meaning • Share Information • Retell Plot Points • Understand Comparisons • Acquire and Use Grade-Level Content Vocabulary • Share and Ask for Information • Acquire Grade-Level Vocabulary • Analyze Expressions • Describe and Explain • Oral Assessment • Speak Using New Language • Use Pre-Taught Vocabulary • Use Accessible Language	**When Students Struggle** • Understand Tragedy • Understand Characters • Identify Subplot • Identify Conflicts • Understand Motivation • Summarize Plot • Identify Cause and Effect • Connect Plot Points • Understand Character Behavior • Summarize Plot • Predict Decisions • Identify Main Ideas • Gather Evidence to Draw Conclusions • Understand Characterization • Understand Conflict • Interpret Behavior • Compare Characters • Interpret Figures of Speech • Review Plot • Analyze Wordplay • Recognize Change in Tone • Paraphrase and Retell • Analyze Attitude • Identify Plot Points • Review Events • Reteach: Internal Conflict	**To Challenge Students** • Write in Blank Verse • Predict Conflict • Consider Points of View • Write in Blank Verse • Adapt a Play Review • Identify Dramatic Irony • Determine Figurative Meanings • Research Cultural Ideas • Consider a Character's Point-of-View • Identify the Plot Device • Analyze Dramatic Irony • Evaluate Character's Actions • Identify and Analyze Satire	**Selection Test**
• Text X-Ray • Identify Cognates		**When Students Struggle** • Reteaching: Analyze Interpretations of Drama		**Selection Test**

A Valediction: Forbidding Mourning — 16, 17

To His Coy Mistress / Twenty-One Love Poems (Poem III) — 18, 19, 20, 21

***from* Speech before the Spanish Armada Invasion / For Army Infantry's First Women, Heavy Packs and the Weight of History** — 22, 23, 24, 25

Independent Reading — 26, 27

End of Unit — 28, 29, 30

PLAN

UNIT 2 Continued

	Instructional Focus	Online Ed Resources
MENTOR TEXT "Hamlet's Dull Revenge" Literary Criticism by René Girard **Lexile 1290L**	**Reading** • Analyze Arguments • Analyze Key Ideas **Writing:** Write an Argument **Speaking and Listening:** Discuss an Interpretation **Vocabulary:** Domain-Specific Words and Phrases **Language Conventions:** Combining Sentences	🔊 Audio **Reading Studio:** Notice & Note **Writing Studio:** Writing Arguments **Speaking and Listening Studio:** Participating in Collaborative Discussions **Vocabulary Studio:** Domain-Specific Words **Grammar Studio:** Conjunctions and Interjections
"Sonnet 30 / Sonnet 75" Poems by Edmund Spenser	**Reading** • Analyze Sonnets • Summarize Poetry **Writing:** Write a Sonnet **Speaking and Listening:** Present a Sonnet	🔊 Audio **Reading Studio:** Notice & Note **Writing Studio:** Writing as a Process **Speaking and Listening Studio:** Giving a Presentation
"A Valediction: Forbidding Mourning" Poem by John Donne	**Reading** • Analyze Metaphysical Conceits • Interpret Ideas in Poetry **Writing:** Write an Essay **Speaking and Listening:** Present the Essay	🔊 Audio **Reading Studio:** Notice & Note **Speaking and Listening Studio:** Giving a Presentation

COLLABORATE & COMPARE

	Instructional Focus	Online Ed Resources
"To His Coy Mistress" Poem by Andrew Marvell "Twenty-One Love Poems" (Poem III) Poem by Adrienne Rich	**Reading** • Interpret Figurative Language • Analyze Speaker **Writing:** Write Letters **Speaking and Listening:** Discuss Similarities/Differences	🔊 Audio **Reading Studio:** Notice & Note **Writing Studio:** Writing as a Process **Speaking and Listening Studio:** Participating in Discussions
Collaborate & Compare	**Reading:** Compare Themes	

138C Unit 2

PLAN

English Learner Support	Differentiated Instruction		Online Ed Assessment
• Text X-Ray • Use Cognates • Recognize Affixes • Use Print Cues to Enhance Understanding • Language Conventions • Summarize Arguments • Oral Assessment	**When Students Struggle** • Identify Evidence **To Challenge Students** • Evaluate the Author's Argument		**Selection Test**
• Text X-Ray • Understand Meter • Acquire Vocabulary • Oral Assessment	**When Students Struggle** • Summarize Poetry • Paraphrase • Analyze Sonnets		**Selection Test**
• Text X-Ray • Learn New Language Structures • Acquire Vocabulary • Oral Assessment	**When Students Struggle** • Paraphrase • Summarize		**Selection Test**
			Selection Test
• Text X-Ray • Analyze Speaker • Draw on Prior Knowledge • Oral Assessment	**When Students Struggle** • Understand Literary Terms • Reteaching: Interpret Figurative Language • Synthesize Ideas	**To Challenge Students** • Write a Metaphor	**Selection Test**
• Perform Critical Analysis	**When Students Struggle** • Synthesize Ideas		

A Celebration of Human Achievement: The English Renaissance **138D**

PLAN

UNIT 2 Continued

	Instructional Focus	**Online Ed Resources**
 from "Speech before the Spanish Armada Invasion" Speech by Queen Elizabeth I **Lexile 1310L**	**Reading** • Analyze Rhetorical Devices • Connect to History **Writing:** Write a Speech **Speaking and Listening:** Present a Speech **Vocabulary:** Multiple-Meaning Words **Language Conventions:** Formal Language	🔊 Audio **Reading Studio:** Notice & Note **Writing Studio:** Writing Arguments **Speaking and Listening Studio:** Giving a Presentation **Vocabulary Studio:** Usage **Grammar Studio:** Spelling
"For Army Infantry's First Women, Heavy Packs and the Weight of History" Article by Dave Philipps **Lexile 1140L**	**Reading** • Analyze Text Features • Summarize and Paraphrase Texts **Writing:** Prepare Notes for a Debate **Speaking and Listening:** Debate **Vocabulary:** Foreign Words and Phrases **Language Conventions:** Dashes and Hyphenation	🔊 Audio **Reading Studio:** Notice & Note **Writing Studio:** Planning an Argument **Speaking and Listening Studio:** Participating in a Collaborative Discussion **Vocabulary Studio:** Foreign Words and Phrases **Grammar Studio:** Dashes and Hyphenations
Collaborate & Compare	**Reading:** Compare Across Genres	

Online Ed INDEPENDENT READING

The Independent Reading selections are only available in the eBook. Go to the Reading Studio for more information on NOTICE & NOTE.	 "Sonnet 18," "Sonnet 29," "Sonnet 130" Poems by William Shakespeare	 "Elizabeth I: The Reality Behind the Mask" Article by Brenda Ralph Lewis **Lexile 1220L**

END OF UNIT

Writing Task: Write a Literary Analysis **Reflect on the Unit**	**Writing:** Write a Literary Analysis **Language Conventions:** Indicate Quotations Properly	**Unit 2 Response Log** **Mentor Text:** Hamlet's Dull Revenge **Writing Studio:** Writing as a Process **Grammar Studio:** Using Quotation Marks

PLAN

English Learner Support	Differentiated Instruction	Online Ed Assessment
• Text X-Ray • Demonstrate Comprehension • Oral Assessment • Summarize • Vocabulary Strategy • Use Formal Language	**When Students Struggle** • Analyze Arguments • Reteaching: Rhetorical Devices	**Selection Test**
• Text X-Ray • Understand Grammar Usage • Shared Reading • Use Contextual Support • Express Ideas • Understand Idioms • Oral Assessment • Vocabulary Strategy • Language Conventions	**When Students Struggle** • Create Outlines • Reteaching: Summarize Texts **To Challenge Students** • Engage in a Debate	**Selection Test**
• Ask Questions	**When Students Struggle** • Organize Findings	
"The Passionate Shepherd to His Love" Poem by Christopher Marlowe	"The Nymph's Reply to the Shepherd" Poem by Sir Walter Raleigh	**Selection Tests**
• Language X-Ray • Understand Academic Language • Write a Group Literary Analysis • Use the Mentor Text • Check Verb Tenses • Use Quotations in Writing	**When Students Struggle** • Draft the Analysis • Use Quotations **To Challenge Students** • Create a Parody	**Unit Test**

A Celebration of Human Achievement: The English Renaissance **138F**

TEACH

DISCUSS THE QUOTATION

Tell students that this quotation is from Act II of the play *Twelfth Night* by William Shakespeare. It is excerpted from a longer line, which continues: "...some are born great, some achieve greatness, and some have greatness thrust upon 'em." The quote reflects the spirit of the Renaissance—a time when people lived life on a grand scale, seeking greatness in the arts, sciences, and exploration as never before.

Ask students to think about what true greatness means. Why might a person be afraid of greatness? What kinds of greatness can be achieved, and what kinds of greatness can a person be born into or have "thrust upon 'em"?

■ English Learner Support

Understand Language Structures Make sure students understand that the quotation uses a nonstandard word order because it reflects an older form of the English language instead of following modern English grammar structures. "Be not afraid of greatness" can be expressed in more modern language as "Do not be afraid of greatness" or "Don't be afraid of greatness." **ALL LEVELS**

UNIT 2

A CELEBRATION OF HUMAN ACHIEVEMENT

THE ENGLISH RENAISSANCE

" Be not afraid of greatness. "

—William Shakespeare

 LEARNING MINDSET

Curiosity Explain to students that if they can find some aspect of a subject that they are interested in or curious about, they will be more motivated to learn. Remind students to look for topics or ideas that especially interest them as they read the historical background essay, author bios, and selections in each unit. What else do they want to learn about the topic? Encourage students to ask additional questions and perform independent research on topics of their choice. Emphasize that research does not have to be a long drawn-out or intimidating process. For a curious learner, a quick Internet search can often yield almost instantaneous results, although the learner must always be cautious and ensure the reliability of the results.

UNIT 2

Discuss the **Essential Questions** with your whole class or in small groups. As you read A Celebration of Human Achievement, consider how the selections explore these questions.

? ESSENTIAL QUESTION:
What can drive someone to seek revenge?

Most of us at one time or another have felt the urge to seek retaliation against someone or something that has harmed either us personally or someone we care about. Revenge is also a major plot element of countless books, movies, and television shows. Clearly, the idea of vengeance is one that appeals to many people. But what factors influence some people to take action while others do not act? And why do people feel the need for revenge in the first place?

? ESSENTIAL QUESTION:
How does time affect our feelings?

"Time heals all wounds. Just sleep on it; you'll feel better in the morning." Chances are you have heard these expressions and others like them many times. The central idea is the same: as time passes, human feelings change. But in what ways? Do feelings fade in strength or do they become more powerful? Are there cases in which feelings are unaffected by time? Can a strong feeling a person has at one time be transformed into a completely different feeling?

? ESSENTIAL QUESTION:
What's the difference between love and passion?

For millennia, writers, poets, artists, and countless others have struggled to define what constitutes true love. Because love takes so many forms, and is expressed differently by each individual, it often blends into and is sometimes confused with other emotions. To some, romantic love and passion are inseparable concepts. What is love, and what is passion? Why is it so difficult for people to distinguish between the two?

? ESSENTIAL QUESTION:
How do you defy expectations?

All of us face them every day: the expectations we have for ourselves and others, and the expectations others and society have for us. High expectations for behavior or achievement can lead to soaring success, if they are met; but can just as easily end in spectacular failure, and crippling blows to self-esteem, if they are unmet or unrealistic. Low expectations, on the other hand, all too often become self-fulfilling prophecies. How are we motivated by the expectations that surround us? What happens when someone chooses to go against the expectations that have been put in place for them?

A Celebration of Human Achievement

TEACH

Connect to the
ESSENTIAL QUESTION

Read aloud the Essential Questions and the paragraphs that follow them. Open the discussion of each idea by having students respond to the questions that conclude each paragraph.

? ESSENTIAL QUESTION:
What can drive someone to seek revenge?

Challenge students to consider the ethics of revenge. Is revenge appropriate in some situations but inappropriate in others? Remind students that personal views on revenge are often shaped by an individual's cultural and/or religious background and experiences.

? ESSENTIAL QUESTION:
How does time affect our feelings?

Have students think of important events in their own lives. How did they feel when the event first happened? How do they feel now that some time has passed?

? ESSENTIAL QUESTION:
What's the difference between love and passion?

Challenge students to define love and passion in their own words. As an option, extend the discussion by displaying dictionary definitions of both words and having students compare and contrast their own definitions with those in the dictionary to deepen their understanding.

? ESSENTIAL QUESTION:
How do you defy expectations?

Explain to students that most people face different expectations in each area of life. Have students consider what expectations they face within their family, as a student, among their friends, and within themselves.

A Celebration of Human Achievement **139**

TEACH

THE ENGLISH RENAISSANCE

The following essay provides students with a historical context for the Unit 2 selections. It presents a brief overview of the major ideological, political, and religious changes that shaped England during the time period 1485–1660.

The Tudor Dynasty and Religious Reform

Explain to students that writers during the English Renaissance were often affected by constantly shifting political and religious influences. As kings and queens rose to power, and as varying forms of Christianity became dominant, writers found themselves either celebrated for their work or censured for it. It was possible for writers to be put to death if they fell out of favor with the ruler of the day, especially if they published ideas that the ruler did not agree with or criticized the political and/or religious groups in power. Ask students to consider how developments in printing technology and increasing literacy rates might have affected the degree of importance that rulers placed on ensuring that writers produced works they agreed with.

COLLABORATIVE DISCUSSION

Ask groups to share their findings with the class.

King Henry VII

THE ENGLISH RENAISSANCE

During the late Middle Ages, Europe suffered from both war and plague. Those who survived wanted to celebrate life and the human spirit. The Renaissance, which literally means "rebirth," was marked by a revival of art and learning, and a rediscovery of classical Greek and Roman ideas. A new emphasis was placed on the individual and human achievement. Artists, writers, and scholars refocused their efforts on exploring the natural world, rather than the spiritual world. Some Europeans even began to question the teachings of the Church, which directed Christians to endure suffering while they awaited their rewards in heaven. After the development of a printing press with movable type in about 1440, Renaissance ideas could be printed in mass and distributed to an increasingly literate population.

The Tudor Dynasty and Religious Reform Although the Renaissance began in the 1300s in Italy and rapidly spread throughout Europe, its influence was delayed in England due to political instability. When King Henry VII assumed the English throne in 1485, the Renaissance finally took hold. King Henry VII was the first in an influential succession of Tudor rulers. A shrewd leader, Henry negotiated favorable treaties, built up the nation's trading fleet, and financed expeditions to the Americas. He also made an alliance with Spain by marrying his son to Princess Catherine of Aragon.

Meanwhile, dissatisfaction with the Roman Catholic Church, and its leader the pope, was spreading in Europe. The great wealth and power of the Church threatened the power of kings, and Church corruption enraged religious reformers. In 1517 Martin Luther, a German monk, responded by writing his 95 Theses and nailing them to a church door. Despite being declared a heretic, Luther's arguments against Church corruption were

COLLABORATIVE DISCUSSION
In a small group, review the timeline and discuss which literary or historical events had the greatest impact.

1485
Henry Tudor becomes King Henry VII, the first ruler of the Tudor dynasty.

1517
Martin Luther begins the Protestant Reformation.

1534
Henry VIII breaks with the Roman Catholic Church and forms the Church of England.

1558
Elizabeth I becomes Queen of England.

1564
William Shakespeare is born.

 ENGLISH LEARNER SUPPORT

Build Background Knowledge To aid comprehension of the essay, provide students with explanations of the following expressions and their definitions:

- *in mass:* in large quantities
- *assumed the throne:* began to rule
- *took hold:* started to have an effect
- *steered a middle course:* held a moderate position, not going to extremes
- *took strong measures:* acted strongly or forcefully
- *pitted. . . against:* set in opposition or competition **ALL LEVELS**

published and spread across Europe. His actions sparked the Reformation, a movement for religious reform, which led to the founding of Christian churches that did not accept the authority of the pope. Christians who belonged to these non-Catholic churches became known as Protestants.

Henry VIII, son of Henry VII, at first remained loyal to the Roman Catholic Church. However, he became obsessed with producing a male heir. When he was only able to produce a female heir, Mary, with his wife, Catherine of Aragon, he asked to annul their marriage. The pope refused, so Henry broke away from the Church, forming the Church of England and declaring himself the head. He divorced Catherine and married Anne Boleyn, who became the mother of his second female heir, Elizabeth.

In all, Henry married six different wives but fathered only one son—the frail and sickly Edward VI, who became king but died when he was just 15. Following Edward, Catherine's daughter Mary succeeded to the throne. To avenge the divorce of her mother, she brought Roman Catholicism back to England and persecuted Protestants, thereby earning the nickname Bloody Mary. When Mary died in 1558, her half-sister Elizabeth became queen.

The Elizabethan Era and the Rise of the Stuarts Elizabeth I was one of the ablest monarchs in English history. During her long reign, England enjoyed a time of unprecedented prosperity and international prestige. The queen kept England out of costly wars, ended the Spanish alliance, and encouraged overseas exploration. In religion, she steered a middle course, reestablishing the Church of England and setting it as a buffer between Catholics and the more radical Protestants known as Puritans. The ideas of the Renaissance flourished, and theater and literature reached new heights. It was during Elizabeth's reign that William Shakespeare began his career, and several of his plays were performed at her court. With Elizabeth's death in 1603, the powerful Tudor dynasty came to an end.

Elizabeth was succeeded by her cousin James Stuart, King of Scotland, who became James I of England. He oversaw a new English translation of the Bible—the King James Bible—but refused to reform the Church of England, angering Puritans, including many in Parliament.

The Defeat of the Monarchy In 1625 James I died and Charles I, his son, became king. In 1629 he dismissed the Puritan-dominated Parliament and

RESEARCH
What about this historical period interests you? Chose a topic, event, or person to learn more about. Then add your own entry to the timeline.

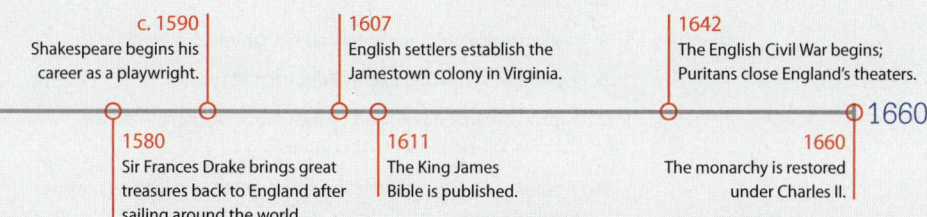

c. 1590 Shakespeare begins his career as a playwright.
1580 Sir Frances Drake brings great treasures back to England after sailing around the world.
1607 English settlers establish the Jamestown colony in Virginia.
1611 The King James Bible is published.
1642 The English Civil War begins; Puritans close England's theaters.
1660 The monarchy is restored under Charles II.

A Celebration of Human Achievement 141

WHEN STUDENTS STRUGGLE...

Take Notes Students may struggle to identify important themes and patterns in the historical background essays. Encourage students to use an outline to record the main ideas and details of the essay, using the boldfaced headings as a starting point to organize the material. Students can then examine their outlines to see whether patterns emerge. For example, after outlining the Unit 2 essay, students might be better able to recognize cause-and-effect relationships between the major political and religious developments of the era.

TEACH

The Elizabethan Era and the Rise of the Stuarts

Renaissance Europeans delighted in the arts and literature, the beauty of nature, human impulses, exploration, and a new sense of mastery over the world. In Elizabethan England, the ideas of exploration and mastery over the world often went hand in hand. New inventions—such as the compass—and advances in astronomy allowed ships to venture into uncharted seas, and Elizabeth encouraged such explorations. During her reign, English explorers expanded the horizon even as English ships took control of the seas. Sir Francis Drake, for example, led an expedition that circumnavigated the globe, and was also one of the commanders who led the English navy in its defeat of the much larger Spanish Armada. Sir Walter Raleigh attempted to found an English colony in Virginia, paving the way for future expansion. Such events contributed greatly to Britain's emergence as a maritime empire with global reach.

The Defeat of the Monarchy

Explain to students that the political upheaval of the English Civil War had a profound effect on the culture of the late English Renaissance. Even before the war, the influence of the Puritans had begun to grow in England. The Puritans believed that the Elizabethan dramas and the rowdy crowds they attracted were highly immoral, and they worked to close all the theaters. However, they were not immediately successful. Shakespeare wrote some of his greatest plays during the reign of Elizabeth's successor James I, while Puritan influence in politics continued to grow. It was not until the defeat of the Royalists and the establishment of a Puritan commonwealth in 1649 that the playhouses were closed and the golden age of drama ended. Most other forms of recreation were also suspended. Under Puritan rule, Sunday became a day of prayer when even walking for pleasure was forbidden.

RESEARCH

To learn more about their chosen topic, encourage students to search for primary sources from the historical period. Have students choose excerpts from a source to present to the class.

A Celebration of Human Achievement **141**

TEACH

CHECK YOUR UNDERSTANDING

Have students answer the questions independently.

Answers:

1. B
2. H
3. D

If students answer any question incorrectly, have them reread the text to confirm their understanding.

---

did not summon it again for 11 years. During that time, he took strong measures against his opponents, persecuting Puritans and attempting to force the practices of the Church of England on Scotland. When the king finally reconvened Parliament, it stripped him of many of his powers. Charles responded with military force, and civil war resulted.

The English Civil War pitted the Royalists against Parliament. Under Oliver Cromwell, the Puritan army, supporting Parliament, defeated the Royalists, and King Charles I was executed in 1649. Parliament established a commonwealth with Cromwell as head, but the Puritan government was just as autocratic as the Stuart kings, and eventually lost public support. In 1660 a new Parliament invited Charles II, the son of Charles I, to return from exile as king, marking the beginning of a period known as the Restoration.

CHECK YOUR UNDERSTANDING

Choose the best answer to each question.

1. Which event led most directly to the formation of the Church of England?
   - A Henry VII made a marriage alliance with Spain.
   - B Henry VIII sought to annul his marriage to Catherine of Aragon.
   - C Martin Luther protested the corruption of the Catholic Church.
   - D The Catholic Church declared Martin Luther a heretic, angering his supporters.

2. Renaissance ideas took hold in England later than in other parts of Europe mainly because —
   - F the Catholic Church discouraged people from pursuing the arts and literature
   - G the Tudor monarchs stunted England's growth as a nation
   - H internal political conflict initially prevented Renaissance ideas from taking root
   - J English Puritans disagreed with the Italian Renaissance worldview

3. Which most accurately describes the religious climate in England during this period?
   - A England was a predominantly Catholic country.
   - B England was a predominantly Puritan country.
   - C England became dominated by the Church of England, which promoted the ideas of Martin Luther.
   - D England had a few main religious groups that each gained power or popularity under specific rulers.

ACADEMIC VOCABULARY

Academic Vocabulary words are words you use when you discuss and write about texts. In this unit, you will learn the following five words:

✓ ambiguous ☐ anticipate ☐ conceive ☐ drama ☐ integrity

Study the Word Network to learn more about the word **ambiguous**.

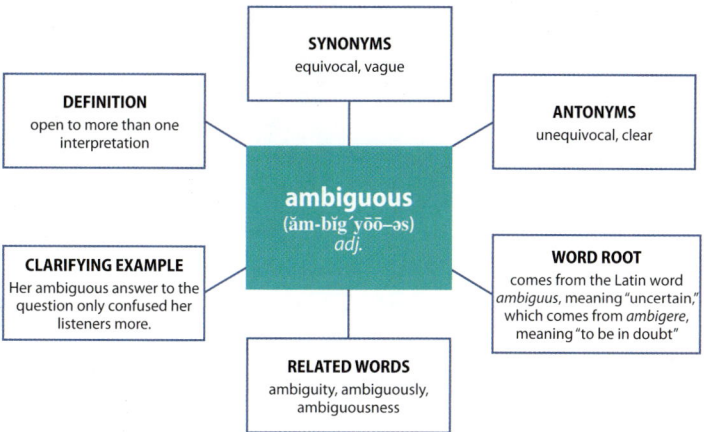

Write and Discuss Discuss your completed Word Network with a partner, making sure to talk through all of the boxes until you both understand the word, its synonyms, antonyms, and related forms. Then fill out a Word Network for the remaining four words. Use a dictionary or online resource to help you complete the activity.

 Go online to access the Word Networks.

RESPOND TO THE ESSENTIAL QUESTION

In this unit, you will explore four different **Essential Questions** related to the literature of the English Renaissance. As you read each selection, you will gather your ideas about one of these questions and write about it in a **Response Log**. At the end of the unit, you will have the opportunity to write a **literary analysis** related to one of the Essential Questions. Filling out the Response Log after you read each text will help you prepare for this writing task.

 You can also go online to access the Response Log.

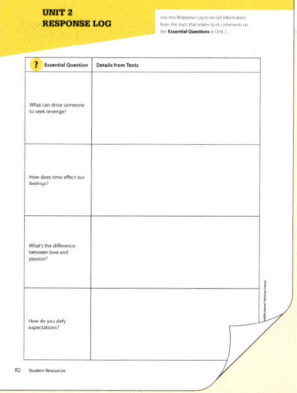

A Celebration of Human Achievement **143**

TEACH

ACADEMIC VOCABULARY

Have students complete Word Networks for the remaining four vocabulary words. Encourage them to include all the categories shown in the completed network if possible, but point out that some words do not have clear synonyms or antonyms.

ambiguous (ăm-bĭg´yo-oəs) *adj.* open to more than one interpretation (Spanish cognate: *ambiguo*)

anticipate (ăn-tĭs´ə-pāt) *v.* to see as a probable occurrence; expect (Spanish cognate: *anticipar*)

conceive (kən-sēv´) *v.* to understand or form in the mind; to devise (Spanish cognate: *concebir*)

drama (drä´mə) *n.* a prose or verse composition intended to be acted out (Spanish cognate: *drama*)

integrity (ĭn-tĕg´rĭ-tē) *n.* the quality of being ethically or morally upright (Spanish cognate: *integridad*)

RESPOND TO THE ESSENTIAL QUESTIONS

Direct students to the Unit 2 Response Log. Explain that students will use it to record ideas and details from the selections that help answer one of the Essential Questions. When they work on the Writing Task at the end of the unit, their Response Logs will help them think about what they have read and make connections between the texts.

PLAN

THE TRAGEDY OF HAMLET
Drama by William Shakespeare

GENRE ELEMENTS
TRAGIC DRAMA
Tell students that a **tragic drama** is a dramatic work that presents the downfall of a dignified character who is involved in historically, morally, or socially significant events. The main character or **tragic hero** has a **tragic flaw** that leads to his or her destruction. The events in a **tragic plot** are set in motion by the character's moral weakness, error in judgment, or inability to cope with uncontrollable circumstances. Succeeding events are linked in a cause-and-effect relationship that lead to a disastrous conclusion, usually death.

LEARNING OBJECTIVES
- Analyze dramatic plot and conflict.
- Conduct research about mental illness in the Renaissance.
- Write a eulogy for a character in Hamlet.
- Discuss a script.
- Explain classical allusions.
- Identify and define paradoxes.
- **Language** Narrate events to analyze dramatic plot.

TEXT COMPLEXITY

Quantitative Measures	Hamlet	Lexile: N/A
Qualitative Measures	**Ideas Presented** Subtle, implied meanings and greater demand for inference.	
	Structures Used More complex with many subplots.	
	Language Used Complex sentence structures with use of archaic and formal language.	
	Knowledge Required Cultural and historical knowledge may make heavier demands.	

144A Unit 2

PLAN

RESOURCES

- Unit 2 Response Log
- 🔊 Selection Audio
- Close Read Screencasts: Modeled Discussions
- Reading Studio: Notice & Note
- Level Up Tutorial: Character Traits
- Writing Studio: Writing a Play
- Speaking and Listening Studio: Participating in Collaborative Discussions
- Vocabulary Studio: Classical Allusions
- Grammar Studio: Paradox
- "Hamlet" Selection Test

SUMMARIES

English

Hundreds of years ago in Denmark, Prince Hamlet returns home from school to attend the funeral of his father, King Hamlet. He then discovers his mother, Gertrude, has married his dead father's brother, Claudius. Soon after, the ghost of the dead king appears to Hamlet and tells him to avenge his death and kill Claudius. Hamlet agonizes over what to do, pretends to be mad, enlists a theater troupe to determine his uncle's guilt, and inadvertently causes one tragedy after the next until the play's ultimate tragic act.

Spanish

Hace cientos de años, en Dinamarca, el príncipe Hamlet regresa de la escuela para asistir al funeral de su padre, el rey Hamlet. Luego, descubre que su madre, Gertrudis, se casó con el hermano de su padre, Claudio. Poco después, el fantasma del rey se le aparece a Hamlet y le dice que debe vengar su muerte matando a Claudio. Hamlet agoniza sobre qué hacer, finge estar demente, recluta a una compañía teatral para determinar la culpa de su tío e inadvertidamente causa una tragedia tras otra hasta el acto final y trágico de la obra.

👥 SMALL-GROUP OPTIONS

Have students work in small groups and pairs to read and discuss the selection.

Activating Academic Vocabulary

- Provide a list of the academic vocabulary words for Unit 2: *ambiguous*, *anticipate*, *conceive*, *drama*, and *integrity*.
- Model how to use two or more academic vocabulary words and phrases to discuss the text.
- Encourage students to use the academic vocabulary as they discuss and write about the text.

Silent Sustained Reading

- Set a timer for thirty minutes.
- Have students read the play silently until the timer rings.
- Suggest that students keep a list of any unfamiliar words they want to look up after reading.
- Ask students to record the title, date, and number of pages read in a reading log.

The Tragedy of Hamlet 144B

PLAN

 **Text X-Ray: English Learner Support**
for The Tragedy of Hamlet

Use the Text X-Ray and the supports and scaffolds in the Teacher's Edition to help guide students at different proficiency levels through the selection.

INTRODUCE THE SELECTION
DISCUSS REVENGE AND MORAL DILEMMA

In this lesson, students will need to be able to discuss the connection between revenge and moral dilemmas. Provide the following explanations:

- To take revenge is to punish someone for a hurt or injury they caused.
- A moral involves right and wrong.
- A moral dilemma is a conflict in which you must choose between two or more actions, and there is a moral reason for each choice.

Explain to students that the central moral dilemma Hamlet faces is whether or not to take revenge for his father's death.

Ask students to give their opinions about Hamlet's moral dilemma. Provide sentence frames, such as: *I think it is wrong to take revenge because _____.*
I think Hamlet should _____ because _____.

CULTURAL REFERENCES

The following words or phrases may be unfamiliar to students:

- *revenge:* harming someone as a reaction to some wrongdoing, especially harming or killing someone
- *nay* (Act I, Scene 1, line 2): no
- *ill-gotten* (Act I, Scene 1, line 141 margin note): gotten through wrong-doing
- *wretch* (Act II, Scene 1, line 169): an unfortunate or unhappy person
- *virtuous* (Act III, Scene 1, line 123 margin note): without sin or bad behavior
- *gallows* (Act V, Scene 1, line 44): a structure used for hanging people to death

LISTENING

Understanding Emotions

Remind students to pay attention to Hamlet's words to explain how his feelings affect the central conflict or moral dilemma he faces.

Have students listen as you read Act I, Scene 2, lines 129–159 (pp. 159–160). Use the following supports with students at varying proficiency levels:

- Provide meanings for: *weary, stale, flat; unweeded garden, self-slaughter,* and *break my heart.* Read these terms aloud and have students echo. **SUBSTANTIAL**
- Provide the word bank from the Beginning activity. Have small groups reread the lines to each other. Tell students to hold their hand up when they hear a phrase that reminds them of a feeling and to name that feeling. For example: *unweeded garden that grows to seed (neglected).* **MODERATE**
- Have partners write a list of words that name emotions. Then, have them use the list and phrases from the text to discuss how Hamlet feels about the death of his father and his mother's new marriage. **LIGHT**

SPEAKING

Defending Opinions

Remind students that they must back up their opinions with reasons that make sense. It is good to include factual examples or text evidence when defending an opinion.

Use the following supports with students at varying proficiency levels:

- After reading each act, provide students with a list of characters and verb phrases describing important events. Match the characters to verb phrases, and read them aloud. Have students echo read. **SUBSTANTIAL**
- After reading each act, elicit words and phrases describing the main events of that act to the board. Have students work together to number them according to the order in which they occur. Then, have students practice retelling the events of that act using the displayed words and phrases for reference. **MODERATE**
- After reading each act, put students in small groups and have them work together to recall the main events of that act. Then, have each student retell the main plot points in order. **LIGHT**

READING

Comparing Words to Identify Paradox

Remind students that they can identify a paradox by noticing antonyms or words that do not usually go together in a phrase.

Use the following supports with students at varying proficiency levels:

- Help students reread the paradoxes on page 277 in the Student Edition. Guide them to identify the words in each phrase that are antonyms or don't usually belong together. For example: *cruel/kind; falsehood/truth.* **SUBSTANTIAL**
- Have pairs explain to each other why each of the phrases from Student Edition page 277 is a paradox. Guide them to use the word *antonym* and phrase *that do not usually go together* in their discussion. **MODERATE**
- Have students review the text and list two more paradoxes. Then, have partners share their lists and explain how they used word meaning to identify each paradox. **LIGHT**

WRITING

Describing Characters

Help students understand that a character's dialogue can reveal what type of person he or she is.

Use the following supports with students at varying proficiency levels:

- After students choose a character, have them refer back to the text to study the chracter's dialogue. Direct them to copy lines of dialogue that reveal something important about the character. Have pairs exchange writing to check spelling accuracy. **SUBSTANTIAL**
- Have students copy several lines of their chosen character's dialogue and write how it reveals something about the character's personality. Then, have them explain their ideas to a partner. **MODERATE**
- Have students use a variety of lines of their character's dialogue to write about what the character is like. Have partners exchange papers and edit for pronoun-antecedent agreement. **LIGHT**

TEACH

CHARACTERISTICS OF SHAKESPEAREAN TRAGEDY

Read the information about Shakespearian tragedy with students. Explain that the **protagonist**, or main character, of a tragedy is a **tragic hero,** who comes to an unhappy end, and that in a classical tragedy this person is usually a person of importance in society, such as a king or queen, and that he or she exhibits extraordinary abilities but also a tragic flaw, a fatal error in judgment or weakness of character that leads directly to his or her downfall. In order for tragedy to involve the audience's emotions, the tragic hero cannot be a villain. He or she must be someone to whom the audience can relate on some level in order to feel sympathy and horror at his or her downfall.

The **plot** of a tragedy involves a conflict between the hero and a person or force, called the **antagonist**, which the hero must battle.

Because few audience members are royalty or nobles, the conflict must be one that on some level represents the kind of dilemma that others have struggled with as well. The tragic hero is battling this conflict merely on a bigger stage.

Inevitably the conflict contributes to the hero's downfall. The plot is built upon a series of causally related events. In most tragedies the tragic hero must make choices that determine his or her fate. Once the hero is on the chosen path, the outcome can be foreseen. These events and choices ultimately lead to the **catastrophe**, or tragic resolution, at which point the plot is usually resolved when the tragic hero meets his or her doom with courage and dignity.

SHAKESPEAREAN DRAMA

Shakespeare wrote *The Tragedy of Hamlet* around 1600. The story originated in an old folktale that was part of Denmark's legendary history. Shakespeare seems to have based his tragedy mainly on an English play about Hamlet from the 1580s. This earlier play had fallen out of fashion among Elizabethan audiences, but Shakespeare's version was a success. Shakespeare transformed the genre of revenge tragedy by introducing a hero whose insights, doubts, and moral dilemmas often overshadow the play's action. *Hamlet*'s psychological complexity helps explain the play's lasting popularity and influence.

The Globe Theatre In Shakespeare's time, most plays were performed in outdoor public theaters. These theaters resembled courtyards, with the stage surrounded on three sides by galleries. The most famous theater in London was the Globe, where Shakespeare and his acting company performed. The Globe was a three-story wooden structure that could hold up to 3,000 people. Poorer patrons, or "groundlings," stood around the stage to watch the performance. Wealthier patrons sat in the covered galleries.

Elizabethan Staging Plays were performed in the afternoon on a platform stage in the theater's center. The stage was mostly bare, which allowed for quick scene changes. A trapdoor gave the stage added flexibility; in *Hamlet*, it was used for the Ghost's entrances and exits and also in a grave scene. Actors were in close proximity to the groundlings, who were often rowdy. Because the theater was viewed as disreputable, women were not allowed to perform; boys played the female roles.

SHAKESPEAREAN TRAGEDY

Renaissance Drama During the Middle Ages, English drama focused mainly on religious themes, teaching moral lessons or retelling Bible stories to a populace that often couldn't read. In the Renaissance, however, renewed interest in ancient Greek and Roman literature led playwrights to model plays on classical drama. The plays were usually comedies and tragedies. **Comedy** was defined as a dramatic work with a happy ending; many comedies had humor, but it was not required. A **tragedy,** in contrast, was a work where the main character, or **tragic hero,** came to an unhappy end. The intention of tragedy is to exemplify the idea that human beings are doomed to suffer, fail, or die because of their own flaws, destiny, or fate. Shakespearean tragedy often differs from classical tragedy because Shakespeare's tragic works are not uniformly serious. He often eased the intensity of the action by using comic relief—a light, mildly humorous scene preceding or following a serious one. Shakespeare also wrote plays classified as **histories,** which present stories about England's monarchs.

WHEN STUDENTS STRUGGLE . . .

Understand Tragedy To help students understand the concept of a tragedy and a tragic hero, ask them to name a famous and well-liked celebrity or politician who suffered a downfall because of his or her actions. Would this figure's story make a good movie? Have students outline a basic plot for this movie using a chart like the one below.

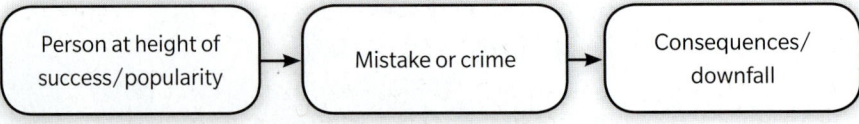

 For additional support, go to the **Reading Studio** and assign the following Level Up tutorial: Types of Drama.

SHAKESPEARE'S CONVENTIONS OF DRAMA

Shakespearean plays are divided into **acts** and **scenes**. **Dialogue** is labeled to show who is speaking. **Stage directions,** written in italics and in parentheses, specify the setting and how the characters should act. Shakespeare also used the following literary devices in his dramas.

Blank Verse Like many plays written before the 19th century, *Hamlet* is a **verse drama,** a play with dialogue consisting mostly of poetry with a fixed pattern of rhythm, or **meter.** Many English verse dramas are written in **blank verse,** or unrhymed **iambic pentameter,** a meter in which the normal line contains five stressed syllables, each preceded by an unstressed syllable.

> A little more than kin and less than kind.

Soliloquy and Aside Shakespeare often used two conventions to express characters' private thoughts and feelings. A **soliloquy** is a speech a character makes while alone to reveal thoughts to the audience. An **aside** is a remark a character quietly makes to the audience or to another character but that others on stage are not supposed to hear. Here is an example from *Hamlet*.

> **Polonius.** Fare you well, my lord.
> **Hamlet** [*aside*]. These tedious old fools.

Dramatic Irony In **dramatic irony,** the audience knows something that one or more characters don't know. For example, the audience knows why Hamlet often behaves strangely in the play, but most characters are confused by this behavior.

SHAKESPEAREAN LANGUAGE

The language Shakespeare used was quite different from today's language.

Shakespearean Language	
Grammatical Forms	The pronouns **thou, thee, thy, thine,** and **thyself** replaced **you.** Old verb forms were used like **art** (*are*) and **cometh** (*comes*).
Unusual Word Order	There is often an unusual word order. For example, Polonius tells Laertes, "Neither a borrower nor a lender be," instead of, "Be neither a borrower nor a lender."
Unfamiliar Vocabulary	The writing used archaic words (**seeling**: "blinding") and words with different modern meanings (**choppy**: "chapped"). He also wrote new words (like **assassination**) commonly used today.

Shakespearean Drama 145

TEACH

BLANK VERSE

Read a longer passage from the play to help students hear the rhythm created by iambic pentameter. Point out that blank verse echoes the natural rhythms of English. Remind them that thoughts are not always expressed in single end-stopped lines (ending with a mark of punctuation). Sometimes, one sentence flows into several lines and can begin or end in the middle of a line. Explain that not all characters speak in blank verse; sometimes rhymed verse and even prose is used.

SOLILOQUY AND ASIDE

Point out that an aside is indicated by the stage directions. Explain that both soliloquies and asides serve the function of revealing a character's thoughts, feelings, attitudes, and personality traits as well as hinting at future plot events.

SHAKESPEAREAN LANGUAGE

Read the description of each characteristic aloud. Then, display lines 19–22 from Scene 1. Point out the unusual grammatical forms and word order. Explain that marginal notes help to clarify meaning; in addition, paraphrasing the lines can help readers understand them more clearly. Display these paraphrased lines as an example:

Marcellus. Good night, Francisco. Who is taking your place? (line 19)

Barnardo. Is that you, Horatio? (line 22)

TO CHALLENGE STUDENTS

Write in Blank Verse Give e students a sense of Shakespeare's genius by having pairs write several lines of blank verse. Suggest that they take these steps:

- Choose a topic. Jot down ideas.
- Rephrase the ideas in lines of iambic pentameter.
- Read them aloud to see how they scan. Mark the stressed and unstressed syllables.

Ask students to share their blank verse with the class. Have them discuss the challenges of creating an entire play in this form.

Shakespearean Drama **145**

TEACH

? **Connect to the ESSENTIAL QUESTION**

The Tragedy of Hamlet is a play about Prince Hamlet's need to get revenge against Claudius for the murder of his father. However, Hamlet struggles psychologically with the idea of revenge, and Hamlet's indecision about killing Claudius and his internal struggle drive the plot of the play more than the action of revenge itself.

ANALYZE & APPLY

THE TRAGEDY OF HAMLET

Drama by **William Shakespeare**

? **ESSENTIAL QUESTION:**

What can drive someone to seek revenge?

QUICK START

Revenge has a central role in the story of *Hamlet*. Is revenge justified in some cases, or is it always misguided? Write a paragraph in response to this question. Then, share your opinion with a partner.

ANALYZE DRAMATIC PLOT

Shakespeare's tragedies have complex plot structures. Critics often refer to distinct stages of a dramatic plot, such as the **exposition,** where the characters and setting are introduced, and the **rising action,** where conflicts arise and suspense builds. The rising action leads to a **climax,** or turning point, where the outcome of the central conflict becomes clear. Events that follow in the **falling action** result in the final outcome, or **resolution.** In Shakespeare's plays, these stages often blend into one another, and a play can have more than one climax.

As the main plot develops, Shakespeare introduces **subplots**—stories that run parallel to the main plot. Subplots may support the main plot by advancing the play's action or by expressing a similar theme. They often involve characters other than the hero and the main opponent. For example, in *Hamlet,* one subplot features a character named Fortinbras, who only makes two brief appearances in the play. However, Fortinbras is important because he serves as a **foil,** a character whose traits contrast with another character, in this case with Hamlet. As you read the play, consider how the subplots connect with the main plot.

ANALYZE CONFLICT

Plots are generally built around **conflict,** a struggle between opposing forces. In tragic drama, conflict often has deadly consequences. The most obvious conflict is external, involving struggles between the main character and opponents.

Hamlet has plenty of violent action, but the play is notable for its exploration of internal conflict, struggles that occur within a character's mind. Prince Hamlet is keenly aware of the potential consequences of his actions. He also understands the consequences of inaction. Shakespeare places him in a situation full of moral dilemmas that are closely tied to the plot and themes of the play. As you read, consider how Hamlet struggles with these questions:

- How can he be certain about what happened to his father?
- How can he live up to his family duties?
- How should he judge his mother's behavior?
- How will his actions affect the fate of his soul as well as his enemy's soul?
- How can he reconcile the corruption and nobility within human nature?

When you finish reading the play, think about whether your views of Hamlet's struggles changed as you learned more about him.

GENRE ELEMENTS: TRAGIC DRAMA

- portrays the downfall of a dignified, courageous character who is generally of importance in society
- hero's downfall occurs because of a character weakness, error in judgment, or circumstances out of his or her control
- events lead to a disastrous or unhappy ending

QUICK START

To support students in thinking about whether revenge is ever justified, provide example situations and ask students whether they think getting revenge would be justified in each one. For example:

- *If someone stole your boyfriend or girlfriend, should you try to get revenge?*
- *What if someone damaged something of yours on purpose?*
- *What if someone started a mean rumor about you?*

Ask volunteers to share their responses to the situations above.

ANALYZE DRAMATIC PLOT

Explain to students that the **plot** is the sequence of significant events and actions in a literary work, such as when a character acts on a major decision, someone dies, or an accident occurs. Direct students to keep track of the major points in the plot as they read. Explain that *The Tragedy of Hamlet* has a main plot as well as **subplots**, which are sequences of events that are happening at the same time as the main action. Explain that the relationship between the main plot and the subplots adds meaning to the text, but that the meaning of the relationship between the main plot and subplot might not become clear until the end of the play.

ANALYZE CONFLICT

Tell students that *The Tragedy of Hamlet* will have multiple **conflicts,** both major and minor, internal and external. Explain that the **external conflicts** will play out in the actions and speech of characters who have opposing desires and interests, which cause them to struggle with each other, while the **internal conflict** will play out in Hamlet's **soliloquies** and conversations with other characters as he struggles in his own mind. Provide students with the following list of types of conflict and at the end of the play, ask them to identify the ones that occur throughout *The Tragedy of Hamlet*:

human vs. self	human vs. nature
human vs. human	human vs. machine
human vs. society	human vs. fate/supernatural

TEACH

ANALYZE SOLILOQUY

Explain that the purpose of a soliloquy is to give the audience insight into the **inner conflicts** and motivations of a character that will affect the **plot.** They also help to develop the play's **theme,** as soliloquies often contain important messages about life. Tell students that Prince Hamlet's soliloquies in *The Tragedy of Hamlet* are some of the most famous and memorable passages in English literature. In these speeches, Hamlet contemplates problems of life and the human condition, and people still find his thoughts relevant hundreds of years after they were written. Point out that Shakespeare's use of literary elements, such as **allusions, metaphors, similes, personification,** and powerful **imagery,** are what make these speeches so powerful and memorable.

- An **allusion** is a reference to a person, place, event or literary work with which the author expects the audience to be familiar.
- A **metaphor** is a figure of speech that compares two different things that have something in common. A **simile** does the same thing, but uses *like* or *as*.
- **Personification** is a figure of speech in which human qualities are attributed to an object, animal, or idea.
- The term **imagery** refers to words and phrases that create vivid sensory connections for the reader. The majority of images are visual, but imagery may also appeal to the senses of smell, hearing, taste, and touch.

Encourage students to take the time to understand these literary devices, using the side notes to help them.

LANGUAGE CONVENTIONS

Review the explanation of **paradox** and explain that one reason Shakespeare's works are so memorable is the clever way he played with words. Explain that a paradox is a way of playing with words by making a statement that gets at a truth while seeming to contradict itself.

ANNOTATION MODEL

Remind students to make notes about the plot, subplots, and conflicts as suggested in Analyze Dramatic Plot and Analyze Conflict on page 147. Point out that they should follow these suggestions and record other ideas they may have while marking up the selection in their write-in text. Their notes in the margin may also include questions about ideas that are unclear. They may want to color-code their annotations by using highlighters.

148   Unit 2

 **GET READY**

ANALYZE SOLILOQUY

A **soliloquy** is a long speech in a play in which a character talks to himself or herself. The character is alone onstage or unaware of the presence of others. Soliloquies help develop characters by revealing their motivations and inner conflicts. They can also express themes and hint at actions to come. Shakespeare uses a variety of techniques in his soliloquies.

Allusions	Act I, Scene 2, 139–140: "So excellent a king, that was to this / Hyperion to a satyr...." Hamlet alludes to the sun god Hyperion to make the point that his father had integrity, unlike his uncle Claudius, whom he compares to a satyr, a mythical figure associated with lechery.
Figures of speech: metaphors, similes, and personification	Act II, Scene I, 59–60: "The slings and arrows of outrageous fortune, / Or to take arms against a sea of troubles...." Shakespeare uses metaphors to express Hamlet's disturbed state of mind.
Powerful imagery; careful word choices	Act II, Scene 2, 393–395: "Now could I drink hot blood / And do such bitter business as the day / Would quake to look on." The imagery and word choices in these lines convey the intensity of Hamlet's feelings.

As you read, think about how Shakespeare uses these literary elements to create memorable and insightful soliloquies.

LANGUAGE CONVENTIONS

A **paradox** is a statement that seems contradictory but actually reveals an element of truth. For example, in Act III, Scene 4, Hamlet says that he "must be cruel only to be kind." Although *cruel* and *kind* have opposite meanings, this paradox suggests that harsh actions are sometimes needed to obtain just outcomes. As you read *Hamlet,* look for other paradoxical statements.

ANNOTATION MODEL   NOTICE & NOTE

As you read *Hamlet*, note elements of the plot and examine conflicts revealed through dialogue. This model shows one reader's note about a soliloquy in Act I, after Hamlet's mother and uncle suggest he has mourned his father's death for too long.

> **Hamlet.** O, that this too, too sullied flesh would melt,
> Thaw, and resolve itself into a dew,
> Or that the Everlasting had not fixed
> His canon 'gainst self-slaughter! O God, God,
> How weary, stale, flat, and unprofitable
> Seem to me all the uses of this world!
> Fie on 't, ah fie! 'Tis an unweeded garden
> That grows to seed. Things rank and gross in nature
> Possess it merely.

Hamlet feels such despair that he wishes he could disappear.

His choice of words expresses his disgust with everything around him.

148   Unit 2

BACKGROUND

William Shakespeare *(1564–1616) is considered the finest writer in the English language, admired for his rhetorical power, poetic brilliance, and profound psychological insight. Four centuries after his death, he continues to occupy a central place in literary studies and in our culture. His plays are regularly performed around the world and have been adapted into many films. Ben Jonson, a rival Elizabethan playwright, showed great foresight when he declared that Shakespeare "was not of an age, but for all time."*

THE TRAGEDY OF HAMLET
Drama by William Shakespeare

Shakespeare was born in Stratford-upon-Avon, a market town in central England. He probably attended Stratford's grammar school, where he would have studied Latin and read classical authors. In 1582 he married Anne Hathaway, who gave birth to their three children within several years. Shakespeare's theatrical career took off in 1594 when he joined the Lord Chamberlain's Men, which became London's most prestigious theater company. Shakespeare, who also acted, soon grew affluent from his share in the company's profits. He bought a large house in Stratford, where his wife and children remained.

Shakespeare's mastered all forms of drama. In the 1590s, he focused on comedies and English history plays, such as A Midsummer Night's Dream and Henry IV. Between 1600 and 1607, he wrote his greatest tragedies, including Hamlet. The final phase of his career saw the creation of darker comedies, such as The Tempest. In addition to his 38 plays, Shakespeare wrote two narrative poems and a highly innovative collection of sonnets.

Shakespeare died in Stratford when he was 52 years old. At the time, some of his plays existed in cheap, often badly flawed editions; others had never appeared in print. In 1623, two theater colleagues published a collected edition of his plays known as the First Folio, which ensured the survival of his remarkable work.

TEACH

BACKGROUND

It is recorded that in 1592, a rival dramatist named Robert Greene jealously referred to Shakespeare as an "upstart crow," showing that already by this time, Shakespeare was gaining recognition for his work. Shakespeare's theater company, the Lord Chamberlain's Men, enjoyed the approval of Queen Elizabeth I. After her death in 1603, King James I became their patron, at which time the company changed its name to the King's Men. Having the patronage of the reigning monarch helped to ensure their domination of the theater scene.

Shakespeare's accomplishments are even more astonishing considering the conditions he had to meet. There had to be enough parts for all of the members of the theater company; the women's parts had to be played by men; and there had to be enough action and excitement to satisfy the demanding audiences of the day. Yet, even working within these parameters, Shakespeare was able to create an astonishing range of plays that all speak to the universal human experience.

LEARNING MINDSET

Effort   Explain to students that part of having a Learning Mindset is being willing to make an effort. Emphasize that success always comes from hard work, and give students positive feedback for making an effort. Even when students struggle, commend them when they keep working through a problem. For example, you might say, "I noticed you really struggled with that passage today, but you didn't give up. That kind of effort is what leads to success, so you should be proud of yourself for that."

TEACH

SETTING A PURPOSE

Direct students to use the Setting a Purpose prompt to focus their reading.

Notice & Note

Use the side margins to notice and note signposts in the text.

SETTING A PURPOSE

As you read, look for clues to Hamlet's attitude toward his mother and uncle, and notice any changes in his attitude over the course of the act.

CHARACTERS

The Ghost
Hamlet, Prince of Denmark, son of the late King Hamlet and Queen Gertrude
Queen Gertrude, widow of King Hamlet, now married to Claudius
King Claudius, brother to the late King Hamlet
Polonius, councillor to King Claudius
Ophelia, daughter of Polonius
Laertes, son of Polonius
Reynaldo, servant to Polonius
Horatio, Hamlet's friend and confidant

COURTIERS AT THE DANISH COURT

    Voltemand
    Cornelius
    Rosencrantz
    Guildenstern
    Osric
    Gentlemen
    A Lord

DANISH SOLDIERS

    Francisco
    Barnardo
    Marcellus

Fortinbras, Prince of Norway
A Captain in Fortinbras's army
Ambassadors to Denmark from England
Players who take the roles of Prologue, Player King, Player Queen, and Lucianus in *The Murder of Gonzago*
Two Messengers
Sailors
Gravedigger
Gravedigger's companion
Doctor of Divinity
Attendants, Lords, Guards, Musicians, Laertes's Followers, Soldiers, Officers

Place: Denmark

WHEN STUDENTS STRUGGLE...

Understand Characters Review the list of characters on page 150. Read each name aloud, and have students repeat them. Then, discuss the identifying details given for the characters. Tell students the list is organized in order of importance. In small groups, have students create a diagram that shows the relationships among the principal characters. Display a blank family tree for structure. Encourage students to refer to their diagram as they read.

 For additional support, go to the **Reading Studio** and assign the following **Level Up tutorial: Characters and Conflict**.

ACT I

NOTICE & NOTE

Scene 1 *A guard platform at Elsinore Castle.*

[*Enter* Barnardo *and* Francisco, *two sentinels.*]

Barnardo. Who's there?

Francisco. Nay, answer me. Stand and unfold yourself.

Barnardo. Long live the King!

Francisco. Barnardo.

5 **Barnardo.** He.

Francisco. You come most carefully upon your hour.

Barnardo. 'Tis now struck twelve. Get thee to bed, Francisco.

Francisco. For this relief much thanks. 'Tis bitter cold, And I am sick at heart.

10 **Barnardo.** Have you had quiet guard?

Francisco. Not a mouse stirring.

Barnardo. Well, good night.
If you do meet Horatio and Marcellus,
The rivals of my watch, bid them make haste.

[*Enter* Horatio *and* Marcellus.]

15 **Francisco.** I think I hear them.—Stand ho! Who is there?

Horatio. Friends to this ground.

Marcellus. And liegemen to the Dane.

Francisco. Give you good night.

Marcellus. O farewell, honest soldier. Who hath relieved you?

20 **Francisco.** Barnardo hath my place. Give you good night.

[*Francisco exits.*]

Marcellus. Holla, Barnardo.

Barnardo. Say, what, is Horatio there?

Horatio. A piece of him.

Barnardo. Welcome, Horatio.—Welcome, good Marcellus.

25 **Horatio.** What, has this thing appeared again tonight?

Barnardo. I have seen nothing.

2 unfold yourself: show who you are.

14 rivals of my watch: the other soldiers on guard duty with me.

16–17 Horatio and Marcellus identify themselves as friendly to Denmark (**this ground**) and loyal subjects of the Danish king (**the Dane**).

The Tragedy of Hamlet: Act I, Scene 1   151

TO CHALLENGE STUDENTS...

Predict Conflict Remind students that the action of a play is driven by conflict, or a struggle between opposing forces. Have students make predictions about possible conflicts based on the details presented for Hamlet, Queen Gertrude, and King Claudius. Have students write down their predictions in a chart, which they can verify and adjust as they read.

TEACH

NOTICE & NOTE

27–33 Marcellus explains that Horatio doubts their story about having twice seen a ghost (**apparition**), so he has brought Horatio to confirm what they saw (**approve our eyes**).

Marcellus. Horatio says 'tis but our fantasy
And will not let belief take hold of him
Touching this dreaded sight twice seen of us.
30 Therefore I have entreated him along
With us to watch the minutes of this night,
That, if again this apparition come,
He may approve our eyes and speak to it.

Horatio. Tush, tush, 'twill not appear.

Barnardo.   Sit down a while,
35 And let us once again assail your ears,
That are so fortified against our story,
What we have two nights seen.

Horatio.   Well, sit we down,
And let us hear Barnardo speak of this.

Barnardo. Last night of all,

40 star . . . pole: the North Star.
41 his: its.

40 When yond same star that's westward from the pole
Had made his course t' illume that part of heaven
Where now it burns, Marcellus and myself,
The bell then beating one—

[*Enter* Ghost.]

Marcellus. Peace, break thee off! Look where it comes again.

46–50 It was commonly believed that a ghost could only speak after it was spoken to, preferably by someone learned enough (**a scholar**) to ask the proper questions.

48 harrows: torments.

50 usurp'st: unlawfully takes over.

52 majesty of buried Denmark: the buried King of Denmark.

53 sometimes: formerly.

45 **Barnardo.** In the same figure like the King that's dead.

Marcellus [*to* **Horatio**]. Thou art a scholar. Speak to it, Horatio.

Barnardo. Looks he not like the King? Mark it, Horatio.

Horatio. Most like. It harrows me with fear and wonder.

Barnardo. It would be spoke to.

Marcellus.   Speak to it, Horatio.

50 **Horatio.** What art thou that usurp'st this time of night,
Together with that fair and warlike form
In which the majesty of buried Denmark
Did sometimes march? By heaven, I charge thee, speak.

Marcellus. It is offended.

Barnardo.   See, it stalks away.

55 **Horatio.** Stay! speak! speak! I charge thee, speak!

[Ghost *exits*.]

Marcellus. 'Tis gone and will not answer.

Barnardo. How now, Horatio, you tremble and look pale.
Is not this something more than fantasy?
What think you on 't?

60 **Horatio.** Before my God, I might not this believe

152 Unit 2

IMPROVE READING FLUENCY

Targeted Passage In lines 45–57, the three characters are reacting to the appearance of the Ghost. After discussing the meaning of the characters' words, divide the class into three groups, each assigned one character's part. Model reading this passage dramatically—with appropriate emotion, stress, and rhythm—and have each group echo you as you read their part. Then, direct the groups to practice reading their parts again in a choral reading. Have volunteers from each group act out the scene as the parts are read.

 Go to the **Reading Studio** for additional support in developing fluency.

Without the sensible and true avouch
Of mine own eyes.

Marcellus. Is it not like the King?

Horatio. As thou art to thyself.
Such was the very armor he had on
65 When he the ambitious Norway combated.
So frowned he once when, in an angry parle,
He smote the sledded Polacks on the ice.
'Tis strange.

Marcellus. Thus twice before, and jump at this dead hour,
70 With martial stalk hath he gone by our watch.

Horatio. In what particular thought to work I know not,
But in the gross and scope of mine opinion
This bodes some strange eruption to our state.

Marcellus. Good now, sit down, and tell me, he that knows,
75 Why this same strict and most observant watch
So nightly toils the subject of the land,
And why such daily cast of brazen cannon
And foreign mart for implements of war,
Why such impress of shipwrights, whose sore task
80 Does not divide the Sunday from the week.
What might be toward that this sweaty haste
Doth make the night joint laborer with the day?
Who is 't that can inform me?

Horatio. That can I.
At least the whisper goes so: our last king,
85 Whose image even but now appeared to us,
Was, as you know, by Fortinbras of Norway,
Thereto pricked on by a most emulate pride,
Dared to the combat; in which our valiant Hamlet
(For so this side of our known world esteemed him)
90 Did slay this Fortinbras, who by a sealed compact,
Well ratified by law and heraldry,
Did forfeit, with his life, all those his lands
Which he stood seized of, to the conqueror.
Against the which a moiety competent
95 Was gagèd by our king, which had returned
To the inheritance of Fortinbras
Had he been vanquisher, as, by the same comart
And carriage of the article designed,
His fell to Hamlet. Now, sir, young Fortinbras,
100 Of unimprovèd mettle hot and full,
Hath in the skirts of Norway here and there
Sharked up a list of lawless resolutes
For food and diet to some enterprise

NOTICE & NOTE

61–62 Without . . . eyes: without seeing the proof (**avouch**) with my own eyes.

ANALYZE DRAMATIC PLOT
Annotate: Mark details in lines 63–68 about the former king's actions.

Infer: What does this exposition suggest about his personality?

65 Norway: the King of Norway.

66 parle: parley, meeting with an enemy.

67 smote: defeated; sledded Polacks: Polish soldiers riding in sleds.

69 jump: exactly.

72–73 This is a bad omen (**bodes some strange eruption**) for Denmark.

74–78 Can anyone explain why the Danes weary themselves each night with sentry duty and why there is so much casting of armaments (**brazen cannon**) and foreign trade (**mart**) for weapons?

81 toward: approaching, in preparation.

90–104 By prior agreement and according to laws governing combat, Hamlet gained all the land that Fortinbras had possessed (**stood seized of**). Hamlet had pledged an equivalent portion (**moiety competent**) of his land, which would have gone to Fortinbras if he won the battle, as was specified in the same agreement. Young Fortinbras, who has an undisciplined character (**unimprovèd mettle**), has gathered hastily (**Sharked up**) in outlying districts (**skirts**) of Norway a troop of lawless desperadoes to serve in some undertaking that requires courage (**hath a stomach in 't**).

The Tragedy of Hamlet: Act I, Scene 1   153

TEACH

✏️ ANALYZE DRAMATIC PLOT

Tell students that in lines 63–68, Horatio is recounting the actions of the late King Hamlet. Have students locate the verbs in these lines and then use a Think Aloud to model how to understand the text, using the side notes to help them:

I see the verb combated. *Whom did he combat? The word order is unusual, but it looks like he combated the* ambitious Norway. *The note in the margin says* Norway *means* the King of Norway.

Then, have students reread the rest of the passage and turn to a partner to explain in their own words what King Hamlet did and what kind of a person they think he was. (Answer: *King Hamlet's battling of "the ambitious Norway" and defeat of the Polish army suggest he was a brave and successful warrior.*)

■ English Learner Support

Demonstrate Comprehension by Retelling Details
To help students answer the question, point out the verbs *combated* and *smote,* and direct students to the side note in Scene 1, page 153, that tells them *smote* means *defeated.* Tell students that the word *combat* means *fight.*

Then, have students complete these sentences orally:

- King Hamlet _____ the King of Norway and the Polish army. (*fought*)
- When King Hamlet _____ the Polish army, _____ won. (*fought/King Hamlet*)
- King Hamlet was scared/angry/brave. (*brave*)

SUBSTANTIAL

WHEN STUDENTS STRUGGLE . . .

Identify Subplot Help students understand the subplot in lines 84–112 by completing a cause-and-effect chart, using the marginal notes as well as the text.

Hamlet defeats Fortinbras, takes land → Fortinbras wants land back and plans attack → Denmark prepares defense against attack

 For additional support, go to the **Reading Studio** and assign the following 📱 Level Up tutorial: Plot: Sequence of Events.

The Tragedy of Hamlet: Act I, Scene 1   **153**

TEACH

 **NOTICE & NOTE**

That hath a stomach in 't; which is no other
105 (As it doth well appear unto our state)
But to recover of us, by strong hand
And terms compulsatory, those foresaid lands
So by his father lost. And this, I take it,
Is the main motive of our preparations,
110 The source of this our watch, and the chief head
Of this posthaste and rummage in the land.

Barnardo. I think it be no other but e'en so.
Well may it sort that this portentous figure
Comes armèd through our watch so like the king
115 That was and is the question of these wars.

Horatio. A mote it is to trouble the mind's eye.
In the most high and palmy state of Rome,
A little ere the mightiest Julius fell,
The graves stood tenantless, and the sheeted dead
120 Did squeak and gibber in the Roman streets;
As stars with trains of fire and dews of blood,
Disasters in the sun; and the moist star,
Upon whose influence Neptune's empire stands,
Was sick almost to doomsday with eclipse.
125 And even the like precurse of feared events,
As harbingers preceding still the fates
And prologue to the omen coming on,
Have heaven and earth together demonstrated
Unto our climatures and countrymen.

[*Enter* Ghost.]

130 But soft, behold! Lo, where it comes again!
I'll cross it though it blast me.—Stay, illusion!

[*It spreads his arms.*]

If thou hast any sound or use of voice,
Speak to me.
If there be any good thing to be done
135 That may to thee do ease and grace to me,
Speak to me.
If thou art privy to thy country's fate,
Which happily foreknowing may avoid,
O, speak!
140 Or if thou hast uphoarded in thy life
Extorted treasure in the womb of earth,
For which, they say, you spirits oft walk in death,
Speak of it.

[*The cock crows.*]

Stay and speak!—Stop it, Marcellus.

---

110 head: source.
111 rummage: bustle.

113 Well . . . sort: it may be fitting.

116 mote: dust speck.
117 palmy: thriving.

119 sheeted: wrapped in shrouds.

120 gibber: chatter.

122 Disasters: menacing signs; **moist star:** the moon, which controls the Earth's tides.

123 Neptune: Roman god of the sea.

125–129 A similar foreshadowing (**precurse**) has occurred in Denmark, where a terrible event (**omen**) was preceded by signs that were like forerunners (**harbingers**) announcing the approach of someone.

130 soft: be quiet, hold off.
131 cross: confront.

138 happily . . . avoid: perhaps (**happily**) may be avoided if known in advance.
141 Extorted: ill-gotten.

Marcellus. Shall I strike it with my partisan?

145 **Horatio.** Do, if it will not stand.

Barnardo. 'Tis here.

Horatio. 'Tis here.

[Ghost *exits*.]

Marcellus. 'Tis gone.
We do it wrong, being so majestical,
150 To offer it the show of violence,
For it is as the air, invulnerable,
And our vain blows malicious mockery.

Barnardo. It was about to speak when the cock crew.

Horatio. And then it started like a guilty thing
155 Upon a fearful summons. I have heard
The cock, that is the trumpet to the morn,
Doth with his lofty and shrill-sounding throat
Awake the god of day, and at his warning,
Whether in sea or fire, in earth or air,
160 Th' extravagant and erring spirit hies
To his confine, and of the truth herein
This present object made probation.

Marcellus. It faded on the crowing of the cock.
Some say that ever 'gainst that season comes
165 Wherein our Savior's birth is celebrated,
This bird of dawning singeth all night long;
And then, they say, no spirit dare stir abroad,
The nights are wholesome; then no planets strike,
No fairy takes, nor witch hath power to charm,
170 So hallowed and so gracious is that time.

Horatio. So have I heard and do in part believe it.
But look, the morn in russet mantle clad
Walks o'er the dew of yon high eastward hill.
Break we our watch up, and by my advice
175 Let us impart what we have seen tonight
Unto young Hamlet; for, upon my life,
This spirit, dumb to us, will speak to him.
Do you consent we shall acquaint him with it
As needful in our loves, fitting our duty?

180 **Marcellus.** Let's do 't, I pray, and I this morning know
Where we shall find him most convenient.

[*They exit*.]

---

144 partisan: a long-handled weapon.

154 started: made a sudden movement.

160 extravagant and erring: wandering out of bounds.

162 made probation: demonstrated.

164–165 ever . . . celebrated: just before Christmas.

168 strike: put forth an evil influence.

169 takes: bewitches.

TEACH

✏️ ANALYZE DRAMATIC PLOT

Explain to students that in Scene 2, lines 1–16, Claudius is talking about the death of King Hamlet—who was his brother—and that after King Hamlet's death, Claudius married the queen. Direct them to look for language that expresses Claudius's feelings about King Hamlet's death. Make sure students read the note on Scene 2, lines 11–12—, which explains the mixed feelings Claudius expresses. For each phrase students mark, ask them to identify whether the emotion is positive or negative. (**Answer:** *Claudius claims he is sorry about his brother's death even though it has meant good fortune for him. There is some doubt, though, as to whether he is sincere in his feelings of grief.*)

■ English Learner Support

Develop Vocabulary To help students complete the activity, first have them circle words in lines 1–16 of Scene 2, page 156, that describe emotions. Provide the following definitions for words that are unfamiliar:

- **woe** (line 4): distress or grief
- **mirth** (line 12): laughter or amusement
- **dirge** (line 12): funeral song mourning the dead
- **dole** (line 13): grief or sorrow **SUBSTANTIAL**

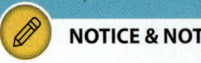 **NOTICE & NOTE**

ANALYZE DRAMATIC PLOT
Annotate: Mark phrases that Claudius uses to convey his feelings about his brother's death in lines 1–16.

Draw Conclusions: Do you think that Claudius is speaking sincerely? Why or why not?

8 our sometime sister: my former sister-in-law. (Claudius uses the royal "we.")

9 jointress: a woman who owns property with her husband.

11–12 With . . . eye: with one eye reflecting good fortune and the other eye, sorrow; **dirge:** a song of mourning.

21 Colleaguèd . . . advantage: connected with this false hope of his superior position.

23 Importing: relating to.

29 impotent: helpless.

30–33 Since Fortinbras has obtained all of his troops and supplies from Norway, Claudius has asked the King of Norway to stop him from proceeding further.

37 To business: to negotiate.

38 dilated articles: detailed instructions.

Scene 2 *A state room at the castle.*

[*Flourish. Enter* Claudius, *King of Denmark,* Gertrude the Queen, *the* Council, *as* Polonius, *and his son* Laertes, Hamlet, *with others, among them* Voltemand *and* Cornelius.]

King. Though yet of Hamlet our dear brother's death
The memory be green, and that it us befitted
To bear our hearts in grief, and our whole kingdom
To be contracted in one brow of woe,
5 Yet so far hath discretion fought with nature
That we with wisest sorrow think on him
Together with remembrance of ourselves.
Therefore our sometime sister, now our queen,
Th' imperial jointress to this warlike state,
10 Have we (as 'twere with a defeated joy,
With an auspicious and a dropping eye,
With mirth in funeral and with dirge in marriage,
In equal scale weighing delight and dole)
Taken to wife. Nor have we herein barred
15 Your better wisdoms, which have freely gone
With this affair along. For all, our thanks.
Now follows that you know. Young Fortinbras,
Holding a weak supposal of our worth
Or thinking by our late dear brother's death
20 Our state to be disjoint and out of frame,
Colleaguèd with this dream of his advantage,
He hath not failed to pester us with message
Importing the surrender of those lands
Lost by his father, with all bonds of law,
25 To our most valiant brother—so much for him.
Now for ourself and for this time of meeting.
Thus much the business is: we have here writ
To Norway, uncle of young Fortinbras,
Who, impotent and bedrid, scarcely hears
30 Of this his nephew's purpose, to suppress
His further gait herein, in that the levies,
The lists, and full proportions are all made
Out of his subject; and we here dispatch
You, good Cornelius, and you, Voltemand,
35 For bearers of this greeting to old Norway,
Giving to you no further personal power
To business with the King more than the scope
Of these dilated articles allow.

[*Giving them a paper.*]

Farewell, and let your haste commend your duty.

Laurence Olivier's 1948 film *Hamlet*. Background: Hamlet (Laurence Olivier). Foreground, left to right: Claudius (Basil Sidney), Gertrude (Eileen Herlie), Polonius (Felix Aylmer).

40 **Cornelius/Voltemand.** In that and all things will we show our duty.

King. We doubt it nothing. Heartily farewell.

[*Voltemand and Cornelius exit.*]

And now, Laertes, what's the news with you?
You told us of some suit. What is 't, Laertes?
You cannot speak of reason to the Dane
45 And lose your voice. What wouldst thou beg, Laertes,
That shall not be my offer, not thy asking?
The head is not more native to the heart,
The hand more instrumental to the mouth,
Than is the throne of Denmark to thy father.
50 What wouldst thou have, Laertes?

Laertes. My dread lord,
Your leave and favor to return to France,
From whence though willingly I came to Denmark
To show my duty in your coronation,

45 lose your voice: waste your breath.

47 native: closely connected.

The Tragedy of Hamlet: Act I, Scene 2   157

TEACH

NOTICE & NOTE

Yet now I must confess, that duty done,
55 My thoughts and wishes bend again toward France
And bow them to your gracious leave and pardon.

King. Have you your father's leave? What says Polonius?

Polonius. Hath, my lord, wrung from me my slow leave
By laborsome petition, and at last
60 Upon his will I sealed my hard consent.
I do beseech you give him leave to go.

King. Take thy fair hour, Laertes. Time be thine,
And thy best graces spend it at thy will.—
But now, my cousin Hamlet and my son—

65 **Hamlet** [*aside*]. A little more than kin and less than kind.

King. How is it that the clouds still hang on you?

Hamlet. Not so, my lord; I am too much in the sun.

Queen. Good Hamlet, cast thy nighted color off,
And let thine eye look like a friend on Denmark.
70 Do not forever with thy vailèd lids
Seek for thy noble father in the dust.
Thou know'st 'tis common; all that lives must die,
Passing through nature to eternity.

Hamlet. Ay, madam, it is common.

Queen. If it be,
75 Why seems it so particular with thee?

Hamlet. "Seems," madam? Nay, it is. I know not "seems."
'Tis not alone my inky cloak, good mother,
Nor customary suits of solemn black,
Nor windy suspiration of forced breath,
80 No, nor the fruitful river in the eye,
Nor the dejected havior of the visage,
Together with all forms, moods, shapes of grief,
That can denote me truly. These indeed "seem,"
For they are actions that a man might play;
85 But I have that within which passes show,
These but the trappings and the suits of woe.

King. 'Tis sweet and commendable in your nature, Hamlet,
To give these mourning duties to your father.
But you must know your father lost a father,
90 That father lost, lost his, and the survivor bound
In filial obligation for some term
To do obsequious sorrow. But to persever
In obstinate condolement is a course
Of impious stubbornness. 'Tis unmanly grief.

60 Upon . . . consent: I reluctantly agreed to his wishes.

64 cousin: kinsman.

65 Hamlet plays off two meanings of **kind:** "loving" and "natural." He does not resemble Claudius in nature or feel a son's affection for him.

67 sun: the sunlight of royal favor (also a pun on **son**, suggesting annoyance at Claudius's use of the word).

68 nighted color: dark mood.

70 vailèd lids: lowered eyes.

74 Hamlet plays off two meanings of **common:** "universal" and "vulgar."

75 particular: special, personal.

77–83 'Tis not . . . truly: My feelings are not limited to my black mourning clothes, heavy sighs, tears, downcast expression, and other outward signs of grief.

89–94 Claudius says that a surviving son must dutifully mourn (**do obsequious sorrow**) for a while, but to remain stubbornly in grief (**obstinate condolement**) beyond that appropriate period is perverse.

158   Unit 2

ENGLISH LEARNER SUPPORT

Use Accessible Language to Learn New Language Tell students that in lines 76–81 of Scene 2, page 158, Hamlet describes the outward appearances of grief, which he calls "the trappings and the suits of woe." Direct their attention to the side note that translates his language into simpler modern English. Using vocabulary cards, have students match words and phrases from the side note to those from the text: *inky cloak/black clothes, suspiration of forced breath/heavy sighs, fruitful river in the eye/tears, visage/expression.* **MODERATE**

95   It shows a will most incorrect to heaven,
     A heart unfortified, a mind impatient,
     An understanding simple and unschooled.
     For what we know must be and is as common
     As any the most vulgar thing to sense,
100 Why should we in our peevish opposition
     Take it to heart? Fie, 'tis a fault to heaven,
     A fault against the dead, a fault to nature,
     To reason most absurd, whose common theme
     Is death of fathers, and who still hath cried,
105 From the first corse till he that died today,
     "This must be so." We pray you, throw to earth
     This unprevailing woe and think of us
     As of a father; for let the world take note,
     You are the most immediate to our throne,
110 And with no less nobility of love
     Than that which dearest father bears his son
     Do I impart toward you. For your intent
     In going back to school in Wittenberg,
     It is most retrograde to our desire,
115 And we beseech you, bend you to remain
     Here in the cheer and comfort of our eye,
     Our chiefest courtier, cousin, and our son.

     Queen. Let not thy mother lose her prayers, Hamlet.
     I pray thee, stay with us. Go not to Wittenberg.
120 **Hamlet.** I shall in all my best obey you, madam.
     King. Why, 'tis a loving and a fair reply.
     Be as ourself in Denmark.—Madam, come.
     This gentle and unforced accord of Hamlet
     Sits smiling to my heart, in grace where of
125 No jocund health that Denmark drinks today
     But the great cannon to the clouds shall tell,
     And the King's rouse the heaven shall bruit again,
     Respeaking earthly thunder. Come away.

     [*Flourish. All but* Hamlet *exit.*]

     Hamlet. O, that this too, too sullied flesh would melt,
130 Thaw, and resolve itself into a dew,
     Or that the Everlasting had not fixed
     His canon 'gainst self-slaughter! O God, God,
     How weary, stale, flat, and unprofitable
     Seem to me all the uses of this world!
135 Fie on 't, ah fie! 'Tis an unweeded garden
     That grows to seed. Things rank and gross in nature
     Possess it merely. That it should come to this:

96 unfortified: unstrengthened against adversity.

99 As . . . sense: as the most common experience.

104 still: always.

105 corse: corpse.

107 unprevailing: not yielding to persuasion.

108–112 Claudius claims that he offers (**impart toward**) Hamlet, who is next in line (**most immediate**) to succeed to the throne, all the love that the most affectionate father feels for his son.

113 Wittenberg University (founded in 1502) was famous for being the school of German theologian Martin Luther, whose challenge to Roman Catholic doctrine started the Reformation.

114 retrograde: contrary.

125–128 Claudius boasts that he will not merely drink a happy toast (**jocund health**) that day, but a deep drink (**rouse**) accompanied by fanfare, which heaven will echo with thunder.

129 sullied: stained, defiled.

132 canon: law.

ANALYZE SOLILOQUY

Annotate: Mark words in lines 129–159 that convey strong feelings.

Analyze: What is Hamlet most upset about in this soliloquy?

The Tragedy of Hamlet: Act I, Scene 2   159

TEACH

ENGLISH LEARNER SUPPORT

Share Information in a Cooperative Learning Interaction Explain to students that in Scene 2, lines 139–156, page 160, Hamlet is telling a story about something that happened before the beginning of the action in the play. Tell students they are going to work together to understand this story. Put students into mixed-ability groups, and have each group read and discuss one of three parts of this passage:

- lines 139–145
- lines 145–153
- lines 153–156

Support students in understanding the events in their assigned passage and have them practice retelling the passage in modern English. Then, form new groups in which each part of this passage is represented by at least one student from the earlier groups. Have the new groups work together to complete a timeline of events that happened during the two months before the beginning of this play.

MODERATE/LIGHT

 **NOTICE & NOTE**

139–140 Hamlet says that comparing his father to Claudius would be like comparing the sun god **Hyperion** to a **satyr** (a mythical creature, half man and half goat, associated with lechery).

141 beteem: allow.

147 or ere: before.

149 Niobe: a Greek mythological figure who continued weeping for her slaughtered children even after she was turned to stone.

155 Had . . . eyes: had stopped reddening her inflamed (**gallèd**) eyes.

157 incestuous: Marriage between a widow and her late husband's brother was often considered incestuous in Shakespeare's time and was prohibited by church law.

163 Horatio refers to himself as a "servant" out of respect for Hamlet.

169 what . . . from: what are you doing away from.

173 truster: believer.

But two months dead—nay, not so much, not two.
So excellent a king, that was to this
140 Hyperion to a satyr; so loving to my mother
That he might not beteem the winds of heaven
Visit her face too roughly. Heaven and earth,
Must I remember? Why, she would hang on him
As if increase of appetite had grown
145 By what it fed on. And yet, within a month
(Let me not think on 't; frailty, thy name is woman!),
A little month, or ere those shoes were old
With which she followed my poor father's body,
Like Niobe, all tears—why she, even she
150 (O God, a beast that wants discourse of reason
Would have mourned longer!), married with my uncle,
My father's brother, but no more like my father
Than I to Hercules. Within a month,
Ere yet the salt of most unrighteous tears
155 Had left the flushing in her gallèd eyes,
She married. O, most wicked speed, to post
With such dexterity to incestuous sheets!
It is not, nor it cannot come to good.
But break, my heart, for I must hold my tongue.

[*Enter* Horatio, Marcellus, *and* Barnardo.]

160 **Horatio.** Hail to your lordship.

Hamlet. I am glad to see you well.
Horatio—or I do forget myself!

Horatio. The same, my lord, and your poor servant ever.

Hamlet. Sir, my good friend. I'll change that name with you.
165 And what make you from Wittenberg, Horatio?—Marcellus?

Marcellus. My good lord.

Hamlet. I am very glad to see you. [*To* Barnardo.] Good even, sir.—
But what, in faith, make you from Wittenberg?

170 **Horatio.** A truant disposition, good my lord.

Hamlet. I would not hear your enemy say so,
Nor shall you do my ear that violence
To make it truster of your own report
Against yourself. I know you are no truant.
175 But what is your affair in Elsinore?
We'll teach you to drink deep ere you depart.

Horatio. My lord, I came to see your father's funeral.

Hamlet. I prithee, do not mock me, fellow student.

WHEN STUDENTS STRUGGLE . . .

Identify External and Internal Conflicts Tell students that conflict is often the basis of action in a drama, as characters try to resolve their conflicts, or problems. To help students understand both Hamlet's character and the conflicts he is experiencing, have them reread Scene 2, lines 65–159, pages 158–160. Then, have students fill out a chart identifying each conflict Hamlet's words reveal and the text that reveals it. Prompt students as needed by directing them to specific passages.

 For additional support, go to the **Reading Studio** and assign the following Level Up tutorial: **Characters and Conflict**.

I think it was to see my mother's wedding.

180 **Horatio.** Indeed, my lord, it followed hard upon.

Hamlet. Thrift, thrift, Horatio. The funeral baked meats
Did coldly furnish forth the marriage tables.
Would I had met my dearest foe in heaven
Or ever I had seen that day, Horatio!
185 My father—methinks I see my father.

Horatio. Where, my lord?

Hamlet. In my mind's eye, Horatio.

Horatio. I saw him once. He was a goodly king.

Hamlet. He was a man. Take him for all in all,
I shall not look upon his like again.

190 **Horatio.** My lord, I think I saw him yesternight.

Hamlet. Saw who?

Horatio. My lord, the King your father.

Hamlet. The King my father?

Horatio. Season your admiration for a while
With an attent ear, till I may deliver
195 Upon the witness of these gentlemen
This marvel to you.

Hamlet. For God's love, let me hear!

Horatio. Two nights together had these gentlemen,
Marcellus and Barnardo, on their watch,
In the dead waste and middle of the night,
200 Been thus encountered: a figure like your father,
Armèd at point exactly, cap-à-pie,
Appears before them and with solemn march
Goes slow and stately by them. Thrice he walked
By their oppressed and fear-surprisèd eyes
205 Within his truncheon's length, whilst they, distilled
Almost to jelly with the act of fear,
Stand dumb and speak not to him. This to me
In dreadful secrecy impart they did,
And I with them the third night kept the watch,
210 Where, as they had delivered, both in time,
Form of the thing (each word made true and good),
The apparition comes. I knew your father;
These hands are not more like.

Hamlet. But where was this?

Marcellus. My lord, upon the platform where we watch.

---

180 hard upon: soon after.

181–182 The funeral . . . tables: Leftovers from the funeral were served cold at the marriage feast.

183 dearest: most hated.

184 Or ever: before.

187 goodly: fine, admirable.

193–194 Season . . . ear: Control your astonishment for a moment and listen carefully.

201 Armèd . . . cap-à-pie: armed properly in every detail, from head to foot.

205 Within his truncheon's length: no farther away than the length of his short staff.

205–206 distilled . . . fear: reduced almost to jelly by fear.

207–208 This . . . did: They told me this in terrified (**dreadful**) secrecy.

210 delivered: asserted.

TEACH

 **NOTICE & NOTE**

215 **Hamlet.** Did you not speak to it?

Horatio. My lord, I did,
But answer made it none. Yet once methought
It lifted up its head and did address
Itself to motion, like as it would speak;
But even then the morning cock crew loud,
220 And at the sound it shrunk in haste away
And vanished from our sight.

Hamlet. 'Tis very strange.

Horatio. As I do live, my honored lord, 'tis true.
And we did think it writ down in our duty
To let you know of it.

225 **Hamlet.** Indeed, sirs, but this troubles me.
Hold you the watch tonight?

All. We do, my lord.

Hamlet. Armed, say you?

All. Armed, my lord.

Hamlet. From top to toe?

All. My lord, from head to foot.

Hamlet. Then saw you not his face?

230 **Horatio.** O, yes, my lord, he wore his beaver up.

Hamlet. What, looked he frowningly?

Horatio. A countenance more in sorrow than in anger.

Hamlet. Pale or red?

Horatio. Nay, very pale.

Hamlet. And fixed his eyes upon you?

235 **Horatio.** Most constantly.

Hamlet. I would I had been there.

Horatio. It would have much amazed you.

Hamlet. Very like. Stayed it long?

Horatio. While one with moderate haste might tell a hundred.

Barnardo/Marcellus. Longer, longer.

240 **Horatio.** Not when I saw 't.

Hamlet. His beard was grizzled, no?

Horatio. It was as I have seen it in his life,
A sable silvered.

Hamlet. I will watch tonight.

217–218 did . . . speak: began to move as if it were going to speak.

219 even then: just then.

230 beaver: movable front piece of a helmet.

238 While . . . hundred: for as long as one could count (**tell**) to one hundred at a moderate pace.

240 grizzled: gray.

242 A sable silvered: black hair with white hair mixed through it.

 ENGLISH LEARNER SUPPORT

Recognize Verb Forms Tell students that as they read the play, they will encounter irregular forms of verbs. Explain that they can use context clues to help them identify the familiar form of the verb. Direct students' attention to the word *crew* in Scene 2, line 219, page 162. Tell students this word means "crowed," based on the clue "loud" that follows it.

SUBSTANTIAL/MODERATE

Perchance 'twill walk again.

Horatio. I warrant it will.

Hamlet. If it assume my noble father's person,
245 I'll speak to it, though hell itself should gape
And bid me hold my peace. I pray you all,
If you have hitherto concealed this sight,
Let it be tenable in your silence still;
And whatsomever else shall hap tonight,
250 Give it an understanding but no tongue.
I will requite your loves. So fare you well.
Upon the platform, 'twixt eleven and twelve,
I'll visit you.

All. Our duty to your Honor.

Hamlet. Your loves, as mine to you. Farewell.

[*All but* Hamlet *exit.*]

255 My father's spirit—in arms! All is not well.
I doubt some foul play. Would the night were come!
Till then, sit still, my soul. Foul deeds will rise,
Though all the earth o'erwhelm them, to men's eyes.

[*He exits.*]

248 tenable: held.
249 whatsomever: whatever;
hap: happen.
251 I...loves: I will reward your devotion.

256 doubt: suspect.

Scene 3 *Polonius's chambers.*

[*Enter* Laertes *and* Ophelia, *his sister.*]

Laertes. My necessaries are embarked. Farewell.
And, sister, as the winds give benefit
And convey is assistant, do not sleep,
But let me hear from you.

Ophelia. Do you doubt that?

5 **Laertes.** For Hamlet, and the trifling of his favor,
Hold it a fashion and a toy in blood,
A violet in the youth of primy nature,
Forward, not permanent, sweet, not lasting,
The perfume and suppliance of a minute,
10 No more.

Ophelia. No more but so?

Laertes. Think it no more.
For nature, crescent, does not grow alone
In thews and bulk, but, as this temple waxes,
The inward service of the mind and soul
Grows wide withal. Perhaps he loves you now,
15 And now no soil nor cautel doth besmirch
The virtue of his will; but you must fear,

6 fashion...blood: a temporary enthusiasm and an amorous whim.
7 in...nature: at the beginning of its prime.
8 Forward: early blooming.
9–10 The...more: a sweet but temporary diversion.
11–14 A growing person does not only increase in strength (**thews**) and size, but as the body grows (**this temple waxes**), the inner life (**inward service**) of mind and soul grows along with it.
15 cautel: deceit.

TEACH

✏️ WORDS OF THE WISER

Explain to students that Words of the Wiser is a signpost in a fiction text that can help them analyze the text and identify **conflicts.** In Words of the Wiser, one character, usually older or more experienced, offers advice to another character. In this scene, Ophelia's older brother Laertes is giving her advice about her relationship with Hamlet. Direct students to think about what conflict Laertes' words are addressing, what choice Ophelia is facing, and what decision he is telling her to make. (**Answer:** *Laertes does not think Ophelia should trust Hamlet's declarations of love because his position as Prince of Denmark means he cannot actually make his own decisions. Laertes thinks if she takes his declarations of love to heart and loses her virginity to him, her honor will be damaged.*)

NOTICE & NOTE

Ophelia (Jean Simmons)

WORDS OF THE WISER

Notice & Note: Mark Laertes' reasons for his concern in lines 10–35.

Summarize: Why does Laertes think that Ophelia should not trust Hamlet's declaration of his love for her?

17 **His . . . weighed:** if you consider his high position.

20 **Carve:** choose.

22–24 **And . . . head:** His choice must be limited (**circumscribed**) by the opinion and consent (**voice and yielding**) of Denmark.

30 **credent:** trustful; **list:** listen to.

31–32 **your chaste . . . importunity:** lose your virginity to his uncontrolled pleading.

34 **keep . . . affection:** Don't go as far as your emotions would lead.

39 **canker galls:** cankerworm destroys; **infants:** early flowers.
40 **buttons:** buds; **disclosed:** opened.

> His greatness weighed, his will is not his own,
> For he himself is subject to his birth.
> He may not, as unvalued persons do,
> 20 Carve for himself, for on his choice depends
> The safety and the health of this whole state.
> And therefore must his choice be circumscribed
> Unto the voice and yielding of that body
> Whereof he is the head. Then, if he says he loves you,
> 25 It fits your wisdom so far to believe it
> As he in his particular act and place
> May give his saying deed, which is no further
> Than the main voice of Denmark goes withal.
> Then weigh what loss your honor may sustain
> 30 If with too credent ear you list his songs
> Or lose your heart or your chaste treasure open
> To his unmastered importunity.
> Fear it, Ophelia; fear it, my dear sister,
> And keep you in the rear of your affection,
> 35 Out of the shot and danger of desire.
> The chariest maid is prodigal enough
> If she unmask her beauty to the moon.
> Virtue itself 'scapes not calumnious strokes.
> The canker galls the infants of the spring
> 40 Too oft before their buttons be disclosed,

164   Unit 2

CLOSE READ SCREENCAST

Modeled Discussions Have students click the *Close Read* icon in their eBooks to access a screencast in which readers discuss and annotate Laertes's warning to his sister (Act I, Scene 3, lines 33–42).

As a class, view and discuss this video. Then, have students pair up to do an independent close read of lines 45–51. Students can record their answers on the Close Read Practice PDF.

 Close Read Practice PDF

And, in the morn and liquid dew of youth,
Contagious blastments are most imminent.
Be wary, then; best safety lies in fear.
Youth to itself rebels, though none else near.

45 **Ophelia.** I shall the effect of this good lesson keep
As watchman to my heart. But, good my brother,
Do not, as some ungracious pastors do,
Show me the steep and thorny way to heaven,
Whiles, like a puffed and reckless libertine,
50 Himself the primrose path of dalliance treads
And recks not his own rede.

Laertes. O, fear me not.

[*Enter* Polonius.]

I stay too long. But here my father comes.
A double blessing is a double grace.
Occasion smiles upon a second leave.

55 **Polonius.** Yet here, Laertes? Aboard, aboard, for shame!
The wind sits in the shoulder of your sail,
And you are stayed for. There, my blessing with thee.
And these few precepts in thy memory
Look thou character. Give thy thoughts no tongue,
60 Nor any unproportioned thought his act.
Be thou familiar, but by no means vulgar.
Those friends thou hast, and their adoption tried,
Grapple them unto thy soul with hoops of steel,
But do not dull thy palm with entertainment
65 Of each new-hatched, unfledged courage. Beware
Of entrance to a quarrel, but, being in,
Bear 't that th' opposèd may beware of thee.
Give every man thy ear, but few thy voice.
Take each man's censure, but reserve thy judgment.
70 Costly thy habit as thy purse can buy,
But not expressed in fancy (rich, not gaudy),
For the apparel oft proclaims the man,
And they in France of the best rank and station
Are of a most select and generous chief in that.
75 Neither a borrower nor a lender be,
For loan oft loses both itself and friend,
And borrowing dulls the edge of husbandry.
This above all: to thine own self be true,
And it must follow, as the night the day,
80 Thou canst not then be false to any man.
Farewell. My blessing season this in thee.

Laertes. Most humbly do I take my leave, my lord.

NOTICE & NOTE

42 Contagious blastments: withering blights, harm or injury, catastrophes.

44 Youth . . . near: Youth by nature is prone to rebel.

46–51 Ophelia warns him not to act like a hypocritical pastor, preaching virtue and abstinence, while leading a life of promiscuity and ignoring his own advice.

58–65 Polonius tells Laertes to write down (**character**) these few rules of conduct (**precepts**) in his memory. He should keep his thoughts to himself and not act on any unfit (**unproportioned**) thoughts, be friendly but not vulgar, remain loyal to friends proven (**tried**) worthy of being accepted, but not shake hands with every swaggering youth (**unfledged courage**) who comes along.

73–74 And they . . . that: Upper-class French people especially show their refinement and nobility in their choice of apparel.

77 husbandry: thrift, proper handling of money.

81 Polonius hopes that his advice will ripen (**season**) in Laertes.

TEACH

NOTICE & NOTE

83 invests: is pressing.

Polonius. The time invests you. Go, your servants tend.

Laertes. Farewell, Ophelia, and remember well
85 What I have said to you.

Ophelia. 'Tis in my memory locked,
And you yourself shall keep the key of it.

Laertes. Farewell.

[*Laertes exits.*]

Polonius. What is 't, Ophelia, he hath said to you?

90 **Ophelia.** So please you, something touching the Lord Hamlet.

91 Marry: a mild oath, shortened from "by the Virgin Mary."

Polonius. Marry, well bethought.
'Tis told me he hath very oft of late
Given private time to you, and you yourself
Have of your audience been most free and bounteous.

95 put on: told to.

95 If it be so (as so 'tis put on me,
And that in way of caution), I must tell you
You do not understand yourself so clearly
As it behooves my daughter and your honor.
What is between you? Give me up the truth.

100–110 tenders: offers (lines 100 and 107). Polonius uses the word in line 107 to refer to coins that are not legal currency (**sterling**). He then warns Ophelia to offer (**tender**) herself at a higher rate (**more dearly**), or she will tender Polonius a fool—meaning either that she will present herself as a fool, that she will make him look like a fool, or that she will give him a grandchild.

100 **Ophelia.** He hath, my lord, of late made many tenders
Of his affection to me.

Polonius. Affection, puh! You speak like a green girl
Unsifted in such perilous circumstance.
Do you believe his "tenders," as you call them?

105 **Ophelia.** I do not know, my lord, what I should think.

Polonius. Marry, I will teach you. Think yourself a baby
That you have ta'en these tenders for true pay,
Which are not sterling. Tender yourself more dearly,
Or (not to crack the wind of the poor phrase,
110 Running it thus) you'll tender me a fool.

Ophelia. My lord, he hath importuned me with love
In honorable fashion—

Polonius. Ay, "fashion" you may call it. Go to, go to!

Ophelia. And hath given countenance to his speech, my lord,
115 With almost all the holy vows of heaven.

116 springes ... woodcocks: snares to catch birds that are easily caught.

117 prodigal: lavishly.

118–121 These blazes ... fire: These blazes, which lose their light and heat almost immediately, should not be mistaken for fire.

Polonius. Ay, springes to catch woodcocks. I do know,
When the blood burns, how prodigal the soul
Lends the tongue vows. These blazes, daughter,
Giving more light than heat, extinct in both
120 Even in their promise as it is a-making,
You must not take for fire. From this time
Be something scanter of your maiden presence.

166 Unit 2

TO CHALLENGE STUDENTS . . .

Consider Points of View What is Prince Hamlet like when looked at through a different lens? Have students analyze the character of Hamlet as he is presented through the eyes of Laertes and Polonius. Have them identify words and phrases that reveal these characters' views of him. Then ask students to discuss these questions in small groups:

- Does the portrayal of Hamlet by Laertes and Polonius match your impression of his character as seen so far in this act? Explain.
- Considering Hamlet is the future king of Denmark, why would Laertes and Polonius oppose his attentions to Ophelia? What might their underlying motives be?

Set your entreatments at a higher rate
Than a command to parle. For Lord Hamlet,
125 Believe so much in him that he is young,
And with a larger tether may he walk
Than may be given you. In few, Ophelia,
Do not believe his vows, for they are brokers,
Not of that dye which their investments show,
130 But mere implorators of unholy suits,
Breathing like sanctified and pious bawds
The better to beguile. This is for all:
I would not, in plain terms, from this time forth
Have you so slander any moment leisure
135 As to give words or talk with the Lord Hamlet.
Look to 't, I charge you. Come your ways.

Ophelia. I shall obey, my lord.

[*They exit.*]

Scene 4 *A guard platform at the castle.*

[*Enter* Hamlet, Horatio, *and* Marcellus.]

Hamlet. The air bites shrewdly; it is very cold.

Horatio. It is a nipping and an eager air.

Hamlet. What hour now?

Horatio. I think it lacks of twelve.

5 **Marcellus.** No, it is struck.

Horatio. Indeed, I heard it not. It then draws near the season
Wherein the spirit held his wont to walk.

[*A flourish of trumpets and two pieces goes off.*]
What does this mean, my lord?

Hamlet. The King doth wake tonight and takes his rouse,
10 Keeps wassail, and the swagg'ring upspring reels;
And, as he drains his draughts of Rhenish down,
The kettledrum and trumpet thus bray out
The triumph of his pledge.

Horatio. Is it a custom?

15 **Hamlet.** Ay, marry, is 't,
But, to my mind, though I am native here
And to the manner born, it is a custom
More honored in the breach than the observance.
This heavy-headed revel east and west
20 Makes us traduced and taxed of other nations.
They clepe us drunkards and with swinish phrase

NOTICE & NOTE

ANALYZE DRAMATIC PLOT

Annotate: Reread lines 116–132. Mark phrases that suggest Polonius's attitude toward Hamlet's courtship of Ophelia.

Analyze: Hamlet's relationship with Ophelia is one of the play's subplots. How does Polonius's speech connect with Hamlet's thoughts about his mother and Claudius in lines 129–159 of Act I, Scene 2?

123–135 Polonius, metaphorically referring to Ophelia as a besieged castle, tells her not to enter into negotiations (**entreatments**) for surrender merely because the enemy wants to meet (**parle**) with her. Hamlet's vows are go-betweens (**brokers**) that are not like their outward appearance; these solicitors (**implorators**) of sinful petitions (**unholy suits**) speak in pious terms in order to deceive. Polonius orders her never to disgrace (**slander**) a moment of her time by speaking to Hamlet.

1 shrewdly: keenly.

2 eager: cutting.

9–13 The King stays up tonight drinking and dancing wildly; as he drinks down a glass of wine, kettledrums and trumpets play.

17 to the manner born: familiar since birth with this custom.

19–24 This drunken festivity makes us slandered and blamed by other nations. They call us drunkards and pigs, soiling our good name. Even when we do something outstanding, the essence of our reputation (**pith and marrow of our attribute**) is lost through drunkenness.

The Tragedy of Hamlet: Act I, Scene 4 167

TEACH

ANALYZE DRAMATIC PLOT

Remind students about the warning Ophelia's brother, Laertes, has already given her about Hamlet, and ask them if they think Polonius is giving her a similar warning. Direct their attention to his statement "These blazes . . . Giving more light than heat . . . You must not take for fire" (lines 118–121) and prompt them to recognize that "these blazes" refer to Hamlet's "vows," or his declarations of love. Ask students to explain what Polonius is saying about Hamlet's words in this sentence and the rest of this passage. (**Answer:** *Polonius believes Hamlet is motivated by lust to make promises and declarations of love that are not really true. In Scene 2, Hamlet says he doesn't think Claudius can really love his mother and that he has other motivations for marrying her.*)

ENGLISH LEARNER SUPPORT

Express Ideas Make sure students understand the warning that Polonius is giving Ophelia about Hamlet in Scene 3, lines 116–136, pages 166–167. Then, have students discuss his warning in pairs or groups, using the prompts below according to students' proficiency levels.

- Ask students: Is Polonius right? Should Ophelia listen to her father? **SUBSTANTIAL**
- Have students complete this statement: I think Polonius is/is not right because . . . **MODERATE**
- Is this a normal warning for a father to give his daughter? Why might Polonius be misjudging Hamlet? **LIGHT**

NOTICE & NOTE

26 mole: defect.

29–32 Hamlet describes reason as a castle whose fortified walls are broken by the excessive growth of a natural trait or by a corrupting habit.

34 nature's . . . star: which they are born with or acquire.

35 His virtues else: their other virtues.

38–40 The dram . . . scandal: A small amount of evil blots out all of a person's good qualities.

45 questionable: capable of responding to questions.

48–50 tell . . . cerements: Tell me why your bones, which were placed in a coffin and received a proper church burial, have escaped from their burial clothes.

57 horridly . . . disposition: disturb us terribly.

61–62 As if . . . alone: as if it has something to tell you on your own.

Soil our addition. And, indeed, it takes
From our achievements, though performed at height,
The pith and marrow of our attribute.
25 So oft it chances in particular men
That for some vicious mole of nature in them,
As in their birth (wherein they are not guilty,
Since nature cannot choose his origin),
By the o'ergrowth of some complexion
30 (Oft breaking down the pales and forts of reason),
Or by some habit that too much o'erleavens
The form of plausive manners—that these men,
Carrying, I say, the stamp of one defect,
Being nature's livery or fortune's star,
35 His virtues else, be they as pure as grace,
As infinite as man may undergo,
Shall in the general censure take corruption
From that particular fault. The dram of evil
Doth all the noble substance of a doubt
40 To his own scandal.

[*Enter* Ghost.]

Horatio.   Look, my lord, it comes.

Hamlet. Angels and ministers of grace, defend us!
Be thou a spirit of health or goblin damned,
Bring with thee airs from heaven or blasts from hell,
Be thy intents wicked or charitable,
45 Thou com'st in such a questionable shape
That I will speak to thee. I'll call thee "Hamlet,"
"King," "Father," "Royal Dane." O, answer me!
Let me not burst in ignorance, but tell
Why thy canonized bones, hearsèd in death,
50 Have burst their cerements; why the sepulcher,
Wherein we saw thee quietly interred,
Hath oped his ponderous and marble jaws
To cast thee up again. What may this mean
That thou, dead corse, again in complete steel,
55 Revisits thus the glimpses of the moon,
Making night hideous, and we fools of nature
So horridly to shake our disposition
With thoughts beyond the reaches of our souls?
Say, why is this? Wherefore? What should we do?

[Ghost *beckons*.]

60 **Horatio.** It beckons you to go away with it
As if it some impartment did desire
To you alone.

Marcellus. Look with what courteous action
It waves you to a more removèd ground.
But do not go with it.

Horatio. No, by no means.

65 **Hamlet.** It will not speak. Then I will follow it.

Horatio. Do not, my lord.

Hamlet. Why, what should be the fear?
I do not set my life at a pin's fee.
And for my soul, what can it do to that,
Being a thing immortal as itself?
70 It waves me forth again. I'll follow it.

Horatio. What if it tempt you toward the flood, my lord?
Or to the dreadful summit of the cliff
That beetles o'er his base into the sea,
And there assume some other horrible form
75 Which might deprive your sovereignty of reason
And draw you into madness? Think of it.
The very place puts toys of desperation,
Without more motive, into every brain
That looks so many fathoms to the sea
80 And hears it roar beneath.

Hamlet. It waves me still.—Go on, I'll follow thee.

Marcellus. You shall not go, my lord.

[*They hold back* Hamlet.]

Hamlet. Hold off your hands.

Horatio. Be ruled. You shall not go.

Hamlet. My fate cries out
And makes each petty arture in this body
85 As hardy as the Nemean lion's nerve.
Still am I called. Unhand me, gentlemen.
By heaven, I'll make a ghost of him that lets me!
I say, away!—Go on. I'll follow thee.

[Ghost *and* Hamlet *exit.*]

Horatio. He waxes desperate with imagination.

90 **Marcellus.** Let's follow. 'Tis not fit thus to obey him.

Horatio. Have after. To what issue will this come?

Marcellus. Something is rotten in the state of Denmark.

Horatio. Heaven will direct it.

Marcellus. Nay, let's follow him.

[*They exit.*]

NOTICE & NOTE

67 **pin's fee:** the value of a pin.

71–76 Horatio is worried that the Ghost might lead Hamlet toward the sea (**flood**) or to the top of the cliff that hangs (**beetles**) over the sea, and then take on some horrible appearance that would drive Hamlet insane.

77 **toys of desperation:** irrational impulses.

84 **arture:** artery.

85 **Nemean lion's nerve:** the sinews of a mythical lion strangled by Hercules.

87 **lets:** hinders.

91 **Have after:** Let's go after him.

WHEN STUDENTS STRUGGLE...

Understand Character Motivation Read aloud Scene 4, lines 83–88, and discuss with students the intensity with which Hamlet expresses his desire to follow the Ghost. Remind them that characters in plays have their own reasons for wanting to do things. Have students work in small groups to identify all of the possible motivations Hamlet might have for following the Ghost. Remind them to consider what they already know about Hamlet.

For additional support, go to the **Reading Studio** and assign the following Level Up tutorial: Character Motivation.

✏️ **NOTICE & NOTE**

Scene 5 *Another part of the fortifications.*

[*Enter* Ghost *and* Hamlet.]

Hamlet. Whither wilt thou lead me? Speak. I'll go no further.

Ghost. Mark me.

Hamlet. I will.

Ghost. My hour is almost come
When I to sulf'rous and tormenting flames
Must render up myself.

Hamlet. Alas, poor ghost!

5 **Ghost.** Pity me not, but lend thy serious hearing
To what I shall unfold.

Hamlet. Speak. I am bound to hear.

Ghost. So art thou to revenge, when thou shalt hear.

Hamlet. What?

10 **Ghost.** I am thy father's spirit.
Doomed for a certain term to walk the night
And for the day confined to fast in fires
Till the foul crimes done in my days of nature
Are burnt and purged away. But that I am forbid
15 To tell the secrets of my prison house,
I could a tale unfold whose lightest word
Would harrow up thy soul, freeze thy young blood,
Make thy two eyes, like stars, start from their spheres,
Thy knotted and combinèd locks to part,
20 And each particular hair to stand an end,
Like quills upon the fearful porpentine.
But this eternal blazon must not be
To ears of flesh and blood. List, list, O list!
If thou didst ever thy dear father love—

7 bound: obligated.

13 crimes: sins.

17 harrow up: tear up, disturb.

18 Make . . . spheres: make your two eyes like stars jump from their assigned places in the universe.

19 knotted . . . locks: carefully arranged hair.

20 an end: on end.

21 fearful porpentine: frightened porcupine.

22–23 The Ghost says he must not describe life beyond death to a living person.

NOTICE & NOTE

25 **Hamlet.** O God!

Ghost. Revenge his foul and most unnatural murder.

Hamlet. Murder?

Ghost. Murder most foul, as in the best it is,
But this most foul, strange, and unnatural.

30 **Hamlet.** Haste me to know 't, that I, with wings as swift
As meditation or the thoughts of love,
May sweep to my revenge.

Ghost.   I find thee apt;
And duller shouldst thou be than the fat weed
That roots itself in ease on Lethe wharf,
35 Wouldst thou not stir in this. Now, Hamlet, hear.
'Tis given out that, sleeping in my orchard,
A serpent stung me. So the whole ear of Denmark
Is by a forgèd process of my death
Rankly abused. But know, thou noble youth,
40 The serpent that did sting thy father's life
Now wears his crown.

Hamlet. O, my prophetic soul! My uncle!

Ghost. Ay, that incestuous, that adulterate beast,
With witchcraft of his wit, with traitorous gifts—
45 O wicked wit and gifts, that have the power
So to seduce!—won to his shameful lust
The will of my most seeming-virtuous queen.
O Hamlet, what a falling off was there!
From me, whose love was of that dignity
50 That it went hand in hand even with the vow
I made to her in marriage, and to decline
Upon a wretch whose natural gifts were poor
To those of mine.
But virtue, as it never will be moved,
55 Though lewdness court it in a shape of heaven,
So, lust, though to a radiant angel linked,
Will sate itself in a celestial bed
And prey on garbage.
But soft, methinks I scent the morning air.
60 Brief let me be. Sleeping within my orchard,
My custom always of the afternoon,
Upon my secure hour thy uncle stole,
With juice of cursèd hebona in a vial,
And in the porches of my ears did pour
65 The leprous distilment, whose effect
Holds such an enmity with blood of man
That swift as quicksilver it courses through

28 as . . . is: which murder in general (**it**) is at the very least.

32–35 I find . . . this: I think you are willing, and you would have to be duller than the thick weed that grows on the banks of Lethe (the river of forgetfulness in the underworld) to not be roused by this.

36 orchard: garden.

37–39 So . . . abused: Thus all of Denmark is deceived by a false account of my death.

ANALYZE DRAMATIC PLOT
Annotate: Mark the secret the Ghost reveals in lines 32–41.

Infer: Why does Hamlet say in line 42 that his soul was "prophetic"?

43 adulterate: adulterous.

54–58 The Ghost compares virtue, which remains pure even if indecency courts it in a heavenly form, with lust, which grows weary of a virtuous marriage and seeks depravity.

63 hebona: a poisonous plant.

64 porches: entrances.

65 leprous distilment: a distilled liquid that causes disfigurement similar to that caused by leprosy.

The Tragedy of Hamlet: Act I, Scene 5   171

APPLYING ACADEMIC VOCABULARY

☐ ambiguous   ☑ anticipate   ☑ conceive   ☐ drama   ☐ integrity

Write and Discuss Have students turn to a partner to discuss the following questions. Guide students to include the academic vocabulary words *anticipate* and *conceive* in their responses. Ask volunteers to share their responses with the class.

- Is it possible Hamlet **anticipated** the Ghost's revelation about his father's murder? Look back to earlier in Act I for evidence of this.
- What plan do you think Hamlet might **conceive** after his encounter with the Ghost?

TEACH

ANALYZE DRAMATIC PLOT

Call students' attention to the fact that the major conflict of the play is about to be introduced. Point out that, up to this point, we know King Hamlet has died, but we don't know how. Direct students to focus on what King Hamlet's ghost says about his death, making sure students understand that "'Tis given out that" means "the story that is told is." Direct their attention to the side note for Scene 5, lines 37–39, page 171, which says that this story is a false account, and ask them to look for the statement that reveals the truth to Hamlet. Ask them who now wears King Hamlet's crown. (**Answer:** When Hamlet learns Claudius murdered his father, he says his soul is "prophetic" because he was troubled by the feeling that something wasn't right about his father's death and did not trust his uncle.)

■ English Learner Support

Develop Vocabulary To help students answer the question, make sure they understand the meaning of the word *prophetic* (of or relating to a prophet or prophecy). Point out that the word *prophetic* has a Spanish cognate *profético*. Then, explain that *prophecy* can mean a prediction about the future or a guess about something. Tell students if Hamlet believes his soul was prophetic, this means he has guessed something. **SUBSTANTIAL**

TEACH

 NOTICE & NOTE

69–71 doth ... blood: The poison curdles the blood like something sour dropped into milk.

72–74 most instant ... body: An eruption of sores (**tetter**) instantly covered my smooth body, leper-like (**lazar-like**), with a vile crust like the bark on a tree.

76 dispatched: deprived.

77–80 The Ghost regrets that he had no chance to receive the last rites of the church; he died with all his sins unabsolved.

84 luxury: lust.

86–89 The Ghost tells Hamlet not to think of revenge against his mother.

90 matin: morning.

94 couple: add.

98 globe: head.

99–105 Hamlet vows to erase from the slate (**table**) of his memory all foolish notes (**fond records**), wise sayings (**saws**) he copied from books, and past impressions (**pressures past**) so that the Ghost's command will live in his mind unmixed with ordinary, insignificant thoughts.

      The natural gates and alleys of the body,
      And with a sudden vigor it doth posset
70 And curd, like eager droppings into milk,
      The thin and wholesome blood. So did it mine,
      And a most instant tetter barked about,
      Most lazar-like, with vile and loathsome crust
      All my smooth body.
75 Thus was I, sleeping, by a brother's hand
      Of life, of crown, of queen at once dispatched,
      Cut off, even in the blossoms of my sin,
      Unhouseled, disappointed, unaneled,
      No reck'ning made, but sent to my account
80 With all my imperfections on my head.
      O horrible, O horrible, most horrible!
      If thou hast nature in thee, bear it not.
      Let not the royal bed of Denmark be
      A couch for luxury and damnèd incest.
85 But, howsomever thou pursues this act,
      Taint not thy mind, nor let thy soul contrive
      Against thy mother aught. Leave her to heaven
      And to those thorns that in her bosom lodge
      To prick and sting her. Fare thee well at once.
90 The glowworm shows the matin to be near
      And 'gins to pale his uneffectual fire.
      Adieu, adieu, adieu. Remember me.

[*He exits.*]

Hamlet. O all you host of heaven! O earth! What else?
      And shall I couple hell? O fie! Hold, hold, my heart,
95 And you, my sinews, grow not instant old,
      But bear me stiffly up. Remember thee?
      Ay, thou poor ghost, whiles memory holds a seat
      In this distracted globe. Remember thee?
      Yea, from the table of my memory
100 I'll wipe away all trivial, fond records,
      All saws of books, all forms, all pressures past,
      That youth and observation copied there,
      And thy commandment all alone shall live
      Within the book and volume of my brain,
105 Unmixed with baser matter. Yes, by heaven!
      O most pernicious woman!
      O villain, villain, smiling, damnèd villain!
      My tables—meet it is I set it down
      That one may smile and smile and be a villain.
110 At least I am sure it may be so in Denmark.

[*He writes.*]

So, uncle, there you are. Now to my word.
It is "adieu, adieu, remember me."
I have sworn 't.
[*Enter* Horatio *and* Marcellus.]

Horatio. My lord, my lord!

115 **Marcellus.** Lord Hamlet.

Horatio. Heavens secure him!

Hamlet. So be it.

Marcellus. Illo, ho, ho, my lord!

Hamlet. Hillo, ho, ho, boy! Come, bird, come!

120 **Marcellus.** How is 't, my noble lord?

Horatio. What news, my lord?

Hamlet. O, wonderful!

Horatio. Good my lord, tell it.

Hamlet. No, you will reveal it.

Horatio. Not I, my lord, by heaven.

Marcellus. Nor I, my lord.

Hamlet. How say you, then? Would heart of man once think it?
125 But you'll be secret?

Horatio/Marcellus. Ay, by heaven, my lord.

Hamlet. There's never a villain dwelling in all Denmark
But he's an arrant knave.

Horatio. There needs no ghost, my lord, come from the grave.
130 To tell us this.

Hamlet. Why, right, you are in the right.
And so, without more circumstance at all,
I hold it fit that we shake hands and part,
You, as your business and desire shall point you
(For every man hath business and desire,
135 Such as it is), and for my own poor part,
I will go pray.

Horatio. These are but wild and whirling words, my lord.

Hamlet. I am sorry they offend you, heartily;
Yes, faith, heartily.

Horatio. There's no offense, my lord.

140 **Hamlet.** Yes, by Saint Patrick, but there is, Horatio,
And much offense, too. Touching this vision here,
It is an honest ghost—that let me tell you.
For your desire to know what is between us,

---

119 Hamlet responds to Marcellus's greeting (**Hillo, ho, ho**) with the call of a falconer to his hawk.

128 arrant knave: thoroughly dishonest person.

131 circumstance: elaboration.

142 honest: genuine.

TEACH

NOTICE & NOTE

O'ermaster 't as you may. And now, good friends,
145 As you are friends, scholars, and soldiers,
Give me one poor request.

Horatio. What is 't, my lord? We will.

Hamlet. Never make known what you have seen tonight.

Horatio/Marcellus. My lord, we will not.

150 **Hamlet.** Nay, but swear 't.

Horatio. In faith, my lord, not I.

Marcellus. Nor I, my lord, in faith.

153 The hilt of a sword, shaped like a cross, was often used for swearing oaths.

Hamlet. Upon my sword.

Marcellus. We have sworn, my lord, already.

Hamlet. Indeed, upon my sword, indeed.

155 **Ghost** [*cries under the stage*]. Swear.

156 truepenny: honest fellow.

Hamlet. Ha, ha, boy, sayst thou so? Art thou there, truepenny?
Come on, you hear this fellow in the cellarage.
Consent to swear.

Horatio. Propose the oath, my lord.

Hamlet. Never to speak of this that you have seen,
160 Swear by my sword.

Ghost [*beneath*]. Swear.

162 *Hic et ubique*: here and everywhere (Latin).

Hamlet. *Hic et ubique*? Then we'll shift our ground.
Come hither, gentlemen,
And lay your hands again upon my sword.
165 Swear by my sword
Never to speak of this that you have heard.

Ghost [*beneath*]. Swear by his sword.

169 pioner: digger, miner.

Hamlet. Well said, old mole. Canst work i' th' earth so fast?
A worthy pioner! Once more remove, good friends.

171 Hamlet tells Horatio to welcome, or accept, the night's events as one would welcome a stranger.
173 your philosophy: the general subject of philosophy (not a particular belief of Horatio's).
174–185 Hamlet reveals that he may have to disguise himself with strange behavior (**antic disposition**); he has them swear not to make any gestures or hints that would give him away.

170 **Horatio.** O day and night, but this is wondrous strange.

Hamlet. And therefore as a stranger give it welcome.
There are more things in heaven and earth, Horatio,
Than are dreamt of in your philosophy. But come.
Here, as before, never, so help you mercy,
175 How strange or odd some'er I bear myself
(As I perchance hereafter shall think meet
To put an antic disposition on)
That you, at such times seeing me, never shall,
With arms encumbered thus, or this headshake,
180 Or by pronouncing of some doubtful phrase,
As "Well, well, we know," or "We could an if we would."

174   Unit 2

WHEN STUDENTS STRUGGLE . . .

Summarize the Plot To aid students' comprehension, suggest they summarize important events in the plot so far. Have pairs work together to complete these steps: 1) Review Act I; 2) Note major events in a sequence chart; 3) Write one or two sentences explaining each event.

Ask students to share their summaries in small groups before beginning Act II.

 For additional support, go to the **Reading Studio** and assign the following **Level Up tutorial: Plot: Sequence of Events**.

Or "If we list to speak," or "There be an if they might,"
Or such ambiguous giving-out, to note
That you know aught of me—this do swear,
185 So grace and mercy at your most need help you.

Ghost [*beneath*]. Swear.

Hamlet. Rest, rest, perturbèd spirit.—So, gentlemen,
With all my love I do commend me to you,
And what so poor a man as Hamlet is
190 May do t' express his love and friending to you,
God willing, shall not lack. Let us go in together,
And still your fingers on your lips, I pray.
The time is out of joint. O cursèd spite
That ever I was born to set it right!
195 Nay, come, let's go together.

[*They exit.*]

NOTICE & NOTE

188–191 Hamlet says that he entrusts himself to them and will do his best to reward them.

193 The . . . joint: Everything is in disorder.

TEACH

✏️ CHECK YOUR UNDERSTANDING

Have students answer the questions independently.

Answers:

1. A
2. H
3. D

If students answer any questions incorrectly, have them reread the text to confirm their understanding. Then, they may proceed to ANALYZE THE TEXT on page 176.

CHECK YOUR UNDERSTANDING

Answer these questions before moving on to the **Analyze the Text** section on the following page.

1 At a public gathering in the castle, Claudius criticizes Hamlet for —

  A continuing to mourn his father's death

  B wanting to return to France

  C associating with friends such as Horatio

  D staying up too late at night

2 How does Hamlet react to hearing about his father's Ghost?

  F He is terrified.

  G He does not believe Horatio.

  H He wants to meet the Ghost.

  J He thinks Horatio is insane.

3 How did King Hamlet die?

  A He was killed in battle.

  B He was murdered by Queen Gertrude.

  C He died of illness.

  D King Claudius poisoned him.

The Tragedy of Hamlet: Act I, Scene 5   175

 ENGLISH LEARNER SUPPORT

Oral Assessment Use the following questions to assess students' comprehension and speaking skills

1. Does Claudius want Hamlet to stop being sad? (*yes*)

2. Does Hamlet want to speak to his father's ghost? (*yes*)

3. Hamlet's father was poisoned by _____. (*Claudius*) **SUBSTANTIAL/MODERATE**

APPLY

ANALYZE THE TEXT

Possible answers:

1. **DOK 2:** *Claudius may want to keep Hamlet close by where he can keep an eye on him and make sure he does not plot against him.*

2. **DOK 3:** *Hamlet is in despair and feels hopeless. He calls "the uses of this world" "weary, stale, flat, and unprofitable" and compares the world to a garden that has gone to seed because it has not been weeded.*

3. **DOK 3:** *Claudius's speeches suggest he is deceitful and manipulative. He says he has married Gertrude and is joyful about the circumstances because it is best for Denmark, but this is not very convincing.*

4. **DOK 2:** *Hamlet plans to act as if he has gone mad to find out the truth about Claudius. The audience will be able to see behind Hamlet's apparent madness, while Claudius and others may just think he has lost his mind.*

5. **DOK 4:** *Gertrude tells Hamlet he shouldn't mourn so long because death is natural and common, and Hamlet tells her his grief is not just a show. This exchange shows Gertrude is concerned about Hamlet but he thinks she does not truly understand his feelings.*

CREATE AND PRESENT

Write a Comparison Direct students to reread the two passages, taking notes as they read. Remind them they will need to make inferences about the relationships based on what the characters say to each other. Tell students they should support their inferences with details from the text.

Present a Comparison Have students cover or turn over their written paragraphs and practice explaining the key points, looking back at their papers only if they need help remembering. Allow them enough time to practice so they can remember everything they want to say before they make their actual presentations.

176 Unit 2

RESPOND

ANALYZE THE TEXT

Support your responses with evidence from the text. 📓 NOTEBOOK

1. **Infer** In Act I, Scene 2, Claudius urges Hamlet to stay at court instead of returning to Wittenberg. What might he be concerned about?

2. **Draw Conclusions** Reread lines 129–159 of Scene 2. What does this soliloquy suggest about Hamlet's state of mind at this point in the play?

3. **Evaluate** Even before the Ghost reveals Claudius's crime, Hamlet has harsh feelings toward him. What do Claudius's speeches in Scene 2 suggest about his character?

4. **Predict** In Scene 5, lines 173–185, Hamlet asks Horatio and Marcellus not to give him away if he starts to act strangely. What does this remark hint about his plans to deal with Claudius?

5. **Notice & Note** Reread Gertrude's advice to Hamlet in Scene 2, lines 68–73, and Hamlet's reaction to it. What does this exchange reveal about Hamlet's relationship with his mother?

CREATE AND PRESENT

Write a Comparison In Act I, we learn about Hamlet's relationship with his uncle, and we also learn about Ophelia's relations with her father. Write a paragraph in which you compare the two relationships.

❏ First, analyze Hamlet's interaction with Claudius in Scene 2, lines 64–128.

❏ Next, analyze Ophelia's interaction with Polonius in Scene 3, lines 89–137.

❏ Summarize the key similarities and differences in these relationships.

Present a Comparison In a small group, present your paragraph that you wrote comparing the relationships between Hamlet and his uncle, and Ophelia and her father.

❏ Try to focus on the main points; don't read directly from your paragraph.

❏ Practice making eye contact with your group members.

❏ Work to avoid filler words like "uh" and "um." Take a silent pause instead and gather yourself before moving forward.

❏ Practice this until you can comfortably deliver a presentation on your paragraph.

176 Unit 2

 LEARNING MINDSET

Problem Solving If students get stuck trying to answer the Analyze the Text questions, remind them it is okay not to know the answer right away. Encourage them to view the questions as problems for them to solve, and apply problem-solving strategies. If they are having trouble with a particular question, they should try looking at the question from a different angle. Remind students that by solving problems they are learning new skills and getting smarter.

SETTING A PURPOSE

As you read, pay attention to subplots that develop and consider how they tie into the arc of the larger story.

NOTICE & NOTE

Notice & Note

Use the side margins to notice and note signposts in the text.

Scene 1 *Polonius's chambers.*

[*Enter old* Polonius *with his man* Reynaldo.]

Polonius. Give him this money and these notes,
       Reynaldo.

Reynaldo. I will, my lord.

Polonius. You shall do marvelous wisely, good
       Reynaldo,
Before you visit him, to make inquire
5 Of his behavior.

Reynaldo.   My lord, I did intend it.

Polonius. Marry, well said, very well said. Look you, sir,
Inquire me first what Danskers are in Paris;
And how, and who, what means, and where they
       keep,
What company, at what expense; and finding
10 By this encompassment and drift of question
That they do know my son, come you more nearer
Than your particular demands will touch it.
Take you, as 'twere, some distant knowledge of him,
As thus: "I know his father and his friends
15 And, in part, him." Do you mark this, Reynaldo?

Reynaldo. Ay, very well, my lord.

Polonius. "And, in part, him, but," you may say, "not
       well.
But if 't be he I mean, he's very wild,
Addicted so and so." And there put on him
20 What forgeries you please—marry, none so rank
As may dishonor him, take heed of that,
But, sir, such wanton, wild, and usual slips
As are companions noted and most known
To youth and liberty.

6–12 Polonius tells him to start by asking general questions, because he will find out more through this roundabout approach (**encompassment**) than by asking specific questions about Laertes.

13 Take you: assume.

19–20 put on . . . please: accuse him of whatever faults you wish to make up; **rank:** gross.

22 wanton: reckless.

23–24 As are . . . liberty: that are commonly associated with youth and freedom.

The Tragedy of Hamlet: Act II, Scene 1 177

TO CHALLENGE STUDENTS . . .

Write in Blank Verse In this scene, Polonius is instructing Reynaldo on what to say to people in Paris to find out what Laertes has been up to by describing a hypothetical meeting and conversation. Have students write this hypothetical scene as it would take place between Reynaldo and an anonymous character in Paris. Rather than just a short dialogue, they should write a whole scene that includes setting notes and stage directions. Encourage students to attempt to write in **blank verse** and mimic Shakespearian language.

TEACH

SETTING A PURPOSE

Direct students to use the Setting a Purpose prompt to focus their reading.

TEACH

 NOTICE & NOTE

24 gaming: gambling.

26 drabbing: going to prostitutes.

28 you . . . charge: You can soften (**season**) the charge by the way you state it.

30 incontinency: habitual sexual misconduct (as opposed to an occasional lapse).

31–36 Polonius tells him to describe Laertes' faults so subtly that they will seem the faults that come with independence (**taints of liberty**), the sudden urges of an excited mind, a wildness in untamed blood that occurs in most men.

37 Wherefore: why.

40 fetch of wit: clever move.

41–46 Polonius wants Reynaldo to put these small stains (**sullies**) on his son's reputation—similar to the way in which cloth might be dirtied when it is handled—and then ask the person whether he has seen Laertes engaged in the offenses Reynaldo has mentioned (**prenominate crimes**).

46 He closes . . . consequence: he agrees with you in the following way.

48 addition: form of address.

59 o'ertook in 's rouse: overcome by drink.

62 *Videlicet:* namely.

Reynaldo. As gaming, my lord.

25 **Polonius.** Ay, or drinking, fencing, swearing,
Quarreling, drabbing—you may go so far.

Reynaldo. My lord, that would dishonor him.

Polonius. Faith, no, as you may season it in the charge.
You must not put another scandal on him
30 That he is open to incontinency;
That's not my meaning. But breathe his faults so quaintly
That they may seem the taints of liberty,
The flash and outbreak of a fiery mind,
A savageness in unreclaimèd blood,
35 Of general assault.

Reynaldo. But, my good lord—

Polonius. Wherefore should you do this?

Reynaldo. Ay, my lord, I would know that.

Polonius. Marry, sir, here's my drift,
40 And I believe it is a fetch of wit.
You, laying these slight sullies on my son,
As 'twere a thing a little soiled i' th' working,
Mark you, your party in converse, him you would sound,
Having ever seen in the prenominate crimes
45 The youth you breathe of guilty, be assured
He closes with you in this consequence:
"Good sir," or so, or "friend," or "gentleman,"
According to the phrase or the addition
Of man and country—

Reynaldo. Very good, my lord.

50 **Polonius.** And then, sir, does he this, he does—what was I about to say? By the Mass, I was about to say something. Where did I leave?

Reynaldo. At "closes in the consequence," at "friend, or so, and gentleman."

55 **Polonius.** At "closes in the consequence"—ay, marry—
He closes thus: "I know the gentleman.
I saw him yesterday," or "th' other day"
(Or then, or then, with such or such), "and as you say,
There was he gaming, there o'ertook in 's rouse,
60 There falling out at tennis"; or perchance
"I saw him enter such a house of sale"—
Videlicet, a brothel—or so forth. See you now

Your bait of falsehood take this carp of truth;
And thus do we of wisdom and of reach,
65 With windlasses and with assays of bias,
By indirections find directions out.
So by my former lecture and advice
Shall you my son. You have me, have you not?

Reynaldo. My lord, I have.

Polonius. God be wi' you. Fare you well.

70 **Reynaldo.** Good my lord.

Polonius. Observe his inclination in yourself.

Reynaldo. I shall, my lord.

Polonius. And let him ply his music.

Reynaldo. Well, my lord.

75 **Polonius.** Farewell.

[*Reynaldo exits*.]

[*Enter Ophelia*.]

How now, Ophelia, what's the matter?

Ophelia. O, my lord, my lord, I have been so affrighted!

Polonius. With what, i' th' name of God?

Ophelia. My lord, as I was sewing in my closet,
Lord Hamlet, with his doublet all unbraced,
80 No hat upon his head, his stockings fouled,
Ungartered, and down-gyvèd to his ankle,
Pale as his shirt, his knees knocking each other,
And with a look so piteous in purport
As if he had been loosèd out of hell
85 To speak of horrors—he comes before me.

Polonius. Mad for thy love?

Ophelia. My lord, I do not know,
But truly I do fear it.

Polonius. What said he?

Ophelia. He took me by the wrist and held me hard.
Then goes he to the length of all his arm,
90 And, with his other hand thus o'er his brow,
He falls to such perusal of my face
As he would draw it. Long stayed he so.
At last, a little shaking of mine arm,
And thrice his head thus waving up and down,
95 He raised a sigh so piteous and profound
As it did seem to shatter all his bulk

NOTICE & NOTE

64–66 we of . . . out: we who have wisdom and intelligence (**reach**) find things out indirectly, through roundabout courses (**windlasses**) and indirect tests (**assays of bias**).

ANALYZE DRAMATIC PLOT
Annotate: Underline phrases in lines 55–68 that sum up Polonius's strategy.

Connect: How do his instructions in this subplot relate to Hamlet's thoughts about the Danish court?

71–73 Polonius tells him to observe Laertes' behavior personally and to see that Laertes practices his music.

78 closet: private room.

79 doublet all unbraced: jacket entirely unfastened.

80 fouled: dirty.

81 down-gyvèd to his ankle: fallen down to his ankles (like a prisoner's ankle chains, or gyves).

83 purport: expression.

96 bulk: body.

The Tragedy of Hamlet: Act II, Scene 1   179

TEACH

ANALYZE DRAMATIC PLOT

Remind students that **subplots** are stories involving minor characters that occur parallel to the **main plot** and have a relationship to the main plot. Thinking about that relationship can help them understand the **theme** of the text. Review with students what Hamlet said about the reputation of Danish court in Act I, Scene 5. Make sure students understand what Polonius is asking Reynaldo to do and why. **(Answer:** *In Act I, Hamlet complains that the Danish court has a reputation among other countries of being careless drunkards. In this scene, Polonius instructs Reynaldo on a plan to find out about Laertes's behavior in Paris to see if he has developed a bad reputation there.)*

WHEN STUDENTS STRUGGLE...

Understand a Character's Motivation Ask students to reread Ophelia's description of Hamlet's appearance and behavior in Scene 1, lines 78–101, page 179. Have them circle details about his appearance and underline details about his actions. Ask students what impression Ophelia got from his appearance and behavior, how this is related to the end of Act I, and what he told Horatio and Marcellus he was going to do.

 For additional support, go to the **Reading Studio** and assign the following Level Up tutorial: Character Motivation.

The Tragedy of Hamlet: Act II, Scene 1   **179**

TEACH

ENGLISH LEARNER SUPPORT

Demonstrate Comprehension Focus students' attention on Scene 1, lines 111–113, page 180. Point out to students that the **syntax,** or word order, is unusual after the phrase *I am sorry that . . .*

Support students in understanding the meaning of these two phrases:

- I had not coted him (*I didn't see him*)
- with better heed and judgment (*with better understanding*)

Have students turn to a partner and answer the questions:

- How does Polonius's opinion of Hamlet change in this passage? **MODERATE**

NOTICE & NOTE

101 to the last . . . me: kept his eyes upon me the whole time.

103–107 Polonius says that the violent nature (**property**) of this love madness (**ecstasy**) often leads people to do something desperate.

113 coted: observed.

114 wrack: ruin, seduce; **beshrew my jealousy:** curse my suspicious nature.

115–118 It is as natural for old people to go too far (**cast beyond ourselves**) with their suspicions as it is for younger people to lack good judgment.

119–120 Polonius decides that although it may anger the King, he must be told about this love because keeping it a secret might create even more grief.

6 Sith . . . man: since neither his appearance nor his personality.

10–18 Because Rosencrantz and Guildenstern were childhood friends with Hamlet and are so familiar with his past and his usual manner (**havior**), Claudius asks them to agree to stay (**vouchsafe your rest**) at court awhile to cheer Hamlet up and find out whether he is troubled by something that Claudius is unaware of.

And end his being. That done, he lets me go,
And, with his head over his shoulder turned,
He seemed to find his way without his eyes,
100 For out o' doors he went without their helps
And to the last bended their light on me.

Polonius. Come, go with me. I will go seek the King.
This is the very ecstasy of love,
Whose violent property fordoes itself
105 And leads the will to desperate undertakings
As oft as any passions under heaven
That does afflict our natures. I am sorry.
What, have you given him any hard words of late?

Ophelia. No, my good lord, but as you did command
110 I did repel his letters and denied
His access to me.

Polonius.   That hath made him mad.
I am sorry that with better heed and judgment
I had not coted him. I feared he did but trifle
And meant to wrack thee. But beshrew my jealousy!
115 By heaven, it is as proper to our age
To cast beyond ourselves in our opinions
As it is common for the younger sort
To lack discretion. Come, go we to the King.
This must be known, which, being kept close,
    might move
120 More grief to hide than hate to utter love.
Come.
[*They exit.*]

Scene 2 *The castle.*

[*Flourish. Enter* King *and* Queen, Rosencrantz *and* Guildenstern *and* Attendants.]

King. Welcome, dear Rosencrantz and Guildenstern.
Moreover that we much did long to see you,
The need we have to use you did provoke
Our hasty sending. Something have you heard
5 Of Hamlet's transformation, so call it,
Sith nor th' exterior nor the inward man
Resembles that it was. What it should be,
More than his father's death, that thus hath put him
So much from th' understanding of himself
10 I cannot dream of. I entreat you both
That, being of so young days brought up with him
And sith so neighbored to his youth and havior,

APPLYING ACADEMIC VOCABULARY

☐ ambiguous   ☐ anticipate   ☐ conceive   ☐ drama   ☑ integrity

Have students turn to a partner to discuss the following questions. Guide students to include the academic vocabulary word *integrity* in their responses. Ask volunteers to share their responses with the class.

In Scene 1, lines 111–119, page 180, how does Polonius change his opinion about Hamlet's **integrity**? What effect does that have on the **conflict** in this **subplot**?

That you vouchsafe your rest here in our court
Some little time, so by your companies
15 To draw him on to pleasures, and to gather
So much as from occasion you may glean,
Whether aught to us unknown afflicts him thus
That, opened, lies within our remedy.

18 opened: revealed.

Queen. Good gentlemen, he hath much talked of you,
20 And sure I am two men there is not living
To whom he more adheres. If it will please you
To show us so much gentry and goodwill
As to expend your time with us awhile
For the supply and profit of our hope,
25 Your visitation shall receive such thanks
As fits a king's remembrance.

22 gentry: courtesy.

24 For . . . hope: to aid and fulfill our wishes.

Rosencrantz.   Both your Majesties
Might, by the sovereign power you have of us,
Put your dread pleasures more into command
Than to entreaty.

Guildenstern.   But we both obey,
30 And here give up ourselves in the full bent
To lay our service freely at your feet,
To be commanded.

29–32 Guildenstern promises that they will devote themselves entirely (**in the full bent**) to the service of the King and Queen.

King. Thanks, Rosencrantz and gentle Guildenstern.

Queen. Thanks, Guildenstern and gentle Rosencrantz.
35 And I beseech you instantly to visit
My too much changèd son. Go, some of you,
And bring these gentlemen where Hamlet is.

Guildenstern. Heavens make our presence and our practices
Pleasant and helpful to him!

38 practices: doings (sometimes used to mean "trickery").

Queen.   Ay, amen!

[*Rosencrantz and* Guildenstern *exit with some* Attendants.]
[*Enter* Polonius.]

40 **Polonius.** Th' ambassadors from Norway, my good lord,
Are joyfully returned.

King. Thou still hast been the father of good news.

42 still: always.

Polonius. Have I, my lord? I assure my good liege
I hold my duty as I hold my soul,
45 Both to my God and to my gracious king,
And I do think, or else this brain of mine
Hunts not the trail of policy so sure
As it hath used to do, that I have found
The very cause of Hamlet's lunacy.

47–48 Hunts . . . do: does not follow the path of political shrewdness as well as it used to.

The Tragedy of Hamlet: Act II, Scene 2 **181**

WHEN STUDENTS STRUGGLE . . .

Identify Cause and Effect Help students to understand how Hamlet's decision to act mad affects the actions of other characters by having them complete this cause-and-effect chart.

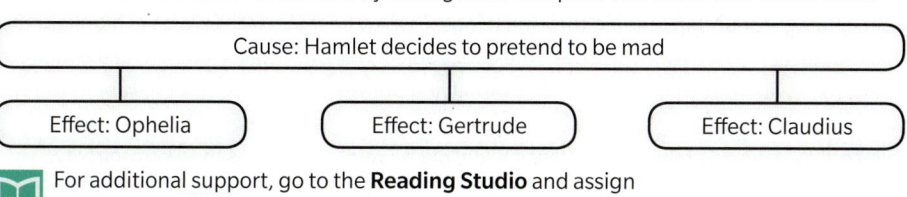

 For additional support, go to the **Reading Studio** and assign the following Level Up tutorial: **Plot: Sequence of Events**.

TEACH

ANALYZE CONFLICT

Remind students that Fortinbras is the King of Norway's nephew, and point out that *your Highness* refers to Claudius. Ask students what Fortinbras was doing and what Norway did when he found out about it. (**Answer:** When Norway found out that Fortinbras was preparing to attack Denmark, he ordered him to stop and then offered to pay him to instead attack Poland and sent a request that Fortinbras be allowed passage through Denmark for that purpose.)

■ English Learner Support

Speak Using Connecting Words Tell students that in lines 61–80 Voltemand gives a summary of events in Norway. He uses adverbs at the beginning of sentences to show the order and relationship of events. Display this passage and ask students to identify these adverbs. (*Upon our first*, line 61; *Whereat*, line 65; *Whereon*, line 72.)

Explain to students that these adverbs are not common to modern English. Have them work in pairs to orally summarize the events Voltemand describes by using their choice of these adverbs:

- at first
- at that point
- at that time
- then
- because of that **MODERATE**

182 Unit 2

NOTICE & NOTE

52 **fruit:** dessert.

56 **the main:** the main matter.

58 **sift him:** question Polonius carefully.

59 **brother:** fellow king.

61 **Upon our first:** as soon as we brought up the matter.

ANALYZE CONFLICT

Annotate: Mark details in lines 60–76 about Fortinbras's plan against Claudius.

Analyze: How was this conflict resolved?

67 **borne in hand:** deceived; **arrests:** orders to desist.

69 **in fine:** finally.

71 **give . . . against:** challenge militarily.

77–80 **give . . . down:** allow troops to move through Denmark for this expedition, under the conditions set down for Denmark's security and Fortinbras's permission.

80 **likes:** pleases.

81 **our more considered time:** a more suitable time for consideration.

---

50 **King.** O, speak of that! That do I long to hear.

Polonius. Give first admittance to th' ambassadors.
My news shall be the fruit to that great feast.

King. Thyself do grace to them and bring them in.
[*Polonius exits.*]
He tells me, my dear Gertrude, he hath found
55 The head and source of all your son's distemper.

Queen. I doubt it is no other but the main—
His father's death and our o'erhasty marriage.

King. Well, we shall sift him.
[*Enter Ambassadors Voltemand and Cornelius with Polonius.*]
 Welcome, my good friends.
Say, Voltemand, what from our brother Norway?

60 **Voltemand.** Most fair return of greetings and desires.
Upon our first, he sent out to suppress
His nephew's levies, which to him appeared
To be a preparation 'gainst the Polack,
But, better looked into, he truly found
65 It was against your Highness. Whereat, grieved
That so his sickness, age, and impotence
Was falsely borne in hand, sends out arrests
On Fortinbras, which he, in brief, obeys,
Receives rebuke from Norway, and, in fine,
70 Makes vow before his uncle never more
To give th' assay of arms against your Majesty.
Whereon old Norway, overcome with joy,
Gives him three-score thousand crowns in annual
  fee
And his commission to employ those soldiers,
75 So levied as before, against the Polack,
With an entreaty, herein further shown,
[*He gives a paper.*]
That it might please you to give quiet pass
Through your dominions for this enterprise,
On such regards of safety and allowance
80 As therein are set down.

King. It likes us well,
And, at our more considered time, we'll read,
Answer, and think upon this business.
Meantime, we thank you for your well-took labor.
Go to your rest. At night we'll feast together.
85 Most welcome home!

182 Unit 2

ENGLISH LEARNER SUPPORT

Develop Learning Strategies Point out that many sentences in Hamlet are long and complicated. Explain that identifying the main subject, verb, and objects in such sentences is a good strategy for understanding their meanings. Display lines 72–80. Have pairs highlight the main subject and verb (*Norway, gives*), the direct objects (*crowns, commission*), and the indirect object (*him*). Then, as a class, identify the modifying phrases and clauses that tell about the subject (*overcome with joy*) and the direct objects (*in annual fee, to employ those soldiers . . .*). Point out that the adjective clause (*that it might please you . . .*) modifies the word *entreaty*. Encourage students to apply this strategy when they encounter long, complicated sentences.
LIGHT

[*Voltemand and Cornelius exit.*]

Polonius. This business is well ended.
My liege, and madam, to expostulate
What majesty should be, what duty is,
Why day is day, night night, and time is time
Were nothing but to waste night, day, and time.
90 Therefore, since brevity is the soul of wit,
And tediousness the limbs and outward flourishes,
I will be brief. Your noble son is mad.
"Mad" call I it, for, to define true madness,
What is 't but to be nothing else but mad?
95 But let that go.

Queen. More matter with less art.

Polonius. Madam, I swear I use no art at all.
That he's mad, 'tis true; 'tis true 'tis pity,
And pity 'tis 'tis true—a foolish figure,
But farewell it, for I will use no art.
100 Mad let us grant him then, and now remains
That we find out the cause of this effect,
Or, rather say, the cause of this defect,
For this effect defective comes by cause.
Thus it remains, and the remainder thus.
105 Perpend.
I have a daughter (have while she is mine)
Who, in her duty and obedience, mark,
Hath given me this. Now gather and surmise.

[*He reads.*] *To the celestial, and my soul's idol, the*
110 *most beautified Ophelia—*

That's an ill phrase, a vile phrase; "beautified" is a
vile phrase. But you shall hear. Thus: [*He reads.*]
In her excellent white bosom, these, etc.—

Queen. Came this from Hamlet to her?

115 **Polonius.** Good madam, stay awhile. I will be faithful.

[*He reads the letter.*]
    Doubt thou the stars are fire,
       Doubt that the sun doth move,
    Doubt truth to be a liar,
       But never doubt I love.
120 *O dear Ophelia, I am ill at these numbers. I have not
art to reckon my groans, but that I love thee
best, O most best, believe it. Adieu.*
       Thine evermore, most dear lady, whilst
       this machine is to him, Hamlet.

NOTICE & NOTE

86–89 To inquire into (**expostulate**) the nature of one's duty to the crown would be a waste of time, like trying to figure out the reason for day, night, and time.

90 brevity . . . wit: intelligent speech should be concise.

91 flourishes: decorations.

95–99 The Queen asks Polonius to make his point without such a display of rhetoric (**art**). He claims to be speaking plainly about the matter, but then he can't resist making a figure of speech that even he describes as foolish.

105 Perpend: consider.

108 gather and surmise: draw your own conclusions.

114–115 The Queen doubts Hamlet would use such formal and flowery language; Polonius assures her he will read the letter accurately.

116 Doubt: suspect.

120 ill at these numbers: bad at writing in verse.

121 reckon: count, put into metrical verse.

123–124 whilst . . . to him: while I am still in this body (**machine**).

TEACH

🗨 ENGLISH LEARNER SUPPORT

Use Accessible Language and Learn New Essential Language Direct students' attention to Scene 2, lines 101–103, page 183.

- Display the word *defect* and give its meaning (n. an imperfect, problem, or flaw).
- Point out that *defective* is the adjective form.
- Point out that the phrase *effect defective* uses unusual **syntax,** because the adjective follows the noun (as is typical in Spanish).

Have students turn to a partner and answer these questions:

- What is the effect in line 101? *(Hamlet's madness)*
- What is the defect in line 102? *(Hamlet's madness)*
- According to the **plot,** what is the cause of "this effect defective"? What does Polonius think it is? *(Hamlet is pretending to be mad, but Polonius thinks he is lovesick for Ophelia.)* **MODERATE**

TEACH

 NOTICE & NOTE

126–128 more above ... ear: In addition, she has told me all the details of his solicitations as they occurred.

137 played ... table-book: kept this knowledge hidden within me.

138 given ... winking: closed the eyes of my heart.

139 with idle sight: saw without really noticing.

142 star: sphere.
143 prescripts: orders.
144 resort: visits.

147–152 Polonius describes the stages of Hamlet's decline: he grew sad, then stopped eating, then suffered from sleeplessness (**a watch**), then turned weak and lightheaded, and finally became mad.

157 The actor playing Polonius might point from his head to his shoulder or make a similar gesture while speaking this line.

160 the center: the Earth's center, the most inaccessible place; **try:** test.

125 This, in obedience, hath my daughter shown me,
And more above, hath his solicitings,
As they fell out by time, by means, and place,
All given to mine ear.

King. But how hath she received his love?

130 **Polonius.** What do you think of me?

King. As of a man faithful and honorable.

Polonius. I would fain prove so. But what might you think,
When I had seen this hot love on the wing
(As I perceived it, I must tell you that,
135 Before my daughter told me), what might you,
Or my dear Majesty your queen here, think,
If I had played the desk or table-book
Or given my heart a winking, mute and dumb,
Or looked upon this love with idle sight?
140 What might you think? No, I went round to work,
And my young mistress thus I did bespeak:
"Lord Hamlet is a prince, out of thy star.
This must not be." And then I prescripts gave her,
That she should lock herself from his resort,
145 Admit no messengers, receive no tokens;
Which done, she took the fruits of my advice,
And he, repelled (a short tale to make),
Fell into a sadness, then into a fast,
Thence to a watch, thence into a weakness,
150 Thence to a lightness, and, by this declension,
Into the madness wherein now he raves
And all we mourn for.

King [*to* Queen].   Do you think 'tis this?

Queen. It may be, very like.

Polonius. Hath there been such a time (I would fain know that)
155 That I have positively said "'Tis so,"
When it proved otherwise?

King.   Not that I know.

Polonius. Take this from this, if this be otherwise.
If circumstances lead me, I will find
Where truth is hid, though it were hid, indeed,
160 Within the center.

King.   How may we try it further?

Polonius. You know sometimes he walks four hours together

184 Unit 2

WHEN STUDENTS STRUGGLE...

Connect Plot Points Point out to students that in 140–152, Polonius is recounting to the King and Queen previous events from Act I, Scene 3, lines 89–137 (pp. 166–167) and Act II, Scene 1, lines 78–101 (pp. 179–180). Have students reread these passages and compare and contrast Polonius's description to what actually happened and what was actually said.

For additional support, go to the **Reading Studio** and assign the following **Level Up tutorial: Plot: Sequence of Events**.

NOTICE & NOTE

Here in the lobby.

Queen. So he does indeed.

Polonius. At such a time I'll loose my daughter to him.
[*To the* King.] Be you and I behind an arras then.
Mark the encounter. If he love her not,
And be not from his reason fall'n thereon,
Let me be no assistant for a state,
But keep a farm and carters.

King. We will try it.

[*Enter* Hamlet *reading on a book.*]

Queen. But look where sadly the poor wretch comes reading.

Polonius. Away, I do beseech you both, away.
I'll board him presently. O, give me leave.

[King *and* Queen *exit with* Attendants.]

How does my good Lord Hamlet?

Hamlet. Well, God-a-mercy.

Polonius. Do you know me, my lord?

Hamlet. Excellent well. You are a fishmonger.

Polonius. Not I, my lord.

163 **loose:** turn loose (as an animal might be released for mating).

164 **arras:** a tapestry hung in front of a wall.

171 **board him presently:** speak to him at once.

ANALYZE CONFLICT
Annotate: As you read lines 172–221, mark insulting comments that Hamlet makes about Polonius.

Infer: Why might he treat Polonius this way?

175 **fishmonger:** fish seller.

The Tragedy of Hamlet: Act II, Scene 2 185

TEACH

 ANALYZE CONFLICT

Direct students to look for the statements Hamlet makes about Polonius in Scene 2, lines 175–178, pages 185–186. Remind them of what he said to Horatio and Marcellus in Act I, Scene 5 about his plan to pretend to be mad. Polonius believes Hamlet has not recognized him and has mistaken him for a fishmonger. Hamlet is using the cover of his pretend madness to insult Polonius. Because *fish* was an impolite reference to women, Hamlet is suggesting Polonius is a pimp. (**Answer:** *Hamlet is trying to convince Polonius he is mad, but he also does not respect or trust him because he is an advisor to Claudius. He may also suspect Polonius's interference in his pursuit of Ophelia and resent him for it.*)

ENGLISH LEARNER SUPPORT

Use Context Have students carefully read Scene 2, lines 163–165, page 185. Point out that in these lines Polonius suggests a plan to the King.

Have students work in pairs and

- Use context clues to find the meaning of the word *encounter* (meeting).

- Explain the reason for Polonius' plan.
MODERATE

TEACH

ENGLISH LEARNER SUPPORT

Demonstrate Comprehension of Complex English Explain to students that dashes have a variety of functions. In dialogue, a dash can be used for these reasons: to indicate an interruption; to show a change in the person being addressed; to show that the speaker has lost his or her train of thought; to signal a sudden change of subject; to include comments that are afterthoughts. Read aloud Scene 2, lines 182–183, page 186, using your voice to show how the dash affects tone and timing.

Ask what the dash in line 183 tells readers. *(The speaker has changed the subject abruptly.)* Have students identify the functions of the dashes in the rest of the dialogue on this page. *(lines 192, 207, and 215: to indicate that Polonius changes from talking to himself to talking to Hamlet; line 218: to add afterthoughts)*

LIGHT

NOTICE & NOTE

Hamlet. Then I would you were so honest a man.

Polonius. Honest, my lord?

Hamlet. Ay, sir. To be honest, as this world goes, is to
180 be one man picked out of ten thousand.

Polonius. That's very true, my lord.

Hamlet. For if the sun breed maggots in a dead dog, being a good kissing carrion—Have you a daughter?

Polonius. I have, my lord.

185 **Hamlet.** Let her not walk i' th' sun. Conception is a blessing, but, as your daughter may conceive, friend, look to 't.

Polonius [*aside*]. How say you by that? Still harping on my daughter. Yet he knew me not at first; he said I
190 was a fishmonger. He is far gone. And truly, in my youth, I suffered much extremity for love, very near this. I'll speak to him again.—What do you read, my lord?

Hamlet. Words, words, words.

195 **Polonius.** What is the matter, my lord?

Hamlet. Between who?

Polonius. I mean the matter that you read, my lord.

Hamlet. Slanders, sir; for the satirical rogue says here that old men have gray beards, that their faces are
200 wrinkled, their eyes purging thick amber and plum-tree gum, and that they have a plentiful lack of wit, together with most weak hams; all which, sir, though I most powerfully and potently believe, yet I hold it not honesty to have it thus set down; for
205 yourself, sir, shall grow old as I am, if, like a crab, you could go backward.

Polonius [*aside*]. Though this be madness, yet there is method in 't.—Will you walk out of the air, my lord?

Hamlet. Into my grave?

210 **Polonius.** Indeed, that's out of the air. [*Aside.*] How pregnant sometimes his replies are! A happiness that often madness hits on, which reason and sanity could not so prosperously be delivered of. I will leave him and suddenly contrive the means of
215 meeting between him and my daughter.—My lord, I will take my leave of you.

183 **a good kissing carrion:** good flesh for kissing. (Hamlet seems to be reading at least part of this sentence from his book.)

185 **Conception:** understanding, being pregnant.

188 **harping on:** sticking to the subject of.

195 **matter:** subject matter. (Hamlet plays off another meaning, "the basis of a quarrel.")

201 **wit:** understanding.

204 **honesty:** good manners.

208 Polonius asks him to come out of the open air.

211 **pregnant:** full of meaning; **happiness:** talent for expression.

186   Unit 2

CLOSE READ SCREENCAST

Modeled Discussions Have students click the *Close Read* icon in their eBooks to access a screencast in which readers discuss and annotate Polonius's attempt to discern the cause of Hamlet's madness (Act II, Scene 2, lines 207–221).

As a class, view and discuss this video. Then, have students pair up to do an independent close read of lines 207–221. Students can record their answers on the Close Read Practice PDF.

Close Read Practice PDF

Hamlet. You cannot, sir, take from me anything that I will more willingly part withal—except my life, except my life, except my life.

220 **Polonius.** Fare you well, my lord.

Hamlet [*aside*]. These tedious old fools.

[*Enter* Guildenstern *and* Rosencrantz.]

Polonius. You go to seek the Lord Hamlet. There he is.

Rosencrantz [*to* Polonius]. God save you, sir.

[*Polonius exits.*]

Guildenstern. My honored lord.

225 **Rosencrantz.** My most dear lord.

Hamlet. My excellent good friends! How dost thou, Guildenstern? Ah, Rosencrantz! Good lads, how do you both?

Rosencrantz. As the indifferent children of the earth.

230 **Guildenstern.** Happy in that we are not overhappy. On Fortune's cap, we are not the very button.

Hamlet. Nor the soles of her shoe?

Rosencrantz. Neither, my lord.

Hamlet. Then you live about her waist, or in the middle
235 of her favors?

Guildenstern. Faith, her privates we.

Hamlet. In the secret parts of Fortune? O, most true! She is a strumpet. What news?

Rosencrantz. None, my lord, but that the world's
240 grown honest.

Hamlet. Then is doomsday near. But your news is not true. Let me question more in particular. What have you, my good friends, deserved at the hands of Fortune that she sends you to prison hither?

245 **Guildenstern.** Prison, my lord?

Hamlet. Denmark's a prison.

Rosencrantz. Then is the world one.

Hamlet. A goodly one, in which there are many confines, wards, and dungeons, Denmark being
250 one o' th' worst.

Rosencrantz. We think not so, my lord.

---

229 indifferent: ordinary.

234–238 Hamlet exchanges sexual puns with his childhood friends. References to Fortune's sexual favors and private parts lead up to the traditional saying that the unfaithful Fortune is a prostitute (**strumpet**).

249 confines: places of confinement; **wards:** cells.

TEACH

✏️ ANALYZE DRAMATIC PLOT

Make sure students understand the meaning of the question in Scene 2, line 273, page 188. To help them understand, have them look at Rosencrantz's reply. Have students paraphrase that question and the ones in Scene 2, lines 278–279, page 188. Ask students to think about the conflicts Hamlet is experiencing and why one or more of them might make him suspicious. (*Answer: Hamlet suspects his friends have been sent by Claudius to check in on him and keep an eye on him.*)

 **NOTICE & NOTE**

260–262 Guildenstern says that the apparently substantial aims of ambition are even less substantial than dreams.

266–267 Hamlet says that according to their logic, only beggars would have real bodies (since they lack ambition), and monarchs and ambitious (**outstretched**) heroes would be the shadows of beggars.

268 fay: faith.

269 wait upon: escort. (Hamlet takes the word to mean "serve" and replies that he would not categorize them with his servants.)

ANALYZE DRAMATIC PLOT
Annotate: Mark Hamlet's questions in lines 270–280.
Infer: What does he suspect is the real purpose of his friends' visit?

278 too dear a halfpenny: too costly at a halfpenny.

279 free: voluntary.

282 Hamlet sarcastically asks them to give him anything but a straight answer.

285 color: disguise.

288–289 conjure you: ask you earnestly.

289–290 consonancy of our youth: our closeness when we were young.

291–292 by what . . . withal: by whatever you hold more valuable, which someone more skillful than me would use to urge you with.

Hamlet. Why, then, 'tis none to you, for there is nothing either good or bad but thinking makes it so. To me, it is a prison.

255 **Rosencrantz.** Why, then, your ambition makes it one. 'Tis too narrow for your mind.

Hamlet. O God, I could be bounded in a nutshell and count myself a king of infinite space, were it not that I have bad dreams.

260 **Guildenstern.** Which dreams, indeed, are ambition, for the very substance of the ambitious is merely the shadow of a dream.

Hamlet. A dream itself is but a shadow.

Rosencrantz. Truly, and I hold ambition of so airy and
265 light a quality that it is but a shadow's shadow.

Hamlet. Then are our beggars bodies, and our monarchs and outstretched heroes the beggars' shadows. Shall we to th' court? For, by my fay, I cannot reason.

Rosencrantz/Guildenstern. We'll wait upon you.

270 **Hamlet.** No such matter. I will not sort you with the rest of my servants, for, to speak to you like an honest man, I am most dreadfully attended. But, in the beaten way of friendship, what make you at Elsinore?

275 **Rosencrantz.** To visit you, my lord, no other occasion.

Hamlet. Beggar that I am, I am even poor in thanks; but I thank you, and sure, dear friends, my thanks are too dear a halfpenny. Were you not sent for? Is it your own inclining? Is it a free visitation? Come,
280 come, deal justly with me. Come, come; nay, speak.

Guildenstern. What should we say, my lord?

Hamlet. Anything but to th' purpose. You were sent for, and there is a kind of confession in your looks which your modesties have not craft
285 enough to color. I know the good king and queen have sent for you.

Rosencrantz. To what end, my lord?

Hamlet. That you must teach me. But let me conjure you by the rights of our fellowship, by the consonancy
290 of our youth, by the obligation of our everpreserved love, and by what more dear a better proposer can charge you withal: be even and

188 Unit 2

IMPROVE READING FLUENCY

Targeted Passage Tell students that reading dialogue aloud can help them to hear and understand the emotions of the characters. Read aloud Scene 2, lines 270–297, pages 188–189, with expression as students follow along in their texts. Ask students what tone they hear in Hamlet's voice. Why? (*He becomes increasingly insistent. He may also sound hopeful that his friends will tell the truth about why they have come to the castle.*) Ask students how Rosencrantz and Guildenstern sound. Why? (*They sound awkward and flustered. They don't know whether to tell the truth or lie.*) Point out to students that this scene shows how much Hamlet suspects about what is going on in the castle.

direct with me whether you were sent for or no.

Rosencrantz [*to* Guildenstern]. What say you?

295 **Hamlet** [*aside*]. Nay, then I have an eye of you.—If you love me, hold not off.

Guildenstern. My lord, we were sent for.

Hamlet. I will tell you why; so shall my anticipation prevent your discovery, and your secrecy to the
300 King and Queen molt no feather. I have of late, but wherefore I know not, lost all my mirth, forgone all custom of exercises, and, indeed, it goes so heavily with my disposition that this goodly frame, the earth, seems to me a sterile promontory; this
305 most excellent canopy, the air, look you, this brave o'er-hanging firmament, this majestical roof, fretted with golden fire—why, it appeareth nothing to me but a foul and pestilent congregation of vapors. What a piece of work is a man, how noble in reason,
310 how infinite in faculties, in form and moving how express and admirable; in action how like an angel, in apprehension how like a god: the beauty of the world, the paragon of animals—and yet, to me, what is this quintessence of dust? Man delights
315 not me, no, nor women neither, though by your smiling you seem to say so.

Rosencrantz. My lord, there was no such stuff in my thoughts.

Hamlet. Why did you laugh, then, when I said "man
320 delights not me"?

Rosencrantz. To think, my lord, if you delight not in man, what Lenten entertainment the players shall receive from you. We coted them on the way, and hither are they coming to offer you service.

325 **Hamlet.** He that plays the king shall be welcome—his Majesty shall have tribute on me. The adventurous knight shall use his foil and target, the lover shall not sigh gratis, the humorous man shall end his part in peace, the clown shall make those laugh
330 whose lungs are tickle o' th' sear, and the lady shall say her mind freely, or the blank verse shall halt for 't. What players are they?

Rosencrantz. Even those you were wont to take such delight in, the tragedians of the city.

335 **Hamlet.** How chances it they travel? Their residence,

NOTICE & NOTE

295 Hamlet reminds them that he is watching.

298–299 shall my . . . discovery: My saying it first will spare you from revealing your secret.

300 molt no feather: will not be diminished.

304 promontory: a rock jutting out from the sea.

305 brave: splendid.

306 fretted: adorned.

308 congregation: gathering.

309 piece of work: work of art or fine craftsmanship.

311 express: exact, expressive.

312 apprehension: understanding.

314 quintessence of dust: essence, or most refined form, of dust.

322 Lenten entertainment: meager, or spare, reception.

323 coted: passed.

325–332 The king shall receive his praise, the knight shall use his sword and shield, the lover shall not sigh for nothing, the eccentric (**humorous**) character shall play his part in peace, the clown shall make those laugh who do so easily, and the lady shall speak without restraint, or else the blank verse (which has five metrical feet) will limp (**halt**) because of it.

TEACH

ENGLISH LEARNER SUPPORT

Take Notes and Analyze Direct students' attention to Scene 2, lines 300–316, page 189, and explain that Hamlet describes two things: the earth and man. Have students sort his statements about each into the graphic organizer:

	Positive	Negative
Earth		
Man		

Then, have students discuss in a group or in pairs:

- What **inner conflict** of Hamlet's does this passage reveal? **LIGHT**

TEACH

ENGLISH LEARNER SUPPORT

Analyze Sayings and Expressions Direct students' attention to Scene 2, lines 363–364, page 190, where Guildenstern says, *O, there has been much throwing about of brains*. Explain to students that this a **figure of speech** and ask them to explain what it means. (*There has been a lot of debate.*)

Define *throw* (to propel through the air) and *brains* (the part of the body that that helps us think). Have students repeat the words. Use them in a sentence, such as: *He likes to throw the ball* and *You use your brain when you take a test*. **SUBSTANTIAL**

Make sure students understand the vocabulary *to throw* and *brains*. Allow students to draw a picture of the figure of speech and then support them in finding the language to describe the expression's literal meaning. **MODERATE**

Have students work in pairs to talk about what the expression means and then cite evidence from the text to explain what the "throwing about of brains" has been about. **LIGHT**

NOTICE & NOTE

337–349 The players had to leave the city due to competition from a company of boy actors—a nest (**aerie**) of young hawks (**little eyases**) who are loudly applauded for their shrill performances. Many fashionable patrons are afraid to attend the public theaters (**common stages**) where adult actors play, fearing satirical attacks from the pens of those who write for the boy actors.

351 escoted: provided for.

351–352 pursue . . . sing: perform only until their voices change.

353 common: adult.

356 succession: future work as actors.

358 tar: provoke.

359–361 no money . . . question: the only profitable plays were satires about this rivalry.

366–367 Ay . . . load: Yes, they've won over the whole theater world.

368–371 Hamlet says that people who made faces (**mouths**) at his uncle while his father was alive now pay up to 100 gold coins for his miniature portrait.

---

both in reputation and profit, was better both ways.

Rosencrantz. I think their inhibition comes by the means of the late innovation.

Hamlet. Do they hold the same estimation they did
340 when I was in the city? Are they so followed?

Rosencrantz. No, indeed are they not.

Hamlet. How comes it? Do they grow rusty?

Rosencrantz. Nay, their endeavor keeps in the wonted pace. But there is, sir, an aerie of children, little
345 eyases, that cry out on the top of question and are most tyrannically clapped for 't. These are now the fashion and so berattle the common stages (so they call them) that many wearing rapiers are afraid of goose quills and dare scarce come thither.

350 **Hamlet.** What, are they children? Who maintains 'em? How are they escoted? Will they pursue the quality no longer than they can sing? Will they not say afterwards, if they should grow themselves to common players (as it is most like, if their means are no better),
355 their writers do them wrong to make them exclaim against their own succession?

Rosencrantz. Faith, there has been much to-do on both sides, and the nation holds it no sin to tar them to controversy. There was for a while no
360 money bid for argument unless the poet and the player went to cuffs in the question.

Hamlet. Is 't possible?

Guildenstern. O, there has been much throwing about of brains.

365 **Hamlet.** Do the boys carry it away?

Rosencrantz. Ay, that they do, my lord—Hercules and his load too.

Hamlet. It is not very strange; for my uncle is King of Denmark, and those that would make mouths at
370 him while my father lived give twenty, forty, fifty, a hundred ducats apiece for his picture in little. 'Sblood, there is something in this more than natural, if philosophy could find it out.

[*A flourish for the* Players.]

Guildenstern. There are the players.

375 **Hamlet.** Gentlemen, you are welcome to Elsinore.

Your hands, come then. Th' appurtenance of welcome
is fashion and ceremony. Let me comply with
you in this garb, lest my extent to the players,
which, I tell you, must show fairly outwards,
380 should more appear like entertainment than yours.
You are welcome. But my uncle-father and aunt-
mother are deceived.

Guildenstern. In what, my dear lord?

Hamlet. I am but mad north-north-west. When the
385 wind is southerly, I know a hawk from a handsaw.

[*Enter* Polonius.]

Polonius. Well be with you, gentlemen.

Hamlet. Hark you, Guildenstern, and you too—at
each ear a hearer! That great baby you see there is
not yet out of his swaddling clouts.

390 **Rosencrantz.** Haply he is the second time come to
them, for they say an old man is twice a child.

Hamlet. I will prophesy he comes to tell me of the
players; mark it.—You say right, sir, a Monday
morning, 'twas then indeed.

395 **Polonius.** My lord, I have news to tell you.

Hamlet. My lord, I have news to tell you: when
Roscius was an actor in Rome—

Polonius. The actors are come hither, my lord.

Hamlet. Buzz, buzz.

400 **Polonius.** Upon my honor—

Hamlet. Then came each actor on his ass.

Polonius. The best actors in the world, either for
tragedy, comedy, history, pastoral, pastoral-comical,
historical-pastoral, tragical-historical,
405 tragical-comical-historical-pastoral, scene individable,
or poem unlimited. Seneca cannot be too
heavy, nor Plautus too light. For the law of writ
and the liberty, these are the only men.

Hamlet. O Jephthah, judge of Israel, what a treasure
410 hadst thou!

Polonius. What a treasure had he, my lord?

Hamlet. Why,

> One fair daughter, and no more,
> The which he lovèd passing well.

NOTICE & NOTE

375–381 Hamlet tells Rosencrantz and Guildenstern that since fashion and ceremony should accompany a welcome, he wants to observe these formalities with them so it will not appear that the players get a better reception than they do.

384–385 Hamlet says he is only mad when the wind blows in a certain direction; at other times, he can tell one thing from another.

389 swaddling clouts: cloth used to wrap a newborn baby.

397 Roscius: a famous Roman actor.

399 Hamlet dismisses the announcement as old news.

406 Seneca: a Roman writer of tragedies.

406–407 Plautus: a Roman writer of comedies; **For the . . . liberty:** for plays that follow strict rules of dramatic composition as well as more loosely written plays.

409–426 Jephthah: a biblical figure who sacrifices his beloved daughter after making a thoughtless vow (see Judges 11). Hamlet quotes lines from a ballad based on this story.

TEACH

WHEN STUDENTS STRUGGLE . . .

Understand Character Behavior Direct students' attention to the statements in Scene 2, lines 381–385, page 191, and make sure they read the side note for lines 384–385. Guide students to understand Hamlet is telling his friends about his pretending to be mad. Then, help students understand why Hamlet's behavior changes at the point Polonius speaks to him.

 For additional support, go to the **Reading Studio** and assign the following **Level Up tutorial: Character Motivation**.

NOTICE & NOTE

415 **Polonius** [*aside*]. Still on my daughter.

Hamlet. Am I not i' th' right, old Jephthah?

Polonius. If you call me "Jephthah," my lord: I have a daughter that I love passing well.

Hamlet. Nay, that follows not.

420 **Polonius.** What follows then, my lord?

Hamlet. Why,
        As by lot, God wot
and then, you know,
    It came to pass, as most like it was—
425 the first row of the pious chanson will show you more, for look where my abridgment comes.

[*Enter the* Players.]

You are welcome, masters; welcome all.—I am glad to see thee well.—Welcome, good friends.—O my old friend! Why, thy face is valanced since I saw
430 thee last. Com'st thou to beard me in Denmark— What, my young lady and mistress! By'r Lady, your ladyship is nearer to heaven than when I saw you last, by the altitude of a chopine. Pray God your voice, like a piece of uncurrent gold, be not

425 the first ... chanson: the first stanza of the religious song.

429 valanced: fringed (with a beard).

431–435 All female roles were played by boys. Hamlet fears that this boy's voice might crack onstage, since he has grown by the height of a thick-soled shoe.

cracked within the ring. Masters, you are all
welcome. We'll e'en to 't like French falconers, fly
at anything we see. We'll have a speech straight.
Come, give us a taste of your quality. Come, a passionate
speech.

First Player. What speech, my good lord?

Hamlet. I heard thee speak me a speech once, but it
was never acted, or, if it was, not above once; for
the play, I remember, pleased not the million: 'twas
caviary to the general. But it was (as I received it,
and others whose judgments in such matters cried
in the top of mine) an excellent play, well digested
in the scenes, set down with as much modesty as
cunning. I remember one said there were no sallets
in the lines to make the matter savory, nor no matter
in the phrase that might indict the author of
affectation, but called it an honest method, as
wholesome as sweet and, by very much, more
handsome than fine. One speech in 't I chiefly
loved. 'Twas Aeneas' tale to Dido, and thereabout
of it especially when he speaks of Priam's slaughter.
If it live in your memory, begin at this line—let me
see, let me see:
    The rugged Pyrrhus, like th' Hyrcanian beast—
'tis not so; it begins with Pyrrhus:
    The rugged Pyrrhus, he whose sable arms,
    Black as his purpose, did the night resemble
    When he lay couchèd in th' ominous horse,
    Hath now this dread and black complexion smeared
    With heraldry more dismal. Head to foot,
    Now is he total gules, horridly tricked
    With blood of fathers, mothers, daughters, sons,
    Baked and impasted with the parching streets,
    That lend a tyrannous and a damnèd light
    To their lord's murder. Roasted in wrath and fire,
    And thus o'ersizèd with coagulate gore,
    With eyes like carbuncles, the hellish Pyrrhus
    Old grandsire Priam seeks.
So, proceed you.

Polonius. 'Fore God, my lord, well spoken, with good
accent and good discretion.

First Player.   Anon he finds him
    Striking too short at Greeks. His antique sword,
    Rebellious to his arm, lies where it falls,
    Repugnant to command. Unequal matched,

436–437 fly . . . see: take on anything.

437 straight: right away.

444 caviary to the general: like caviar, which is unappreciated by most people.

446 digested: arranged.

447 modesty: restraint.

448 cunning: skill; **sallets:** spicy bits, racey jests.

454–455 Pyrrhus, son of the Greek hero Achilles, killed King Priam to revenge the death of his father during the Trojan War. Aeneas tells the story to Dido, the Queen of Carthage, in Virgil's *Aeneid*.

458 Hyrcanian beast: a tiger.

462 couchèd: concealed; **ominous horse:** wooden horse used by the Greeks to enter Troy.

465 total gules: all red; **tricked:** adorned.

467 The blood is baked and crusted (**impasted**) from the heat of the burning streets.

470 o'ersizèd: smeared over.

471 carbuncles: fiery red stones.

479 Repugnant to: resisting.

TO CHALLENGE STUDENTS . . .

Adapt a Play Review In Scene 2, lines 441–443, page 193, Hamlet evaluates a play. Have students rewrite his remarks as a short, modern play review. Provide them with models to follow. Tell them they can use their imaginations to invent some characteristics of the play, but their evaluations should generally match the one Hamlet gives.

TEACH

 **NOTICE & NOTE**

482 unnervèd: strengthless;
senseless Ilium: the inanimate fortress of Troy.

485 Takes . . . ear: captures Pyrrhus' attention.

488–490 So . . . nothing: Pyrrhus stood still like a tyrant in a painting, suspended between his intentions and taking the actions that would fulfill them.

492 rack: mass of high clouds.

497 Cyclops: one-eyed giants who worked for Vulcan, the Roman god of metalworking.

498 Mars: Roman god of war; **for proof eterne:** to last for eternity.

502 synod: assembly.

503 fellies: section of a wheel's rim.

504 nave: hub of a wheel.

508–509 He's for . . . sleeps: Unless he's hearing a comic song and dance (**jig**) or a bawdy tale, he falls asleep.

509 Hecuba: Priam's wife.

510 moblèd: her face was muffled.

514 bisson rheum: blinding tears; **clout:** cloth.

516 o'erteemèd: worn out from childbearing.

519 'Gainst . . . pronounced: would have proclaimed treasonous statements against Fortune's rule.

480 *Pyrrhus at Priam drives, in rage strikes wide;*
But with the whiff and wind of his fell sword
Th' unnervèd father falls. Then senseless Ilium,
Seeming to feel this blow, with flaming top
Stoops to his base, and with a hideous crash
485 *Takes prisoner Pyrrhus' ear. For lo, his sword,*
Which was declining on the milky head
Of reverend Priam, seemed i' th' air to stick.
So as a painted tyrant Pyrrhus stood
And, like a neutral to his will and matter,
490 *Did nothing.*
But as we often see against some storm
A silence in the heavens, the rack stand still,
The bold winds speechless, and the orb below
As hush as death, anon the dreadful thunder
495 *Doth rend the region; so, after Pyrrhus' pause,*
Arousèd vengeance sets him new a-work,
And never did the Cyclops' hammers fall
On Mars's armor, forged for proof eterne,
With less remorse than Pyrrhus' bleeding sword
500 *Now falls on Priam.*
Out, out, thou strumpet Fortune! All you gods
In general synod take away her power,
Break all the spokes and fellies from her wheel,
And bowl the round nave down the hill of heaven
505 *As low as to the fiends!*

Polonius. This is too long.

Hamlet. It shall to the barber's with your beard.—
Prithee say on. He's for a jig or a tale of bawdry, or
he sleeps. Say on; come to Hecuba.

510 **First Player.** *But who, ah woe, had seen the moblèd queen—*

Hamlet. "The moblèd queen"?

Polonius. That's good. "Moblèd queen" is good.

First Player. *Run barefoot up and down, threat'ning*
  the flames
With bisson rheum, a clout upon that head
515 *Where late the diadem stood, and for a robe,*
About her lank and all o'erteemèd loins
A blanket, in the alarm of fear caught up—
Who this had seen, with tongue in venom steeped,
'Gainst Fortune's state would treason have pronounced.
520 *But if the gods themselves did see her then*
When she saw Pyrrhus make malicious sport

194 Unit 2

WHEN STUDENTS STRUGGLE . . .

Summarize a Plot Explain to students that the text in italics is a speech Hamlet and First Player are quoting that tells the story of a Greek mythological figure named Pyrrhus. Make sure students read and understand the side note on page 195. Divide students into groups and assign each a chunk of Scene 2 that you summarized in modern English: 1) Lines 460–472 (p. 193), 2) Lines 476–490 (pp. 193–194), and 3) Lines 491–500 (p. 194). Then, form new groups in which each chunk of text is represented by at least one student and have them work together to understand the story. Ask how this story relates to Hamlet's internal conflict.

 For additional support, go to the **Reading Studio** and assign the following **Level Up tutorial: Plot: Sequence of Events**.

In mincing with his sword her husband's limbs,
The instant burst of clamor that she made
(Unless things mortal move them not at all)
525 Would have made milch the burning eyes of heaven
And passion in the gods.

Polonius. Look whe'er he has not turned his color and
has tears in 's eyes. Prithee, no more.

Hamlet. 'Tis well. I'll have thee speak out the rest of
530 this soon.—Good my lord, will you see the players
well bestowed? Do you hear, let them be well used,
for they are the abstract and brief chronicles of the
time. After your death you were better have a bad
epitaph than their ill report while you live.

535 **Polonius.** My lord, I will use them according to their
desert.

Hamlet. God's bodykins, man, much better! Use every
man after his desert and who shall 'scape whipping?
Use them after your own honor and dignity.
540 The less they deserve, the more merit is in your
bounty. Take them in.

Polonius. Come, sirs.

Hamlet. Follow him, friends. We'll hear a play tomorrow.
[*As* Polonius *and* Players *exit,* Hamlet *speaks to*
545 *the* First Player.] Dost thou hear me, old friend?
Can you play "The Murder of Gonzago"?

First Player. Ay, my lord.

Hamlet. We'll ha 't tomorrow night. You could, for a
need, study a speech of some dozen or sixteen
550 lines, which I would set down and insert in 't,
could you not?

First Player. Ay, my lord.

Hamlet. Very well. Follow that lord—and look you mock
him not. [*First Player exits.*] My good friends, I'll leave
555 you till night. You are welcome to Elsinore.

Rosencrantz. Good my lord.

Hamlet. Ay, so, good-bye to you.

[*Rosencrantz and* Guildenstern *exit.*]

   Now I am alone.
O, what a rogue and peasant slave am I!
Is it not monstrous that this player here,
560 But in a fiction, in a dream of passion,

525 milch: milky, moist with tears.

527 whe'er: whether.

532 abstract: summary.

537 God's bodykins: by God's little body.

548 ha 't: have it.

ANALYZE SOLILOQUY
Annotate: As you read lines 558–590, mark phrases Hamlet uses to describe himself.

Interpret: What internal conflict does the speech express?

TEACH

NOTICE & NOTE

561–562 Could . . . wanned: could force his soul into such agreement with his thoughts that his soul made his face turn pale.

564–565 his whole . . . conceit: all of his activity creating outward appearances that express his thoughts.

571 cleave . . . speech: pierce everyone's ears with horrible words.

572 appall the free: terrify the innocent.

575 muddy-mettled: weak-spirited; **peak:** mope.

576 John-a-dreams: a dreamy idler; **unpregnant of:** not roused to action by.

579 defeat: destruction.

582–583 gives . . . lungs: calls me a complete liar.

584 'Swounds: by Christ's wounds (an oath).

585 pigeon-livered: meek as a pigeon.

587 kites: birds of prey.

588 offal: entrails.

589 kindless: unnatural.

591 brave: admirable.

595 drab: prostitute.

596 scullion: kitchen servant.

597 About: get to work.

599 cunning of the scene: skill of the performance.

600 presently: immediately.

601 malefactions: crimes.

606 tent . . . quick: probe him in his most vulnerable spot; **blench:** flinch.

Could force his soul so to his own conceit
That from her working all his visage wanned,
Tears in his eyes, distraction in his aspect,
A broken voice, and his whole function suiting
565 With forms to his conceit—and all for nothing!
For Hecuba!
What's Hecuba to him, or he to Hecuba,
That he should weep for her? What would he do
Had he the motive and the cue for passion
570 That I have? He would drown the stage with tears
And cleave the general ear with horrid speech,
Make mad the guilty and appall the free,
Confound the ignorant and amaze indeed
The very faculties of eyes and ears. Yet I,
575 A dull and muddy-mettled rascal, peak
Like John-a-dreams, unpregnant of my cause,
And can say nothing—no, not for a king
Upon whose property and most dear life
A damned defeat was made. Am I a coward?
580 Who calls me "villain"? breaks my pate across?
Plucks off my beard and blows it in my face?
Tweaks me by the nose? gives me the lie i' th' throat
As deep as to the lungs? Who does me this?
Ha! 'Swounds, I should take it! For it cannot be
585 But I am pigeon-livered and lack gall
To make oppression bitter, or ere this
I should have fatted all the region kites
With this slave's offal. Bloody, bawdy villain!
Remorseless, treacherous, lecherous, kindless villain!
590 O vengeance!
Why, what an ass am I! This is most brave,
That I, the son of a dear father murdered,
Prompted to my revenge by heaven and hell,
Must, like a whore, unpack my heart with words
595 And fall a-cursing like a very drab,
A scullion! Fie upon 't! Foh!
About, my brains!—Hum, I have heard
That guilty creatures sitting at a play
Have, by the very cunning of the scene,
600 Been struck so to the soul that presently
They have proclaimed their malefactions.
For murder, though it have no tongue, will speak
With most miraculous organ. I'll have these players
Play something like the murder of my father
605 Before mine uncle. I'll observe his looks;
I'll tent him to the quick. If he do blench,

196 Unit 2

ENGLISH LEARNER SUPPORT

Demonstrate Comprehension by Taking Notes To help students take notes about Hamlet's conflict, display these sentence stems and ask students to copy them into their notes:

- Hamlet does not want to kill his uncle because . . .
- The Ghost may not have . . .
- If he . . ., he will be a murderer.

Ask students to complete the sentence stems. **LIGHT/MODERATE**

I know my course. The spirit that I have seen
May be a devil, and the devil hath power
T' assume a pleasing shape; yea, and perhaps,
610 Out of my weakness and my melancholy,
As he is very potent with such spirits,
Abuses me to damn me. I'll have grounds
More relative than this. The play's the thing
Wherein I'll catch the conscience of the King.

[*He exits.*]

NOTICE & NOTE

612–613 **grounds . . . this:** a more solid basis for acting than the Ghost's words.

ANALYZE DRAMATIC PLOT
Annotate: Mark details in lines 597–614 that explain why Hamlet wants to test Claudius's guilt.

Connect: What does this explanation demonstrate about his character?

CHECK YOUR UNDERSTANDING

Answer these questions before moving on to the **Analyze the Text** section on the following page.

1 What does Polonius think is causing Hamlet's moodiness?
  A He suspects Hamlet is plotting revenge against Claudius.
  B He believes Hamlet has a mental illness.
  C He realizes Hamlet is still grieving for his father.
  D He knows Hamlet is lovesick for Ophelia.

2 Why have Claudius and Gertrude invited Rosencrantz and Guildenstern to Elsinore?
  F They want Rosencrantz and Guildenstern to spy on Polonius.
  G They want Rosencrantz and Guildenstern to cheer up Hamlet.
  H Rosencrantz and Guildenstern will manage their land.
  J Rosencrantz and Guildenstern have committed crimes.

3 How does Hamlet plan to test Claudius's guilt?
  A He will ask Claudius to watch a play that depicts a murder similar to that of his father.
  B He hopes to get Claudius to admit to the crime by holding him at knife point.
  C He asks his mother to coax it out of Claudius over dinner.
  D He will confront Claudius as if he already has evidence proving his guilt.

The Tragedy of Hamlet: Act II, Scene 2 197

TEACH

ANALYZE DRAMATIC PLOT

Point out to students that Hamlet is explaining his plan to attempt to resolve his internal conflict. In Scene 2, lines 608–612, pages 196–197, he explains his specific reason for needing to test Claudius's guilt. Ask students to think about what might have happened if Hamlet had avenged the murder of his father as the Ghost told him to do rather than looking for further proof of his guilt. (**Answer:** *Hamlet wants some other evidence that Claudius murdered his father. This shows Hamlet is generally cautious and distrustful, as he worries that the ghost of his father is actually a trick of the devil.*)

CHECK YOUR UNDERSTANDING

Have students answer the questions independently.

Answers:
1. D
2. G
3. A

If students answer any questions incorrectly, have them reread the text to confirm their understanding. Then, they may proceed to ANALYZE THE TEXT on page 198.

 ENGLISH LEARNER SUPPORT

Oral Assessment

1. Polonius says Hamlet is lovesick for _____. (*Ophelia*)
2. King and Queen want Rosencrantz and Guilderstern to cheer up _____. (*Hamlet*)
3. Hamlet wants Claudius to watch a _____. (*play*) **ALL LEVELS**

The Tragedy of Hamlet: Act II, Scene 2 **197**

APPLY

ANALYZE THE TEXT

Possible answers:

1. **DOK 4:** *Student answers may vary. Hamlet does tell his friends in Act I that he intends to pretend to be mad However, he is also very upset having learned of his father's murder, so some aspects of his behavior may not be completely fabricated.*

2. **DOK 2:** *Hamlet wants to leave the court because he does not like his uncle and disapproves of his mother's marriage to him. However, his mother and Claudius are requiring him to stay there, and he realizes his uncle is keeping him there to keep an eye on him.*

3. **DOK 4:** *Hamlet is conflicted because he does not have the feelings of love and admiration for his fellow man that he thinks he should.*

4. **DOK 3:** *In the story told by the First Player, Pyrrhus goes to find King Priam—who killed his father—and avenge him. Like Hamlet, Pyrrhus at first hesitated before killing the old man, but then ultimately gained his courage and killed him. Hamlet, on the other hand, has not been able to find the courage to act.*

5. **DOK 3:** *Shakespeare expects his audience to appreciate the power of drama to reveal truth.*

CREATE AND DISCUSS

Discuss with a Small Group Have students go through their notes, including answers to GRQs and other annotations they have made as they read, to look for details about Hamlet's decision-making. Give them some time to gather their thoughts independently before putting them in groups. Encourage students to listen carefully to their classmates' ideas. Remind them to use language of discussion such as *I found the same thing* and *I have something different to add.*

 RESPOND

ANALYZE THE TEXT

Support your responses with evidence from the text. NOTEBOOK

1. **Evaluate** In Act II, Scene 1, lines 78–101, Ophelia describes what happened when Hamlet visited her. Did he just pretend to be mad in that encounter, or could he have been genuinely disturbed because of what he learned about his father's murder? Consider the following:
   - his warning to Horatio and Marcellus at the end of Act I
   - his relationship with Ophelia
   - the details in her description
   - his behavior with other characters in Act II

2. **Interpret** In Scene 2, line 246, Hamlet tells Rosencrantz and Guildenstern that "Denmark's a prison." How does this statement reflect his situation at the Danish court?

3. **Analyze** Reread Hamlet's speech in Scene 2, lines 309–316. What internal conflict does he express here?

4. **Compare** The speech recited by the First Player in Scene 2, lines 475–505, tells the story of Pyrrhus. How does this Greek mythological figure serve as a foil for Hamlet?

5. **Draw Conclusions** At the end of Act II, Hamlet reveals his plan for testing Claudius's guilt. Why might Shakespeare have chosen a theatrical performance for this purpose?

CREATE AND DISCUSS

Discuss with a Small Group Hamlet is not quick to act; instead, he takes time to think through each decision he makes before moving forward. Why is Hamlet so cautious?

- ❏ Gather evidence from the text about Hamlet's pretending to be mad and his plan to test Claudius's guilt.
- ❏ In a small group, discuss why Hamlet takes these measures. Consider what might happen if he tried to immediately take revenge.
- ❏ As group members share ideas and supporting evidence, reflect on and adjust your earlier remarks if their reasons and evidence lead you to change your mind.
- ❏ Respond using appropriate vocabulary and tone.
- ❏ Summarize the group discussion and present your ideas to the class.

 ENGLISH LEARNER SUPPORT

Take Notes and Collaborate with Peers Have students gather their notes for the discussion into one place and practice in pairs reading aloud and paraphrasing them. Have them make a place in their notebooks to write down their peers' ideas and provide them with language to ask for help and clarification:

- *I'd like to write that down. Can you repeat it?*
- *Can you show me that on the page?* **MODERATE**

SETTING A PURPOSE

As you read, notice how conflicts build to a turning point that leads Hamlet to commit to a course of action.

NOTICE & NOTE

Notice & Note

Use the side margins to notice and note signposts in the text.

ACT III

Scene 1 *The castle.*

[*Enter* King, Queen, Polonius, Ophelia, Rosencrantz, Guildenstern, *and* Lords.]

King. And can you by no drift of conference
Get from him why he puts on this confusion,
Grating so harshly all his days of quiet
With turbulent and dangerous lunacy?

5 **Rosencrantz.** He does confess he feels himself distracted,
But from what cause he will by no means speak.

Guildenstern. Nor do we find him forward to be sounded,
But with a crafty madness keeps aloof
When we would bring him on to some confession
10 Of his true state.

Queen.   Did he receive you well?

Rosencrantz. Most like a gentleman.

Guildenstern. But with much forcing of his disposition.

Rosencrantz. Niggard of question, but of our demands
   Most free in his reply.

15 **Queen.** Did you assay him to any pastime?

Rosencrantz. Madam, it so fell out that certain players
We o'erraught on the way. Of these we told him,
And there did seem in him a kind of joy
To hear of it. They are here about the court,
20 And, as I think, they have already order
This night to play before him.

Polonius.   'Tis most true,
And he beseeched me to entreat your Majesties
To hear and see the matter.

King. With all my heart, and it doth much content me
25 To hear him so inclined.

1 drift of conference: steering of conversation.

7 forward to be sounded: interested in being questioned.

12 forcing of his disposition: effort.

13–14 Niggard . . . reply: Reluctant to talk, but willing to answer our questions.

15 assay: tempt.

17 o'erraught: overtook.

The Tragedy of Hamlet: Act III, Scene 1 **199**

TEACH

SETTING A PURPOSE

Direct students to use the Setting a Purpose prompt to focus their reading.

TO CHALLENGE STUDENTS . . .

Identify Dramatic Irony Tell students that one of the conventions of Shakespeare's plays is **dramatic irony,** in which the audience knows something that one or more characters do not know. Have them read lines 15–25 and identify what is significant that the audience knows that the characters do not. Ask them to explain what the purpose of **dramatic irony** might be in this scene. (*The audience knows Hamlet has planned to have the actors do a play resembling the murder of his father as a test for the King, and that Hamlet plans to observe the King to see if he gives away his guilt. The* **dramatic irony** *here adds suspense.*)

Have students watch for other instances of **dramatic irony** in this act.

The Tragedy of Hamlet: Act III, Scene 1 **199**

TEACH

ANALYZE SOLILOQUY

Point out to students they will likely recognize the famous first line to this soliloquy in Scene 1, lines 57–69, pages 200–201. Remind students that a soliloquy is a speech that a character gives that no other characters can hear. One function of a soliloquy is to express a character's **inner conflict**, which contributes to the **theme** about life.

Make sure students understand Hamlet is contemplating the reasons for and against suicide, and have them look for the reasons he gives to continue living despite life's struggles. (**Answer:** *Hamlet says that despite the struggle and pain of life, people choose to continue to endure them out of the fear of what might wait for them in death, which is unknown:* For in that sleep of death what dreams may come,/When we have shuffled off this mortal coil,/Must give us pause.)

ENGLISH LEARNER SUPPORT

Take Notes and Summarize Make sure that students understand Hamlet is thinking out loud about the question of *to be* and *not to be* and that they know *to be* means to continue living and *not to be* means to die. Help students understand this **inner conflict** by having them work in mixed-proficiency groups to complete this chart with words from the text. (Examples are given.)

To be (continue living)	Not to be (death)
• slings and arrows of outrageous fortune	• what dreams may come
• heartache and the thousand natural shocks	• The undiscovered country from whose bourn no traveler returns

Elicit familiar vocabulary to describe Hamlet's feelings about life (example: *pain, sad*) and death (*fear*) **SUBSTANTIAL**

Have students compare the lists and discuss why or why not Hamlet should choose life or death. **MODERATE**

In a complete sentence or sentences, have students summarize the idea that Hamlet expresses about life versus death. **LIGHT**

 **NOTICE & NOTE**

26 **give . . . edge:** sharpen his interest.

29 **closely:** privately.

31 **Affront:** meet.

32 **espials:** spies.

35 **as he is behaved:** according to his behavior.

43 **Gracious:** Your Grace (addressing the King).

44–49 Polonius tells Ophelia to read a religious book to provide an excuse for being alone. He remarks that many people are guilty of using worship and a devout appearance to cover their sins.

50–55 Claudius compares the heavy makeup that covers up the flaws on a prostitute's cheek to the beautiful words that cover his crime.

57 **To be:** to exist, to continue living.

59 **slings:** something thrown or shot.

ANALYZE SOLILOQUY

Annotate: Mark figurative language in lines 57–89 that expresses how Hamlet feels about life.

Interpret: What reason does he give for continuing to endure life's problems?

Good gentlemen, give him a further edge
And drive his purpose into these delights.

Rosencrantz. We shall, my lord.

[*Rosencrantz and Guildenstern and Lords exit.*]

King. Sweet Gertrude, leave us too,
For we have closely sent for Hamlet hither,
30 That he, as 'twere by accident, may here
Affront Ophelia.
Her father and myself (lawful espials)
Will so bestow ourselves that, seeing unseen,
We may of their encounter frankly judge
35 And gather by him, as he is behaved,
If 't be th' affliction of his love or no
That thus he suffers for.

Queen. I shall obey you.
And for your part, Ophelia, I do wish
That your good beauties be the happy cause
40 Of Hamlet's wildness. So shall I hope your virtues
Will bring him to his wonted way again,
To both your honors.

Ophelia. Madam, I wish it may.

[*Queen exits.*]

Polonius. Ophelia, walk you here.—Gracious, so please you,
We will bestow ourselves. [*To Ophelia.*] Read on this book,
45 That show of such an exercise may color
Your loneliness.—We are oft to blame in this
('Tis too much proved), that with devotion's visage
And pious action we do sugar o'er
The devil himself.

50 **King** [*aside*]. O, 'tis too true!
How smart a lash that speech doth give my conscience.
The harlot's cheek beautied with plast'ring art
Is not more ugly to the thing that helps it
Than is my deed to my most painted word.
55 O heavy burden!

Polonius. I hear him coming. Let's withdraw, my lord.

[*They withdraw.*]

[*Enter Hamlet.*]

Hamlet. To be or not to be—that is the question:
Whether 'tis nobler in the mind to <u>suffer</u>
<u>The slings and arrows of outrageous fortune,</u>
60 Or to take arms against a sea of troubles
And, by opposing, end them. To die, to sleep—

200 Unit 2

NOTICE & NOTE

No more—and by a sleep to say we end
The heartache and the thousand natural shocks
That flesh is heir to—'tis a consummation
65 Devoutly to be wished. To die, to sleep—
To sleep, perchance to dream. Ay, there's the rub,
For in that sleep of death what dreams may come,
When we have shuffled off this mortal coil,
Must give us pause. There's the respect
70 That makes calamity of so long life.
For who would bear the whips and scorns of time,
Th' oppressor's wrong, the proud man's contumely,
The pangs of despised love, the law's delay,
The insolence of office, and the spurns
75 That patient merit of th' unworthy takes,
When he himself might his quietus make
With a bare bodkin? Who would fardels bear,
To grunt and sweat under a weary life,
But that the dread of something after death,
80 The undiscovered country from whose bourn
No traveler returns, puzzles the will
And makes us rather bear those ills we have
Than fly to others that we know not of?
Thus conscience does make cowards of us all,
85 And thus the native hue of resolution
Is sicklied o'er with the pale cast of thought,
And enterprises of great pitch and moment
With this regard their currents turn awry
And lose the name of action.— Soft you now,
90 The fair Ophelia.— Nymph, in thy orisons
Be all my sins remembered.

Ophelia. Good my lord,
How does your Honor for this many a day?

Hamlet. I humbly thank you, well.

Ophelia. My lord, I have remembrances of yours
95 That I have longèd long to redeliver.
I pray you now receive them.

Hamlet. No, not I. I never gave you aught.

Ophelia. My honored lord, you know right well you did,
And with them words of so sweet breath composed
100 As made the things more rich. Their perfume lost,
Take these again, for to the noble mind
Rich gifts wax poor when givers prove unkind.
There, my lord.

Hamlet. Ha, ha, are you honest?

64 **consummation:** final ending.

66 **rub:** obstacle.

68 **shuffled . . . coil:** cast aside the turmoil of life.

69–70 **There's . . . life:** That is the consideration that makes us endure misery (**calamity**) for such a long time.

71 **time:** life in this world.

72 **contumely:** insults, expressions of contempt.

73 **despised:** unreturned.

74 **office:** officials.

74–75 **spurns . . . takes:** the insults that people of merit receive from the unworthy.

76–77 **When . . . bodkin:** when he might settle his accounts (**his quietus make**) with merely a dagger (**a bare bodkin**)—that is, end his unhappiness by killing himself.

77 **fardels:** burdens.

80 **bourn:** boundary.

81 **puzzles:** paralyzes.

85 **native hue:** natural color.

86 **cast:** shade.

87–89 **pitch and moment:** height and importance; **With this regard:** for this reason.

89 **Soft you:** be quiet, enough.

90 **orisons:** prayers.

104 **honest:** truthful, chaste.

IMPROVE READING FLUENCY

Targeted Passage Explain to students that in this speech in Scene 1, lines 57–84, pages 200–201, Hamlet is debating with himself why anyone would continue to suffer through life rather than end it all by suicide, and ask them to imagine the emotional turmoil he is feeling. Divide the passage into chunks: lines 57–65, lines 65–77, and lines 77–83. Assign small groups one chunk each and have them do a choral reading, practicing for several rounds while attempting to express Hamlet's emotion through emphasis, pace, and the rise and fall of volume.

 Go to the **Reading Studio** for additional support in developing fluency.

TEACH

✏️ NOTICE & NOTE

108 your honesty . . . beauty: Your chastity should not allow itself to be influenced by your beauty.

110 commerce: dealings.

114 his: its.

115 This . . . paradox: This once went against the common viewpoint.

116 time: the present age.

118–120 Hamlet's metaphor is of grafting a branch onto a fruit tree: If virtue is grafted onto his sinful nature, the fruit of the grafted tree will still taste of his old nature.

122 nunnery: convent (sometimes used as a slang word for "brothel").

123 indifferent honest: reasonably virtuous.

127 beck: command.

---

105 **Ophelia.** My lord?

Hamlet. Are you fair?

Ophelia. What means your lordship?

Hamlet. That if you be honest and fair, your honesty should admit no discourse to your beauty.

110 **Ophelia.** Could beauty, my lord, have better commerce than with honesty?

Hamlet. Ay, truly, for the power of beauty will sooner transform honesty from what it is to a bawd than the force of honesty can translate beauty into his
115 likeness. This was sometime a paradox, but now the time gives it proof. I did love you once.

Ophelia. Indeed, my lord, you made me believe so.

Hamlet. You should not have believed me, for virtue cannot so inoculate our old stock but we shall relish
120 of it. I loved you not.

Ophelia. I was the more deceived.

Hamlet. Get thee to a nunnery. Why wouldst thou be a breeder of sinners? I am myself indifferent honest, but yet I could accuse me of such things that it
125 were better my mother had not borne me: I am very proud, revengeful, ambitious, with more offenses at my beck than I have thoughts to put

202 Unit 2

WHEN STUDENTS STRUGGLE . . .

Understand a Character's Behavior Direct students' attention to Scene 1, lines 94–96, page 201, and review with students the sequence of events in this **subplot** so far. Ask: *Why is Ophelia giving back Hamlet's "remembrances"? How does Hamlet's behavior change from lines 90–94 to lines 104–132? What words can describe Hamlet's emotions in this scene?*

 For additional support, go to the **Reading Studio** and assign the following **Level Up tutorial: Making Inferences About Characters**.

them in, imagination to give them shape, or time to
act them in. What should such fellows as I do
130 crawling between earth and heaven? We are arrant
knaves all; believe none of us. Go thy ways to a
nunnery. Where's your father?

Ophelia. At home, my lord.

Hamlet. Let the doors be shut upon him that he may
135 play the fool nowhere but in 's own house. Farewell.

Ophelia. O, help him, you sweet heavens!

Hamlet. If thou dost marry, I'll give thee this plague
for thy dowry: be thou as chaste as ice, as pure as
snow, thou shalt not escape calumny. Get thee to a
140 nunnery, farewell. Or if thou wilt needs marry,
marry a fool, for wise men know well enough what
monsters you make of them. To a nunnery, go, and
quickly too. Farewell.

Ophelia. Heavenly powers, restore him!

145 **Hamlet.** I have heard of your paintings too, well
enough. God hath given you one face, and you
make yourselves another. You jig and amble, and
you lisp; you nickname God's creatures and make
your wantonness your ignorance. Go to, I'll no
150 more on 't. It hath made me mad. I say we will
have no more marriage. Those that are married
already, all but one, shall live. The rest shall keep
as they are. To a nunnery, go.

[*He exits.*]

Ophelia. O, what a noble mind is here o'erthrown!
155 The courtier's, soldier's, scholar's, eye, tongue, sword,
Th' expectancy and rose of the fair state,
The glass of fashion and the mold of form,
Th' observed of all observers, quite, quite down!
And I, of ladies most deject and wretched,
160 That sucked the honey of his musicked vows,
Now see that noble and most sovereign reason,
Like sweet bells jangled, out of time and harsh;
That unmatched form and stature of blown youth
Blasted with ecstasy. O, woe is me
165 T' have seen what I have seen, see what I see!

King [*advancing with* Polonius]. Love? His affections do
not that way tend;
Nor what he spake, though it lacked form a little,
Was not like madness. There's something in his soul

NOTICE & NOTE

139 calumny: slander, defamation.

142 monsters: horned cuckolds (men whose wives are unfaithful).

148 nickname: find new names for.

148–149 make . . . ignorance: use ignorance as an excuse for your waywardness.

155–158 Ophelia starts her description of Hamlet's former self by evoking the princely ideal of statesman, soldier, and scholar. He was the hope and ornament (**expectancy and rose**) of Denmark, a model of behavior and appearance for other people, respected (**observed**) by all who looked upon him.

163–164 blown . . . ecstasy: youth in full bloom withered by madness.

166 affections: feelings.

168–171 Claudius says that Hamlet's melancholy broods on something like a bird sits on an egg; he fears that some danger will hatch from it.

TEACH

ENGLISH LEARNER SUPPORT

Analyze Sayings and Expressions Direct students' attention to Ophelia's soliloquy in Scene 1, lines 154–165, page 203. Remind students that a soliloquy is a speech given by a character that no other characters can hear, and that it reveals **inner conflicts, themes,** and character traits.

Read the passage aloud with appropriate expression and tone.

Prompt students to say what Ophelia's emotions are in this passage (*sorrow, regret*).

Tell students that in his soliloquys, Shakespeare uses a lot of **figurative language,** meaning that the words represent other meanings rather than being literal. Display these figures of speech from the soliloquy:

- *glass of fashion*
- *rose of the fair state*
- *sucked the honey of his misguided vows*
- *like sweet bells jingled out of time and harsh*

Put students in same-level groups and assign one phrase to each group to discuss the meaning. Students should get the meanings of unfamiliar vocabulary from other students or the dictionary. Then, have them use what they know about the play to interpret these figures of speech. When students are confident they understand their group's assigned figure of speech, rearrange the groups into mixed-level groups and have students explain the meanings of the phrases to other students. **MODERATE/LIGHT**

 **NOTICE & NOTE**

O'er which his melancholy sits on brood,
170 And I do doubt the hatch and the disclose
Will be some danger; which for to prevent,
I have in quick determination
Thus set it down: he shall with speed to England
For the demand of our neglected tribute.
175 Haply the seas, and countries different,
With variable objects, shall expel
This something-settled matter in his heart,
Whereon his brains still beating puts him thus
From fashion of himself. What think you on 't?

180 **Polonius.** It shall do well. But yet do I believe
The origin and commencement of his grief
Sprung from neglected love.— How now, Ophelia?
You need not tell us what Lord Hamlet said;
We heard it all.— My lord, do as you please,
185 But, if you hold it fit, after the play
Let his queen-mother all alone entreat him
To show his grief. Let her be round with him;
And I'll be placed, so please you, in the ear
Of all their conference. If she find him not,
190 To England send him, or confine him where
Your wisdom best shall think.

King.   It shall be so.
Madness in great ones must not unwatched go.

[*They exit.*]

Scene 2 *The castle.*

[*Enter* Hamlet *and three of the* Players.]

Hamlet. Speak the speech, I pray you, as I pronounced
it to you, trippingly on the tongue; but if you mouth
it, as many of our players do, I had as lief the town-crier
spoke my lines. Nor do not saw the air too
5 much with your hand, thus, but use all gently; for in
the very torrent, tempest, and, as I may say, whirlwind
of your passion, you must acquire and beget
a temperance that may give it smoothness. O, it
offends me to the soul to hear a robustious, periwig-
10 pated fellow tear a passion to tatters, to very rags,
to split the ears of the groundlings, who for the
most part are capable of nothing but inexplicable
dumb shows and noise. I would have such a fellow
whipped for o'erdoing Termagant. It out-
15 Herods Herod. Pray you, avoid it.

177 This . . . heart: this unknown thing that has settled in his heart.

187 be round: speak plainly.

189 find him not: does not learn what is disturbing him.

3 I had as lief: I would just as soon.

9 robustious: boisterous.

9–10 periwig-pated: wig-wearing.

11 groundlings: the spectators who paid the cheapest price for admittance to the theater and stood in an open area in front of the stage.

14–15 Termagant, Herod: noisy, violent figures from early drama.

Player. I warrant your Honor.

Hamlet. Be not too tame neither, but let your own discretion be your tutor. Suit the action to the word, the word to the action, with this special observance, that you o'erstep not the modesty of nature. For anything so o'erdone is from the purpose of playing, whose end, both at the first and now, was and is to hold, as 'twere, the mirror up to nature, to show virtue her own feature, scorn her own image, and the very age and body of the time his form and pressure. Now this overdone or come tardy off, though it makes the unskillful laugh, cannot but make the judicious grieve, the censure of the which one must in your allowance o'erweigh a whole theater of others. O, there be players that I have seen play and heard others praise (and that highly), not to speak it profanely, that, neither having th' accent of Christians nor the gait of Christian, pagan, nor man, have so strutted and bellowed that I have thought some of nature's journeymen had made men, and not made them well, they imitated humanity so abominably.

Player. I hope we have reformed that indifferently with us, sir.

Hamlet. O, reform it altogether. And let those that play your clowns speak no more than is set down for them, for there be of them that will themselves laugh, to set on some quantity of barren spectators to laugh too, though in the meantime some necessary question of the play be then to be considered. That's villainous and shows a most pitiful ambition in the fool that uses it. Go make you ready.

[*Players exit.*]

[*Enter Polonius, Guildenstern, and Rosencrantz.*]

How now, my lord, will the King hear this piece of work?

Polonius. And the Queen too, and that presently.

Hamlet. Bid the players make haste. [*Polonius exits.*] Will you two help to hasten them?

Rosencrantz. Ay, my lord.

[*They exit.*]

Hamlet. What ho, Horatio!

---

20 modesty: moderation.

21 is from: strays from.

24 scorn: something scornful.

25–26 the very ... pressure: a true impression of the present.

26 come tardy off: done inadequately.

27 the unskillful: those lacking in judgment.

28–30 the censure ... others: You should value the opinion of a single judicious theatergoer over an entire audience that lacks judgment.

38 indifferently: fairly well.

42 of them: some among them.

43 barren: dull-witted.

The Tragedy of Hamlet: Act III, Scene 2 205

APPLYING ACADEMIC VOCABULARY

☐ ambiguous    anticipate   ☐ conceive   drama   ☐ integrity

Have students turn to a partner to discuss the following questions. Guide students to include the academic vocabulary words *anticipate* and *drama* in their responses. Ask volunteers to share their responses with the class.

- What direction does Hamlet give to the player about the **drama** they will enact?
- What reaction does the audience **anticipate** from Claudius when he sees the play?

TEACH

 NOTICE & NOTE

[*Enter* Horatio.]

55 **Horatio.** Here, sweet lord, at your service.

Hamlet. Horatio, thou art e'en as just a man
As e'er my conversation coped withal.

Horatio. O, my dear lord—

Hamlet.   Nay, do not think I flatter,
For what advancement may I hope from thee
60 That no revenue hast but thy good spirits
To feed and clothe thee? Why should the poor be flattered?
No, let the candied tongue lick absurd pomp
And crook the pregnant hinges of the knee
Where thrift may follow fawning. Dost thou hear?
65 Since my dear soul was mistress of her choice
And could of men distinguish, her election
Hath sealed thee for herself. For thou hast been
As one in suffering all that suffers nothing,
A man that Fortune's buffets and rewards
70 Hast ta'en with equal thanks; and blessed are those
Whose blood and judgment are so well commeddled
That they are not a pipe for Fortune's finger
To sound what stop she please. Give me that man
That is not passion's slave, and I will wear him
75 In my heart's core, ay, in my heart of heart,
As I do thee.—Something too much of this.—
There is a play tonight before the King.
One scene of it comes near the circumstance
Which I have told thee of my father's death.
80 I prithee, when thou seest that act afoot,
Even with the very comment of thy soul
Observe my uncle. If his occulted guilt
Do not itself unkennel in one speech,
It is a damnèd ghost that we have seen,
85 And my imaginations are as foul
As Vulcan's stithy. Give him heedful note,
For I mine eyes will rivet to his face,
And, after, we will both our judgments join
In censure of his seeming.

Horatio.   Well, my lord.
90 If he steal aught the whilst this play is playing
And 'scape detecting, I will pay the theft.

[*Sound a flourish.*]

Hamlet. They are coming to the play. I must be idle.
Get you a place.

[*Enter Trumpets and Kettle Drums. Enter* King, Queen,

56–57 Hamlet says that Horatio is as honorable as any man he has ever dealt with.

62 candied: flattering.

63 crook . . . knee: bend the ready joint of the knee (kneel down).

64 thrift: profit.

68 one . . . nothing: one who experiences everything but is harmed by nothing.

71 blood: passions; **commeddled:** blended.

72 pipe: small wind instrument.

73 stop: a hole in a wind instrument that controls sound.

81 Even . . . soul: with your most searching observation.

82–86 Hamlet says that if Claudius's hidden (**occulted**) guilt does not reveal (**unkennel**) itself with the speech Hamlet wrote, then the Ghost is in league with the devil and Hamlet's thoughts about Claudius are as foul as the forge of the Roman god of metalworking.

89 censure of his seeming: judgment of how he looks and behaves.

92 be idle: play the fool, be unoccupied.

206 Unit 2

WHEN STUDENTS STRUGGLE . . .

Connect Plot Points Focus students' attention on lines 77–89 and read the passage aloud. Ask students to identify what Hamlet tells Horatio to do (*Observe my uncle*). Explain to students what these phrases refer to:

- **that act afoot** (*the scene in which the alleged murder is reenacted*)
- **occulted guilt** (*the king's hidden guilt for the murder*)

📖 For additional support, go to the **Reading Studio** and assign the following ⬆ **Level Up tutorial: Plot: Sequence of Events**.

Polonius, Ophelia, Rosencrantz, Guildenstern, and other Lords *attendant with the* King's guard *carrying torches.*]

King. How fares our cousin Hamlet?

95 **Hamlet.** Excellent, i' faith, of the chameleon's dish. I eat the air, promise-crammed. You cannot feed capons so.

King. I have nothing with this answer, Hamlet. These words are not mine.

100 **Hamlet.** No, nor mine now. [*To* Polonius.] My lord, you played once i' th' university, you say?

Polonius. That did I, my lord, and was accounted a good actor.

Hamlet. What did you enact?

105 **Polonius.** I did enact Julius Caesar. I was killed i' th' Capitol. Brutus killed me.

Hamlet. It was a brute part of him to kill so capital a calf there.—Be the players ready?

Rosencrantz. Ay, my lord. They stay upon your patience.

110 **Queen.** Come hither, my dear Hamlet, sit by me.

Hamlet. No, good mother. Here's metal more attractive.

[Hamlet *takes a place near* Ophelia.]

Polonius [*to the* King]. Oh, ho! Do you mark that?

Hamlet. Lady, shall I lie in your lap?

Ophelia. No, my lord.

115 **Hamlet.** I mean, my head upon your lap?

Ophelia. Ay, my lord.

Hamlet. Do you think I meant country matters?

Ophelia. I think nothing, my lord.

Hamlet. That's a fair thought to lie between maids' legs.

120 **Ophelia.** What is, my lord?

Hamlet. Nothing.

Ophelia. You are merry, my lord.

Hamlet. Who, I?

Ophelia. Ay, my lord.

125 **Hamlet.** O God, your only jig-maker. What should a man do but be merry? For look you how cheerfully my mother looks, and my father died within 's two hours.

NOTICE & NOTE

94–97 Hamlet, taking **fares** to mean "feeds," answers that he eats promises. (Chameleons were said to feed on air.)

108 calf: fool.

111 metal more attractive: a substance more magnetic.

117 country matters: something coarse or indecent, which a rustic from the country might propose.

CONTRASTS AND CONTRADICTIONS

Notice & Note: Mark Hamlet's remarks about Ophelia in lines 111–119.

Compare: How does his attitude toward her in this scene compare with his attitude in Scene 1, lines 104–153?

125 Hamlet sarcastically refers to himself as the best jig (comical song and dance) performer.

TEACH

CONTRASTS AND CONTRADICTIONS

Review with students the way Hamlet behaved toward Ophelia in Scene 1 and the emotions they inferred from his behavior. Point out that in the staging of the play, Hamlet lays at Ophelia's feet. Then, have students answer the question by comparing Hamlet's attitude toward Ophelia here with that in Scene 1. To help them, direct them to Ophelia's reaction. (**Answer:** *In this scene, Hamlet's attitude is disrespectful and crude but not cruel and accusatory as in Scene 1. Ophelia takes him to be "merry" but still thinks Hamlet is mad.*)

TEACH

ENGLISH LEARNER SUPPORT

Write to Narrate with Increasing Specificity and Detail Focus students' attention on the stage directions following line 135. Explain to students that this paragraph describes the action of the play that the characters are watching. Read each sentence and have students turn to a partner and show their understanding using their own words and pantomime.

Have students find and circle the words *poison, dead,* and *body*. **SUBSTANTIAL**

Have students fill in the blanks:

- At the beginning, the Queen _____ the King. (loves)
- Then, the King _____ in the garden (goes to sleep).
- While he is asleep, a man _____ him and takes _____ (poisons/his crown).
- The Queen acts as if she is _____ that he is dead. (upset, sad)
- But in the end she _____ the poisoner. (accepts the love of)

Have students write a short paragraph narrating in their own words the events as pantomimed in the stage directions. **MODERATE**

When students have finished writing, have them turn to a partner and explain why Hamlet wants Claudius to watch this scene. **LIGHT**

NOTICE & NOTE

129–130 Hamlet sarcastically suggests giving up his mourning clothes for luxurious clothing trimmed with furs.

134 not thinking on: being forgotten; **hobby-horse:** a horse-and-rider figure who once performed in morris and may-day dances. Such traditions had been disappearing.

Dumb show: a scene without dialogue.

138 miching mallecho: sneaking misdeed. (The Spanish word *malhecho* means "misdeed.")

139 Belike: perhaps; **argument:** plot.

148 naught: naughty, indecent.

152 posy of a ring: a motto inscribed in a ring.

Ophelia. Nay, 'tis twice two months, my lord.

Hamlet. So long? Nay, then, let the devil wear black, for
130 I'll have a suit of sables. O heavens, die two months
ago, and not forgotten yet? Then there's hope a great
man's memory may outlive his life half a year. But,
by'r Lady, he must build churches, then, or else shall
he suffer not thinking on, with the hobby-horse, whose
135 epitaph is "For oh, for oh, the hobby-horse is forgot."

[*The trumpets sound. Dumb show follows.*]

[*Enter* a King *and* a Queen, *very lovingly, the* Queen *embracing him and he her. She kneels and makes show of protestation unto him. He takes her up and declines his head upon her neck. He lies him down upon a bank of flowers. She, seeing him asleep, leaves him. Anon comes in another* man, *takes off his crown, kisses it, pours poison in the sleeper's ears, and leaves him. The* Queen *returns, finds the* King *dead, makes passionate action. The* poisoner *with some three or four come in again, seem to condole with her. The dead body is carried away. The* poisoner *woos the* Queen *with gifts. She seems harsh awhile but in the end accepts his love.*]

[Players *exit.*]

Ophelia. What means this, my lord?

Hamlet. Marry, this is miching mallecho. It means mischief.

Ophelia. Belike this show imports the argument of the play.

[*Enter* Prologue.]

140 **Hamlet.** We shall know by this fellow. The players cannot keep counsel; they'll tell all.

Ophelia. Will he tell us what this show meant?

Hamlet. Ay, or any show that you will show him. Be not you ashamed to show, he'll not shame to tell
145 you what it means.

Ophelia. You are naught, you are naught. I'll mark the play.

Prologue.
    For us and for our tragedy,
150   Here stooping to your clemency,
    We beg your hearing patiently.

[*He exits.*]

Hamlet. Is this a prologue or the posy of a ring?

Ophelia. 'Tis brief, my lord.

Hamlet. As woman's love.

[*Enter the Player King and Queen.*]

155 **Player King.** *Full thirty times hath Phoebus' cart gone round*
Neptune's salt wash and Tellus' orbèd ground,
And thirty dozen moons with borrowed sheen
About the world have times twelve thirties been
Since love our hearts and Hymen did our hands
160 *Unite commutual in most sacred bands.*

Player Queen. *So many journeys may the sun and moon*
Make us again count o'er ere love be done!
But woe is me! You are so sick of late,
So far from cheer and from your former state,
165 *That I distrust you. Yet, though I distrust,*
Discomfort you, my lord, it nothing must.
For women fear too much, even as they love,
And women's fear and love hold quantity,
In neither aught, or in extremity.
170 *Now what my love is, proof hath made you*
know, And, as my love is sized, my fear is so:
Where love is great, the littlest doubts are fear;
Where little fears grow great, great love grows there.

Player King. *Faith, I must leave thee, love, and shortly too.*
175 *My operant powers their functions leave to do.*
And thou shalt live in this fair world behind,
Honored, beloved; and haply one as kind
For husband shalt thou—

Player Queen. O, confound the rest!
Such love must needs be treason in my breast.
180 *In second husband let me be accurst.*
None wed the second but who killed the first.

Hamlet. That's wormwood!

Player Queen. *The instances that second marriage move*
Are base respects of thrift, but none of love.
185 *A second time I kill my husband dead*
When second husband kisses me in bed.

Player King. *I do believe you think what now you speak,*
But what we do determine oft we break.
Purpose is but the slave to memory,
190 *Of violent birth, but poor validity,*
Which now, the fruit unripe, sticks on the tree
But fall unshaken when they mellow be.
Most necessary 'tis that we forget

NOTICE & NOTE

155–160 The Player King says that they have been united in love and marriage for 30 years. **Phoebus' cart:** the sun god's chariot; **Neptune's salt wash:** the ocean; **Tellus:** Roman goddess of the earth; **Hymen:** god of marriage.

165 distrust you: am worried about you.

168–169 And women's ... extremity: Women love and fear in equal measure, loving and fearing either too much or hardly at all.

175 My ... do: My vital powers are no longer functioning.

176 behind: after I'm gone.

182 wormwood: a bitter herb.

183–184 The instances ... love: People marry a second time for profit, not for love.

189–190 Our intentions are dependent on our memory; they are powerful at first but have little durability (**validity**).

193–194 Most ... debt: We inevitably forget promises we have made to ourselves.

The Tragedy of Hamlet: Act III, Scene 2 209

TEACH

NOTICE & NOTE

197–200 When the violence of extreme grief or joy ceases, so too does the willingness to act upon these emotions. People who feel extreme grief also feel extreme joy, and one passion is likely to follow another without much cause (**on slender accident**).

201 for aye: forever.

205 The great . . . flies: When a great man's fortune falls, his closest friend abandons him.

206 advanced: moving up in life.

207 hitherto: to this extent.

210 Directly seasons him: immediately changes him into.

213 devices still: plans always.

218 Sport . . . night: May the day deny (**lock from**) me its pastimes and night its rest.

220 An anchor's cheer: a religious hermit's fare.

221–222 May each obstacle that turns the face of joy pale meet and destroy everything that I wish to see prosper (**what I would have well**).

231 doth protest too much: overstates her case, makes too many assurances.

233 argument: plot.

To pay ourselves what to ourselves is debt.
195 What to ourselves in passion we propose,
The passion ending, doth the purpose lose.
The violence of either grief or joy
Their own enactures with themselves destroy.
Where joy most revels, grief doth most lament;
200 Grief joys, joy grieves, on slender accident.
This world is not for aye, nor 'tis not strange
That even our loves should with our fortunes change;
For 'tis a question left us yet to prove
Whether love lead fortune or else fortune love.
205 The great man down, you mark his favorite flies;
The poor, advanced, makes friends of enemies.
And hitherto doth love on fortune tend,
For who not needs shall never lack a friend,
And who in want a hollow friend doth try
210 Directly seasons him his enemy.
But, orderly to end where I begun:
Our wills and fates do so contrary run
That our devices still are overthrown;
Our thoughts are ours, their ends none of our own.
215 So think thou wilt no second husband wed,
But die thy thoughts when thy first lord is dead.

Player Queen. Nor earth to me give food, nor heaven light,
Sport and repose lock from me day and night,
To desperation turn my trust and hope,
220 An anchor's cheer in prison be my scope.
Each opposite that blanks the face of joy
Meet what I would have well and it destroy.
Both here and hence pursue me lasting strife,
If, once a widow, ever I be wife.

225 **Hamlet.** If she should break it now!

Player King. 'Tis deeply sworn. Sweet, leave me here awhile.
My spirits grow dull, and fain I would beguile
The tedious day with sleep.

[*Sleeps.*]

Player Queen.   *Sleep rock thy brain,*
And never come mischance between us twain.

[*Player Queen exits.*]

230 **Hamlet.** Madam, how like you this play?

Queen. The lady doth protest too much, methinks.

Hamlet. O, but she'll keep her word.

King. Have you heard the argument? Is there no offense in 't?

210 Unit 2

IMPROVE READING FLUENCY

Targeted Passage The "play within a play" in this scene is written in rhyming iambic pentameter. Direct students' attention to the Player Queen's speech in Scene 2, lines 217–224, page 210. Read pairs of rhyming lines aloud and have students echo you while tapping on their desks to mark the stressed syllables. After a few rounds of practice, have students read the verse aloud round-robin style, with each student taking a pair of lines while the others keep the beat by tapping on their desks. Have them start out with a slow beat and then get a little faster with each round.

 Go to the **Reading Studio** for additional support in developing fluency.

NOTICE & NOTE

235 **Hamlet.** No, no, they do but jest, poison in jest. No offense i' th' world.

King. What do you call the play?

Hamlet. "The Mousetrap." Marry, how? Tropically. This play is the image of a murder done in Vienna.
240 Gonzago is the duke's name, his wife Baptista. You shall see anon. 'Tis a knavish piece of work, but what of that? Your Majesty and we that have free souls, it touches us not. Let the galled jade wince; our withers are unwrung.

[*Enter* Lucianus.]

245 This is one Lucianus, nephew to the king.

Ophelia. You are as good as a chorus, my lord.

Hamlet. I could interpret between you and your love, if I could see the puppets dallying.

Ophelia. You are keen, my lord, you are keen.

250 **Hamlet.** It would cost you a groaning to take off mine edge.

Ophelia. Still better and worse.

Hamlet. So you mis-take your husbands.—Begin, murderer. Pox, leave thy damnable faces and begin.

238 **Tropically:** metaphorically.

242 **free:** guilt-free.

243–244 **Let . . . unwrung:** a proverbial expression that means, "Let the guilty flinch; our consciences do not bother us."

246 **chorus:** a character who explains what will happen in a play.

247–252 An "interpreter" is a narrator in a puppet show. Hamlet says that he could explain what is going on between Ophelia and her lover if he caught them together. When she comments that he is **keen** (sharp, penetrating), he responds with wordplay (using **keen** to mean "sexually aroused") that she finds even more witty but also more offensive.

253 **mis-take:** take falsely. A reference to the marriage vow to take a husband "for better, for worse."

TEACH

ENGLISH LEARNER SUPPORT

Narrate and Explain Explain to students that in Scene 2, lines 232–244, page 211, Hamlet and Claudius are discussing the *argument* (line 234), or **plot,** of the play they are watching. Have students turn to a partner and practice telling the plot of this "play within a play." Then, have them answer these questions:

- Why does Hamlet say to Claudius, *Your Majesty and we that have free souls, it touches us not*?
- What is a *galled jade*?
- How is this exchange significant to the play's central conflict?

LIGHT

TEACH

 ANALYZE CONFLICT

Remind students the **plot** is driven by the conflicts in the play, and one conflict is the mutual suspicion and distrust between Claudius and Hamlet. Another conflict is Hamlet's **internal conflict** over whether to believe the Ghost about Claudius murdering his father, and he has arranged for Claudius to view this play as a way to resolve the inner conflict by testing his guilt. Remind students that up to this point Claudius wished to keep Hamlet close by in Denmark so as to keep an eye on him. Then ask them to predict whether that might change and why. (**Answer:** *Claudius now probably realizes Hamlet has somehow found out about his crime and may expose him. Therefore, it is likely Claudius will want to get rid of Hamlet somehow.*)

 **NOTICE & NOTE**

257 Time is my ally (**Confederate**) and only witness.

259 Hecate's ban: the curse of Hecate, goddess of witchcraft.

261 usurp: steal.

267 false fire: the discharge of a gun loaded without shot.

273 ungallèd: uninjured.

ANALYZE CONFLICT
Annotate: Reread lines 255–271. Mark Claudius's reaction to Hamlet's comments and the performance.

Predict: How might this incident affect Claudius's plans for Hamlet?

277–279 turn Turk with me: turn against me. Elizabethan theater costumes often included feathers worn on hats and ribbon rosettes on shoes. A fellowship is a share or partnership in a theater company.

282 Damon: in Roman mythology the friend of Pythias.

285 pajock: either "peacock," which had a reputation for lust and cruelty, or "patchock," a savage person. (Presumably the rhyme Horatio hints at is **ass**.)

---

255 Come, the croaking raven doth bellow for revenge.

   Lucianus. *Thoughts black, hands apt, drugs fit, and*
       time agreeing,
   Confederate season, else no creature seeing,
   Thou mixture rank, of midnight weeds collected,
   With Hecate's ban thrice blasted, thrice infected,
260 *Thy natural magic and dire property*
   On wholesome life usurp immediately.

   [*Pours the poison in his ears.*]

   Hamlet. He poisons him i' th' garden for his estate. His name's Gonzago. The story is extant and written in very choice Italian. You shall see anon how
265 the murderer gets the love of Gonzago's wife.

   [*Claudius rises.*]

   Ophelia. The King rises.

   Hamlet. What, frighted with false fire?

   Queen. How fares my lord?

   Polonius. Give o'er the play.

270 **King.** Give me some light. Away!

   Polonius. Lights, lights, lights!

   [*All but* Hamlet *and* Horatio *exit.*]

   Hamlet. *Why, let the strucken deer go weep,*
       The hart ungallèd play.
   For some must watch, while some must sleep:
275   *Thus runs the world away.*
   Would not this, sir, and a forest of feathers (if the rest of my fortunes turn Turk with me) with two Provincial roses on my razed shoes, get me a fellowship in a cry of players?

280 **Horatio.** Half a share.

   Hamlet. A whole one, I.
   For thou dost know, O Damon dear,
       This realm dismantled was
   Of Jove himself, and now reigns here
285   *A very very—pajock.*

   Horatio. You might have rhymed.

   Hamlet. O good Horatio, I'll take the ghost's word for a thousand pound. Didst perceive?

   Horatio. Very well, my lord.

290 **Hamlet.** Upon the talk of the poisoning?

212 Unit 2

WHEN STUDENTS STRUGGLE...

Predict a Character's Decisions Review what the Ghost told Hamlet in Act I. Then have students carefully reread Scene 2, lines 256–265, and work in pairs to answer these questions:

- What problem is Hamlet trying to solve by having Claudius watch this play?
- What does Claudius probably realize at this moment about Hamlet?
- What might Claudius want to do now that he didn't want to do before?

 For additional support, go to the **Reading Studio** and assign the following Level Up tutorial: **Character Motivation**.

212 Unit 2

Horatio. I did very well note him.

Hamlet. Ah ha! Come, some music! Come, the recorders!
　For if the King like not the comedy,
295　*Why, then, belike he likes it not, perdy.*
Come, some music!

[*Enter* Rosencrantz *and* Guildenstern.]

Guildenstern. Good my lord, vouchsafe me a word with you.

Hamlet. Sir, a whole history.

300 **Guildenstern.** The King, sir—

Hamlet. Ay, sir, what of him?

Guildenstern. Is in his retirement marvelous distempered.

Hamlet. With drink, sir?

Guildenstern. No, my lord, with choler.

305 **Hamlet.** Your wisdom should show itself more richer to signify this to the doctor, for for me to put him to his purgation would perhaps plunge him into more choler.

Guildenstern. Good my lord, put your discourse into
310 some frame and start not so wildly from my affair.

Hamlet. I am tame, sir. Pronounce.

Guildenstern. The Queen your mother, in most great affliction of spirit, hath sent me to you.

Hamlet. You are welcome.

315 **Guildenstern.** Nay, good my lord, this courtesy is not of the right breed. If it shall please you to make me a wholesome answer, I will do your mother's commandment. If not, your pardon and my return shall be the end of my business.

320 **Hamlet.** Sir, I cannot.

Rosencrantz. What, my lord?

Hamlet. Make you a wholesome answer. My wit's diseased. But, sir, such answer as I can make, you shall command—or, rather, as you say, my mother.
325 Therefore no more but to the matter. My mother, you say—

Rosencrantz. Then thus she says: your behavior hath struck her into amazement and admiration.

---

293 recorders: flute-like wooden wind instruments.

295 perdy: by God (from the French **par dieu**).

302 distempered: upset. (Hamlet takes it in the sense of "drunk.")

304 choler: anger. (Hamlet takes it in the sense of "biliousness.")

307 purgation: cleansing of the body of impurities; spiritual cleansing through confession.

310 frame: order; **start:** shy away like a nervous or wild horse.

318 pardon: permission to leave.

328 admiration: wonder.

NOTICE & NOTE

Hamlet. O wonderful son that can so 'stonish a mother!
330 But is there no sequel at the heels of this mother's admiration? Impart.

Rosencrantz. She desires to speak with you in her closet ere you go to bed.

Hamlet. We shall obey, were she ten times our mother.
335 Have you any further trade with us?

Rosencrantz. My lord, you once did love me.

Hamlet. And do still, by these pickers and stealers.

Rosencrantz. Good my lord, what is your cause of distemper? You do surely bar the door upon your
340 own liberty if you deny your griefs to your friend.

Hamlet. Sir, I lack advancement.

Rosencrantz. How can that be, when you have the voice of the King himself for your succession in Denmark?

345 **Hamlet.** Ay, sir, but "While the grass grows"—the proverb is something musty.

[*Enter the* Players *with recorders*.]

O, the recorders! Let me see one. [*He takes a recorder and turns to* Guildenstern.] To withdraw with you: why do you go about to recover the
350 wind of me, as if you would drive me into a toil?

Guildenstern. O, my lord, if my duty be too bold, my love is too unmannerly.

Hamlet. I do not well understand that. Will you play upon this pipe?

355 **Guildenstern.** My lord, I cannot.

Hamlet. I pray you.

Guildenstern. Believe me, I cannot.

Hamlet. I do beseech you.

Guildenstern. I know no touch of it, my lord.

360 **Hamlet.** It is as easy as lying. Govern these ventages with your fingers and thumb, give it breath with your mouth, and it will discourse most eloquent music. Look you, these are the stops.

Guildenstern. But these cannot I command to any
365 utt'rance of harmony. I have not the skill.

Hamlet. Why, look you now, how unworthy a thing

---

332 closet: private room.

337 pickers and stealers: hands (from the Church catechism, "To keep my hands from picking and stealing").

345–346 The rest of the stale (**musty**) proverb is "the horse starves," suggesting that Hamlet cannot wait so long.

348–350 withdraw: speak privately. Hamlet uses a hunting metaphor: The hunter moves to the windward side of the prey, causing it to flee toward a net (**toil**).

360 ventages: stops, or finger holes, on the recorder.

you make of me! You would play upon me, you would seem to know my stops, you would pluck out the heart of my mystery, you would sound me
370 from my lowest note to the top of my compass; and there is much music, excellent voice, in this little organ, yet cannot you make it speak. 'Sblood, do you think I am easier to be played on than a pipe? Call me what instrument you will, though
375 you can fret me, you cannot play upon me.

[*Enter* Polonius.]

God bless you, sir.

Polonius. My lord, the Queen would speak with you, and presently.

Hamlet. Do you see yonder cloud that's almost in
380 shape of a camel?

Polonius. By th' Mass, and 'tis like a camel indeed.

Hamlet. Methinks it is like a weasel.

Polonius. It is backed like a weasel.

Hamlet. Or like a whale.

385 **Polonius.** Very like a whale.

Hamlet. Then I will come to my mother by and by.

[*Aside.*] They fool me to the top of my bent.—I will come by and by.

Polonius. I will say so.

390 **Hamlet.** "By and by" is easily said. Leave me, friends.

[*All but* Hamlet *exit*.]

'Tis now the very witching time of night,
When churchyards yawn and hell itself breathes out
Contagion to this world. Now could I drink hot blood
And do such bitter business as the day
395 Would quake to look on. Soft, now to my mother.
O heart, lose not thy nature; let not ever
The soul of Nero enter this firm bosom.
Let me be cruel, not unnatural.
I will speak daggers to her, but use none.
400 My tongue and soul in this be hypocrites:
How in my words somever she be shent,
To give them seals never, my soul, consent.

[*He exits.*]

369–375 sound me: play upon me like an instrument, investigate me; **compass:** an instrument's range; **organ:** musical instrument; **fret me:** annoy me (also punning on **frets,** the raised bars for fingering a stringed instrument).

387 fool . . . bent: make me play the fool to the limits of my ability.

388 by and by: before long.

397 Nero: a Roman emperor who put his mother to death.

401–402 Hamlet tells himself that however much she is rebuked (**shent**) in his words, he must not put those words into action (**give them seals**).

The Tragedy of Hamlet: Act III, Scene 2 215

ENGLISH LEARNER SUPPORT

Demonstrate Comprehension by Summarizing For Scene 2, lines 395–402, page 215, explain to students that Hamlet is preparing to speak to his mother, and that he is now sure Claudius murdered his father. Ask them to think about why he might be angry at and suspicious of his mother. Provide the meanings of these words and phrases: *Let me*: Allow me to/I should/I promise to; *Firm bosom*: Hard heart; *Daggers*: knives

Have students work with a partner to summarize in their own words what Hamlet will and won't do. **MODERATE**

TEACH

NOTICE & NOTE

Scene 3 *The castle.*

[*Enter* King, Rosencrantz, *and* Guildenstern.]

King. I like him not, nor stands it safe with us
To let his madness range. Therefore prepare you.
I your commission will forthwith dispatch,
And he to England shall along with you.
5   The terms of our estate may not endure
Hazard so near 's as doth hourly grow
Out of his brows.

Guildenstern.   We will ourselves provide.
Most holy and religious fear it is
To keep those many many bodies safe
10 That live and feed upon your Majesty.

Rosencrantz. The single and peculiar life is bound
With all the strength and armor of the mind
To keep itself from noyance, but much more
That spirit upon whose weal depends and rests
15 The lives of many. The cess of majesty
Dies not alone, but like a gulf doth draw
What's near it with it; or it is a massy wheel
Fixed on the summit of the highest mount,
To whose huge spokes ten thousand lesser things
20 Are mortised and adjoined, which, when it falls,
Each small annexment, petty consequence,
Attends the boist'rous ruin. Never alone
Did the king sigh, but with a general groan.

King. Arm you, I pray you, to this speedy voyage,
25 For we will fetters put about this fear,
Which now goes too free-footed.

Rosencrantz.   We will haste us.

[Rosencrantz *and* Guildenstern *exit*.]

[*Enter* Polonius.]

Polonius. My lord, he's going to his mother's closet.
Behind the arras I'll convey myself
To hear the process. I'll warrant she'll tax him home;
30 And, as you said (and wisely was it said),
'Tis meet that some more audience than a mother,
Since nature makes them partial, should o'erhear
The speech of vantage. Fare you well, my liege.
I'll call upon you ere you go to bed
35 And tell you what I know.

King.   Thanks, dear my lord.

[Polonius *exits*.]

---

1 him: his behavior.

3 forthwith dispatch: have prepared at once.

5 The terms of our estate: my position as king.

6 near 's: near us.

11 single and peculiar: individual and private.

13 noyance: harm.

14 weal: well-being.

15 cess: cessation, decease.

16 gulf: whirlpool.

17–22 Rosencrantz alludes to Fortune's massive (**massy**) wheel, with the king traditionally shown on the top; when the king falls, everyone connected with him plunges as well.

24 Arm you: prepare yourself.

29 process: proceedings; **tax him home:** strongly rebuke him.

31 meet: fitting.

33 of vantage: in addition.

216   Unit 2

TO CHALLENGE STUDENTS...

Determine Figurative Meanings How do comparisons help authors convey ideas and emotions? Have students discuss the simile in Scene 3, lines 15–17, page 216, with a partner. *(The downfall or death of a king is compared to a whirlpool that draws in others. This shows the importance of the throne to the well-being of the country.)* Have students use this simile and the metaphor that follows to answer these questions in small groups:

- What do these figures of speech illustrate about the Renaissance view of the monarchy?
- How do these figures of speech provide insight into the motives of Rosencrantz and Guildenstern? How should they be classified in the play—as villains or pawns of the King?

NOTICE & NOTE

O, my offense is rank, it smells to heaven;
It hath the primal eldest curse upon 't,
A brother's murder. Pray can I not,
Though inclination be as sharp as will.
40 My stronger guilt defeats my strong intent,
And, like a man to double business bound,
I stand in pause where I shall first begin
And both neglect. What if this cursèd hand
Were thicker than itself with brother's blood?
45 Is there not rain enough in the sweet heavens
To wash it white as snow? Whereto serves mercy
But to confront the visage of offense?
And what's in prayer but this twofold force,
To be forestallèd ere we come to fall,
50 Or pardoned being down? Then I'll look up.
My fault is past. But, O, what form of prayer
Can serve my turn? "Forgive me my foul murder"?
That cannot be, since I am still possessed
Of those effects for which I did the murder:
55 My crown, mine own ambition, and my queen.
May one be pardoned and retain th' offense?
In the corrupted currents of this world,
Offense's gilded hand may shove by justice,
And oft 'tis seen the wicked prize itself
60 Buys out the law. But 'tis not so above:

37 primal eldest curse: the curse of Cain (the son of Adam and Eve who murdered his brother Abel).

46–47 Whereto . . . offense: What purpose does mercy serve other than to oppose condemnation?

56 th' offense: the benefits of the crime.

57–64 In the corrupt ways (**currents**) of this world, a rich offender can push aside justice, and often the law is bribed with stolen wealth. But that isn't the case in heaven, where there is no evasion (**shuffling**); the true nature of every deed lies exposed, and we must testify against ourselves.

The Tragedy of Hamlet: Act III, Scene 3 217

WHEN STUDENTS STRUGGLE . . .

Identify Main Ideas To help students better comprehend the meaning of the King's speech:

- Read these sets of lines aloud as students follow along: 36–43, 51–56, 66–72.
- Give students time to work with a partner to identify the main idea.
- Call on pairs to state the main idea. Then record it in a class chart.

  For additional support, go to the **Reading Studio** and assign the following Level Up tutorial: Main Idea and Supporting Details.

TEACH

✏️ ANALYZE SOLILOQUY

Remind students that sometimes a **soliloquy** occurs when there is more than one character on stage but the other characters cannot hear the speaker. Explain that Claudius does not hear Hamlet speaking. Direct their attention to the stage direction that shows that Hamlet raises his sword and prepares to kill Claudius. Then, ask them to imagine Hamlet in that moment. Explain that Hamlet's speech reveals an **inner conflict** he experiences at that moment. Have them reread line 75 and the side note and ask them what Hamlet thinks needs to be looked at carefully and why. Review with students what the Ghost told Hamlet in Act I, Scene 5, lines 10–14, and ask them to compare King Hamlet's fate to the fate Hamlet expects for Claudius if he kills him in that moment. (**Answer:** *In Act I, the Ghost tells Hamlet he is now doomed to spend a certain amount of time paying for his crimes in the afterlife. Hamlet realizes Claudius has just purged his soul and would therefore go directly to Heaven if he were to die at that moment. That would be a kinder fate than the one his father suffered, which Hamlet does not think is fair.*)

 **NOTICE & NOTE**

64 rests: remains.

68 limèd: trapped like a bird caught in quicklime (a sticky substance).

69 engaged: entangled; **Make assay:** make an attempt (addressed to himself).

ANALYZE SOLILOQUY
Annotate: As you read lines 73–96, mark the reason why Hamlet delays killing Claudius.

Analyze: How does this decision relate to what the Ghost told Hamlet about his death in Act I?

73 pat: conveniently.

75 would be scanned: needs to be looked at carefully.

79 hire and salary: something Claudius should pay me to do.

80–84 Hamlet complains that his father was killed without allowing him spiritual preparation (**grossly**). He was immersed in worldly pleasures and his sins were in full bloom. Only heaven knows how his final account stands, but from Hamlet's perspective his father's sins seem a heavy burden.

86 seasoned: prepared.

88 know thou a more horrid hent: wait to be grasped on a more horrible occasion.

95 stays: awaits me.

96 physic: medicine (referring to the postponement of revenge or to Claudius's act of prayer).

There is no shuffling; there the action lies
In his true nature, and we ourselves compelled,
Even to the teeth and forehead of our faults,
To give in evidence. What then? What rests?
65 Try what repentance can. What can it not?
Yet what can it, when one cannot repent?
O wretched state! O bosom black as death!
O limèd soul, that, struggling to be free,
Art more engaged! Help, angels! Make assay.
70 Bow, stubborn knees, and heart with strings of steel
Be soft as sinews of the newborn babe.
All may be well.

[*He kneels.*]

[*Enter* Hamlet.]

Hamlet. Now might I do it pat, now he is a-praying,
And now I'll do 't.

[*He draws his sword.*]
                    And so he goes to heaven,
75 And so am I revenged. That would be scanned:
A villain kills my father, and for that,
I, his sole son, do this same villain send
To heaven.
Why, this is hire and salary, not revenge.
80 He took my father grossly, full of bread,
With all his crimes broad blown, as flush as May;
And how his audit stands who knows save heaven.
But in our circumstance and course of thought
'Tis heavy with him. And am I then revenged
85 To take him in the purging of his soul,
When he is fit and seasoned for his passage?
No.
Up sword, and know thou a more horrid hent.

[*He sheathes his sword.*]

When he is drunk asleep, or in his rage,
90 Or in th' incestuous pleasure of his bed,
At game a-swearing, or about some act
That has no relish of salvation in 't—
Then trip him, that his heels may kick at heaven,
And that his soul may be as damned and black
95 As hell, whereto it goes. My mother stays.
This physic but prolongs thy sickly days.

[*Hamlet exits.*]

King [*rising*]. My words fly up, my thoughts remain
    below;

218 Unit 2

TO CHALLENGE STUDENTS . . .

Research Cultural Ideas in Literature *The Tragedy of Hamlet* repeatedly visits the subject of the afterlife. Have students do research on common ideas of the afterlife during the Renaissance, and give a presentation on how these ideas would have been perceived by Shakespeare's audience. Students should answer these questions:

- Would the ideas about the afterlife in *Hamlet* have been familiar to Shakespeare's audience?
- Would Hamlet's fears about the afterlife have been common at that time?
- Where would Shakespeare's audience have gotten their ideas about the afterlife?

Words without thoughts never to heaven go.

[*He exits.*]

Scene 4 *The Queen's private chamber.*

[*Enter* Queen *and* Polonius.]

Polonius. He will come straight. Look you lay home to him.
Tell him his pranks have been too broad to bear with
And that your Grace hath screened and stood between
Much heat and him. I'll silence me even here.
5 Pray you, be round with him.

Hamlet [*within*]. Mother, mother, mother!

Queen. I'll warrant you. Fear me not. Withdraw,
I hear him coming.

[Polonius *hides behind the arras*.]

[*Enter* Hamlet.]

Hamlet. Now, mother, what's the matter?

10 **Queen.** Hamlet, thou hast thy father much offended.

Hamlet. Mother, you have my father much offended.

Queen. Come, come, you answer with an idle tongue.

Hamlet. Go, go, you question with a wicked tongue.

Queen. Why, how now, Hamlet?

Hamlet. What's the matter now?

15 **Queen.** Have you forgot me?

Hamlet. No, by the rood, not so.
You are the Queen, your husband's brother's wife,
And (would it were not so) you are my mother.

Queen. Nay, then I'll set those to you that can speak.

Hamlet. Come, come, and sit you down; you shall not budge.
20 You go not till I set you up a glass
Where you may see the inmost part of you.

Queen. What wilt thou do? Thou wilt not murder me?
Help, ho!

Polonius [*behind the arras*]. What ho! Help!

25 **Hamlet.** How now, a rat? Dead for a ducat, dead.

[*He kills* Polonius *by thrusting a rapier through the arras*.]

Polonius [*behind the arras*]. O, I am slain!

Queen. O me, what hast thou done?

Hamlet. Nay, I know not. Is it the King?

NOTICE & NOTE

1 **straight:** right away; **lay home to:** strongly rebuke.

2 **broad:** unrestrained.

5 **round:** blunt.

12 **idle:** foolish.

15 **forgot me:** forgotten who I am; **rood:** cross.

20 **glass:** mirror.

25 **Dead for a ducat:** I'll wager a ducat that I kill him; I'll kill him for a ducat.

CLOSE READ SCREENCAST

Modeled Discussions Have students click the *Close Read* icon in their eBooks to access a screencast in which readers discuss and annotate Hamlet's murder of Polonius (Act III, Scene 4, lines 19–32).

As a class, view and discuss this video. Then, have students pair up to do an independent close read of lines 19–32. Students can record their answers on the Close Read Practice PDF.

 Close Read Practice PDF

TEACH

NOTICE & NOTE

ANALYZE DRAMATIC PLOT
Annotate: Mark Gertrude's reaction to Hamlet's accusations in lines 28–41.

Draw Conclusions: Do you think she knew that Claudius murdered her husband? Why or why not?

34 too busy: too much of a busybody.

38–39 If . . . sense: if habitual wickedness (**damnèd custom**) has not so hardened (**brazed**) your heart that it has become armor (**proof**) and fortification against feeling (**sense**).

47 contraction: the marriage contract.

48 sweet religion: marriage vows.

49 rhapsody: senseless jumble.

Queen. O, what a rash and bloody deed is this!

Hamlet. A bloody deed—almost as bad, good mother,
30 As kill a king and marry with his brother.

Queen. As kill a king?

Hamlet. Ay, lady, it was my word.

[*He pulls* Polonius' *body from behind the arras.*]
Thou wretched, rash, intruding fool, farewell.
I took thee for thy better. Take thy fortune.
Thou find'st to be too busy is some danger.

[*To* Queen.]
35 Leave wringing of your hands. Peace, sit you down,
And let me wring your heart; for so I shall
If it be made of penetrable stuff,
If damnèd custom have not brazed it so
That it be proof and bulwark against sense.

40 **Queen.** What have I done, that thou dar'st wag thy tongue
In noise so rude against me?

Hamlet. Such an act
That blurs the grace and blush of modesty,
Calls virtue hypocrite, takes off the rose
From the fair forehead of an innocent love
45 And sets a blister there, makes marriage vows
As false as dicers' oaths—O, such a deed
As from the body of contraction plucks
The very soul, and sweet religion makes
A rhapsody of words! Heaven's face does glow
50 O'er this solidity and compound mass

WHEN STUDENTS STRUGGLE . . .

Gather Evidence to Draw Conclusions Tell students thay a good way to help them draw conclusions is by taking notes about major situations that happen throughout Hamlet. Have them use list major events in Act III and ask them how those events could help them draw conclusions.

 For additional support, go to the **Reading Studio** and assign the following Level Up tutorial: **Making Inferences About Characters.**

With heated visage, as against the doom,
Is thought-sick at the act.

Queen.   Ay me, what act
That roars so loud and thunders in the index?

Hamlet. Look here upon this picture and on this,
55 The counterfeit presentment of two brothers.
See what a grace was seated on this brow,
Hyperion's curls, the front of Jove himself,
An eye like Mars' to threaten and command,
A station like the herald Mercury
60 New-lighted on a heaven-kissing hill,
A combination and a form indeed
Where every god did seem to set his seal
To give the world assurance of a man.
This was your husband. Look you now what follows.
65 Here is your husband, like a mildewed ear
Blasting his wholesome brother. Have you eyes?
Could you on this fair mountain leave to feed
And batten on this moor? Ha! Have you eyes?
You cannot call it love, for at your age
70 The heyday in the blood is tame, it's humble
And waits upon the judgment; and what judgment
Would step from this to this? Sense sure you have,
Else could you not have motion; but sure that sense
Is apoplexed; for madness would not err,
75 Nor sense to ecstasy was ne'er so thralled,
But it reserved some quantity of choice
To serve in such a difference. What devil was 't
That thus hath cozened you at hoodman-blind?
Eyes without feeling, feeling without sight,
80 Ears without hands or eyes, smelling sans all,
Or but a sickly part of one true sense
Could not so mope. O shame, where is thy blush?
Rebellious hell,
If thou canst mutine in a matron's bones,
85 To flaming youth let virtue be as wax
And melt in her own fire. Proclaim no shame
When the compulsive ardor gives the charge,
Since frost itself as actively doth burn,
And reason panders will.

90 **Queen.** O Hamlet, speak no more!
Thou turn'st my eyes into my very soul,
And there I see such black and grainèd spots
As will not leave their tinct.

Hamlet.   Nay, but to live

NOTICE & NOTE

49–52 Heaven's face looks down shamefully and is sick with sorrow.

53 index: introduction.

55 counterfeit presentment: portraits.

57 Hyperion: the sun god; **front:** brow.

59–60 A station . . . hill: a stance like that of the winged messenger of the gods.

65–66 Hamlet uses the metaphor of a **mildewed ear** of grain that is blighting (**Blasting**) a nearby healthy plant.

68 batten on: grow fat from feeding on; **moor:** barren land.

70 heyday in the blood: sexual excitement.

72–78 Hamlet says that her senses must be paralyzed, because madness would let her choose correctly between Claudius and Hamlet's father. He wonders what devil tricked her in a game.

80 sans all: without the other senses.

82 so mope: be so dazed.

83–89 If hell can stir up rebellion in an older woman's bones, then in young people virtue should be like a candle melting in its own flame.

92 grainèd: ingrained, indelible.

93 leave their tinct: lose their color, fade.

ENGLISH LEARNER SUPPORT

Draw Inferences Have students reread the Queen's reaction to Hamlet's speech in lines 90–93. Have them answer the following questions in pairs:

- What does she see in her *very soul*? *(black and grainèd spots)*
- What do these represent? *(her guilt)*
- What does Gertrude's reaction to Hamlet's speech suggest? *(she'll always feel guilty)*

SUBSTANTIAL/LIGHT

NOTICE & NOTE

94 enseamèd: greasy, sweaty.

In the rank sweat of an enseamèd bed,
95 Stewed in corruption, honeying and making love
Over the nasty sty!

Queen. O, speak to me no more!
These words like daggers enter in my ears.
No more, sweet Hamlet!

Hamlet. A murderer and a villain,
100 A slave that is not twentieth part the tithe
Of your precedent lord; a vice of kings,
A cutpurse of the empire and the rule,
That from a shelf the precious diadem stole
And put it in his pocket—

105 **Queen.** No more!

Hamlet. A king of shreds and patches—

[*Enter* Ghost.]

Save me and hover o'er me with your wings,
You heavenly guards!— What would your gracious figure?

Queen. Alas, he's mad.

110 **Hamlet.** Do you not come your tardy son to chide,
That, lapsed in time and passion, lets go by
Th' important acting of your dread command?
O, say!

Ghost. Do not forget. This visitation
115 Is but to whet thy almost blunted purpose.
But look, amazement on thy mother sits.
O, step between her and her fighting soul.
Conceit in weakest bodies strongest works.
Speak to her, Hamlet.

Hamlet. How is it with you, lady?

120 **Queen.** Alas, how is 't with you,
That you do bend your eye on vacancy
And with th' incorporal air do hold discourse?
Forth at your eyes your spirits wildly peep,
And, as the sleeping soldiers in th' alarm,
125 Your bedded hair, like life in excrements,
Start up and stand an end. O gentle son,
Upon the heat and flame of thy distemper
Sprinkle cool patience! Whereon do you look?

Hamlet. On him, on him! Look you how pale he glares.
130 His form and cause conjoined, preaching to stones,
Would make them capable. [*To the Ghost*.] Do not look upon me,

---

100 tithe: tenth part.

101 vice: buffoon. (The Vice was a clownish villain in medieval morality plays.)

102 cutpurse: thief.

103 diadem: crown.

106 shreds and patches: referring to the patchwork costume of clowns or fools.

111 lapsed in time and passion: having let time pass and my passion cool.

116 amazement: bewilderment, shock.

118 Conceit: imagination.

122 incorporal: immaterial.

124–126 Like soldiers awakened by an alarm, your smoothly laid (**bedded**) hair—as if there were life in this outgrowth (**excrements**)—jumps up and stands on end.

130 conjoined: joined together.

131 them capable: the stones responsive.

Lest with this piteous action you convert
My stern effects. Then what I have to do
Will want true color—tears perchance for blood.

135 **Queen.** To whom do you speak this?

Hamlet. Do you see nothing there?

Queen. Nothing at all; yet all that is I see.

Hamlet. Nor did you nothing hear?

Queen. No, nothing but ourselves.

140 **Hamlet.** Why, look you there, look how it steals away!
My father, in his habit as he lived!
Look where he goes even now out at the portal!

[Ghost *exits*.]

Queen. This is the very coinage of your brain.
This bodiless creation ecstasy
145 Is very cunning in.

Hamlet.   Ecstasy?
My pulse as yours doth temperately keep time
And makes as healthful music. It is not madness
That I have uttered. Bring me to the test,
And I the matter will reword, which madness
150 Would gambol from. Mother, for love of grace,
Lay not that flattering unction to your soul
That not your trespass but my madness speaks.
It will but skin and film the ulcerous place,
Whiles rank corruption, mining all within,
155 Infects unseen. Confess yourself to heaven,
Repent what's past, avoid what is to come,
And do not spread the compost on the weeds
To make them ranker. Forgive me this my virtue,
For, in the fatness of these pursy times,
160 Virtue itself of vice must pardon beg,
Yea, curb and woo for leave to do him good.

Queen. O Hamlet, thou hast cleft my heart in twain!

Hamlet. O, throw away the worser part of it,
And live the purer with the other half!
165 Good night. But go not to my uncle's bed.
Assume a virtue if you have it not.
That monster, custom, who all sense doth eat,
Of habits devil, is angel yet in this,
That to the use of actions fair and good
170 He likewise gives a frock or livery
That aptly is put on. Refrain tonight,

NOTICE & NOTE

133–134 convert . . . effects: alter the stern impression I give.

135 want: lack.

LANGUAGE CONVENTIONS
Annotate: Mark the paradox in lines 158–161.
Interpret: What truth does this statement suggest?

142 in his habit as he lived: in the clothes he wore when alive.

145 Madness (**ecstasy**) is very skillful at creating this kind of hallucination (**bodiless creation**).

148–155 Hamlet tells his mother to make him repeat his description word for word, a test that madness would skip (**gambol**) away from. He asks her not to use his madness rather than her misdeeds to explain this visitation; such a soothing ointment (**unction**) would merely cover up the sore on her soul, allowing the infection within to grow unseen.

158 this my virtue: my virtuous talk.

159 fatness: grossness; **pursy:** flabby, bloated.

161 curb: bow; **leave:** permission.

167–171 Custom, which consumes our awareness of the evil we habitually do, can also make us grow used to performing good actions.

The Tragedy of Hamlet: Act III, Scene 4 223

 ENGLISH LEARNER SUPPORT

Express Ideas Using Single Words and Short Phrases Give students these definitions and have them repeat them aloud:

- *virtue:* Moral excellence and righteousness; goodness
- *vice:* A practice or habit considered to be evil, degrading, or immoral

Ask students for examples of each one. Tie the discussion of these two words with opposite meanings into the idea of paradox, a statement that contradicts itself, but that shares with us some underlying truth. **MODERATE**

Ask students for examples of *virtue* and *vice* from the text. **LIGHT**

NOTICE & NOTE

And that shall lend a kind of easiness
To the next abstinence, the next more easy;
For use almost can change the stamp of nature
175 And either . . . the devil or throw him out
With wondrous potency. Once more, good night,
And, when you are desirous to be blest,
I'll blessing beg of you. For this same lord

[*Pointing to* Polonius.]

I do repent; but heaven hath pleased it so
180 To punish me with this and this with me,
That I must be their scourge and minister.
I will bestow him and will answer well
The death I gave him. So, again, good night.
I must be cruel only to be kind.
185 This bad begins, and worse remains behind.
One word more, good lady.

Queen. What shall I do?

Hamlet. Not this by no means that I bid you do:
Let the bloat king tempt you again to bed,
Pinch wanton on your cheek, call you his mouse,
190 And let him, for a pair of reechy kisses
Or paddling in your neck with his damned fingers,
Make you to ravel all this matter out
That I essentially am not in madness,
But mad in craft. 'Twere good you let him know,
195 For who that's but a queen, fair, sober, wise,
Would from a paddock, from a bat, a gib,
Such dear concernings hide? Who would do so?
No, in despite of sense and secrecy,
Unpeg the basket on the house's top,
200 Let the birds fly, and like the famous ape,
To try conclusions, in the basket creep
And break your own neck down.

Queen. Be thou assured, if words be made of breath
And breath of life, I have no life to breathe
205 What thou hast said to me.

Hamlet. I must to England, you know that.

Queen. Alack,
I had forgot! 'Tis so concluded on.

Hamlet. There's letters sealed; and my two schoolfellows,
Whom I will trust as I will adders fanged,
210 They bear the mandate; they must sweep my way
And marshal me to knavery. Let it work,
For 'tis the sport to have the enginer

174 stamp of nature: the traits we are born with.

175 A word seems to be missing in this line after *either*.

180 this: Polonius.
181 their scourge and minister: heaven's agent of retribution.
182 answer well: explain.
185 remains behind: is still to come.

188 bloat: bloated.
189 mouse: a term of endearment.
190 reechy: filthy.
191 paddling in: fingering on.

194 in craft: by clever design or action.
194–202 Although Hamlet has asked his mother not to let Claudius use sexual attentions to unravel the secret that Hamlet is only pretending to be mad, he now sarcastically urges her to go ahead and tell Claudius. He refers to a story about an ape that died trying to imitate the flight of birds it released from a cage, hinting that the Queen will get hurt if she lets out her secret.

208–211 Rosencrantz and Guildenstern have been commanded to escort Hamlet to some treachery.

212–213 to have . . . petard: to have the maker of military devices blown up (**hoist**) by his own bomb (**petard**).

224 Unit 2

Hoist with his own petard; and 't shall go hard
But I will delve one yard below their mines
215 And blow them at the moon. O, 'tis most sweet
When in one line two crafts directly meet.
This man shall set me packing.
I'll lug the guts into the neighbor room.
Mother, good night indeed. This counselor
220 Is now most still, most secret, and most grave,
Who was in life a foolish prating knave.—
Come, sir, to draw toward an end with you.
Good night, mother.

[*They exit*, Hamlet *tugging in* Polonius.]

NOTICE & NOTE

213–214 and 't ... I will: unless I have bad luck I will; **mines:** tunnels.

216 crafts: plots, crafty schemes.

217 Polonius's death will force Hamlet to leave in a hurry.

222 to draw toward an end: to finish up.

CHECK YOUR UNDERSTANDING

Answer these questions before moving on to the **Analyze the Text** section on the following page.

1 Claudius decides to send Hamlet to England because he —

  A feels threatened by Hamlet

  B needs Hamlet to negotiate a treaty

  C hopes the long voyage will cure Hamlet

  D wants to keep Hamlet away from Ophelia

2 Why does Hamlet avoid killing Claudius in this act?

  F Claudius is always surrounded by heavily armed guards.

  G Hamlet is still uncertain about whether Claudius is guilty.

  H He doesn't want to send Claudius to heaven while praying.

  J Someone else must kill Claudius so Hamlet won't be blamed.

3 Why does Hamlet kill Polonius in Gertrude's room?

  A He is angry that Polonius kept Ophelia from him.

  B He thinks the hidden Polonius might be Claudius.

  C Polonius is having an affair with Gertrude.

  D Polonius took part in his father's murder.

The Tragedy of Hamlet: Act III, Scene 4 225

TEACH

CHECK YOUR UNDERSTANDING

Have students answer the questions independently.

Answers:

1. A
2. H
3. B

If students answer any questions incorrectly, have them reread the text to confirm their understanding. Then, they may proceed to ANALYZE THE TEXT on page 226.

ENGLISH LEARNER SUPPORT

Oral Assessment To show their comprehension, have students answer the following questions:

1. Is Claudius afraid of Hamlet? *(yes)*
2. Does Hamlet want Claudius to go to heaven? *(no.)*
3. Hamlet kils _____. *(Polonius)*

APPLY

ANALYZE THE TEXT

Possible answers:

1. **DOK 4:** *In Scene 1, Hamlet is cruel and insulting toward Ophelia, but this seems to be out of genuine hurt, which suggests that the feelings he expressed for her before were true. Later in Scene 2, he is crude and irreverent toward her, suggesting his increasing disgust. These scenes suggest Hamlet is not emotionally stable and in control, but rather is subject to poor judgment and rash behavior.*

2. **DOK 4:** *Hamlet admires Horatio's steadiness in the face of life's ups and downs and his ability to be objective. Shakespeare uses Horatio as a foil to Hamlet while helping him to be certain of his uncle's guilt. This certainty pushes Hamlet toward his resolve to confront his mother and avenge his father's murder.*

3. **DOK 4:** *The climax of the play occurs in Act I, Scene 4, when Hamlet confronts his mother about the murder of his father and kills Polonius. This is the turning point because Hamlet cannot turn back from this action. It therefore resolves his conflict of indecision about whether to proceed with avenging his father's death.*

4. **DOK 4:** *Hamlet decides not to kill Claudius when he has the opportunity because he thinks Claudius would go to heaven, which does not suit his need for revenge. Later, he stabs Polonius without thinking in a state of rage, thinking he is killing Claudius. This combination of events shows revenge to be both confusing and irrational.*

5. **DOK 4:** *These two passages reveal Claudius to be filled with regret and grief for his crime and for the death of his brother. This contrasts with the opening of the play when he acts as if he is no longer grieving his brother's death and is focusing on the positive outcome as well as the impression he gives of having a guilty conscience for his misdeeds.*

CREATE AND PRESENT

Perform a Scene Remind students that this text was written to be performed on stage. You may have students select their favorite scenes and group them accordingly. To build confidence in struggling students, suggest that groups do a choral reading of every part in the scene before breaking up the parts. Have students practice their parts in groups before planning their staging. Tell students that the reading of parts before practicing staging is called a "table read."

RESPOND

ANALYZE THE TEXT

Support your responses with evidence from the text. 📓 NOTEBOOK

1. **Evaluate** Review Hamlet's dialogue with Ophelia in Act III, Scene 1, and during the performance by the players in Scene 2. Do these encounters lead you to adjust ideas you formed earlier about his character? Explain why or why not.

2. **Analyze** Reread lines 58–76 in Scene 2. What does Hamlet admire about Horatio? How does Shakespeare use Horatio to help develop the play's plot?

3. **Analyze** In Shakespeare's plays, a climax or turning point usually occurs in the third act when something happens that clarifies the outcome of the central conflict. Where does this climax occur in Act III of *Hamlet*? Explain your response.

4. **Synthesize** Soon after Hamlet decides against killing Claudius while he is praying, he mistakes Polonius for the King and kills him without hesitation. What does this combination of events suggest about revenge?

5. **Notice & Note** Shakespeare reveals Claudius's true thoughts to the audience in his aside in Scene 1, lines 50–55, and his soliloquy in Scene 3, lines 35–72. How does your impression of him in these moments differ from the way he presents himself earlier in the play?

CREATE AND PRESENT

Perform a Scene Act out a brief scene or a section of a longer scene.

- ❏ In a small group, choose a scene and decide which role will be played by each member.
- ❏ Read the scene aloud. Discuss the stated and implied motivations of the characters.
- ❏ Decide where performers will enter or exit and where they will stand while reciting the dialogue. Read the stage directions to determine if any sound or lighting effects are needed.
- ❏ Practice the performance. There is no need for performers to memorize their parts, but they should read them several times to become familiar with the language. Each performer should use a tone of voice appropriate to his or her character.
- ❏ Perform the scene in front of the class. You might also videotape the performance and upload it to the Internet.

SETTING A PURPOSE

As you read, notice how new events create conflict and complicate the plot of the play.

NOTICE & NOTE

Notice & Note

Use the side margins to notice and note signposts in the text.

ACT IV

Scene 1 *The Castle.*

[*Enter* King and Queen, *with* Rosencrantz and Guildenstern.]

King. There's matter in these sighs; these profound heaves
You must translate; 'tis fit we understand them.
Where is your son?

Queen. Bestow this place on us a little while.

[Rosencrantz *and* Guildenstern *exit*.]

5 Ah, mine own lord, what have I seen tonight!

King. What, Gertrude? How does Hamlet?

Queen. Mad as the sea and wind when both contend
Which is the mightier. In his lawless fit,
Behind the arras hearing something stir,
10 Whips out his rapier, cries "A rat, a rat,"
And in this brainish apprehension kills
The unseen good old man.

King.   O heavy deed!
It had been so with us, had we been there.
His liberty is full of threats to all—
15 To you yourself, to us, to everyone.
Alas, how shall this bloody deed be answered?
It will be laid to us, whose providence
Should have kept short, restrained, and out of haunt
This mad young man. But so much was our love,
20 We would not understand what was most fit,
But, like the owner of a foul disease,
To keep it from divulging, let it feed
Even on the pith of life. Where is he gone?

Queen. To draw apart the body he hath killed,

1 matter: significance.

11 brainish apprehension: frenzied belief.

17–19 Claudius worries that the death will be blamed on him (**laid to us**) because he should have had the foresight (**providence**) to keep Hamlet restrained (**short**) and isolated (**out of haunt**).

22 divulging: being revealed.

The Tragedy of Hamlet: Act IV, Scene 1   227

LEARNING MINDSET

Persistence Remind students that an important part of learning is to keep trying when something is challenging. Challenges are how we grow and learn, but we can't learn from them if we give up. Reassure students that even if they think they are stuck, by continuing to make an effort they will eventually make progress. They should keep in mind that any progress they make in learning registers as a reward in their brains, so learning becomes pleasurable. Tell students that when they feel stuck and frustrated, they should take a moment to relax and tell themselves "I know I can do this if I keep at it."

TEACH

ENGLISH LEARNER SUPPORT

Look for Language Patterns Direct students' attention to Scene 1, lines 26–32. Explain that Gertrude has just told Claudius about Hamlet killing Polonius, and Claudius is planning what they will do in response. Point out that Claudius uses three auxiliary, or helper, verbs. Have students identify and mark the auxiliary verbs. *(will, shall, must)*. Students may not recognize *shall*. Explain that this word is not often used in modern English, but they may see it in older texts, like the King James translation of the Bible. Tell them that *shall* generally indicates an obligation or order but can also indicate a strong expectation.

Use the following supports with students at varying proficiency levels:

- After students identify and mark the auxiliary verbs, have them look for the main verbs that go with them. *(shall touch, will ship, must countenance and excuse)* **SUBSTANTIAL**

- After students identify and mark the auxiliary verbs, have them look for the main verbs that go with them. Then, instruct them to identify the subjects and objects of the verbs and work in pairs to explain in their own words what Claudius's plan is. **MODERATE**

- After students identify and mark the auxiliary verbs, have them look for the main verbs that go with them. Then instruct students to explain what Claudius wants to do and why he wants to do this. *(He wants to get rid of Hamlet because he suspects Hamlet knows he killed King Hamlet and wants to prevent him from plotting against him. He is also worried that he will be blamed for the murder and about how that will affect him.)* **LIGHT**

 **NOTICE & NOTE**

25–26 O'er ... mineral: vein of gold in a mine.

25 O'er whom his very madness, like some ore
    Among a mineral of metals base,
    Shows itself pure: he weeps for what is done.

    King. O Gertrude, come away!
    The sun no sooner shall the mountains touch
30 But we will ship him hence; and this vile deed
    We must with all our majesty and skill
    Both countenance and excuse.—Ho, Guildenstern!

32 countenance: accept.

    [*Enter* Rosencrantz *and* Guildenstern.]
    Friends both, go join you with some further aid.
    Hamlet in madness hath Polonius slain,
35 And from his mother's closet hath he dragged him.
    Go seek him out, speak fair, and bring the body
    Into the chapel. I pray you, haste in this.

33 some further aid: others who can help.

    [Rosencrantz *and* Guildenstern *exit.*]
    Come, Gertrude, we'll call up our wisest friends
    And let them know both what we mean to do
40 And what's untimely done. . . .
    Whose whisper o'er the world's diameter,
    As level as the cannon to his blank
    Transports his poisoned shot, may miss our name
    And hit the woundless air. O, come away!
45 My soul is full of discord and dismay.

    [*They exit.*]

40–44 Some words are missing after "untimely done" in line 40. Many editors insert "So haply slander" or a similar phrase. Claudius is hoping that slander, which hits as directly as a cannon fired at point-blank range hits its target, will miss the royal household.

Scene 2 The Castle.

[*Enter* Hamlet.]

Hamlet. Safely stowed.

Gentlemen [*within*]. Hamlet! Lord Hamlet!

Hamlet. But soft, what noise? Who calls on Hamlet? O, here they come.

[*Enter* Rosencrantz, Guildenstern, *and others.*]

5 **Rosencrantz.** What have you done, my lord, with the dead body?

6 Compounded: mixed. Hamlet alludes to Genesis 3.19: "dust thou art, and unto dust shalt thou return."

Hamlet. Compounded it with dust, whereto 'tis kin.

Rosencrantz. Tell us where 'tis, that we may take it thence
And bear it to the chapel.

Hamlet. Do not believe it.

10 **Rosencrantz.** Believe what?

228 Unit 2

WHEN STUDENTS STRUGGLE . . .

Understand Characterization Direct students to Scene 1, lines 38–45. Note the missing words mentioned in the side note for lines 40–44. Read the passage aloud, substituting the words as suggested in the note. Discuss the concerns that the King mentions here. *(He is worried about what others will think and say about the death of Polonius and about how it will affect his power as King.)*

 For additional support, go to the **Reading Studio** and assign the following **Level Up tutorial: Character Motivation**.

Hamlet. That I can keep your counsel and not mine own. Besides, to be demanded of a sponge, what replication should be made by the son of a king?

Rosencrantz. Take you me for a sponge, my lord?

15 **Hamlet.** Ay, sir, that soaks up the King's countenance, his rewards, his authorities. But such officers do the King best service in the end. He keeps them like an ape an apple in the corner of his jaw, first mouthed, to be last swallowed. When he needs
20 what you have gleaned, it is but squeezing you, and, sponge, you shall be dry again.

Rosencrantz. I understand you not, my lord.

Hamlet. I am glad of it. A knavish speech sleeps in a foolish ear.

25 **Rosencrantz.** My lord, you must tell us where the body is and go with us to the King.

Hamlet. The body is with the King, but the King is not with the body. The King is a thing—

Guildenstern. A "thing," my lord?

30 **Hamlet.** Of nothing. Bring me to him. Hide fox, and all after!

[*They exit.*]

Scene 3 *The castle.*

[*Enter* King *and two or three.*]

King. I have sent to seek him and to find the body.
How dangerous is it that this man goes loose!
Yet must not we put the strong law on him.
He's loved of the distracted multitude,
5 Who like not in their judgment, but their eyes;
And, where 'tis so, th' offender's scourge is weighed,
But never the offense. To bear all smooth and even,
This sudden sending him away must seem
Deliberate pause. Diseases desperate grown
10 By desperate appliance are relieved
Or not at all.

[*Enter* Rosencrantz.]

How now, what hath befallen?

Rosencrantz. Where the dead body is bestowed, my lord,
We cannot get from him.

King. But where is he?

NOTICE & NOTE

12 **demanded of:** questioned by.

13 **replication:** response.

15 **countenance:** favor.

17–18 **like an ape . . . jaw:** as an ape keeps food in the corner of its mouth.

23 **sleeps in:** is meaningless to.

27–30 Hamlet may be playing off the idea that the king occupies two "bodies": his own mortal body and the office of kingship. Claudius is a king of no account (**Of nothing**); the office of kingship does not belong to him.

30 **Hide fox . . . after:** a cry from a children's game such as hide-and-seek.

4–5 **He's loved . . . eyes:** He's loved by the confused masses, who choose not by judgment but by appearance.

6 **scourge:** punishment.

7 **To bear . . . even:** to manage everything smoothly and evenly.

9 **Deliberate pause:** carefully thought out.

9–11 **Diseases . . . all:** Desperate diseases require desperate remedies.

APPLYING ACADEMIC VOCABULARY

❑ ambiguous   ❑ anticipate   ❑ conceive   ❑ drama   ☑ **integrity**

Write and Discuss Have students turn to a partner to discuss the following question. Guide students to include the academic vocabulary word *integrity* in their responses. Ask volunteers to share their responses with the class.

- How do Claudius's actions reveal his lack of **integrity**?

TEACH

NOTICE & NOTE

Rosencrantz. Without, my lord; guarded, to know your pleasure.

15 **King.** Bring him before us.

Rosencrantz. Ho! Bring in the lord.

[*They enter with* Hamlet.]

King. Now, Hamlet, where's Polonius?

Hamlet. At supper.

King. At supper where?

Hamlet. Not where he eats, but where he is eaten. A
20 certain convocation of politic worms are e'en at
him. Your worm is your only emperor for diet. We
fat all creatures else to fat us, and we fat ourselves
for maggots. Your fat king and your lean beggar is
but variable service—two dishes but to one table.
25 That's the end.

King. Alas, alas!

Hamlet. A man may fish with the worm that hath eat
of a king and eat of the fish that hath fed of that
worm.

30 **King.** What dost thou mean by this?

Hamlet. Nothing but to show you how a king may go
a progress through the guts of a beggar.

King. Where is Polonius?

Hamlet. In heaven. Send thither to see. If your messenger
35 find him not there, seek him i' th' other place
yourself. But if, indeed, you find him not within
this month, you shall nose him as you go up the
stairs into the lobby.

King [*to* Attendants]. Go, seek him there.

40 **Hamlet.** He will stay till you come.

[Attendants *exit*.]

King. Hamlet, this deed, for thine especial safety
(Which we do tender, as we dearly grieve
For that which thou hast done) must send thee hence
With fiery quickness. Therefore prepare thyself.
45 The bark is ready, and the wind at help,
Th' associates tend, and everything is bent
For England.

Hamlet. For England?

King. Ay, Hamlet.

19–21 Hamlet says that a group of crafty (**politic**) worms are dining on him.

21 Your . . . diet: Worms have the last word when it comes to eating.

24 but variable service: only different courses (of a meal).

32 progress: royal journey.

42 tender: regard, hold dear.

45–47 Claudius says that the sailing vessel (**bark**) is ready, the wind is favorable (**at help**), his fellow travelers wait (**tend**) for him, and everything is ready (**bent**).

230 Unit 2

50 **Hamlet.** Good.

  King. So is it, if thou knew'st our purposes.

  Hamlet. I see a cherub that sees them. But come, for
    England.
   Farewell, dear mother.

  King. Thy loving father, Hamlet.

  Hamlet. My mother. Father and mother is man and wife,
55 Man and wife is one flesh, and so, my mother.—
   Come, for England.

  [*He exits.*]

  King. Follow him at foot; tempt him with speed aboard.
   Delay it not. I'll have him hence tonight.
   Away, for everything is sealed and done
60 That else leans on th' affair. Pray you, make haste.

  [*All but the* King *exit.*]

   And England, if my love thou hold'st at aught
   (As my great power thereof may give thee sense,
   Since yet thy cicatrice looks raw and red
   After the Danish sword, and thy free awe
65 Pays homage to us), thou mayst not coldly set
   Our sovereign process, which imports at full,
   By letters congruing to that effect,
   The present death of Hamlet. Do it, England,
   For like the hectic in my blood he rages,
70 And thou must cure me. Till I know 'tis done,
   Howe'er my haps, my joys were ne'er begun.

  [*He exits.*]

  Scene 4 *Near the coast of Denmark.*

  [*Enter* Fortinbras *with his army over the stage.*]

  Fortinbras. Go, Captain, from me greet the Danish king.
   Tell him that by his license Fortinbras
   Craves the conveyance of a promised march
   Over his kingdom. You know the rendezvous.
5 If that his Majesty would aught with us,
   We shall express our duty in his eye;
   And let him know so.

  Captain. I will do 't, my lord.

  Fortinbras. Go softly on.

  [*All but the* Captain *exit.*]

  [*Enter* Hamlet, Rosencrantz, Guildenstern, *and others.*]

NOTICE & NOTE

52 cherub: angel of knowledge.

ANALYZE DRAMATIC PLOT

Annotate: In lines 61–71, mark what Claudius wants the English king to do.

Draw Conclusions: Why might he want this action done in England instead of Denmark?

57 at foot: closely.

60 leans on: is related to.

61–68 Claudius says that if the King of England values his friendship, he will not ignore Claudius's command to have Hamlet killed immediately.

69 hectic: fever.

71 Howe'er my haps: whatever my fortunes.

2 license: permission.

3 the conveyance of: escort during.

5–7 Fortinbras says that if the King wishes to see him, he will show his respect in person (**in his eye**).

9 softly: slowly, carefully.

The Tragedy of Hamlet: Act IV, Scene 4   231

TEACH

🌐 ENGLISH LEARNER SUPPORT

Use Accessible Language Focus students' attention on Claudius's instructions to Rosencrantz and the others in Scene 3, lines 57–60, page 231. Tell them that Claudius wants Rosencrantz and the others to get Hamlet onto a ship as soon as possible. Point out that this passage uses antiquated, or old and out-of-use, language: *at foot, aboard, hence,* and *make haste.*

Supply students with the following modern equivalents. Working in pairs, have students use context clues to match the modern equivalent to each antiquated word or phrase:

hurry (*make haste*)
closely (*at foot*)
away from here (*hence*)
on a ship (*aboard*) **SUBSTANTIAL/MODERATE**

✏️ ANALYZE DRAMATIC PLOT

Review with students what has happened so far in this act. Make sure students understand that Claudius is now sending Hamlet to England. Point out that in the speech in Scene 3, lines 61–71, page 231, Claudius reveals what he has written in a sealed letter to the King of England that he is sending with Hamlet. Have them look for what Claudius says in the letter and what he wants the King of England to do. Review with students what Claudius said about Hamlet in Scene 3, lines 4–7, page 229, about Hamlet's popularity with the citizens of Denmark. (**Answer:** *Claudius wants Hamlet killed in England so the citizens of Denmark won't think he did it and be angry, as they might be angrier about Hamlet's death than that he killed Polonius.*)

TO CHALLENGE STUDENTS...

Consider a Character's Point-of-View Claudius makes a very hasty decision to send Hamlet away to England. He makes this decision based on various things that he thinks, knows, or suspects about Hamlet. Looking back at previous events in the play, think about what Claudius thinks, knows, or suspects about Hamlet that has led him to take this action. In a group, discuss the following questions:

- Is Claudius right about everything he thinks about Hamlet?
- Is there anything about Hamlet that he would be uncertain about?
- How might Claudius's action change if Claudius knew or thought something else?

TEACH

✏️ ANALYZE SOLILOQUY

Remind students that a **soliloquy** can have a number of functions in a play, including revealing a character's traits and inner **conflicts,** which in turn influence the **plot** and **theme.** Explain that one way that characters are developed is through the use of **foils,** or other characters that have contrasting traits to the main characters. Point out that Fortinbras is a **foil** for Hamlet.

Focus students' attention on Scene 4, lines 49–50, page 234, and make sure they understand what "this army of such mass and charge" refers to. (*Fortinbras's army*) If necessary, direct them to look back at the description of the setting and the stage direction at the opening of Scene 4. Ask students to think about what Fortinbras is doing and to read Hamlet's words carefully to determine what Hamlet thinks about Fortinbras's actions. (**Answer:** *Hamlet admires that Fortinbras is decisive in his action; he does not hesitate to lead an army into battle and is willing to fight for the sake of honor without a thought to future consequences.*)

■ English Learner Support

Understand General Meaning Divide the class into mixed-proficiency pairs or groups and assign each pair or group a chunk of Hamlet's **soliloquy** from Scene 4:

- Lines 35–41 (starting with *What is*)
- Lines 41–48 (starting with *Now whether* and up to *To do 't.*)
- Lines 49–58 (up to *at the stake*)

Provide prereading vocabulary as needed. Then, have students in each pair or group read their assigned chunk of text together to determine the main idea. Higher-proficiency students should clarify meanings for lower-proficiency students using accessible English, and lower-proficiency students should ask questions of higher-proficiency students to help them understand the main idea.

Then, rearrange the class into new groups, composed of students who have studied the three different chunks of text, and have them share with each other the main idea of the chunks they read. **ALL LEVELS**

NOTICE & NOTE

10 **powers:** forces.

16 **the main:** the main part.

18 **Truly . . . addition:** to speak plainly.

21 **To pay . . . it:** I would not pay even five ducats a year to rent it.

23 **ranker:** higher; **in fee:** outright.

27 **Will not . . . straw:** are not enough to settle this trifling dispute.

28 **impostume:** puss-filled swelling.

29 **without:** on the outside.

ANALYZE SOLILOQUY

Annotate: Mark statements describing Fortinbras in lines 34–68.

Interpret: What does Hamlet admire about Fortinbras?

34 **inform against:** denounce.

36 **market:** profit.

38–41 **Sure He . . . unused:** God would not have given us such a considerable power of reasoning to let it grow moldy from lack of use.

42–43 **Bestial . . . event:** beast-like forgetfulness or cowardly hesitation from thinking too carefully about the outcome.

48 **gross:** obvious.

232 Unit 2

---

10 **Hamlet.** Good sir, whose powers are these?

Captain. They are of Norway, sir.

Hamlet. How purposed, sir, I pray you?

Captain. Against some part of Poland.

Hamlet. Who commands them, sir?

15 **Captain.** The nephew to old Norway, Fortinbras.

Hamlet. Goes it against the main of Poland, sir,
Or for some frontier?

Captain. Truly to speak, and with no addition,
We go to gain a little patch of ground
20 That hath in it no profit but the name.
To pay five ducats, five, I would not farm it;
Nor will it yield to Norway or the Pole
A ranker rate, should it be sold in fee.

Hamlet. Why, then, the Polack never will defend it.

25 **Captain.** Yes, it is already garrisoned.

Hamlet. Two thousand souls and twenty thousand ducats
Will not debate the question of this straw.
This is th' impostume of much wealth and peace,
That inward breaks and shows no cause without
30 Why the man dies.—I humbly thank you, sir.

Captain. God be wi' you, sir.

[*He exits.*]

Rosencrantz. Will 't please you go, my lord?

Hamlet. I'll be with you straight. Go a little before.

[*All but* Hamlet *exit.*]

How all occasions do inform against me
35 And spur my dull revenge. What is a man
If his chief good and market of his time
Be but to sleep and feed? A beast, no more.
Sure He that made us with such large discourse,
Looking before and after, gave us not
40 That capability and godlike reason
To fust in us unused. Now whether it be
Bestial oblivion or some craven scruple
Of thinking too precisely on th' event
(A thought which, quartered, hath but one part wisdom
45 And ever three parts coward), I do not know
Why yet I live to say "This thing's to do,"
Sith I have cause, and will, and strength, and means
To do 't. Examples gross as earth exhort me:

NOTICE & NOTE

Witness this army of such mass and charge,
50 Led by a delicate and tender prince,
Whose spirit with divine ambition puffed
Makes mouths at the invisible event,
Exposing what is mortal and unsure
To all that fortune, death, and danger dare,
55 Even for an eggshell. Rightly to be great
Is not to stir without great argument,
But greatly to find quarrel in a straw
When honor's at the stake. How stand I, then,
That have a father killed, a mother stained,
60 Excitements of my reason and my blood,
And let all sleep, while to my shame I see
The imminent death of twenty thousand men
That for a fantasy and trick of fame
Go to their graves like beds, fight for a plot
65 Whereon the numbers cannot try the cause,
Which is not tomb enough and continent
To hide the slain? O, from this time forth
My thoughts be bloody or be nothing worth!

[*He exits*.]

Scene 5 *The castle.*

[*Enter* Horatio, Queen, *and a* Gentleman.]

Queen. I will not speak with her.

Gentleman. She is importunate,
Indeed distract; her mood will needs be pitied.

Queen. What would she have?

5 **Gentleman.** She speaks much of her father, says she hears
There's tricks i' th' world, and hems, and beats her heart,
Spurns enviously at straws, speaks things in doubt
That carry but half sense. Her speech is nothing,
Yet the unshaped use of it doth move
10 The hearers to collection. They aim at it
And botch the words up fit to their own thoughts;
Which, as her winks and nods and gestures yield them,
Indeed would make one think there might be thought,
Though nothing sure, yet much unhappily.

15 **Horatio.** 'Twere good she were spoken with, for she may strew
Dangerous conjectures in ill-breeding minds.

Queen. Let her come in.

---

52 Makes mouths ... event: makes scornful faces at the unforeseeable outcome.

55–58 True greatness does not lie in refraining from action when there is no great cause but in the willingness to fight whenever honor is at stake.

63 fantasy and trick of fame: illusion of honor.

65–67 Whereon ... slain: The disputed land does not have enough room for so many men to battle on and is too small a burial ground to hold those who will be killed.

3 distract: distracted; **mood ... pitied:** state of mind must be pitied.

6 tricks: deception.

7 Spurns enviously at straws: takes offense at trifles; **in doubt:** without clear meaning.

8–11 Although Ophelia speaks nonsense, her confused manner of speaking moves her listeners to gather some meaning by patching her words together to fit their conjectures.

16 ill-breeding: intent on making trouble.

TEACH

EL ENGLISH LEARNER SUPPORT

Describe a Person and Retell Stories Have students look at the image of Ophelia on page 235 and work in groups to describe her appearance and her character, as well as the events in the play so far in which she has been involved. When describing her character, students should cite evidence from the text. After students have had a chance to discuss in groups, ask volunteers to share their ideas and write them on the board. Encourage students to copy the notes into their notebooks. **LIGHT**

WHEN STUDENTS STRUGGLE...

Understand Internal Conflict Help students understand the significance of Hamlet's **soliloquy** in Scene 4, lines 34–68, pages 232–233, by reviewing the events that came before it in the main **plot:** The Ghost revealed his father's murder and asked him to avenge it; Hamlet confirmed Claudius's guilt and confronted his mother; then he hesitated instead of killing Claudius. Ask students to think about Hamlet's **inner conflict** and how his comments about Fortinbras relate to this struggle.

  For additional support, go to the **Reading Studio** and assign the following **Level Up tutorial: Characters and Conflict**.

TEACH

NOTICE & NOTE

[Gentleman *exits*.]

[*Aside*] To my sick soul (as sin's true nature is),
Each toy seems prologue to some great amiss.
So full of artless jealousy is guilt,
It spills itself in fearing to be spilt.

[*Enter* Ophelia *distracted*.]

Ophelia. Where is the beauteous Majesty of Denmark?

Queen. How now, Ophelia?

Ophelia [*sings*]. How should I your true love know
   From another one?
   By his cockle hat and staff
   And his sandal shoon.

Queen. Alas, sweet lady, what imports this song?

Ophelia. Say you? Nay, pray you, mark.
[*Sings*.] He is dead and gone, lady,
   He is dead and gone;
   At his head a grass-green turf,
   At his heels a stone.
Oh, ho!

Queen. Nay, but Ophelia—

Ophelia. Pray you, mark.

[*Sings*.] White his shroud as the mountain snow—

[*Enter* King.]

Queen. Alas, look here, my lord.

Ophelia [*sings*]. Larded all with sweet flowers;
Which bewept to the ground did not go
   With true-love showers.

King. How do you, pretty lady?

Ophelia. Well, God dild you. They say the owl was a baker's daughter. Lord, we know what we are but know not what we may be. God be at your table.

King. Conceit upon her father.

Ophelia. Pray let's have no words of this, but when they ask you what it means, say you this:
[*Sings*.] Tomorrow is Saint Valentine's day,
   All in the morning betime,
And I a maid at your window,
   To be your Valentine.
Then up he rose and donned his clothes
   And dupped the chamber door,

19 toy: trifle; **amiss:** misfortune.

20–21 Guilt is so full of clumsy suspicion (**artless jealousy**) that it reveals (**spills**) itself through fear of being revealed.

26 cockle hat: a hat with a scallop shell (worn by pilgrims to show that they had been to an overseas shrine).

27 shoon: shoes.

28 imports: means.

39 Larded: decorated.

41 showers: tears.

43 God dild you: God yield, or reward, you.

43–44 Ophelia refers to a legend about a baker's daughter who was turned into an owl because she refused to give Christ bread.

46 Conceit: brooding.

49–67 This song refers to the ancient custom that the first maiden a man sees on St. Valentine's Day will be his sweetheart.

54 dupped: opened.

CLOSE READ SCREENCAST

Modeled Discussions Have students click the *Close Read* icon in their eBooks to access a screencast in which readers discuss and annotate Hamlet's steeling of himself to act (Act IV, Scene 4, lines 58–68, page 234).

As a class, view and discuss this video. Then, have students pair up to do an independent close read of lines 58–68. Students can record their answers on the Close Read Practice PDF.

 Close Read Practice PDF

NOTICE & NOTE

The Tragedy of Hamlet: Act IV, Scene 5 235

TEACH

ENGLISH LEARNER SUPPORT

Share Information Explain to students that when Ophelia appears in Scene 5, she sings verses of a song. Her behavior appears crazy, and Claudius and Gertrude do not understand why she is acting this way. Focus students' attention on the verses Ophelia sings in lines 24–27 and 30–33 (page 234) and read them aloud.

Next, assign students to two mixed-level groups and have them work to understand these verses, using the side notes and their own knowledge of vocabulary and sentence structure. Encourage lower-proficiency students to ask questions of higher-proficiency students to help them understand the verses.

Then, bring the two groups together and have them take turns explaining what Ophelia is singing about in each verse. Guide them in answering these questions:

- What themes is Ophelia singing about in these two verses? *(She's singing about death and love.)*
- How does her singing relate to previous **plot** events? *(The subjects of the verses relate to her troubled relationship with Hamlet and her father's death.)*
- What explanation can you give for her behavior? *(The stress of Hamlet's cruel treatment of her and the death of her father have caused her to go insane.)*

ALL LEVELS

WHEN STUDENTS STRUGGLE . . .

Interpret a Character's Behavior Direct students' attention to Scene 5, lines 22–56. Ask students to observe Ophelia closely during this scene. Remind students about the **subplot** involving Ophelia, and ask them to recount the events of that **subplot** that directly affect her.

 For additional support, go to the **Reading Studio** and assign the following **Level Up tutorial: Making Inferences About Characters**.

235

TEACH

ENGLISH LEARNER SUPPORT

Retell Plot Points Direct students' attention to Scene 5, lines 79–89, page 236, and read those lines aloud as students follow along. Point out that in lines 79–80, Claudius says *sorrows* (unfortunate, sad events) come "in battalions" (that is, many of them come at once). In the following lines, Claudius recounts the events in the play so far that trouble him.

Use the following supports with students at varying proficiency levels:

- Have students identify the people whom Claudius mentions by marking names, pronouns, and other identifiers. Ask them to say what has happened to those people and to identify words that tell those events. (For example, students may identify *your son* in line 81 and recognize the word *gone* as meaning that he has left.) **SUBSTANTIAL**

- Supply students with this list of **plot** points and ask them to identify the line or lines in which Claudius mentions them:
  - Polonius is killed. *(line 80)*
  - Hamlet leaves. *(line 81)*
  - Ophelia goes mad. *(line 85–86)*
  - Laertes returns from Paris. *(line 89)* **MODERATE**

- Have students identify and summarize the four **plot** points that Claudius recounts in lines 79–89. **LIGHT**

 **NOTICE & NOTE**

59 Gis: Jesus.

62 Cock: a substitution for "God" in oaths.

63 tumbled: had sexual intercourse with.

79 spies: soldiers sent ahead as scouts.

82 muddied: confused.

84–85 Claudius says that he has only acted foolishly (**greenly**) by burying Polonius in haste and secrecy.

89–95 Laertes, who has secretly returned from France, is clouded by suspicion and does not lack gossipers who spread rumors of his father's death. And in the absence of facts, the need for some explanation means that Claudius will be accused of the crime.

---

55 *Let in the maid, that out a maid*
    Never departed more.

King. Pretty Ophelia—

Ophelia. Indeed, without an oath, I'll make an end on 't:
[*Sings.*] *By Gis and by Saint Charity,*
60   *Alack and fie for shame,*
Young men will do 't, if they come to 't;
    By Cock, they are to blame.
Quoth she "Before you tumbled me,
    You promised me to wed."
65 He answers:
"So would I 'a done, by yonder sun,
    An thou hadst not come to my bed."

King. How long hath she been thus?

Ophelia. I hope all will be well. We must be patient,
70 but I cannot choose but weep to think they would
lay him i' th' cold ground. My brother shall know
of it. And so I thank you for your good counsel.
Come, my coach! Good night, ladies, good night,
sweet ladies, good night, good night.

[*She exits.*]

75 **King.** Follow her close; give her good watch, I pray you.

[*Horatio exits.*]

O, this is the poison of deep grief. It springs
All from her father's death, and now behold!
O Gertrude, Gertrude,
When sorrows come, they come not single spies,
80 But in battalions: first, her father slain;
Next, your son gone, and he most violent author
Of his own just remove; the people muddied,
Thick, and unwholesome in their thoughts and
    whispers
For good Polonius' death, and we have done but
    greenly
85 In hugger-mugger to inter him; poor Ophelia
Divided from herself and her fair judgment,
Without the which we are pictures or mere beasts;
Last, and as much containing as all these,
Her brother is in secret come from France,
90 Feeds on his wonder, keeps himself in clouds,
And wants not buzzers to infect his ear
With pestilent speeches of his father's death,
Wherein necessity, of matter beggared,
Will nothing stick our person to arraign

NOTICE & NOTE

95   In ear and ear. O, my dear Gertrude, this,
     Like to a murd'ring piece, in many places
     Gives me superfluous death.

     [*A noise within.*]

     Queen. Alack, what noise is this?

     King. Attend!
100 Where is my Switzers? Let them guard the door.

     [*Enter a* Messenger.]

     What is the matter?

     Messenger.   Save yourself, my lord.
     The ocean, overpeering of his list,
     Eats not the flats with more impiteous haste
     Than young Laertes, in a riotous head,
105 O'erbears your officers. The rabble call him "lord,"
     And, as the world were now but to begin,
     Antiquity forgot, custom not known,
     The ratifiers and props of every word,
     They cry "Choose we, Laertes shall be king!"
110 Caps, hands, and tongues applaud it to the clouds,
     "Laertes shall be king! Laertes king!"

     [*A noise within.*]

     Queen. How cheerfully on the false trail they cry.
     O, this is counter, you false Danish dogs!

     King. The doors are broke.

     [*Enter* Laertes *with others.*]

115 **Laertes.** Where is this king?—Sirs, stand you all without.

     All. No, let's come in!

     Laertes. I pray you, give me leave.

     All. We will, we will.

     Laertes. I thank you. Keep the door. [*Followers exit.*] O,
        thou vile king,
120 Give me my father!

     Queen.   Calmly, good Laertes.

     Laertes. That drop of blood that's calm proclaims me
        bastard,
     Cries "cuckold" to my father, brands the harlot
     Even here between the chaste unsmirchèd brow
     Of my true mother.

     King.   What is the cause, Laertes,
125 That thy rebellion looks so giant-like?—

96 murd'ring piece: a cannon that can kill many men simultaneously with its scattered shot.

97 Gives . . . death: kills me over and over.

100 Switzers: Swiss bodyguards.

102–105 Laertes is overpowering Claudius's officers as quickly as the ocean, rising above its boundary (**list**), floods the level ground.

106–108 as the world . . . word: as if the world had just begun, and ancient tradition and custom, which should confirm and support everything one says, were both forgotten.

110 Caps: caps thrown into the air.

113 counter: a hunting term that means "to follow a trail in the wrong direction."

121–124 Laertes says that no true son could be calm about his father's murder—that being calm would in effect prove that son to be a bastard.

122 cuckold: a man whose wife is unfaithful.

124 true: faithful.

The Tragedy of Hamlet: Act IV, Scene 5   237

WHEN STUDENTS STRUGGLE . . .

Compare Characters Ask students to reread Scene 5, lines 102–124, page 237. Revisit the definition of **foil.** Have students work in pairs to compare Laertes and Hamlet by answering the following questions: How is Laertes's situation similar to Hamlet's at the beginning of the play? What action is Laertes taking in this scene?

   For additional support, go to the **Reading Studio** and assign the following **Level Up tutorial: Character Traits.**

TEACH

ANALYZE CONFLICT

Remind students that at this point (Scene 5, lines 135–141, page 238) Laertes believes Claudius is responsible for his father's death and has come to confront him. Ask students to recount the way Hamlet first reacted when the Ghost revealed Claudius had murdered his father. Direct students to think about what evidence Hamlet had of Claudius's guilt and what evidence Laertes has, as well as what each character's attitude is about the consequences of revenge. (**Answer:** Hamlet reacted with grief and anger but also with uncertainty. He felt an obligation toward his father to act but was also worried about the consequences. Laertes, on the other hand, reacts swiftly with passionate anger and declares that he has no concern for the consequences, only with doing right by his father by getting revenge.)

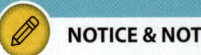 **NOTICE & NOTE**

126–129 Claudius tells Gertrude not to fear for his personal safety; so much divinity protects (**doth hedge**) a king that treason can only peer (**peep**) from afar at what it would like to do.

135 juggled with: played with, deceived.

ANALYZE CONFLICT
Annotate: Mark emotionally charged language in lines 135–141.

Compare: How does Laertes' speech compare with Hamlet's reaction when he first learned about his father's murder?

144 husband: manage, conserve.

148 swoopstake: a gambling term that means taking all the stakes on the gambling table.

153 pelican: traditionally thought to feed its young with its own blood.

157 sensibly: feelingly.
158 level: plain.

Let him go, Gertrude. Do not fear our person.
There's such divinity doth hedge a king
That treason can but peep to what it would,
Acts little of his will.—Tell me, Laertes,
130 Why thou art thus incensed.—Let him go,
     Gertrude.—
Speak, man.

Laertes. Where is my father?

King. Dead.

Queen. But not by him.

King.   Let him demand his fill.

135 **Laertes.** How came he dead? I'll not be juggled with.
To hell, allegiance! Vows, to the blackest devil!
Conscience and grace, to the profoundest pit!
I dare damnation. To this point I stand,
That both the worlds I give to negligence,
140 Let come what comes, only I'll be revenged
Most throughly for my father.

King. Who shall stay you?

Laertes. My will, not all the world.
And for my means, I'll husband them so well
145 They shall go far with little.

King.   Good Laertes,
If you desire to know the certainty
Of your dear father, is 't writ in your revenge
That, swoopstake, you will draw both friend and
     foe,
Winner and loser?

150 **Laertes.** None but his enemies.

King. Will you know them, then?

Laertes. To his good friends thus wide I'll ope my arms
And, like the kind life-rend'ring pelican,
Repast them with my blood.

King.   Why, now you speak
155 Like a good child and a true gentleman.
That I am guiltless of your father's death
And am most sensibly in grief for it,
It shall as level to your judgment 'pear
As day does to your eye.
          [*A noise within*] Let her come in.

160 **Laertes.** How now, what noise is that?

[*Enter* Ophelia.]

O heat, dry up my brains! Tears seven times salt
Burn out the sense and virtue of mine eye!
By heaven, thy madness shall be paid with weight
Till our scale turn the beam! O rose of May,
165 Dear maid, kind sister, sweet Ophelia!
O heavens, is 't possible a young maid's wits
Should be as mortal as an old man's life?
Nature is fine in love, and, where 'tis fine,
It sends some precious instance of itself
170 After the thing it loves.

Ophelia [*sings*]. *They bore him barefaced on the bier,*
  Hey non nonny, nonny, hey nonny,
  And in his grave rained many a tear.
Fare you well, my dove.

175 **Laertes.** Hadst thou thy wits and didst persuade revenge,
It could not move thus.

Ophelia. You must sing "A-down a-down"—and you
"Call him a-down-a."—O, how the wheel becomes
it! It is the false steward that stole his master's
180 daughter.

Laertes. This nothing's more than matter.

Ophelia. There's rosemary, that's for remembrance.
Pray you, love, remember. And there is pansies,
that's for thoughts.

185 **Laertes.** A document in madness: thoughts and
remembrance fitted.

Ophelia. There's fennel for you, and columbines.
There's rue for you, and here's some for me; we
may call it herb of grace o' Sundays. You must
190 wear your rue with a difference. There's a daisy. I
would give you some violets, but they withered all
when my father died. They say he made a good end.
[*Sings.*] *For bonny sweet Robin is all my joy.*

Laertes. Thought and afflictions, passion, hell itself
195 She turns to favor and to prettiness.

Ophelia [*sings*].
And will he not come again?
And will he not come again?
  No, no, he is dead.
  Go to thy deathbed.
200 *He never will come again.*

His beard was as white as snow,

NOTICE & NOTE

162 virtue: power.

163–164 In his vow to revenge Ophelia's madness, Laertes uses the image of weights being placed on a scale to make it tilt in the opposite direction.

168–169 fine in: refined by; **instance:** token (suggesting that Ophelia has sent her sanity into the grave with her father).

175 persuade: argue rationally for.

176 move thus: have such an effect.

177–178 Ophelia assigns refrains to the others so they can join in the singing.

178 the wheel: perhaps referring to the refrain or a spinning wheel that accompanies the singing.

181 This . . . matter: This nonsense has more meaning than rational speech.

182–192 Rosemary was used to symbolize remembrance at funerals. **Pansies,** a name derived from the French word for thought, **pensée,** was associated with courtship. Ophelia also mentions **fennel** (flattery), **columbines** (adultery or ingratitude), **rue** (repentance, sorrow), the **daisy** (dissembling, false love), and **violets** (faithfulness).

185–186 Laertes finds a lesson (**document**) in Ophelia's linking of thoughts and remembrance.

194 Thought: melancholy; **passion:** suffering.

TEACH

ENGLISH LEARNER SUPPORT

Understand Comparisons Point out that Ophelia enters just before Scene 5, lines 161–170, page 239, and Laertes expresses his grief and sorrow that his sister has gone mad. Focus students' attention on his question in lines 166–167:

O heavens, is 't possible a young maid's wits
Should be as mortal as an old man's life?

Point out the word *as*, and explain that Laertes is expressing his grief by making a comparison. Have students identify which two things he is comparing. *("a young maid's wits" and "an old man's life")* Provide definitions for the words *wits* (sanity, the opposite of madness) and *mortal* (likely to die). Then, discuss the meaning of this comparison. *(Laertes feels Ophelia's sanity has "died" like an old man's life.)* **SUBSTANTIAL/MODERATE**

TEACH

 **NOTICE & NOTE**

202 flaxen: pale yellow; **poll:** head.

204 cast away: scatter uselessly.

           All flaxen was his poll.
              He is gone, he is gone,
              And we cast away moan.
205 *God 'a mercy on his soul.*
        And of all Christians' souls, I pray God. God be
        wi' you.

[*She exits.*]

Laertes. Do you see this, O God?

King. Laertes, I must commune with your grief,
210 Or you deny me right. Go but apart,
       Make choice of whom your wisest friends you will,
       And they shall hear and judge 'twixt you and me.

213 collateral: indirect.

214 find us touched: find me implicated.

       If by direct or by collateral hand
       They find us touched, we will our kingdom give,
215 Our crown, our life, and all that we call ours,
       To you in satisfaction; but if not,
       Be you content to lend your patience to us,
       And we shall jointly labor with your soul
       To give it due content.

221–222 The traditional burial ceremony (**ostentation**) for a knight included hanging his helmet, sword, and a tablet displaying his coat of arms (**hatchment**) over the tomb.

224 That I . . . question: so that I must demand an explanation.

      Laertes.   Let this be so.
220 His means of death, his obscure funeral
       (No trophy, sword, nor hatchment o'er his bones,
       No noble rite nor formal ostentation)
       Cry to be heard, as 'twere from heaven to earth,
       That I must call 't in question.

      King.   So you shall,
225 And where th' offense is, let the great ax fall.
       I pray you, go with me.

[*They exit.*]

Scene 6 *The castle.*

[*Enter* Horatio *and others.*]

Horatio. What are they that would speak with me?

Gentleman. Seafaring men, sir. They say they have letters for you.

Horatio. Let them come in. [*Gentleman exits.*] I do not
5 know from what part of the world I should be
  greeted, if not from Lord Hamlet.

[*Enter* Sailors.]

Sailor. God bless you, sir.

Horatio. Let Him bless thee too.

240   Unit 2

IMPROVE READING FLUENCY

Targeted Passage To develop reading fluency, have pairs of students read Scene 5, lines 209–226, page 240, aloud, taking turns reading each sentence. Direct them to pay attention to punctuation as they read—to commas, to know where to pause; and to periods, to alert them when to change readers. When pairs have read through the entire passage, have them read the same passage aloud again, this time changing who reads first. Encourage them to provide each other with feedback about phrasing and pacing.

 Go to the **Reading Studio** for additional support in developing fluency.

Sailor. He shall, sir, an 't please Him. There's a letter
for you, sir. It came from th' ambassador that was
bound for England—if your name be Horatio, as I
am let to know it is.

[*He hands* Horatio *a letter.*]

Horatio [*reads the letter*]. Horatio, when thou shalt
have overlooked this, give these fellows some means
to the King. They have letters for him. Ere we
were two days old at sea, a pirate of very warlike
appointment gave us chase. Finding ourselves too
slow of sail, we put on a compelled valor, and in the
grapple I boarded them. On the instant, they got
clear of our ship; so I alone became their prisoner.
They have dealt with me like thieves of mercy, but
they knew what they did: I am to do a good turn
for them. Let the King have the letters I have sent,
and repair thou to me with as much speed as thou
wouldst fly death. I have words to speak in thine
ear will make thee dumb; yet are they much too
light for the bore of the matter. These good fellows
will bring thee where I am. Rosencrantz and
Guildenstern hold their course for England; of
them I have much to tell thee. Farewell.
He that thou knowest thine, Hamlet.

Come, I will give you way for these your letters
And do 't the speedier that you may direct me
To him from whom you brought them.

[*They exit.*]

Scene 7 *The castle.*

[*Enter* King *and* Laertes.]

King. Now must your conscience my acquittance seal,
And you must put me in your heart for friend,
Sith you have heard, and with a knowing ear,
That he which hath your noble father slain
Pursued my life.

Laertes. It well appears. But tell me
Why you proceeded not against these feats,
So criminal and so capital in nature,
As by your safety, greatness, wisdom, all things else,
You mainly were stirred up.

NOTICE & NOTE

9 an 't: if it.

10 th' ambassador: Hamlet.

ANALYZE DRAMATIC PLOT
Annotate: Mark details in lines 13–31 that explain why Hamlet is back in Denmark.

Evaluate: Is Shakespeare's use of the letter an effective way to advance the plot? Why or why not?

14 overlooked: read; **means:** means of access.

16–17 pirate . . . appointment: pirate ship well equipped for warfare.

21 thieves of mercy: merciful thieves.

22 they knew what they did: their actions were calculated.

24 repair: come.

27 light . . . bore: inadequate for the importance.

32 way: means of access.

1 my acquittance seal: confirm my innocence.

3 Sith: since.

7 capital: punishable by death.

8 safety: concern for your safety.

9 mainly: greatly.

The Tragedy of Hamlet: Act IV, Scene 7 241

TEACH

ANALYZE DRAMATIC PLOT

Explain that sometimes playwrights rely on outside events to advance the **plot.** In some cases, this may include highly improbable events. Point out that earlier in the play, Shakespeare has Hamlet shipped off to England, and then he must find a way to have Hamlet return to the action of the play.

Tell students that the letter Hamlet sends to Horatio (Scene 6, lines 13–31, page 241) is a **plot device,** something used to advance the **plot.** Have students carefully read this letter and then summarize the events in the letter and discuss their plausibility. (**Answer:** *Hamlet's letter says that the ship he was traveling on was attacked by pirates; that he was the only one captured; and that the ship carrying Rosencrantz and Guildenstern continued to England, while Hamlet persuaded the pirates to bring him back to Denmark and release him. It advances the plot because Claudius must now take some other action to get rid of Hamlet, and because it gives Laertes the opportunity to seek his revenge against Hamlet. Students may recognize the pirate attack as a rather implausible turn of events, but one that is necessary to advance the plot by bringing Hamlet back to the Danish court.*)

ENGLISH LEARNER SUPPORT

Acquire and Use Grade-Level Content Vocabulary Supply students with definitions for the following vocabulary words, providing images where possible:

- pirate *(criminal of the sea)*
- sail *(move or travel by boat)*
- boarded *(got onto a ship)*
- ship *(boat)*
- prisoner *(someone being held by force)*
- mercy *(kind treatment)*

Have students practice the pronunciation of each word by echoing you. Then, have students work in pairs to retell the events described in the letter using these words. **SUBSTANTIAL/MODERATE**

TO CHALLENGE STUDENTS . . .

Identify the Plot Device Hamlet's letter to Horatio (Scene 6, lines 13–31, p. 241) announces his return and describes the events that have led to it. The pirate attack is an example of a classic plot device. Have students research classic plot devices and identify what type of plot device this is and what purpose it serves. (*The pirate attack described in the letter is an example of* deus ex machina, *an unlikely event unrelated to the plot or theme that serves the purpose of solving a plot problem. In this case it solves the problem of how Hamlet, the hero of the play, will return after being sent off to England.*) Then, ask students to think of other examples of *deus ex machina* in books, plays, or movies with which they may be familiar.

The Tragedy of Hamlet: Act IV, Scene 7 241

TEACH

 NOTICE & NOTE

11 **unsinewed:** weak.

15 **conjunctive:** closely joined.

16 **star . . . sphere:** In Shakespeare's time, it was believed that each planet moves around the Earth in a hollow sphere.

18 **count:** account, indictment.

19–25 Claudius says that the common people (**general gender**), through their love for Hamlet, act like a spring with such a high concentration of lime that wood placed in it will become petrified; they change his limitations (**gyves**) into attractive qualities, so that the strong wind of their approval would blow back any arrows that Claudius might shoot at Hamlet.

27 **terms:** condition.

28–30 **Whose worth . . . perfections:** If praises can recall Ophelia's former self, her worth placed her at the top of the age.

45 **naked:** destitute, defenseless.

10 **King.** O, for two special reasons,
   Which may to you perhaps seem much unsinewed,
   But yet to me they're strong. The Queen his mother
   Lives almost by his looks, and for myself
   (My virtue or my plague, be it either which),
15 She is so conjunctive to my life and soul
   That, as the star moves not but in his sphere,
   I could not but by her. The other motive
   Why to a public count I might not go
   Is the great love the general gender bear him,
20 Who, dipping all his faults in their affection,
   Work like the spring that turneth wood to stone,
   Convert his gyves to graces, so that my arrows,
   Too slightly timbered for so loud a wind,
   Would have reverted to my bow again,
25 But not where I have aimed them.

   Laertes. And so have I a noble father lost,
   A sister driven into desp'rate terms,
   Whose worth, if praises may go back again,
   Stood challenger on mount of all the age
30 For her perfections. But my revenge will come.

   King. Break not your sleeps for that. You must not think
   That we are made of stuff so flat and dull
   That we can let our beard be shook with danger
   And think it pastime. You shortly shall hear more.
35 I loved your father, and we love ourself,
   And that, I hope, will teach you to imagine—

   [*Enter a* Messenger *with letters*.]

   How now? What news?

   Messenger.   Letters, my lord, from Hamlet.
   These to your Majesty, this to the Queen.

   King. From Hamlet? Who brought them?

40 **Messenger.** Sailors, my lord, they say. I saw them not.
   They were given me by Claudio. He received them
   Of him that brought them.

   King.   Laertes, you shall hear them.—
   Leave us.

   [Messenger *exits*.]

   [*Reads*.] High and mighty, you shall know I am set
45 naked on your kingdom. Tomorrow shall I beg
   leave to see your kingly eyes, when I shall (first

242   Unit 2

WHEN STUDENTS STRUGGLE . . .

Interpret Figures of Speech In Scene 7, lines 10–25, p. 242, Claudius answers Laertes's question. Point out that Laertes's question is in lines 7–8, and have a volunteer explain what the question is. Then, point out that Claudius uses a number of metaphors and similes in his explanation.

📖 For additional support, go to the **Reading Studio** and assign the following **Level Up tutorial: Figurative Language**.

242   Unit 2

*asking your pardon) thereunto recount the occasion
of my sudden and more strange return.* **Hamlet.**
What should this mean? Are all the rest come back?
50 Or is it some abuse and no such thing?

Laertes. Know you the hand?

King. 'Tis Hamlet's character. "Naked"—
And in a postscript here, he says "alone."
Can you advise me?

55 **Laertes.** I am lost in it, my lord. But let him come.
It warms the very sickness in my heart
That I shall live and tell him to his teeth
"Thus didst thou."

King.   If it be so, Laertes
(As how should it be so? how otherwise?),
60 Will you be ruled by me?

Laertes.   Ay, my lord,
So you will not o'errule me to a peace.

King. To thine own peace. If he be now returned,
As checking at his voyage, and that he means
No more to undertake it, I will work him
65 To an exploit, now ripe in my device,
Under the which he shall not choose but fall;
And for his death no wind of blame shall breathe,
But even his mother shall uncharge the practice
And call it accident.

70 **Laertes.** My lord, I will be ruled,
The rather if you could devise it so
That I might be the organ.

King.   It falls right.
You have been talked of since your travel much,
And that in Hamlet's hearing, for a quality
75 Wherein they say you shine. Your sum of parts
Did not together pluck such envy from him
As did that one, and that, in my regard,
Of the unworthiest siege.

Laertes. What part is that, my lord?

80 **King.** A very ribbon in the cap of youth—
Yet needful too, for youth no less becomes
The light and careless livery that it wears
Than settled age his sables and his weeds,
Importing health and graveness. Two months since

NOTICE & NOTE

50 Claudius wonders if this is a deception and no such thing has occurred.

52 **character:** handwriting.

61 **So:** as long as.

63 **checking at:** turning away from.

65 **device:** devising.

68 **uncharge the practice:** not blame the plot.

72 **organ:** agent, instrument.

75–84 The rest of Laertes' qualities combined did not inspire as much envy in Hamlet as this one, which ranks lowest in Claudius's regard. Yet this quality is important even if only a mere decoration (**very ribbon**), because light, carefree clothes (**livery**) are as well-suited to youth as more richly trimmed or sober clothes (**his sables and his weeds**) are to old age, suggesting well-being and dignity.

The Tragedy of Hamlet: Act IV, Scene 7   243

IMPROVE READING FLUENCY

Targeted Passage Focus students' attention on Scene 7, lines 62–69, p. 243, in which Claudius tells Laertes what he will do about Hamlet's return to Denmark. Read the passage aloud with appropriate pauses and stress. Then, read it again and have students echo after each natural pause. After several rounds of practice, have students read the chunks individually, round-robin style, as a whole class or in groups.

 Go to the **Reading Studio** for additional support in developing fluency.

TEACH

ENGLISH LEARNER SUPPORT

Share and Ask for Information Point out to students that when Claudius finds out Hamlet has come back to Denmark, he decides to make a new plan to have him killed. In Scene 7, lines 73–108, pages 243–244, Claudius introduces this plan to Laertes. Have students focus their attention on three chunks of this text:

- lines 73–78
- lines 98–105
- lines 105–108

Read each chunk of text aloud, and have students identify the words they know by marking them and making an annotation. Make sure students pay attention to the side notes and mark the words they recognize there as well.

Then, organize students into same-level groups to share the words they know and discuss what they think each chunk of text means, as well as what information Claudius is giving Laertes about Hamlet. Use the following supports with students at varying proficiency levels:

- Have the lower-proficiency groups form questions to ask the higher-proficiency groups, including questions about word meanings and any other clarifications they need to help figure out what Claudius is telling Laertes. **SUBSTANTIAL/MODERATE**
- Have students explain why this information might be significant and predict what Claudius's plan is. **LIGHT**

NOTICE & NOTE

87 can well: are skillful.

90–91 encorpsed . . . beast: as if he and the horse shared the same body, a double-natured beast (like the mythical centaur, half man and half horse).

91–93 His feats surpassed the ability of Claudius's imagination to reconstruct them.

96 brooch: ornament.

98 made confession of: testified about.

100 art . . . defense: skill and practice in fencing.

103 'scrimers: fencers.

108 play: fence.

114 begun by time: created by circumstance.

119 nothing . . . still: Nothing remains at the same level of goodness.

120 pleurisy: excess.
121 his own too-much: its own excess.

85 Here was a gentleman of Normandy.
  I have seen myself, and served against, the French,
  And they can well on horseback, but this gallant
  Had witchcraft in 't. He grew unto his seat,
  And to such wondrous doing brought his horse
90 As had he been encorpsed and demi-natured
  With the brave beast. So far he topped my thought
  That I in forgery of shapes and tricks
  Come short of what he did.

  Laertes.   A Norman was 't?

  King. A Norman.

95 **Laertes.** Upon my life, Lamord.

  King.   The very same.

  Laertes. I know him well. He is the brooch indeed
  And gem of all the nation.

  King. He made confession of you
  And gave you such a masterly report
100 For art and exercise in your defense,
  And for your rapier most especial,
  That he cried out 'twould be a sight indeed
  If one could match you. The 'scrimers of their nation
  He swore had neither motion, guard, nor eye,
105 If you opposed them. Sir, this report of his
  Did Hamlet so envenom with his envy
  That he could nothing do but wish and beg
  Your sudden coming-o'er, to play with you.
  Now out of this—

  Laertes.   What out of this, my lord?

110 **King.** Laertes, was your father dear to you?
  Or are you like the painting of a sorrow,
  A face without a heart?

  Laertes.   Why ask you this?

  King. Not that I think you did not love your father,
  But that I know love is begun by time,
115 And that I see, in passages of proof,
  Time qualifies the spark and fire of it.
  There lives within the very flame of love
  A kind of wick or snuff that will abate it,
  And nothing is at a like goodness still;
120 For goodness, growing to a pleurisy,
  Dies in his own too-much. That we would do

We should do when we would; for this "would"
   changes
And hath abatements and delays as many
As there are tongues, are hands, are accidents;
125 And then this "should" is like a spendthrift sigh,
That hurts by easing. But to the quick of th' ulcer:
Hamlet comes back; what would you undertake
To show yourself indeed your father's son
More than in words?

Laertes.   To cut his throat i' th' church.

130 **King.** No place indeed should murder sanctuarize;
Revenge should have no bounds. But, good Laertes,
Will you do this? Keep close within your chamber.
Hamlet, returned, shall know you are come home.
We'll put on those shall praise your excellence
135 And set a double varnish on the fame
The Frenchman gave you; bring you, in fine, together
And wager on your heads. He, being remiss,
Most generous, and free from all contriving,
Will not peruse the foils, so that with ease,
140 Or with a little shuffling, you may choose
A sword unbated, and in a pass of practice
Requite him for your father.

Laertes.   I will do 't,
And for that purpose I'll anoint my sword.
I bought an unction of a mountebank
145 So mortal that, but dip a knife in it,
Where it draws blood no cataplasm so rare,
Collected from all simples that have virtue
Under the moon, can save the thing from death
That is but scratched withal. I'll touch my point
150 With this contagion, that, if I gall him slightly,
It may be death.

King.   Let's further think of this,
Weigh what convenience both of time and means
May fit us to our shape. If this should fail,
And that our drift look through our bad performance,
155 'Twere better not assayed. Therefore this project
Should have a back or second that might hold
If this did blast in proof. Soft, let me see.
We'll make a solemn wager on your cunnings—
I ha 't!
160 When in your motion you are hot and dry
(As make your bouts more violent to that end)
And that he calls for drink, I'll have prepared him

NOTICE & NOTE

121–122 That we . . . would: If one wishes to do something, one should act right away.

123 abatements: lessenings.

125–126 spendthrift sigh . . . easing: an allusion to the idea that sighing brings temporary relief but weakens the heart.

130 should murder sanctuarize: should protect a murderer from punishment.

134 put on those shall: arrange for people to.

136 in fine: finally.

137 remiss: carelessly unsuspicious.

138 generous: noble-minded.

141 unbated: not blunted; **pass of practice:** treacherous thrust.

144–149 Laertes bought from a quack doctor an ointment (**unction**) so deadly that no medical dressing (**cataplasm**) can save anyone scratched by it.

150 gall: injure.

153 fit us to our shape: suit our purposes.
153–155 If the plot should fail and our intentions are exposed, it would be better if we never attempted it.
156 back: backup.
157 blast in proof: blow up while tested.
158 cunnings: skills.
159 ha 't: have it.

The Tragedy of Hamlet: Act IV, Scene 7   245

APPLYING ACADEMIC VOCABULARY

☐ ambiguous   ☐ anticipate   ☑ conceive   ☐ drama   ☑ integrity

Write and Discuss Have students turn to a partner to discuss the following questions. Guide students to include the academic vocabulary words *conceive* and *integrity* in their responses. Ask volunteers to share their responses with the class.

- What plan do Claudius and Laertes **conceive** in lines 130–165 in response to finding out Hamlet has returned to Denmark alive?
- What does Laertes's willingness to participate in this plan say about his **integrity**?

TEACH

ENGLISH LEARNER SUPPORT

Analyze Sayings and Expressions To increase comprehension, provide language support for the passage in which the King explains his backup plan for killing Hamlet (Scene 7, lines 151–165, pages 245–246).

Ask students to paraphrase the following phrases and discuss their meaning. Students should use the side notes to assist them. Help students to understand the meaning of the passage as necessary.

- Line 152: "convenience both of time and means" (*opportunities*)
- Line 154: "our drift look through our bad performance" (*our plan is revealed*)
- Line 164: "venomed stuck" (*a thrust with a poisoned fencing sword*)
- Line 165: "Our purpose may hold there." (*We may still accomplish our purpose.*) **MODERATE**

NOTICE & NOTE

163 **A chalice for the nonce:** a cup of wine for the occasion.
164 **stuck:** thrust.

169 **askant:** slanting over.
170 **his hoar:** its gray.
171 **Therewith . . . make:** she used the willow twigs to make elaborate wreaths.
172 **long purples:** orchids.
173 **liberal:** free-spoken.
174 **cold:** chaste.
175 **pendant boughs:** overhanging branches; **coronet:** made into a wreath or crown.
176 **envious sliver:** malicious branch.
180 **lauds:** hymns.
181 **incapable:** unaware.
182 **native and endued:** naturally adapted.

A chalice for the nonce, whereon but sipping,
If he by chance escape your venomed stuck,
165 Our purpose may hold there.—But stay, what noise?

[*Enter* Queen.]

Queen. One woe doth tread upon another's heel,
So fast they follow. Your sister's drowned, Laertes.

Laertes. Drowned? O, where?

Queen. There is a willow grows askant the brook
170 That shows his hoar leaves in the glassy stream.
Therewith fantastic garlands did she make
Of crowflowers, nettles, daisies, and long purples,
That liberal shepherds give a grosser name,
But our cold maids do "dead men's fingers" call them.
175 There on the pendant boughs her coronet weeds
Clamb'ring to hang, an envious sliver broke,
When down her weedy trophies and herself
Fell in the weeping brook. Her clothes spread wide,
And mermaid-like awhile they bore her up,
180 Which time she chanted snatches of old lauds,
As one incapable of her own distress
Or like a creature native and endued
Unto that element. But long it could not be
Till that her garments, heavy with their drink,
185 Pulled the poor wretch from her melodious lay
To muddy death.

Laertes. Alas, then she is drowned.

Queen. Drowned, drowned.

246 Unit 2

WHEN STUDENTS STRUGGLE . . .

Review the Plot Guide students' comprehension of **plot** by having them complete a sequence chart that includes the important events in Act IV. Ask students to quickly skim Act IV for ideas about important events. Sort them chronologically.

For additional support, go to the **Reading Studio** and assign the following **Level Up tutorial: Plot: Sequence of Events**.

246 Unit 2

Laertes. Too much of water hast thou, poor Ophelia,
And therefore I forbid my tears. But yet
190 It is our trick; nature her custom holds,
Let shame say what it will. When these are gone,
The woman will be out.—Adieu, my lord.
I have a speech o' fire that fain would blaze,
But that this folly drowns it.

[*He exits.*]

King.   Let's follow, Gertrude.
195 How much I had to do to calm his rage!
Now fear I this will give it start again.
Therefore, let's follow.

[*They exit.*]

189–192 Laertes says that tears are a natural trait (**trick**), which shame cannot prevent. When all his tears are shed, the womanly part of him will be gone.

CHECK YOUR UNDERSTANDING

Answer these questions before moving on to the **Analyze the Text** section on the following page.

1. Why is Fortinbras traveling through Denmark?
   A He wants to overtake the kingdom.
   B He is spying on the king and queen.
   C He is on his way to invade Poland.
   D He wants to open trade routes with Denmark and Poland.

2. Why is Ophelia behaving irrationally?
   F She is sad that Hamlet is traveling to England.
   G She is upset about Fortinbras's visit to Denmark.
   H She misses her brother.
   J She is distraught over her father's death.

3. What happens to Hamlet's ship on the way to England?
   A It capsizes during a storm.
   B It is captured by pirates.
   C It is attacked by a fleet of Fortinbras's ships.
   D It springs a leak and sinks off the coast of England.

TEACH

CHECK YOUR UNDERSTANDING

Have students answer the questions independently.

Answers:
1. C
2. J
3. B

If students answer any questions incorrectly, have them reread the text to confirm their understanding. Then, they may proceed to ANALYZE THE TEXT on page 248.

ENGLISH LEARNER SUPPORT

Oral Assessment To show their comprehension, have students answer the following questions:

1. Fortinbras is going to invade _____. *(Poland)*
2. Ophelia is mad because her father _____. *(was killed)*
3. Hamlet's ship was captured by _____. *(pirates)* **ALL LEVELS**

APPLY

ANALYZE THE TEXT

Possible answers:

1. **DOK 2:** *In Act IV, Hamlet's killing of Polonius results in Claudius taking action to send him away to England, Ophelia going mad, and Laertes seeking revenge, as well as Claudius making a plan with Laertes to kill Hamlet after he returns to Denmark. Earlier in the play, Hamlet feared the unintended consequences if he were to kill Claudius to avenge his father's death. These events show that such acts of revenge do have serious consequences.*

2. **DOK 3:** *In Scene 1, Gertrude reports to Claudius that Hamlet has killed Polonius. However, she alters the story to say Hamlet thought there was a rat behind the arras and went to kill it because of his madness. She does not tell Claudius the truth because Hamlet has instructed her not to. Gertrude also wants to protect Hamlet from the consequences of his crime by making it seem like he did it out of madness rather than a desire to kill a person.*

3. **DOK 4:** *In this scene, Hamlet sees Fortinbras's resolve in defending his honor and berates himself for not having similar courage. While earlier he made the excuse that he could not be certain of Claudius's guilt and the consequences of taking action, he now feels more shame for his inaction because he sees that Fortinbras is willing to go into battle "for a fantasy and trick of fame."*

4. **DOK 2:** *The songs Ophelia sings seem to reference the death of her father as well as her troubled relationship with Hamlet and his departure for England.*

5. **DOK 3:** *Both Fortinbras and Laertes serve as foils to Hamlet in Act IV as they take decisive action rather than deliberating and agonizing in indecision as Hamlet does. Laertes, in particular, serves as a foil because his situation is so similar to Hamlet's in that his father has been killed and he seeks revenge.*

CREATE AND PRESENT

Write a Journal Entry Remind students to consider the purpose of a journal entry. Encourage them to reflect on the feelings Rosencrantz or Guildenstern would have had, rather than just recounting events.

Present a News Briefing Provide a model news briefing for students to follow and have them identify the tone, the structure, and other elements of the genre.

248 Unit 2

RESPOND

ANALYZE THE TEXT

Support your responses with evidence from the text.   NOTEBOOK

1. **Cause/Effect** Which events in Act IV result from Hamlet's killing of Polonius? How does this sequence of events help explain why Hamlet was slow to take action earlier in the play?

2. **Draw Conclusions** Does Gertrude seem sincere in Scene 1 when she tells Claudius that Hamlet killed Polonius in a fit of insanity, or is she trying to protect him? Consider the following:
   - Hamlet's instructions to her at the end of Act III
   - how closely her description matches Hamlet's actual behavior

3. **Evaluate** Reread Hamlet's soliloquy in Scene 4, lines 48–58. This isn't the first time that Hamlet has berated himself for not taking revenge. Is he just repeating himself, or do you sense a change in his attitude? Explain.

4. **Interpret** Ophelia sings fragments of songs when she appears in Scene 5 suffering from mental illness. How do the songs reflect her experiences in the play?

5. **Compare** Shakespeare often highlights the traits of his main characters through the use of foils, characters with contrasting traits. How do Fortinbras and Laertes serve as foils in Act IV?

CREATE AND PRESENT

Write a Journal Entry Write a journal entry by either Rosencrantz or Guildenstern about their mission to take Hamlet to England.

❏ Describe Hamlet's behavior toward his old friends and the events that led to Claudius's decision to send him away.

❏ Consider the limited knowledge that Rosencrantz and Guildenstern have about these events. Only include information that your character would be aware of.

❏ Use an informal, intimate style appropriate for a journal entry.

Present a News Briefing Imagine you are a journalist tracking the rapid development of events in Act IV of Hamlet. Write a news briefing to present.

❏ Make sure to cover all the important developments in chronological order.

❏ Make sure your news briefing is free from bias and opinion.

❏ Practice reading your news briefing until you feel comfortable with the information.

❏ Read your news briefing to a small group and respond to questions from your classmates.

248 Unit 2

LEARNING MINDSET

Problem Solving Remind students that as they have worked through this challenging text, they have made progress and learned by solving problems. As they have solved problems, they have gained the skills they need to solve more difficult problems. Ask students to take a moment to reflect on the problems they have solved so far and what they understand now that they didn't before. As they move to answering the Analyze the Text questions, reassure them that even if they don't know an answer right away, they have the skills they need to solve these problems because of the effort they have already made.

SETTING A PURPOSE

As you read, notice how Shakespeare creates sharp contrasts in the mood of the scenes.

Notice & Note

Use the side margins to notice and note signposts in the text.

ACT V

Scene 1 *A churchyard.*

[*Enter* Gravedigger *and* Another.]

Gravedigger. Is she to be buried in Christian burial, when she willfully seeks her own salvation?

Other. I tell thee she is. Therefore make her grave straight. The crowner hath sat on her and finds it
5 Christian burial.

Gravedigger. How can that be, unless she drowned herself in her own defense?

Other. Why, 'tis found so.

Gravedigger. It must be se offendendo; it cannot be else.
10 For here lies the point: if I drown myself wittingly, it argues an act, and an act hath three branches—it is to act, to do, to perform. Argal, she drowned herself wittingly.

Other. Nay, but hear you, goodman delver—

15 **Gravedigger.** Give me leave. Here lies the water; good. Here stands the man; good. If the man go to this water and drown himself, it is (will he, nill he) he goes; mark you that. But if the water come to him and drown him, he drowns not himself. Argal, he
20 that is not guilty of his own death shortens not his own life.

Other. But is this law?

Gravedigger. Ay, marry, is 't—crowner's 'quest law.

Other. Will you ha' the truth on 't? If this had not
25 been a gentlewoman, she should have been buried out o' Christian burial.

Gravedigger. Why, there thou sayst. And the more pity that great folk should have count'nance in this

1 Christian burial: Suicides were not allowed Christian funeral rites. The Gravedigger assumes that Ophelia killed herself.

2 salvation: probably a blunder for *damnation*.

4 straight: immediately; **crowner:** coroner; **sat on her:** held an inquest into her death; **finds it:** gave a verdict allowing.

9 se offendendo: a blunder for *se defendendo*, a legal term meaning "in self-defense."

12 Argal: a blunder for Latin *ergo*, "therefore."

13 wittingly: intentionally.

14 goodman: a title used before the name of a profession or craft; **delver:** digger.

17 will he, nill he: willy-nilly, whether he wishes it or not.

23 'quest: inquest.

27 thou sayst: you speak the truth.

28 count'nance: privilege.

SETTING A PURPOSE

Direct students to use the Setting a Purpose prompt to focus their reading.

TEACH

ENGLISH LEARNER SUPPORT

Acquire Grade-Level Vocabulary Focus students' attention on Scene 1, lines 42–61, page 250. Supply students with the following vocabulary, using images to support the meanings:

- **grave** *(a hole where a dead person is buried)*
- **mason** *(someone who builds brick walls)*
- **shipwright** *(someone who builds ships)*
- **carpenter** *(someone who makes things with wood)*
- **gallows** *(a structure for hanging people)*
- **tenant** *(someone who lives in or uses a building)*

Have students practice the pronunciation of each word by echoing you and then practicing in pairs. Review the meaning of each word using visual clues and spoken prompts. **ALL LEVELS**

 **NOTICE & NOTE**

30 even-Christian: fellow Christians.

32 hold up: keep up.

34 bore arms: had a coat of arms (the sign of a gentleman).

41 Go to: go on (an expression of impatience).

44 frame: structure.

48–50 Now, thou . . . to thee: Since you blasphemously say that the gallows is stronger than the church, you may be headed for the gallows.

53 unyoke: stop work for the day.

56 Mass: by the Mass.

57–58 The Gravedigger tells him to stop beating his brains to figure it out, because a beating won't make a slow donkey pick up its pace.

62–123 The Gravedigger sings a version of a popular Elizabethan song, with some added grunts (**O** and **a**), as he works.

world to drown or hang themselves more than
30 their even-Christian. Come, my spade. There is no
ancient gentlemen but gard'ners, ditchers, and
grave-makers. They hold up Adam's profession.

Other. Was he a gentleman?

Gravedigger. He was the first that ever bore arms.

35 **Other.** Why, he had none.

Gravedigger. What, art a heathen? How dost thou
understand the scripture? The scripture says Adam
digged. Could he dig without arms? I'll put another
question to thee. If thou answerest me not to the
40 purpose, confess thyself—

Other. Go to!

Gravedigger. What is he that builds stronger than
either the mason, the shipwright, or the carpenter?

Other. The gallows-maker; for that frame outlives a
45 thousand tenants.

Gravedigger. I like thy wit well, in good faith. The gallows
does well. But how does it well? It does well
to those that do ill. Now, thou dost ill to say the
gallows is built stronger than the church. Argal, the
50 gallows may do well to thee. To 't again, come.

Other. "Who builds stronger than a mason, a shipwright,
or a carpenter?"

Gravedigger. Ay, tell me that, and unyoke.

Other. Marry, now I can tell.

55 **Gravedigger.** To 't.

Other. Mass, I cannot tell.

[*Enter* Hamlet *and* Horatio *afar off.*]

Gravedigger. Cudgel thy brains no more about it, for
your dull ass will not mend his pace with beating.
And, when you are asked this question next, say "a
60 grave-maker." The houses he makes lasts till doomsday.
Go, get thee in, and fetch me a stoup of liquor.

[*The* Other Man *exits and the* Gravedigger *digs and sings.*]

In youth when I did love, did love,
    Methought it was very sweet
To contract—O—the time for—a—my behove,
65   O, methought there—a—was nothing—a—meet.

Hamlet. Has this fellow no feeling of his business? He sings in grave-making.

Horatio. Custom hath made it in him a property of easiness.

70 **Hamlet.** 'Tis e'en so. The hand of little employment hath the daintier sense.

Gravedigger [*sings*].
　　But age with his stealing steps
　　Hath clawed me in his clutch,
　　And hath shipped me into the land,
75　As if I had never been such.

[*He digs up a skull.*]

Hamlet. That skull had a tongue in it and could sing once. How the knave jowls it to the ground as if 'twere Cain's jawbone, that did the first murder! This might be the pate of a politician which this
80 ass now o'erreaches, one that would circumvent God, might it not?

Horatio. It might, my lord.

Hamlet. Or of a courtier, which could say "Good morrow, sweet lord! How dost thou, sweet lord?"
85 This might be my Lord Such-a-one that praised my Lord Such-a-one's horse when he went to beg it, might it not?

Horatio. Ay, my lord.

Hamlet. Why, e'en so. And now my Lady Worm's,
90 chapless and knocked about the mazard with a sexton's spade. Here's fine revolution, an we had the trick to see 't. Did these bones cost no more the breeding but to play at loggets with them? Mine ache to think on 't.

Gravedigger [*sings*].
95　A pickax and a spade, a spade,
　　For and a shrouding sheet,
　　O, a pit of clay for to be made
　　For such a guest is meet.

[*He digs up more skulls.*]

Hamlet. There's another. Why may not that be the
100 skull of a lawyer? Where be his quiddities now, his quillities, his cases, his tenures, and his tricks? Why does he suffer this mad knave now to knock him about the sconce with a dirty shovel and will not

---

NOTICE & NOTE

68–69 Custom . . . easiness: Habit has made it easy for him.

71 hath the daintier sense: is more sensitive.

77 jowls: dashes.

79–81 The skull, which the Gravedigger gets the better of, might have been the head (**pate**) of a schemer who would have tried to get the better of God.

90 chapless: missing the lower jaw; **mazard:** head.

91 revolution: turn of Fortune's wheel; **an:** if.

92 trick: ability.

92–94 Hamlet asks whether the cost of bringing up these people was so low that one may play a game with their bones.

100 quiddities: subtle arguments, quibbles.

101 quillities: subtle distinctions; **tenures:** terms for the holding of property.

103 sconce: head.

TEACH

ENGLISH LEARNER SUPPORT

Analyze Expressions Explain that Shakespeare often used words with multiple meanings as part of his wordplay and puns. In Scene 1, lines 107–109, page 251, he uses the word *fine* to indicate four different meanings in a single sentence. Remind students that they may need to use a dictionary to find another meaning of a word if it isn't familiar.

- "Is this the fine . . . " (*This is an archaic use indicating the end result of something—the lawyer's life.*)
- ". . . of his fines . . . " (*This is another archaic usage related to documents in the sale of real estate.*)

In a group, discuss and paraphrase the meanings of these wordplays and puns.
LIGHT

 **NOTICE & NOTE**

104–114 Hamlet lists different legal terms related to the buying and holding of property. **Fines** were documents involved in the transfer of estates; Hamlet also uses the word to refer to the "end result" of the lawyer's legal work and his "elegant" head filled with "small particles" of dirt. He plays similarly off the meanings of other terms.

119 assurance in that: safety in legal documents.

120 sirrah: a term used to address inferiors.

125 out on 't: outside of it.

130 quick: living.

139 absolute: strict, precise.

140 by the card: accurately; **equivocation:** use of words that are vague or have more than one meaning.

142–144 The present age has grown so refined (**picked**) that hardly any distinction remains between a peasant and a courtier; the peasant walks so closely that he chafes (**galls**) the courtier's sore heel (**kibe**).

tell him of his action of battery? Hum, this fellow
105 might be in 's time a great buyer of land, with his statutes, his recognizances, his fines, his double vouchers, his recoveries. Is this the fine of his fines and the recovery of his recoveries, to have his fine pate full of fine dirt? Will his vouchers vouch him
110 no more of his purchases, and double ones too, than the length and breadth of a pair of indentures? The very conveyances of his lands will scarcely lie in this box, and must th' inheritor himself have no more, ha?

115 **Horatio.** Not a jot more, my lord.

Hamlet. Is not parchment made of sheepskins?

Horatio. Ay, my lord, and of calves' skins too.

Hamlet. They are sheep and calves which seek out assurance in that. I will speak to this fellow.—
120 Whose grave's this, sirrah?

Gravedigger. Mine, sir.

[*Sings.*] O, a pit of clay for to be made
    For such a guest is meet.

Hamlet. I think it be thine indeed, for thou liest in 't.

125 **Gravedigger.** You lie out on 't, sir, and therefore 'tis not yours. For my part, I do not lie in 't, yet it is mine.

Hamlet. Thou dost lie in 't, to be in 't and say it is thine. 'Tis for the dead, not for the quick; therefore thou liest.

130 **Gravedigger.** 'Tis a quick lie, sir; 'twill away again from me to you.

Hamlet. What man dost thou dig it for?

Gravedigger. For no man, sir.

Hamlet. What woman then?

135 **Gravedigger.** For none, neither.

Hamlet. Who is to be buried in 't?

Gravedigger. One that was a woman, sir, but, rest her soul, she's dead.

Hamlet. How absolute the knave is! We must speak
140 by the card, or equivocation will undo us. By the Lord, Horatio, this three years I have took note of it: the age is grown so picked that the toe of the peasant comes so near the heel of the courtier, he

252 Unit 2

WHEN STUDENTS STRUGGLE . . .

Analyze Wordplay Explain to students that Shakespeare uses a lot of wordplay. To help them understand wordplay in this scene, ask them to focus on the shifting meanings of the word *lie* in Scene 1, lines 124–131, page 252. Have students use a chart like the one below to record the meaning and other possible meanings of the word *lie* (or any form of it).

Line #	Meaning	Other Possible Meanings
124	Recline, as in "lie down"	To say something that is not true

 For additional support, go to the **Reading Studio** and assign the following **Level Up tutorial: Multiple-Meaning Words**.

galls his kibe.—How long hast thou been grave
145 maker?

Gravedigger. Of all the days i' th' year, I came to 't that
day that our last King Hamlet overcame Fortinbras.

Hamlet. How long is that since?

Gravedigger. Cannot you tell that? Every fool can tell
150 that. It was that very day that young Hamlet was
born—he that is mad, and sent into England?

Hamlet. Ay, marry, why was he sent into England?

Gravedigger. Why, because he was mad. He shall
recover his wits there. Or if he do not, 'tis no great
155 matter there.

Hamlet. Why?

Gravedigger. 'Twill not be seen in him there. There the
men are as mad as he.

Hamlet. How came he mad?

160 **Gravedigger.** Very strangely, they say.

Hamlet. How "strangely"?

Gravedigger. Faith, e'en with losing his wits.

Hamlet. Upon what ground?

Gravedigger. Why, here in Denmark. I have been sexton
165 here, man and boy, thirty years.

Hamlet. How long will a man lie i' th' earth ere he rot?

Gravedigger. Faith, if he be not rotten before he die
(as we have many pocky corses nowadays that will
scarce hold the laying in), he will last you some eight
170 year or nine year. A tanner will last you nine year.

Hamlet. Why he more than another?

Gravedigger. Why, sir, his hide is so tanned with his
trade that he will keep out water a great while; and
your water is a sore decayer of your whoreson
175 dead body. Here's a skull now hath lien you i' th'
earth three-and-twenty years.

Hamlet. Whose was it?

Gravedigger. A whoreson mad fellow's it was. Whose
do you think it was?

180 **Hamlet.** Nay, I know not.

Gravedigger. A pestilence on him for a mad rogue! He
poured a flagon of Rhenish on my head once. This

163 ground: cause. (The Gravedigger takes it in the sense of "land.")

168 pocky: rotten, infected with syphilis.

169 scarce hold the laying in: barely hold together until they are buried.

174–175 your . . . body: Water is a terrible (**sore**) decayer of vile (**whoreson**) corpses.

175 lien you: lain.

TEACH

ENGLISH LEARNER SUPPORT

Describe and Explain Have students look at the image and write questions about it. Then, have them practice reading their questions aloud. Finally, have them work in pairs to read and answer each other's questions. Make sure they do not show the written questions to their partners, as the purpose of the activity is to practice listening as well as speaking. Encourage students to point to places in the text that help them answer the questions.

Possible questions:

- *Who is he?*
- *Where is he?*
- *What is he holding?*
- *Why is he holding that?*
- *What is he saying?* **ALL LEVELS**

 **NOTICE & NOTE**

same skull, sir, was, sir, Yorick's skull, the King's jester.

185 **Hamlet.** This?

Gravedigger. E'en that.

Hamlet [*taking the skull*]. Let me see. Alas, poor Yorick! I knew him, Horatio—a fellow of infinite jest, of most excellent fancy. He hath bore me on his back
190 a thousand times, and now how abhorred in my

imagination it is! My gorge rises at it. Here hung
those lips that I have kissed I know not how oft.
Where be your gibes now? your gambols? your
songs? your flashes of merriment that were wont to
195 set the table on a roar? Not one now to mock your
own grinning? Quite chapfallen? Now get you to
my lady's chamber, and tell her, let her paint an
inch thick, to this favor she must come. Make her
laugh at that.—Prithee, Horatio, tell me one thing.

200 **Horatio.** What's that, my lord?

Hamlet. Dost thou think Alexander looked o' this
fashion i' th' earth?

Horatio. E'en so.

Hamlet. And smelt so? Pah!

[*He puts the skull down.*]

205 **Horatio.** E'en so, my lord.

Hamlet. To what base uses we may return, Horatio!
Why may not imagination trace the noble dust of
Alexander till he find it stopping a bunghole?

Horatio. 'Twere to consider too curiously to consider so.

210 **Hamlet.** No, faith, not a jot; but to follow him thither,
with modesty enough and likelihood to lead it, as
thus: Alexander died, Alexander was buried,
Alexander returneth to dust; the dust is earth; of
earth we make loam; and why of that loam whereto
215 he was converted might they not stop a beer barrel?
Imperious Caesar, dead and turned to clay,
Might stop a hole to keep the wind away.
O, that that earth which kept the world in awe
Should patch a wall t' expel the winter's flaw!

[*Enter* King, Queen, Laertes, Lords attendant, *and the corpse of*
Ophelia, *with a* Doctor of Divinity.]

220 But soft, but soft awhile! Here comes the King,
The Queen, the courtiers. Who is this they follow?
And with such maimèd rites? This doth betoken
The corse they follow did with desp'rate hand
Fordo its own life. 'Twas of some estate.
225 Couch we awhile and mark.

[*They step aside.*]

Laertes. What ceremony else?

Hamlet. That is Laertes, a very noble youth. Mark.

---

193 gibes: taunts; **gambols:** pranks.

196 chapfallen: down in the mouth, missing the lower jaw.

197–198 let her . . . come: Even if she covers her face with an inch of makeup, eventually she will have this appearance (**favor**).

201 Alexander: Alexander the Great.

208 bunghole: a hole in a keg or barrel for pouring liquid.

209 curiously: minutely, closely.

211 modesty: moderation.

214 loam: a mixture of clay, sand, and straw used for plastering.

216 Imperious: imperial.

219 flaw: gust of wind.

222 maimèd: incomplete.

224 Fordo: destroy; **some estate:** high rank.

225 Couch . . . mark: Let us conceal ourselves awhile and observe.

ANALYZE DRAMATIC PLOT
Annotate: Mark details in lines 220–225 that reflect a change in Hamlet's tone.

Predict: Hamlet does not seem to have heard about Ophelia's death. How do you predict he will react to this news?

TEACH

NOTICE & NOTE

229–233 The priest says he has performed her funeral rites to the extent allowed under church law. The manner of her death was suspicious, and if the King's orders hadn't overruled the procedures, she would have remained buried in unsanctified ground until Judgment Day.

233 For: instead of.

234 Shards: pieces of broken pottery; **should be:** would have been.

235 virgin crants: wreaths placed on the coffin as a sign of virginity.

236 strewments: flowers strewn on a grave.

236–237 bringing . . . burial: being laid to rest in consecrated ground with church bells tolling.

240–241 such rest . . . souls: pray for her to have the same rest as those who died in peace.

245 howling: in hell.

252–253 thy most . . . thee of: deprived you of your excellent mind.

257 Pelion: In Greek mythology, giants placed Mount Pelion on top of Mount Ossa in an attempt to reach the top of Mount Olympus, home of the gods.

260–261 wand'ring stars: planets; **wonder-wounded:** struck with amazement.

Laertes. What ceremony else?

Doctor. Her obsequies have been as far enlarged
230 As we have warranty. Her death was doubtful,
And, but that great command o'ersways the order,
She should in ground unsanctified been lodged
Till the last trumpet. For charitable prayers
Shards, flints, and pebbles should be thrown on her.
235 Yet here she is allowed her virgin crants,
Her maiden strewments, and the bringing home
Of bell and burial.

Laertes. Must there no more be done?

Doctor.   No more be done.
We should profane the service of the dead
240 To sing a requiem and such rest to her
As to peace-parted souls.

Laertes.   Lay her i' th' earth,
And from her fair and unpolluted flesh
May violets spring! I tell thee, churlish priest,
A minist'ring angel shall my sister be
245 When thou liest howling.

Hamlet [to Horatio].   What, the fair Ophelia?

Queen. Sweets to the sweet, farewell!

[*She scatters flowers.*]

I hoped thou shouldst have been my Hamlet's wife;
I thought thy bride-bed to have decked, sweet maid,
250 And not have strewed thy grave.

Laertes.   O, treble woe
Fall ten times treble on that cursèd head
Whose wicked deed thy most ingenious sense
Deprived thee of!—Hold off the earth awhile,
Till I have caught her once more in mine arms.

[*Leaps in the grave.*]

255 Now pile your dust upon the quick and dead,
Till of this flat a mountain you have made
T' o'ertop old Pelion or the skyish head
Of blue Olympus.

Hamlet [*advancing*]. What is he whose grief
Bears such an emphasis, whose phrase of sorrow
260 Conjures the wand'ring stars and makes them stand
Like wonder-wounded hearers? This is I,
Hamlet the Dane.

Laertes [*coming out of the grave*].

IMPROVE READING FLUENCY

Targeted Passage Focus students' attention on Scene 1, lines 238–245, page 256. Using the side notes for support, have students work with a partner to discuss what Laertes and the doctor are arguing about. Ask them to consider what each character's attitude and emotions are. Have them read the lines aloud, each taking a part, and attempt to evoke the characters' attitudes. Next, demonstrate a dramatic reading of the lines, asking students to listen carefully to compare their readings to yours. Then, have them practice reading the lines in pairs again, adjusting their readings to match yours.

                                The devil take thy soul!

Hamlet. Thou pray'st not well.

[*They grapple.*]
        I prithee take thy fingers from my throat,
265   For though I am not splenitive and rash,
        Yet have I in me something dangerous,
        Which let thy wisdom fear. Hold off thy hand.

King. Pluck them asunder.

Queen. Hamlet! Hamlet!

270 **All.** Gentlemen!

Horatio. Good my lord, be quiet.

[*Hamlet and Laertes are separated.*]

Hamlet. Why, I will fight with him upon this theme
        Until my eyelids will no longer wag!

Queen. O my son, what theme?

275 **Hamlet.** I loved Ophelia. Forty thousand brothers
        Could not with all their quantity of love
        Make up my sum. What wilt thou do for her?

King. O, he is mad, Laertes!

Queen. For love of God, forbear him.

280 **Hamlet.** 'Swounds, show me what thou't do.
        Woo't weep, woo't fight, woo't fast, woo't tear thyself,
        Woo't drink up eisel, eat a crocodile?
        I'll do 't. Dost thou come here to whine?
        To outface me with leaping in her grave?
285   Be buried quick with her, and so will I.
        And if thou prate of mountains, let them throw
        Millions of acres on us, till our ground,
        Singeing his pate against the burning zone,
        Make Ossa like a wart. Nay, an thou'lt mouth,
290   I'll rant as well as thou.

Queen.   This is mere madness;
        And thus awhile the fit will work on him.
        Anon, as patient as the female dove
        When that her golden couplets are disclosed,
        His silence will sit drooping.

Hamlet.   Hear you, sir,
295   What is the reason that you use me thus?
        I loved you ever. But it is no matter.
        Let Hercules himself do what he may,
        The cat will mew, and dog will have his day.

NOTICE & NOTE

265 **splenitive:** quick-tempered.

ANALYZE CONFLICT
Annotate: In lines 272–290, mark statements that explain the cause of Hamlet's anger.

Draw Conclusions: Is Hamlet's response consistent with his earlier treatment of Ophelia? Why or why not?

279 **forbear him:** leave him alone.

281 **Woo't:** wilt thou.
282 **eisel:** vinegar.

285 **quick:** alive.

288 **Singeing his . . . zone:** burning its head in the sphere of the sun's orbit.

289 **Ossa:** See note to line 257, **an thou'lt mouth:** if you rant.

290 **mere:** utter.

292–294 Soon Hamlet will fall as silent as a dove after its twin baby birds (**couplets**) are hatched.

The Tragedy of Hamlet: Act V, Scene 1   257

TEACH

ENGLISH LEARNER SUPPORT

Demonstrate Comprehension Explain to students that in Scene 2, lines 12–25, Hamlet tells the story of what happened while he was on the ship with Rosencrantz and Guildenstern. Set the scene for them with drawings or images of a ship and a sealed letter. As you read the lines aloud, direct students to act out the action of the story using a prop letter. Direct students' attention to line 19, *an exact command,* and ask students to explain what the command is. Finally, have students demonstrate their comprehension by writing the contents of the letter Hamlet finds.
SUBSTANTIAL/MODERATE

 **NOTICE & NOTE**

299 wait upon: accompany.

[*Hamlet exits.*]

King. I pray thee, good Horatio, wait upon him.

[*Horatio exits.*]

300 [*To Laertes.*] Strengthen your patience in our last
    night's speech.
We'll put the matter to the present push.—
Good Gertrude, set some watch over your son.—
This grave shall have a living monument.
An hour of quiet shortly shall we see;
305 Till then in patience our proceeding be.

[*They exit.*]

301 to the present push: into immediate action.

Scene 2 *The hall of the castle.*

[*Enter* Hamlet *and* Horatio.]

Hamlet. So much for this, sir. Now shall you see the
    other.
You do remember all the circumstance?

Horatio. Remember it, my lord!

1 see the other: hear the rest of the story.

Hamlet. Sir, in my heart there was a kind of fighting
5   That would not let me sleep. Methought I lay
Worse than the mutines in the bilboes. Rashly—
And praised be rashness for it: let us know,
Our indiscretion sometime serves us well
When our deep plots do pall; and that should learn us
10 There's a divinity that shapes our ends,
Rough-hew them how we will—

6 mutines: mutineers; **bilboes:** shackles, chains.
8 indiscretion: hasty actions.
9 pall: falter; **learn:** teach.
10–11 There's a . . . will: A divine power guides our destinies, despite our clumsy attempts to fashion them ourselves.

Horatio.   That is most certain.

Hamlet. Up from my cabin,
My sea-gown scarfed about me, in the dark
Groped I to find out them; had my desire,
15 Fingered their packet, and in fine withdrew
To mine own room again, making so bold
(My fears forgetting manners) to unfold
Their grand commission; where I found, Horatio,
A royal knavery—an exact command,
20 Larded with many several sorts of reasons
Importing Denmark's health and England's too,
With—ho!—such bugs and goblins in my life,
That on the supervise, no leisure bated,
No, not to stay the grinding of the ax,
25 My head should be struck off.

13 scarfed: wrapped.
14 them: Rosencrantz and Guildenstern.
15 Fingered: stole; **in fine:** finally.

20 Larded: embellished.
21 Importing: concerning.
22 bugs . . . life: imaginary terrors in my remaining alive.
23 on the supervise: upon reading this; **no leisure bated:** without hesitation.
24 stay: wait for.

Horatio.   Is 't possible?

258   Unit 2

WHEN STUDENTS STRUGGLE . . .

Paraphrase and Retell Point out that significant action has occurred offstage. Here, with Horatio as his confidant, Hamlet tells us about the adventure at sea. Read Hamlet's story, stopping after each detail to paraphrase for students. Then, have students turn to a partner and practice retelling the story.

 For additional support, go to the **Reading Studio** and assign the following **Level Up tutorial: Paraphrasing.**

NOTICE & NOTE

Hamlet. Here's the commission. Read it at more leisure.
[*Handing him a paper.*]
But wilt thou hear now how I did proceed?

Horatio. I beseech you.

Hamlet. Being thus benetted round with villainies,
30   Or I could make a prologue to my brains,
     They had begun the play. I sat me down,
     Devised a new commission, wrote it fair—
     I once did hold it, as our statists do,
     A baseness to write fair, and labored much
35   How to forget that learning; but, sir, now
     It did me yeoman's service. Wilt thou know
     Th' effect of what I wrote?

Horatio.   Ay, good my lord.

Hamlet. An earnest conjuration from the King,
     As England was his faithful tributary,
40   As love between them like the palm might flourish,
     As peace should still her wheaten garland wear
     And stand a comma 'tween their amities,
     And many suchlike ases of great charge,
     That, on the view and knowing of these contents,
45   Without debatement further, more or less,
     He should those bearers put to sudden death,
     Not shriving time allowed.

Horatio.   How was this sealed?

Hamlet. Why, even in that was heaven ordinant.
     I had my father's signet in my purse,
50   Which was the model of that Danish seal;
     Folded the writ up in the form of th' other,
     Subscribed it, gave 't th' impression, placed it safely,
     The changeling never known. Now, the next day
     Was our sea-fight; and what to this was sequent
55   Thou knowest already.

Horatio. So Guildenstern and Rosencrantz go to 't.

Hamlet. Why, man, they did make love to this employment.
     They are not near my conscience. Their defeat
     Does by their own insinuation grow.
60   'Tis dangerous when the baser nature comes
     Between the pass and fell incensèd points
     Of mighty opposites.

Horatio. Why, what a king is this!

Hamlet. Does it not, think thee, stand me now upon—

30–31 Before Hamlet had time to consider what to do, his brains started working out a plan.

33–36 Like a politician, Hamlet once considered it beneath him to write neatly (as a clerk would), but his handwriting gave him substantial service.

39 tributary: a nation controlled by another.

41 still: always; **wheaten garland:** symbol of peace and prosperity.

42 stand . . . amities: join their friendships.

43 suchlike . . . charge: similar legal phrases of great import beginning with "whereas." (Hamlet is ridiculing official language.)

47 shriving time: time for confession and absolution of sins.

48 ordinant: controlling events.

50 model: likeness.

52 Subscribed . . . impression: signed and sealed it.

53 changeling: substitution.

54 what to this was sequent: what followed.

58 defeat: destruction.

59 insinuation: worming their way in.

60–62 'Tis . . . opposites: It is dangerous for inferior people to come between the fiercely thrusting sword points of mighty antagonists.

The Tragedy of Hamlet: Act V, Scene 2   259

TEACH

ENGLISH LEARNER SUPPORT

Demonstrate Comprehension Read Scene 2, lines 29–37, page 259, and explain to students that in these lines Hamlet explains what he did in response to finding the letter ordering his execution. Point out that the phrase *devised a new commission* means "made a new letter." In lines 38–47, Hamlet describes what he wrote in the letter. Have students work in pairs or in a group to answer these questions:

- What is the purpose of what Hamlet says he wrote in lines 38–45?
- Who are "the bearers"?
- What does the letter ask the King of England to do? **LIGHT**

TO CHALLENGE STUDENTS . . .

Evaluate Character's Actions Have students evaluate Hamlet's actions in response to finding the letter, and answer the following questions in a group:

- Were Hamlet's actions just?
- Do Hamlet's actions reflect any change in his character?
- Do you feel Rosencrantz and Guildenstern deserved their fate? Explain.

TEACH

NOTICE & NOTE

66 The Danish king was elected by a small group of electors.

68 cozenage: deception.

69 quit: pay back.

70–71 come In: grow into.

74–75 Hamlet says that although he only has a short time in which to act, a man's life is also brief, lasting no longer than it takes to count to one.

78 image: likeness.

80 bravery: showiness.

88–89 Let a . . . mess: If a man owns a lot of livestock, no matter how much he resembles them, he may eat at the king's table.

89 chough: chattering bird.

93–106 Men commonly wore their hats indoors but removed them in the presence of superiors. Hamlet mocks not only this show of respect but also Osric's insistence on agreeing with everything Hamlet says.

98 indifferent: somewhat.

100 complexion: temperament.

65 He that hath killed my king and whored my mother,
Popped in between th' election and my hopes,
Thrown out his angle for my proper life,
And with such cozenage—is 't not perfect conscience
To quit him with this arm? And is 't not to be damned
70 To let this canker of our nature come
In further evil?

Horatio. It must be shortly known to him from England
What is the issue of the business there.

Hamlet. It will be short. The interim's mine,
75 And a man's life's no more than to say "one."
But I am very sorry, good Horatio,
That to Laertes I forgot myself,
For by the image of my cause I see
The portraiture of his. I'll court his favors.
80 But, sure, the bravery of his grief did put me
Into a tow'ring passion.

Horatio.   Peace, who comes here?

[*Enter* Osric, *a courtier.*]

Osric. Your lordship is right welcome back to Denmark.

Hamlet. I humbly thank you, sir. [*Aside to* Horatio.]
Dost know this waterfly?

85 **Horatio** [*aside to* Hamlet]. No, my good lord.

Hamlet [*aside to* Horatio]. Thy state is the more gracious, for 'tis a vice to know him. He hath much land, and fertile. Let a beast be lord of beasts and his crib shall stand at the king's mess. 'Tis a chough,
90 but, as I say, spacious in the possession of dirt.

Osric. Sweet lord, if your lordship were at leisure, I should impart a thing to you from his Majesty.

Hamlet. I will receive it, sir, with all diligence of spirit. Put your bonnet to his right use: 'tis for the head.

95 **Osric.** I thank your lordship; it is very hot.

Hamlet. No, believe me, 'tis very cold; the wind is northerly.

Osric. It is indifferent cold, my lord, indeed.

Hamlet. But yet methinks it is very sultry and hot for
100 my complexion.

Osric. Exceedingly, my lord; it is very sultry, as 'twere—I cannot tell how. My lord, his Majesty bade me signify to you that he has laid a great

260 Unit 2

WHEN STUDENTS STRUGGLE . . .

Analyze Change in Character's Attitude Focus students' attention on Scene 2, lines 65–72, page 260. Read these lines aloud and ask students to identify Hamlet's opinion about whether he should kill Claudius. The,n have them look for the details he uses to support this claim. Have students discuss these questions: How has Hamlet's attitude changed about killing Claudius? Why might he now have a different attitude? What new reason does he have? (*Claudius has tried to have him killed.*)

 For additional support, go to the **Reading Studio** and assign the following **Level up tutorial: Character Motivation**.

wager on your head. Sir, this is the matter—

105 **Hamlet.** I beseech you, remember.

[*He motions to* Osric *to put on his hat.*]

Osric. Nay, good my lord, for my ease, in good faith. Sir, here is newly come to court Laertes—believe me, an absolute gentleman, full of most excellent differences, of very soft society and great showing.
110 Indeed, to speak feelingly of him, he is the card or calendar of gentry, for you shall find in him the continent of what part a gentleman would see.

Hamlet. Sir, his definement suffers no perdition in you, though I know to divide him inventorially would
115 dozy th' arithmetic of memory, and yet but yaw neither, in respect of his quick sail. But, in the verity of extolment, I take him to be a soul of great article, and his infusion of such dearth and rareness as, to make true diction of him, his semblable is his mirror,
120 and who else would trace him, his umbrage, nothing more.

Osric. Your lordship speaks most infallibly of him.

Hamlet. The concernancy, sir? Why do we wrap the gentleman in our more rawer breath?

125 **Osric.** Sir?

Horatio [*aside to* Hamlet]. Is 't not possible to understand in another tongue? You will to 't, sir, really.

Hamlet [*to* Osric]. What imports the nomination of this gentleman?

130 **Osric.** Of Laertes?

Horatio [*aside*]. His purse is empty already; all 's golden words are spent.

Hamlet. Of him, sir.

Osric. I know you are not ignorant—

135 **Hamlet.** I would you did, sir. Yet, in faith, if you did, it would not much approve me. Well, sir?

Osric. You are not ignorant of what excellence Laertes is—

Hamlet. I dare not confess that, lest I should compare
140 with him in excellence. But to know a man well were to know himself.

Osric. I mean, sir, for his weapon. But in the imputation

NOTICE & NOTE

110–112 Among his compliments, Osric calls Laertes the map or guide (**card or calendar**) of good breeding, one who contains in him (**the continent of**) all the qualities a gentleman would look for.

113–121 Hamlet, mocking Osric's flowery speech, says that nothing has been lost in Osric's definition of Laertes, but the calculations needed to make an inventory of Laertes' excellences would be dizzying, and even then one would fail to capture him. He goes on to say that the only true likeness (**semblable**) of Laertes is his reflection in a mirror, and anyone who wanted to copy him would be nothing more than his shadow (**umbrage**).

123–124 Hamlet asks why they are speaking about Laertes.

128 What imports . . . of: for what purpose are you mentioning.

131 all 's: all his.

136 approve: commend.

142–143 In the reputation others have given him, his merit (**meed**) is unmatched.

TEACH

TO CHALLENGE STUDENTS . . .

Identify and Analyze Satire Provide the definition of satire—ridiculing ideas, customs, behaviors, or institutions to improve society. Explain that Hamlet's interactions with Osric are repeated instances of satire. This use of satire at the expense of the upper classes was another reason Shakespeare was popular with those at the lower end of the social ladder. Have students carefully read Scene 2, lines 82–121, pages 260–261, and discuss in a group how Shakespeare uses satire. Then ask students to give a short presentation to the rest of the class on the use of satire in this passage.

TEACH

ENGLISH LEARNER SUPPORT

Demonstrate Comprehension Explain to students that in Scene 2, lines 147–169, page 262, Osric is explaining that the king has made a *wager* that involves him. Supply the meaning of the word *wager* (bet) and point out that the words *impawn* and *stake* (from the side notes) have the same meaning. If students need more help understanding the words, use visual supports that they will recognize such as an image of a poker table and a casino. Make sure they understand that a bet is made on the outcome of some event or contest.

Have students work in small same-level groups and read the text carefully to answer these questions?

- What items has the King put up in this bet? *(six Barbary horses)*
- What items has Laertes put up? *(six French swords with their accessories)*
- What event or contest are they betting on? *(a duel between Hamlet and Laertes)* **LIGHT**

NOTICE & NOTE

145 Rapier and dagger: a type of fencing with a rapier (sword) held in the right hand and a dagger in the left.

147–153 Against Claudius's wager, Laertes has staked six rapiers and daggers, along with their accessories, such as straps (**hangers**) to hold the swords onto a sword belt (**girdle**), and so forth. Three of the hangers are fancifully designed, well adjusted, finely crafted, and have an elaborate design.

155–156 Horatio jokes that he knew Hamlet would seek explanation in a marginal note.

159 cannon by our sides: an affected term for "hanger," *carriage* normally refers to the wheeled base of a cannon.

165 laid: wagered.
166 passes: bouts, exchanges; **him:** Laertes.
169 vouchsafe the answer: accept the challenge.

174 breathing time of day: usual time for exercise.
175 foils: swords with blunt tips.

182 commend: present to your favor.

---

laid on him by them, in his meed he's unfellowed.

Hamlet. What's his weapon?

145 **Osric.** Rapier and dagger.

Hamlet. That's two of his weapons. But, well—

Osric. The King, sir, hath wagered with him six Barbary horses, against the which he has impawned, as I take it, six French rapiers and poniards, with their
150 assigns, as girdle, hangers, and so. Three of the carriages, in faith, are very dear to fancy, very responsive to the hilts, most delicate carriages, and of very liberal conceit.

Hamlet. What call you the "carriages"?

155 **Horatio** [*aside to* Hamlet]. I knew you must be edified by the margent ere you had done.

Osric. The carriages, sir, are the hangers.

Hamlet. The phrase would be more germane to the matter if we could carry a cannon by our sides. I
160 would it might be "hangers" till then. But on. Six Barbary horses against six French swords, their assigns, and three liberal-conceited carriages— that's the French bet against the Danish. Why is this all "impawned," as you call it?

165 **Osric.** The King, sir, hath laid, sir, that in a dozen passes between yourself and him, he shall not exceed you three hits. He hath laid on twelve for nine, and it would come to immediate trial if your lordship would vouchsafe the answer.

170 **Hamlet.** How if I answer no?

Osric. I mean, my lord, the opposition of your person in trial.

Hamlet. Sir, I will walk here in the hall. If it please his Majesty, it is the breathing time of day with me.
175 Let the foils be brought, the gentleman willing, and the King hold his purpose, I will win for him, an I can. If not, I will gain nothing but my shame and the odd hits.

Osric. Shall I deliver you e'en so?

180 **Hamlet.** To this effect, sir, after what flourish your nature will.

Osric. I commend my duty to your lordship.

Hamlet. Yours. [Osric *exits.*] He does well to commend

it himself. There are no tongues else for 's turn.

185 **Horatio.** This lapwing runs away with the shell on his head.

Hamlet. He did comply, sir, with his dug before he sucked it. Thus has he (and many more of the same breed that I know the drossy age dotes on) only
190 got the tune of the time, and, out of an habit of encounter, a kind of yeasty collection, which carries them through and through the most fanned and winnowed opinions; and do but blow them to their trial, the bubbles are out.

[*Enter a* Lord.]

195 **Lord.** My lord, his Majesty commended him to you by young Osric, who brings back to him that you attend him in the hall. He sends to know if your pleasure hold to play with Laertes, or that you will take longer time.

200 **Hamlet.** I am constant to my purposes. They follow the King's pleasure. If his fitness speaks, mine is ready now or whensoever, provided I be so able as now.

Lord. The King and Queen and all are coming down.

205 **Hamlet.** In happy time.

Lord. The Queen desires you to use some gentle entertainment to Laertes before you fall to play.

Hamlet. She well instructs me.

[Lord *exits.*]

Horatio. You will lose, my lord.

210 **Hamlet.** I do not think so. Since he went into France, I have been in continual practice. I shall win at the odds; but thou wouldst not think how ill all's here about my heart. But it is no matter.

Horatio. Nay, good my lord—

215 **Hamlet.** It is but foolery, but it is such a kind of gaingiving as would perhaps trouble a woman.

Horatio. If your mind dislike anything, obey it. I will forestall their repair hither and say you are not fit.

Hamlet. Not a whit. We defy augury. There is a special
220 providence in the fall of a sparrow. If it be now, 'tis not to come; if it be not to come, it will be now; if it be not now, yet it will come. The readiness is all.

---

185 lapwing: A bird that supposedly left its nest soon after hatching and ran around with its shell on its head—probably a reference to Osric's hat.

187–194 After joking that Osric paid courtesies to his mother's nipple before nursing, Hamlet complains that Osric and his type, popular in this worthless age, have only picked up a fashionable manner of speaking (**the tune of the time**) and a frothy collection of phrases that help them move through refined society (**fanned and winnowed opinions**), but the bubbles burst as soon as they are tested.

201–202 If his . . . whensoever: I am ready at his convenience.

205 In happy time: a polite phrase of welcome.

206 use some gentle entertainment: show some courtesy.

215 gaingiving: misgiving.

218 repair: coming.

TEACH

NOTICE & NOTE

219–224 Hamlet rejects **augury** (attempting to foresee the future by interpreting omens) and declares that since the death of even a sparrow is not left to chance, he is ready to accept any circumstances he encounters; his death will come sooner or later. He concludes that since man knows nothing about the life he leaves behind, what does it matter if he leaves early?

227 presence: royal assembly.

229 sore distraction: severe confusion.

230 exception: disapproval.

237 faction: party.

240 purposed evil: intentional harm.
242 That I have: as if I had.

244–250 Laertes is satisfied in regard to his own feelings (**nature**), but in regard to his honor he will wait until men experienced in such matters have given their authoritative judgment (**voice and precedent**) in favor of reconciliation, which would allow him to keep his reputation undamaged (**name ungored**).

253 frankly: without any hard feelings.

255 foil: metallic background used to display a jewel (punning on **foils,** referring to the blunted swords).

Since no man of aught he leaves knows, what is 't
to leave betimes? Let be.

[*A table prepared. Enter Trumpets, Drums, and* Officers *with cushions,*
King, Queen, Osric, *and all the state, foils, daggers, flagons of wine,*
and Laertes.]

225 **King.** Come, Hamlet, come and take this hand from me.

[*He puts* Laertes' *hand into* Hamlet's.]

Hamlet [*to* Laertes]. Give me your pardon, sir. I have
done you wrong;
But pardon 't as you are a gentleman. This presence
knows,
And you must needs have heard, how I am punished
With a sore distraction. What I have done
230 That might your nature, honor, and exception
Roughly awake, I here proclaim was madness.
Was 't Hamlet wronged Laertes? Never Hamlet.
If Hamlet from himself be ta'en away.
And when he's not himself does wrong Laertes,
235 Then Hamlet does it not; Hamlet denies it.
Who does it, then? His madness. If 't be so,
Hamlet is of the faction that is wronged;
His madness is poor Hamlet's enemy.
Sir, in this audience
240 Let my disclaiming from a purposed evil
Free me so far in your most generous thoughts
That I have shot my arrow o'er the house
And hurt my brother.

Laertes. I am satisfied in nature,
245 Whose motive in this case should stir me most
To my revenge; but in my terms of honor
I stand aloof and will no reconcilement
Till by some elder masters of known honor
I have a voice and precedent of peace
250 To keep my name ungored. But till that time
I do receive your offered love like love
And will not wrong it.

Hamlet. I embrace it freely
And will this brothers' wager frankly play.—
Give us the foils. Come on.

Laertes. Come, one for me.

255 **Hamlet.** I'll be your foil, Laertes; in mine ignorance
Your skill shall, like a star i' th' darkest night,
Stick fiery off indeed.

264 Unit 2

APPLYING ACADEMIC VOCABULARY

❏ **ambiguous**   ❏ **anticipate**   ☑ **conceive**   ❏ **drama**   ❏ **integrity**

Write and Discuss Have students turn to a partner to discuss the following question. Guide students to include the academic vocabulary word *conceive* in their responses. Ask volunteers to share their responses with the class.

- Hamlet and Horatio are arguing about whether Hamlet should agree to the fencing match. What plan have Claudius and Laertes **conceived** that Hamlet is unaware of?

Laertes. You mock me, sir.

Hamlet. No, by this hand.

King. Give them the foils, young Osric. Cousin Hamlet,
260 You know the wager?

Hamlet. Very well, my lord.
Your Grace has laid the odds o' th' weaker side.

King. I do not fear it; I have seen you both.
But, since he is better, we have therefore odds.

Laertes. This is too heavy. Let me see another.

265 **Hamlet.** This likes me well. These foils have all a length?

Osric. Ay, my good lord.

[*Prepare to play.*]

King. Set me the stoups of wine upon that table.—
If Hamlet give the first or second hit
Or quit in answer of the third exchange,
270 Let all the battlements their ordnance fire.
The King shall drink to Hamlet's better breath,
And in the cup an union shall he throw,
Richer than that which four successive kings
In Denmark's crown have worn. Give me the cups,
275 And let the kettle to the trumpet speak,
The trumpet to the cannoneer without,
The cannons to the heavens, the heaven to earth,
"Now the King drinks to Hamlet." Come, begin.
And you, the judges, bear a wary eye.

[*Trumpets the while.*]

280 **Hamlet.** Come on, sir.

Laertes. Come, my lord.

[*They play.*]

Hamlet. One.

Laertes. No.

Hamlet. Judgment!

285 **Osric.** A hit, a very palpable hit.

Laertes. Well, again.

King. Stay, give me drink.—Hamlet, this pearl is thine.
Here's to thy health.

[*He drinks and then drops the pearl in the cup. Drum, trumpets, and shot.*]

Give him the cup.

---

257 Stick fiery off: stand out brilliantly.

260–261 Hamlet comments that Claudius has bet on (**laid the odds o'**) the weaker fencer. Claudius expresses confidence in Hamlet, but says he has arranged a handicap (**odds**) for Laertes because he has improved.

265 likes me: pleases me; **have all a length:** are all the same length.

269 quit ... exchange: gets back at Laertes by scoring the third hit.

272 union: pearl.

275 kettle: kettledrum.

TEACH

ENGLISH LEARNER SUPPORT

Demonstrate Comprehension Focus students' attention on Scene 2, lines 226–244, page 245. Point out that Hamlet is asking Laertes for forgiveness. Hamlet is attempting to solve one of the central conflicts of the play, that he killed Polonius and now Laertes is seeking revenge against him. Have students work in groups to read the text carefully and answer the following questions:

- What reason does Hamlet give for his actions? *(He was mad at the time.)*
- Who does Hamlet blame? *(Hamlet blames himself because he was mad.)*
- What action does Hamlet compare his actions to? *(Shooting an arrow over a house and accidentally hurting his brother.)*
- Will this resolve the conflict? Why or why not? *(Probably not. Laertes is planning to kill him in the fencing match.)*

MODERATE/LIGHT

WHEN STUDENTS STRUGGLE . . .

Identify Plot Points Explain that Shakespeare uses the king's directions to remind the audience of important elements of the plot. Ask students to examine Scene 2, lines 267–279, page 266, and identify lines that notify the audience of an important bit of stagecraft needed to advance the plot. *(In lines 271–274, the king suggests he will give Hamlet a cup containing a valuable pearl for his success in any of the first three rounds of swordplay; the pearl is meant to mark the cup that is poisoned to cause Hamlet's death.)*

For additional support, go to the **Reading Studio** and assign the following Level Up tutorial: **Characters and Conflict**.

 **NOTICE & NOTE**

Hamlet. I'll play this bout first. Set it by awhile.
290 Come. [*They play.*] Another hit. What say you?

Laertes. A touch, a touch. I do confess 't.

King. Our son shall win.

Queen. He's fat and scant of breath.
Here, Hamlet, take my napkin; rub thy brows.
The Queen carouses to thy fortune, Hamlet.

[*She lifts the cup.*]

295 **Hamlet.** Good madam.

King. Gertrude, do not drink.

Queen. I will, my lord; I pray you pardon me.

[*She drinks.*]

King [*aside*]. It is the poisoned cup. It is too late.

Hamlet. I dare not drink yet, madam—by and by.

300 **Queen.** Come, let me wipe thy face.

Laertes [*to* Claudius]. My lord, I'll hit him now.

King. I do not think 't.

Laertes [*aside*]. And yet it is almost against my conscience.

Hamlet. Come, for the third, Laertes. You do but dally.
I pray you pass with your best violence.
305 I am afeard you make a wanton of me.

Laertes. Say you so? Come on. [*Play.*]

Osric. Nothing neither way.

Laertes. Have at you now!

[Laertes *wounds* Hamlet. *Then in scuffling they change rapiers, and* Hamlet *wounds* Laertes.]

King. Part them. They are incensed.

310 **Hamlet.** Nay, come again.

[*The* Queen *falls.*]

Osric. Look to the Queen there, ho!

Horatio. They bleed on both sides.—How is it, my lord?

Osric. How is 't, Laertes?

Laertes. Why as a woodcock to mine own springe, Osric.

[*He falls.*]

315 I am justly killed with mine own treachery.

Hamlet. How does the Queen?

---

292 fat: sweaty.
293 napkin: handkerchief.

304 pass: thrust.
305 make a wanton of me: indulge me as if I were a spoiled child.

314 Laertes says he's been caught like a **woodcock** (a proverbially stupid bird) in his own trap.

NOTICE & NOTE

Hamlet dueling with Laertes (Terence Morgan)

The Tragedy of Hamlet: Act V, Scene 2 267

TEACH

ENGLISH LEARNER SUPPORT

Describe and Explain Have students describe what is happening in the image and name the characters that they expect to be in this image. Have them explain what Claudius's plan is and predict what they think will happen. Supply these questions to guide their answers:

- Who is that?
- What are they doing?
- Why are they doing that?
- Who is watching?
- What will happen?   **SUBSTANTIAL/LIGHT**

IMPROVE READING FLUENCY

Targeted Passage To help students understand the events in Scene 2, lines 289–319, pages 266 and 268, divide the students into groups, assigning each a part: Hamlet, Laertes, Osric, Claudius, and Gertrude. Read the lines aloud with appropriate dramatic expression and have the groups echo your parts. Then, have each group practice its part in a choral reading. Finally, put students into new groups in which each has one of the parts and have them act out the scene. Struggling students can share a part and read together.

TEACH

ANALYZE DRAMATIC PLOT

Point out that in this passage, Hamlet is dying and giving his last request to his trusted friend, Horatio, who has witnessed all of these events. To explain his request, have students think about what they know of Hamlet's character and what is important to him. Remind them of what Claudius has said about the people of Denmark's opinion of Hamlet. (**Answer:** *Hamlet asks Horatio to tell his story to the people so they know the truth of what happened. Hamlet is beloved by the people of Denmark, and his reputation is very important to him. He will want them to know he died honorably and with good cause.*)

 **NOTICE & NOTE**

King. She swoons to see them bleed.

Queen. No, no, the drink, the drink! O, my dear Hamlet!
The drink, the drink! I am poisoned. [*She dies.*]

Hamlet. O villainy! Ho! Let the door be locked.

[*Osric exits.*]

320 Treachery! Seek it out.

Laertes. It is here, Hamlet. Hamlet, thou art slain.
No med'cine in the world can do thee good.
In thee there is not half an hour's life.
The treacherous instrument is in thy hand,
325 Unbated and envenomed. The foul practice
Hath turned itself on me. Lo, here I lie,
Never to rise again. Thy mother's poisoned.
I can no more. The King, the King's to blame.

Hamlet. The point envenomed too! Then, venom, to thy work. [*Hurts the King.*]

330 **All.** Treason, treason!

King. O, yet defend me, friends! I am but hurt.

Hamlet. Here, thou incestuous, murd'rous, damnèd Dane,
Drink off this potion. Is thy union here?

[*Forcing him to drink the poison.*]

Follow my mother.

[*King dies.*]

Laertes. He is justly served.
335 It is a poison tempered by himself.
Exchange forgiveness with me, noble Hamlet.
Mine and my father's death come not upon thee,
Nor thine on me.

[*Dies.*]

Hamlet. Heaven make thee free of it. I follow thee.—
340 I am dead, Horatio.—Wretched queen, adieu.—
You that look pale and tremble at this chance,
That are but mutes or audience to this act,
Had I but time (as this fell sergeant, Death,
Is strict in his arrest), O, I could tell you—
345 But let it be.—Horatio, I am dead.
Thou livest; <u>report me and my cause aright
To the unsatisfied.</u>

---

325 unbated: not blunted; **practice:** trick.

333 union: a pun on the meanings "pearl" and "marriage." (Claudius is joining his wife in death.)

335 tempered: mixed.

342 mutes: silent observers (literally, actors without speaking parts).

343 fell sergeant: cruel arresting officer.

ANALYZE DRAMATIC PLOT
Annotate: Mark Hamlet's instructions to Horatio in lines 340–356.

Analyze: Why is this request so important to Hamlet?

Horatio. Never believe it.
I am more an antique Roman than a Dane.
Here's yet some liquor left.

[*He picks up the cup.*]

Hamlet. As thou'rt a man,
350 Give me the cup. Let go! By heaven, I'll ha 't.
O God, Horatio, what a wounded name,
Things standing thus unknown, shall I leave behind me!
If thou didst ever hold me in thy heart,
Absent thee from felicity awhile
355 And in this harsh world draw thy breath in pain
To tell my story.

[*A march afar off and shot within.*]

What warlike noise is this?

[*Enter Osric.*]

Osric. Young Fortinbras, with conquest come from Poland,
To th' ambassadors of England gives
This warlike volley.

Hamlet. O, I die, Horatio!
360 The potent poison quite o'ercrows my spirit.
I cannot live to hear the news from England.
But I do prophesy th' election lights
On Fortinbras; he has my dying voice.
So tell him, with th' occurrents, more and less,
365 Which have solicited—the rest is silence.
O, O, O, O!

[*Dies.*]

Horatio. Now cracks a noble heart. Good night, sweet prince,
And flights of angels sing thee to thy rest.

[*March within.*]

Why does the drum come hither?

[*Enter Fortinbras with the English Ambassadors with Drum, Colors, and Attendants.*]

370 **Fortinbras.** Where is this sight?

Horatio. What is it you would see?
If aught of woe or wonder, cease your search.

Fortinbras. This quarry cries on havoc. O proud Death,
What feast is toward in thine eternal cell
375 That thou so many princes at a shot
So bloodily hast struck?

NOTICE & NOTE

348 **more an antique Roman:** a reference to the Roman idea that suicide can be an honorable action following a defeat or the death of a loved one.

354 **Absent thee from felicity:** deny yourself the pleasure of death.

357–359 Fortinbras, returning triumphant from Poland, has saluted the English ambassadors with a volley of gunfire.

360 **o'ercrows:** triumphs over (like the winner in a cockfight).

362–363 Hamlet predicts that Fortinbras will be elected the new Danish king and gives him his vote (**voice**).

364 **occurrents:** occurrences.

365 **solicited:** prompted, brought about. (Hamlet dies before finishing this thought.)

373 This heap of dead bodies (**quarry**) proclaims a massacre (**cries on havoc**).

374 **toward:** in preparation.

The Tragedy of Hamlet: Act V, Scene 2 269

TEACH

EL ENGLISH LEARNER SUPPORT

Speak Using New Language Focus students' attention on Scene 2, lines 345–356, pages 268–269.

Have students find the words "tell my story."

Ask students to identify the exact text where Hamlet makes his request. *(line 346: report me and my cause aright; line 356: tell my story.)*

Then, direct students' attention to lines 351–352, where Hamlet explains his reason for this request. Ask students to think about the meaning of the phrase *wounded name* and offer their explanations for what it means. Have each student practice answering this sentence stem:

Hamlet wants Horatio to . . . because . . .

CLOSE READ SCREENCAST

Modeled Discussions Students have heard modeled discussions in the Close Read Screencasts for Acts I–IV. Now have them pair up and do an independent close read of the following passage: Hamlet's dying words (Act V, Scene 2, lines 351–365). As a class, discuss the passage.

TEACH

ENGLISH LEARNER SUPPORT

Describe and Explain Focus students' attention on Scene 2, lines 379–380, page 270. Have students review earlier events in the play to explain why Rosencrantz and Guildenstern are dead. To help them explain, have them work in groups to answer these questions:

- Who are Rosencrantz and Guildenstern? *(two old friends and servants of Hamlet)*
- Where did they die? *(England)*
- Who killed them? *(The King of England had them executed.)*
- Why did they get killed? *(They delivered to the King of England a letter that ordered him to kill the bearers of the letter.)* **ALL LEVELS**

NOTICE & NOTE

381 **his:** Claudius's.

384 **so jump upon this bloody question:** so soon after this bloody quarrel.

387 **stage:** platform.

390 **carnal, bloody, and unnatural acts:** Claudius's murder of his brother and marriage to Gertrude.

391 **accidental judgments, casual slaughters:** punishments that occurred by chance.

392 **put on:** instigated; **forced:** contrived.

395 **deliver:** tell the story of.

398–399 Fortinbras says he has some unforgotten claims to Denmark, and this is a favorable time to present them.

401 **from his mouth . . . more:** the words of Hamlet, whose decision will influence other votes.

402 **presently:** immediately.

403–404 **lest more . . . happen:** lest other trouble occur in addition to these plots and accidents.

406 **put on:** enthroned, and so put to the test.

407 **passage:** death.

411 **field:** field of battle.

Ambassador.   The sight is dismal,
And our affairs from England come too late.
The ears are senseless that should give us hearing
To tell him his commandment is fulfilled,
380 That Rosencrantz and Guildenstern are dead.
Where should we have our thanks?

Horatio.   Not from his mouth,
Had it th' ability of life to thank you.
He never gave commandment for their death.
But since, so jump upon this bloody question,
385 You from the Polack wars, and you from England,
Are here arrived, give order that these bodies
High on a stage be placed to the view,
And let me speak to th' yet unknowing world
How these things came about. So shall you hear
390 Of carnal, bloody, and unnatural acts,
Of accidental judgments, casual slaughters,
Of deaths put on by cunning and forced cause,
And, in this upshot, purposes mistook
Fall'n on th' inventors' heads. All this can I
395 Truly deliver.

Fortinbras.   Let us haste to hear it
And call the noblest to the audience.
For me, with sorrow I embrace my fortune.
I have some rights of memory in this kingdom,
Which now to claim my vantage doth invite me.

400 **Horatio.** Of that I shall have also cause to speak,
And from his mouth whose voice will draw on more.
But let this same be presently performed
Even while men's minds are wild, lest more mischance
On plots and errors happen.

405 **Fortinbras.**   Let four captains
Bear Hamlet like a soldier to the stage,
For he was likely, had he been put on,
To have proved most royal; and for his passage,
The soldier's music and the rite of war
Speak loudly for him.
410 Take up the bodies. Such a sight as this
Becomes the field but here shows much amiss.
Go, bid the soldiers shoot.

[*They exit, marching, after the which a peal of ordnance are shot off.*]

270   Unit 2

WHEN STUDENTS STRUGGLE . . .

Review Events In the final scene of the play, several people have died. Have students name the deceased and trace the events that lead to their deaths. Have them use a chart like below:

| Gertrude is dead. | → | Why? | → | Why? | → | Why? |

 For additional support, go to the **Reading Studio** and assign the following **Level Up tutorial: Plot: Sequence of Events**.

270   Unit 2

CHECK YOUR UNDERSTANDING

Answer these questions before moving on to the **Analyze the Text** section on the following page.

1. Why does the Gravedigger question Ophelia's burial in a churchyard?
   A He heard she wasn't a Christian.
   B He thinks she committed suicide.
   C He is too tired to dig her grave.
   D He believes her funeral wasn't arranged properly.

2. What sets off the argument between Hamlet and Laertes at Ophelia's funeral?
   F Hamlet is offended by Laertes' passionate display of grief.
   G Laertes is offended that Hamlet came to the funeral.
   H Hamlet thinks Laertes has returned to Denmark to kill him.
   J Laertes wants Ophelia to have a longer funeral service.

3. Why does Hamlet accept the fencing challenge from Laertes even though he has misgivings about it?
   A He fears that Laertes would mock him if he refused.
   B He wants to make a good impression on Osric.
   C He hopes his mother will forgive him if he wins.
   D He thinks that he cannot avoid his destiny.

TEACH

CHECK YOUR UNDERSTANDING

Have students answer the questions independently.

Answers:

1. B
2. F
3. D

If students answer any questions incorrectly, have them reread the text to confirm their understanding. Then, they may proceed to ANALYZE THE TEXT on page 272.

ENGLISH LEARNER SUPPORT

Oral Assessment Use the following questions to assess students' comprehension and speaking skills.

1. The grave digger thinks Ophelia _____. *(committed suicide)*
2. Does Laertes's grief make Hamlet angry? *(yes)*
3. Does Hamlet think he will win the fencing match with Laertes? *(no)* **ALL LEVELS**

APPLY

ANALYZE THE TEXT

Possible answers:

1. **DOK 4:** *The Gravedigger's scene provides comic relief, but it also offers a meditation on the nature of death. All are reduced to dust and bones, no matter what their status. This scene shows Hamlet no longer seeks death, but now accepts it as life's natural conclusion.*

2. **DOK 3:** *Hamlet shows he has become a man of action rather than reflection. He altered the king's letter to cause the deaths of Rosencrantz and Guildenstern (lines 38–47), and then escaped from the ship.*

3. **DOK 4:** *Student answers will vary. Students may cite various strengths and weaknesses of Hamlet's that may or may not have made him a good king. For example, his hesitance to act without sufficient cause and with a mind to the consequences may be seen as a good quality in a king, but his indecisiveness may not.*

4. **DOK 4:** *Example: In Scene 1, lines 57–89, Hamlet ponders what lies after death. Shakespeare uses parallel structure to echo the balancing of Hamlet's thoughts. He employs metaphors and personification to contrast Hamlet's images of what life has to offer with what is unknown about death, describing "the slings and arrows of outrageous fortune," "a sea of troubles," "the whips and scorns of time," and concluding that "conscience does make cowards of us all." His fear of the unknown ultimately "puzzles the will" and makes "enterprises of great pitch" "lose the name of action."*

5. **DOK 4:** *Student answers will vary. Review with them the characteristics of a revenge plot. If they say this is not a satisfying ending, ask them to give an alternate ending they think would be better and explain why.*

RESEARCH

Help students find the information they are looking for by working as a class to suggest search terms and phrases. Remind students that this time period is called the Renaissance. Possible searches include:

mental illness in the Renaissance; attitudes toward . . . ; treatment of . . . ; understanding of

Extend/Connect Encourage students to seek out summaries of other plays as well as essays on the subject of madness in Shakespeare.

 **RESPOND**

ANALYZE THE TEXT

Support your responses with evidence from the text. 📓 NOTEBOOK

1. **Analyze** Act V begins with the Gravedigger joking about his profession and Hamlet's witty comments about Yorick's skull. Why might Shakespeare have chosen to include this dark humor in the scene?

2. **Compare** At the start of Scene 2, Hamlet tells Horatio how he handled the plot to have him executed in England. How do his actions on the ship contrast with his earlier behavior? What does this change suggest about the internal conflict he has struggled with for much of the play?

3. **Evaluate** In his closing speech, Fortinbras says that Hamlet was likely to "have proved most royal." Do you agree that Hamlet would probably have made a good king? Why or why not?

4. **Analyze** Briefly analyze one of the play's soliloquies. First, summarize the ideas expressed in the soliloquy and explain how they relate to the plot. Then, discuss how Shakespeare uses literary elements such as figurative language and imagery to make the speech moving and memorable. Choose one of the following:
   - Act I, Scene 2, lines 129–159
   - Act II, Scene 2, lines 558–614
   - Act III, Scene 1, lines 57–89
   - Act IV, Scene 4, lines 34–68

5. **Critique** At the end of *Hamlet*, all of the main characters are dead, and a foreigner is poised to take over Denmark's throne. Is this a satisfying resolution to the revenge plot? Why or why not?

RESEARCH

RESEARCH TIP
Use your sources to find sources. If you have an article that is exactly what you are looking for, use that article's references page to find more relevant sources.

Hamlet pretends to be mad in the play, and Ophelia actually loses her sanity. Do some research on ideas about mental illness in the Renaissance.

QUESTION	ANSWER
What did physicians think caused madness?	*Either supernatural forces or environmental or social conditions such as bad air or poor education*
What medical treatments were used on mentally ill people?	*Prayer, exorcism, physical restraints, cutting a hole in the skull, physical beating*
How were the mentally ill viewed by society?	*They were condemned for having weak faith or morals.*

Extend Research how Shakespeare portrays madness in other plays. Synthesize this information with what you learned from your other sources.

RESPOND

CREATE AND DISCUSS

Write a Eulogy A eulogy is a speech given at a funeral. Typically, a eulogy highlights a person's most important accomplishments and characteristics across their lifespan. Write a eulogy for a character in *Hamlet*.

- ❏ Many characters die in *Hamlet*. Pick the character you understand the best or feel a personal connection to in some way.
- ❏ Take note of his or her accomplishments or characteristics. Find a central idea you can focus on in the eulogy.
- ❏ Use a somber and formal tone and style appropriate for an audience of mourners.

Discuss the Script *Hamlet* is the longest of Shakespeare's plays, and directors often revise the text so their productions won't run too long. In a small group, discuss cuts you would make if you were staging the play.

- ❏ List all the subplots, and discuss how each one contributes to and advances the action of the play. Critique and evaluate each subplot to determine whether it can be shortened or cut.
- ❏ Identify long speeches, such as the soliloquies and the speeches of the First Player. Discuss how they reveal conflicts and support the play's themes. Consider what would be lost if they were shortened.
- ❏ Discuss the comic dialogue involving the Gravedigger and Osric in Act V. Is this dialogue necessary to advance the action, or can it be trimmed or cut out completely?

Go to **Participating in Collaborative Discussions** in the **Speaking and Listening Studio** for help.

RESPOND TO THE ESSENTIAL QUESTION

 What can drive someone to seek revenge?

Gather Information Review your annotations and notes on *Hamlet*. Then, add relevant information to your Response Log. As you determine which information to include, think about:

- how an internal conflict can either spur action or lead to inaction
- how forgiveness can be an antidote to revenge

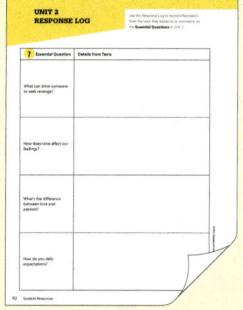

ACADEMIC VOCABULARY
As you write and discuss what you learned from the play, be sure to use the Academic Vocabulary words. Check off each of the words that you use.

- ❏ ambiguous
- ❏ anticipate
- ❏ conceive
- ❏ drama
- ❏ integrity

APPLY

VOCABULARY STRATEGY:
Classical Allusion

Explain that a **classical allusion** is similar to the cultural references students are familiar with now. Shakespeare's audience was familiar with certain stories, particularly ancient mythology, in the way that we are now familiar with popular books, movies, and recent events. By referencing these stories, Shakespeare took advantage of the meanings that the audience associated with them to convey meanings in his plays and enrich the audience's experience.

Have students look back at the text for classical allusions and choose one they find interesting. Tell them that by finding out more about the story, they can get closer to understanding the play in the way Shakespeare's original audience would have.

RESPOND

VOCABULARY STRATEGY:
Classical Allusion

A **classical allusion** is a reference to a historical or fictional figure, event, or creative work from the ancient world. Shakespeare uses classical allusions several times in *Hamlet*. In Act III, Scene 4, Hamlet compares his father to Hyperion and Jove:

See what a grace was seated on this brow: / Hyperion's curls, the front of Jove himself.

Hyperion is the ancient Greek god of the sun, and Jove is the Roman god of thunder. These classical allusions allow readers and audience members to understand the depth of reverence Hamlet feels for his father.

Practice and Apply Read the classical allusions from *Hamlet* in the chart below. Explain how each allusion relates to its context in the play. Do research if needed.

ALLUSION	EXPLANATION
Act I, Scene 2 . . . A little month, or ere those shoes were old / With which she follow'd my poor father's body, / Like Niobe, all tears . . .	*Immediately after her husband's death, Gertrude's grief was extreme as that of Niobe, who continued to cry for her slaughtered children even after Zeus turned her to stone.*
Act I, Scene 2 . . . My father's brother, but no more like my father / Than I to Hercules . . .	*Hamlet compares Claudius to his dead father, saying that Claudius is no more like his father than he himself is to Hercules, a figure of Greek mythology legendary for his strength and heroism.*
Act I, Scene 4 My fate cries out / And makes each petty arture in this body / As hardy as the Nemean lion's nerve.	*The reference to the Nemean Lion is also part of the Hercules myth. Here, Hamlet is saying that he will need the same strength as the Nemean Lion in order to face his father's ghost.*
Act II, Scene 2 What's Hecuba to him, or he to Hecuba, / That he should weep for her?	*Hamlet is speaking of the actor's ability to show grief despite the fact that the play is fiction and those emotions are not real to him. Earlier in the scene, Hamlet had asked First Player to recite a monologue about Hecuba's grief at the death of her husband.*

ENGLISH LEARNER SUPPORT

Use Pre-taught Vocabulary For the Practice and Apply activity, students will need to review the scene in the play where the allusion occurs, read the side note, and possibly access a text for additional research. Have students work in same-level groups and choose one or two of the allusions from a scene they are most familiar with. Pre-teach the necessary vocabulary for the side note and, If they select a research text, support their reading by pre-teaching the necessary vocabulary. For lower proficiency learners, supply language to help them express the relationship between the play and the allusion: *in the same way that; just as; as much as*, etc. For beginners, have them identify the character and mythological figure being compared (*example: Gertrude and Niobe.*) **ALL LEVELS**

RESPOND

LANGUAGE CONVENTIONS:
Paradox

A **paradox** is a statement that seems contradictory but actually reveals an element of truth. Shakespeare uses this literary device frequently in *Hamlet*. By expressing ideas paradoxically, he is able to convey subtle meanings and reinforce the audience's understanding of the duplicitous nature of many of the characters and their actions.

In Act I, Scene 2, Claudius's first speech features examples of paradox and **oxymoron** (a paradox condensed into a brief phrase):

> Have we (as 'twere with a defeated joy,
> With an auspicious and a dropping eye,
> With mirth in funeral and with dirge in marriage,
> In equal scale weighing delight and dole)
> Taken to wife.

He speaks of "defeated joy," "mirth in funeral," "dirge in marriage," and "weighing delight and dole." These paradoxical expressions tell those assembled that he views his marriage and accession to the throne as a mixed blessing, achieved at the expense of his brother's life. The use of paradox also hints at his own contradictory nature: outwardly virtuous, inwardly scheming and self-centered.

Hamlet also uses paradoxical language in the play. For example, in Act II, Scene 2, lines 309–320, he describes humankind in idealistic terms ("how noble in reason, how infinite in faculties . . . in action how like an angel, in apprehension how like a god") but ends the speech with the dismissive remark, "and yet, to me, what is this quintessence of dust? Man delights not me. . . ." This paradox emphasizes Hamlet's obsession with human corruption.

Note these other instances of paradox in the play:

- **Hamlet:** "it is a custom / More honored in the breach than the observance" (Act I, Scene 4, lines 17–18)
- **Polonius:** "Your bait of falsehood takes this carp of truth; / And thus do we of wisdom and of reach, / With windlasses and with assays of bias, / By indirections find directions out." (Act II, Scene 1, lines 63–66)
- **Hamlet:** "I must be cruel only to be kind." (Act III, Scene 4, line 184)

Practice and Apply Review the context of each example of paradox listed above. With a partner, discuss the meaning of each paradox and examine how it deepens the audience's understanding of the character or situation.

The Tragedy of Hamlet 275

APPLY

LANGUAGE CONVENTIONS:
Paradox

Emphasize that paradoxical expressions, including oxymorons, are ways to grab the attention of the audience because they combine clearly opposing attributes of a situation. Discuss the idea that Hamlet himself is a paradoxical character who exhibits widely divergent characteristics: impulsiveness and careful planning, tenderness and extreme violence, attraction to Ophelia and disgust with Ophelia, etc.

Practice and Apply

Possible answers:

Individual insertions of paradoxes into the funeral speeches will vary. Invite volunteers to share with the class paradoxical references or expressions they have used in their funeral speeches.

1. *(Hamlet) This paradox is in reference to excessive drinking that occurs at the King's late-night celebrations. By saying that among the people, the habit of excessive drinking is more honored in the breach than in the observance, Hamlet suggests Danish citizens are not excessive drinkers.*

2. *(Polonius) Polonius says that by asking misleading questions that are false accusations against his son, they will find out the truth of his behavior.*

3. *(Hamlet) Hamlet says this to his mother, meaning that to force her to face the truth and save herself, he has to be cruel.*

ENGLISH LEARNER SUPPORT

Use Accessible Language Explain to students that they can often identify a paradox by looking for words with opposite meanings. For example, *breach* is the opposite of *observance*. Have students look at the example paradoxes give for Practice and Apply and look for the words that have opposite meanings. For beginners, supply one of the words and ask them to look for the word that means its opposite. If necessary, supply the meanings of several words in the sentence. **ALL LEVELS**

The Tragedy of Hamlet **275**

PLAN

from HAMLET
Film Clip by BBC Shakespeare

GENRE ELEMENTS
FILM ADAPTATION

Tell students to think about how a **film adaptation** of a play is both like and unlike a play that is performed live on a stage. Each director has a personal vision of the film he or she wants to make. This vision is determined by the way the director interprets the play, the film's purpose and intended audience, previous versions of the play, and the subject matter of the play. To realize his or her vision, the director must make decisions that include **casting**, **set design**, and **lighting**.

LEARNING OBJECTIVES

- Analyze interpretations of drama.
- Conduct research about another film adaptation of *Hamlet*.
- Write a narrative about revenge.
- Produce and present a movie trailer about a story.
- **Language** With teacher and partner support, narrate the action in a film.

TEXT COMPLEXITY

Quantitative Measures	Hamlet Film Clip	Lexile: N/A
Qualitative Measures	**Ideas Presented** Subtle, implied meanings and greater demand for inference.	
	Structures Used Complex plot lines.	
	Language Used Complex sentence structures with use of archaic and formal language.	
	Knowledge Required Cultural and historical references may make heavier demands.	

PLAN

RESOURCES

Online Ed

- Unit 2 Response Log
- Reading Studio: Notice and Notes
- Level Up Tutorial: Elements of Drama
- Writing Studio: Writing Narratives
- Speaking and Listening Studio: Using Media in a Presentation
- ✓ "Hamlet Film Clip" Selection Test

SUMMARIES

English

In this scene, Hamlet has come home to attend his father's funeral. Hamlet's mother and her new husband, Hamlet's uncle, tell him he should not feel depressed, but Hamlet is upset about his father's death and his mother's hasty wedding. Horatio comes and tells Hamlet that he has seen the ghost of his father.

Spanish

En esta escena, Hamlet ha vuelto a casa para ir al funeral de su padre. La madre de Hamlet y su nuevo esposo, el tío de Hamlet, le dicen que no debe deprimirse, pero Hamlet está enfadado por la muerte de su padre y la precipitada boda de su madre. Horacio le dice a Hamlet que ha visto al fantasma de su padre.

 SMALL-GROUP OPTIONS

Have students work in small groups and pairs to view and discuss the selection.

Double-Entry Journal

- Show students how to create a two-column double-entry journal by drawing a line from top to bottom on a page. The left column head will be *Quotes from the Film* and the right head will be *My Notes*.
- Encourage students to pause the film repeatedly as they view it, and tell them to copy important or confusing lines in the left column of their journals.
- Then, have students write their own questions, restatements, or interpretations in the right column next to the quoted material.
- Have students exchange journals and help answer each other's questions.

Send a Problem

- After watching the first minute and a half of the film, pose this question: *How would you describe Hamlet's mood?*
- Call on a student to respond. Wait up to 11 seconds for a response.
- If the student has no response, he or she must call on another student by name to answer the same question.
- Have students continue asking each other for assistance as needed. Monitor responses and ask more questions as appropriate.

Hamlet Film Clip **276B**

PLAN

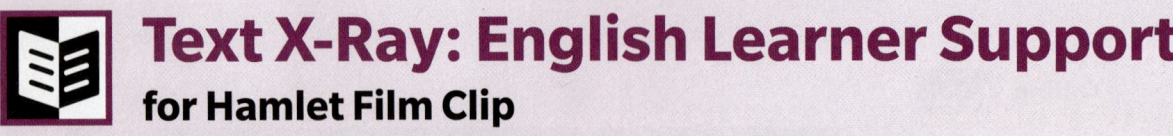

Text X-Ray: English Learner Support
for Hamlet Film Clip

Use the Text X-Ray and the supports and scaffolds in the Teacher's Edition to help guide students at different proficiency levels through the selection.

INTRODUCE THE SELECTION
DISCUSS FILM ADAPTATION

In this lesson, students will need to be able to discuss the choices a director makes in order to adapt a play into a film, including **casting, set design,** and **lighting.**

Remind students that directors make many choices about what the camera sees, how close or wide a shot will be, and how long a shot will be, as well as how to cut together or edit shots into one continuous scene.

Ask students to discuss other techniques directors can use to adapt scenes into film. Provide sentence frames, such as: *The director can use a wide shot to show _____. The director can use a close-up shot to show _____.*

CULTURAL REFERENCES

The following words or phrases may be unfamiliar to students:

- *fie*: an expression of outrage or disgust
- *most immediate to the throne*: next in line to be king
- *the Everlasting*: God
- *on't*: on it
- *good even*: good evening
- *methinks*: I think
- *in my mind's eye*: in my imagination
- *hold my peace*: not speak

LISTENING

Understand Implicit Ideas

Remind students that characters may be saying a familiar saying, but in the old British plays, it's difficult to understand what they mean.

Play the film clip and pause after every minute or so. Use the following supports with students at varying proficiency levels:

- Repeat certain lines and ask explain their meaning. Choose one word with which to focus and have students write the word. (*"Let not thou mother lose her prayers"* means let her prayers be heard.) **SUBSTANTIAL**
- Ask general content questions to assess listening comprehension. For example: *All that loves must die.* (Everybody has to die at some point.) **MODERATE**
- Have partners ask and answer questions about what they heard. For example: *What do you think Claudius really means when he says _____?* **LIGHT**

276C Unit 2

PLAN

SPEAKING

Narrate Action

Tell students that the action in a film is what the characters do. Remind them that a character's gestures, actions, and facial expressions are clues to help them better understand the plot.

Use the following supports with students at varying proficiency levels:

- Help students write the names of the characters on separate index cards. Then, as you say short sentences about each character's actions in the order that they happen, have students repeat each sentence and hold up the appropriate character card. For example: *This character sits on a throne as she speaks. (Queen Gertrude)* **SUBSTANTIAL**
- Have partners watch the film again and pause it as they take turns describing the actions of the characters in the order that they happen. **MODERATE**
- Have partners watch the clip again. Then, have them take turns narrating the action in their own words. **LIGHT**

READING

Use Think Alouds to Improve Comprehension

Remind students that it is a good idea to pause as they read the subtitles, so they can ask themselves questions about what they see on screen. Model how to use Think Alouds as you read the subtitles.

Use the following supports with students at varying proficiency levels:

- Pause the clip after Hamlet's line: *"Seems," madam? Nay, it is! I know not "seems."* Have students read the line with you. Then, model a Think Aloud: *I watch Hamlet's face and listen to his tone to see how he is feeling when he says this. He sounds and looks angry. I think he wants his mother to know that it doesn't "seem" like he's upset, he's actually very upset.* Ask yes/no questions to assess students' comprehension of the Think Aloud. **SUBSTANTIAL**
- Model the Think Aloud described above. The,n tell partners to take turns reading the next two subtitles and use clues from the film to recite their own brief Think Alouds. **MODERATE**
- Model the Think Aloud described above. Then, have partners choose three places to pause the film clip and recite their own Think Alouds. **LIGHT**

WRITING

Write Dialogue

Tell students that dialogue in modern stories attempts to sound the way people naturally speak. Guide students to write dialogue for their stories about revenge.

Use the following supports with students at varying proficiency levels:

- Work with students to write words about revenge. Provide words, such as *avenge, payback, punish,* and *retaliate*. Write the words on the board and have students copy it. **SUBSTANTIAL**
- Work with students to improvise a brief dialogue about revenge. Provide words and expressions relating to revenge, such as *avenge, payback, punish, retaliate,* and *get back at*. Write two of their dialogues on the board and have students copy them. **MODERATE**
- Have partners study examples of dialogue in modern stories. Then tell them to use these examples as models as they write a page of dialogue about a situation related to revenge. **LIGHT**

Hamlet Film Clip

TEACH

? Connect to the ESSENTIAL QUESTION

The film clip from *Hamlet* (2009) shows how Hamlet, driven by his sorrow over his father's death and his mother's speedy marriage to his uncle, is determined to get revenge on the person who killed his father.

QUICK START

Encourage students to brainstorm as they discuss possible adaptations of *Hamlet* with a partner. They could start by coming up with lists of their favorite actors and then narrow down the list to choose actors who would be best for the roles in the play. Then, they could try to come up with fun settings for the play (the future, the Wild West, Mars, etc.).

ANALYZE INTERPRETATIONS OF DRAMA

Discuss with students the importance of **casting** in a film. Explain that each actor interprets a role differently and that casting directors often are looking for actors who have experience playing the particular types of characters that will be in a film. Point out that the **set design** of a film adaptation is an important part of the mood the film creates; it provides the backdrop for the events in the film and affects the way viewers experience those events. **Lighting** is also very important for creating mood, as the amount of lighting affects the atmosphere and the viewer's ability to see what is happening in a scene.

ANALYZE & APPLY

MEDIA

from HAMLET

Film Clip by **BBC Shakespeare**

? ESSENTIAL QUESTION:

What can drive someone to seek revenge?

QUICK START

If you were hired to direct a film adaptation of *Hamlet*, what actors would you cast in the important roles? Would you keep the play's historical setting or chose another time and place? Discuss your choices with a partner.

ANALYZE INTERPRETATIONS OF DRAMA

GENRE ELEMENTS: FILM
- sometimes interprets a literary source such as a play or novel
- uses elements such as visual images, sound, music, and lighting to convey ideas and emotions
- often reflects the director's personal vision

Shakespeare's plays present challenges and opportunities for directors who want to adapt them into films. Shakespeare sometimes included descriptions of characters or setting in the dialogue, but his texts have few stage directions. As a result, directors have a great deal of freedom to imagine a play's details. The director must make decisions that include casting, set design, and lighting.

Casting refers to the selection of actors. Actors may be chosen based on their appearance or age. For example, directors casting Hamlet would most likely choose actors of different ages for the roles of Hamlet and his mother. The choice of actors is crucial to the success of a production; the actors determine how the audience responds to the film as a whole. Directors may stay true to type or cast against type, perhaps choosing a female Hamlet or an actor whose ethnicity differs from what would be expected for a character.

Set design refers to the scenery, props, and physical location that create the setting for the film. The set design may be traditional, modern, futuristic, or primitive, or it may spring from the imagination of the director. The setting in which the action of the film takes place is important to the director's interpretation. It also affects how the audience reacts.

Lighting can have a major influence on the mood and perception of characters and action. Dim lighting conveys an air of mystery or gloominess and obscures actors' features and actions. Bright lighting cheers up the atmosphere and highlights actors' movements and expressions.

276   Unit 2

 ENGLISH LEARNER SUPPORT

Identify Cognates   Draw students' attention to the word *drama* in the skill heading on page 274. Discuss with students the meaning of the word *(a work to be performed by actors on stage or film)*. Explain that the word *drama* in Spanish has the same meaning. Then, explain that there are other words in English derived from the word *drama* that have Spanish cognates as well. Say the word *dramatic* and ask students to discuss its meaning. Tell students that the word *dramatico* in Spanish has the same meaning.   **ALL LEVELS**

276   Unit 2

GET READY

BACKGROUND

This BBC adaptation of Hamlet, produced in 2009, was based on a highly acclaimed stage production by the Royal Shakespeare Company. The film stars David Tennant as Hamlet and Patrick Stewart as both Claudius and the Ghost. Director Gregory Doran came up with interesting ways to bring the film into the present; for example, some of the action is viewed through closed-circuit cameras used for surveillance in the castle. The clip you will view is from Act I, Scene 2 of the play.

SETTING A PURPOSE

Pay attention to the elements that make the film version unique, and generate a list of questions as you watch. NOTEBOOK.

OBSERVATIONS	QUESTIONS

For more online resources log in to your dashboard and click on the "*from* HAMLET" title from the selection menu.

As needed, pause the video to make notes about what impresses you or about ideas you might want to talk about later. Replay or rewind so that you can clarify anything you do not understand.

Hamlet (film version) 277

TEACH

BACKGROUND

After students read the Background notes on page 277, have them review the discussion of set design on the previous page. How might the use of closed-circuit cameras change the mood of the adaptation? Does this decision by the director resemble anything they would have liked to do in their own adaptations?

SETTING A PURPOSE

Direct students to use the Setting a Purpose prompt to focus their reading.

For **listening** and **reading support** for students at varying proficiency levels, see the **Text X-Ray** on page 276D.

WHEN STUDENTS STRUGGLE...

Reteaching: Analyze Interpretations of Drama Review with students the main points of adapting drama for the screen. Then, have them complete a chart in which they will note the purpose and importance of each aspect of an adaptation.

| Casting | Set Design | Lighting |

 For additional support, go to the **Reading Studio** and assign the following Level Up tutorial: Elements of Drama.

Hamlet (film version) **277**

APPLY

ANALYZE THE MEDIA

Possible answers:

1. **DOK 4:** *The setting of the clip is a parlor area in a large castle. The time, based on the costumes, looks as if it is the twentieth or twenty-first century.*

2. **DOK 2:** *Because the lights are somewhat dim, a gloomy and tense mood is evoked; this mood is supported by the content, which concerns the murder of Hamlet's father and his mother's cold, hasty marriage to his uncle.*

3. **DOK 4:** *The clip emphasizes that Hamlet is tormented by his grief and that he has a complex relationship with Gertrude and Claudius, fueled by his distrust of both of them.*

4. **DOK 3:** *The director's decision to briefly show the action as if through a closed-circuit camera reminds us of the time setting but also creates a mood of secrecy, or spying.*

5. **DOK 4:** *The director uses the camera in this scene in a way that shows the immediacy of Hamlet's relationship with his old friends; the scene is effective in that it represents a departure from our relentless focus on Hamlet's emotions thus far.*

RESEARCH

Encourage students to use online resources to find other film adaptations of *Hamlet*. Have the class work in pairs as they watch their chosen adaptation. Once they have watched the adaptation, ask them to fill out the graphic organizer on page 276. Answers will vary, depending on the adaptation chosen, but responses for the 2009 BBC adaptation could be as follows:

Casting—an intense lead chosen to play Hamlet; a more relaxed actor chosen for Claudius

Set Design—modern sets, including closed-circuit camera

Lighting—extremes, from glaringly bright to quite dim

Extend Explain to students that a review is a statement of their opinion of something's quality. Remind them that their opinions must be supported by details and evidence. If possible, provide students with examples of published reviews that they can use as models.

RESPOND

ANALYZE THE MEDIA

Support your responses with evidence from the film clip.

1. **Identify** Describe the setting of the BBC *Hamlet* adaptation. What time and place are indicated by the set and costumes?

2. **Interpret** What mood is evoked by the lighting of this film?

3. **Analyze** What does this adaptation emphasize about Hamlet's personality and his relationships with Gertrude and Claudius? Explain.

4. **Draw Conclusions** Why might the director have chosen to briefly show the action as if we were viewing it through a security camera?

5. **Critique** Reread lines 160–180 in Act I, Scene 2 of the play. What choices did the director make in adapting this passage to the film? How effective are these choices? Explain.

RESEARCH

RESEARCH TIP
To begin researching start by searching the subject, directors, or common setting of the film. Once you locate a possible searchable resource, evaluate the resource, avoid any review based resources or Wikipedia-like platforms to ensure it is credible. Once you find a valid resource take notes and gather only the most usable and factual information.

With a partner, research another film adaptation of *Hamlet* and compare the choices that the directors made in casting, set design, and lighting. If possible, find a clip of the film that shows Act 1, Scene 2. Use a chart such as the one below to record your comparisons.

	BBC *HAMLET* (2009)	OTHER ADAPTATIONS
Casting		
Set Design		
Lighting		

Extend View the entire 2009 BBC adaptation of *Hamlet*. Then write a review of the film. Share your review with the class.

ENGLISH LEARNER SUPPORT

Oral Assessment To gauge comprehension and speaking skills, ask:

- Who is in the scene? *(Hamlet, Gertrude, Claudius)* **SUBSTANTIAL**
- What is the lighting like in this scene? How does this make you feel? *(The lighting is dim; students' reactions may vary)* **MODERATE**
- What effect does filming with a security camera have on part of the scene? *(The security camera creates a feeling of secrecy, as if someone is spying.)* **LIGHT**

CREATE AND PRESENT

Write a Narrative Imagine why someone might want to seek revenge. Then, write a narrative story about a case of revenge.

- ❏ Establish the story by introducing the event. Where did the story take place? Who is involved?
- ❏ Organize the plot in a logical order.
- ❏ Include dialogue and vivid images to portray the experience.
- ❏ Review your story to edit and add more details if necessary.

Produce a Movie Trailer With a partner, create a trailer for a movie that dramatizes your story.

- ❏ Create a storyboard for a trailer depicting events in your story.
- ❏ Film a video of the trailer storyboard, with voiceover narration.
- ❏ Present your trailer to the class.

RESPOND TO THE ESSENTIAL QUESTION

 What can drive someone to seek revenge?

Gather Information Review your notes on the film clip as it compares to the play. Then, add relevant information to your Response Log. As you determine which information to include, think about:

- the elements of a film adaptation
- the use of literary devices such as metaphors
- the central theme of revenge established through the play and film clip
- the mental state of the character Hamlet as it pertains to the plot

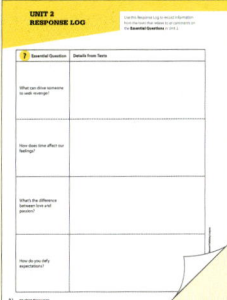

RESPOND

 Go to the **Writing Studio** to find out more about writing narratives.

 Go to the **Speaking and Listening Studio** to find out more about using media in a presentation.

ACADEMIC VOCABULARY
As you write and discuss what you learned from the film clip, be sure to use the Academic Vocabulary words. Check off each of the words that you use.

- ❏ ambiguous
- ❏ anticipate
- ❏ conceive
- ❏ drama
- ❏ integrity

Hamlet (film version) 279

APPLY

CREATE AND PRESENT

Write a Narrative After students have written drafts of their narratives, encourage them to read their drafts to a partner. Ask partners to provide constructive feedback to improve the narratives.

Produce a Movie Trailer Have students share their storyboards with another pair of students before creating their videos.

- Ask the other pair of students to provide concrete suggestions for improvement of the storyboards.
- Encourage the students to listen carefully to the suggestions and incorporate them into their storyboards, when possible.
- Tell the students to make notes of any suggestions that might affect the filming of the videos.

RESPOND TO THE ESSENTIAL QUESTION

Allow time for students to add details from "Hamlet Film Clip" to their Unit 2 Response Logs.

For **writing** and **speaking support** for students at varying proficiency levels, see the **Text X-Ray** on page 276D.

Hamlet (film version) **279**

PLAN

HAMLET'S DULL REVENGE
Literary Criticism by René Girard

This literary criticism serves as a mentor text, a model for students to follow for the Unit 2 Writing Task: Writing a Literary Analysis.

GENRE ELEMENTS
LITERARY CRITICISM

Tell students that reading a **literary criticism** can be very useful when they want to develop their own interpretations and opinions of a piece of literature. Reading a literary criticism can enrich the original experience of reading the literature. In this lesson, students will analyze the arguments and key ideas in a criticism of Hamlet.

LEARNING OBJECTIVES

- Analyze arguments and key ideas.
- Conduct research on theories of René Girard.
- Write an argument.
- Summarize an argument.
- Define domain-specific words and phrases.
- Combine sentences.
- **Language** Rephrase key ideas in an argument.

TEXT COMPLEXITY

Quantitative Measures	Hamlet's Dull Revenge	Lexile: 1290L
Qualitative Measures	**Ideas Presented** Multiple levels of complex meaning.	
	Structures Used Complex, but mostly explicit. Exhibits traits of literary criticism.	
	Language Used Increased academic, unfamiliar, and domain-specific words.	
	Knowledge Required Cultural and literary knowledge essential to understanding.	

PLAN

Online

RESOURCES

- Unit 2 Response Log
- 🔊 Selection Audio
- 📖 Reading Studio: Notice & Note
- Level Up Tutorial: Analyzing Arguments
- Writing Studio: Writing Arguments
- 💬 Speaking and Listening Studio: Participating in Collaborative Discussions
- Vocabulary Studio: Domain-Specific Words
- ❗ Grammar Studio: Module 2 Lesson 7: Conjunctions and Interjections
- ✅ "Hamlet's Dull Revenge" Selection Test

SUMMARIES

English

In this work of literary criticism, René Girard explains and supports his complex argument about the motives Shakespeare had for writing *Hamlet*. Girard backs his claims with an analysis of many plot points and quotes from the original play.

Spanish

En este trabajo de crítica literaria, René Girard explica y apoya su complejo argumento sobre los motivos de Shakespeare al escribir *Hamlet*. Girard apoya sus afirmaciones con un análisis de muchos puntos de la trama y de citas de la obra original.

SMALL-GROUP OPTIONS

Have students work in small groups and pairs to read and discuss the selection.

Think-Pair-Share

- After students have read paragraphs 1–3 of the selection, pose this question to the class: *What is Shakespeare's double purpose for writing* Hamlet *according to Girard?*
- Have students think about the question individually and take notes.
- Invite pairs to discuss their ideas about the question.
- Ask pairs to share their responses with the class.

Pinwheel Discussion

- Arrange students in a group of eight with four students seated facing in and four students seated facing out.
- After reading a paragraph of the selection, pose a question to students for discussion. For example: *Why does Hamlet think of his crime as a link in a chain?*
- Students in the inner circle remain stationary throughout the discussion. Students in the outer circle move to their right after discussing each question.

Hamlet's Dull Revenge **280B**

PLAN

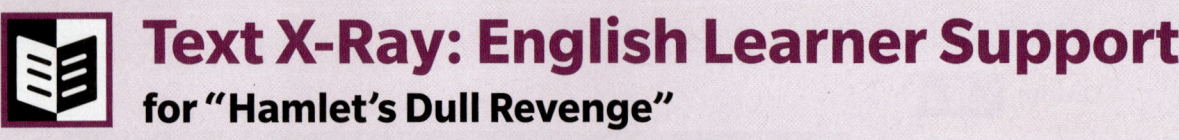

Text X-Ray: English Learner Support
for "Hamlet's Dull Revenge"

Use the Text X-Ray and the supports and scaffolds in the Teacher's Edition to help guide students at different proficiency levels through the selection.

INTRODUCE THE SELECTION
DISCUSS VALUE AND VALIDITY

In this lesson, students will need to be able to identify and discuss the difference between the value and validity of a work of literary criticism.

Provide the following explanations:
- The value of something is its importance.
- The validity of something is how sound, just, or well-founded it is.

Point out the Latin root *val* in both words. Explain that the root means "strength or worth."

Ask students to discuss value and validity of a literary criticism using sentence frames, such as: *Value, in terms of literary criticism, means _____. When speaking of literary criticism, validity means_____.*

CULTURAL REFERENCES

The following words or phrases may be unfamiliar to students:
- *thriller* (paragraph 1): a genre characterized by giving viewers a great feeling of suspense or excitement
- *in the margins* (paragraph 1): not the main point or idea
- *to stir up* (paragraph 10): to excite
- *to rise to such a pitch* (paragraph 13): to become very intense

LISTENING

Seek Clarification

Have students read aloud from their graphic organizers from the Get Ready activity. As other students listen, guide them to ask for clarification as needed.

Use the following supports with students at varying proficiency levels:
- Provide students with a large question mark printed on an index card. Have students hold up the card if they need clarification or to have something repeated. Provide a question bank for students to refer to as they ask their question, such as: *Can you repeat that? What did you mean?* **SUBSTANTIAL**
- Have students raise a finger to indicate that they need clarification. Pause the speaker, and have students voice their question. Provide sentence starters, such as: *Why did you say _____? I don't understand what you mean by _____.* **MODERATE**
- As students listen, have them take notes about things that did not sound clear. Then, have them restate their notes as questions they can pose to each speaker. **LIGHT**

PLAN

SPEAKING

Rephrase Key Ideas

Help students use simpler language to rephrase key ideas of an argument.

Use the following supports with students at varying proficiency levels:

- Read aloud the first sentence. Model how to rephrase the key idea more simply. Define any unfamiliar words. For example: Hamlet *belongs to the genre of the revenge tragedy* (Hamlet *is a revenge tragedy*). **SUBSTANTIAL**
- Model how to orally rephrase the key idea in the first sentence in simpler language. Then, have partners chunk and define the next sentence, then identify the key idea. Direct partners to use their definitions and work together to orally rephrase the key ideas in the first paragraph. Allow students to use dictionaries as needed. **MODERATE**
- Model how to rephrase the key idea in the first sentence in simpler language. Then, ask partners to work together to orally rephrase the key ideas in the text in paragraph 2. **LIGHT**

READING

Use Affixes, Base Words, and Roots to Determine Meaning

Tell students that they can often determine the meaning of a word by first identifying its parts.

Use the following supports with students at varying proficiency levels:

- Write the word *inescapable* from paragraph 1 on the board. Underline the prefix *in-* and explain that it means *"not."* Underline the suffix *-able* and explain that it means "able to be." Explain that the base word *escape* means "to break free." Then, elicit the meaning of *inescapable*. **SUBSTANTIAL**
- Repeat the Beginning activity. Then, have students use lists of affixes and roots to identify and define three more longer, unfamiliar words in paragraph 2. **MODERATE**
- Have students look for words in paragraphs 1–3 that have affixes or Latin and Greek roots. Direct students to use the word parts to help them define 5 of those words. **LIGHT**

WRITING

Summarize Ideas

Guide students to identify and compare ideas to help them figure out the most important point in an argument. Remind them that a summary tells the most important information with the fewest words.

Use the following supports with students at varying proficiency levels:

- Reread paragraph 4 to students and help students write a sentence that summarizes the most important idea. Ask yes/no questions to help students identify the sentence's subject and verb. Review how to use subject-verb agreement. **SUBSTANTIAL**
- Have partners reread paragraph 4 and discuss the most important idea. Ask them to work together to write a one-sentence summary of it. Remind them to use correct subject-verb agreement. **MODERATE**
- Have partners reread paragraphs 1–5 and write a three-sentence summary of the most important ideas. Remind them to use correct subject-verb agreement. **LIGHT**

TEACH

? Connect to the ESSENTIAL QUESTION

"Hamlet's Dull Revenge" offers one literary critic's analysis of Shakespeare's motivation for writing *Hamlet* and his treatment of the genre of revenge theater. The piece argues that Hamlet as a character struggled to find motivation for revenge and had to draw inspiration from others.

MENTOR TEXT

At the end of the unit, students will be asked to write a literary analysis. "Hamlet's Dull Revenge" provides a model for how a writer can support a claim about a literary text or genre with reasons and evidence.

ANALYZE & APPLY

HAMLET'S DULL REVENGE

Literary Criticism by **René Girard**

? ESSENTIAL QUESTION:

What can drive someone to seek revenge?

QUICK START

The essay you are about to read discusses the genre of revenge tragedy. In your notebook, summarize the plot of a film that centers on revenge. Does the main character face only external obstacles, or does he or she have conflicted feelings about the act of revenge? Share your observations in a small group.

ANALYZE ARGUMENTS

An argument is designed to persuade the reader to agree with the **claim**, or position the author is taking. In order to persuade effectively, the author must back up his or her claim with **reasons** that are supported by **evidence**. In "Hamlet's Dull Revenge," René Girard makes an argument about Shakespeare's motives for writing *Hamlet*. To assess the validity of Girard's argument, you will need to ask questions about the claim he is making, his reasons for the claim, and the evidence he uses to support those reasons. As you read, use a graphic organizer like the one below to analyze Girard's argument.

QUESTION	MY NOTES
What is Girard's claim?	
What reasons does Girard use to support his claim?	
What textual evidence does Girard use to support his reasoning?	
Are there any inconsistencies in the structure of Girard's argument?	

ANALYZE KEY IDEAS

Key ideas are the reasons, or points, that the author wants the reader to understand. In an argument, the claim the author makes is backed up with reasons supported by evidence. Typically, the author divides the argument into sections. In each section, the author provides details that support a specific line of reasoning, or key idea. In turn, each section provides support for the claim the author is making in the argument.

Girard's literary analysis contains several key ideas that he uses to support his claim. By paying attention to how Girard structures his claim and key ideas, the reader can better understand the complex argument Girard is making about Shakespeare's motives for writing *Hamlet*.

GET READY

GENRE ELEMENTS: LITERARY CRITICISM
- focuses on a literary work or genre as the subject
- describes an aspect or aspects of the subject, such as its origins, characteristics, or effects
- often makes interpretive claims or judgments that are backed by evidence

Hamlet's Dull Revenge 281

TEACH

QUICK START

As an option, extend the Quick Start by asking each group to decide, based on the film examples they generated, whether revenge is usually portrayed positively or negatively. What determines whether the person seeking revenge is viewed as the protagonist or the antagonist?

ANALYZE ARGUMENTS

Inform students that an argument usually begins with a **claim**, a statement of the author's position on an issue. To find the claim, students should look for a central idea in the first few paragraphs. Then, they can verify whether this idea is the author's claim by reading on to see whether the idea is supported by **reasons** and **evidence** throughout the entire argument. Types of evidence include specific **details** and **examples** that prove the line of reasoning is valid.

ANALYZE KEY IDEAS

Have students read the definition of **key ideas.** In an argument, both the overall claim and the supporting reasons are types of key ideas, or important points. Sometimes key ideas are stated directly, but other times readers must **infer** them by reading the details in a section of the argument and then determining the major point or reason being advanced in that section.

Inform students that although the piece they are about to read is an argument supported by key ideas and evidence, it does not always follow the typical pattern described on p. 281 in which the author presents each key idea and its supporting evidence one at a time. Instead, Girard presents his key ideas over a series of paragraphs, with some of the key ideas and supporting evidence overlapping.

WHEN STUDENTS STRUGGLE . . .

Identify Key Ideas Using Evidence Because Girard does not present his key ideas one at a time, students may find it easier to identify the key ideas if they work backwards, first identifying a piece of evidence the author is using as support and then asking the question, "What idea does this piece of evidence support?" to infer the key idea. One of the primary types of evidence used in a literary criticism is direct quotations from the work being discussed.

 For additional support, go to the **Reading Studio** and assign the following Level Up tutorial: **Evidence**.

Hamlet's Dull Revenge **281**

TEACH

CRITICAL VOCABULARY

Encourage students to read all answer choices before selecting a response. Remind struggling students that although words may appear as possible responses multiple times, each word will only be used once as the correct answer.

Answers:

1. *c*
2. *b*
3. *a*
4. *a*
5. *b*

■ English Learner Support

Use Cognates Tell students that several of the critical vocabulary words have Spanish Cognates: *genre/género, emulation/emulación, hierarchy/jerarquía.*
ALL LEVELS

LANGUAGE CONVENTIONS

Review the information about combining sentences. Explain that when sentences are combined using a coordinating conjunction, a comma is used before the conjunction. Read aloud or display the sample sentence. Ask students to identify the two complete sentences that make it up. Then, read aloud or display the two separate sentences. Discuss how the flow of a single compound sentence is different from the flow of two separate sentences. *Using two sentences sounds choppier. A single sentence is smoother to read, and the use of a comma instead of a period makes it clear that the two thoughts are closely related to each other, part of the same idea.*

ANNOTATION MODEL

Remind students of the order that claims, key ideas, and evidence are usually presented in an argument, as discussed on page 281. Point out that they may follow this suggestion or use their own system for marking up the selection in their write-in text. They may want to color-code their annotations by using highlighters. Their notes in the margin may include questions about ideas that are unclear or topics they want to learn more about.

282   Unit 2

GET READY

CRITICAL VOCABULARY

genre   double entendre   entail   emulation   hierarchy

To see how many Critical Vocabulary words you already know, answer the following questions.

1. Which refers to competitive imitation?
   a. hierarchy   b. double entendre   c. emulation

2. Which word refers to a category?
   a. hierarchy   b. genre   c. double entendre

3. Which refers to an expression with two meanings?
   a. double entendre   b. emulation   c. entail

4. Which refers to a ranking of status?
   a. hierarchy   b. emulation   c. genre

5. Which word is most closely associated with "involve"?
   a. genre   b. entail   c. double entendre

LANGUAGE CONVENTIONS

Coordinating Conjunctions Combining sentences can improve the clarity and flow of your writing. Complete sentences can be combined using coordinating conjunctions, such as *and, but,* and *or.* Note this example:

Hamlet is a revenge tragedy, but it is also a criticism of revenge tragedies.

As you read "Hamlet's Dull Revenge," note places where the author chooses to combine or not to combine sentences.

ANNOTATION MODEL   NOTICE & NOTE

As you read, note how the author uses a traditional argument structure of claims and evidence to organize his key ideas. You can also mark up evidence that supports your own ideas. In the model, you can see one reader's notes about "Hamlet's Dull Revenge."

> Shakespeare can turn this tedious chore into the most brilliant feat of theatrical **double entendre** because <u>the tedium of revenge is really what he wants to talk about</u>, and he wants to talk about it in the usual Shakespearean fashion; <u>he will denounce the revenge theater and all its works</u> with the utmost daring without denying his mass audience the *katharsis* it demands, <u>without depriving himself of the dramatic success</u> which is necessary to his own career as a dramatist.

Claim: Shakespeare's motive for writing Hamlet is to criticize revenge theater.

Evidence: He writes a revenge play about the tedium of revenge plays, but includes elements of revenge plays to keep the audience's interest.

282   Unit 2

BACKGROUND

René Girard (1923–2015) *was born in France and moved to the United States in 1950. He became well known as an influential writer and theorist. Girard's primary theory was that humans are motivated by desire, and their desires are based on imitating the desires of others, a concept he called* mimesis. *His theory of mimesis has influenced other writers, been used to explain economic concepts, and even inspired the founder of a major technology company to invest in social media before it became a major industry. Girard received international recognition for his many achievements in and contributions to the fields of literature, philosophy, and anthropology.*

HAMLET'S DULL REVENGE

Literary Criticism by René Girard

SETTING A PURPOSE

As you read, pay attention to details that show how Girard views Shakespeare as a writer and Hamlet as a character.

1 **H**amlet belongs to the **genre** of the revenge tragedy, as hackneyed and yet inescapable in Shakespeare's days as the "thriller" in ours to a television writer. In *Hamlet* Shakespeare turned this necessity for a playwright to go on writing the same old revenge tragedies into an opportunity to debate almost openly for the first time the questions I have tried to define. The weariness with revenge and *katharsis*[1] which can be read, I believe, in the margins of the earlier plays must really exist because, in *Hamlet*, it moves to the center of the stage and becomes fully articulated.

2 Some writers who were not necessarily the most unimaginative found it difficult, we are told, to postpone for the whole duration of the lengthy Elizabethan play an action which had never been in doubt in the first place and which is always

---
[1] **katharsis:** catharsis, the elimination of tension through the release of repressed emotions

Notice & Note

Use the side margins to notice and note signposts in the text.

genre
(zhän´rə) *n.* a category within an art form, based on style or subject.

TEACH

BACKGROUND

After students read the Background note, explain that Girard believed mimesis led to competition, which over time could build to destructive levels. In the essay, Girard applies his theory of mimesis to literature. Therefore, the essay is considered literary criticism. As a genre, literary criticism has several possible purposes: It might evaluate, interpret, analyze, or describe an aspect of an author's work, an entire work, or all of an author's writing. Although Girard analyzed many of Shakespeare's works, in this essay he focuses only on *Hamlet*. He presents a theory about Shakespeare's purposes for writing the play that he thinks explains the inconsistencies or oddities that other critics have found in it, especially Hamlet's reluctance to avenge his father's death.

SETTING A PURPOSE

Direct students to use the Setting a Purpose prompt to focus their reading.

CRITICAL VOCABULARY

genre: The author compares revenge tragedies to television "thrillers."

ASK STUDENTS what these two genres have in common. *(Both forms have predictable elements but still create excitement and suspense for the audience.)*

ENGLISH LEARNER SUPPORT

Recognize Affixes Explain that prefixes and suffixes (together called affixes) are word parts that change a word's meaning. Some words can have more than one affix. Write *unimaginative* (paragraph 2) on the board. Have students identify and define the base word. (*imagine,* "to create a mental image of something") Explain that the prefix *un-* means "not," and the suffix *-ive* means "tending toward." Thus, the word means, roughly, "not tending to create mental images." (Example: An unimaginative playwright is not very creative.) Distribute a list of affixes and their meanings. As they read, students can look for words with affixes, and then find the base words. Explain that even if students don't know the meaning of an affix, identifying the base word can help their understanding of the essay. **MODERATE**

TEACH

ANALYZE ARGUMENTS

Remind students that **evidence** for reasoning in an argument includes specific examples or facts that demonstrate why the line of reasoning is valid. Usually, a main idea or line of reasoning can be described in general terms, while the evidence supporting the line of reasoning is more specific. Have students consider how Girard moves from general, universal statements in paragraph 4 to specific examples from *Hamlet* in paragraph 5. (**Answer:** *Hamlet realizes that revenge is a cycle where violence leads to more violence and that no one person is truly superior and has the right to pass judgment and execute vengeance. His father, Claudius's victim, was not an innocent man. If Hamlet kills Claudius to avenge his father's death, he will be killing a guilty man who was, in turn, also killing a guilty man, and at the same time he himself will become guilty of murder.*)

 ENGLISH LEARNER SUPPORT

Use Print Cues to Enhance Understanding
Explain to students that italics are used in the essay for different purposes. For example:

- to indicate direct quotations
- to emphasize certain words and phrases
- to distinguish a work *(Hamlet)* from a character's name (Hamlet)
- to indicate words from other languages

ASK STUDENTS to scan the essay to look for italicized words. Then, have them use context to determine which purpose the italics serve in each case.
LIGHT

CRITICAL VOCABULARY

double entendre: The author suggests that Shakespeare has two goals in mind for his play.

ASK STUDENTS to explain the *double entendre* that the author describes. (*Shakespeare's first goal is to denounce revenge theater, and his second is to give his audience what it wants, thus making his revenge play a success.*)

entail: A justifiable act of revenge assumes certain facts about the person who will be targeted.

ASK STUDENTS what the decision to get revenge on a victim entails. (*The revenge seeker must be sure of the guilt of an intended victim and the innocence of that victim's victim.*)

284 Unit 2

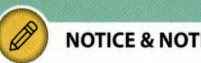 **NOTICE & NOTE**

double entendre
(dŭb´əl än-tän´drə) *n.* an expression having a double meaning.

entail
(ĕn-tāl´) *v.* involve as a consequence.

ANALYZE ARGUMENTS
Annotate: Mark the specific evidence in paragraph 5 that supports the author's reasoning in paragraph 4.

Summarize: According to Girard, why might Hamlet not "believe" in the justice of his own cause?

---

the same anyway. Shakespeare can turn this tedious chore into the most brilliant feat of theatrical **double entendre** because the tedium of revenge is really what he wants to talk about, and he wants to talk about it in the usual Shakespearean fashion; he will denounce the revenge theater and all its works with the utmost daring without denying his mass audience the *katharsis* it demands, without depriving himself of the dramatic success which is necessary to his own career as a dramatist.

3   If we assume that Shakespeare really had this double goal in mind, we will find that some unexplained details in the play become intelligible and that the function of many obscure scenes becomes obvious.

4   In order to perform revenge with conviction, you must believe in the justice of your own cause. This is what we noted before, and the revenge seeker will not believe in his own cause unless he believes in the guilt of his intended victim. And the guilt of that intended victim **entails** in turn the innocence of that victim's victim. If the victim's victim is already a killer and if the revenge seeker reflects a little too much on the circularity of revenge, his faith in vengeance must collapse.

5   This is exactly what we have in *Hamlet*. It cannot be without a purpose that Shakespeare suggests the old Hamlet, the murdered king, was a murderer himself. In the various sources of the play there may be indications to that effect, but Shakespeare would have omitted them if he had wanted to strengthen the case for revenge. However nasty Claudius may look, he cannot look nasty enough if he appears in a context of previous revenge; he cannot generate, as a villain, the absolute passion and dedication which is demanded of Hamlet. The problem with Hamlet is that he cannot forget the context. As a result, the crime by Claudius looks to him like one more link in an already long chain, and his own revenge will look like still another link, perfectly identical to all the other links.

6   In a world where every ghost, dead or alive, can only perform the same action, revenge, or clamor for more of the same from beyond the grave, all voices are interchangeable. You can never know with certainty which ghost is addressing whom. It is one and the same thing for Hamlet to question his own identity and to question the ghost's identity, and his authority.

7   To seek singularity in revenge is a vain enterprise but to shrink from revenge, in a world which looks upon it as a "sacred duty" is to exclude oneself from society, to become a nonentity once more. There is no way out for Hamlet and he shifts endlessly from one impasse to the other, unable to make up his mind because neither choice makes sense.

8   If all characters are caught in a cycle of revenge that extends in all directions beyond the limits of its action, *Hamlet* has no beginning

284 Unit 2

APPLYING ACADEMIC VOCABULARY

☐ ambiguous   ☐ anticipate   ☐ conceive   ☑ drama   ☐ integrity

Write and Discuss Have students turn to a partner to discuss the following questions. Guide students to include the academic vocabulary word *drama* in their responses. Ask volunteers to share their responses with the class.

- What type of **drama** was popular in Shakespeare's day?
- How was the **drama** of Shakespeare's day similar to and/or different from popular entertainment today?

and no end. The play collapses. The trouble with the hero is that he does not believe in his play half as much as the critics do. He understands revenge and the theater too well to assume willingly a role chosen for him by others. His sentiments are those, in other words, which we have surmised in Shakespeare himself. What the hero feels in regard to the act of revenge, the creator feels in regard to revenge as theater.

9   The public wants vicarious victims and the playwright must oblige. Tragedy is revenge. Shakespeare is tired of revenge, and yet he cannot give it up or he gives up his audience and his identity as a playwright. Shakespeare turns a typical revenge topic, *Hamlet*, into a meditation on his predicament as a playwright. . . .

10   What Hamlet needs, in order to stir up his vengeful spirit, is a revenge theater more convincing than his own, something less half-hearted than the play Shakespeare is actually writing. Fortunately for the hero and for the spectators who are eagerly awaiting their final bloodbath, Hamlet has many opportunities to watch rousing spectacles during his play and he tries to generate even more, in a conscientious effort to put himself in the right mood for the murder of Claudius. Hamlet must receive from someone else, a mimetic[2] model, the impulse which he does not find in himself. This is what he tried to achieve with his mother, we found, and he did not succeed. He is much more successful with the actor who impersonates for him the role of Hecuba. It becomes obvious, at this point, that the only hope for Hamlet to accomplish what his society—or the spectators—require, is to become as "sincere" a showman as the actor who can shed real tears when he pretends to be the queen of Troy!

> Is it not monstrous that this player here,
> But in a fiction, in a dream of passion,
> Could force his soul so to his own conceit
> That from her working all his visage wanned,
> Tears in his eyes, distraction in's aspect,
> A broken voice, and his whole function suiting
> With forms to his conceit? And all for nothing!
> For Hecuba!
> What's Hecuba to him or he to Hecuba,
> That he should weep for her? What would he do
> Had he the motive and the cue for passion
> That I have?

Another catchy example for Hamlet comes from the army of Fortinbras on its way to Poland. The object of the war is a worthless speck of land. Thousands of people must risk their lives:

---

[2] **mimetic:** relating to imitation

LANGUAGE CONVENTIONS

Annotate: Underline sentences that have been combined in paragraph 9, and circle the coordinating conjunctions.

Annotate: How does the author's decision to combine these sentences affect the flow of the paragraph?

QUOTED WORDS

Notice & Note: A block quote is often used when quoting several lines of text. Circle the block quote in paragraph 10.

Evaluate: How does the block quote help support the point the author is making?

TEACH

ANALYZE ARGUMENTS

Tell students that every choice a writer makes is for a reason. When a writer structures an argument, he or she considers carefully the order in which to present the reasons and evidence. Often, the lines of reasoning a writer uses do not have equal support, and one line of reasoning may be stronger than another. Stronger and weaker lines of reasoning are placed strategically within the argument so that the strongest lines of reasoning are the ones that the reader is most likely to notice and remember. (**Answer:** *Girard feels that the example of Laertes is the piece of evidence that best supports his argument that Hamlet needs a model of action to motivate his revenge. Girard saves the example of Laertes for last because it is his strongest point and the point on which he has the most to say. Girard started with the actor playing Hecuba because Hamlet draws that comparison himself and it effectively introduces Girard's main point. He then put the example of Fortinbras in the middle because it supports his idea, but the connection is not as strong as the other two examples. Starting and ending with the strongest examples make the argument seem more solid to the reader.*)

ANALYZE KEY IDEAS

Remind students that key ideas should support the overall claim the author makes. Encourage students to consider reasons why a literary critic like Girard would want to emphasize the differences between his own analysis and those of other critics. (**Answer:** *Girard tries to separate himself from other critics when he says "it never occurs to most critics that Shakespeare himself could question the validity of revenge." He feels that the analysis he is offering is new and fresh, superior to what many other literary critics offer. To Girard, other literary critics are often "simple and unreflective" formalists, like Laertes.*)

CRITICAL VOCABULARY

emulation: The author explains that Hamlet is moved to action by Laertes's example.

ASK STUDENTS to explain why Hamlet is especially driven toward emulation of Laertes. (*Laertes is Hamlet's peer—he is about Hamlet's age and is a privileged member of the court. When Hamlet sees him react with such passion to the death of his sister, Hamlet feels ashamed that he has not had a similarly passionate response to his own father's murder.*)

NOTICE & NOTE

Even for an eggshell. Rightly to be great
Is not to stir without great argument,
But greatly to find quarrel in a straw
When Honor's at the stake.

11 The scene is as ridiculous as it is sinister. It would not impress Hamlet so much if the hero truly believed in the superiority and urgency of his cause. His words constantly betray him, here as in the scene with his mother. As a cue for passion, his revenge motif is no more compelling, really, than the cue of an actor on the stage. He too must *greatly . . . find quarrel in a straw*, he too must stake everything *even for an eggshell*.

12 The effect of the army scene obviously stems, at least in part, from the large number of people involved, from the almost infinite multiplication of the example which cannot fail to increase its mimetic attraction enormously. Shakespeare is too much a master of mob effects not to remember at this point the cumulative effect of mimetic models. In order to whip up enthusiasm for the war against Claudius, the same irrational contagion is needed as in the war against Poland. The type of mimetic incitement from which Hamlet "benefits" at this point resembles very much the kind of spectacle which governments never fail to organize for their citizenry when they have decided it is time to go to war: a rousing military parade.

13 But it is not the actor, ultimately, or the army of Fortinbras; it is Laertes, I believe, who determines Hamlet to act. Laertes provides the most persuasive spectacle not because he provides the "best" example but because his situation parallels that of Hamlet. Being Hamlet's peer, at least up to a point, his passionate stance constitutes the most powerful challenge imaginable. In such circumstances, even the most apathetic man's sense of **emulation** must rise to such a pitch that the sort of disaster that the fulfillment of the revenge demands can finally be achieved.

14 The simple and unreflective Laertes can shout to Claudius "give me my father" and then leap into his sister's grave in a wild demonstration of grief. Like a well-adjusted gentleman or a consummate actor, he can perform with the utmost sincerity all the actions his social milieu demands, even if they contradict each other. He can mourn the useless death of a human being at one minute and the next he can uselessly kill a dozen more if he is told that his honor is at stake. The death of his father and sister are almost less shocking to him than the lack of pomp and circumstance at their burial. At the rites of Ophelia, Laertes keeps asking the priest for "more ceremony." Laertes is a formalist[3] and he reads the tragedy of which he is a part very much like the formalists of all stripes. He does not question the

---
[3] **formalist:** one who strictly adheres to accepted rules and conventions

ANALYZE ARGUMENTS

Annotate: Mark the words and phrases in paragraph 13 that show how the author feels about the final piece of evidence he is about to present in support of his claim.

Analyze: Why do you think the author chose to discuss the examples of the actor playing Hecuba, Fortinbras' army, and Laertes in that particular order?

emulation
(ĕm-yə-lā´shən) *n.* competitive imitation.

ANALYZE KEY IDEAS

Annotate: Mark details in paragraph 14 that the author uses to draw comparisons between Laertes and literary critics.

Infer: How does the author seem to feel about his own analysis of *Hamlet* compared to other critics?

IMPROVE READING FLUENCY

Targeted Passage Have students work with partners to practice reading informational text. First, use paragraph 11 to model how to read informational text. Have students follow along as you read the text with appropriate pausing, tone, and inflection. Then, have partners take turns reading paragraphs 12 and 13. Encourage students to provide feedback and support for pausing appropriately. Remind students that when they read aloud, commas, semicolons, colons, and periods signal different types of pauses. Then, have students switch and repeat the exercise so that each student has an opportunity to practice reading both paragraphs.

 Go to the **Reading Studio** for additional support in developing fluency.

validity of revenge. He does not question the literary *genre*. He does not question the relationship between revenge and mourning. These are not valid critical questions to him; they never enter his mind, just as it never occurs to most critics that Shakespeare himself could question the validity of revenge.

15   Hamlet watches Laertes leap into Ophelia's grave and the effect on him is electrifying. The reflective mood of the conversation with Horatio gives way to a wild imitation of the rival's theatrical mourning. At this point, he has obviously decided that he, too, would act according to the demands of society, that he would become another Laertes in other words. He, too, as a result, must leap into the

ANALYZE ARGUMENTS

Annotate: Mark the details the author cites in paragraph 15 to support the idea that Hamlet's actions are inspired by Hamlet's observations of Laertes.

Analyze: How is the reasoning and evidence presented in paragraph 15 related to the author's overall claim about Shakespeare's double purpose for writing?

Hamlet's Dull Revenge   287

TEACH

ANALYZE ARGUMENTS

Remind students that the overall argument Girard is making is not just about the content of *Hamlet*, but about Shakespeare's purpose for writing. Encourage them to consider parallels between Hamlet as a character who does not believe in revenge and Shakespeare as a writer who (according to Girard) does not believe in revenge theater. (**Answer:** *In paragraph 15 Girard uses Hamlet's own words to show that Hamlet is inspired by the example of Laertes and determines to show grief and seek revenge in the way that society wants him to. Even if it involves behavior that he does not agree with, he will do what he is supposed to and do it well. In a similar way, Girard notes early in the essay that Shakespeare is tired of traditional revenge theater, but also has to find inspiration within that genre because it is what his audience wants. The result is Hamlet: a revenge play that is even more brilliant and compelling than other revenge plays because the main character does not believe in revenge.*)

■ English Learner Support

Summarize Arguments   Make sure students understand that paragraph 15 contains important details that support the author's claim that Hamlet draws inspiration from the examples of others. Have students summarize the evidence presented, identifying the cause and effect relationship that forms the backbone of Girard's reasoning: Hamlet observes Laertes's example of grief (cause), and he decides that his own actions must be different as a result (effect). **MODERATE**

TO CHALLENGE STUDENTS

Evaluate the Author's Argument   Near the beginning of his essay, Girard says that his analysis will help clarify "some unexplained details" and "the function of many obscure scenes."

Ask students to identify the details and scenes from *Hamlet* that Girard cites as evidence in his argument. Do the students agree that these parts of the play are "unexplained" and "obscure" *without* Girard's explanation that Shakespeare sought to denounce revenge theater and the very idea of revenge? Have students formulate some thoughts independently and then share their ideas in pairs or small groups.

TEACH

ANALYZE KEY IDEAS

In a well-structured essay, key ideas are always backed up by evidence or supporting details. In the genre of literary criticism, the details that provide the strongest support for a key idea are generally those that come directly from the text being analyzed. Draw students' attention to places where Girard includes direct quotations and then refers back to those quotation in his explanation, re-quoting specific phrases as needed to make his point. (**Answer:** According to Girard, Hamlet changes from being uncertain and lacking motivation to showing overwhelming passion and near madness because he is inspired by the extreme emotions of mimetic models. He then changes from being passionate to being calm and quiet because the passion has changed into "cool determination" to act in the way that society wants him to and accomplish the revenge.)

CRITICAL VOCABULARY

hierarchy: At Ophelia's funeral, Laertes shows a higher degree of passion than Hamlet has been able to muster.

ASK STUDENTS how Hamlet confuses the hierarchy between him and Laertes. (*Laertes's passion is the model that Hamlet imitates, not the reverse, thus, Laertes's "passion" is at the higher level.*)

 **NOTICE & NOTE**

grave of one who has already died, even as he prepares other graves for those still alive:

> 'Swounds, show me what thou'lt do.
> Woo't weep? Woo't fight? Woo't fast? Woo't tear thyself?
> Woo't drink up eisel? Eat a crocodile?
> I'll do't. Dost thou come here to whine?
> To outface me with leaping in her grave?
> Be buried quick with her, and so will I.
> ....
> I'll rant as well as thou. . . .

ANALYZE KEY IDEAS
Annotate: Mark details in paragraphs 16 and 17 that indicate Hamlet undergoes a change.

Infer: According to Girard, what is the reason Hamlet changes?

16   Shakespeare can place these incredible lines in the mouth of Hamlet without undermining the dramatic credibility of what follows. Following the lead of Gertrude, the spectators will ascribe the outburst to "madness."

> This is mere madness.
> And thus awhile the fit will work on him.
> Anon, as patient as the female dove
> When that her golden couplets are disclosed,
> His silence will sit drooping.

A little later Hamlet himself, now calmly determined to kill Claudius, will recall the recent outburst in most significant words:

> I am very sorry, good Horatio,
> That to Laertes I forgot myself,
> For by the image of my cause I see
> The portraiture of his. I'll court his favors.
> But, sure, the bravery of his grief did put me
> Into a towering passion.

hierarchy
(hī′ə-rär′kē) *n.* a ranking of status within a group.

17   Like all victims of mimetic suggestion, Hamlet reverses the true **hierarchy** between the other and himself. He should say: "by the image of *his* cause I see the portraiture of *mine*." This is the correct formula, obviously, for all the spectacles that have influenced Hamlet. The actor's tears and the military display of Fortinbras were already presented as mimetic models. In order to realize that Laertes, too, functions as a model, the last two lines are essential. The cool determination of Hamlet, at this point, is the transmutation[4] of the "towering passion" which he had vainly tried to build up before and which Laertes has finally communicated to him through the "bravery of his grief." This transmutation is unwittingly predicted by Gertrude when she compares Hamlet to the dove who becomes quiet after she

---
[4] **transmutation:** an alteration or conversion into another form

288   Unit 2

WHEN STUDENTS STRUGGLE. . .

Identify Evidence To help students understand this part of the argument, point out the indented block quotations. Explain that these are used to show that Hamlet needs to find a model in order to make his revenge. Summarize the main point of these quotations: Paragraph 10, *Is it not monstrous . . .* Hamlet wonders if he can be as sincere as the actor seems to be; Paragraph 10, *Even for an eggshell . . .* Hamlet acknowledges that Fortinbras is able to act.

 For additional support, go to the **Reading Studio** and assign the following Level Up tutorial: Analyzing Arguments.

has laid her eggs. Gertrude only thinks of Hamlet's previous changes of mood, as sterile as they were sudden, but her metaphor suggests a more tangible accomplishment, the birth of something portentous:

> Anon, as patient as the female dove
> When that her golden couplets are disclosed,
> His silence will sit drooping.

CHECK YOUR UNDERSTANDING

Answer these questions before moving on to the **Analyze the Text** section.

1. According to Girard, Shakespeare's two goals in writing *Hamlet* were to criticize revenge theater and —
   - **A** to show that revenge is pointless
   - **B** to expose the ways people imitate each other
   - **C** to create a new genre of theater
   - **D** to write the kind of play that his audience wanted

2. According to Girard's analysis, which statement about the character of Hamlet is true?
   - **F** Hamlet struggles with killing Claudius because he does not fully believe in revenge.
   - **G** Hamlet subconsciously imitates the example of Laertes because Laertes is his older brother.
   - **H** Hamlet's mood changes from one of passion to one of calm because he is exhausted by the speech he makes to Laertes.
   - **J** Hamlet finds the sight of Fortinbras' army depressing because he realizes they are dedicated to a worthless cause.

3. Which quotation from the selection shows that Girard believes using mimetic models as a motivating force can be dangerous?
   - **A** *Hamlet must receive from someone else, a mimetic model, the impulse which he does not find in himself.*
   - **B** *Hamlet watches Laertes leap into Ophelia's grave and the effect on him is electrifying.*
   - **C** *Like all victims of mimetic suggestion, Hamlet reverses the true hierarchy between the other and himself.*
   - **D** *The actor's tears and the military display of Fortinbras were already presented as mimetic models.*

TEACH

CHECK YOUR UNDERSTANDING

Have students answer the questions independently.

Answers:

1. D
2. F
3. C

If students answer any questions incorrectly, have them reread the text to confirm their understanding. Then, they may proceed to ANALYZE THE TEXT on page 290.

ENGLISH LEARNER SUPPORT

Oral Assessment To assess students' comprehension and speaking skills, ask:.

1. Does Shakespeare want his audience to enjoy *Hamlet*? *(yes)*
2. Hamlet does not fully believe in _____. *(revenge.)*
3. Who does Hamlet copy? *(Laertes)* **SUBSTANTIAL/MODERATE**

APPLY

ANALYZE THE TEXT

Possible answers:

1. **DOK 3:** *Girard develops the idea that Shakespeare uses Hamlet to analyze both the concept of revenge and the genre of revenge theater. Hamlet's own reluctance to participate in revenge is compared to Shakespeare's reluctance to produce another work of revenge theater.*

2. **DOK 4:** *Girard speaks about Shakespeare in a tone that indicates he respects Shakespeare and believes that he is a truly great and talented playwright. In paragraph 2, he refers to Hamlet as a "brilliant feat" and describes Shakespeare's style as one of "utmost daring."*

3. **DOK 3:** *Because Laertes does not question the act of revenge like Hamlet does, he represents traditional revenge theater and the audiences and playwrights that do not question or get tired of the genre of revenge theater. Girard backs up his interpretation with examples from the text that show different Laertes's and Hamlet's initial reactions to revenge are and how Hamlet's own decisions about revenge are affected by Laertes.*

4. **DOK 4:** *When Hamlet's passionate speeches end and he becomes silent, his silence is "something portentous" that predicts that the revenge will take place. According to Girard, Hamlet's views on revenge mirror Shakespeare's views on revenge theater. Girard believes that Shakespeare was tired of revenge tragedies before he even started writing Hamlet. However, just like Hamlet becomes determined to avenge his father, Shakespeare determines that he will write Hamlet as a revenge tragedy despite his feelings about the genre. His acceptance of the fact that his audience wants revenge tragedies is "something portentous" that predicts the writing of Hamlet itself.*

5. **DOK 4:** *The quotations show how each model—The actor playing Hecuba, Fortinbras's army, and Laertes—is a catalyst for Hamlet's introspection and eventual shift from inaction to determination to avenge his father's death.*

RESEARCH

Remind students that in addition to evaluating sources for bias, they must also evaluate for credibility. The best sources are both credible and unbiased.

Connect Students may note that Claudius's imitation of the former king, possibly a murderer himself, created the destructive rivalry which resulted in Claudius murdering his brother (Hamlet's father) before the play begins.

290 Unit 2

RESPOND

ANALYZE THE TEXT

Support your responses with evidence from the text. NOTEBOOK

1. **Draw Conclusions** What key idea does Girard begin to develop in paragraphs 4–9?

2. **Analyze** What is Girard's tone toward Shakespeare and his play? Explain how his feelings are revealed through his language.

3. **Critique** According to Girard, what is the relationship between the character of Laertes and traditional revenge theater? How well does Girard back up his interpretation of Laertes' role? Explain.

4. **Analyze** *Portend* means to predict that something is likely to occur. What is the "something portentous" that Gertrude's birth metaphor refers to in paragraph 17? In Girard's view, how might the phrase be applied to Shakespeare's play as well?

5. **Notice & Note** Review the lines spoken by Hamlet quoted in Girard's essay. Do these lines effectively support his perspective on Hamlet's state of mind? Explain.

RESEARCH TIP
When conducting research about a scholarly work, be sure to evaluate sources for bias. As you consider the information presented, ask yourself, "Is the information obviously designed to make me agree or disagree with a certain point of view, or is it presented in an objective, or neutral, way? Is the philosophy presented as one possible explanation, or as undeniable fact?"

RESEARCH

In his analysis of *Hamlet*, Girard makes frequent references to the idea of mimesis and theories of human motivation. With a partner, research the theories of René Girard. Use what you learn to answer these questions:

QUESTION	ANSWER
In what book did Girard first describe his theory of mimesis?	*Deceit, Desire, and the Novel (1961)*
How is Girard's concept of mimesis different from imitation?	*Girard's concept of mimesis involves rivalry, which Girard believed was a natural and destructive result of individuals having the same desires. Imitation does not always involve rivalry, and can at times be positive.*
Why do some critics and scholars find it difficult to classify Girard's works and ideas?	*Girard's theories cover many different disciplines, including literature, philosophy, anthropology, and religion.*

Connect In "Hamlet's Dull Revenge," Girard claims that Hamlet's desires and actions are affected by mimetic models. Now that you have learned more about Girard's theory of mimesis, consider what you know about other characters in *Hamlet*. With a partner, discuss whether the actions of any of the other characters in the play can be explained using Girard's theory.

290 Unit 2

WHEN STUDENTS STRUGGLE . . .

Reteaching: Analyze Arguments Review what students have learned about analyzing an argument. Tell them that as they read an argument, they should be able to identify

- the claim that the argument makes
- the reasons that support the claim
- the pieces of evidence that support the reasoning

 For additional support, go to the **Reading Studio** and assign the following Level Up tutorial: Analyzing Arguments.

CREATE AND DISCUSS

Write an Argument Write an argumentative essay that answers the following question: Does Girard succeed in presenting a valid interpretation of Shakespeare's play *Hamlet*? Review your annotations and your responses to the analysis questions before you begin.

- ❏ Write a sentence or two summarizing Girard's interpretation.
- ❏ Decide whether or not he convincingly supports this interpretation of the play in his essay.
- ❏ Give reasons for your claim and use details from the essay to provide evidence for your argument.

Discuss an Interpretation Now that you have evaluated Girard's argument, discuss your thoughts about his argument with a partner.

- ❏ Take turns summarizing the findings of your own argumentative essays.
- ❏ Compare and contrast your opinions with those of your partner. Which parts of Girard's argument do you both agree on? Which parts do you disagree on? Cite evidence to support your positions.
- ❏ Ask your partner respectful clarifying questions when you do not understand a point he or she is trying to make.

RESPOND TO THE ESSENTIAL QUESTION

 What can drive someone to seek revenge?

Gather Information Review your annotations and notes on "Hamlet's Dull Revenge." Then, add relevant information to your Response Log. As you determine which information to include, think about:

- how society shapes ideas and expectations about revenge
- when or whether revenge is justified
- how revenge contributes to cycles of violence

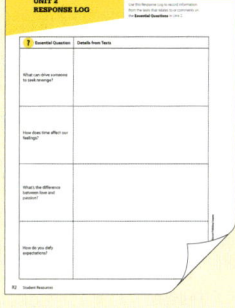

RESPOND

Go to **Writing Arguments** in the **Writing Studio** to help with the development of your essay.

Go to **Participating in Collaborative Discussions** in the **Speaking and Listening Studio** to find out more.

ACADEMIC VOCABULARY
As you write and discuss what you learned from the literary criticism, be sure to use the Academic Vocabulary words. Check off each of the words that you use.

- ❏ ambiguous
- ❏ anticipate
- ❏ conceive
- ❏ drama
- ❏ integrity

Hamlet's Dull Revenge 291

APPLY

CREATE AND DISCUSS

Write an Argument Begin with a class discussion that elicits students' own interpretations of Hamlet. Encourage students to validate their own opinions with reasons and textual evidence. Explain that there is no single "correct" interpretation, and that students need not agree with Girard's claim in order to address its validity. When writing their arguments, students should cite Girard's central ideas and the examples he uses to support them.

 For **writing** and **speaking support** for students at verying proficiency levels, see the **Text X-Ray** on page 280D.

Discuss an Interpretation Remind students that when they compare their opinions about Girard's argument, they should be discussing the *validity* of his argument, not whether they personally agree with his analysis.

RESPOND TO THE ESSENTIAL QUESTION

Allow time for students to add details from "Hamlet's Dull Revenge" to their Unit 2 Response Logs.

Hamlet's Dull Revenge **291**

APPLY

CRITICAL VOCABULARY

Answers:

1. **entail**, *because it refers to a necessary or required consequence*
2. **genre**, *of which* drama *and* novel *are examples*
3. **emulation**, *which connotes copying someone else in a spirit of competition*
4. **hierarchy**, *which refers to organization by status or rank*
5. **double entendre**, *because it indicates more than one meaning*

VOCABULARY STRATEGY:
Domain-Specific Words and Phrases

Practice and Apply Remind students that when they are looking for context clues to a word's meaning, they may need to consider several sentences before or after the sentence in which the word appears.

Answers:

1. **tragedy:** root word: *tragic = very sad;* context clue: *genre = category of literature;* definition: *a drama or literary work in which the main character is brought to ruin or suffers extreme sorrow*
2. **Elizabethan:** word parts: *contains the name Elizabeth;* definition: *of or relating to Elizabeth I of England or her reign*
3. **vicarious:** context clue: *used to describe people in a play, not real people;* definition: *experienced or felt by watching someone else rather than by doing something oneself*
4. **motif:** context clue: *used in a phrase with revenge, one of the main themes of the essay and of Hamlet;* definition: *a recurrent thematic element in an artistic or literary work*
5. **metaphor:** context clue: *previous sentence speaks of Gertrude comparing Hamlet to a dove;* definition: *a figure of speech in which a word or phrase that ordinarily designates one thing is used to designate another, thus making an implicit comparison*

292   Unit 2

 **RESPOND**

WORD BANK
genre
double entendre
entail
emulation
hierarchy

 Go to the **Vocabulary Studio** for more.

CRITICAL VOCABULARY

Practice and Apply Work with a partner to answer the questions below. Discuss which Critical Vocabulary word is most closely associated with the italicized word in each sentence and why.

1. Which word is most closely associated with *requirement*? Why?
2. Which word goes with *drama* or *novel*? Why?
3. Which word is associated with *rivalry*? Why?
4. Which word goes with *rank*? Why?
5. Which word might be associated with *ambiguity*? Why?

VOCABULARY STRATEGY:
Domain-Specific Words and Phrases

To convey his precise meaning, Girard uses **domain-specific words**, terms that are related to the field, or domain, of literary criticism. The Critical Vocabulary words *genre* and *double entendre* are two examples of this specialized vocabulary. Many times domain-specific words are footnoted. If the words are not explained, following these steps will help you define them:

1. Look closely at the context in which the term is used for familiar phrases or words that give clues to its meaning.
2. Identify word parts—roots, prefixes, or suffixes—as well as the word's part of speech, and use them to help define the term.
3. Consult a print or digital dictionary to determine the exact meaning of the term, referring to a specialized dictionary if necessary.

Practice and Apply Work with a partner to define each of the following words that Girard uses in his essay: *tragedy, Elizabethan, vicarious, motif, metaphor*. Make sure that the definition you determine relates to literature or literary criticism. Complete the graphic organizer to show the process that you use.

WORD	STRATEGY: FOOTNOTES, CONTEXT CLUES, WORD PARTS	DICTIONARY DEFINITION
tragedy		
Elizabethan		
vicarious		
motif		
metaphor		

292   Unit 2

 ENGLISH LEARNER SUPPORT

Vocabulary Strategy Vocabulary Strategy Students may be able to use cognates to determine the meanings of some domain-specific words, for example *tragedy/tragedia, vicarious/vicario,* and *metaphot/metáfora*. However, because words sometimes have multiple definitions, some domain-specific and others not domain-specific, students must use caution and avoid false cognates. For example, the word *motif* appears to have the Spanish cognate *motivo*. However, although *motivo* can be translated as *motif*, it more often refers to a motive, reason, or cause. **ALL LEVELS**

RESPOND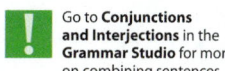

APPLY

LANGUAGE CONVENTIONS:
Combining Sentences

A series of short sentences can result in a flat, terse style that fails to clearly show the relationship between ideas. One way writers can combine their sentences is by connecting two or more complete sentences with one of these coordinating conjunctions:

COORDINATING CONJUNCTION	SAMPLE SENTENCE
and: builds upon or adds to an idea	Shakespeare was tired of writing revenge tragedies, *and* his boredom with the genre is demonstrated in *Hamlet*.
but: shows opposition or contrast	Shakespeare could have written a play that was not a tragedy, *but* he chose instead to write what his audience wanted.
or: identifies a choice	Hamlet had to avenge his father's death, *or* he would risk harsh criticism from society.

In the essay "Hamlet's Dull Revenge," Girard uses coordinating conjunctions to build compound sentences that show how the ideas in each sentence relate to each other. By combining ideas, he creates a smooth, rhythmical prose.

Read this sentence from the essay:

> Shakespeare is tired of revenge, and yet he cannot give it up, or he gives up his audience and his identity as a playwright.

This compound sentence could have been written as a series of simple sentences:

> Shakespeare is tired of revenge. Yet he cannot give it up. He would give up his audience and his identity as a playwright.

Breaking the sentence into three separate statements takes away from Girard's style and meaning. The first two sentences convey the correct meaning and are grammatically correct, but they have a choppy rhythm. The meaning of the third sentence is completely lost without the conjunction "or," which indicates that Shakespeare has a choice between giving up revenge as a topic or giving up his audience and his identity.

Practice and Apply Return to the argumentative essay you wrote for the Create and Discuss activity for this selection. Find a place where you can improve the clarity of your writing by combining sentences to connect ideas, show opposition, or identify choices with a coordinating conjunction. Record your original sentences and write your new combined sentence. Remember to include a comma before the conjunction. When you have finished, share your changes with a partner.

Go to **Conjunctions and Interjections** in the **Grammar Studio** for more on combining sentences.

LANGUAGE CONVENTIONS:
Combining Sentences

Review the information about combining sentences with students. Explain that sometimes the decision to combine or not combine sentences is purely a stylistic choice, meaning that it improves or affects flow but does not impact meaning. This is most often true of sentences combined using *and*. Using *but* and *or* to combine sentences, on the other hand, often adds to or changes the meaning of a sentence. Sentences that have been combined using *but* and *or* usually cannot be separated and retain all of the intended meaning.

Practice and Apply Have partners discuss whether sentences have been combined correctly and effectively. *(Students' sentences will vary.)*

ENGLISH LEARNER SUPPORT

Language Conventions Use the following supports with students at varying proficiency levels:

- Have students find sentences in "Hamlet's Dull Revenge" that have been combined using *and*, *but*, and *or* and copy them in their notebooks. Make sure they recognize the simple sentences that have been combined. **SUBSTANTIAL**

- Have students write original sentences and then combine them. Have them meet with a partner to compare sentences. **MODERATE**

- Have students write three combined sentences, using *and*, *but*, and *or* one time each. Then have them explain to a partner why they chose a specific conjunction to convey a certain meaning. **LIGHT**

PLAN

SONNET 30/ SONNET 75
Poems by Edmund Spenser

GENRE ELEMENTS
SONNET

Tell students that all **sonnets** are **poems,** but not all poems are sonnets. Explain that the word **poem** originates from a Greek word meaning "to make" and that a poem is a literary creation made of arrangements of words in rhythmical lines. A sonnet, however, has only 14 lines and a strict rhyme scheme. In this lesson, students will analyze sonnets about love and passion.

LEARNING OBJECTIVES

- Analyze sonnets and summarize poetry.
- Conduct research about Edmund Spenser's literary career.
- Write a sonnet.
- Present a sonnet.
- **Language** React to a presentation using connecting words.

TEXT COMPLEXITY

Quantitative Measures	Sonnet 30/Sonnet 75	**LEXILE: N/A**
Qualitative Measures	**Ideas Presented** Subtle, implied meaning. Abstract ideas and use of symbolism.	
	Structures Used Sonnet structure.	
	Language Used Implied meanings, with figurative, archaic and formal language. Complex sentence structures.	
	Knowledge Required Familiar themes.	

294A Unit 2

PLAN

RESOURCES

Online Ed

- Unit 2 Response Log
- 🔊 Selection Audio
- 📖 Reading Studio: Notice & Note
- 📈 Level Up Tutorial: Elements of Poetry
- 📝 Writing Studio: Writing as a process
- 💬 Speaking and Listening Studio: Giving a presentation
- ✅ "Sonnet 30/Sonnet 75" Selection Test

SUMMARIES

English

In Sonnet 30, the speaker cannot understand why the intensity of his love does not melt his beloved's icy coldness or why her coldness does not cool his burning desire. Instead, his passion makes her grow colder, while her coldness intensifies his heat. He concludes that love defies the laws of nature.

In Sonnet 75, the speaker hopes to immortalize his beloved by writing her name in the sand, but the waves wash it away. She tells him that his effort is pointless: he cannot immortalize her because she is mortal. The speaker replies that his poetry will allow her – and their love – to live forever.

Spanish

En el Soneto 30, el narrador no entiende por qué la intensidad de su amor no derrite el helado corazón de su amada o por qué la frialdad de ella no enfría su ardiente deseo. En vez de eso, su pasión hace que ella se enfríe, mientras que la frialdad de ella intensifica su calor. Concluye que el amor desafía las leyes de la naturaleza.

En el Soneto 75, el narrador espera inmortalizar a su amada escribiendo su nombre en la arena, pero las olas lo borran. Ella le dice que su esfuerzo es en vano: él no puede inmortalizarla porque ella es mortal. El narrador responde que su poesía permitirá que ella, y su amor, vivan por siempre.

👥 SMALL-GROUP OPTIONS

Have students work in small groups and pairs to read and discuss the selection.

Numbered Heads Together

- After students have read both sonnets, pose this question to the class: *Why might an author want to write more than one poem about love and passion?*
- Have students form groups of four and number off 1-2-3-4 within the group.
- Students discuss their responses to the question in their groups.
- Call a number from 1–4. The student with that number will then respond for the group.

Three-Minute Review

- After students read each sonnet, set a timer for three minutes.
- Have students work independently to write clarifying questions about what they read.
- After three minutes, ask volunteers to share their questions.
- Briefly discuss answers to each question.

PLAN

Text X-Ray: English Learner Support
for "Sonnet 30" and "Sonnet 75"

Use the Text X-Ray and the supports and scaffolds in the Teacher's Edition to help guide students at different proficiency levels through the selection.

INTRODUCE THE SELECTION
DISCUSS DESIRE AND PASSION

In this lesson, students will need to be able to discuss why poets often write about desire and passion.

Remind students that poets often use literary devices, such as metaphor, paradox, and imagery, when they write about desire and passion. Review that *desire* is the "wish for something" and *passion* is an "intense emotion."

Ask students to discuss why poets are fascinated with the subjects of desire and passion using sentence frames, such as: *Poets use imagery to write about passion because _____. Poets may use paradox to talk about desire because _____.*

CULTURAL REFERENCES

The following words or phrases may be unfamiliar to students:

- *pow'r* (line 13): power
- *the course* (line 14): the sequence of events
- *baser* (line 9): lower quality

LISTENING

Distinguish Intonation

Remind students that much of the pleasure of reading a sonnet is listening to the music of the words and rhythm of the lines.

Use the following supports with students at varying proficiency levels:

- Read aloud each line of Sonnet 30 and have students repeat it, matching your intonation and phrasing. Repeat any words that students have difficulty pronouncing. **SUBSTANTIAL**
- Have partners take turns rereading Sonnet 30 to each other. Guide them to correct each other's pronunciation, intonation, and phrasing, as necessary. **MODERATE**
- Have partners take turns rereading both sonnets to each other. Then, have them retell each line in their own words and compare the differences in rhythm and intonation. **LIGHT**

PLAN

SPEAKING

Compare Sonnets

Have students use academic vocabulary to compare and contrast the two sonnets.

Use the following supports with students at varying proficiency levels:
- Provide a list of questions that students can use to compare the two sonnets in a discussion. For example: *How are these sonnets alike? How are these sonnets different? Which sonnet has stronger imagery?* Have students ask you each question and then repeat your answers. **SUBSTANTIAL**
- Have each partner ask the other several compare-and-contrast questions about the two sonnets. Elicit that they will be asking about ways that the sonnets are alike and different. **MODERATE**
- Have students form a small group. Each student states one comparison or contrast sentence about the sonnets in a round robin until the topic has been exhausted. **LIGHT**

READING

Use Peer Support

Pair more-fluent readers with less-fluent readers and guide them to help each other develop vocabulary. Review familiar question stems, such as: *How do you pronounce _____? What does _____ mean?*

Use the following supports with students at varying proficiency levels:
- Have the more-fluent reader read aloud the first four lines of Sonnet 75 as the less-fluent reader follows along. Direct the less-fluent reader to read aloud the words they can. **SUBSTANTIAL**
- Have the less-fluent reader read aloud Sonnet 75. Guide the more-fluent reader to correct pronunciation and intonation as necessary. Have the pair write a list of unfamiliar words or phrases and work together to define them. **MODERATE**
- Have partners silently reread the two sonnets. Then, have them take turns asking and answering questions about unfamiliar words or language structures. **LIGHT**

WRITING

Use Connecting Words

Tell students that the use of connecting words will make their writing sound smoother and more like natural speech.

Use the following supports with students at varying proficiency levels:
- Provide a list of connecting words and phrases, such as: *and, but, since, or, even if, so that* and have students copy it. Model how to use a word to connect two short sentences in order to describe a reaction to a sonnet presentation: *The sonnet is about love and I liked it.* **SUBSTANTIAL**
- Have students copy the list from the Beginning activity. Then, have them use several of the terms as they write a two-sentence reaction to one of the sonnet presentations. **MODERATE**
- Have small groups create a list of connecting words and phrases. After a speaker presents a sonnet, have students take notes in order to write a 2–3 sentence reaction using connecting words. Direct students to write reactions to at least two sonnets. **LIGHT**

TEACH

Connect to the
ESSENTIAL QUESTION

Ask a volunteer to read aloud theEssential Question. Explain that the poems "Sonnet 30," and "Sonnet 75" by the English poet Edmund Spenser will present some interesting comparisons between love and passion. Explain to students that as they read, they should consider the differences between these two strong emotions.

ANALYZE & APPLY

SONNET 30
SONNET 75

Poems by **Edmund Spenser**

ESSENTIAL QUESTION:

What's the difference between love and passion?

GET READY

QUICK START

In the two sonnets you will be reading, Spenser deals with both love and passion. What is the difference between love and passion? How would you define each one? What are examples of each? Use the chart to record your initial thoughts. Discuss with your classmates.

LOVE	PASSION

ANALYZE SONNETS

What makes a poem a sonnet? A **sonnet** has fourteen lines and usually follows one of two forms. The Petrarchan, or Italian, sonnet (named after poet Francesco Petrarch) is divided into two parts of eight and six lines. The Shakespearean, or Elizabethan, sonnet consists of three quatrains (four-line units) plus one rhyming couplet at the end. Although the rhyming pattern is the same in each quatrain, the ending rhymes in a Shakespearean sonnet are unique within each grouping—ABAB CDCD EFEF GG. Spenser uses a variation of this rhyme scheme by interlocking the patterns between quatrains—ABAB BCBC CDCD EE.

Sonnets are also written in a particular meter, or rhythm, called **iambic pentameter. Iambic** is a repeating pattern of one unstressed syllable followed by a stressed syllable. **Pentameter** means that the pattern occurs five times in each line. The syllables are marked in the following example:

My lóve is líke to íce, and Í to fíre;

Most sonnets include a turn (sometimes called the "volta"), or a shift in thought. Since the first two quatrains often present questions or a problem, the poet might turn his thoughts to answering the question or to contradicting an idea previously stated. This turn usually occurs in the third quatrain or the couplet. The turn can resolve the poem or can be followed by a resolution.

As you read each sonnet, notice and mark each quatrain. Indicate the rhyme scheme by placing a letter at the end of each line. Notice the interlocking pattern connecting one quatrain to the next. Find the turn and the resolution in each sonnet. Use the graphic organizer to record your observations.

	TURN	RESOLUTION
Sonnet 30		
Sonnet 75		

GENRE ELEMENTS: SONNET

- consists of 14 lines
- groups the main ideas into three quatrains (four-line units) and one couplet (two rhymed lines) at the end
- written in iambic pentameter
- focuses on one sentiment or emotion
- includes a "turn," or shift in the poet's thoughts, somewhere after the second quatrain
- often includes a revelation or resolution in the couplet

Sonnet 30 / Sonnet 75   295

 ENGLISH LEARNER SUPPORT

Understand Meter Direct students' attention to the term *iambic pentameter.* Explain that the word *iamb* means a poetic meter. In poetry, a meter includes two syllables. Then, explain that the word *pentameter* includes the Greek root for "five." So, an iambic pentameter has five poetic meters. **ALL LEVELS**

TEACH

QUICK START

Have students read the Quick Start question. Then, invite them to share their favorite examples of love songs or romantic movies. Encourage students to describe the song or film of their choice and determine if it is primarily focused on love or passion. Then, have students work together to brainstorm definitions of love and passion.

ANALYZE SONNETS

Help students understand the terms and concepts related to analyzing **sonnets.** Introduce the terms **quatrain** and **couplet** to discuss the format of these kinds of poems. Explain that quatrains can be like the paragraphs in a story. Together, the four lines focus on one main idea.

Also examine both the rhyme scheme and rhythm common to sonnets. Explain that an **iambic pentameter** is a repeating pattern of syllables. Tell students that an iamb is an unstressed syllable followed by a stressed syllable, such as in the word *below*. Then explain that a pentameter includes five of these syllable pairs. Have them read the example in the student edition, following the markings that show which syllables are stressed.

Explain to students that poets use the conventions of sonnets to convey their ideas (such as a shift in thought in the third quatrain or couplet). Tell students that knowing the structure, format, and style of sonnets can help them understand the meaning of a poem and interpret the ideas the poet conveys. Then, have them complete the graphic organizer as they read the two sonnets.

Sonnet 30 / Sonnet 75   **295**

TEACH

SUMMARIZE POETRY

Explain to students that summarizing a poem can help them understand difficult phrases and interpret the poet's meaning. Explain that a summary should only include the most important points and not minor details that are part of the poem. Direct them to the chart and explain that they can use it to break down a sonnet, quatrain by quatrain, to identify the key ideas of the poem.

Suggest that students use these questions to help them summarize poetry:

- How does the poem begin? How does it end?
- Which lines stand out?
- How can I rephrase key lines in my own words?
- What is the most important point the poet makes?

 ## ANNOTATION MODEL

Remind students to focus on the key idea in each quatrain or couplet to summarize each sonnet as a whole. Point out that they may follow this suggestion or use their own system for marking up the selection in their write-in text. They may want to color-code their annotations by using highlighters. Their notes in the margin may include questions about ideas that are unclear or topics they want to learn more about.

296 Unit 2

 **GET READY**

SUMMARIZE POETRY

You can often clarify the meaning of a poem by rephrasing it using simpler language. You might **paraphrase** a difficult passage by restating it in your own words. It is important to maintain the passage's meaning and logical order when you paraphrase. Another option would be to **summarize** the entire poem, restating only the key ideas or themes. A summary is much shorter than the original text because it leaves out most details. As you read each sonnet, use a chart like this to help you summarize the idea in each part of the poem.

"Sonnet 75"	
Part of Poem	**Key Idea**
1st Quatrain	Whenever I write my beloved's name in the sand, the waves wash it away.
2nd Quatrain	
3rd Quatrain	
Couplet	

ANNOTATION MODEL NOTICE & NOTE

As you read, notice how Spenser uses images to express ideas. Paraphrase or summarize the key idea in each quatrain or couplet. This model shows one reader's notes about the first quatrain of "Sonnet 30."

> My love is like to (ice,) and I to (fire;)
> How comes it then that this her cold so great
> Is not dissolved through my so (hot desire,)
> But harder grows the more I her entreat?

Why doesn't my flaming desire melt my beloved's coldness?
She only grows icier the more I plead with her.

296 Unit 2

WHEN STUDENTS STRUGGLE...

Summarize Poetry Have students complete the graphic organizer to summarize the first three quatrains (12 lines).

Lines	Summary
1–4	My beloved and I are like fire and ice.
5–8	Yet our opposite natures don't seem to affect one another.
9–12	She remains cold; however, this does not lessen my fiery passion.

 For additional support, go to the **Reading Studio** and assign the following Level Up tutorial: Summarizing.

BACKGROUND

Edmund Spenser (1552?–1599) was a highly innovative poet who rose from humble origins to become one of the most admired Elizabethan writers. He invented a sonnet form based on an intricate pattern of rhymes, called the Spenserian sonnet, and a special stanza form called the Spenserian stanza. Both influenced later poets. Spenser's greatest work is The Faerie Queene, *an allegorical epic that uses stories of adventurous knights to convey a message about how to lead a virtuous life.*

SONNET 30
SONNET 75
Poems by Edmund Spenser

Spenser was born in London. He attended Cambridge University as a "sizar," or poor scholar. Several years after his graduation, he published his first major work, The Shepheardes Calender. In 1580, Spenser moved to Ireland to serve as secretary to the lord deputy of Ireland. He became a wealthy landowner in Ireland and wrote most of his remaining works there. Spenser's courtship of his second wife in 1594 inspired him to write a sonnet sequence (a series of related sonnets) called Amoretti, which means "little love poems." The sequence includes "Sonnet 30" and "Sonnet 75."

In 1598, Spenser fled his estate when it was attacked by Irish rebels. He managed to reach London, but he died shortly afterward. In recognition of his literary achievements, he was buried near Geoffrey Chaucer in what is now called the Poets' Corner of Westminster Abbey.

SETTING A PURPOSE

As you read, notice how Spenser uses vivid imagery and figurative language to convey ideas about passion and love in his poems.

NOTICE & NOTE

Notice & Note

Use the side margins to notice and note signposts in the text.

Sonnet 30 / Sonnet 75 297

TEACH

BACKGROUND

After students read the Background note, explain that a sonnet sequence is a series of loosely connected poems. William Shakespeare wrote them as well. "Sonnet 30" and "Sonnet 75" were taken from a sequence called *Amoretti*, which means "little love poems" in Italian. The series was first published in 1595, and included 89 poems by Edmund Spenser, focused on his second wife.

SETTING A PURPOSE

Direct students to use the Setting a Purpose prompt to focus their reading.

 ENGLISH LEARNER SUPPORT

Acquire Vocabulary Explain to students that this poem was written long ago, and that many of the words will be unfamiliar to modern-day readers. Review the meaning of the following words: *dissolved* (line 3), *entreat* (line 4), *exceeding* (line 5), *miraculous* (line 9), *kindle* (line 12), and *alter* (line 14). Help students look up the words in the dictionary and find synonyms for each word. Then, replace the unfamiliar words with synonyms and reread the lines. Have students work with a partner to summarize the lines. **LIGHT**

Sonnet 30 / Sonnet 75 **297**

TEACH

 ANALYZE SONNETS

Remind students that sonnets follow a strict structure. Have them consider how changing the order of words would affect the structure of the poem. (**Answer:** *In the first quatrain, Spenser sets up a conflict between himself and his beloved. They have opposite natures which are represented by the contrasting elements fire and ice. Ice represents her, and fire represents him.*)

 **NOTICE & NOTE**

Sonnet 30

My love is like to ice, and I to fire:
How comes it then that this her cold so great
Is not dissolved through my so hot desire,
But harder grows the more I her entreat?
5   Or how comes it that my exceeding heat
Is not delayed by her heart-frozen cold:
But that I burn much more in boiling sweat,
And feel my flames augmented manifold?
What more miraculous thing may be told
10   That fire which all things melts, should harden ice:
And ice which is congealed with senseless cold,
Should kindle fire by wonderful device.
Such is the pow'r of love in gentle mind,
That it can alter all the course of kind.

8 augmented manifold: greatly increased

11 congealed: solidified.

14 kind: nature.

ANALYZE SONNETS
Annotate: Circle the rhyming pair in the first and third lines. Underline the rhyming pair in the second and fourth lines.

Identify: What conflict does Spencer set up in the first quatrain? What contrasting elements are used to represent each side of the conflict?

298   Unit 2

WHEN STUDENTS STRUGGLE...

Paraphrase   To help students understand *augmented manifold* and *congealed*, paraphrase lines 8 and 11 and have students follow along in the graphic organizer.

Line	Meaning
8	And feel my passion greatly increased
11	And ice which solidifies with extreme cold

 For additional support, go to the **Reading Studio** and assign the following Level Up tutorial: **Paraphrasing**.

298   Unit 2

NOTICE & NOTE

CHECK YOUR UNDERSTANDING

Answer these questions about "Sonnet 30" before moving on to the next selection.

1. The speaker wonders why the more he pleads with his beloved —
   - A the closer she draws near to him
   - B the colder she becomes
   - C the more her ice melts
   - D the further she runs from him

2. The speaker asks why his beloved's coldness does not —
   - F cool his desire
   - G dissolve their relationship
   - H delay their marriage
   - J fade away

3. The speaker concludes that —
   - A their love is dying
   - B his beloved is preparing to leave him
   - C he should give up on his beloved
   - D love has supernatural powers

Sonnet 30 / Sonnet 75

TEACH

CHECK YOUR UNDERSTANDING

Have students answer the questions independently.

Answers:

1. B
2. F
3. D

If students answer any questions incorrectly, have them reread the text to confirm their understanding. Then, they may proceed to the next sonnet.

ENGLISH LEARNER SUPPORT

Oral Assessment Use the following questions to assess students' comprehension and speaking skills.

1. What does the poet notice about his beloved the more he pleads with her? *(She becomes colder with him.)*

2. How does the poet respond to the coldness of his beloved? *(His feeling for her grows stronger.)*

3. What does the poet conclude about the relationship with his beloved? *(Their love has supernatural powers.)* **ALL LEVELS**

TEACH

✏️ SUMMARIZE POETRY

Guide students to identify the comparison in the text. (**Answer:** *Silly man, you write my name in vain. Because I'm only human and will one day be gone just like my name in the sand has been wiped away.*)

✏️ ANALYZE SONNETS

Remind students that turn is when a poet shifts his or her thinking on a subject. Where does this happen in the poem? (**Answer:** *The poet states that he can make his beloved immortal by writing about her and their love. And his words will live on long after they have both died.*)

EL ENGLISH LEARNER SUPPORT

Acquire Vocabulary Explain to students that Spenser uses words that were standard in the 16th century, but modern-day readers may find them unfamiliar. Help students understand the meanings of the following words.

- *dost* (line 5) "do"
- *whenas* (line 13) "when"

Help students replace the words in the poem with modern-day synonyms and reread the lines. **ALL LEVELS**

✏️ NOTICE & NOTE

1 **strand:** beach.

5 **assay:** try.

SUMMARIZE POETRY
Annotate: Mark the lines in which the poet's beloved compares herself to the writing in the sand.
Summarize: Write a paraphrase of her comparison.

8 **eke:** also

9 **quod:** said.

ANALYZE SONNETS
Annotate: Mark the phrase that expresses the turn.
Interpret: What does the poet state he can do for his beloved?

Sonnet 75

One day I wrote her name upon the strand,
But came the waves and washéd it away:
Again I wrote it with a second hand,
But came the tide, and made my pains his prey.
5 "Vain man," said she, "that dost in vain assay,
A mortal thing so to immortalize.
For I myself shall like to this decay,
<u>And eke my name be wipéd out likewise.</u>"
"Not so," quod I, "let baser things devise
10 To die in dust, but you shall live by fame:
<u>My verse your virtues rare shall eternize,</u>
And in the heavens write your glorious name,
Where whenas death shall all the world subdue,
Our love shall live, and later life renew."

300 Unit 2

WHEN STUDENTS STRUGGLE...

Analyze Sonnets Have students answer the following questions to analyze Sonnet 75. 1) What is the rhyme scheme? (*ABAB BCBC CDCD EE*), 2) What happens at the turn? (*The poet decided to make his beloved immortal by writing about her and their love.*), 3) What happens at the resolution? (*The poet realizes that both he and his beloved will live on long after they have died in the words of his poetry.*)

📖 For additional support, go to the **Reading Studio** and assign the following Level Up tutorial: Analyze Sonnets.

300 Unit 2

NOTICE & NOTE

CHECK YOUR UNDERSTANDING

Answer these questions before moving on to the **Analyze the Text** section on the following page.

1. What is the setting of this sonnet?
   A The speaker's beach house
   B On board a ship
   C Along the beach
   D In heaven

2. What does the speaker's beloved say about his efforts to write her name in the sand?
   F She asks him to keep trying so that she can see her name written in the sand.
   G She says it is pointless because, just as she will die someday, her name will be wiped out and forgotten.
   H She scolds him for doing such a ridiculous thing.
   J She praises his efforts for immortalizing her name.

3. Why does the speaker say that his beloved's name, as well as their love, will last forever?
   A Because he has written about them in his poetry
   B Because they have become famous
   C Because songs about her virtues will be sung throughout eternity
   D Because the heavens will declare her glorious name

TEACH

CHECK YOUR UNDERSTANDING

Have students answer the questions independently.

Answers:

1. C
2. G
3. A

If students answer any questions incorrectly, have them reread the text to confirm their understanding. Then, they may proceed to ANALYZE THE TEXT on page 302.

ENGLISH LEARNER SUPPORT

Oral Assessment Use the following questions to assess students' comprehension and speaking skills.

1. What is the setting of this sonnet? *(It is set along a beach.)*

2. What does the poet's beloved say about his writing her name in the sand? *(She says it is a waste because water washes it away.)*

3. Why does the poet claim their love will last forever? *(His poems will keep her name and their love alive.)* **ALL LEVELS**

APPLY

ANALYZE THE TEXT

Possible answers:

1. **DOK 2:** *The conflict in Sonnet 30 is one of unrequited love, between fire (passion) and ice (disinterest). In Sonnet 75, the problem is how to make love eternal in the face of death.*

2. **DOK 4:** *Sonnet 30's use of an ABAB BCBC CDCD EE rhyme scheme helps to connect ideas across the quatrains. For example, line 4 ends in the word entreat and line 5 ends in the word heat. This pattern connects the metaphor that the poet is like fire with his beloved's response to the fiery passion he offers her. This creates a tension throughout the poem.*

3. **DOK 4:** *In Sonnet 30, the turn occurs in the third quatrain. The poet comes to realize the conflict between him and his beloved shows that love is powerful enough to overcome their conflicting natures and points of view on the relationship.*

4. **DOK 2:** *In Sonnet 75, the poet repeats the image of an ocean, using terms such as waves and tide. An ocean is powerful and everlasting. This can be compared to poetry, which conveys powerful ideas to readers and lasts long after a poet has died.*

5. **DOK 3:** *Sonnet 30 focuses more on passion than love. The poet's beloved has a "heart-frozen cold." He has strong affection for her, but she does not seem to return the feeling. This does not seem like love. On the other hand, in Sonnet 75 the poet and his beloved have a strong connection. They engage in a conversation and understand one another. The poet intends to make their love immortal by writing about her "virtues," which suggests he knows her very well.*

RESEARCH

Discuss with students that it would be helpful to learn about Spenser's career to complete the graphic organizer. Explain that poets and authors often repeat themes throughout their work, and one piece may shape or influence another.

Extend Remind students that Spenser wrote during the Renaissance, which was a period that included many other poets who remain renowned today, such as William Shakespeare. Have them consider how Spenser's peers may have influenced his work.

RESPOND

ANALYZE THE TEXT

Support your responses with evidence from the text.  NOTEBOOK

1. **Summarize** In both sonnets, the first two quatrains introduce a conflict or problem. Summarize the conflict or problem in each poem.

2. **Analyze** How does Spenser's use of an interlocking rhyming pattern in "Sonnet 30" help to connect his ideas across quatrains?

3. **Analyze** Identify the turn in "Sonnet 30." How does this turn resolve the speaker's confusion about the effects of love?

4. **Identify Patterns** In "Sonnet 75," what image is repeated in the first quatrain? How does this underscore the speaker's resolution about the power of poetry?

5. **Compare** Which poem, "Sonnet 30" or "Sonnet 75," seems to focus more on passion? on love? Explain, using details from the poems.

RESEARCH

RESEARCH TIP
Before you begin researching answers to these questions, make a list of key words to use in your search. Rank the search terms on your list from more-specific to less-specfic. If at first you're having difficulty finding answers, broaden your search to include the less-specific key words.

Spenser was one of the greatest poets of the English Renaissance. With a partner, research his literary career. Use what you learn to answer these questions.

QUESTION	ANSWER
Who is represented by the title character of Spenser's epic *The Fairie Queene*?	*Named "Gloriana," the Fairy Queen represents the virtue glory and is modeled after Queen Elizabeth I.*
Which event inspired Spenser's poem "Epithalamion"?	*Spenser's wedding in 1594 to his second wife inspired the writing of the poem.*
What name did Spenser use for a character who represents him in several of his poems?	*Spenser was represented by the character Colin Clout in several poems.*

Extend "Sonnet 30" and "Sonnet 75" belong to a series of related sonnets called *Amoretti*, which means "little love poems." Read several other sonnets in this series and discuss them with a partner.

302 Unit 2

WHEN STUDENTS STRUGGLE...

Reteaching: Comprehension Support To help students engage with the text, invite them to sketch images described in the text, using the Draw It strategy. To help students focus on the imagery the selection includes, use the **What's Most Important** strategy.

 For additional support, go to the **Reading Studio** and assign the following **Level Up tutorial: Reading for Details**.

CREATE AND PRESENT

Write a Sonnet Write a sonnet that expresses your idea of love or that contrasts your ideas of love and passion. Before you begin, review your notes from the Quick Start activity and reflect on what you have learned from Spenser's sonnets. You may choose to work with a partner.

- ❏ Decide on the theme. What do you want to say about love or passion?
- ❏ Start with a question, conflict, or problem that will lead to a resolution.
- ❏ Decide how your first two quatrains will present your question, problem, or conflict.
- ❏ Determine a "turn" for the third quatrain of your sonnet and a resolution for the closing couplet. How will you show a new perspective or shift in thought? How will the third quatrain lead into the couplet?
- ❏ Decide if you will follow the Shakespearean or the Spenserian rhyme scheme. Maintain iambic pentameter and your chosen rhyme scheme.

Present the Sonnets As a class, present the sonnets you have created, using presentational software to project background visuals and transitions.

- ❏ In teams, plan the design and content of the presentation. Include an introductory screen and select a corresponding image for each sonnet.
- ❏ Practice reading your sonnets. Work on making eye contact and using your voice to express the appropriate level of emotion. As you practice with others, offer feedback to enhance the presentation.
- ❏ Pick a date, time, and meeting place for your formal readings. Invite other students to watch the presentation.

RESPOND

Go to **Writing as a Process** in the **Writing Studio** to help with planning and drafting the sonnet.

Go to **Using Media in a Presentation** in the **Speaking and Listening Studio** to find out more.

RESPOND TO THE ESSENTIAL QUESTION

 What's the difference between love and passion?

Gather Information Review your annotations and notes on "Sonnet 30" and "Sonnet 75." Then, add relevant information to your Response Log. As you determine which information to include, think about:

- the distinctions made between love and passion in Spenser's sonnets
- the relationship between true love and desire
- appropriate expressions of love and passion

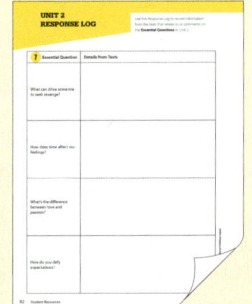

ACADEMIC VOCABULARY

As you write and discuss what you learned from the sonnets, be sure to use the Academic Vocabulary words. Check off each of the words that you use.

- ❏ ambiguous
- ❏ anticipate
- ❏ conceive
- ❏ drama
- ❏ integrity

Sonnet 30 / Sonnet 75   303

APPLY

CREATE AND PRESENT

Write a Sonnet Have students review their notes from the Quick Start activity. Then, guide them to consider what they want to say about love or passion in their own poems. Explain that each poem should include a theme that relates to love. The theme is the author's main message. Guide them to brainstorm a list of ideas expressed in the form of a complete sentence.

Some examples of common ideas related to love include:
- Love conquers all.
- All is fair in love and war.
- Better to have lost in love than never to have loved at all.

Then, have students choose one main message and determine how they will express it using the conventions of a sonnet.

Present the Sonnets Provide time for students to practice and present their sonnets in small groups. Following critiques, students should revise their work based on the suggestions of their peers.

RESPOND TO THE ESSENTIAL QUESTION

Allow time for students to add details from "Sonnet 30" and "Sonnet 75" to their Unit 2 Response Logs.

APPLYING ACADEMIC VOCABULARY

❏ **ambiguous**   ✓ **anticipate**   ❏ **conceive**   ❏ **drama**   ❏ **integrity**

Write and Discuss Have students turn to a partner to discuss the following questions about Sonnet 30 or Sonnet 75. Guide them to include the academic vocabulary word *anticipate* in their responses. Ask volunteers to share their responses with the class.

- Could a reader **anticipate** the ending of this poem? Why or why not?
- What strategies can readers use to **anticipate** how a text will end?

PLAN

A VALEDICTION: FORBIDDING MOURNING
Poem by John Donne

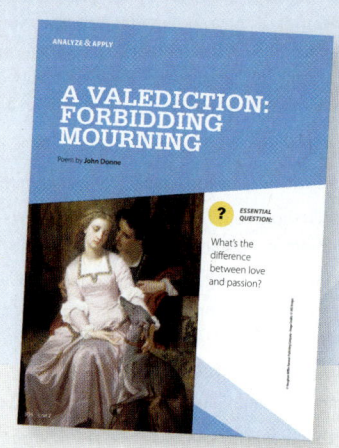

GENRE ELEMENTS
LYRIC POETRY
Tell students that *lyric* is the singular for *lyrics*, which are the words of a song. In the olden days, **lyric poems** were played on an instrument called a lyre, but today we don't generally sing lyric poems. Unlike narrative and dramatic poems, the lyric poem is shorter and delivers a personal, emotional message from the poet to the reader. In this lesson, students will analyze how a poet uses a metaphysical conceit in a lyric poem.

LEARNING OBJECTIVES
- Analyze metaphysical conceits and interpret ideas in poetry.
- Conduct research about the works of John Donne.
- Write a poem containing a metaphysical conceit.
- Present a poem.
- **Language** Describe images related to familiar concepts.

TEXT COMPLEXITY

Quantitative Measures	A Valediction: Forbidding Mourning	**LEXILE: N/A**
Qualitative Measures	**Ideas Presented** Subtle, implied meaning. Abstract ideas and use of irony, hyperbole, paradox, and symbolism.	
	Structures Used Lyric poem structure.	
	Language Used Implied meanings, with figurative, archaic and formal language. Complex sentence structures.	
	Knowledge Required Familiar themes.	

304A Unit 2

PLAN

RESOURCES

Online

- Unit 2 Response Log
- Selection Audio
- Reading Studio: Notice and Notes
- Level Up Tutorial: Elements of Poetry
- Writing Studio: Writing a Poem
- Speaking and Listening Studio: Giving a Presentation
- "A Valediction" Selection Test

SUMMARIES

English

The speaker of this poem urges his wife not to mourn his absence, for their love is strong enough to endure the separation. He compares their love to a compass, with one lover remaining stationary while the other revolves around his or her stability, making a perfect circle.

Spanish

El narrador de este poema insta a su esposa a no lamentar su ausencia, porque su amor es suficientemente fuerte para soportar la separación. Compara su amor con una brújula, en la cual un amante se mantiene fijo, mientras que el otro gira alrededor de su estabilidad, creando un círculo perfecto.

SMALL-GROUP OPTIONS

Have students work in small groups and pairs to read and discuss the selection.

Reciprocal Teaching
- Have students read the poem.
- After reading, ask students to write 3–5 questions about the poem, using these stems: *What does the poet mean by ____? Why did the poet ____? How does the poet use ____ to ____? How does the ____ affect the ____?*
- Form teams of three students.
- Each student offers two questions for group discussion.
- Group reaches consensus on the answers and finds supporting text evidence.

Think Pair Share
- After reading the poem, pose this question: *What kind of musical style would best accompany the poem if it were sung?*
- Have students think about the question individually and take notes.
- Then, have pairs listen, discuss, and formulate a shared response to the question. Direct them to include at least two reasons to support their chosen musical style.
- Finally, have pairs share their responses with the class.

A Valediction: Forbidding Mourning **304B**

PLAN

 **Text X-Ray: English Learner Support**
for "A Valediction: Forbidding Mourning"

Use the Text X-Ray and the supports and scaffolds in the Teacher's Edition to help guide students at different proficiency levels through the selection.

INTRODUCE THE SELECTION
DISCUSS METAPHYSICAL CONCEITS

In this lesson, students will need to be able to discuss the use of metaphysical conceits. Provide the following explanations:

- The Greek root *meta* means "beyond."
- *Metaphysical* refers to what is abstract, supernatural, or spiritual.
- A *conceit* in literature is an exaggerated comparison.

Explain to students that a metaphysical conceit in this poem compares an abstract, spiritual concept to a physical object.

Ask students to discuss things they could compare in a metaphysical conceit. Provide sentence frames, such as: *I can compare ____ with ____. One example of a metaphysical idea is ____. One example of a physical object is ____.*

CULTURAL REFERENCES

The following words or phrases may be unfamiliar to students:

- *pass . . . away* (line 1): die
- *compass* (line 26): hinged device for drawing circles
- *wilt* (line 33): will

LISTENING

Take Dictation

Remind students that lyric poems are designed to be read aloud because of their musicality and rhythm. Direct students to listen for rhyming sounds as you read the poem aloud.

Use the following supports with students at varying proficiency levels:

- Read aloud line 5 of the poem. Then, slowly reread it, repeating as necessary. Have students write down what they hear. After reading, write the line on the board and have students make corrections to their work, as needed. **SUBSTANTIAL**
- Have one student read the first stanza to another. Then, have the speaker slowly reread the stanza, one line at a time, while the listener writes down what they hear. Direct listeners to ask speakers to repeat words as needed. Then, have them switch roles and repeat the activity for the second stanza. Have them check their work and make any necessary corrections. **MODERATE**
- Have partners do the Intermediate activity. Tell them to repeat the activity for the entire poem. **LIGHT**

304C Unit 2

PLAN

SPEAKING

Use a Visual Aid

As students prepare to write their essays for the assignment on page 311, have them use drawings to sketch out their ideas. Ask them to describe their drawings to a partner or in a small group.

Use the following supports with students at varying proficiency levels:

- Provide a list of familiar concepts related to Donne's poem, such as friendship or loss. Have students draw simple pictures for each concept. Help students use nouns to tell what is in their drawings. **SUBSTANTIAL**
- Have partners ask each other *wh-* questions about their drawings. For example: *Who is in your drawing? What are they doing? What idea does the drawing show?* **MODERATE**
- Have partners describe their drawings to each other. Encourage them to refer to Donne's poem as they explain parts of the drawings. **LIGHT**

READING

Identify Central Idea

Remind students that they should look for comparisons, key words, mood, and other clues to help them identify the central idea in poems.

Use the following supports with students at varying proficiency levels:

- Have small groups reread the poem. Guide them to read aloud and circle any words or phrases they think give clues to the central idea in the poem. **SUBSTANTIAL**
- Have pairs reread the poem. Have them use a chart to record clues to the central idea, such as key words, mood, images, and comparisons. Have pairs exchange charts and discuss their findings. **MODERATE**
- As students reread the poem, have them take notes about the central idea. Then, have them write a sentence stating the poem's central idea. **LIGHT**

WRITING

Use Sentence Patterns

As students review their paragraphs from the Quick Start activity, have them look for ways to vary their sentence patterns.

Use the following supports with students at varying proficiency levels:

- Write these sentences on the board: *I walk today. I walked yesterday.* Point out the difference between present and past tense. Have students copy the sentences. **SUBSTANTIAL**
- Review how to add *-ed* to present-tense verbs to make them past tense. Have students write three simple sentences using the verbs *walk, cook, paint*. Have them exchange papers and rewrite each other's sentences in the past tense. **MODERATE**
- Have students practice revising simple past tense sentences into past continuous by adding the past form of "to be" (was, were) to a verb + *-ing*. For example: *I tried to sleep. I was trying to sleep.* **LIGHT**

TEACH

? Connect to the ESSENTIAL QUESTION

Ask a volunteer to read aloud the essential question. Have students look at the image on page 304 and explain that the poem "A Valediction: Forbidding Mourning" written by John Donne will present some interesting comparisons between love and passion.

ANALYZE & APPLY

A VALEDICTION: FORBIDDING MOURNING

Poem by **John Donne**

? ESSENTIAL QUESTION:

What's the difference between love and passion?

GET READY

QUICK START

Saying goodbye to someone can be difficult, even if the parting is only temporary. Write a paragraph about a time when you had to be separated from someone you cared about. Use a chart like this one to help you plan your paragraph.

Cause of the separation	
How I felt at the time	
How I feel thinking back on it	

ANALYZE METAPHYSICAL CONCEITS

John Donne was a central figure in a literary group known as the metaphysical poets. In contrast to the ornate, exuberant style of earlier Renaissance poets, they used a more conversational style to explore subjects such as religious devotion, death, physical love, and relationships. Many metaphysical poems are in the form of an argument, giving the poet an opportunity to show off his wit and intellectual subtlety.

The metaphysical poets were admired and sometimes criticized for making unexpected comparisons. A **metaphysical conceit** is an elaborate metaphor or simile in which the comparison is unusually striking and original. It shows likeness in two things that at first seem to have no connection whatsoever. The example below is taken from lines 1–8 of "A Valediction: Forbidding Mourning," where the death of virtuous people is compared to a couple saying goodbye temporarily. The center shows how these two disparate things are made to seem alike in the poem.

GENRE ELEMENTS: LYRIC POETRY
- expresses strong feelings or thoughts
- has a musical quality
- deals with intense emotions surrounding events such as death, love, or loss
- include forms such as ode, elegy, sonnet

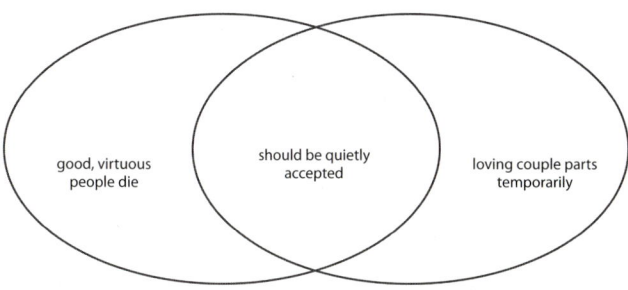

As you read the poem, look for other examples of metaphysical conceits.

A Valediction: Forbidding Mourning 305

TEACH

QUICK START

Write "Does absence make the heart grow fonder?" on the board. Read it to students then have students read the Quick Start activity. After using the graphic organizer to plan and write their paragraph, give students the option to share with the class. After sharing, have students brainstorm emotions felt during and after separation. Chose a student to record answers.

ANALYZE METAPHYSICAL CONCEITS

Review with students that a **metaphor** is a figure of speech that compares two things that have something in common without using *like* or *as*, as in a **simile.** Have students generate a list of common metaphors, by adding to the following examples displayed on the board.

Drowned in a sea of grief
Stench of failure
Broken heart

Explain that **metaphysical conceit** is an extended metaphor that compares two essentially dissimilar things on several qualities. For example, Donne compares physical love to a flea in his poem "The Flea."

Discuss the Venn diagram in the student edition that shows how craftly Donne uses a **metaphysical conceit** to compare death of a virtuous person with the separation of a loving couple.

A Valediction: Forbidding Mourning 305

TEACH

INTERPRET IDEAS IN POETRY

Tell students that poetry is filled with literary techniques that give poets opportunity to express their message in very creative ways.

Instruct students to read this section and give the following examples of each type of literary technique.

Paradox- this statement is false, sweet as a lemon, "I must be cruel, only to be kind" (Hamlet)

Figurative Language- blue as the ocean, you are what you eat

Irony- Titanic, the unsinkable ship, sinking on its first voyage

Consider dividing the class into groups to have each group try to identify these techniques in this selection.

 ## ANNOTATION MODEL

Remind students to look at the annotation model on page 306 which illustrates how someone can notate vivid language and literary techniques while reading.

Point out that they may follow this suggestion or use their own system for marking up the selection in their write-in text. They may want to color-code their annotations by using highlighters. Their notes in the margin may include questions about ideas that are unclear or topics they want to learn more about.

 **GET READY**

INTERPRET IDEAS IN POETRY

John Donne is known for his highly creative expression of ideas. In many of his poems, the speaker presents an ingenious argument in verse. This complexity of thought makes his poetry rewarding but also sometimes difficult to interpret. To better understand the meaning of "A Valediction: Forbidding Mourning," examine Donne's use of the following literary techniques to express ideas:

Paradox: a statement that seems contradictory or absurd but actually reveals some element of truth

Figurative Language: language that communicates ideas beyond the literal meaning of words, often through comparisons of two unlike things, as in similes and metaphors

Irony: a contrast between expectation and reality

ANNOTATION MODEL NOTICE & NOTE

As you read, note the author's use of metaphysical conceits as well as other techniques that require interpretation. This model shows how one reader responded to lines 1–8 of "A Valediction: Forbidding Mourning."

> As virtuous men pass mildly away,
>   And whisper to their souls to go,
> Whilst some of their sad friends do say
>   The breath goes now, and some say, No;
>
> So let us melt, and make no noise,
>   No tear-floods, nor sigh-tempests move,
> 'Twere profanation of our joys
>   To tell the laity our love.

A virtuous person dying quietly is likened to "us" melting, making no noise.

Donne's word choices suggest a comparison between love and religion.

WHEN STUDENTS STRUGGLE . . .

Paraphrase To help students sort through all the footnotes in the poem, have pairs of them complete this graphic organizer.

Lines	Meaning
1–2	Good men die willingly.
3–4	Friends may accept or not accept the death.

 For additional support, go to the **Reading Studio** and assign the following **Level Up tutorial: Paraphrasing**.

BACKGROUND

John Donne (1572–1631) was born in London, England. He had planned for a career in government, but his secret marriage to his patron's niece in 1601 got him into trouble. Eventually he became an Anglican priest whose eloquent sermons drew large crowds to St. Paul's Cathedral. "A Valediction: Forbidding Mourning" was written for his wife, Anne, who was upset about his approaching trip to France. (A valediction is a speech or poem that bids farewell.) Anne's death when she was just 33 inspired many of Donne's later spiritual poems.

A VALEDICTION: FORBIDDING MOURNING
Poem by John Donne

SETTING A PURPOSE

As you read, notice the subtle and often surprising ideas the speaker expresses in the argument he makes to his wife.

As virtuous men pass mildly away,
    And whisper to their souls to go,
Whilst some of their sad friends do say
    The breath goes now, and some say, No;

5 So let us melt, and make no noise,
    No tear-floods, nor sigh-tempests move,
'Twere profanation of our joys
    To tell the laity our love.

Moving of th' earth brings harms and fears,
10   Men reckon what it did and meant;
But trepidation of the spheres,
    Though greater far, is innocent.

Notice & Note

Use the side margins to notice and note signposts in the text.

5 melt: part; dissolve our togetherness.

7 profanation (prŏf′-ə-nā′shən): an act of contempt for what is sacred.

8 laity (lā′ĭ-tē): persons who do not understand the "religion" of love.

9 moving of th' earth: an earthquake.

11 trepidation of the spheres: apparently irregular movements of heavenly bodies.

12 innocent: harmless.

A Valediction: Forbidding Mourning   307

WHEN STUDENTS STRUGGLE . . .

Summarize Have students complete the graphic organizer to summarize every two stanzas (8 lines).

Lines	Summary
1–8	Wife should not show emotions at the impending separation
9–16	Compares earthquakes to heavenly bodies

 For additional support, go to the **Reading Studio** and assign the following **Level Up tutorial: Summarizing**.

TEACH

BACKGROUND

After students read the Background note, explain that John Donne is considered the pioneer of **metaphysical poetry.** He rejected the conventions of the Elizabethan style characterized by its musical quality and themes of love. He preferred a more colloquial, conversational style. Because he was an intellectual, educated at Oxford and Cambridge Universities, and an Anglican priest, he was well read and chose to analyze subjects such as religion, death, and love with a philosophical and logical flare. Death was a prominent theme in Donne's writing. During the Renaissance, medical knowledge was limited and life expectancy was less than 50 years. Of the 12 children he had, two were stillborn and 3 died at the ages of 3, 7, and 19 as well as his wife at the age of 33. Donne's work is filled with surprising twists, unexpected images and comparisons, making his poetry have a much deeper meaning than on the surface.

SETTING A PURPOSE

Direct students to use the Setting a Purpose prompt to focus their reading.

ENGLISH LEARNER SUPPORT

Learn New Language Structures: To help students better understand the concept of a paradox, provide the following statement: To succeed, you may need to fail first. Ask for volunteers to put this statement in their own words. Explain that students can first recognize this as a paradox because succeed and fail are antonyms, or words with opposite meanings. The statement seems like a contradiction until we think of situations where failure typically comes before success. For example, when learning to ride a bike, an individual typically falls down many times before being successful.
MODERATE

For **listening** and **reading support** for students at varying proficiency levels, see the **Text X-Ray** on pages 304C–D.

A Valediction: Forbidding Mourning   307

TEACH

ANALYZE METAPHYSICAL CONCEIT

Remind students of the definition of a **metaphysical conceit.** Show students a compass. Discuss how it moves apart and can come together, without becoming completely apart. (**Answer:** The compass is connected together and as one remains stationary, the other leg may move. The moving parts work together as a unit, but in the end, one leg will always circle back to the other leg. The speaker is telling his wife that their relationship is solid, and that she is the base to which he will circle around and return.)

ENGLISH LEARNER SUPPORT

Acquire Vocabulary Explain to students that Donne uses words that were standard in the 16th and 17th centuries, but modern-day readers find them unfamiliar. Help students understand the meanings of the following words.

- *Thy* (lines 27 and 35) "Your"
- *be* (line 25) "are"
- *doth* (lines 28 and 30) "does"
- *wilt* (line 33) "will"

Help students to use the dictionary or thesaurus to find synonyms for each word. Replace the words in the poem with the synonyms and reread the lines. Have students work with a partner to summarize the lines. **LIGHT**

NOTICE & NOTE

13 sublunary (sŭb-lōō′nə-rē) **lovers' love:** the love of earthly lovers, which, like all things beneath the moon, is subject to change and death.

14 soul . . . sense: essence is sensuality.

16 elemented: composed.

19 Inter-assuréd of the mind: confident of each other's love.

22 endure not yet: do not, nevertheless, suffer.

24 like . . . beat: Unlike less valuable metals, gold does not break when beaten thin.

26 twin compasses: the two legs of a compass used for drawing circles.

ANALYZE METAPHYSICAL CONCEITS
Annotate: Mark phrases in lines 25–36 that describe the motion of the two legs of a compass.

Analyze: What does this conceit suggest about the relationship between the speaker and his wife?

32 as that comes home: when the moving foot returns to the center as the compass is closed.

34 obliquely (ō-blēk′lē)**:** not in a straight line.

35 firmness: constancy; **just:** perfect.

Dull sublunary lovers' love
  (Whose soul is sense) cannot admit
15 Absence, because it doth remove
  Those things which elemented it.

But we by a love so much refined
  That our selves know not what it is,
Inter-assuréd of the mind,
20 Care less, eyes, lips, and hands to miss.

Our two souls therefore, which are one,
  Though I must go, endure not yet
A breach, but an expansion,
  Like gold to airy thinness beat.

25 If they be two, they are two so
  As stiff twin compasses are two;
Thy soul, the fixed foot, makes no show
  To move, but doth, if th' other do.

And though it in the center sit,
30 Yet when the other far doth roam,
It leans and hearkens after it,
  And grows erect, as that comes home.

Such wilt thou be to me, who must
  Like th' other foot, obliquely run;
35 Thy firmness makes my circle just,
  And makes me end where I begun.

308 Unit 2

APPLYING ACADEMIC VOCABULARY

☑ **ambiguous** ☐ **anticipate** ☐ **conceive** ☐ **drama** ☐ **integrity**

Write and Discuss Have students turn to a partner to discuss the following questions. Guide students to include the academic vocabulary word **ambiguous** in their responses. Ask volunteers to share their responses with the class.

- In what ways can this poem be considered **ambiguous**?
- What strategies can you use to clear up the **ambiguous** parts of the poem?

NOTICE & NOTE

CHECK YOUR UNDERSTANDING

Answer these questions before moving on to the **Analyze the Text** section on the following page.

1. The speaker in the poem is —
   A terminally ill
   B going on a journey
   C abandoning his family
   D begging his wife to return

2. Which words best describe the speaker's tone?
   F Cold and belittling
   G Sad and regretful
   H Happy and excited
   J Calm and consoling

3. What is an important idea in the poem?
   A Couples need their own personal space.
   B Husbands and wives should not separate.
   C True love is not endangered by physical separation.
   D Women did not travel during the Elizabethan period.

TEACH

CHECK YOUR UNDERSTANDING

Have students answer the questions independently.

Answers:

1. B
2. J
3. C

If students answer any questions incorrectly, have them reread the text to confirm their understanding. Then, they may proceed to ANALYZE THE TEXT on page 310.

ENGLISH LEARNER SUPPORT

Oral Assessment Use the following questions to assess students' comprehension and speaking skills.

1. Why did the speaker of the poem write to his wife? *(He is going away and he doesn't want her to mourn.)*

2. How would you describe the way the speaker talks to his wife? *(He is caring, calm, supporting.)*

3. What does this poem say about the effect of separation of two people and the love they have for one another? *(True love will stand the test of time and separation.)* **LIGHT**

APPLY

ANALYZE THE TEXT

Possible answers:

1. **DOK 4:** *It is a natural expectation that a person mourns when someone dies or when physical separation occurs. It is ironic that Donne expects that virtuous men and his wife not mourn at these events.*

2. **DOK 4:** *Donne likens earthquakes to shallow love, to those connected to earthly things. He connects his and his wife's love to motions of the heavenly bodies, innocent, unnoticed and refined. The conceit expresses that a silent, quiet, steady love, is one that endures, not the one that attracts loud attention.*

3. **DOK 2:** *The couple's love is so strong that when they separate (breech), they don't break apart, their love just fills more space (expands). Using gold as a simile shows the value of connection their souls have made.*

4. **DOK 4:** *He exaggerated sorrow by using terms "tear-flood" and "sigh-tempests." He states that publicizing their sorrow would cheapen their love. By exaggerating, the tone of the poem takes on an argumentative, convincing tone, although gentle and firm.*

5. **DOK 4:** *He viewed marriage as something sacred, and he talks about it in spiritual terms. He talks not about people who die, but "virtuous" people who die. As a devoutly religious person, wouldn't he expect those virtuous people to go "mildly away" to heaven? So, his poem is not sad, it reflects his spiritual belief system.*

RESEARCH

Discuss with students the ethical use of the Internet and websites. Encourage students when searching for John Donne's poems, to find different recitations of the same poem and compare the effect of each.

Extend Donne is a prolific writer and is a master of using figurative language techniques. Listening to his poetry gives a person a different perspective in understanding his intended meaning. When listening to his poems, seek out the musical quality and try to visualize images based on his word choices.

310 Unit 2

RESPOND

ANALYZE THE TEXT

Support your responses with evidence from the text. 📓 NOTEBOOK

1. **Analyze** What is ironic about the speaker's comparison in lines 1–8 of the poem?

2. **Analyze** Reread lines 9–20. Explain how Donne compares earthquakes and planetary motion with different kinds of love. What idea does this metaphysical conceit express?

3. **Interpret** Reread lines 21–24. What paradox does Donne express in this stanza? How does the simile comparing their souls to gold help explain the paradox?

4. **Analyze** What hyperbole, or exaggeration for emphasis, does Donne include in lines 5–8? How does this hyperbole affect the speaker's tone?

5. **Connect** John Donne was a very spiritual man who made sacrifices to marry his wife. How is this reflected in his view of his marriage?

RESEARCH TIP
You can hear many poems read aloud online on YouTube. It's an easy search by author or by performer.

RESEARCH

John Donne wrote about subjects such as love and death with great originality and sophistication. With a partner, research other works written by Donne and answer the following questions.

QUESTION	ANSWER
What phrase contained in a John Donne sermon became the title of a novel by Ernest Hemingway?	*For Whom The Bell Tolls*
Which swashbuckling acquaintance of Donne's was knighted by Queen Elizabeth I and eventually executed in the Tower of London?	*Sir Walter Raleigh*
By what other name is John Donne's famous poem "Holy Sonnet 10" known?	*Death Be Not Proud*

Extend Many professional readings of Donne's poems have been recorded. Listen to a variety of his poems read aloud. Appreciate the rhythm and rhymes of poems such as "The Canonization" and "Holy Sonnet 10." With a partner, discuss the tone and the mood of each poem, and how hearing the poem read aloud affected you.

310 Unit 2

WHEN STUDENTS STRUGGLE . . .

Reteaching: Interpret Ideas in Poetry To help students identify and understand **paradox** in "A Valediction: Forbidding Mourning" have them use these steps: 1) Identify the apparent contradictory elements of the paradox; 2) Examine the surrounding words and phrases. Example: Our two souls that are one (Two people so closely united cannot be separated by space.)

📖 For additional support, go to the **Reading Studio** and assign the following Level Up tutorial: **Figurative Language**.

RESPOND

CREATE AND PRESENT

Write an Essay Write a reflective essay that is inspired by the Donne poem. In the light of your own experience, examine the poet's viewpoints on such ideas as love, family relationships, or coping with separation or loss.

- ❑ To develop your reflective essay, think about any expectations you may have for significant relationships in the future. As you reflect on your life, include any insights you might have gained from reading "A Valediction: Forbidding Mourning."
- ❑ Reread the poem more than once as a way to enhance your interpretation. Think about any life lessons it may offer.
- ❑ Choose a line from the poem that is striking or memorable to you. Consider making the line the theme of your essay.

Present the Essay As a class, read your essays aloud. Use the following suggestions to help prepare.

- ❑ Practice reading your essay aloud, using an engaging tone to draw listeners into your reflections. Speak at a pace that will hold the interest of your audience.
- ❑ As you read, make eye contact with your audience and use facial expressions and gestures to help reinforce the essay's points.

 Go to **Writing Informative Texts** in the **Writing Studio** to help develop your essay.

 Go to **Giving a Presentation** in the **Speaking and Listening Studio** for help.

RESPOND TO THE ESSENTIAL QUESTION

 What's the difference between love and passion?

Gather Information Review your annotations and notes on "A Valediction: Forbidding Mourning." Then, add relevant information to your Response Log. As you determine which information to include, think about:

- the sacrifices one might make for love
- how well passion can withstand trials, such as separation
- personal characteristics that are needed to make love long-lasting

ACADEMIC VOCABULARY

As you write and discuss what you learned from the poem, be sure to use the Academic Vocabulary words. Check off each of the words that you use.

- ❑ ambiguous
- ❑ anticipate
- ❑ conceive
- ❑ drama
- ❑ integrity

A Valediction: Forbidding Mourning 311

APPLY

CREATE AND PRESENT

Write an Essay As students prepare to write their essays, tell them to reread the poem and write down memorable lines, images, and comparisons. Ask them to think about what the lines and comparisons suggest about love and relationships. Encourage students to think about how the ideas or lessons from the poem could apply to their own experiences or the experiences of people they know.

For **writing** and **speaking support** for students at varying proficiency levels, see the **Text X-Ray** on page 304D.

Present the Essay Provide time for students to practice reading their essays aloud. Encourage them to videotape themselves so they can self-analyze style, tone, intonation and eye contact.

RESPOND TO THE ESSENTIAL QUESTION

Allow time for students to add details from "A Valediction: Forbidding Mourning" to their Unit 2 Response Logs.

TO CHALLENGE STUDENTS

Analyze Perspective Pretend you are Donne's wife as you read "A Valediction: Forbidding Mourning." With a partner, write a response to your husband to let him know how you feel about his message.

PLAN

TO HIS COY MISTRESS
Poem by Andrew Marvell

TWENTY-ONE LOVE POEMS (POEM III)
Poem by Adrienne Rich

GENRE ELEMENTS
LYRIC POETRY
Remind students that **lyric poetry** deals with strong emotions and has a musical quality. It often contains **figurative language,** such as **similes, metaphors,** and **hyperbole.** In this lesson, students will interpret the figurative language used in an Early Modern English poem and a modern American poem.

LEARNING OBJECTIVES
- Interpret figurative language and analyze speaker.
- Conduct research about Cavalier and Metaphysical schools of poetry.
- Write a letter.
- Discuss letters.
- **Language** Use first-person point of view.

TEXT COMPLEXITY

Quantitative Measures	To His Coy Mistress/Twenty-One Love Poems (Poem III)	Lexile: NA
Qualitative Measures	**Ideas Presented** Multiple levels; use of symbolism; greater demand for inference	
	Structures Used More complex; lyrical and poetic	
	Language Used Implied meanings; allusive, figurative, and formal language; complex sentence structures	
	Knowledge Required Mostly familiar themes	

PLAN

RESOURCES

Online

- Unit 2 Response Log
- 🔊 Selection Audio
- 📖 Reading Studio: Notice and Notes
- Level Up Tutorial: Figurative Language; Synthesizing Information
- Writing Studio: Writing as a Process
- Speaking and Listening Studio: Participating in Collaborative Discussions
- ✓ "To His Coy Mistress" and "Twenty-One Love Poems (Poem III)" Selection Test

SUMMARIES

English

In "To His Coy Mistress," the speaker tells his sweetheart that they should love each another now because time is fleeting. "In Twenty-One Love Poems (Poem III)," the speaker reminds her beloved that because they are no longer young, they have an even greater urgency to love each other, as death is closer than it was when they were younger.

Spanish

En "Para su tímida amante", el narrador le dice a su enamorada que deberían amarse ahora porque el tiempo es fugaz. En "Veintiún poemas de amor (poema III)", el narrador le recuerda a su amada que debido a que ya no son jóvenes, tienen una urgencia mayor de amarse, puesto que la muerte está más cerca que cuando eran jóvenes.

 SMALL-GROUP OPTIONS

Have students work in small groups or pairs to read and discuss the selections.

Activating Academic Vocabulary

- Provide a list of academic vocabulary words and phrases, such as: *speaker, figurative language, metaphor, simile, hyperbole, tone, word choice, imagery, detail, convey, lyrical, compare, line,* and *stanza*.
- After reading ten lines of one of the poems, model how to use one or more of the academic vocabulary words and phrases to discuss the poems.
- Encourage students to use the academic vocabulary words as they discuss the poems.

Double-Entry Journal

- Have students use notebooks to record their double-entry notes.
- Show students how to create a two-column format by drawing a line from top to bottom on each page. Label the left column *Quotes from the Poem* and the right column *My Notes*.
- Tell students to copy important or confusing lines in the left column. Then, have students write their own questions, restatements, or interpretations in the right column, next to the quoted material.
- Encourage students to exchange their double-entry journals with other students, who should respond to the notes.

PLAN

Text X-Ray: English Learner Support
for "To His Coy Mistress" and "Twenty-One Love Poems (Poem III)"

Use the Text X-Ray and the supports and scaffolds in the Teacher's Edition to help guide students at different proficiency levels through the selections.

INTRODUCE THE SELECTIONS
DISCUSS SPEAKERS

In this lesson, students will need to be able to discuss how poems give clues about their speakers.

Provide the following explanation:

The **speaker** of a poem is the person who is talking in the poem. The poem is from his or her point of view. A poem's speaker is like a character in a story.

Guide students to practice this concept by using details from various poems they read previously in the text and using them to describe the speaker.

Provide sentence frames, such as: *I think the speaker in [poem] is _____ because _____. The speaker's use of the phrase _____ makes me think that s/he is _____.*

CULTURAL REFERENCES

The following words or phrases may be unfamiliar to students:

- *Time's winged chariot* ("To His Coy Mistress," line 22): time is moving fast
- *marble vault* ("To His Coy Mistress," line 26): burial chamber or grave
- *warp in time* ("Twenty-One Love Poems [Poem III]," lines 2–3): a change in the measurement of time in which people and events from one part of history are imagined to be in another part
- *cress* ("Twenty-One Love Poems [Poem III]," line 12): a plant of the mustard family, with pungent-tasting leaves

LISTENING

Identify Figurative Language

Review with students the definitions of *simile*, *metaphor*, and *hyperbole*.

Use the following supports with students at varying proficiency levels:

- Have students write *simile*, *metaphor*, and *hyperbole* on three separate index cards. Slowly read aloud one example of each from the poems and have students hold up the card that names the literary device they hear. **SUBSTANTIAL**
- Have students work in pairs. Direct one partner to read aloud an example of figurative language from "To His Coy Mistress." Have the other partner tell whether the example is a simile, metaphor, or hyperbole. Have partners switch roles to repeat the activity. **MODERATE**
- Have students work in pairs. Direct one partner to read aloud an example of figurative language from "To His Coy Mistress." Have the other partner tell whether the example is a simile, metaphor, or hyperbole. Have partners switch roles to repeat the activity for passages from both "To His Coy Mistress" and "Twenty-One Love Poems (Poem III)." **LIGHT**

312C Unit 2

PLAN

SPEAKING

Compare Tone

Explain that comparing tone in poetry can help us see the different ways authors view and write about a single subject.

Use the following supports with students at varying proficiency levels:

- Rephrase the first stanza of "Twenty-One Love Poems (Poem III)" in simpler language. Then, ask students to discuss how they would describe the tone. Have students talk about the stanza using sentence frames such as: *The speaker is no longer ____. The lovers will help each other ____ and ____.* **SUBSTANTIAL**
- Have partners reread the first stanzas of both poems and rephrase them in simpler language. Then, have them ask each other questions about the speakers' tones. For example: *What is the tone of the first line? Why do you think so?* **MODERATE**
- Have partners discuss and compare the tones of both poems. Remind them to use examples from the poems to support their ideas. Direct them to ask each other clarifying questions as needed. **LIGHT**

READING

Use Accessible Language

Remind students that using a dictionary as they read can help them better understand the meaning of a poem.

Use the following supports with students of varying proficiency levels:

- Have students work in pairs to read lines 1-5 of "Twenty-One Love Poems (Poem III)," circling and reading aloud words they know. Have them underline unfamiliar words and ask for help with their meanings. **SUBSTANTIAL**
- Have pairs work together to use accessible language to create a dictionary for 6–10 unfamiliar words in the poems. Then, have students silently reread the poems, using their dictionaries. After reading, have students discuss how the dictionary helped them better understand the poem. **MODERATE**
- Have students use accessible language to create dictionaries for 10–15 unfamiliar words in the poems. Direct them to list synonyms for each word, in addition to their definitions. **LIGHT**

WRITING

Use First Person

Remind students that when they write in the first-person point of view, they will use the pronouns *I*, *me*, and *my*. The first-person speaker tells about his or her feelings, thoughts, and experiences.

Use the following supports with students of varying proficiency levels:

- Have students practice writing from the first-person point of view. Provide sentence starters, such as: *I feel ____. I think ____. ____ belongs to me. I will give you my ____.* **SUBSTANTIAL**
- Have students write five sentences from the first-person point of view. Encourage them to use each of these pronouns at least once: *I, me, my*. Have partners exchange papers to check for pronoun agreement. **MODERATE**
- Have students write a scenes from the first-person point of view. Tell students that in each scene, the narrator should take his or her beloved on a date. Remind students that a first-person narrator will not know the feelings and thoughts of another character. **LIGHT**

TEACH

? Connect to the ESSENTIAL QUESTION

Discuss the Essential Question with the class. Ask students how they feel the element of time affects the way they feel or behave in different situations. Do they feel a sense of urgency when they have a limited amount of time, or are they not really impacted by time? Tell students that in "To His Coy Mistress," Marvell's speaker wants to enjoy love while he and his beloved are still young. In "Twenty-One Love Poems (Poem III)," Rich's speaker feels a sense of urgency because she and her beloved are older and, therefore, feel their time is limited. Remind students to keep track of how each author addresses the topic of time in their work.

COMPARE THEMES

Point out that the **theme** of a poem is the idea that the poem expresses about a subject or uses the subject to explore. Ask students to predict the themes of the two poems based on their titles. Why do they think these might be the themes? How do they think the poets might use figurative language and imagery to convey their themes? Tell students that they should keep their predictions in mind as they read the poems to determine if their predictions were correct.

COLLABORATE & COMPARE

POEM

TO HIS COY MISTRESS

by **Andrew Marvell**
pages 315–317

COMPARE THEMES

As you read each poem, think about the theme, or the central message, and how the author uses figurative language and imagery to convey this theme. Then, think about how the themes of the two poems relate to each other. After you read both poems, you will collaborate on a small group project.

 ESSENTIAL QUESTION:

How does time affect our feelings?

POEM

TWENTY-ONE LOVE POEMS (POEM III)

by **Adrienne Rich**
pages 318–319

QUICK START

Sometimes it is better to have patience and take your time with something, while at other times it is better to take advantage of an opportunity while you have it. With a partner, discuss a situation in which it is best to be patient and one in which it is best to act right away. How do the situations differ?

INTERPRET FIGURATIVE LANGUAGE

Figurative language is language that communicates ideas beyond the literal meaning of words. Poets often rely on types of figurative language, including metaphors, similes, personification, and hyperbole, to express ideas in an imaginative yet concrete way. A poet's use of figurative language can transform descriptions, making them more surprising and memorable.

This chart shows examples of figurative language from one of the poems you are about to read.

FIGURATIVE LANGUAGE	EXAMPLE
A **simile** compares two dissimilar things using the word *like* or *as*.	Now therefore, while the youthful hue Sits on thy skin like morning dew —"To His Coy Mistress," lines 33–34
A **metaphor** compares two things directly, without using *like* or *as*.	But at my back I always hear Time's winged chariot hurrying near —"To His Coy Mistress," lines 21–22
Hyperbole is any expression that greatly exaggerates facts or ideas for humorous effect or for emphasis.	An hundred years should go to praise Thine eyes, and on thy forehead gaze —"To His Coy Mistress," lines 13–14

To interpret each poem's use of figurative language, read the poem to grasp its overall meaning. Then, read a second time, focusing your attention on the figurative language:

- Note what is being compared or exaggerated in each instance.
- Consider the effect the poet may be trying to achieve.
- Think about what the comparison reveals, and note your conclusions about the comparison's possible meaning.

GENRE ELEMENTS: LYRIC POETRY
- expresses strong feelings or thoughts
- has a musical quality
- deals with intense emotions surrounding events like death, love, or loss
- includes forms such as ode, elegy, and sonnet

To His Coy Mistress / Twenty-One Love Poems (Poem III) 313

TEACH

ANALYZE SPEAKER

Review the literary terms associated with analyzing the speaker **(speaker, tone, word choice)** and read through the examples in the table on page 314. List the elements in a poem that help reveal tone—direct statements, use of details, and word choice. As they read each poem, encourage students to look for details and word choices that reveal characteristics about the speaker, such as gender, age, personality, outlook on life, etc.

■ English Learner Support

Analyze Speaker Provide students with sentence frames they can use to describe or analyze the speaker in each poem, such as:

- The speaker's tone toward the subject of _____ is _____.
- The speaker's word choice of _____ conveys _____.
- The poet's use of specific details in lines _____ shows _____. **SUBSTANTIAL/MODERATE**

✏ ANNOTATION MODEL

Remind students of the types of **figurative language** listed in the chart on page 313. Point out the bulleted list under this chart, and tell students to refer to this list as they make their annotations. Encourage students to try to paraphrase what the poet is saying in their own words in the margins. Their notes in the margin may also include their conclusions about the speaker, as well as questions about any ideas that are unclear.

 **GET READY**

ANALYZE SPEAKER

A poem's **speaker,** like the narrator of a story, is the voice that talks to the reader. The choice of speaker can have a great effect on how a lyric poem develops. Some speakers just offer observations and insights. Other speakers are more like fictional characters who are directly involved in the experience portrayed in the poem. A speaker may express the poet's own thoughts and feelings, but you should not assume that the speaker is the same as the poet, even if he or she uses the pronouns *I* and *me*.

Both poems in this lesson have a speaker who addresses a loved one. As you read each poem, pay attention to the speaker's tone, or attitude, toward this person as well as toward love itself. Notice the word choices and imagery that convey the speaker's tone. You can use a chart like this one to record observations about the speaker.

What do we learn about the speaker?	
What is the speaker's tone?	
What words and images convey this tone?	

ANNOTATION MODEL   NOTICE & NOTE

As you read, mark examples of figurative language. Note each speaker's tone, marking word choices and other elements that help convey the tone. In the model, you can see how one reader annotated the first few lines of "To His Coy Mistress."

> Had we but world enough, and time,
> This (coyness,) lady, were no crime.
> We would sit down, and think which way
> To walk, and pass our long love's day.
> Thou by the Indian Ganges' side
> Shouldst rubies find; I by the tide
> Of Humber would complain.

Although he addresses his "mistress," the speaker's tone is pretty formal. "Coyness" suggests he is gently teasing her.

These references to places they would walk to are examples of hyperbole.

314 Unit 2

BACKGROUND

Andrew Marvell (1621–1678) was known during his lifetime for his political activities rather than for his poetry. He managed to maintain ties with political figures on both sides of the English Civil War. From 1659 until his death, he served in Parliament. His poetry wasn't published while he was alive, but he did circulate it among friends. "To His Coy Mistress" exemplifies Marvell's graceful use of language and his intellectual depth and wit. The poem develops the ancient theme of carpe diem (Latin for "seize the day"), a call for people to live for the moment. It was only in the 20th century that Marvell gained recognition as a major poet.

TO HIS COY MISTRESS
Poem by Andrew Marvell

PREPARE TO COMPARE

As you read, note the kind of language used to reveal the character of the speaker, as well as the language used by the speaker to express his emotions and desires. Think about the impression he is trying to make.

Had we but world enough, and time,
This coyness, lady, were no crime.
We would sit down, and think which way
To walk, and pass our long love's day.
5   Thou by the Indian Ganges' side
Shouldst rubies find; I by the tide
Of Humber would complain. I would
Love you ten years before the flood,
And you should, if you please, refuse
10 Till the conversion of the Jews.
My vegetable love should grow
Vaster than empires and more slow;

Notice & Note

Use the side margins to notice and note signposts in the text.

5 Ganges (găn´jēz): a great river of northern India.

7 Humber: a river of northern England, flowing through Marvell's hometown; **complain:** sing melancholy love songs.

8 flood: the biblical Flood.

10 till . . . Jews: In Marvell's day, Christians believed that all Jews would convert to Christianity just before the Last Judgment and the end of the world.

3 vegetable love: a love that grows like a plant (an oak tree, for example)—slowly but with the power to become very large.

APPLYING ACADEMIC VOCABULARY

☐ ambiguous    anticipate    conceive   ☐ drama   ☐ integrity

Write and Discuss Have students turn to partners to discuss the following questions. Guide students to include the academic vocabulary words *anticipate* and *conceive* in their responses. Ask volunteers to share their responses with the class.

- Does the speaker **anticipate** that his life will pass slowly or quickly?
- How does the speaker **conceive** death?

TEACH

BACKGROUND

After students read the background note on Andrew Marvell, reinforce the idea that Marvell's poetry is a clever blend of the Metaphysical and Cavalier schools of thought. Explain that Metaphysical poets tended to address grand themes and important subjects in their work, with a focus on spirituality and the religious experience. Cavalier poetry, in contrast, tended to focus on secular ideas and was much simpler stylistically. Both schools, however, shared a love of lyrical language and rich details, and they were both influenced by Elizabethan poets, including William Shakespeare. Let students know that later in the lesson, they will have a chance to delve a little deeper into the two schools of thought.

ENGLISH LEARNER SUPPORT

Draw on Prior Knowledge It may be helpful to start your poetry instruction by finding out what kinds of experiences your students have had with poetry. Do they know any poems in their native language? Is there a particular poem from their country or heritage they like? Would they be willing to share a translation? Who are the famous poets from their country? Have they themselves written any poems? If so, were the poems in English or in their native language? You may also wish to have students look at bilingual collections of poetry in English and their native language, if these are readily available.   **ALL LEVELS**

PREPARE TO COMPARE

Direct students to use the Prepare to Compare prompt to focus their reading.

ANALYZE SPEAKER

Remind students that the **speaker** in a lyric poem is the person, who may or may not be the poet, who expresses his or her thoughts and feelings. Point out that the poet's **word choice** reveals **tone**, or the speaker's attitude toward the poem's subject. (*Answer: By using words like "I would love you ten years before the flood . . ." and "My vegetable love should grow vaster than empires . . ." the speaker establishes a tone of admiration and devoted love.*)

For **speaking support** for students at varying proficiency levels, see the **Text X-Ray** on page 312D.

TEACH

INTERPRET FIGURATIVE LANGUAGE

Remind students that a **simile** is a figure of speech that makes a comparison, showing similarities between two different things. Encourage students to first identify the topics, items, or concepts being compared in lines 33–40, as this will make the process of interpreting the comparisons simpler. (**Answer:** *The first simile compares the lady's youthfulness to morning dew, which expresses how refreshing her presence is to the speaker. The second simile emphasizes the attraction between the two—the speaker wants to demonstrate his love toward the subject the way "amorous birds of prey" do.*)

 For **reading support** for students at varying proficiency levels, see the **Text X-Ray** on page 312D.

 **NOTICE & NOTE**

19 state: dignity.

INTERPRET FIGURATIVE LANGUAGE

Annotate: Mark the similes in lines 33–40.

Analyze: What comparison is created by each simile? What does each comparison reveal or help express?

35 transpires: breathes.

40 slow-chapped: slow-jawed.

44 thorough: through.

  An hundred years should go to praise
  Thine eyes, and on thy forehead gaze;
15 Two hundred to adore each breast,
  But thirty thousand to the rest;
  An age at least to every part,
  And the last age should show your heart.
  For, lady, you deserve this state,
20 Nor would I love at lower rate.
    But at my back I always hear
  Time's wingéd chariot hurrying near;
  And yonder all before us lie
  Deserts of vast eternity.
25 Thy beauty shall no more be found,
  Nor, in thy marble vault, shall sound
  My echoing song; then worms shall try
  That long-preserved virginity,
  And your quaint honor turn to dust,
30 And into ashes all my lust:
  The grave's a fine and private place,
  But none, I think, do there embrace
    Now therefore, while the youthful hue
  Sits on thy skin like morning dew,
35 And while thy willing soul transpires
  At every pore with instant fires,
  Now let us sport us while we may,
  And now, like amorous birds of prey,
  Rather at once our time devour
40 Than languish in his slow-chapped power.
  Let us roll all our strength and all
  Our sweetness up into one ball,
  And tear our pleasures with rough strife
  Thorough the iron gates of life:
45 Thus, though we cannot make our sun
  Stand still, yet we will make him run.

316 Unit 2

IMPROVE READING FLUENCY

Targeted Passage Use lines 1–20 to model how to read lines of a poem. Have students follow along in their books as you read the lines with proper emphasis and phrasing, pausing where punctuation is used. Then, have partners take turns reading aloud the rest of the stanzas from lines 21–46. Encourage students to give feedback to each other when reading unfamiliar words. Explain that when they are reading aloud for an audience, they should pace their reading, so the audience has time to appreciate the figurative language used.

 Go to the **Reading Studio** for additional support in developing fluency.

CHECK YOUR UNDERSTANDING

Answer these questions about "To His Coy Mistress" before moving on to the next selection.

1. Which sentence best summarizes the speaker's message in lines 1–20?
   A She is so beautiful that it will take him a very long time to properly love every part of her.
   B If they had all the time in the world, he would be happy for them to take their time in love.
   C He hopes that they will spend a lot of time together and do a lot of traveling.
   D He's in no rush about their relationship because the world is so big and they have so much time.

2. What do the lines *And yonder all before us lie / Deserts of vast eternity* mean?
   F Time stretches on forever.
   G We have to travel across the desert to see each other.
   H If we wait too long, our feelings for each other will dry up.
   J We're both going to be dead one day.

3. Read these lines of the poem: *And while thy willing soul transpires / At every pore with instant fires*. What emotion do these lines evoke?
   A The excitement of youthful love
   B Sorrow for the fate of the soul
   C The discomfort of a high fever
   D Anger at time for going by so fast

To His Coy Mistress / Twenty-One Love Poems (Poem III) 317

TEACH

CHECK YOUR UNDERSTANDING

Have students answer the questions independently.

Answers:
1. B
2. J
3. A

If students answer any questions incorrectly, have them reread the text to confirm their understanding. Then, they may proceed to the next selection.

ENGLISH LEARNER SUPPORT

Oral Assessment Use the following questions to assess students' comprehension and speaking skills.

1. Does the speaker wish he had more time? *(He wishes they had all the time in the world for him to express his love for her.)*

2. Does the speaker say he will die? *(yes)*

3. By "instant fires" in line 36, the speaker means his _____. *(excitement or passion)*
   SUBSTANTIAL/MODERATE

TEACH

BACKGROUND

After students have read the background note on Adrienne Rich, tell them that Rich's work has explored issues of identity, sexuality, and politics and has spanned over seven decades. Rich's poetry and essays reflected her commitment to social justice, her role in the anti-war movement, and her radical feminism. Unlike Marvell, Rich used irregular lines and stanza lengths in her work and often integrated "non-poetic" language in her poems. Ask students to watch for these elements as they read "Twenty-One Love Poems (Poem III)."

PREPARE TO COMPARE

Direct students to use the Prepare to Compare prompt to focus their reading.

ANALYZE SPEAKER

In "Twenty-One Love Poems (Poem III)," the speaker uses **figurative language,** including **metaphors,** to convey a specific tone and message. Remind students that a **metaphor** compares two things directly, without using *like* or *as*. (**Answer:** Mark "we're not young," "weeks have to do time," "years of missing each other," "streets at twenty." The speaker and her lover are middle aged and have met fairly recently; they have a passionate relationship.)

 **NOTICE & NOTE**

BACKGROUND

Adrienne Rich *(1929–2012) was a widely admired poet and one of the leading feminist writers in the United States. She started writing poetry at a young age. In 1951, the same year she graduated from Radcliffe College, she published her first book of poems. She went on to publish over 20 more volumes. Rich's poetry, which combines personal and political content, reflects her passionate interest in social activism and women's rights. She won numerous literary awards for her work.*

TWENTY-ONE LOVE POEMS (POEM III)

Poem by Adrienne Rich

Notice & Note

Use the side margins to notice and note signposts in the text.

ANALYZE SPEAKER
Annotate: Mark references to age and time in lines 1–5.

Infer: What can you infer from this passage about the speaker's relationship with her lover?

PREPARE TO COMPARE

Now that you have read "To His Coy Mistress," read this poem and notice how the speaker phrases her sense of urgency and her description of her own experience of love. Later, you will compare the two poems.

Since we're not young, weeks have to do time
for years of missing each other. Yet only this odd warp
in time tells me we're not young.
Did I ever walk the morning streets at twenty,
5 my limbs streaming with a purer joy?
did I lean from any window over the city
listening for the future
as I listen here with nerves tuned for your ring?
And you, you move toward me with the same tempo.
10 Your eyes are everlasting, the green spark
   of the blue-eyed grass of early summer,
   the green-blue wild cress washed by the spring.
   At twenty, yes: we thought we'd live forever.
   At forty-five, I want to know even our limits.
15 I touch you knowing we weren't born tomorrow,
   and somehow, each of us will help the other live,
   and somewhere, each of us must help the other die.

318 Unit 2

TO CHALLENGE STUDENTS

Write a Metaphor Explain to students that lines 10–12 are an extended **metaphor**—a metaphor that is developed over a series of lines in a poem. Ask students to write their own extended metaphors, using these lines as a model. Suggest that their metaphors might compare someone's eyes, hair, or mouth to something else. Ask students to share their extended metaphors in pairs or small groups.

318 Unit 2

CHECK YOUR UNDERSTANDING

Answer these questions before moving on to the **Analyze the Text** section on the following page.

1. Which of these statements is true?
   A The speaker thinks that her lover is too young for her.
   B The speaker feels the same now as she did when she was young.
   C The speaker's emotions are more intense now than they were when she was young.
   D The speaker regrets that she is too old to love as intensely as she would have when she was young.

2. Which line from "Twenty-One Love Poems (Poem III)" tells us the most about her lover's feelings toward the speaker?
   F *Did I ever walk the morning streets at twenty,*
   G *Your eyes are everlasting, the green spark*
   H *At twenty, yes: we thought we'd live forever.*
   J *And you, you move toward me with the same tempo.*

3. What does the speaker mean when she says, *At forty-five, I want to know even our limits*?
   A They should stay together long enough to face death together.
   B There is always a limit to love, no matter how old you are.
   C Being in love means they can get away with anything.
   D Love is eternal, so there's no reason to worry about death.

To His Coy Mistress / Twenty-One Love Poems (Poem III)   319

CHECK YOUR UNDERSTANDING

Have students answer the questions independently.

Answers:

1. C
2. J
3. A

If students answer any questions incorrectly, have them reread the text to confirm their understanding. Then, they may proceed to ANALYZE THE TEXTS on page 320.

ENGLISH LEARNER SUPPORT

Oral Assessment Use the following questions to assess students' comprehension and speaking skills.

1. In lines 4–8, does the speaker say she loves more intensely now or when she was younger? *(She loves more intensely now than when she was younger.)*

2. How does the speaker say she knows that her lover loves her too? *("you move toward me with the same tempo")*

3. Based on lines 15–17, what does the speaker mean by "even our limits" in line 14? *(death)* **SUBSTANTIAL/MODERATE**

APPLY

ANALYZE THE TEXTS

Possible answers:

1. **DOK 2:** *1. If we had all the time in the world, I wouldn't mind your being coy and would be happy to take my time in love. 2. But, time is passing fast and when we are dead it will be too late. 3. So, let's take advantage of the moment and love while we can.*

2. **DOK 4:** *The author talks about how, if it were possible, he would be happy to take hundreds and even thousands of years to allow their love to develop. He says he'd be willing to love her "ten years before the flood" and allow her to keep refusing him until "the conversion of the Jews." He does this to argue that the problem is not that he is impatient, but that time is fleeting.*

3. **DOK 2:** *Answers will vary. Students might respond that Marvell didn't expect readers to take the speaker's passionate argument seriously because the figurative language.*

4. *is so clever and because the poem contains more images of death than of love.*

5. **DOK 2:** *She is satisfied and content with her lover's response, because she moves toward her "with the same tempo," meaning she matches her emotional intensity rather than holding back.*

6. **DOK 4:** *The last line of the poem makes the overall tone of the poem much more somber and also much more intense because it acknowledges that while the poet may feel young in her feelings of love, she and her lover are old enough that they might face death together.*

RESEARCH

Remind students to use specific search terms or phrases when conducting research. For example, they might search for "similarities and differences between Metaphysical and Cavalier poetry." Tell students that the simpler their search terms, the more results they will yield, so they should normally use search terms that are as specific as possible.

Extend Ask students to work in pairs to complete this activity. While one partner identifies the ways in which Marvell's poem fits the characteristics of a Metaphysical poem, the other can identify the ways in which the poem aligns with Cavalier poetry. Then, have students share their results with each other and answer the questions together.

RESPOND

ANALYZE THE TEXTS

Support your responses with evidence from the text. 📓 NOTEBOOK

1. **Summarize** In "To His Coy Mistress," the speaker develops his argument in three sections: lines 1–20, 21–32, and 33–46. Summarize the main idea in each section of the poem.

2. **Analyze** In the first stanza of "To His Coy Mistress," how does the speaker use hyperbole to support his argument?

3. **Draw Conclusions** Marvell titled his poem "To His Coy Mistress" instead of "To My Coy Mistress," putting distance between himself and the speaker. Do you think he intended readers to take the speaker's passion seriously? Explain why or why not.

4. **Interpret** In "Twenty-One Love Poems (Poem III)," how does the speaker's use of figurative language reveal her affection for her beloved?

5. **Analyze** What is the overall tone of "Twenty-One Love Poems (Poem III)"? How does the poem's final line contribute to the tone?

RESEARCH

RESEARCH TIP
If you find a source that has a lot of text and you don't have time to read all of it, use the search function [ctrl + f for PC; cmd + f for Apple] to skip to keywords that you are looking for.

At the time that Andrew Marvell wrote "To His Coy Mistress," there were two significant schools of poetry in England: Cavalier and Metaphysical. These two schools, although distinct, shared certain characteristics. Do some research to compare and contrast these two schools of poetry.

SCHOOLS	DIFFERENCES	SIMILARITIES
Cavalier	*About romantic love, war, honor, and duty to the king. Simple language.*	*Both schools of poetry were inspired by Elizabethan poets, and both adopted the lyrical form.*
Metaphysical	*About intellectual ideas and analysis of feelings. Philosophical and spiritual.*	*Theme of carpe diem* *Subject matter is love and devotion*

Extend While Andrew Marvell is usually considered a metaphysical poet, his poetry also has qualities of Cavalier poetry. In what ways might "To His Coy Mistress" be considered Cavalier poetry and in what ways might it be considered Metaphysical poetry?

WHEN STUDENTS STRUGGLE . . .

Reteaching: Interpret Figurative Language Remind students that **hyperbole** is a phrase that exaggerates ideas for humorous effect or emphasis. For example, in "To His Coy Mistress," the speaker says he would praise his beloved's eyes for a "hundred years", which expresses the depth of his love. Help students find other examples in the text and discuss them. *("ten years before the flood," "Till the conversion of the Jews," "thirty thousand to the rest")*

 For additional support, go to the **Reading Studio** and assign the following 📖 **Level Up tutorial: Figurative Language**.

CREATE AND DISCUSS

Write Imagine that the speaker of "To His Coy Mistress" finds his old poem to his mistress in a coat pocket 25 years after he had written it. Imagine that he has decided to write her a letter reflecting on the poem. Write that letter.

- ❏ Write in the first person, as if you were the speaker.
- ❏ Consider the perspective of the speaker of "Twenty-One Love Poems (Poem III)."
- ❏ Predict how the speaker's attitude toward love may have changed.
- ❏ Cite specific ideas, images, or lines from his poem.

Discuss In a group, share the letter you wrote and read or listen to other students' writing. Then, compare letters and critique the tone of each. Evaluate how well your letters portray the speaker's feelings, and provide feedback on qualities you think are most realistic.

RESPOND TO THE ESSENTIAL QUESTION

 How does time affect our feelings?

Gather Information Review your annotations and notes on "To His Coy Mistress" and "Twenty-One Love Poems (Poem III)." Then, add relevant details to your Response Log. As you determine which information to include, think about:

- how each author describes the passage of time
- the way that getting older affects the experience of love
- the speakers' emotional responses to time

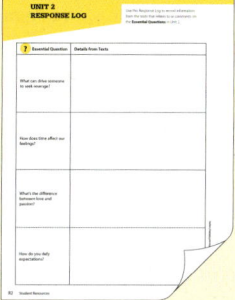

RESPOND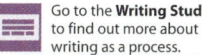

 Go to the **Writing Studio** to find out more about writing as a process.

 Go to the **Speaking and Listening Studio** to find out more about participating in collaborative discussions.

ACADEMIC VOCABULARY

As you write and discuss what you learned from the two lyric poems, be sure to use the Academic Vocabulary words. Check off each of the words that you use.

- ❏ ambiguous
- ❏ anticipate
- ❏ conceive
- ❏ drama
- ❏ integrity

APPLY

CREATE AND DISCUSS

Write Point out that the list on page 321 should serve as a guideline for students' letters. Tell students that before they write their letters, they should brainstorm some ideas about how a person might change over the course of 25 years. How might time affect the way a paerson feels, thinks, and behaves? Encourage students to incorporate these ideas into their letters.

For **writing support** for students at varying proficiency levels, see the **Text X-Ray** on page 312D.

Discuss As they listen to each other's letters, tell students to feel free to take notes or write down questions they might have so that they can ask them at the end. Encourage students to note similarities and differences in their letters, and then discuss how word choice affected the tone of each letter.

RESPOND TO THE ESSENTIAL QUESTION

Allow time for students to add details from "To His Coy Mistress" and "Twenty-One Love Poems (Poem III)" to their Unit 2 Response Logs.

APPLY

COMPARE THEMES

Before students complete their graphic organizers, ask them if they have ever heard someone use the expression *carpe diem*. Ask them to provide examples of when this expression might be used, making connections to their own lives. Then, ask them to consider how this theme is developed in "To His Coy Mistress" and "Twenty-One Love Poems (Poem III)." How do the speakers' ages affect how they develop this theme?

ANALYZE THE TEXTS

Possible answers:

1. **DOK 2:** Both speakers are afraid they will not have enough time to enjoy their love before they get old and die.

2. **DOK 3:** The speaker in "Twenty-One Love Poems (Poem III)" is being more reasonable because she has less time left, while the other speaker is young and still has plenty of time.

3. **DOK 4:** The speaker in "To His Coy Mistress" is afraid of death and is anxious to be with his beloved because of that fear. The other speaker accepts the inevitability of death and wants her and her beloved to face it together.

4. **DOK 4:** In both texts, being in love causes people to think about how quickly time passes because they want to have so much more time with their beloved than they know is possible. Being in love seems to accelerate time and make the moment of our deaths seem closer. In both texts, however, being in love puts the speakers in touch with their feelings of youthfulness.

RESPOND

Collaborate & Compare

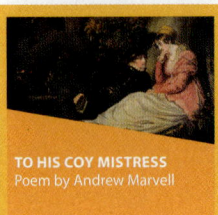

TO HIS COY MISTRESS
Poem by Andrew Marvell

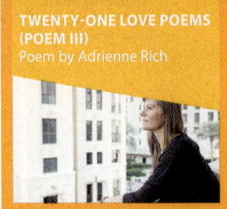

TWENTY-ONE LOVE POEMS (POEM III)
Poem by Adrienne Rich

COMPARE THEMES

The poems "To His Coy Mistress" and "Twenty-One Love Poems (Poem III)" express the ancient literary theme of *carpe diem*, Latin for "seize the day." This was one of the most popular themes of Cavalier poetry. *Carpe diem* is often taken to mean that one should enjoy life as much as possible for the present moment. Compare how the poems develop this theme. What reasons do they give for the necessity of enjoying the present moment?

REASONS WE MUST "SEIZE THE DAY"
"To His Coy Mistress"   *Time is moving very fast. But at my back I always hear / Time's wingéd chariot hurrying near*
"Twenty-One Love Poems (Poem III)"   *We have to make up for lost time: Weeks have to do time / for years of missing each other*

ANALYZE THE TEXTS

Discuss these questions in your group.

1. **Compare** How does the speaker of each poem feel about the passage of time? How are the speakers' feelings similar? How do they differ?

2. **Evaluate** Which speaker is more reasonable in his or her urgency about the relationship? Why do you think this is the case?

3. **Analyze** How does each speaker respond to the inevitability of death?

4. **Synthesize** According to these two texts, how does being in love affect our perception of age and the passing of time?

ENGLISH LEARNER SUPPORT

Perform Critical Analysis Use the following questions to help students analyze and compare the selections:

1. What common themes do the poems "To His Coy Mistress" and "Twenty-One Love Poems (Poem III)" address?

2. How is figurative language used in each poem to develop these themes?

3. In what ways are the two poems similar, and in what ways are they different?
   MODERATE/LIGHT

COLLABORATE AND PRESENT

Now your group can continue exploring the ideas in these texts by discussing the pros and cons of *carpe diem* and living for the moment. Work together to gain an understanding of the arguments pro and con, and then come to an agreement about your position as a group. Follow these steps:

1. **Get some ideas on paper.** Have everyone in the group take some time to think and jot down their answers to the questions, "Is it really best to live for the day? Why or why not?"

2. **Share ideas.** Have everyone in the group explain their thoughts, both pro and con, about living for the moment, and record these thoughts in a chart like the one below.

LIVING FOR THE MOMENT	
Pros	**Cons**
You don't miss out on the fun of being young.	*If you don't think about how your current actions affect your future, you will be very unhappy later.*

3. **Discuss and debate.** Identify the points on which you agree. Then, identify points on which you disagree, and resolve disagreements by presenting and evaluating the evidence. Decide which conclusion (pro or con) is best supported by the evidence.

4. **Present to the class.** Now, present your ideas to the class. Explain why you believe it is or is not better to live for the moment. Remember to provide evidence or examples to support your position.

RESPOND

Go to the **Listening and Speaking Studio** for more on participating in collaborative discussions.

Collaborate & Compare 323

APPLY

COLLABORATE AND PRESENT

Explain to students that while some people prefer to live in the moment, others like to plan for the future. Ask students to think of times when it might be useful to "seize the day," as well as times when "seizing the day" may not be such a good idea.

1. **Get some ideas on paper.** Walk around as students jot down their answers to the questions, "Is it really best to live for the day? Why or Why not?" If students appear stuck, ask them additional questions, such as "When might it be important to act quickly?" and "Why can it be important to plan for the future?"

2. **Share ideas.** As students complete their graphic organizers, encourage them to think carefully about each pro and con and make sure they have considered as many scenarios as possible.

3. **Discuss and debate.** Remind students that when one person is sharing, the rest of the group should be listening. Encourage students to provide evidence for their positions, especially if they disagree.

4. **Present to the class.** Before students present to the class, remind them to speak clearly and to use eye contact as way to connect with the audience. If time permits, give students a few minutes to practice before they present.

WHEN STUDENTS STRUGGLE...

Synthesize Ideas If students struggle with how to organize the ideas they want to present to the class, provide them with a and anticipate questions their peers might ask:

Ideas	Evidence from Selections or Life	Potential Questions from Classmates
Idea 1:		

 For additional support, go to the **Reading Studio** and assign the following Level Up tutorial: Synthesizing Information.

PLAN

FROM SPEECH BEFORE THE SPANISH ARMADA INVASION

Speech by Queen Elizabeth I

GENRE ELEMENTS
SPEECH

Remind students that **speeches** use **persuasive techniques** in order to call an audience to action. Some persuasive techniques are **ethos,** which develops the speaker's credibility, **logos,** which evokes a rational response from the audience, and **pathos,** which evokes an emotional response. In this lesson, students will analyze the persuasive techniques and rhetorical devices in a political speech.

LEARNING OBJECTIVES

- Analyze rhetorical devices and connect to history.
- Conduct research about the Spanish Armada.
- Write a speech with rhetorical devices.
- Present a speech.
- Understand vocabulary usage.
- Spell commonly misspelled words.
- **Language** Discuss persuasive techniques in speeches.

TEXT COMPLEXITY

Quantitative Measures	Speech before the Spanish Armada	Lexile: 1310L
Qualitative Measures	**Ideas Presented** Much is explicit. Simple, single meaning. Purpose is clear.	
	Structures Used Primarily explicit.	
	Language Used Complex sentence structures with use of archaic and formal language.	
	Knowledge Required Cultural and historical references may make heavier demands.	

PLAN

Online

RESOURCES

- Unit 2 Response Log
- Selection Audio
- Reading Studio: Notice and Notes
- Level Up Tutorial: Persuasive Techniques
- Writing Studio: Writing Arguments
- Speaking and Listening Studio: Giving a Presentation
- Vocabulary Studio: Vocabulary Usage
- Grammar Studio: Module 15: Lesson 2: Spelling
- "Speech Before the Spanish Armada Invasion" Selection Test

SUMMARIES

English
In this speech before an armed fleet of Spanish ships invades England, Queen Elizabeth I assures her subjects that she stands with them against Spain. She praises their courage and forecasts victory.

Spanish
En este discurso, dado frente a una flota de barcos españoles invasores la reina inglesa, Isabel I, les asegura a sus súbditos que ella está con ellos en contra de España. Alaba su valentía y pronostica la victoria.

SMALL-GROUP OPTIONS

Have students work in small groups and pairs to read and discuss the selection.

Reciprocal Teaching
- Have students read the speech.
- After reading, ask students to write 3–5 questions about the section, using these stems: *Why does Queen Elizabeth say _____? Why did the _____? Who is going to _____?*
- Form teams of three students.
- Have each student offer two questions for group discussion.
- The group reaches consensus on the answers and finds supporting text evidence.

Think-Pair-Share
- After reading the speech, pose this question: *What words show Queen Elizabeth's feelings and attitude toward the event she describes?*
- Have students think about the question individually and take notes.
- Then, have pairs listen, discuss, and formulate a shared response to the question.
- Finally, have pairs share their responses with the class.

Speech Before the Spanish Armada Invasion   **324B**

PLAN

 **Text X-Ray: English Learner Support** for "Speech before the Spanish Armada Invasion"

Use the Text X-Ray and the supports and scaffolds in the Teacher's Edition to help guide students at different proficiency levels through the selection.

INTRODUCE THE SELECTION

DISCUSS INVASION, TREACHERY, AND VALOR

In this lesson, students will need to be able to understand what happens during an invasion. Provide the following explanation:

- An *invasion* is an attempt by one group to conquer another.
- *Treachery* is an act of betrayal, such as an attempt to help an enemy.
- *Valor* is courage or bravery.

Write related word families for the above terms on the board and have students practice using them as they discuss the Spanish invasion of England. Provide sentence frames, such as: _____ invaded _____. Queen Elizabeth did not want her subjects to act _____. She hoped her subjects would act with _____.

CULTURAL REFERENCES

The following words or phrases may be unfamiliar to students:

- *take heed* (line 2): to listen to and follow
- *(in the) heat of* (line 9): during the most intense or active stage of an event
- *to lay down for* (line 10): to give up or surrender for
- *take up arms* (line 17): to hold a weapon
- *crowns* (line 19): British coins

LISTENING

Identify Rhetorical Devices

Help students distinguish among the types of rhetorical devices: *repetition, analogy, rhetorical questions,* and *antithesis.*

Use the following supports with students at varying proficiency levels:

- Write the four types of rhetorical devices on the board and define them. Slowly read aloud definitions and have students name the matching rhetorical device. **SUBSTANTIAL**
- Have partners quiz each other about the meanings of the four rhetorical devices. Guide them to turn each definition into a question. For example: *Which rhetorical device repeats a word, phrase, or similar grammatical construction? (repetition)* **MODERATE**
- One partner finds an example of a rhetorical device in the speech and reads it aloud. The other partner names the rhetorical device. Have them switch roles to repeat the activity. **LIGHT**

PLAN

SPEAKING

Discuss Persuasive Techniques

Write and define a list of academic and informal words and phrases that can be used to discuss persuasive techniques, such as *ethos, logos, pathos,* speaker's credibility, appeals to reason, appeals to emotion.

Use the following supports with students at varying proficiency levels:

- Have students write *ethos, logos,* and *pathos* on separate cards and review their meanings. Read aloud phrases from the text and have students say aloud the appropriate term to tell if the speaker is saying it to develop credibility or appeal to the audience's reason or emotion. **SUBSTANTIAL**
- Have partners take turns reading aloud the speech, phrase by phrase. After each phrase, have them say if it develops the speaker's credibility or appeals to the audience's reason or emotion. **MODERATE**
- Have partners ask and answer questions about the speech using terms from the list. For example: *How does the phrase _____ appeal to the audience's sense of reason?* **LIGHT**

READING

Identify Rhetorical Devices

After students write their speeches from the Respond activity, have them exchange their work to check for proper use of rhetorical devices.

Use the following supports with students at varying proficiency levels:

- Have a Beginner read the speech silently with an Advanced partner. Have the Advanced partner point out examples of rhetorical devices in the speech and explain why they are used correctly. **SUBSTANTIAL**
- After reading, have partners write brief comments about the use of rhetorical devices in the speech. Suggest that they tell their opinions of the devices used. **MODERATE**
- After reading, have partners write a list of the rhetorical devices used in the speech and a brief explanation of why the device will help to emphasize ideas or strengthen the speech. **LIGHT**

WRITING

Use Word Webs

After students choose an issue to discuss in their speech, have them use word webs to record related concepts, events, people, and ideas.

Use the following supports with students at varying proficiency levels:

- Help students write their issue in a center circle of the web. Then, help them use a thesaurus to find related words, concepts, and ideas to list in the outer circles. **SUBSTANTIAL**
- Direct students to write their issue in the center of their word web. Have small groups brainstorm related words, concepts, events, people, and ideas to include in each other's webs. **MODERATE**
- As students research their issue, have them take notes to write related keywords, concepts, events, people, and ideas in their word webs. **LIGHT**

TEACH

 Connect to the
ESSENTIAL QUESTION

This excerpt from "Speech Before the Spanish Armada Invasion" provides an example of how Queen Elizabeth I defied the expectations of her countrymen time and again, leading her country in a long reign of success and prosperity.

COMPARE ACROSS GENRES

Point out that each selection features women defying the expectations of society. This was much more difficult during Queen Elizabeth I's time, though today's women still face barriers through which they need to break. Explain that each selection is geared toward a different audience, and therefore uses different language to make similar points.

COLLABORATE & COMPARE

SPEECH

from SPEECH BEFORE THE SPANISH ARMADA INVASION

by **Queen Elizabeth I**
pages 327–329

COMPARE ACROSS GENRES

As you read, consider the historical context, time period, and purpose of each text. Next, consider similarities and differences in how each audience is addressed. Finally, make note of the topics and ideas shared by both texts. After you have finished reading, you will collaborate on a small group project.

 ESSENTIAL QUESTION:

How do you defy expectations?

ARTICLE

FOR ARMY INFANTRY'S FIRST WOMEN, HEAVY PACKS AND THE WEIGHT OF HISTORY

by **Dave Philipps**
pages 337–343

324 Unit 2

from Speech Before the Spanish Armada Invasion

QUICK START

Trust is an important factor in motivating people. Think about a time in your life when you tried to motivate someone to take an action you desired. What strategies did you use? Were your efforts successful? Why or why not?

ANALYZE RHETORICAL DEVICES

Elizabeth I was a brilliant speaker who captivated audiences through her command of **rhetorical devices**—techniques that communicate ideas and strengthen arguments. The following devices are often found in persuasive writing:

- **Repetition**—the repeated use of a word or phrase
- **Parallelism**—the use of similar grammatical constructions to express ideas that are related or equal in importance
- **Antithesis**—the use of similar grammatical constructions to express sharply contrasting ideas
- **Rhetorical question**—a question to which no answer is expected
- **Analogy**—a comparison made between two dissimilar things to explain an unfamiliar subject in terms of a familiar one

As you read the speech, pay attention to Elizabeth's use of rhetorical devices.

CONNECT TO HISTORY

Some writing becomes clearer and more meaningful when you make historical connections. A literary work's **historical context** includes the events and social conditions that inspired or influenced its creation. The cultural beliefs and values of a particular period are also part of the historical context.

The background note preceding Queen Elizabeth's speech discusses the event that inspired her address to English soldiers. As you read the text, you should also consider that women's lives in 16th-century England were severely restricted. Most women received a very limited education, suitable for running a household. Women had to be subservient to their fathers and husbands. Elizabeth I was a remarkable exception: Her father, Henry VIII, provided her with an excellent education, and after the deaths of her father, brother, and older sister, she inherited the throne. Because she never married, Elizabeth remained free to make her own decisions.

As you read the speech, pay attention to details that relate to the Spanish Armada invasion. Also notice how in crafting her speech, Elizabeth took into account her audience's views about women and the English monarchy. Consult outside sources such as an encyclopedia if you would like additional information about the historical context of the speech.

GET READY

GENRE ELEMENTS: SPEECH
- addresses a specific audience
- often explicitly states the speaker's purpose
- uses rhetorical devices and persuasive techniques
- may include a call to action

TEACH

QUICK START

Ask students to share their motivational-moment stories, prompting the other students to listen proactively for strategies and how effective those strategies were toward motivating others to action. Challenge students to consider how small changes in strategies could have led to different results, asking them to offer those alternatives up for group discussion.

ANALYZE RHETORICAL DEVICES

Help students understand each type of **rhetorical device** by explaining how each device uses a particular aspect of language to meet a specific goal. Like other types of figurative language, rhetorical devices can be difficult for some readers. Remind them that identifying these devices can help them better understand the point a speaker or author is trying to make and that learning to use rhetorical devices in their own writing will lend clarity to their communications and strength to their arguments.

CONNECT TO HISTORY

Remind students that the time in which people lived influenced how they were educated and how others responded to them. Being a single female queen, Elizabeth I had to prove herself over and over. Ask students to consider how her armies and her council might have reacted to her leading a country into war. Point out that because Elizabeth was educated as if she were a male, she was able to speak and act in ways that were powerful and convincing. As students read the speech, have them think about her upbringing and her word choice and how that wording might have affected the soldiers. Ask students to consider how Elizabeth's education and experiences led her to deliver such a motivational speech.

 ENGLISH LEARNER SUPPORT

Demonstrate Comprehension Review rhetorical devices with students, providing specific examples of each type of device. Place students in small same-first-language groups, if possible. Direct each group to answer these questions:

- Are there similar types of devices in your own language? What are some examples?

Ask each group to share its answers with the whole class and moderate a discussion on figurative wording used in other languages. **ALL LEVELS**

TEACH

CRITICAL VOCABULARY

Encourage students to read all the sentences before deciding which word best completes each one. Remind them to look for context clues to help them understand the meaning of each word.

Answers:

1. *treachery*
2. *feeble*
3. *valor*
4. *realm*
5. *scorn*

LANGUAGE CONVENTIONS

Review the information on **formal language.** Explain that there are numerous differences between informal and formal language. Read the following example:

- **Informal Version (text):** Ya'll, Ash-Ash can't party with her peeps tonight cuz she's gotta work in AM.
- **Formal Version:** Hello everyone. Ashley cannot attend her friend's party because she has to work early the next morning.

Challenge students to point out the differences, ensuring that the following items are noted: word choice, style, grammar, and mechanics.

ANNOTATION MODEL

Review rhetorical devices with students, asking them to pay attention to the speech, identifying language used by Elizabeth to persuade her armies to fight their opponents successfully. Explain the impact these word choices had and why she chose to use this wording. Point out that they may follow this suggestion or use their own system for marking up the selection in their write-in text. They may want to color-code their annotations by using highlighters. Their notes in the margin may include questions about ideas that are unclear or topics they want to learn more about.

326   Unit 2

GET READY

CRITICAL VOCABULARY

treachery   feeble   scorn   realm   valor

Replace the boldfaced word in each of the following sentences with a Critical Vocabulary word from the list.

1. **Dishonesty** isn't a concern among the queen's loyal people. _____
2. The queen is a **weak** woman but leads like a fearless king. _____
3. The people's **heroism** gives the queen confidence that her subjects can and will defeat their enemies. _____
4. Outsiders are attempting to invade, but Queen Elizabeth I is willing to fight in order to protect her **kingdom.** _____
5. The act of invading the queen's land is viewed with **disdain.** _____

LANGUAGE CONVENTIONS

Formal Language   Writing in emails, texts, and letters to friends often uses informal language. On the other hand, textbooks, reports, and speeches are usually written using formal language. **Formal language** includes sophisticated vocabulary and complex sentence structures. It also follows all writing, grammar, and mechanical rules; it doesn't include slang or contractions. It is less personal and more professional. Queen Elizabeth's speech uses formal language to address her subjects before they went into battle against a formidable enemy. Although the sentiments expressed in the speech are personal and bring her closer to her audience, the language is formal, which fits the situation and her education and rank as queen.

ANNOTATION MODEL   NOTICE & NOTE

As you read, note the queen's tone and the rhetorical devices she uses to appeal to her audience. In the model, you can see one reader's notes about the beginning of the speech.

We have been (persuaded) by some that are careful of our safety, to take heed how we commit our selves to armed multitudes, for fear of treachery; <u>but I assure you I do not desire to live to distrust my faithful and loving people.</u> Let tyrants fear, I have always so behaved myself that, under God, <u>I have placed my chiefest strength and safeguard in the loyal hearts and good-will of my subjects;</u>	She uses "we" to refer to herself. "Persuaded" here means that they tried to persuade her, not that she agreed. Elizabeth uses a calm, confident tone in addressing her soldiers. This must have reassured them in a time of emergency.

326   Unit 2

BACKGROUND

Queen Elizabeth I *(1533–1603) enjoyed great popularity, but her life was often in danger. Before becoming queen, she found herself imprisoned by her sister, Mary I, who suspected her of treason. After she took the throne, Elizabeth became the target of assassination plots by Catholics opposed to her Protestant rule. One of the most dangerous events came in 1588, when a fleet of Spanish ships known as the Armada set sail to invade England. Elizabeth delivered the following speech near Tilbury Fort, where her troops were preparing to defend against the invasion. Unknown to her, the Armada had already been defeated at sea.*

NOTICE & NOTE

SPEECH BEFORE THE SPANISH ARMADA INVASION
Speech by Queen Elizabeth I

PREPARE TO COMPARE

As you read, note the ways Queen Elizabeth I reveals her commitment to her subjects and kingdom. Consider closely the words she chooses to express her loyalty and dedication, as well as her suggestions about women. This analysis will help you compare this speech with the article "For Army Infantry's First Women, Heavy Packs and the Weight of History."

My Loving People,

We have been persuaded by some that are careful of our safety, to take heed how we commit our selves to armed multitudes, for fear of **treachery**; but I assure you I do not desire to live to
5   distrust my faithful and loving people. Let tyrants fear, I have always so behaved myself that, under God, I have placed my chiefest strength and safeguard in the loyal hearts and good-will of my subjects; and therefore I am come amongst you, as you see, at this time, not for my recreation and disport,[1] but
10   being resolved, in the midst and heat of the battle, to live or die amongst you all; to lay down for my God, and for my kingdom,

---
[1] **disport:** entertainment.

Notice & Note
Use the side margins to notice and note signposts in the text.

treachery
(trĕch´ə-rē) *n.* an act of betrayal.

CONNECT TO HISTORY
Annotate: In lines 1-7, mark Elizabeth's reason for ignoring warnings about her safety.

Connect: Why were some people worried about her giving this speech?

Speech Before the Spanish Armada Invasion 327

WHEN STUDENTS STRUGGLE . . .

Analyze Arguments Challenge students to write the beginning of Elizabeth's speech in their own words and share their versions with partners. Discuss with students these questions:
- Why is she addressing the soldiers?
- What words does she use to inspire them and how does she show she supports them?

 For additional support, go to the **Reading Studio** and assign the following **Level Up tutorial: Persuasive Techniques**.

TEACH

✏️ ANALYZE RHETORICAL DEVICES

Remind students that **repetition** is a common **rhetorical device.** Queen Elizabeth uses repetition to strengthen the points she is trying to make. (**Answer:** *In repeating the words "myself," "by your," and "of my," she connects herself to her people.*)

CRITICAL VOCABULARY

feeble: Some people think female rulers are *feeble*, or weak, but Queen Elizabeth proved that false.

ASK STUDENTS to describe the difference between a feeble and strong ruler. (*A feeble ruler would be bad for the country, while a strong ruler would do great things for the country.*)

scorn: It is common to feel *scorn*, or disdain, for someone who has disappointed you.

ASK STUDENTS how it feels when someone is disappointed in something you've done. (*When someone is disappointed in you, it can make you feel sad and wish you had behaved differently.*)

realm: The whole *realm*, or kingdom, celebrated when Elizabeth was born.

ASK STUDENTS how a country would celebrate a princess's birth. (*There would likely be a huge party with great food, music, and entertainment.*)

valor: Soldiers who fight for their country show great heroism, or *valor*, in doing so.

ASK STUDENTS to describe what heroism means to them. (*Heroism means that you are brave and will do whatever you need to when called upon to do so.*)

328 Unit 2

 NOTICE & NOTE

feeble
(fē´bəl) *adj.* lacking strength.

scorn
(skôrn) *n.* contempt or disdain.

realm
(rĕlm) *n.* kingdom.

ANALYZE RHETORICAL DEVICES
Annotate: Mark instances of repetition and parallelism in lines 16–26.

Analyze: What ideas are emphasized by the queen's use of these devices?

valor
(văl´ər) *n.* courage, bravery.

and my people, my honor and my blood, even in the dust. I know I have the body but of a weak and **feeble** woman; but I have the heart and stomach of a king, and of a king of England too, and think foul
15 **scorn** that Parma or Spain, or any prince of Europe,² should dare to invade the borders of my **realm**; to which rather than any dishonor shall grow by me, I myself will take up arms, I myself will be your general, judge, and rewarder of every one of your virtues in the field. I know already, for your forwardness you have deserved rewards and
20 crowns; and We do assure you in the word of a prince, they shall be duly paid you. In the mean time, my lieutenant general shall be in my stead,³ than whom never prince commanded a more noble or worthy subject; not doubting but by your obedience to my general, by your
25 concord⁴ in the camp, and your **valor** in the field, we shall shortly have a famous victory over those enemies of my God, of my kingdom, and of my people.

---

² **Parma or Spain . . . Europe:** the duke of Parma, the king of Spain, or any other monarch of Europe. Alessandro Farnese, duke of the Italian city of Parma, was a skillful military leader whom Philip II, king of Spain, often relied upon. Philip's plan was to send the Spanish fleet to join the army under Parma's command in the Netherlands and invade England.
³ **my lieutenant general . . . stead:** Elizabeth refers to Robert Dudley, the Earl of Leicester. He was a courtier who, for a time, was Elizabeth's favorite.
⁴ **concord** (kŏn´kôrd): friendly and peaceful relations; harmony; agreement.

328 Unit 2

APPLYING ACADEMIC VOCABULARY

☐ ambiguous   ☑ anticipate   ☐ conceive   ☐ drama   ☑ integrity

Write and Discuss Have students turn to partners to discuss the following questions. Guide students to include the academic vocabulary words *anticipate* and *integrity* in their responses. Ask volunteers to share their responses with the class.

- What might the soldiers have anticipated after Elizabeth's speech?
- How does the queen demonstrate integrity in her actions?

NOTICE & NOTE

CHECK YOUR UNDERSTANDING

Answer these questions before moving on to the **Analyze the Text** section on the following page.

1. How does Queen Elizabeth I address her subjects?
   - A Angrily
   - B Fearfully
   - C Aggressively
   - D Passionately

2. The people of England need _____ from their leader.
   - F Food
   - G Security
   - H Clean water
   - J Warm clothes

3. What is Queen Elizabeth I willing to do in order to defend her kingdom?
   - A Give up her position as queen
   - B Die for her people
   - C Learn from other European monarchs
   - D Move to another country

Speech Before the Spanish Armada Invasion 329

TEACH

CHECK YOUR UNDERSTANDING

Have students answer the questions independently.

Answers:

1. D
2. G
3. B

If students answer any questions incorrectly, have them reread the text to confirm their understanding. Then, they may proceed to ANALYZE THE TEXT on page 330.

ENGLISH LEARNER SUPPORT

Oral Assessment Use the following questions to assess students' comprehension and speaking skills.

1. What emotion does Queen Elizabeth I show in her speech? *(passion)*
2. What do people need most from their leaders? *(safety)*
3. What would the queen do to protect her people? *(She would die in battle for them.)*

MODERATE/LIGHT

APPLY

ANALYZE THE TEXT
Possible answers:

1. **DOK 1:** *She says that tyrants live in fear of their subjects, but because she has been a good ruler she trusts them completely. This appeals to their patriotism because they wouldn't want to be seen as disloyal to a ruler who treats them well.*

2. **DOK 3:** *She uses antithesis, contrasting the weakness of her body with the strength of her character. It emphasizes that a ruler's mental qualities are much more important than physical ones.*

3. **DOK 4:** *She probably wanted to inspire bravery in her soldiers, who would not want to be seen as less courageous than a woman.*

4. **DOK 3:** *She assures the soldiers that they will be rewarded for their service, and she assigns her lieutenant general to lead them instead of trying to do that herself.*

5. **DOK 4:** *Answers will vary. Students might point to her use of antithesis in lines 11–13 and her talk of taking up arms as an effective reversal of gender stereotype.*

RESEARCH

Remind students to use sources ending in .edu, .org, or .gov for the most-reliable results. Explain that the information they are looking for can also be found through reputable historical or scholarly articles, though each one should be evaluated for credibility and bias. Help students locate an article on the English defeat of the Spanish Armada. Instruct them on how to evaluate the site and article to ensure it is valid, credible, and free of obvious bias. Challenge them to consider the reasons why some sites may cover historical events with a distinct bias or represent the past inaccurately.

Extend Guide students in a discussion on potential reasons why some "news sites" would alter historical facts to misrepresent events that occurred. Challenge them to consider reasons why some of the news and information they read on the Internet is biased for or against the subjects about which its articles are written.

RESPOND

ANALYZE THE TEXT
Support your responses with evidence from the text.  NOTEBOOK

1. **Interpret** What difference does Queen Elizabeth point out between herself and a tyrant in lines 2–8? How does she use this contrast to appeal to her audience's sense of patriotism?

2. **Analyze** What rhetorical device does Elizabeth use to describe herself in lines 12–14? How does this device help her address doubts the soldiers may have had about her ability to lead them?

3. **Connect** In lines 16–18, Elizabeth says that to avoid dishonor, she would take up arms and lead the soldiers into battle. Traditionally, women were not allowed to have professions in this time period, including military roles. Why might she have made this declaration?

4. **Cite Evidence** Which details in lines 19–23 reveal that in addition to being inspirational, Elizabeth was a practical leader?

5. **Evaluate** Given the historical circumstances, do you consider this to be an effective speech? Explain why or why not.

RESEARCH

RESEARCH TIP
Start your Internet research with a few keywords like "Elizabeth I," "Spanish Armada," or even "Spanish Armada loss." As you conduct your research, rely on websites that end in .edu, .org, and .gov. These websites are more likely to have been reviewed for accuracy. Be sure to note website URLs and sources during your research.

The defeat of the Spanish Armada was one of the most important events of the English Renaissance. With a partner, do research on what led up to the attempted invasion and why it failed. Use what you learn to answer these questions.

QUESTION	ANSWER
Why did Spain's king want to invade England?	
What was the plan for the invasion?	
How was the Armada defeated?	

Extend Find another speech by Elizabeth I. With a partner, compare it with her Armada speech, analyzing the ideas she expresses and her use of rhetorical devices

---

WHEN STUDENTS STRUGGLE . . .

Reteaching: Rhetorical Devices Remind students that rhetorical devices are often used in persuasive speeches to add depth or effect. Assign small groups a different device (repetition, analogy, rhetorical question, or antithesis). Have them identify all uses of their assigned device within the speech, and rewrite it by removing the rhetorical device. Have groups share their rewrites and decide which would be most effective in leading an army into a successful battle.

 For additional support, go to the **Reading Studio** and assign the following Level Up tutorial: *Revising at the Sentence Level*.

RESPOND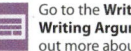

CREATE AND PRESENT

Write a Speech Write a speech about an issue that is important to you. Your speech should be crafted to appeal to a specific audience—for example, an assembly at your school or a community meeting. Use a variety of rhetorical devices such as repetition and rhetorical questions to help make your speech compelling and persuasive.

❏ Review your Quick Start activity notes.
❏ Choose an issue that you are passionate about.
❏ Identify and address an audience that faces the same issue.
❏ Commit to your purpose and revisit it throughout your speech.

Present a Speech The queen used her words to gain her people's trust and establish herself as a capable leader. Imagine her facial expressions, gestures, and tone as she delivered her speech. Then, use some of those same strategies for delivery in your own presentation.

❏ Practice reading aloud quietly; then try a more assertive tone.
❏ Share your speech with a small group. Revise your word choices and approach based on their feedback.
❏ Then, present your speech. Pause now and then to give your audience time to think, make eye contact with each member of the audience, and include natural gestures.

 Go to the **Writing Studio: Writing Arguments** to find out more about persuasive techniques.

 Go to the **Speaking and Listening Studio** to find out more about giving a presentation.

RESPOND TO THE ESSENTIAL QUESTION

? How do you defy expectations?

Gather Information Review your notes on "Speech Before the Spanish Armada Invasion." Then, add relevant details to your Response Log. As you decide which information to include, think about:

- how rhetorical devices may be used to motivate people to action
- how connections to historical context help explain and clarify texts
- the relationship between women and power in history

ACADEMIC VOCABULARY
As you write and discuss what you learned from the speech, be sure to use the Academic Vocabulary words. Check off each of the words that you use.

❏ ambiguous
❏ anticipate
❏ conceive
❏ drama
❏ integrity

APPLY

CREATE AND PRESENT

Write a Speech As a class, brainstorm ideas students can use for their persuasive speeches. After brainstorming, review how to outline the main ideas and supporting details of a speech, as well as how to write an effective call to action.

 For **writing support** for students at varying proficiency levels, see the **Text X-Ray** on pages 324D.

Present a Speech Remind students how to deliver a speech using appropriate verbal and nonverbal techniques—such as making eye contact or varying their tone or volume to emphasize key points. Pair students and have them practice their speeches. Listeners should offer constructive feedback to help the speakers improve the speeches.

RESPOND TO THE ESSENTIAL QUESTION

Allow time for students to add details from "Speech Before the Spanish Armada Invasion" to their Unit 2 Response Logs.

🅔🅛 ENGLISH LEARNER SUPPORT

Summarize Place students in small groups. Task each group with summarizing the queen's speech in two to three complete sentences. Remind each group to ensure their sentences are written correctly, following all rules of grammar and mechanics. Ask groups to share each of their summaries. Ask students to point out what elements make the summary strong.
MODERATE/LIGHT

APPLY

CRITICAL VOCABULARY

Answers:

1. *feeble*
2. *treachery*
3. *realm*
4. *valor*
5. *scorn*

VOCABULARY STRATEGY:
Mutiple-Meaning Words

Answers:

1. *B*
2. *B*
3. *A*

 **RESPOND**

WORD BANK
treachery
feeble
scorn
realm
valor

CRITICAL VOCABULARY

Practice and Apply Answer each question by using one of the Critical Vocabulary words in a complete sentence.

1. How might someone describe you if you cannot lift a lightweight object?
2. Which word would be used to describe someone's dishonesty?
3. Which word could you use to describe a kingdom?
4. If you were brave enough to save an entire country what word would be used to describe you?
5. What word would be used to describe a person's feelings towards something contemptible?

 Go to the **Vocabulary Studio** for more on words with multiple meanings.

VOCABULARY STRATEGY:
Multiple-Meaning Words

Many words have more than one meaning. To make sense of what you read, you need to make sure that you understand which meaning a writer intended. This is particularly true with words used as more than one part of speech or words appearing in older texts. For example, the noun *stomach* usually refers to a digestive organ or to the abdomen, but Elizabeth uses it to mean "courage" or "pride."

As you read texts from earlier periods, be alert to the nuances of meaning in words. If you encounter an unfamiliar word or a familiar word used in a way you find confusing, examine the **context**—the surrounding words, phrases, and sentences—for clues to the writer's meaning.

Practice and Apply Read each word. Then select the correct meaning of the word as it is used in "Speech Before the Spanish Armada Invasion."

1. tyrant _____
   a. an extremely oppressive, harsh, arbitrary person
   b. an absolute ruler who governs without restrictions, especially one who seized power illegally

2. subject _____
   a. prone or disposed
   b. one who is under the rule of another or others

3. general _____
   a. highest or superior in rank
   b. prevalent

332   Unit 2

ENGLISH LEARNER SUPPORT

Vocabulary Strategy Give students additional practice in determining the meanings of multiple-meaning words. Write the following sentences on the board:

- The **body** of water was quite large. The dog's **body** was furry.
- Make a **column** for each item in the list. Shelia wrote a newspaper **column** about the town meeting.

Work with students to find the meanings of each word and then determine how it is used in the sentence. Underline or circle context clues to help students understand how to use the context of a sentence to determine which meaning is used. **ALL LEVELS**

RESPOND

APPLY

LANGUAGE CONVENTIONS:
Formal Language

Different writing situations call for different levels of formality. For personal communication such as emails and texts, most people tend to use casual or informal language. **Formal language** is often used in academic and professional work; it is also used during formal occasions such as speeches. Queen Elizabeth I uses formal language in her speech marking the occasion when her armed forces went to war with the Spanish Armada. In her speech, the queen uses language that is appropriate for the seriousness of the occasion and the sophistication of her audience. Here is an example from the speech:

> I know already, for your forwardness you have deserved rewards and crowns; and We do assure you in the word of a prince, they shall be duly paid you.

Notice that the passage contains key elements of formal language, including complex vocabulary and sentence structure. Note that it does not use slang or contractions.

Practice and Apply Rewrite the following sentences using formal language. An example sentence has been done for you.

Informal: The battle went back and forth for hours before the guys upstairs decided that we'd just kick back and rest a bit.
Formal: The battle raged on for several hours before the military personnel in charge determined that the soldiers who had been on the frontlines could be relieved for a short rest.

Informal: A battlefield is a really rough place, and I don't think it's any place I want to stick around.

Formal:

Informal: During a battle, people are all over the place with their swords and horses, and everything's just a big, huge mess.

Formal:

Go to **Writing Arguments: Formal Style** in the **Writing Studio** for more help.

LANGUAGE CONVENTIONS:
Formal Language

Review the information on **formal language** with students. Explain that, in their daily lives, students most often use informal language, which includes slang or contractions. In school, and later at work, students will be required to write more formally, following all grammatical and mechanical rules.

Read aloud the example sentence from the queen's speech and challenge students to point out each instance of formality, including word choice, style, grammar, and mechanics.

Practice and Apply Display the example sentence and read it aloud. Then, read the revised version. Have students explain the differences between the two. Pair students and have them rewrite the two sentences so they are formal.

Once both partners have rewritten the sentences, they should exchange and review each other's new versions. Direct them to edit the new sentences to ensure formal style, grammar, and mechanics are properly used. (*Students' sentence rewrites will vary. Possible answer: A battlefield is a dangerous place that I do not believe is where I ever would like to be. During a battle, soldiers and military personnel fill the battle-zone, wielding swords and riding their horses; during battles, the entire field is filled with the sounds and sights of war.*)

Speech Before the Spanish Armada Invasion

ENGLISH LEARNER SUPPORT

Use Formal Language Note that Spanish speakers might use language that does not follow formal usage rules. For example, Spanish requires double negatives in many sentence structures. Point out to students that in formal language, only one negative is used.

Give students additional practice in speaking using formal language. Place students into pairs or small groups and have them take turns reading the speech aloud. Challenge students to use proper pacing when they are reading and direct group members to assist with pronunciations when needed. Work with students who have difficulty with the language or who seem to be struggling with reading aloud. **MODERATE/LIGHT**

PLAN

FOR ARMY INFANTRY'S FIRST WOMEN, HEAVY PACKS AND THE WEIGHT OF HISTORY

Article by Dave Philipps

GENRE ELEMENTS
ARTICLE
Remind students that authors of articles use text features such as titles, subheads, and photographs to give readers important information. Articles may also reference well-known events or ideas to help provide context for their issues. In this lesson, students will analyze text features and summarize an article in their own words.

LEARNING OBJECTIVES
- Analyze text features and summarize a text.
- Conduct research about famous female military leaders.
- Write notes for a debate.
- Conduct a debate.
- Identify foreign words and phrases.
- Use dashes and hyphenation.
- **Language** Rephrase a classmate's arguments for a debate.

TEXT COMPLEXITY

Quantitative Measures	For Army Infantry's First Women, Heavy Packs and the Weight of History	**Lexile: 1140L**
Qualitative Measures	**Ideas Presented** Much is explicit, but moves to some implied meaning. Requires some inferential thinking.	
	Structures Used More deviation from chronological or sequential order.	
	Language Used Explicit, literal, contemporary, familiar language.	
	Knowledge Required Subjects mostly familiar, with some references to historical and specialized knowledge.	

PLAN

Online

RESOURCES

- Unit 2 Response Log
- 🔊 Selection Audio
- 📖 Reading Studio: Notice and Notes
- 📊 Level Up Tutorial: Elements of an Argument
- 📝 Writing Studio: Planning an Argument
- 💬 Speaking and Listening Studio: Participating in Collaborative Discussions
- ⚛ Vocabulary Studio: Foreign Words and Phrases
- ❗ Grammar Studio: Module 14 Lesson 3: Dashes and Hyphenations
- ✅ "Army Infantry's First Women" Selection Test

SUMMARIES

English

In 2013, the Obama administration ordered the military to open all combat positions to women. In 2017, the first group of women graduated from the U.S. Army infantry training. In this article, army personnel and recent graduates discuss how army life has changed and stayed the same.

Spanish

En 2013, la administración de Obama ordenó al ejército abrir todos los puestos de combate a las mujeres. En 2017, el primer grupo de mujeres se graduó del entrenamiento de infantería del Ejército de Estados Unidos. En este artículo, miembros del ejército y recién graduados discuten cómo la vida en el ejército ha cambiado y qué sigue igual.

SMALL-GROUP OPTIONS

Have students work in small groups and pairs to read and discuss the selection.

Three-Minute Review

- As you read the text, pause after every 2–3 paragraphs.
- Direct students to reread the paragraphs and write clarifying questions. Set a timer for three minutes.
- After three minutes, ask: *What did you notice about the sentences you reread in the text?*
- Invite volunteers to share clarifying questions.
- Guide small groups to discuss and answer the questions.

Think-Pair-Share

- After reading the "Not 'treated special'," section, pose this question: *How do you think the other army privates felt about Private Donovan shaving her head?*
- Call on a student to respond. Wait up to 11 seconds.
- If the student has no response, s/he must call on another student by name to answer the same question.
- Have students continue asking each other for assistance as needed. Monitor responses and ask more questions as appropriate.

For Army Infantry's First Women, Heavy Packs and the Weight of History **334B**

PLAN

Text X-Ray: English Learner Support
For Army Infantry's First Women, Heavy Packs and the Weight of History

Use the Text X-Ray and the supports and scaffolds in the Teacher's Edition to help guide students at different proficiency levels through the selection.

INTRODUCE THE SELECTION
DISCUSS MOTIVATIONS AND EXPECTATIONS

In this lesson, students will need to be able to discuss society's expectations of women and the motivations women have to overturn those expectations.

Provide the following explanations:
- A motivation is a reason to act.
- An expectation is an expected standard of behavior.

Guide students to use the terms as they discuss why some women want to join combat in the army and why some people in society may be against it.

Provide sentence frames, such as: *In our society, one expectation of women is for them to _____. One motivation for a woman to join the army infantry is _____.*

CULTURAL REFERENCES

The following words or phrases may be unfamiliar to students:
- *taken pains* (paragraph 3): tried very hard to do something
- *to the pound* (paragraph 3): of the same weight
- *play down the significance* (paragraph 4): lower the importance
- *business as usual* (paragraph 5): the situation remains the same
- *making history* (paragraph 8): being the first to do something important in history

LISTENING

Rephrase Arguments

Review that a claim is a statement of opinion, and an argument is made up of facts and evidence that support that opinion.

Use the following supports with students at varying proficiency levels:
- As more fluent English speakers state their arguments to support their claims, have beginners write down key words they hear. Use the words in short sentences and have students copy them as you say them. **SUBSTANTIAL**
- As partners listen to each other's arguments, have them take notes about key ideas. Then, have them rephrase the argument. Provide a sentence starter: *[Name of student]'s argument supports his/her claim because _____.* **MODERATE**
- After listening to a partner's argument, have the other partner write it in their own words. **LIGHT**

PLAN

SPEAKING

Use Photographs

Review the photographs that accompany the text. Have students work together to create a word bank of vocabulary based on the images to use in a discussion of women in the military.

Use the following supports with students at varying proficiency levels:

- Have students repeat the words from the word bank as they point to related elements in the photographs. Use the words in simple sentences related to women in the military and have students repeat them. **SUBSTANTIAL**
- Have partners use the words from the word bank in simple sentences related to women in the military. Provide a sentence starter, such as: *The photograph shows how _____.* **MODERATE**
- Have partners ask each other questions about women in the military using the word bank and photographs. Have students answer in complete sentences. For example: *What do women do in the military? (Women do hard physical exercise in the military.)* **LIGHT**

READING

Distinguish Dashes and Hyphens

Review the purposes of dashes and hyphens in a text. Create a two-column chart on the board to record places in the text where dashes and hyphens are used.

Use the following supports with students of varying proficiency levels:

- Have students search pages 338 and 339 for dashes and hyphens. Have them circle those that they find. **SUBSTANTIAL**
- Have pairs read the text aloud to each other to identify places where the author uses a dash or a hyphen. Have students explain to each other why the author used each of the punctuation marks. **MODERATE**
- Have students create a similar two-column chart to fill in as they reread the article. Then, have them explain to partners how the text would change if the author did not use the dashes or hyphens. **LIGHT**

WRITING

Write with Foreign Words and Phrases

Brainstorm a list of foreign words and phrases and write it on the board.

Use the following supports with students of varying proficiency levels:

- Help students create dictionaries of foreign words and phrases in their notebooks. Provide definitions, and have students copy them. Then, have students add sketches or definitions in their own language. **SUBSTANTIAL**
- Help students define the words and phrases on the list. Then, have them use each term in a short sentence. **MODERATE**
- Have partners discuss the definitions of the words and phrases on the list. Then, have them work together to write a funny paragraph using as many terms from the list as possible. **LIGHT**

TEACH

? Connect to the
ESSENTIAL QUESTION

Explain that a stereotype is an idea or image of a person or idea held by society. Stereotypes are often limiting and do not offer true or complete descriptions of any of the people to whom they are ascribed. "For Army Infantry's First Women, Heavy Packs and the Weight of History" describes how women "defy expectations" by being in the military. Ask students if they would consider a person who broke through stereotypes to be brave. Challenge students to think of times when they broke stereotypes or defied the expectations someone had of them.

COMPARE ACROSS GENRES

Ask students to discuss some typical stereotypes of women in America. Challenge them to contrast these ideas with stereotypes of individuals seeking to engage in military combat. Remind students that as they read, they should consider how these women were motivated to overcome expectations and face new challenges.

COLLABORATE & COMPARE

ARTICLE

FOR ARMY INFANTRY'S FIRST WOMEN, HEAVY PACKS AND THE WEIGHT OF HISTORY

by **Dave Philipps**
pages 337–342

COMPARE ACROSS GENRES

As you read, think about why expectations for women in our culture might make some people question whether they should take combat roles in the military. What motivates some women to overcome these expectations, and what challenges are they willing to face as they do so? After you read this article and the speech, you will collaborate on a small group project.

 ESSENTIAL QUESTION:

How do you defy expectations?

SPEECH

from
SPEECH BEFORE THE SPANISH ARMADA INVASION

by **Queen Elizabeth I**
pages 327–328

For Army Infantry's First Women, Heavy Packs and the Weight of History

QUICK START

Sometimes we choose to do difficult things—or even things that will make us miserable—because we perceive that they will serve some greater purpose. With a partner or in a small group, think of a time you have challenged yourself by doing something difficult. Why did you do it? Was it worth it?

ANALYZE TEXT FEATURES

Some texts, especially articles in periodicals, include text features that help readers understand the text's organizational structure and readily identify its main ideas. These **text features** include titles, subtitles, subheadings, pull quotes, boldface type, and bulleted and numbered lists.

Before you read, preview the article's text features to make predictions about the text's organization and ideas. Then, as you read, confirm or adjust your predictions. You can use a chart such as the one below to record predictions.

TEXT FEATURES	
TYPE OF FEATURE	PREDICTION
Title	
Subtitle	
Subheadings	

GENRE ELEMENTS: ARTICLE
- provides information about a topic
- uses evidence, including facts and quotations, to support ideas
- may rely on text features to clarify organizational structure

SUMMARIZE AND PARAPHRASE TEXTS

A summary can help clarify how ideas in a text fit together. When you **summarize,** you briefly restate the main ideas and most important details in a text. A summary should follow the order of the original text and be accurate and objective. If you come across passages that are confusing or difficult, you can **paraphrase** the passage, restating ideas and information in your own words. A paraphrase is usually the same length as the original text but contains simpler language.

As you read the article, note ideas and details to include in a summary, and look out for difficult passages that you can simplify by paraphrasing.

TEACH

QUICK START

Ask students to share their narratives, first by describing the difficult tasks, then explaining the greater purposes their actions served, and finally sharing whether or not they believed their actions to be worth their efforts. Prompt the other students to listen proactively and offer constructive comments or ask questions about the stories shared by their peers.

ANALYZE TEXT FEATURES

Explain that **text features** can be useful in reading informational items like articles or texts. Subtitles and subheadings provide an **organizational structure** and give insight into what the reader can expect from each section. Pull quotes are used to emphasize particularly noteworthy statements. Boldface type often indicates a word of importance, such as a new vocabulary word. Bulleted and numbered lists are typically presented to summarize key points within the article. Remind students to use the text features to help them preview what they will be reading and predict what each section may be about.

SUMMARIZE AND PARAPHRASE TEXTS

Tell students that, when **summarizing** a text, they must restate the information in their own words. Summaries should be shorter than the original text and include only the most important information. Explain that students can use the text features as their organizational guide for a summary. For each subtitle and subheading, they can prepare a short statement or bullet point that identifies the key details. Reviewing and combining each of these statements will provide an organized and comprehensive summary. Remind them that maintaining objectivity and accuracy is important when writing a summary.

TEACH

CRITICAL VOCABULARY

Encourage students to review all of the possible choices before deciding which word best completes each blank. Remind them to look for context clues to help them understand the meaning of each word.

Answers:

1. *chow*
2. *scrounge*
3. *rotation*
4. *espirit de corps*
5. *infantry*
6. *chafe*
7. *smart*

LANGUAGE CONVENTIONS

Review the information on **hyphens** and **dashes**. Then, review some other hyphen uses: to join parts of a compound with *all-, ex-, self-,* or *elec-*; to join parts of compound numbers; to join parts of a fraction; to join a prefix to a word beginning with a capital letter; to indicate that a word is divided in half at the end of a line. Em dashes are often used to indicate an abrupt break in thought or to emphasize an idea.

■ English Learner Support

Understand Grammar Usage Using a hyphen to join compound adjectives before a noun may be difficult for speakers of Haitian, Creole, Hmong, Khmer, Spanish, and Vietnamese. In these languages, adjectives commonly come after the nouns they modify. For example, *She lives in an apartment first floor.* Point out that in English, adjectives come before nouns and when two adjectives modify the same noun, they come before the noun and are hyphenated: *She lives in a first-floor apartment.* **ALL LEVELS**

ANNOTATION MODEL

Review the annotations used on page 336. Point out that students may follow this suggestion or use their own system for marking up the selection in their write-in text. They may want to color-code their annotations by using highlighters. Their notes in the margin may include questions about ideas that are unclear or topics they want to learn more about.

336 Unit 2

 **GET READY**

CRITICAL VOCABULARY

infantry   smart   esprit de corps   rotation   chow
scrounge   chafe

Write the Critical Vocabulary word next to its meaning:

1. Food: _____
2. Search: _____
3. Regular variation in a sequence: _____
4. A feeling or spirit shared by a group: _____
5. Soldiers trained to fight on foot: _____
6. To annoy or irritate: _____
7. Feel pain or distress: _____

LANGUAGE CONVENTIONS

Hyphens and dashes look similar but have very different uses. **Hyphens** (-) are used in hyphenated compounds, including some compound modifiers, which are created when two words work together to modify a noun (for example, first-year cadet). An **em dash** (—) is punctuation that can be used instead of a comma, semicolon, or parentheses. An **en dash** (–) has many uses, often to signify the word *to* or *between* in ranges of numbers.

ANNOTATION MODEL NOTICE & NOTE

As you read, note main ideas and important details, and look for text features that support your understanding.

> (FORT BENNING, GA.)— The first group of women graduated from United States Army infantry training last week, but with soldiers obscured by body armor, camouflage face paint and smoke grenades, it was almost impossible to distinguish the mixed-gender squads in the steamy woods from those of earlier generations.

This feature shows where the article was reported.

The opening detail about it being hard to tell women apart from men may support one of the writer's main ideas.

336 Unit 2

BACKGROUND

Dave Philipps *(1977–) is a journalist who has written about veterans and the military community for* The New York Times. *He has focused on the unintended consequences of wars in Iraq and Afghanistan, including the presence of women in combat zones. In these wars, women found themselves engaging in combat, although they did not hold official combat positions. They held dangerous frontline roles and often engaged in fierce firefights, even leading battles. Because official combat positions are crucial to career advancement, women felt they were being unfairly held back. Under the Obama administration, these positions were gradually opened to women.*

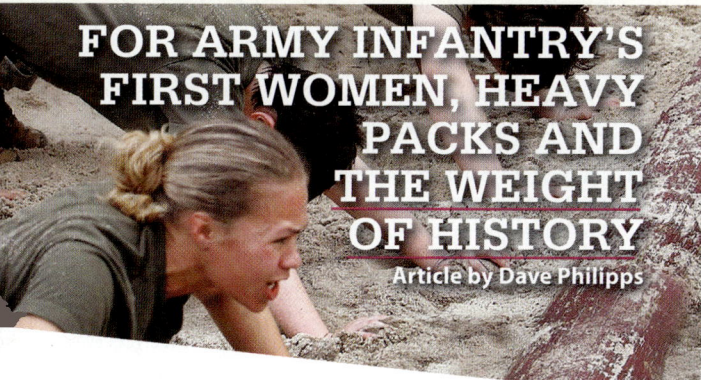

FOR ARMY INFANTRY'S FIRST WOMEN, HEAVY PACKS AND THE WEIGHT OF HISTORY

Article by Dave Philipps

PREPARE TO COMPARE

As you read, look for details about attitudes toward women serving in combat and how women have overcome them. This analysis will help you compare the article with "Speech Before the Spanish Armada Invasion."

NOTICE & NOTE

Use the side margins to notice and note signposts in the text.

> **The Army has sought to play down the significance of the mixed-gender milestone. But female grunts see it as monumental and revolutionary.**

1 FORT BENNING, Ga. — The first group of women graduated from United States Army **infantry** training in May of 2017 but with soldiers obscured by body armor, camouflage face paint and smoke grenades, it was almost impossible to distinguish the mixed-gender squads in the steamy woods from those of earlier generations.

2 That's just how the Army wants it.

3 After the Obama administration ordered the military in 2013 to open all combat positions to women, the Army developed gender-neutral performance standards to ensure that recruits entering the infantry were all treated the same. Still **smarting** over accusations that it had lowered standards to help the first

infantry
(ĭn′fən-trē) *n.* the branch of an army made up of units trained to fight on foot.

smart
(smärt) *v.* to suffer acutely, as from mental distress, wounded feelings, or remorse.

🗨 ENGLISH LEARNER SUPPORT

Understand Grammar Usage Direct students' attention to the hyphenated words in paragraphs 1 (mixed-gender) and 3 (gender-neutral). Remind them that hyphens are used with compound nouns, or when two words are put together to make a new word. Ask them to define each of the hyphenated words based only on the literal meanings of each word-part.
ALL LEVELS

TEACH

BACKGROUND

After students read the Background note, explain the ongoing debate of women in the military and in combat roles particularly. Women disguised as men have been serving in the armed forces and women have served in other ways, such as camp cooks, laundresses, or nurses, since the time of the Revolutionary War. Women were finally allowed to become active military members during late World War I (1917–1918). In 1948, Congress passed the Women's Armed Services Integration Act, which granted women permanent status to serve in the military, though only in non-combat roles.

Women continued to serve in non-combat roles until the Persian Gulf War (1991–1992) when it was necessary to deploy them to combat zones, though they still were not able to hold official combat positions. Women continued to earn higher levels of authorization including piloting planes in combat, but were still not allowed to enter military infantry or be officially accepted into combat-prep positions until awarded the opportunity under President Barack Obama in 2013.

PREPARE TO COMPARE

Direct students to use the Prepare to Compare prompt to focus their reading.

CRITICAL VOCABULARY

infantry: When people picture soldiers, they typically picture foot soldiers, or the *infantry*.

ASK STUDENTS to describe the meaning of the word *infantry*. *(The infantry are soldiers who fight in close combat.)*

smart: It *smarts*, or hurts people's feelings, when their abilities are dismissed.

ASK STUDENTS to explain why it smarts when a person insults you. *(When a person insults me, I become upset.)*

TEACH

SUMMARIZE AND PARAPHRASE TEXTS

Remind students that a **summary** states the most important details in the writer's own words. Work with students to summarize paragraphs 3 and 4: Paragraph 3: *To prove that male and female recruits are treated equally, they are required to perform exactly the same tasks.* Paragraph 4: *Though making history, the female graduates are treated no differently than other recruits.* Explain to students that paragraph 2 provides a direct answer to the question. (**Answer:** *The Army wants no distinction between male and female infantry troops and for the entry of females to not affect training in any way. Therefore they are not emphasizing the historic entry of women into the infantry. Women recognized the revolutionary change and were glad that they could finally pursue a combat career and the career advancement that was now open to them.*)

ENGLISH LEARNER SUPPORT

Shared Reading Place students into pairs and assign each pair a selection of paragraphs from the article. Students should take turns reading two paragraphs aloud. After reading through the paragraphs once, have students read the paragraphs again, each reading the parts read by his or her partner the first time.
ALL LEVELS

NOTICE & NOTE

SUMMARIZE AND PARAPHRASE TEXTS
Annotate: Reread paragraphs 3–8. Mark phrases that express the main ideas.
Summarize: Briefly summarize this passage of text.

women graduate from its elite Ranger School in 2015, the Army has taken pains to avoid making any exceptions for infantry boot camp. To the pound, men and women lug the same rucksacks, throw the same grenades and shoulder the same machine guns.

4 The Army has also sought to play down the significance of the new female infantrymen — as they are still known — not mentioning, when families gathered . . . for their graduation, that the 18 women who made it through would be the first in more than two centuries for the American infantry.[1]

5 "It's business as usual," the battalion commander overseeing the first class, Lt. Col. Sam Edwards, said as he watched a squad of soldiers run past — including one with French braids and a grenade launcher. "I've tried to not change a thing."

6 Female grunts[2] in the battalion see things differently. In interviews during a series of visits to observe training, many said the fact that they could finally pursue a combat career, and have it treated as no big deal, was for them revolutionary. Now many who dreamed of going into the infantry are no longer barred from the core combat positions that are the clearest career routes to senior leadership.

7 Just before graduation, one female drill sergeant pulled aside a group of female privates, who ranged from high school athletes to a single mother with a culinary[3] degree, and gave them her unofficial assessment out of officers' earshot.

8 "This is a big deal," she said as she looked into one recruit's eyes. She said they were making history.

'Misery is a great equalizer'

9 Rain pounded the roughly 150 troops of Alpha Company, who ranged in age from 17 to 34, as they stood in formation during a tornado warning, waiting to hear if it was too stormy to train.

10 If the downpour let up, they would practice rushing out of armored vehicles. If not, they would tramp back to the foxholes where they had slept the night before and bail out the standing brown water with canteen cups.

11 Either way, by day's end they would be wet, tired, hungry and cold: the four pillars of misery the Army has long relied on to help whip recruits into cohesive fighting teams.

12 "Misery is a great equalizer," one male recruit said with a resigned grin.

13 The rain eventually let up and the sergeants ran the platoons through repeated ambush drills. By the end, while some of the troops

---

[1] **The Army has also sought .. the American infantry:** Congress authorized the raising of the first infantry battalion units in 1775, shortly after the outbreak of the American Revolution, as part of the Continental Army.
[2] **grunt:** *slang.* infantry soldier.
[3] **culinary** (kŭl´ə-nĕr-ē, kyo͞o´lə)**:** of or relating to a kitchen or to cookery.

WHEN STUDENTS STRUGGLE . . .

Create Outlines Direct students to develop outlines for paragraphs 1–12. Remind them to begin with the headings and subheadings included before those paragraphs and to provide one-to two-statement summaries for each paragraph corresponding to those text features. Explain that creating an outline and summarizing will help them identify the key ideas and supporting details within the article, and that these mini-summaries can later be used to prepare a comprehensive summary of the article.

For additional support, go to the **Reading Studio** and assign the following **Level Up tutorial: Taking Notes and Outlining**.

had buzz cuts and some had their hair in buns, they all shared the drooping weariness that grunts have worn for as long as there's been an infantry.

'She's a hoss'

14 In the woods, after hours of mock raids, Pvt. Kayla Padgett rested her rifle against her rucksack and turned to her platoon, assembling them in three neat rows.

15 It was 90 degrees. A tick crawled along the back of her shirt. The night before, the platoon had slept in the dirt. Everyone was dog tired. Many were covered in ant bites. But as platoon guide, it was her job to make them ready.

16 "All right, hustle it up, let's count off," she said.

17 One by one the platoon of mostly men each shouted until all were accounted for.

18 "O.K., good," Private Padgett said, scanning the group with her blue eyes. "If you haven't done so, keep loading up ammo, all your magazines."

19 Over the years, countless voices have warned that women could never handle the demands of the infantry, and would destroy its all-male **esprit de corps**. None of the recruits or drill sergeants interviewed at Fort Benning shared that fear. They all pointed to women like Private Padgett.

20 The 23-year-old track champion from North Carolina could throw a 20-pound hammer more than 60 meters while on the team at East Carolina University, and showed up at basic training in better shape than many of the men. She is now on her way to Airborne School, and wants to eventually become a Ranger.

21 "She's a hoss," her drill sergeant, Joseph Sapp, said as he watched her. After a tour in Iraq and four in Afghanistan, he has served with his share of soldiers. "Forget male-female; she's one of the best in the company. She's one you're happy to have."

'Not 'treated special'

22 In the new integrated infantry companies, women and men train together in mixed-gender squads from before dawn until after dusk: practicing the same raids, kicking in the same doors, doing the same push-ups when their squad messes up. No one gets out of a **rotation** serving **chow**.

23 At night, they sleep in rooms separated by gender, in identical metal bunks with identically scratchy green blankets. To graduate, all must pass tests of the same infantry skills, including hurling a grenade 35 meters, dragging a 268-pound dummy 15 meters, running five miles in less than 45 minutes and completing a 12-mile march carrying 68 pounds.

NOTICE & NOTE

ANALYZE TEXT FEATURES
Annotate: Circle the subheading 'She's a hoss.' Then, in paragraph 20, underline details that support the key idea of this section.

Evaluate: How well does the subheading help you predict the details and key idea of this section? Did you need to correct your prediction?

esprit de corps
n. a spirit of devotion and loyalty among group members.

LANGUAGE CONVENTIONS
Annotate: Mark the words *male-female* in paragraph 21.

Analyze: What is the mark between *male* and *female* called and why is it used here? What does the speaker mean by "Forget male-female"?

rotation
n. regular and uniform variation in a sequence or series.

chow
n. food; victuals.

TEACH

ANALYZE TEXT FEATURES

Subheadings are **text features** used to mark minor sections. These sections give details that support the main idea. (**Answer:** *The subheading says the section will be about a lady who is very strong. The description in paragraph 20 proves it.*)

LANGUAGE CONVENTIONS

Hyphens are used in many compound words. (**Answer:** *The mark between "male-female" is a hyphen and it connects the two words into one new word. The phrase means it doesn't matter what gender Padgett is, she's as tough as they come.*)

ENGLISH LEARNER SUPPORT

Use Contextual Support Help students use context clues to determine the meaning of the idiom "she's a hoss" from paragraph 21. Direct them to use context clues from the "She's a hoss" section to help them learn that the phrase means someone who is very tough.
LIGHT

CRITICAL VOCABULARY

esprit de corps: Groups with similar experiences often feel an *esprit de corps*, or loyalty, to other group members.

ASK STUDENTS to name groups they are loyal to. (*Answers will vary.*)

rotation: People in the infantry work in a *rotation*, meaning they take turns serving food.

ASK STUDENTS to give examples of rotational shifts in their own lives. (*Examples: work shifts or school days*)

chow: In the army, soldiers' meals are often called *chow*.

ASK STUDENTS to list other words meaning *chow*. (*Other words include eats, fare, fodder, grub, noms*)

TEACH

24 Hair is one of the few places where standards still diverge. All men get their heads shaved on arrival. Women don't. Not wanting to be held to a different standard, though, many of the women decided a few weeks into training to shave in solidarity. They would earn back their hair, just like the men.

25 "I loved my hair, but didn't want anyone to look at me and think I was being treated special," said Pvt. Irelynn Donovan.

'I wanted to make history'

26 Private Donovan, 20, grew up outside Philadelphia with five older brothers. She was the only girl on her junior high football team. When assigned to write an essay about an adult she admired, she chose her grandfather, who had served two tours in Vietnam.

27 "She's just always been a badass," said her mother, Cristine Zalewski.

28 She always wanted to join the infantry, despite a ban on women. On her forearm is a tattoo of flowers wrapped around a saying uttered by her single mother, who sometimes had to **scrounge** for change in the house to pay bills: "We'll find a way"

scrounge
(skrounj) *v.intr.* to obtain by salvaging or foraging; round up.

CRITICAL VOCABULARY

scrounge: When she was young and hungry, she sometimes had to *scrounge*, or forage, for food because her mother couldn't afford to buy a lot of food.

ASK STUDENTS for examples of things for which a person would scrounge. *(Examples include change in the couch cushions or floor of the car, berries in a wooded area.)*

IMPROVE READING FLUENCY

Targeted Passage Direct students to listen as you read paragraph 32 aloud, and ask them to pay close attention to the pace of your reading and the intonations and expressions you use. After you have modeled how to read the paragraph, place students into pairs to practice reading the paragraph aloud to each other. Remind them to practice pacing, intonation, and expression, and direct partners to provide feedback on their performances. Challenge them to offer constructive suggestions for how to read the passage aloud the most fluently.

 Go to the **Reading Studio** for additional support in developing fluency.

NOTICE & NOTE

29 As soon as the ban was lifted in 2016, Irelynn Donovan went to a local recruiter.

30 "I wanted to make history," she said. "Pave the way, if not for me, then for others."

31 During training, she wrote home complaining that she was exhausted and tired of being yelled at. "Everything is **chafing**," she wrote. But she became a standout, nailing the physical tests for both men and women when she did 79 push-ups in two minutes.

'Hey, the infantry's tough, man'

32 Afghanistan and Iraq were turning points for the Army's thinking on women in combat. The wars forced thousands of women who were not technically combat troops into fire fights. Nearly 14,000 women were awarded the Combat Action Badge for engaging with the enemy. Today most of the men leading the Army have served with women in combat for years.

33 "We saw it can work," said Maj. Gen. Jeffrey Snow, who heads Army Recruiting Command at Fort Knox, Ky. "And now we have a

chafe
(chāf) *v.intr.* to annoy or irritate.

SUMMARIZE AND PARAPHRASE TEXTS
Annotate: Mark key details in paragraph 32.
Interpret: Write a few sentences paraphrasing this paragraph.

For Army Infantry's First Women, Heavy Packs and the Weight of History 341

TEACH

✎ SUMMARIZE AND PARAPHRASE TEXTS

Explain to students that a summary includes only the key points of a passage. A paraphrase is restating the information in different words and includes not only key points but also important details. (**Possible answer:** *How the government saw women's roles in combat changed during wars in Afghanistan and Iran. While women weren't officially combat troops, they were often forced into fire fights and thousands received a special honor for being in combat. Leaders who are serving now are more used to serving with women than older leaders, so they accept the situation.*)

EL ENGLISH LEARNER SUPPORT

Express Ideas Place students in pairs or small groups. Assign each group a heading or subheading from the article. For their assigned passages, students in each group should take turns reading the selection aloud. After each student has read the section, that student should provide two statements to the group: (1) A summary of the passage; and (2) A sentence describing what he or she believes the author is trying to convey with the passage. Direct the group partners to offer constructive feedback on the summaries and idea-sharing. **LIGHT**

APPLYING ACADEMIC VOCABULARY

☑ **ambiguous** ☐ anticipate ☐ conceive ☐ drama ☑ **integrity**

Write and Discuss Have students discuss the following questions with partners. Have them use the academic vocabulary words *ambiguous* and *integrity* in their responses.

- Why would the female recruits want to be seen as no different than their male counterpart?
- In what ways do these first female recruits break stereotypes of "the typical woman"?

CRITICAL VOCABULARY

chafe: Everything was *chafing*, or causing an irritation, because the clothes she was wearing were not her typical clothes and the work she was doing was new to her.

ASK STUDENTS for examples of things that cause chafing. (*Examples: wool sweaters, scratchy socks, tight shoes*)

TEACH

CONTRASTS AND CONTRADICTIONS

Explain to students that the description of Private Donovan's physical accomplishments as the highest female fitness score contrasts with the gift of flowers, which are often given to female performers such as actresses, opera singers, and ballerinas. (**Answer:** *She's likely to feel embarrassment at being given a token of achievement usually given for "feminine" achievements.*)

ENGLISH LEARNER SUPPORT

Understand Idioms Explain that writers of informal articles often use idioms, or common figures of speech whose meaning is different from the literal meaning of the words. Point out the idiom "take it in stride" in paragraph 42. Explain that this phrase does not mean that the women are walking. The phrase means that they did not let the commander's words upset them. Then, note the idiom "shrank in embarrassment" in the same paragraph. Explain that this phrase means the woman was embarrassed—she did not get smaller.
ALL LEVELS

NOTICE & NOTE

generation that just wants to accomplish the mission and have the most talented people to do it."

34 The Army is determined not to sacrifice performance for the sake of inclusion, and many women have not been able to meet the standard. Of the 32 who showed up at infantry boot camp in February, 44 percent dropped out. For the 148 men in the company, the dropout rate was just 20 percent.

35 Commanders say the higher dropout rate among females is in line with other demanding boot camps for military police and combat engineers, which have been open to women for years. In part, they say, it is a consequence of size. A 5-foot-2 woman has to carry the same weight and perform the same tasks as a man who stands a foot taller, and is more likely to be injured.

36 Why did so many more women fail? One female recruit summed it up by saying simply, "Hey, the infantry's tough, man."

37 "Is it fair?" said the brigade commander overseeing gender-integrated infantry training at Fort Benning, Col. Kelly Kendrick. "I don't care about fair. I care if you can meet the standard."

38 Male soldiers acknowledged in interviews that the women who remain, like Chonell Morgan, 18, are some of the toughest soldiers in the company. During a punishment run the platoons were ordered to undertake on a hot afternoon, Private Morgan, who is from Apple Valley, Calif., was near the front of the pack.

39 The daughter of a NASA engineer, she postponed plans for college when she heard the infantry was opening to women. Her mother is still upset about the decision, but her father, Lorenzo Morgan, who served in the Army in the 1980s, said, "You have to let your children be who they want to be."

AN UNSPOKEN ACCOMPLISHMENT

40 After 14 weeks of running and crawling in the dirt, Alpha Company marched onto the parade grounds in crisp dress uniforms and carefully creased berets.

41 The company commander's voice booming over loudspeakers welcomed them to the infantry, but he gave no nod to the women now joining the ranks.

42 The women appeared to take it in stride. Private Donovan, who had won the award for the highest female fitness score in the company, finishing just behind the top man, pushed through the crowd toward her family, then shrank in embarrassment when her mother greeted her with a bouquet of flowers.

43 "Mom," she muttered, looking to see if anyone noticed, "you don't bring flowers to infantry graduation."

CONTRASTS AND CONTRADICTIONS

Notice & Note: Mark details in paragraphs 42–43 that indicate Private Donovan's feelings.

Infer: Why does she respond this way to her mother's gift?

TO CHALLENGE STUDENTS

Engage in a Debate Place students in small groups and direct them to identify both sides of the debate of women in combat positions. Have them identify each of the ways the author shows support for this premise, and then identify the counterarguments to those ideas found within the article. Groups should refine their lists to no more than three major argument and counterargument sections.

After groups have refined their lists, assign half of the groups to debate the pro-women stance and the other half to debate the anti-women stance. Remind groups of the etiquette for a respectful debate.

CHECK YOUR UNDERSTANDING

Answer these questions before moving on to the **Analyze the Text** section on the following page.

1. In paragraph 2, what does the sentence "That's just how the Army wants it" refer to?

   A The soldiers are wearing body armor.

   B Women graduated from U.S. infantry training.

   C Infantry was being trained in the woods of Georgia.

   D It was almost impossible to distinguish the female and male soldiers.

2. In paragraph 5, the speaker is quoted as saying, "It's business as usual." Which sentence from the text contradicts this statement?

   F "This is a big deal," she said as she looked into one recruit's eyes.

   G "I've tried to not change a thing."

   H "Misery is a great equalizer," one male recruit said with a resigned grin.

   J "I wanted to make history," she said. "Pave the way, if not for me, then for others."

3. Which detail from the section with the subheading "Not 'treated special'" best supports the main idea of that section?

   A Hair is one of the few places where standards still diverge.

   B To graduate, all must pass tests of the same infantry skills. . . .

   C At night, they sleep in rooms separated by gender. . . .

   D Not wanting to be held to a different standard, though, many of the women decided a few weeks into training to shave in solidarity.

TEACH

CHECK YOUR UNDERSTANDING

Have students answer the questions independently.

Answers:

1. D
2. F
3. B

If students answer any questions incorrectly, have them reread the text to confirm their understanding. Then, they may proceed to ANALYZE THE TEXT on page 344.

ENGLISH LEARNER SUPPORT

Oral Assessment Use the following questions to assess students' comprehension and speaking skills.

1. What does the Army expect from both male and female soldiers? *(That they will be able to perform the same tasks.)*

2. Explain what the opposite of "business as usual" means. *(The opposite is something that is important.)*

3. Describe what being "not treated special" means. *(Not being treated special means that everyone is treated exactly the same.)* **MODERATE/LIGHT**

APPLY

ANALYZE THE TEXT

Possible answers:

1. **DOK 1:** *The author highlights how being in the infantry is good for career advancement in the military. One woman indicated she wanted to make history.*

2. **DOK 4:** *There has been resistance to women serving in the infantry because it was assumed that they would lack the strength and stamina needed for successful hand-to-hand combat. The Army has opened its ranks and allowed women to compete with the exact same standards as the male recruits to prove equality.*

3. **DOK 2:** *The women who graduated from the infantry that day were the first women to go through infantry training. Until recently, women were not allowed to hold combat roles in the U.S. military; that began to change because of the wars in Iraq and Afghanistan.*

4. **DOK 4:** *The quotes used as subheadings highlight the key ideas within each section while engaging the readers. It is an effective approach to organization because each quote comes directly from one of the subjects in the article and provides mini-summaries for each section.*

5. **DOK 4:** *The U.S. Army sought to normalize having women in infantry training and downplayed the significance of the first female graduates. For the women, however, it is clear that this historical moment is an important accomplishment in their lives and that they will serve as examples for all the female recruits who follow them.*

RESEARCH

Remind students that they should confirm any information they find by checking multiple websites and texts, assessing the credibility of each one.

Extend There have been a few famous female military leaders who have proven themselves strong leaders despite the expectations of their gender. These females set the precedent for other women in demonstrating that women have the ability to serve in the military. Historically, these women were forced into these positions through birth, like Queen Elizabeth, or through circumstance and calling, like Joan of Arc. Later women felt compelled to stand with their male counterparts and protect the country and people who they loved. All of these women displayed deep integrity, impressive strength, and tremendous bravery, and they are role models for not just other women, but for all people.

344 Unit 2

RESPOND

ANALYZE THE TEXT

Support your responses with evidence from the text. 📓 NOTEBOOK

1. **Identify** What are two reasons offered in the text that explain why women want to join the infantry?

2. **Analyze** Why has there been resistance to having women serve in the infantry? What has the U.S. Army done to overcome that resistance?

3. **Summarize** What is the historical significance of the infantry graduation described in the article's final section?

4. **Evaluate** The article's subheadings consist of quotations from people noted by the author. Does this approach communicate organization and key ideas effectively? Explain why or why not.

5. **Notice & Note** How do the women's attitudes about their success in infantry training compare with the Army's official position about them?

RESEARCH

RESEARCH TIP
Don't rely on a single source for your research. Many sources are incomplete or inaccurate. Compare information from multiple sources, and if you find an inaccuracy in a source, consider that source generally unreliable.

Although most women in history have served in domestic roles, such as housekeeping and child rearing, rather than roles suited to the battlefield, history does note some famous female military leaders. Carry out research to discover the facts about some of these women warriors.

MILITARY LEADER	TIME AND PLACE	MILITARY EXPERIENCE
Boudicca	60/61 CE - Rome	No experience. Led revolt against Rome. 80,000+ died.
Joan of Arc	Early-mid 1400s - France	No experience. Led French forces. Restored throne to the King.
Zenobia	240 CE - Rome	Queen of Palmyra. Rebelled against Rome's authority.
Nakano Takeko	Mid-1800s - Japan	With a band of 20 women, broke a siege at Battle of Aizu.
Grace O'Malley	mid-1500s - Ireland	A pirate for 40 years. A politician. Rebelled against English rule.

Extend What motivated these women to become military leaders and what personal qualities might have caused them to do something so unconventional?

344 Unit 2

WHEN STUDENTS STRUGGLE...

Reteaching: Summarize Texts Tell students that a summary is a brief retelling of a text's main idea and key supporting details. It is shorter and is written in the student's own words. Explain that summaries ensure that students remember the text. Have students complete the outlines they began at the beginning of this selection. Have them first list the headings and subheadings, then add summaries. Then, have them write short summaries of the article.

 For additional support, go to the **Reading Studio** and assign the following 📈 Level Up tutorial: Taking Notes and Outlining.

CREATE AND DEBATE

Prepare Notes for a Debate In teams of three or four, brainstorm ideas and research supporting information to prepare to debate either for or against allowing women to serve in all roles in the military.

- ❏ Decide which position your team will defend.
- ❏ Brainstorm ideas and information to support your argument. You may need to do some research.
- ❏ Anticipate opposing claims so that you can be prepared to argue against them.

Debate Your team will be matched with another to debate the topic, with each team assigned to be either in favor of allowing women to serve in all roles in the military or against that position. Teams will alternate turns, with each speaker refuting (disagreeing with) the arguments of the previous speaker.

DEBATE PLANNING	
In Favor	Against

RESPOND

Go to the **Writing Studio: Writing Arguments** to find out more about planning an argument.

Go to the **Speaking and Listening Studio: Analyzing and Evaluating a Presentation** to find out more about tracing a speaker's argument.

RESPOND TO THE ESSENTIAL QUESTION

 How do you defy expectations?

Gather Information Review your annotations and notes on "For Army Infantry's First Women, Heavy Packs and the Weight of History" and "Speech Before the Spanish Armada Invasion." Then, add relevant details to your Response Log. As you determine which information to include, think about:

- how each author discusses expectations
- the arguments against those expectations
- the motivations of the women to defy expectations

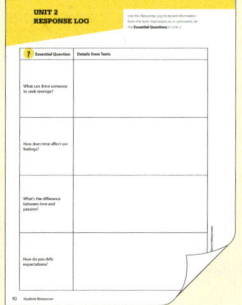

ACADEMIC VOCABULARY

As you write and discuss what you learned from the article, be sure to use the Academic Vocabulary words. Check off each of the words that you use.

- ❏ ambiguous
- ❏ anticipate
- ❏ conceive
- ❏ drama
- ❏ integrity

APPLY

CREATE AND DEBATE

Prepare Notes for a Debate Advise groups of students to use graphic organizers to prepare for the debate. Direct them to find all the reasons agreeing with the claim first, then look for related arguments disagreeing with the claim. Students should write one or two persuasive statements about both sides of each point-of-debate. Challenge them to consider possible counterpoints to each of their persuasive statements, which could be used to strengthen their own arguments.

For **writing support** for students at varying proficiency levels, see the **Text X-Ray** on page 334D.

Debate Separate groups into pro and con teams. Provide groups with five to ten minutes to prepare for the debate. Encourage them to select their best speakers and to provide support to the speakers when needed during the debate. Remind them to stick to the topics under discussion, to maintain professionalism and detachment of emotion, and to remain respectful at all times during the debate.

RESPOND TO THE ESSENTIAL QUESTION

Allow time for students to add details from "For Army Infantry's First Women, Heavy Packs and the Weight of History" to their Unit 2 Response Logs.

APPLY

CRITICAL VOCABULARY

Answers:

1. scrounge
2. chow
3. espirit de corps
4. rotation
5. it would smart
6. infantry
7. it would chafe

VOCABULARY STRATEGY:
Foreign Words and Phrases

Answers:

1. Word/Phrase: faux pas; Meaning: socially forbidden
2. Word/Phrase: spiel; Meaning: an explanation or speech repeated often
3. Word/Phrase: hoi polloi; Meaning: common people
4. Word/Phrase: kaput; Meaning: broken permanently

 RESPOND

WORD BANK
infantry
smart
esprit de corps
rotation
chow
scrounge
chafe

CRITICAL VOCABULARY

Practice and Apply Answer each question by using one of the Critical Vocabulary words in a complete sentence.

1. What might you do if you don't have enough change for the bus?
2. What do you get at the cafeteria?
3. Why do members of a team feel close to each other?
4. What's a fair way to divide up household chores?
5. How might someone feel after getting into trouble?
6. Who might go to fight a battle in the woods?
7. Why might a wet wool suit be uncomfortable?

 Go to the **Vocabulary Studio** for more on understanding word origins.

VOCABULARY STRATEGY:
Foreign Words and Phrases

Sometimes you will come across a word or phrase that is borrowed from another language. The article you just read, for example, includes the phrase *esprit de corps*, a French phrase that translates to "group spirit."

Often, a text provides clues that a word is of non-English origin. Foreign words and phrases frequently use accent marks (à) or unusual letter combinations or pronunciations. Foreign words and phrases may also be set in italic font.

Practice and Apply In each sentence, mark the foreign word or phrase. Then, write it next to the correct origin and translation of the word in the graphic organizer provided. Finally, use your own words to write the meaning of each word, based on how it is used in the sentence.

1. My grandmother believes it is a faux pas to wear white after Labor Day.
2. We've all heard your spiel on that, so there's no sense in repeating it.
3. She's royalty, but she mingles with the hoi polloi with such gracefulness.
4. Well that's it; my car is kaput!

FOREIGN WORD OR PHRASE	ORIGIN AND TRANSLATION	MEANING IN USAGE
hoi polloi	Greek: the many	*common people*
kaput	German: broken	*broken permanently*
spiel	Yiddish: game	*an explanation or speech repeated often*
faux pas	French: false step	*socially forbidden*

346 Unit 2

 ENGLISH LEARNER SUPPORT

Vocabulary Strategy Ask students if their native language used any words or phrases from other countries. Tell students the below phrases, origins, and meanings and discuss them:

- *bon voyage:* French; have a nice trip
- *bona fide:* Latin; genuine
- *prima donna:* Latin; conceited or temperamental person
- *pro bono:* Latin; without charge; donated
- *status quo:* Latin; the existing condition   **ALL LEVELS**

LANGUAGE CONVENTIONS:
Dashes and Hyphenation

Dashes and hyphenation can make your writing more interesting, sophisticated, and precise. It is important to understand exactly how these marks function in a text and to know when it is best to use them.

An *em dash* (—), also called simply a *dash,* can function similarly to a comma, colon, semicolon, or parentheses. Use a dash or pair of dashes to set off text that explains, contrasts, or amplifies.

In this example, dashes set off explanatory text:

> The Army has also sought to play down the significance of the new female infantrymen—<u>as they are still known</u>—not mentioning, when families gathered last week for their graduation, that the 18 women who made it through would be the first in more than two centuries for the American infantry.

In the following sentence, the dash sets off an idea that contrasts with the idea before it.

> "It's business as usual," the battalion commander overseeing the first class, Lt. Col. Sam Edwards, said as he watched a squad of soldiers run past—<u>including one with French braids and a grenade launcher.</u>

This helps the author convey one of the text's key ideas: having women in infantry training contrasts with our image of women in a way that is still surprising, despite the Army's efforts to normalize the change.

Hyphens are used to create compound nouns and compound modifiers. Hyphens help clarify which word is modifying which. In this example, the compound modifier is made up of an adjective, *mixed,* and a noun, *gender.*

> It was almost impossible to distinguish the <u>mixed-gender</u> squads in the steamy woods from those of earlier generations.

Without the hyphen, it would be unclear that there is a squad of mixed gender (male and female), not a "gender squad" that is mixed. It's unlikely that a reader would misunderstand in this instance, but use of hyphens in compound modifiers before a noun is recommended for better readability and to ensure precision.

Practice and Apply Write a short description of an unusual situation or a way that someone you know, or have heard of, has overcome expectations. Use dashes to set off explanations, surprises, or contrasts. Make your writing descriptive and precise by using hyphenated compound modifiers.

RESPOND

Go to the **Grammar Studio: Other Marks of Puncuation** for more on dashes and hyphenation.

APPLY

LANGUAGE CONVENTIONS:
Dashes and Hyphenation

Review the information on dashes and hyphenation with students. Explain that learning to properly use these punctuation marks can improve the clarity of their writing.

Explain that dashes can serve as replacements for various other punctuation marks, such as commas, colons, semicolons, and parentheses. Discuss how one or two dashes are used to explain, contrast, or amplify parts of a sentence. Display the first sentence on page 349 and read it aloud. Ask students to explain how the underlined section gives an explanation. Repeat the activity for the second example sentence, with students explaining how the underlined section offers a contrasting idea. Explain how the author's use of dashes helps him better convey his ideas.

Explain that hyphens serve as connectors to create compound modifiers and compound nouns. Hyphens are also used with some prefixes, to write out numbers above nineteen, and to create fractions. Remind students that some compound nouns are not hyphenated and are always one word (*basketball*) or two words (*high school*). Using hyphens creates more precise wording and increases readability. Review the example sentence and have students provide additional examples.

Practice and Apply Direct students to write short narratives about overcoming expectations. Their writing should include introductions to the person or situation involved, as well as a short, but detailed, overviews of the events. Encourage them to use dashes and to hyphenate words to make their writing clearer, easier to understand, and more enjoyable.

After students have completed their narratives, place students in pairs to share their work. Encourage partners to offer constructive suggestions on the use of dashes and hyphens.

 ENGLISH LEARNER SUPPORT

Language Conventions Use the following supports with students at varying proficiency levels:

- Pair students and have them find sentences in the article that use hyphenated words. Have students copy the sentences into their notebooks and orally explain why each word is hyphenated. **SUBSTANTIAL**

- Have students work with partners to write three original sentences. Two sentences should use hyphens in different ways. One sentence should use dashes. Have pairs exchange papers and identify the hyphenated words and explain why they are hyphenated. Then, they should discuss the effect of the dashes. **MODERATE**

- Ask students to work independently to write several sentences using dashes and hyphenated words in different ways. Then, pair students and have them discuss their sentences, explaining why words were hyphenated and the purpose of the dashes (i.e. to explain, contrast, or emphasize ideas). **LIGHT**

APPLY

COMPARE ACROSS GENRES

Before completing their graphic organizers, ask students how knowing the historical context of a written work is important to gaining the full measure of what the author is saying. List with the class ways Queen Elizabeth I's time period differed from today. Have them consider how modern women are still earning their places on battlefields. Also, consider how Elizabeth's male armies might have felt having a woman lead them into battle.

ANALYZE THE TEXTS

Possible answers:

1. **DOK 3:** *Queen Elizabeth says she is physically weak: "I know I have the body but of a weak and feeble woman," but that she is still fit to fight because she has "the heart and stomach of a king." This implies that "the heart and stomach" of a woman would not be fit for battle. In "Infantry's First Women," females show that they have the same strength and capability their male peers have, proving they too can be successful on the battlefield.*

2. **DOK 3:** *Queen Elizabeth seems to agree that women are not fit to be on the battlefield, but considers herself the exception because she has "the heart and stomach of a king." In "Infantry's First Women," the author gives arguments that women should not be in battle: "Over the years, countless voices have warned that women could never handle the demands of the infantry, and would destroy its all-male espirit de corps." However, he gives evidence that this is not a valid assertion, such as the example of Private Padgett, who "showed up at basic training in better shape than many of the men."*

3. **DOK 2:** *Queen Elizabeth's motives are to stand with her subjects for the good of England and protect the country. The women in "Infantry's First Women" share this love of and need to protect their country. The women differ in that, in the queen's case, she felt compelled to earn the loyalty of her subjects by speaking to them before battle, while "Infantry's" women fought with those defending the country, and were more motivated by personal goals like career advancement and wanting to "make history."*

4. **DOK 4:** *In both texts, the demands of war put pressure on normal stereotypes. Although Queen Elizabeth was a woman, she was the ruler and had to go to battle to lead just as a king would. The women of "Infantry's First Women" have had the opportunity to serve in combat roles because the demands of the wars have put them onto the battlefields already where they've proven women's exemplary capabilities in battle conditions.*

348   Unit 2

RESPOND

Collaborate & Compare

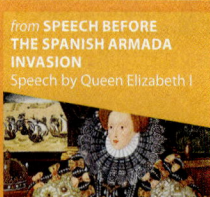

from SPEECH BEFORE THE SPANISH ARMADA INVASION
Speech by Queen Elizabeth I

FOR ARMY INFANTRY'S FIRST WOMEN, HEAVY PACKS AND THE WEIGHT OF HISTORY
Article by Dave Philipps

COMPARE ACROSS GENRES

Two texts may express similar ideas even though they are written in different genres and address different topics. Sometimes these ideas are explicitly stated. But often the reader must infer the author's general views and values from details in the text.

In a small group, collaborate with classmates to state each author's attitude toward women serving in traditionally male roles. Then, identify ideas and information in each text to support your inferences.

POSITION ABOUT WOMEN IN NONTRADITIONAL ROLES	
"Speech Before the Spanish Armada Invasion"	**"For Army Infantry's First Women Heavy Packs and the Weight of History"**
SUPPORT	
Women do not belong in battle unless by no other choice, though they can still inspire the loyalty of the troops toward great success.	*No matter the opposition they've faced, women have proven they can be as capable as men in battle.*
Lines 11 - 13: "I know I ... too ...."	*Political history of banning women from combat*
Lines 17 - 18: "I myself ... the field." *Lines 20 - 21: "... my lieutenant ... my stead ...."*	*Women proved themselves in combat in Iraq and Afghanistan wars* *Private Padgett's story*

ANALYZE THE TEXTS

Discuss these questions in your group.

1. **Cite Evidence** How does each author portray the ability of women to demonstrate courage and leadership?

2. **Compare** Which author has the more traditional view of differences between men and women?

3. **Cause and Effect** What motivates the women in these texts to overcome stereotypes about their gender?

4. **Synthesize** How do these texts support the right of women to serve in traditionally male roles?

348   Unit 2

 ENGLISH LEARNER SUPPORT

Ask Questions Use the following questions to help students compare the selections:

1. Why does Queen Elizabeth want to address her soldiers? Why do the women in "Infantry's First Women" want to fight? *(Queen Elizabeth believes that as a ruler, it is her duty to be in the battle field. The women want to defend their country and improve their careers.)*

2. How do Queen Elizabeth and the women in "Infantry's First Women" feel as women with male soldiers? *(Queen Elizabeth feels she has the heart of a king, so she should be addressing the troops. The women in the article feel they are equal to the men.)* **ALL LEVELS**

RESPOND

RESEARCH AND SHARE

Now, your group can continue exploring the ideas in these texts by carrying out research and presenting your findings to the class.

1. **Choose a Topic** In your group, brainstorm other ways that women have overcome stereotypes concerning their roles in society, either historically or currently. Think about jobs that were not open to women before, rights that women did not always have, and academic subjects or recreational activities for which women were not expected to express an interest. Discuss which examples your group finds most interesting and select one topic to research.

2. **Gather Sources** Look for multiple sources that contain information about your group's topic. Try to find sources that discuss the topic in a variety of ways, rely on different kinds of details, or take different perspectives on the topic.

   ❏ Look for sources that present a position. Remember that authors sometimes imply a position through their use of details and evidence.

   ❏ Watch for extreme or inflammatory language. This is usually an indication that an author is biased and is distorting or altering facts to support a position. Check the provided facts against other sources.

3. **Take Notes** For each source, summarize the author's conclusion and note the details used to support it. Always record source information, such as author, title, publisher, and date of publication.

TOPIC:

Source	Position	Details
Sample Source A: Women as CEOs are TOPS!	Women can be as (or more) successful than men in the corporate world.	Three examples of successful companies run by female CEOs
Sample Source B: Men Still Dominate in the Boardroom	More women hold top positions in the corporate world. Men dominate the top tier.	Statistics on top global 1,000 CEOs

4. **Share Your Findings** Tell the class about the stereotype your group researched, providing details on what your research revealed about how women have overcome that stereotype. Explain and summarize the information you discovered in your sources. If you found examples of authors who altered or distorted facts to support a position, be sure to note this, explaining what led you to this conclusion.

Go to the **Speaking and Listening Studio** for more on giving a presentation.

APPLY

RESEARCH AND SHARE

Explain to groups that each member should have the opportunity to share their ideas. Listeners should remain quiet while others are talking and then add his or her own ideas or ask clarifying questions.

1. **Choose an Example** Circulate and listen to each group as it brainstorms. Take opportunities to clarify any historical or contextual inaccuracies you might hear. Challenge students to think more deeply about the stereotypes of women, as well as women vs. men.

2. **Gather Sources** As the students search for sources, recommend search strategies or phrases to use in the search bar. Help them determine which sources present unbiased and fair viewpoints, and how to tell which sources are valid.

3. **Take Notes** Explain to students that an author's position may have to be inferred. Direct students to consult with their groups if they are having difficulty determining an author's position or in identifying details to support that position.

4. **Share Your Findings** Encourage students to listen actively while others present their findings. After each presentation, have students discuss or debate the research, reminding them to do so with respect and consideration for the subject and each other.

WHEN STUDENTS STRUGGLE...

Organize Findings Students struggling with sharing their work with the class can use a graphic organizer, such as the following, to help them outline their presentations.

Title of Article / Author	Summary	Position	Supporting Details

 For additional support, go to the **Reading Studio** and assign the following **Level Up tutorial: Taking Notes and Outlining**.

INDEPENDENT READING

READER'S CHOICE

Select and Preview Have students review their Unit 2 Response Log and think about what they've already learned about the theme of revenge. As they choose their Independent Reading selections, encourage them to consider what more they want to know.

NOTICE NOTE

Explain that some selections may contain multiple signposts; others may contain only one. Moreover, the same type of signpost may occur many times in the same text.

LEARNING MINDSET

Curiosity Explain to students that curiosity is valuable and is an important part of a learning mindset. It is often the first step toward meeting the challenge of learning a new skill. Encourage students to think about the titles of the Independent Reading selections and the illustrations that accompany them. Then ask students to share what they are curious to learn about each of the selections.

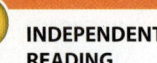 **INDEPENDENT READING**

? ESSENTIAL QUESTIONS

Review the four Essential Questions for this Unit on page 139.

Reader's Choice

Select and Preview Select one or more of these options from your eBook to continue your exploration of the Essential Questions.

- Read the descriptions to see which text is most interesting to you.
- Think about which genres you enjoy reading.

Notice & Note

In this unit, you practiced noticing and noting the signposts and asking big questions about nonfiction. As you read independently, these signposts and others will aid your understanding. Below are the key questions to ask when you read literature and nonfiction.

Reading Literature: Stories, Poems, and Plays	
Signpost	Key Question
Contrasts and Contradictions	Why did the character act that way?
Aha Moment	How might this action or event change things?
Tough Questions	What does this piece of writing make me wonder about?
Words of the Wiser	What is the lesson for the character?
Again and Again	Why might the author keep bringing up this issue or topic?
Memory Moment	Why is this memory important?

Reading Nonfiction: Essays, Articles, and Arguments	
Signpost	Key Question(s)
Big Questions	What surprised me? What did the author think I already knew? What challenged, changed, or confirmed what I already knew?
Contrasts and Contradictions	What is the difference, and why does it matter?
Extreme or Absolute Language	Why did the author use this type of language?
Numbers and Stats	Why did the author use these numbers or amounts?
Quoted Words	Why was this person quoted or cited, and what did this quotation add?
Word Gaps	Do I know this word from some other source? Does the word seem like technical talk for this topic? Do clues in the sentence help me understand the word?

ENGLISH LEARNER SUPPORT

Develop Fluency Select a passage from the text that matches students' reading abilities, and read it aloud while students follow along silently.

- Have students read a short and simple passage several times. Work with them to identify words that summarize the main concept, and say these words aloud. Have students repeat the words. **SUBSTANTIAL**
- Divide students into groups of four and read the passage silently several times. Have each student identify a word or phrase that summarizes the main concept, and have the students share them with the rest of the group. **MODERATE**
- Allow more fluent readers to select their own passages. Set a period of time for them to read silently. Then, have them write a summary of what they've read using keywords or phrases from the passage. **LIGHT**

INDEPENDENT READING

You can preview these texts in Unit 2 of your eBook.
Then check off the text or texts that you select to read on your own.

POETRY

Sonnet 18, Sonnet 29, Sonnet 130
William Shakespeare

Three sonnets reveal Shakespeare's thoughts about true love.

ARTICLE

Elizabeth I: The Reality Behind the Mask
Brenda Ralph Lewis

Discover the real Queen Elizabeth I, who exercised great skill to disguise her true personality.

POETRY

The Passionate Shepherd to His Love
Christopher Marlowe

Find out what a shepherd will promise to entice his beloved.

POETRY

The Nymph's Reply to the Shepherd
Sir Walter Raleigh

A wise and cautious young woman responds to the shepherd's invitation.

Collaborate and Share With a partner, discuss what you learned from at least one of your independent readings.

- Give a brief synopsis or summary of the text.
- Describe any signposts that you noticed in the text and explain what they revealed to you.
- Describe what you most enjoyed or found most challenging about the text. Give specific examples.
- Decide if you would recommend the text to others. Why or why not?

 Go to the **Reading Studio** for more resources on **Notice & Note.**

INDEPENDENT READING

MATCHING STUDENTS TO TEXTS

Use the following information to guide students in choosing their texts.

Sonnet 18, Sonnet 29, Sonnet 130
Genre: poem
Overall Rating: Challenging

Elizabeth I: The Reality Behind the Mask   **Lexile: 1220L**
Genre: article
Overall Rating: Challenging

The Passionate Shepherd to His Love
Genre: poem
Overall Rating: Challenging

The Nymph's Reply to the Shepherd
Genre: poem
Overall Rating: Challenging

Collaborate and Share To assess how well students read the selections, walk around the room and listen to their conversations. Encourage students to focus and be specific in their comments.

 for Assessment

- Independent Reading Selection Tests

 Encourage students to visit the **Reading Studio** to download a handy bookmark of **NOTICE & NOTE** signposts.

WHEN STUDENTS STRUGGLE . . .

Keep a Reading Log As students read their selected texts, have them keep a reading log for each selection to note signposts and their thoughts about them. Use their logs to assess how well they are noticing and reflecting on elements of their texts.

Reading Log for (title)		
Location	**Signpost I Noticed**	**My Notes about It**

PLAN

UNIT 2 Task

- **WRITE A LITERARY ANALYSIS**

MENTOR TEXT
HAMLET'S DULL REVENGE
Literary Criticism
by René Girard

LEARNING OBJECTIVES

Writing Task
- Write a literary analysis of a scene in a play.
- Use strategies and graphic organizers to plan and organize a literary analysis.
- Use the Mentor Text as a model for writing a clear thesis statement and strong conclusion.
- Present key ideas or reasons in logical order.
- Support key ideas with evidence from the play.
- Quote passages from the play.
- Use a graphic organizer to plan a draft.
- Use genre characteristics to help write a first draft.
- Use a Revision Guide and peer review to revise a draft.
- Edit a draft to indicate quotations properly.
- Publish writing to share it with an audience.
- Use a rubric to evaluate writing.
- **Language** Defend claims with reasons and evidence.

Assign the Writing Task in **Ed.**

RESOURCES

- Unit 2 Response Log
- Writing Studio: Writing as a Process
- Grammar Studio: Module 14 : Lesson 5: Using Quotation Marks

352A Unit 2

Language X-Ray: English Learner Support

Use the instruction below and the supports and scaffolds in the Teacher's Edition to help you guide students of different proficiency levels.

INTRODUCE THE WRITING TASK

Explain that a literary analysis has a tone like other forms of writing. Point out that their analysis could have an informal tone, but if they want their ideas taken seriously, they must use a formal tone.

Discuss the difference between lighter and more serious tones in a literary analysis. Have students consider which tone would be appropriate for a given audience.

Have students brainstorm sentences about *Hamlet* that are written in an informal tone and then sentences written in a more serious tone. Write both types of sentences on the board. Have students discuss the difference in tone and decide which type of sentences they will use in their literary analyses.

WRITING

Defend Claims

Remind students that they will defend their claims with reasons as well as text evidence. Explain that a reason could be their own opinion and that evidence could be a quote or retelling of the text.

Use the following supports with students at varying proficiency levels:

- Provide sentence frames to help students support claims in their literary analyses. For example: *This scene is significant to the story because ____.* Have students copy the frames and complete them. **SUBSTANTIAL**
- Work with small groups to develop a list of questions they can ask about the reasons for the claims in their literary analyses. For example: *Why is this scene significant?* Then have individual students write answers to the questions. Accept simple sentences as responses. **MODERATE**
- Have partners write down questions they can ask about how Girard supports his claims in "Hamlet's Dull Revenge." Then have partners write down answers to each other's questions. **LIGHT**

SPEAKING

Ask for Clarification

Have students check each other's use of quotation marks for accuracy.

Use the following supports with students at varying proficiency levels:

- Provide a word bank of terms and phrases students can use as they seek clarification about each other's use of quotation marks. **SUBSTANTIAL**
- Have partners review each other's literary analyses and then make a list of words and phrases to use when asking for clarification about the use of quotation marks. **MODERATE**
- Have partners review each other's literary analyses and ask for clarification about the use of quotation marks to see whether the punctuation has been used correctly. **LIGHT**

WRITING

WRITE A LITERARY ANALYSIS

Introduce students to the Writing Task by reading the introductory paragraph on page 352 with them. Remind students to refer to the notes they recorded in the Unit 2 Response Log as they plan and draft their literary analyses. The Response Log should contain ideas about revenge from a variety of perspectives. Drawing on these different perspectives will make their own writing more interesting and well-informed.

 For **writing support** for students at varying proficiency levels, see the **Language X-Ray** on page 352B.

USE THE MENTOR TEXT

Point out that the students' literary analyses will be similar to the literary criticism article "Hamlet's Dull Revenge" by René Girard, in that they will be analyzing *Hamlet* and focusing on the theme of revenge. Their literary analyses will be shorter than Girard's article, however, and will focus on a specific scene in *Hamlet*.

WRITING PROMPT

Review the prompt on page 352 with students. Encourage them to ask questions about any part of the assignment which is unclear. Make sure they understand the purpose of their literary analysis is to answer the question "What can drive someone to seek revenge?," using examples from a scene in *Hamlet*.

 **WRITING TASK**

Write a Literary Analysis

Go to the **Writing Studio** for help with writing arguments and using textual evidence.

In this unit, you have read just a few great works from the English Renaissance, with a focus on Shakespeare, the dominant literary figure of the period. Your next writing task will focus on what you have learned about the theme of revenge in *Hamlet*. Write a literary analysis of a scene in *Hamlet* that shows the hero struggling to overcome an internal or external conflict. You can use "Hamlet's Dull Revenge" by René Girard as a mentor text.

As you write your literary analysis, you can use the notes from your Response Log to answer the question, "What can drive someone to seek revenge?" which you filled out after reading the texts in this unit.

Writing Prompt

Read the information in the box below.

This is the topic or context for your literary analysis.

> Probably more has been written about *Hamlet* than any of Shakespeare's other plays. Despite the fact that it was written more than four hundred years ago, it continues to fascinate readers and stimulate thoughts about revenge.

Think carefully about the following question.

How might this Essential Question relate to a literary analysis?

> What can drive someone to seek revenge?

Mark the words that shows which type of conflicts you will explore in your analysis.

Write a literary analysis of a scene in *Hamlet* that shows the hero struggling to overcome an internal or external conflict.

Be sure to—

Review these points as you write, and again when you finish. Make any needed changes.

- ☐ make a clear thesis statement, or claim
- ☐ present key ideas, or reasons, in a logical order
- ☐ support key ideas with details and evidence from the text
- ☐ quote passages from the text
- ☐ end your analysis with a strong conclusion

352 Unit 2

 LEARNING MINDSET

Asking for Help Encourage students to ask for help from peers, teachers, and parents to get "unstuck" and move forward. Reinforce the recognition that asking for help does not equal failure and it is important to ask for help if they are struggling with the planning or drafting of their analyses. Remind students they should support each other as learners and work together.

352 Unit 2

WRITING TASK

1 Plan

Plan your analysis carefully before you start to write, using the chart below. First note the genre—literary analysis. Your topic deals with questions about revenge, conflict, and human relationships in *Hamlet*. Think of scenes from the play that contain some sort of conflict or other interaction. Consider the type of interaction involved in each scene. Are there internal or external conflicts? Are these forces struggling against each other? Gather ideas for your analysis of the scene. Perhaps you want to comment on how the scene developed; its significance to the story; what it reveals about Hamlet; how it might lead to another scene in the play; or how the characters are affected by the scene. As you explore the topic for your literary analysis, use any background reading or class discussions to help you generate ideas.

Informative Essay Planning Table	
Genre	Literary analysis
Topic	
Possible scenes	
Ideas about scenes	
Ideas from background reading	
Ideas from class discussion	

Go to the **Writing Studio: Using Textual Evidence** for help planning your literary analysis.

Notice & Note
From Reading to Writing

As you plan your literary analysis, apply what you've learned about signposts to your own writing. Remember that writers use common features called signposts to help convey their message to readers.

Think how you can incorporate **Quoted Words** into your essay.

Go to the **Reading Studio** for more resources on **Notice & Note**.

Use the notes from your Response Log as you plan your literary analysis.

Background Reading Review the notes you have taken in your Response Log that relate to the question, "What can drive someone to seek revenge?" Texts in this unit provide background reading that will help you formulate ideas and offer evidence you will use in your literary analysis.

Write a Literary Analysis 353

WRITING

1 PLAN

Allow time for students to discuss the topic with partners or in small groups and then to complete the planning table on page 353 independently.

■ **English Learner Support**

Understand Academic Language Make sure students understand the words and phrases used in the chart on page 353, such as *genre, topic, scene,* and *background reading*. Work with them to fill in the blank sections, providing text they can copy into their charts as needed, according to each student's proficiency level. **SUBSTANTIAL**

▶ **NOTICE & NOTE**
From Reading to Writing

Remind students to use **Quoted Words** to include the opinions or conclusions of experts in their analyses. Students can also use Quoted Words to provide additional support for a point they want to make. Remind students to format direct quotations correctly and to credit their sources.

Background Reading As students plan their analyses, remind them to refer to the notes they took in the Response Log. They may also review the selections to find additional examples to support ideas they want to include in their writing.

TO CHALLENGE STUDENTS . . .

Create a Parody Challenge students to think about how they might create a parody of a scene about Hamlet's seeking revenge. Have students work together in groups to brainstorm creative and comical ideas about such a scene. Then, have students write the scene using the ideas they have brainstormed. If time allows, students may act out the scene in class. Encourage students to write in their Response Logs about how the parody relates to the Essential Question, "What can drive someone to seek revenge?"

Write a Literary Analysis **353**

WRITING

Organize Your Ideas Tell students to use their ideas from their planning activities as they fill out the chart on page 354. They should fill out the chart completely with the elements they plan to use for their analyses. Point out that each student's analysis should include the following:

- An interaction in a specific scene
- The conflict within that scene
- A claim related to the topic that serves as a thesis statement
- Detailed reasons to support the claim
- Evidence from the text

Students' analyses should also reflect the theme about how a person is driven to seek revenge. Remind students that by thinking about and organizing their ideas before they begin to write their analyses, they can best decide how to draft their analyses and include all the essential elements.

② DEVELOP A DRAFT

Remind students to use the chart on page 354 as a guide as they draft their analyses. Point out that they can still make adjustments to their ideas, such as reasons and supporting evidence, as they write their draft. For example, they may decide that a particular quote from the text does not adequately support an idea and choose a more appropriate quote.

■ English Learner Support

Write a Group Literary Analysis Guide students to simplify the writing task by working together to write their literary analyses. Encourage those students with greater English proficiency to assist those who may need more support. **SUBSTANTIAL/MODERATE**

WRITING TASK

Go to **Writing Arguments: What is a Claim?** for more help.

Organize Your Ideas After you have gathered ideas from your planning activities, you need to organize them in a way that will help you draft your literary analysis. Choose your scene and identify the type of interaction. Next, decide what the focus of your analysis of the interaction will be. Write a clear thesis statement, or claim, and identify reasons that support it to help develop key ideas. Then find evidence in the text to support your key ideas. You can use the chart below to organize the elements of your analysis.

Topic: Analysis of a Scene in *Hamlet*		
Thesis Statement:		
Key Idea	Key Idea	Key Idea
Evidence	Evidence	Evidence

② Develop a Draft

You might prefer to draft your literary analysis online.

Once you have completed your planning, you will be ready to draft your literary analysis. Refer to your Graphic Organizer and your planning chart as well as any notes you took as you studied the texts in this unit. These will provide a map for you to follow as you write. Using a word processor or online writing application makes it easier to make changes or move sentences around later when you are ready to revise your first draft.

WHEN STUDENTS STRUGGLE . . .

Draft the Analysis Even when working from a chart to organize ideas, students may struggle to get started on their drafts. Suggest that in addition to the chart on page 354, students may want to use a graphic organizer to plot out specific reasons which support their claim. They can then list evidence under each reason, including relevant quotes from the text or literary experts, and refer to this graphic organizer as they develop their writing. Remind students that they don't have to write everything perfectly for their first drafts. They will revise and edit their writing later.

For additional support, go to the **Reading Studio** and assign the following **Level Up tutorial: Revising to Add Supporting Details**.

WRITING TASK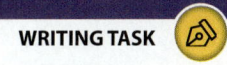

Use the Mentor Text

Author's Craft
State your thesis clearly at the beginning of your literary analysis; tell your reader what you are writing about and the claim you are making. Girard's first paragraph of "Hamlet's Dull Revenge" states his claim about Shakespeare's purpose for writing *Hamlet*.

WRITING

WHY THIS MENTOR TEXT?
"Hamlet's Dull Revenge" provides a good example of a literary analysis. Use the instruction below to help students use the mentor text as a model for writing their own literary analyses with a claim or thesis statement that helps answer the Essential Question: "What can drive someone to seek revenge?"

Hamlet belongs to the **genre** of the revenge tragedy, as hackneyed and yet inescapable in Shakespeare's days as the "thriller" in ours . . . In *Hamlet* Shakespeare turned this necessity for a playwright to go on writing the same old revenge tragedies into an opportunity to debate almost openly for the first time the questions I have tried to define. The weariness with revenge and *katharsis* . . . must really exist because, in *Hamlet*, it moves to the center of the stage and becomes fully articulated.

Girard claims that Shakespeare is trying to make a statement about revenge and revenge theater rather than just producing another clichéd revenge tragedy.

Apply What You've Learned After you've chosen the scene you want to focus on and identified the claim you want to make, begin your analysis with a thesis statement. What interesting insight will you offer your reader?

Genre Characteristics
You must provide key ideas and evidence from the text to support your thesis. In the text below, Girard makes the point that Hamlet is searching for a model of revenge because he lacks inspiration and passion.

The scene is as ridiculous as it is sinister. . . . [Hamlet's] words constantly betray him, . . . his revenge motif is no more compelling, really, than the cue of an actor on the stage. He too must *greatly . . . find quarrel in a straw*, he too must stake everything *even for an eggshell*.

Girard cites a particular instance in the play to support his point. The words in italics are directly quoted from the play.

Apply What You've Learned When you are providing key ideas that support your thesis, be sure to offer evidence from the text to convince your reader. Cite direct evidence from the text, such as quotations, for your major points, and use several pieces of evidence when possible.

USE THE MENTOR TEXT

Making a Claim or Thesis Statement Ask a volunteer to read aloud the first quotation from "Hamlet's Dull Revenge" on page 355. Discuss how Girard's word choice and the specific details in his thesis statement or claim capture the reader's attention and offer interesting insights on Shakespeare's purpose in writing *Hamlet*. Invite students to offer their own insights about *Hamlet* and the topic of revenge. Then, direct students to use these insights to come up with a thesis statement for their own analyses.

Offering Details and Evidence from the Text To help students understand how details and evidence are used in "Hamlet's Dull Revenge" to support the author's thesis statement, point out the major points in the article and have students identify how Girard presents specific evidence to support each point. Then, have them look for specific details and evidence in *Hamlet* to support their own thesis statements.

Write a Literary Analysis 355

 ENGLISH LEARNER SUPPORT

Use the Mentor Text Use the following supports with students at varying proficiency levels:

- Have students read silently the first quotation from "Hamlet's Dull Revenge" on page 355. Tell them to circle any words or phrases they do not understand. Then, provide assistance as needed as they work in pairs to determine the meanings of these words and phrases. **MODERATE**

- Discuss with students Girard's phrase from paragraph 2 "the tedium of revenge is really what he [Shakespeare] wants to talk about." Ask them what is meant by "tedium of revenge" and what insight into Shakespeare's purpose this phrase provides.
LIGHT

Write a Literary Analysis **355**

WRITING

3 REVISE

On Your Own Have students answer each question in the chart on page 356 to determine how they can use the revision tips and techniques to improve their drafts. Invite volunteers to model their revision techniques.

With a Partner Have students ask peer reviewers to evaluate their thesis statements and supporting evidence by answering the following questions:

- Is my thesis interesting and insightful?
- Is my thesis well supported by details and evidence?
- Are any pieces of evidence unclear? Do any details fail to support my thesis?
- What questions do you have about my main points?

Students should use the reviewer's feedback to add relevant facts, details, examples, or quotations to further develop their theses and supporting points.

 **WRITING TASK**

3 Revise

Go to **Writing as a Process: Revising and Editing** for more help.

On Your Own Once you have written your draft, you'll want to go back and look for ways to improve your literary analysis. As you reread and revise, think about whether you have achieved your purpose. The Revision Guide will help you focus on specific elements to strengthen your writing.

Revision Guide

Ask Yourself	Tips	Revision Techniques
1. Did I state my thesis clearly and in an interesting way?	Highlight your thesis statement, or claim.	If necessary, add a sentence or two to clarify your thesis. Add an interesting example or related quotation to hook your reader.
2. Do I have enough support for my thesis?	Circle key ideas and underline details and evidence that provide support.	Read your thesis statement aloud, followed by your key ideas. Are your ideas well-supported? If not, look for more evidence in the text.
3. Are my thoughts logically organized?	Outline your key ideas and check for the most logical order.	Reorder ideas if needed so that each idea flows easily to the next.
4. Did I include sufficient evidence from the text?	Underline any specific quotations or examples you used.	Add more direct evidence from the text to strengthen your claim.
5. Did I effectively present my claim to the redaer by the end of the essay?	Review the key points and ideas of your analysis.	Fill in any noticeable gaps or weak points with more relevant details.
6. Is my conclusion strong?	Highlight your conclusion.	Add text that summarizes your key ideas to support your conclusion.

ACADEMIC VOCABULARY

As you conduct your **peer review**, be sure to use these words.

- ☐ ambiguous
- ☐ anticipate
- ☐ conceive
- ☐ drama
- ☐ integrity

With a Partner Once you and your partner have worked through the Revision Guide on your own, exchange papers and evaluate each other's draft in a **peer review**. Offer revision suggestions for at least three of the items mentioned in the chart. Explain why you think your partner's draft should be revised and what your specific suggestions include.

When receiving feedback from your partner, listen attentively and ask questions to make sure you fully understand his or her suggestions for revision.

356   Unit 2

 ENGLISH LEARNER SUPPORT

Check Verb Tenses In such languages as Vietnamese, verbs do not change form to express a different tense. As a result, some English learners may struggle with English verb tenses. Remind students to review their analyses to make sure that verb tenses have been used consistently. For example, a student may switch from present to past tense while expressing an idea in a paragraph. Tell students that such paragraphs should be revised so all verbs are either in the present or past tense.   **MODERATE**

4 Edit

After you write and revise your literary analysis, it is time to edit some of the finer details. Ensure the proper use of standard English conventions. Look for ways to improve word choice, and be sure to correct all spelling and grammatical errors.

WRITING TASK

! Go to the **Quotation Marks** lesson in the **Grammar Studio** to learn more.

Language Conventions

Indicate Quotations Properly When you are citing words that aren't your own, you must use correct punctuation and format. Even if the words are a short phrase that you want to incorporate, place quotation marks around the phrase. Quotation marks may be appropriate for just one word if that word was used in a particular way or held special significance. Notice that writers use block quotes—setting off the material from the main text in a separate paragraph—when quoting several lines of text. Look at Girard's use of quotation marks, spacing, and indentation in the chart below.

Type of quotation	Example
One word	The only hope for Hamlet to accomplish what his society—or the spectators—require, is to become as "sincere" a showman as the actor who can shed real tears . . . .
Phrase	The cool determination of Hamlet, at this point, is the transmutation of the "towering passion" which he had vainly tried to build up before . . . ;

Block quote	. . . her metaphor suggests a more tangible accomplishment, the birth of something portentous:
	    Anon, as patient as the female dove
	    When that her golden couplets are
	      disclosed,
	    His silence will sit drooping.

Do not use block quotes with fewer than three lines of poetry. Instead, set off the quoted lines within your paragraph with quotation marks, and place a slash mark between each two lines: "Anon, as patient as the female dove/When that her golden couplets are disclosed . . . ."

5 Publish

Finalize your literary analysis and share it with an audience. Consider these options:

- Save your analysis as a writing sample to include in your college application.
- Research various literary journals and their submission guidelines. Choose at least one and submit your paper.

Write a Literary Analysis 357

WHEN STUDENTS STRUGGLE . . .

Use Quotations Some students may have difficulty deciding when and how to use quotations from a text in their writing. To help them better understand quotations, ask them to underline all the direct quotes in a section of the mentor text "Hamlet's Dull Revenge." Discuss with students why Girard might have decided to use these quotations. Remind them that quotation marks must be used whenever they are incorporating words which are not their own into their writing, just as Girard did in his article. The only exception is a longer quote, which can be cited properly by using an indented block quote.

 For additional support, go to the **Reading Studio** and assign the following **Level Up tutorial: Punctuating Quotations**.

WRITING

4 EDIT

Suggest that students read their drafts aloud to assess how clearly and smoothly they have presented their ideas. Have them check for correct spelling and any grammatical errors.

LANGUAGE CONVENTIONS

Indicate Quotations Properly Review the information on page 358 about using quotations properly. Then, discuss the examples in the chart. To practice how to punctuate and format quotations properly, use the following excerpt from *Hamlet* (Act III, Scene I):

> To be, or not to be—that is the question:
> Whether 'tis nobler in the mind to suffer
> The slings and arrows of outrageous fortune,
> Or to take arms against a sea of troubles,
> And, by opposing, end them. To die, to sleep—

Show students how to quote two lines and three lines or more lines. For example:

Two lines: "Whether 'tis nobler in the mind to suffer/The slings and arrows of outrageous fortune"

Three or more lines (block quote):

> Whether 'tis nobler in the mind to suffer
> The slings and arrows of outrageous fortune,
> Or to take arms against a sea of troubles,
> And by opposing end them?

■ English Learner Support

Use Quotations in Writing Explain to students that quotation marks are used to cite words which are not their own. To reinforce this idea, provide sentence frames for students to fill in with quotations (for example, Claudius says to Hamlet," _____ "). **SUBSTANTIAL/MODERATE**

5 PUBLISH

Students can present their literary analyses as blog posts on a school website. Encourage others to read the analyses and write comments about them. The authors can then respond to the comments.

Write a Literary Analysis 357

WRITING

USE THE SCORING GUIDE

Allow students time to read the scoring guide and ask questions about any words, phrases, or ideas that are unclear. Then, ask each student to evaluate his or her literary analysis in each of the three categories in the scoring guide: Organization/Progression, Development of Ideas, and Use of Language and Conventions. After students have completed their own evaluations, have them ask partners to read their literary analyses and explain whether they agree with the evaluation.

WRITING TASK

Use the scoring guide to evaluate your essay.

Writing Task Scoring Guide: Literary Analysis

	Organization/Progression	Development of Ideas	Use of Language and Conventions
4	• Structure is clearly organized and appropriate. • Includes strong thesis statement; all ideas are related to the thesis. • Ideas are in logical order and connected with meaningful transitions.	• Effective development with credible and compelling analysis. • Includes sufficient relevant textual evidence. • Thoughtful and engaging content; demonstrates thorough understanding of the text.	• Precise and appropriate word choice. • Strong and varied sentences. • Consistent command of spelling, punctuation, grammar, and usage conventions.
3	• Structure is for the most part organized and appropriate. • Includes clear thesis statement; most ideas are related to the thesis; minor lapses in unity or focus. • Ideas are generally presented in logical order and connected with sufficient transitions.	• Sufficient development with largely convincing analysis. • Includes sufficient relevant textual evidence; at times could be more complete. • Thoughtful content; demonstrates good understanding of the text.	• For the most part, clear and specific word choice. • Reasonably varied sentences. • Adequate command of spelling, punctuation, grammar, and usage conventions.
2	• Structure is evident but not always appropriate or clear. • Thesis statement is weak or unclear; some irrelevant information affects unity and focus. • Ideas are not always in logical order or connected with sufficient transitions.	• Minimal development with superficial analysis. • Includes textual evidence that is sometimes irrelevant or inaccurate; underdeveloped ideas. • Content reflects little thoughtfulness; demonstrates limited understanding of the text.	• For the most part, general or imprecise word choice. • Some awkward sentences. • Partial command of spelling, punctuation, grammar, and usage conventions.
1	• Structure is inappropriate to the purpose. • Thesis statement is missing, unclear, or illogical; contains irrelevant information. • Weak progression of ideas; includes repetition and wordiness; lacks sufficient transitions.	• Weak development with ineffective analysis. • Includes little if any relevant textual evidence; overall vague development. • Vague or confused response to the text; demonstrates lack of understanding of the text.	• Vague or limited word choice. • Simplistic or awkward sentences. • Little or no command of spelling, punctuation, grammar, and usage conventions.

Reflect on the Unit

By completing your literary analysis, you have a writing product that pulls together and expresses your thoughts about the reading you have done in this unit. Now is a good time to reflect on what you have learned.

Reflect on the Essential Questions

- Review the four Essential Questions on page 139. How have your answers to these questions changed in response to the texts you read in this unit?

- What are some examples from the texts you read that explore individual human nature or celebrate human achievement?

Reflect on Your Reading

- Which selections were the most interesting or surprising to you?

- From which selection did you learn the most about human nature or human achievement?

Reflect on the Writing Task

- What difficulties did you encounter while working on your literary analysis? How might you avoid them next time?

- Which parts of the literary analysis were the easiest to write? The hardest to write? Why?

- What improvements did you make to your literary analysis as you were revising?

UNIT 2 SELECTIONS
- *The Tragedy of Hamlet*
- *Hamlet* film clip
- "Hamlet's Dull Revenge"
- "Sonnet 30" and "Sonnet 75"
- "A Valediction: Forbidding Mourning"
- "To His Coy Mistress"
- "Twenty-One Love Poems (Poem III)"
- "Speech Before the Spanish Armada Invasion"
- "For Army Infantry's First Women, Heavy Packs and the Weight of History"

LEARNING MINDSET

Problem Solving Explain to students that an important part of developing a learning mindset and growing mentally is the ability to solve problems effectively. Remind students that everyone runs into problems when learning something new and every problem solved helps their minds grow. Discuss how everyone solves problems in their own way; for example, by asking for help, waiting for further instruction, etc. As students reflect on the unit, encourage them to ask the following questions: What problems did I face when writing my analysis? How did I address these problems? How did I find the answers to my problems?

REFLECT ON THE UNIT

Have students reflect on the questions independently and write some notes in response to each one. Then, have students meet with partners or in small groups to discuss their reflections. Circulate during these discussions to identify the questions that are generating the liveliest conversations. Wrap up with a whole-class discussion focused on these questions.

UNIT 3

Instructional Overview and Resources

		Instructional Focus	Online Ed Resources
	Unit Introduction **Tradition and Reason: The Restoration and the 18th Century**	Unit 3 Essential Question Unit 3 Academic Vocabulary	**Stream to Start:** Tradition and Reason: The Restoration and the 18th Century **Unit 3 Response Log**

ANALYZE & APPLY

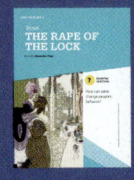	from **"The Rape of the Lock"** Poem by Alexander Pope	**Reading** • Analyze Satire • Analyze Heroic Couplet • Analyze Mock Epic **Writing:** Write a Rhymed Satirical Poem **Speaking and Listening:** Discuss a Poem	🔊 **Audio** **Reading Studio:** Notice & Note **Speaking and Listening Studio:** Participating in Collaborative Discussions
	**"A Modest Proposal"** Satire by Jonathan Swift **Lexile 1590L**	**Reading** • Analyze Satirical Devices • Understand Author's Purpose **Writing:** Write a Satirical Essay **Speaking and Listening:** Discuss a Satirical Essay **Vocabulary:** Context Clues **Language Conventions:** Active and Passive Voice	🔊 **Audio** **Close Read Screencast:** Modeled Discussion **Reading Studio:** Notice & Note **Writing Studio:** Writing as a Process **Speaking and Listening Studio:** Participating in Collaborative Discussions **Vocabulary Studio:** Using Context Clues **Grammar Studio:** Using Active and Passive Voice
	**"Satire Is Dying Because the Internet Is Killing It"** Editorial by Arwa Mahdawi **Lexile 1240L**	**Reading** • Analyze Development of Ideas • Analyze Tone **Writing:** Write a Satire **Speaking and Listening:** Discuss the Editorial **Vocabulary:** Context Clues **Language Conventions:** Effective Words, Nouns, and Adjectives	🔊 **Audio** **Reading Studio:** Notice & Note **Writing Studio:** Writing as a Process **Speaking and Listening Studio:** Participating in Collaborative Discussions **Vocabulary Studio:** Using Antonyms **Grammar Studio:** Using Effective Adjectives

SUGGESTED PACING: 30 DAYS

Unit Introduction	from The Rape of the Lock	A Modest Proposal	Satire Is Dying Because the Internet Is Killing It	from The Journal and Letters of Fanny Burney: An Encounter with King George III
1	2 3 4	5 6 7	8 9 10	11 12 13 14

PLAN

English Learner Support	Differentiated Instruction	Assessment
• Understand Archaic Language • Build Background Knowledge	**When Students Struggle** • Identify Main Ideas	
• Text X-Ray • Acquire New Vocabulary • Analyze Mock Epic • Analyze Satire • Use Contextual Support • Oral Assessment	**When Students Struggle** • Heroic Couplets • Understand Irony • Reteaching: Analyze Satire **To Challenge Students** • Analyze Point of View • Analyze Narrator	**Selection Test**
• Text X-Ray • Use Cognates • Draw Inferences • Explore Connotations • Draw Inferences about Author's Purpose • Expand Vocabulary • Analyze Illustrations	• Improve Reading Fluency • Identify Relative Clauses • Evaluate Complex Word Structures • Oral Assessment • Vocabulary Strategy • Language Conventions	**When Students Struggle** • Analyze Types of Literature • Make a Tax Chart **To Challenge Students** • Write a Satire Video	**Selection Test**
• Text X-Ray • Use Cognates • Express Ideas and Opinions • Oral Assessment • Vocabulary Strategy • Using Effective Words, Concrete Nouns, and Adjectives	**When Students Struggle** • Understand Irony and Overstatement • Draw on Prior Knowledge • Reteaching: Analyze Tone	**Selection Test**

from **A Vindication of the Rights of Woman/ Education Protects Woman from Abuse**
15 16 17 18 19

from **A Journal of the Plague Year/** *from* **Inferno: A Doctor's Ebola Story**
20 21 22 23 24 25

Independent Reading
26 27

End of Unit
28 29 30

UNIT 3

UNIT 3 Continued

	Instructional Focus	 Resources
 *from* **"The Journal and Letters of Fanny Burney: An Encounter with King George III"** Diary by Fanny Burney **Lexile 1380L**	**Reading** • Connect to History • Make Inferences **Writing:** Write a Diary Entry **Speaking and Listening:** Discuss a Diary Entry **Vocabulary:** Context Clues **Language Conventions:** Reflexive and Intensive Pronouns	Audio **Reading Studio:** Notice & Note **Writing Studio:** Writing Narratives **Speaking and Listening Studio:** Participating in Collaborative Discussions **Vocabulary Studio:** Using Context Clues **Grammar Studio:** Understanding Special Pronoun Problems

COLLABORATE & COMPARE

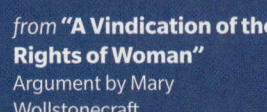 *from* **"A Vindication of the Rights of Woman"** Argument by Mary Wollstonecraft **Lexile 1350L**	**Reading** • Evaluate Arguments • Analyze Counterarguments **Writing:** Write an Argument **Speaking and Listening:** Give a Persuasive Speech **Vocabulary:** Literary Allusions **Language Conventions:** Coordinating and Subordinating Conjunctions	Audio **Reading Studio:** Notice & Note **Writing Studio:** Writing Arguments **Speaking and Listening Studio:** Giving a Presentation **Grammar Studio:** Coordinating and Subordinating Conjunctions
 **"Education Protects Woman from Abuse"** Article by Olga Khazan **Lexile 1160L**	**Reading** • Make Predictions • Analyze Graphic Features **Writing:** Write an Analysis **Speaking and Listening:** Adapt and Present **Vocabulary:** Greek Roots and Prefixes **Language Conventions:** Direct and Indirect Quotations	Audio **Reading Studio:** Notice & Note **Writing Studio:** Writing Informative Texts, Using Textual Evidence **Speaking and Listening Studio:** Giving a Presentation **Vocabulary Studio:** Analyzing Word Structure
Collaborate & Compare	**Reading:** Compare across Genres	**Speaking and Listening Studio:** Giving a Presentation

PLAN

English Learner Support	Differentiated Instruction	Assessment
• Text X-Ray • Use Cognates • Identify Affixes • Use Synonyms • Understand Language Structure • Use Context Clues • Understand Idioms • Improve Reading Fluency • Oral Assessment • Acquire New Vocabulary • Language Conventions	**When Students Struggle** • Build Background • Make Inferences • Paraphrase Text • Reteach: Read for Details **To Challenge Students** • Analyze Author's Craft • Analyze Allusion	**Selection Test**
• Text X-Ray • Use Cognates • Use Support to Enhance Understanding • Improve Reading Fluency • Summarizing • Oral Assessment • Vocabulary Strategy • Language Conventions	**When Students Struggle** • Summarize Arguments **To Challenge Students** • Understand Logical Fallacies	**Selection Test**
• Text X-Ray • Use Cognates • Analyze Maps • Improve Reading Fluency • Oral Assessment • Vocabulary Strategy • Language Conventions	**When Students Struggle** • Analyze Graphic Features • Reteaching: Understand Direct Quotations **To Challenge Students** • Conduct Research	**Selection Test**
• Summarize	**When Students Struggle** • Take Notes	

PLAN

UNIT 3 Continued

	Instructional Focus	Online Ed Resources
from **A Journal of the Plague Year** Novel by Daniel Defoe **Lexile 1470L**	**Reading** • Analyze Historical Setting • Analyze Narrator **Writing:** Write Notes for a Problem-Solution Essay **Speaking and Listening:** Discuss **Vocabulary:** Denotation and Connotation **Language Conventions:** Participles and Participial Phrases	🔊 **Audio** **Reading Studio:** Notice & Note **Writing Studio:** Writing Informative Texts **Speaking and Listening Studio:** Participating in Collaborative Discussions **Vocabulary Studio:** Denotations and Connotations **Grammar Studio:** Participles and Participial Phrases
Mentor Text *from* **Inferno: A Doctor's Ebola Story** Memoir by Steven Hatch, M.D. **Lexile 1150L**	**Reading** • Analyze Author's Perspective • Connect to Memoirs **Writing:** Take Informal Notes **Speaking and Listening:** Create an Informational Poster **Vocabulary:** Classical Allusions **Language Conventions:** Subordinate Clauses	🔊 **Audio** **Reading Studio:** Notice & Note **Writing Studio:** Organizing Ideas **Speaking and Listening Studio:** Types of Media: Audio, Video, and Images **Vocabulary Studio:** Classical Allusions **Grammar Studio:** Kinds of Clauses
Collaborate & Compare	**Reading:** Compare across Genres	

Online Ed — INDEPENDENT READING

The Independent Reading selections are only available in the eBook.

📖 Go to the Reading Studio for more information on NOTICE & NOTE.

 "Elegy Written in a Country Churchyard"
Poem by Thomas Gray

 "One Below Gas Station, Virginia Cemetery Restored"
Article by Wyatt Andrews
Lexile 840L

END OF UNIT

Writing Task: Write a Personal Narrative **Speaking and Listening Task:** Present a Narrative **Reflect on the Unit**	**Writing:** Write a Personal Narrative **Language Conventions:** Direct and Indirect Quotations **Speaking and Listening:** Present a Narrative	**Unit 3 Response Log** **Mentor Text:** *from* Inferno: A Doctor's Ebola Story **Writing Studio:** Writing Narratives **Grammar Studio:** Quotation Marks

PLAN

English Learner Support	Differentiated Instruction	Online Ed Assessment
• Text X-Ray • Use Cognates • Use Grammatical Structures • Use Concept Mapping • Internalize Multiple-Meaning Words • Improve Reading Fluency • Paraphrase • Oral Assessment • Analyze Expressions • Language Conventions	**When Students Struggle** • Analyze Historical Setting **To Challenge Students** • Eighteenth-Century Social Customs	**Selection Test**
• Text X-Ray • Use Cognates • Summarize Using Five-Word Summary • Internalize New Vocabulary • Understand Relative Clauses • Improve Reading Fluency • Understand Figurative Language • Retell • Oral Assessment • Vocabulary Strategy • Language Conventions	**When Students Struggle** • Analyze Author's Perspective • Reteaching: Analyze Author's Perspective **To Challenge Students** • Research Epidemics in the United States	**Selection Test**
• Ask Questions	**When Students Struggle** • Present to a Group	

"On Her Loving Two Equally"
Poem by Aphra Behn

"King George's Letters Betray Madness, Computer Finds"
Article by Mindy Weisberger
Lexile 1470L

Selection Tests

• Language X-Ray • Understand Academic Language • Write a Group Essay • Internalize Basic Vocabulary • Use Synonyms • Use Quotation Marks • Adapt the Essay	**When Students Struggle** • Draft the Narrative • Use Direct Quotations • Take Notes **To Challenge Students** • Conduct Research	**Unit Test**

TEACH

DISCUSS THE QUOTATION

Tell students that this quotation is from Mary Wollstonecraft's work *A Vindication of the Rights of Woman*, published in 1792. The book, which students will read excerpts from later in the unit, was the first text to catalog the injustices and indignities suffered by women of Wollstonecraft's time. This quotation reflects the emphasis that Enlightenment thinkers—both men and women—placed on knowledge and reason. To them, it was not enough for people simply to act in or believe a certain way because it was expected by society; people's actions should be based on understanding and reason.

Ask students to think about what it means for something—a behavior, a belief, a decision—to be "founded on knowledge." What is the opposite or the alternative to something being "founded on knowledge"?

■ English Learner Support

Understand Archaic Language Make sure students understand that the phrase *to deserve the name* roughly means "to be called such" or "to be considered real." In simple modern language, the quotation might read: "True virtue must be based on knowledge." **ALL LEVELS**

UNIT 3

TRADITION AND REASON

THE RESTORATION AND THE 18TH CENTURY

" Virtue, to deserve the name, must be founded on knowledge.

—Mary Wollstonecraft

360 Unit 3

LEARNING MINDSET

Setting Goals Explain that students will gain more from the selections, activities, and inquiries in each unit if they set their own learning goals. Encourage students to formulate their individual learning goals for Unit 3 as they consider the Unit Opener. What do they hope to know or understand better by the end of this unit? How will the information presented in this unit contribute to their overall understanding of British literature and their learning goals for the class? What specific steps can they take as they complete the unit tasks to ensure that they meet their goals?

UNIT 3

Discuss the **Essential Questions** with your whole class or in small groups. As you read Tradition and Reason, consider how the selections explore these questions.

? ESSENTIAL QUESTION:

How can satire change people's behavior?

If you have ever read an "Opinion" news column or watched a television show about current events, chances are you have encountered satire. Satire uses exaggeration, irony, and/or humor to make an often serious point about a public figure, event, issue, or situation. Is satire the most effective way for a critic or comic to make a point? Who are the intended audiences of satires? What kinds of reactions do satires evoke from their audiences and, occasionally, their subjects?

? ESSENTIAL QUESTION:

What is your most memorable experience?

Memory is extremely personal. After all, there are no two people alive who have the exact same memories. The things we remember about our lives often depend on who we are, what we value, and the emotions we experience during an event. What makes an experience memorable? Does an experience have to be life-changing or have long-term importance to be memorable?

? ESSENTIAL QUESTION:

What keeps women from achieving equality with men?

In many parts of the world, women are regarded as second-class citizens and do not have the same access to education, health care, and protection under law as men. Even in lands where gender inequality is supposedly a thing of the past, many women do not receive equal pay for equal work, and women are severely underrepresented in positions of influence. What lies at the root of gender inequality? What must change for gender equality to become a reality?

? ESSENTIAL QUESTION:

Why are plagues so horrifying?

Few events strike fear into humans like the threat of disease. Many people take daily precautions to avoid sickness and maintain themselves in the best possible health. When an epidemic or a pandemic occurs, however, avoiding sickness can mean the difference between life and death. How have plagues, both historical and contemporary, shaped the modern world? Have human attitudes toward plagues changed as a result of modern medicine? Why do plague accounts simultaneously fascinate and repel people?

TEACH

Connect to the ESSENTIAL QUESTIONS

Read aloud the Essential Questions and the paragraphs that follow them. Open the discussion of each idea by having students respond to the questions that conclude each paragraph.

? ESSENTIAL QUESTION:

How can satire change people's behavior?

Ask students to brainstorm examples of satire they are familiar with and identify: 1) who or what is the subject of the satire; and 2) what point the author or performer of the satire is trying to make. Encourage students to think about what makes a satire effective. Satires often elicit strong reactions *from* people, but can they also motivate people to action?

? ESSENTIAL QUESTION:

What is your most memorable experience?

Have students answer the question in their notebooks. Then, take a brief class poll: What kinds of emotions do you usually associate with a memorable experience? *(positive, neutral, negative)* How often do you think about the experience? *(constantly, often, occasionally, rarely, almost never)* Use the poll results as the basis for a class discussion of the types of experiences that are most memorable and have the most lasting impact, and why.

? ESSENTIAL QUESTION:

What keeps women from achieving equality with men?

Challenge students to identify additional ways in which women have not yet achieved social or political equality with men. Which beliefs or assumptions about the differences between men and women contribute to these inequalities? Ask students how they believe gender equality can be achieved and steps they can take to help create a society in which women and men benefit equally.

? ESSENTIAL QUESTION:

Why are plagues so horrifying?

Have students identify examples of modern plagues or health scares they have seen on the news (or possibly know from personal experience). How did they feel about these events? How might the experience of a modern-day plague be similar to and/or different from the experiences people faced with historical plagues?

TEACH

THE RESTORATION AND THE 18TH CENTURY

The following essay provides students with a historical context for the Unit 3 selections.

The Reign of Charles II Tell students the differences between Tories and Whigs extended beyond ideas about royal authority. The Tories consisted mainly of landowning aristocrats and conservative Anglicans. They had little tolerance for Protestant dissenters and no desire for war with France. The Whigs included wealthy merchants, financiers, and some nobles. They favored leniency toward Protestant dissenters and also wanted to curb French expansion in Europe and North America, which they considered a threat to England's commercial interests.

Royalty and the People Anti-Catholic sentiment in Parliament had an immense influence on the English monarchy. A year before the death of King William III (who ruled alone after Mary's death), Parliament passed the Act of Settlement, which permanently barred Catholics from the throne. The throne passed to Mary's Protestant sister Anne after William's death; however, Anne outlived all of her surviving children. When she died, the succession passed to a distant Protestant cousin: George, the ruler of Hanover in Germany, instead of to a closer Catholic relative. George spoke no English and was viewed with contempt by many Tories. Because of the language barrier, he relied heavily on his Whig ministers, so Robert Walpole, head of the Whig party, assumed an influential position as prime minister.

COLLABORATIVE DISCUSSION

Ask groups to share their ideas with the class. As an option, assign groups different historical events from the essay or the timeline and ask each group to consider the influence its assigned event had on writing and literature. Have each group share its findings with the class.

THE RESTORATION AND THE 18TH CENTURY

The year 1660 marked Charles II's ascent to the English throne following more than a decade of exile, during which the country had experienced the Puritan rule of Oliver Cromwell's short-lived Commonwealth. The period that immediately followed this return of the Stuart monarchs became known as the Restoration. At the same time, in England and throughout Europe, other important changes led to the late 1600s and the 1700s being known as the Age of Reason.

The Reign of Charles II Under Charles II, England turned its back on the grim era of Puritan rule and entered a lively period in which upper-class social and political life copied the sophistication and splendor of the French court of Louis XIV. The upper classes attended elegant parties and enjoyed going to the theater, where they were amused by comedies of manners that poked fun at their own glamorous but artificial society. Charles was also an astute politician, and his reign brought relative stability to England. A period of increased growth and prosperity began and led eventually to the growth of the English middle class.

The Restoration brought about the realization that English monarchs would have to share their authority with Parliament, whose influence had increased substantially. Charles at first had widespread support in Parliament, weathering both the Great Plague of 1665 and the Great Fire of London a year later. Soon, though, two factions arose that would become the nation's chief political parties: the Tories, who supported royal authority; and the Whigs, who wanted to limit royal authority.

Royalty and the People Political conflict increased after Charles' death in 1685. Charles had reestablished Anglicanism as the state religion, but his successor James II wanted England to return to Roman Catholicism. When Parliament forced James to abdicate in 1688, the crown passed peacefully to his Protestant daughter Mary and her husband William, demonstrating the power of Parliament over the monarchy. The next year, Parliament passed the English Bill of Rights, which strictly limited royal authority.

The first prime minister, Robert Walpole, was appointed in 1721. The position of prime minister became influential, and although the monarchy remained, people recognized that the time of absolute monarchs was over.

COLLABORATIVE DISCUSSION
In a small group, discuss how historical events influenced writing and literature during the late 1600s and the 1700s.

1660 The Stuart monarchy is restored under Charles II.
1665 The Great Plague of London kills thousands.
1666 The Great Fire of London destroys a large section of the city.
1687 Sir Isaac Newton defines the law of gravity.
1690 John Locke publishes *Two Treatises of Government*.
1707 England, Wales, and Scotland unite as Great Britain.
1718 Smallpox inoculation introduced.
1719 Daniel Defoe publishes *Robinson Crusoe*.
1721 Walpole is prime minister.

362 Unit 3

 ENGLISH LEARNER SUPPORT

Build Background Knowledge To aid comprehension of the essay, provide students with the following definitions and have them use them in sample sentences.

- *poke fun at:* to make a joke about something or someone, usually in a friendly way
- *astute:* mentally sharp or clever, showing understanding of a situation
- *weathering:* dealing with something dangerous or unpleasant without being greatly harmed
- *factions:* groups within a larger group that have different ideas and opinions
- *abdicate:* to leave the position of being king or queen
- *formulate:* to create, invent, or produce by careful thought and effort
- *methodology:* a set of methods, rules, or procedures
- *advocate:* a person who argues for or supports a cause

ALL LEVELS

The Age of Reason The period including the late 1600s and the 1700s is called the Enlightenment or the Age of Reason because it was during this time that people increasingly made use of scientific thought to understand the world. Sir Isaac Newton formulated the laws of gravity and motion, and developed the scientific method—a process that scientists could use to test hypotheses about how the world works. Newton's findings suggested that the universe operates according to logical principles, an idea that inspired such philosophers as John Locke to apply the rules of logic and reasoning to human nature and society.

During the 1700s, it became common for male writers, artists, politicians, and others to gather in public places and exchange ideas, conduct business, and share gossip. Educated women held private gatherings for the same purpose so that they too could be included in the intellectual life of the day. More women started writing and publishing their work. Some, most notably Mary Wollstonecraft, became advocates for women's rights.

An Era of Change The spirit of the Enlightenment brought about many improvements in living conditions. For example, the practice of inoculation against disease was introduced by Lady Mary Wortley Montagu, and a vaccine for smallpox was developed. The middle class grew and prospered, and ordinary men and women had more money, leisure time, and education than ever before.

For writers, that meant a broad new audience eager to read and willing to pay for literature. The middle classes wanted writing that reflected their

RESEARCH
What about this historical period interests you? Choose a topic, event, or person to learn more about. Then add your own entry to the timeline.

TEACH

The Age of Reason Tell students that John Locke is generally considered to be one of history's most influential—and controversial—philosophers. He believed that people could create a perfect society through the use of reason. Therefore, he encouraged people to use their intelligence to rid themselves of unjust authorities. Rejecting the "divine right" of kings, a system of belief that had prevailed for centuries and provided the justification of absolute monarchy, Locke instead provided a logical justification for the forced abdication of James II (and later the American Revolution) by asserting the right of citizens to revolt against an unfair government.

An Era of Change Prior to the rise of the middle class, reading for leisure had been a pastime reserved mainly for the elite. Poetry and literature contained sophisticated allusions to classical Greek and Roman works that would have been part of an aristocratic education but were unfamiliar to most middle-class readers. The 17th century saw the rise of new literary styles that appealed to the middle classes, but also a resurgence of classical styles intended for the elites. Such satirists as Alexander Pope and Jonathan Swift produced neoclassical works modeled after Roman satirists that commented on moral, political, and philosophical issues of the day. Ask students whether they notice any similar divisions or differences between contemporary styles of entertainment. Do they see certain types of entertainment directed toward specific socioeconomic classes or other distinct groups within society?

RESEARCH

To learn more about their chosen topic, encourage students to search for primary sources from the historical period. Have students choose excerpts from a source to present to the class.

WHEN STUDENTS STRUGGLE...

Identify Main Ideas Students may have difficulty determining the main ideas and details presented in the historical background essay. Have students use a chart like the one below to identify at least one main idea and two supporting details for each subheading of the essay.

Subheading:	
Main Idea:	**Detail:**
	Detail:

TEACH

✎ CHECK YOUR UNDERSTANDING

Have students answer the questions independently.

Answers:

1. D
2. G
3. A

If students answer any question incorrectly, have them reread the text to confirm their understanding.

---

own concerns and experiences. Thus prose journalism experienced a rise in popularity. Some nonfiction journalists, diarists, and letter writers turned to fictional topics, leading to the birth of the novel. While much poetry was at first still written in a classical style, toward the end of the 1700s some poets began to move toward a simpler and freer poetic style. In the century to come, both prose and poetry would continue to evolve as the new era of Romanticism blossomed.

CHECK YOUR UNDERSTANDING

Choose the best answer to each question.

1 Why was the reign of Charles II known as the Restoration?

  A Parliament passed laws that restored and increased the power of the monarchy.

  B Charles II restored Roman Catholicism as the state religion of England.

  C Peaceful relations between the English and French courts were restored.

  D The Commonwealth ended and the Stuart monarchy was restored.

2 Which factor contributed most to the development of rival political parties in England?

  F Disagreements over how Charles II handled the Great Plague and the Great Fire of London

  G Differing ideas about how much authority the monarchy should have

  H Conflicts between Catholics and Protestants about the appointment of a prime minister

  J Opposing views of the use of reason in society

3 Which best represents how an Enlightenment philosopher would have viewed the Great Plague of 1665?

  A "The Great Plague is a natural event that can be explained through the use of reason."

  B "The Great Plague is a sign that God is displeased with the English people for returning to Anglicanism."

  C "The inability of the king to prevent the Great Plague shows the limits of absolute monarchy."

  D "The devastation caused by the Great Plague indicates a need for the English Bill of Rights."

ACADEMIC VOCABULARY

Academic Vocabulary words are words you use when you discuss and write about texts. In this unit, you will learn the following five words:

✓ encounter   ☐ exploit   ☐ persist   ☐ subordinate   ☐ widespread

Study the Word Network to learn more about the word **encounter**.

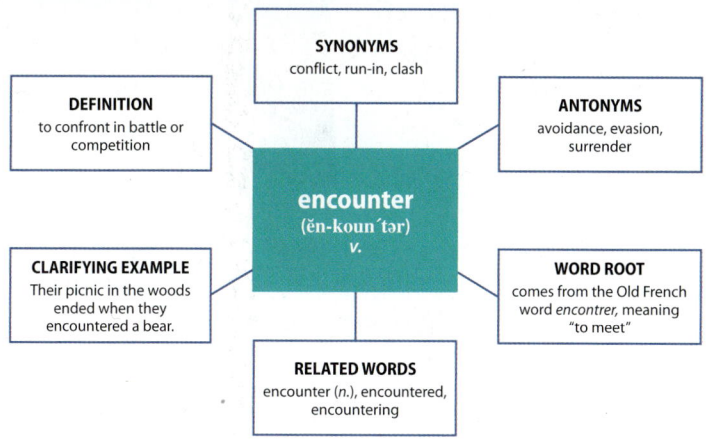

Write and Discuss Discuss your completed Word Network with a partner, making sure to talk through all of the boxes until you both understand the word, its synonyms, antonyms, and related forms. Then fill out a Word Network for the remaining four words. Use a dictionary or online resource to help you complete the activity.

 Go online to access the Word Networks.

RESPOND TO THE ESSENTIAL QUESTIONS

In this unit, you will explore four different **Essential Questions** about the Restoration period and the Enlightenment. As you read each selection, you will gather your ideas about one of these questions and write about it in a **Response Log**. At the end of the unit, you will have the opportunity to write a **personal narrative** related to one of the Essential Questions. Filling out the Response Log after you read each text will help you prepare for this writing task.

 You can also go online to access the Response Log.

Tradition and Reason 365

TEACH

ACADEMIC VOCABULARY

Have students complete Word Networks for the remaining four vocabulary words; encourage them to include all the categories shown in the completed network if possible, but point out that some words do not have clear synonyms or antonyms.

encounter (ĕn-koun´tər) *n.* to control in battle or competition (Spanish cognate: *encuentro*)

exploit (ĭk-sploit´) *v.* to take advantage of; to use for selfish or unethical purposes (Spanish cognate: *explotar*)

persist (pər-sĭst´) *v.* to hold firmly to a purpose or task in spite of obstacles (Spanish cognate: *persistir*)

subordinate (sə-bôr´dn-ĭt) *adj.* subject to the authority or control of another (Spanish cognate: *subordinado*)

widespread (wīd´sprĕd´) *adj.* occurring or accepted widely

RESPOND TO THE ESSENTIAL QUESTION

Direct students to the Unit 3 Response Log. Explain that students will use it to record ideas and details from the selections that help answer one of the Essential Questions. When they work on the Writing Task at the end of the unit, their Response Logs will help them think about what they have read and make connections between the texts.

Tradition and Reason **365**

PLAN

THE RAPE OF THE LOCK
Poem by Alexander Pope

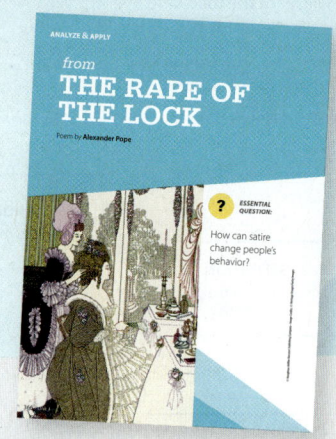

GENRE ELEMENTS
SATIRE

Tell students that while **satire** is humorous, it is not pointless; it always has a very clear message. Satire is a particular kind of comedy that manages to both offend and entertain as it tries to get readers to view its topic in a new light. Remind students that a **mock epic poem** does not mock the form of the epic poem, but makes fun of the subject of the poem. In this lesson, students will analyze the techniques used in a mock epic poem and evaluate its power over an audience.

LEARNING OBJECTIVES

- Analyze satire, heroic couplets, and mock epics.
- Conduct research about 18th century aristocratic culture.
- Write a rhymed satirical poem.
- Discuss a poem.
- **Language** Compare satirical techniques.

TEXT COMPLEXITY

	The Rape of the Lock	LEXILE: N/A
Quantitative Measures		
Qualitative Measures	**Ideas Presented** Multiple levels, subtle, implied meanings and purpose. Use of irony, satire, and exaggeration.	
	Structures Used More complex.	
	Language Used Complex sentence structures with use of allusive, figurative, ironic, archaic, and formal language.	
	Knowledge Required Cultural and historical knowledge may make heavier demands.	

366A Unit 3

PLAN

Online

RESOURCES

- Unit 3 Response Log
- 🔊 Selection Audio
- 📖 Reading Studio: Notice & Note
- Level Up Tutorial: Irony
- 💬 Speaking and Listening Studio: Participating in Collaborative Discussions
- ✅ "The Rape of the Lock" Selection Test

SUMMARIES

English

These excerpts from Pope's mock epic describe a quarrel between members of the British aristocracy. A baron watches Belinda while she wins a game of cards; then, despite attempted intervention by supernatural powers, he snips off a ringlet of her hair without her consent. Belinda is horrified and attacks the baron. The stolen lock ascends to the heavens, where it becomes a star that immortalizes the fair lady.

Spanish

Estos pasajes del cuento heroicoburlesco de Pope describen una riña entre miembros de la aristocracia británica. Un barón ve a Belinda mientras ésta gana un juego de cartas; luego, a pesar de la aparente intervención de poderes sobrenaturales, le corta un rizo de su cabello sin su consentimiento. Horrorizada, Belinda ataca al barón. El mechón robado sube a los cielos, donde se convierte en una estrella que inmortaliza a la hermosa dama.

SMALL-GROUP OPTIONS

Have students work in small groups and pairs to read and discuss the selection.

Activating Academic Vocabulary

- Provide a list of Academic Vocabulary words and phrases, such as: *satire, exaggeration, irony, critique, comment, issue, distinguish, what is stated, what is meant, humor, purpose.*
- After reading the first 40 lines of the poem, model how to use one or more Academic Vocabulary words and phrases to discuss the text.
- Encourage students to use the Academic Vocabulary as they discuss and write about the text.

Silent Sustained Reading

- Set a timer for 30 minutes.
- Have students read the play silently until the timer rings.
- Suggest that students keep a list of any unfamiliar words they want to look up after reading.
- Ask students to record the title, date, and number of pages read in a reading log.

PLAN

Text X-Ray: English Learner Support
for *The Rape of the Lock*

Use the Text X-Ray and the supports and scaffolds in the Teacher's Edition to help guide students at different proficiency levels through the selection.

INTRODUCE THE SELECTION
DISCUSS *IRONY* AND *EXAGGERATION*

In this lesson, students will need to be able to discuss the use of verbal irony and exaggeration in a mock epic poem. Provide the following explanations:

- Irony is humor that involves saying one thing while meaning the opposite.
- Exaggeration happens when something is overstated or made to seem more important than it is.

Explain to students that irony and exaggeration are both literary techniques that add humor to a text.

Ask students to talk about ironic or exaggerated situations or events from their lives that they think are funny. Provide sentence frames, such as: *It is ironic when my [friend/parent] says ____ but really means ____. One example of exaggeration I saw on TV was ____.*

CULTURAL REFERENCES

The following words or phrases may be unfamiliar to students:

- *crowned with* (line 1): covered with
- *ball* (line 12): formal dance party
- *a reputation dies* (line 16): people think less of a person
- *sentence* (line 21): an official judgment or decision

LISTENING

Identify Types of Rhymes

Remind students that not all rhymes in Pope's rhyme scheme are exact or full rhymes. Some rhymes may have two different long vowel sounds or they may only share the same ending consonant sound. Have students listen closely to identify the sounds that are being "rhymed."

Use the following supports with students at varying proficiency levels:

- Have students listen as you read lines 1–8. Name ending pairs of words, and have students give the thumbs-up if the words are an exact rhyme (flowers/towers) or thumbs-down if they are a surprising rhyme (foredoom/home). **SUBSTANTIAL**
- Have partners take turns reading aloud couplets through line 8 to each other. Have them tell what sounds they hear being rhymed in each pair of end words. Direct them to point out any silent letters or consonant clusters. **MODERATE**
- Have partners take turns reading aloud couplets through line 28 to each other. Have them tell what sounds they hear being rhymed in each pair of end words. Direct them to identify any silent letters, consonant clusters, or different spellings of the same sound. **LIGHT**

PLAN

SPEAKING

Compare Satirical Techniques

Remind students that authors use a variety of techniques when writing a satire, such as irony, exaggeration, ridicule, dark humor, mockery, and scornful or lighthearted and playful tones.

Use the following supports with students at varying proficiency levels:

- Write a list of satirical techniques and work with students to carefully pronounce each one. Review how to pronounce words with silent letters and consonant clusters, as well as short and long vowels. **SUBSTANTIAL**
- Have partners choose a school issue to satirize and then say a few words about how they could use each type of satirical technique from the list. **MODERATE**
- Have small groups choose a school or community issue to satirize. Then, have them discuss and compare how effective each technique from the list would be in a satire about the issue. **LIGHT**

READING

Use Rhyme

Remind students that most rhymes share the same vowel sound, but the spellings of these sounds may be different. For example: *eyes/dies*.

Use the following supports with students of varying proficiency levels:

- Help students reread the end words of couplets in lines 9–18. Have students copy the pairs of end words and underline the vowels in each that are spelled the same. Have them circle any vowel sounds that are spelled differently. **SUBSTANTIAL**
- Have pairs reread lines 9–18 and discuss the way the rhymes are spelled and how they sound. Guide them to use the phrase *sound the same but are spelled differently* in their discussion. **MODERATE**
- Have students reread lines 9–18 and use the rhyming words in new rhyming couplets. Have partners exchange their work and check for spelling accuracy. **LIGHT**

WRITING

Dictate Rhymes

Tell students to listen carefully to what sounds they hear in a rhyme. Remind them that sometimes one letter may have different sounds. For example: *short and long e; hard and soft g*. Review that different letters may share the same sound. For example: *s and soft c*.

Use the following supports with students of varying proficiency levels:

- Read aloud several pairs of rhyming words from the text. Have students repeat the rhyming sound they hear. Then have them write that sound. **SUBSTANTIAL**
- Have partners take turns reading aloud a pair of rhyming words from a couplet in the text. Have the listener repeat and write the rhyming sound they hear. Have the speaker check for accuracy. **MODERATE**
- Have partners take turns reading aloud a couplet from the text. Have the listener repeat, name, and write the rhyming sound they hear. Have the speaker check for accuracy. **LIGHT**

TEACH

Connect to the ESSENTIAL QUESTION

Satire is an important way people make arguments against things in a society which are either harmful, unnecessary, or both. Satire can be aimed at policies or social norms. "The Rape of the Lock" is a satire that highlighted one man's behavior in an attempt to reconcile a family by changing their behavior.

ANALYZE & APPLY

from THE RAPE OF THE LOCK

Poem by **Alexander Pope**

? ESSENTIAL QUESTION:

How can satire change people's behavior?

GET READY

QUICK START

Think of a time when you overreacted to an incident but later realized that what happened was not very important. What made you see that you had overreacted?

ANALYZE SATIRE

Satire is a literary technique in which institutions, practices, or behaviors are ridiculed for the purpose of bringing about reform. Authors write satire to comment on social and political issues and to advocate for improving society. Satirists often use exaggeration and irony to cast a critical eye on human follies and shortcomings. The success of satire depends on readers' ability to distinguish what is stated from what is really meant.

There are two types of satire, named for the Roman satirists Horace and Juvenal. **Juvenalian** satire uses a scathing, scornful tone and dark humor to criticize incompetence or corruption with scorn and outrage. Jonathon Swift's *A Modest Proposal* is an example of Juvenalian satire. *The Rape of the Lock,* on the other hand, is an example of **Horatian** satire, which uses a playful, lighthearted tone to correct foolishness and vice with a combination of gentle mockery and sympathetic understanding.

GENRE ELEMENTS: SATIRE
- ridicules customs, behaviors, or institutions
- purpose is to improve society
- intended to be humorous
- often uses exaggeration
- employs verbal irony

HORATIAN SATIRE	JUVENALIAN SATIRE
Purpose is to improve society	Purpose is to improve society
Lighthearted	Scornful
Gentle humor	Dark humor
Example: Alexander Pope's *The Rape of the Lock*	Example: Jonathan Swift's *A Modest Proposal*

ANALYZE HEROIC COUPLETS

A **heroic couplet** is a pair of rhymed lines in **iambic pentameter,** a metrical pattern of five feet (units). Each foot consists of two syllables, the first unstressed and the second stressed.

> O thoughtless mortals! ever blind to fate,
> Too soon dejected, and too soon elate:

Pope's adherence to the heroic couplet structure creates some of the unusual syntax in *The Rape of the Lock*. Pope also uses surprising rhymes for a humorous effect.

The Rape of the Lock 367

TEACH

QUICK START

Discuss the Quick Start question with students, and encourage them to think about how a situation can get out of hand. Ask questions like, "Why did you react so strongly to something that wasn't very serious?" Have students offer suggestions for how such a situation can be resolved.

ANALYZE SATIRE

Satire may be gently witty, mildly abrasive, or bitterly critical, and it often uses exaggeration that is used to force readers to see something in a more critical light. Help students understand the importance of humor as an element in satire. Point out that humor can be deployed in different ways, such as through exaggeration, use of irony, or extension to the ridiculous. Review with students the definition of **irony** (using words to convey the opposite of their literal meaning) and **exaggeration** (to represent something beyond its normal bounds). Then, discuss the two types of satire. Explain that **Horatian** satire is more playful and amusing, while **Juvenalian** satire is bitter, critical, and scornful. Pope uses Horatian satire in *The Rape of the Lock* to satirize the trivial pursuits of the idle wealthy.

ANALYZE HEROIC COUPLETS

A **heroic couplet** consists of two rhyming lines written in iambic pentameter. The term *heroic* comes from the fact that English poems having heroic themes and elevated style have often been written in iambic pentameter. Point out to students that **iambic pentameter** is the most commonly used meter in English poetry; it is the meter used in blank verse and in the sonnet. Write out an example of a rhyming couplet in iambic pentameter on the board, such as this one written by John Milton:

> "How soon hath Time, the subtle thief of youth,
> Stol'n on his wing my three-and-twentieth year!
> My hasting days fly on with full career,
> But my late spring no bud or blossom shew'th."

Have students practice reading it aloud. Remind students to follow the unstressed/stressed pattern when reading.

WHEN STUDENTS STRUGGLE . . .

Heroic Couplets To reinforce the distinguishing characteristics of heroic couplets, return to the couplet in the side column of this page. Students should realize quickly that *year* and *career* rhyme, as do *youth* and *shew'th*. Write the lines on the board. Use scansion marks to verify the iambic pentameter, marking the stressed syllables of *soon, Time, sub-, thief,* and *youth*, and *on, wing, three, twen-,* and *year*. Ask students to add their own marks to verify iambic pentameter in the two lines that follow.

The Rape of the Lock **367**

TEACH

ANALYZE MOCK EPIC

A **mock epic** uses the lofty style and conventions of epic poetry to satirize a trivial subject. In *The Rape of the Lock*, Pope makes fun of a silly quarrel by narrating it in a grandiose manner. Explain to students that they should look for epic characteristics—such as formal language, boasting speeches, supernatural intervention in human affairs, and elaborate descriptions of weapons and battles—as they read the poem.

Have students think back to examples of epic poetry they have read, such as *Beowulf*. Tell them to recall that the use of **syntax** varied throughout the poem. Remind students that, regardless of syntax, sentences in epic poems still must express clear, complete thoughts.

ANNOTATION MODEL

Remind students of the annotation ideas on page 368, which suggest underlining important details and circling words that signal how the Pope uses comparisons and rhymes to achieve a humorous effect. Point out that they may follow this suggestion or use their own system for marking up the selection in their write-in text. They may want to color-code their annotations by using highlighters. Their notes in the margin may include questions about ideas that are unclear or topics they want to learn more about.

 **GET READY**

ANALYZE MOCK EPIC

The Rape of the Lock is a **mock epic,** a form of satire that uses the grandiose style of epic poetry to portray a trivial subject. Mock epics include formal language, supernatural intervention in human affairs, boastful speeches, and elaborate descriptions of weapons and battles to emphasize the subject's insignificance.

In *The Rape of the Lock,* Pope uses elevated language—including **diction** (word choice) and **syntax** (word order)—to shape the reader's perception of how a woman reacts to someone cutting off a lock of her hair. To better understand difficult words and unusual syntax in the poem:

- Use the side notes provided for historical background and unfamiliar words.
- Visualize the action and images.
- Paraphrase sentences with unusual syntax by rearranging words in a more familiar sentence structure.

Here is an example of how you might paraphrase elevated language.

ELEVATED LANGUAGE	PARAPHRASE
"Hither the heroes and the nymphs resort"	The men and young women gather here.

ANNOTATION MODEL   NOTICE & NOTE

As you read, look for juxtapositions, comparisons, and rhymes that Pope makes to achieve a humorous effect. Use paraphrasing to note the meaning of elevated language. This model shows one reader's notes about the excerpt from *The Rape of the Lock*.

> Close by those meads, forever crowned with flowers,
> Where Thames with pride surveys his rising towers,
> There stands a structure of majestic frame,
> Which from the neighboring Hampton takes its name.
> Here Britain's statesmen oft the fall foredoom
> Of foreign tyrants and of nymphs at home;
> Here thou, great Anna! whom three realms (obey,)
> Dost sometimes counsel take—and sometimes (tea.)

Paraphrase: The majestic Hampton Court stands near the meadows by the Thames River, which are always in bloom.

The elevated diction and the rhyming of "obey" and "tea" create a funny contrast between the serious and the trivial. That dash in the last line is like a pause for comic effect.

BACKGROUND

Alexander Pope (1688–1744) is considered one of the best poets and satirists of the early 18th century. He is especially celebrated for his masterful use of the heroic couplet. The Rape of the Lock is based on an actual dispute between two prominent families, the Fermors and the Petres, that resulted when Lord Petre snipped a lock of hair from Arabella Fermor. The feud spiraled out of proportion, and Pope composed the poem in response to a friend's request that he intervene to "laugh them together again."

from THE RAPE OF THE LOCK
Poem by Alexander Pope

SETTING A PURPOSE

As you read, look for ways that Pope makes fun of the aristocracy through his description of this incident, including his use of elevated language and other characteristics of epic poetry.

In the first of the poem's five cantos, a Muse is evoked for inspiration (a tradition in epic poetry) and Belinda is warned of impending danger by Ariel, a spirit sent to protect Belinda. In Canto 2, Belinda rides up the Thames River to a Hampton Court party and is noticed by the scheming Baron, who resolves to possess one of the two curly locks spiraling down Belinda's back.

from CANTO 3

Close by those meads, forever crowned with flowers,
Where Thames with pride surveys his rising towers,
There stands a structure of majestic frame,
Which from the neighboring Hampton takes its name.
5   Here Britain's statesmen oft the fall foredoom
Of foreign tyrants and of nymphs at home;
Here thou, great Anna! whom three realms obey,
Dost sometimes counsel take—and sometimes tea.

Notice & Note

Use the side margins to notice and note signposts in the text.

1 **meads:** meadows.

2 **Thames** (tĕmz): a river that flows through southern England.

3–4 **structure . . . name:** the royal palace of Hampton Court, about 15 miles from London.

6 **nymphs** (nĭmfs): maidens; young women.

7 **Anna . . . obey:** Queen Anne, who rules over the three realms of England, Scotland, and Wales.

TEACH

ANALYZE HEROIC COUPLETS

Inform students that the reference to an Indian screen refers to a wooden divider that would be ornately carved and decorated. (**Answer:** The glory of the British Queen is a lofty subject of public and historic importance, while an Indian screen is just a decorative item. Comparing them emphasizes that, at Hampton Court, trivial and important things are often mixed up.)

ENGLISH LEARNER SUPPORT

Acquire New Vocabulary Explain that many words have multiple meanings, some of which are outdated. Help students use context clues to determine the most appropriate meaning of each of these words:

- *Burns* (line 26): "feels strong emotion"
- *routed* (line 35): "defeated"
- *livid* (line 44): "ash-gray"
- *look* (line 44): "appearance"
- *ill* (line 45): "disaster" **MODERATE**

For **reading support** for students at varying proficiency levels, see the **Text X-Ray** on page 366C.

 **NOTICE & NOTE**

ANALYZE HEROIC COUPLETS

Annotate: In lines 13–14, mark the two words that are rhymed for humorous effect.

Analyze: What makes the pairing of these two things humorous?

17 snuff: powdered tobacco that is inhaled.

24 toilet: the process of dressing, fixing one's hair, and otherwise grooming oneself.

27 ombre (ŏm´bər): a popular card game of the day, similar to bridge.

30 King . . . face: the king of diamonds, the only king shown in profile in a deck of cards.

31 refulgent (rĭ-fŭl´jənt) **Queen:** resplendent or shining queen of diamonds. The Baron is leading his highest diamonds in an effort to win.

34 promiscuous (prə-mĭs´kyōō-əs): confused; **level green:** the green cloth-covered card table.

36 Afric's sable sons: Africa's black soldiers.

41 Knave: jack.

43 the virgin's: Belinda's.

46 Codille (kō-dēl´): a losing hand of cards in ombre.

47 distempered: disordered.

48 nice: delicate; subtle; **trick:** a single round of cards played and won.

Hither the heroes and the nymphs resort,
10 To taste awhile the pleasures of a court;
    In various talk the instructive hours they passed,
    Who gave the ball, or paid the visit last;
    One speaks the glory of the British Queen,
    And one describes a charming Indian screen;
15 A third interprets motions, looks, and eyes;
    At every word a reputation dies.
    Snuff, or the fan, supply each pause of chat,
    With singing, laughing, ogling, and all that.

    Meanwhile declining from the noon of day,
20 The sun obliquely shoots his burning ray;
    The hungry judges soon the sentence sign,
    And wretches hang that jurymen may dine;
    The merchant from the Exchange returns in peace,
    And the long labors of the toilet cease.
25 Belinda now, whom thirst of fame invites,
    Burns to encounter two adventurous knights,
    At ombre singly to decide their doom,
    And swells her breast with conquests yet to come. . . .

    The Baron now his Diamonds pours apace;
30 The embroidered King who shows but half his face,
    And his refulgent Queen, with powers combined,
    Of broken troops an easy conquest find.
    Clubs, Diamonds, Hearts, in wild disorder seen,
    With throngs promiscuous strew the level green.
35 Thus when dispersed a routed army runs,
    Of Asia's troops, and Afric's sable sons,
    With like confusion different nations fly,
    Of various habit, and of various dye,
    The pierced battalions disunited fall
40 In heaps on heaps; one fate o'erwhelms them all.

    The Knave of Diamonds tries his wily arts,
    And wins (oh, shameful chance!) the Queen of Hearts.
    At this, the blood the virgin's cheek forsook,
    A livid paleness spreads o'er all her look;
45 She sees, and trembles at the approaching ill,
    Just in the jaws of ruin, and Codille.
    And now (as oft in some distempered state)
    On one nice trick depends the general fate.
    An Ace of Hearts steps forth: The King unseen
50 Lurked in her hand, and mourned his captive Queen.
    He springs to vengeance with an eager pace,

370   Unit 3

TO CHALLENGE STUDENTS . . .

Analyze Narrator Pair students to discuss these questions about Pope's narrator:

- In what way does the narrator's tone shift between lines 41–54 and lines 55–58?
- The narrator's purpose in lines 41–54 is to describe the card game. What is the narrator's purpose in lines 55–58?
- In lines 55–58, what event is the narrator foreshadowing?

And falls like thunder on the prostrate Ace.
The nymph exulting fills with shouts the sky,
The walls, the woods, and long canals reply.

55 O thoughtless mortals! ever blind to fate,
Too soon dejected, and too soon elate:
Sudden these honors shall be snatched away,
And cursed forever this victorious day.

For lo! the board with cups and spoons is crowned,
60 The berries crackle, and the mill turns round;
On shining altars of Japan they raise
The silver lamp; the fiery spirits blaze:
From silver spouts the grateful liquors glide,
While China's earth receives the smoking tide.
65 At once they gratify their scent and taste,
And frequent cups prolong the rich repast.
Straight hover round the fair her airy band;
Some, as she sipped, the fuming liquor fanned,
Some o'er her lap their careful plumes displayed,
70 Trembling, and conscious of the rich brocade.
Coffee (which makes the politician wise,
And see through all things with his half-shut eyes)
Sent up in vapors to the Baron's brain
New stratagems, the radiant Lock to gain.
75 Ah, cease, rash youth! desist ere 'tis too late,
Fear the just Gods, and think of Scylla's fate!
Changed to a bird, and sent to flit in air,
She dearly pays for Nisus' injured hair!

But when to mischief mortals bend their will,
80 How soon they find fit instruments of ill!
Just then, Clarissa drew with tempting grace
A two-edged weapon from her shining case:
So ladies in romance assist their knight,
Present the spear, and arm him for the fight.
85 He takes the gift with reverence, and extends
The little engine on his fingers' ends;
This just behind Belinda's neck he spread,
As o'er the fragrant steams she bends her head.
Swift to the Lock a thousand sprights repair,
90 A thousand wings, by turns, blow back the hair,
And thrice they twitched the diamond in her ear,
Thrice she looked back, and thrice the foe drew near.
Just in that instant, anxious Ariel sought
The close recesses of the virgin's thought;

ANALYZE MOCK EPIC

Annotate: In lines 59–70, mark and label two different examples of the characteristics of a mock epic.

Interpret: What actions, real and imaginary, is Pope describing?

61 shining altars of Japan: small lacquered tables. In mock-epic style, Pope elevates the tables to altars.

64 China's earth ... tide: China cups receive the hot coffee.

66 repast (rĭ-păst´): meal.

67 the fair: Belinda; **her airy band:** the Sylphs (sĭlfs), supernatural creatures attending Belinda. Epic heroes and heroines are generally aided by higher powers.

74 new stratagems (străt´ə-jəmz) **... gain:** new schemes for acquiring a lock of Belinda's hair.

76–78 Scylla's (sĭl´əz) **fate ... Nisus'** (nī´səs) **injured hair:** In ancient Greek legend, Scylla was turned into a bird because she betrayed her father, King Nisus, by giving his enemy the purple lock of his hair on which his safety depended.

89 sprights (sprīts): the Sylphs.

93 Ariel (âr´ē-əl): Belinda's special guardian among the Sylphs.

TEACH

ANALYZE SATIRE

Help students observe the juxtaposition between Belinda's reaction and the expected reaction when a husband may die. Encourage them to question what this reveals about the author's opinion of this part of society. (**Answer:** *The exaggeration highlights the vanity of aristocrats and the folly of losing control of emotions.*)

NOTICE & NOTE

95 nosegay: a small bouquet of flowers.

> 95 As on the nosegay in her breast reclined,
>   He watched the ideas rising in her mind,
>   Sudden he viewed, in spite of all her art,
>   An earthly lover lurking at her heart.
>   Amazed, confused, he found his power expired,
> 100 Resigned to fate, and with a sigh retired.

101 the Peer: the Baron; **forfex:** a fancy term for scissors.

>   The Peer now spreads the glittering forfex wide,
>   To enclose the Lock; now joins it, to divide.
>   Even then, before the fatal engine closed,
>   A wretched Sylph too fondly interposed;
> 105 Fate urged the shears, and cut the Sylph in twain
>   (But airy substance soon unites again):
>   The meeting points the sacred hair dissever
>   From the fair head, forever and forever!

ANALYZE SATIRE
Annotate: In lines 109–114, mark phrases that exaggerate Belinda's reaction to having her lock cut.

Analyze: What human folly or flaw is highlighted by this exaggeration?

>   Then flashed the living lightning from her eyes,
> 110 And screams of horror rend the affrighted skies.
>   Not louder shrieks to pitying heaven are cast,
>   When husbands, or when lapdogs breathe their last;
>   Or when rich china vessels fallen from high,
>   In glittering dust and painted fragments lie!

APPLYING ACADEMIC VOCABULARY

❑ encounter ❑ exploit ☑ persist ❑ subordinate ☑ widespread

Write and Discuss Have students turn to a partner to discuss the following questions. Guide students to include the Academic Vocabulary words *persist* and *widespread* in their responses. Ask volunteers to share their responses with the class.

- Why did the Baron **persist**, despite the efforts of the sylphs to stop him?
- Will the news of the Baron's theft become **widespread**? Why or why not?

115 "Let wreaths of triumph now my temples twine,"
   The victor cried, "the glorious prize is mine!
   While fish in streams, or birds delight in air,
   Or in a coach and six the British fair,
   As long as *Atalantis* shall be read,
120 Or the small pillow grace a lady's bed,
   While visits shall be paid on solemn days,
   When numerous wax-lights in bright order blaze,
   While nymphs take treats, or assignations give,
   So long my honor, name, and praise shall live!

125   "What time would spare, from steel receives its date,
   And monuments, like men, submit to fate!
   Steel could the labor of the Gods destroy,
   And strike to dust the imperial towers of Troy;
   Steel could the works of mortal pride confound,
130 And hew triumphal arches to the ground.
   What wonder then, fair nymph! thy hairs should feel,
   The conquering force of unresisted steel?"

In Canto 4, following an epic tradition, a melancholy sprite descends to the Underworld—which Pope calls the "Cave of Spleen"—and returns to the party with a vial of grief and "flowing tears" and a bag of "sobs, sighs, and passions," which are emptied over Belinda's head, fanning her fury even further.

from CANTO 5

   "To arms, to arms!" the fierce virago cries,
   And swift as lightning to the combat flies.
135 All side in parties, and begin the attack;
   Fans clap, silks rustle, and tough whalebones crack;
   Heroes' and heroines' shouts confusedly rise,
   And bass and treble voices strike the skies.
   No common weapons in their hands are found,
140 Like Gods they fight, nor dread a mortal wound. . . .

   See, fierce Belinda on the Baron flies,
   With more than usual lightning in her eyes;
   Nor feared the chief the unequal fight to try,
   Who sought no more than on his foe to die.

145   But this bold lord with manly strength endued,
   She with one finger and a thumb subdued:
   Just where the breath of life his nostrils drew,
   A charge of snuff the wily virgin threw;

NOTICE & NOTE

115 wreaths . . . twine: In epics, victors or champions traditionally wore laurel wreaths as a kind of crown.

118 coach and six: a coach drawn by six horses.

119 Atalantis: *The New Atalantis* by Delarivier Manley, a thinly disguised account of scandal among the rich.

ANALYZE SATIRE

Annotate: In lines 117–124, mark the activities of the aristocracy that are mentioned.

Analyze: What do these details suggest about the aristocracy?

125 date: end.

127–128 the labor of the Gods . . . towers of Troy: Troy, an ancient city famous for its towers, whose walls were said to have been built by the Greek gods Apollo and Poseidon.

133 virago (və-rä′gō): a woman who engages in warfare or other fighting. She has come to Belinda's aid at Ariel's request.

136 whalebones: elastic material from whales' mouths, used in corsets or support undergarments.

145 endued (ĕn-do̅o̅d′): endowed; provided with.

TEACH

ENGLISH LEARNER SUPPORT

Use Contextual Support Have groups of three students reread lines 163–168. Have each student take one of the lines and paraphrase it. Assist students as needed. Then, have them explain to their group how they came to their paraphrases for each line.

MODERATE/LIGHT

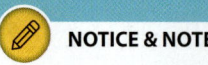

NOTICE & NOTE

149 Gnomes (nōmz): supernatural creatures bent on causing mischief.

152 And the high . . . nose: In other words, he sneezes.

154 bodkin (bŏd´kĭn): a long, ornamental hairpin.

157 seal rings: signet rings bearing a person's family crest or initials.

159 Her infant grandame's (grăn´dāmz) **. . . grew:** It was next melted down and turned into a whistle used by Belinda's grandmother as a child. Pope is here making fun of family heirlooms.

168 burn in Cupid's flames: burn with passion.

170 rebound: echo.

171–172 Othello . . . pain: In Shakespeare's *Othello*, the deeply jealous Othello demands the handkerchief that he believes is a sign of his wife's infidelity.

179 mounted to the lunar sphere: climbed up to the moon.

182 beaux' (bōz): the wits of fops.

184 riband (rĭb´ənd): ribbon.

185 Muse (myōōz): the goddess who inspires the writing of the poem. In typical epic fashion, the narrator opens the poem by addressing his Muse and continues to address her throughout the poem.

188 trail of hair: The word *comet* comes from a Greek word that means "long haired."

The Gnomes direct, to every atom just,
150 The pungent grains of titillating dust.
Sudden, with starting tears each eye o'erflows,
And the high dome re-echoes to his nose.

"Now meet thy fate," incensed Belinda cried,
And drew a deadly bodkin from her side.
155 (The same, his ancient personage to deck,
Her great-great-grandsire wore about his neck,
In three seal rings; which after, melted down,
Formed a vast buckle for his widow's gown:
Her infant grandame's whistle next it grew,
160 The bells she jingled, and the whistle blew;
Then in a bodkin graced her mother's hairs,
Which long she wore, and now Belinda wears.)

"Boast not my fall," he cried, "insulting foe!
Thou by some other shalt be laid as low.
165 Nor think to die dejects my lofty mind:
All that I dread is leaving you behind!
Rather than so, ah, let me still survive,
And burn in Cupid's flames—but burn alive."

"Restore the Lock!" she cries; and all around
170 "Restore the Lock!" the vaulted roofs rebound.
Not fierce Othello in so loud a strain
Roared for the handkerchief that caused his pain.
But see how oft ambitious aims are crossed,
And chiefs contend till all the prize is lost!
175 The lock, obtained with guilt, and kept with pain,
In every place is sought, but sought in vain:
With such a prize no mortal must be blessed,
So Heaven decrees! with Heaven who can contest?

   Some thought it mounted to the lunar sphere,
180 Since all things lost on earth are treasured there.
There heroes' wits are kept in ponderous vases,
And beaux' in snuffboxes and tweezer cases.
There broken vows and death-bed alms are found,
And lovers' hearts with ends of riband bound. . . .

185   But trust the Muse—she saw it upward rise,
Though marked by none but quick, poetic eyes. . . .
A sudden star, it shot through liquid air,
And drew behind a radiant trail of hair. . . .

IMPROVE READING FLUENCY

Targeted Passage Read aloud lines 149–162, and direct the class in a choral reading exercise. Have students practice reading in iambic pentameter. Point out the author's use of an apostrophe in line 151 to truncate the word *overflows* into a two-syllable word.

 Go to the **Reading Studio** for additional support in developing fluency.

Then cease, bright nymph! to mourn thy ravished hair,
190 Which adds new glory to the shining sphere!
Not all the tresses that fair head can boast
Shall draw such envy as the Lock you lost.
For, after all the murders of your eye,
When, after millions slain, yourself shall die:
195 When those fair suns shall set, as set they must,
And all those tresses shall be laid in dust,
This Lock the Muse shall consecrate to fame,
And 'midst the stars inscribe Belinda's name.

NOTICE & NOTE

193 murders of your eye: men struck down by your glance.

ANALYZE MOCK EPIC
Annotate: Mark the supernatural intervention in lines 185–198 that resolves the conflict.

Paraphrase: What does this mock epic element suggest about the power of Pope's satire?

CHECK YOUR UNDERSTANDING

Answer these questions before moving on to the **Analyze the Text** section on the following page.

1 In Canto 3, which two common activities of the aristocracy does Pope describe?
  A Watching a mock battle and drinking coffee
  B Playing cards and drinking coffee
  C Dueling and decorating parlors
  D Playing cards and reciting epic poetry

2 Reread lines 71–74: *Coffee . . . Sent up in vapors to the Baron's brain / New stratagems, the radiant Lock to gain*. Which sentence best paraphrases this statement?
  F Drinking coffee has made the Baron want to steal the lock of hair.
  G The coffee gave the Baron new ideas about how to steal the lock of hair.
  H The smell of the coffee made the lock of hair seem more attractive.
  J The lock of hair looked more radiant because of the steam of the coffee.

3 What happens to the lock of hair at the end of the poem?
  A The lock becomes lost and then turns into a star.
  B Belinda screams at the Baron until he is forced to return it.
  C It becomes lost and goes to the moon with the other lost things.
  D When Belinda dies, it turns to dust.

The Rape of the Lock 375

TEACH

ANALYZE MOCK EPIC

Remind students that when Pope wrote the poem, he had a specific audience and purpose in mind: to convince members of the aristocracy that they were acting silly. (**Answer:** *This element suggests that Pope can immortalize people through his satire.*)

CHECK YOUR UNDERSTANDING

Have students answer the questions independently.

Answers:

1. *B*
2. *G*
3. *A*

If they answer any questions incorrectly, have them reread the text to confirm their understanding. Then they may proceed to ANALYZE THE TEXT on page 376.

ENGLISH LEARNER SUPPORT

Oral Assessment

1. What two activities are the characters doing in lines 27–54 and 59–78? (*They are playing cards and drinking coffee.*)

2. How can you rephrase lines 71–74? (*Drinking coffee helped give the Baron a new idea for how to steal the hair.*)

3. Reread lines 195–198. What happens to the lock of hair the Baron cut? (*It turns into a star.*)

   ALL LEVELS

The Rape of the Lock 375

APPLY

ANALYZE THE TEXT

Possible answers:

1. **DOK 2:** *He satirizes the superficiality of the aristocrat's conversation, the destructive power of gossip, and the heartlessness of judges.*

2. **DOK 3:** *He wanted to humiliate her because of the way she beat him at cards.*

3. **DOK 2:** *He satirizes pride by having the Baron boast in ridiculously exaggerated terms about snipping off a lock of hair.*

4. **DOK 4:** *He describes them fighting like gods, but details such as "Fans clap, silks rustle, and tough whalebones crack" and Belinda's use of snuff to make the Baron sneeze emphasize the silliness of the quarrel.*

5. **DOK 4:** *Most students will respond that the ending offers an effective conclusion to the Horatian satire because Pope uses words such as glory and fame, suggesting that Belinda has satisfied the "thirst for fame" that he refers to earlier in line 25. The last sentence of the poem contains a series of subordinate clauses, which builds up momentum leading to the declaration of Belinda's immortality.*

RESEARCH

Remind students that they must be careful about the online sources they use for research. Sources that are reliable will typically link to other reliable sources. Internet sources which are not verified or fact checked might or might not link to reliable sources. Also, tell students to copy a hyperlink and paste it into a word format first in order to verify that it is going to take them where they want to go, and not to a website that may harm their computer.

Extend Encourage students to consider how this question can be applied to the present day as well.

RESPOND

ANALYZE THE TEXT

Support your responses with evidence from the text. 📓 NOTEBOOK

1. **Interpret** Poets often use heroic couplets to express complete thoughts in a witty and concise way. What flaws or problems in British society does Pope satirize in the following heroic couplets?
   • lines 11–12 ("In various talk . . . the visit last;")
   • lines 15–16 ("A third interprets . . . reputation dies.")
   • lines 21–22 ("The hungry judges . . . jurymen may dine.")

2. **Draw Conclusions** What motivates the Baron to cut Belinda's lock?

3. **Interpret** In lines 115–132, the Baron boasts about his conquest. What flaw does Pope satirize through exaggeration in the speech? Explain.

4. **Analyze** Reread lines 133–152. How does Pope use this mock epic battle to emphasize the foolishness of the quarrel?

5. **Evaluate** Does the poem's ending provide an effective conclusion to Pope's Horatian satire, or is it too scornful of Belinda? Discuss Pope's use of diction and syntax in your response.

RESEARCH

RESEARCH TIP
When reading a source on a very unfamiliar subject, use hyperlinks provided in the text for background information that will help you make sense of it. Keep the source you are reading open, and open the new one in a separate tab or window. You can do this by hovering your cursor over the link and right clicking or pressing *ctrl+click* to open a context menu and selecting "Open in new tab" or "Open in new window."

Pope includes a lot of details about 18th century aristocratic culture in *The Rape of the Lock*. With a partner, do research to learn more about fashions and trends in Britain at the time Pope wrote the poem.

QUESTION	ANSWER
What women's hairstyles were fashionable in the early 18th century?	*Women in the early 18th century frequently wore elaborate and ornate hairstyles with lots of curls, and they frequently used white powder to color their hair.*
How did aristocratic men and women dress?	*Aristocratic men wore heels, tights, ruffled shirts, and other formal types of clothing. Aristocratic women usually wore large dresses, petticoats, and corsets.*
What types of entertainment were popular?	*Plays and other performances were the most popular form of entertainment in the early 18th century.*

Extend With a partner, discuss what 18th century fashions and entertainment suggest about the gender roles of men and women in aristocratic society. Consider how these attitudes about gender are reflected in *The Rape of the Lock*.

376 Unit 3

WHEN STUDENTS STRUGGLE . . .

Reteaching: Analyze Satire Help students understand how the use of irony introduces humor into satire by violating expectations. The use of irony also serves to draw attention to the problem or problems the author is satirizing by showing how a behavior, policy, or institution does not make sense.

 For additional support, go to the **Reading Studio** and assign the following 📖 **Level Up tutorial: Irony.**

RESPOND

CREATE AND DISCUSS

Write a Rhymed Satirical Poem Think of a behavior common in our culture that you disapprove of. Write a short rhymed poem satirizing that behavior.

- Before you start composing, generate ideas through a short free write.
- Invent an imaginary incident as an example.
- Create humor through the use of elevated language, rhyme, and juxtaposition.

Discuss a Poem Alexander Pope's poem *The Rape of the Lock* makes fun of a young woman for being very upset that a man cut off a lock of her hair as a joke. With your group, talk about whether you think the woman's anger is justified.

- Listen as other students explain their ideas, and consider everyone's point of view.
- When you disagree with someone, calmly explain why you disagree.
- Think of questions you can ask your group to further explore this issue.

Go to **Participating in Collaborative Discussions** in the **Speaking and Listening Studio** to find out more about.

RESPOND TO THE ESSENTIAL QUESTION

 How can satire change people's behavior?

Gather Information Review your annotations and notes on *The Rape of the Lock*. Then, add relevant information to your Response Log. As you determine which information to include, think about:

- how the use of humor affects the audience
- whether serious matters can be addressed through humor
- how the people being made fun of might respond to satire

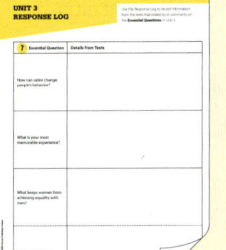

ACADEMIC VOCABULARY

As you write and discuss what you learned from *The Rape of the Lock*, be sure to use the Academic Vocabulary words. Check off each of the words that you use.

- encounter
- exploit
- persist
- subordinate
- widespread

APPLY

CREATE AND DISCUSS

Write a Rhymed Satirical Poem Before students begin writing, have students work with a partner to discuss their ideas and brainstorm other ideas. As they write their poems, encourage students to use the techniques that Pope used in his poem, such as irony or absurdity. Have students focus on why they disapprove of this cultural behavior. Encourage them to exaggerate examples of this behavior to highlight what is wrong with it.

Discuss a Poem Remind students to ask questions to clarify meaning of elements they do not understand in their classmates' poems or comments. The process of asking and answering questions can help everyone understand an issue more clearly and can lead to new ideas.

RESPOND TO THE ESSENTIAL QUESTION

Allow time for students to add details from *The Rape of the Lock* to their Unit 3 Response Logs.

PLAN

A MODEST PROPOSAL
Satire by Jonathan Swift

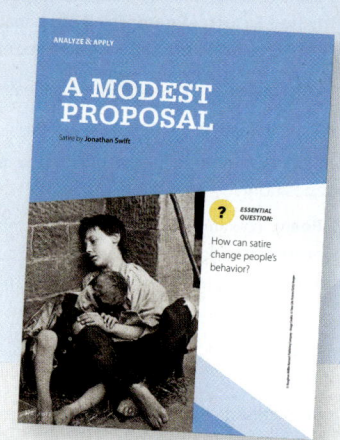

GENRE ELEMENTS
SATIRE
Tell students that some satires **parody,** or humorously imitate, other, more serious genres. In this text, Swift parodies a persuasive essay and uses the same techniques found in that genre, such as claims and supporting arguments based on facts. The **juxtaposition,** or contrast, of the serious format and absurdist content is what makes his essay so effective as a satire. In this lesson, students will analyze how satire can be used to promote an author's beliefs.

LEARNING OBJECTIVES
- Analyze satirical devices and understand the author's purpose.
- Conduct research about 18th-century life in Ireland.
- Write a satirical essay.
- Discuss an essay.
- Use context clues.
- Use active and passive voice.
- **Language** React to a satirical essay by stating an opinion.

TEXT COMPLEXITY

	A Modest Proposal	Lexile: 1590L
Quantitative Measures		
Qualitative Measures	**Ideas Presented** Multiple levels of complex meanings.	
	Structures Used Organization of main ideas and details is highly complex; not explicit, must be inferred by the reader.	
	Language Used Ambiguous language requiring inferences.	
	Knowledge Required Cultural and historical knowledge essential to understanding.	

PLAN

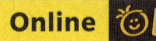

RESOURCES

- Unit 3 Response Log
- 🔊 Selection Audio
- Close Read Screencasts: Modeled Discussions
- 📖 Reading Studio: Notice & Note
- Level Up Tutorial: Author's Purpose
- Writing Studio: Writing as a Process
- 💬 Speaking and Listening Studio: Participating in Collaborative Discussions
- Vocabulary Studio: Context Clues
- Grammar Studio: Module 8 Lesson 7: Active Voice and Passive Voice
- ✓ *A Modest Proposal* Selection Test

SUMMARIES

English

In this satire, Swift first identifies a problem: Ireland's poor are leading wretched lives. He then offers a proposal for relieving this burden, decreasing the population, finding a new source of food, and curbing begging. The solution is to breed a certain portion of Irish children to be eaten. Swift provides statistics and detailed reasons supporting the plan, which serves as a harsh social critique of England's treatment of the Irish.

Spanish

En esta sátira, Swift primero identifica un problema: los pobres irlandeses tienen vidas desdichadas. Ofrece una propuesta para aliviar esta carga: reducir la población, encontrar una nueva fuente de comida y frenar la mendicación. La solución es criar a una porción de los niños de Irlanda para ser comidos. Swift ofrece estadísticas y razones específicas que apoyan este plan, que sirve como una dura crítica social del trato de los ingleses a los irlandeses.

👥 SMALL-GROUP OPTIONS

Have students work in small groups and pairs to read and discuss the selection.

Double-Entry Journal

- Have students use a notebook for recording their double-entry notes.
- Show students how to create a two-column chart by drawing a line from top to bottom on each page. The left head is *Quotes from the Text* and the right head is *My Notes*.
- Encourage students to pause as needed and copy important or confusing lines into the left column.
- Students then write their own questions, restatements, or interpretations in the right column next to the quoted material.

Send a Problem

- After reading the first paragraph, pose this question: *How can you describe the tone of this essay?*
- Call on a student to respond. Wait up to 11 seconds.
- If the student has no response, s/he must call on another student by name to answer the same question.
- Have students continue asking each other for assistance as needed. Monitor responses and ask more questions as appropriate.

PLAN

Text X-Ray: English Learner Support
for *A Modest Proposal*

Use the Text X-Ray and the supports and scaffolds in the Teacher's Edition to help guide students at different proficiency levels through the selection.

INTRODUCE THE SELECTION
DISCUSS *UNDERSTATEMENT* AND *HYPERBOLE*

In this lesson, students will need to be able to discuss how understatement and hyperbole are used to add humor in a satirical essay.

Provide the following explanations:

- *Understatement* is a compound word made up of two smaller words: *under* and *statement*. When you make an understatement, you are saying less than the obvious.
- *Hyperbole* is an overstatement or exaggeration of the facts. It is the opposite of *understatement*.

Have students practice using understatement and hyperbole as they talk about familiar situations and events. Provide sentence frames, such as: *It is an understatement to say that _____. When [friend] says _____ about _____, it is an example of hyperbole.*

CULTURAL REFERENCES

The following words or phrases may be unfamiliar to students:

- *crop failure* (Background): when all the fields of a particular type of food fail to produce that food because of an insect, fungus, or other problem
- *all parties* (paragraph 2): everyone involved in a situation
- *turned my thoughts . . . upon* (paragraph 4): thought about
- *shillings* (paragraph 4): British money
- *on the contrary* (paragraph 4): in an opposite way
- *in season* (paragraph 13): available

LISTENING

Understand Implicit Ideas

Remind students that they can ask themselves questions to clarify the implied meaning behind what is literally stated in a text.

Use the following supports with students at varying proficiency levels:

- Read aloud paragraph 9 from the text. Model how to ask clarifying questions about what they heard, such as: *Does the author literally mean that a young healthy child is a most delicious food? Is the author using understatement?* Have students repeat each question. Then, have them repeat any new academic vocabulary. **SUBSTANTIAL**
- Ask general content questions to assess listening comprehension. Read aloud paragraph 9, then ask: *What does Swift really mean by "I make no doubt that it will equally serve in a fricassee or a ragout?"* **MODERATE**
- Have partners each choose a paragraph to read aloud to each other. Have them ask and answer questions about what they heard. For example: *What do you think Swift really means when he says _____?* **LIGHT**

378C   Unit 3

PLAN

SPEAKING

React to Ideas

Remind students that a satirical essay may use absurd or outrageous ideas to get people to relax enough to change their views and their behaviors related to a serious political issue. Have students discuss their opinions of the use of satire in politics.

Use the following supports with students at varying proficiency levels:

- Provide sample questions, such as: *How do you feel about satire?* Provide a choice of answers, such as: *I find satire entertaining. I find satire offensive.* Check understanding of the statements and then have them pose the question for a partner to answer. Then, have them practice saying them with a partner. For example: *How do you feel about satire? Did you find this essay offensive? I found the humor very entertaining.* **SUBSTANTIAL**
- Have partners discuss Swift's proposal to cook and eat poor children. Direct them to state their reaction and then ask their partner for his or her reaction. Provide sentence frames, such as: *I find the proposal _____, because _____.* **MODERATE**
- Have partners discuss paragraph 10. Direct them to state their reaction and then ask their partner for his or her reaction. Tell them to use complete sentences. **LIGHT**

READING

Use Think-Alouds

Remind students it's a good idea to pause as they read to ask themselves questions about the author's purpose. Model how to use Think-Alouds as you read sections of the text.

Use the following supports with students at varying proficiency levels:

- Read aloud paragraph 12. Have students reread the sentence with you. Then, model a Think-Aloud: *I can use a dictionary to look up* devour. Devour *means "to eat." I ask myself, did the landlord really eat the parents? I think the author is exaggerating.* Ask: *Did the landlord eat the parents?* **SUBSTANTIAL**
- Model the Think-Aloud from the Beginning activity. Have partners take turns reading a sentence and then saying a brief Think-Aloud about it. **MODERATE**
- Model the Think-Aloud from the Beginning activity. Have students reread paragraph 14 and recite a Think-Aloud in at least two places they have a question about. Have them take notes to use in their Think-Alouds. **LIGHT**

WRITING

Use Spelling Rules

Review common English spelling rules with students, such as *i before e, except after c*.

Use the following supports with students at varying proficiency levels:

- Write one spelling rule on the board such as *i before e, except after c* and provide examples that follow it, such as *receive, believe*. Have students copy the rule and the examples. **SUBSTANTIAL**
- Write two spelling rules on the board and provide examples of each. Have students write several sentences that show examples of each rule. **MODERATE**
- Have partners research and write a list of five spelling rules. Then, have them exchange drafts of their essays and look for correct usage of each rule. Have them correct any words or phrases that do not follow the rules. **LIGHT**

A Modest Proposal **378D**

TEACH

? **Connect to the ESSENTIAL QUESTION**

Ask a volunteer to read aloud the Essential Question. Discuss how the image relates to the question. How might satire change the lives of the children depicted in the photograph? Ask students to think about ways their lives might be changed.

ANALYZE & APPLY

A MODEST PROPOSAL

Satire by **Jonathan Swift**

? **ESSENTIAL QUESTION:**

How can satire change people's behavior?

 LEARNING MINDSET

Curiosity Mindset Discuss the value of curiosity with your students. Explain that being curious is an important part of having a learning mindset because it is a first step toward taking on the challenges that come with learning new skills. Encourage students to think about the title of the selection and the photograph that accompanies the title. Then, ask students to share what they are curious to learn about in the selection.

QUICK START

Poverty is a problem that affects all societies. What proposals for fighting poverty have you heard about? List a few ideas in your notebook, ranking them in order of their likelihood of success. Discuss your list with a partner.

ANALYZE SATIRICAL DEVICES

Swift's essay is an example of Juvenalian satire, which uses a scornful tone and dark humor to criticize problems such as corruption or incompetence. Swift relies on a variety of rhetorical devices to develop his satire. As you read, use a chart like this one to identify examples of these devices in the essay.

DEVICE	EXAMPLE
Verbal irony occurs when a writer says the opposite of what is meant.	The title is ironic because the actual proposal is outrageous, not modest.
Understatement occurs when a writer says less than is expected or appropriate.	
Exaggeration (also called **overstatement** or **hyperbole**) occurs when a writer exaggerates the truth for emphasis or humorous effect.	
Contradiction occurs when a writer expresses two ideas that are in opposition to one another.	
Paradox is a statement that seems contradictory or absurd but actually reveals some element of truth.	

GENRE ELEMENTS: SATIRE

- ridicules customs, behaviors, or institutions
- purpose is to improve society
- can be gently humorous (Horatian) or scornful (Juvenalian)
- uses satirical devices, like irony and exaggeration

UNDERSTAND AUTHOR'S PURPOSE

Swift wrote *A Modest Proposal* in the form of an argument for a public policy. The unnamed narrator who makes this argument bears some resemblance to Swift: both men have previously tried to promote ideas to help Ireland's poor. Despite this ambiguity, Swift's purpose clearly isn't to persuade people to accept the narrator's claim. Instead, he uses the structure of an argument to attack British policies and the callousness of wealthy people in Ireland and England. As you read *A Modest Proposal*, consider whether Swift's satirical argument is an effective way to achieve his intended purpose.

TEACH

QUICK START

Have students read the Quick Start question, and then encourage them to work in pairs to come up with a list of proposals they have heard. They may also try to find such proposals on the internet, adding the web addresses to their lists. When the pairs are finished, have them present what they consider to be their best findings to the rest of the class. Do some proposals make more sense than others? Do students notice common themes running through the proposals?

ANALYZE SATIRICAL DEVICES

Explain to students that there are many different kinds of satire, and that they differ in their purposes and the techniques they use. As students complete the graphic organizer, you will need to explain the meanings of the different devices they are looking for in the selection. Give some examples of **understatement** in conversation, such as the sentence, "I was not thrilled to hear that." Offer sentences like, "That was the best book in the world" as you explain what **exaggeration** is. Quote the opening of Charles Dickens's *A Tale of Two Cities* for an example of **contradiction:** "It was the best of times; it was the worst of times." Discuss the meanings of statements such as "I didn't have time to write a postcard, so I wrote a letter instead" when you go over the meaning of **paradox.**

UNDERSTAND AUTHOR'S PURPOSE

Tell students that a writer usually writes for one or more of these purposes: to inform, to entertain, to express himself or herself, or to persuade readers to believe or do something. For example, the **author's purpose** of a news report is to inform; the purpose of an editorial is to persuade the readers or audience to do or believe something.

Explain that understanding an author's purpose in writing a text will help their comprehension and analysis of the piece. Help students to make the connection between Swift's experiences as a politically active writer and the form of his argument; he used his own experiences to try to effect change, not in literal public policy but in the minds of his readers.

TEACH

CRITICAL VOCABULARY

Remind students that they will make better choices for words to complete the sentences if they read all of the sentences before completing each one. Reinforce the importance of context clues in determining meaning.

Answers:

1. scrupulous
2. rudiments
3. encumbrance
4. prodigious
5. inducement
6. collateral
7. sustenance

■ English Learner Support

Use Cognates Tell students that several of the critical vocabulary words have Spanish cognates: *prodigious/prodigioso, sustenance/sustento, rudiment/rudimento, scrupulous/escrupuloso.* **ALL LEVELS**

LANGUAGE CONVENTIONS

Review the text about active and passive voice, reinforcing their main difference: In active voice, the subject is doing something, and in passive voice, the subject is being done to someone.

Read aloud the two example sentences. Discuss with students the different tone the sentences have. Do they find one sentence more interesting than another? *(Answers will vary.)*

 ANNOTATION MODEL

Remind students of the annotation ideas on page 380, which suggests underlining passages where Swift uses satirical devices and making notes about those devices. Point out that they may follow this suggestion or use their own system for marking up the selection in their write-in text. They may want to color-code their annotations by using highlighters. Their notes in the margin may include questions about ideas that are unclear or topics they want to learn more about.

380 Unit 3

 **GET READY**

CRITICAL VOCABULARY

| sustenance | rudiment | scrupulous | inducement |
| prodigious | collateral | encumbrance | |

To see how many Critical Vocabulary words you already know, use them to complete the sentences.

1. Although some governing rulers are _____ and decent, others are less so.
2. Irony, overstatement, paradox, and other devices are the _____ of satire.
3. During famine, having a large family would be a(n) _____.
4. There were a(n) _____ number of starving children in Ireland.
5. According to Swift, earning good market prices for their children would be a(n) _____ for mothers to have more of them.
6. During a famine, higher food prices are a(n) _____ effect.
7. The narrator of *A Modest Proposal* suggests that one-year-old children would provide the most satisfying _____ for those with enough money to afford the treat.

LANGUAGE CONVENTIONS

In this lesson, you will learn how to differentiate between passive and active voice. In the active voice, the subject performs the action; while in the passive voice, the subject is the receiver of the action.

Active Voice: Poor families in Ireland starved because of the ruling classes' laws.
Passive Voice: Unfair laws were voted on by the ruling classes.

As you read *A Modest Proposal*, note places where the author chooses to use active or passive voice, and how it affects the meaning of what he's saying.

ANNOTATION MODEL **NOTICE & NOTE**

As you read, note how the narrator uses satirical devices like contradiction and overstatement. In the model, you can see one reader's notes for *A Modest Proposal*.

> I think it is agreed by all parties that this <u>prodigious number of children</u> in the arms, or on the backs, or at the heels of their mothers, and frequently of their fathers, is in the present deplorable state of the kingdom a <u>very great additional grievance</u>; and therefore whoever could find out a fair, cheap, and easy method of making these children <u>sound, useful members of the commonwealth</u> would deserve so well of the public as to have <u>his statue set up</u> for a preserver of the nation.

The narrator refers to children as a "grievance," contradicting his earlier sympathetic statements.

The sentence about the statue being erected is a humorous exaggeration.

380 Unit 3

BACKGROUND

In the 1720s Catholics in Ireland suffered from the repressive rule of England, which stripped them of their rights and plunged many into poverty. Their misery increased with a series of crop failures that forced people to beg or face starvation. After his 1713 appointment as dean of St. Patrick's Cathedral in Dublin, Ireland, Jonathan Swift wrote a series of publications attacking England's unjust policies. *A Modest Proposal*, his last major work about Ireland, is one of the greatest satires ever written. For Irish Catholics and many Protestants, Swift became a national hero.

NOTICE & NOTE

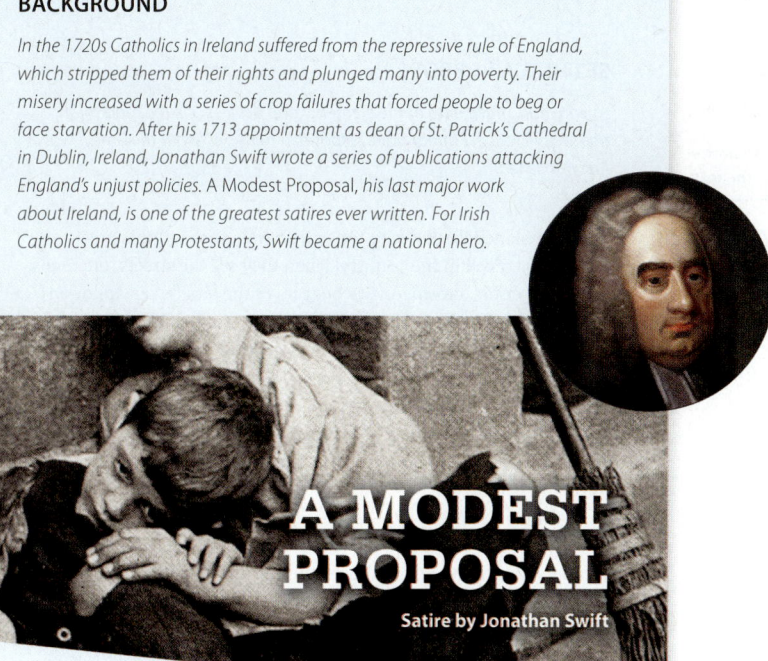

A MODEST PROPOSAL
Satire by Jonathan Swift

Jonathan Swift *(1667–1745) was born of Anglo-Irish parents in Dublin. His father died two months shy of his birth, leaving the family dependent on Swift's uncles for support. After graduating from Trinity College, Swift moved to England. He became ordained as an Anglican priest and started to write satires.*

Swift's first two satires, The Battle of the Books *and* A Tale of the Tub, *quickly established his acerbic style. Whether lampooning modern thinkers and scientists, religious abuses, or humanity in general, Swift raged at the arrogance, phoniness, and shallowness he saw infecting the intellectual and moral life of the time. Though most of his publications were anonymous, people began to recognize his witty and often harsh political writing through his contributions to London periodicals.*

Although, at first, Swift felt exiled when he returned to Ireland to become dean of St. Patrick's Cathedral, he soon regained his interest in politics and in satirical writing. His most famous work is Gulliver's Travels. *This satire is now usually appreciated as a fantasy story, but Swift's main purpose in writing it was to satirize British institutions and human follies. After his death, he was buried in St. Patrick's. Swift wrote his own epitaph for his memorial tablet, saying that he lies "where savage indignation can no longer tear his heart."*

TEACH

BACKGROUND

After students have read the Background note, go over a few significant facts about Swift's life. He was primarily the author of sharp, aggressive satires which often took the form of fantasy stories to ridicule authorities and encourage readers to think in ways that would lead to social change. Mention that his most famous book, *Gulliver's Travels*, can be enjoyed as an imaginative tale, but it had a broader political purpose: to point out the more absurd and unjust side of human nature and to ridicule the social structures he saw around him. *A Modest Proposal* makes an outrageous recommendation to suggest that the government itself is being outrageous in prioritizing economic well-being over social well-being.

CLOSE READ SCREENCAST

Modeled Discussion Have students click the *Close Read* icon in their eBooks to access a screencast in which readers discuss and annotate the following key passages:

- development of the narrator's persona (paragraph 4)
- one of the reasons in favor of the proposal (paragraph 24)

As a class, view and discuss this video. Then, have students pair up to do an independent close read of an additional passage—the narrator's final plea to readers (paragraph 32). Students can record their answers on the Close Read Practice PDF.

 Close Read Practice PDF

TEACH

SETTING A PURPOSE

Direct students to use the Setting a Purpose prompt to focus their reading.

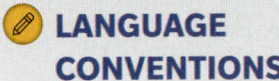

LANGUAGE CONVENTIONS

Remind students that active voice is used when a subject is doing something, and passive voice is when something is being done to the subject. To help students understand the difference, use these sentence frames: [name] ____ is eating ____ [food] ____ (active voice) and [food] ____ is/are being ____ [eaten] ____ by ____ [name] ____ (passive voice).
(**Answer:** *The use of passive voice at the beginning of the essay helps to establish the formal, detached tone of the narrator.*)

ENGLISH LEARNER SUPPORT

Draw Inferences Guide students to make inferences about Swift's attitude toward the Irish government, based on the information presented. Remind them that when they make inferences, they look at all the information an author presents and then make a decision supported by that information. **MODERATE**

UNDERSTAND AUTHOR'S PURPOSE

Remind students that the **author's purpose** is the primary reason the author wrote a text. (**Answer:** *The comparison underscores Swift's point that the poor are treated no better than animals.*)

CRITICAL VOCABULARY

sustenance: If the people of Ireland have little *sustenance*, this means they have little food.

ASK STUDENTS what foods they consider to be the most basic forms of sustenance.

prodigious: The *prodigious* numbers of children in Ireland caused government authorities a great deal of economic concern at the time the essay was written.

ASK STUDENTS when was the last time they saw a prodigious number of people.

 **NOTICE & NOTE**

Notice & Note
Use the side margins to notice and note signposts in the text.

LANGUAGE CONVENTIONS
Annotate: Mark an example of passive voice in the second sentence.
Analyze: Why might Swift have chosen to use passive voice here?

sustenance
(sŭs′tə-nəns) *n.* something, especially food, that sustains life or health.

prodigious
(prə-dĭj′əs) *adj.* enormous.

UNDERSTAND AUTHOR'S PURPOSE
Annotate: In paragraph 4, mark the sentence where the narrator compares mothers and their children to farm animals.
Analyze: How does this comparison serve the author's purpose?

SETTING A PURPOSE

As you read, make note of the elements and devices of satire and think about how readers might have responded to this essay at the time it was first published.

1. It is a melancholy object to those who walk through this great town[1] or travel in the country, when they see the streets, the roads, and cabin doors, crowded with beggars of the female sex, followed by three, four, or six children, all in rags and importuning[2] every passenger for an alms. These mothers, instead of being able to work for their honest livelihood, are forced to employ all their time in strolling to beg **sustenance** for their helpless infants, who, as they grow up, either turn thieves for want[3] of work, or leave their dear native country to fight for the Pretender[4] in Spain, or sell themselves to the Barbadoes.[5]

2. I think it is agreed by all parties that this **prodigious** number of children in the arms, or on the backs, or at the heels of their mothers, and frequently of their fathers, is in the present deplorable state of the kingdom a very great additional grievance; and therefore whoever could find out a fair, cheap, and easy method of making these children sound, useful members of the commonwealth would deserve so well of the public as to have his statue set up for a preserver of the nation.

3. But my intention is very far from being confined to provide only for the children of professed beggars; it is of a much greater extent, and shall take in the whole number of infants at a certain age who are born of parents in effect as little able to support them as those who demand our charity in the streets.

4. As to my own part, having turned my thoughts for many years upon this important subject, and maturely weighed the several schemes of other projectors,[6] I have always found them grossly mistaken in their computation. It is true, a child just dropped from its

---
[1] **this great town:** Dublin, Ireland.
[2] **importuning** (ĭm-pôr-to͞on′ĭng) ... **alms** (ämz): begging from every passerby for a charitable handout.
[3] **want:** lack; need.
[4] **Pretender:** James Edward Stuart, who claimed the English throne, from which his now deceased father, James II, had been removed in 1688. Because James II and his son were Catholic, the common people of Ireland were loyal to them.
[5] **sell ... Barbadoes:** To escape poverty, some Irish migrated to the West Indies, obtaining money for their passage by agreeing to work as slaves on plantations there for a set period.
[6] **projectors:** persons who propose public projects or plans.

382 Unit 3

 ENGLISH LEARNER SUPPORT

Explore Connotations Explain to students the connotation of the phrase *in rags*. Start by asking students what rags are, what they look like, and how they get that way. Then, discuss why someone might wear clothes that look like rags. Lead students to the understanding that the connotation of the phrase is *great poverty, their clothes are worn to shreds and they must beg for every last ounce of food*. For instance, you might also say, "I felt so ragged after the trip was over," meaning you felt exhausted. This is the mood Swift is trying to create with the use of this phrase. **ALL LEVELS**

dam[7] may be supported by her milk for a solar year, with little other nourishment; at most not above the value of two shillings, which the mother may certainly get, or the value in scraps, by her lawful occupation of begging; and it is exactly at one year old that I propose to provide for them in such a manner as instead of being a charge upon their parents or the parish, or wanting food and raiment for the rest of their lives, they shall on the contrary contribute to the feeding, and partly to the clothing, of many thousands.

5   There is likewise another great advantage in my scheme, that it will prevent those voluntary abortions, and that horrid practice of women murdering their bastard children, alas, too frequent among us, sacrificing the poor innocent babes, I doubt,[8] more to avoid the expense than the shame, which would move tears and pity in the most savage and inhuman breast.

6   The number of souls in this kingdom being usually reckoned one million and a half, of these I calculate there may be about two hundred thousand couples whose wives are breeders; from which number I subtract thirty thousand couples who are able to maintain their own children, although I apprehend there cannot be so many under the present distresses of the kingdom; but this being granted, there will remain an hundred and seventy thousand breeders. I again subtract fifty thousand for those women who miscarry, or whose children die by accident or disease within the year. There only remain an hundred and twenty thousand children of poor parents annually born. The question therefore is, how this number shall be reared and provided for, which, as I have already said, under the present situation of affairs, is utterly impossible by all the methods hitherto proposed. For we can neither employ them in handicraft or agriculture; we neither build houses (I mean in the country) nor cultivate land. They can very seldom pick up a livelihood by stealing till they arrive at six years old, except where they are of towardly parts;[9] although I confess they learn the **rudiments** much earlier, during which time they can however be looked upon only as probationers, as I have been informed by a principal gentleman in the county of Cavan, who protested to me that he never knew above one or two instances under the age of six, even in a part of the kingdom so renowned for the quickest proficiency in that art.

---

[7] **dam** (dăm): female parent. The term is used mostly for farm animals.
[8] **doubt:** suspect.
[9] **are of towardly** (tôrd´lē) **parts:** have a promising talent.

UNDERSTAND AUTHOR'S PURPOSE
Analyze: In paragraph 6, mark each number from the narrator's calculations.

Infer: Why would Swift include these calculations in his essay?

rudiment:
(ro͞o´də-mənt) *n.* fundamental element, principle, or skill.

A Modest Proposal   383

TEACH

✏ UNDERSTAND AUTHOR'S PURPOSE

Explain to students that the author's purpose can be determined by looking at the stylistic and content decisions the author has made and by determining the reasons behind them. Have students look for the numbers the narrator lists, explaining that the numbers are written out, and mark them. (**Answer:** *Swift includes the numbers to show the enormity of the problem facing Ireland, which his narrator will exploit to advance his argument.*)

WHEN STUDENTS STRUGGLE . . .

Analyze Types of Literature Remind students this is a satire. Explain the basic qualities that make it a satire, and then fill out the graphic organizer as a class for clarification.

A Modest Proposal **is a satire because . . .**

_____
_____

📖 For additional support, go to the **Reading Studio** and assign the following 🎬 **Level Up tutorial: Prose Forms.**

CRITICAL VOCABULARY

rudiment: The writer uses the word *rudiment* here to describe the most basic points of being a thief, which is to suggest the children are dishonest from a very young age.

ASK STUDENTS what might be the rudiments of being a thief or pickpocket. (*Possible answers could include being sneaky, being observant, or learning how to move quickly.*)

A Modest Proposal   **383**

TEACH

UNDERSTAND AUTHOR'S PURPOSE

Explain to students that Swift is making a parallel between the children in Ireland and cattle you might cut up to eat by mentioning all their different body parts. (**Answer:** *Swift wanted to shock his readers and also probably make them feel uncomfortable because these gruesome details are funny.*)

■ English Learner Support

Draw Inferences about Author's Purpose Explain to students what a satire is. Discuss the fact that first, a satire makes fun of something. Then, explain there might be different reasons to make fun of something. In this case, a person writes a satire to change someone's opinion on a subject, usually through techniques like humor or exaggeration. Discuss the different forms of humor with students, for reinforcement. Then, remind them that the selection is a satire, and that it has a definite purpose. Brainstorm with students what some of those purposes might be, then draw a two-box cause-and-effect chart on the board, with boxes connected by arrows. Have students determine the purpose of the selection and what the desired result will be. **LIGHT**

For **listening and speaking support** for students at varying proficiency levels, see the **Text X-Ray** on page 378C–D.

 **NOTICE & NOTE**

7   I am assured by our merchants that a boy or girl before twelve years old is no salable commodity; and even when they come to this age they will not yield above three pounds, or three pounds and half a crown at most on the Exchange; which cannot turn to account[10] either to the parents or the kingdom, the charge of nutriment and rags having been at least four times that value.

8   I shall now therefore humbly propose my own thoughts, which I hope will not be liable to the least objection.

9   I have been assured by a very knowing American of my acquaintance in London, that a young healthy child well nursed is at a year old a most delicious, nourishing, and wholesome food, whether stewed, roasted, baked, or boiled; and I make no doubt that it will equally serve in a fricassee[11] or a ragout.

UNDERSTAND AUTHOR'S PURPOSE

Annotate: In paragraph 10, mark words and phrases normally used to describe the preparation of meat.

Draw Conclusions: What effects do you think Swift wanted to have on readers by including these details?

10   I do therefore humbly offer it to public consideration that of the hundred and twenty thousand children, already computed, twenty thousand may be reserved for breed,[12] whereof only one fourth part to be males, which is more than we allow to sheep, black cattle, or swine; and my reason is that these children are seldom the fruits of marriage, a circumstance not much regarded by our savages, therefore one male will be sufficient to serve four females. That the remaining hundred thousand may at a year old be offered in sale to the persons of quality and fortune through the kingdom, always advising the mother to let them suck plentifully in the last month, so as to render them plump and fat for a good table. A child will make two <u>dishes</u> at an entertainment for friends; and when the family dines alone, the <u>fore or hind quarter</u> will make a reasonable dish, and seasoned with a <u>little pepper or salt</u> will be very good <u>boiled</u> on the fourth day, especially in winter.

11   I have reckoned upon a medium that a child just born will weigh twelve pounds, and in a solar year if tolerably nursed increaseth to twenty-eight pounds.

12   I grant this food will be somewhat dear, and therefore very proper for landlords, who, as they have already devoured most of the parents, seem to have the best title to the children.

13   Infant's flesh will be in season throughout the year, but more plentiful in March, and a little before and after. For we are told by a grave author, an eminent French physician,[13] that fish being a prolific[14] diet, there are more children born in Roman Catholic countries about nine months after Lent[15] than at any other season;

---

[10] **turn to account:** earn a profit; benefit; prove useful.
[11] **fricassee** (frĭk′ə-sē′) . . . **ragout** (ră-gōō′): types of meat stews.
[12] **reserved for breed:** kept for breeding (instead of being slaughtered).
[13] **grave . . . physician:** François Rabelais (răb′ə-lā), a 16th-century French satirist.
[14] **prolific:** promoting fertility.
[15] **Lent:** Catholics traditionally do not eat meat during Lent, the 40 days leading up to Easter, but instead eat a lot of fish.

384   Unit 3

APPLYING ACADEMIC VOCABULARY

☐ encounter   ☑ exploit   ☐ persist   ☐ subordinate   ☑ widespread

Write and Discuss Have students work with a partner to discuss the following questions. Guide students to include the academic vocabulary words *exploit* and *widespread* in their responses. Ask volunteers to share their responses with the class.

- In Swift's view, how do some people feel the poor **exploit** the public?
- How **widespread** does Swift suggest poverty is at the time of the essay's writing?

NOTICE & NOTE

therefore, reckoning a year after Lent, the markets will be more glutted than usual, because the number of popish infants is at least three to one in this kingdom; and therefore it will have one other **collateral** advantage, by lessening the number of Papists[16] among us.

14   I have already computed the charge of nursing a beggar's child (in which list I reckon all cottagers, laborers, and four fifths of the farmers), to be about two shillings per annum, rags included; and I believe no gentleman would repine to give ten shillings for the carcass of a good fat child, which, as I have said, will make four dishes of excellent nutritive meat, when he hath only some particular friend or his own family to dine with him. Thus the squire will learn to be a good landlord, and grow popular among the tenants; the mother will have eight shillings net profit, and be fit for work till she produces another child.

15   Those who are more thrifty (as I must confess the times require) may flay the carcass; the skin of which artificially dressed will make admirable gloves for ladies, and summer boots for fine gentlemen.

16   As to our city of Dublin, shambles[17] may be appointed for this purpose in the most convenient parts of it, and butchers we may be assured will not be wanting; although I rather recommend buying the children alive, and dressing them hot from the knife as we do roasting pigs.

17   A very worthy person, a true lover of his country, and whose virtues I highly esteem, was lately pleased in discoursing on this matter to offer a refinement upon my scheme. He said that many gentlemen of this kingdom, having of late destroyed their deer, he conceived that the want of venison might be well supplied by the bodies of young lads and maidens, not exceeding fourteen years of age nor under twelve, so great a number of both sexes in every county being now ready to starve for want of work and service; and these to be disposed of by their parents, if alive, or otherwise by their nearest relations. But with due deference to so excellent a friend and so deserving a patriot, I cannot be altogether in his sentiments; for as to the males, my American acquaintance assured me from frequent experience that their flesh was generally tough and lean, like that of our schoolboys, by continual exercise, and their taste disagreeable; and to fatten them would not answer the charge. Then as to the females, it would, I think with humble submission, be a loss to the public, because they soon would become breeders themselves; and

---

[16] **popish** (pō´pĭsh) . . . **Papists:** hostile or contemptuous terms referring to Roman Catholics.
[17] **shambles:** slaughterhouses.

collateral
(kə-lăt´ər-əl) *adj.* concomitant or accompanying.

ANALYZE SATIRICAL DEVICES
Annotate: In paragraph 17, mark the words and phrases the narrator uses to describe the man who suggested a change to the proposal.

Identify: What satirical device is Swift using in these descriptions?

A Modest Proposal   385

TEACH

 ANALYZE SATIRICAL DEVICES

Explain that when writers seem to go overboard in the excessive words they use, sometimes they intend to say the opposite of what they seem to be saying. Make the point that in a satire, the author's point of view has to be considered very carefully. (**Answer:** *Swift is using irony; he means the opposite of what he says.*)

> **EL ENGLISH LEARNER SUPPORT**
>
> **Expand Vocabulary** Draw students' attention to the discussion of how exaggeration is often done for effect. Review with students the difference between the words *effect* and *affect,* indicating that an *effect* is a change made by one thing to another, while the word *affect* is a verb describing the making of such a change.
> **MODERATE**

 For **reading support** for students at varying proficiency levels, see the **Text X-Ray** on page 378D.

TO CHALLENGE STUDENTS . . .

Write a Satire Video Discuss with students issues they consider to be significant in their school and which require change of some sort. Have students work in small groups to write scripts for their own short satire videos in which they address these issues. Encourage the students to be humorous in their approaches, if they feel that would be more effective.

CRITICAL VOCABULARY

collateral: The word *collateral* is used here to describe something that comes as a result of something else, as a sort of secondary result. In this case, eating children is shown to not only reduce the general population but to reduce the number of Roman Catholics.

ASK STUDENTS what other collateral effects of following Swift's plan might be. (*Possible answers could include more living space for city inhabitants or fewer beggars in the city streets.*)

A Modest Proposal   **385**

TEACH

ENGLISH LEARNER SUPPORT

Analyze Illustrations Have students look at the illustration. Discuss with them what the picture shows and what it is meant to represent. Have students work in pairs to find three to five words words in the text that describe the picture. Then, have them write descriptions of the picture, or say the descriptions aloud for the class, using these words. **MODERATE**

 NOTICE & NOTE

IMPROVE READING FLUENCY

Targeted Passage Have students work in pairs to read the previous page aloud. First, use paragraph 16 to model how to read informational text. Have students follow along in their books as you read the text with appropriate phrasing and emphasis. Then, have partners take turns reading aloud the following paragraphs. You could have students' alternate sentences, given their length. Encourage students to provide feedback and support as they read the sentences, noting that semicolons and commas are places for natural pauses. Remind students that when they are reading aloud for an audience, they should pace their reading and read expressively, so listeners can understand difficult concepts.

 Go to the **Reading Studio** for additional support in developing fluency.

besides, it is not improbable that some **scrupulous** people might be apt to censure such a practice (although indeed very unjustly) as a little bordering upon cruelty; which, I confess, hath always been with me the strongest objection against any project, how well soever intended.

18   But in order to justify my friend, he confessed that this expedient was put into his head by the famous Psalmanazar, a native of the island Formosa,[18] who came from thence to London above twenty years ago, and in conversation told my friend that in his country when any young person happened to be put to death, the executioner sold the carcass to persons of quality as a prime dainty; and that in his time the body of a plump girl of fifteen, who was crucified for an attempt to poison the emperor, was sold to his Imperial Majesty's prime minister of state, and other great mandarins of the court, in joints from the gibbet,[19] at four hundred crowns. Neither indeed can I deny that if the same use were made of several plump young girls in this town, who without one single groat[20] to their fortunes cannot stir abroad without a chair,[21] and appear at the playhouse and assemblies in foreign fineries which they never will pay for, the kingdom would not be the worse.

19   Some persons of a desponding spirit are in great concern about that vast number of poor people who are aged, diseased, or maimed, and I have been desired to employ my thoughts what course may be taken to ease the nation of so grievous an **encumbrance**. But I am not in the least pain upon that matter, because it is very well known that they are every day dying and rotting by cold and famine, and filth and vermin, as fast as can be reasonably expected. And as to the younger laborers, they are now in almost as hopeful a condition. They cannot get work, and consequently pine away for want of nourishment to a degree that if at any time they are accidentally hired to common labor, they have not strength to perform it; and thus the country and themselves are happily delivered from the evils to come.

20   I have too long digressed, and therefore shall return to my subject. I think the advantages by the proposal which I have made are obvious and many, as well as of the highest importance.

21   For first, as I have already observed, it would greatly lessen the number of Papists, with whom we are yearly overrun, being the principal breeders of the nation as well as our most dangerous enemies; and who stay at home on purpose to deliver the kingdom

---

[18] **Psalmanazar** (săl′mə-nă′zər) . . . **Formosa** (fôr-mō′sə): a French imposter in London who called himself George Psalmanazar and pretended to be from Formosa (now Taiwan), where, he said, cannibalism was practiced.
[19] **gibbet** (jĭb′ĭt): gallows.
[20] **groat:** an old British coin worth four pennies.
[21] **cannot stir . . . chair:** cannot go outside without using an enclosed chair carried on poles by two men.

NOTICE & NOTE

scrupulous
(skrōō′pyə-ləs) *adj.* conscientious and exact; having scruples.

encumbrance
(ĕn-kŭm′brəns) *n.* a burden or impediment.

ANALYZE SATIRICAL DEVICES
Annotate: In paragraph 19, mark the example of verbal irony.

Infer: What is ironic about the narrator saying that he is not pained about the fact that so many people are dying?

TEACH

ANALYZE SATIRICAL DEVICES

Explain to students that verbal irony occurs when a speaker or character says one thing, but the author means the opposite. (**Answer:** *The narrator's statement that he is happy so many people are dying is verbally ironic because Swift himself is clearly not happy about it, which is why he wrote the essay in the first place.*)

CRITICAL VOCABULARY

scrupulous: The author uses the word *scrupulous* here to describe people who would have moral principles and would object to eating children as a means to solve the problems of overpopulation.

ASK STUDENTS what qualities a person might have that would cause someone to call them *scrupulous*. (*Answers might include goodness, kindness, a desire to help other people, and concern for others' safety.*)

encumbrance: The word *encumbrance* is used here to describe the responsibility that poor people who are ill place on the government and on those more fortunate than they are.

ASK STUDENTS if there are parts of their daily lives that they consider to be encumbrances. (*Answers may vary but could include chores or other similar tasks.*)

ENGLISH LEARNER SUPPORT

Identify Relative Clauses Read this sentence to students: "I think the advantages by the proposal which I have made are obvious and many, as well as of the highest importance." Explain to students that the phrase "which I have made" is a relative clause, describing the proposal the speaker has made; also explain that people add phrases such as these to their sentences to make their meanings clearer. Have students fill out a two-column chart. In the left column, have students write the words "which," "where," and "how"; in the right column, have students write phrases formed with these words. **LIGHT**

TEACH

CONTRASTS AND CONTRADICTIONS

Discuss with students the fact that these signposts often cue places in the text where they should notice a compare-and-contrast structure, in which the similarities and differences of two different elements or positions are highlighted. The signpost may also signal contradictions. (**Answer:** *One would not expect people considered "fine gentlemen" to view human flesh as high cuisine, and yet the speaker suggests this would be a possibility.*)

CRITICAL VOCABULARY

inducement: The word *inducement* is used here to mean a point of persuasion; Swift suggests that the idea of being able to market children as food would make the prospect of marrying and having children more appealing.

ASK STUDENTS what other things might possibly serve as inducements to marriage. (*Answers might include love, the need for companionship, or a desire for stability.*)

NOTICE & NOTE

to the Pretender, hoping to take their advantage by the absence of so many good Protestants, who have chosen rather to leave their country than stay at home and pay tithes against their conscience to an Episcopal curate.[22]

22 Secondly, the poorer tenants will have something valuable of their own, which by law may be made liable to distress,[23] and help to pay their landlord's rent, their corn and cattle being already seized and money a thing unknown.

23 Thirdly, whereas the maintenance of an hundred thousand children, from two years old and upwards, cannot be computed at less than ten shillings a piece per annum, the nation's stock will be thereby increased fifty thousand pounds per annum, besides the profit of a new dish introduced to the tables of all gentlemen of fortune in the kingdom who have any refinement in taste. And the money will circulate among ourselves, the goods being entirely of our own growth and manufacture.

24 Fourthly, the constant breeders, besides the gain of eight shillings sterling per annum by the sale of their children, will be rid of the charge of maintaining them after the first year.

25 Fifthly, this food would likewise bring great custom to taverns, where the vintners will certainly be so prudent as to <u>procure the best receipts</u>[24] <u>for dressing it to perfection</u>, and consequently <u>have their houses frequented by all the fine gentlemen</u>, who justly value themselves upon their knowledge in good eating; and a skillful cook, who understands how to oblige his guests, <u>will contrive to make it as expensive as they please</u>.

26 Sixthly, this would be a great **inducement** to marriage, which all wise nations have either encouraged by rewards or enforced by laws and penalties. It would increase the care and tenderness of mothers toward their children, when they were sure of a settlement for life to the poor babes, provided in some sort by the public, to their annual profit instead of expense. We should see an honest emulation among the married women, which of them could bring the fattest child to the market. Men would become as fond of their wives during the time of their pregnancy as they are now of their mares in foal, their cows in calf, or sows when they are ready to farrow; nor offer to beat or kick them (as is too frequent a practice) for fear of a miscarriage.

27 Many other advantages might be enumerated. For instance, the addition of some thousand carcasses in our exportation of barreled beef, the propagation of swine's flesh, and improvement in the art

> **CONTRASTS AND CONTRADICTIONS**
>
> **Notice & Note:** Mark phrases in paragraph 25 that describe how the narrator expects people to take advantage of his proposal.
>
> **Analyze:** How do these details contradict your sense of the way any normal person would react to such a practice?

inducement
(ĭn-do͞os′mənt, -dyo͞os′-) *n.*
an incentive.

---

[22] **Protestants . . . curate** (kyo͝or′ĭt): Swift is criticizing absentee Anglo-Irish landowners who lived—and spent their income from their property—in England.
[23] **distress:** seizure of a person's property for the payment of debts.
[24] **receipts:** recipes.

APPLYING ACADEMIC VOCABULARY

☑ encounter ☐ exploit ☑ persist ☑ subordinate ☐ widespread

Write and Discuss Have students work with a partner to discuss the following questions. Guide students to include the academic vocabulary words *encounter, persist,* and *subordinate* in their responses. Ask volunteers to share their responses with the class.

- What might Swift's reactions be when he **encounters** a beggar?
- Why might the problem of poverty **persist** in Ireland?
- In what sense are the lower classes **subordinate** to the upper classes in this selection?

of making good bacon, so much wanted among us by the great destruction of pigs, too frequent at our tables, which are no way comparable in taste or magnificence to a well-grown, fat, yearling child, which roasted whole will make a considerable figure at a lord mayor's feast or any other public entertainment. But this and many others I omit, being studious of brevity.

28   Supposing that one thousand families in this city would be constant customers for infants' flesh, besides others who might have it at merry meetings, particularly weddings and christenings, I compute that Dublin would take off annually about twenty thousand carcasses, and the rest of the kingdom (where probably they will be sold somewhat cheaper) the remaining eighty thousand.

29   I can think of no one objection that will possibly be raised against this proposal, unless it should be urged that the number of people will be thereby much lessened in the kingdom. This I freely own, and it was indeed one principal design in offering it to the world. I desire the reader will observe, that I calculate my remedy for this one individual kingdom of Ireland and for no other that ever was, is, or I think ever can be upon earth. Therefore let no man talk to me of other expedients: *of taxing our absentees at five shillings a pound: of using neither clothes nor household furniture except what is of our own growth and manufacture: of utterly rejecting the materials and instruments that promote foreign luxury: of curing the expensiveness of pride, vanity, idleness, and gaming in our women: of introducing a vein of parsimony,[25] prudence, and temperance: of learning to love our country, in the want of which we differ even from Laplanders and the inhabitants of Topinamboo:[26] of quitting our animosities and factions, nor acting any longer like the Jews, who were murdering one another at the very moment their city was taken:[27] of being a little cautious not to sell our country and conscience for nothing: of teaching landlords to have at least one degree of mercy toward their tenants: lastly, of putting a spirit of honesty, industry, and skill into our shopkeepers; who, if a resolution could now be taken to buy only our native goods, would immediately unite to cheat and exact upon us in the price, the measure, and the goodness, nor could ever yet be brought to make one fair proposal of just dealing, though often and earnestly invited to it.*

---

[25] **parsimony** (pär´sə-mō-nē): frugality; thrift.
[26] **Topinamboo** (tŏp ĭ-năm´bōō): an area in Brazil supposedly inhabited by wild savages.
[27] **Jews . . . taken:** In AD 70, during a Jewish revolt against Roman rule, the inhabitants of Jerusalem, by fighting among themselves, made it easier for the Romans to capture the city.

TEACH

✏️ UNDERSTAND AUTHOR'S PURPOSE

Explain to students that when Swift uses the word *expedients*, he is referring to raising taxes and other similar, more humane responses to the problems Ireland is facing with its population. Have them underline the words that explain the narrator's dismissal of these ideas. (**Answer:** *Swift is making the point that approaching solutions to problems with mere expediency in mind can be very dangerous since the idea of eating the children is, in a sense, more expedient than any other possible solution and yet it is savage.*)

✏️ ANALYZE SATIRICAL DEVICES

Explain to students that Swift is introducing a paradox in this paragraph. The first step to understanding the paradox is to understand the question Swift's narrator is asking those who disagree with him. Have the students mark the sentences that show that question. (**Answer:** *The question is paradoxical because it is no more practical to make the proposal the narrator has made than it is to do the opposite; neither solution does anything to put clothes on people who have none.*)

NOTICE & NOTE

UNDERSTAND AUTHOR'S PURPOSE
Annotate: Underline the statement in paragraph 30 that explains why the narrator dismisses the "expedients" listed in the previous paragraph.

Draw Conclusions: What point does Swift make in describing his own proposals in these paragraphs?

ANALYZE SATIRICAL DEVICES
Annotate: In paragraph 32, mark the question the narrator suggests that people who object to his proposal should ask.

Analyze: What is paradoxical about this question?

---

30   Therefore I repeat, let no man talk to me of these and the like expedients,[28] till he hath at least some glimpse of hope that there will ever be some hearty and sincere attempt to put them in practice.

31   But as to myself, having been wearied out for many years with offering vain, idle, visionary thoughts, and at length utterly despairing of success, I fortunately fell upon this proposal, which, as it is wholly new, so it hath something solid and real, of no expense and little trouble, full in our own power, and whereby we can incur no danger in disobliging England. For this kind of commodity will not bear exportation, the flesh being of too tender a consistence to admit a long continuance in salt, although perhaps I could name a country which would be glad to eat up our whole nation without it.

32   After all, I am not so violently bent upon my own opinion as to reject any offer proposed by wise men, which shall be found equally innocent, cheap, easy, and effectual. But before something of that kind shall be advanced in contradiction to my scheme, and offering a better, I desire the author or authors will be pleased maturely to consider two points. First, as things now stand, how they will be able to find food and raiment for an hundred thousand useless mouths and backs. And secondly, there being a round million of creatures in human figure throughout this kingdom, whose sole subsistence put into a common stock[29] would leave them in debt two millions of pounds sterling, adding those who are beggars by profession to the bulk of farmers, cottagers, and laborers, with their wives and children who are beggars in effect; I desire those politicians who dislike my overture, and may perhaps be so bold to attempt an answer, that they will first ask the parents of these mortals whether they would not at this day think it a great happiness to have been sold for food at a year old in the manner I prescribe, and thereby have avoided such a perpetual scene of misfortunes as they have since gone through by the oppression of landlords, the impossibility of paying rent without money or trade, the want of common sustenance, with neither house nor clothes to cover them from the inclemencies of the weather, and the most inevitable prospect of entailing the like or greater miseries upon their breed forever.

33   I profess, in the sincerity of my heart, that I have not the least personal interest in endeavoring to promote this necessary work, having no other motive than the public good of my country, by advancing our trade, providing for infants, relieving the poor, and giving some pleasure to the rich. I have no children by which I can propose to get a single penny; the youngest being nine years old, and my wife past childbearing.

---

[28] **let no man . . . expedients:** Swift had written pamphlets in support of these proposals, but his efforts were unsuccessful.
[29] **common stock:** ordinary stock in a company or business venture.

 ENGLISH LEARNER SUPPORT

Evaluate Complex Word Structures   Read this sentence from paragraph 33 to students: "I profess, in the sincerity of my heart, that I have not the least personal interest in endeavoring to promote this necessary work, having no other motive than the public good of my country, by advancing our trade, providing for infants, relieving the poor, and giving some pleasure to the rich." Explain to students that the sentence contains numerous gerunds, which are forms of verbs ending in –*ing*. First, have students find all the gerunds in the sentence. Then, have them work in pairs to fill out a two-column table. Write the gerunds in the sentence in the left column. Write the roots of each gerund in the right column. Have students discuss what letters, if any, were deleted to change the root into a gerund.   **MODERATE**

NOTICE & NOTE

CHECK YOUR UNDERSTANDING

Answer these questions before moving on to the **Analyze the Text** section on the following page.

1. The narrator's proposal for easing poverty in Ireland is to —
   A eat disadvantaged children
   B put disadvantaged children to work
   C raise taxes to pay for social services
   D ration children's food

2. According to Swift's narrator, the proposal will benefit Irish parents by —
   F allowing them to eat their children if necessary
   G saving them the difficulties of parenting
   H turning mouths to feed into valuable property
   J encouraging them to have more children

3. Which idea does the narrator dismiss as impractical?
   A Preparing stews from children's flesh
   B Making gloves from the skin of children
   C Greatly reducing Ireland's population
   D Selling adolescents for food

A Modest Proposal 391

TEACH

CHECK YOUR UNDERSTANDING

Have students answer the questions independently.

Answers:

1. A
2. H
3. D

If they answer any questions incorrectly, have them reread the text to confirm their understanding. Then they may proceed to ANALYZE THE TEXT on page 392.

ENGLISH LEARNER SUPPORT

Oral Assessment Use the following questions to assess students' comprehension and speaking skills.

1. What does the narrator say people should do to make less poverty in Ireland? *(eat their young.)*

2. Who will benefit by turning mouths to feed into valuable property? *(Irish parents)*

3. Selling adolescents for food is a ___ idea. *(bad)* **MODERATE**

A Modest Proposal **391**

APPLY

ANALYZE THE TEXT

Possible answers:

1. **DOK 3:** *Answers may vary.*

2. **DOK 4:** *Understatement: "some scrupulous people might be apt to censure such as practice . . . as a little bordering on cruelty" (17); exaggeration: "they are every day dying and rotting by cold and famine, and filth and vermin, as fast as can be reasonably expected" (19). These devices draw attention to the callous attitude toward the Irish poor by rich landlords and the English government.*

3. **DOK 4:** *The digression enables the narrator to describe in detail the actual living conditions of the poor in Ireland, thus clarifying the great gulf between the rich and the impoverished there.*

4. **DOK 4:** *Swift's distaste for purely scientific reasoning is shown here by the fact that the solution the narrator proposes is, on the surface, a reasonable one according to scientific principles; in reality, however, it is grotesque.*

5. **DOK 2:** *Answers may vary but could suggest that the contradictions call the plight of the poor into relief, given the extreme measures that seem to be necessary to solve the problem.*

RESEARCH

Remind students that when they search for information on the Internet, they should make sure information sources are solid and credible before using them.

Extend Discuss with students the ways satires attempt to change the minds of their readers through criticism and commentary. Then, have them work in pairs to discuss the effectiveness of this satire. When they research Swift's other work, remind them that the full texts of most of Swift's works should be available online.

RESPOND

ANALYZE THE TEXT

Support your responses with evidence from the text. 📓 NOTEBOOK

1. **Evaluate** Is Swift's parody of an argument an effective way to achieve his purpose? Explain why or why not.

2. **Analyze** Identify examples of understatement and exaggeration in paragraphs 17 and 19. What effect do these satirical devices have on the reader?

3. **Analyze** Swift's narrator says that he has "digressed" in paragraph 20. Explain how this digression actually serves his purpose of exposing injustice.

4. **Connect** The period from the late 1600s through the 1700s is known as the Enlightenment, a time when many writers promoted scientific reasoning as a means of solving social problems. Swift was often critical of such writers. How is this attitude reflected in *A Modest Proposal*?

5. **Notice & Note** Review the many contrasts and contradictions between accepted behavior and Swift's "modest proposal." Do you think these stark contrasts and contradictions make the satire more powerful? Why or why not?

RESEARCH

RESEARCH TIP
When using the Internet to search for information about a historical event, make sure to use only reliable sources, such as those ending .edu. Academic institutions are less likely to have an agenda—and more likely to be reliable—than commercial sites.

Swift offers his proposal as a consideration for easing the suffering of those living in Ireland under England's rule. With a partner, research what life was like in Ireland during the 18th century. Use what you learn to answer these questions.

QUESTION	ANSWER
What living conditions did most Irish people experience during English rule in this period?	*Answers will vary depending on research results but should indicate that they had poor, dirty living conditions.*
How did English policies harm the Irish people?	*Answers will vary but should indicate that individuals were taxed too highly and there were no provisions in place for the poor.*

Extend Swift presented this proposal in the form of Juvenalian satire to strengthen his message about the suffering in Ireland. With a partner, discuss how this reinforced the points he was trying to make. Then study another work by Swift to determine whether he uses the same type of satire in that text.

LEARNING MINDSET

Try Again Discuss how complex the purpose of this satire is. Explain that readers may not understand every part of the satire after reading it. If that is the case, reassure students that it is okay to go back and read it a second time. Students should also be encouraged to ask questions if there is something they still don't understand.

CREATE AND DISCUSS

Write a Satirical Essay Write a short satirical essay that addresses a problem in your school or community. Before you begin drafting, review your notes and analysis of Swift's use of satirical devices such as irony and exaggeration. Then, model your essay on his style.

- ❏ Identify a problem or behavior that will be the target of your satire.
- ❏ Think of a solution to the problem or a way to reform the behavior.
- ❏ Draft your essay using satirical devices to show the problem or behavior in a critical light.

Discuss the Satirical Essay Now that you have written your own satirical essay, discuss the process with a partner.

- ❏ Take turns sharing your essays.
- ❏ Evaluate your partner's use of satirical devices and the strength of the argument.
- ❏ Offer constructive suggestions on ways your partner could polish the essay to make it more effective.

RESPOND TO THE ESSENTIAL QUESTION

How can satire change people's behavior?

Gather Information Review your annotations and notes on *A Modest Proposal*. Then, add relevant information to your Response Log. As you determine which information to include, think about:

- current examples of the use of satire to change people's behavior
- satirical devices used in the examples you identified
- whether these satires caused a change in your behavior or in the behavior of others

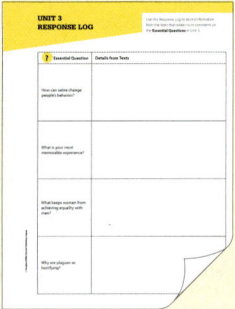

RESPOND

Go to the **Writing Studio** to find out more about writing as a process.

Go to the **Speaking and Listening Studio** to find out more about participating in collaborative discussions.

ACADEMIC VOCABULARY

As you write and discuss what you learned from the satirical essay, be sure to use the Academic Vocabulary words. Check off each of the words that you use.

- ❏ encounter
- ❏ exploit
- ❏ persist
- ❏ subordinate
- ❏ widespread

A Modest Proposal 393

APPLY

CREATE AND DISCUSS

Write a Satirical Essay Indicate to students that the bulleted list on page 393 could help them shape their draft of their satire. The first bullet could be the introduction, and the second and third bullets could help form the body.

 For **writing support** for students at varying proficiency levels, see the **Text X-Ray** on page 378D.

Discuss the Satirical Essay Remind students that when they are commenting on other students' essays, they have to make sure their comments are constructive. This means the comments have to be intended to be helpful for the satire, and not merely critical.

RESPOND TO THE ESSENTIAL QUESTION

Allow time for students to add details from *A Modest Proposal* to their Unit 3 Response Logs.

A Modest Proposal **393**

APPLY

CRITICAL VOCABULARY

Answers:

1. knowing how to grow plants; because the purpose of farming is growing food

2. offer a break on rent; because the landlord would want to treat the tenant fairly

3. a rise in umbrella sales; because as more rain falls, more people need umbrellas for protection

4. getting a skateboard; because it encourages the skateboard owner to go outside and ride it

5. a salad; because vegetables do not contain as much sugar as cake

6. not earning a high hourly wage; because having less money makes it harder to provide for a family

7. the state of Texas; because being a larger state, it has a higher population, being a larger state

VOCABULARY STRATEGY:
Context Clues

Answers:

1. liable
2. reckoned
3. inclemency

 **RESPOND**

CRITICAL VOCABULARY

WORD BANK
sustenance   scrupulous
prodigious   encumbrance
rudiment   inducement
collateral

Practice and Apply Choose the situation that fits the meaning of the Critical Vocabulary word. Explain your decision.

1. Which is a rudiment of farming—knowing how to grow plants or knowing how to cook harvested food?

2. Which would a scrupulous landlord be more likely to do for a tenant who is out of work—offer a break on rent or ask for rent earlier than it is due?

3. Which is a collateral effect of heavy rains—a rise in umbrella sales or a decline in raincoat sales?

4. Which is an inducement to exercise more—getting a guitar or getting a skateboard?

5. Which of these provides healthier sustenance—a salad or a cake?

6. Which of these is an encumbrance to maintaining your household—not getting a bigger office at work or not earning a high hourly wage?

7. Which of these is more prodigious—the state of Texas or the state of Rhode Island?

VOCABULARY STRATEGY:
Context Clues

WORD BANK
inclemency
liable
reckoned

Go to the **Vocabulary Studio** for more on using context clues.

Context clues are often found in the words and sentences around an unknown term. A context clue may consist of a definition or a restatement of the meaning of the unfamiliar word, an example following the word, a comparison or contrast, or a nearby synonym. The unknown word's position or function in a sentence can also be a clue.

For example, the placement and suffix of the Critical Vocabulary word *prodigious* in paragraph 2 tells you that it is an adjective. Knowing this makes the word easier to define.

After using context clues to get a preliminary understanding of a word, you can verify the word's meaning by looking it up in a dictionary.

Practice and Apply Use context clues in each sentence to help you identify the correct words to complete the sentences. Check your answers in a dictionary.

1. The farmer was _____ for the loan payment on the farm, even though he was not responsible for the failure of his crops.

2. He _____ the cost of raising a child, computing it to the penny.

3. The _____ of the winter weather, with frequent snow and ice storms, added to the misery of the homeless.

394   Unit 3

 ENGLISH LEARNER SUPPORT

Vocabulary Strategy Have students look at the last sentence of paragraph 23. Discuss the meaning of circulate, based on the words surrounding it. Explain that the phrase among ourselves is a clue to the word's meaning. But also indicate that in a discussion of money, the word takes on a special significance. Ask students what the word circulate means when used to describe the movement of the blood through the body. **ALL LEVELS**

RESPOND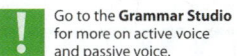

APPLY

LANGUAGE CONVENTIONS:
Active and Passive Voice

Swift uses both active and passive voice in his essay. When a verb is in the **active voice**, the subject performs the action. When the verb is in the **passive voice**, the subject is the receiver of the action. The passive voice is formed with the verb *to be* and the past participle of a verb. Typically, the active voice is preferred because it conveys more energy and is more direct. To develop a more stilted, formal tone fitting for the narrator of his proposal, however, Swift turns to the passive voice.

Read these sentences from the essay.

> It is agreed by all parties that this prodigious number of children . . . is . . . a very great additional grievance.

> I am assured by our merchants that a boy or girl before twelve years old is no salable commodity.

Swift could have chosen to use the active voice in both sentences:

> All parties agree that this prodigious number of children is a very great additional grievance.

> Our merchants assure me that a boy or girl before twelve years old is no salable commodity.

Altering the verb from passive to active makes the writing more vigorous and less like the bureaucratic language that might be used in a real proposal. Sometimes, the passive voice is preferred for other reasons as explained in the chart.

USE OF PASSIVE VOICE	
PURPOSE	**EXAMPLE**
to emphasize the receiver of the action	The truce was shattered by the accidental firing.
when the doer of the action is not known or not important or when the writer or speaker wants to conceal the identity of the doer	The window was broken.

Practice and Apply Write four sentences about *A Modest Proposal* in the passive voice. Exchange sentences with a partner and rewrite each other's sentences in the active voice. Compare the differences between the two versions.

Go to the **Grammar Studio** for more on active voice and passive voice.

LANGUAGE CONVENTIONS:
Active and Passive Voice

Review the information about active and passive voice with students. Explain that the choice of these voices is a conscious choice Swift made, to make a point to the reader. In the active voice, someone or something is completing an action. In the passive voice, someone is having something done to them. The active voice is a means of suggesting ideas or asserting opinions; the passive voice comes in handy when he wants to characterize the downtrodden state of Ireland's poor.

Try to demonstrate the uses of active and passive voice by having students rewrite the following passive sentences in active voice.

It is agreed by all parties that this prodigious number of children . . . is . . . a very great additional grievance.

I am assured by our merchants that a boy or girl before twelve years old is no salable commodity.

Written in the active voice, the sentences have an entirely different effect.

All parties agree that this prodigious number of children is a very great additional grievance.

Our merchants assure me that a boy or girl before twelve years old is no salable commodity.

Discuss with the students what differences in tone they notice when they rewrite the sentences.

Practice and Apply Have partners discuss the use of the passive and active voice in their sentences.

ENGLISH LEARNER SUPPORT

Language Conventions Use the following supports with students at varying proficiency levels:

Have students read the first sentence in paragraph 29. Explain why this is a passive sentence. Have them write the sentence. **SUBSTANTIAL**

Have students rewrite "it should be urged" from the first sentence in paragraph 29 to make it active. Explain that to make it active, they should start with "Urge . . ." **MODERATE**

PLAN

SATIRE IS DYING BECAUSE THE INTERNET IS KILLING IT

Editorial by Arwa Mahdawi

GENRE ELEMENTS
EDITORIAL

Tell students that an **editorial** expresses an opinion, often on a controversial subject. Editorial writers often hook their readers with a strong and surprising opening claim. Then, they develop their claim with a series of arguments, often saving the strongest and most surprising for last. In this lesson, students will analyze the development of ideas and tone in an editorial.

LEARNING OBJECTIVES

- Analyze development of ideas and tone.
- Conduct research on satires.
- Write a satire.
- Discuss an editorial.
- Use context clues and antonyms.
- Identify effective words, adjectives, and concrete nouns.
- **Language** Use formal and informal language to adapt tone.

TEXT COMPLEXITY

Quantitative Measures	Satire Is Dying Because the Internet Is Killing It	Lexile: 1240L
Qualitative Measures	**Ideas Presented** Much is explicit, but irony and satire are also used.	
	Structures Used Primarily explicit; development of arguments with statistics and examples.	
	Language Used Contemporary and ironic language, with academic and domain-specific words.	
	Knowledge Required Cultural references essential to understanding.	

PLAN

Online

RESOURCES

- Unit 3 Response Log
- Selection Audio
- Reading Studio: Notice & Note
- Level Up Tutorial: Irony; Navigating and Evaluating Web Sites; Tone
- Writing Studio: Writing as a Process
- Speaking and Listening Studio: Participating in Collaborative Discussions
- Vocabulary Studio: Antonyms
- Grammar Studio: Module 2 Lesson 3: Adjectives
- "Satire Is Dying Because the Internet Is Killing It" Selection Test

SUMMARIES

English

In this editorial, Arwa Mahdawi makes the claim that satire is a necessary literary genre that keeps people thinking. She argues that Facebook's new satire tag is a mistake and that people need to learn to identify satire on their own.

Spanish

En este editorial, Arwa Mahdawi afirma que la sátira es un género literario necesario que pone a pensar a la gente. Alega que la etiqueta de sátira de Facebook es un error porque la gente debe aprender a identificar las sátiras por cuenta propia.

SMALL-GROUP OPTIONS

Have students work in small groups and pairs to read and discuss the selection.

Think-Pair-Share

- After students have read paragraphs 1–2 of the selection, pose this question to the class: *Why does Facebook care about helping people identify satire?*
- Have students think about the question individually and make notes.
- Invite pairs to discuss their ideas about the question and prepare a shared response.
- Ask pairs to share their responses with the class.

Pinwheel Discussion

- Arrange students in groups of eight—four students seated in a circle facing out with four students seated facing them.
- After reading a paragraph of the selection, pose a question to students for discussion. For example: *Why does the author use the attention span of a goldfish as an example?*
- Students in the inner circle remain stationary throughout the discussion. Students in the outer circle move to their right after discussing the question.
- Provide additional questions for students to discuss during each rotation.

Satire Is Dying Because the Internet Is Killing It **396B**

PLAN

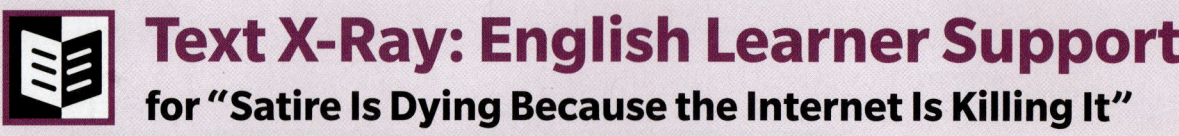

Text X-Ray: English Learner Support
for "Satire Is Dying Because the Internet Is Killing It"

Use the Text X-Ray and the supports and scaffolds in the Teacher's Edition to help guide students at different proficiency levels through the selection.

INTRODUCE THE SELECTION
DISCUSS *SATIRE-BLINDNESS*

In this lesson, students will need to be able to discuss the effects of satire-blindness.

Provide the following explanations:
- A satirical news story is not real, truthful news.
- Satire-blindness is the inability to recognize what news is not true.

Ask students to discuss their opinions of satire-blindness, using sentence frames, such as: *I experienced satire-blindness once when I read ____ and thought ____. Satire-blindness can cause trouble when ____.*

CULTURAL REFERENCES

The following words or phrases may be unfamiliar to students:
- *career move* (paragraph 3): change in employment
- *Marilyn* (paragraph 4): reference to a famous Hollywood actress from the 1950s, Marilyn Monroe.
- *demand eyeballs for their dollars* (paragraph 5): want people to view something because money was spent on it
- *clickbait* (paragraph 5): attractive or entertaining content that gets viewers to click on a link so that advertisers can make money

LISTENING

Understand Main Ideas

Remind students that the **main idea** is the most important point that a writer wants to make. Tell them that they can ask themselves *who, what, where, when,* and *why* questions in order to understand what an editorial is about and to determine the main idea.

Use the following supports with students at varying proficiency levels:
- Read aloud the first paragraph of the editorial and ask questions about the main idea. Accept one-word answers or have students point to the words in the text that answer the question. For example: *Who has a new innovation? (Facebook) What is the newest innovation? (satire tag)* **SUBSTANTIAL**
- Have partners take turns reading aloud the first two paragraphs of the editorial. Then, have them take turns asking each other *who, what, when, where,* and *why* questions about what they just heard. **MODERATE**
- Have partners take turns reading aloud the first two paragraphs of the editorial. Then, have them take turns asking each other *who, what, when, where,* and *why* questions about what they just heard. When they finish, have them state the main idea of each paragraph. **LIGHT**

PLAN

SPEAKING

Adapt Tone

Review the difference between formal and informal language. Explain that the degree of formality they use will help develop the tone of what they say.

Use the following supports with students at varying proficiency levels:

- Model the difference between formal and informal language when discussing a social issue. Say two sentences: *You guys should register to vote. People need to take responsibility and register to vote.* Have students repeat the sentences and identify which is formal and which is informal. **SUBSTANTIAL**
- Model the difference between formal and informal language, as above. Then, have partners choose a social issue. Tell them to say a few informal and formal sentences about their issue. **MODERATE**
- Have partners choose one of the social issues from the Intermediate activity to discuss. Instruct one student to use informal language and the other to use formal language. Then, have them switch roles and repeat the activity. **LIGHT**

READING

Use Graphic Organizers

Tell students that they can use graphic organizers to help them keep track of unfamiliar words as they read. After reading, they can use reference materials and classroom support to define the words, and then reread the text again.

Use the following supports with students of varying proficiency levels:

- Reread the first paragraph of the editorial with students. Model how to use a word web to keep track of any unfamiliar words. Write the word *virtual* in the center of the web. Help small groups use peer support to fill in the web with related words and phrases. **SUBSTANTIAL**
- Have students reread the first two paragraphs of the editorial. Tell them to use a two-column chart to keep track of any unfamiliar words. After reading, guide them to use reference materials to help them write definitions in their charts. Then, have them reread the paragraphs, noting if their comprehension of the content has changed. **MODERATE**
- Model the use of a Frayer Model. Guide students to draw a square of four boxes and write the word *algorithms* in a circle in the center. Have them label the other four boxes: Definition, Characteristics, Examples, Non-examples. Tell pairs to discuss their completed Frayer Models. **LIGHT**

WRITING

Use Antonyms

Tell students that it is important to know whom they want to read their work before they begin writing. Knowing the audience will help them decide the purpose, form, and tone for their satires.

Use the following supports with students of varying proficiency levels:

- Help students discuss possible audiences for their satires using sentence frames, such as: *The audience for my satire is _____. I think _____ need to know about [social issue]. The best form for this audience is _____.* Have students copy and complete the frames. **SUBSTANTIAL**
- Have students write three sentences that explain (1) who their audience is, (2) why the audience is the best for the issue students choose to satirize, and (3) why they will choose a particular genre for their satires. **MODERATE**
- Have students write a paragraph explaining their audience, message, genre, and how the audience will influence the tone. Have pairs exchange feedback. **LIGHT**

TEACH

 Connect to the ESSENTIAL QUESTION

Engage students in a discussion around the Essential Question, making sure they understand that satire is a technique employed by writers to criticize or expose corruption or shortcomings in an individual or a society by using humor, irony, exaggeration, or ridicule. Tell students that satire can take different forms, including plays, poems, short stories, and essays. At times, writers of satirical works use fictional characters to represent the individual or systems they want to critique. Ask students to think of other reasons an author might use satire to engage in social commentary.

ANALYZE & APPLY

SATIRE IS DYING BECAUSE THE INTERNET IS KILLING IT

Editorial by **Arwa Mahdawi**

ESSENTIAL QUESTION:

How can satire change people's behavior?

QUICK START

What are your favorite sources of satire? Do you generally look for satires in print publications, on the Internet, or on television? With a partner, discuss the kind of satires you enjoy most.

ANALYZE DEVELOPMENT OF IDEAS

In a nonfiction selection, the **main idea** is the most important point the writer wants to make about the topic. This main idea is usually developed through several key points, each of which is supported by details. An author may state a main idea outright; however, more often the reader must infer the main idea from key points and details in the selection.

To develop the main idea stated in its title, "Satire Is Dying Because the Internet Is Killing It," author Arwa Mahdawi presents a series of key points, drawing connections between them. Details and examples support the key points and make the selection meaningful and interesting to readers.

Use a graphic organizer like this one to help analyze how an author develops ideas in a nonfiction selection.

GENRE ELEMENTS: EDITORIAL

- expresses an opinion, often on a controversial subject
- often found on the editorial page of a newspaper
- presents an argument and uses rhetorical techniques to persuade readers

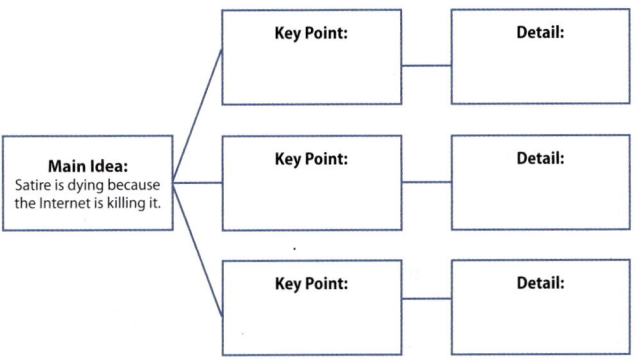

ANALYZE TONE

Tone is the attitude that a writer expresses toward a subject. In nonfiction, tone is often developed through **diction,** or word choice and syntax. The details a writer includes may also contribute to tone. The tone of a text may be intimate or distant, serious or humorous, ironic or earnest, understated or hyperbolic.

To identify the tone in a selection, you might try reading it aloud. What attitude toward the subject and audience do the words, sentence structures, and details convey? An author's tone can powerfully shape readers' perceptions of a selection's topic.

As you read "Satire Is Dying Because the Internet Is Killing It," analyze and evaluate the author's tone. What is the overall tone, and does it help the author to achieve her purpose?

TEACH

QUICK START

After students have shared which sources of satire they enjoy most, ask them to identify some topics they have seen or heard addressed through satire. If they need some ideas to get them started, offer some suggestions (e.g., presidential elections, education, economic issues). Let students know that satire is quite common, but at times, it can be difficult to distinguish between a satirical piece and a serious piece of work.

ANALYZE DEVELOPMENT OF IDEAS

Remind students that a nonfiction selection is usually intended to teach or inform the audience about a specific topic. Normally, the author introduces a thesis or **main idea** at the beginning and develops the idea through several key points. These key points are then supported by details. Remind students that even though identifying the main idea can be challenging if it is not stated outright, they should be able to infer it from the key points and details. Tell students that the main idea of "Satire Is Dying Because the Internet Is Killing It" is easy to identify because it is stated in the title. As they read, they should identify key points that support this main idea and specific details that support the key points. Point out that a graphic organizer like the one on page 397 can help them connect and organize their ideas.

ANALYZE TONE

Remind students that **tone** is the writer's attitude toward a subject. This should not be confused with **mood,** which is the feeling the writer creates for the audience. Tell students that to identify tone, they should pay attention to the writer's **diction** and syntax. What words does the writer use? Do they seem serious or humorous? Encourage students to identify the writer's purpose in the selection and then to think about how the writer's tone helps her to achieve this purpose.

TEACH

CRITICAL VOCABULARY

Encourage students to read all the sentences before deciding which word best completes each one. Remind them to look for context clues that match the precise meaning of each word.

Answers:

1. *accolades*
2. *spoof*
3. *finite*
4. *meme*
5. *curate*
6. *monetize*
7. *algorithm*
8. *eschews*
9. *satire*

■ English Learner Support

Use Cognates Tell students that some of the Critical Vocabulary words have Spanish cognates: *algorithm/algoritmo, finite/finito, satire/sátira*. **ALL LEVELS**

LANGUAGE CONVENTIONS

Review the definitions of **adjectives** (words that modify nouns and pronouns) and **concrete nouns** (nouns naming something material and nonabstract). Then, ask students to provide examples of each.

Discuss the effect that highly effective words, evocative adjectives, and concrete nouns have on a sentence. Read one or two sentences from the selection, and ask students to identify the highly effective words, evocative adjectives, and concrete nouns in the sentence. Challenge them to think about how the sentences would be different if other, more neutral words were used. How would this impact the **tone**?

✎ ANNOTATION MODEL

Before students begin reading, review the definition of *overstatement* (exaggeration) and *irony* (the opposite of its literal meaning). Tell students that these literary devices are used to create a sarcastic or humorous **tone**. Encourage students to mark overstated or ironic words or phrases as they read the selection. They may want to color-code their annotations by using highlighters. Their notes in the margin may include questions about ideas that are unclear or topics they want to learn more about.

398 Unit 3

 **GET READY**

CRITICAL VOCABULARY

| algorithm | accolade | curate | eschew | finite |
| satire | spoof | monetize | meme | |

To see how many Critical Vocabulary words you already know, use them to complete the sentences.

1. At this company, the highest _____ is accompanied with a bonus.
2. The _____ they performed poked fun at his self-importance.
3. There are only a(n) _____ number of solutions to the problem.
4. Micha posted a(n) _____ that promised to break the Internet.
5. Darcy was asked to _____ the newest exhibit at the Austen Museum.
6. She tried to _____ her knitting skills selling hats in an online shop.
7. To solve the problem quickly, Joaquin wrote a(n) _____.
8. Since Christian hates chores, he _____ them whenever possible.
9. Although he claimed to enjoy _____, the principal was not happy.

LANGUAGE CONVENTIONS

Effective Words A part of Arwa Mahdawi's style is her use of highly effective words, evocative adjectives, and concrete nouns to critique the digital generation. For example, she uses adjectives like *satire-blindness* and compares the human attention span to that of goldfish. As you read, note how she uses distinctive wording to convey her ideas and perspective.

ANNOTATION MODEL NOTICE & NOTE

As you read the selection, note how the author develops her argument by overstating certain elements and by using irony to create a humorous tone. This model shows one reader's notes about an excerpt from the editorial.

> Forget self-driving cars or virtual reality nano-technology algorithms, <u>the newest innovation</u> to emerge from Silicon Valley is square brackets. Facebook is testing a "satire tag" that will clearly label fake news stories from well-known satire sites like the *Onion* as [satire]. <u>No longer will you need to rely on outdated technology such as common sense</u> to realize that content like Area Facebook User Incredibly Stupid is [satire], the square brackets will do it for you.

The author refers to square brackets as "the newest innovation," even though they aren't as innovative as technology such as self-driving cars, and calls common sense "outdated." This establishes an ironic tone.

398 Unit 3

BACKGROUND

Arwa Mahdawi *is a Palestinian/British writer based in New York. She writes about pop culture, race, technology, and women's issues. In "Satire Is Dying Because the Internet Is Killing It," she laments the death of satire and points out both reported and underlying reasons for the apparent decline. This editorial was published on August 19, 2014, in the Opinion section of* The Guardian.

SATIRE IS DYING BECAUSE THE INTERNET IS KILLING IT

Editorial by Arwa Mahdawi

SETTING A PURPOSE

As you read, notice the author's diction, or word choice, and how it conveys her viewpoints about the "satire tag."

1   Forget self-driving cars or virtual reality nano-technology[1] algorithms, the newest innovation to emerge from Silicon Valley[2] is square brackets. Facebook is testing a "satire tag" that will clearly label fake news stories from well-known **satire** sites like the *Onion* as [satire]. No longer will you need to rely on outdated technology such as common sense to realize that content like Area Facebook User Incredibly Stupid is [satire], the square brackets will do it for you.

2   It should perhaps be noted that Facebook isn't introducing the satire tag because it thinks we're all morons, but rather because it knows we're all morons. In a statement, the social network explained that it had "received feedback that people wanted a clearer way to distinguish satirical articles from others".

---

[1] **nano-technology** the study of technology and engineering functions at a molecular level.
[2] **Silicon Valley** located in the Bay Area in California; home to many start-up and global technology companies like Facebook.

Notice & Note

Use the side margins to notice and note signposts in the text.

LANGUAGE CONVENTIONS
Annotate: Mark effective words, nouns, and adjectives in paragraphs 1 and 2 that illustrate the author's view of using satire tags in news.

Evaluate: What effect does the author's choice of language create?

algorithm
(ăl′gə-rĭth′-əm) *n.* a finite set of unambiguous instructions that, given some set of initial conditions, can be performed in a prescribed sequence to achieve a certain goal and that has a recognizable set of end conditions.

satire
(săt′īr) *n.* a literary work in which human foolishness or vice is attacked through irony, derision, or wit.

Satire Is Dying Because the Internet Is Killing It 399

WHEN STUDENTS STRUGGLE . . .

Understand Irony and Overstatement Ask students to define *irony* and *overstatment* in their own words, then use a graphic organizer (below) to identify examples of both. Challenge students to think about how they know the sentence is irony or overstatement.

Example from Selection	Irony or Overstatement?	How Do I know?

 For additional support, go to the **Reading Studio** and assign the following Level Up tutorial: Irony.

TEACH

BACKGROUND

After students read the background note, explain that many essayists use their work as a platform to discuss important topics or issues that affect society and the way we live. Tell students that Arwa Mahdawi has written satires on topics from presidential elections to healthcare to food snacks, and her ability to write about such a diverse range of subjects has garnered her quite a loyal following and fan base.

SETTING A PURPOSE

Direct students to use the Setting a Purpose prompt to focus their reading.

 For **reading support** for students at varying proficiency levels, see the **Text X-Ray** on page 396D.

LANGUAGE CONVENTIONS

Remind students that **effective words, concrete nouns,** and evocative **adjectives** can help set the writer's **tone** and create an overall effect that either draws readers in or alienates them. (**Answer:** *Words and phrases like "the newest innovation" and "outdated technology such as common sense" allow the reader to reflect on the importance of common sense and how foolish it is that some online users can't tell real news from a satire.*)

 For **listening support** for students at varying proficiency levels, see the **Text X-Ray** on page 396C.

CRITICAL VOCABULARY

algorithm: The author uses the word *algorithms* to describe the complex set of instructions that go into the creation of new technologies.

ASK STUDENTS what "newest innovation" the author compares to self-driving cars and virtual reality nano-technology algorithms. (*The author compares the "newest innovation" of square brackets to self-driving cars and virtual reality nano-technology algorithms.*)

satire: The author uses the word *satire* to distinguish between fake news and real news stories.

ASK STUDENTS what the author means by a "satire tag." (*A satire tag is a tag in square brackets that labels fake news stories from known satire sites.*)

Satire Is Dying Because the Internet Is Killing It 399

TEACH

ANALYZE DEVELOPMENT OF IDEAS

Tell students that the term *clickbait* is used to describe online content that attracts readers because of its entertainment value. (**Answer:** *It might be useful to change the business model of the Internet so companies aren't relying solely on advertising to make money. If executives become less concerned with the number of clicks their headlines get, they are more likely to put out quality content and fewer items that are considered clickbait.*)

CRITICAL VOCABULARY

accolade: In the text, this describes Kim Jong-un's supposed achievement as "sexiest man alive."

ASK STUDENTS whether the *Onion* article's proclamation about Kim Jong-un was a true accolade. (*It was not a true accolade but a spoof.*)

spoof: The author says that the *Onion* article was a *spoof*, or parody, of the sexiest-man-alive awards.

ASK STUDENTS whether the *People's Daily* understood that the *Onion* article was a spoof. (*It did not seem to understand that it was a spoof, as it ran a slideshow of Kim Jong-un, complete with quotes from the* Onion *spoof.*)

curate: The author says she curated, or gathered, a list of headlines to illustrate how difficult it can be to distinguish between fake and real news.

ASK STUDENTS if they think the author is serious when she says that her list of headlines was "carefully curated." (*She isn't serious because she should have been able to pull these headlines together easily.*)

monetize: In social media, the number of clicks is monetized, or converted into income.

ASK STUDENTS to describe the drawbacks of monetizing clicks. (*They'd rather focus on money than on serious news.*)

eschew: The author says that people with short attention spans eschew, or avoid, quality content for entertainment.

ASK STUDENTS what it means when it says "eschew meaning for memeing." (*We choose reaction over reflection.*)

meme: The author describes *memes* as reactions that lack reflection.

ASK STUDENTS what attitude the author seems to have about memeing. (*She seems to disapprove of memeing, as she says that people "eschew meaning for memeing."*)

400   Unit 3

 NOTICE & NOTE

accolade
(ăk´ə-lād, -läd) *n.* a special acknowledgment; an award.

spoof
(spoof) *n.* a satirical imitation; a parody or send-up.

ANALYZE DEVELOPMENT OF IDEAS
Annotate: Mark the statements in paragraphs 4 and 5 that explain why it has become so difficult to discern between satire and real news on the Internet.

Draw Conclusions: What might be one solution to this problem?

curate
(kyoor´ ĭt) *tr.vb.* to gather and present to the public.

monetize
(mŏn´ ĭ-tīz, mŭn-) *tr.vb.* to convert into a source of income.

eschew
(ĕ-shoo´, ĕs-choo´) *tr.vb.* to avoid using, accepting, participating in, or partaking of.

meme
(mēm) *n.* a unit of cultural information, such as a cultural practice or idea, that is transmitted verbally or by repeated action from one mind to another.

400   Unit 3

3   Some of those people may well be journalists who have had embarrassing lapses of satire-blindness in the past. The *Washington Post*, for example, was once fooled into reporting that Sarah Palin[3] was, in a somewhat unlikely career move, taking a job at *al-Jazeera*[4]. And the English-language arm of China's *People's Daily* fell for an *Onion*[5] article proclaiming the North Korean ruler, Kim Jong-un, the sexiest man alive, even using the **accolade** as an opportunity to run a 55-image slideshow of him, complete with quotes from the *Onion* **spoof**. Although, it's possible this may itself have been satire—I'm unsure.

4   And that's the problem. The Internet has become so weird, so saturated with cats and lists and Buzzfeed[6] quizzes that it's difficult to know what's serious and what's a spoof any more. I challenge you, for example, to identify the *Onion* piece from these headlines:

• U.S. Adults Are Dumber than the Average Human
• Hazelnut Prices Soar, Fueling Fears of Nutella Shortage
• Tips for Being an Unarmed Black Teen[7]
• Serial Chicken Smuggler Caught in Norway
• Definitive Proof Kale Is the Marilyn of Foods

5   The point of this carefully **curated** list is that you often can't tell the difference between satire and real news online. There are several reasons for this. The first is the underlying business model of the Internet. We don't like to pay for stuff online so the Internet is funded by advertising; advertising executives demand eyeballs for their dollars; content providers resort to clickbait headlines and shareable content to secure eyeballs and ad dollars; users get addicted to an endless stream of clickbait.

6   The manner in which we've **monetized** digital media means we often reward reaction over reflection and **eschew** meaning for **meme**-ing. News can't just be news; it has to be entertainment. Indeed, the third law of modern media states that for every moderately important news item published, there will be an obligatory roundup of the funniest Twitter reactions to said news story, generally in slideshow format to maximize clicks.

7   The second big contributor to satire-blindness is our diminishing attention span. The average American attention span in 2000 was

---

[3] **Sarah Palin:** American politician who served as governor of Alaska and as the Republican Party nominee for vice-president in 2008 alongside presidential nominee, John McCain.
[4] *al-Jazeera:* media network that reports on news from the Middle East and worldwide.
[5] **the** *Onion:* an American digital media company and news satire organization.
[6] **Buzzfeed:** an American digital media company that reports on social news and entertainment.
[7] **"Tips for Being an Unarmed Black Teen"** is the only headline from the Onion.

WHEN STUDENTS STRUGGLE . . .

Draw on Prior Knowledge Ask students to think about their own experiences with online content and clickbait. Ask them to reflect on the type of content they are drawn to on the web and why they are attracted to those sites. Then in pairs, ask them to discuss their experiences and their reasons for choosing certain content.

For additional support, go to the **Reading Studio** and assign the following **Level Up** tutorial: Navigating and Evaluating Web Sites.

12 seconds; in 2013, it was eight seconds. This is less than the average attention span of a goldfish (nine seconds).

8   As Vladimir Nabokov[8] once said, "Satire is a lesson, parody is a game." But if there's one thing we've learned from the Internet, it's that everyone prefers games to lessons. The problem with satire in an age of **finite** attention and infinite content is that it makes you stop and think. It interrupts the speed and simplicity of the discover-click-share cycle that makes platforms like Facebook lots of money. By introducing satire tagging, Facebook has helpfully gone some way in eliminating the unhelpful friction of thought and, in doing so, made life easier for us all.

---

[8] **Vladimir Nabokov:** Russian-American novelist, well known for his modern classic, *Lolita*.

NOTICE & NOTE

ANALYZE TONE
Annotate: Mark specific evidence in paragraph 7 that supports the author's overall tone.

Summarize: What does the author say about humans' attention span and how it affects their ability to engage with satire?

finite
(fī´nĭt) *adj.* having bounds; limited.

CHECK YOUR UNDERSTANDING

Answer these questions before moving on to the **Analyze the Text** section on the following page.

1   What is a "satire tag," as described in this editorial?

  A   A trick of social media companies to pass fake stories off as real news

  B   A way social media sites help people distinguish satire from parody

  C   A label social media sites are considering to alert readers to satire

  D   A form of social media advertising

2   Mahdawi cites which of the following as a reason why it is difficult to tell a real news story from a satire?

  F   Increasing attention spans

  G   Overvaluing of entertainment

  H   Innovative technologies across sectors

  J   Reduction in social media marketing dollars

3   In paragraph 8, the author explains that the problem with satire is that it makes you stop and think. What is her purpose for this statement?

  A   She wants readers to find better ways of sorting their online content.

  B   She wants readers to take a stand against satire in the news.

  C   She wants readers to recognize the value and importance of satire.

  D   She wants readers to know that satire is too difficult to understand.

Satire Is Dying Because the Internet Is Killing It   401

ENGLISH LEARNER SUPPORT

Oral Assessment Use the following questions to assess students' comprehension and speaking skills.

1. What does the author mean by a "satire tag"? *(a tag to clearly label fake news as satire)*

2. Mahdawi believes that _____ of entertainment makes it difficult to tell a real news story from satire. *(overvaluing)*

3. The author says that the "problem with satire" is that it makes you stop and think. Does she really mean satire is a problem? *(No, she thinks satire is important because it makes you stop and think.)* **SUBSTANTIAL/MODERATE**

TEACH

ANALYZE TONE

Explain that research suggests that the amount of time people spend online is a contributor to our diminishing attention spans. (**Answer:** *The author says that because human attention span has decreased from 12 seconds to 8 seconds since 2013, humans probably have a difficult time engaging with satirical texts, which require critical thinking.*)

ENGLISH LEARNER SUPPORT

Express Ideas and Opinions Tell students that they can come up with their own ideas and opinions about the editorial based on whether or not they think the evidence or details provided are effective.

• Ask students to share their opinions about the argument presented in the editorial. Ask students if they agree or disagree with the writer and to state why. **SUBSTANTIAL**

• Ask students to identify one point in the editorial with which they strongly agree or disagree. Provide students with a sentence frame such as, *I agree/disagree with _____ because _____*. **MODERATE**

• Ask students to identify one point in the editorial about which they agree or disagree and give a reason why. **LIGHT**

CHECK YOUR UNDERSTANDING

Have students answer the questions independently.

Answers:

1. C

2. G

3. C

If they answer any questions incorrectly, have them reread the text to confirm their understanding. Then they may proceed to ANALYZE THE TEXT on page 402.

CRITICAL VOCABULARY

finite: The author uses the word *finite*, or limited, to describe our attention spans in contrast to the infinite amount of information available.

ASK STUDENTS how finite the human attention span is, according to this editorial. *(eight seconds, or less than the attention span of a goldfish)*

APPLY

ANALYZE THE TEXT
Possible answers:

1. **DOK 1:** *At the beginning of the editorial, the author's tone is sarcastic. She asks readers to "Forget self-driving cars or virtual reality nano-technology algorithms," insinuating that these improvements in technology aren't as innovative as whatever she is about to describe.*

2. **DOK 2:** *Details in paragraph 3 support the idea that people are having a difficult time distinguishing real news from satire on the Internet, which is killing satire. For example, the* Washington Post *was fooled into reporting fake news about Sarah Palin, and the* People's Daily *was fooled into reporting that the leader of North Korea had been named the "sexiest man alive."*

3. **DOK 3:** *The author quotes Vladimir Nabokov's quote, "Satire is a lesson, parody is a game," which suggests that she believes readers have an easier time understanding parody. She also says that "everyone prefers games to lessons." Because satire requires critical thinking and a different kind of attention than what people in the Internet age are used to giving, parody is an easy way out.*

4. **DOK 4:** *The final statement illustrates the author's annoyance with the concept of satire tagging. Her choice of words, such as the "unhelpful friction of thought," seem to mock the notion of people needing to be told that what they are reading is indeed a satire. In general, thought processes are very complex and not ordinarily thought of as "unhelpful," so it is clear she is making fun of the idea.*

5. **DOK 5:** *The author likely employs this approach because she wants her readers to realize just how unreasonable it is to require satirical stories to be tagged. For example, in the first paragraph she refers to common sense as an "outdated technology." By overstating ideas and using irony, she gets the reader to think about the validity of her points. Ironically, she is also able to use her own writing, a piece of satire, to get people to think about the topic.*

RESEARCH
Remind students that they should confirm any information they find by checking multiple websites and assessing the credibility of each one.

Extend Tell students that they can find other editorials by Mahdawi by searching on her name or by going to the website of *The Guardian*, where she frequently contributes. Tell students that Mahdawi has written editorials on many different topics, and they do not have to limit themselves to her editorials on technology.

RESPOND

ANALYZE THE TEXT
Support your responses with evidence from the text. NOTEBOOK

1. **Evaluate** Reread paragraphs 1 and 2. What tone does the author establish at the beginning of the editorial through her word choices and syntax? Do you think this tone is effective? Explain why or why not.

2. **Identify** What details in paragraph 3 support the author's main idea?

3. **Interpret** The author quotes Vladimir Nabokov, who said that "Satire is a lesson, parody is a game." What point does she make with this quotation?

4. **Infer** At the end of the editorial, the author says that social media has "made life easier for us all." Does she intend to praise it with this statement? Explain why or why not.

5. **Draw Conclusions** Throughout the editorial, the author uses elements of satire, such as irony and overstatement. Why do you think she uses these elements of satire?

RESEARCH

RESEARCH TIP
Be sure to use credible and accurate sources when conducting research. Websites with URLs that end in .edu are often good sources of information on academic subjects like Swift's satire.

As you have learned, satire is a form of social commentary that uses ridicule to get people to think about issues in a different way. With a partner, identify three contemporary satires and determine whether they are true satires or parodies. Share your findings with the class.

TITLE OF WORK	AUTHOR	SOCIAL TOPICS THE WORK ADDRESSES	THE AUTHOR'S ATTITUDE TOWARD THE TOPIC

Extend Research another article by Arwa Mahdawi. Then, compare and contrast it with "Satire Is Dying Because the Internet Is Killing It." What are similarities and differences between the two pieces of writing? Share your findings with a partner.

WHEN STUDENTS STRUGGLE . . .

Reteaching: Analyze Tone Remind students that **tone** is the attitude that a writer expresses toward a subject. As students read another article by Mahdawi, encourage them to analyze the tone she uses in that article. How does the tone relate to the subject of the article? How does it relate to Mahdawi's purpose in writing the article? Then, have them compare the tone of that article to the tone in "Satire Is Dying Because the Internet Is Killing It."

For additional support, go to the **Reading Studio** and assign the following **Level Up tutorial: Tone.**

CREATE AND DISCUSS

Write a Satire Write your own brief satirical work about a social issue that interests you. Your satire can be structured as an essay, editorial, poem, play, or song lyric. Make sure you have a clear central, or main, idea that is developed by examples and details. Also, be sure to craft a certain tone and incorporate techniques like overstatement and irony.

- ❏ Identify a clear central idea. Is your intended purpose clear?
- ❏ Who is your audience? Will they understand your main idea?
- ❏ What is the tone you want to convey? Is it clear? Do you want to set different tones at different points? How will you achieve this?
- ❏ What details will you use to support your main idea?
- ❏ What elements of satire have you included?

Discuss the Editorial In a small group, discuss whether or not you agree with the author's viewpoint expressed in this editorial.

- ❏ Take turns sharing your thoughts.
- ❏ Support your opinions with evidence and examples from the text.

RESPOND TO THE ESSENTIAL QUESTION

 How can satire change people's behavior?

Gather Information Review your annotations and notes on "Satire Is Dying Because the Internet Is Killing It." Then, add relevant details to your Response Log. As you determine which information to include, think about:

- the characteristics of a satire
- how an author of a satire might appeal to readers' emotions
- how language can be used to convey a certain tone

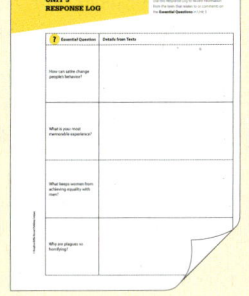

RESPOND

Go to **Writing as a Process** in the **Writing Studio** for help with planning and drafting the satire.

 Go to the **Speaking and Listening Studio** to find out more about participating in collaborative discussions.

ACADEMIC VOCABULARY

As you write and discuss what you learned from the editorial, be sure to use the Academic Vocabulary words. Check off each of the words that you use.

- ❏ encounter
- ❏ exploit
- ❏ persist
- ❏ subordinate
- ❏ widespread

APPLY

CREATE AND DISCUSS

Write a Satire Point out that the list on page 409 can serve as a guideline for students' satires. Tell students that before they write their pieces of satire, they can brainstorm some ideas that interest them. For example, what social issues have they heard about recently that they would like more information on? If students struggle to come up with ideas, guide them by providing some topics (women's rights, education, environmentalism, equitable health for all, etc.). Once they come up with a topic, encourage them to identify a specific aspect of the issue they would like to address so their writing process is more manageable. Remind students to think about their audience, what message they want to convey, what **tone** will effectively convey the message, and how best to structure the satire.

Discuss the Editorial Remind students to listen carefully and respectfully as each group member shares, even if they do not agree with what is being shared. Tell them that when they do not understand a comment made by another group member, they should ask questions to clarify meaning.

RESPOND TO THE ESSENTIAL QUESTION

Allow time for students to add details from "Satire Is Dying Because the Internet Is Killing It" to their Unit 3 Response Logs.

For **writing support** for students at varying proficiency levels, see the **Text X-Ray** on page 369D.

APPLY

CRITICAL VOCABULARY

Possible answers:

1. formulas
2. laughter
3. make more money
4. make fun of something
5. organizing the paintings
6. cooking for celebrities
7. high-school students
8. meat
9. spent it carelessly

VOCABULARY STRATEGY:
Antonyms

Answers:

1. increased, she went for a run
2. but voluntary for associate members
3. used to receiving praise and flattery
4. rainy; dried up and cracked

 **RESPOND**

WORD BANK

algorithm	monetize
satire	eschew
accolade	meme
spoof	finite
curate	

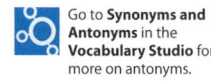 Go to **Synonyms and Antonyms** in the **Vocabulary Studio** for more on antonyms.

CRITICAL VOCABULARY

Practice and Apply Complete each sentence in a way that reflects the meaning of the Critical Vocabulary word.

1. An engineer might use an *algorithm* to create . . .
2. A typical response to a *satire* might be . . .
3. The *accolades* she received for her work made it possible to . . .
4. The purpose of a *spoof* is to . . .
5. To *curate* the exhibition, she spent hours . . .
6. The chef *monetized* his skills by . . .
7. The *meme* was passed around by . . .
8. As a vegetarian, she *eschewed* . . .
9. Although money was a *finite* commodity, he . . .

VOCABULARY STRATEGY: Context Clues

The **context** of an unfamiliar word—other words, sentences, and paragraphs around the word—often gives clues to its meaning. Sometimes an **antonym,** a word that is opposite of the unfamiliar word, appears in the context. An example of this kind of clue appears in "Satire Is Dying Because the Internet Is Killing It":

> The problem with satire in an age of finite attention and infinite content is that it makes you stop and think.

Understanding the word *finite* means "having bounds," you can guess that the word *infinite* means "having no boundaries or limits." Using a print or digital resource can also help you clarify meanings of unfamiliar words.

Practice and Apply In each of the sentences below, underline the antonyms and additional words or phrases that provide clues to the meaning of the italicized words from the selection.

1. As the medicine caused Maxine's fatigue to *diminish*, her energy increased, and she went for a run.
2. The federal organization passed a law indicating that attendance at meetings was *obligatory* for all executive members but voluntary for associate members.
3. Because the director is used to receiving praise and flattery for his work, he was not amused by the witty *parody* of his film.
4. As the rainy season subsided, the once-*saturated* ground dried up and cracked.

 ENGLISH LEARNER SUPPORT

Vocabulary Strategy Give students additional practice in determining the meanings of unfamiliar words from the selection, using context clues. Ask students to identify two Critical Vocabulary words they still find challenging and use a reference book to define each word. Then, ask them to write a sentence using the words. Ask students to exchange their sentences with a partner who chose two different words and see if they can determine the meaning of each other's words using the clues in the sentences. **LIGHT**

LANGUAGE CONVENTIONS:
Effective Words

The use of highly **effective words,** including adjectives and concrete nouns, helps the writer convey ideas clearly and connect with the audience. Whether trying to establish a serious or silly tone, the right choice of words allows a writer to capture the audience's attention and to convey a perspective.

Effective words help writers to infuse their writing with certain meanings. The "weight" of the words a writer might choose can depend on the intensity of the writer's tone and the ideas he or she wants to emphasize. These words might be understood according to their **connotation,** the shade of meaning that might connect to a neutral, positive, or negative feeling.

Neutral: He offered a decent excuse for his actions.
Positive: He offered a valid excuse for his actions.
Negative: He offered a lame excuse for his actions.

An **adjective** modifies nouns and pronouns. Well-chosen adjectives can also convey the "weight" of a writer's ideas.

bad judgment   keen understanding   flagrant injustice

A **concrete noun** names something that can be perceived by the senses. The use of such words might reflect the writer's effort to express ideas plainly and concisely. Concrete writing, which aims to give its audience a clear understanding of what it is about, is most engaging when it includes sensory details.

Vague: I really like satire a lot.
Concrete: I am swept up by fiery satire that seems to singe off my eyelashes.

Practice and Apply Copy paragraph 5 from the selection into your notebook. Then, underline all the effective words, circle the adjectives, and highlight the concrete nouns that you think enable the author to get her point across. Think about how her writing would have been different had she chosen a different set of words, and rewrite the paragraph using your own language.

RESPOND

Go to **Adjectives** in the **Grammar Studio** to learn more.

APPLY

LANGUAGE CONVENTIONS:
Effective Words

Review the information on **effective words, concrete nouns,** and **adjectives**. Remind students that not only do these words allow writers to effectively convey their ideas and **tone**, they also help the writer create vivid images that capture the audience's attention. Point out that the right words can make a story or an essay come alive. Remind students that when writing, authors have the choice to include words or phrases that have literal meanings or figurative meanings. In addition, certain words have very specific **connotations**, so writers need to take those connotations into account as they choose which words to use.

Work through the examples of positive, neutral, and negative **connotations** and discuss how each of the adjectives changes the meaning or the overall **tone**. Then review the impact of adjectives and concrete nouns on sentences. Ask students to come up with their own sentences that incorporate effective words, concrete nouns, and adjectives before asking them to complete the Practice and Apply activity.

Practice and Apply Have partners discuss what they underlined, circled, and highlighted in paragraph 5 and how they think the author's use of these specific words affected the overall meaning and **tone** of that paragraph. Then ask them to share their rewrites of the paragraph with each other and discuss how the meaning changed.

ENGLISH LEARNER SUPPORT

Language Conventions Use the following supports with students at varying proficiency levels:

- Write a sentence on the board using a neutral adjective (e.g., I am feeling alright.). Explain to students that "alright" is neutral because it doesn't really tell us if the person is feeling good or bad. Provide students with examples of words they might use instead (e.g., terrible, excited, angry) and explain that these words paint a better picture of how a person feels. **ALL LEVELS**

PLAN

from THE JOURNAL AND LETTERS OF FANNY BURNEY: AN ENCOUNTER WITH KING GEORGE III

Diary by Fanny Burney

GENRE ELEMENTS
DIARY

Tell students that since most **diaries** are private documents, they may include thoughts and opinions that the writer would not normally share in public. Also, since the diary is written from a particular person's point of view about his or her experiences, it is more **subjective** and biased than an **objective**, factual piece of news reporting. In this lesson, students will connect the personal events recounted in a diary to historical events.

LEARNING OBJECTIVES

- Connect to history and make inferences.
- Conduct research about the novels of Fanny Burney.
- Write a diary entry.
- Discuss a diary entry.
- Use context clues and synonyms.
- Use reflexive and intensive pronouns.
- **Language** Justify inferences using connecting words.

TEXT COMPLEXITY

Quantitative Measures	An Encounter with King George III	Lexile: 1380L

Qualitative Measures		
	Ideas Presented Much is explicit, but moves to some implied meaning. Requires some inferential reasoning.	
	Structures Used Primarily clear and chronological.	
	Language Used Archaic and formal language. Complex sentence structures.	
	Knowledge Required Cultural and historical references make heavier demands.	

PLAN

Online Ed

RESOURCES

- Unit 3 Response Log
- Selection Audio
- Reading Studio: Notice & Note
- Level Up Tutorial: First-Person Point of View
- Writing Studio: Narrative Techniques
- Speaking and Listening Studio: Preparing for Discussion
- Vocabulary Studio: Context Clues and Synonyms
- Grammar Studio: Module 2: Lesson 2: Pronouns
- "An Encounter with King George III" Selection Test

SUMMARIES

English

In this excerpt from her diary, Fanny Burney records that she has been ordered to avoid contact with King George III, whose mental health is fragile. At the start of a walk recommended by her doctor, Burney realizes that the king has spotted her, and she tries unsuccessfully to escape an encounter. Her concerns evaporate during their friendly exchange, however. Burney concludes that the king's health has improved and that he welcomes normal conversation.

Spanish

En este pasaje de su diario, Fanny Burney documenta que se le ordenó evitar el contacto con el rey Jorge III, cuya salud mental era frágil. Al inicio de un paseo recomendado por su doctor, Burney entiende que el rey la ha visto e intenta escapar del encuentro sin éxito. Pero sus preocupaciones se evaporan durante un intercambio amigable. Burney concluye que la salud del rey ha mejorado y por eso le ha dado paso a conversaciones normales.

SMALL-GROUP OPTIONS

Have students work in small groups and pairs to read and discuss the selection.

Numbered Heads Together

- After students have read through to paragraph 18, pose these questions to the class: *What is Burney feeling at this moment? Why is she feeling like this?*
- Have students form groups of four and number off 1-2-3-4 within the group.
- Have students discuss their responses to the question in their groups.
- Call a number from 1 to 4. The student with that number will then respond for the group.

Three-Minute Review

- After students read the text, set a timer for three minutes.
- Have students work independently to write clarifying questions about what they read.
- After three minutes, ask volunteers to share their questions.
- Briefly discuss answers to each question.

An Encounter with King George III **406B**

PLAN

Text X-Ray: English Learner Support
for "An Encounter with King George III"

Use the Text X-Ray and the supports and scaffolds in the Teacher's Edition to help guide students at different proficiency levels through the selection.

INTRODUCE THE SELECTION
DISCUSS AUTHORITY AND MENTAL ILLNESS

In this lesson, students will need to be able to discuss the challenges a person might face when encountering a person of authority who has a mental illness.

Tell students that *mental* means having to do with the mind and a person with *mental illness* may have trouble telling reality from fantasy. Review that an *authority* is someone in power with the right to command others.

Ask students to use prior knowledge and sentence frames as they discuss how an authority's mental illness could be problematic, such as: *A policeman with mental illness can be a problem because _____.*

CULTURAL REFERENCES

The following words or phrases may be unfamiliar to students:

- *to look sharp* (paragraph 6): to see things more clearly
- *Vesuvius* (paragraph 10): a volcano in Italy
- *received . . . intelligence* (paragraph 13): found out information
- *pages* (paragraph 32): male servants

LISTENING

Recognize Sounds

Help students recognize and distinguish sounds and intonation as they read aloud lines of dialogue from the text.

Use the following supports with students at varying proficiency levels:

- Read aloud a line of dialogue from the text and have students listen for your intonation and phrasing. Then, have students repeat it. **SUBSTANTIAL**
- Have partners take turns rereading lines of dialogue, listening for intonation and phrasing. Guide them to correct each other's pronunciation, intonation, and phrasing. **MODERATE**
- Have partners write out a conversation using lines from the text to create a short dialogue between the characters. Then, have them read aloud the conversation, listening for opportunities to correct each other's pronunciation, intonation, and phrasing, as necessary. **LIGHT**

PLAN

SPEAKING

Justify Inferences

Have students use connecting words as they justify their inferences. Provide a word bank, such as *because, since, as a result, however, in spite of, yet, on the other hand, or, rather*.

Use the following supports with students at varying proficiency levels:

- Model how to use a connecting word to justify an inference: *I think the king trusts Fanny **because** he likes her father.* Have students repeat your inference, emphasizing the connecting word. **SUBSTANTIAL**
- Provide the following inferences/reasons: *The king trusts Fanny/he likes her father. Fanny will not be afraid of the king the next time she meets him/he behaved well.* Guide them to connect each inference with a reason for it, using words from the bank. **MODERATE**
- Have one partner state an inference, such as: *I think the king trusts Fanny.* The other partner asks for justification: *Why do you think that?* The speaker responds using a connecting word from the bank: *Since the king likes Fanny's father's music, I think he also likes Fanny.* **LIGHT**

READING

Use Peer Support

Pair more-fluent readers with less-fluent readers and guide them to help each other develop vocabulary. Review familiar question stems, such as *How do you pronounce _____? What does _____ mean?*

Use the following supports with students at varying proficiency levels:

- Have a student read aloud a paragraph of the text as a partner follows along. Have students work together to fill in the question stems with words from the text that are unfamiliar or difficult to pronounce. **SUBSTANTIAL**
- Have a student read aloud several pages of the text. Guide a partner to correct pronunciation and intonation as necessary. Have the pair write a list of unfamiliar words or phrases and work together to define them. **MODERATE**
- Have partners silently reread the text. Then, have them take turns asking and answering questions about unfamiliar words or language structures. **LIGHT**

WRITING

Use Visual Support

Tell students that if they want to film the action described in the text, they can create a storyboard of images showing the sequence of events the camera could capture.

Use the following supports with students at varying proficiency levels:

- Work with students to help them identify the sequence of events in the diary entry. Write short phrases for students to copy, such as *Fanny sees king. Fanny runs.* Then, have students sketch visuals and write the phrases as captions. **SUBSTANTIAL**
- Have students create simple storyboards to show the action of the scene described in the diary. Guide them to label each image with a short caption. **MODERATE**
- Have students write detailed descriptions of images that show the action of the scene for their diary entry. Direct them to include details about the setting and characters. **LIGHT**

TEACH

? Connect to the ESSENTIAL QUESTION

Maximize student participation and focus attention by asking students to independently read and reflect on the Essential Question. Invite students to share their individual responses to the Essential Question with a partner. Ask for volunteers to share their most memorable experience with the entire class. Encourage students to use descriptive details when recounting their experiences. Follow-up questions might include these: How did the experience make the student feel? What effect did the experience have on the student's life? How does the experience continue to influence the student's life? Tell students the selection they are about to read is a firsthand account of one of Fanny Burney's most memorable experiences.

ANALYZE & APPLY

from THE JOURNAL AND LETTERS OF FANNY BURNEY: AN ENCOUNTER WITH KING GEORGE III

Diary by **Fanny Burney**

? ESSENTIAL QUESTION:

What is your most memorable experience?

WHEN STUDENTS STRUGGLE...

Build Background Explain that a **diary** is a form of prose known as literary nonfiction. A diary is a personal daily account of one's life experiences and impressions. Some are published because they provide a useful perspective on historical events or insight into the life of particular eras. As students read, ask them to make notes of details that reveal the personal, social, political, and economic contexts of 18th-century England.

 For additional support, go to the **Reading Studio** and assign the following Level Up tutorial: **Historical and Cultural Context.**

QUICK START

What are your most memorable experiences, and why are they memorable? What do you think makes experiences memorable? With a partner, discuss your answers to these questions.

CONNECT TO HISTORY

A diary documents the events in a person's life. To fully appreciate a diary entry from the distant past, readers need some background knowledge of the **historical context** in which the diary was written. Often, this context is not provided in the diary itself but requires some outside research to fully understand.

Footnotes will explain some details. To learn more about a topic mentioned in a diary, you need to do research. As you read this diary entry, you might go online to find information about King George's illness, the king's reign, or Fanny Burney's career.

In Burney's diary, she writes about having a personal encounter with King George III. This would have been an unusual experience for someone like Burney, who was not a member of the royal family or the aristocracy; she had been invited to the court several years earlier to serve Queen Charlotte as second keeper of the robes. As you read the diary, consider how this context helps you understand her reaction to the king.

MAKE INFERENCES

Fanny Burney's diary provides a rare personal account of the illness of King George, including details about his behavior and how it affected life at the royal court. As you read the selection, use text clues and your own knowledge to **make inferences,** or logical guesses, about the king's condition and the reactions of those around him. For example, you can infer from these lines that Burney avoids the king because she is worried about getting into trouble:

> This morning, when I received my intelligence of the king from Dr. John Willis, I begged to know where I might walk in safety? "In Kew gardens," he said, "as the king would be in Richmond."

As you read, record your inferences in a chart like the one below.

DETAILS FROM THE TEXT	MY INFERENCES
"…I thought I saw the person of his majesty! Alarmed past all possible expression, I waited not to know more, but turning back, ran off with all my might" (Lines 18–22).	Burney is terrified of the king. She may be afraid because he has displayed erratic or angry behavior in the past.

GENRE ELEMENTS: DIARY

- written in first-person point of view
- usually written in chronological order with separate entries for each day
- documents historical events from the perspective of the person experiencing them
- subjective and dependent on the perception of the writer

TEACH

QUICK START

Ask a volunteer to read the questions aloud. Prior to having students share their responses with a partner, engage students in a 3–5 minute Quick Write activity. Have students write their personal responses to the questions either in a journal or on a separate piece of paper. Use a timer to stop the activity after the allotted time has expired. Allow time for students to share their Quick Write activity with a partner. Point out that unforgettable memories are often created because of the strong emotions associated with an experience, good or bad.

CONNECT TO HISTORY

Engage students in a discussion of how literature offers readers critical information about historical time periods, social movements, and cultural trends. Point out to students that since a diary is meant to be personal, it often reveals intense feelings and thoughts that people had intended to be private. Instruct students to note information related to the historical context in which Burney recorded her thoughts in the diary. Remind students to use the footnotes throughout the selection to develop a better understanding of the circumstances under which Burney wrote.

MAKE INFERENCES

Tell students that an **inference** is a logical assumption that is based on observed facts and one's own knowledge and experience. Point out to students that writers do not tell their readers everything. They expect readers to bring their own personal experiences and backgrounds to a text in order to construct meaning and extend thinking. Ask students to closely read the sentences from the selection. Which detail from the sentences best supports the inference that Burney wants to avoid the king because she is worried about getting into trouble? Ask students to mark the detail in their text. Assist students in creating a chart on which they can record their inferences as they read. Teachers may also choose to display an inference chart in the classroom on which they can record text details and inferences to model the skill for students.

TEACH

CRITICAL VOCABULARY

Encourage students to read all the sentences before deciding which word best completes each one. Remind them to look for context clues that match the precise meaning of each word.

Answers:

1. *salutation*
2. *malady*
3. *undaunted*
4. *expound*
5. *anecdote*
6. *assent*

■ English Learner Support

Use Cognates Identify and display the Spanish cognates of the following Critical Vocabulary words: *salutation/el saludo* (paragraph 20); *expound/exponer* (paragraph 25); *assent/el asentimiento* (paragraph 29); *malady/el mal* (paragraph 32); and *anecdote/la anécdota* (paragraph 34). Students may work in small groups to generate a list of additional cognates of their home languages. These lists can be combined to create a class compilation list.
ALL LEVELS

LANGUAGE CONVENTIONS

Explain to students that **reflexive** and **intensive pronouns** differ in function and usage. Read aloud the example sentence for the reflexive pronoun, emphasizing the words *I* and *myself* to indicate how the reflexive pronoun (*myself*) reflects back on the earlier pronoun (*I*).

Review the information about an intensive pronoun. Read aloud the example sentence for an intensive pronoun, stressing the word *himself* to demonstrate the emphasis on the antecedent (*prince*). Discuss how the use of an intensive pronoun contributes to the tone of a sentence.

ANNOTATION MODEL

Remind students of the annotation ideas in Make Inferences on page 407, which suggest recording details from the text in a chart in order to make inferences about the circumstances of the king's court. Point out that they may follow this suggestion or use their own system for marking up the selection in their write-in text. They may want to color-code their annotations by using highlighters. Their notes in the margin may include questions about ideas that are unclear or topics they want to learn more about.

 **GET READY**

CRITICAL VOCABULARY

| malady | salutation | assent |
| undaunted | expound | anecdote |

To see how many Critical Vocabulary words you already know, use them to complete the sentences.

1. Sharice greeted the passengers as they boarded the plane, but they did not return her _____.
2. This particular _____ can be cured with antibiotics.
3. Though she lost her first race, she continued her training _____.
4. Would you care to _____ on that?
5. In her witty _____, Rebecca narrated the story.
6. The vote indicated _____ to the proposed changes.

LANGUAGE CONVENTIONS

Reflexive and Intensive Pronouns A **reflexive pronoun** follows a verb or a preposition and reflects back on an earlier noun or pronoun. Reflexive pronouns end in *-self* or *-selves*. Note the example:

> I cut my hair myself.

An **intensive pronoun** also ends in *-self* or *-selves* but has a different use. Intensive pronouns emphasize the antecedent. Note the example:

> The prince himself sent me the wedding invitation!

As you read Burney's diary entry, pay attention to how she uses reflexive and intensive pronouns and how this contributes to her tone and style.

ANNOTATION MODEL **NOTICE & NOTE**

As you read the selection, note how the author, who was not only a diarist but also a novelist, uses many of the techniques of fiction. This model shows one reader's notes about an excerpt from the diary.

> What an adventure had I this morning! one that has occasioned me the severest personal terror I ever experienced in my life.

The author captures readers' attention by introducing the conflict immediately.

BACKGROUND

Frances "Fanny" Burney (1752–1840) became a successful published novelist at a time when writing for a living was considered unsuitable for a lady. However, Burney's popular novels gained her entrance to the men's world of English literature and paved the way for other women writers. Her success led to her becoming a prominent member of the British social scene. Burney was invited to the royal court of King George III and Queen Charlotte in 1785, where she remained for five years until problems with her health led to her resignation. She documented who and what she observed in a diary that was published several years after her death.

AN ENCOUNTER WITH KING GEORGE III

Diary by Fanny Burney

SETTING A PURPOSE

As you read, pay attention to how King George III and his illness are characterized.

Kew Palace, Monday February 2, 1789

1 What an adventure had I this morning! one that has occasioned me the severest personal terror I ever experienced in my life.

2 Sir Lucas Pepys[1] still persisting that exercise and air were absolutely necessary to save me from illness, I have continued my walks, varying my gardens from Richmond to Kew,[2] according to the accounts I received of the movements of the king. For this I had her majesty's permission, on the representation of Sir Lucas.

3 This morning, when I received my intelligence of the king from Dr. John Willis,[3] I begged to know where I might

---

[1] **Sir Lucas Pepys** (pēps): a physician who was an old friend of the Burney family.
[2] **gardens from Richmond to Kew:** the gardens at Richmond House and Kew House, two adjoining royal residences west of London that were often used by George III and his family.
[3] **Dr. John Willis:** a clergyman and physician who attended George III during his illness. His son, John Willis, also a physician, assisted in treating the king.

Notice & Note

Use the side margins to notice and note signposts in the text.

CONNECT TO HISTORY

Annotate: Mark paragraph 2 where Fanny's diary entry connects to what you just learned about her in the Background feature.

Analyze: How does this part of the diary connect to biographical details from Fanny's life?

An Encounter with King George III 409

TEACH

BACKGROUND

After students read the Background note, tell them that Fanny was the middle child in a large family. Both of her parents were musicians, and her father had a doctorate in music from Oxford. Fanny did not learn to read until she was 8 years old but started writing when she was 16. After the death of her mother, she devoted herself to her father's career, acting as his secretary and helping him write his ambitious history of music. Dr. Burney's growing reputation first brought her into contact with leading artists and intellectuals. With the spotlight on her father, Burney wrote for herself in secret and published all four of her novels anonymously. Even her father didn't know she was writing until after the runaway success of her first novel, *Evelina* (1778).

SETTING A PURPOSE

Direct students to use the Setting a Purpose prompt to focus their reading.

CONNECT TO HISTORY

Explain that knowing the **historical** and **cultural context** in which a literary work was written helps readers better understand, interpret, and analyze the work. To fully appreciate a literary work, like a diary, it helps readers to know and apply information about an author's background as they read the text. (**Answer:** *Fanny eventually had to leave the court due to illness. In paragraph 2, Fanny's doctor tries to help her find a way to recover.*)

TO CHALLENGE STUDENTS . . .

Analyzing Author's Craft Explain that word choice, sentence length, tone, imagery, and use of dialogue all contribute to an author's style. **Style** is the distinctive way in which a work of literature is written. Explain that style refers not so much to what an author writes but how an author writes it. Utilize a Think-Pair-Share activity to examine Burney's style of writing. Think: Have students read paragraphs 1 and 2, marking words that reflect Burney's deliberate word choices. Pair: Ask students to partner with a peer to share the rationale behind the words identified. Share: Discuss as a class how Burney's style contributes to the overall mood and tone of the diary entry. What effect do the opening lines of the diary have on readers?

An Encounter with King George III **409**

TEACH

LANGUAGE CONVENTIONS

Remind students that **reflexive pronouns** end in *-self* or *-selves*. Other reflexive pronouns include *himself, herself, yourself, itself,* and *themselves*. Reflexive pronouns are always the object of a sentence and can never be the subject. (**Answer:** *Because kings did not do very many tasks themselves, it suggests the king takes a personal interest.*)

MAKE INFERENCES

Remind students to use text details, clues, and their own knowledge to make **inferences,** or logical guesses, about the effects of the king's condition on those around him. (**Answer:** *The king keeps the royal court on edge because the style and intensity of his illness is not predictable. His mood changes from day to day.*)

ENGLISH LEARNER SUPPORT

Identify Affixes Explain that many languages around the world share some basic linguistic characteristics, such as using word parts like prefixes and suffixes. The prefixes *re-* and *dis-* serve similar functions in both English and Spanish.

Prefix	Meaning	English Word	Spanish Word
dis-	not	dislike	disparejo
re-	again	redo	rehacer

Ask students to locate the words *recollected* and *disobedience* within the text. Discuss the meaning of each word.

recollected means to remember <u>again</u>.
disobedience means act of <u>not</u> obeying.

Have students create a list of other words that include the prefixes *re-* and *dis-* and discuss the meanings of the words. **ALL LEVELS**

CRITICAL VOCABULARY

malady: When people are ill or not well, they are said to have a *malady* or ailment.

ASK STUDENTS to describe what symptoms or behaviors they might notice if their close friend was not feeling well. (*If a friend was not feeling well, he or she might be quiet, pale, weak, and tired.*)

410 Unit 3

 **NOTICE & NOTE**

4 walk in safety? "In Kew gardens," he said, "as the king would be in Richmond."

4 "Should any unfortunate circumstance," I cried, "at any time, occasion my being seen by his majesty, do not mention my name, but let me run off without call or notice."

5 This he promised. Everybody, indeed, is ordered to keep out of sight.

6 Taking, therefore, the time I had most at command, I strolled into the gardens. I had proceeded, in my quick way, nearly half the round, when I suddenly perceived, through some trees, two or three figures. Relying on the instructions of Dr. John, I concluded them to be workmen and gardeners; yet tried to look sharp, and in so doing, as they were less shaded, I thought I saw the person of his majesty!

LANGUAGE CONVENTIONS
Annotate: Mark the reflexive pronouns that Burney uses in paragraph 7.
Analyze: What distressful prospect does she face here?

7 Alarmed past all possible expression, I waited not to know more, but turning back, ran off with all my might. But what was my terror to hear myself pursued!—to hear the voice of the king himself loudly and hoarsely calling after me, "Miss Burney! Miss Burney!"

8 I protest I was ready to die. I knew not in what state he might be at the time; I only knew the orders to keep out of his way were universal; that the queen would highly disapprove any unauthorized meeting, and that the very action of my running away might deeply, in his present irritable state, offend him. Nevertheless, on I ran, too terrified to stop, and in search of some short passage, for the garden is full of little labyrinths, by which I might escape.

9 The steps still pursued me, and still the poor hoarse and altered voice rang in my ears:—more and more footsteps resounded frightfully behind me,—the attendants all running, to catch their eager master, and the voices of the two Doctor Willises loudly exhorting him not to heat himself so unmercifully.

10 Heavens, how I ran! I do not think I should have felt the hot lava from Vesuvius—at least not the hot cinders—had I so run during its eruption. My feet were not sensible that they even touched the ground.

MAKE INFERENCES
Annotate: Mark the sentence in paragraph 13 that tells you about the king's illness.
Analyze: What can you infer about the king based on this sentence?

malady
(măl´ə-dē) *n.* a disease, disorder, or ailment.

11 Soon after, I heard other voices, shriller, though less nervous, call out "Stop! stop! stop!"

12 I could by no means consent; I knew not what was purposed, but I recollected fully my agreement with Dr. John that very morning, that I should decamp if surprised, and not be named.

13 My own fears and repugnance, also, after a flight and disobedience like this, were doubled in the thought of not escaping; <u>I knew not to what I might be exposed, should the **malady** be then high,[4] and take the turn of resentment.</u> Still, therefore, on I flew; and

---

[4] **be then high:** then be greater, or worse, than usual.

410 Unit 3

TO CHALLENGE STUDENTS . . .

Analyze Allusion Point out the **allusion** to Vesuvius that Burney uses in paragraph 10. An allusion is an indirect reference to a person, place, event or literary work with which the author believes the reader will be familiar. Point out to students that the effect of an allusion is dependent on the reader's background knowledge and experiences. Activate student background and formulate ideas by asking students to freewrite for three minutes. Challenge students to work in small groups to rewrite paragraph 10 in order to insert an allusion to a modern-day event without changing the overall meaning and purpose of the paragraph. Invite a student from each group to read the original paragraph to the class.

such was my speed, so almost incredible to relate or recollect, that I fairly believe no one of the whole party could have overtaken me, if these words, from one of the attendants, had not reached me: "Doctor Willis begs you to stop!"

14 "I cannot! I cannot!" I answered, still flying on, when he called out "You must, ma'am; it hurts the king to run."

15 Then, indeed, I stopped—in a state of fear really amounting to agony. I turned round, I saw the two doctors had got the king between them, and three attendants of Dr. Willis's were hovering about. They all slackened their pace, as they saw me stand still; but such was the excess of my alarm, that I was wholly insensible[5] to the effects of a race which, at any other time, would have required an hour's recruit.[6]

16 As they approached, some little presence of mind happily came to my command; it occurred to me that, to appease the wrath of[7] my flight, I must now show some confidence. I therefore faced them as **undauntedly** as I was able, only charging the nearest of the attendants to stand by my side.

17 When they were within a few yards of me, the king called out, "Why did you run away?"

18 Shocked at a question impossible to answer, yet a little assured by the mild tone of his voice, I instantly forced myself forward, to meet him, though the internal sensation, which satisfied me this was a step the most proper to appease his suspicions and displeasure, was so violently combated by the tremor of my nerves, that I fairly think I may reckon it the greatest effort of personal courage I have ever made.

19 The effort answered:[8] I looked up, and met all his wonted benignity of countenance,[9] though something still of wildness in his eyes. Think, however, of my surprise, to feel him put both his hands round my two shoulders, and then kiss my cheek!

20 I wonder I did not really sink, so exquisite was my affright when I saw him spread out his arms! Involuntarily, I concluded he meant to crush me; but the Willises, who have never seen him till this fatal illness, not knowing how very extraordinary an action this was from him, simply smiled and looked pleased, supposing, perhaps, it was his customary **salutation**!

21 I believe, however, it was but the joy of a heart unbridled, now, by the forms and proprieties of established custom and sober reason. To see any of his household thus by accident, seemed such a near

---

undaunted
(ŭn-dôn′tĭd, -dän′-) *adj.* not discouraged or disheartened; resolutely courageous.

salutation
(săl′yə-tā′shən) *n.* a polite expression of greeting or goodwill.

---

[5] **wholly insensible:** completely unaware.
[6] **recruit** (rĭ-krōōt′): recovery; renewal of strength.
[7] **appease the wrath of:** make up for the fury of.
[8] **answered:** met the situation; worked.
[9] **his wonted benignity** (wôn′tĭd bĭ-nĭg′nĭ-tē) **of countenance** (koun′tə-nəns): the customary kindness of his facial expression.

An Encounter with King George III   411

TEACH

ENGLISH LEARNER SUPPORT

Use Synonyms Show students how to substitute a synonym for unknown or unfamiliar words they encounter while reading. Explain that a synonym is a word that has a meaning similar to that of another word. Refer to the definitions of both words that appear on the page. Read paragraphs 16 and 20 aloud to students to model correct pronunciation of words and speaking patterns. Ask students to generate a list of possible synonyms that could be substituted in the text for each word.

Vocabulary Word	Synonyms
undaunted	bravely, courageously, boldly, fearlessly
salutation	greetings, welcome, introductions

ALL LEVELS

CRITICAL VOCABULARY

undaunted: Rescue workers are neither intimidated nor discouraged by dangerous conditions because of their *undaunted* courage and selflessness.

ASK STUDENTS to make a list of characteristics associated with heroes. *(Heroes are steadfast, brave, resolute, resilient, and unstoppable, etc.)*

salutation: As a sign of goodwill and friendship, the youth ambassadors exchanged pleasant *salutations* during their first meeting.

ASK STUDENTS to describe how they might greet or welcome a close family relative or friend. *(Most people would smile warmly, make eye contact, embrace, give a kiss on the cheek, or extend a friendly handshake.)*

An Encounter with King George III   411

WHEN STUDENTS STRUGGLE...

Make Inferences Have student continue to record text details and their inferences on the chart that was introduce in the Get Ready section. Use the chart below to model how text details support the inferences readers make while interacting with text.

Details from the Text	My Inferences

 For additional support, go to the **Reading Studio** and assign the following Level Up tutorial: Making Inferences.

TEACH

CONNECT TO HISTORY

Explain to students that members of royalty must follow strict protocols. Discuss how the king's behavior went against the rules of decorum. Ask students what Burney's reaction tells them about the king's statement and how kings were expected to behave at the time. (**Answer:** *Burney is shocked by the king's statement that he is her friend. This implies that it would be very unusual and even shocking for a king to speak so intimately with someone in Burney's position.*)

ENGLISH LEARNER SUPPORT

Understand Language Structure Have students scan paragraphs 26 through 30 to identify the author's use of em dashes throughout the paragraphs. Explain that em dashes create strong feelings and build anticipation in the reader. Emdashes are punctuation marks that cause the reader to pause. Read aloud paragraphs 26 through 30, using appropriate pauses and emphasis to indicate the use of emdashes. Use choral reading to reread paragraphs 27 through 30. Have students read along with the teacher while the teacher's voice acts as a model.
MODERATE/LIGHT

CRITICAL VOCABULARY

expound: If a teacher asked a student to *expound* on his answer, the student would explain his answer in great detail.

ASK STUDENTS to describe how they might deliver an argument for a public debate. (*Students would systematically present information they gathered from researching a particular controversial topic.*)

assent: If everyone in a meeting nods their head in agreement with a decision, they acknowledge their approval or acceptance of the decision.

ASK STUDENTS if the majority of the student body *assent* to a policy requiring school uniforms. (*Answers will vary.*)

412 Unit 3

 **NOTICE & NOTE**

approach to liberty and recovery, that who can wonder it should serve rather to elate than lessen what yet remains of his disorder!

22 He now spoke in such terms of his pleasure in seeing me, that I soon lost the whole of my terror; astonishment to find him so nearly well, and gratification to see him so pleased, removed every uneasy feeling, and the joy that succeeded, in my conviction of his recovery, made me ready to throw myself at his feet to express it.

23 What a conversation followed! When he saw me fearless, he grew more and more alive, and made me walk close by his side, away from the attendants, and even the Willises themselves, who, to indulge him, retreated. I own[10] myself not completely composed, but alarm I could entertain no more.

24 Everything that came uppermost in his mind he mentioned; he seemed to have just such remains of his flightiness as heated his imagination without deranging his reason, and robbed him of all control over his speech, though nearly in his perfect state of mind as to his opinions.

25 What did he not say!—He opened his whole heart to me,— **expounded** all his sentiments, and acquainted me with all his intentions.

26 The heads of his discourse[11] I must give you briefly, as I am sure you will be highly curious to hear them, and as no accident can render of much consequence what a man says in such a state of physical intoxication. He assured me he was quite well—as well as he had ever been in his life; and then inquired how I did, and how I went on? and whether I was more comfortable? If these questions, in their implication, surprised me, imagine how that surprise must increase when he proceeded to explain them! He asked after the coadjutrix,[12] laughing, and saying "Never mind her!—don't be oppressed—I am your friend! don't let her cast you down!—I know you have a hard time of it—but don't mind her!"

27 Almost thunderstruck with astonishment, I merely curtsied to his kind "I am your friend," and said nothing.

28 Then presently he added, "Stick to your father—stick to your own family—let them be your objects."

29 How readily I **assented**!

30 Again he repeated all I have just written, nearly in the same words, but ended it more seriously: he suddenly stopped, and held me to stop too, and putting his hand on his breast, in the most solemn manner, he gravely and slowly said, "I will protect you!—I promise you that—and therefore depend upon me!"

expound
(ĭk-spound´) *v.* to explain in detail; elucidate.

CONNECT TO HISTORY
Annotate: Mark the king's comments in paragraph 26 and then mark in paragraph 27 the author's reaction to his comment.
Analyze: What does Burney's reaction tell you about the king's statement and how kings were expected to behave at the time?

assent
(ə-sĕnt´) *intr.v.* to express agreement or acceptance, as of a proposal.

---
[10] **own:** admit.
[11] **heads of his discourse:** main points of his conversation.
[12] **coadjutrix** (kō-ə-jū´trĭks): Elizabeth Juliana Schwellenberg, First Keeper of the Robes to Queen Charlotte and Fanny's immediate superior. She was known to be bossy and difficult toward the rest of the royal household staff and gave Fanny a terrible time.

APPLYING ACADEMIC VOCABULARY

☑ encounter   ☑ exploit   ☐ persist   ☐ subordinate   ☐ widespread

Write and Discuss Have students turn to a partner to discuss the following questions. Guide students to include the Academic Vocabulary words *encounter* and *exploit* in their responses. Ask volunteers to share their responses with the class.

- How might a person react to an unexpected **encounter** with a member of a royal family? How might a king's illness be used to **exploit** information from him?

31 I thanked him; and the Willises, thinking him rather too elevated,[13] came to propose my walking on. "No, no, no!" he cried, a hundred times in a breath; and their good humor prevailed, and they let him again walk on with his new companion.

32 He then gave me a history of his pages,[14] animating almost into a rage, as he related his subjects of displeasure with them, particularly with Mr. Ernst, who he told me had been brought up by himself. I hope his ideas upon these men are the result of the mistakes of his malady.

33 Then he asked me some questions that very greatly distressed me, relating to information given him in his illness, from various motives, but which he suspected to be false, and which I knew he had reason to suspect; yet was it most dangerous to set anything right, as I was not aware what might be the views of their having been stated wrong. I was as discreet as I knew how to be, and I hope I did no mischief; but this was the worst part of the dialogue.

34 He next talked to me a great deal of my dear father, and made a thousand inquiries concerning his "History of Music."[15] This brought him to his favorite theme, Handel;[16] and he told me innumerable **anecdotes** of him, and particularly that celebrated tale of Handel's saying of himself, when a boy, "While that boy lives, my music will never want a protector." And this, he said, I might relate to my father. Then he ran over most of his oratorios, attempting to sing the subjects of several airs and choruses,[17] but so dreadfully hoarse that the sound was terrible.

35 Dr. Willis, quite alarmed at this exertion, feared he would do himself harm, and again proposed a separation. "No! no! no!" he exclaimed, "not yet; I have something I must just mention first."

36 Dr. Willis, delighted to comply, even when uneasy at compliance, again gave way. The good king then greatly affected me. He began upon my revered old friend, Mrs. Delany;[18] and he spoke of her with such warmth—such kindness! "She was my friend!" he cried, "and I loved her as a friend! I have made a memorandum when I lost her—I will show it you."

anecdote
(ăn´ĭk-dōt) *n.* a short account of an interesting or humorous incident.

[13] **elevated:** excited.
[14] **pages:** young male servants attending a king or someone else of high rank.
[15] **"History of Music":** Fanny's father, Dr. Charles Burney, was a music historian best known for his *General History of Music*, the third and fourth volumes of which were published in 1789, the same year in which the events in this selection occurred.
[16] **Handel** (hăn´dl): George Frideric Handel (1685–1759), the great composer and a favorite of the king's father, George II.
[17] **oratorios** (ôr-ə-tôr´ē-ōz) . . . **choruses:** long, dramatic musical compositions that contain arias (or "airs"), choruses, and other portions to be sung but that differ from operas in not being performed with stage action, scenery, and costumes.
[18] **Mrs. Delany:** Mary Delany, an elderly friend of Fanny's who had recently died.

TEACH

ENGLISH LEARNER SUPPORT

Use Context Clues Have students identify unfamiliar words such as *prevailed* and *companion* in paragraph 31, *discreet* in paragraph 33, and *inquiries* and *dreadfully* in paragraph 34. Invite students to make a list of new words they encounter in their reading. Allow time for students to collaborate and look for context clues that hint at the meanings of the unknown words. Challenge students to guess at the word's meaning based on context clues before they consult a dictionary.
ALL LEVELS

WHEN STUDENTS STRUGGLE . . .

Paraphrase Text Explain to students that paraphrasing helps readers focus on the most important details of a text. Have students reread paragraph 34 until they believe they understand the full meaning and intention of Burney's words. Next, have students use a notecard to cover the paragraph. Once the paragraph cannot be seen, ask students to work in pairs to write out the main gist of the paragraph. Have students check their writing against Burney's original writing.

 For additional support, go to the **Reading Studio** and assign the following **Level Up tutorial: Paraphrasing.**

CRITICAL VOCABULARY

anecdote: At holiday parties, family members may share funny and embarrassing *anecdotes* or stories to entertain guests.

ASK STUDENTS to describe how their friends would respond if someone started telling an anecdote about something funny that happened in class. (*Friends would listen very closely so that they did not miss any of the good parts of the story.*)

TEACH

CONTRASTS AND CONTRADICTIONS

Explain to students that contrasts and contradictions can help students understand similarities and differences between two or more ideas, characters, themes, etc. Help students connect with text by asking them under what circumstances might they or someone they know open their heart to someone. Ask students to share their impressions of the king's behavior. Did his actions or words surprise them? Did the king act as one would expect a king to act? Ask students to recall what the king does to astound the narrator. Is this how a king is supposed to act? (**Answer:** *Kings are not expected to discuss matters of state with keepers of robes.*)

ENGLISH LEARNER SUPPORT

Understand Idioms Discuss with students the phrase, "–as soon as I get loose again!" from paragraph 41. This is an example of an idiom. An idiom is a common figure of speech whose meaning is different from the literal meaning of its words. Utilize Think-Pair-Share strategy to have students guess what the king means when he says "–as soon as I get loose again!" Have students talk about situations where they might use the phrase. Then, have students practice writing their own sentences using the phrase. Invite students to share their sentences with the class by reading them aloud. **LIGHT**

 **NOTICE & NOTE**

37 He pulled out a pocketbook,[19] and rummaged some time, but to no purpose. The tears stood in his eyes—he wiped them, and Dr. Willis again became very anxious. "Come, sir," he cried, "now do you come in and let the lady go on her walk,—come, now you have talked a long while,—so we'll go in,—if your majesty pleases."

38 "No, no!" he cried, "I want to ask her a few questions;—I have lived so long out of the world, I know nothing!"

39 This touched me to the heart. . . . He then told me he was very much dissatisfied with several of his state officers, and meant to form an entire new establishment. He took a paper out of his pocketbook, and showed me his new list.

CONTRASTS AND CONTRADICTIONS

Notice and Note: In paragraphs 39–40, mark what the king does that astounds the narrator.

Compare: How does this contrast with the behavior that would be expected from a king?

40 This was the wildest thing that passed; and Dr. John Willis now seriously urged our separating; but he would not consent; he had only three more words to say, he declared, and again he conquered.

41 He now spoke of my father, with still more kindness, and told me he ought to have had the post of master of the band, and not that little poor musician Parsons,[20] who was not fit for it: "But Lord Salisbury,"[21] he cried, "used your father very ill in that business, and so he did me! However, I have dashed out his name, and I shall put your father's in,—as soon as I get loose again!"

42 This again—how affecting was this!

43 "And what," cried he, "has your father got, at last? nothing but that poor thing at Chelsea?[22] O fie! fie! fie! But never mind! I will take care of him! I will do it myself!" Then presently he added, "As to Lord Salisbury, he is out already, as this memorandum will show you, and so are many more. I shall be much better served; and when once I get away, I shall rule with a rod of iron!"

44 This was very unlike himself, and startled the two good doctors, who could not bear to cross him, and were exulting at my seeing his great amendment,[23] but yet grew quite uneasy at his earnestness and volubility.

45 Finding we now must part, he stopped to take leave, and renewed again his charges about the coadjutrix. "Never mind her!" he cried, "depend upon me! I will be your friend as long as I live!—I here

---

[19] **pocketbook:** a case or folder for carrying money or papers in one's pocket.
[20] **he ought . . . Parsons:** Dr. Burney applied for the position of Master of the King's Band when it became vacant, but the post was instead given to a William Parsons.
[21] **Lord Salisbury** (sôlz´bĕr-ē): James Cecil, Marquess of Salisbury, who served as the royal household's Lord Chamberlain from 1783 to 1804, would have been involved in deciding who obtained the position of Master of the King's Band.
[22] **that poor thing at Chelsea** (chĕl´sē): Instead of Master of the King's Band, Dr. Burney was made organist in the chapel on the grounds of Chelsea Hospital, a refuge for old and disabled soldiers located in London.
[23] **amendment:** change for the better; improvement.

IMPROVE READING FLUENCY

Targeted Passage Supporting students as they practice reading aloud with appropriate pacing, intonation, and pacing will improve their comprehension. Read paragraphs 37–40 aloud to students to model how to read both narration and dialogue within literary nonfiction. After listening to the teacher read, have students work with partners to practice reading the targeted passage independently. Have students take turns listening and reading. Encourage students to give helpful feedback and support.

 Go to the **Reading Studio** for additional support in developing fluency.

pledge myself to be your friend!" And then he saluted me again just as at the meeting, and suffered me to go on.

46   What a scene! how variously was I affected by it! but, upon the whole, how inexpressibly thankful to see him so nearly himself—so little removed from recovery!

NOTICE & NOTE

CHECK YOUR UNDERSTANDING

Answer these questions before moving on to the **Analyze the Text** section on the following page.

1 What does Burney do when she sees King George III in the gardens?

   A She greets him and starts a conversation.

   B She quickly runs away.

   C She joins him for his walk.

   D She does nothing and continues on her walk.

2 Which member of Burney's family does the king speak kindly of?

   F Her father

   G Her mother

   H Her sister-in-law

   J Her brother

3 What did Burney note was the *"wildest thing that had passed"*?

   A The king read a eulogy for a mutual friend who had died.

   B His doctors wanted him to continue with his walk, but the king refused to listen.

   C The king talked about Burney's father's work in music.

   D The king shared with Burney plans for changing his state officers and forming a new establishment.

An Encounter with King George III   415

TEACH

CHECK YOUR UNDERSTANDING

Have students answer the questions independently.

Answers:

1. B
2. F
3. D

If they answer any questions incorrectly, have them reread the text to confirm their understanding. Then they may proceed to ANALYZE THE TEXT on page 416.

ENGLISH LEARNER SUPPORT

Oral Assessment Divide students into small groups of three. Have students respond to a series of true-false questions delivered orally by the teacher. Students may indicate their answers to the questions either by raising their hand or writing their responses on paper.

1. What does Burney do when she sees King George III in the gardens? *(runs away)*

2. Which member of Burney's family does the king speak kindly of? *(Burney's father)*

3. Burney thought the *"wildest thing"* that had happened was _____. *(The king shared his plans to change state officers and to form a new establishment.)* **ALL LEVELS**

An Encounter with King George III   **415**

APPLY

ANALYZE THE TEXT

Possible answers:

1. **DOK 2:** *It can be inferred that the king's condition is precarious and very worrisome to those charged with taking care of him.*

2. **DOK 4:** *Burney very deliberately plans her morning walk around the grounds of the royal palace to avoid an encounter with the king. When she does unexpectedly cross paths with the king, she runs away. The king frantically pursues Burney and commands her to stop. It is not until she hears the voices of his attendants, does she turn to acknowledge the presence of the king. While Burney is acutely aware that the king's behavior is uncharacteristic of him, she relishes the memorable experience of interacting with King George III.*

3. **DOK 3:** *Hugging Burney seems impulsive and inappropriate, especially considering his position as king.*

4. **DOK 4:** *It is customary for people to share intimate details of their lives with those they deeply trust and know well. Most likely, people only open their hearts to someone they know will not gossip, break confidentiality, or betray them with the information. This level of trust is especially important to a ruler or a member of the royal family.*

5. **DOK 4:** *Based on Burney's account of the events in her diary, readers understand that King George III suffers from a complex condition that impedes his judgment and ability to self-regulate. In paragraph 25, Burney recounts that the king " . . . –expounded all his sentiments, and acquainted me with all his intentions."*

RESEARCH

Remind students that they should confirm any information they find by checking multiple websites and assessing the credibility of each one.

Connect Have students work with partners to research the British royal family. Have them take and compare notes on how the British monarchy and their roles today are similar and different since the time of King George III.

416   Unit 3

 **RESPOND**

ANALYZE THE TEXT

Support your responses with evidence from the text. NOTEBOOK

1. **Infer** In paragraphs 36–38, Dr. Willis is distressed by the king's behavior. What can be inferred from his concern?

2. **Draw Conclusions** Summarize the events in each of the following scenes. To what extent is Burney's initial "terror" of the king justified?
   - her plans for a morning walk (paragraphs 2–4)
   - her flight from the king (paragraphs 7–8)
   - her "disobedience" (paragraphs 10–11)
   - the king's treatment of her (paragraphs 19–20)

3. **Evaluate** Reread paragraph 19. What do the king's appearance and actions toward Burney reveal about him?

4. **Connect** Consider your own familiarity with diaries or journals. Based on reading this account, what insights have you gained into the importance of diaries to life in the 18th century?

5. **Synthesize** Using information from Burney's diary, what is your understanding of George III's condition? Cite specific details in your response.

RESEARCH

RESEARCH TIP
The best search terms are specific. In addition to an author's name, you will want to include a word such as *novels* to help you find the information you need.

It is often said that novelists should write what they know. Do some research on Burney's novels and think about how her life experiences may have contributed to these novels. Use the chart below for your notes.

NOVEL	HOW DOES BURNEY "WRITE WHAT SHE KNOWS" IN THIS NOVEL?
Evelina	*In Evelina, the protagonist learns how to navigate London's social scene. This is similar to how Burney learned to navigate the British social scene to break into writing.*

Connect Do some research about the current British royal family. Based on what you have learned from reading this selection, what has changed about the British monarchy and their roles and responsibilities since the time of King George III?

416   Unit 3

WHEN STUDENTS STRUGGLE . . .

Reteach: Read for Details Explain to students that when reading for details, they must adjust their reading rate and do a close read of each and every sentence. Remind students that when approaching complex texts, students should be prepared to reread as needed. Invite students to share their notes they made from the Get Ready section. Provide students feedback to strengthen their ability to identify relevant text details to support their inferences.

For additional support, go to the **Reading Studio** and assign the following **Level Up tutorial: Reading for Details.**

CREATE AND DISCUSS

Write a Diary Entry Imagine that you are a royal court doctor described in Burney's diary entry. You may also choose another person present at the scene. Write your own diary entry depicting the scene from your perspective. Think about how Burney may have misunderstood the motivations of others present in the garden, and try to portray the scene from a new perspective.

- ❏ Choose one of the king's attendants as your character.
- ❏ Relate the enounter from his first-person point of view.
- ❏ Be sure to represent your character's personality in the entry.

Discuss a Diary Entry With a partner, take turns reading your diary entries. Then discuss them. How do your entries compare? In reading aloud, use the enunciation and speaking rate to match your character.

- ❏ Consider how different perspectives affect the narration of the event.
- ❏ Think about your character's view of the king and of Burney.

RESPOND

 Go to **Writing Narratives** in the **Writing Studio** for help in writing your diary entry.

Go to **Participating in Collaborative Discussions** in the **Speaking and Listening Studio** for more.

ACADEMIC VOCABULARY

As you write and discuss what you learned from the diary entry, be sure to use the Academic Vocabulary words. Check off each of the words that you use.

- ❏ encounter
- ❏ exploit
- ❏ persist
- ❏ subordinate
- ❏ widespread

RESPOND TO THE ESSENTIAL QUESTION

 What is your most memorable experience?

Gather Information Review your annotations and notes on *The Journal and Letters of Fanny Burney: An Encounter with King George III*. Then, add relevant information to your Response Log. As you determine which information to include, think about:

- how Burney sets up her story by providing background information about herself and the king
- how Burney works in her own thoughts and feelings as she tells the story
- how Burney uses sensory details to make the memory vivid and exciting

APPLY

CREATE AND DISCUSS

Write a Diary Entry Direct students to look back at the text when Burney is in the garden. Have them think about how they would have felt being a doctor witnessing the events that took place in the garden.

Discuss a Diary Entry As they listen to each other's diary entries, tell students to feel free to take notes or write down questions they might have so that they can ask them at the end. Encourage students to note similarities and differences in their diary entries, and then discuss how word choice affected the tone of each entry.

RESPOND TO THE ESSENTIAL QUESTION

Allow time for students to add details from "An Encounter with King George III" to their Unit 3 Response Logs.

APPLY

CRITICAL VOCABULARY

Answers:

1. A
2. B
3. C
4. A
5. B
6. C

VOCABULARY STRATEGY: SYNONYMS

Answers:

1. Overpowering surprise (synonym: "thunderstruck")
2. To exercise authority over ("cast your down")
3. act of yielding (synonym: "gave way")

 **RESPOND**

WORD BANK
malady
undaunted
salutation
expound
assent
anecdote

CRITICAL VOCABULARY

Practice and Apply Circle the letter of the best answer to each question. Then explain your answer.

1. Which is an example of a **malady**?
   a. the flu
   b. a song
   c. a vehicle

2. Which is an example of an **anecdote**?
   a. a cure for poison
   b. a story told to illustrate a point in a speech
   c. a law or regulation

3. Which is an example of **expounding**?
   a. firing someone from their job
   b. throwing a bad fish overboard
   c. explaining instructions in further detail

4. Which is an example of a **salutation**?
   a. Hello
   b. Mrs.
   c. King

5. Which is an example of someone who is **undaunted**?
   a. a person who flees at danger
   b. a person who keeps trying no matter what
   c. a person who speaks to himself or herself

6. Which is an example of giving **assent**?
   a. arguing
   b. explaining
   c. agreeing

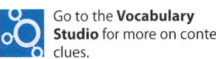 Go to the **Vocabulary Studio** for more on context clues.

VOCABULARY STRATEGY: Context Clues

Synonyms are words similar in meaning to another word. *Happy* and *content* are synonyms. A synonym is one kind of **context clue** you can use when trying to figure out the meaning of an unfamiliar word. In this example from Burney's diary, notice how the word *anecdotes* has a corresponding synonym:

> This brought him to his favorite theme, Handel; and he told me innumerable anecdotes of him, and particularly that celebrated tale of Handel's saying of himself, when a boy, "While that boy lives, my music will never want a protector."

Practice and Apply Find each of these words in the selection. Define it and identify the synonym used as a context clue that helped you identify its meaning as it is used in the diary entry.

1. astonishment (paragraph 27)
2. oppressed (paragraph 26)
3. compliance (paragraph 36)

418 Unit 3

 ENGLISH LEARNER SUPPORT

Acquire New Vocabulary Explain that a syllable is the sound of a vowel that is created when pronouncing the letters *a, e, i, o* and *u*. The number of times that the sound of a vowel is heard is the number of syllables in a word. Model the proper pronunciation of each vocabulary word. Repeat each vocabulary word, making sure to produce each syllable. (*an-ec-dote; as-sent; ex-pound; mal-a-dy; sal-u-ta-tion; un-daunt-ed*) Invite students to echo the pronunciations of words as they record the syllables of each word in their notebooks. Invite students to work in pairs to continue practicing the pronunciation of each word in casual conversation with each other. **SUBSTANTIAL/MODERATE**

LANGUAGE CONVENTIONS:
Reflexive and Intensive Pronouns

There are pronouns that are naturally suited to such personal writing as diary entries, memoirs, and autobiographies. These pronouns are formed by adding *-self* or *-selves* to certain personal pronouns. The forms are the same but differ in how they are used.

REFLEXIVE AND INTENSIVE PRONOUNS	
SINGULAR	**PLURAL**
myself	ourselves
yourself	yourselves
himself, herself, itself	themselves

A **reflexive pronoun** follows a verb or a preposition and reflects back on an earlier noun or pronoun.

> The king threw himself into the chase.

A reflexive pronoun may serve as a direct object, an indirect object, an object of a preposition, or a predicate nominative.

> DIRECT OBJECT   He might have hurt himself running.
>
> INDIRECT OBJECT   All were surprised when she made herself stop.
>
> OBJECT OF A PREPOSITION   We are proud of ourselves for showing respect.
>
> PREDICATE NOMINATIVE   The king is not himself these days.

An **intensive pronoun** intensifies or emphasizes the nouns and pronouns to which they refer.

> The queen herself stepped in to handle the matter.
>
> I myself saw no reason to interfere.

Reflexive and intensive pronouns are used throughout Fanny Burney's diary entry. Note the italicized pronouns in this example:

> But what was my terror to hear myself pursued! —to hear the voice of the king himself loudly and hoarsely calling after me, "Miss Burney! Miss Burney!"

Practice and Apply Write a narrative paragraph in which you use both reflexive and intensive pronouns.

RESPOND

Go to **Special Pronoun Problems** in the **Grammar Studio** to learn more.

APPLY

LANGUAGE CONVENTIONS:
Reflexive and Intensive Pronouns

Review the information about reflexive and intensive pronouns with students. Explain that using reflexive and intensive pronouns shifts the tone and style of the text.

Practice and Apply Have students share their paragraphs with a partner. As partners read through a peer's writing, they can mark reflexive and intensive pronouns. Ask student volunteers to read their writings aloud to the class.

ENGLISH LEARNER SUPPORT

Language Conventions Use the following with students at varying proficiency levels:

- Have students find other reflexive and intensive pronouns in the selection and copy them in their notebooks. Make sure they recognize the difference between reflexive and intensive pronouns.
- Locate the reflexive and intensive pronouns Burney uses in paragraph 7. Reread the paragraph aloud for students to model correct pronunciation and enunciation. Have students record the reflexive and intensive pronouns in a chart in their notebooks. Students can add to their charts as they read the example sentences in the Language Conventions activity.
- Have students work with partners to write their original sentences with reflexive and intensive pronouns. Then, have them meet with another pair to compare their sentences. **INTERMEDIATE**

PLAN

from A VINDICATION OF THE RIGHTS OF WOMAN

Argument by Mary Wollstonecraft

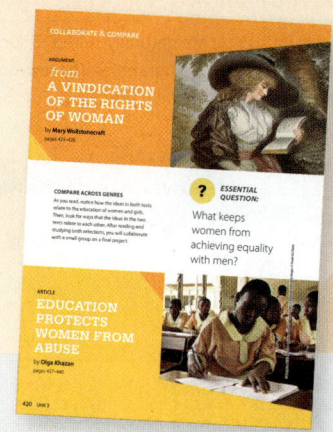

GENRE ELEMENTS
ARGUMENT

Remind students that an **argument** expresses a position on an issue and supports the position with reasons and evidence. Explain that including **counterarguments** in an argument shows that the writer has a deep understanding of the issue he or she is writing about. When writing an argument, it is important to research other points of view and imagine that someone opposes all your claims. In this lesson, students will evaluate arguments and counterarguments.

LEARNING OBJECTIVES

- Evaluate arguments and analyze counterarguments.
- Conduct research about the works of Jean-Jacques Rousseau and Dr. John Gregory.
- Write an argument.
- Give a persuasive speech.
- Identify literary allusions.
- Use coordinating and subordinating conjunctions.
- **Language** Respond respectfully to counterarguments.

TEXT COMPLEXITY

Quantitative Measures	A Vindication of the Rights of Woman	Lexile: 1350L
Qualitative Measures	**Ideas Presented** More than one purpose; implied, easily identified from context.	
	Structures Used Organization of main ideas and details complex but mostly explicit.	
	Language Used Complex and varied sentence structure.	
	Knowledge Required Complex social studies concepts and literary allusions.	

PLAN

RESOURCES

Online Ed

- Unit 3 Response Log
- 🔊 Selection Audio
- Reading Studio: Notice & Note
- Level Up Tutorial: Elements of an Argument
- Writing Studio: Writing Arguments
- Speaking and Listening Studio: Giving a Presentation
- Vocabulary Studio: Literary Allusions
- Grammar Studio: Module 2: Lesson 7: Conjunctions and Interjections
- "A Vindication of the Rights of Woman" Selection Test

SUMMARIES

English

In these essay excerpts, Wollstonecraft posits that society educates women not to be strong or useful but only to be pleasing to men. Given that charm fades, she suggests, such training leads to misery. She appeals to reason as she argues that women should cultivate strength of body and mind and should develop their character so that they may become worthy wives, mothers, and companions.

Spanish

En estos pasajes de ensayos, Wollstonecraft plantea que la sociedad educa a las mujeres solo para complacer a los hombres, y no para ser fuertes o útiles. Debido a que los encantos desaparecen, sugiere que este entrenamiento lleva al sufrimiento. Apela a la razón mientras argumenta que las mujeres deben cultivar la fuerza mental y física y deben desarrollar su carácter para convertirse en esposas, madres y compañeras dignas.

SMALL-GROUP OPTIONS

Have students work in small groups and pairs to read and discuss the selection.

Reciprocal Teaching

- Have students read Wollstonecraft's argument.
- After reading, ask students to write three to five questions about the selection, using these stems: *Why does Wollstonecraft say _____? What does Wollstonecraft believe about _____? What example does Wollstonecraft use to _____?*
- Form teams of three students.
- Have each student offer two questions for group discussion.
- Direct the groups to reach consensus on the answers and find supporting text evidence.

Think-Pair-Share

- After students read Wollstonecraft's argument, pose this question: *What words show Wollstonecraft's attitude toward the treatment of women?*
- Have students think about the question individually and make notes.
- Then, have pairs listen, discuss, and formulate a shared response to the question.
- Finally, have pairs share their responses with the class.

PLAN

Text X-Ray: English Learner Support
for *A Vindication of the Rights of Woman*

Use the Text X-Ray and the supports and scaffolds in the Teacher's Edition to help guide students at different proficiency levels through the selection.

INTRODUCE THE SELECTION
DISCUSS GENDER EQUALITY, RIGHTS, AND PRIVILEGES

In this lesson, students will need to be able to discuss how gender was related to rights and privileges in the 18th century. Provide the following explanation:

- *Gender equality* happens when people of all sexes have the same rights and privileges. *Gender inequality* is when people don't have the same rights and privileges based on their sex.

Point out the prefix *in-* and tell students it means *no* or *without*.

Have students use prior knowledge to discuss the importance of gender equality and what happens when a group doesn't have the same rights as another group. Provide sentence frames, such as *One right that shows gender equality is _____*.

CULTURAL REFERENCES

The following words or phrases may be unfamiliar to students:

- *bloom of beauty* (paragraph 7): *the years in a person's life when they look their best*
- *youth is the season for love* (paragraph 9): *the time to be in love is when you are young*
- *charms* (paragraph 10): *pleasing qualities of a person*
- *a weaker frame* (paragraph 14): *a less strong body*

LISTENING

Respond to Counterarguments

Tell students that it will be easier to persuade someone who does not agree with their claim if they show respect for the opposing opinion. Help students listen for keywords and phrases in counterarguments and respectfully restate them in their response.

Use the following supports with students at varying proficiency levels:

- State a claim and a counterargument, such as *Dogs are great pets* and *Dogs need too much exercise*. Tell students that *too much exercise* is a key phrase because it gives a reason why dogs are not great pets. Have students come up with their own claims about the best pets. **SUBSTANTIAL**
- Have a student state a claim about the best pet and a student state a counterargument. Have the first student identify keywords that they can use to respond to the counterargument. **MODERATE**
- Have a student state a claim about the best pet and a student give a counterargument. Have the first student use keywords from the counterargument to respond with a new counterargument, such as *I know you don't like birds because they make noise, but others like bird songs*. **LIGHT**

PLAN

SPEAKING

Use Register

Review the Give a Persuasive Speech activity on Student Edition page 431. Remind students that they need to pay attention to the tone and style they use when they give a persuasive speech.

Use the following supports with students at varying proficiency levels:

- Model an example of stating a claim in formal and informal register and have students repeat each one. Informal: *It's hard to do tons of homework every night.* Formal: *Studies have shown that more than two hours of homework a night is unproductive.* **SUBSTANTIAL**
- Have students rewrite the claim of their argument in informal speech. Then, have them orally present the formal and informal versions to a partner. Have the partner give feedback about what was and was not effective about each register. **MODERATE**
- Have students rewrite several sentences of their argument in formal register and then write several sentences in an informal register. Have them orally present both sets of sentences. Ask listeners to hold up a finger when they hear a switch in register. **LIGHT**

READING

Identify Reasons

Review the Write an Argument activity on Student Edition page 431. After students write their arguments, have them exchange their work with a partner to check for supporting reasons.

Use the following supports with students at varying proficiency levels:

- Write a simple claim and a supporting reason on the board. Read both aloud. Point to the claim and say *This is the claim.* Point to the reason and say *This is the reason that supports the claim.* **SUBSTANTIAL**
- After reading each other's arguments, have partners put a check next to supporting reasons they find. **MODERATE**
- After reading each other's arguments, have partners write a list of supporting reasons they find and an explanation of why each reason does or does not strengthen the argument. **LIGHT**

WRITING

Use Correct Verb Tense

As students draft and edit their argument essays, remind them how to use past, present, and future verb tenses in their writing.

Use the following supports with students at varying proficiency levels:

- Explain how to write the verb *achieve* in present, past, and future tenses. Then, use it in simple sentences and have students copy them. For example, have students write about what women could achieve if there was gender equality in all areas. **SUBSTANTIAL**
- Review how to identify past, present, and future verb tenses. Tell students that many past tense verbs end in *-ed*. Future tense verbs often have a word like *will, shall,* or *is* before the verb. Have partners edit each other's arguments for correct use of verbs. **MODERATE**
- As students write arguments, have them include each verb tense. Give ideas for sentence stems they can use to switch verb tense. For example: *In the past, ____. In the future, ____.* **LIGHT**

TEACH

 Connect to the ESSENTIAL QUESTION

Consider what equality means. Ask students to think about how education, or the lack thereof, impacts a person's ability to be truly equal. In addition to education, challenge students to explore other ways that equality can be better achieved across genders.

COMPARE ACROSS GENRES

Explain that the word *vindication* means "justification," so the first title, *A Vindication of the Rights of Woman*, tells us that Wollstonecraft will be providing justifications for women's rights. Ask students to consider what those rights are, and encourage them to debate to what extent women have those rights in comparison to men. Challenge them to consider how opportunities for education have changed the lives of women, both historically and in today's world. Ask them to think about the value of education and what it might mean to those to whom it is denied. What does the second title tell us about this topic?

COLLABORATE & COMPARE

ARGUMENT

from A VINDICATION OF THE RIGHTS OF WOMAN

by **Mary Wollstonecraft**
pages 423–428

COMPARE ACROSS GENRES

As you read, notice how the ideas in both texts relate to the education of women and girls. Then, look for ways that the ideas in the two texts relate to each other. After reading and studying both selections, you will collaborate with a small group on a final project.

 ESSENTIAL QUESTION:

What keeps women from achieving equality with men?

ARTICLE

EDUCATION PROTECTS WOMEN FROM ABUSE

by **Olga Khazan**
pages 437–440

 LEARNING MINDSET

Effort Remind students that effort is necessary for growth. Emphasize that hard work leads to success, and praise students for making an effort. For example, you might say, "I know that the language in this essay can be difficult, and I noticed you put a lot of effort into reading it. When you hit a difficult passage, you didn't give up. That attitude will help you succeed."

from *A Vindication of the Rights of Woman*

QUICK START

Think about opportunities for education today. Discuss with a partner of the opposite gender how educational opportunities have improved for women over the years.

EVALUATE ARGUMENTS

Many writers express their opinions on important issues by presenting a formal **argument**. When you read an argument, you should determine whether it is valid by evaluating the argument's main elements.

First, identify the author's **claim**. Is the opinion presented clearly and in detail?

Next, consider the reasons the author gives to support the claim. Are the **reasons** logical? Do they support the claim? As you evaluate the author's reasons, watch out for errors in logic, or **fallacies**. Common fallacies include:

- **Oversimplification** Treating a complex problem as if it were simple
- **Hasty Generalization** Making a generalization that is too broad or is drawn from too little information
- **False Cause-and-Effect** The mistaken assumption that because one event followed another, the first event caused the second one to occur
- **Red Herring** Irrelevant or false reasoning used to divert attention away from an issue

Finally, examine the author's **evidence**. Does the author give relevant facts and sufficient details to support his or her reasons? Is the information verified by reliable sources?

As you read Wollstonecraft's essay, analyze and evaluate the elements of her argument and look out for any logical fallacies.

ANALYZE COUNTERARGUMENTS

Writers often include **counterarguments** in which they anticipate opposing views and refute them. Mary Wollstonecraft provides several counterarguments that acknowledge her opponents' perspectives. This makes readers who might disagree with her more likely to be open to her ideas.

Examine the counterargument in paragraph 3: "In the government of the physical world it is observable that the female in point of strength is, in general, inferior to the male.... But not content with this natural preeminence, men endeavor to sink us still lower merely to render us alluring objects for a moment...." Wollstonecraft asserts that men have a physical advantage over women and wrongly use this advantage to treat women as mere ornaments.

As you read, identify other counterarguments the author uses. Try to imagine how these counterarguments might have swayed her audience.

GET READY

GENRE ELEMENTS: ARGUMENT

- expresses a position on an issue
- supports the position with reasons and evidence
- considers other points of view, anticipating and answering possible objections raised by opponents
- may be spoken or written

A Vindication of the Rights of Woman   421

TEACH

QUICK START

Place students in mixed-gender pairs or small groups. Encourage them to discuss educational opportunities—both in the United States and around the world. Then, challenge them to consider how opportunities for education have changed over the years, both here and abroad. Ask them to consider how different the world might be had those changes not occurred.

EVALUATE ARGUMENTS

Explain that formal **arguments** include certain elements. These elements include the author's **claim,** which is the point that the author is trying to make, as well as the **reasons** that support that claim. Explain that sometimes the reasons given to support an idea are logical, but sometimes they are logical **fallacies,** which can be misleading. Tell students that reviewing the **evidence**—the details that the author gives in support of his or her reasons—will allow them to determine if an author is being logical. Tell students that they will evaluate Wollstonecraft's argument as they read her essay.

ANALYZE COUNTERARGUMENTS

Tell students that identifying and refuting opposing views through **counterarguments** is an excellent way to address all points of view on a subject. Explain that doing this can help nullify the arguments of potential opponents and may even change opponents into supporters. Challenge students to identify the counterarguments used in Wollstonecraft's essay and to consider how the use of counterarguments helped make her overall argument stronger.

For **listening support** for students at varying proficiency levels, see the **Text X-Ray** on page 420C.

A Vindication of the Rights of Woman   **421**

TEACH

CRITICAL VOCABULARY

Encourage students to review all of the possible choices before deciding which word best answers each question. Remind them to look for words or phrases that match the precise meaning of each word.

Answers:

1. dissimulation
2. congenial
3. prerogative
4. vindication
5. Utopian
6. evanescent
7. abrogate
8. inculcate

■ English Learner Support

Use Cognates Tell students that several of the Critical Vocabulary words have Spanish cognates: *dissimulation/ disimulación, prerogative/prerrogativa, vindication/ vindicación, Utopian/utópico, evanescent/evanescente, abrogate/abrogar, inculcate/inculcar.* **ALL LEVELS**

LANGUAGE CONVENTIONS

Review conjunctions by explaining that there are two types of conjunctions: (1) **coordinating conjunctions,** that connect two ideas or sentences together; and (2) **subordinating conjunctions,** where one part of the sentence is dependent on the other part and cannot stand alone. Give students lists of coordinating conjunctions (*and, but, for, nor, or, so, yet*) and subordinating conjunctions (*after, although, as, as if, because, before, if, since, so that, than, though, unless, until, when, whenever, where, wherever, while*). In small groups, challenge them to devise four sentences—two with one type of conjunction and two with the other. Ask groups to present one of each. Have students give feedback.

ANNOTATION MODEL

Review page 422 with the students, focusing on the underlined items. Ask students why they think the reader has underlined these particular items. Point out that they may follow this annotation method or use their own system for marking up the selection in their write-in text. They may want to use highlighters to color-code their annotations. Their notes in the margin may include questions about ideas that are unclear or summaries of important points.

 **GET READY**

CRITICAL VOCABULARY

| vindication | prerogative | evanescent | dissimulation |
| abrogate | inculcate | congenial | Utopian |

Answer the questions using a Critical Vocabulary word in a complete sentence.

1. Which word means deceit or pretense?
2. Which word is the opposite of disagreeable?
3. Which word means a right or privilege?
4. Which word means justification?
5. Which word suggests something that is unattainable?
6. Which word suggests something temporary?
7. Which word means to revoke, or take away?
8. Which word suggests instruction?

LANGUAGE CONVENTIONS

Conjunctions help create varied sentences and clarify the relationships between ideas. **Coordinating conjunctions** connect independent clauses (clauses that can stand alone as complete sentences). **Subordinating conjunctions** connect dependent clauses (clauses that can't stand alone as complete sentences).

ANNOTATION MODEL NOTICE & NOTE

As you read, note how Wollstonecraft develops her argument. This model shows one reader's notes about an excerpt from *A Vindication of the Rights of Woman.*

> I have turned over various books written on the subject of education, and patiently observed the conduct of parents and the management of schools; but what has been the result?—a profound conviction that <u>the neglected education of my fellow-creatures is the grand source of the misery I deplore</u>; and that women, in particular, are rendered weak and wretched by a variety of concurring causes, originating from one hasty conclusion. The conduct and manners of women, in fact, evidently prove that their minds are not in a healthy state; for, <u>like the flowers which are planted in too rich a soil</u>, strength and usefulness are sacrificed to beauty; and the flaunting leaves, after having pleased a fastidious eye, fade, disregarded on the stalk, long before the season when they ought to have arrived at maturity.

She seems to be describing the problem first—the misery of women.

She is identifying a cause-effect relationship: Neglected education causes women's misery.

She uses a simile to help readers understand the problem—women are raised to be beautiful rather than productive.

BACKGROUND

Mary Wollstonecraft *(1759–1797) is considered by many to be the mother of feminism. Inspired by the ideas of liberal reformers, she wrote about the rights of women and others. Her 1790 book,* A Vindication of the Rights of Man, *attacked class and privilege; she followed that with* A Vindication of the Rights of Woman *in 1792.*

In the 18th century, the daughters of English gentlemen were mostly taught reading, languages, playing the piano, singing, drawing, and needlework. This was thought to be adequate preparation for their lives as wives, mothers, governesses, or companions to wealthy ladies.

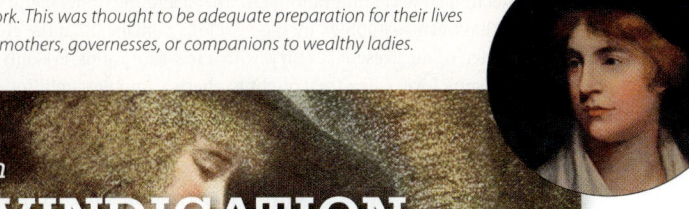

from
A VINDICATION OF THE RIGHTS OF WOMAN

Argument by Mary Wollstonecraft

PREPARE TO COMPARE

As you read, make note of Wollstonecraft's evaluation of women's education at the time, her suggestion for needed changes, and her conclusions about how these changes would affect the lives of women. This information will help you compare her argument with the article "Education Protects Women from Abuse," which follows it.

Notice & Note

Use the side margins to notice and note signposts in the text.

vindication
(vĭn-dĭ-kā′shən) *n.* justification.

1   After considering the historic page, and viewing the living world with anxious solicitude, the most melancholy emotions of sorrowful indignation have depressed my spirits, and I have sighed when obliged to confess, that either nature has made a great difference between man and man, or that the civilization which has hitherto taken place in the world has been very partial. I have turned over various books written on the subject of education, and patiently observed the conduct of parents and the management of schools; but what has been the result?—a profound conviction that the neglected education of my fellow-creatures is the grand source of the misery I deplore; and that women, in particular, are rendered weak and wretched by a variety of concurring causes, originating from one hasty conclusion. The conduct and manners of women, in fact, evidently prove that their minds are not in a healthy state;

TEACH

ANALYZE COUNTERARGUMENTS

Select a student to read paragraph 4 aloud. Direct the remainder of the class to take notes on the **counterargument** found in this paragraph. After the oral reading, place students in pairs or small groups where they should identify the counterargument and discuss how Wollstonecraft refutes the counterargument in this paragraph and paragraphs 6–8. (**Answer:** *The view that more education will make women too masculine is the counterargument she is refuting in these paragraphs. She does so by pointing out that the virtues which strengthen human character, body, and mind will make women better wives and mothers, not more masculine.*)

CRITICAL VOCABULARY

abrogate: The Nineteenth Amendment prohibits states from abrogating, or revoking, voting rights for women.

ASK STUDENTS what "law of nature" is not abrogated in favor of women, according to Wollstonecraft. (*the law that women, in terms of physical strength, are inferior to men*)

prerogative: The prerogative, or right, of women to be educated is something Wollstonecraft believed strongly in.

ASK STUDENTS what prerogative men have that women do not, according to Wollstonecraft. (*the degree of physical superiority that they enjoy*)

424   Unit 3

 **NOTICE & NOTE**

for, like the flowers which are planted in too rich a soil, strength and usefulness are sacrificed to beauty; and the flaunting leaves, after having pleased a fastidious eye, fade, disregarded on the stalk, long before the season when they ought to have arrived at maturity. One cause of this barren blooming I attribute to a false system of education, gathered from the books written on this subject by men who, considering females rather as women than human creatures, have been more anxious to make them alluring mistresses than affectionate wives and rational mothers; and the understanding of the sex has been so bubbled by this specious homage,[1] that the civilized women of the present century, with a few exceptions, are only anxious to inspire love, when they ought to cherish a nobler ambition, and by their abilities and virtues exact respect.

2   In a treatise,[2] therefore, on female rights and manners, the works which have been particularly written for their improvement must not be overlooked; especially when it is asserted, in direct terms, that the minds of women are enfeebled by false refinement; that the books of instruction, written by men of genius, have had the same tendency as more frivolous productions; and that . . . they are treated as a kind of subordinate beings, and not as a part of the human species, when improvable reason is allowed to be the dignified distinction which raises men above the brute creation, and puts a natural scepter in a feeble hand.

3   Yet, because I am a woman, I would not lead my readers to suppose that I mean violently to agitate the contested question respecting the quality or inferiority of the sex; but as the subject lies in my way, and I cannot pass it over without subjecting the main tendency of my reasoning to misconstruction, I shall stop a moment to deliver, in a few words, my opinion. In the government of the physical world it is observable that the female in point of strength is, in general, inferior to the male. This is the law of nature; and it does not appear to be suspended or **abrogated** in favor of woman. A degree of physical superiority cannot, therefore, be denied—and it is a noble **prerogative**! But not content with this natural preeminence, men endeavor to sink us still lower merely to render us alluring objects for a moment; and women, intoxicated by the adoration which men, under the influence of their senses, pay them, do not seek to obtain a durable interest in their hearts, or to become the friends of the fellow creatures who find amusement in their society.

4   I am aware of an obvious inference: from every quarter have I heard exclamations against masculine women; but where are they to be found? If by this appellation men mean to inveigh against their ardor[3] in hunting, shooting, and gaming, I shall most cordially join

---

abrogate
(ăb´rə-gāt) *v.* to revoke or nullify.

prerogative
(prĭ-rŏg´ə-tĭv) *n.* an exclusive right or privilege held by a person or group, especially a hereditary or official right.

ANALYZE COUNTERARGUMENTS

Annotate: Read paragraphs 4 and 6–8. Mark the sections in which Wollstonecraft addresses counterarguments, or anticipated opposing views.

Interpret: What opposing view is Wollstonecraft acknowledging in these paragraphs? How does she refute it?

---

[1] **bubbled by this specious homage** (spē´shəs hŏm´ĭj): deceived by this false honor.
[2] **treatise:** a formal, detailed article or book on a particular subject.
[3] **If by . . . inveigh** (ĭn-vā´) **against their ardor:** by this term ("masculine women") men mean to condemn some women's enthusiasm.

in the cry; but if it be against the imitation of manly virtues, or, more properly speaking, the attainment of those talents and virtues, the exercise of which ennobles the human character, and which raise females in the scale of animal being, when they are comprehensively termed mankind; all those who view them with a philosophic eye must, I should think, wish with me, that they may every day grow more and more masculine. . . .

5   My own sex, I hope, will excuse me, if I treat them like rational creatures, instead of flattering their *fascinating* graces, and viewing them as if they were in a state of perpetual childhood, unable to stand alone. I earnestly wish to point out in what true dignity and human happiness consists—I wish to persuade women to endeavor to acquire strength, both of mind and body, and to convince them that the soft phrases, susceptibility of heart, delicacy of sentiment, and refinement of taste, are almost synonymous with epithets[4] of weakness, and that those beings who are only the objects of pity and that kind of love, which has been termed its sister, will soon become objects of contempt. . . .

6   The education of women has, of late, been more attended to than formerly; yet they are still reckoned a frivolous sex, and ridiculed or pitied by the writers who endeavor by satire or instruction to improve them. It is acknowledged that they spend many of the first years of their lives in acquiring a smattering of accomplishments;[5] meanwhile strength of body and mind are sacrificed to libertine[6] notions of beauty, to the desire of establishing themselves—the only way women can rise in the world—by marriage. And this desire making mere animals of them, when they marry they act as such children may be expected to act: they dress; they paint, and nickname God's creatures. Surely these weak beings are only fit for a seraglio![7] Can they be expected to govern a family with judgment, or take care of the poor babes whom they bring into the world?

7   If then it can be fairly deduced from the present conduct of the sex, from the prevalent fondness for pleasure which takes place of ambition and those nobler passions that open and enlarge the soul; that the instruction which women have hitherto received has only tended, with the constitution of civil society, to render them insignificant objects of desire—mere propagators of fools!—if it can be proved that in aiming to accomplish them, without cultivating their understandings, they are taken out of their sphere of duties, and made ridiculous and useless when the short-lived bloom of beauty is over, I presume that *rational* men will excuse me for endeavoring to persuade them to become more masculine and respectable.

---

[4] **epithets** (ĕp´ə-thĕts): descriptive terms.
[5] **accomplishments:** This term, when applied to women, designated only those achievements then considered suitable for middle- and upper-class women, such as painting, singing, playing a musical instrument, and embroidery.
[6] **libertine** (lĭb´ər-tēn): indecent or unseemly.
[7] **seraglio** (sə-răl´yō): harem.

NOTICE & NOTE

EVALUATE ARGUMENTS

Annotate: Mark in paragraph 5 the specific words that indicate the author's claim.

Evaluate: How does the author make her claim clear? How does the placement of her claim affect the strength of her argument?

LANGUAGE CONVENTIONS

Annotate: Circle the coordinating conjunction in the first sentence of paragraph 6. Underline the independent clauses that have been joined together by the conjunction.

Interpret: How does the conjunction clearly show the relationship between the two clauses?

A Vindication of the Rights of Woman   425

APPLYING ACADEMIC VOCABULARY

☐ encounter   ☑ exploit   ☐ persist   ☑ subordinate   ☐ widespread

Write and Discuss Have students turn to a partner to discuss the following questions. Guide students to include the Academic Vocabulary words *exploit* and *subordinate* in their responses. Ask volunteers to share their responses with the class.

- In what ways were women kept **subordinate** to men during Wollstonecraft's time?
- Why are uneducated women easier to control, and how does this **exploit** them?

TEACH

EVALUATE ARGUMENTS

Explain that paragraph 5 includes a direct call to action for the women reading the essay. Explain that Wollstonecraft is giving women support to make their own arguments to men about the value of education. (**Answer:** *She uses specific words to indicate her claim—"I earnestly wish to point out" and "I wish to persuade women." The claim comes later than one might expect, and keeps the reader from considering all her reasons in order, which weakens the beginning of her argument. Some may feel that the placement is effective since the first part of the argument lays the groundwork for her claim.*)

English Learner Support

Use Support to Enhance Understanding Analyze with students how Wollstonecraft presents her **argument** in paragraph 5. Have them consider why she might address women as well as men, and why she might address them differently. Have students mark each instance where Wollstonecraft is talking directly to women to help them understand the argument, such as when she says, "I wish to persuade women." **LIGHT**

LANGUAGE CONVENTIONS

Remind students that coordinating conjunctions connect two separate sentences, or independent clauses, together. If necessary, provide students with a list of coordinating conjunctions (*and, but, for, nor, or, so, yet*). (**Answer:** *It shows the reader that women are still regarded as a "frivolous sex" in spite of the fact that more time and attention has been spent on the education of women than ever before.*)

A Vindication of the Rights of Woman   425

TEACH

CRITICAL VOCABULARY

inculcate: In Wollstonecraft's time, women were inculcated, or instilled, with the importance of being good wives and mothers.

ASK STUDENTS what Wollstonecraft thought Rousseau and most male writers had inculcated about female education. *(that female education should be directed toward making women pleasing to men)*

evanescent: According to Wollstonecraft, love is a passion that is evanescent, or likely to vanish.

ASK STUDENTS why Wollstonecraft thinks a wife's love might become evanescent. *(if she has been taught only to please men and her husband no longer acts as if he loves her)*

congenial: Friends are usually congenial, or agreeable and sympathetic.

ASK STUDENTS why Wollstonecraft thinks women might dream of the "happiness enjoyed by congenial souls." *(if they feel neglected by their husbands and have relied on their husbands for all their happiness)*

426 Unit 3

 **NOTICE & NOTE**

8 Indeed the word masculine is only a bugbear:⁸ there is little reason to fear that women will acquire too much courage or fortitude; for their apparent inferiority with respect to bodily strength, must render them, in some degree, dependent on men in the various relations of life; but why should it be increased by prejudices that give a sex to virtue, and confound simple truths with sensual reveries?⁹

From Chapter 2

9 Youth is the season for love in both sexes; but in those days of thoughtless enjoyment provision should be made for the more important years of life, when reflection takes place of sensation. But Rousseau,¹⁰ and most of the male writers who have followed his steps, have warmly **inculcated** that the whole tendency of female education ought to be directed to one point: to render them¹¹ pleasing.

10 Let me reason with the supporters of this opinion who have any knowledge of human nature, do they imagine that marriage can eradicate the habitude of life? The woman who has only been taught to please will soon find that her charms are oblique sunbeams, and that they cannot have much effect on her husband's heart when they are seen every day, when the summer is passed and gone. Will she then have sufficient native energy to look into herself for comfort, and cultivate her dormant faculties? or, is it not more rational to expect that she will try to please other men; and, in the emotions raised by the expectation of new conquests, endeavor to forget the mortification her love or pride has received? When the husband ceases to be a lover—and the time will inevitably come, her desire of pleasing will then grow languid, or become a spring of bitterness; and love, perhaps, the most **evanescent** of all passions, gives place to jealousy or vanity.

11 I now speak of women who are restrained by principle or prejudice; such women, though they would shrink from an intrigue with real abhorrence, yet, nevertheless, wish to be convinced by the homage of gallantry that they are cruelly neglected by their husbands; or, days and weeks are spent in dreaming of the happiness enjoyed by **congenial** souls till their health is undermined and their spirits broken by discontent. How then can the great art of pleasing be such a necessary study? it is only useful to a mistress; the chaste wife, and serious mother, should only consider her power to please as the polish of her virtues, and the affection of her husband as one of the comforts that render her talk less difficult and her life happier. But, whether she be loved or neglected, her first wish should be to make

inculcate
(ĭn-kŭl´kāt, ĭn´kŭl-) *v.* to impress (something) upon the mind of another by frequent instruction or repetition; instill.

evanescent
(ĕv-ə-nĕs´ənt) *adj.* vanishing or likely to vanish like vapor.

congenial
(kən-jēn´yəl) *adj.* agreeable, sympathetic.

---

⁸ **bugbear:** an object of exaggerated fear.
⁹ **confound . . . reveries** (rĕv´ə-rēz): confuse simple truths with men's sexual daydreams.
¹⁰ **Rousseau** (ro͞o-sō´): The Swiss-born French philosopher Jean-Jacques Rousseau (1712–1778) presented a plan for female education in his famous 1762 novel *Émile*.
¹¹ **them:** that is, females.

426 Unit 3

IMPROVE READING FLUENCY

Targeted Passage Direct students to listen as you read paragraph 9 aloud, and ask them to pay close attention to the pace of your reading and the intonations and expressions you use. After you have modeled how to read the paragraph, place students into pairs to practice reading the paragraph aloud to each other. Remind them to practice pacing, intonation, and expression, and direct partners to provide feedback on their performances. Encourage them to offer constructive suggestions for how to read the passage more fluently.

 Go to the **Reading Studio** for additional support in developing fluency.

herself respectable, and not to rely for all her happiness on a being subject to like infirmities with herself.

12   The worthy Dr. Gregory fell into a similar error. I respect his heart; but entirely disapprove of his celebrated Legacy to his Daughters.[12] . . .

13   He actually recommends **dissimulation**, and advises an innocent girl to give the lie to her feelings, and not dance with spirit, when gaiety of heart would make her feet eloquent without making her gestures immodest. In the name of truth and common sense, why should not one woman acknowledge that she can take more exercise than another? or, in other words, that she has a sound constitution; and why, to damp innocent vivacity, is she darkly to be told that men will draw conclusions which she little thinks of? Let the libertine draw what inference he pleases; but, I hope, that no sensible mother will restrain the natural frankness of youth by instilling such indecent cautions. Out of the abundance of the heart the mouth speaketh; and a wiser than Solomon[13] hath said, that the heart should be made clean, and not trivial ceremonies observed, which it is not very difficult to fulfil with scrupulous exactness when vice reigns in the heart.

14   Women ought to endeavor to purify their heart; but can they do so when their uncultivated understandings make them entirely dependent on their senses for employment and amusement, when no noble pursuit sets them above the little vanities of the day, or enables them to curb the wild emotions that agitate a reed over which every passing breeze has power? To gain the affections of a virtuous man, is affectation necessary? Nature has given woman a weaker frame than man; but, to ensure her husband's affections, must a wife, who by the exercise of her mind and body whilst she was discharging the duties of a daughter, wife, and mother, has allowed her constitution to retain its natural strength, and her nerves a healthy tone, is she, I say, to condescend to use art and feign a sickly delicacy in order to secure her husband's affection? Weakness may excite tenderness, and gratify the arrogant pride of man; but the lordly caresses of a protector will not gratify a noble mind that pants for, and deserves to be respected. Fondness is a poor substitute for friendship! . . .

15   Besides, the woman who strengthens her body and exercises her mind will, by managing her family and practicing various virtues, become the friend, and not the humble dependent of her husband; and if she, by possessing such substantial qualities, merit his regard, she will not find it necessary to conceal her affection, nor to pretend

dissimulation
(dĭ-sĭm´yə-lā-shən) *n.* deceit or pretense.

---

[12] **Dr. Gregory . . . Daughters:** In his 1774 work *A Father's Legacy for His Daughters*, John Gregory (1724–1773) offered a plan for female education that remained popular for decades.

[13] **a wiser than Solomon:** King David, reputed author of many psalms in the Bible and the father of King Solomon, who was known for his wisdom. The words that follow draw on ideas in Psalm 24, which states that only those with "clean hands and a pure heart" shall ascend into Heaven.

TEACH

EXTREME LANGUAGE

Explain to students that extreme or exaggerated language is sometimes used in **arguments** to make strong points. (**Answer:** *Examples of extreme language in paragraph 6 include "paltry crown," "let her grovel contentedly," and "scarcely raised . . . above the animal kingdom." The author uses extreme, nearly insulting language to suggest that women who are satisfied with their lives have somehow demeaned themselves. Such language shows her strong feelings about the subject and her ultimate purpose to persuade women.*)

 EVALUATE ARGUMENTS

Point out the metaphor in paragraph 19, "Liberty is the mother of virtue." Explain that metaphors, or comparisons, can create powerful images in the reader's mind. (**Answer:** *The author uses this metaphor effectively to make an emotional appeal with the idea of liberty versus slavery. It helps to persuade the reader that if women are not allowed the freedom of education, then they will never realize their full potential.*)

CRITICAL VOCABULARY

Utopian: Wollstonecraft hopes that her ideas about women are not just Utopian dreams—ideal but impractical.

ASK STUDENTS where Wollstonecraft thinks she got her Utopian dreams. (*She thinks God ["that Being"] impressed them on her soul.*)

428   Unit 3

 **NOTICE & NOTE**

EXTREME LANGUAGE

Notice & Note: What examples of extreme or exaggerated language do you find in paragraph 16? Why might it be considered extreme? Mark the words and phrases you find.

Evaluate: What does this type of language reveal about the author's purpose?

Utopian
(yo͞o-tō´pē-ən) *adj.* excellent or ideal but impracticable; visionary.

EVALUATE ARGUMENTS

Annotate: Mark the metaphor in paragraph 19.

Analyze: How does this metaphor contribute to the author's argument? How does it support her purpose?

---

to an unnatural coldness of constitution to excite her husband's passions. . . .

16   If all the faculties of woman's mind are only to be cultivated as they respect her dependence on man; if, when a husband be obtained, she have arrived at her goal, and meanly proud rests satisfied with such a **paltry crown**, **let her grovel contentedly**, **scarcely raised by her employments above the animal kingdom**; but, if, struggling for the prize of her high calling, she look beyond the present scene, let her cultivate her understanding without stopping to consider what character the husband may have whom she is destined to marry. Let her only determine, without being too anxious about present happiness, to acquire the qualities that ennoble a rational being, and a rough inelegant husband may shock her taste without destroying her peace of mind. She will not model her soul to suit the frailties of her companion, but to bear with them: his character may be a trial, but not an impediment to virtue. . . .

17   These may be termed **Utopian** dreams. Thanks to that Being who impressed them on my soul, and gave me sufficient strength of mind to dare to exert my own reason, till, becoming dependent only on him for the support of my virtue, I view, with indignation, the mistaken notions that enslave my sex.

18   I love man as my fellow; but his scepter, real, or usurped, extends not to me, unless the reason of an individual demands my homage; and even then the submission is to reason, and not to man. In fact, the conduct of an accountable being must be regulated by the operations of its own reason; or on what foundation rests the throne of God?

19   It appears to me necessary to dwell on these obvious truths, because females have been insulated, as it were; and, while they have been stripped of the virtues that should clothe humanity, they have been decked with artificial graces that enable them to exercise a short-lived tyranny. Love, in their bosoms, taking place of every nobler passion, their sole ambition is to be fair, to raise emotion instead of inspiring respect; and this ignoble desire, like the servility in absolute monarchies, destroys all strength of character. **Liberty is the mother of virtue**, and if women be, by their very constitution, slaves, and not allowed to breathe the sharp invigorating air of freedom, they must ever languish like exotics,[14] and be reckoned beautiful flaws in nature.

---

[14] **languish** (lăng´gwĭsh) **like exotics:** wilt like plants grown away from their natural environment.

428   Unit 3

WHEN STUDENTS STRUGGLE . . .

Summarize Arguments Have students make a graphic organizer, like the one below, that explains Wollstonecraft's **argument** (**claims, reasons, evidence,** and **counterarguments**).

Para #	Claim	Reason	Evidence	Counterargument

 For additional support, go to the **Reading Studio** and assign the following Level Up tutorial: **Elements of an Argument.**

NOTICE & NOTE

CHECK YOUR UNDERSTANDING

Answer these questions before moving on to the **Analyze the Text** section on the following page.

1 Wollstonecraft argues that women should be educated to strengthen what two things?

　A　Body and soul

　B　Beauty and usefulness

　C　Mind and body

　D　Beauty and emotions

2 Which of the following is an opposing view on which the author builds a counterargument?

　F　Education will make women too conceited.

　G　The behavior of women proves their lack of intelligence.

　H　Women lack the desire for higher education.

　J　The point of female education is to make women pleasing to men.

3 According to Wollstonecraft, what is one main cause of women's misery?

　A　Their physical weaknesses

　B　An obligation to respect their husbands

　C　Their suppressed emotions

　D　A false system of education

A Vindication of the Rights of Woman　429

TEACH

CHECK YOUR UNDERSTANDING

Have students answer the questions independently.

Answers:

1. C
2. J
3. D

If they answer any questions incorrectly, have them reread the text to confirm their understanding. Then they may proceed to ANALYZE THE TEXT on page 430.

 ENGLISH LEARNER SUPPORT

Oral Assessment Use the following questions to assess students' comprehension and speaking skills.

1. What two things are made stronger by educating women, according to Wollstonecraft? *(minds and bodies)*

2. What is a different viewpoint that Wollstonecraft uses to build her argument? *(to make women pleasing to men)*

3. What is the main source of women's "misery," according to Wollstonecraft? *(a false system of education)* **SUBSTANTIAL/MODERATE**

A Vindication of the Rights of Woman　**429**

APPLY

ANALYZE THE TEXT

Possible answers:

1. **DOK 2:** *Wollstonecraft refers to the "hasty conclusion," or hasty generalization, that women's education should be aimed at making them pleasing to men.*

2. **DOK 3:** *Using the writings of a famous French philosopher well known for his ideas of liberty and equality draws the reader's attention. As she succeeds in successfully countering his ideas, the reader is inclined to view her argument with respect.*

3. **DOK 4:** *Because his plan was popular, Gregory's writings support the author's claim that these particular ideas for female education were common. She also cites his specific recommendation that women conceal their true feelings and restrain their movements for the sake of propriety; this supports her argument that Dr. Gregory's plan is unhealthy.*

4. **DOK 2:** *She can become a respected friend of her husband rather than a weak dependent. She will no longer have to hide her true feelings, and she will be better able to manage her family.*

5. **DOK 4:** *The desire of women to get married is "making mere animals of them." She also claims that marriage is "the only way women can rise in the world." Although most women did aspire to marry, the author's language suggests that women had no other choice. She leaves no room for other possibilities. Her exaggeration also suggests that marriage leaves all women mindless. By using this kind of language, she likely wishes to get women's attention in order to persuade them.*

RESEARCH

Remind students that they should confirm any information they find by checking multiple websites and assessing the credibility of each one.

Extend After completing their research and the chart, place students in pairs or small groups. Have group members share their findings, with other members noting comparisons to their own. Once all members have shared their findings, challenge students to identify which writer's ideas make the most sense and then write two reasons to defend their choices. Once these are written, ask group members to share their choices and reasoning.

430 Unit 3

RESPOND

ANALYZE THE TEXT

Support your responses with evidence from the text. 📓 **NOTEBOOK**

1. **Interpret** In paragraph 1, the author identifies a logical fallacy, saying that "women, in particular, are rendered weak and wretched by a variety of concurring causes, originating from one hasty conclusion." What is the hasty conclusion to which Wollstonecraft refers?

2. **Critique** How does the author's counterargument to Rousseau's view in paragraphs 9–11 help her to achieve her purpose?

3. **Evaluate** Reread paragraphs 12–13. How does Dr. Gregory's plan for women's education provide evidence to support the author's argument?

4. **Interpret** Wollstonecraft presents her counterargument to Gregory's ideas in paragraphs 14–15. According to Wollstonecraft, how will strengthening her body and mind improve a woman's marriage?

5. **Notice & Note** In paragraph 6, Wollstonecraft makes a claim about the way women gain stature in the world and how this affects them. How might her statements in this paragraph be considered a use of extreme or exaggerated language? What does she most likely wish to accomplish by using this kind of language?

RESEARCH

RESEARCH TIP
Since you'll be searching for specific content included in two texts, be sure to include the titles of the works in the search bar rather than just the authors' names. If you find summaries of their works, use only those from reliable sources.

In support of her argument, Wollstonecraft refers to two writers of her day—Jean-Jacques Rousseau and Dr. John Gregory. She summarizes their general ideas for female education and then presents counterarguments for each one.

But what were some of their other specific ideas on this topic? How did the two men differ in their opinions? Conduct research to find out more about these authors and the works to which Wollstonecraft refers in her essay. Use the chart to record your findings.

ROUSSEAU'S IDEAS ABOUT WOMEN'S EDUCATION—FROM HIS NOVEL *ÉMILE*	GREGORY'S IDEAS ABOUT WOMEN'S EDUCATION—FROM *A FATHER'S LEGACY FOR HIS DAUGHTERS*
- A woman's main purpose in life is to be a wife and mother. - Her education should be seen as relative to men. - Education is for pleasing man. - A woman learns to keep home.	- A woman should shun reading that "warms the imagination." - Too much reading brings discontent and interferes with natural intuition. - She needs education to perform her work well.

Extend In a small group, compare notes from your research and discuss which writers' ideas you believe have more merit.

430 Unit 3

LEARNING MINDSET

Try Again Tell students that sometimes they may think they know the answer to a question, but then find out they got it incorrect. Remind them that it's OK to make mistakes—it's how we learn. If they get an answer wrong, encourage them to go back to the text and reread until they figure it out.

RESPOND

APPLY

CREATE AND PRESENT

Write an Argument Use what you have learned from reading and studying Wollstonecraft's essay to write your own argument. Choose a topic related to education or to the essential question: What keeps women from achieving equality with men?

When you write your argument, remember the basic structure of an argument:

- State your claim, or thesis, clearly in your introduction.
- Support your claim with logical reasons. Make sure to avoid relying on logical fallacies.
- Use quotations and other evidence from the text and your research to support your reasons.
- Anticipate any opposing views to your argument and prepare counterarguments.

Give a Persuasive Speech Once you have written your argument, prepare to present it as a persuasive speech to your class. Practice first with a partner. Critique each other using the following criteria:

- clear and logical presentation of argument
- effective use of logical, ethical, and emotional appeals
- appropriate volume and tone of voice
- appropriate use of eye contact, facial expressions, and gestures

 Go to **Writing Arguments** in the **Writing Studio** for more help.

 Go to **Giving a Presentation** in the **Speaking and Listening Studio** to find out more about making a speech.

RESPOND TO THE ESSENTIAL QUESTION

 What keeps women from achieving equality with men?

Gather Information Review your annotations and notes on *A Vindication of the Rights of Woman*. Then, add relevant details to your Response Log. As you determine which information to include, think about:

- The importance of education for all people
- The meaning of true equality
- How education affects relationships between men and women

ACADEMIC VOCABULARY

As you write and discuss what you learned from the argument, be sure to use the Academic Vocabulary words. Check off each of the words that you use.

- ❏ encounter
- ❏ exploit
- ❏ persist
- ❏ subordinate
- ❏ widespread

CREATE AND PRESENT

Write an Argument Direct students to brainstorm topics on which they could write an **argument** that relates to the Essential Question: What keeps women from achieving equality with men?

Remind students that the basic structure of an argument should be followed, including the **claim** (or thesis), logical **reasons** to support the claim, credible **evidence** to support the reasons, and inclusion of **counterarguments.** Encourage students to outline their arguments to ensure that each item is included.

Remind students to avoid using logical **fallacies,** such as oversimplifying things, making hasty generalizations, providing false causes and effects, or dropping red herrings.

For **reading** and **writing support** for students at varying proficiency levels, see the **Text X-Ray** on page 420D.

Give a Persuasive Speech Once students have completed their arguments, place them in pairs to practice delivery. Partners should give feedback on each of the criteria on page 437 and offer constructive suggestions for improvement. After practice, have students present their arguments to the class. Direct the other students to listen attentively to identify the **claim,** supporting **reasons** and **evidence,** and **counterarguments.**

For **speaking support** for students at varying proficiency levels, see the **Text X-Ray** on page 420D.

RESPOND TO THE ESSENTIAL QUESTION

Allow time for students to add details from "A Vindication of the Rights of Woman" to their Unit 3 Response Logs.

APPLY

CRITICAL VOCABULARY

Answers:

1. *prerogative*
2. *evanescent*
3. *abrogate*
4. *Utopian*
5. *inculcate*
6. *dissimulation*
7. *congenial*
8. *vindication*

VOCABULARY STRATEGY:
Literary Allusions

Answers:

1. *Paragraph 9 (Rousseau); Explanation: French philosopher who presented a plan for female education in his novel* Emile. *How It Strengthens Her Argument: Provides evidence of the attitude toward education for women.*

2. *Paragraph 12 (Dr. Gregory—A Father's Legacy for his Daughters); Explanation: Dr. John Gregory offers a popular plan for female education in* A Father's Legacy for his Daughters. *How It Strengthens Her Argument: Provides further evidence of a popular attitude.*

3. *Paragraph 13 (King Solomon and reference to a clean heart); Explanation: Words inspired from Psalm 24. King David was the author of many psalms and his son Solomon was noted for his great wisdom. How It Strengthens Her Argument: Contrasts the idea of deceit—which is recommended to women—with the ideas of truth presented in the Bible.*

4. *Paragraph 13 ("Out of the abundance of the heart the mouth speaketh."); Explanation: The author quotes the words of Jesus in Matthew 12:34. How It Strengthens Her Argument: One with a pure heart will speak truth not deceit.*

432 Unit 3

 RESPOND

WORD BANK
vindication evanescent
abrogate congenial
prerogative dissimulation
inculcate Utopian

CRITICAL VOCABULARY

Practice and Apply Fill in each blank with the most appropriate Critical Vocabulary word.

1. Your friends might try to persuade you to stay, but you have the _____ to change your mind.

2. We lingered on the porch as long as possible in order to enjoy the _____ beauty of the setting sun.

3. His attorney assured him that his actions would not _____ the agreement.

4. The business soon dropped its _____ plans for total participation.

5. Parents should _____ their children with moral values and principles.

6. True friends should avoid any sort of _____ in order to maintain an honest relationship.

7. Although I felt quite homesick during my first week at the university, my discomfort began to fade as my roommate became a _____ companion.

8. When the mayor's innocence was proven, the town rejoiced over his _____.

VOCABULARY STRATEGY:
Literary Allusions

Allusions are indirect references to a person, place, event, or literary work. Writers make allusions to things they assume will be familiar to their readers.

Practice and Apply Wollstonecraft makes four references to literary works to support her argument. How does each allusion strengthen her argument? Use the footnotes in the selection and record answers in the chart below. The last entry in the chart is not footnoted. Can you identify the allusion?

ALLUSION/REFERENCE	EXPLANATION	HOW IT STRENGTHENS HER ARGUMENT
Paragraph 9	*A French philosopher*	*Gives proof of attitude*
Paragraph 12	*Plan to educate women*	*Evidence of popular idea*
Paragraph 13	*Words from Psalm 24*	*Contrasts deceit/truth*
Paragraph 13: "Out of the abundance of the heart the mouth speaketh."	*The author quotes the words of Jesus in Matthew 12:34.*	*One with a pure heart will speek truth not deceit.*

432 Unit 3

 ENGLISH LEARNER SUPPORT

Vocabulary Strategy Point out that two of the Critical Vocabulary words end in -*ation*. Explain that this suffix is used to turn verbs into nouns. Ask students to identify the verbs that *vindication* and *dissimulation* are derived from (*vindicate* and *dissimulate*). Then, have students list other words that end in -*ation* and identify the verbs these words are derived from.
SUBSTANTIAL

RESPOND

Go to the **Grammar Studio** for more on coordinating and subordinating conjunctions.

LANGUAGE CONVENTIONS:
Coordinating and Subordinating Conjunctions

Wollstonecraft expresses her ideas in long, detailed sentences that rely heavily on coordinating and subordinating conjunctions to connect words, phrases, and clauses smoothly in a way that shows the relationships between ideas.

The charts list the coordinating and subordinating conjunctions and explain how they are used.

COORDINATING CONJUNCTIONS	PURPOSE	SAMPLE SENTENCE
and, but, for, nor, or, so, yet	connect words or groups of words that have the same function in a sentence (examples: two subjects, two phrases, two independent clauses)	She read many books on education, but they did not provide satisfactory answers to her questions.

SUBORDINATING CONJUNCTIONS	PURPOSE	SAMPLE SENTENCE
after, although, as, as if, because, before, if, since, so that, than, though, unless, until, when, whenever, where, wherever, while	introduce subordinate clauses—clauses that cannot stand alone as complete sentences	Although many men read her essay, some were not convinced by the argument she made for the need to enhance the education of women.

Examine the following sentence from Wollstonecraft's essay:

> I love man as my fellow; but his scepter, real, or usurped, extends not to me, unless the reason of an individual demands my homage; and even then the submission is to reason, and not to man.

Find the conjunctions between the clauses and identify each one as coordinating or subordinating. What if the author had chosen to write the same ideas in separate sentences, without the use of these conjunctions? Write the resulting sentences below. What effect does removing the conjunctions have on the presentation of ideas?

Practice and Apply Write a brief paragraph providing instructions on how to perform a complex task. Include the correct usage of at least two coordinating conjunctions and two subordinating conjunctions. Remember that the clauses joined by coordinating conjunctions must be able to stand alone as sentences—that is, they must be independent clauses.

A Vindication of the Rights of Woman   433

APPLY

LANGUAGE CONVENTIONS:
Coordinating and Subordinating Conjunctions

Review the information on **coordinating** and **subordinating conjunctions.** Explain that conjunctions help show the relationships between ideas. Read both charts aloud to students. Challenge volunteers to explain the difference between the two types of conjunctions and give their own examples.

Read the sentence from Wollstonecraft's essay ("I love man as my fellow . . .") aloud. Direct students to identify each conjunction and what type it is. (*but*–coordinating; *unless*–subordinating; *and*–coordinating) Challenge students to consider how this excerpt would be different if Wollstonecraft had not used the conjunctions. Have volunteers write the separate sentences on the board and then read them aloud to determine how the sentences sound without the conjunctions.

Practice and Apply Direct students to write short paragraphs explaining how to do something. Help students get started by brainstorming examples of things they could write about. Tell students that their paragraphs must include two examples of each type of conjunction. Remind students that **coordinating conjunctions** join two standalone sentences (independent clauses), while **subordinating conjunctions** connect clauses that cannot stand alone.

After students have completed their paragraphs, place students in pairs to share their work. Encourage partners to offer constructive suggestions on the use of conjunctions.

 ENGLISH LEARNER SUPPORT

Language Conventions Place students into small groups and ask them to locate three examples of each type of conjunction within the essay. Direct students to copy the sentences they find and then underline the **coordinating conjunctions** and circle the **subordinating conjunctions.** Once students have located and identified all six conjunctions, have them share their findings with their group.   **SUBSTANTIAL/MODERATE**

PLAN

EDUCATION PROTECTS WOMEN FROM ABUSE
Article by Olga Khazan

GENRE ELEMENTS
ARTICLE

Remind students that an **article** provides factual information on a topic or recent event and often includes text features. Point out that authors often use **pull quotes** in articles to give readers a clue about an important idea or point. A pull quote is a brief quote from the text that will catch readers' attention by being surprising or particularly engaging or thought provoking. In this lesson, students will use a variety of text features to make predictions about an article's content.

LEARNING OBJECTIVES

- Make predictions and analyze graphic features.
- Conduct research about the education of women and girls worldwide.
- Write an analysis of graphic features.
- Create and present a graphic.
- Identify Greek roots and prefixes.
- Use direct and indirect quotations.
- **Language** Discuss and retell information from graphic features.

TEXT COMPLEXITY

Quantitative Measures	Education Protects Women from Abuse	Lexile: 1160L
Qualitative Measures	**Ideas Presented** Much is explicit, but moves to some implied meaning. Requires some inferential thinking.	
	Structures Used Argument structure.	
	Language Used Explicit, literal, contemporary language; complex sentence structures.	
	Knowledge Required Subjects mostly familiar, with some historical and cultural references.	

434A Unit 3

PLAN

RESOURCES

- Unit 3 Response Log
- 🔊 Selection Audio
- 📖 Reading Studio: Notice & Note
- 📈 Level Up Tutorial: Reading Graphic Aids; Paraphrasing; Taking Notes and Outlining
- 📝 Writing Studio: Using Textual Evidence
- 💬 Speaking and Listening Studio: Giving a Presentation
- ⚛ Vocabulary Studio: Greek Roots and Prefixes
- ❗ Grammar Studio: Module 14: Lesson 5: Quotation Marks
- ✓ "Education Protects Women from Abuse" Selection Test

SUMMARIES

English

In 2014 the militant Islamist group Boko Haram kidnapped nearly 300 Nigerian schoolgirls from school in an attempt to halt their education and force them into child marriage. In this article, Olga Khazan provides statistical evidence that education helps to protect women from physical and sexual abuse.

Spanish

En 2014, el grupo militante islámico Boko Haram secuestró a casi 300 colegialas nigerianas en un intento de detener su educación y forzarlas a matrimonios precoces. En este artículo, Olga Khazam da pruebas estadísticas de que la educación protege a las mujeres del abuso físico y sexual.

SMALL-GROUP OPTIONS

Have students work in small groups to read and discuss the selection.

Three-Minute Review

- As you read the text aloud, pause after every 1–2 paragraphs.
- Direct students to reread the paragraphs and write clarifying questions. Set a timer for three minutes.
- After three minutes, ask: "How is this article different from other types of text you have read?"
- Invite volunteers to share clarifying questions.
- Guide small groups to discuss and answer the questions.

Jigsaw with Experts

- Divide the text into three sections, each containing at least one graphic feature.
- Have students count off, or assign students a numbered section.
- After reading their sections, have students form groups with other students who read the same section. Each expert group should discuss its section and how the graphic feature(s) contributes to its meaning. Encourage them to use the Academic Vocabulary.
- Then, have students form new groups with a representative from each section. These groups should discuss all the sections and the selection as a whole.

PLAN

Text X-Ray: English Learner Support
for "Education Protects Women from Abuse"

Use the Text X-Ray and the supports and scaffolds in the Teacher's Edition to help guide students at different proficiency levels through the selection.

INTRODUCE THE SELECTION
DISCUSS MISOGYNY AND DOMESTIC VIOLENCE

In this lesson, students will need to be able to discuss how misogyny contributes to domestic violence.

Provide the following explanations:
- *Misogyny* is a type of prejudice aimed at women.
- *Domestic violence* is any physically abusive act that occurs in the home.

Guide students to use the terms and what they already know as they discuss why it is important for societies to change laws and attitudes that contribute to misogyny and domestic violence.

Provide sentence frames, such as: *One example of misogyny in our country is _____. One attitude about women that contributes to domestic violence is _____.*

CULTURAL REFERENCES

The following words or phrases may be unfamiliar to students:
- *went after* (paragraph 1): to chase or pursue in order to capture
- *youth bulge* (paragraph 3): a disproportional number of young people in the population (in relation to older people)
- *child marriage* (paragraph 4): a forced situation where a young person, usually female, must marry an adult
- *men's groups* (paragraph 11): community associations that focus on men's issues

LISTENING

Retell Key Ideas

Have student pairs choose one of the graphic features to discuss. Point out that titles give essential information about the main point of a graphic.

Use the following supports with students at varying proficiency levels:
- Read aloud the title of the graphic on page 438 about the share of women who have experienced physical or sexual violence. Tell students that this title is the main idea of the graphic. Point to the graphic as you state facts from it, such as: *43 percent of women in South Asia have experienced violence from an intimate partner*. Have students repeat your statements. Discuss with students that sexual violence includes unwanted sexual acts. An intimate partner is a person who has an ongoing physical or sexual activity with a partner. **SUBSTANTIAL**
- Have one partner retell a few key ideas from the graphic in his or her own words. Have the other partner take notes about what was heard. **MODERATE**
- Have one partner discuss the key ideas in the graphic, and have the other partner write what was said in his or her own words. **LIGHT**

PLAN

SPEAKING

Use Visuals

Review the photographs and other graphic features that accompany the text. Have students create a word bank of vocabulary based on the images. Then, have them use the word bank to discuss ideas they could include in a film about the importance of educating women.

Use the following supports with students at varying proficiency levels:

- Have students repeat the words from the word bank as they point to related elements in the visuals. Use the words in simple sentences relating to the education of women, and have students repeat them. **SUBSTANTIAL**
- Have partners use the words from the word bank in simple sentences as they discuss what to include in the film. Provide a sentence starter, such as: *My film will have a scene about ____ because ____.* **MODERATE**
- Have partners ask each other questions about what they could include in their film, using the word bank and visuals from the text. For example: *What will be the first scene of your film? How can you use the statistics about physical abuse in your film?* Have students answer the questions. **LIGHT**

READING

Evaluate Sources

As students conduct their research about educational inequality, remind them to make inferences about the sources they find.

Use the following supports with students of varying proficiency levels:

- Help students do an online search for sources. Then, have students repeat the names of sources you find. Ask either/or questions. For example: *What section of this site tells me about this source, About Us or Join Us?* (About Us) *Which is the more trusted source, [a university] or [a personal blog]?* (university) **SUBSTANTIAL**
- Have students read about the sources they find as they do research. Have them take notes about each source and then make an inference about the credibility of each source. **MODERATE**
- Have students read the sources they find. Then, have them write a brief paragraph explaining why they used some sources and not others for their research. **LIGHT**

WRITING

Rewrite Direct Quotes

Review the difference between direct and indirect quotes. Work with students to rewrite direct quotes in their own words.

Use the following supports with students of varying proficiency levels:

- Write on the board a statement from the selection about the education of women. Place it in quotes. Tell students this is a direct quote. Show how to write it as an indirect quote. Have students copy both. **SUBSTANTIAL**
- Have one student give a direct quote about an opinion regarding the education of women. Have the partner write the quote. Then, have students work together to rewrite the quote as an indirect quote. Repeat the activity with the partner giving the next direct quote. **MODERATE**
- Have speakers take turns giving direct quotes. Have listeners write the quotes, using one of the tag and punctuation examples from the chart on page 445 as a model. Then, have students rewrite each direct quote as an indirect quote. **LIGHT**

TEACH

 Connect to the ESSENTIAL QUESTION

Have students consider how different beliefs have held women back for centuries and are still holding them back in many parts of today's world. Some societies have moved closer to the ideal of equality, while others seem to be moving backward toward a less equal society.

COMPARE ACROSS GENRES

Explain to students that historically—and still today—many women have not been provided opportunities to become educated. In the past, the education of women was dismissed as unimportant, while today, girls in some parts of the world risk their very lives to learn. Tell students to explore how each of these authors addresses the topic of education for women and look for similarities and differences in their approaches.

COLLABORATE & COMPARE

ARTICLE

EDUCATION PROTECTS WOMEN FROM ABUSE

by **Olga Khazan**
pages 437–440

COMPARE ACROSS GENRES

Now that you've read excerpts from *A Vindication of the Rights of Woman*, read "Education Protects Women from Abuse" and explore how the article connects to some of the same ideas. As you read, think about how the author of "Education Protects Women from Abuse" presents and supports her point of view. After you are finished, you will collaborate with a small group on a final project that involves an analysis of both texts.

 ESSENTIAL QUESTION:

What keeps women from achieving equality with men?

ARGUMENT

from A VINDICATION OF THE RIGHTS OF WOMAN

by **Mary Wollstonecraft**
pages 423–428

434 Unit 3

Education Protects Women from Abuse

QUICK START

Imagine you have been invited to promote a United Nations program designed to achieve gender equality and empower all women and girls. In your notebook, list different approaches to empower and educate women to combat inequality. Discuss your ideas with a partner.

MAKE PREDICTIONS

Text features are design elements of a text. They may include titles, subtitles, headings, pull quotes, and boldfaced or italicized text. You will often find a variety of text features in magazine and newspaper articles because they help attract readers' attention. Readers can use text features to make predictions about an article's subject matter, key ideas, and the author's purpose.

In "Education Protects Women from Abuse," Olga Khazan offers strong opinions about the issue she discusses. Use the chart to make predictions about the article based on its text features.

TEXT FEATURE	PREDICTIONS
Title: Education Protects Women from Abuse	*The text will most likely give details showing that better education of women leads to lower rates of abuse.*
Subtitle: Extremists hate smart girls because smart girls are less likely to be kept down.	*The text will discuss political extremist groups that are against the education of women.*
Pull Quote: Girls' schooling . . . has a protective effect against domestic violence, rape, and child marriage.	*The article will focus on the protective effect of girls' schooling.*

ANALYZE GRAPHIC FEATURES

A **multimodal text** combines two or more ways of communicating meaning, such as text, graphic features, and audio. This approach offers the reader a rich learning experience. For example, graphic features can provide at-a-glance information that is difficult to convey in text. Graphic features may include illustrations, photographs, charts, graphs, and maps.

The author of "Education Protects Women from Abuse" integrates two graphic features into her analysis. The first feature is a **thematic map,** a map focused on a specific theme or subject. The second feature is a **scatter plot graph,** which is a type of graph that uses points to show the relationship between two sets of data. As you read the article, note how the information in these features supports the author's ideas about education.

GET READY

GENRE ELEMENTS: ARTICLE
- provides factual information on a topic or recent event
- includes evidence to support ideas
- often contains text features
- appears in print or online newspapers or magazines

TEACH

QUICK START

Place students in pairs. Encourage them to brainstorm approaches to empower women, with the goal of achieving greater levels of equality globally. Challenge them to consider innovative ways to address this issue, as well as how each approach might need to be modified for different parts of the world. Encourage pairs to share their ideas with the whole class. Direct students to listen proactively and to offer constructive feedback on the ideas shared.

MAKE PREDICTIONS

Explain to students that **text features** include titles, subtitles, headings, pull quotes, and differentiated text (like boldface or italics). Tell students that these features can help the reader predict what an article will be about before they begin to read. The features can also indicate what the writer thinks is most important. Use the title of the article as an example, challenging students to make predictions about the article based on its title. Encourage students to make predictions based on the subtitle and pull quote, as well, and then confirm their predictions as they read Khazan's article.

ANALYZE GRAPHIC FEATURES

Explain to students that **graphic features,** including the map and graph in Khazan's article, create a richer learning experience for the reader. These features can clarify difficult points, present facts more succinctly, and provide an easier way to convey complex information to readers. As they read, have students consider how this article would be more difficult to understand without the map and graph.

TEACH

CRITICAL VOCABULARY

Encourage students to review all of the possible choices before deciding which word best completes each blank. Remind them to look for context clues to help them understand the meaning of each word.

Answers:

1. *misogyny*
2. *condone*
3. *autonomy*
4. *extremist*
5. *inoculate*
6. *mire*
7. *manacle*

■ English Learner Support

Use Cognates Tell students that one of the Critical Vocabulary words has a Spanish cognate: *autonomy/autonomía.* **ALL LEVELS**

LANGUAGE CONVENTIONS

Review with students the information on direct and indirect quotations. Explain that a quotation is direct when it includes the speaker's exact wording. It is indirect when the speaker's words are paraphrased. Display these examples:

Example #1: "No place is less safe for a woman than her own home."

Example #2: A woman has more to fear in her own home than she does anywhere else.

Explain that the first item is a direct quote from a 2014 World Bank report, while the second is a paraphrase. Challenge students to consider which might have more impact on a reader and why. *(The direct quote would likely make a greater impact on the reader because it is worded more strongly.)*

ANNOTATION MODEL

Read aloud the article's subtitle, and ask a student to read the excerpt in the Annotation Model. Point out that the reader made a note linking the subtitle to the excerpt. Tell students that they may want to make similar notes or use their own system for marking up the selection in their write-in text. They may also want to color-code their annotations by using highlighters. Their notes in the margin may include questions about ideas that are unclear or topics they want to learn more about.

436   Unit 3

 **GET READY**

CRITICAL VOCABULARY

| extremist | manacle | autonomy | misogyny |
| mire | condone | inoculate | |

To see how many Critical Vocabulary words you already know, use the words to complete the sentences.

1. A person who says disparaging things about women displays _____.
2. A police officer should not _____ the act of speeding.
3. The freed prisoner was thrilled to once again have personal _____.
4. The members of the _____ group used riots to get media attention.
5. Gaining knowledge is a good way to _____ yourself against fear of the unknown.
6. The amount of information available on the Internet can _____ even the most skilled researchers in hours of useless searching.
7. The man would _____ his rival by digging up details about the past.

LANGUAGE CONVENTIONS

Direct and Indirect Quotations In this lesson, you will learn about properly citing others' ideas using direct and indirect quotations. As you read "Education Protects Women from Abuse," look for places where the author uses the exact words of a speaker or writer in a **direct quotation** or uses her own words to paraphrase another writer's work in an **indirect quotation.**

ANNOTATION MODEL NOTICE & NOTE

As you read, note how the author uses text features and graphic features. Consider and make note of how these choices add to your experience as a reader and your understanding of the author's purpose for writing. You can mark up evidence that supports your ideas. In the model, you can see one reader's notes about the author's use of the subtitle: "Extremists hate smart girls because smart girls are less likely to be kept down."

> The horrifying kidnapping of nearly 300 Nigerian schoolgirls by the extremist group <u>Boko Haram</u> was made even more horrifying by the fact that the group specifically targeted the girls for trying to improve their lives. <u>Boko Haram</u> went after the girls for the same reason the <u>Taliban</u> went after Malala Yousafzai: <u>Extremists fear smart women</u>.

Boko Haram and the Taliban must be some of the "extremists" referred to in the subtitle.

436   Unit 3

BACKGROUND

Boko Haram is a militant Islamist group that arose in northeastern Nigeria in 2002. Boko Haram can be roughly translated as "Western education is forbidden." In 2014 Boko Haram sparked international outrage by kidnapping an estimated 276 girls, stating that the girls would be enslaved and married off. In 2015 a coalition of military forces from Nigeria and several other African nations in the region, successfully reclaimed much of the territory the group had gained in its attacks, but Boko Haram remains an influential force in northeastern Nigeria.

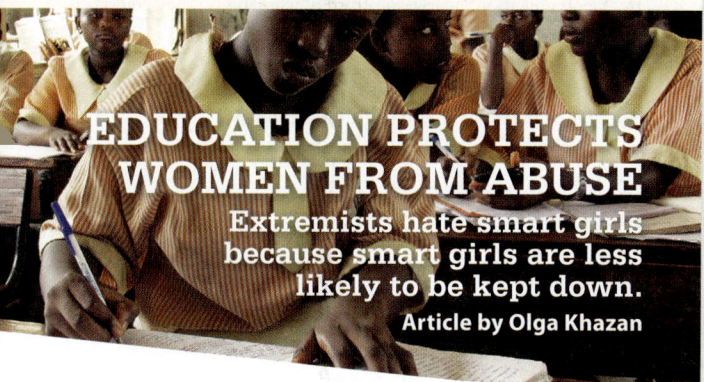

EDUCATION PROTECTS WOMEN FROM ABUSE

Extremists hate smart girls because smart girls are less likely to be kept down.

Article by Olga Khazan

PREPARE TO COMPARE

As you read, pay attention to the ideas that the author presents about women's education and rights. Note details and features of the text that help you understand the author's purpose for writing. This will help you compare this text with the excerpt from A Vindication of the Rights of Woman.

1   The horrifying kidnapping of nearly 300 Nigerian schoolgirls by the **extremist** group Boko Haram was made even more horrifying by the fact that the group specifically targeted the girls for trying to improve their lives. Boko Haram went after the girls for the same reason the Taliban went after Malala Yousafzai: Extremists fear smart women.

2   "If you want to **mire** a nation in backwardness, **manacle** your daughters," wrote *New York Times* columnist Nick Kristof. . . .

> "Girls' schooling . . . has a <u>protective effect</u> against domestic violence, rape, and child marriage."

Notice & Note

Use the side margins to notice and note signposts in the text.

extremist
(ĭk-strē´mĭst) *adj.* advocating or resorting to measures beyond the norm, especially in politics.

mire
(mīr) *v.* to hinder, entrap, or entangle.

manacle
(măn´ə-kəl) *v.* to restrain the action or progress of something or someone.

MAKE PREDICTIONS

Annotate: Mark the words in the pull quote that provide clues to the author's purpose.

Analyze: Why do you think this quotation was chosen as a pull quote?

APPLYING ACADEMIC VOCABULARY

☐ encounter ☐ exploit ☑ persist ☐ subordinate ☑ widespread

Write and Discuss Have students turn to a partner to discuss the following questions. Guide students to include the Academic Vocabulary words *persist* and *widespread* in their responses. Ask volunteers to share their responses with the class.

- How **widespread** are the attacks and kidnappings by Boko Haram?
- Why do you think the kidnappings **persist** even when officials are warned in advance?

TEACH

LANGUAGE CONVENTIONS

Remind students that **direct quotations** often make powerful statements that would be less powerful if they were paraphrased. (**Answer:** *The idea that women face the most danger in the place where they should feel safest makes a powerful statement about what life is like for many women around the world.*)

ANALYZE GRAPHIC FEATURES

Remind students that a **graphic feature,** like the **thematic map,** can provide a great deal of information in a concise and attention-grabbing way. (**Answer:** *The author could have listed the statistics in the text as a paragraph or bullet points. If the information was listed in a sentence or bullet points, it would not be as visually appealing to the reader. It would also be harder for the reader to understand which countries were included in the various regions.*)

■ **English Learner Support**

Analyze Maps Organize students into pairs and direct them to review the thematic map on page 438. Explain that the map shows the percentages of women around the world who have experienced some violence from an intimate partner. Ask them to interpret the map by writing one statement about each region represented and the percentage next to it. Once pairs have finished their sentences, call on volunteers to share their insights about each region. **MODERATE/LIGHT**

 For **listening support** for students at varying proficiency levels, see the **Text X-Ray** on page 434C.

CRITICAL VOCABULARY

condone: One-third of women worldwide condone, or overlook, domestic violence.

ASK STUDENTS to describe the relationship between condoning domestic violence and experiencing it. (*According to the article, women who condone domestic violence are more likely to experience it.*)

438 Unit 3

NOTICE & NOTE

3   Kristof listed some of the better-known positive externalities of having an educated female population: Fewer children, and thus less risk of a "youth bulge" and, later, civil war. Not to mention a more skilled labor force and a stronger economy.

4   But a . . . report suggests that the benefit of girls' schooling extends even further—that it has a protective effect against domestic violence, rape, and child marriage.

5   "No place is less safe for a woman than her own home," reads a World Bank report released in 2014. Roughly 30 percent of the world's women have experienced physical or sexual violence at the hands of their partners, and across 33 developing countries surveyed by the organization, nearly one-third of women said they could not refuse sex with their partner.

LANGUAGE CONVENTIONS
Annotate: Mark the direct quotation in paragraph 5.
Analyze: Why does the author most likely include the direct quotation?

ANALYZE GRAPHIC FEATURES
Annotate: Mark the sentence in paragraph 5 that is supported by the thematic map.
Synthesize: How else could the author have chosen to present the information in the map? Would another kind of presentation have been as effective?

Share of Women Who Have Experienced Physical or Sexual Violence by an Intimate Partner

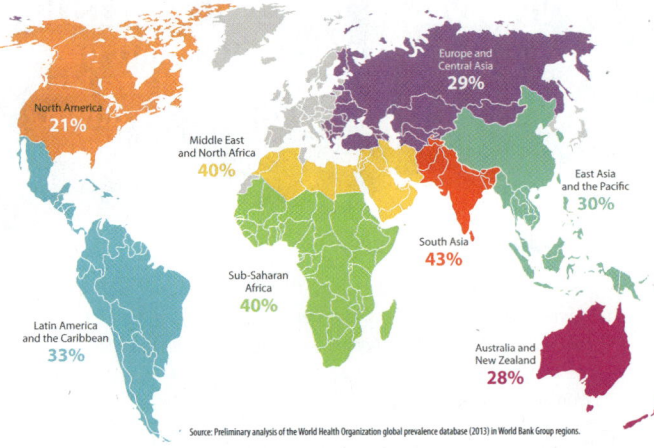

Source: Preliminary analysis of the World Health Organization global prevalence database (2013) in World Bank Group regions.

6   "Yes, it's normal, being beaten, yelled at. If you tell [anyone], your peers will ask you, is this your first time to be beaten? Some of us are used to it, just like the way we are used to eating *ugali*,"[1] one Tanzanian woman said in a World Bank focus group.

7   To make matters worse, one in three women said they thought wife-beating was justifiable, and women who **condoned** domestic violence were more likely to experience it.

condone
(kən-dōn´) *v.* to overlook, forgive, or disregard (an offense) without protest or censure.

---
[1] **ugali:** (u:´ga:li) *n.* a type of maize porridge eaten in east and central Africa.

438   Unit 3

TO CHALLENGE STUDENTS . . .

Conduct Research Place students in small groups and direct them to conduct research about women's education around the world. Ask them to find out where women have the most education and where they have the least education. Challenge them to compare those findings to the **graphic features** (**thematic map** and **scatterplot graph**) in the article and identify any relationships. After their analyses are complete, ask groups to present their findings. Encourage the other students to listen attentively and ask questions about the information presented.

NOTICE & NOTE

Education Protects Women from Abuse 439

TEACH

WHEN STUDENTS STRUGGLE...

Analyze Graphic Features Have students use a graphic organizer to help them gain insights into the **thematic map** and **scatterplot graph** on pages 438 and 440.

	Title	Main Idea	Details
Map			
Graph			

 For additional support, go to the **Reading Studio** and assign the following **Level Up tutorial: Reading Graphic Aids.**

Education Protects Women from Abuse **439**

TEACH

ANALYZE GRAPHIC FEATURES

Remind students that a **scatterplot graph** is another type of **graphic feature** used to enhance the text. This type of feature can provide valuable insights from which conclusions can be drawn. (**Answer:** *The graph shows a trend of fewer women believing that domestic abuse is justified. The information in paragraphs 8 and 9 suggests that a better education for women is correlated with lower rates of abuse. Thus, it is reasonable to conclude that education of women is improving in the countries represented in the graph.*)

MAKE PREDICTIONS

Remind students that **direct quotations** often present information in a powerful way. Ask students to share the predictions they made before they began to read and compare those predictions to what they have learned from reading the article. (**Answer:** *Answers will vary substantially based on individual student predictions.*)

CRITICAL VOCABULARY

autonomy: Better-educated women are more likely to feel that they have autonomy, or can be independent.

ASK STUDENTS to describe how education impacts a woman's sexual autonomy. (*Each additional year of schooling is associated with a 1-percent increase in sexual autonomy, according to the World Bank.*)

inoculate: Khazan believes that better-educated women help protect, or inoculate, societies from extremist viewpoints that keep women from achieving equality.

ASK STUDENTS what female education seems to inoculate society against, according to Khazan. (*Khazan says female education seems to inoculate society against misogyny.*)

misogyny: Boko Haram promotes misogyny, or hatred and mistrust of women.

ASK STUDENTS how Boko Haram's misogyny has impacted education in Nigeria. (*Boko Haram has kidnapped schoolgirls, making girls nervous to attend class.*)

440 Unit 3

NOTICE & NOTE

ANALYZE GRAPHIC FEATURES

Annotate: Mark details in paragraphs 8 and 9 that demonstrate the effect of education on abuse.

Draw Conclusions: Based on the data presented in the graph and the information in the text, what conclusions can you draw about the education of women in the countries listed?

autonomy
(ô-tŏn´ə-mē) *n.* the condition or quality of being autonomous; independence.

MAKE PREDICTIONS
Annotate: Mark the direct quotation in paragraph 10.

Evaluate: Now that you have nearly finished reading the selection, look back at the predictions you made in the table on page 435. Were your predictions correct? Why or why not?

inoculate
(ĭ-nŏk´yə-lāt) *v.* to safeguard as if by inoculation; to protect.

misogyny
(mĭ-sŏj´ə-nē) *n.* hatred or mistrust of women.

440 Unit 3

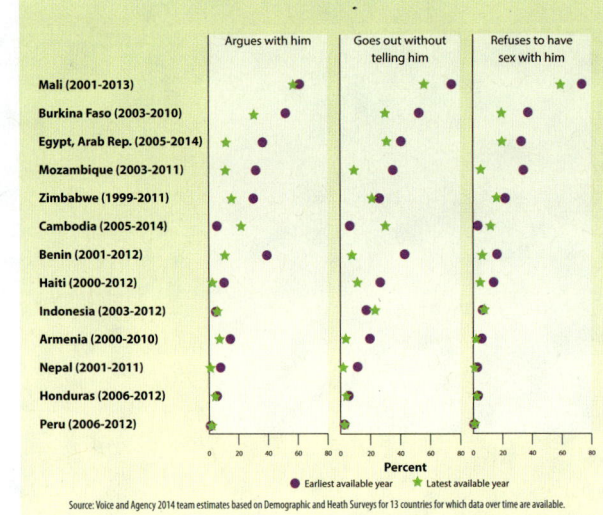

Change in the Percent of Women Who Believe a Husband Is Justified in Beating His Wife if She . . .

Source: Voice and Agency 2014 team estimates based on Demographic and Health Surveys for 13 countries for which data over time are available.

8 But the Bank also found that better-educated women were more likely to not be sexually or physically abused. Each additional year of schooling was associated with a 1-percent increase in their ability to refuse sex with their partner.

9 "The strongest correlate of women's sexual **autonomy** in a relationship is her level of education," the report notes. "Overall, 87 percent of women with a higher education say they can refuse sex. Women with some or completed secondary education have an 11 and 36 percent lower risk of violence, respectively, compared with women with no education."

10 One of the most lasting, damaging impacts of the Boko Haram kidnapping could be making Nigerian girls nervous about attending class. According to recent interviews with some of the escaped girls, when the group arrived at the school in northern Nigeria, they were shouting, "We are Boko Haram. We will burn your school. You shall not do school again. You shall do Islamic school."

11 Of course, it's also crucial to change social norms and laws in countries with high levels of domestic violence, and working with men's groups can go a long way as well. But since female education seems to **inoculate** societies against **misogyny**, it's both unsurprising and heartbreaking that Boko Haram would target classrooms.

IMPROVE READING FLUENCY

Targeted Passage Direct students to listen as you read paragraph 10. Ask them to pay close attention to the pace of your reading, as well as the intonation and expression you use. After you have modeled how to read the paragraph, place students into pairs to practice reading the paragraph aloud to each other. Remind them to practice pacing, intonation, and expression, and direct partners to provide feedback on their performances.

Go to the **Reading Studio** for additional support in developing fluency.

NOTICE & NOTE

CHECK YOUR UNDERSTANDING

Answer these questions before moving on to the **Analyze the Text** section on the following page.

1. Why did the author most likely include the thematic map?

   A To emphasize the geopolitical cause of abuse

   B To make a point about the importance of maps

   C To present complex information in an effective way

   D To show that extremist groups are an international threat

2. Which quotation from the selection best supports the claim made by the title of the article?

   F *But a ... report suggests that the benefit of girls' schooling extends even further—that it has a protective effect against domestic violence, rape, and child marriage.*

   G *To make matters worse, one in three women said they thought wife-beating was justifiable, and women who condoned domestic violence were more likely to experience it.*

   H *Of course, it's also crucial to change social norms and laws in countries with high levels of domestic violence, and working with men's groups can go a long way as well.*

   J *One of the most lasting, damaging impacts of the Boko Haram kidnapping could be making Nigerian girls nervous about attending class.*

3. According to the graph, in which country have women's beliefs about justification for domestic violence changed the least?

   A Mozambique

   B Zimbabwe

   C Haiti

   D Peru

Education Protects Women from Abuse 441

ENGLISH LEARNER SUPPORT

Oral Assessment Use the following questions to assess students' comprehension and speaking skills.

1. What does the map on page 438 show? *(the percentage of women worldwide who have been beaten or sexually abused by their partners)*

2. Explain the title of the article in your own words. *(Possible answer: The more educated a woman is, the less likely she is to be abused.)*

3. According to the graph on page 440, in which country have attitudes about wife beating changed the least? *(Peru)* **MODERATE/LIGHT**

TEACH

CHECK YOUR UNDERSTANDING

Have students answer the questions independently.

Answers:

1. C
2. F
3. D

If they answer any questions incorrectly, have them reread the text to confirm their understanding. Then they may proceed to ANALYZE THE TEXT on page 442.

APPLY

ANALYZE THE TEXT
Possible answers:

1. **DOK 2:** *The reports showed that about one-third of women have experienced domestic or sexual violence, and that domestic violence is considered normal and even justified by some women. Higher levels of education were associated with lower risk of domestic violence, and lower levels of education were associated with increased risk. The findings support the author's purpose of showing that education protects women from abuse.*

2. **DOK 4:** *The graph shows that, overall, women are less likely to believe that domestic violence is justified than they were in years past. One exception is in Indonesia, where the percentage slightly increased of women who believe abuse is justified when a woman argues with her husband or goes out without telling him.*

3. **DOK 3:** *The scatterplot graph shows change over time, while the map does not.*

4. **DOK 3:** *The subtitle and the pull quote both reference the education of girls and its effects. The features were effective in emphasizing the author's message.*

5. **DOK 4:** *The main idea of the map is to show the prevalence of domestic violence against women worldwide and compare rates between regions. It provides evidence for the idea that abuse is widespread and shows that areas generally thought to have better education systems also have lower abuse rates. The main idea of the scatterplot graph is that although the percentage of women who condone domestic violence has decreased, there are still large numbers of women who believe it is justified. This shows that more education of women helps change perspectives but also that much more education is still needed.*

RESEARCH

Remind students that they should confirm any information they find by checking multiple websites and assessing the credibility of each one.

Extend After completing their research and the chart, place students into small groups. Have group members take turns sharing their statistics with each other. Encourage them to comment on the statistics. Challenge them to determine if the findings support the author's claim, and if so, which statistics best support the claim. Ask groups to share the statistics they found most enlightening.

 For **reading support** for students at varying proficiency levels, see the **Text X-Ray** on page 434D.

442 Unit 3

RESPOND

ANALYZE THE TEXT
Support your responses with evidence from the text. 📝 NOTEBOOK

1. **Summarize** Review paragraphs 4–9. In your own words, summarize the findings of the World Bank report. Explain how the findings relate to the author's purpose.

2. **Analyze** Examine the scatter plot graph. What is the overall trend or pattern in women's opinions regarding domestic violence? Do any countries listed go against the trend?

3. **Compare** Compare the information presented in the map with the information presented in the scatter plot graph. Both present data about domestic violence in different parts of the world. What is an important kind of information presented in the scatter plot graph that the map does not show?

4. **Critique** Review the subtitle and the pull quote. Is the author's use of these text features effective? Why or why not?

5. **Analyze** What are the main ideas of the two graphic features? How does each graphic feature relate to the main idea of the article?

RESEARCH TIP
When using a search engine to conduct research, choose search terms carefully to obtain relevant results. To research statistical information on education inequality, consider including the term "statistics" in your search phrase.

RESEARCH
Inequalities in levels of education for women and men have been extensively researched and reported on by many global organizations. Research some statistics on the education of women and girls worldwide. Use the chart to record your findings.

STATISTIC	SOURCE
31 million girls are out of school worldwide.	*unesco.org*
Women make up more than 2/3 of the world's illiterate people.	*unwomen.org*
In Arab states and Sub-Saharan Africa, almost 2/3 of out-of-school girls are never expected to attend school.	*unicef.org*
One additional year of school can increase women's earnings by 10–20%.	*globalpartnership.org*

Extend Share the statistics you found with a small group. Discuss whether the statistics support the author's claim about the effect of education on the abuse of women.

442 Unit 3

WHEN STUDENTS STRUGGLE...

Reteaching: Understand Direct Quotations Have students create a graphic organizer, like below, that lists each **direct quotation** from the article. Tell them to write the main idea of each quote to help them better understand why the author included it.

Direct Quotation	Main Idea

 For additional support, go to the **Reading Studio** and assign the following 📖 Level Up tutorial: Paraphrasing.

CREATE AND ADAPT

Write an Analysis Write a three- or four-paragraph essay in which you analyze and evaluate the author's use of graphic features in "Education Protects Women from Abuse." Consider reviewing your notes and annotations of the text before you begin.

- ❏ Introduce your essay by identifying the author's purpose for writing the article.
- ❏ Then, describe the graphic features the author chose to use and explain how they relate to and/or support the author's purpose for writing. Support your ideas with evidence from the text.
- ❏ In your final paragraph, state your conclusion about the effectiveness of the graphic features.

Adapt and Present With a small group, discuss your opinions about what makes a graphic feature effective. Then, adapt information from the article into an effective graphic.

- ❏ Review the article with your group to identify statistics that are presented in a text format but could be adapted to a visual format.
- ❏ Create a graphic that could be used to replace one of the statistics in the article.
- ❏ Present your graphic to the class. Explain possible pros and cons of using your graphic to replace the text.

RESPOND TO THE ESSENTIAL QUESTION

What keeps women from achieving equality with men?

Gather Information Review your annotations and notes on "Education Protects Women from Abuse." Then, add relevant information to your Response Log. As you determine which information to include, think about:

- how abuse is related to inequality
- how education is related to inequality
- how views of the role of women vary from one society to another

RESPOND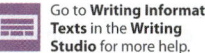

Go to **Writing Informative Texts** in the **Writing Studio** for more help.

Go to **Giving a Presentation** in the **Speaking and Listening Studio** for more help.

ACADEMIC VOCABULARY

As you write and discuss what you learned from "Education Protects Women from Abuse," be sure to use the Academic Vocabulary words. Check off each of the words that you use.

- ❏ encounter
- ❏ exploit
- ❏ persist
- ❏ subordinate
- ❏ widespread

APPLY

CREATE AND ADAPT

Write an Analysis To prepare students to start writing their analyses, tell them that their introductions should outline the author's purpose. Then, explain that the body of their analyses should include a description of each graphic feature, along with analyses of the purpose of each feature and how each supported the author's message. Tell them to include a conclusion that provides an evaluation of the effectiveness of the author's use of these graphic features.

Adapt and Present Tell groups to review the article and identify statistics that could be translated into a graphic feature. Encourage them to consider different ways that the statistics could be presented and decide, as a group, which would be the most effective method. Then, give students time to create the graphic itself and prepare it for presentation to the class.

RESPOND TO THE ESSENTIAL QUESTION

Allow time for students to add details from "Education Protects Women from Abuse" to their Unit 3 Response Logs.

APPLY

CRITICAL VOCABULARY

Answers:

1. condone
2. autonomy
3. extremist
4. inoculate
5. manacle
6. misogyny
7. mire

VOCABULARY STRATEGY:
Greek Roots and Prefixes

Answers:

1. Word: misogyny; Prefixes/Roots: mis, gyn; Definition: hatred or mistrust of women
2. Word: autonomy; Prefixes/Roots: auto, nomos; Definition: the condition or quality of being self-governing; independence

 RESPOND

WORD BANK

extremist   autonomy
mire   inoculate
manacle   misogyny
condone

CRITICAL VOCABULARY

Practice and Apply With a partner, discuss and then write down an answer to each of the following questions. Then, work together to write a sentence for each Critical Vocabulary word.

1. Which vocabulary word goes with the idea of excusing behavior?
2. Which vocabulary word is associated with personal freedom?
3. Which vocabulary word could be used to describe outrageous actions?
4. Which vocabulary word goes with the word *safeguard*?
5. Which vocabulary word goes with the idea of holding back or restricting something?
6. Which vocabulary word is associated with gender relations?
7. Which vocabulary word is associated with becoming stuck?

VOCABULARY STRATEGY:
Greek Roots and Prefixes

One of the languages that had a significant impact on the development of the English language was Greek. Knowing the meanings of Greek prefixes and roots can help you determine the meanings of unfamiliar words.

For example, the word **physical** contains the Greek root **phys,** meaning "body." The word *physical* means "relating to the body." When the author of the selection refers to *physical* abuse, she is specifying abuse that involves violence against the human body, as opposed to other forms of abuse.

Practice and Apply Examine the Greek word parts listed below. Use the word parts and the Critical Vocabulary words from this selection to complete the chart. Then, with a partner, brainstorm a list of other English words that use these word parts.

auto: self, same, one   *mis:* bad, wrong, to hate
gyn: woman, female   *nomos:* law

 Go to the **Vocabulary Studio: Analyzing Word Structure** for more on Greek roots and prefixes.

WORD	PREFIXES AND ROOTS	DEFINITION
misogyny	mis, gyn	hatred or mistrust of women
autonomy	auto, nomos	the condition or quality of being self-governing; independence

---

ENGLISH LEARNER SUPPORT

Vocabulary Strategy Give students additional practice in determining the meanings of unfamiliar words with Greek roots and prefixes. Write the following words on the board: *acronym, chronological, heterogeneous, lexicology.* Have pairs of students copy the words, underline the prefixes, and write definitions for the words. Tell them to confirm their definitions by looking up each word in a print or online dictionary. **ALL LEVELS**

RESPOND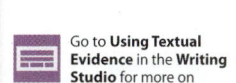

LANGUAGE CONVENTIONS:
Direct and Indirect Quotations

Direct quotations are a writer's or speaker's exact words. When included in texts, they are set off by quotation marks. **Indirect quotations** are a writer's restatement of another writer's or speaker's words. They are not punctuated with quotation marks. For detailed instruction on punctuating direct quotations, you can consult a style guide such as the Modern Language Association (MLA) Handbook or the Publication Manual of the American Psychological Association (APA).

Khazan includes a direct quotation from a Tanzanian woman in her article:

> "Yes, it's normal, being beaten, yelled at. If you tell [anyone], your peers will ask you, is this your first time to be beaten? Some of us are used to it, just like the way we are used to eating *ugali*," one Tanzanian woman said in a World Bank focus group.

The author could have instead chosen to present the woman's comments as an indirect quotation:

> A Tanzanian woman told a World Bank focus group that being beaten and yelled at was normal, and that some Tanzanian women are so accustomed to domestic abuse that it seems as normal to them as the food they eat.

Notice the difference between the two versions. In the first, the reader hears the woman's own voice as she matter-of-factly describes being beaten as part of everyday life. The second version conveys the idea that some women view domestic abuse as normal, but it does not have the same impact as the woman's own words.

The chart below shows ways to integrate and punctuate direct quotations, using tags or phrases such as "she said" that indicate the speaker or writer:

PUNCTUATION OF DIRECT QUOTATIONS	
with tag at beginning	The woman said, "In my country, very few girls finish school."
with tag interrupting the quotation	"In my country," the woman said, "very few girls finish school."
with tag after the quotation	"In my country, very few girls finish school" the woman said.
to introduce a long quotation	One woman spoke about her personal experience in the education system: "I entered school at the age of 6. . . ."

Practice and Apply Return to the article. Find a paragraph that includes at least one direct quotation. Rewrite the paragraph using an indirect quotation. When you have finished, share your new paragraph with a partner and work together to analyze how the changes you made affect that part of the article.

 Go to **Using Textual Evidence** in the **Writing Studio** for more on using direct and indirect quotations.

Education Protects Women from Abuse 445

APPLY

LANGUAGE CONVENTIONS:
Direct and Indirect Quotations

Review with students the information on page 445 about **direct and indirect quotations.** Explain that using **direct quotations** in your writing can strengthen your arguments by providing powerful statements in the original speaker's own words.

Read the direct quotation on page 445 aloud. Then, read the **indirect quotation,** which paraphrases the quote. Challenge students to explain the differences between the two and evaluate the impact each would have on readers. Encourage them to debate which is more impactful and why.

Explain to students that each type of quotation requires specific punctuation. Indirect quotations are punctuated like normal sentences, while direct quotations are punctuated with quotation marks. Also point out that most direct quotations have short tags at the beginning, in the middle, or at the end of the quote. Review the chart on page 445 with students and point out the punctuation and tags for each quotation.

Practice and Apply Direct students back to Khazan's article to identify a paragraph with a direct quotation that interests them. Challenge students to rewrite the paragraph by paraphrasing the quote (i.e., turning it from a direct to an indirect quotation).

After students have finished their paragraphs, place them in pairs to share their work. Encourage pairs to discuss how paraphrasing changed the paragraphs and whether the change strengthened or weakened the author's message.

For **writing support** for students at varying proficiency levels, see the **Text X-Ray** on page 434D.

 ENGLISH LEARNER SUPPORT

Language Conventions Place students into pairs, and then display the following two sentences. Explain that each is a direct quotation and that they should paraphrase each one into an indirect quotation. Remind them to use correct punctuation.

Sentence #1: "The content of a book holds the power of education and it is with this power that we can shape our future and change lives." –*Malala Yousafzai*

Sentence #2: "If you educate a man, you educate an individual. But if you educate a woman, you educate a nation." –*African Proverb*

Once the paraphrases are complete, ask volunteers to share their indirect quotations with the class. **MODERATE/LIGHT**

APPLY

COMPARE ACROSS GENRES

Before students complete their graphic organizers, ask them to consider how each genre (one an argument, one an informational article) presents a similar message, but in different ways. Have them analyze the themes of the two selections, and then challenge them to write a sentence expressing an overall theme for both selections.

ANALYZE THE TEXTS

Possible answers:

1. **DOK 2:** *Wollstonecraft most likely expected people to be shocked by her ideas because she lived in a time when the ideas of women were not generally respected, and women were not thought of as scholars and thinkers. She had to structure her writing as an argument to defend her ideas as valid in a society that was most likely going to disagree with her. Khazan most likely expected her work to be accepted because, although she acknowledges the lack of education of women worldwide, her article was written for educated Westerners. Khazan can report facts and figures and does not need to argue her point, because her ideas are already acknowledged and accepted by many in society.*

2. **DOK 3:** *According to Wollstonecraft, lack of education harms women by keeping them dependent on men, by encouraging shallow and frivolous behavior, and by destroying noble character traits such as virtue. Khazan focuses primarily on how education or a lack thereof is related to physical and/or sexual abuse and the attitudes women have toward abuse.*

3. **DOK 2:** *When Khazan refers to women as a group, she is speaking of women worldwide. In some places, Wollstonecraft seems to be referring to all women, but much of her argument deals with middle- and upper-class women who would have been similar to her in background and social position. She does not address poor or working-class women or women in other countries or parts of the world.*

4. **DOK 4:** *Wollstonecraft would be appalled by the information in Khazan's article and might even use it to support her own arguments. The statistics Khazan cites about the number of women who are uneducated and abused worldwide supports Wollstonecraft's assertion that "neglected education" leads to "misery" for women.*

446   Unit 3

RESPOND

Collaborate & Compare

COMPARE ACROSS GENRES

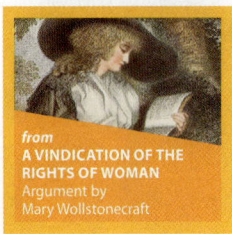

from
A VINDICATION OF THE RIGHTS OF WOMAN
Argument by
Mary Wollstonecraft

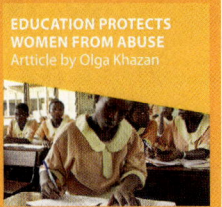

EDUCATION PROTECTS WOMEN FROM ABUSE
Article by Olga Khazan

A Vindication of the Rights of Woman and "Education Protects Women from Abuse" reflect two different genres, or types of writing. Wollstonecraft presents her *Vindication* as an argument, while Khazan presents her ideas in an informational article. Despite the difference in genre, both authors address similar themes related to the education of women.

When you compare the ideas in two or more texts, you also synthesize those ideas, making connections, expanding on key concepts, and even developing new questions. In a small group, complete the Venn diagram with similarities and differences in the ideas presented by Wollstonecraft and Khazan.

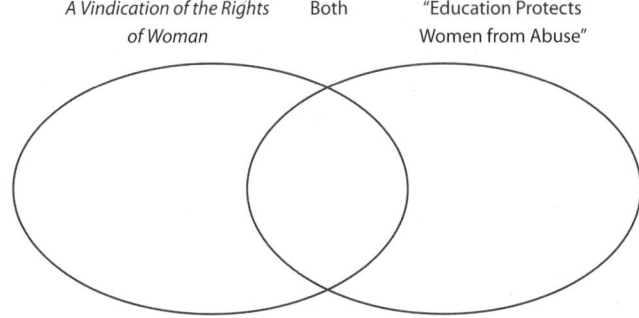

A Vindication of the Rights of Woman   Both   "Education Protects Women from Abuse"

ANALYZE THE TEXTS

Discuss these questions in your group.

1. **Infer** How did Wollstonecraft and Khazan most likely expect their works to be received? How might their expectations have influenced their writing styles? Explain your response.

2. **Contrast** How do Wollstonecraft's and Khazan's interpretations of how lack of education harms women differ?

3. **Interpret** Both Wollstonecraft and Khazan are concerned about the education of women. However, they are writing in very different times and cultures. When Khazan refers to "women" as a group, who is she describing? Does the word *women* used by Wollstonecraft define the same group?

4. **Synthesize** How do you think Mary Wollstonecraft would respond to the information and statistics Khazan presents in her article? Cite evidence to support your response.

446   Unit 3

ENGLISH LEARNER SUPPORT

Summarize Give students additional practice in understanding Khazan's article by placing students into small groups. Have each group member read a paragraph from the article aloud and then provide a summary of the reading. Encourage other group members to discuss the summary and provide feedback. Have them continue until the entire article has been read and summarized. **LIGHT**

RESPOND

COLLABORATE AND PRESENT

Now your group can continue exploring the ideas in these texts by collaborating to compare the texts and present your analyses. Follow these steps:

1. **Determine Central Ideas** In your group, discuss the main ideas of each text, making sure that everyone contributes. Narrow down the ideas presented and try to reach an agreement on one central or controlling idea for each selection.

2. **Identify Supporting Details** Next, identify at least two lines of reasoning each author uses to develop her central idea and at least two specific details she uses to support each line of reasoning. You can use a table to organize your ideas.

SELECTION AND CONTROLLING IDEA	LINES OF REASONING	SUPPORTING DETAILS
A Vindication of the Rights of Woman: The education women receive is inadequate and needs to be reformed.	Education women currently receive makes them irrational and frivolous.	Minds aren't developed through true education.
		Women ready for marriage but not anything else.
	Women who are better educated will make better wives.	Educated women can better care for their children.
		Educated women are better companions to husbands.
"Education Protects Women from Abuse": Educating women is one of the best ways to combat high abuse rates among women.	Rates of domestic abuse among women worldwide are very high.	30% of women have been abused by intimate partners.
		As many as 1/3 of women think wife-beating is ok.
	Better education is correlated with lower likelihood of abuse.	More education means a higher ability to refuse sex.
		Women are 36% less likely to endure domestic violence.

3. **Compare and Analyze** With your group, discuss the similarities and differences between the central ideas of the selections and the ways in which each author develops and supports those ideas. Then analyze how the central idea and techniques used by each author reflect her purposes for writing.

4. **Present to the Class** Present your group's findings to the class. Be sure to include your group's conclusions about both the central idea and the author's purpose of each selection, highlighting the primary similarities and differences that you identified. You may adapt the charts you created or use other visuals to convey your ideas to the class.

Go to **Giving a Presentation** in the **Speaking and Listening Studio** for more on presenting.

Collaborate & Compare 447

APPLY

COLLABORATE AND PRESENT

Point out that these two selections are from very different eras and are written in very different styles, but they deliver similar messages.

1. **Determine Central Ideas** Walk around the room and listen to each group as the students brainstorm. Use this as an opportunity to clarify or focus groups as necessary. Challenge students to think about overarching ideas, rather than minor points.

2. **Identify Supporting Details** As students work to identify the lines of reasoning and the supporting details used in each selection, provide guidance in understanding the difference between lines of reasoning (the principal reasons used to support an idea) and supporting details (specific facts or examples a writer gives).

3. **Compare and Analyze** Encourage students to discuss, as a group, the similarities and differences between the selections. Challenge them to think about why each author used specific techniques and how these techniques are related to the author's purpose.

4. **Present to the Class** Have each group presents its analysis to the class. Encourage groups to include the central ideas and the author's purpose for each selection, as well as the similarities and differences they noted. Tell students to listen actively while each group presents its findings and then compare each group's findings to their own.

WHEN STUDENTS STRUGGLE . . .

Take Notes If students have difficulty following their classmates' presentations, direct them to take notes as each group presents its findings. Suggest they use a graphic organizer to help with their note taking. Offer the chart below as one possibility:

Group	Main Idea Presented	Supporting Ideas Presented

 For additional support, go to the **Reading Studio** and assign the following Level Up tutorial: **Taking Notes and Outlining.**

Collaborate & Compare 447

PLAN

from A JOURNAL OF THE PLAGUE YEAR
Novel by Daniel Defoe

GENRE ELEMENTS
NOVEL

Tell students that a **novel** includes all the basic elements of fiction, but often has more characters and a more complex plot than a short story. **Novel excerpts** are parts of a novel that can stand alone, or be read without having to read the entire novel. Novel excerpts often give a good sense of character, setting, and the main problem or conflict in the plot. In this lesson, students will analyze how a historical setting affects the plot.

LEARNING OBJECTIVES

- Analyze historical setting and narrator.
- Conduct research about the bubonic plague of 1665.
- Write notes for a problem-solution essay.
- Discuss a presentation.
- Identify denotations and connotations.
- Use participles and participial phrases.
- **Language** Discuss denotations and connotations.

TEXT COMPLEXITY

Quantitative Measures	A Journal of the Plague Year	Lexile: 1470L
Qualitative Measures	**Ideas Presented** Simple, single meaning. Literal, explicit, and direct.	
	Structures Used Primarily explicit. Largely chronological.	
	Language Used Archaic and formal language. Complex sentence structures.	
	Knowledge Required Experience may be less familiar to many. Historical references may make heavier demand.	

448A Unit 3

PLAN

Online Ed

RESOURCES

- Unit 3 Response Log
- Selection Audio
- Reading Studio: Notice & Note
- Level Up Tutorial: Analyze Historical Setting
- Writing Studio: Writing Informative Texts
- Speaking and Listening Studio: Participating in Collaborative Discussions
- Vocabulary Studio: Denotations and Connotations
- Grammar Studio: Module 3: Lesson 3: Participles and Participial Phrases
- *A Journal of the Plague Year* Selection Test

SUMMARIES

English

In these excerpts, the narrator, a saddle maker known only as H.F., describes plague-ridden London as a city altered by sorrow and the constant fear of death. He describes the pits in which the dead are buried and explains how people react to their own illness, the illness of family and friends, and the persistent threat of contagion.

Spanish

En estos pasajes, el narrador, un fabricante de monturas conocido únicamente como H.F., describe Londres durante la peste como una ciudad alterada por el dolor y el constante miedo a la muerte. Describe las fosas en que los muertos son enterrados y explica cómo la gente reacciona a su propia enfermedad, la enfermedad de familiares y amigos, y la amenaza persistente del contagio.

SMALL-GROUP OPTIONS

Have students work in small groups and pairs to read and discuss the selection.

Reciprocal Teaching

- Have students read the text.
- After reading, ask students to write three to five questions about the text, using these frames: *What does the narrator mean by ____? Why did the narrator describe ____? How does the narrator use description to ____? How do the details about ____ affect the ____?*
- Form teams of three students.
- Have each student offer two questions for group discussion.
- Have the group reach consensus on the answers and find supporting text evidence.

Think-Pair-Share

- After reading the text, pose this question: *What kind of person is the narrator?*
- Have students think about the question individually and take notes.
- Then, have pairs listen, discuss, and formulate a shared response to the question. Direct them to include at least two reasons to support their inference.
- Finally, have pairs share their responses with the class.

A Journal of the Plague Year **448B**

PLAN

 **Text X-Ray: English Learner Support**
for *A Journal of the Plague Year*

Use the Text X-Ray and the supports and scaffolds in the Teacher's Edition to help guide students at different proficiency levels through the selection.

INTRODUCE THE SELECTION
DISCUSS PLAGUE AND INFECTIONS

In this lesson, students will need to be able to discuss how infections can lead to plagues.

Provide the following explanations:
- An *infection* is a disease. "*To be infectious*" means "to cause an infection."
- A *plague* occurs when a serious or fatal disease infects a great number of people.

Explain to students that during the time of the bubonic plague, there were no modern conveniences to keep germs at bay—like flush toilets, washing machines, and dishwashers; living conditions were less sanitary in general. Many medicines were not yet invented or available.

Ask students to discuss why it is less likely that a plague will happen in a society that benefits from modern hygiene. Provide sentence frames, such as *Modern hygiene makes it less likely a plague will happen because _____. Plagues were caused by circumstances such as _____ that are not a problem today.*

CULTURAL REFERENCES

The following words or phrases may be unfamiliar to students:
- *the face of London* (paragraph 1): the general appearance of London
- *the whole the face of things* (paragraph 1): everything
- *pierce the stoutest heart* (paragraph 1): upset even the most unfeeling or calmest person
- *such as no tongue can express* (paragraph 6): like nothing that words can describe
- *running that hazard* (paragraph 7): taking the risk
- *dead-cart* (paragraph 8): cart full of dead bodies

LISTENING

Listen for Details

Draw students' attention to the first paragraph. Explain that the first paragraph of an excerpt introduces the setting. Understanding details about the setting will help them better understand the selection.

Have students listen as you read aloud paragraph 1. Use the following supports with students at varying proficiency levels:

- Reread the first few sentences of paragraph 1. Tell students the setting of this selection is in London during a time of great sorrow from widespread disease. Ask them yes–no questions about the setting and have them give a thumbs up for "yes" and a thumbs down for "no." **SUBSTANTIAL**
- Have students reread paragraph 1, explaining words and phrases as needed. Ask students questions that elicit details about the setting. For example: *Where is the narrator?* (London) *What do the people look like?* (sad and sorrowful) *How do they act?* (They shriek and cry.) **MODERATE**
- After students reread the paragraph, have groups discuss the setting, tone, and how people looked and acted. **LIGHT**

448C   Unit 3

PLAN

SPEAKING

Discuss Word Meanings

Tell students they can find the *denotation* of a word by looking it up in the dictionary. They can find the *connotation*, or feelings associated with the word, by looking at how an author uses it to make a reader feel a certain way.

Review the Vocabulary Strategy on Student Edition page 460. Create a four-column chart labeled *Word*, *Meaning*, *Positive*, and *Negative*. Use the following supports with students at varying proficiency levels:

- Write a list of words, such as *shy*, *quiet*, *smart*. Help students use a dictionary to find the meaning for each word, and write it in the chart. Then, ask questions to help students understand connotations. For example: *Which is a better way to describe a shy person, bashful or antisocial? Which is a better way to describe a smart person, clever or sly?* **SUBSTANTIAL**
- Have partners choose five words from the text. Help students find the meaning for each word, and write it in the chart. Have them discuss the connotation of the words they chose. **MODERATE**
- Have partners fill in the chart with five words from the text. Then, have pairs share their charts with other pairs. Have them ask questions, like *Why is bashful a positive connotation for shy?* **LIGHT**

READING

Decode Words

Remind students that paying attention to cognates, affixes, roots, and base words can help them sound out words as they read.

Use the following supports with students at varying proficiency levels:

- Have students chorally reread the first paragraph with you. Point out any cognates *(particular; horror)*, affixes, and root words, and model how to use them to help in pronunciation. For example: *The root word is strange. The suffix is -ly. I pronounce the word strangely.* **SUBSTANTIAL**
- Have students reread the first paragraph and make a list of any cognates. Then, have them list any words with an affix. Tell them to circle the base word and underline the affix. **MODERATE**
- Have students reread the text and make a list of any cognates, affixes, and roots they find. Tell partners to discuss the meanings of the words on their list, focusing on correct pronunciation. **LIGHT**

WRITING

Write Notes for an Essay

Read the prompt on Student Edition page 459. Explain that a problem-solution essay gives one or more solutions. Answer questions to ensure students understand the task.

Use the following supports with students at varying proficiency levels:

- Create a scene in which you just discovered a new disease. On the board, list ways you would tell people about the disease and what could be done to stop it. Then, have students write the list. **SUBSTANTIAL**
- List ideas for preventing and limiting the spread of a new disease. Have the students write about how to control the spread of the disease. Offer this sentence frame: *One way to stop the spread is _____.* **MODERATE**
- Pair students and have them brainstorm a scenario and then come up with possible solutions for limiting the spread of the disease. Have students work together to write notes. **LIGHT**

TEACH

? Connect to the ESSENTIAL QUESTION

A Journal of the Plague Year chronicles the personal reactions to the bubonic plague that broke out in London in 1665. The narrator must make a difficult choice when faced with this horrifying situation.

COMPARE ACROSS GENRES

Point out that both selections are told through the eyes of a narrator. Although *A Journal of the Plague Year* is a fictional account of the bubonic plague in London and *Inferno: A Doctor's Ebola Story* is a memoir based on actual experiences by the author while in Africa, both use details to develop a sense of reality and make events seem authentic and intimate. Have students think about how the authors use details, setting, and the narrator to shape the reader's perception of the event.

COLLABORATE & COMPARE

NOVEL

from
A JOURNAL OF THE PLAGUE YEAR

by **Daniel Defoe**
pages 451–456

COMPARE ACROSS GENRES

As you read, carefully note details about the setting, the narrator, and the plague being described. How does the author use setting to develop the plot and theme? How does the text's point of view affect your impression of events? Later, your answers will help guide you and your group as you compare this text to *Inferno: A Doctor's Ebola Story*.

? ESSENTIAL QUESTION:

Why are plagues so horrifying?

MEMOIR

from
INFERNO: A DOCTOR'S EBOLA STORY

by **Steven Hatch, M.D.**
pages 465–470

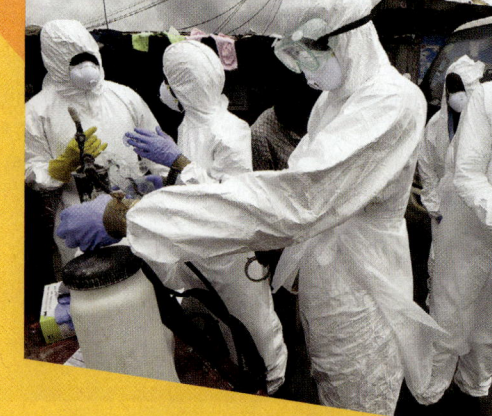

from A Journal of the Plague Year

QUICK START

How do you think you would behave during a major epidemic? Would you flee to a safer place or stay to help others? With a partner, discuss how fear of a dangerous illness can affect people's behavior.

ANALYZE HISTORICAL SETTING

Daniel Defoe's *A Journal of the Plague Year* is a work of fiction. However, the novel realistically portrays historical events in London in the summer of 1665, during the darkest days of the city's outbreak of bubonic plague. In the novel, Defoe incorporates details from mortality records, city maps, and other historical documents to help him achieve **verisimilitude,** or the appearance of truth and actuality. Presented as an eyewitness account, the novel purposefully blurs the line between fact and fiction.

As you read, notice details—such as dates and times, geographical names and information, and numbers and statistics—that establish the novel's historical setting. Note how these details help drive the plot and shape the text's theme.

ANALYZE NARRATOR

Novelists relate the events of their stories through the voices of their narrators. In *A Journal of the Plague Year,* Daniel Defoe uses a first-person **narrator**, a character in the novel who relates events in his own words, using the pronouns *I*, *me*, and *my*. The perspective of Defoe's narrator affects a reader's impression of what is happening.

As you read, identify details that reveal the character of the narrator, as well as his perspective. Use a chart like the one below to help you analyze Defoe's narrator and to note how that narrator affects your impression of events.

GENRE ELEMENTS: NOVEL
- includes the basic elements of fiction—plot, characters, conflict, setting, and theme
- often includes more characters and a more complex plot than a short story
- story may be told by one or more narrators
- setting may be real, as in a historical novel, or imagined

DETAIL ABOUT NARRATOR	CHARACTERISTIC REVEALED	EFFECT ON MY IMPRESSIONS
Includes names of streets, dates, statistics	Detailed	Overly objective ~~Unemotional~~
Wants to watch people buried at night at pit.	Morbid	Takes risks
Says scene is impossible to describe.	Might have some emotion after all.	Devastation is so great, even narrator is affected.

A Journal of the Plague Year 449

WHEN STUDENTS STRUGGLE . . .

Analyze Setting Have students use a graphic organizer to record varied settings.

Detail	Location
London	Paragraph 1
Aldgate, Whitechapel	Paragraph 2
4th of Sept. 20th of Sept. 1,114 bodies	Paragraph 3

 For additional support, go to the **Reading Studio** and assign the following Level Up tutorial: Setting.

TEACH

QUICK START

Tell students that people's behavior often changes when confronted with a catastrophe—sometimes they change in a surprising way. Ask students to think about the last time they experienced the threat of a natural disaster. Were they surprised about some people's behavior? Have them complete the Quick Start activity.

ANALYZE HISTORICAL SETTING

Remind students that a story's **setting** is the time and place in which action occurs. A story's **setting** may also encompass the larger historical and cultural contexts that form the background for a narrative. Explain that Defoe's writing anticipates the realism and psychological depth of the modern novel.

Tell students that in order to analyze a **historical setting,** a reader must

- examine how the author uses **word choice** to create images that develop the mood and tone of the written piece
- note how characters react to the setting
- identify how the author provides an appearance of truth by weaving in details based on historical documents that define time, location, and historical facts (**verisimilitude**).

ANALYZE NARRATOR

Explain to students that the narrator in this text is the main character. To analyze a narrator, a reader must think about the narrator's actions, dialogue, observations, inner thoughts, perspective, and word choice. Remind students that the narrator in *A Journal of the Plague Year* is intentionally creating very specific impressions. Tell students to complete the graphic organizer as they read through the text.

A Journal of the Plague Year **449**

TEACH

CRITICAL VOCABULARY

Encourage students to read all the sentences before deciding which word best completes each one. Remind them to look for context clues that match the precise meaning of each word.

Answers:

1. *discourse*
2. *visitation*
3. *promiscuous*
4. *huddle*
5. *summon*
6. *abate*

■ English Learner Support

Use Cognates Tell students that one of the Critical Vocabulary words has a Spanish cognate: *discourse/discurso*.
ALL LEVELS

LANGUAGE CONVENTIONS

Review the definition of a participle. Tell students that authors use participles to create powerful mental images. Explain to students that Defoe uses participles very effectively throughout *A Journal of the Plague Year*.

The **wailing** *man threw himself into the river* is an effective participle because the verb *wail* creates a vivid image.

ANNOTATION MODEL

Remind students of the Annotation Model on page 450 which suggests underlining important details that assist them in analyzing the historical setting and narrator.

Point out that they may follow this suggestion or use their own system for marking up the selection in their write-in text. They may want to color-code their annotations by using highlighters. Their notes in the margin may include questions about setting or plot that isn't clear.

450   Unit 3

 **GET READY**

CRITICAL VOCABULARY

| visitation | discourse | huddle |
| summon | promiscuously | abate |

To preview the Critical Vocabulary words, fill in the blanks with the correct vocabulary word.

1. During their heated _____, Mike and Mary were able to solve their disagreements and continue with plans for the project.
2. There are rules limiting _____ at the college dorm.
3. Joline leaves her laundry strewn _____ across the floor of her room.
4. When it rains, we _____ under the awning to stay warm and dry.
5. Don't worry about the time; a bell will _____ us for our next class.
6. Although you are miserable today, your cold symptoms will _____ soon and you will feel much better.

LANGUAGE CONVENTIONS

A participle is a verb form that functions as an adjective, modifying nouns and pronouns. Most participles are present participle forms that end in *-ing* or past participle forms that end in *-ed* or *-en*.

> The <u>wailing</u> man threw himself into the river.
> <u>Confused</u>, he swam in circles.

As you read the excerpt from *A Journal of the Plague Year*, watch for participles.

ANNOTATION MODEL   NOTICE & NOTE

In the model, you can see how one reader marked the text to analyze the historical setting by noting the narrator's language and use of details.

| The face of <u>London</u> was now indeed strangely altered, I mean the whole mass of buildings, city, liberties, <u>suburbs, Westminster, Southwark,</u> and altogether; for as to the particular part called the city, or within the walls, that was not yet much infected. <u>But in the whole the face of things, I say, was much altered; sorrow and sadness sat upon every face; and though some parts were not yet overwhelmed, yet all looked deeply concerned</u>; and, as we saw it apparently coming on, so everyone looked on himself and his family as in the <u>utmost danger</u>. | *The story takes place in London and surrounding areas. The disaster is widespread.*

 Emotions are seen on faces, so the author uses the words "the whole face of things, I say, was much altered" to describe the generally sad atmosphere.

 All are extremely concerned, so the danger must be great. |

450   Unit 3

ENGLISH LEARNER SUPPORT

Use Grammatical Structures Write a list of verbs on the board and have students act them out. Explain to students that these verbs can be made into adjectives by adding *-ing* or *-ed* to describe a noun or pronoun. Help students form phrases or sentences orally using the participles. **MODERATE**

BACKGROUND

Daniel Defoe (c. 1660–1731) is considered a pioneer of modern journalism and the father of the English novel. He was five years old when the bubonic plague broke out in London in 1665, and he and his family survived the epidemic and the great fire of London the following year. In *A Journal of the Plague Year*, Defoe chronicles the epidemic through the eyes of his narrator, a saddle maker known as H. F. After agonizing over whether to leave the city, H. F. reads a passage in the Bible and decides to stay to do what he can for those in need.

from
A JOURNAL OF THE PLAGUE YEAR
Novel by Daniel Defoe

PREPARE TO COMPARE

As you read, look for details in the text that help describe and develop the historical setting. Also, take time to analyze the narrator so that you can determine the effect his perspective has on the development of the plot and theme. Your analysis will help you compare this narrator's perspective with the perspective of the author of the memoir that follows this selection.

1   The face of London was now indeed strangely altered, I mean the whole mass of buildings, city[1], liberties[2], suburbs, Westminster, Southwark, and altogether; for as to the particular part called the city, or within the walls, that was not yet much infected. But in the whole face of things, I say, was much altered; sorrow and sadness sat upon every face; and though some parts were not yet overwhelmed, yet all looked deeply concerned; and, as we saw it apparently coming on, so every one looked on himself and his family as in the utmost danger. Were it possible to represent those times exactly to those that did not see them, and give the reader due ideas of the horror that everywhere presented itself, it must make just impressions upon their minds and fill

---
[1] **city:** the portion of London once within the old city walls with Westminster to the west and Southwark to the south.
[2] **liberties:** densely populated area just outside the city walls.

Notice & Note

Use the side margins to notice and note signposts in the text.

ANALYZE HISTORICAL SETTING

Annotate: In paragraph 1, mark the words or phrases that evoke emotions about the plague.

Analyze: How does the use of this evocative language help readers understand the setting?

A Journal of the Plague Year   451

TEACH

BACKGROUND

Defoe did not write his first novel, *Robinson Crusoe* (1719), until he was nearly 60 years old. It was tremendously successful, and he quickly published two Crusoe sequels, following them with several other novels, including *Moll Flanders* (1722), *A Journal of the Plague Year* (1722), *Colonel Jack* (1722), and *Roxana* (1724). During his lifetime, Defoe was not highly regarded by his literary contemporaries. Jonathan Swift, for example, stated witheringly, "There is no enduring him." By the mid-19th century, however, critics had come to appreciate Defoe's ability to plumb the depths of human emotions and to recreate in his fiction all the rich detail of real life.

PREPARE TO COMPARE

Direct students to use the Prepare to Compare prompt to focus their reading.

ANALYZE HISTORICAL SETTING

Tell students that in order to fully understand the historical setting, readers should note the **mood** by identifying words that convey strong emotions. (**Answer:** *The narrator wants the reader to understand that normal life has ceased to exist, tragedy is everywhere, the smell of impending doom prevails, and fear permeates the existence of all people. People are heard wailing. It seems dark, streets are quiet, and people are consumed with self-preservation.*)

For **listening and reading support** for students at varying proficiency levels, see the **Text X-Ray** on page 448C–D.

EL ENGLISH LEARNER SUPPORT

Use Concept Mapping Help students to visualize the setting and effects of the plague by using a concept map. Read aloud paragraph 1, and work with students to identify the words and phrases that describe the setting and effects of the plague. Write the words on the map. Ask students to describe what they visualize.   **MODERATE**

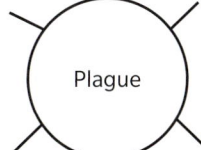

A Journal of the Plague Year   **451**

TEACH

✏️ ANALYZE NARRATOR

Remind students to pay close attention to the narrator's words, thoughts, and observations in order to understand his **motivations,** or what he wants. (**Answer:** *He is highly curious and apt to take risks.*)

■ **English Learner Support**

Internalize Multiple-Meaning Words Make sure that students understand the meanings in context of these words and phrases:

- *suffering* (paragraph 3): "allowing"
- *drove* (paragraph 4): "forced"
- *content* (paragraph 4): "satisfied" **ALL LEVELS**

CRITICAL VOCABULARY

visitation: At a *visitation,* such as a wake, people pay respect to a deceased person.

ASK STUDENTS what they might see and hear at a visitation. *(people talking about memories, pictures of the deceased person, music, a coffin, crying, whispering)*

summon: In this text, people worry if they will be *summoned*—or called upon to die—by the plague.

ASK STUDENTS what other people might be summoned and why. *(Nurses and doctors might be summoned to help the sick; police might be summoned to help control areas; clergy might be summoned to bury the dead.)*

✏️ NOTICE & NOTE

visitation
(vĭz-ĭ-tā´shən) *n.* an instance of being visited.

summon
(sŭm´ən) *v.* to bring into existence or readiness.

them with surprise. London might well be said to be all in tears; the mourners did not go about the streets indeed, for nobody put on black or made a formal dress of mourning for their nearest friends; but the voice of mourning was truly heard in the streets. The shrieks of women and children at the windows and doors of their houses, where their dearest relations were perhaps dying, or just dead, were so frequent to be heard as we passed the streets, that it was enough to pierce the stoutest heart in the world to hear them. Tears and lamentations were seen almost in every house, especially in the first part of the **visitation**; for towards the latter end men's hearts were hardened, and death was so always before their eyes, that they did not so much concern themselves for the loss of their friends, expecting that themselves should be **summoned** the next hour. . . .

2   I went all the first part of the time freely about the streets, though not so freely as to run myself into apparent danger, except when they dug the great pit in the churchyard of our parish of Aldgate.³ A terrible pit it was, and I could not resist my curiosity to go and see it. As near as I may judge, it was about forty feet in length, and about fifteen or sixteen feet broad, and, at the time I first looked at it, about nine feet deep; but it was said they dug it near twenty feet deep afterwards in one part of it, till they could go no deeper for the water; for they had, it seems, dug several large pits before this. For though the plague was long a-coming to our parish, yet, when it did come, there was no parish in or about London where it raged with such violence as in the two parishes of Aldgate and Whitechapel. . . .⁴

3   They had supposed this pit would have supplied them for a month or more when they dug it, and some blamed the churchwardens for suffering such a frightful thing, telling them they were making preparations to bury the whole parish, and the like; but time made it appear the churchwardens knew the condition of the parish better than they did, for the pit being finished the 4th of September, I think, they began to bury in it the 6th, and by the 20th, which was just two weeks, they had thrown into it 1,114 bodies when they were obliged to fill it up, the bodies being then come to lie within six feet of the surface. . . .

ANALYZE NARRATOR
Annotate: In paragraph 4, mark details that help you understand more about the narrator.

Infer: What can you infer about the narrator's motivations and character?

4   It was about the 10th of September that my curiosity led, or rather drove, me to go and see this pit again, when there had been near 400 people buried in it; and I was not content to see it in the daytime, as I had done before, for then there would have been nothing to have been seen but the loose earth; for all the bodies that were thrown in were immediately covered with earth by those they called the buriers, which at other times were called bearers; but I resolved to go in the night and see some of them thrown in.

5   There was a strict order to prevent people coming to those pits, and that was only to prevent infection. But after some time that order

---

³ **parish of Aldgate:** the street and area known as Aldgate take their name from the nearby old gate, or Aldgate.
⁴ **Whitechapel:** an area just east of Aldgate and the old city walls.

was more necessary, for people that were infected and near their end, and delirious also, would run to those pits, wrapt in blankets or rugs, and throw themselves in, and, as they said, bury themselves. I cannot say that the officers suffered any willingly to lie there; but I have heard that in a great pit in Finsbury, in the parish of Cripplegate, it lying open then to the fields, for it was not then walled about, [some] came and threw themselves in, and expired there, before they threw any earth upon them; and that when they came to bury others and found them there, they were quite dead, though not cold.

6   This may serve a little to describe the dreadful condition of that day, though it is impossible to say anything that is able to give a

NOTICE & NOTE

ANALYZE HISTORICAL SETTING

Annotate: In paragraph 5, mark the phrases that indicate why people were not allowed to go to the burial pit.

Analyze: How does this information add to your understanding of the setting?

A Journal of the Plague Year 453

TEACH

ANALYZE HISTORICAL SETTING

Tell students that in paragraph 5, the **setting** is further developed through characters' actions and their reactions to the time, place, mood, and tone. (**Answer:** *It is important for the narrator to explain that people were desperate, delirious, and without hope. People's actions, in this way, help to define the setting. This also helps the reader to understand the devastating effects a plague has on society.*)

ENGLISH LEARNER SUPPORT

Paraphrase Read aloud paragraph 5 to students. Pause at intervals so that students can paraphrase the text. Answer questions and clarify as needed. After the paragraph, model a summary statement for students. Ask them comprehension questions such as:

1. Could any person go to the burial pits? Why or why not? *(They might get infected or try to throw themselves in.)*

2. What did delirious people do? *(throw themselves into the pit)*

3. What does it mean to be "walled about"? *(have a fence or wall around something)* **MODERATE**

IMPROVE READING FLUENCY

Targeted Passage Direct students to paragraph 5 and instruct them that you will model how to read the paragraph with expression. Tell them you will use the punctuation that the author uses to help you chunk or group words appropriately. Direct students when to echo read.

 Go to the **Reading Studio** for additional support in developing fluency.

A Journal of the Plague Year **453**

TEACH

ANALYZE HISTORICAL SETTING

Remind students that **setting** impacts characters, **plot**, and **conflict**. Authors reveal setting and its effects in many ways, including conversations and interactions between characters. (**Answer:** *The sexton explains that by entering the burial pit, the narrator would be exposing himself to a great sermon that will call him to repentance. This conversation explains that this is a time in history that gave cause for people to begin to question the meaning of their lives, their belief systems, and even their existence. The main hope is that one can learn from tragedy.*)

AGAIN AND AGAIN

Tell students that this signpost clues the reader that certain images and ideas will be repeated for effect. The author intentionally echoes words, phrases, and images to emphasize a point. Ask students to look at Defoe's word choice in paragraph 8 to find several images that have already been referenced in previous paragraphs. (**Answer:** *The repetition of death and the images of the surrounding death indicate how far-reaching the perils of the plague extend. No one can really describe the agony unless it is witnessed or experienced.*)

LANGUAGE CONVENTIONS

Remind students that participles are verb forms that end in *-ing* or *-ed*. Participles act as adjectives. (**Answer:** *The grieving man is not infected, nor distempered. He is oppressed and heavily weighted down with the death of his family.*)

CRITICAL VOCABULARY

discourse: The *discourse*, or conversation, took place between the narrator and the sexton.

ASK STUDENTS to paraphrase the discourse between the narrator and the sexton. (*The narrator told the sexton that he was curious to see the burial pit. The sexton told him that he could enter, but he warned the narrator that the sights would be a loud lesson about life, death, and humanity.*)

454   Unit 3

NOTICE & NOTE

ANALYZE HISTORICAL SETTING

Annotate: Mark phrases in paragraph 7 that highlight the purpose of the conversation between the narrator and the sexton.

Analyze: What does this conversation reveal about the time period and cultural setting?

discourse
(dĭs´kôrs) *n.* verbal exchange or conversation.

AGAIN & AGAIN

Notice & Note: Recurring or similar use of imagery often emphasizes an important point. In paragraph 8, mark imagery used to describe death and suffering.

Analyze: What idea is being emphasized through this use of imagery?

LANGUAGE CONVENTIONS

Annotate: Mark the participles in the first sentence of paragraph 9.

Analyze: What details do these participles add to the description of the grieving man?

---

true idea of it to those who did not see it, other than this, that it was indeed very, very, very dreadful, and such as no tongue can express.

7   I got admittance into the churchyard by being acquainted with the sexton[5] who attended, who, though he did not refuse me at all, yet earnestly persuaded me not to go, telling me very seriously, for he was a good, religious, and sensible man, that it was indeed their business and duty to venture, and to run all hazards, and that in it they might hope to be preserved; but that I had no apparent call to it but my own curiosity, which, he said, he believed I would not pretend was sufficient to justify my running that hazard. I told him I had been pressed in my mind to go, and that perhaps it might be an instructing sight, that might not be without its uses. "Nay," says the good man, "if you will venture upon that score, name of God go in; for, depend upon it, 't will be a sermon to you, it may be, the best that ever you heard in your life. 'T is a speaking sight," says he, "and has a voice with it, and a loud one, to call us all to repentance;" and with that he opened the door and said, "Go, if you will."

8   His **discourse** had shocked my resolution a little, and I stood wavering for a good while, but just at that interval I saw two links[6] come over from the end of the Minories,[7] and heard the bellman, and then appeared a dead-cart, as they called it, coming over the streets; so I could no longer resist my desire of seeing it, and went in. There was nobody, as I could perceive at first, in the churchyard, or going into it, but the buriers and the fellow that drove the cart, or rather led the horse and cart; but when they came up to the pit they saw a man go to and again, muffled up in a brown cloak, and making motions with his hands under his cloak, as if he was in a great agony, and the buriers immediately gathered about him, supposing he was one of those poor delirious or desperate creatures that used to pretend, as I have said, to bury themselves. He said nothing as he walked about, but two or three times groaned very deeply and loud, and sighed as he would break his heart.

9   When the buriers came up to him they soon found he was neither a person infected and desperate, as I have observed above, or a person distempered[8] in mind, but one oppressed with a dreadful weight of grief indeed, having his wife and several of his children all in the cart that was just come in with him, and he followed in an agony and excess of sorrow. He mourned heartily, as it was easy to see, but with a kind of masculine grief that could not give itself vent by tears; and calmly defying the buriers to let him alone, said he would only see the bodies thrown in and go away, so they left importuning him. But no sooner was the cart turned round and the bodies shot into

---

[5] **sexton:** a church officer or employee responsible for the care and upkeep of church property, sometimes charged with ringing bells and digging graves.
[6] **links:** torches.
[7] **Minories:** a street running from Aldgate to the Tower of London.
[8] **distempered:** afflicted with distemper, or disorder, of the mind; deranged; mentally disturbed.

454   Unit 3

ENGLISH LEARNER SUPPORT

Internalize Multiple-Meaning Words   Make sure that students understand the meanings in context of these words and phrases:

- *preserved* (paragraph 7): "protected"
- *call* (paragraph 7): "reason"   **ALL LEVELS**

the pit **promiscuously**, which was a surprise to him, for he at least expected they would have been decently laid in, though indeed he was afterwards convinced that was impracticable; I say, no sooner did he see the sight but he cried out aloud, unable to contain himself. I could not hear what he said, but he went backward two or three steps and fell down in a swoon. The buriers ran to him and took him up, and in a little while he came to himself, and they led him away to the Pie Tavern over against the end of Houndsditch,[9] where, it seems, the man was known, and where they took care of him. He looked into the pit again as he went away, but the buriers had covered the bodies so immediately with throwing in earth, that though there was light enough, for there were lanterns, and candles in them, placed all night round the sides of the pit, upon heaps of earth, seven or eight, or perhaps more, yet nothing could be seen.

10   This was a mournful scene indeed, and affected me almost as much as the rest; but the other was awful and full of terror. The cart had in it sixteen or seventeen bodies; some were wrapt up in linen sheets, some in rags, some little other than naked, or so loose that what covering they had fell from them in the shooting out of the cart, and they fell quite naked among the rest; but the matter was not much to them, or the indecency much to any one else, seeing they were all dead, and were to be **huddled** together into the common grave of mankind, as we may call it, for here was no difference made, but poor and rich went together; there was no other way of burials, neither was it possible there should, for coffins were not to be had for the prodigious numbers that fell in such a calamity as this....

11   I had some little obligations, indeed, upon me to go to my brother's house, which was in Coleman Street parish,[10] and which he had left to my care, and I went at first every day, but afterwards only once or twice a week.

12   In these walks I had many dismal scenes before my eyes, as particularly of persons falling dead in the streets, terrible shrieks and screechings of women, who, in their agonies, would throw open their chamber windows and cry out in a dismal, surprising manner. It is impossible to describe the variety of postures in which the passions of the poor people would express themselves.... People in the rage of the distemper, or in the torment of their swellings,[11] which was indeed intolerable, running out of their own government,[12] raving and distracted, and oftentimes laying violent hands upon themselves, throwing themselves out at their windows, shooting themselves, etc.; mothers murdering their own children in their lunacy, some dying of mere grief as a passion, some of mere fright and surprise without any

---

[9] **Houndsditch:** a street on the site of an old ditch running northwest along the city wall between Aldgate and Bishopgate.
[10] **Coleman Street parish:** an area about half a mile west of the narrator's parish.
[11] **swellings:** Bubonic plague is characterized by the painful swelling of inflamed lymph glands, or buboes.
[12] **running out of their own government:** losing the ability to govern, or control, themselves.

NOTICE & NOTE

promiscuously
(prə-mĭs´kyōō-əs-lə) *adv.*
lacking standards of selection; acting without careful judgment; indiscriminate.

ANALYZE HISTORICAL SETTING

Annotate: Mark details in paragraph 9 that describe the setting.

Analyze: What do these details add to your understanding of the setting's time and location?

huddle
(hŭd´l) *v.* crowded together, as from cold or fear (in this case, death)

ANALYZE NARRATOR

Annotate: In paragraph 12, mark details that reveal the narrator's perspective on events.

Compare: How does the narrator's perspective affect your impression of the events he describes?

A Journal of the Plague Year 455

TO CHALLENGE STUDENTS...

Eighteenth-Century Social Customs To help students understand the chaos that descended on London during the outbreak, have them research social customs in 18th-century England. Students may want to focus on burial and mourning customs, as well as how society looked upon and cared for the sick. Then have students work in groups to discuss their findings and how Defoe wove these social customs into his work.

TEACH

ANALYZE HISTORICAL SETTING

Tell students that in paragraph 9, the narrator begins to expound on the **mood** and **tone** by describing the agonizing reaction of one man's experience in the burial pit. *(Answer: This event brings the tragedy to a personal level. Readers can more readily connect with personal trials than to general descriptions of events. To read about how bodies are indiscriminately dumped into the pits adds the idea of inhumanity and the plague.)*

ANALYZE NARRATOR

Remind students that a character's **perspective** is his or her attitude toward events. Authors often use the character's observations and words to reveal perspective. *(Answer: The narrator reports on what he observes in a very objective, unemotional voice. This matter-of-fact discourse may assist the reader in reading about such a terrible plight with controlled emotion, as if they were watching a documentary.)*

Remind students to add to the graphic organizer on page 449 to keep track of their thinking.

CRITICAL VOCABULARY

promiscuous: The bodies were indiscriminately dumped into the burial pit, without ceremony.

ASK STUDENTS how choosing something randomly is similar to the *promiscuous* way they buried bodies. *(When you choose something randomly, there is no standard of selection just as there was no standard of laying the bodies in the pit.)*

huddle: The closeness of the bodies that are buried in a common grave reminded the narrator of people *huddling*, or crowding together out of fear.

ASK STUDENTS to think of a time that people might huddle. *(when it's cold outside).*

A Journal of the Plague Year **455**

TEACH

✏️ ANALYZE HISTORICAL SETTING

Remind students that Defoe weaves fact and fiction to create his narrative. This **verisimilitude** lends a sense of reality to the story. (**Answer:** *By including the name of the river, Thames, the Stillyard stairs, and Falcon stairs that the infected man uses to access the river and even the direction the tide is moving, it gives the reader a sense of reality and authenticity, thus achieving verisimilitude.*)

CRITICAL VOCABULARY

abate: The waters lessened, or *abated*, the fever and swelling of lymph glands are lessened or reduced.

ASK STUDENTS how they can abate a fever. (*drink a lot of fluids, take aspirin, or take a cool bath.*)

456   Unit 3

✏️ NOTICE & NOTE

ANALYZE HISTORICAL SETTING

Annotate: Mark each aspect of the setting used in the narrator's description of events surrounding the infected man.

Evaluate: Do the details of the setting create a sense of verisimilitude in the description? Explain why or why not.

abate
(ə-bāt´) *v.* reduced in amount, degree, or intensity; lessen.

456   Unit 3

infection at all, others frighted into idiotism and foolish distractions, some into despair and lunacy, others into melancholy madness. . . .

13   I heard of one infected creature who, running out of his bed in his shirt in the anguish and agony of his swellings, of which he had three upon him, got his shoes on and went to put on his coat; but the nurse resisting, and snatching the coat from him, he threw her down, ran over her, ran downstairs and into the street, directly to the <u>Thames</u> in his shirt, the nurse running after him, and calling to the watch to stop him; but the watchman, frighted at the man, and afraid to touch him, let him go on; upon which he ran down to the <u>Stillyard stairs</u>, threw away his shirt, and plunged into the Thames, and, being a good swimmer, swam quite over the river; and the <u>tide being coming in</u>, as they call it, that is, <u>running westward</u>, he reached the land not till he came about the <u>Falcon stairs</u>, where landing, and finding no people there, it being in the night, he ran about the streets there, naked as he was, for a good while, when, it being by that time high water, he takes the river again, and swam back to the <u>Stillyard</u>, landed, ran up the streets again to his own house, knocking at the door, went up the stairs and into his bed again; and that this terrible experiment cured him of the plague, that is to say, that the violent motion of his arms and legs stretched the parts where the swellings he had upon him were, that is to say, under his arms and his groin, and caused them to ripen and break, and that the cold of the water **abated** the fever in his blood.

APPLYING ACADEMIC VOCABULARY

☐ encounter   ☐ exploit   ☑ persist   ☐ subordinate   ☑ widespread

Write and Discuss Have students turn to a partner to discuss the following questions. Guide students to include the academic vocabulary word *persist* and *widespread* in their responses. Ask volunteers to share their responses with the class.

- What might cause a disease to become **widespread**?
- Why might an epidemic **persist**?

NOTICE & NOTE

CHECK YOUR UNDERSTANDING

Answer these questions before moving on to the **Analyze the Text** section on the following page.

1. Why was there an order to keep people away from the burial pit?
   A To stop mourners from crowding the site
   B To protect citizens from wild animals
   C To keep people from discovering the mass grave
   D To prevent the spread of infection

2. How is the narrator able to get in to see the pit?
   F He bribes the sexton.
   G He knows the sexton.
   H He sneaks past an officer.
   J He goes at night.

3. How does the man at the end of the story supposedly cure himself of the plague?
   A He goes to the doctor.
   B He drinks a lot of fluids.
   C He swims in the river.
   D He takes herbal remedies.

A Journal of the Plague Year 457

TEACH

CHECK YOUR UNDERSTANDING

Have students answer the questions independently.

Answers:
1. D
2. G
3. C

If they answer any questions incorrectly, have them reread the text to confirm their understanding. Then they may proceed to the next selection.

 ENGLISH LEARNER SUPPORT

Oral Assessment Use the following questions to assess students' comprehension and speaking skills.

1. Why is no one allowed to visit the burial pit? *(to keep the disease from spreading and to keep people from jumping in the pit)*

2. Why does the sexton let the narrator see the pit? *(The sexton knows the narrator.)*

3. What did the infected man at the end of the story do? What happens to the man? *(He jumps in the Thames River. The water cooled his fever. The motions of swimming broke open the sores so they could heal.)*
   MODERATE/LIGHT

A Journal of the Plague Year **457**

APPLY

ANALYZE THE TEXT

Possible answers:

1. **DOK 3:** *Details include the hardening of men's hearts because death was so widespread. People were more worried about becoming ill themselves and perhaps dying. Relationships deteriorated and the culture became one of self-preservation.*

2. **DOK 2:** *The setting is about the tragedy of inescapable death. A person's social or economic position in life cannot save someone from death or an incurable disease. In the end, in death, everyone is equal. Another theme is that widespread tragedy is so incomprehensible, that people do not or cannot behave rationally.*

3. **DOK 4:** *The narrator details real times, place names, and dates in his descriptions, making his writing realistic and authentic. The fact that the narrator is more removed and observant rather than emotional makes it less realistic.*

4. **DOK 4:** *Phrases such as "sermon, speaking sight with a loud voice and call us to repentance" impress upon the reader that the events being described by the narrator should trigger deep emotion, compassion, and trepidation. Devastation such as this surely was an act of God. It affects the reader because it makes them feel the tragedy.*

5. **DOK 4:** *The narrator repeated death and reference to the dead, and used synonyms for shrieking, groaning, and mourning several times. The narrator discussed the sounds of death and what it looked like for an individual and for a whole community. These techniques were effective in helping the reader understand the magnitude of the plague.*

RESEARCH

Have students think about what they read and go back through the notes to determine what they would like to know more about. Remind students to use keyword searches and reliable sources. Explain that they might come up with more questions based on their initial research. Help students complete the graphic organizer on this page with questions related to the bubonic plague.

Extend Have students use the questions they asked and their notes to brainstorm more topics related to the bubonic plague. Remind students to take turns speaking and to listen closely as they share ideas.

RESPOND

ANALYZE THE TEXT

Support your responses with evidence from the text. 📓 **NOTEBOOK**

1. **Draw Conclusions** Reread paragraph 1. Which details suggest that the plague affects family relationships and friendships? What conclusions can you draw about the plague's impact on relationships?

2. **Infer** Review the narrator's description of the mass grave in paragraphs 3 and 4. What do details about the historical setting reveal about a possible theme, or message about life or human nature, in the text?

3. **Evaluate** What qualities and characteristics of the narrator help make the historical novel seem realistic? What qualities and characteristics make it seem less than realistic? Explain.

4. **Analyze** List details of the narrator's conversation with the church sexton in paragraph 7. How does the narrator's description of this conversation affect your impression of events?

5. **Notice & Note** Describe images that the narrator repeats again and again in the novel excerpt. What effect does this repetition have on your understanding of events?

RESEARCH TIP
Once you have chosen a topic, formulate a specific question about that topic to guide your research.

RESEARCH

As you studied this fictional journal, did you have any questions about the plague that you would like to have answered? Were you curious about England's history before the event or how London recovered? Generate at least three questions that you have about the plague. Use the categories below to guide you, writing your questions in the row of the chart next to the corresponding category.

Burial and mourning customs	*What are burial and mourning customs of London in 1664? What was the role of religion then?*
Beliefs about caring for the sick/poor	*During the plague, how were the rich treated versus the poor?*
Medicine and treatments	*How was medicine practiced in this time? How were the sick treated?*
Economic consequences	*How did the plague affect the economy? How did it benefit it?*
My own category	

Extend Research one of the following topics that are related to the bubonic plague: Pied Piper, positive outcomes of bubonic plague, literature about bubonic plague, CDC (Centers for Disease Control and Prevention). Once you complete your research, share what you learned with a small group.

CREATE AND DISCUSS

Write Notes for a Problem-Solution Essay As Daniel Defoe emphasizes in his novel, epidemics can strike indiscriminately and unpredictably. Even today, despite advances in medicine, diseases capable of triggering epidemics remain threats to public health.

Imagine that you are a public health official. You have just discovered several cases of a highly infectious disease that you fear may develop into an epidemic. Write notes for a problem-solution essay that proposes ways that you might work with different sectors of society—such as the media, politicians, and the elderly—to limit the spread of the disease.

Discuss Share your notes with others in a small group of classmates and discuss which ideas might work best to fight the epidemic. Then, organize your group's final ideas into a structure you could use for a presentation.

- ❏ As a group, set an agenda and establish clear goals for your discussion.
- ❏ Set a time limit for each group member to present his or her ideas.
- ❏ Listen closely and respectfully to all speakers.
- ❏ Take notes to record everyone's ideas and suggestions.
- ❏ Take a vote on the best way(s) your group has come up with to limit the spread of an infectious disease.
- ❏ Work together to organize a presentation of your group's ideas.

RESPOND

 Go to the **Writing Studio: Writing Informative Texts** for help with writing notes for a problem-solution essay.

 Go to the **Speaking and Listening Studio** to find out more about participating in collaborative discussions.

RESPOND TO THE ESSENTIAL QUESTION

 Why are plagues so horrifying?

Gather Information Review your annotations and notes on *A Journal of the Plague Year*. Then, add relevant details to your Response Log. As you determine which information to include, think about:

- how people cope with the fear of getting sick and dying
- how social, religious, and economic structures can be affected
- how people take desperate measures to protect themselves and their families

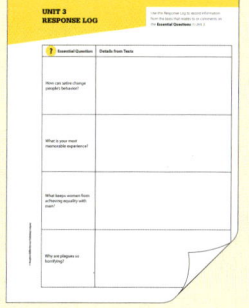

ACADEMIC VOCABULARY

As you write and discuss what you learned from *A Journal of the Plague Year*, be sure to use the Academic Vocabulary words. Check off each of the words that you use.

- ❏ encounter
- ❏ exploit
- ❏ persist
- ❏ subordinate
- ❏ widespread

APPLY

CREATE AND DISCUSS

Write Notes for a Problem-Solution Essay Have students think of other epidemics they have heard of, such as the bird flu, and consider how health officials dealt with the situation. How did the health officials share the news with the public? What did they recommend the public do? What did they recommend the politicians do?

For **writing support** for students at varying proficiency levels, see the **Text X-Ray** on page 448D.

Discuss Tell students to compare their notes with others and determine which steps would be most effective. Once the steps have been determined, tell students to organize their ideas as if they were preparing the ideas for a presentation.

RESPOND TO THE ESSENTIAL QUESTION

Allow time for students to add details from *A Journal of the Plague Year* to their Unit 3 Response Logs.

APPLY

CRITICAL VOCABULARY

Answers:

1. visitation
2. summon
3. discourse
4. promiscuously
5. huddle
6. abate

VOCABULARY STRATEGY:
Denotation and Connotation

Answers:

1. **visitation:** *act of making a visit; holiday, vacation; viewing, wake, procession*
2. **summoned:** *to order or call; mobilized, assembled, called; subpoenaed, ordered, commanded*
3. **discourse:** *conversation; talk, confer, speak, chat; lecture, sermon, complaint*
4. **promiscuous:** *without standards of selection of choosing; random, arbitrary; immoral, indiscriminate*
5. **abate:** *to lesson; subside, reduce; terminate*

 For **speaking support** for students at varying proficiency levels, see the **Text X-Ray** on page 448D.

 **RESPOND**

WORD BANK

visitation	promiscuously
summon	huddle
discourse	abate

CRITICAL VOCABULARY

Practice and Apply Write the Critical Vocabulary word that has the same or nearly the same meaning as the given word or phrase.

1. the act of going to a place _____
2. order, call to act upon _____
3. conversation _____
4. indiscriminately _____
5. crowd together _____
6. reduce _____

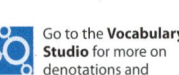 Go to the **Vocabulary Studio** for more on denotations and connotations.

VOCABULARY STRATEGY:
Denotation and Connotation

Dictionary definitions provide the meaning of words, or their **denotations**. However, words also have emotional associations, or connotations. **Connotations** can be positive or negative. The denotation of the word *huddle*, for example, is "to group together." However, *huddle* generally has a negative connotation, an association with crouching together in fear or misery.

Practice and Apply Complete the table below. Under the *Denotation* heading, write a short definition for the vocabulary word. Then, add synonyms that have positive and negative connotations to the chart. Use a thesaurus to help identify synonyms, if needed.

VOCABULARY WORD	DENOTATION (MEANING)	SYNONYMS WITH POSITIVE CONNOTATIONS	SYNONYMS WITH NEGATIVE CONNOTATIONS
huddle	crowd together	nestle, snuggle	crouch, bunch
visitation	act of making a visit	holiday, vacation	viewing, wake, procession
summon	to order or call	mobilized, assembled, called	subpoenaed, ordered, commanded
discourse	conversation	talk, confer, speak, chat	lecture, sermon, complaint
promiscuously	without standards of choosing	random, arbitrary	immoral, indiscriminate
abate	to lesson	subside, reduce	terminate

 ENGLISH LEARNER SUPPORT

Analyze Expressions Explain to students that some words have a positive or friendly effect, while other words have a negative or unfriendly effect. It is important to choose words carefully so that meaning is clear. Discuss the connotations of the following words. Then ask students to think of other words that have positive and negative connotations. **LIGHT**

Positive	Negative
interested	nosy
conversational	chatty
remind	nag

RESPOND

LANGUAGE CONVENTIONS:
Participles and Participial Phrases

A **participle** is a verb form that can be used as an adjective. A present participle ends in -ing, and a past participle usually ends in -ed or -d, although some past participles are formed irregularly and end in -t or -n.

A **participial phrase** consists of a participle together with its modifiers and complements. The entire phrase is used as an adjective.

Writers often use participial phrases to add detail that will make their meaning more precise. They also use participial phrases to vary their sentence structure and keep the attention of their readers.

Defoe's use of participles helps to create a clear picture of what happened in London during the plague.

Here, Defoe uses the past participle *altered* to describe London's appearance:

> The face of London was now indeed strangely <u>altered</u>.

Here, he uses the participial phrase *muffled up in a brown coat* to describe a plague victim:

> . . . they saw a man go to and again, <u>muffled up in a brown coat</u>, and making motions with his hands. . . .

Practice and Apply

1. Write a sentence about the plague that uses a participle to describe something.

2. Rewrite this sentence from the excerpt so that at least one of the verbs is used as a participle.

> He said nothing as he walked about, but two or three times groaned very deeply and loud, and sighed as he would break his heart.

Go to **Participles and Participial Phrases** in the **Grammar Studio** for more.

APPLY

LANGUAGE CONVENTIONS:
Participles and Participial Phrases

Review the information about **participles** with students. Remind them that even though participles look like verbs in the present or future tense, they act like adjectives. Explain that when they write, they should place participles and participial phrases as near as they can to the noun or pronoun they modify. When participial phrases are placed too far away from the word they modify, they are dangling participles. A dangling participle has no subject and does not logically modify any of the words in the sentence in which it appears.

Practice and Apply After students write their sentence, have partners discuss the sentences to see if the participles and participial phrases were used correctly. *(Students' sentences will vary. For example: Groaning and walking about, he said nothing; broken hearted, he sighed.)*

 ENGLISH LEARNER SUPPORT

Language Conventions Use the following supports with students at varying proficiency levels:

- Help students understand the difference between verbs and participles. Write the following sentences on the board: *The girl <u>was crying</u> because she scraped her knee.* (verb) *Lisa put a bandage on the <u>crying</u> girl's scraped knee.* (participle) **SUBSTANTIAL**

- Have students work with a partner to review the selection and find another sentence with a participle or participial phrase. Have students explain what the participle or participial phrase is modifying. **MODERATE**

- Have students work with a partner to complete the Practice and Apply activity. Then, have pairs exchange papers and identify what the participle or participial phrase is modifying. **LIGHT**

PLAN

from INFERNO: A DOCTOR'S EBOLA STORY
Memoir by Steven Hatch, M.D.

This memoir serves as a mentor text, a model for students to follow when they come to the Unit 3 Writing Task: Write a Personal Narrative.

GENRE ELEMENTS
MEMOIR

Tell students that a **memoir** is like an **autobiography**; both are narratives of actual events in a person's life. Memoirs describe the author's thoughts and feelings about specific events and people, and they may reflect on something the author realized over time. Memoirs often focus on specific time periods and may portray social issues or historical events.

LEARNING OBJECTIVES

- Analyze author's perspective and connect to memoirs.
- Conduct research about how the brain processes information.
- Take informal notes.
- Create an informational poster.
- Understand classical allusions.
- Use subordinate clauses.
- **Language** Identify words and phrases that show author's perspective.

TEXT COMPLEXITY

Quantitative Measures	Inferno: A Doctor's Ebola Story	Lexile: 1150L
Qualitative Measures	**Ideas Presented** Simple, single meaning. Literal, explicit, and direct.	
	Structures Used Clear, mostly chronological and conventional.	
	Language Used Explicit, literal, contemporary, familiar language.	
	Knowledge Required Situations and subjects easily envisioned.	

462A Unit 3

PLAN

Online

RESOURCES

- Unit 3 Response Log
- Selection Audio
- Reading Studio: Notice & Note
- Level Up Tutorial: Reading for Details
- Reading Studio: Notice & Note
- Writing Studio: Organizing Ideas
- Speaking and Listening Studio: Types of Media: Audio, Video, and Images
- Vocabulary Studio: Classical Allusions
- Grammar Studio: Module 4: Lesson 1: Kinds of Clauses
- *Inferno: A Doctor's Ebola Story* Selection Test

SUMMARIES

English
In this excerpt from Dr. Steven Hatch's memoir, he describes the ordeal of one of his patients, George Beyan, who was able to triumphantly survive the Ebola outbreak, only to suffer some bad news when his family showed symptoms of the virus. Hatch convinces George to return to the ward to nurse his sick son, Williams. Hatch describes how the medical team struggled to remain professional as they became emotionally involved with the Beyan family and then witnessed Willams's death.

Spanish
Este pasaje de la autobiografía del Dr. Steven Hatch, describe la terrible experiencia de uno de sus pacientes, George Beyan, quien sobrevivió triunfantemente al brote del Ébola, solo para enterarse de que su familia mostraba síntomas del virus. Hatch convence a George de regresar a la sala para cuidar de su hijo enfermo, Williams. Hatch describe cómo el equipo médico luchó por mantener una conducta profesional mientras se involucraban emocionalmente con la familia Beyan y luego presenciaban la muerte de Williams.

SMALL-GROUP OPTIONS

Have students work in small groups and pairs to read and discuss the selection.

Activating Academic Vocabulary

- Provide a list of Academic Vocabulary words and phrases, such as: *memoir, author's perspective, personal experience, historical significance, setting, events, point of view, voice, reaction,* and *reflection*.
- After reading the first paragraph, model how to use one or more Academic Vocabulary words or phrases to discuss the text.
- Encourage students to use the Academic Vocabulary as they discuss and write about the text.

Silent Sustained Reading

- Set a timer for 30 minutes.
- Have students read the text silently until the timer rings.
- Suggest that students keep a list of any unfamiliar words they want to look up after reading.
- Ask students to record the title, date, and number of pages read in a Reading Log.

Inferno: A Doctor's Ebola Story **462B**

PLAN

Text X-Ray: English Learner Support
for *Inferno: A Doctor's Ebola Story*

Use the Text X-Ray and the supports and scaffolds in the Teacher's Edition to help guide students at different proficiency levels through the selection.

INTRODUCE THE SELECTION
DISCUSS SYMPTOMS AND PROGNOSIS

In this lesson, students will need to be able to discuss how doctors use symptoms to determine a patient's prognosis. Provide the following explanations:

- A *symptom* is a sign of illness.
- A *prognosis* is an opinion of the course or outcome of a disease.

Explain to students that doctors carefully observe patients' symptoms in order to give a prognosis.

Ask students to talk about a hypothetical situation where a person had symptoms they were experiencing and how a doctor used them to determine prognosis. Provide sentence frames, such as: *One symptom a man (woman) had was _____. As his/her symptoms improved, the doctor was _____.*

CULTURAL REFERENCES

The following words or phrases may be unfamiliar to students:

- *Robert Mapplethorpe* (paragraph 2): controversial American photographer who made highly-stylized black-and-white images
- *positive; negative tests* (paragraph 3): patients who test positive have a disease; patients who test negative do not have it
- *in tow* (paragraph 4): accompanying or going with
- *waiting game* (paragraph 4): a situation where you don't take action as you wait for results
- *decontamination shower* (paragraph 5): shower that is meant to kill germs or bacteria
- *fend for himself* (paragraph 6): take care of himself
- *utterly out of my mind* (paragraph 8): crazy to think something
- *heaping spoonfuls* (paragraph 10): a lot
- *bounced around* (paragraph 12): went from feeling better to feeling worse
- *a canvas on which everyone painted different impressions* (paragraph 13): something about which everyone had a different opinion

LISTENING

Identify Main Ideas

Explain that when reading an informational text, it is important to understand the main idea. Direct students' attention to the first paragraph, which often hints at the main idea.

Read aloud paragraph 1. Use the following supports with students at varying proficiency levels:

- Reread the paragraph. Tell them the main idea is that the doctors are upset by illness and death.
  SUBSTANTIAL
- Pair students and have them read aloud paragraph 1. Then, have them say what they think the main idea of the excerpt is. Give a sentence frame: *I think the main idea is that Dr. Hatch _____.*
  MODERATE
- Have students work in groups to read paragraphs 1 and 15–18. Ask them to use the sections to find the main idea. (*Doctors are used to death, but the doctors were upset about Williams's death.*)
  LIGHT

462C Unit 3

PLAN

SPEAKING

Give Opinions

Have students discuss how they feel about the actions of the author during the events described in the memoir.

Use the following supports with students at varying proficiency levels:

- Read aloud paragraphs 21–22. Write a word bank on the board of verbs and verb phrases that describe Hatch's actions, and help students define the terms. Use verbs in sentences that state an opinion of Hatch's actions and have the students repeat it. **SUBSTANTIAL**
- Have small group members take turns reading aloud paragraphs 7–9. Then, have them name something Hatch did and then state their opinion of it. Have them support the opinions with reasons. For example: *Hatch asked George to take care of Williams. I did/didn't like when he did this because _____.* **MODERATE**
- Have students read aloud paragraphs 7–9 in pairs. Then have them discuss their opinions of Hatch's actions. Students should respond to and build on each other's ideas with constructive comments. Such as: You said *Hatch shouldn't have asked George to take care of Williams. Who should he have asked?* **LIGHT**

READING

Identify Author's Perspective

Remind students that authors of memoirs describe how they reacted to and reflected on events to let readers know their point of view. Tell students that a reaction is how an author responds to something. A reflection is what an author learned from the experience.

Use the following supports with students of varying proficiency levels:

- Read phrases from the text to students that show students examples of sentences telling how the author reacted or reflected on an event. Have students try to share their own examples on reacting or reflecting about an event at school. **SUBSTANTIAL**
- Have pairs read the first two paragraphs and identify phrases that tell how the author reacts or reflects on the events that are happening. Have students restate the phrases in their own words and explain why they tell readers the author's perspective. **MODERATE**
- Have students read the first three pages of the text and write a list of any phrases that tell how the author reacts or reflects on the events. Have pairs exchange lists and discuss which shows reaction and which shows reflection, and how both show author's perspective. **LIGHT**

WRITING

Identify Key Ideas

Have students reread the writing assignment on Student Edition page 473.

Use the following supports with students at varying proficiency levels:

- Have students sketch images for an informational poster. Help them write a few words to describe the main idea of their images. **SUBSTANTIAL**
- Have partners write their ideas for their poster and discuss their ideas with a partner. Guide them to ask for clarification if something is not clear. For example: *Can you please explain why _____?* **MODERATE**
- Have partners write key ideas they want to include on their informational posters. Then, have students turn their ideas into imperative sentences. Ask students to add or discuss visual aids they can use. **LIGHT**

TEACH

Connect to the
ESSENTIAL QUESTION
Tell students to think about how the bubonic plague was represented in *A Journal of the Plague Year*. Now have students brainstorm what they know about Ebola. Tell students that the next selection will discuss a doctor's perspective of the Ebola epidemic in Africa and what makes plagues so horrifying.

MENTOR TEXT
At the end of the unit, students will be asked to write a personal narrative. *Inferno: A Doctor's Ebola Story* provides a model for how a writer can share his or her perspective on an important event in his or her life by using select details and word choice.

COMPARE ACROSS GENRES
Tell students that this selection, also written in the first-person, is a memoir. Have students note the use of details that the author uses to portray his experiences witnessing the plague. Students should also seek to understand Hatch's message and perspective so it can be compared to the narrator in *A Journal of the Plague Year*.

COLLABORATE & COMPARE

MEMOIR

from
INFERNO: A DOCTOR'S EBOLA STORY

by **Steven Hatch, M.D.**
pages 465–470

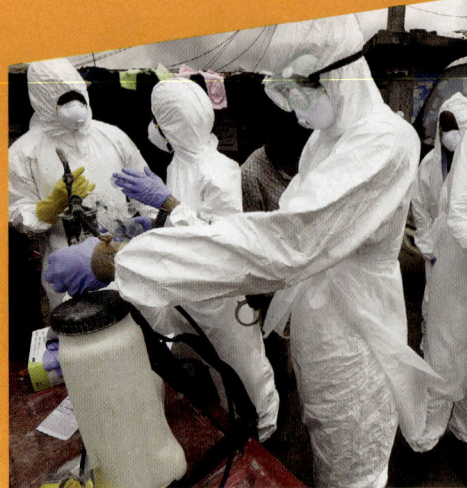

COMPARE ACROSS GENRES
As you read, note the details Hatch uses to portray the experience of witnessing a plague. This will help you later when you compare this text to the excerpt from Defoe's *A Journal of the Plague Year*.

ESSENTIAL QUESTION:

Why are plagues so horrifying?

NOVEL

from
A JOURNAL OF THE PLAGUE YEAR

by **Daniel Defoe**
pages 451–456

from Inferno: A Doctor's Ebola Story

QUICK START

Think of an important decision you have made. Were you guided by logic and facts or by gut feelings? With a partner, discuss how you made the decision and what happened.

ANALYZE AUTHOR'S PERSPECTIVE

An **author's perspective** is a unique combination of ideas, values, feelings, and beliefs that influence the way the writer looks at a topic. In *Inferno*, Steven Hatch sometimes directly addresses the significance of his perspective as a doctor and as an American in an African country:

> Say what you will about the potential for cross-cultural misunderstandings . . . but there is simply no mistaking the absolute, unadulterated joyous state of George Beyan in Daniel's portrait.

In the above statement, Hatch acknowledges the potential for cultural misinterpretation of George Beyan's emotions.

As you read a nonfiction narrative, pause to ask questions about how the author's background, beliefs, and experiences shape his or her perception of people and events. Ask yourself about how the author assesses

- the motives governing the actions and behaviors of people
- the emotional condition and responses of others
- the moral or ethical value of decisions
- the significance and meaning of words and actions

As you read the following excerpt, note comments and clues that provide insight into the author's perspective.

CONNECT TO MEMOIRS

Memoir is a form of autobiographical writing in which the author describes significant personal experiences in a first-person narrative. In addition to recording details of events, memoirs express the author's thoughts and feelings at the time of the events and also upon later reflection.

In their memoirs, authors often address issues of wide social, philosophical, or historical significance. Readers, therefore, can deepen their understanding by connecting the text to their own experiences, to the experiences of people they know, and to their own social and historical contexts.

In *Inferno*, Hatch describes an Ebola outbreak in Liberia through his experience as a doctor in an Ebola treatment unit. His narrative, based on firsthand historical experience, provides valuable insight into how local, extraordinary events can still reflect the universal experience of people across cultures and across the globe.

GENRE ELEMENTS: MEMOIR

- is a narrative of actual events
- recounts author's personal experience in the first-person point of view
- describes author's thoughts and feelings
- author often reflects on events with an understanding gained over time
- may portray and discuss issues of wide social and historical significance

GET READY

TEACH

QUICK START

Ask students to think about what is involved in making decisions. Are the decisions made always the right ones? Have students read and complete the Quick Start activity.

ANALYZE AUTHOR'S PERSPECTIVE

Explain to students that an **author's perspective** is the way the author feels about an event or an experience. Many facets of a text must be considered to truly understand an author's perspective. To identify the perspective, a reader must

- analyze the clues that are given about the author's background, attitudes, and belief systems
- examine the author's inner thoughts that reflect morals and cultural differences
- look deeper to interpret how the author reacts to situations
- study the significance of word choice that describe events

CONNECT TO MEMOIRS

Explain to students that **memoirs** can provide a firsthand account of historical events, allowing readers to generalize from an individual's experience to learn about an event from a more personal perspective. In Hatch's memoir, readers view through his eyes to the horrors of Ebola and how people reacted to it. Tell students to think about which of Hatch's experiences would have been similar for other doctors in Africa. They should also consider what they know about Ebola and what they learn from Hatch. They can use a graphic organizer to record Hatch's experiences and any generalizations they can make from his experiences.

TEACH

CRITICAL VOCABULARY

Encourage students to read all the sentences before deciding which word best completes each one. Remind them to look for context clues that match the precise meaning of each word.

Answers:

1. veracity
2. prognosis
3. plateaued
4. pyrrhic victory
5. ersatz
6. vexation
7. abyss
8. vigilance

■ English Learner Support

Use Cognates Tell students that two of the Critical Vocabulary words have Spanish cognates: *abyss/abismo, vigilance/vigilancia.* **ALL LEVELS**

LANGUAGE CONVENTIONS

Review the information about **subordinate, relative,** and **independent clauses.** Tell them that during the editing portion of the writing process, writers look to combine sentences by turning one of the independent clauses into a subordinate clause. Subordinate clauses can improve flow and clarity and show important relationships between ideas.

ANNOTATION MODEL

Remind students of the annotation model on page 464, which suggests underlining important details that will assist them in analyzing the author's perspective in memoirs. Point out that they may follow this suggestion or use their own system for marking up the selection in their write-in text. They may want to color-code their annotations by using highlighters. Their notes in the margin may include questions about ideas that are unclear or topics they want to learn more about.

464   Unit 3

 **GET READY**

CRITICAL VOCABULARY

| abyss | veracity | vexation | plateau |
| ersatz | pyrrhic victory | vigilance | prognosis |

To see how many Critical Vocabulary words you already know, choose the best word to complete each sentence.

1. We can't help but doubt the _____ of the claims.
2. The doctor gave me a worrisome _____.
3. Your running times may _____ after months of improvement.
4. We won, but it was a(n) _____.
5. A(n) _____ medical clinic sprang up at the site of the disaster.
6. His _____ at her rudeness was obvious.
7. Facing the difficulty of the situation was like staring into the _____.
8. We value her constant _____ against many potential threats.

LANGUAGE CONVENTIONS

Writers use subordinate clauses to add descriptive details to their texts. A **subordinate clause** has a subject and verb but does not express a complete idea, so it cannot stand alone as a sentence. Subordinate clauses must be connected to at least one **independent clause.**

Some subordinate clauses, **relative clauses,** function as adjectives. Relative clauses use **relative pronouns,** such as *that, which, who, whom,* or *whose,* as their subjects.

ANNOTATION MODEL  **NOTICE & NOTE**

As you read, ask questions about how the author's background and experience influence his perception of people and events. This model shows one reader's notes about the beginning of *Inferno*.

> Death was part of the daily routine, but some deaths affected us more than others. Each of us grew attached to certain patients as we would have done in any hospital, but one loss hit us all with equal force. We had cared for George Beyan, a quiet man in his mid-thirties who had acquired the virus by tending to a sick friend. George had made the slow recovery after emerging from the abyss in mid-October and waited around for the virus to clear, hardly making a noise as he sat outside listening to Radio Gbargna in the hot sun.

Hatch is a doctor. He works in hospitals and is used to dealing with patients and growing attached to them at times.

What is it about this case that made it significant enough for the author to write about it? What effect did the case have on him?

464   Unit 3

BACKGROUND

Dr. Steven Hatch is an infectious disease and immunology specialist from the United States who spent six weeks as a volunteer at the Ebola Treatment Unit in Liberia during the outbreak of 2013–2014. Fear that the outbreak would spread to the United States was high, and controversy erupted when an American nurse and doctor contracted the virus in Liberia and were flown back to the United States for treatment. Hatch's memoir details his experience, including the extreme measures he had to take to avoid infection, the suffering he witnessed, and the bureaucratic struggles he and the rest of the medical staff faced.

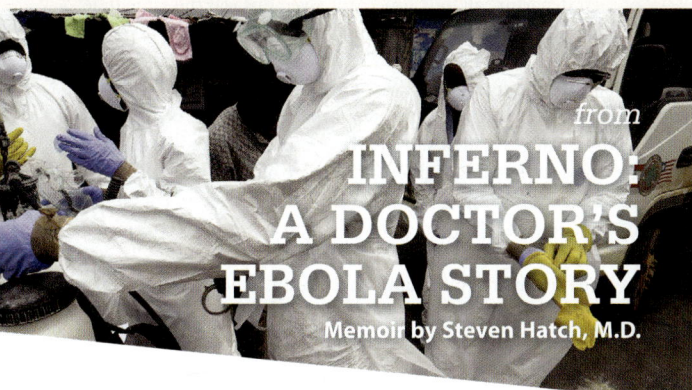

from
INFERNO: A DOCTOR'S EBOLA STORY
Memoir by Steven Hatch, M.D.

PREPARE TO COMPARE

As you read, make note of the kinds of details Hatch uses to describe his experience as a witness to a devastating plague. Your notes will help you later when you compare this text to A Journal of the Plague Year.

1   Death was part of the daily routine, but some deaths affected us more than others. Each of us grew attached to certain patients as we would have done in any hospital, but one loss hit us all with equal force. We had cared for George Beyan, a quiet man in his mid-thirties who had acquired the virus by tending to a sick friend. George had made the slow recovery after emerging from the **abyss** in mid-October and waited around for the virus to clear, hardly making a noise as he sat outside listening to Radio Gbarnga in the hot sun.

2   Daniel Berehulak had featured George in a photo essay in the *Times* that ran at the end of October. He had created an **ersatz** studio in the lone unused office of the compound taking portraits of the patients and the staff. He used sheets as a white background and the portraits shared a highly formal quality; they reminded me of the work of Robert Mapplethorpe. Say what you will about the potential for cross-cultural misunderstandings, as well as the risks of projecting oneself onto another's inner mental

NOTICE & NOTE

Notice & Note

Use the side margins to notice and note signposts in the text.

abyss
(ə-bĭs´) *n.* an immeasurably deep chasm, depth, or void.

ersatz
(ĕr´zäts, ĕr-zäts´) *adj.* being an usually inferior imitation or substitute; artificial.

Inferno: A Doctor's Ebola Story   465

TEACH

ANALYZE AUTHOR'S PERSPECTIVE

Remind students that someone's **perspective** is his or her attitude toward an event or person. Explain that a person's perspective is not always fixed and may differ from other people's perspectives. Culture and previous experience can affect someone's perspective. (**Answer:** Students' answers will vary, but they should compare Hatch's cultural barrier as an American to his experience in observing Liberian people and offer arguments as to why that experience may or may not be enough to prevent a cultural misunderstanding in this instance.)

CRITICAL VOCABULARY

veracity: The portrait of George has *veracity* because it is an accurate depiction of his ecstatic happiness of getting well.

ASK STUDENTS when they should question someone's veracity. *(when someone doesn't use facts to support an argument)*

pyrrhic victory: The victory is George winning the battle against Ebola; it is a *pyrrhic victory* because he loses his son in the meantime.

ASK STUDENTS to give an example of a pyrrhic victory. *(You get to be the starting pitcher because your best friend who was the pitcher broke his arm.)*

466   Unit 3

 **NOTICE & NOTE**

veracity
(və-răs′ĭ-tē) *n.* conformity to fact or truth; accuracy.

state by looking at their facial expressions, but there is simply no mistaking the absolute, unadulterated joyous state of George Beyan in Daniel's portrait. "I got up in the morning, I prayed. In the evening, I prayed. At dinner, I prayed. Prayed to get well," the caption quotes him as saying. "Yesterday, they said, 'You, you're free.' I danced, I jumped." The picture attests to the **veracity** of his statement.

3   George got the news of his impending freedom from the Navy lab one late afternoon. As much as patients understandably wanted to get the hell out of such confinement upon hearing the news, almost nobody left the day they received it. Coordinating the discharge paperwork and setting up a plan for them to return by alerting family of their departure all took time. Moreover, this was the same time that some of the staff were busying themselves with the patients in the suspect ward whose tests returned as negative, as they were prioritized to leave the high-risk area as soon as possible to avoid further risk of exposure. Others were working on taking the patients whose tests returned positive to the confirmed ward. Patients like George, who had lingered for weeks, were not going to suffer any ill effects from hanging out in the ETU[1] another night. For all their understandable jubilation, in terms of the tasks to be performed at that hour, they were not the top priority.

4   George savored his triumph over death, dancing and jumping, but bad news was about to arrive in the form of his wife and two sons, one aged five, the other a toddler. They all had some form of symptoms. That night he stood at the boundary talking to his wife across the one-meter divide that separated the suspect from the confirmed ward, the boys in tow. The following day would be a waiting game for the blood tests.

pyrrhic victory
n. a victory that is offset by staggering losses.

ANALYZE AUTHOR'S PERSPECTIVE

Annotate: In paragraph 5, underline the author's assessment of George's mental state. Then, circle one reason the author may have misjudged George's emotional state and one reason he may not have misjudged it.

Evaluate: How accurate do you think Hatch's assessment of George's mental state is? Why?

5   That next morning we sent George through the decontamination shower as he returned to freedom after nearly three weeks in isolation. I assumed he would have regarded this as a **pyrrhic victory** since his entire family now awaited word as to whether they would have to endure a similar experience, but I was surprised by the serenity of his appearance as he sat outside the main staff quarters. There is always the chance that given the cultural barriers I was misinterpreting his reaction, but I had seen anxiety, dread, and fear on enough Liberian faces to sense that this was different. Having lived through what he had just lived through, however, it was certainly not for me to judge him. Daniel took him into his studio, and his reaction was captured for posterity.

---
[1] **ETU:** Ebola Treatment Unit.

466   Unit 3

 ENGLISH LEARNER SUPPORT

Internalize New Vocabulary Review the following terms in paragraph 5 to clarify any misinterpretation. Expand on how the words are used in the text:

- *decontamination shower:* the need for a special shower to remove virus or germs
- *return to freedom:* George was not in jail but in isolation
- *main staff quarters:* where medical staff live (quarters = housing)
- *cultural barriers:* barriers are not physical in this case; they refer to not understanding cultural differences   **MODERATE**

6   The question arose as to whether he should return home in the morning or spend the afternoon waiting for his family's test results. George chose to wait. He was going home with his family, you could almost hear him think. Only fate had a crueler plan in store for him. We again got the call from the Navy guys in the late afternoon. His wife and younger son tested negative, but his elder son, Williams, was positive, and shortly we would need to escort him over to the confirmed side. He was obviously ill and was too young to fend for himself. He was going to need help or he would surely die. The women on the confirmed side could not be expected to provide essentially twenty-four-hour nursing support to this child, busy as they were with other children, to say nothing of their own illnesses. And we would not allow his mother to take him to the confirmed side, even if she wanted to.

7   That left only one obvious choice: We would have to ask George to return to the confirmed ward to nurse Williams. We knew that this was asking an enormous amount of him. Yet we also knew that this would not endanger him and that it was Williams's best chance for survival. After a brief team conference where we all agreed this was the best course to pursue, I walked over to hand George the news and our singular and extremely unpleasant request.

8   Although he did not explicitly say so when I first explained the situation, I had the distinct impression that he thought I was utterly out of my mind. He gave a little shake of his head at first and said quietly that he wasn't going back *in there*. I told him his wife couldn't care for Williams and that I couldn't ask anyone in the confirmed ward—people whom he knew well by this point—to take on such a responsibility. And Williams needed help. After a brief exchange I realized that he was more than simply dreading returning inside, as if the posttraumatic stress of moving back into the nightmarish prison from which he was so recently set free was only the beginning of his **vexations**. I saw that same fear in his eyes that I saw every day with patients in the suspect ward.

9   But what was he concerned about? He was, after all, cured, possessing Ebola-specific antibodies and lymphocytes, which now made him immune to a repeat infection. But . . . did he know that? As I spoke with him, I sat there puzzling this over. Surely he knew at some intuitive level that he was not at risk of getting sick again while he spent day after day convalescing, although maybe he had thought a reset button had been pressed when he emerged from the decontamination shower. But how to explain a concept like acquired immunity to someone who probably had no formal education beyond grade school?

NOTICE & NOTE

LANGUAGE CONVENTIONS
Annotate: Mark the sentence in paragraph 6 that includes a subordinate clause.
Infer: What is implied by this subordinate clause?

CONTRASTS AND CONTRADICTIONS
Notice & Note: In paragraph 8, mark details about George's reaction to Hatch's request.
Compare: How does George's reaction compare with your expectations?

vexation
(vĕk-sā′shən) *n.* a source of irritation or annoyance.

Inferno: A Doctor's Ebola Story   467

APPLYING ACADEMIC VOCABULARY

☑ encounter   ☐ exploit   ☐ persist   ☑ subordinate   ☐ widespread

Write and Discuss Have students turn to a partner to discuss the following questions. Guide students to write their responses and to include the Academic Vocabulary words *encounter* and *subordinate*. Ask volunteers to share their responses with the class.

- How do you act in situations in which you **encounter** someone who feels superior to you?
- How would you treat someone who is a **subordinate**?

TEACH

LANGUAGE CONVENTIONS

Remind students that a subordinate clause has a subject and verb but does not express a complete thought. Subordinate clauses often add details or show relationships. (**Answer:** *The clause implies that mothers sometimes try to get into the confirmed side to care for their sick children.*)

■ **English Learner Support**

Understand Relative Clauses Speakers of Vietnamese may omit relative pronouns when using relative clauses. For example: *My grandfather was a generous man helped everyone.* Relative pronouns are not required in Vietnamese. Help students understand that when using relative clauses, they need a relative pronoun.

CONTRASTS AND CONTRADICTIONS

Explain that this signpost indicates that the author might be setting up for a contradiction. An author might use a contradiction to emphasize a point or make the reader think. Ask students what word signifies this pattern in paragraph 8?. *(although)* (**Answer:** *Students might respond that they would expect a father not to hesitate to take care of his son.*)

CRITICAL VOCABULARY

vexation: One of George's *vexations* is that he is afraid of returning to the ward.

ASK STUDENTS when they last felt a vexation. *(exam time, going to the doctor, getting caught by a parent for doing something wrong)*

TEACH

✏️ CONNECT TO MEMOIRS

Have students think about a time when they had opposing emotions and the turmoil it caused. Tell them that in paragraph 14, Dr. Hatch describes such turmoil. (**Answer:** *Hatch is portraying the struggle between rationality and emotion when trying to predict the outcome of something over which we have no control.*)

CRITICAL VOCABULARY

vigilance: The medical staff was *vigilant*, or very alert, as they watched over Williams.

ASK STUDENTS when vigilance is appropriate. (*a football coach analyzing plays; a mother watching a toddler in the park*)

plateau: When Williams *plateaued*, he didn't get any worse (or better).

ASK STUDENTS who else can plateau. (*a person dieting, an athlete, an actor*)

prognosis: Hatch had to control his emotions to understand Williams's *prognosis*, or possible outcome of the disease.

ASK STUDENTS what the prognosis would be for a cold. (*5–7 days of symptoms, but full recovery*)

 **NOTICE & NOTE**

10   "Look, George," I said. "You're like Superman." It crossed my mind that he might not be familiar with Superman, but I plowed ahead. "You have . . . *special blood* now. The virus cannot hurt you. You can go back in there and you won't be sick. And your son needs you right now." Some more give-and-take took place, and along with heaping spoonfuls of reassurance, we convinced him to perform the nearly unthinkable act of walking back into the high-risk area and receiving his sick son from his uninfected wife.

11   In the coming days everyone on the staff, Liberian and expat, followed Williams's progress carefully. Nobody said anything, but it was easy to see when we discussed everyone's status as we ran the boards that we were monitoring Williams with heightened **vigilance** and had attached special emotional importance to his prospects for survival. We also carefully observed Williams because he had taken a less typical clinical course. Most patients were on a clear trajectory: either up, or down. We could usually tell within about a twenty-four-hour window whether they were getting worse and would likely die, or had weathered the storm and would likely survive.

12   However, Williams behaved differently: He **plateaued**, then bounced around. His wet symptoms were not as profound as they were in so many other patients. We would see him on morning rounds inside the ward, lying in bed listless, unable even to sit up and take fluids while his fever raged out of control, the heat draining his small body of the water and electrolytes that would be critical to his survival. Then only hours later George would be seen escorting him by the hand outside to sit on the plastic chairs while he idly munched on some cookies, and the afternoon rounds would include chattering among the staff about how he had turned the corner.

13   But over this time his clinical picture had become a canvas onto which everyone painted different impressions: The more sanguine among us would view every stirring as an indicator of impending improvement, while those more naturally predisposed to pessimism noted that he wasn't looking like the true survivors, who often had made such progress within twenty-four hours of their worst moments that one didn't need to be a medical professional to see they would leave the unit intact.

14   I am much more naturally predisposed to pessimism. When I try to think scientifically, I do my best to check this pessimism, along with any other emotions, at the door, <u>lest they interfere with good clinical judgment</u>. For me, in order to understand his **prognosis**, those emotions had to be corralled, which meant

vigilance
(vĭj´ə-ləns) *n.* alert watchfulness.

plateau
(plă-tō´) *intr.v.* to reach a stable level; level off.

CONNECT TO MEMOIRS
Annotate: In paragraph 14, mark the explanation of why Hatch tries to restrain his emotions when evaluating a patient.

Connect: How does his conflicted view of Williams's prognosis reflect a common human struggle?.

prognosis
(prŏg-nō´sĭs) *n.* a prediction of the probable course and outcome of a disease.

468   Unit 3

IMPROVE READING FLUENCY

Targeted Passage   Have students work with partners to read paragraphs 10–12. First, use paragraph 10 to model how to read aloud. Have students follow along in their books as you read the text with appropriate phrasing and emphasis. Then, have partners take turns reading aloud paragraphs 11 and 12. Encourage students to provide feedback and support for pronouncing multisyllabic words. Remind students that when they are reading aloud for an audience, they should pace their reading so the audience has time to understand difficult concepts.

📖   Go to the **Reading Studio** for additional support in developing fluency.

ignoring the small blips of improvement that would get reported and celebrated. Instead, a simple mental equation needed to be performed, and the equation went like this: Fever equaled fluid loss, fluid loss equaled dehydration, and dehydration equaled circulatory collapse. Which, no matter how many ways I turned it over in my head, equaled death. I couldn't explain why he was able to hold on and have moments where he seemed to look, if not well, then definitely better. But unless we could figure out a way to get a lot of fluid into him, I just couldn't see how this would lead to a happy outcome. I didn't say so during rounds, but I wasn't in the mind of putting forth a huzzah just because he was able to hold down a little orange juice. Still, with each passing night, I felt the longer he survived, the more likely it was that he was going home.

15   Then one morning I came in, and I knew something terrible had happened. Everyone was silent. Steve Whiteley, the most unflappable person in the ETU, hardly made eye contact with anyone. The national staff moved about their tasks quietly, and the expat office space felt oppressive. Sheri Fink had been working through the night on a story, and I searched her bloodshot eyes for an explanation, but none came.

16   "Sheri, *what happened*?" I asked.

17   "Williams died last night," she replied in a monotone voice. I blinked, surprised to hear this news, a part of me thinking, No, *that can't be right, he looked good yesterday*, and then was surprised at my surprise, as if the hemispheres of my brain were unhappily squabbling about what to do with this information. I should have surmised instantly why such a pall[2] had been cast over the ETU, and yet it made no sense to me in the moment. I shook my head once as if to rid my ears of what I had just heard, even though I knew not only that it was true but that I had sized it up pretty accurately in the previous days.

18   What she didn't tell me right away, and I would learn only a few days later, was that after Williams had died, George had stayed up the entire night, wailing for his lost son, speaking to him, entreating him to come back, wishing for him to be alive. His lamentations rang throughout the compound for hours. We all knew that the ETU was a place of hellish misery, for by the time that Williams died, about thirty souls that had come to the Bong ETU had been committed to the earth. And we knew there were more to follow, as we fed one new body each day into the maw of the beast. Despite that knowledge, we were able to keep on with our jobs and not let our spirits flag. Our cheer and hope were among our only weapons in the darkness.

---

[2] **pall:** (pôl) a gloomy effect or atmosphere.

NOTICE & NOTE

ANALYZE AUTHOR'S PERSPECTIVE

Annotate: Mark descriptive details in paragraph 18 that describe George's behavior the night that Williams dies. Then, mark details that explain why the author and others are able to keep working under the circumstances.

Analyze: What do these details illustrate about the differences in perspective among the plague's victims and the author?

Inferno: A Doctor's Ebola Story   469

TEACH

ANALYZE AUTHOR'S PERSPECTIVE

Tell students they can analyze the **author's perspective** by looking for inner thoughts that reflect moral and cultural differences. Have them mark details in paragraph 18, about George and the medical staff, to prepare for a comparison. (**Answer:** *The victims' perspective comes from feelings of hopelessness. They likely had limited knowledge of the sickness, its causes, and why the doctors couldn't save them. The medical professionals are supportive but know their role is in preventing the spread of the disease, not in curing all the victims. They became doctors in a foreign country because they valued life, and although they buried many victims, they counted on maintaining hope. Their perspective comes from working hard to prevent the spread of the disease and to support the ill.*)

ENGLISH LEARNER SUPPORT

Understand Figurative Language Help students understand the following figurative language by having them pair up and act out the meaning of each phrase.

- *mental equation* (paragraph 14): an understanding when thinking about all the facts
- *turned it over in my head* (paragraph 14): thought about something
- *wasn't in the mind* (paragraph 14): didn't want to
- *putting forth a huzzah* (paragraph 14): make something seem important
- *unflappable person* (paragraph 15): someone who doesn't get upset much or is usually very calm
- *hemispheres of my brain were unhappily squabbling* (paragraph 15): couldn't make sense of the situation
- *rid my ears of* (paragraph 17): did not hear
- *committed to the earth* (paragraph 18): died
- *maw of the beast* (paragraph 18): another person died
- *not let our spirits flag* (paragraph 18): become upset

ALL LEVELS

WHEN STUDENTS STRUGGLE . . .

Analyze Author's Perspective Remind students that an inference is an educated guess using details in the text. Have students use the graphic organizer below to help them make inferences about the author.

What Dr. Hatch Says	What I Think Dr. Hatch Believes

For additional support, go to the **Reading Studio** and assign the following **Level Up tutorial: Reading for Details.**

Inferno: A Doctor's Ebola Story   **469**

TEACH

✏️ ANALYZE AUTHOR'S PERSPECTIVE

Remind students that another way to analyze the author's perspective is to look deeper into the author's actions and to make some **inferences,** or educated guesses based on the details in the text. In paragraph 12, Dr. Hatch describes his own behavior at the funeral of Williams. (**Answer:** *Because Williams is not Hatch's family member and because Hatch is also sensitive to the cultural differences that might make his crying at this moment inappropriate, Hatch shows respect and reverence to George.*)

■ English Learner Support

Retell Read paragraphs 19–21 aloud to students. Call on students to retell the story in their own words. Assist students with comprehension, but do not correct grammar or pronunciation. Discuss the passage using these questions:

1. In what ways was Dr. Hatch feeling guilty about the death of Williams? (*Hatch was the one who asked George to take care of his son.*)
2. How were the rounds that morning different than any other? (*Everyone was very quiet.*)
3. Describe the burial of Williams. (*The ceremony lasted only a few minutes.*)

MODERATE/LIGHT

 For **speaking support** for students at varying proficiency levels, see the **Text X-Ray** on page 462D.

NOTICE & NOTE

19 Yet what made the passing of Williams Beyan harder than the others was not only that we had all become deeply emotionally invested in his survival, but that we had asked George to cross back over in order to help achieve this. If there was a literal place that could be called hell on earth, for George Beyan, the confirmed ward was it, and we had willingly cajoled him into returning to that place of his nightmares only to provide him with one even worse. We asked him to make such sacrifices knowing that this might happen. Indeed, *I* was the one who had asked it of him.

20 Rounds that morning were unlike any other, with the raucous banter that usually accompanied the handoff absent, and the morning meeting a quiet recitation of pertinent items. Everyone silently went about their tasks. I asked Godfrey, who was in charge of burials, when they would inter Williams. He told me it would happen around eleven. I turned to Sambhavi Cheemalapati, who was running the ETU while Sean was on his R & R, and told her that we needed to go. She reluctantly agreed.

AUTHOR'S PERSPECTIVE
Annotate: Mark two reasons that Hatch gives in paragraph 21 for preventing himself from crying at Williams's funeral.

Analyze: What do Hatch's reasons reveal about his personal and cultural perspective?

21 George came back out a second time through the decontamination chamber, glistening from the light bleach shower, and Sambhavi, Godfrey, and I formed the back of a small processional led by two members of the burial team, an empty cart, a sprayer, and George. We moved around the peripheral road of the ETU, stopping at the back fence abutting the morgue, and the staff retrieved Williams's body, covered in two shiny white body bags. George began to wail again, and I struggled like mad to stop the tears from flowing down my face, for this was not my loss, and I didn't dare guess whether such a show of emotion would be considered appropriate. Eventually I had to bite the tip of my tongue so hard to prevent my tears that it bled. We put Williams in the ground in a ceremony that lasted no more than two or three minutes. Godfrey, I believe, spoke some official words.

22 It was the only funeral I attended in the outbreak. Sambhavi, Godfrey, and I had to return to work.

470 Unit 3

TO CHALLENGE STUDENTS...

Research Epidemics in the United States Have students make a timeline of the major epidemics in the United States. Include where the disease originated, how many people died, how it spread, and if a vaccine was discovered.

NOTICE & NOTE

CHECK YOUR UNDERSTANDING

Answer these questions before moving on to the **Analyze the Text** section on the following page.

1. What reason does the author give that George is not immediately released when his results come back as negative?
   A He has to stay because his son has just been admitted.
   B The staff is too busy with other tasks to process his release.
   C The staff believes he might get sick again in a few days.
   D He is afraid to be released because he thinks he might infect his family.

2. Which quotation from the selection shows the author using his experience as a doctor to assess someone's mental state?
   F *He was obviously ill and was too young to fend for himself.*
   G *He was going home with his family, you could almost hear him think.*
   H *His wet symptoms were not as profound as they were in so many other patients.*
   J *I saw that same fear in his eyes that I saw every day with patients in the suspect ward.*

3. Which paragraph explains the statement in paragraph 1 that "one loss hit us all with equal force"?
   A Paragraph 11
   B Paragraph 13
   C Paragraph 14
   D Paragraph 19

Inferno: A Doctor's Ebola Story   471

TEACH

CHECK YOUR UNDERSTANDING

Have students answer the questions independently.

Answers:

1. B
2. J
3. D

If they answer any questions incorrectly, have them reread the text to confirm their understanding. Then they may proceed to the next selection.

ENGLISH LEARNER SUPPORT

Oral Assessment Use the following questions to assess students' comprehension and speaking skills.

1. Why did it take so long to release George? *(The staff was busy with other patients.)*
2. How did Dr. Hatch use his experience to determine George's mental condition? *(He saw that George's reaction was the same as he had seen in other patients' eyes.)*
3. Why was Williams's death so upsetting? *(George had been cured and should have been able to leave, but he returned to care for his son.)* **SUBSTANTIAL/MODERATE**

Inferno: A Doctor's Ebola Story   **471**

APPLY

ANALYZE THE TEXT

Possible answers:

1. **DOK 3:** *The* Times *photo and caption present George looking joyous, and they describe his jubilation at surviving the virus. However, as we learn from Hatch's account, George has also just received very worrisome news about his family possibly being infected, and will soon face suffering and grief again.*

2. **DOK 3:** *The staff attached particular emotional importance to Williams's survival in part because they had sent his father, George, back into the confirmed ward after his own recovery to look after the young boy. Williams's case was also special in that it did not follow the same course as usual, and therefore became a "canvas" onto which staff members projected their own tendencies toward optimism and pessimism. This shows the staff to be sensitive to patients' and their families emotional needs.*

3. **DOK 4:** *As a doctor, Hatch knows he should avoid letting his emotions interfere with his judgment. This perspective helps us understand how emotionally involved he became with Williams and George because he came to believe Williams would recover.*

4. **DOK 2:** *Hatch conveys the emotional impact of Williams's death mainly through the unusual silence of the staff that morning, as compared to the usual "raucous banter." He describes the morning meeting as "quiet," and says the staff "silently" went about their tasks. He also says one staff member "hardly made eye contact with anyone" and another staff member's eyes were bloodshot.*

5. **DOK 4:** *Students might respond that they felt greater sympathy for George as they read further because they learned more about what it was like in the confirmed ward, and they saw how emotionally devastated George was after the experience.*

RESEARCH

Remind students that when they conduct their research, they should use more than one source. Students should evaluate each source to make sure it is credible. Remind students how to evaluate sources.

Extend In their research, students may come across the terms *right-brained* and *left-brained* to describe how one side of the brain might dominate another, thus determining areas of cognitive superiority. Students should use what they have learned in their discussions.

RESPOND

ANALYZE THE TEXT

Support your responses with evidence from the text. 📝 **NOTEBOOK**

1. **Compare** Review paragraphs 2 and 5, which provide details about George's photo and caption in the *Times*. How is George's portrayal in the *Times* similar to Hatch's portrayal of him in the memoir? How do the two portrayals differ?

2. **Draw Conclusions** Why did the medical staff at the ETU take particular interest in the case of Williams Beyan? What does their interest reveal about them?

3. **Analyze** In paragraphs 13 and 14, how does your understanding of the author's perspective provide insight into his reaction to the course of Williams's illness?

4. **Interpret** In paragraph 20, how does the author use details to convey the emotional effect of Williams's death on the staff?

5. **Notice & Note** What were your thoughts when you first learned of George's reluctance to return to the confirmed ward? Did your thoughts change by the end of the excerpt? Explain why or why not.

RESEARCH

RESEARCH TIP
When you carry out a search, scroll to the bottom of the results page and look for a list of suggested additional search topics. Often, these suggested topics are highly specific and relevant to your inquiry. They also may guide you to interesting, unexpected aspects of the topic.

In paragraph 17, Hatch describes his mental response to the news of Williams's death by saying it was "as if the hemispheres of my brain were unhappily squabbling about what to do with this information." Research popular theories of how the right and left hemispheres of the brain process information. Then, record what you discover in the chart below.

LEFT HEMISPHERE	RIGHT HEMISPHERE
Analytical thought	Art awareness
Uses logic	Creativity
Language	Imagination
Reasoning	Intuition
Number skills	Insight
Right-hand control	Music awareness
	3-D forms
	Left-hand control

Extend Use what you have discovered to explain why Hatch would describe his response in this way. Base your explanation only on research from reliable sources of information on the brain.

WHEN STUDENTS STRUGGLE . . .

Reteaching: Analyze Author's Perspective Review with students that an author's perspective is how he or she views events or a situation. An author's perspective can be influenced by his or her values, culture, upbringing, or experiences. Readers have to pay close attention to the details an author provides to determine his or her perspective. Have students work in pairs to discuss Dr. Hatch's perspective on Ebola or Williams. They should identify details that support their ideas.

 For additional support, go to the **Reading Studio** and assign the following **Level Up tutorial: Reading for Details**.

APPLY

CREATE AND RESEARCH

Take Informal Notes Remind students that note-taking does not involve writing in complete sentences. Students should look for main ideas and supporting ideas and record them with meaningful phrases. Students should note the source for each piece of information.

 For **writing support** for students at varying proficiency levels, see the **Text X-Ray** on page 462D.

Create an Informational Poster As students work within a group, members should analyze their strengths so they conduct their [online?] research, they should access [use?] more than one source. each member makes a contribution to the poster. Encourage students to use photographs, illustrations, or diagrams, along with text.

RESPOND TO THE ESSENTIAL QUESTION

Allow time for students to add details from *Inferno: A Doctor's Ebola Story* to their Unit 3 Response Logs.

CREATE AND RESEARCH

Take Informal Notes Carry out research to gather information about the steps that are taken to control Ebola outbreaks.

- ❏ Make sure you are using trusted websites, such as those with .org and .gov addresses, with reputable and reliable authors and hosts.
- ❏ Scan for headings to locate the specific information you are interested in.
- ❏ Take informal notes by writing down key words and phrases.

Create an Informational Poster With a group, combine and organize the notes you have gathered through research, and create a poster that tells people what they should do if there is an Ebola outbreak in their community.

- ❏ Make instructions clear and accurate.
- ❏ Use short, imperative sentences.
- ❏ Use visual aids.

RESPOND

 Go to the **Writing Studio** to find out more about taking notes during research.

 Go to the **Speaking and Listening Studio** for more on presentations and working with a group.

RESPOND TO THE ESSENTIAL QUESTION

? Why are plagues so horrifying?

Gather Information Review your annotations and notes on *Inferno: A Doctor's Ebola Story*. Then, add relevant information to your Response Log. As you determine which information to include, think about:

- how emotions such as fear and hope affect our judgments
- how our understanding of a particular moment changes with time and experience
- how our perception of others' emotions and reactions are influenced by our own perspectives

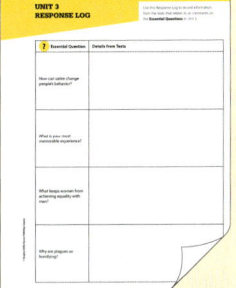

ACADEMIC VOCABULARY

As you write and discuss what you learned from *Inferno: A Doctor's Ebola Story*, be sure to use the Academic Vocabulary words. Check off each of the words that you use.

- ❏ encounter
- ❏ exploit
- ❏ persist
- ❏ subordinate
- ❏ widespread

APPLY

CRITICAL VOCABULARY

Answers:

1. in danger of getting into a situation you can't return from.
2. Student answers will vary. Accept any sensible answer.
3. Student answers will vary. Accept any sensible answer.
4. Student answers will vary. Accept any sensible answer.
5. Student answers will vary. Accept any sensible answer.
6. Student answers will vary. Accept any sensible answer.
7. Student answers will vary. Accept any sensible answer.
8. Student answers will vary. Accept any sensible answer.

VOCABULARY STRATEGY:
Classical Allusions

Answers:

1. The illness of Ebola can seem like a bottomless pit, metaphorically, because it is a place of darkness from which return is a long, uncertain journey. The abyss could also be used to describe the confirmed ward, as Hatch later explains that the confirmed ward was "hell on earth" to George.

2. Although George survives the Ebola virus, he suffers the loss of his son, whom he has to care for within the confirmed ward in an effort to save him. Although the death of George's son was not directly caused by his own survival, he may feel surviving the virus was not worth having to return to the confirmed ward to endure watching his son die.

RESPOND

WORD BANK
- abyss
- ersatz
- veracity
- pyrrhic victory
- vexation
- vigilance
- plateau
- prognosis

Go to the **Vocabulary Studio: Understanding Word Origins** for more on words from classical mythology.

CRITICAL VOCABULARY

Practice and Apply Respond to each question or prompt by using the Critical Vocabulary word in a complete sentence.

1. What does it mean to be "on the edge of an **abyss**"?
2. Give an example of a **pyrrhic victory**.
3. Name a job that requires **vigilance**.
4. How do you determine the **veracity** of a source?
5. What's the most common cause of **vexation** for you?
6. At what time of day does your energy **plateau**?
7. Name something that could be used as an **ersatz** chair.
8. What would you do if your doctor gave you a scary **prognosis**?

VOCABULARY STRATEGY:
Classical Allusions

The title of Steven Hatch's memoir contains an allusion to Dante's epic poem *The Divine Comedy*, in which the first part, *Inferno*, is a detailed description of punishments in an underworld. The English language uses many such **classical allusions**, or indirect references to classical works of literature.

For example, this excerpt from *Inferno: A Doctor's Ebola Story* contains other classical allusions:

> George had made the slow recovery after emerging from the *abyss* in mid-October and waited around for the virus to clear, hardly making a noise as he sat outside listening to Radio Gbarnga in the hot sun.

The word *abyss* is derived from both ancient Greek and Latin and means "an extremely deep or bottomless hole." It is used in classical literature and translations of the New Testament to refer to hell.

> I assumed he would have regarded this as a *pyrrhic victory* since his entire family now awaited word as to whether they would have to endure a similar experience. . . .

The phrase *pyrrhic victory* refers to the victory of King Pyrrhus over the Romans, in which Pyrrhus lost a large portion of his army, including many of his closest friends, as described in Plutarch's classical poem *Pyrrhus*.

Practice and Apply Answer the following questions in complete sentences, citing evidence from the text to support your answers.

Why does Hatch say that George emerged from the abyss?

In what ways might George's recovery be considered a pyrrhic victory?

ENGLISH LEARNER SUPPORT

Vocabulary Strategy Many of the Critical Vocabulary words contain the letter *v*. Speakers of Spanish, Cantonese, Korean, and Khmer may have difficulty pronouncing these words. The sound may not exist in their native languages, may be pronounced somewhat differently, or may be confused with another sound. Read aloud the words *veracity, vexation, vigilance,* and *victory,* and have students repeat the words. Work on pronouncing the /v/.

ALL PROFIENCIES

RESPOND

LANGUAGE CONVENTIONS:
Subordinate Clauses

Subordinate clauses add detail to a text by answering questions such as *where, when, how, what kind*, and *which one*. They cannot stand on their own and must be connected to at least one independent clause, sometimes through the use of a **subordinating conjunction.** Here are some examples of subordinating conjunctions and what they indicate.

SUBORDINATING CONJUNCTIONS	WHAT THEY INDICATE
until, when, after, before, as, as soon as, while, whenever	Time relationship
because, as, if, since, unless	Cause/effect or conditional relationship
even though, although, while, whereas	Contrast
where, wherever	Place

Some subordinate clauses function as adjectives, with relative pronouns such as *who, that*, or *which* as their subjects. In this case, the clause is also called a **relative clause,** and it provides information about a noun.

Practice and Apply Summarize some of the specific events in *Inferno* in your own words, incorporating subordinate clauses. Write at least four sentences that use a subordinating conjunction with a clause or that use a relative pronoun as the subject of a clause. For example:

> Williams's father, *who* had survived Ebola infection, stayed with him in the confirmed ward.

> *Although* the staff members were used to seeing people die, they were especially upset about Williams's death.

Student answers will vary

Have students compare summary sentences to check for accuracy and to identify subordinate and independent clauses.

Go to the **Grammar Studio** for more on types of clauses.

Inferno: A Doctor's Ebola Story

APPLY

LANGUAGE CONVENTIONS:
Subordinate Clauses

Tell students that writers use **subordinate clauses** to connect ideas and clarify relationships. Remind students that the coordinating conjunction that begins a subordinate clause indicates the purpose of the clause. Review the different subordinating conjunctions and what the conjunctions indicate. Review the examples in the Practice and Apply section. The clause "who had survived Ebola infection" is a relative clause that provides information about Williams's father—he had survived Ebola. The clause "Although the staff were used to seeing people die" indicates a conditional relationship—the staff were used to seeing death, but this one upset them more than most.

Practice and Apply Tell students that to help them summarize, they can reread each paragraph and make a summary statement. In that statement, include **independent** and **subordinate clauses.**

ENGLISH LEARNER SUPPORT

Language Conventions Use the following supports with students at varying proficiency levels:

- Have students find a sentence in *Inferno: A Doctor's Ebola Story* that uses a subordinate clause and have volunteers share what they found. Work with students to identify the subordinating conjunction and what it indicates. **SUBSTANTIAL**

- Have students work with partners to write two original sentences with subordinate clauses. Have pairs exchange sentences and identify the subordinate clause and what the conjunction indicates. **MODERATE**

- Have students work individually to write one complex sentence for each relationship in the chart (time, cause/effect, contrast, and place). Have students exchange sentences and discuss the effect of the subordinate clause. **LIGHT**

Inferno: A Doctor's Ebola Story

APPLY

COMPARE ACROSS GENRES

Before students begin working, discuss the types of details each author used, including statistics, facts, descriptions, and dialogue. Students should consider each author's language and word choices as they compare the texts.

ANALYZE THE TEXTS

Possible answers:

1. **DOK 3:** *Defoe's narrator is a resident of London who is there because it is his home and he feels an obligation to stay and help his neighbors. The author of Inferno has travelled to a foreign land to help strangers because he is a doctor and has special skills and knowledge that can help them. These perspectives influence how they feel about the number of people who are dying and how the disease is spreading. The narrator is more objective but is also tormented. The doctor is trying to be aware of the culture and understand the differences.*

2. **DOK 4:** *Defoe describes the "voice of mourning" in the streets of London as people watch their loved ones die or the cry of the man at the burial pit when his family is thrown in. Hatch describes George's wailing when his son dies, but also the unusual quiet of the staff that morning because Williams's death hit everyone harder than the others.*

3. **DOK 2:** *Death becomes routine and ubiquitous; the many burials had to be handled quickly, without the usual sacredness and ceremony. In Journal, the bodies were buried at night in a mass grave, with bodies on top of bodies. In Inferno, Williams's burial lasted three or four minutes and was attended by only a few hospital staff. This was an exception, implying that other burials had fewer, if any, mourners in attendance. In both texts, it is human nature to do what is necessary to keep others alive.*

4. **DOK 4:** *Both texts gave extreme examples of the fear of dying and the hope of recovery. Both fear and hope can cloud a people's judgment, causing them to behave irrationally, or to have unreasonable expectations. In an epidemic when people have very little, if any, control over what happens, it is natural to give in to fear or to cling to hope, even against all logic and evidence. Fear, however, can keep people out of danger, while hope can allow people to press on and keep working to save as many as possible, since they must face death and suffering on a daily basis.*

476 Unit 3

RESPOND

Collaborate & Compare

COMPARE ACROSS GENRES

Compare and Contrast Details Both Daniel Defoe and Steven Hatch use a variety of details to convey the experience of witnessing a plague to readers. With your group, use a chart like the one below to gather information with which to compare and contrast the types of details used by the two authors.

from
A JOURNAL OF THE PLAGUE YEAR
Novel by Daniel Defoe

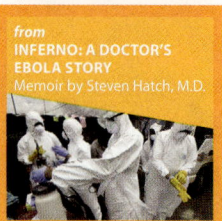
from
INFERNO: A DOCTOR'S EBOLA STORY
Memoir by Steven Hatch, M.D.

	A JOURNAL OF THE PLAGUE YEAR	INFERNO: A DOCTOR'S EBOLA STORY
Images	voice of mourning muffled up in brown coat	decontamination shower hellish misery
Sounds	shrieking wailing	wail lamentations rang
Statistics	size of pit # of people buried	lingered for weeks
Dialogue	'T's a speaking sight	What happened?
Emotional Language	dead-cart melancholy madness	cheer and hope weapons of darkness
Metaphors/Comparisons	face of London	you are like superman clinic like a canvas
Examples and Anecdotes	man witnessing his family dumped into pit	Williams sickness was different than others

What similarities and differences do you notice in how the two authors use details in their texts? Which use of details did you find more effective? Why?

ANALYZE THE TEXTS

Discuss these questions in your group.

1. **Contrast** How do the motivations of Defoe's narrator differ from those of the author of *Inferno*? How do these differences affect their perspectives on the events they describe?

2. **Analyze** How do Defoe and Hatch appeal to the sense of hearing to convey the impact and effects of each plague on those who witness it?

3. **Infer** What do the burial scenes in each text reveal about how humans respond to the high number of deaths during a lethal epidemic? What message about human nature is suggested by how humans respond?

4. **Synthesize** Identify examples of both fear and hope in the two texts. What do the texts suggest about the significance of these emotions during an epidemic?

476 Unit 3

  ENGLISH LEARNER SUPPORT

Ask Questions Put students in trios. Together, they should decide on how to respond verbally to the following questions. Each should take turns in responding to the group.

1. What motivated the narrator in *A Journal of the Plague Year*? What motivated Dr. Hatch in *Inferno*? How are they alike? How are they different?

2. Describe the fear that occurred in both stories. Describe the hope that occurred in both stories. What do both texts tell you about fear and hope that develops during an epidemic? **MODERATE/LIGHT**

RESPOND

RESEARCH AND SHARE

Now your group can continue exploring the ideas in these texts by researching other examples of how epidemics and plagues are portrayed in literature and the media.

1. **Brainstorm as a group.** Share ideas about how plagues and epidemics have been portrayed through literature and media. The representations can be fictional or nonfictional and can include books, movies, or television shows. Make a list of all the examples you discuss.

2. **Assign a topic to each group member to research.** Assign or have each member of the group choose one book, show, or movie to explore.

3. **Gather information.** Use summaries, reviews, and other sources, including excerpts and clips, to learn about the book, show, or movie you are to research. Note who the narrator or central character is, what details are used to portray the epidemic (such as statistics, visual descriptions, or individual stories), and identify the historical and/or scientific background.

Title of book, movie, or show:	
Brief description of epidemic:	
Scientific or historical background:	
Details about narrator or central character:	Details used to portray epidemic:

RESEARCH TIP
When looking for works of literature about a particular topic, use the "advanced search" feature of an online library catalogue or a city library's website to search by subject.

4. **Share with your group.** Have individual members of your group explain the books, shows, or movies they have researched. Then, discuss the various ways that epidemics are portrayed in literature and media, as well as the kinds of reactions these portrayals create in readers and viewers.

Collaborate & Compare   477

APPLY

RESEARCH AND SHARE

1. **Brainstorm as a group.** Provide students with Internet service and the use of computers to help them identify the titles of books, movies, and television shows. Remind them that the brainstorming process is indiscriminate, meaning all ideas are included. Encourage students to come up with as many ideas as possible so they have ample options to choose from.

2. **Assign a topic to each group member to research.** Students should analyze the brainstormed list and select a topic they want to research. Remind students that they each should take a different topic. Encourage students to research an epidemic they don't know much about.

3. **Gather information.** Explain to students that the Internet will be a great resource for their research, but they should choose websites carefully. To verify information, more than one website should be used.

4. **Share with your group.** Remind students that this is an informal presentation, but they need to prepare. Encourage them to provide a visual. They should also provide a list of their references, so others can learn more about the topic.

WHEN STUDENTS STRUGGLE . . .

Present to a Group Encourage students to make note cards for their presentations. Suggest they summarize each fact they learned or idea they want to share. They should include the source on each card. Writing down each talking point will help them remember what they learned and what they want to share.

 For additional support, go to the **Reading Studio** and assign the following **Level Up tutorial: Summarizing.**

Collaborate & Compare   **477**

INDEPENDENT READING

READER'S CHOICE

Setting a Purpose Have students review their Unit 3 Response Logs and think about what they've already learned about literature of the Restoration and Enlightenment eras. As they choose their Independent Reading selections, encourage them to consider what more they want to know.

NOTICE & NOTE

Explain that some selections may contain multiple signposts; others may contain only one. And the same type of signpost can occur many times in the same text.

LEARNING MINDSET

Plan and Predict Remind students that planning is essential to completing work efficiently and thoroughly. Encourage students to make a plan for completing an assignment, including mapping the steps by predicting outcomes toward the final goal. Explain that planning will help students learn to discipline themselves, which will help them in the future.

INDEPENDENT READING

ESSENTIAL QUESTIONS: Review the four Essential Questions for this unit on page 361.

Reader's Choice

Select and Preview Select one or more of these options from your eBook to continue your exploration of the Essential Questions.

- Read the descriptions to see which text seizes your interest.
- Think about which genres you enjoy reading.

Notice Note

In this unit, you practiced noticing and noting the signposts and asking big questions about nonfiction. As you read independently, these signposts and others will aid your understanding. Below are the key questions to ask when you read literature and nonfiction.

Reading Literature: Stories, Poems, and Plays	
Signpost	**Key Question**
Contrasts and Contradictions	Why did the character act that way?
Aha Moment	How might this moment change things?
Tough Questions	What does this make me wonder about?
Words of the Wiser	What's the lesson for the character?
Again and Again	Why might the author keep bringing this up?
Memory Moment	Why is this memory important?

Reading Nonfiction: Essays, Articles, and Arguments	
Signpost	**Key Question(s)**
Big Questions	What surprised me? What did the author think I already knew? What challenged, changed, or confirmed what I already knew?
Contrasts and Contradictions	What is the difference, and why does it matter?
Extreme or Absolute Language	Why did the author use this language?
Numbers and Stats	Why did the author use these numbers or amounts?
Quoted Words	Why was this person quoted or cited, and what did their words add?
Word Gaps	Do I know this word from someplace else? Does it seem like technical talk for this topic? Do clues in the sentence help me understand the word?

478 Unit 3

ENGLISH LEARNER SUPPORT

Develop Fluency Select a passage from the text that matches students' reading abilities. Read the passage aloud while students follow along silently.

- Echo-read the passage by reading aloud one sentence and then having students repeat the sentence back to you. Then, have the students read the passage silently several times. Check their comprehension by asking yes/no questions about the passage. **SUBSTANTIAL**
- Have students read and then reread the passage silently. Ask students to time their reading to track improvements over time. **MODERATE**
- Allow more fluent readers to select their own texts. Set a specific time for students to read silently (for example, 30 minutes). Check their comprehension by having them write a summary of what they've read. **LIGHT**

 Go to the **Reading Studio** for additional support in developing fluency.

INDEPENDENT READING

You can preview these texts in Unit 3 of your eBook.
Then check off the text or texts that you select to read on your own.

POETRY

Elegy Written in a Country Churchyard
Thomas Gray

A young poet contemplates his own mortality, asking why people are remembered after death.

ARTICLE

Once Below Gas Station, Virginia Cemetery Restored
Wyatt Andrews

Who is buried beneath our feet? And why do people feel a need to identify those strangers from the past?

POEM

On Her Loving Two Equally
Aphra Behn

She loves two very different men. How can she resolve her equally strong affections for them both?

ARTICLE

King George's Letters Betray Madness, Computer Finds
Mindy Weisberger

Historians use a computer to detect signs of mental illness in the letters of America's last king.

Collaborate and Share With a partner, discuss what you learned from at least one of your independent readings.
- Give a brief synopsis or summary of the text.
- Describe any signposts that you noticed in the text and explain what they showed you.
- Describe what you most enjoyed or found most challenging about the text. Give specific examples.
- Decide if you would recommend the text to others. Why or why not?

 Go to the **Reading Studio** for more resources on **Notice & Note.**

Independent Reading   479

INDEPENDENT READING

MATCHING STUDENTS TO TEXTS

Use the following information to guide students in choosing their texts.

Elegy Written in a Country Churchyard
Genre: poem
Overall Rating: Challenging

King George's Letters Betray Madness, Computer Finds   Lexile: 1470L
Genre: article
Overall Rating: Challenging

On Her Loving Two Equally
Genre: poem
Overall Rating: Challenging

Once Below Gas Station, Virginia Cemetery Restored   Lexile: 840L
Genre: article
Overall Rating: Accessible

Collaborate and Share To assess how well students read the selections, walk around the room and listen to their conversations. Encourage students to focus and be specific in their comments.

Online Ed for Assessment
- Independent Reading Selection Tests

 Encourage students to visit the **Reading Studio** to download a handy bookmark of **NOTICE & NOTE** signposts.

WHEN STUDENTS STRUGGLE...

Keep a Reading Log As students read their selected texts, have them keep a reading log for each selection to note signposts and their thoughts about them. Use their logs to assess how well they are noticing and reflecting on elements of their texts.

Reading Log for (title)		
Location	Signpost I Noticed	My Notes About It

Independent Reading   479

PLAN

UNIT 3 Tasks

- **WRITE A PERSONAL NARRATIVE**
- **PRESENT A NARRATIVE**

MENTOR TEXT

from **INFERNO: A DOCTOR'S EBOLA STORY**

Memoir by Steven Hatch, M.D.

LEARNING OBJECTIVES

Writing Task
- Write a personal narrative connected to a wider issue.
- Use strategies and graphic organizers to plan and organize a personal narrative.
- Use the Mentor Text as a model for writing.
- Use narrative techniques.
- Use direct and indirect quotations.
- Use a Revision Guide and peer review to revise a draft.
- Edit draft to indicate quotations properly.
- Use a rubric to evaluate writing.
- Publish writing to share with an audience.
- **Language** Share reflections about a personal experience.

Speaking Task
- Adapt an essay as a presentation.
- Identify the needs of an audience.
- Choose visuals and audio.
- Practice effective verbal and nonverbal techniques.
- Provide and consider advice for improvement.
- Deliver a presentation.
- **Language** Ask for advice using the sentence stem: *How can I improve my _____?*

Assign the Writing Task in **Ed**.

RESOURCES
- Unit 3 Response Log
- Writing Studio: Writing Narratives
- Speaking and Listening Studio: Giving a Presentation
- Grammar Studio: Quotation Marks

PLAN

Language X-Ray: English Learner Support

Use the instruction below and the supports and scaffolds in the Teacher's Edition to help you guide students of different proficiency levels.

INTRODUCE THE WRITING TASK

Explain that a **memoir** has a tone, just like other forms of writing. Review with students that their memoirs can have a conversational tone, but the use of narrative techniques will help their memoirs sound more like literature. Discuss the difference between an informal tone and a more literary tone. Have students consider ways to make their language more formal.

Brainstorm possible statements about experiences, and write them on the board. Provide sentence frames, such as: *One thing I learned from ____ was ____. It seemed to me then that ____.*

WRITING

Share Reflections

Remind students that a **reflection** explains what they have learned or how they felt about their personal experience. Tell them to think about each event in their narrative and how they felt before, during, and after it.

Use the following supports with students at varying proficiency levels:

- Provide sentence frames to help students articulate their reflections about their personal experience. For example: *Before I ____, I felt ____. As I ____, I felt ____. After I ____, I felt ____.* Have students copy the frames and help them complete as neededm. **SUBSTANTIAL**
- Have partners ask each other questions about their reflections. For example: *How did you feel before you ____? How did your thinking change as you ____?* Have students write simple sentences in response. **MODERATE**
- Have students review the ways Hatch wrote his reflections. Then, have them use his sentences as a model for their own reflections. **LIGHT**

SPEAKING

Ask for Advice

Have students use informal language to ask each other for advice on how to improve their presentations. Guide them to use the sentence stem: *How can I improve my ____?*

Use the following supports with students at varying proficiency levels:

- Provide a word bank of terms and phrases students can use as they seek advice, such as: *delivery, pronunciation, enunciation, speaking rate.* Help students use a dictionary to define unfamiliar terms. **SUBSTANTIAL**
- Provide the sentence stem as a model, and then have students make a list of questions they can ask each other about improving the delivery of their presentations. **MODERATE**
- Have partners observe each other's presentations. Then have presenters ask observers questions about ways to improve both their deliveries and the content of their presentations. **LIGHT**

Unit 3 Tasks **480B**

WRITING

WRITE A PERSONAL NARRATIVE

Introduce students to the Writing Task by reading the introductory paragraph with them. Remind students to refer to the notes they recorded in their Unit 3 Response Logs as they plan and draft their narratives. Their Response Logs should contain ideas about narratives from personal experiences, including notes on Steven Hatch's memoir *Inferno: A Doctor's Ebola Story*, and how to connect personal experiences to a topic of importance to the reader.

 For **writing support** for students at varying proficiency levels, see the **Language X-Ray** on page 480B.

USE THE MENTOR TEXT

Students should use the mentor text, Steven Hatch's memoir *Inferno: A Doctor's Ebola Story* as a model. Point out that while their stories may be similar in style, topic, or length to the mentor text, they will write an original narrative using their own important personal experience and connecting it to a topic of significance for the reader.

WRITING PROMPT

Review the prompt with students. Encourage them to ask questions about any part of the assignment that is unclear. Make sure they understand that the purpose of their personal narratives is to answer the question using their own experience and connecting it to a topic of importance for the reader.

 **WRITING TASK**

Write a Personal Narrative

 Go to the **Writing Studio** for help writing narratives.

This unit focuses on literature from the Restoration and 18th century. Although writers in these periods often addressed social issues and historical events, there were also important portrayals of personal experiences, especially in memoirs and journals. For this writing task, you will write about an important personal experience and connect that experience to a topic of wider significance that may be important to a reader. You can use the excerpt from Steven Hatch's memoir *Inferno: A Doctor's Ebola Story* as a mentor text.

As you write your personal narrative, you can use the notes from your Response Log that you filled out after reading the texts in this unit.

Writing Prompt

Read the information in the box below.

> We often gain a better understanding of the significance and meaning of an event after we've had some time to reflect, especially if that event is of historical significance.

This is the context for your personal narrative.

Think carefully about the following question.

> What is your most memorable experience?

How might the Essential Question relate to a personal narrative?

Write a personal narrative about a significant experience you have had.

How might this significant experience relate to a personal narrative?

Be sure to—
- ❏ tell a story that has a beginning, middle, and end
- ❏ use conventions of storytelling, including characterization, scene, and dialogue
- ❏ include concrete sensory details to bring the reader into the experience
- ❏ describe your thoughts and feelings both at the time you had the experience and now as you remember it
- ❏ use the story to relate a "big idea," something of wider social, philosophical, or historical significance that will interest the reader

Review these points as you write and again when you finish. Make any needed changes.

480 Unit 3

 LEARNING MINDSET

Seeking Challenges Remind students that trying hard is important, but trying things that *are* hard is just as important. Explain that taking risks and trying new things without being afraid to fail is part of a growth mindset. Encourage students to view the process of writing a personal narrative or any difficult task as a challenge. Tell students to remember that they can ask for help from a friend or teacher if they need ideas or are struggling with coming up with ideas, the planning of, or drafting of their narratives.

1 Plan

Before you begin your writing, take some time to plan your draft. You should already know which story you want to tell. It's also important to make choices about which details to include, as you don't want to try to include every single detail or clutter your writing with unimportant information. Choose details that best convey something important about the experience, such as an emotion or a mood. You should also think about the significance of this experience that you want to convey. You should always know how your story is going to end *before* you start writing, as your text should be designed to lead your reader to that point.

Personal Narrative Planning Chart	
Genre	Personal narrative
Memorable experience	one-sentence summary of the experience
Something I learned or understood better because of the experience	the "big idea" or larger significance for the reader
Details I recall	images, sounds, tastes, smells, the weather, things that people did and said, etc

Background Reading Review the notes you have taken in your Response Log that relate to the question "What is your most memorable experience?" Texts in this unit provide background reading that will help you understand the wider significance of personal experiences.

WRITING TASK

Go to the **Writing Narratives: Narrative Context** for help planning your personal narrative.

Notice & Note
From Reading to Writing

As you plan your personal narrative, apply what you've learned about signposts to your own writing. Remember that writers use common features called signposts to help convey their message to readers.

Think how you can incorporate **Contrasts and Contradictions** into your essay.

Go to the **Reading Studio** for more resources on **Notice & Note**.

Use the notes from your Response Log as you plan your personal narrative.

Write a Personal Narrative 481

WRITING

1 PLAN

Allow time for students to discuss the topic with partners or in small groups and then to complete the planning table independently.

■ English Learner Support

Understand Academic Language Make sure students understand words and phrases used in the graphic organizer, such as *genre, memorable experience,* and *recall*. Use examples as needed. Work with students to fill in the blank sections of the graphic organizer with their own ideas. Provide text that they can copy as needed.
SUBSTANTIAL

▶ NOTICE & NOTE

From Reading to Writing

Remind students to incorporate **Contrasts and Contradictions** into their writing. They should find places in the narrative to illustrate the difference between two or more elements in the text. Using phrases such as *on the other hand, by contrast,* and *however* can signal contrast to the reader. Other contrasts or contradictions are made internally by the reader when thinking about things the writer suggests *don't happen* or *aren't the way I thought they would be*.

Background Reading As students plan their narratives, remind them to refer to the notes they took in their Response Logs. They may also review the selections to find additional ideas and examples to support ideas they want to include in their writing.

TO CHALLENGE STUDENTS . . .

Conduct Research Challenge students to incorporate facts and examples from another text that is a personal narrative. They might start by thinking of examples of autobiographies that relate a personal experience. If they cannot think of an appropriate text, they may search online or at the library. Encourage them to add details from their chosen text to their Response Logs and think about how these details support their answers to the Essential Question.

Write a Personal Narrative 481

WRITING

Organize Your Ideas Tell students that the ideas from the elements of their personal narrative should answer the questions as they fill out the chart. They should be able to completely fill the chart with details they plan to include in their narratives. Point out that the narrative should have an opening "hook," a beginning, details that develop their personal story, a climax, and a closing that conveys their experience, thoughts, or feelings to the reader. The events in the narrative should alternate with the student's reflection on the events to help the reader understand the writer's thoughts and feelings. By thinking about these questions before drafting the narrative, students can best decide how to organize their narratives and include all the essential elements.

② DEVELOP A DRAFT

Remind students to use the chart as they draft their narratives. Point out that they can still make minor adjustments to the elements, such as enhancing the development of the story, as they write their drafts. For example, they may decide that a particular event in the narrative does not support the idea being developed. They can make changes, or even remove details of an event.

■ English Learner Support

Write a Group Essay Simplify the writing task, and provide direct support by working together to write an informative paragraph that answers the Essential Question.
SUBSTANTIAL

 **WRITING TASK**

Go to the **Writing Narratives: Narrative Structure** for help organizing your ideas.

Organize Your Ideas After you have gathered ideas from your planning activities, you need to organize them in a way that will help you draft your personal narrative. You can use the chart below to decide on the elements of your story.

Introduction: How can you grab your readers attention? What is your story about? Where does it take place? Who is involved?	*This is how you will open the narrative. This may or may not be the beginning of the story, but it should catch the reader's attention.*
Second Paragraph: What happens at the beginning of your story?	*Begin to describe the experience and your thoughts at the time, as well as the emotions you felt.*
Third Paragraph: How does your story develop? Are there any twists or turns?	*Tell your personal story here and describe your thoughts and feelings about your experience.*
Fourth Paragraph What is the climax, or ending, of your story?	*This is the climax of your story, the part that is most significant and meaningful.*
Conclusion: Why does your story matter? What has changed, and what does it mean for the future?	*This is what you are leading your reader to with the story. It can be a thought about your feelings or a telling detail that you remember.*

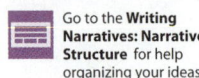 You might prefer to draft your personal narrative online.

② Develop a Draft

Once you have completed your planning activities, you will be ready to begin drafting your personal narrative. Refer to your Graphic Organizers and any notes you took as you studied the texts in the collection. These will provide a kind of map for you to follow as you write. Using a word processor or online writing application makes it easier to make changes or move sentences around later when you are ready to revise your first draft.

482 Unit 3

WHEN STUDENTS STRUGGLE . . .

Draft the Narrative Even when working from a chart to organize ideas and story elements, students may struggle to get started on their drafts. Remind students that they don't have to start with the beginning of the story. Encourage them to start by developing a part of the narrative they feel most confident about, such as a scene that describes the "big idea" of the story. Once they have this part written, they may feel more confident to take on the rest of the narrative. Remind students that they don't have to write everything perfectly for the first draft, because they will revise and edit their writing later.

WRITING

WRITING TASK

Use the Mentor Text

Author's Craft
The first few sentences of your opening paragraph should "hook" readers and grab their attention, making them curious about the story to come. In a personal narrative, the introduction may include a description of the place where the story took place, a quote, a thought, or even an interesting fact.

> Death was part of the daily routine, but some deaths affected us more than others. Each of us grew attached to certain patients as we would have done in any hospital, but one loss hit us all with equal force. We had cared for George Beyan, a quiet man in his mid-thirties who had acquired the virus by attending a sick friend.
>
> *This is the hook. It seizes the reader's attention because it is shocking. The reader wants to continue reading to find out what was significant about this particular death.*

Apply What You've Learned Brainstorm a few ideas for how you might open your personal narrative and try writing a sentence for each one. Think of a surprising or unusual detail you could use to open the story, and make the reader curious to keep reading.

Genre Characteristics
Your personal narrative should have a "big idea," something that you learned from or understood differently after the experience. Help the reader understand this "big idea" by reflecting on events.

> If there was a literal place that could be called hell on earth, for George Beyan, the confirmed ward was it, and we had willingly cajoled him into returning to that place of his nightmares only to provide him with one even worse. We asked him to make sacrifices knowing that this might happen. Indeed, I was the one who had asked it of him.
>
> *The author is reflecting on his decision to convince George to go back to the confirmed ward and the terrible experience the man had as a result.*

Apply What You've Learned As you tell your story, alternate narration of events with reflection, and give the reader insight into your inner thoughts and feelings, especially at moments when your understanding of the experience changed.

Write a Personal Narrative 483

WHY THIS MENTOR TEXT?

The memoir *Inferno: A Doctor's Ebola Story* provides a good example of a personal narrative. Use the instruction below to help students use the mentor text as a model for writing a personal narrative of their own that clearly develops a narrative based on the student's personal experience, includes reflection, and connects to the reader.

USE THE MENTOR TEXT

Author's Craft Ask a volunteer to read aloud the opening paragraph of the selection from *Inferno: A Doctor's Ebola Story*. Discuss how the writer's word choices and specific details capture readers' attention from the beginning and draw them into the narrative. Invite students to offer examples of an interesting description that could be used to open their own personal narratives. Discuss strategies students might use to develop their narratives, such as drawing on an experience taken from their lives and bringing out an important point or message from the event.

Genre Characteristics To help students understand how reflection is used to convey the "big idea" to the reader in *Inferno: A Doctor's Ebola Story*, have them locate paragraph 19 in the text. Have students take note of the author's thoughts and feelings as he reflects on his decision. Have students contrast a statement that shares the author's thoughts and feelings with another that simply relates the events. Discuss how using reflection helps the reader enter into the narrative and imagine other details that aren't specifically provided in the narration.

ENGLISH LEARNER SUPPORT

Internalize Basic Vocabulary Use the following supports with students at varying proficiency levels:

- List these words and read them aloud to students: *death, patient, hospital, virus*. Then, read the introduction aloud, using gestures to help students understand what is happening. Ask: *Are these words sad? How do you feel about this story?* **SUBSTANTIAL**

- Read the introduction aloud and invite students to ask about any words or phrases that are unclear. Ask students whether this text makes them want to read more, and why. **MODERATE**

- Have students read the introduction and identify words that add to the feeling of loss. Then, ask them to brainstorm other situations that could be used to introduce the general topic of death. **LIGHT**

Write a Personal Narrative 483

WRITING

3 REVISE

Have students answer each question in the chart to determine how they can use the revision tips and techniques to improve their drafts. Invite volunteers to model their revision techniques.

With a Partner Have students ask peer reviewers to evaluate their personal narratives by answering the following questions:

- Does my opening grab the reader's attention?
- Can the reader understand my emotions?
- Will the reader come away with a "big idea"?

Students should use the reviewer's feedback to make their story's opening engaging, use reflection to convey emotion, and further clarify their story's "big idea."

WRITING TASK

Go to the **Writing Narratives: The Language of Narratives** for help revising your personal narrative.

3 Revise

On Your Own Once you have written your draft, you'll want to go back and look for ways to improve your personal narrative. As you reread and revise, think about whether you have conveyed the significance of your experience. The Revision Guide will help you focus on specific elements to make your writing stronger.

Revision Guide

Ask Yourself	Tips	Revision Techniques
1. Does my opening paragraph grab the reader's attention?	**Think** about whether you as a reader would want to keep going after the first sentence.	**Add** an interesting detail to your opening to engage your reader's curiosity.
2. Do I include enough sensory details?	**Highlight** the sensory details you used.	**Add** such sensory details as images, sounds, smells, and physical sensations.
3. Does the reader understand my emotions?	**Look** for the moments where you describe your emotions.	**Elaborate** on emotional moments with details that "show" emotion rather than just telling.
4. Is my story organized and logical?	Go through your draft and make a short note to **summarize** each of your paragraphs.	**Break up** and **reorder** paragraphs so the story flows logically.
5. Is my "big idea" clearly conveyed to the reader?	**Write** a sentence or two that summarizes your "big idea."	**Add** reflection, emotions, and details to bring out the "big idea" throughout the story.

ACADEMIC VOCABULARY

As you conduct your **peer review**, be sure to use these words.

- ❏ encounter
- ❏ exploit
- ❏ persist
- ❏ subordinate
- ❏ widespread

With a Partner Once you and your partner have worked through the Revision Guide on your own, exchange personal narratives and evaluate each other's draft in a **peer review.** Focus on providing revision suggestions for at least three of the items mentioned in the chart. Explain why you think your partner's draft should be revised and what your specific suggestions are.

When receiving feedback from your partner, listen attentively and ask questions to make sure you fully understand the revision suggestions.

484   Unit 3

ENGLISH LEARNER SUPPORT

Use Synonyms Explain that writers often connect ideas by referring back to a noun with a synonym. Have students identify the pair of synonyms in this passage:

> What she didn't tell me right away, and I would learn only a few days later, was that after Williams had died, George had stayed up the entire night, wailing for his lost son, speaking to him, entreating him to come back, wishing for him to be alive. His lamentations rang throughout the compound for hours. *(wailing, lamentations)*

Encourage students to find opportunities to link ideas with synonyms in their essays.
LIGHT

④ Edit

Once you have addressed the narrative flow, development of the "big idea," and other elements of your personal narrative, you can look to improve the finer points of your draft. Edit for proper use of standard English conventions, including syntax, sentence structure, grammar, and spelling.

Language Conventions

One way to really give life to your personal narrative is to include **direct quotations.** Look at your writing to see whether there are places you could add direct quotations or revise to change **indirect quotations** to direct ones.

Indirect Quotation	Direct Quotation
After half an hour of walking around the island, I asked him whether he was sure there was a beach this way.	"Are you sure there's a beach this way?" I asked after half an hour of walking around the island.

! Go to the **Quotation Marks** lesson in the **Grammar Studio** to learn more.

When you write direct quotations, make sure you punctuate them correctly. If you are quoting a conversation, use a paragraph break when the speaker changes.

> We'd been hiking around the rocky edge of the island for half an hour, with no sign of a beach. "Are you sure there's a beach this way?" I asked.
>
> "That's what the locals told me," he retorted. "Why would they lie?"
>
> "Maybe that's a joke for them around here," I said, slightly out of breath from jumping between the rocks. "They send tourists walking around the whole island looking for a beach that isn't there."

⑤ Publish

Finalize your personal narrative and choose a way to share it with your audience. Consider these options:

- Upload it as an article to an open web platform.
- Submit it to a school or local publication.

WRITING TASK

④ EDIT

Suggest that students read their drafts aloud to assess how clearly and smoothly their narrative flows. Have students evaluate whether they have correctly used direct and indirect quotations appropriately when describing events.

LANGUAGE CONVENTIONS

Use Direct and Indirect Quotations Appropriately
Review the information about direct and indirect quotations with students. Then, discuss the example sentences in the chart, asking students to note the differences in each one. To emphasize how using direct quotations can improve writing, rewrite the sentences to use direct quotations and discuss the differences.

- I impatiently asked the guide for directions to the nearest beach. (*"Where is the nearest beach, please?" I impatiently asked the guide.*)
- He told me it was a mile farther to the south and motioned toward the road. (*He motioned toward the road, stating, "About another mile farther to the south."*)

■ English Learner Support

Use Quotation Marks Discuss the correct form for using quotation marks in direct quotations and for starting a new paragraph each time they quote a different person. Encourage students to use the proper form for direct quotations as they edit their essays. **MODERATE**

⑤ PUBLISH

Students can present their personal narratives as blog posts on their school website. Encourage others to read the narratives and to write comments about them. The authors can then respond to the comments.

WHEN STUDENTS STRUGGLE...

Use Direct Quotations Some students may have difficulty understanding how to use direct quotations appropriately when writing a narrative. Ask them to identify the subject in the example of the indirect quotation sentence in the chart on this page and then discover the question or statement made by the subject. Help them to identify when it may be better to write something as a direct quotation rather than an indirect one. Clarify that while using indirect quotations is generally acceptable, direct quotations should be used to add variety and interest to their writing.

WRITING

USE THE SCORING GUIDE

Allow students time to read the scoring guide and to ask questions about any words, phrases, or ideas that are unclear. Then, have partners exchange final drafts of their personal narratives. Ask them to score their partner's writing using the scoring guide. Each student should write a paragraph explaining the reasons for the score he or she awarded in each category.

 **WRITING TASK**

Use the scoring guide to evaluate your essay.

Writing Task Scoring Guide: Narrative Essay

	Organization/Progression	Development of Ideas	Use of Language and Conventions
4	• The introduction and conclusion are engaging and appropriate, and every part of the narrative is on topic. • Sentences and paragraphs flow smoothly, with every detail adding to the quality of the narrative.	• The writer's imaginative and creative use of details and elaboration effectively supports the important ideas in the narrative.	• The writer's voice and personality are evident, and the writer's word choice and language are vivid and expressive. • The writer shows consistent command of grammar with only minor errors in punctuation or spelling.
3	• The introduction and conclusion add to the narrative, and most of the narrative is on topic. • Most sentences and paragraphs include effective transitions, and most of the details support the focus of the narrative.	• Some details and elaboration help to support important ideas in the narrative.	• The writer's style is mostly effective and appropriate, and parts of the narrative are expressive and engaging. • The writer shows moderate command of grammar with occasional errors in spelling and grammar.
2	• The introduction and conclusion are weak, and sometimes the narrative wanders from the topic. • Few transitions are included; some points are irrelevant and don't contribute to the focus of the narrative.	• Details are present but don't really support the important ideas. Details are often unnatural and disconnected.	• The writing is formulaic and simple, with no varied sentence structure or expressive language. • The writer makes many mistakes that 12th-grade students should not be making.
1	• The introduction or conclusion is missing, and the narrative is often off topic. • Sentences are choppy and paragraphs are disjointed. There is repetition and unnecessary wordiness.	• Very few details are present, and no information is given to support the important ideas.	• The writing is confusing, with simple and awkward sentences. • The writer makes many errors in grammar and spelling.

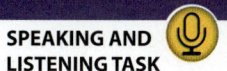

SPEAKING AND LISTENING TASK

Present a Narrative

You will now adapt your narrative essay for presentation to your classmates. You will also listen to their presentations, will ask questions to better understand their ideas, and will help them improve their work.

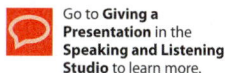

Go to **Giving a Presentation** in the **Speaking and Listening Studio** to learn more.

1 Adapt Your Essay for Presentation

Review your personal narrative, and use the chart below to guide you as you adapt your essay and create a script and presentation materials.

Presentation Planning Chart		
Title and Introduction	Is there a clever title or creative way you can introduce your presentation that will draw your audience's attention?	
Audience	What might you need to explain to the audience? What details in your essay might be of particular interest to the audience? What is the best way to present these details to convey your "big idea" to the audience?	
Effective Language and Organization	Which parts of your essay should be condensed for a presentation format? Which parts could you elaborate on? Could any of the language in your narrative be revised to make it more vivid or engaging?	
Visuals and Audio	Which kinds of visuals or props can you include to enrich your presentation? Would sound-effects or music help to enhance your presentation?	

Present a Narrative 487

SPEAKING AND LISTENING

PRESENT A NARRATIVE

Introduce students to the Speaking and Listening Task by discussing what makes reading a story different from hearing someone tell the same story. Point out that people read at different rates, and a reader may also stop and reread a passage to better understand it. Have students consider how a speaker can share their narratives in a way that helps listeners follow and understand it. Remind students that the way they say things and relate events can make them sound more interesting and engaging.

1 ADAPT YOUR ESSAY FOR PRESENTATION

Have students read the questions in the chart. Then, work with the class to list some general principles for presenting information orally. *(Examples: Use short sentences. Repeat important ideas. Use humor or interesting examples to keep the audience engaged.)* Point out that visuals, such as slides, can serve the same purpose as subheadings in a text. Students can use them to highlight the main ideas of their presentations for the audience.

For **speaking support** for students at varying proficiency levels, see the **Language X-Ray** on page 480B.

 ENGLISH LEARNER SUPPORT

Adapt the Essay Use the following supports with students at varying proficiency levels:

- Help students identify several key sentences in their essays. Then, have them include these sentences in visuals that illustrate the ideas. **SUBSTANTIAL**
- Review the questions in the chart to ensure students' understanding. Then, have students work in pairs to apply the questions to their essays. **MODERATE**
- Have students discuss the questions in the chart with partners before writing their answers independently. **LIGHT**

Write a Personal Narrative **487**

SPEAKING AND LISTENING

② PRACTICE WITH A PARTNER OR GROUP

Review the information and tips with the class, ensuring that all the terms and ideas are clear. Remind students that the purpose of practicing their presentations is to gain useful feedback from their peers. Emphasize that speaking before a group makes most people feel nervous, so everyone should be as supportive and helpful as possible.

③ DELIVER YOUR PRESENTATION

Set aside time for all students to give their presentations. When everyone has finished, ask students to share their thoughts on how their classmates' feedback helped them improve their performance.

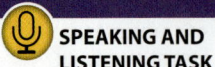 **SPEAKING AND LISTENING TASK**

As you work to improve your presentations, be sure to follow discussion rules:
- ❏ listen closely to each other
- ❏ don't interrupt
- ❏ stay on topic
- ❏ ask only helpful and relevant questions
- ❏ provide only clear, thoughtful, and direct answers

② Practice with a Partner or Group

Once you've completed the draft of your presentation, practice with a partner or group to improve both the presentation and your delivery.

Practice Effective Verbal Techniques

- ❏ **Enunciation** Replace words that you stumble over, and rearrange sentences so your delivery is smooth.
- ❏ **Voice Modulation and Pitch** Use your voice to display enthusiasm and emphasis.
- ❏ **Speaking Rate** Speak slowly enough that listeners understand you. Pause now and then to let them consider important points.
- ❏ **Volume** Remember that listeners at the back of the room need to hear you.

Practice Effective Nonverbal Techniques

- ❏ **Eye Contact** Try to let your eyes rest on each member of the audience at least once.
- ❏ **Facial Expression** Smile, frown, or raise an eyebrow to show your feelings or to emphasize points.
- ❏ **Gestures** Stand tall and relaxed, and use natural gestures—shrugs, nods, or shakes of your head—to add meaning and interest to your presentation.

Provide and Consider Advice for Improvement

As a listener, pay close attention. Take notes about ways that presenters can improve their presentations and use verbal and nonverbal techniques more effectively. Summarize each presenter's personal narrative to confirm your understanding, and ask questions to clarify any confusing details.

As a presenter, listen closely to questions and consider ways to revise your presentation to make sure your narrative is clear and logical. Remember to ask for suggestions about how you might change elements of your presentation to make it more clear and more interesting.

③ Deliver Your Presentation

Use the advice you received during practice to make final changes to your presentation. Then, using effective verbal and nonverbal techniques, present your personal narrative to your classmates.

WHEN STUDENTS STRUGGLE . . .

Take Notes If students have difficulty taking notes during their classmates' presentations, divide the task among several students. One student may focus on the list of effective verbal techniques, checking off techniques that are used well and jotting down brief notes about those that need improvement. Another student may do the same for the list of effective nonverbal techniques. A third may listen for key ideas and write those down. This student may choose to listen with eyes closed to tune out distractions.

Reflect on the Unit

By completing your personal narrative, you have created a writing product that pulls together and expresses your thoughts about the reading you have done in this unit. Now is a good time to reflect on what you have learned.

Reflect on the Essential Questions

- Review the four Essential Questions on page 361. How have your answers to these questions changed in response to the texts you've read in this unit?

- What are some examples from the texts you've read that show how personal experiences can have social and historical significance?

Reflect on Your Reading

- Which selections were the most interesting or surprising to you?

- From which selection did you learn the most about the importance of personal experiences?

Reflect on the Writing Task

- What difficulties did you encounter while working on your personal narrative? How might you avoid them next time?

- Which part of the personal narrative was the easiest to write? The hardest to write? Why?

- What improvements did you make to your personal narrative as you were revising?

UNIT 3 SELECTIONS
- *The Rape of the Lock*
- *A Modest Proposal*
- "Satire Is Dying Because the Internet Is Killing It"
- from *The Journal and Letters of Fanny Burney: An Encounter with King George III*
- *A Vindication of the Rights of Woman*
- "Education Protects Women from Abuse"
- from *A Journal of the Plague Year*
- from *Inferno: A Doctor's Ebola Story*

REFLECT ON THE UNIT

Have students reflect on the questions independently and write some notes in response to each one. Then, have students meet with partners or in small groups to discuss their reflections. Circulate during these discussions to identify the questions that are generating the liveliest conversations. Wrap up with a whole-class discussion focused on these questions.

LEARNING MINDSET

Self-Reflection Explain to students that an important part of developing a learning mindset and growing mentally is the ability to recognize strengths and weaknesses. As students reflect on the unit, encourage them to ask themselves the following questions: *What did I learn about my writing ability? Did I ask for help if I felt weak in a certain area? How did I handle errors? Am I proud of the work I turned in?*

UNIT 4

Instructional Overview and Resources

		Instructional Focus	Online Ed Resources
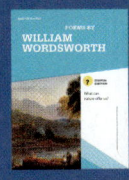	**Unit Introduction** **Emotion and Experimentation: The Flowering of Romanticism**	Unit 4 Essential Question Unit 4 Academic Vocabulary	**Stream to Start:** Emotion and Experimentation: The Flowering of Romanticism **Unit 4 Response Log**

ANALYZE & APPLY

	Poems by William Wordsworth Lexile N/A	**Reading** • Analyze Romantic Poetry • Analyze Imagery **Writing:** Write a Summary **Speaking and Listening:** Discuss	Audio **Reading Studio:** Notice & Note **Writing Studio:** Writing as a Process **Speaking and Listening Studio:** Participating in Collaborative Discussions
	**"Ode on a Grecian Urn"** Poem by John Keats Lexile N/A	**Reading** • Analyze Stanza Structure • Analyze Rhyme Scheme **Writing:** Write a Poem Using Apostrophe **Speaking and Listening:** Present Your Poem	Audio **Reading Studio:** Notice & Note **Writing Studio:** Writing as a Process **Speaking and Listening Studio:** Giving a Presentation
	**from Frankenstein** Novel by Mary Shelley Lexile 890L	**Reading** • Analyze Science Fiction • Analyze Motivation **Writing:** Write a Science Fiction Story **Speaking and Listening:** Discuss **Vocabulary:** Antonyms **Language Conventions:** Sensory Language	Audio **Reading Studio:** Notice & Note **Writing Studio:** Writing Narratives **Speaking and Listening Studio:** Participating in Collaborative Discussions **Vocabulary Studio:** Antonyms
	**MENTOR TEXT** **"Frankenstein: Giving Voice to the Monster"** Essay by Langdon Winner Lexile 1350L	**Reading** • Evaluate an Essay • Monitor Comprehension **Writing:** Write a Reflective Essay **Speaking and Listening:** Discuss Your Essay **Vocabulary:** Latin Roots **Language Conventions:** Parallel Structure	Audio **Reading Studio:** Notice & Note **Writing Studio:** Writing as a Process **Speaking and Listening Studio:** Participating in Collaborative Discussions **Vocabulary Studio:** Latin Roots **Grammar Studio:** Sentence Structure

SUGGESTED PACING: 30 DAYS

Unit Introduction	Poems by William Wordsworth	Ode on a Grecian Urn	from Frankenstein	Frankenstein: Giving Voice to the Monster
1	2 3 4 5 6	7 8 9	10 11 12 13 14	15 16 17

PLAN

English Learner Support	Differentiated Instruction	Assessment
• Text X-Ray • Use Imagery • Retell Material • Use Vocabulary Support • Acquire New Vocabulary • Demonstrate Comprehension • Oral Assessment • Identify Affixes	**When Students Struggle** • Analyze Imagery **To Challenge Students** • Analyze Historical Context • Research Context	**Selection Test**
• Text X-Ray • Acquire Grade-Level Vocabulary • Distinguish Sounds • Oral Assessment	**When Students Struggle** • Visualize Imagery • Reteaching: Apostrophe	**Selection Test**
• Text X-Ray • Use Cognates • Analyze Events • Examine Motivation • Compare and Contrast • Identify Sensory Language • Oral Assessment • Use Antonyms • Use Sensory Language	**When Students Struggle** • Develop an Outline • Reteaching: Outline Plot **To Challenge Students** • Analyze Cause and Effect	**Selection Test**
• Text X-Ray • Use Cognates • Acquire New Vocabulary • Compare Quotes • Oral Assessment • Vocabulary Strategy • Language Conventions	**When Students Struggle** • Identify Parallel Structure • Reteaching: Monitor Comprehension **To Challenge Students** • Debate the Issue	**Selection Test**

Ode to the West Wind / Song of a Thatched Hut Damaged in Autumn Wind
18 19 20 21

***from* Songs of Innocence / *from* Songs of Experience**
22 23 24 25

Independent Reading
26 27

End of Unit
28 29 30

Emotion and Experimentation **490B**

PLAN

UNIT 4 Continued

		Instructional Focus	Resources

COLLABORATE & COMPARE

	Instructional Focus	Resources
 **"Ode to the West Wind"** Lyric Poem by Percy Bysshe Shelley **Lexile N/A** **"Song of a Thatched Hut Damaged in Autumn Wind"** Lyric Poem by Du Fu **Lexile N/A**	**Reading** • Analyze Form • Analyze Diction **Writing:** Create a Visual Representation **Speaking and Listening:** Present Your Image	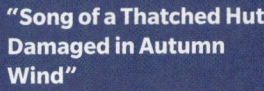 **Audio** **Reading Studio:** Notice & Note **Speaking and Listening Studio:** Giving a Presentation
Collaborate & Compare	**Reading:** Compare Themes	**Speaking and Listening Studio:** Giving a Presentation
 **from Songs of Innocence** Lyric Poetry by William Blake **Lexile N/A** **from Songs of Experience** Lyric Poetry by William Blake **Lexile N/A**	**Reading** • Analyze Symbols • Understand Historical Background **Writing:** Write an Essay **Speaking and Listening:** Make a Podcast	**Audio** **Reading Studio:** Notice & Note **Writing Studio:** Writing Informative Texts **Speaking and Listening Studio:** Participating in Collaborative Discussions
Collaborate & Compare	**Reading:** Compare Poems	

INDEPENDENT READING

The Independent Reading selections are available only in the eBook. 📖 Go to the Reading Studio for more information on Notice & Note.	 "William Blake: Visions and Verses" Article by Rachel Galvin **Lexile 1130L**	 "Frost at Midnight" Poem by Samuel Taylor Coleridge

END OF UNIT

Writing Task: Write an Explanatory Essay **Reflect on the Unit**	**Writing:** Writing Explanatory Essays **Language Conventions:** Sensory Language	**Unit 4 Response Log** **Mentor Text:** "Frankenstein: Giving Voice to the Monster" **Writing Studio:** Writing Informative Texts **Grammar Studio:** Adjective Phrases and Adverb Phrases

PLAN

English Learner Support	Differentiated Instruction	Online Ed Assessment
• Text X-Ray • Analyze Diction • Draw on Prior Knowledge • Monitor Oral and Written Language • Demonstrate Comprehension • Oral Assessment	**When Students Struggle** • Use Context Clues • Reteaching: Analyze Form **To Challenge Students** • Analyze Allusions • Write an Alliteration	**Selection Test**
• Perform Critical Analysis	**When Students Struggle** • Summarize	
• Text X-Ray • Use Inductive Reasoning • Use Prereading Supports • Oral Assessment • Understand Nonstandard English • Read Linguistically Accommodated Content • Demonstrate English Comprehension	**When Students Struggle** • Understand Diction and Tone **To Challenge Students** • Structure a Debate	**Selection Test**
• Perform Critical Analysis	**When Students Struggle** • Craft a Coherent Message	
"Walking with Wordsworth" Article by Bruce Stutz **Lexile 1280L**	from "A Defence of Poetry" Essay by Percy Bysshe Shelley **Lexile 1140L** — "The Skylark" Poem by John Clare	**Selection Tests**
• Language X-Ray • Understand Academic Language • Write a Group Essay • Use the Mentor Text • Use Adjectives • Use Sensory Words	**When Students Struggle** • Draft the Essay • Use Sensory Language **To Challenge Students** • Discuss in a Group	**Unit Test**

Emotion and Experimentation **490D**

TEACH

DISCUSS THE QUOTATION

Tell students that this quotation is from the epic poem *Jerusalem*, which the poet William Blake began composing around 1804. The quotation expresses the immense ideological shift that took place in the arts and literature as poets, writers, philosophers, and others turned from the Enlightenment's focus on logic and reason to embrace a new and in many ways opposite school of thought, Romanticism.

Ask students to think about the distinction Blake makes between reason and creation. Why might Blake and others have thought that artistic creation and expression are separate from reason? Ask students whether they agree with this view, or if they feel that reason and artistic expression complement each other.

■ English Learner Support

Learn Multiple-Meaning Words Make sure students understand that in the context of the quotation, *business* does not refer to an economic enterprise or secular job, but instead to someone's primary concern, interest, or endeavor. **MODERATE**

UNIT 4

EMOTION AND EXPERIMENTATION

THE FLOWERING OF ROMANTICISM

"I will not Reason and Compare; my business is to Create."

—William Blake

490 Unit 4

🧠 LEARNING MINDSET

Effort Explain that effort, rather than raw intelligence or "smarts," is one of the most important factors that determine how much students benefit from education. Students who are willing to work hard to engage and understand new material, despite the challenges they personally face throughout the learning process, experience personal and academic growth. Students who put forth minimal effort, even if they initially "succeed" at memorizing facts and passing tests, do not demonstrate a growth mindset and will be less prepared to deal with future academic challenges.

UNIT 4

Discuss the **Essential Questions** with your whole class or in small groups. As you read Emotion and Experimentation, consider how the selections explore these questions.

? ESSENTIAL QUESTION:
What can nature offer us?

As the 19th century dawned, England's cities underwent tremendous growth. Urban life had advantages, but some observers worried about the negative consequences of so many people leaving the countryside and losing contact with the natural world. Today, the idea of going outside and "back to nature" holds great appeal for many. Why are people drawn to nature? What does nature offer that we cannot find anywhere else?

? ESSENTIAL QUESTION:
How do you define beauty?

Beauty was a topic of great interest during the Romantic period. Writers, artists, and others sought to discover beauty not only in such conventional places as nature, the arts, and the human form, but also in such abstract concepts as emotions, ideals, and the human spirit. Some writers even explored the idea of beauty in failure and tragedy. What does it mean for something to be described as beautiful? How do definitions of beauty vary from person to person and from culture to culture?

? ESSENTIAL QUESTION:
How can science go wrong?

The Enlightenment ushered in a new era of scientific progress and confidence in the power of humanity over the natural world. With advances, however, came new responsibilities and new dilemmas, many of which still concern scientists and society today. What happens when scientific discoveries or experiments result in harm or get out of control? When do the risks of pursuing scientific advancement outweigh the benefits to society? Who gets to define ethical scientific practices?

? ESSENTIAL QUESTION:
What shapes your outlook on life?

One hallmark of Romanticism was its focus on individual feelings and personal experiences. As humans, we are often shaped by our most emotionally intense experiences. Still, it is not experience alone that molds perspective. Two people can live through the same event and come away from it with completely different perspectives, based on their outlooks on life or how they view and interact with the world. If experience cannot account for all of the differences in perspective, what can?

Emotion and Experimentation   491

TEACH

Connect to the
ESSENTIAL QUESTIONS

Read aloud the Essential Questions and the paragraphs that follow them. Open the discussion of each idea by having students respond to the questions that conclude each paragraph.

? ESSENTIAL QUESTION:
What can nature offer us?

Challenge students to think about how their view of nature and their interactions with nature are shaped by where they live. How might people who come from urban, suburban, or rural areas view nature and what it has to offer in different ways?

? ESSENTIAL QUESTION:
How do you define beauty?

Remind students that ideas about beauty vary not only between people and cultures, but also across time. Encourage students to consider how standards of beauty are set and also how they evolve. How are definitions of beauty changing in the modern world?

? ESSENTIAL QUESTION:
How can science go wrong?

Extend the discussion by having students identify examples of science gone wrong from recent history. What dangers did the event cause, and/or what ethical dilemmas did it raise? Was it possible to fix or resolve the issues created? Are future similar events avoidable, or does the root problem remain?

? ESSENTIAL QUESTION:
What shapes your outlook on life?

Explain that some people see themselves as having control over their lives and being able to shape their own circumstances, while others see themselves as having little control and being subject to external factors. Encourage students to think about how both internal and external factors have shaped their own outlooks and the outlooks of others.

Emotion and Experimentation   **491**

TEACH

THE FLOWERING OF ROMANTICISM

The following essay provides students with a historical context for the Unit 4 selections. It presents a brief overview of events occurring in England and abroad during the late 1700s and early 1800s that significantly reshaped British society and contributed to the rise of the short-lived but powerfully influential Romantic era of literature.

A Time of Revolution Explain that at this time in Britain as in France, the social ills afflicted mainly the lower classes of society. The new working-class industrial centers in the north and west of England had no representation in Parliament, and archaic laws denied rights to many religious groups. The nation's growing cities suffered from crime and poor sanitation, among other problems. The criminal justice system inflicted such harsh penalties as hanging for minor theft and imprisonment for debt. In addition, Britain's overseas empire faced a host of troubles, from corruption in India to the evils of the slave trade. Yet for nearly 25 years, all efforts toward reform were suppressed due to fear aroused by the excesses of the French Revolution and then by the threat of Napoleonic invasion.

COLLABORATIVE DISCUSSION

Ask groups to share their reasoning with the class, providing support for their opinions.

THE FLOWERING OF ROMANTICISM

The literary movement known as Romanticism developed in reaction to many social influences: the unrest of the French Revolution, the economic excesses of the Industrial Revolution, and the widespread poverty and oppression of workers.

A Time of Revolution During the American Revolution and, later, the French Revolution, George III ruled Britain. He was not a very capable king, and many blamed the loss of the American colonies chiefly on his inflexible attitude toward the colonists. In 1788, the year before the French Revolution began, George III suffered a major attack of mental illness; in 1811 he was declared permanently insane. His son George ruled as prince regent until the king's death in 1820.

Initially, many British citizens, including most of the early Romantic writers and poets, felt sympathy for the French Revolution and its ideals of liberty, equality, and brotherhood. The Romantics saw the revolution as a turning point in human history, a move toward an ideal civilized society in which those who had previously struggled under oppression would find relief. When the revolution turned radical and violent, however, British sympathy dissipated, and the Romantics turned elsewhere for inspiration.

During the Reign of Terror, radical revolutionaries persecuted and massacred thousands of French aristocrats and middle-class citizens. The British upper and middle classes were all too aware that England's lower classes faced many of the same social ills as the French lower classes. The British ruling classes were afraid that any efforts at reform could lead to anarchy as it had in France. As a result, British leaders grew more conservative, suppressing reform and outlawing writing or speech that was critical of the government.

War with France In 1793 Britain entered into a war with France that would last for more than 25 years. It was during this conflict that General Napoleon Bonaparte took control of France's government, made himself emperor, and then proceeded to conquer much of continental Europe. Britain was continually threatened with invasion until the British fleet destroyed the French navy in 1805. After that, Britain was able to loosen Napoleon's hold on Europe, and Napoleon was finally defeated at Waterloo in 1815.

COLLABORATIVE DISCUSSION
In a small group, discuss how the events on the timeline influenced British society. Was this influence mainly direct or indirect?

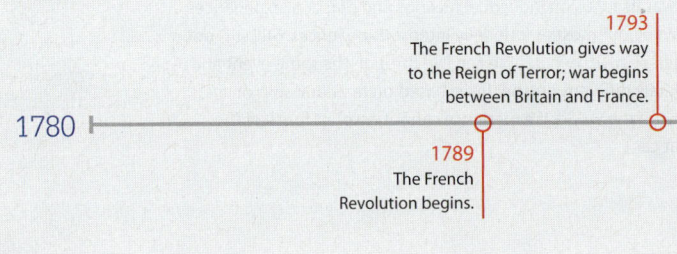

492 Unit 4

 ENGLISH LEARNER SUPPORT

Build Background Knowledge To aid comprehension of the essay, provide students with the following definitions.

- *capable:* having the necessary qualities or abilities
- *dissipate:* to disappear or go away
- *suppress:* to slow or stop something from growing or developing
- *outlaw:* to make something illegal
- *appalling:* very bad to a shocking and disgusting extent
- *sympathize:* to feel sorry for someone
- *plight:* a very bad or difficult situation **ALL LEVELS**

The Downside of Industry During this period, England was an industrial as well as an agricultural country. The Industrial Revolution and improvements in farming brought increased prosperity to the middle and upper classes, but brought degrading poverty to the families employed in the factories and mills. Living and working conditions were appalling. There were no laws to regulate work safety, hours, wages, or child labor. At the time, Britain operated under the doctrine of *laissez-faire* economics, which means that an economy works best without government intervention.

Shortly after George III's son took control as regent, an economic depression resulted in the loss of many factory jobs. Advances in technology caused even more job losses, as fewer workers were needed to run textile mills. In the ensuing Luddite Riots, unemployed mill workers rioted, smashing the machines they blamed for taking their jobs. Frightened by the violence, Parliament, instead of working to solve the root causes of the violence, passed laws that made the rioters' actions punishable by death. Labor unions were illegal, and workers had little power in Parliament. Some workers organized anyway, but were quickly put down by the government.

The Romantics Romantic writers often sympathized with the oppressed lower classes and wrote about their plight. Lord Byron, a Romantic poet

RESEARCH
What about this historical period interests you? Choose a topic, event, or person to learn more about. Then add your own entry to the timeline.

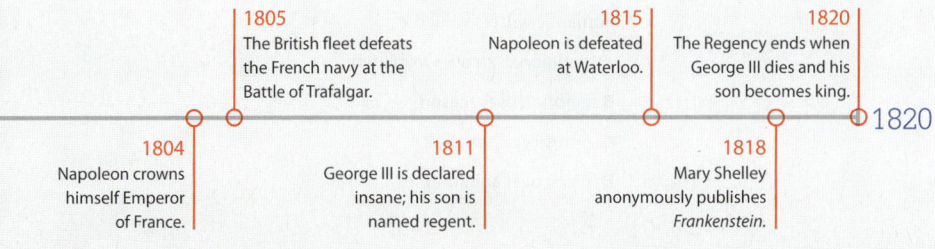

TEACH

War with France Britain's struggles against France during this period led to changes for Ireland that had far-reaching effects. Near the end of the 18th century, rebellious Irishmen, encouraged by the promise of French assistance, rose up against their British-controlled rulers. Though the rebellion was put down after poor weather prevented a major landing by the French, the threat of a French invasion of Britain, by way of Ireland, remained. Hoping to ease the situation, Prime Minister William Pitt persuaded Parliament to pass the Act of Union in 1800. Ireland would be represented in the British Parliament, and all the British Isles would be joined as the United Kingdom of Great Britain and Ireland.

The Downside of Industry High rates of unemployment due to newer and more efficient equipment were aggravated further by the return of veterans from the war with France after the decisive battle at Waterloo in 1815. In addition, to keep cheap foreign grain from glutting the market after the war, the government passed a Corn Law that taxed imported grain. These taxes protected the income of large landowners and small farmers, but they also devastated the poor and unemployed by keeping food prices high. Ask students to consider how what they have learned about Britain's policies at home during this time period connects to what they already know about Britain's policies toward the American colonies in the mid-1700s prior to the American Revolution.

RESEARCH

To learn more about their chosen topic, encourage students to search for primary sources from the historical period. Have students choose excerpts from a source to present to the class.

WHEN STUDENTS STRUGGLE . . .

Identify Cause and Effect Students may have difficulty tracing the sequence of events in Britain and France and understanding the relationships between events. Encourage students to look for cause-and-effect relationships between events occurring in the two countries. Students should first identify at least 2-3 events (causes) that took place in France. Then, for each event, students should identify at least one effect that the event had on Britain. Students may find it helpful to mark causes and effects in the text with different colors or to track them in a T-chart, with "Causes" on the left side and "Effects" on the right side.

TEACH

The Romantics Explain that the Romantic movement is generally divided into two parts, an earlier movement beginning in the 1780s and established by 1798 that included such poets as William Blake, William Wordsworth, and Samuel Taylor Coleridge; and a second generation of Romantic poets that arrived on the literary scene during the Regency, including Lord Byron, Percy Bysshe Shelley, and John Keats. Although one of the hallmarks of the Romantic period was the rich and emotionally intense works of its poets, the movement also included essayists, novelists, philosophers, and artists.

Some students will likely be familiar with Jane Austen, one of the most famous prose writers of the era. Tell students that although Romanticism dominated the literary scene from 1798 to 1832, Austen seems to have been largely untouched by the movement. Her work does contain Romantic elements in that it focuses on the details of daily life and is preoccupied with character and personality. In many ways, however, Austen remained a neoclassical writer.

CHECK YOUR UNDERSTANDING

Have students answer the questions independently.

Answers:

1. C
2. J
3. B

If students answer any question incorrectly, have them reread the text to confirm their understanding.

---

and a member of Parliament, openly expressed his sympathy for the poor to other members of the British government. In fact, he was one of only three members of Parliament to vote against the law punishing the Luddite rioters with death.

Such political efforts, however, yielded few results. Many of the Romantic writers reacted to the harsh realities of industrialization by turning to nature for truth and beauty. They revolted against the order, propriety, and traditionalism of the Age of Reason and rejected the classical tradition that venerated the achievements of ancient Greece and Rome. The Romantics were influenced by the same forces that gave rise to the American and French revolutions and by the agitation for political, social, and economic change taking place in their own country. For the Romantics, emotion became more important than reason. Thus, they preferred styles of writing that allowed self-expression, like lyric poetry, which came to dominate English literature during this time.

CHECK YOUR UNDERSTANDING

Choose the best answer to each question.

1. Which event caused many British citizens to lose sympathy for the French Revolution?
   A Britain's loss of the American colonies in an earlier revolution
   B The takeover of the French government by Napoleon Bonaparte
   C The execution of French aristocrats during the Reign of Terror
   D The defeat of the French navy by the British fleet

2. Which factor contributed most directly to the Luddite Riots?
   F Instigation by Romantic writers like Lord Byron
   G Appointment of George III's son as regent in his father's place
   H Discontent over the outlawed status of labor unions
   J Loss of factory jobs due to advances in technology

3. Romantic writers valued —
   A traditionalism over revolution
   B emotion over reason
   C industry over nature
   D order over agitation

ACADEMIC VOCABULARY

Academic Vocabulary words are words you use when you discuss and write about texts. In this unit, you will learn the following five words:

☑ appreciate ☐ insight ☐ intensity ☐ invoke ☐ radical

Study the Word Network to learn more about the word **appreciate**.

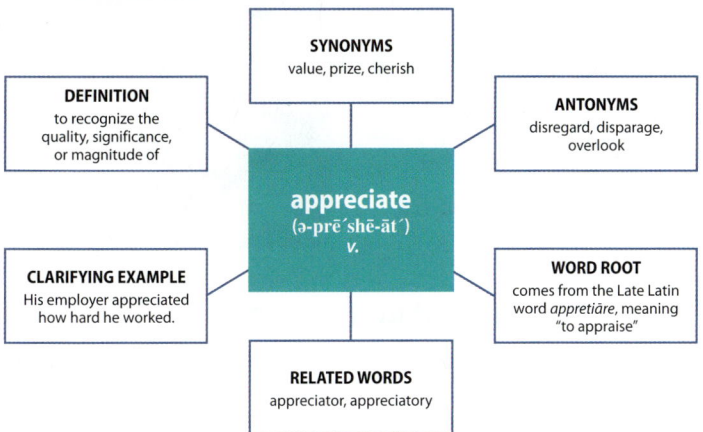

Write and Discuss Discuss your completed Word Network with a partner, making sure to talk through all of the boxes until you both understand the word, its synonyms, antonyms, and related forms. Then fill out a Word Network for the remaining four words. Use a dictionary or online resource to help you complete the activity.

 Go online to access the Word Networks.

RESPOND TO THE ESSENTIAL QUESTIONS

In this unit, you will explore four different **Essential Questions** about Emotion and Experimentation. As you read each selection, you will gather your ideas about one of these questions and write about it in a **Response Log**. At the end of the unit, you will have the opportunity to write an **explanatory essay** related to one of the Essential Questions. Filling out the Response Log after you read each text will help you prepare for this writing task.

 You can also go online to access the Response Log.

Emotion and Experimentation 495

PLAN

POEMS BY WILLIAM WORDSWORTH

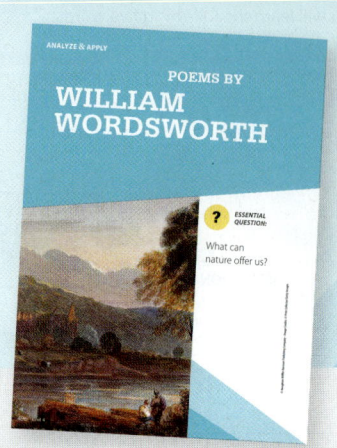

GENRE ELEMENTS
LYRIC POETRY

Tell students that lyric poetry is usually written in the first person and expresses the feelings and thoughts of the speaker. It uses sound devices to create a musical quality. **Romantic** lyric poetry uses strong **imagery** that appeals to the five senses: sight, hearing, smell, touch, and taste. In this lesson, students will analyze how imagery creates sensory experiences for the reader of romantic poetry.

LEARNING OBJECTIVES

- Analyze romantic poetry and imagery.
- Conduct research about places in England that were settings for Wordsworth's poems.
- Write a summary.
- Participate in a discussion.
- **Language** Identify the sense a spoken word appeals to.

TEXT COMPLEXITY

Quantitative Measures	Poems by William Wordsworth	Lexile: N/A
Qualitative Measures	**Ideas Presented** Multiple levels, use of symbolism.	
	Structures Used More complex, lyrical and poetic.	
	Language Used Implied meanings, allusive, figurative, and formal language. Complex sentence structures.	
	Knowledge Required Mostly familiar themes.	

PLAN

Online

RESOURCES

- Unit 4 Response Log
- 🔊 Selection Audio
- 📖 Reading Studio: Notice & Note
- 📈 Level Up Tutorial: Figurative Language
- ✏️ Writing Studio: Writing as a Process
- 💬 Speaking and Listening Studio: Participating in Collaborative Discussions
- ✓ "Poems by William Wordsworth" Selection Test

SUMMARIES

English

"Lines Composed a Few Miles Above Tintern Abbey" is a long meditative poem in which the speaker describes a lovely landscape that he first visited five years before and now revisits with his sister. "Composed upon Westminster Bridge, September 3, 1802" is a sonnet in which the speaker expresses pleasure in viewing London from a bridge in early morning. "I Wandered Lonely As a Cloud" is a lyric poem in which the speaker takes joy in encountering a field of daffodils and later finds comfort in recalling them.

Spanish

"Líneas compuestas unas millas arriba de Tintern Abbey" es un poema meditativo largo en el cual la voz narrativa describe un precioso paisaje que visitó hace cinco años y que ahora visita con su hermana. "Compuesto en el puente de Westminster, 3 de septiembre de 1802" es un soneto en que la voz narrativa se complace al ver Londres desde un puente, temprano en la mañana. "Deambulé solo como una nube" es un poema lírico en que la voz narrativa se alegra al encontrarse en un campo de narcisos y luego se conforta al recordarlos.

 SMALL-GROUP OPTIONS

Have students work in small groups and pairs to read and discuss the selections.

Activating Academic Vocabulary

- Provide a list of academic vocabulary words and phrases, such as: *speaker, image, appeals to my sense of, visual, hearing, sight, sound device, taste, touch, smell, figurative language, metaphor, simile, hyperbole, tone, word choice, make a connection between, line,* and *stanza.*
- After reading 10 lines of one of the poems, model how to use one or more academic vocabulary words and phrases to discuss the poems.
- Encourage students to use the academic vocabulary as they discuss and write about the poems.

Double-Entry Journal

- Have students use a notebook for recording their double-entry notes.
- Show students how to create a two-column format by drawing a line from top to bottom on each page. The left head should be *Quotes from the Poems,* and the right head should be *My Notes.*
- Encourage students to copy important or confusing lines or verses in the left column.
- Then, have students write their own questions, restatements, or interpretations in the right column next to the quoted material.

PLAN

 **Text X-Ray: English Learner Support**
for Poems by William Wordsworth

Use the Text X-Ray and the supports and scaffolds in the Teacher's Edition to help guide students at different proficiency levels through the selections.

INTRODUCE THE SELECTION

DISCUSS ROMANTICISM

In this lesson, students will need to be able to discuss the characteristics of a romantic poem.

Provide the following explanation:
- *Romanticism* is a 19th-century literary movement.
- *Romantic* poets wrote about personal experiences, often having to do with nature.

Point out the endings of the two terms, and pronounce the terms with students. Explain that the meaning of "romantic" as a literary term is different from the common meaning, which generally refers to a love relationship.

Have students discuss *romanticism* by providing sentence frames, such as: *If I were a romantic poet, I would write about _____. I prefer romanticism to realism because I like _____.*

CULTURAL REFERENCES

The following words or phrases may be unfamiliar to students:
- *Hermit* (Tintern Abbey, line 21): a person who lives alone and keeps himself or herself away from the rest of the world
- *City* (Westminster Bridge, line 4): refers to London
- *oft* (I Wandered, line 19): often

LISTENING

Identify Sensory Language

Review with students the five senses: sight, sound, taste, touch, and smell.

Use the following supports with students at varying proficiency levels:
- Have students write the senses on separate index cards. Slowly read aloud an example of each type of sensory language from the poems and have students hold up the card that names the sense the sensory language appeals to. Then, have them repeat the line you read. **SUBSTANTIAL**
- Direct one partner to read aloud one example of sensory language from one of the poems. Have the other partner tell which sense it appeals to. Have students switch roles and repeat the activity. **MODERATE**
- Direct one partner to read aloud an example of sensory language from one of the poems. Have the other partner tell which sense it appeals to. Have students switch roles and repeat the activity. Then, have them discuss which words helped them identify the sense. **LIGHT**

PLAN

SPEAKING

Rephrase Formal Language

Have students use a dictionary and thesaurus to help them find simpler, more informal words for formal language.

Use the following supports with students at varying proficiency levels:
- Rephrase the first four lines of "Lines Composed a Few Miles Above Tintern Abbey" in simpler language. Define any difficult words, such as *inland* and *murmur*. Have students repeat your rephrasing several times. For example: *Five long years have passed. Again I hear the soft sound of the mountain streams.* **SUBSTANTIAL**
- Have partners reread lines 1–14 of "Lines Composed a Few Miles Above Tintern Abbey" and rephrase them in simpler language. Then, ask *wh-* questions to monitor comprehension. For example: *Where is the speaker? What does he see?* **MODERATE**
- Have partners rephrase lines 1–22 of "Lines Composed a Few Miles Above Tintern Abbey" in simpler, less formal language. Have them discuss how changing formal language to informal language affects their response to the poem. **LIGHT**

READING

Use Accessible Language

Remind students that using a dictionary as they read can help them better understand the meaning of a poem.

Use the following supports with students at varying proficiency levels:
- Read lines 1–4 aloud and have students echo read only with you. **SUBSTANTIAL**
- Have students use drawings, accessible language, and peer support to create a dictionary for 10 unfamiliar words in the poems. Then, have students silently reread the poems, using their dictionaries. After reading, have students discuss how the dictionary helped them better understand the poem. **MODERATE**
- Have students use accessible language to create dictionaries for 10–15 unfamiliar words in the poems. Direct them to list synonyms for each word, in addition to definitions. **LIGHT**

WRITING

Describe Settings

Remind students that when they want to describe how a setting looks, sounds, and smells, they can use adjectives, which are words that describe nouns. Provide some simple examples, such as: *red, tall, loud, sweet*.

Use the following supports with students at varying proficiency levels:
- Have students name any adjectives they can think of, and record them in a list on the board. Discuss the sense each adjective appeals to. Then, provide sentence starters to help students use the adjectives, such as: _____ *can describe how a setting* _____. **SUBSTANTIAL**
- Have students write a list of adjectives to describe the setting in "Lines Composed a Few Miles Above Tintern Abbey." Have them write what sense each adjective appeals to. **MODERATE**
- Have students write a list of adjectives they could use to describe the setting in "Lines Composed a Few Miles Above Tintern Abbey." Then, have them write a list of nouns that are in the setting. **LIGHT**

TEACH

Connect to the
ESSENTIAL QUESTION

Discuss the Essential Question with students by asking them to define *nature*. Ask questions such as: What does nature mean to you? Can nature mean different things to different people? How has nature inspired people to do great things? Encourage students to reflect on their own experiences as they read Wordsworth's poems.

ANALYZE & APPLY

POEMS BY WILLIAM WORDSWORTH

 ESSENTIAL QUESTION:

What can nature offer us?

LEARNING MINDSET

Seeking Challenges Remind students that seeking challenges is an essential part of academic growth and that by taking on challenges, we give ourselves the chance to improve our abilities. Encourage students to view the poems in this selection as an opportunity to study something that may be unfamiliar and, in doing so, to learn new ways of thinking and viewing the world.

GET READY

QUICK START

Think about a time you were in nature and were fully absorbed in the present moment. What do you remember seeing, hearing, and smelling? How did it make you feel?

ANALYZE ROMANTIC POETRY

Romanticism was a literary movement that flourished in Britain and Europe in the 19th century. Unlike the neoclassical poets who preceded them, the Romantics emphasized the importance of the individual's subjective experiences rather than issues that concerned society as a whole. Their philosophy valued emotion, spontaneity, and imagination over reason, analysis, and orderliness.

Romantic poets wrote about personal experiences, often using simple, unadorned language. Many Romantic poems celebrate the beauty and grandeur of the natural world. The Romantics rejected the forces of industrialization that were beginning to transform Europe and tended to idealize the distant past. They looked to nature for inspiration and also for insight into their creative processes.

You are about to read three poems by William Wordsworth, one of the key figures of the Romantic movement. As you read, use a chart such as this one to note details that display the characteristics of Romantic poetry.

**GENRE ELEMENTS:
LYRIC POETRY**

- usually written in the first person
- expresses the feelings and thoughts of the speaker
- uses sound devices such as rhythm and repetition to create a musical quality
- often deals with intense emotions surrounding events like death, love, or loss

DETAILS FROM THE POEMS	CHARACTERISTICS OF ROMANTIC POETRY

TEACH

QUICK START

Begin the discussion with the class by asking students to share some of the places they think of when they think about their experiences in nature. Ask them which features of nature they enjoy most. Compare and contrast students' ideas.

ANALYZE ROMANTIC POETRY

Help students understand **Romanticism** by explaining the social context in which it came about. The urbanization of England gave rise to feelings of isolation and detachment among many in the late 18th and 19th centuries, including the Romantics, who rejected the changes that were taking place. They valued introspection, or the examination of oneself, and their focus on nature reflected their desire both to reconnect with a more idyllic way of life and to focus their attention on their own understanding. The shift from the language conventions of the neoclassicists to a simpler style, as well as the shift in focus to everyday life, reflected the Romantics' yearning for a more egalitarian society. Encourage students to look for these elements as they read the poems in this selection.

TEACH

ANALYZE IMAGERY

Remind students that **imagery** is any language that is used by an author to help the reader better imagine a scene. Point out that imagery focuses on sensory experiences. To demonstrate imagery, provide sentences with and without imagery, such as: "The airplane flew through the sky on a sunny day, " and "The shimmering airplane caught the sun as it spread its wings high above me." Emphasize that making careful observations about the use of imagery will help them understand the subject, mood, and theme of each poem.

■ English Learner Support

Use Imagery Have pairs of students take turns using **imagery** to describe a scene, with all five of the senses. Encourage them to provide suggestions to improve each other's sensory language. **MODERATE**

ANNOTATION MODEL

Point out that the annotation model on page 498 highlights **imagery** using underlines. Tell students that they may follow this suggestion or use their own system for marking up the selection in their write-in text. They may want to color-code their annotations by using highlighters. Their notes in the margin may include questions about ideas that are unclear, as well as their own ideas about what they are reading.

 **GET READY**

ANALYZE IMAGERY

Imagery is language that creates vivid sensory experiences for the reader. Visual imagery, which appeals to the sense of sight, is the most common form of imagery used in literature, but writers also use words and phrases to appeal to the senses of hearing, touch, smell, and taste to deepen their readers' understanding of and connection to their works. For example, in "Lines Composed a Few Miles Above Tintern Abbey," Wordsworth refers to the "soft inland murmur" of the Wye River. This auditory image describes the sound of the moving water and also suggests its calming effect.

As you read Wordsworth's poems, look for sensory language and create mental images of the sights and sounds of the landscapes and experiences the poet describes. Also notice how Wordsworth develops the subject, mood, and theme of each poem through imagery. Consider the following lines from "Lines Composed a Few Miles Above Tintern Abbey":

> Therefore let the moon
> Shine on thee in thy solitary walk;
> And let the misty mountain winds be free
> To blow against thee:

The visual image of the moon shining and the tactile image of the misty winds blowing against his sister as she walks alone help develop the solemn, reverent mood of the poem. This imagery also reflects the poet's ideas related to the spiritual nourishment that the natural world can provide and the importance of the individual's unique experience.

ANNOTATION MODEL NOTICE & NOTE

As you read, note passages in the poems that reflect characteristics of Romanticism, and examine how Wordsworth uses imagery to develop ideas about nature and the experiences of individuals. This model shows one reader's notes about "Lines Composed a Few Miles Above Tintern Abbey."

> Five years have passed; five summers, with the length
> Of five long winters! and again I hear
> <u>These waters, rolling from their mountain-springs</u>
> With a soft inland murmur. Once again
> Do I behold these steep and lofty cliffs,
> That on a <u>wild secluded scene impress</u>
> <u>Thoughts of more deep seclusion; and connect</u>
> The landscape with the quiet of the sky.

These images suggest the grandeur of the wilderness near Tintern Abbey.

The speaker draws a connection between the landscape and the turning inward of his thoughts.

BACKGROUND

William Wordsworth (1770–1850) helped launch the Romantic movement in England. Rebelling against the formal diction and lofty writings of many poets of the time, Wordsworth used simple language to celebrate subjects drawn mostly from nature and everyday life.

As a child, Wordsworth happily explored the countryside near his home. When he was seven, his mother died, and he was sent to boarding school. Fortunately, he was able to continue spending time outdoors there, developing his deep love for the natural world and writing poetry. He went to Cambridge University, graduating in 1791.

POEMS BY WILLIAM WORDSWORTH

A walking tour of France in 1790 interested Wordsworth in the political changes happening as a result of the French Revolution. In 1791 Wordsworth returned to France and fell in love with a French woman, Annette Vallon. Lacking money, he returned to England in 1792, but when war broke out between France and England he was prevented from reuniting with Annette and their newborn baby.

In 1795 Wordsworth and his sister set up a home together in a rural area in Dorset. There they befriended the poet Samuel Taylor Coleridge. Wordsworth and Coleridge collaborated on a book of poetry, Lyrical Ballads (1798), that ushered in the Romantic movement.

In many of his poems, Wordsworth describes specific natural settings and often shares his thoughts and feelings about them. In "Lines Composed a Few Miles Above Tintern Abbey," Wordsworth reflects on his memories of the beauty of the Wye River Valley in Wales, an area he hiked through extensively. Near this valley are the ruins of Tintern Abbey, a medieval monastery that captivated public imagination with its picturesque decay.

In 1802 Wordsworth married childhood friend Mary Hutchinson. Over the next two decades, he struggled to find readers and critical acceptance for his work. In the 1820s his reputation gradually improved, and by the 1830s he was hugely popular. In 1843 his immense achievement as a poet was recognized when he was named England's poet laureate.

TEACH

BACKGROUND

Wordsworth and his sister were traveling to the city of Bristol to see to the publication of *Lyrical Ballads* when they visited the area around Tintern Abbey. Wordsworth reportedly composed his poem mentally and memorized it while still traveling. On reaching Bristol, he wrote out the poem, and titled it "Lines Written a Few Miles Above Tintern Abbey, on Revisiting the Banks of the Wye During a Tour, July 13, 1798." He then added the poem to the manuscript of *Lyrical Ballads*. In later editions, Wordsworth changed the title from *Written* to *Composed*, as seen in the title on page 500. Discuss with students possible reasons for the change in wording.

TEACH

SETTING A PURPOSE

Direct students to use the Setting a Purpose prompt to focus their reading.

ANALYZE ROMANTIC POETRY

Point out that Wordsworth contrasts his feelings about the landscape with his feelings about city life. Ask students to look for words and phrases that indicate how he feels about life in the city. ("lonely rooms," "din/Of towns and cities," "weariness," "the heavy and the weary weight/ Of all this unintelligible world"). **(Answer:** *His memories of the landscape have helped him cope with the loneliness and stress of city life and have helped him connect to something meaningful.)*

> For **speaking support** and **writing support** for students at varying proficiency levels, see the **Text X-Ray** on page 496D.

NOTICE & NOTE

Notice & Note
Use the side margins to notice and note signposts in the text.

9 repose: lie at rest.

14 copses (kŏpˊsĭz): thickets of small trees.

16 pastoral (păsˊtər-əl): rural and serene.

20 vagrant: wandering.

ANALYZE ROMANTIC POETRY

Annotate: Mark words and phrases in lines 27–49 that describe the speaker's feelings about the landscape.

Analyze: Why are these feelings important for the speaker?

SETTING A PURPOSE

As you read, pay attention to the ideas expressed in the poems about how people are affected by nature and by city life. Also notice how Wordsworth uses imagery to appeal to the reader's senses.

Lines Composed a Few Miles Above Tintern Abbey

Five years have passed; five summers, with the length
Of five long winters! and again I hear
These waters, rolling from their mountain-springs
With a soft inland murmur. Once again
5 Do I behold these steep and lofty cliffs,
That on a wild secluded scene impress
Thoughts of more deep seclusion; and connect
The landscape with the quiet of the sky.
The day is come when I again repose
10 Here, under this dark sycamore, and view
These plots of cottage ground, these orchard tufts,
Which at this season, with their unripe fruits,
Are clad in one green hue, and lose themselves
'Mid groves and copses. Once again I see
15 These hedgerows, hardly hedgerows, little lines
Of sportive wood run wild; these pastoral farms,
Green to the very door; and wreaths of smoke
Sent up, in silence, from among the trees!
With some uncertain notice, as might seem
20 Of vagrant dwellers in the houseless woods,
Or of some Hermit's cave, where by his fire
The Hermit sits alone.

      These beauteous forms,
Through a long absence, have not been to me
As is a landscape to a blind man's eye;
25 But oft, in lonely rooms, and 'mid the din
Of towns and cities, I have owed to them,
In hours of weariness, sensations sweet,
Felt in the blood, and felt along the heart;
And passing even into my purer mind,
30 With tranquil restoration—feelings too
Of unremembered pleasure; such, perhaps,
As have no slight or trivial influence
On that best portion of a good man's life,
His little, nameless, unremembered, acts
35 Of kindness and of love. Nor less, I trust,
To them I may have owed another gift,

500   Unit 4

ENGLISH LEARNER SUPPORT

Retell Material Have students select two unfamiliar words in lines 1–22 and look up their definitions. Then, have them paraphrase the sentences these words are in. Encourage them to share their paraphrases with a partner and ask the partner to critique the paraphrase. **MODERATE**

Of aspect more sublime; that blessed mood,
In which the burthen of the mystery,
In which the heavy and the weary weight
40 Of all this unintelligible world,
Is lightened—that serene and blessed mood,
In which the affections gently lead us on—
Until, the breath of this corporeal frame
And even the motion of our human blood
45 Almost suspended, we are laid asleep
In body, and become a living soul;
While with an eye made quiet by the power
Of harmony, and the deep power of joy,
We see into the life of things.

                          If this
50 Be but a vain belief, yet, oh! how oft—
In darkness and amid the many shapes
Of joyless daylight; when the fretful stir
Unprofitable, and the fever of the world,
Have hung upon the beatings of my heart—
55 How oft, in spirit, have I turned to thee,
O sylvan Wye! thou wanderer through the woods,
How often has my spirit turned to thee!

    And now, with gleams of half-extinguished thought
With many recognitions dim and faint,
60 And somewhat of a sad perplexity,
The picture of the mind revives again;
While here I stand, not only with the sense
Of present pleasure, but with pleasing thoughts
That in this moment there is life and food
65 For future years. And so I dare to hope,
Though changed, no doubt, from what I was when first
I came among these hills; when like a roe
I bounded o'er the mountains, by the sides
Of the deep rivers, and the lonely streams,
70 Wherever nature led—more like a man
Flying from something that he dreads than one
Who sought the thing he loved. For nature then
(The coarser pleasures of my boyish days,
And their glad animal movements all gone by)
75 To me was all in all.—I cannot paint
What then I was. The sounding cataract
Haunted me like a passion; the tall rock,
The mountain, and the deep and gloomy wood,
Their colors and their forms, were then to me

NOTICE & NOTE

38 burthen: burden.

43 corporeal (kôr-pôr´ē-əl): bodily.

56 sylvan: located in a wood or forest; **Wye:** a river near Tintern Abbey.

67 roe: deer.

76 cataract (kăt´ə-răkt): waterfall.

ANALYZE IMAGERY
Annotate: Mark the auditory and visual imagery in lines 76–78.

Analyze: How does this imagery affect the reader's understanding of the speaker's experience?

Poems by William Wordsworth 501

TEACH

ENGLISH LEARNER SUPPORT

Acquire New Vocabulary Students may be unfamiliar with some of the vocabulary in lines 80–99. Provide the following definitions to aid their comprehension:

rapture (line 85): extreme happiness or joy
mourn (line 86): to be sad over loss
murmur (line 86): complain or grumble
subdue (line 93): overpower or keep under control
sublime (line 95): great or noble **SUBSTANTIAL**

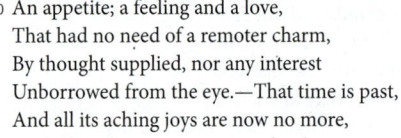

> 80 An appetite; a feeling and a love,
>   That had no need of a remoter charm,
>   By thought supplied, nor any interest
>   Unborrowed from the eye.—That time is past,
>   And all its aching joys are now no more,
> 85 And all its dizzy raptures. Not for this
>   Faint I, nor mourn nor murmur; other gifts
>   Have followed; for such loss, I would believe,
>   Abundant recompense. For I have learned
>   To look on nature, not as in the hour
> 90 Of thoughtless youth; but hearing oftentimes
>   The still, sad music of humanity,
>   Nor harsh nor grating, though of ample power
>   To chasten and subdue. And I have felt
>   A presence that disturbs me with the joy
> 95 Of elevated thoughts; a sense sublime
>   Of something far more deeply interfused,
>   Whose dwelling is the light of setting suns,
>   And the round ocean and the living air,

86 Faint I: I lose heart.

88 recompense (rĕk´əm-pĕns): compensation.

93 chasten (chā´sən): scold; make modest.

IMPROVE READING FLUENCY

Targeted Passage Tell students that the poem is written in blank verse, which uses iambic pentameter as the basic meter. Model how to read lines 83–88 in the cadence of iambic pentameter, using the unstressed/stressed syllable pattern. Then, either in pairs or small groups, have students take turns reading lines, beginning with line 88 "For I have learned. . ." Encourage students to provide feedback and support with pronunciation as each student reads.

Go to the **Reading Studio** for additional support in developing fluency.

And the blue sky, and in the mind of man:
100 A motion and a spirit, that impels
All thinking things, all objects of all thought,
And rolls through all things. Therefore am I still
A lover of the meadows and the woods,
And mountains; and of all that we behold
105 From this green earth; of all the mighty world
Of eye, and ear—both what they half create,
And what perceive; well pleased to recognize
In nature and the language of the sense
The anchor of my purest thoughts, the nurse,
110 The guide, the guardian of my heart, and soul
Of all my moral being.

    Nor perchance,
If I were not thus taught, should I the more
Suffer my genial spirits to decay:
For thou art with me here upon the banks
115 Of this fair river; thou my dearest Friend,

ANALYZE IMAGERY
Annotate: Mark images of nature in lines 93–102.
Analyze: How do these images support the speaker's idea about a force that affects all things?

111 perchance: by chance; perhaps.
113 genial (jēn´yəl): relating to genius; creative.
115 thou my dearest Friend: Wordsworth´s sister, Dorothy.

TEACH

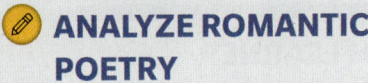

ANALYZE ROMANTIC POETRY

Remind students that one of the most important themes in Romantic literature is the beauty of nature. Also point out that Wordsworth is using personification (referring to nature as if it is a person) in lines 122–128. (**Answer:** *Nature has the power to teach people how to look beyond their everyday struggles and appreciate the true beauty of the world.*)

NOTICE & NOTE

ANALYZE ROMANTIC POETRY

Annotate: Mark the verbs used in lines 123–134 to describe nature's actions.

Analyze: What romantic idea does Wordsworth express in this passage?

146 exhortations: words of encouraging advice.

149 past existence: the speaker's own past experience five years before (see lines 116–119).

> My dear, dear Friend; and in thy voice I catch
> The language of my former heart, and read
> My former pleasures in the shooting lights
> Of thy wild eyes. Oh! yet a little while
> 120 May I behold in thee what I was once,
> My dear, dear Sister! and this prayer I make,
> Knowing that Nature never did betray
> The heart that loved her; 'tis her privilege,
> Through all the years of this our life, to <u>lead</u>
> 125 From joy to joy: for she can so <u>inform</u>
> The mind that is within us, so <u>impress</u>
> With quietness and beauty, and so <u>feed</u>
> With lofty thoughts, that neither evil tongues,
> Rash judgments, nor the sneers of selfish men,
> 130 Nor greetings where no kindness is, nor all
> The dreary intercourse of daily life,
> Shall e'er prevail against us, or disturb
> Our cheerful faith, that all which we behold
> Is full of blessings. Therefore let the <u>moon</u>
> 135 <u>Shine on thee</u> in thy solitary walk;
> <u>And let the misty mountain winds be free</u>
> <u>To blow against thee</u>: and, in after years,
> When these wild ecstasies shall be matured
> Into a sober pleasure; when thy mind
> 140 Shall be a mansion for all lovely forms,
> Thy memory be as a dwelling place
> For all sweet sounds and harmonies; oh! then,
> If solitude, or fear, or pain, or grief
> Should be thy portion, with what healing thoughts
> 145 Of tender joy wilt thou remember me,
> And these my exhortations! Nor, perchance—
> If I should be where I no more can hear
> Thy voice, nor catch from thy wild eyes these gleams
> Of past existence—wilt thou then forget
> 150 That on the banks of this delightful stream
> We stood together; and that I, so long
> A worshiper of Nature, hither came
> Unwearied in that service; rather say
> With warmer love—oh! with far deeper zeal
> 155 Of holier love. Nor wilt thou then forget,
> That after many wanderings, many years
> Of absence, these steep woods and lofty cliffs,
> And this green pastoral landscape, were to me
> More dear, both for themselves and for thy sake!

504   Unit 4

APPLYING ACADEMIC VOCABULARY

☑ **appreciate**   ☐ insight   ☐ intensity   ☑ **invoke**   ☐ radical

Write and Discuss Have students turn to a partner to discuss the following questions. Guide students to include the academic vocabulary words *appreciate* and *invoke* in their responses. Ask volunteers to share their responses with the class

- Why does Wordsworth think he **appreciates** nature more now than in his youth?
- What does Wordsworth **invoke** in his prayer in line 121?

CHECK YOUR UNDERSTANDING

Answer these questions about "Lines Composed a Few Miles Above Tintern Abbey" before moving on to the next selection.

1. How did the speaker's memories of the valley affect him during the past five years?
   A They tormented him.
   B They restored his spirit.
   C They made him resent city life.
   D They caused him to avoid nature.

2. What has the speaker lost since he last visited the valley?
   F His ability to run up the mountains
   G His memory of where the ruined abbey stood
   H His career in the city
   J His passionate reaction to nature

3. What does the speaker observe in his sister?
   A She responds to nature the same way he used to.
   B She fears hurting herself in the valley.
   C She shares his memories of the valley.
   D She behaves recklessly on their hike.

TEACH

CHECK YOUR UNDERSTANDING

Have students answer the questions independently.

Answers:

1. B
2. J
3. A

If they answer any questions incorrectly, have them reread the text to confirm their understanding. Then they may proceed to the next selection on page 506.

ENGLISH LEARNER SUPPORT

Oral Assessment Use the following questions to assess students' comprehension and speaking skills.

1. Did memories of the valley help the speaker? *(yes)*

2. Does the speaker still enjoy the valley? *(He reacts less passionately to nature but appreciates its beauty more deeply.)*

3. The speaker's _____ is like the poet when he was younger. *(sister)* **ALL LEVELS**

TEACH

✏️ ANALYZE ROMANTIC POETRY

Help students recognize the superlative way the poet describes his feelings. Point out the repetition of the word *Ne'er/never* and the exclamation point. (**Answer:** *The language conveys Wordsworth's deep love for nature. It shows how nature is a calming influence on him in the chaos of the industrial world.*)

NOTICE & NOTE

Composed upon Westminster Bridge, September 3, 1802

ANALYZE ROMANTIC POETRY

Annotate: Mark language in lines 9–14 that conveys the emotions of the speaker.

Analyze: What emotions does this language convey?

9 steep: soak; saturate.

12 The river: Westminster Bridge spans the Thames (tĕmz)—the principal river in London.

13 houses: possibly a pun on the Houses of Parliament, near Westminster Bridge.

Earth has not anything to show more fair:
Dull would he be of soul who could pass by
A sight so touching in its majesty;
This City now doth, like a garment, wear
5 The beauty of the morning; silent, bare,
Ships, towers, domes, theaters, and temples lie
Open unto the fields, and to the sky;
All bright and glittering in the smokeless air.
Never did sun more beautifully steep
10 In his first splendor, valley, rock, or hill;
Ne'er saw I, never felt, a calm so deep!
The river glideth at his own sweet will:
Dear God! the very houses seem asleep;
And all that mighty heart is lying still!

506   Unit 4

WHEN STUDENTS STRUGGLE . . .

Analyze Imagery Remind students that a simile is a comparison between unlike things using the words *like* or *as*. Then, have students identify the simile in lines 4–5 ("This City now doth, like a garment, wear/The beauty of the morning; silent, bare, . . .") Ask them what the City is "wearing." (*the beauty of the morning*)

📖 For additional support, go to the **Reading Studio** and assign the following **Level Up tutorial: Figurative Language.**

CHECK YOUR UNDERSTANDING

Answer these questions about "Composed upon Westminster Bridge, September 3, 1802" before moving on to the next selection.

1. What time of day does "Composed Upon Westminster Bridge, September 3, 1802" describe?

   A Dawn

   B Dusk

   C Midnight

   D Midday

2. Which of the following best describes the speaker's meaning in lines 2 and 3?

   F He prefers being in the city to being in nature.

   G He believes people should stop to appreciate the world around them.

   H He thinks his soul is better than the souls of other people.

   J He feels saddened by the majestic view.

3. How does the scene he describes in the poem make the speaker feel?

   A Excited

   B Melancholy

   C Peaceful

   D Disappointed

Poems by William Wordsworth 507

TEACH

CHECK YOUR UNDERSTANDING

Have students answer the questions independently.

Answers:

1. A
2. G
3. C

If they answer any questions incorrectly, have them reread the text to confirm their understanding. Then, they may proceed to the next selection on page 508.

ENGLISH LEARNER SUPPORT

Oral Assessment Use the following questions to assess students' comprehension and speaking skills.

1. The poet is writing about a _____. (city)

2. Does the poet write about the city in the morning, afternoon, or night? (morning)

3. The scene makes the speaker feel _____. (calm) **ALL LEVELS**

TEACH

ANALYZE IMAGERY

Point out that Wordsworth describes the daffodils as "dancing," and then discuss what impression this creates. (**Answer:** *It conveys a vivid impression of so many colorful flowers moving in the wind.*)

ENGLISH LEARNER SUPPORT

Identify Affixes Tell students that the suffix *-ly* signals either an adjective or an adverb. Remind them that adverbs modify verbs, while adjectives modify nouns. Ask students to identify how the word "sprightly" is used in line 12. **MODERATE**

 **NOTICE & NOTE**

I Wandered Lonely As a Cloud

I wandered lonely as a cloud
That floats on high o'er vales and hills,
When all at once I saw a crowd,
A host, of golden daffodils;
5   Beside the lake, beneath the trees,
Fluttering and dancing in the breeze.

Continuous as the stars that shine
And twinkle on the milky way,
They stretched in never-ending line
10 Along the margin of a bay:
Ten thousand saw I at a glance,
Tossing their heads in sprightly dance.

The waves beside them danced; but they
Outdid the sparkling waves in glee;
15 A poet could not but be gay,
In such a jocund company;
I gazed—and gazed—but little thought
What wealth the show to me had brought:

2 vales: valleys.

ANALYZE IMAGERY
Annotate: Mark the imagery that describes nature in lines 1–12.
Analyze: How do these images help the reader understand the speaker's experience?

16 jocund (jŏk´ənd): merry.

508   Unit 4

TO CHALLENGE STUDENTS...

Research Context Have students do research into the origin of "I Wandered Lonely as a Cloud" in order to answer the following questions: When and where was this poem written? What inspired Wordsworth to compose the poem? When was the final version of the poem published? Ask students to share any thoughts or conclusions they have about the poem based on the information they gathered.

For oft, when on my couch I lie
20 In vacant or in pensive mood,
They flash upon that inward eye
Which is the bliss of solitude;
And then my heart with pleasure fills,
And dances with the daffodils.

CHECK YOUR UNDERSTANDING

Answer these questions before moving on to the **Analyze the Text** section on the following page.

1 What sight captures the speaker's attention in "I Wandered Lonely As a Cloud"?

A Clouds

B Daffodils

C Dancers

D Waves

2 The tone of the poem is best described as —

F lonely

G joyful

H solemn

J humorous

3 What does Wordsworth mean in line 21 when he says that the daffodils "flash upon that inward eye"?

A They remind him that he is alone.

B They keep him awake at night.

C They make him feel pensive.

D They appear in his imagination.

TEACH

CHECK YOUR UNDERSTANDING

Have students answer the questions independently.

Answers:

1. B

2. G

3. D

If they answer any questions incorrectly, have them reread the text to confirm their understanding. Then, they may proceed to ANALYZE THE TEXT on page 510.

ENGLISH LEARNER SUPPORT

Oral Assessment Use the following questions to assess students' comprehension and speaking skills.

1. In the poem, the speaker describes _____. *(daffodils)*

2. The daffodils make the speaker feel_____. *(Possible answers: happy, joyful, gleeful, "gay," "jocund")*

3. Does the speaker picture the daffodils in his mind? *(yes)*
   ALL LEVELS

APPLY

ANALYZE THE TEXT

Possible answers:

1. **DOK 4:** Wordsworth shares personal experiences of nature and provides subjective emotional responses to it. He celebrates "vagrant dwellers" (line 20) and a hermit (lines 21–22), individuals outside accepted society.

2. **DOK 3:** He used to react passionately to the beauty of nature, without thinking about it; now his response is more measured and he draws pleasure by thinking about how nature has affected his life.

3. **DOK 4:** In lines 4–5, Wordsworth describes the city as a person putting on the beauty of the morning like a garment. The personification helps readers visualize how the morning light adds beauty to the city.

4. **DOK 2:** He didn't appreciate how much pleasure this sight would bring to him later in life when he remembered the scene.

5. **DOK 4:** They all celebrate something exciting or unexpected that the speaker encounters outdoors; they strongly express an individual's emotional response to a personal experience; and they are all written using plain language.

RESEARCH

Remind students to evaluate sources for reliability before using them. Westminster Bridge and Tintern Abbey are both well-known landmarks, and there are many informational sources available for researching them. Recommend that students look for government or scholarly websites as they research these places.

Extend Advise students that the Lake District is now a national park in England. Encourage students to use the park's official website in their research.

510   Unit 4

RESPOND

ANALYZE THE TEXT

Support your responses with evidence from the text. NOTEBOOK

1. **Analyze** What details in lines 1–22 of "Lines Composed a Few Miles Above Tintern Abbey" suggest that Wordsworth preferred to celebrate the individual in his work rather than society?

2. **Draw Conclusions** In "Lines Composed a Few Miles Above Tintern Abbey," how has the speaker's relationship with nature changed over time?

3. **Analyze** How does Wordsworth use imagery in "Composed upon Westminster Bridge, September 3, 1802" to support the mood and theme of the poem?

4. **Interpret** Reread lines 17–24 of "I Wandered Lonely As a Cloud." What is the "wealth" that the speaker doesn't initially appreciate when he sees the daffodils?

5. **Synthesize** Which characteristics of romanticism do all three of these poems share?

RESEARCH

RESEARCH TIP
Before you begin researching, identify keywords from the research prompt to help start your online search.

Tintern Abbey and Westminster Bridge are real places in England. With a partner, research these places to find out more about them.

- Read some background information about the history of these places.
- Search for images so you can see what each place looks like.
- Do a map search so you can see where the locations are in reference to the rest of England.

Use a chart like the one below to record the results of your research.

PLACE	HISTORY	APPEARANCE	LOCATION
Tintern Abbey	The abbey was used from 1131 to 1536.	Large stone ruin with arched windows.	Near the Wye river in Wales.
Westminster Bridge	Proposed in 1664, the bridge was not finished until 1747 due to opposition.	The bridge is an arch bridge. It used to be made of stone arches. Iron is now used.	The bridge is in Central London, crossing the Thames River at Parliament.

Extend The poem "I Wandered Lonely As a Cloud" describes the scenery of the Lake District, another real place in England. Research the Lake District, add a row to your chart, and record information about its history, appearance, and location.

510   Unit 4

LEARNING MINDSET

Asking for Help Encourage students to ask peers, teachers, parents, or other responsible adults for help. Explain that asking for help from others will allow them to get "unstuck" and move forward. Reinforce that asking for help does not equal failure. Rather, seeking help is a way of "trying smarter."

RESPOND

CREATE AND DISCUSS

Write a Summary Write a summary of "Lines Composed a Few Miles Above Tintern Abbey." To do this, you will briefly retell the events and experiences described in the poem in your own words.

- ❏ Introduce the speaker and the other people mentioned in the poem.
- ❏ Describe the setting of the poem, and explain the effect it has on the speaker.
- ❏ Explain how the imagery in the poem engages the reader's senses and conveys meaning.
- ❏ Include a statement of the poem's theme, or central message.

Discuss Consider the ideas Wordsworth expresses in his poetry about nature and the comfort it can provide. With a partner, discuss any of your own experiences in nature that you've found meaningful or helpful in your life.

- ❏ Listen thoughtfully as your partner tells you about his or her experiences.
- ❏ Ask questions about any ideas or details that are unclear or need elaboration.
- ❏ Brainstorm to come up with ideas as to how you and your partner might seek out additional meaningful experiences in nature.

Go to the **Writing Studio: Writing as a Process** for more help with writing a summary.

Go to **Participating in Collaborative Discussions** in the **Speaking and Listening Studio** for more help.

RESPOND TO THE ESSENTIAL QUESTION

 What can nature offer us?

Gather Information Review your annotations and notes on the poems by William Wordsworth. Then, add relevant information to your Response Log. As you determine which information to include, think about:

- the mental and emotional solace Wordsworth finds in nature
- the role of memory in Wordsworth's poems
- what you value about your own memories of experiences with nature

ACADEMIC VOCABULARY

As you write and discuss what you learned from the poem, be sure to use the Academic Vocabulary words. Check off each of the words that you use.

- ❏ appreciate
- ❏ insight
- ❏ intensity
- ❏ invoke
- ❏ radical

APPLY

CREATE AND DISCUSS

Write a Summary Review with students the characteristics of Romanticism on page 497 and tell them to keep these characteristics in mind as they write their summaries. Encourage them to provide details and examples to support their statements

Discuss Encourage students to describe not only the natural settings they have experienced but also the feelings that being in nature produced. Have them compare their feelings to those Wordsworth describes in his poetry.

RESPOND TO THE ESSENTIAL QUESTION

Allow time for students to add details from "Poems by William Wordsworth" to their Unit 4 Response Logs.

PLAN

ODE ON A GRECIAN URN
Poem by John Keats

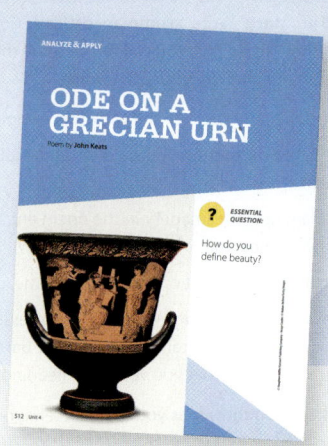

GENRE ELEMENTS
ODE
Explain that an **ode** is a lyric poem with a serious tone that develops a single theme and appeals to both the imagination and the intellect. Point out that odes often address a place or thing as though it were a person. The speaker in an ode speaks directly to the place or thing, giving it praise or thanks. Adjectives describe the place or thing, and verbs bring it to life. An ode often repeats lines, which gives it a particular rhythm. In this lesson, students will analyze how a poet uses apostrophe in an ode.

LEARNING OBJECTIVES
- Analyze stanza structure, rhyme scheme, and apostrophe.
- Conduct research about John Keats' connection to ancient Greece.
- Write a poem using apostrophe.
- Present a poem.
- **Language** Discuss and use ideas for apostrophes.

TEXT COMPLEXITY

Quantitative Measures	**Ode on a Grecian Urn**	Lexile: N/A
Qualitative Measures	**Ideas Presented** Abstract ideas and use of apostrophe and symbolism.	
	Structures Used Ode structure.	
	Language Used Figurative, archaic, and formal language; complex sentence structures.	
	Knowledge Required Cultural and historical references make heavier demands.	

PLAN

RESOURCES

Online

- Unit 4 Response Log
- 🔊 Selection Audio
- 📖 Reading Studio: Notice & Note
- 📊 Level Up Tutorials: Figurative Language; Imagery
- 📝 Writing Studio: Writing as a Process
- 💬 Speaking and Listening Studio: Giving a Presentation
- ✓ "Ode on a Grecian Urn" Selection Test

SUMMARIES

English
The speaker of this poem contemplates the scenes and figures depicted on a Grecian urn, as well as the immortality that the urn affords to the figures. The poet uses apostrophe to address both the urn itself and the figures portrayed on it.

Spanish
La voz narrativa de este poema contempla las escenas y figuras representadas en una urna griega, además de la inmortalidad que la urna le da a las figuras. El poeta utiliza apóstrofes para dirigirse a la urna y las figuras.

SMALL-GROUP OPTIONS

Have students work in small groups and pairs to read and discuss the selection.

Reciprocal Teaching
- Have students read the poem.
- After reading, ask students to write three to five questions about the poem, using these stems: *What does the poet mean by _____? Why did the poet _____? How does the poet use _____ to _____? How does the _____ affect the _____?*
- Form teams of three students.
- Have each student offer two questions for group discussion.
- Direct the groups to reach consensus on the answers and find supporting text evidence.

Think-Pair-Share
- After students read the poem, pose these questions: *If you made a film of this poem, what images would you use? Why?*
- Have students think about the questions individually and make notes.
- Then, have pairs listen, discuss, and formulate a shared response to the questions. Direct them to include at least two reasons to support their chosen images.
- Finally, have pairs share their responses with the class.

Ode on a Grecian Urn **512B**

PLAN

Text X-Ray: English Learner Support
for "Ode on a Grecian Urn"

Use the Text X-Ray and the supports and scaffolds in the Teacher's Edition to help guide students at different proficiency levels through the selection.

INTRODUCE THE SELECTION
DISCUSS BEAUTY AND TRUTH

In this lesson, students will need to be able to discuss the concepts of beauty and truth as they relate to the meaning of a poem. Provide the following explanations:

- *Beauty* refers to the pleasing qualities of something.
- *Truth* is something factual or believable.

Write word families for both terms on the board. For example: *beauty, beautiful, beautifully; truth, truthful, true, truly*. Have students practice using these words in sentences.

Then, have students use the terms to discuss the relationship between beauty and truth in art. Ask questions, such as: *What beautiful art have you seen? What truth did you learn from that art?* Provide sentence frames, such as:
I saw _____ and it was beautiful because _____. I learned something true from _____ because _____.

CULTURAL REFERENCES

The following words or phrases may be unfamiliar to students:

- *unravish'd bride* (line 1): still a virgin even though she is married
- *foster-child* (line 2): not a natural-born child
- *mad pursuit* (line 9): crazy thing to do

LISTENING

Take Dictation

Remind students that an ode sounds pleasing when read aloud because of its rhythm and rhyme scheme. Direct students to listen for rhyming sounds as you read the poem aloud.

Use the following supports with students at varying proficiency levels:

- Read the first eight lines of the poem aloud, emphasizing any rhyming words. Then, slowly reread each line. Have students write down the rhyming words they hear. After reading, write the rhyming words on the board and have students make corrections to their work, as needed. **SUBSTANTIAL**

- Have one student read lines 1–8 to another. Then, have the speaker slowly reread the lines, while the listener writes down any rhyming words he or she hears. Direct listeners to ask speakers to repeat words as needed. Then, have them switch roles and repeat the activity for lines 11–20. Have them check their work and make any necessary corrections. **MODERATE**

- Have one student read lines 1–8 to another. Then, have the speaker slowly reread the lines, while the listener writes down any rhyming words he or she hears. Direct listeners to ask speakers to repeat words as needed. Then, have them switch roles and repeat the activity for the entire poem, taking turns reading and listening to 8–10 lines at a time. When they have finished reading, have them check their work and make any necessary corrections. **LIGHT**

PLAN

SPEAKING

Discuss Apostrophes

Remind students that they can write an apostrophe about any common object. Recite the lines of "Twinkle, Twinkle, Little Star" as an example: *Twinkle, twinkle, little star, How I wonder what you are. Up above the world so high, Like a diamond in the sky.*

Use the following supports with students at varying proficiency levels:

- Have students name classroom objects, and list their responses on the board. Have students copy the name of each object and sketch its image. Have students point to their images and say one or two words to them. For example: *You are _____.* **SUBSTANTIAL**
- Have partners point to classroom objects and speak to them using sentences frames, such as: *Why are you _____? I think _____.* Guide them to try to express strong emotions. **MODERATE**
- Have partners choose a classroom object and hold a discussion with it. Have them address it in the style of a romantic poet and use sensory language to ask it questions about its life. For example: *Oh, slender and intelligent pencil! How do you feel about waking up each day in my soft and cozy backpack?* **LIGHT**

READING

Adapt Text

Provide students with simplified versions of the poem that include summaries of each stanza.

Use the following supports with students at varying proficiency levels:

- Have students echo read the simplified version of the poem with you. **SUBSTANTIAL**
- Have students record themselves reading Keats's poem. Next, have them practice reading the simplified poem and make several recordings of it until fluency improves. Then have them read and record Keats's poem again. Have them discuss how their fluency improved and why. **MODERATE**
- Have students record themselves reading Keats's poem several times. Have them chart and discuss their fluency rates. **LIGHT**

WRITING

Vary Sentence Lengths

Before students write their descriptions for the Quick Start activity on page 513, remind them to vary their sentence lengths.

Use the following supports with students at varying proficiency levels:

- Provide a classroom object to describe. Have students use one or two words to describe the object. For example: *red, blue, painting.* **SUBSTANTIAL**
- Provide a classroom object to describe. Write on the board several sentences of different lengths about the object. Then have partners use the sentences to help them write a brief description. After writing, have them read their descriptions to each other and then revise sentence lengths to make the descriptions sound smoother. **MODERATE**
- Have students read their descriptions to a partner. Then have them discuss the rhythm and flow of the writing. Encourage partners to give suggestions for revising sentence length to make the writing sound smoother and more like natural speech. **LIGHT**

TEACH

Connect to the
ESSENTIAL QUESTION

Explain to students that "Ode on a Grecian Urn" addresses the subject of beauty. Keats tries to express what it is about this urn that captures his attention and moves him. At the end, he offers a simple definition of beauty as the message he receives from the urn.

Ask students to think about what Keats defines as beauty and whether they think beauty is an objective quality that can be defined or whether it is a subjective, individual experience. Invite students to write down their own ideas about what beauty is.

ANALYZE & APPLY

ODE ON A GRECIAN URN

Poem by **John Keats**

ESSENTIAL QUESTION:

How do you define beauty?

QUICK START

Write a description of your favorite artwork or a prized possession. Discuss the feelings you associate with this object and why you find it so appealing. Include at least four sensory details in your description.

ANALYZE STANZA STRUCTURE

A **stanza** is a group of lines that form a unit in a poem. In traditional poetic forms, stanzas often contain the same number of lines and have the same rhyme scheme and meter. Stanzas often function like paragraphs in prose, each presenting a discrete idea.

Although odes can vary in structure, the five stanzas of "Ode on a Grecian Urn" have a regular structure of ten lines of **iambic pentameter,** a metrical pattern of five feet, or units. Each iambic foot consists of two syllables, the first unstressed and the second stressed.

> Thou still unravish'd bride of quietness,
>
> Thou foster-child of silence and slow time,

Keats sometimes varies the meter to emphasize certain words and to keep the poem from sounding monotonous. You can gain insight into the meaning of the poem by reading it aloud and noticing which words are stressed. As you read, also notice the main idea expressed in each stanza.

ANALYZE RHYME SCHEME

The **rhyme scheme** of a poem is the pattern of **end rhyme** that helps establish the structure and unity of a stanza and adds to the poem's musicality. A rhyme scheme is described using letters, such as *abab* or *aabb*, where lines that rhyme are given the same letter. Certain poetic forms, such as the various types of sonnets, follow a set rhyme scheme.

Keats's "Ode on a Grecian Urn" has a complex rhyme scheme. The first four lines of each stanza rhyme *abab*. The next six lines follow one of these patterns: *cdedce, cdeced,* or *cdecde*. Because of these variations, the rhyming becomes subtler and more unexpected as you move farther along in a stanza. While reading the poem, notice how the rhyme scheme appeals to your sense of hearing.

GET READY

GENRE ELEMENTS: ODE

- lyric poem that develops a single theme
- has a serious tone
- appeals to both the imagination and the intellect
- may commemorate an event or praise people or nature's beauty

TEACH

QUICK START

Make sure students understand that they should choose a specific object, such as a work of art or something that they own, rather than a category of objects. For example, rather than writing about bicycles in general, they should write about their own particular bicycle. Direct students to write about that object's sensory qualities using concrete and specific details.

ANALYZE STANZA STRUCTURE

To help students understand the components of **stanza** structure, use visuals that show syllables as building blocks to feet, feet as building blocks to lines, and lines as building blocks to stanzas. Read aloud the sample lines on page 513, and have students mark the stressed syllables by clapping or tapping their fingers on their desks. Explain that marking the meter of poetry in this way can help them hear the words the way the author intended. Point out that each stanza has a main idea and that by noting the main idea in each stanza, they can determine the overall **theme** of the poem.

ANALYZE RHYME SCHEME

Read aloud the information about **rhyme scheme** on page 513. Make sure students understand that *scheme* means "pattern." Explain that a poem's rhyme scheme is the pattern of **end rhymes,** or rhyming syllables that fall at the ends of lines. The rhyme scheme of a poem is designated by assigning a letter of the alphabet to each line, beginning with *a*. Lines that rhyme are given the same letter. The rhyme scheme of a poem makes it easier to memorize and adds a musical quality to the poem.

TEACH

ANALYZE APOSTROPHE

Read aloud the information on **apostrophe.** Clarify that the word *apostrophe* as a literary term is different from the punctuation mark used to indicate possessives. Point out that an apostrophe, in this case, is a figure of speech, and ask students to name other figures of speech they have learned about *(metaphor, simile, personifications, etc.).* Explain to students that this literary device is often used to express an admiration for nature, especially among the romantic poets.

ENGLISH LEARNER SUPPORT

Acquire Grade-Level Vocabulary Point out that "Ode on a Grecian Urn" is written in the second person, as Keats is addressing the subject he is talking about. Explain that he uses archaic language, including the archaic pronouns *thou* and *thy.*

Write the following pronouns and their modern equivalents on the board:

thou–you
thy–your
thine–yours

Pronounce each of these pronouns and have students echo you. Suggest to students that they may wish to annotate their write-in texts when they see these words, to indicate their modern equivalents.
ALL LEVELS

 ANNOTATION MODEL

Explain that one way to annotate a poem is to note the figures of speech, such as **apostrophe,** that the author uses. Point out that students may follow the suggested annotation method or use their own system for marking up the selection in their write-in texts. They may want to color-code their annotations by using highlighters. Their notes in the margin may include questions about ideas that are unclear or their own observations about the poem.

 **GET READY**

ANALYZE APOSTROPHE

Apostrophe is a figure of speech in which the speaker addresses an object, abstract concept, or absent or imaginary person as if present and able to understand. Poets often use apostrophe to express strong emotions. This device was especially popular among the Romantic poets. In "Ode on a Grecian Urn," Keats uses apostrophe to address both the urn itself and the figures portrayed on it.

> O Attic shape! Fair attitude! with brede
> Of marble men and maidens overwrought,

Here the speaker addresses the urn as one might speak to an admired person, heightening the reader's sense of his emotional response to seeing the urn. As you read the poem, pay attention to the shifting focus of the apostrophe.

ANNOTATION MODEL   **NOTICE & NOTE**

As you read, note words and phrases that convey ideas about the artwork discussed in the poem. Also notice how the rhyme scheme and meter emphasize important words. In the model, you can see one reader's notes about the opening lines of "Ode on a Grecian Urn."

> Thou still <u>unravish'd bride</u> of quietness,
> Thou <u>foster-child</u> of silence and slow time,
> <u>Sylvan historian</u>, who canst thus express
> A flowery tale more sweetly than our rhyme:
> What leaf-fring'd legend haunts about thy shape
> Of deities or mortals, or of both,
> In Tempe or the dales of Arcady?
> What men or gods are these? What maidens loath?
> What mad pursuit? What struggle to escape?
> What pipes and timbrels? What wild ecstasy?

The speaker uses phrases that compare the urn to specific types of people. This helps give the impression that he is addressing something that can understand him.

BACKGROUND

John Keats (1795–1821) only lived to age 25, yet he produced some of the most famous poems in the English language. Keats's life was marred by illness and tragedy. His father died in a riding accident when he was young. Later, both his mother and brother died of tuberculosis, and Keats himself became ill with the disease at 22. His poor health prevented him from marrying his sweetheart, Fanny Brawne. It was during his illness, however, that he produced some of his greatest work. "Ode on a Grecian Urn" was probably inspired by ancient Greek urns that Keats saw at the British Museum. Such urns were often painted with mythological scenes, as described in this poem.

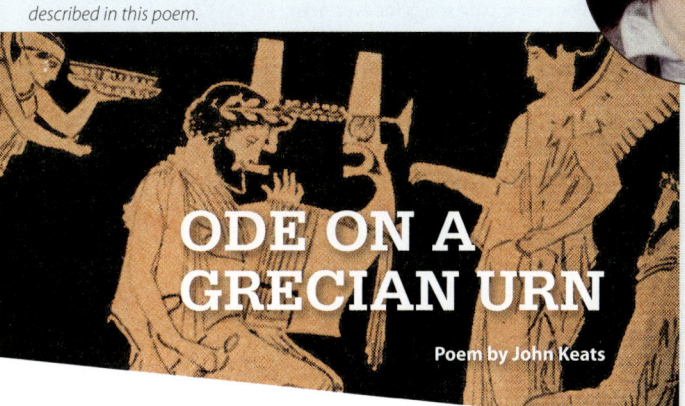

ODE ON A GRECIAN URN

Poem by John Keats

SETTING A PURPOSE

As you read, notice the ideas that the speaker associates with images on the urn.

Thou still unravish'd bride of quietness,
    Thou foster-child of silence and slow time,
Sylvan historian, who canst thus express
    A flowery tale more sweetly than our rhyme:
5 What leaf-fring'd legend haunts about thy shape
    Of deities or mortals, or of both,
      In Tempe or the dales of Arcady?
    What men or gods are these? What maidens loath?
What mad pursuit? What struggle to escape?
10   What pipes and timbrels? What wild ecstasy?

Heard melodies are sweet, but those unheard   A
    Are sweeter; therefore, ye soft pipes, play on;   B
Not to the sensual ear, but, more endear'd,   A
    Pipe to the spirit ditties of no tone;   B
15 Fair youth, beneath the trees, thou canst not leave   C
    Thy song, nor ever can those trees be bare;   D

Notice & Note

Use the side margins to notice and note signposts in the text.

3 **Sylvan:** pertaining to trees or woods.

5 **haunts about:** surrounds.

7 **Tempe** (tĕm´pē) . . . **Arcady** (är´kə-dē): two places in Greece that became traditional literary settings for an idealized rustic life. Tempe is a beautiful valley; Arcady (Arcadia) is a mountainous region.

8 **loath:** unwilling; reluctant.

10 **timbrels:** tambourines.

Ode on a Grecian Urn   515

TEACH

BACKGROUND

John Keats had literary ambitions from a very young age and was a passionate admirer of William Shakespeare. He began writing poetry at the age of 18 and was a very driven and determined writer, but his first two books, *Poems* and *Endymion*, did not do well. Keats kept writing anyway. In 1818, he became ill after a walking tour, showing the first signs of tuberculosis. He watched his brother Tom die of the same disease and anguished over not being able to marry his sweetheart because of his illness. It was during this time of emotional and physical suffering that Keats produced his most beloved and remembered poems, which convey his love for Fanny Brawne, his desire for immortality, and his deep appreciation for the beauty of the natural world. Keats was known to be especially sensitive and perceptive and may have possessed a faculty called *synesthesia*, in which a person experiences stimulation of one sense with another sense, such as seeing sounds or hearing smells.

SETTING A PURPOSE

Direct students to use the Setting a Purpose prompt to focus their reading.

 For **listening** and **reading support** for students at varying proficiency levels, see the **Text X-Ray** on pages 512C and 512D.

WHEN STUDENTS STRUGGLE . . .

Visualize Imagery Tell students to visualize what the writer is describing, then have them describe the images in their own words. They can use the chart below for details of the images.

Lines	Image
11–14	Someone playing an instrument made of pipes

 For additional support, go to the **Reading Studio** and assign the following Level Up tutorial: Imagery.

Ode on a Grecian Urn   **515**

TEACH

✏️ ANALYZE RHYME SCHEME

Remind students that **rhyme scheme** refers to the pattern of **end rhyme** in a **stanza.** Have students read lines 11–20 aloud and label the pairs of rhyming words with letters *a, b, c, d,* and *e*. Then, ask students to express the rhyme scheme as a string of letters. (**Answer:** *The rhyme scheme is ababcdeced.*)

■ English Learner Support

Distinguish Sounds Remind students that two words or syllables rhyme when they share the same or very similar vowel sounds and consonant endings. Provide examples such as *sun/run* and *red/bed*. Point out that in English, a vowel can have multiple sounds, so words that have the same vowels might not rhyme and words might rhyme even when they have different vowels. Provide this list of words and have students match the ones that rhyme: *fun, yawn, done, loan, gone, phone*. For beginners, read the words aloud and have them echo you.

Then, read lines 11–20 aloud, and have students repeat the end rhymes. Ask students to identify the pairs of rhymes in these lines. **ALL LEVELS**

✏️ ANALYZE APOSTROPHE

Remind students that in **apostrophe**, the speaker is speaking directly to, rather than about, the subject. Explain that there are several images in lines 11–20, and ask students to look for the ones that the speaker is speaking directly to. Tell them to look for the second-person pronouns (*thou, thy,* and *thine*) and then read carefully to determine whom or what those pronouns refer to. Then, have students look for the words that the speaker uses to describe these images and think about the emotions that are associated with those words. (**Answer:** *To the mysterious priest, he is expressing wonder and curiosity. To the little town, he is expressing empathy and sorrow for it because it is now abandoned forever.*)

✏️ ANALYZE STANZA STRUCTURE

Remind students that in **iambic pentameter**, there should be one unstressed syllable followed by a stressed one, but Keats varied that pattern slightly. Have them try to read it in strict iambic pentameter, identifying places where exceptions to iambic pentameter are necessary. (**Answer:** *Student answers may vary, but they will probably identify the stresses on "Thou," and "Cold," as variations in the meter.*)

 **NOTICE & NOTE**

ANALYZE RHYME SCHEME
Annotate: Mark the end rhymes in lines 11–20.
Analyze: What is the rhyme scheme in this stanza?

29 cloy'd: having had too much of something; oversatisfied.

ANALYZE APOSTROPHE
Annotate: In lines 32–40, mark the two images that the author addresses.
Interpret: What emotions does the author express about each of these images?

41 Attic: pure and classical; in the style of Attica, the part of Greece where Athens is located; **brede** (brēd): interwoven design.

45 Pastoral (păs'tər-əl): an artistic work that portrays rural life in an idealized way.

ANALYZE STANZA STRUCTURE
Annotate: In lines 41–45, mark the syllables that are stressed.
Identify: Where in the passage does Keats vary the metrical pattern to emphasize certain words?

> Bold lover, never, never canst thou kiss, E
> Though winning near the goal—yet, do not grieve; C
> She cannot fade, though thou hast not thy bliss, E
> 20 For ever wilt thou love, and she be fair! D
>
> Ah, happy, happy boughs! that cannot shed
> Your leaves, nor ever bid the spring adieu;
> And, happy melodist, unwearièd,
> For ever piping songs for ever new;
> 25 More happy love! more happy, happy love!
> For ever warm and still to be enjoyed,
> For ever panting, and for ever young;
> All breathing human passion far above,
> That leaves a heart high-sorrowful and cloy'd,
> 30 A burning forehead, and a parching tongue.
>
> Who are these coming to the sacrifice?
> To what green altar, O mysterious priest,
> Lead'st thou that heifer lowing at the skies,
> And all her silken flanks with garlands drest?
> 35 What little town by river or sea shore,
> Or mountain-built with peaceful citadel,
> Is emptied of this folk, this pious morn?
> And, little town, thy streets for evermore
> Will silent be; and not a soul to tell
> 40 Why thou art desolate, can e'er return.
>
> O Attic shape! Fair attitude! with brede
> Of marble men and maidens overwrought,
> With forest branches and the trodden weed;
> Thou, silent form, dost tease us out of thought
> 45 As doth eternity: Cold Pastoral!
> When old age shall this generation waste,
> Thou shalt remain, in midst of other woe
> Than ours, a friend to man, to whom thou say'st,
> "Beauty is truth, truth beauty,"—that is all
> 50 Ye know on earth, and all ye need to know.

IMPROVE READING FLUENCY

Targeted Passage Direct students' attention to lines 31–38. Remind them that keeping in mind the meter of the poem as they read will help them understand how the poet expected the lines to be read. Have them mark the stressed syllables and then try reading the lines quietly to themselves. Then, model reading the lines aloud with the correct rhythm and intonation, and have students echo you.

 Go to the **Reading Studio** for additional support in developing fluency.

CHECK YOUR UNDERSTANDING

Answer these questions before moving on to the **Analyze the Text** section on the following page.

1 In line 3, the phrase "Sylvan historian" refers to —
   A a Greek writer
   B a man pictured on the urn
   C the reader of the poem
   D the Grecian urn

2 In line 20, why does the author say, "For ever wilt thou love, and she be fair"?
   F True love is everlasting.
   G Their images are frozen in time.
   H They exist only in each other's memories.
   J Their love is immortalized in song.

3 What is the urn's message, delivered in its last two lines?
   A Beauty and truth are unable to stand the test of time.
   B Beauty and truth are equivalent and eternal.
   C Beauty and truth both are important.
   D Beauty and truth are often confused.

TEACH

CHECK YOUR UNDERSTANDING

Have students answer the questions independently.

Answers:
1. D
2. G
3. B

If they answer any questions incorrectly, have them reread the text to confirm their understanding. Then they may proceed to ANALYZE THE TEXT on page 518.

ENGLISH LEARNER SUPPORT

Oral Assessment   Use the following questions to assess students' comprehension and speaking skills.

1. Who or what is the *Sylvan historian* in line 3? *(the urn)*
2. Will the lovers on the urn always be the same? *(Yes, because they are frozen on the urn.)*
3. How does the speaker think truth and beauty are related? *(They are both the same thing.)*
   ALL LEVELS

APPLY

ANALYZE THE TEXT
Possible answers:

1. **DOK 4:** *Possible answers:* "unravished bride"—the urn's purity; "Sylvan historian"—the urn tells stories about woodlands from the distant past.

2. **DOK 2:** *Music that we imagine is even sweeter than music we hear played on instruments because the imagined music is flawless and eternal.*

3. **DOK 2:** *Happy* and *for ever* are repeated; the repetition helps develop the idea that timeless and eternal pleasures bring more happiness than pleasures that change and decay.

4. **DOK 3:** *Possible answer:* The variation helps keep readers' attention while still maintaining the poem's overall stanza structure.

5. **DOK 4:** *The poem celebrates the immortality of the images represented on the urn. Keats may have been preoccupied with thoughts of impermanence and mortality because of his illness and the recent deaths of his mother and brother.*

RESEARCH
Have students do independent research to find out more about Keats' works and the classical art and literature that influenced him. Encourage them to use credible, scholarly sites.

Extend Remind students that "Ode on a Grecian Urn" is a sonnet, and have them review its **stanza** structure and **rhyme scheme.** Encourage them also to think about the main ideas in this poem. Then, have them apply what they have learned about analyzing poetry to "Ode to Psyche" and explain what qualities the two poems share and how the ideas they express are related.

RESPOND

ANALYZE THE TEXT
Support your responses with evidence from the text. 📓 NOTEBOOK

1. **Analyze** In lines 1–4, Keats addresses the urn as an "unravish'd bride" and a "Sylvan historian." What characteristics of the urn do these phrases in the apostrophe convey?

2. **Interpret** Reread lines 11–14. How do you interpret the statement, "Heard melodies are sweet, but those unheard / Are sweeter"?

3. **Identify Patterns** What words are repeated in stanza 3? What idea does this repetition help develop in the stanza?

4. **Draw Conclusions** Why might Keats have chosen to vary the rhyme scheme in the last six lines of the stanzas?

5. **Connect** How might Keats's personal circumstances have contributed to the sentiments expressed in the poem?

RESEARCH

RESEARCH TIP
When looking for information in an online source or digital document, use Ctrl + F to do a search of the page. Put phrases in quotation marks to search only for that exact phrase.

Like most educated people of his era, Keats studied classical literature. He was also inspired by Greek art and philosophy. With a partner, research Keats's connections to ancient Greece. Use what you learn to answer these questions.

QUESTION	ANSWER
What artworks in the British Museum probably inspired "Ode on a Grecian Urn"?	*The Elgin Marbles*
What characteristics of the Greek goddess Psyche does Keats emphasize in his poem "Ode to Psyche"?	*youth and beauty*
In the poem "On First Looking into Chapman's Homer," what does Keats admire about the translation of the Greek epics referred to in the title?	*Chapman's "loud and bold" language*

Extend Read "Ode to Psyche." With a partner, discuss the poem's ideas and also its formal qualities, such as stanza structure and rhyme scheme. Compare the poem with "Ode on a Grecian Urn."

518 Unit 4

WHEN STUDENTS STRUGGLE . . .

Reteaching: Analyze Apostrophe Remind students the purpose of **apostrophe.** To help students understand how Keats uses apostrophe, have them complete this graphic organizer:

Who/What Is Addressed	Emotional Language	What Emotions Are Expressed

 For additional support, go to the **Reading Studio** and assign the following Level Up tutorial: Figurative Language.

518 Unit 4

RESPOND

CREATE AND PRESENT

Write a Poem Using Apostrophe Is there an inanimate object or abstract idea that you have strong feelings about? Perhaps you love winter or are upset about the closing of a local restaurant. Write a poem addressing that inanimate object or abstract idea to express your feelings.

- ❏ Address the object or idea directly. Use apostrophe to express strong emotion.
- ❏ Include several stanzas. Decide whether you will use regular patterns of rhyme and meter or if you'll write in free verse, with no regular patterns.
- ❏ Use sensory details to create a vivid experience for your reader.

Present Your Poem Give a dramatic reading of your poem for a group or the whole class.

- ❏ Practice your dramatic reading and revise the text as necessary for dramatic effectiveness and ease of speech.
- ❏ Make notations to remind yourself to emphasize certain words or phrases.
- ❏ When giving your presentation, use voice inflection, facial expressions, gestures, and eye contact.

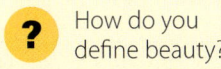
Go to the **Speaking and Listening Studio** to find out more about giving a presentation.

RESPOND TO THE ESSENTIAL QUESTION

How do you define beauty?

Gather Information Review your annotations and notes on "Ode on a Grecian Urn." Then, add relevant information to your Response Log. As you determine which information to include, think about:

- whether beauty is subjective or objective
- what emotions beauty inspires
- whether your experiences change how you perceive beauty

ACADEMIC VOCABULARY

As you write and discuss what you learned from the poem, be sure to use the Academic Vocabulary words. Check off each of the words that you use.

- ❏ appreciate
- ❏ insight
- ❏ intensity
- ❏ invoke
- ❏ radical

APPLY

CREATE AND PRESENT

Write a Poem Using Apostrophe Explain to students that this is a chance for them to practice the literary device known as **apostrophe** and express their own emotions at the same time. Direct students to spend some time brainstorming ideas about things they feel strongly about. Once they have chosen subjects for their apostrophes, encourage them to jot down images, physical details, descriptive adjectives, and other words or phrases that they associate with their subjects. Encourage them to use their imaginations as they think of what they want to say to the chosen objects, concepts, places, or persons to express their feelings.

Present Your Poem Direct students to think about the primary emotions and messages of their poems and how to best convey those emotions. Have students practice in pairs or small groups before giving their presentations to the class. Encourage them to revise their poems, or how they present them, based on the feedback they receive.

RESPOND TO THE ESSENTIAL QUESTION

Allow time for students to add details from "Ode on a Grecian Urn" to their Unit 4 Response Logs.

PLAN

from FRANKENSTEIN
Novel by Mary Shelley

GENRE ELEMENTS
NOVEL

Tell students that even though a **science fiction novel** portrays things that don't actually exist, it still has a logic that makes sense. Science fiction uses what is known about real science to speculate on what could possibly happen one day. In this lesson, students will analyze how a character deals with a moral dilemma caused by scientific progress.

LEARNING OBJECTIVES

- Analyze science fiction and motivation.
- Conduct research about scientific and medical knowledge in the early 19th century.
- Write a science fiction story.
- Participate in a discussion.
- Use antonyms.
- Use sensory language.
- **Language** Discuss sensory words.

TEXT COMPLEXITY

Quantitative Measures	Frankenstein	Lexile: 890L
Qualitative Measures	**Ideas Presented** Much is explicit, but moves to some implied meaning. Requires some inferential reasoning.	
	Structures Used Primarily explicit, excerpt structure with support from italicized summaries. Largely chronological, with one dream sequence.	
	Language Used Archaic, formal, and figurative language. Complex sentence structures.	
	Knowledge Required Science fiction concepts may make heavier demand.	

520A Unit 4

PLAN

Online Ed

RESOURCES

- Unit 4 Response Log
- 🔊 Selection Audio
- 📖 Reading Studio: Notice & Note
- 📈 Level Up Tutorial: Taking Notes and Outlining
- 📝 Writing Studio: Writing Narratives
- 💬 Speaking and Listening Studio: Participating in Collaborative Discussions
- 🔵 Vocabulary Studio: Antonyms
- ❗ Grammar Studio: Module 8 Lesson 8: Mood
- ✅ *Frankenstein* Selection Test

SUMMARIES

English
In these excerpts, the narrator, Victor Frankenstein, brings a creature to life from dead human remains. He struggles with being responsible for the so-called monster he created, especially when the monster murders his younger brother.

Spanish
En estos pasajes, el narrador, Víctor Frankenstein, le da vida a una criatura hecha de restos humanos. Le remuerde ser responsable por el supuesto monstruo que creó, especialmente cuando el monstruo asesina a su hermano menor.

👥 SMALL-GROUP OPTIONS

Have students work in small groups and pairs to read and discuss the selection.

Reciprocal Teaching
- Have students read the text.
- After reading, ask students to write three to five questions about the text, using these frames: *What does Frankenstein mean by _____? How does the author use description to _____? How do the details about _____ affect _____? Why did Frankenstein _____?*
- Form teams of three students.
- Have each student offer two questions for group discussion.
- Have each group reach a consensus on the answers and find supporting text evidence.

Think-Pair-Share
- After reading the text, pose this question: *What kind of person is Victor Frankenstein?*
- Have students think about the question individually and take notes.
- Then, have pairs listen, discuss, and formulate a shared response to the question. Direct them to include at least two reasons to support their inference.
- Finally, have pairs share their response with the class.

Frankenstein **520B**

PLAN

Text X-Ray: English Learner Support
for *Frankenstein*

Use the Text X-Ray and the supports and scaffolds in the Teacher's Edition to help guide students at different proficiency levels through the selection.

INTRODUCE THE SELECTION
DISCUSS ACCOUNTABILITY AND ETHICS

In this lesson, students will need to be able to discuss why scientists might need to be accountable for their discoveries and achievements.

Provide the following explanations:

- When you are *accountable,* you take responsibility for your actions.
- *Ethics* are a code of moral behavior. When your behavior is *ethical,* you do not cause harm.

Have students ask questions and make statements about accountability and ethics. Provide sentence stems, such as: *Is it ethical to _____? You need to be accountable for your actions when you _____.*

CULTURAL REFERENCES

The following words or phrases may be unfamiliar to students:

- *in vain* (paragraph 3): without success
- *took refuge* (paragraph 4): found a safe place
- *mortal combat* (paragraph 7): physical fight to the death
- *begone* (paragraph 8): go away

LISTENING

Identify Literary Devices

Remind students that authors use literary devices such as imagery and repetition to help readers visualize the setting and understand the characters' states of mind.

Use the following supports with students at varying proficiency levels:

- Slowly read aloud paragraph 13. Ask students to identify the repeated word (*begone*) and repeat it after you. Describe the meaning of this word, and explain that repeating it shows the narrator's strong feelings of disgust toward the creature he created. **SUBSTANTIAL**

- Read aloud the part of paragraph 14 beginning with "Listen to my tale." Have students take notes to identify repeated words (*listen* or *listen to me; destroy*). Ask what the repetition helps them understand (for example, the creature's fear and desire to be heard). **MODERATE**

- Read aloud paragraph 14 and have students note examples of imagery (*desert mountains, dreary glaciers, caves of ice, bleak skies*). Ask what the imagery helps show about the creature. (*He is lonely and feels the setting reflects his isolation.*) **LIGHT**

520C Unit 4

PLAN

SPEAKING

Use Sensory Words

Remind students that sensory words include words related to the five senses. Remind them that using sensory words when they speak can help make their language more descriptive.

Use the following supports with students at varying proficiency levels:

- Ask students to identify the five senses and give an example of a word that describes that appeals to each sense. For example, sight/blue, hear/squeak, feel/soft, taste/sweet, smell/stinky. **SUBSTANTIAL**
- Have partners create a list of two words for each sense. Then have them recite their lists to the class.
- Have partners create a list of three words related to each sense. Have them create one sentence from each sense. Then have them present their sentences to the class. **MODERATE**
- Have partners create a short skit using sensory words in every line of the play. Let them have fun with it (allowing silliness in their sentences), but challenge them to have a plot for their play. **LIGHT**

READING

Use Graphic Organizers

Tell students that they can use graphic organizers to help them keep track of unfamiliar words as they read. After reading, they can use reference materials and classroom support to define the words, then reread the text again.

Use the following supports with students of varying proficiency levels:

- Model how you use a word web to keep track of any unfamiliar words you want to know more about as you reread the first paragraph. Write the word *agitated* in the center of the web. Model how to use reference materials to fill in the web with related words and phrases. Have students copy the completed web into their notebooks **SUBSTANTIAL**
- Have students reread the first two paragraphs. Tell them to use a two-column chart to keep track of any unfamiliar words they encounter. After reading, guide them to ask one another for definitions and to use reference materials to help write definitions in their charts. **MODERATE**
- Show students how to draw and use a Frayer Model. Have them label the other four boxes: Definition; Characteristics; Examples; Non-examples. Tell pairs to discuss their completed Frayer Models. **LIGHT**

WRITING

Identify and Use Antonyms

Review the list of prefixes in the Vocabulary Strategy activity on page 532. Help students use the prefixes to identify and write more antonyms.

Use the following supports with students of varying proficiency levels:

- Model how to turn the words *appear, possible,* and *sense* into their antonyms by adding a prefix. Have students copy your work. Then have students write pairs of words that are antonyms. *(appear/disappear; possible/impossible; sense/nonsense)* **SUBSTANTIAL**
- Have partners work together to use prefixes from the list to turn *appear, possible,* and *sense* into their antonyms. Then have them use the words and their antonyms together in sentences. For example: *The dog disappeared and then appeared again.* **MODERATE**
- Have students do the Intermediate activity. Then have them exchange sentences and revise for correct spelling, verb tense, and standard grammatical usage. **LIGHT**

Frankenstein **520D**

TEACH

 Connect to the ESSENTIAL QUESTION

Science has come a long way since Mary Shelley's time, and it has demonstrated value in improving and saving lives. However, when ethical standards are not applied, and scientists exhibit hubris, as Dr. Frankenstein did, things can go terribly wrong.

ANALYZE & APPLY

from FRANKENSTEIN

Novel by **Mary Shelley**

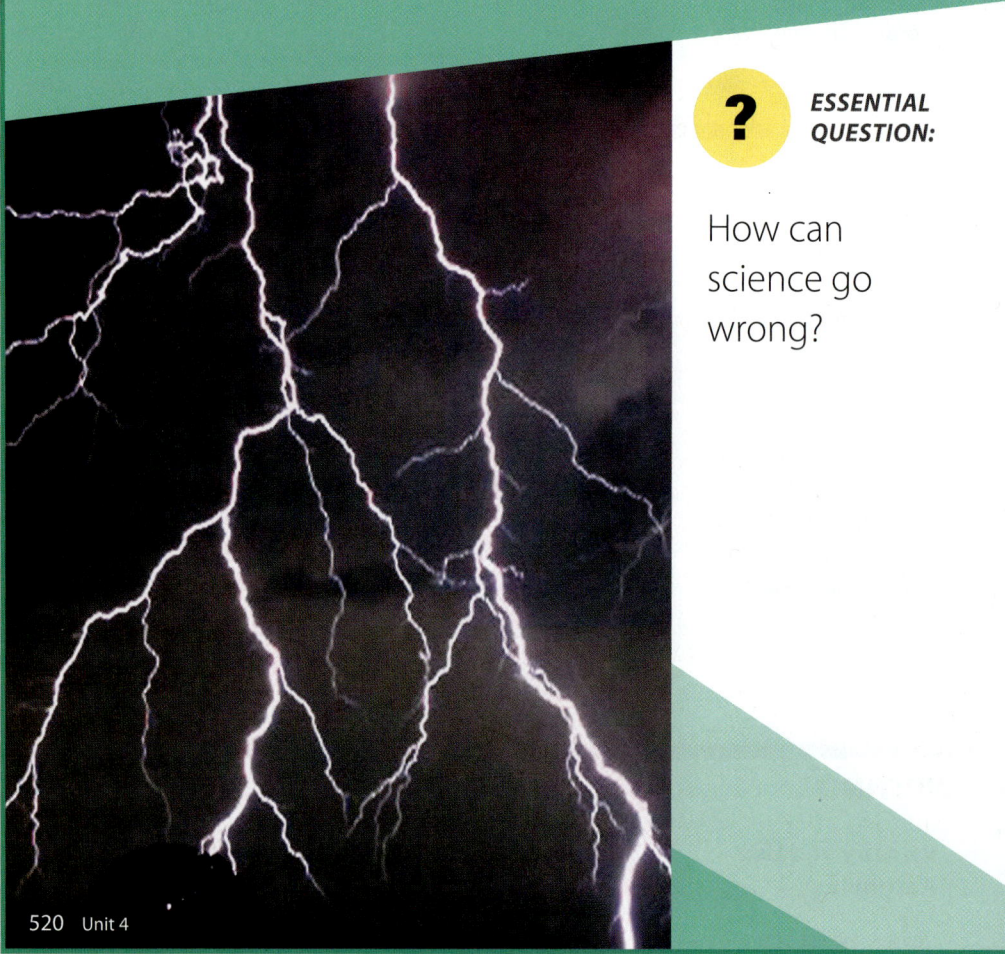

ESSENTIAL QUESTION:

How can science go wrong?

QUICK START

The name *Frankenstein* is often used to describe scientific research that has gotten out of control. To what extent should scientists be held accountable for the results of their discoveries? Discuss this question with a partner.

ANALYZE SCIENCE FICTION

Frankenstein is a work of gothic horror that is also considered one of the first science fiction novels. **Science fiction** is a literary genre based on imagined scientific or technological developments, such as time travel or encounters with extraterrestrial life. Mary Shelley said that the idea for the book came to her in a dream after spending several stormy nights discussing ghost stories and medical experiments with a group of friends. She wrote a story about a scientist who creates a man from human remains, which she later expanded into the novel *Frankenstein*.

As you read, use a chart like the one below to note how imaginary advances in science or medicine influence important elements of the novel.

Elements of Science Fiction in *Frankenstein*	
Plot	The plot is based on scientific and technology experiments that were not possible now or at the time.
Characters	A mad scientist and his created monster are both standard elements of sci-fi.
Theme	Themes related to sci-fi include: science vs morality, new technologies/sciences vs "the old way of doing things," and alienation from society.

GENRE ELEMENTS: NOVEL
- a long fictional prose narrative
- includes the same fictional elements as a short story
- usually has a more complex plot and a wider range of characters than a short story
- may be written in subgenres such as science fiction, historical fiction, or mystery

ANALYZE MOTIVATION

Motivation is the stated or implied reason behind a fictional character's behavior. Sometimes motivation is directly expressed in a story, but usually readers must infer a character's motivation from dialogue, thoughts, and actions. Characters' motivations often influence the plot and theme of a work, so careful readers look closely for relationships among these elements.

In Shelley's novel, Victor Frankenstein struggles with the moral dilemma of whether to accept or abandon the creature he has created. As you read, analyze the motivations that contribute toward this dilemma. Also, analyze the motivations underlying the creature's behavior toward Frankenstein.

TEACH

QUICK START

Have students read the Quick Start question and invite them to share with a partner their ideas about scientific accountability. Encourage them to write down their main points to share with the class. Challenge them to respectfully debate differences of opinion, and to listen proactively to what the fellow students believe.

ANALYZE SCIENCE FICTION

Explain the elements of science fiction to students, ensuring they understand that there are many different types of works that can fit into the classification, although they all share similar qualities. Challenge them to complete the chart, filling in the plot, characters, and theme of *Frankenstein* as they read through the story. Remind them to consider how each of these includes elements of the genre.

ANALYZE MOTIVATION

Explain that a character's motivation is the reason (or reasons) for the actions he or she takes in a story. Explain that this can be found through careful analysis of what the character says and does, especially as it relates to the other major characters. Challenge them to pay careful attention to each character's motivations as they read the excerpt from *Frankenstein*. Display this sentence from the selection:

I had desired it with an ardor that far exceeded moderation; but now that I had finished, the beauty of the dream vanished, and breathless horror and disgust filled my heart.

Challenge students to examine how Victor is feeling in this moment, and what that says about his motivations for conducting this experiment.

TEACH

CRITICAL VOCABULARY

Encourage students to read all the sentences before deciding which words best complete each one. Remind them to look for context clues that match the precise meaning of each word.

Answers:

1. ardor; inanimate
2. tumult; precipice
3. inarticulate; infuse
4. odious; misdeed

■ English Learner Support

Use Cognates Tell students that one of the Critical Vocabulary words has a Spanish cognate: *odious/odioso*.
ALL LEVELS

LANGUAGE CONVENTIONS

Review the information on **sensory language**. Explain that this type of descriptive language is used to deepen the reader's experience by further immersion in the world within the story. Read the sentence from *Frankenstein* aloud. Challenge students to identify the sensory language, as well as how it impacts the meaning and tone of the story.

ANNOTATION MODEL

Review elements of horror and science fiction with students. Challenge them to brainstorm what some of these elements might be, in addition to those discussed in this section. Review the notes on the classic horror setting and the sci-fi details. Point out that they may follow this suggestion or use their own system for marking up the selection in their write-in text. They may want to color-code their annotations by using highlighters. Their notes in the margin may include questions about ideas that are unclear or topics they want to learn more about.

 **GET READY**

CRITICAL VOCABULARY

| infuse | ardor | inarticulate | precipice |
| inanimate | tumult | misdeed | odious |

To see how many Critical Vocabulary words you already know, use them to complete the sentences.

1. Because of his _____ for his experiment, he would stop at nothing to discover how to make the _____ creature come to life.

2. Frankenstein's mind was in a _____ about what he had created, and he felt that he was standing at the edge of a terrifying _____ in the history of science.

3. Though at first the creature was _____, he later learned to speak and even to _____ his speech with the tones and cadences used in real human conversation.

4. The _____ creature, cast out from human society, was determined to find his creator and deny that he had committed any _____.

LANGUAGE CONVENTIONS

Sensory Language In this lesson, you will examine how sensory language is used to help re-create sensory experiences for the reader. Sensory language includes descriptive words or phrases that appeal to one or more of the five senses: sight, hearing, smell, taste, and touch.

In this sentence from *Frankenstein*, Mary Shelley uses sensory language that helps the reader feel the cold wind that the narrator experiences in the novel:

> I was troubled: a mist came over my eyes, and I felt a faintness seize me; but I was quickly restored by the cold gale of the mountains.

As you read the excerpt from *Frankenstein*, note places where the author uses sensory language.

ANNOTATION MODEL NOTICE & NOTE

As you read, make note of any elements of horror and science fiction. In the model, you can see one reader's notes on a passage from *Frankenstein*.

> It was <u>on a dreary night</u> of November that I beheld the accomplishment of my toils. With anxiety that almost amounted to agony, I collected <u>the instruments of life</u> around me, that I <u>might infuse a spark of being</u> into the lifeless thing that lay at my feet.

Shelley opens with a classic horror story phrase to describe the setting.

The details about bringing something dead to life ("the instruments of life" and "might infuse a spark of being") tell me this is a science fiction story.

BACKGROUND

Mary Shelley (1797–1851) was the daughter of two famous writers, the early feminist Mary Wollstonecraft and the philosopher William Godwin. Shelley's education benefited from access to her father's vast library and the many scientific and literary people she encountered during her upbringing. When she was 19, she married the poet Percy Bysshe Shelley. Although her literary reputation was long overshadowed by those of her parents and husband, in recent decades Shelley has gained increased recognition as an important writer. Written in 1818, *Frankenstein* was first published anonymously, then later under Shelley's name.

FRANKENSTEIN
Novel by Mary Shelley

SETTING A PURPOSE

As you read, pay attention to Victor Frankenstein's reactions to the creature he created, and consider whether his reactions are out of proportion based on the creature's words and behavior.

A young Swiss scientist named Victor Frankenstein sets out to learn the secret of creating life. For two years he devotes himself to studying chemistry and human anatomy. Finally, after assembling a creature from human remains, he prepares to use an electrical charge to bring it to life.

1 It was on a dreary night of November that I beheld the accomplishment of my toils. With an anxiety that almost amounted to agony, I collected the instruments of life around me, that I might **infuse** a spark of being into the lifeless thing that lay at my feet. It was already one in the morning; the rain pattered dismally against the panes, and my candle was nearly burnt out, when, by the glimmer of the half-extinguished light, I saw the dull yellow eye of the creature open; it breathed hard, and a convulsive motion agitated its limbs.

Notice & Note

Use the side margins to notice and note signposts in the text.

ANALYZE SCIENCE FICTION
Annotate: In paragraph 1, mark the words and phrases that suggest scientific endeavors.

Explain: How do these details support the categorization of *Frankenstein* as one of the first works of science fiction?

infuse
(ĭn-fyōōz´) *v.* to fill or cause to be filled with something.

Frankenstein 523

TEACH

ANALYZE MOTIVATION

Remind students that a character's actions speak directly toward his motivations, and indicate what he hopes will be the outcome of his efforts. (**Answer:** *The doctor hoped that by using beautiful parts and pieces, his creation would also be beautiful. He wanted to be God-like and create something in his own image, so he endeavored to make the creature as perfect as he felt Adam must have been.*)

CRITICAL VOCABULARY

inanimate: Anything that is not living can be considered *inanimate*.

ASK STUDENTS to explain why a book is an inanimate object. (*A book cannot move on its own.*)

ardor: When people have an *ardor* for a sport, they are extremely enthusiastic about it.

ASK STUDENTS why they think Dr. Frankenstein had an ardor for infusing life into an inanimate body. (**Possible answer:** *He might have seen it as a challenge to bring an object to life.*)

tumult: When his creator rejected him, the creature's mind was in a *tumult*, or state of agitation.

ASK STUDENTS to describe what a tumultuous state of mind would feel like. (*agitated, upset, worried*)

inarticulate: Babies are *inarticulate* since they babble until they can form words. Victor's monster learned to articulate, or speak clearly, much more quickly than a baby would.

ASK STUDENTS to give examples of times when a person might be inarticulate. (*Examples: when a person is rendered in awe or is shocked, when a person is nervous about a situation, etc.*)

524 Unit 4

NOTICE & NOTE

ANALYZE MOTIVATION
Annotate: In paragraph 2, mark the words or phrases that demonstrate the great care Frankenstein took in building his creation.

Analyze: Why would Frankenstein have taken such pains to make his creation?

inanimate
(ĭn-ăn´ə-mĭt) *adj.* not having the qualities associated with active, living organisms.

ardor
(är´dər) *n.* intensity of emotion, especially strong desire, enthusiasm, or devotion.

tumult
(tōō´mŭlt) *n.* a state of agitation of the mind or emotions.

inarticulate
(ĭn-är-tĭk´yə-lĭt) *adj.* uttered without the use of normal words or syllables; incomprehensible as speech or language.

524 Unit 4

2   How can I describe my emotions at this catastrophe, or how delineate the wretch whom, with such infinite pains and care, I had endeavored to form? His limbs were in proportion, and I had selected his features as beautiful. Beautiful! Great God! His yellow skin scarcely covered the work of muscles and arteries beneath; his hair was of a lustrous black, and flowing; his teeth of a pearly whiteness; but these luxuriances only formed a more horrid contrast with his watery eyes, that seemed almost of the same color as the dun white sockets in which they were set, his shriveled complexion, and straight black lips.

3   The different accidents of life are not so changeable as the feelings of human nature. I had worked hard for nearly two years, for the sole purpose of infusing life into an **inanimate** body. For this I had deprived myself of rest and health. I had desired it with an **ardor** that far exceeded moderation; but now that I had finished, the beauty of the dream vanished, and breathless horror and disgust filled my heart. Unable to endure the aspect of the being I had created, I rushed out of the room, and continued a long time traversing my bed-chamber, unable to compose my mind to sleep. At length lassitude succeeded to the **tumult** I had before endured; and I threw myself on the bed in my clothes, endeavoring to seek a few moments of forgetfulness. But it was in vain: I slept indeed, but I was disturbed by the wildest dreams. I thought I saw Elizabeth, in the bloom of health, walking in the streets of Ingolstadt. Delighted and surprised, I embraced her; but as I imprinted the first kiss on her lips, they became livid with the hue of death; her features appeared to change, and I thought that I held the corpse of my dead mother in my arms; a shroud enveloped her form, and I saw the grave-worms crawling in the folds of the flannel. I started from my sleep with horror; a cold dew covered my forehead, my teeth chattered, and every limb became convulsed; when, by the dim and yellow light of the moon, as it forced its way through the window-shutters, I beheld the wretch, the miserable monster whom I had created. He held up the curtain of the bed; and his eyes, if eyes they may be called, were fixed on me. His jaws opened, and he muttered some **inarticulate** sounds, while a grin wrinkled his cheeks.

4   He might have spoken, but I did not hear; one hand was stretched out, seemingly to detain me, but I escaped, and rushed downstairs. I took refuge in the courtyard belonging to the house which I inhabited; where I remained during the rest of the night, walking up and down in the greatest agitation, listening attentively, catching and fearing each sound as if it were to announce the approach of the demoniacal corpse to which I had so miserably given life. . . .

ENGLISH LEARNER SUPPORT

Analyze Events Have pairs take turns reading paragraph 3 aloud. Direct students to make and fill in a graphic organizer like the one below. Have pairs share their completed organizers.

What Happened	To Whom It Happened	What Was Said	What Feelings Were Shown

MODERATE

After fleeing from his creation, Victor Frankenstein falls seriously ill and is cared for by a friend. He learns that the creature has killed his younger brother, William, and framed a family servant for the murder. Frankenstein returns home, but he is unable to save her. Tormented by guilt, he sets out for a hike in the Swiss Alps, hoping to relieve his despair.

5   It was nearly noon when I arrived at the top of the ascent. For some time I sat upon the rock that overlooks the sea of ice. A mist covered both that and the surrounding mountains. Presently a breeze dissipated the cloud, and I descended upon the glacier. The surface is very uneven, rising like the waves of a troubled sea, descending low, and interspersed by rifts that sink deep. The field of ice is almost a league in width, but I spent nearly two hours in crossing it. The opposite mountain is a bare perpendicular rock. From the side where I now stood Montanvert was exactly opposite, at the distance of a league; and above it rose Mont Blanc, in awful majesty. I remained in a recess of the rock, gazing on this wonderful and stupendous scene. The sea, or rather the vast river of ice, wound among its dependent mountains, whose aerial summits hung over its recesses. Their icy and glittering peaks shone in the sunlight over the clouds. My heart, which was before sorrowful, now swelled with something like joy; I exclaimed — "Wandering spirits, if ye indeed wander, and do not rest in your narrow beds, allow me this faint happiness, or take me as your companion, away from the joys of life."

6   As I said this, I suddenly beheld the figure of a man, at some distance, advancing towards me with superhuman speed. He bounded over the crevices of the ice, among which I had walked with caution; his stature also, as he approached, seemed to exceed that of man.

7   I was troubled: a mist came over my eyes, and I felt a faintness seize me; but I was quickly restored by the cold gale of the mountains. I perceived, as the shape came nearer (sight tremendous and abhorred!), that it was the wretch whom I had created. I trembled with rage and horror, resolving to wait his approach, and then close with him in mortal combat. He approached; his countenance bespoke bitter anguish, combined with disdain and malignity, while its unearthly ugliness rendered it almost too horrible for human eyes. But I scarcely observed this; anger and hatred had at first deprived me of utterance, and I recovered only to overwhelm him with words expressive of furious detestation and contempt.

LANGUAGE CONVENTIONS
Annotate: Mark the language that evokes the senses in paragraph 5.
Infer: What impression of the setting does the sensory language help convey?

ANALYZE MOTIVATION
Annotate: Mark words in paragraph 7 that show how Frankenstein feels about his creation and what he plans to do to it.
Infer: Why might Frankenstein feel this way and resolve to take this action?

Frankenstein 525

WHEN STUDENTS STRUGGLE...

Develop an Outline Direct students to develop an outline for paragraphs 1–7, providing one-statement summaries for each paragraph. Explain that this will enable them to easily keep track of the events within the story, and can be used later to create a clear plot outline for the excerpt.

  For additional support, go to the **Reading Studio** and assign the following Level Up tutorial: Taking Notes and Outlining.

TEACH

LANGUAGE CONVENTIONS

Remind students that sensory language is language that helps you to see, hear, feel, touch, taste, or smell something within a story. (**Answer:** *These details give the impression that the valley is a very remote and rugged place.*)

ANALYZE MOTIVATION

Remind students that characters may not even be aware of their true motivations until a situation arises that makes those intentions known. (**Answer:** *The doctor is horrified that he created such a monster and resolves to kill it because he feels responsible. However, the word "troubled" suggests he feels some conflict about destroying his creation.*)

■ **English Learner Support**

Examine Motivation Provide students with this short description, directing them to visualize what you are reading.

The man walked slowly toward the bus stop. His feet dragged and his face wore a deep frown. His head was filled with thoughts of what the day might bring.

Explain to students that the man is walking to work, and ask them to consider what his actions might mean about how he feels about going. (*Examples: he doesn't want to go, he is worried about something at work*) Help them understand that motivation sometimes can be found by examining descriptions of a character's actions. **ALL LEVELS**

TEACH

✏️ ANALYZE MOTIVATION

Remind students that all creatures' primary motivation is to be alive and to do what needs to be done to stay that way. (**Answer:** *The creature asks to be allowed to live in peace. He is motivated by the survival instinct common to all living things.*)

■ English Learner Support

Compare and Contrast Direct students to use a graphic organizer to compare and contrast each character, using paragraphs 10, 11, and 13 to analyze Victor, and paragraphs 9 and 12 to analyze the creature. Challenge students to use the descriptions provided to explain what each character is doing (with relation to the other character), how each character is feeling, and the meaning expressed by the words each character is saying. Encourage students to share their findings to gain deeper insight into the story and each character. Challenge them to consider this analysis when examining each character's motivations.
LIGHT

CRITICAL VOCABULARY

misdeed: When Victor realizes what he had done, he is horrified by his *misdeed*, and tries to escape his wrongdoing.

ASK STUDENTS to give examples of misdeeds that made them regret their actions. *(Examples: breaking a rule or law, stealing, etc.)*

526 Unit 4

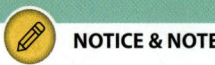 **NOTICE & NOTE**

8 "Devil!" I exclaimed, "do you dare approach me? and do you not fear the fierce vengeance of my arm wreaked on your miserable head? Begone, vile insect! or rather stay, that I may trample you to dust! and, oh, that I could, with the extinction of your miserable existence, restore those victims whom you have so diabolically murdered!"

ANALYZE MOTIVATION
Annotate: Mark the words or phrases in paragraph 9 that show what the creature asks of Frankenstein.
Draw Conclusions: What does the creature ask for, and what motivates his request?

9 "I expected this reception," said the demon. "All men hate the wretched; how then must I be hated, who am miserable beyond all living things! Yet you, my creator, detest and spurn me, thy creature, to whom thou art bound by ties only dissoluble by the annihilation of one of us. You purpose to kill me. How dare you sport thus with life? <u>Do your duty towards me, and I will do mine towards you and the rest of mankind. If you will comply with my conditions, I will leave them and you at peace</u>; but if you refuse, I will glut the maw of death, until it be satisfied with the blood of your remaining friends."

10 "Abhorred monster! fiend that thou art! the tortures of hell are too mild a vengeance for thy crimes. Wretched devil! you reproach me with your creation; come on then, that I may extinguish the spark which I so negligently bestowed."

11 My rage was without bounds; I sprang on him, impelled by all the feelings which can arm one being against the existence of another. He easily eluded me, and said, —

12 "Be calm! I entreat you to hear me, before you give vent to your hatred on my devoted head. Have I not suffered enough, that you seek to increase my misery? Life, although it may only be an accumulation of anguish, is dear to me, and I will defend it. Remember, thou hast made me more powerful than thyself; my height is superior to thine; my joints more supple. But I will not be tempted to set myself in opposition to thee. I am thy creature, and I will be even mild and docile to my natural lord and king, if thou wilt also perform thy part, the which thou owest me. Oh, Frankenstein, be not equitable to every other, and trample upon me alone, to whom thy justice, and even thy clemency and affection, is most due. Remember, that I am thy creature: I ought to be thy Adam; but I am rather the fallen angel, whom thou drivest from joy for no **misdeed**. Everywhere I see bliss, from which I alone am irrevocably excluded. I was benevolent and good; misery made me a fiend. Make me happy, and I shall again be virtuous."

misdeed
(mĭs-dēd´) *n.* a wrong or illegal deed; a wrongdoing.

13 "Begone! I will not hear you. There can be no community between you and me; we are enemies. Begone, or let us try our strength in a fight, in which one must fall."

14 "How can I move thee? Will no entreaties cause thee to turn a favorable eye upon thy creature, who implores thy goodness and compassion? Believe me, Frankenstein: I was benevolent; <u>my soul glowed with love and humanity</u>: but am I not alone, miserably alone?

526 Unit 4

APPLYING ACADEMIC VOCABULARY

☐ appreciate   ☐ insight   ☑ intensity   ☐ invoke   ☑ radical

Write and Discuss Have students turn to a partner to discuss the following questions. Guide students to include the academic vocabulary words *intensity* and *radical* in their responses. Ask volunteers to share their responses with the class.

- Describe the **intensity** of a person who would be obsessed with creating life.
- Consider the doctor's actions and explain why he would have been considered a **radical** by other scientists of his time.

You, my creator, abhor me; what hope can I gather from your fellow-creatures, who owe me nothing? They spurn and hate me. The desert mountains and dreary glaciers are my refuge. I have wandered here many days; the caves of ice, which I only do not fear, are a dwelling to me, and the only one which man does not grudge. These bleak skies I hail, for they are kinder to me than your fellow-beings. If the multitude of mankind knew of my existence, they would do as you do, and arm themselves for my destruction. Shall I not then hate them who abhor me? I will keep no terms with my enemies. I am miserable, and they shall share my wretchedness. Yet it is in your power to recompense me, and deliver them from an evil which it only remains for you to make so great, that not only you and your family, but thousands of others, shall be swallowed up in the whirlwinds of its rage. Let your compassion be moved, and do not disdain me. Listen to my tale: when you have heard that, abandon or commiserate me, as you shall judge that I deserve. But hear me. The guilty are allowed, by human laws, bloody as they may be, to speak in their own defense, before they are condemned. Listen to me, Frankenstein. You accuse me of murder; and yet you would, with a satisfied conscience, destroy your own creature. Oh, praise the eternal justice of man! Yet I ask you not to spare me: listen to me; and then, if you can, and if you will, destroy the work of your hands."

15 "Why do you call to my remembrance circumstances of which I shudder to reflect that I have been the miserable origin and author? Cursed be the day, abhorred devil, in which you first saw light! Cursed (although I curse myself) be the hands that formed you! You have made me wretched beyond expression. You have left me no power to consider whether I am just to you or not. Begone! relieve me from the sight of your detested form."

16 "Thus I relieve thee, my creator," he said, and placed his hated hand before my eyes, which I flung from me with violence; "thus I take from thee a sight which you abhor. Still thou canst listen to me, and grant me thy compassion. By the virtues that I once possessed, I demand this from you. Hear my tale; it is long and strange, and the temperature of this place is not fitting to your fine sensations; come to the hut upon the mountain. The sun is yet high in the heavens; before it descends to hide itself behind yon snowy **precipices**, and illuminate another world, you will have heard my story, and can decide. On you it rests, whether I quit forever the neighborhood of man, and lead a harmless life, or become a scourge to your fellow-creatures, and the author of your own speedy ruin."

NOTICE & NOTE

ANALYZE SCIENCE FICTION
Annotate: In paragraph 14, mark the words or phrases that show that the creature believes he should be treated the same as all humans.

Evaluate: Do you find the creature's argument convincing? Why or why not?

precipice
(prĕs´ə-pĭs) *n.* an overhanging or extremely steep mass of rock; the brink of a dangerous or disastrous situation.

Frankenstein 527

TEACH

ANALYZE SCIENCE FICTION

Remind students that science fiction often includes imaginary or impossible beings, like the creature in *Frankenstein*. (**Answer:** *Answers will vary. Students might sympathize with the creature's argument that he deserves the rights of humans since Frankenstein intended him to be a person.*)

IMPROVE READING FLUENCY

Targeted Passage Have students work with partners to read paragraph 16. First, use paragraph 15 to model how to read the text, demonstrating the pace that should be used when reading aloud a difficult text. Then, have students take turns reading the assigned paragraph. Encourage students to provide feedback and support, and remind them to apply the proper pacing to their oral readings.

 Go to the **Reading Studio** for additional support in developing fluency.

CRITICAL VOCABULARY

precipice: Part of this excerpt includes Victor and the creature walking near a *precipice,* or rock overhang, while facing a moral precipice of their own.

ASK STUDENTS to describe a situation where they might feel they are facing a precipice. (**Possible answer:** *Individuals might feel they are facing a precipice when confronted with choosing between two difficult decisions or faced with a choice that will greatly affect their lives.*)

Frankenstein **527**

TEACH

AHA MOMENT

Stories often include moments where the characters learn something important about themselves, the people around them, or the situations in which they find themselves. Explain to students that these moments are often pivotal in the characters' lives. (**Answer:** *Answers will vary. Students might say he was wrong to abandon the creature so soon after creating him; if he had protected the creature and taught him right from wrong, he may not have committed crimes.*)

ENGLISH LEARNER SUPPORT

Identify Sensory Language Place students in pairs or small groups and direct them to the last three sentences of the excerpt. One group member should read the sentences aloud, with other group members recording each sensory word as it is read. Direct the reader to read the sentences aloud a second time, ensuring all students have the chance to record all words. Then, encourage students to share their lists until a complete list has been created.

ALL LEVELS

CRITICAL VOCABULARY

odious: The science experiment gone wrong left the lab with an *odious* stink that lasted for days.

ASK STUDENTS to describe items that have an odious nature. (*Examples: rotten food, a pile of garbage, a dirty person*)

528   Unit 4

 **NOTICE & NOTE**

AHA MOMENT

Notice & Note: What does Frankenstein realize for the first time in paragraph 17? Mark the sentence where he expresses this thought.

Evaluate: Is Frankenstein partly responsible for the creature's behavior? Why or why not?

odious
(ō′dē-əs) *adj.* extremely unpleasant; repulsive.

17   As he said this, he led the way across the ice: I followed. My heart was full, and I did not answer him; but, as I proceeded, I weighed the various arguments that he had used, and determined at least to listen to his tale. I was partly urged by curiosity, and compassion confirmed my resolution. I had hitherto supposed him to be the murderer of my brother, and I eagerly sought a confirmation or denial of this opinion. <u>For the first time, also, I felt what the duties of a creator towards his creature were, and that I ought to render him happy before I complained of his wickedness.</u> These motives urged me to comply with his demand. We crossed the ice, therefore, and ascended the opposite rock. The air was cold, and the rain again began to descend: we entered the hut, the fiend with an air of exultation, I with a heavy heart and depressed spirits. But I consented to listen; and, seating myself by the fire which my **odious** companion had lighted, he thus began his tale.

528   Unit 4

TO CHALLENGE STUDENTS...

Analyze Cause and Effect Help students identify situational causes within the story, then identify the intended and actual effects. Have have them use this graphic organizer to help them find additional cause and effect relationships within the selection.

Cause	Intended Effect	Actual Effect

NOTICE & NOTE

CHECK YOUR UNDERSTANDING

Answer these questions before moving on to the **Analyze the Text** section on the following page.

1. Why does Frankenstein feel disgusted by the creature soon after bringing him to life?

   A The creature acts violently.

   B The creature chases him.

   C The creature has an ugly appearance.

   D The creature is physically weak.

2. How does Frankenstein react when the creature finds him in the Swiss Alps?

   F He is afraid of the creature.

   G He tries to run away.

   H He feels guilty for creating the creature.

   J He wants to kill the creature.

3. The creature demands that Frankenstein —

   A listen to his story

   B protect him from his enemies

   C be his companion

   D improve his appearance

Frankenstein 529

TEACH

CHECK YOUR UNDERSTANDING

Have students answer the questions independently.

Answers:

1. C
2. J
3. A

If they answer any questions incorrectly, have them reread the text to confirm their understanding. Then they may proceed to ANALYZE THE TEXT on page 530.

ENGLISH LEARNER SUPPORT

Oral Assessment Use the following questions to assess students' comprehension and speaking skills.

1. Is the creature ugly? *(yes)*

2. The creature finds Frankenstein in the _____. *(Swiss Alps)*

3. The creature wants the doctor to _____. *(listen to his story)*

MODERATE / LIGHT

Frankenstein **529**

APPLY

ANALYZE THE TEXT

Possible answers:

1. **DOK 2:** *Although he brought the creature to life instead of turning it into a corpse, he is similarly horrified by the corpse-like appearance of the creature, whom he expected to be perfect and beautiful.*

2. **DOK 3:** *He thinks he is not guilty because after Frankenstein abandoned him, he was completely alone and despised by all people. He says he only hates people because they hate him, and if Frankenstein shows him compassion, he will lead a good life.*

3. **DOK 4:** *He is torn between his wish to destroy the monster and his desire to understand him better. His earlier abandonment of the creature and his wish to create a perfect being contributed to the dilemma.*

4. **DOK 4:** *Some students might say it was unrealistic for the creature to find Frankenstein in such a large, wild area. But most students will probably find the setting effective because it completely isolates the two characters, and it reflects the harshness and isolation the creature has experienced since Frankenstein brought him to life.*

5. **DOK 4:** *Answers will vary. Students might relate the story to developments such as nuclear weapons, stem cell research, genetic engineering, or artificial intelligence.*

RESEARCH

Remind students that they should confirm any information they find by checking multiple websites and assessing the credibility of each one.

Extend Scientists had known about electricity for years, since Benjamin Franklin introduced it. However, there had been no way to harness it until Edison and Tesla made this possible and began to slowly electrify the world. Scientists mainly looked at electricity as something to learn more about and to harness for commercial uses.

 **RESPOND**

ANALYZE THE TEXT

Support your responses with evidence from the text. NOTEBOOK

1. **Interpret** In paragraph 3, Frankenstein dreams that Elizabeth, a woman he loves, turns into a corpse after he kisses her. How does this dream reflect his experience in the previous paragraph?

2. **Draw Conclusions** Why does the creature think that he should be forgiven for his crimes? Cite evidence for your conclusion.

3. **Analyze** What moral dilemma does Frankenstein experience in the Swiss Alps? What actions and motivations have contributed to this dilemma?

4. **Critique** Did Shelley choose an effective setting for the confrontation between Frankenstein and the creature? Explain why or why not.

5. **Notice & Note** In paragraph 17, Frankenstein says, "For the first time, also, I felt what the duties of a creator towards his creature were." How does this realization relate to scientific and technological developments today?

RESEARCH

RESEARCH TIP
When researching a subject at a specific time period, use specific search terms like "science early 19th century" or "science and *Frankenstein*." Using specific search terms makes it easier to find relevant information quickly.

Scientific understanding was much different during Mary Shelley's time than it is today. With a partner, research scientific and medical knowledge in the early 19th century. Use the following questions to guide your research.

QUESTION	ANSWER
What did scientists know about electricity by the early 19th century?	*Scientists had known about electricity since Ben Franklin's time, but were just learning to harness it for commercial use.*
What methods did scientists use to generate electricity?	*They used lightning, chemical reactions, or other methods.*
What ideas did scientists have about the relationship between electricity and life?	*Some scientists believed that electricity could restore life or take it away, depending on how it was used.*

Extend With a small group, discuss how the information you learned about early 19th-century science relates to *Frankenstein*.

WHEN STUDENTS STRUGGLE . . .

Reteaching: Outline Plot Direct students to complete the plot outlines they began at the beginning of this selection. Remind them to provide a one-sentence summary statement for each paragraph of the excerpt. Once they have completed their paragraph summaries, direct them to create a plot-line graph that lists all the key events within the excerpt. Have them share these plot outlines in small groups and identify which one is the most comprehensive and best written.

 For additional support, go to the **Reading Studio** and assign the following Level Up tutorial: Taking Notes and Outlining.

RESPOND

CREATE AND DISCUSS

Write a Science Fiction Story Write a short science fiction story that addresses a moral or ethical issue. The story can be set in the present and involve an imagined scientific or technological development, or it can be set in the future.

- ❏ Identify an imagined scientific or technological advance or invention and evaluate the moral and ethical dilemmas involved with this innovation.
- ❏ Consider the motivations of your characters as you develop the story.
- ❏ Use details to develop the characters and the setting of your story.
- ❏ Think about ways you can use sensory language to give your readers a vivid experience.

Discuss Have a discussion about the possible negative effects and dangers of the rapid advancement of science, medicine, and technology.

- ❏ Discuss possible ways in which people might respond to and address the issues brought on by major advancements in science, medicine, and technology.
- ❏ Listen carefully to your classmates, ask questions, and comment respectfully on others' ideas.
- ❏ As a group, summarize the key points of the discussion and identify points of agreement.

 Go to **Writing Narratives** in the **Writing Studio** for more about writing short stories.

 Go to **Participating in Collaborative Discussions** in the **Speaking and Listening Studio** for more help with having a discussion.

RESPOND TO THE ESSENTIAL QUESTION

How can science go wrong?

Gather Information Review your annotations and notes on the excerpt from *Frankenstein*. Then, add relevant information to your Response Log. As you determine which information to include, think about:

- how scientific and medical technologies require ethical consideration
- how science fiction can reflect human nature
- how science can be used for both good and bad purposes

ACADEMIC VOCABULARY

As you write and discuss what you learned from the novel, be sure to use the Academic Vocabulary words. Check off each of the words that you use.

- ❏ appreciate
- ❏ insight
- ❏ intensity
- ❏ invoke
- ❏ radical

APPLY

CREATE AND DISCUSS

Write a Science Fiction Story Brainstorm ideas for stories with students, recording the notes for all to see. Encourage them to let their imaginations go wild in considering scientific or technological development they could use for their stories. Challenge them to consider the moral dilemmas that might accompany those developments, and how that would play into their characters' motivations. Encourage them to use sensory language as they write.

For **writing support** for students at varying proficiency levels, see the **Text X-Ray** on page 520D.

Discuss After writing is complete, ask students to engage in a discussion on the dangers of moving too quickly with scientific and technological advancements, and challenge them to consider the negative consequences in doing so. Encourage them to debate, ensuring they maintain respectful discourse with their fellow students. Ask one student to summarize the key points of the discussion, as well as points of agreement reached by the group.

RESPOND TO THE ESSENTIAL QUESTION

Allow time for students to add details from *Frankenstein* to their Unit 4 Response Logs.

APPLY

CRITICAL VOCABULARY

Answers:

1. poor
2. love
3. refuse to eat
4. contains lemons
5. rock
6. punished
7. no
8. moving to a new city

VOCABULARY STRATEGY:
Antonyms

Answers:

1. nonviolent
2. illegitimate
3. irresponsible
4. immobile
5. inconclusive
6. irreverent
7. disorderly
8. unintelligible

 **RESPOND**

WORD BANK

infuse	inarticulate
inanimate	misdeed
ardor	precipice
tumult	odious

CRITICAL VOCABULARY

Practice and Apply Use your understanding of the Critical Vocabulary words to answer each question.

1. If a person is **inarticulate**, would that person make an excellent or a poor public speaker?
2. If someone feels **ardor** toward another person, does that person hate or love the other?
3. Would an **odious** meal be one you look forward to eating or one you refuse to eat?
4. If tea is **infused** with lemons, does that mean it is made of lemons or it contains lemons?
5. Which is an **inanimate** object, a rock or a bird?
6. Would a **misdeed** be more likely to be punished or celebrated?
7. If you were afraid of heights, would you be likely to stand near a **precipice**?
8. Which would be more likely to cause a **tumult**, going on a vacation or moving to a new city?

 Go to the **Vocabulary Studio** for more on antonyms.

VOCABULARY STRATEGY:
Antonyms

An **antonym** is a word with a meaning opposite that of another word. Some antonyms are formed by adding a prefix that means "not" to a word to create one with the opposite meaning. For example, the word *inanimate* is formed by adding the prefix *in-* to the adjective *animate,* which means "living."

Practice and Apply Add the prefix *dis-, il-, im-, in-, ir-, non-,* or *un-* to each word below to create its antonym.

1. violent
2. legitimate
3. responsible
4. mobile
5. conclusive
6. reverent
7. orderly
8. intelligible

 ENGLISH LEARNER SUPPORT

Use Antonyms For students who are struggling with which prefixes to add to words to make them mean the opposite of the original words, provide them with the following list of prefixes: *dis-, il-, im-, in-, ir-, non-, un-*. Direct them to use a print or online dictionary to look up the meanings of each one. Then, ask them to use the dictionary or other online resources to come up with at least 5 words using each of the listed prefixes. Direct students to write 14 sentences, two for each prefix, using the words they found. Remind them to write sentences that clarify, or give insight into, the meaning of the words. **LIGHT**

RESPOND

LANGUAGE CONVENTIONS:
Sensory Language

Sensory language includes descriptive words and phrases that appeal to one or more of the reader's senses, creating a more vivid experience for the reader. In *Frankenstein*, Mary Shelley often uses sensory words and phrases to provide descriptions that elicit feelings of horror in the reader. For instance, read the following sentence from the novel.

> It was already one in the morning; the rain pattered dismally against the panes, and my candle was nearly burnt out, when, by the glimmer of the half-extinguished light, I saw the dull yellow eye of the creature open; it breathed hard, and a convulsive motion agitated its limbs.

Notice that in this sentence, Shelley appeals to the senses of sight ("dull yellow eye") and hearing ("rain pattered dismally"). Now compare that sentence to the following paraphrased version.

> It was already one in the morning. Rain was falling, and my candle was nearly burnt out. I saw the creature's eye open. It breathed hard and moved its limbs.

Which version is more effective at establishing a mood and bringing the reader into the story? Why?

Practice and Apply Revisit the science fiction story you wrote. Identify settings, characters, and events in the story that lack vivid description. Look for opportunities to enhance your reader's experience by using sensory language. Revise your story to help bring your reader into the action of the story by adding details that appeal to the senses. Share your revisions with a partner.

Go to the **Writing Studio: Writing Narratives** for more on the language of narratives.

APPLY

LANGUAGE CONVENTIONS:
Sensory Language

Review the information on sensory language. Explain what a more-vivid experience is for a reader, and how sensory language contributes to that. Explain that writers use these types of descriptions to immerse readers into a story more than just plain language would allow.

Read the first example sentence from the novel aloud. Challenge students to consider which senses are addressed in the sentence, and encourage them to identify the senses of sight and hearing.

Read the second, paraphrased sentence aloud. Challenge students to compare the two and identify reasons why the first is more effective at establishing mood—and bringing the reader deeper into the story.

Practice and Apply Once students have completed their rewrites, place them in pairs or small groups. Direct students to orally share their stories and encourage other group members to point out the examples of sensory language used by each writer. Challenge groups to identify the best sentence among all stories that exemplifies the use of this type of language, and share that with the whole class.

ENGLISH LEARNER SUPPORT

Use Sensory Language For students who are struggling with sensory language, provide them with these simple sentences: 1) The rain felt cold and wet. 2) The wind was chilly and it smelled like snow. 3) The blanket was soft and smelled like flowers.

Ask students to identify the sensory words used in each sentence. **SUBSTANTIAL**

PLAN

MENTOR TEXT

FRANKENSTEIN: GIVING VOICE TO THE MONSTER

Essay by Langdon Winner

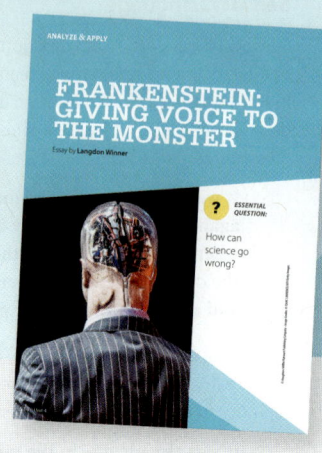

This essay serves as a **mentor text,** a model for students to follow when they come to the Unit 4 Writing Task: Write an Explanatory Essay.

GENRE ELEMENTS

ESSAY

Explain that an **essay** is a short piece of nonfiction that offers an opinion on a subject. Tell students that authors of essays often build a persuasive argument by referencing works of fiction, mythology, historical events, or quotes from experts in the field being discussed. In this lesson, students will evaluate an essay and monitor their comprehension of it.

LEARNING OBJECTIVES

- Evaluate an essay and monitor comprehension.
- Conduct research on the future of automation and employment.
- Write a reflective essay.
- Discuss and respond to essays.
- Use Latin roots.
- Use parallel structure.
- **Language** Rephrase key ideas in an essay.

TEXT COMPLEXITY

Quantitative Measures	Frankenstein: Giving Voice to the Monster	Lexile: 1350L
Qualitative Measures	**Ideas Presented** Multiple levels of complex meaning.	
	Structures Used Complex, but mostly explicit. Exhibits traits of persuasive argument.	
	Language Used Increased academic and domain-specific words.	
	Knowledge Required Cultural and literary knowledge essential to understanding.	

PLAN

Online Ed

RESOURCES

- Unit 4 Response Log
- Selection Audio
- Close Read Screencast: Modeled Discussion
- Reading Studio: Notice & Note
- Level Up Tutorial: Making Inferences; Classifying Sentences by Structure
- Writing Studio: Writing as a Process
- Speaking and Listening Studio: Participating in Collaborative Discussions
- Vocabulary Studio: Latin Roots
- Grammar Studio: Module 4: Lesson 5: Sentence Structure
- "Frankenstein: Giving Voice to the Monster" Selection Test

SUMMARIES

English
In this essay, Langdon Winner uses examples from Mary Shelley's *Frankenstein* to discuss the responsibility scientists have to fully consider the effects of technological advancements, particularly in the field of artificial intelligence.

Spanish
En este ensayo, Langdon Winner usa ejemplos de *Frankenstein* de Mary Shelley para discutir la responsabilidad que los científicos tienen de considerar los efectos de los avances tecnológicos, especialmente en el campo de la inteligencia artificial.

SMALL-GROUP OPTIONS

Have students work in small groups to read and discuss the selection.

Jigsaw With Experts
- Divide the text into three parts: paragraphs 1–5, 6–12, and 13–19.
- Have students count off, or assign students a numbered reading section.
- After reading their sections, have students form groups with other students who read the same section. Each expert group should discuss its section. Encourage students to use academic vocabulary in their discussions.
- Then, have students form new groups with at least one representative from each section. These groups should discuss all the sections and the selection as a whole.

Pinwheel Discussion
- Arrange students in a group of eight, with four students seated facing in and four students seated facing out.
- After reading two or three paragraphs of the selection, pose questions to students for discussion. For example: *What facts surprise you? Why?*
- Students in the inner circle remain stationary throughout the discussion. Students in the outer circle move to their right after discussing each question.
- Provide additional questions for students to discuss during each rotation.

Frankenstein: Giving Voice to the Monster **534B**

PLAN

 **Text X-Ray: English Learner Support**
for "Frankenstein: Giving Voice to the Monster"

Use the Text X-Ray and the supports and scaffolds in the Teacher's Edition to help guide students at different proficiency levels through the selection.

INTRODUCE THE SELECTION
DISCUSS ARTIFICIAL INTELLIGENCE

In this lesson, students will need to be able to discuss how scientific and technological advancements can lead to problems.

Provide the following explanation: *Artificial intelligence (AI)* refers to the development of smart machines that may be superior to the human brain.

Ask students to discuss examples of artificial intelligence and how it might both help and cause problems for humans. Provide sentence frames, such as *One known example of artificial intelligence is _____. This form of AI can help people by _____. It can be a problem because _____.*

CULTURAL REFERENCES

The following words or phrases may be unfamiliar to students:

- *products of human hands* (paragraph 1): things made by people
- *age-old conception* (paragraph 1): a belief held for hundreds or thousands of years
- *to shed light* (paragraph 4): to clarify or explain something unknown
- *to give voice* (paragraph 8): to allow a point of view to be expressed
- *to speak his mind* (paragraph 8): to give his opinions or say what he is thinking about

LISTENING

Seek Clarification

As partners discuss the Quick Start questions on page 535, guide them to ask for clarification as needed.

Use the following supports with students at varying proficiency levels:

- Provide students with a large question mark printed on an index card. Have students hold up the card if they need clarification or want to have something repeated during the discussion. Provide a question bank for students to refer to as they ask their questions, such as *Can you repeat that? What did you mean by _____?* **SUBSTANTIAL**
- During the discussion, have students raise their hands to indicate that they need clarification. Tell the speaker to pause, and have the student ask his or her question. After the speaker responds, have the other student indicate whether further clarification is needed. **MODERATE**
- As students discuss the questions, have them take notes about things that do not seem clear to them. Then, have them restate their notes as questions that they can pose to each other. **LIGHT**

SPEAKING

Rephrase Key Ideas

Help students use simpler language to rephrase the key ideas of an argument.

Use the following supports with students at varying proficiency levels:

- Define these words for students: *artificial, creatures, achieve, sentience, conception*. Then, have them repeat simplified versions of the sentences after you. **SUBSTANTIAL**
- Model how to rephrase the key idea in paragraph 1 in simpler language. Then, have partners work together to identify the key idea in paragraph 2 and rephrase it. Allow students to use dictionaries as needed. **MODERATE**
- Ask pairs to work together to identify the key ideas in paragraphs 1–5. Then, have them state two or three key ideas of this section in their own words. **LIGHT**

READING

Use Pre-Reading Supports

Review how to use footnotes and the dictionary format of pre-taught vocabulary words to increase comprehension.

Use the following supports with students at varying proficiency levels:

- Point out the small number 1 after *Daedalus* in paragraph 3. Direct students to the corresponding footnote at the bottom of the page. Review how to use the pronunciation key and how to identify which part of the footnote tells who *Daedalus* was and which part tells what he did. Paraphrase the two sentences in the footnote. **SUBSTANTIAL**
- Have students discuss the definition of *sentient* in the left column next to paragraph 5. Have partners use sentence frames to explain what each part of the definition tells them. For example: *The letters* adj. *mean that sentient is an* ____. **MODERATE**
- Have students review the essay's footnote and vocabulary definitions. Then, have them discuss how their reading experience would be different without the footnote and definitions. **LIGHT**

WRITING

Use Informal and Formal Tones

Guide students to identify and compare language used to create informal and formal tones. Explain that before they choose a tone for their reflective essays, they need to consider the audience and purpose of the essay.

Use the following supports with students at varying proficiency levels:

- Dictate decodable words from the essay for students to sound out and write. **SUBSTANTIAL**
- Have partners discuss the differences in tone between the following two sentences: (1) *I think artificial intelligence is cool.* (2) *Artificial intelligence has many positive effects.* Then, have them write their own formal and informal sentences about artificial intelligence. **MODERATE**
- Have students write the first paragraph of their reflective essay in a formal tone. Then, have them rewrite it in an informal tone. **LIGHT**

TEACH

? Connect to the ESSENTIAL QUESTION

The essay "Frankenstein: Giving Voice to the Monster" provides an analysis of Mary Shelley's novel as it relates to contemporary issues in science and technology. Shelley's insight into the relationship between Victor Frankenstein and his creature seemingly offers a glimpse into the future of robotics and artificial intelligence, and the responsibility of those who manage such technology.

MENTOR TEXT

At the end of the unit, students will be asked to write an explanatory essay. "Frankenstein: Giving Voice to the Monster" provides a model of how a **formal essay** can be structured to support an author's opinion.

ANALYZE & APPLY

FRANKENSTEIN: GIVING VOICE TO THE MONSTER

Essay by **Langdon Winner**

? ESSENTIAL QUESTION:

How can science go wrong?

QUICK START

Imagine a world in which robots do all of the work. Would such a development make life better? Might there be disadvantages to a fully automated society? Would there be possible dangers to consider? Discuss these questions with a partner.

EVALUATE AN ESSAY

An essay is a brief work of nonfiction that offers an opinion on a subject. A **formal essay** is well organized and has a clear main idea. Formal essays are usually serious and impersonal in tone. Most formal essays are written to inform or persuade or to express ideas. An **informal essay** may be more loosely structured; the tone is conversational, reflecting the personality of the author. The purpose of an informal essay is often to express ideas and feelings or to entertain.

In "Frankenstein: Giving Voice to the Monster," Langdon Winner offers an interesting perspective on the relevance of Mary Shelley's novel today. As you read his essay, notice how he uses his analysis of the novel to support his ideas about science and technology.

MONITOR COMPREHENSION

Some texts are more difficult than others due to their complex ideas, writing style, or unfamiliar content. When you **monitor comprehension,** you check to make sure that you understand what you are reading. One method is to ask questions about a text before, during, and after reading. The following types of questions can help clarify and deepen your understanding:

- **Literal questions** can be answered directly from statements in the text. You might also ask literal questions before you start reading; for example, you might ask yourself what you already know about the topic of an essay or what your purpose is in reading it.

- **Inferential questions** have answers that are not directly stated in the text. Readers make inferences and draw conclusions based on details in a text and their own knowledge and experience.

- **Evaluative questions** are generally asked after reading a text. You might ask whether you agree with ideas in an essay or how effectively you think the author presented them.

As you read this essay, mark up statements that you have trouble understanding, and make note of any questions you have about the content. Review and try to answer your questions after you finish reading.

GET READY

GENRE ELEMENTS: ESSAY
- is a short piece of nonfiction
- offers an opinion on a subject
- formal essays have a serious and impersonal tone
- informal essays are loosely structured and have a conversational tone

TEACH

CRITICAL VOCABULARY

Encourage students to read all the sentences before deciding which word best completes each one. Remind them to look for context clues that match the precise meaning of each word.

Answers:
1. artifice, sentient
2. ominous, prescient
3. recoil, calamity
4. domain, succinct

■ English Learner Support

Use Cognates Tell students that two of the Critical Vocabulary words have Spanish cognates: *artifice/artifice* and *succinct/sucinto*. **ALL LEVELS**

LANGUAGE CONVENTIONS

Parallel Structure Review the information about **parallel structure** on page 536. Read aloud the example sentence, using appropriate phrasing and emphasis to highlight the use of parallel structure. Read paragraph 4 from the text aloud to give another example. Explain that in this example, the repetition of the phrase *"what it means to be"* shows parallelism.

ANNOTATION MODEL

Remind students of the types of questions they can ask themselves to **monitor comprehension,** which are listed on page 535 (**literal, inferential,** and **evaluative**). Tell students that as they read, they may want to circle words they don't understand and underline ideas they have questions about and then write their questions in the margins. Explain that they may follow this model or use their own system for marking up the selection in their write-in text. They may also want to color-code their annotations by using highlighters. Their notes in the margin may include questions about ideas that are unclear or their own observations about the text.

536   Unit 4

 **GET READY**

CRITICAL VOCABULARY

| sentient | recoil | ominous | domain |
| artifice | succinct | calamity | prescient |

To see how many Critical Vocabulary words you already know, use them to complete the sentences.

1. The magician used _____ to trick all of the _____ beings in the room.

2. A(n) _____ mood filled the room as the seer used his _____ powers to direct the detectives to the missing child.

3. The nauseated medical student fought the urge to _____ in horror at the sight of the bloody _____.

4. "Welcome to my _____," said the teacher. "Please keep your comments _____ as I dislike long, rambling explanations."

LANGUAGE CONVENTIONS

Parallel Structure In this lesson, you'll learn about parallel structure—the use of similar grammatical constructions to express ideas that are related or equal in importance. Notice the parallel phrases in this example:

> Mary Shelley's insights on these matters were . . . some of the <u>most ominous hazards</u> and <u>most ghastly calamities</u>. . . .

The repeated grammatical construction of the adjective *most* plus a second adjective and a noun emphasizes that the two phrases are related and equally important. As you read Winner's essay, notice other uses of parallelism.

ANNOTATION MODEL   NOTICE & NOTE

As you read the essay, practice monitoring your comprehension by taking notes, marking the text, and asking questions. The model below shows one reader's notes in response to the text.

> The possibility that artificial creatures, products of human hands, might achieve (sentience) and take on an active role in society is <u>an age-old conception in world cultures</u>, the subject of myths, stories, moral fables, and philosophical speculation.
>
> In Greek mythology one finds the tale of (Pygmalion) who carves a statue named Galatea with whom he falls in love and who <u>eventually comes to life</u>.

What does this word mean?

Why has this been a common theme in literature? What does this say about humans? Does it reflect the need to create?

The writer uses this detail to support his point in the sentence above.

536   Unit 4

BACKGROUND

Langdon Winner (1944–present) is a professor and political theorist. He has taught in colleges and universities and lectured on several continents. He currently serves as the humanities and social sciences department chair at Rensselaer Polytechnic Institute in Troy, New York. His essay "Frankenstein: Giving Voice to the Monster" was presented in Geneva in 2016 at the "Frankenstein's Shadow" conference, honoring the 200th anniversary of the writing of Mary Shelley's novel.

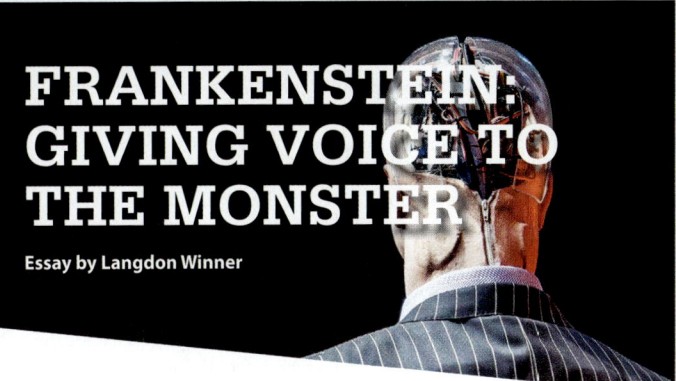

FRANKENSTEIN: GIVING VOICE TO THE MONSTER

Essay by Langdon Winner

SETTING A PURPOSE

As you read, note Winner's ideas about the novel *Frankenstein* and how he connects those ideas to society today.

1   The possibility that artificial creatures, products of human hands, might achieve sentience and take on an active role in society is an age-old conception in world cultures, the subject of myths, stories, moral fables, and philosophical speculation.

2   In Greek mythology one finds the tale of Pygmalion who carves a statue named Galatea with whom he falls in love and who eventually comes to life. In Jewish folklore there are stories of the Golem, an artificial creature animated with surprising results. Norse legends include reports of clay giants able to move on their own accord. An ancient Chinese text describes the work of Yan Shi who in the 10th century B.C. crafted a humanoid figure with lifelike qualities.

3   Both Plato and Aristotle draw upon the myth of the statues of Daedalus[1], mythical creations that could move, perform certain

---

[1] **Daedalus** (dĕd´l-əs): Greek Mythology; A renowned craftsman, sculptor, and inventor and builder of the Labyrinth. He fashioned the wings with which he and his son Icarus escaped from Crete after their imprisonment by Minos.

NOTICE & NOTE

Notice & Note

Use the side margins to notice and note signposts in the text.

EVALUATE AN ESSAY

Annotate: Reread paragraph 2. Mark the examples of myths and legends.

Analyze: What is the author's purpose for listing these examples?

Frankenstein: Giving Voice to the Monster   537

TEACH

BACKGROUND

The essay's author, Langdon Winner, is a political theorist, writer, and professor of science and technology studies. His views on technology and innovation are the subject of much debate. He studies the political issues surrounding modern technology and promotes the advancement of technology that is socially responsible.

Winner says, "To an astonishing degree, today's technological society is based upon a collection of bad habits inherited from a reckless industrial past." Discuss with students the meaning and implications of Winner's quote about technology.

SETTING A PURPOSE

Direct students to use the Setting a Purpose prompt to focus their reading.

 EVALUATE AN ESSAY

Draw a two-column chart on the board. Have students name each of the myths and legends mentioned in paragraph 2, and write them in the first column. Then, have students identify the countries or cultures where these myths and legends originated, and write those in the second column. (**Answer:** *They support his idea in paragraph 1 that cultures around the world and throughout time have created myths and legends about artificial creatures.*)

 For **speaking** and **reading support** for students at varying proficiency levels, see the **Text X-Ray** on page 534D.

IMPROVE READING FLUENCY

Targeted Passage Direct students' attention to paragraphs 2 and 3. Point out that these paragraphs contain proper nouns whose pronunciations may be unfamiliar to them. Tell them to be prepared to read aloud by first identifying the words they may need help pronouncing. Encourage them to determine the correct pronunciation of each word by looking the words up in a dictionary or by asking the teacher or peers for assistance. Then have partners take turns reading the paragraphs to each other. Encourage them to provide support for pronunciation and feedback about pacing and intonation.

 Go to the **Reading Studio** for additional support in developing fluency.

Frankenstein: Giving Voice to the Monster   **537**

TEACH

✏️ MONITOR COMPREHENSION

Remind students that **inferential questions** are questions that have answers not directly stated in the text. To answer these questions, the reader must make inferences, or draw conclusions, from details in the text and their own knowledge and experience. (**Answer:** Sample response: What does this idea imply about current developments in technology? The author feels troubled by recent developments in computer technology.)

■ English Learner Support

Acquire New Vocabulary Make sure students understand the vocabulary in paragraph 5. If necessary, explain the following words:

pivotal—of crucial importance
spawned—produced or gave rise to
monstrosity—something horrible
manifestations—instances or expressions
unsettling—disturbing or upsetting
artificial—made by humans
humanoid—having human characteristics **SUBSTANTIAL**

CRITICAL VOCABULARY

sentient: The author uses the word *sentient* to describe the idea that artificial beings may one day be able to think and feel on their own.

ASK STUDENTS what problems might arise from the creation of sentient nonhuman beings, such as the creature in Shelley's *Frankenstein*. (*Possible answer: These beings might be difficult to control.*)

artifice: The author uses the word *artifice* to indicate something that seems like a clever idea (like Frankenstein's creature) but that can go terribly wrong if not carefully executed.

ASK STUDENTS to think about the awesome responsibility scientists have to ensure that innovation and artifice is handled responsibly and does not result in harm. Have them share about the factors scientists and inventors should consider when implementing groundbreaking technology in artificial intelligence. (*The author would have scientists consider whether by creating beings that surpass human capapbilities, their technological innovations and artifice will be truly helpful to the human species or potentially harmful.*)

538 Unit 4

 **NOTICE & NOTE**

kinds of work and would wander off on their own unless tied down by a rope. In the *Politics* Aristotle uses the metaphor in his defense of slavery: ". . . if every tool could perform its own work when ordered, or by seeing what to do in advance, like the statues of Daedalus in the story . . . master-craftsmen would have no need of assistants and masters no need of slaves."

4   World literature, not to mention modern science fiction, contains a great many stories of this kind, ones that are often used to shed light upon basic questions about what it means to be alive, what it means to be conscious, what it means to be human, what membership in society entails.

5   Within this tradition of thought Mary Shelley's *Frankenstein* plays a pivotal role. Within popular culture, of course, its story has spawned an astonishing range of novels, stories, movies, television programs, advertisements, toys, and costumes, most of which center upon images of monstrosity, horror and the mad scientist. Beyond these familiar manifestations, however, the novel offers a collection of deeply unsettling reflections upon the human condition, ones brought to focus by <u>modern dreams of creating **sentient**, artificial, humanoid beings</u>.

6   In direct, provocative ways the book asks: What is the relationship between the creator and the thing created? What are the larger responsibilities of those who seek power through scientific knowledge and technological accomplishment? What happens when those responsibilities are not recognized or otherwise left unattended?

7   Questions of this kind concern particular projects that involve attempts to create artificial devices that exhibit features and abilities similar to or even superior to ones associated with human beings. In a larger sense, however, the problems posed by the novel point to situations in which scientific technologies introduced into nature and society seem to run out of control, to achieve a certain autonomy, taking on a life of their own beyond the plans and intentions of the persons involved in their creation.

8   As she addresses issues of this kind, the genius of Mary Shelley is to give voice not only to Victor Frankenstein, his family, friends and acquaintances, but to the creature that sprang from his work and after a time learns to speak, read and form his thoughts, eager to speak his mind about his situation. I do not know whether this is the first time in world literature that one finds a serious dialogue between an artificial creation and its creator. But first instance or not, it is a literary device that Shelley uses with stunning effectiveness.

9   At their climatic meeting high in the Alps, the creature's observations and arguments painfully articulate the perils of unfinished, imperfect, carelessly prepared **artifice**, suddenly released

MONITOR COMPREHENSION
Annotate: Mark the reference to technology in the last sentence of paragraph 5.

Infer: What inferential question can you develop in response to this statement? How would you answer it?

sentient
(sĕn´shənt) *adj.* having sense perception; conscious.

artifice
(är´tə-fĭs) *n.* cleverness or ingenuity in making or doing something.

538 Unit 4

APPLYING ACADEMIC VOCABULARY

☐ appreciate   insight   ☐ insanity   ☐ invoke    radical

Write and Discuss Have students turn to a partner to discuss the following questions. Guide students to include the Academic Vocabulary words *insight* and *radical* in their responses. Ask volunteers to share their responses with the class.

- What **insights** does Winner share about science and technology?
- Why might the idea of Frankenstein's monster seem less **radical** today than it did in the 19th century?

NOTICE & NOTE

into the world, emphasizing the obligations of the creator as well as the consequences of insensitivity and neglect.

I am thy creature, and I will be even mild and docile to my natural lord and king if thou wilt also perform thy part, that which thou owest me.

You propose to kill me. How dare you sport thus with life? Do your duty towards me, and I will do mine toward you and the rest of mankind. If you will comply with my conditions I will leave them and you at peace; but if you refuse, I will glut the maw of death, until it be satiated with the blood of your remaining friends.

10   The creature goes on to explain that his greatest desire is to be made part of the human community, something that has been strongly, even brutally, denied him to that point. His stern admonition to Victor is to recognize that the invention of something powerful, ingenious, even marvelous cannot be the end of the work at hand. Thoughtful care must be given to its place in the sphere of human relationships.

11   At first Victor **recoils** and bitterly denounces the creature's demands that he recognize, affirm and fulfill his obligations. But as the threat of violent revenge becomes clear, Victor finally yields to the validity of the argument. "For the first time," he admits, "I felt what the duties of a creator towards his creature were, and that I ought to render him happy before I complained of his wickedness."

12   Following that flash of recognition the story careens toward a disastrous conclusion. Within the wreckage that envelops both Victor and his creature, the book reveals crucial insight, one before its time and with profound implications for similar projects in the future. It can be stated **succinctly** as follows: The quest for power through scientific technology often tends to override and obscure the recognition of the profound responsibilities that the possession of such power entails.

13   Put even more simply: The impulse to power and control typically comes first, while the recognition of personal and collective moral obligation arrives later, if ever at all. Within that unfortunate gap—between aspirations to power through science and belated recognitions of responsibility—arise generations of monstrosity.

14   Mary Shelley's insights on these matters were well ahead of their time and foreshadow some of the most **ominous** hazards and most ghastly **calamities** found along the path to modernity from the early 19th century up to the present day. . . .

15   One could offer a great many historical and contemporary illustrations of what I would call "Frankenstein's problem." An

EVALUATE AN ESSAY
Annotate: Reread the author's analysis of a passage from *Frankenstein* in paragraphs 10–12. Mark words and phrases with strong connotations.

Evaluate: Identify the author's tone. How does his choice of words contribute to the persuasiveness of his essay?

recoil
(rĭ-koil′) *v.* to shrink back, as in fear or repugnance.

succinct
(sək-sĭngkt′) *adj.* characterized by clear, precise expression in few words; concise and terse.

LANGUAGE CONVENTIONS
Annotate: Mark the author's use of parallel structure in the first sentence of paragraph 13.

Evaluate: How does parallelism strengthen the connection between ideas here?

ominous
(ŏm′ə-nəs) *adj.* menacing; threatening.

calamity
(kə-lăm′ĭ-tē) *n.* an event that brings terrible loss, lasting distress, or severe affliction; a disaster.

Frankenstein: Giving Voice to the Monster   539

TEACH

EVALUATE AN ESSAY

Remind students that **connotations** are the feelings that may be attached to the meanings of words. An author's word choice is instrumental in determining the **tone** of the piece. (**Answer:** *The tone of the essay is serious and even cautionary. His word choices help the reader grasp the serious tone of the novel as well as of the dilemma discussed in the essay, illustrate his thesis that the novel directly speaks to the modern dilemma of science and responsibility, and emphasize the real and serious risks society faces today.*)

LANGUAGE CONVENTIONS

Parallel Structure Have students review the example of **parallel structure** given on page 536. Then, have them read paragraph 13 to find the author's use of parallelism and answer the question. (**Answer:** *It reinforces the idea that scientists are neglecting to consider their moral obligations and sometimes never consider them.*)

CRITICAL VOCABULARY

recoil: The author uses the word *recoil*, or shrinking away in fear and disgust, to emphasize Victor's reaction to the creature.

ASK STUDENTS to think of examples when the word *recoil* might be used and describe the feeling the word evokes in each case. (*Possible examples: A hiker may recoil from seeing a snake on the trail out of fear of being bitten. A person may recoil in disgust after removing the lid from a filthy trash can.*)

succinct: The author uses the word *succinct* to describe a statement as clear and concise.

ASK STUDENTS to list times when it is important to make communication succinct. (*Possible answers: when delivering a speech, when giving directions, in an emergency*)

ominous: An ominous feeling is one of foreboding because of potential danger.

ASK STUDENTS to explain how Mary Shelley's novel foreshadowed ominous possibilities in the future. (*The same thing could happen in modern times with robotics and artificial intelligence.*)

calamity: The author uses the word *calamities* to describe the terrible disasters that have occurred in history.

ASK STUDENTS to identify examples of modern-day calamities. (*Possible examples: natural disasters, such as hurricanes and fires, violent attacks, acts of war*)

Frankenstein: Giving Voice to the Monster   539

WHEN STUDENTS STRUGGLE . . .

Identify Parallel Structure Some students may have difficulty identifying the features of parallelism. Ask them to circle the phrases in the first sentence of paragraph 13 that relate to time (*comes first, arrives later*). Explain that this repetition of time phrases indicates **parallel structure**. Help them identify other examples of parallelism in the text and write them down.

 For additional support, go to the **Reading Studio** and assign the following Level Up tutorial: Classifying Sentences by Structure.

TEACH

QUOTED WORDS

The author shares quotes from well-known, respected, and knowledgeable people in the fields of artificial intelligence and technology. Point out that an expert opinion is often persuasive and convincing because of the person's reputation. Have students study the quotes to determine how they support the author's opinion. (**Answer:** Answers will vary. Students will probably find the quotes to be effective support because Hawking and Gates are such famous figures in science and technology, and Sinclair has practical experience in dealing with inventions.)

■ English Learner Support

Compare Quotes Tell students that the word *distress* in paragraph 15 means "worry" or "anxiety." As students read the quotes by Hawking, Gates, and Sinclair, guide them in finding words and phrases that indicate that these experts feel distress about the future of AI. (*Hawking:* "warned," "could spell the end of the human race," "Humans . . . would be superseded by AI," "outsmarting," "out-inventing," "out-manipulating," "weapons we cannot even understand," "whether it can be controlled at all"; *Gates:* "concerned," "concern"; *Sinclair* "surpassing humans," "very difficult for us to survive") **MODERATE/LIGHT**

CRITICAL VOCABULARY

domain: The author uses the word *domain* to describe an area of activity in scientific inquiry, specifically the area of computerization, robotics, and artificial intelligence.

ASK STUDENTS what domains of expertise Stephen Hawking, Bill Gates, and Clive Sinclair have. (*Stephen Hawking, physics; Bill Gates, computer science; Clive Sinclair, inventions/electronics*)

prescient: The word *prescient* describes the ability to know that something will happen before it happens.

ASK STUDENTS why the author considers Shelley's Frankenstein to be prescient. (*It illustrated that humans can lose control of the things they create, which is a present-day concern due to the rise of artificial intelligence.*)

540 Unit 4

 **NOTICE & NOTE**

domain
(dō-mān´) *n.* a sphere of activity, influence, or knowledge.

QUOTED WORDS

Notice & Note: Mark the names of notable people the author quotes in paragraphs 16–18.

Critique: Do these quotations provide effective support for the author's opinion about artificial intelligence? Why or why not?

prescient
(prĕsh´ənt) *adj.* of or relating to prescience—which means knowledge of actions or events before they occur.

appropriate, highly practical, obviously troubling set of developments at present are found within a particular **domain** of scientific inquiry and application, a zone of works not all that dissimilar from the one the fictional Victor Frankenstein explored—today's realm of advanced computerization, smart algorithms, artificial intelligence (AI) and robotics. . . . During the past several years, notable scientists, engineers and luminaries in the technology business sector have stepped forward to express distress at what they see as dire risks that research in AI presents to the human species overall.

16 In a BBC interview last year, Stephen Hawking warned, "The development of full artificial intelligence could spell the end of the human race. . . . Humans, limited by slow biological evolution, couldn't compete and would be superseded by AI. . . . One can imagine such technology outsmarting financial markets, out-inventing human researchers, out-manipulating human leaders, and developing weapons we cannot even understand. Whereas the short-term impact of AI depends on who controls it, the long-term impact depends on whether it can be controlled at all."

17 In a live exchange on the internet, Microsoft cofounder Bill Gates offered similar views. "I am in the camp that is concerned about super intelligence," Gates wrote. "First the machines will do a lot of jobs for us and not be super intelligent. . . . A few decades after that though the intelligence is strong enough to be a concern."

18 In the same vein, British inventor Clive Sinclair recently told the BBC, "Once you start to make machines that are rivaling and surpassing humans with intelligence, it's going to be very difficult for us to survive. It's just an inevitability." . . .

19 Studies of and speculation about issues of this kind has inspired the creation of a collection of new research centers at leading universities. Among them are the Cambridge Center for the Study of Existential Risk and The Future of Life Institute at MIT. Taken together the shelf of books on AI and Robots, the systematic studies of the future of automation and employment, and the excited warnings about artificial devices superseding human beings as the key actors on the stage of world history are, in my view, a contemporary realization of the **prescient** concerns and warnings at the heart of Mary Shelley's book—concerns and warnings about the headlong flight from responsibility.

540 Unit 4

TO CHALLENGE STUDENTS . . .

Debate the Issue Have students form two teams to represent both sides of a debate on the use of artificial intelligence. Do the benefits of using artificial intelligence outweigh the drawbacks, or are there too many potentially negative consequences to consider its use? Have each team take one of the two positions and conduct research online or at the library to find evidence in support of their position. Then, have students conduct a debate about this issue.

Check Your Understanding

Answer these questions before moving on to the **Analyze the Text** section on the following page.

1. According to the author, the genius of Shelley is in —

   A setting the climactic meeting place in the Alps

   B giving a voice to Frankenstein's creature

   C anticipating the novel's effect on popular culture

   D introducing the concept of a mad scientist

2. What is one of the deeper questions posed by Shelley's novel?

   F Who should participate in scientific development?

   G What is the relationship between nature and society?

   H What scientific projects should never be attempted?

   J What responsibilities accompany scientific development?

3. The attitude that Gates, Hawking, and Sinclair share about the future of artificial intelligence is one of —

   A concern and caution

   B hope and excitement

   C annoyance and dismay

   D doubt and negativity

CHECK YOUR UNDERSTANDING

Have students answer the questions independently.

Answers:

1. B
2. J
3. A

If they answer any questions incorrectly, have them reread the text to confirm their understanding. Then they may proceed to ANALYZE THE TEXT on page 542.

ENGLISH LEARNER SUPPORT

Oral Assessment Use the following questions to assess students' comprehension and speaking skills:

1. Did the author like *Frankenstein*? *(yes)*
2. Does the author think technology can cause problems? *(yes)*
3. Do Hawking, Gates, and Sinclair worry about artificial intelligence? *(yes)*
   SUBSTANTIAL/MODERATE

APPLY

ANALYZE THE TEXT

Possible answers:

1. **DOK 2:** *Frankenstein was the first novel to raise questions about science and moral responsibility, an issue that has led to many calamities and is especially relevant to current research into artificial intelligence.*

2. **DOK 4:** *Winner supports his opinion effectively with evidence from the text in the form of quotations and summaries in paragraphs 9–12. He also uses evocative language with strong connotations that sets an appropriate tone.*

3. **DOK 3:** *His conclusion effectively summarizes his view of Shelley's novel and how it relates to our modern situation. The final paragraph also includes examples of current studies on the issue, which implies an element of hope for the future.*

4. **DOK 3:** *Answers will vary. Sample questions: What safeguards can prevent artificial intelligence from getting out of control? How advanced is artificial intelligence today? Why is society pushing to develop artificial intelligence quickly if the risks are so great?*

5. **DOK 4:** *Possible answers: Yes, because offering a balance of views would have made the conclusion more credible; no, because the author's point is that leaders in science and technology have expressed concerns similar to Shelley's, not that everyone shares this view.*

RESEARCH

Remind students that they should confirm any information they find by checking multiple websites and assessing the credibility of each one. Tell them to make sure that any statistical information they find is up to date.

Extend Students should review the jobs that are being replaced, or are in danger of being replaced, by automation and think about their own career plans. Have students share whether their first choice of career is one of these "endangered" jobs and, if so, whether they are now rethinking their choice. How many students think they might forego their first choice based on the information they gathered in their research? How many would stay with their choice of career?

542   Unit 4

RESPOND

ANALYZE THE TEXT

Support your responses with evidence from the text. 📓 NOTEBOOK

1. **Identify** What is the main idea of this essay?
2. **Evaluate** Does the author provide sufficient support for his opinion that Shelley's genius was to "give voice to the monster"? Why or why not?
3. **Critique** How effective is the author's conclusion to the essay? Explain.
4. **Question** Review your markups and notes on "Frankenstein: Giving Voice to the Monster." What questions do you have after reading this essay? What kind of research or investigation might help you answer these questions?
5. **Notice and Note** Reread paragraphs 16–18. Do you think that the author should have included a quotation from someone with a different view of the future of artificial intelligence? Explain why or why not.

RESEARCH

RESEARCH TIP
Look for sources that include up-to-date research and provide evidence in the form of facts, statistics, and logical reasoning.

Winner suggests that some problems resulting from the development of artificial intelligence might be related to the "future of automation and employment." He quotes Bill Gates, who also mentions the issue of machines doing many of our jobs. Research these concerns. What jobs are currently being replaced by machines? What jobs are in danger of being replaced in the future? Use the chart below to record your findings.

JOBS ALREADY REPLACED OR ARE BEING REPLACED	JOBS IN DANGER OF BEING REPLACED IN THE NEAR FUTURE	JOBS PROBABLY NOT IN DANGER OF BEING REPLACED
some assembly line and factory jobs; telemarketers; some packing and warehouse jobs; etc.	jobs requiring only a high school education; cashiers; receptionists; couriers and delivery jobs; etc.	human resource managers; sales managers; public relations mangers; event planners; creative writers; etc.

Extend Use the information you found to think about your own plans for a future career. Write a brief paragraph explaining how the research might influence your planning for the future.

542   Unit 4

WHEN STUDENTS STRUGGLE . . .

Reteaching: Monitor Comprehension Guide students to ask **inferential questions** about artificial intelligence and the author's attitude toward the scientists who work in this field. Remind students that when they make inferences, they look at all of the information an author presents and then draw conclusions based on this information and their own knowledge and experience.

📖 For additional support, go to the **Reading Studio** and assign the following Level Up tutorial: Making Inferences.

RESPOND

CREATE AND DISCUSS

Write a Reflective Essay Respond to Winner's essay with a **reflective essay** in which you make connections between the text and yourself. Use your own point of view to express your personal reaction to the ideas presented in the essay.

- ❏ Record your personal reactions to the text. Use the annotations and notes you made while reading. How does the text relate to your life?
- ❏ Use a topical outline or a chart to organize your thoughts.
- ❏ Begin your essay with a hook, such as an anecdote or an interesting example.
- ❏ As you write, stay organized. Maintain a personal tone appropriate to your purpose and audience, using academic vocabulary as applicable.
- ❏ Conclude by sharing what you discovered about yourself, important insights you gained, or a decision you made as a result of your reflection upon the essay.

Discuss Your Essay Use your reflective essay to generate discussion in a small group.

- ❏ Read your essay to the members of your group.
- ❏ Ask each member of the group to give a brief oral response to your essay.
- ❏ Encourage the group to discuss ideas and questions raised in your essay.
- ❏ Listen and respond appropriately as other group members read their essays.

Go to the **Writing Studio: Writing as a Process** for help with writing your reflective essay.

Go to the **Speaking and Listening Studio** to find out more about participating in collaborative discussions.

RESPOND TO THE ESSENTIAL QUESTION

 How can science go wrong?

Gather Information Review your annotations and notes on "Frankenstein: Giving Voice to the Monster." Then, add relevant information to your Response Log. As you determine which information to include, think about:

- possible dangers and problems related to the development of artificial intelligence
- society's responsibility in controlling scientific developments
- how Shelley's novel relates to Winner's ideas

ACADEMIC VOCABULARY

As you write and discuss what you learned from the essay, be sure to use the Academic Vocabulary words. Check off each of the words that you use.

- ❏ appreciate
- ❏ insight
- ❏ intensity
- ❏ invoke
- ❏ radical

Frankenstein: Giving Voice to the Monster 543

APPLY

CREATE AND DISCUSS

Write a Reflective Essay Introduce students to the writing task by reading aloud the introductory paragraph on page 543 with them. Remind students to refer to the notes they recorded in their Unit 4 Response Logs and in their write-in texts as they plan and draft their essays. Encourage them to look for ideas and questions about artificial intelligence and the responsibility that comes with new technologies. Tell them that they can use these ideas and questions as the basis for their reflection.

 For **writing support** for students at varying proficiency levels, see the **Text X-Ray** on page 534D.

Discuss Your Essay Remind students that speaking and listening are critical components of literacy. As they listen to each other's essays, they should feel free to write down questions they might have so they can ask them at the end. Encourage students to be respectful as they make comments and ask questions about each other's essays.

RESPOND TO THE ESSENTIAL QUESTION

Allow time for students to add details from "Frankenstein: Giving Voice to the Monster" to their Unit 4 Response Logs.

Frankenstein: Giving Voice to the Monster **543**

APPLY

CRITICAL VOCABULARY

Encourage students to read all the sentences before deciding which word best completes each one. Remind them to look for context clues that match the precise meaning of each word.

Answers:

1. *artifice*
2. *ominous*
3. *calamity*
4. *succinct*

VOCABULARY STRATEGY:
Latin Roots

Answers:

1. **artis:** *"art"; artifact, artisan, artless*
2. **dominus:** *"master"; dominate*
3. **scire:** *"to know"; prescience, conscience, omniscient*
4. **omen:** *"foreboding"; omen*

 **RESPOND**

WORD BANK

sentient   ominous
artifice   calamity
recoil   domain
succinct   prescient

CRITICAL VOCABULARY

Practice and Apply Choose the word that completes the sentence.

1. The politician used _____ to make it appear as if he wanted to enrich the people when, in fact, he wanted only to enrich himself.
   a. artifice   b. sentient

2. Despite the _____ clouds on the near horizon, the skipper pressed onward toward the stricken vessel.
   a. prescient   b. ominous

3. When the dam broke above the village, _____ ensued.
   a. calamity   b. recoil

4. The professor delivered a _____ lecture that ended well before the class period was over.
   a. succinct   b. domain

VOCABULARY STRATEGY:
Latin Roots

Knowing Latin roots can give you clues to the meanings of unfamiliar words. For example, knowing that the Latin root *sent* means "to feel" could help you figure out the meaning of *sentient*, which means "capable of feeling." When the author speaks of sentient beings, you know that he means beings that are aware of their surroundings and capable of emotions. Another word in the essay with the same root is *sentience*, which refers to the state of being sentient.

Practice and Apply The following words are all based on a Latin root. Write the root for each word and then the meaning of the root. Use a dictionary to help you. Notice how the definition of the word is related to its root. Can you think of other words that might be based on each root?

1. artifice *artis —"art"; artifact, artisan, artless*
2. domain *dominus — "master"; dominate*
3. prescient *scire — "to know"; prescience, conscience, omniscient*
4. ominous *omen — "foreboding"; omen*

Go to the **Vocabulary Studio: Analyzing Word Structure** for more on Latin roots.

 ENGLISH LEARNER SUPPORT

Vocabulary Strategy Give students additional practice in determining the meaning of words based on their roots. Have pairs of students copy the words, underline the roots, and guess the definitions. Have them confirm their definitions by looking up each word in a dictionary. Write the following words on the board:

- *inspect, multicolored, fracture, dictation*
  SUBSTANTIAL/MODERATE
- *artificial, dominion, nescient, omnipotent* **LIGHT**

LANGUAGE CONVENTIONS:
Parallel Structure

Parallel structure, or parallelism, is the use of similar grammatical constructions to express ideas that are closely related or equal in importance. The grammatical constructions may include phrases, clauses, or sentences. Parallel structure helps writers organize, clarify, and emphasize their thoughts. It can also affect the meaning and tone of a sentence or passage. Read this sentence from Langdon Winner's essay:

> World literature, . . . contains a great many stories of this kind, ones that are often used to shed light upon basic questions about <u>what it means to be</u> alive, <u>what it means to be</u> conscious, <u>what it means to be</u> human, <u>what membership in society entails</u>.

Winner uses a series of noun clauses beginning with *what* that are the objects of the preposition *about*. The repetition of this grammatical construction gives equal weight to the "basic questions" he identifies in world literature. The parallelism also gives the sentence a pleasing rhythm that makes it more memorable. Consider that he could have written the sentence like this:

> World literature, . . . contains a great many stories of this kind, ones that are often used to shed light upon basic questions about what it means to be alive, conscious, and human, and what membership in society entails.

In this sentence without parallel structure, the relationship between the questions is less clear. The sentence is also less memorable because it lacks a strong rhythm.

Writers can use parallel structure not only within sentences but also in groups of sentences. For example, Winner starts the first two sentences in paragraph 2 with "In Greek mythology" and "In Jewish folklore," using parallelism to tie together examples from different cultural traditions to support his idea.

Practice and Apply Underline the parallel structures in the sentences below. Then, use each sentence as a model to write two sentences of your own with the same parallel structures.

1. "One can imagine such technology outsmarting financial markets, out-inventing human researchers, out-manipulating human leaders, and developing weapons we cannot even understand."

2. "Whereas the short-term impact of AI depends on who controls it, the long-term impact depends on whether it can be controlled at all."

RESPOND

Go to the **Grammar Studio: Sentence Fragments and Run-on Sentences** for more on parallel structure.

APPLY

LANGUAGE CONVENTIONS:
Parallel Structure

Review the information on **parallel structure** on page 545. Point out that parallel structure may involve words, phrases, or clauses, and that all three are evident in Winner's essay. Walk through the examples on page 545 and discuss how each example emphasizes or creates connections between ideas.

Practice and Apply Ask students to write their own sentences that include words, phrases, or clauses in a parallel structure. Then, have partners share their sentences with each other. Tell them to identify each use of parallelism in their partner's sentences and discuss whether each usage involved words, phrases, or clauses.

 ENGLISH LEARNER SUPPORT

Language Conventions Use the following supports with students at varying proficiency levels:

- Have students find and circle phrases in paragraph 4 that have **parallel structure. SUBSTANTIAL**

- Have students find sentences in the text that have a parallel structure. Then, have them rewrite the sentences using different words but maintaining the parallel structure and overall meaning. **MODERATE**

- Have students identify a section of Winner's essay that could be made stronger by the use of parallelism. Ask students to rewrite a sentence or two in this section, adding parallel words, phrases, or clauses. **LIGHT**

PLAN

ODE TO THE WEST WIND
Lyric Poem by Percy Bysshe Shelley

SONG OF A THATCHED HUT DAMAGED IN AUTUMN WIND
Lyric Poem by Du Fu

GENRE ELEMENTS
LYRIC POEM
Remind students that **lyric poetry** deals with the thoughts and feelings of the speaker. It has a musical quality and often contains figurative language, such as similes, metaphors, and imagery. Lyric poetry can be in a variety of forms and cover many subjects. In this lesson, students will analyze the forms of lyric poetry and compare their diction and theme.

LEARNING OBJECTIVES
- Analyze form and diction.
- Conduct research about times and places of the poets Percy Bysshe Shelley and Du Fu.
- Create a visual representation.
- Present an image.
- Collaborate and present a theme comparison.
- **Language** Discuss the diction of poems.

TEXT COMPLEXITY

Quantitative Measures	Ode to the West Wind / Song of a Thatched Hut Damaged in Autumn Wind	Lexile: N/A
Qualitative Measures	**Ideas Presented** Multiple levels, use of symbolism. Greater demand for inference.	
	Structures Used More complex, lyrical and poetic.	
	Language Used Implied meanings, allusive, figurative, and formal language. Complex sentence structures.	
	Knowledge Required Mostly familiar themes, with some geographical references.	

PLAN

Online

RESOURCES

- Unit 4 Response Log
- Selection Audio
- Reading Studio: Notice & Note
- Level Up Tutorials: Using Context Clues, Elements of Poetry, Summarizing
- Writing Studio: Task, Purpose, and Audience
- Speaking and Listening Studio: Knowing Your Audience
- "Ode to the West Wind" and "Song of a Thatched Hut Damaged in Autumn Wind" Selection Test

SUMMARIES

English

In "Ode to the West Wind," the speaker praises the west wind, a symbol of autumn and a catalyst of storms. Wearied by life, he asks the wind to lift him, fill him with its spirit, drive his thoughts across the universe, and make him its instrument and prophet of a new day. In "Song of a Thatched Hut Damaged in Autumn Wind," the speaker reminds us that it's natural for everything to be impermanent, but it's still important to dream and try to achieve those dreams.

Spanish

En "Oda al viento del oeste", la voz narrativa elogia al viento del oeste, un símbolo del otoño y catalizador de tormentas. Cansado de la vida, le pide al viento que lo levante, que lo llene de su espíritu, esparza sus pensamientos a lo largo del universo y haga de él su instrumento y profeta de un nuevo día. En "Canción de tejado dañado en un otoño salvaje", la voz narrativa nos recuerda que es natural que nada sea permanente, pero que es importante soñar y tratar de alcanzar esos sueños.

SMALL-GROUP OPTIONS

Have students work in small groups and pairs to read and discuss the selections.

Three-Minute Review

- After reading aloud Section I of "Ode to the West Wind," set a timer for three minutes and have students work independently.
- During this time, ask students to reread the material and write clarifying questions or copy down unfamiliar words.
- After three minutes, have students share observations about the poem or any of the questions or notes they wrote.
- Briefly discuss students' observations and clarify material as needed.

Final Word

- Have students read "Song of a Thatched Hut Damaged in Autumn Wind."
- After reading, ask one student to describe his or her impression of the poem.
- Have other students briefly give their impressions in turn.
- Return to the original student and ask if he or she would like to revise his or her initial impression based on the responses of the group.
- Continue the activity with students until all have had an opportunity to revise their first impression.

Ode to the West Wind / Song of a Thatched Hut   **546B**

PLAN

Text X-Ray: English Learner Support
for "Ode to the West Wind" and "Song of a Thatched Hut Damaged in Autumn Wind"

Use the Text X-Ray and the supports and scaffolds in the Teacher's Edition to help guide students at different proficiency levels through the selections.

INTRODUCE THE SELECTION
DISCUSS PERSONIFICATION AND ALLITERATION

In this lesson, students will need to be able to discuss how poems use personification and alliteration to create specific effects.

Provide the following explanation:

- *Personification* is when a writer attributes human qualities to an object, animal, or idea.
- *Alliteration* is the repetition of consonant sounds at the beginning of words. Alliteration creates a musical quality to poems.

Guide students' reading by telling them they will be looking for examples of personification and alliteration in the poems. They should make note of examples they find and prepare to describe their findings with the class.

- Write sentence frames on the board, such as: *The author of "Ode to the West Wind" personifies the ____. An example of alliteration in [poem] is ____.*

CULTURAL REFERENCES

The following words or phrases may be unfamiliar to students:

- *thou* (Ode, line 2): archaic way of saying *you*
- *pestilence* (Ode, line 5): a fatal epidemic disease
- *thine* (Ode, line 9): archaic way of saying *yours*
- *o'er* (Ode, line 10): contraction for *over*
- *didst* (Ode, line 29): archaic way of saying *did*
- *the sense faints picturing them* (Ode, line 36): too beautiful to look at
- *cleave* (Ode, line 38): split
- *ne'er* (Ode, line 51): contraction for *never*
- *thatched roof* (Song, line 2): a type of roof made from plant material
- *took advantage* (Song, line 6): exploited or used to get something, usually unfairly

LISTENING

Identify Alliteration

Review with students that when they listen for alliteration, they are listening for similar consonant sounds.

Use the following supports with students at varying proficiency levels:

- Slowly read aloud the first line of "Ode to the West Wind." Have students listen for alliteration. Elicit that the letter *w* is repeated at the beginning of *wild, west,* and *wind*. Have students repeat the words, emphasizing the initial /w/. Repeat the activity for other alliteration in the poem. **SUBSTANTIAL**
- Have pairs find examples of alliteration in "Ode to the West Wind." One partner will read an example and the other will tell what consonant sound is repeated. Have them switch roles and repeat the activity. **MODERATE**
- Have pairs find examples of alliteration in "Ode to the West Wind." One partner will read an example and the other will tell what consonant sound is repeated. Have them switch roles and repeat the activity. Then, have them find examples in the second selection. **LIGHT**

PLAN

SPEAKING

Analyze Diction

Review diction and explain that understanding diction in poetry can help the reader understand the author's ideas.

Use the following supports with students at varying proficiency levels:

- Reread *"the leaves dead are driven"* from "Ode to the West Wind." Then, ask questions about diction: *Do we usually say "the leaves dead" or "the dead leaves?"* (the dead leaves) Have students hold up one finger for the first phrase and two fingers for the second phrase. *Which phrase shows inverted syntax?* (the leaves dead) **SUBSTANTIAL**
- Have partners read aloud stanzas 1–3 of "Ode to the West Wind" and share examples of inverted syntax. Have students work together to restate the examples into more natural speech. **MODERATE**
- Have partners choose one of the poems and discuss the diction. Have them use examples from the poem to discuss inverted and natural syntax, plain and elevated vocabulary, and concrete and abstract words. **LIGHT**

READING

Create Dictionaries

Remind students that using a dictionary as they read can help them better understand the meaning of a poem.

Focus on "Ode to the West Wind." Use the following supports with students at varying proficiency levels:

- Have students circle and read aloud familiar words in the poem with a partner. **SUBSTANTIAL**
- Have pairs read the poem. They should identify 6 unfamiliar words. Then, have them work together to use accessible language to create a dictionary for the words. **MODERATE**
- Have students read the poem and identify 10 unfamiliar words. Then, have them work together to write definitions to create dictionaries for the words. Challenge them to list synonyms for the words. **LIGHT**

WRITING

Use Connecting Words

Read the Create and Present prompt on SE page 563. Tell students before they create a visual representation, they need to write down their ideas.

Use the following supports with students at varying proficiency levels:

- Ask students yes–no questions about how the poets described the wind. Such as, *Did the poet say the wind was strong?* (yes) Then, have students draw what they think the wind looked like. **SUBSTANTIAL**
- Have students work with a partner to write words or phrases that the poets used to describe the wind. Students should note which words or phrases are positive or negative. Then, have students create a visual based on their list of words. **MODERATE**
- Have students work individually to write a list of words or phrases the poets used to describe the wind. Then, have them create visuals based on their lists. Pair students to discuss their visuals. **LIGHT**

TEACH

 Connect to the
ESSENTIAL QUESTION

Tell students that in Percy Bysshe Shelley's "Ode to the West Wind" and Du Fu's "Song of a Thatched Hut Damaged in Autumn Wind," the poets' outlooks are shaped by their relationships and perceptions of the government and their outlook on life.

COMPARE THEMES

Point out that both of these poems have similar topics. Remind students that the theme is the message about life or human nature that the author wants to share. Poets use imagery, figurative language, and word choice to develop their themes. Tell students to keep this information in mind as they read the poems and prepare to compare.

COLLABORATE & COMPARE

POEM
ODE TO THE WEST WIND
by **Percy Bysshe Shelley**
pages 549–552

COMPARE THEMES

As you read, notice how both poets describe the effects of the wind in autumn. What can you infer about the poems' themes based on their imagery, figurative language, diction, and other elements? Once you have read both poems, you will collaborate with a small group on a research project.

 ESSENTIAL QUESTION:

What shapes your outlook on life?

POEM
SONG OF A THATCHED HUT DAMAGED IN AUTUMN WIND
by **Du Fu**
pages 554–555

546 Unit 4

GET READY

QUICK START

People constantly learn from nature. Think about a lesson you have learned by observing some aspect of nature, such as a seasonal change. With a partner, discuss the lesson you learned and why it is important.

ANALYZE FORM

In poetry, **form** refers to the arrangement of words into structural patterns, including the length of a poem's lines and their grouping into stanzas. Form can also refer to a poem's rhyme scheme, meter, or its traditional poetic type, such as sonnet or ode. The form of a poem helps support its mood and theme.

Prior to the 20th century, poets usually relied on traditional forms to express their ideas and feelings. One popular form that you have already encountered is the **sonnet,** which has 14 lines and a regular rhyme scheme. Another traditional form is the **ode,** a complex lyric that develops a serious theme. Odes typically have a dignified or reflective tone, and they often commemorate events or praise people, ideas, or elements of nature. Shelley's "Ode to the West Wind," a famous example, employs a complex rhyme scheme and regular meter.

During the 20th century, poets increasingly turned away from traditional forms, often producing **free verse**—poems that do not have regular patterns of rhyme and meter. This form usually gives their poems a rhythm closer to that of everyday speech. Instead of following a fixed structure, lines are organized according to a plan developed by the poet. The poet Du Fu wrote "Song of a Thatched Hut Damaged in Autumn Wind" in a traditional Chinese form; however, the translation you are about to read is composed in free verse.

As you read the two poems, notice these characteristics of their forms:

GENRE ELEMENTS: LYRIC POETRY

- expresses the personal thoughts and feelings of a single speaker
- has a musical quality
- is marked by imagination and evocative language
- creates a strong, unified impression
- can be in a variety of forms covering many subjects

"Ode to the West Wind"	• Follows a regular meter • Written in terza rima, a series of three-line stanzas linked by rhyme • Highly melodic with a dignified tone
"Song of a Thatched Hut Damaged in Autumn Wind"	• Free verse translation • Lines not grouped in stanzas • Rhythms approximate speech • Includes alliteration, figurative language, and other poetic devices

Ode to the West Wind / Song of a Thatched Hut 547

TEACH

ANALYZE DICTION

Review the terms associated with analyzing **diction** (**syntax, inverted syntax**) and ask students to provide examples of how syntax might affect reader's perceptions of the subject or topic of a poem. Challenge them to think about different poems they have read or heard and how diction impacted their overall experience of the poet's message. Remind students that as they read, they can refer to the bullet points on page 556 to help them answer questions about Shelley and Du Fu's use of specific vocabulary and language to convey their themes.

■ English Learner Support

Analyze Diction Provide students with language frames they can use to evaluate the speaker's diction in each of the selections. Consider using the following frames:

- The speaker uses _____ diction to show _____.
- The speaker uses plain language to explain _____. He uses formal language to explain _____.
- The syntax in lines _____ is _____.

Ask students to discuss their ideas in small groups.

ANNOTATION MODEL

Remind students to refer to the table on page 548 to help them differentiate between different forms in poetry. Tell them that while contemporary poetry may have words, phrases, and language that feel more modern or familiar, older poems may sound elevated and more formal, though the diction may reflect common language at the time they were written. Ask students to try to explain what the poet is saying in their own words (paraphrase) in the margins as they read. Point out that they may follow this suggestion or use their own system for marking up the selection in their write-in text. They may want to color-code their annotations by using highlighters. Their notes in the margin may include questions about ideas that are unclear or topics they want to learn more about.

 **GET READY**

ANALYZE DICTION

Careful control of language is especially important in poetry. To shape the perception of readers, poets must choose appropriate **diction,** a term that refers to both word choice and **syntax,** the order or arrangement of words. Traditionally, poets used a special diction, **inverted syntax,** which reverses the expected order of words. Inverted syntax can help maintain patterns of rhyme and meter. Poets also tended to choose elevated and vivid vocabulary. In contrast, the syntax of modern poetry is usually closer to natural speech, though poets still rely on concrete, vivid words, and distinct poetic elements to appeal to readers' senses.

Use the following questions to help guide your analysis of diction:

- Does the poet use plain or elevated vocabulary?
- Does the poet choose mostly concrete words, which name specific things, or abstract words that identify concepts?
- Does the poet select words with strong connotations, or associated feelings?
- Is the writer's syntax formal or informal? inverted or natural?

ANNOTATION MODEL

 NOTICE & NOTE

As you read, note elements of each poem's form and mark distinctive examples of the poet's diction. In the model, you can see one reader's notes about lines 1–6 of "Ode to the West Wind."

> O wild West Wind, (thou) breath of Autumn's being,
> Thou, from whose unseen presence <u>the leaves dead</u>
> Are driven, like ghosts from an (enchanter fleeing.)
>
> Yellow, and black, and pale, and hectic red,
> (Pestilence-stricken multitudes:) O thou,
> Who (chariotest) to their dark wintry bed

The poem includes elevated and abstract vocabulary.

The syntax is formal. The phrase "the leaves dead" is an example of inverted syntax.

Words like "dead" and "hectic" and "Pestilence-stricken" have strong, serious connotations.

BACKGROUND

Percy Bysshe Shelley (1792–1822) led a turbulent life. As an adolescent, he embraced radical political and social views, which alienated him from his aristocratic relatives. Shelley wrote "Ode to the West Wind" in the autumn of 1819 when he and his family were living in Florence, Italy. Earlier that year, English workers demonstrating for reform were killed by soldiers in the Peterloo Massacre. This event outraged Shelley, who opposed all injustice and dreamed of changing the world through poetry. In 1822, shortly before he would have turned 30, he drowned when his sailboat sank in a storm off the coast of Italy.

ODE TO THE WEST WIND
Poem by Percy Bysshe Shelley

PREPARE TO COMPARE

As you read, note the ways in which the poet describes and personifies the autumn wind. Think about what this suggests about the poet's view of nature and how these details contribute to the theme of the poem.

I

O wild West Wind, thou breath of Autumn's being,
Thou, from whose unseen presence the leaves dead
Are driven, like ghosts from an enchanter fleeing,

Yellow, and black, and pale, and hectic red,
5   Pestilence-stricken multitudes: O thou,
Who chariotest to their dark wintry bed

The wingèd seeds, where they lie cold and low,
Each like a corpse within its grave, until
Thine azure sister of the Spring shall blow

Mark the end of lines 1-14 in the first stanza with the following letters: aba bcb, cdc, ded, ee.

NOTICE & NOTE

Notice & Note

Use the side margins to notice and note signposts in the text.

ANALYZE FORM
Annotate: Use letters to mark the patterns of end rhyme in lines 1–14.

Analyze: What is the rhyme scheme? How does rhyme link each stanza to the next?

4 hectic: feverish.

9 sister . . . Spring: the reviving south wind of spring.

Ode to the West Wind / Song of a Thatched Hut 549

ENGLISH LEARNER SUPPORT

Monitor Oral and Written Language Provide students with opportunities to speak and write frequently as they familiarize themselves with the concept of form in poetry. Ask students to write two short poems, one in which they practice rhyme, and the other, free verse. Allow students to pair up and read their poems to each other, discuss their forms, and provide each other with feedback. **LIGHT**

TEACH

BACKGROUND

While enrolled at Oxford, Shelley coauthored and published "The Necessity of Atheism," which got him expelled from the university after less than a year's enrollment. Shelley could have been reinstated had his father intervened, but this would have required him to disavow the pamphlet and declare himself Christian, so he refused. This, and his marriage to 16-year-old Harriet Westbrook, led to a complete break between him and his father. Throughout his life, he surrounded himself with influential thinkers and philosophers, and he regularly challenged English ideals and systems through his works. In his first major poem, *Queen Mab* (1813), Shelley continued to attack social institutions, the monarchy, and the church. In 1814 Shelley met and fell in love with another radical thinker, Mary Wollstonecraft Godwin. Abandoning Harriet, Shelley eloped to France with Mary, returning to England several weeks later. In 1819 despite his grief over the deaths of his two infant children, Shelley wrote many of his greatest poems, including "Ode to the West Wind" and the verse drama *Prometheus Unbound*.

ENGLISH LEARNER SUPPORT

Draw on Prior Knowledge It may help to start your poetry instruction by finding out if students have read poems in their native languages as well as in English translations. If so, ask them if the message or theme was consistent across the two poems or if some meaning was lost in the translation. If you have bilingual collections of poetry in English and students' native languages, you may give students the option of reading both to support comprehension. **ALL LEVELS**

PREPARE TO COMPARE

Direct students to use the Prepare to Compare prompt to focus their reading.

ANALYZE FORM

Remind students that to determine the rhyme scheme, they can look at the words at the end of each line to see which ones rhyme in the poem. Have students mark the end of each line as they read. (**Answer:** *The rhyme scheme is aba bcb, cdc, ded, ee. This scheme is repeated in the rest of the poem.*)

Ode to the West Wind / Song of a Thatched Hut **549**

TEACH

NOTICE & NOTE

IMPROVE READING FLUENCY

Targeted Passage Have students work with partners to read page 549 in their books. First, use lines 1–3 to model how to read the lines of the poem. Have students follow along in their books as you read the text with appropriate phrasing and emphasis, pausing where punctuation is used. Make sure students can identify which lines and words rhyme. Then, have partners take turns reading aloud each line on this page. Encourage students to provide feedback and support when pronouncing unfamiliar words. Remind students to pace their reading and emphasize important details and pauses so the person who is listening understands the speaker's tone. Encourage students to pause and discuss ideas or details they think are important and why the poet might have included them.

10 Her clarion o'er the dreaming earth, and fill
       (Driving sweet buds like flocks to feed in air)
       With living hues and odors plain and hill:

     Wild Spirit, which art moving everywhere;
     Destroyer and preserver; hear, oh, hear!

II

15   Thou on whose stream, mid the steep sky's commotion,
       Loose clouds like earth's decaying leaves are shed,
       Shook from the tangled bough of Heaven and Ocean,

     Angels of rain and lightning: there are spread
     On the blue surface of thine aëry surge,
20   Like the bright hair uplifted from the head

     Of some fierce Maenad, even from the dim verge
     Of the horizon to the zenith's height,
     The locks of the approaching storm. Thou dirge

     Of the dying year, to which this closing night
25   Will be the dome of a vast sepulcher,
     Vaulted with all thy congregated might

     Of vapors, from whose solid atmosphere
     Black rain, and fire, and hail will burst: oh, hear!

III

     Thou who didst waken from his summer dreams
30   The blue Mediterranean, where he lay,
     Lulled by the coil of his crystálline streams,

     Beside a pumice isle in Baiae's bay,
     And saw in sleep old palaces and towers
     Quivering within the wave's intenser day,

35   All overgrown with azure moss and flowers
     So sweet, the sense faints picturing them! Thou
     For whose path the Atlantic's level powers

     Cleave themselves into chasms, while far below
     The sea-blooms and the oozy woods which wear
40   The sapless foliage of the ocean, know

     Thy voice, and suddenly grow gray with fear,
     And tremble and despoil themselves: oh, hear!

NOTICE & NOTE

10 clarion: a trumpet with a clear, ringing tone.

ANALYZE DICTION
Annotate: Mark words and phrases in lines 15–28 that are examples of elevated language.

Analyze: How does Shelley's use of elevated language in this description shape your impression of the wind?

18 Angels: messengers.

19 aëry: airy.

20–22 Like . . . height: The clouds lie in streaks from the horizon upward, looking like the streaming hair of a maenad (mē´năd)—a wildly dancing female worshiper of Dionysus, the Greek god of wine.

23 dirge: funeral song.

25 sepulcher (sĕp´əl-kər): tomb.

31 crystálline (krĭs´tə-lĭn) **streams:** the different-colored currents of the Mediterranean Sea.

32 pumice (pŭm´ĭs): a light volcanic rock; **Baiae's** (bī´ēz´) **bay:** the Bay of Naples, site of the ancient Roman resort of Baiae.

37 level powers: surface.

Ode to the West Wind / Song of a Thatched Hut 551

TEACH

ANALYZE DICTION
Tell students that **elevated language** tends to be formal and often uses more elaborate figures of speech. Explain that when a poet uses elevated language, it can reveal the way he or she feels about certain subjects. Elevated language is also often used to express religious ideas or spiritual experiences. (**Answer:** *Shelley's description in these lines give the impression that the wind is a godlike force.*)

ENGLISH LEARNER SUPPORT

Demonstrate Comprehension Give students frequent opportunities to participate in shared reading in small groups to demonstrate their comprehension of increasingly complex English texts.

- Have groups of students circle the two words in line 15 with the long /e/ sound. Then, tell them to underline the two words in the second stanza that rhyme with the word "shed" in the first stanza. **SUBSTANTIAL**

- In pairs, ask students to take turns reading the poem, stanza by stanza. Provide them with a graphic organizer to help them organize the main ideas and supporting details in each stanza. Have them identify keywords that reflect the speaker's tone in each stanza. **MODERATE**

- In pairs, have students take turns reading the poem, stanza by stanza. As they read, they should circle the poet's main idea in each stanza and underline details that directly support these ideas. Have students discuss why they think the poet uses specific words in the poem and their overall impact on his message. **LIGHT**

WHEN STUDENTS STRUGGLE . . .

Use Context Clues As students read "Ode to the West Wind," tell them to use context clues to determine the meaning of unfamiliar words. Have them use a graphic organizer like below.

Lines from the Poem	Context Clues	Meaning
Lines 19–21	*blue surface, aery surge*	clouds

 For additional support, go to the **Reading Studio** and assign the following Level Up tutorial: Using Context Clues.

TEACH

 ANALYZE FORM

Remind students that Shelley uses a **couplet** in the last two lines of each section of the poem. Ask students to go back through each section to identify the couplet and think about how it emphasizes Shelley's main idea. *(Answer: He emphasizes the idea that the troubles he has endured have weighed him down and humbled him, but he was once as wild and proud as the wind.)*

 **NOTICE & NOTE**

ANALYZE FORM

Annotate: A couplet is two lines of verse that rhyme and form a unit. Mark the words that rhyme at the end of the couplet in section IV.

Analyze: What idea does Shelley emphasize with the rhymed words in this couplet?

50 skyey (skī´ē) **speed:** the swiftness of clouds moving across the sky.

51 vision: something impossible to achieve.

57 lyre: a reference to the Aeolian harp; an instrument whose strings make musical sounds when the wind blows over them.

62 impetuous (ĭm-pĕch´ōō-əs): violently forceful; impulsive.

65 incantation: recitation, as of a magic spell.

IV

If I were a dead leaf thou mightest bear;
If I were a swift cloud to fly with thee;
45 A wave to pant beneath thy power, and share

The impulse of thy strength, only less free
Than thou, O uncontrollable! If even
I were as in my boyhood, and could be

The comrade of thy wanderings over Heaven,
50 As then, when to outstrip thy skyey speed
Scarce seemed a vision; I would ne'er have striven

As thus with thee in prayer in my sore need.
Oh, lift me as a wave, a leaf, a cloud!
I fall upon the thorns of life! I bleed!

55 A heavy weight of hours has chained and bowed
One too like thee: tameless, and swift, and proud.

V

Make me thy lyre, even as the forest is:
What if my leaves are falling like its own!
The tumult of thy mighty harmonies

60 Will take from both a deep, autumnal tone,
Sweet though in sadness. Be thou, Spirit fierce,
My spirit! Be thou me, impetuous one!

Drive my dead thoughts over the universe
Like withered leaves to quicken a new birth!
65 And, by the incantation of this verse,

Scatter, as from an unextinguished hearth
Ashes and sparks, my words among mankind!
Be through my lips to unawakened earth

The trumpet of a prophecy! O Wind,
70 If Winter comes, can Spring be far behind?

TO CHALLENGE STUDENTS . . .

Analyze Allusions Have students in a group learn more about the Maenads (line 21) and about Baiae (line 32). Have the group discuss why Shelley used these allusions. Ask questions:

- How do these allusions shape the meaning of the lines in which they appear? How do they influence the ode's overall message?
- What do the allusions suggest about Shelley's views of poetry? of nature?

To extend this activity, have them include in the discussion the references to Heaven (line 17), angels (line 18), the Mediterranean Sea (lines 29–36), and the Atlantic Ocean (lines 36–42).

NOTICE & NOTE

CHECK YOUR UNDERSTANDING

Answer these questions about "Ode to the West Wind" before moving on to the next selection.

1. In section I, the speaker refers to the west wind as a "preserver" because it —
   A blows away the dead leaves
   B spreads seeds that will bloom in the spring
   C brings in the warm spring wind
   D protects flocks of sheep from harm

2. In section IV, what does the speaker regret about his adult years?
   F He has lost his appreciation of the seasons.
   G Winter is hard for him to bear.
   H He is all alone in the world.
   J He has become less free and vigorous.

3. Which of the following themes can be inferred from the poem?
   A Life is full of contradictions.
   B Society lacks beauty and grace.
   C The wind is the only constant in life.
   D The world needs to be reawakened.

Ode to the West Wind / Song of a Thatched Hut 553

TEACH

CHECK YOUR UNDERSTANDING

Have students answer the questions independently.

Answers:
1. B
2. J
3. D

If they answer any questions incorrectly, have them reread the text to confirm their understanding. Then they may proceed to the next selection.

 ENGLISH LEARNER SUPPORT

Oral Assessment Use the questions to assess students' comprehension and speaking skills.

1. In Section I of the "Ode to the West Wind," does the speaker think the wind is good or bad? *(The wind is good because it spreads seeds around and gives them life.)*

2. Does the speaker look forward to spring? *(yes)*

3. Does the speaker think the world should change? *(Yes. The world needs to be reawakened.)*
   SUBSTANTIAL/MODERATE

TEACH

BACKGROUND

Du Fu is known by many names, including Tu Fu, Du Gongbu, and Du Shaoling. During the 740s, Du Fu was a well-regarded member of a group of high officials, even though he had no money or an official position. Later on in life, he attracted imperial attention by submitting his literary works, which earned him a small position in the royal court. While his early works celebrated nature's beauty, his later pieces addressed war and what he perceived to be senseless and inhumane social acts. Du Fu conveys his social views in "Song of a Thatched Hut Damaged in Autumn Wind."

PREPARE TO COMPARE

Direct students to use the Prepare to Compare prompt to focus their reading.

ANALYZE DICTION

Remind students that a poet uses specific words, phrases, and figurative language to convey a clear message. The words are intended to create a specific feeling and **mood**—the feeling or atmosphere a writer creates for the reader—as well as to convey the speaker's **tone,** or attitude, toward the subject. (**Answer:** *Du Fu's word choice conveys a tone of sadness and despair.*)

ANALYZE FORM

Review the definition of **simile** with students and challenge them to offer examples of ones they have read or heard (e.g., "She sells sea shells at the sea shore"). Challenge students to think how similes might enrich the poem. (**Answer:** *"Rain like yarn spins down forever" helps readers visualize how heavily the rain falls; "we'd be calm as mountains" provides a vivid contrast with the flimsiness of the hut.*)

NOTICE & NOTE

BACKGROUND

Du Fu (712–770) is considered by many literary critics to be the greatest figure in Chinese poetry. He was born into a scholarly family and received a traditional Confucian education, but he failed his imperial examinations. As a result, he spent much of his youth traveling and writing poetry. Du Fu is often described as a poet-historian whose body of work addresses a wide range of personal, political, and social issues.

SONG OF A THATCHED HUT DAMAGED IN AUTUMN WIND

Poem by Du Fu

PREPARE TO COMPARE

As you read the poem, look for images and details that help develop its theme.

Wind howled angrily in high autumn's September
and tore off three layers of reed from my thatched roof.
The reeds flew over the river and scattered on the bank.
Some flew high and hung from the trees.
5   Some flew low and swirled and sank into pools.
The kids from the southern village took advantage of my old age,
played pirate and stole my reeds while I watched them
openly carrying armfuls into the bamboo groves.
My lips cracked, my throat dried, and I couldn't yell out.
10 I returned home and leaned on my stick, sighing.
In a moment the wind stopped and clouds stood ink black,
the autumnal sky stretched into darkness in desert silence.
My cotton quilt is tattered from use and cold as iron.
In an ugly dream, my small son rips the lining with his feet.
15 The roof is leaking by my bed's headboard and nowhere is dry.

Notice & Note
Use the side margins to notice and note signposts in the text.

ANALYZE DICTION
Annotate: Mark the words or phrases in lines 10–14 that suggest how the speaker feels.
Analyze: What tone do these word choices help convey?

554   Unit 4

TO CHALLENGE STUDENTS...

Write an Alliteration Provide students with an interesting topic, or ask them to identify their own topics about which they can write a short poem that employs alliteration. Ask students to share their poems in small groups or pairs and discuss why they chose to repeat certain consonants or words, the effect they were trying to achieve, and whether or not they think they achieved their overall goal.

The rain like yarn spins down forever.
I've had little sleep since the An Lushan Rebellion.[1]
Such a wet and long night, when will it end!
I wish I had a house with thousands of rooms
20 to shelter all the cold people under the sky and give them happy faces.
We'd be calm as mountains when it stormed and rained.
Oh, let this big house appear before my eyes
and I will die of cold in my damaged hut, happy.

---

[1] **An Lushan Rebellion:** a rebellion lasting almost a decade that began in 755 as a revolt by a disgruntled general in the Tang Dynasty's army.

NOTICE & NOTE

ANALYZE FORM

Annotate: Mark the similes in lines 16–23.

Analyze: How does the use of this literary element enrich the poem?

CHECK YOUR UNDERSTANDING

Answer these questions before moving on to the **Analyze the Text** section on the following page.

1. In "Song of a Thatched Hut Damaged in Autumn Wind," what happens to the speaker's roof?
   A It has been stolen by children.
   B The wind destroys it.
   C It leaks during heavy rains.
   D It was damaged during a rebellion.

2. The speaker wishes for "a house with thousands of rooms" because he wants to —
   F protect his family
   G use the space as a hotel
   H house anyone who needs shelter
   J hide from rebellious soldiers

3. What theme is expressed in the last two lines of the poem?
   A Wealth is just an illusion.
   B Poor people will always struggle.
   C We need comfort to be happy.
   D Imagination can ease our sufferings.

Ode to the West Wind / Song of a Thatched Hut 555

TEACH

CHECK YOUR UNDERSTANDING

Have students answer the questions independently.

Answers:
1. B
2. H
3. D

If they answer any questions incorrectly, have them reread the text to confirm their understanding. Then they may proceed to ANALYZE THE TEXTS on page 556.

ENGLISH LEARNER SUPPORT

Oral Assessment Use the following questions to assess students' comprehension and speaking skills.

1. The wind blows the _____ off the speaker's home. *(roof)*
2. The speaker wants a big _____. *(house for shelter)*
3. The speaker wants to shelter _____. *(anyone who needs it)*

SUBSTANTIAL/MODERATE

APPLY

ANALYZE THE TEXTS

Possible answers:

1. **DOK 2:** *Life and nature go through cycles, with destruction followed by renewal. Shelley may have wanted to suggest that the tragic deaths at the Peterloo Massacre could lead to a renewal of justice in England.*

2. **DOK 4:** *The diction is formal. Shelley often uses elevated language and inverted syntax to emphasize certain details, for example, the wind's power and grace. He says, "Wild Spirit, which art moving everywhere; Destroyer and preserver; hear, oh, hear!" This emphasizes the awe and respect he has for nature.*

3. **DOK 4:** *It is a complex poem that develops a serious theme about death and rebirth. It uses dignified language to celebrate the freedom and power of the west wind.*

4. **DOK 4:** *Answers will vary. Some students may feel that the poem doesn't sound poetic enough. Others will say that the translator's choices make it easy for readers to empathize with the old man.*

5. **DOK 4:** *The reference to the rebellion informs us that in addition to suffering from old age, poverty, and natural events, the speaker has been harmed by civil war. This insight increases our sympathy for him and our admiration of his effort to use imagination to rise above his circumstances.*

RESEARCH

Remind students to focus their research by entering key dates during the time periods and geographical regions in which the poets lived. Tell students that they may yield a wide range of search results if, for example, they search the poets' names. However, if they search terms like "Shelley and social uprisings during the 1790s in England," they are more likely to find information they can use.

Extend Provide students with a list of social or political topics they might find interesting. If they have their own ideas, allow them to experiment as long as their topics are appropriate for the classroom. Once students have written their poems, ask them to pair up and share their work with each other. Ask students to discuss the tone and mood they were trying to achieve and whether or not the form and diction they employed helped them to successfully achieve their intentions.

556 Unit 4

RESPOND

ANALYZE THE TEXTS

Support your responses with evidence from the text. **NOTEBOOK**

1. **Infer** In the last line of "Ode to the West Wind," Shelley poses the question, "If Winter comes, can Spring be far behind?" What theme does this question help convey? How might this theme relate to disturbing political events such as the Peterloo Massacre.

2. **Analyze** How would you describe the diction of "Ode to the West Wind"? What purpose does this use of diction serve? Explain.

3. **Analyze** Which elements of Shelley's poem fit the characteristics of an ode? Why might he have chosen this form to express his ideas?

4. **Evaluate** The translator of "Song of a Thatched Hut Damaged in Autumn Wind" created a free-verse English version of the poem, with plain vocabulary and conversational syntax. Do you think that this was an effective choice? Explain why or why not.

5. **Connect** Du Fu refers to the An Lushan Rebellion in line 17 of his poem. How does this historical reference deepen the poem's meaning?

RESEARCH TIP
When researching information online, be sure to use various types of reliable sources. For example, you may use a combination of primary sources, which are firsthand accounts of events, and secondary sources, which are secondhand accounts created at a later date.

RESEARCH

As you read in their biographies, both Shelley and Du Fu wrote poetry as social or political commentary. Research the times and places in which the poets wrote these two poems. What historical, social, or political events occurred around those times, and how might these events have informed the poets' works? Use the chart below to organize your findings and to explain the connections you discover.

	HISTORICAL CONTEXT	CONNECTIONS
Percy Bysshe Shelley	*Shelley reacted to neo-classicism and the Industrial Revolution. Incited by democratic ideas causing revolution in France and America.*	*This might have left Shelley devastated and feeling powerless, hence writing a poem asking the wind to help him disperse his ideas.*
Du Fu	*The An Lushan Rebellion, lasting 10 years, left devastating social and economic impacts on the Tang dynasty in China.*	*Some difficulty and poverty the speaker in "Song of a Thatched Hut Damaged in Autumn Wind" faced may be a result of dire situations the rebellion left behind.*

Extend Find another poem by Shelley or Du Fu that addresses a social or political issue. Discuss the poem with a partner, comparing it to the two poems you read in this lesson.

556 Unit 4

WHEN STUDENTS STRUGGLE...

Reteaching: Analyze Form Remind students that form refers to the arrangement of words into structural patterns. Have students create a T-chart to compare the form of the poems. They should take into consideration the line lengths, rhyme scheme, poetic type, and grouping of stanzas. Students should realize that the two poems are very different, even though they focus on similar topics.

 For additional support, go to the **Reading Studio** and assign the following Level Up tutorial: Elements of Poetry.

CREATE AND PRESENT

Create a Visual Representation In both selections, the wind is personified in different ways—that is, it is given some human characteristics. Develop a visual representation of the wind in each poem.

- ❏ Think about the similarities and differences in the two poems. How does each poet describe the wind?
- ❏ Identify the human characteristics ascribed to the wind in each selection. Are these descriptions positive or negative?
- ❏ Think about how you can represent these characteristics visually.

Present Your Image Pair up with a partner, and take turns presenting your visual representations.

- ❏ Identify two elements of your visual representation that you would like to present.
- ❏ Present your visual to your partner, and explain two of your choices in creating it. For instance, explain why you chose a certain color or style.
- ❏ Take turns giving each other feedback. If it makes sense, incorporate your partner's feedback into your visual representation.

RESPOND TO THE ESSENTIAL QUESTION

 What shapes your outlook on life?

Gather Information Review your annotations and notes on "Ode to the West Wind" and "Song of a Thatched Hut Damaged in Autumn Wind." Then, add relevant information to your Response Log. As you determine which information to include, think about:

- how nature affects the way you perceive the world
- the experiences that have shaped the way you relate to people and the world around you
- the relationship between the natural world and human society

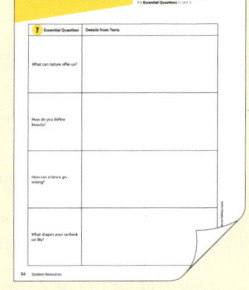

RESPOND

 Go to the **Speaking and Listening Studio** to find out more about giving a presentation.

ACADEMIC VOCABULARY

As you write and discuss what you learned from the poems, be sure to use the Academic Vocabulary words. Check off each of the words that you use.

- ❏ appreciate
- ❏ insight
- ❏ intensity
- ❏ invoke
- ❏ radical

APPLY

CREATE AND PRESENT

Create a Visual Representation Point out that the list on page 557 can serve as a guideline for students' visual representations. Review the definition of **personification** with students, making sure they understand the different ways in which the wind is personified in the selections. Tell students that before they draw their visuals, they can brainstorm some ideas or adjectives they want to capture. Ask them to think about how the description of the wind in the two poems make them feel as they draw.

For **writing support** for students at varying proficiency levels, see the **Text X-Ray** on page 546D.

Present Your Image Before students present their images to their partners, remind them to plan their presentations. What do they want to share first? What makes sense to share next? Challenge them to identify the mood they want to create and then plan the presentation accordingly.

RESPOND TO THE ESSENTIAL QUESTION

Allow time for students to add details from "Ode to The West Wind"/"Song of a Thatched Hut Damaged in Autumn Wind" to their Unit 4 Response Logs.

APPLY

COMPARE THEMES

Before students complete the graphic organizer on page 558, ask them to take a few moments to discuss the impact that imagery, figurative language, and diction has on each poem. This will allow students to organize their ideas and to determine a clear starting point. After students complete the graphic organizer, ask them to review their responses with their partners and come to a consensus about each of the selection's overall theme and message.

ANALYZE THE TEXT

Possible answers:

1. **DOK 2:** *The images are similar in that the winds are described as powerful and capable of destruction; however, "Ode to the West Wind" focuses on mostly positive qualities, whereas "Song of a Thatched Hut Damaged in Autumn Wind" focuses on the damage that is done to the hut.*

2. **DOK 2:** *In "Ode to the West Wind," nature is venerated and treated with awe. For example, the poet describes the wind as a "Wild Spirit" that moves "everywhere." He also calls the wind "Destroyer and preserver." In "Song of a Thatched Hut Damaged in Autumn Wind," nature is seen as harsh, as the wind "howled angrily" right before it blows the roof off the hut.*

3. **DOK 4:** *Sample answer: The approach used in "Song of a Thatched Hut Damaged in Autumn Wind" was more effective because the language is more relatable.*

4. **DOK 3:** *Humans might learn to stand in and harness their power to do great things. We might also embrace the idea that life is a cycle of death and rebirth.*

RESPOND

ODE TO THE WEST WIND
Poem by Percy Bysshe Shelley

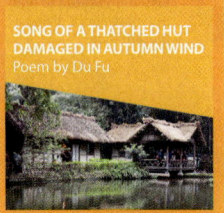

SONG OF A THATCHED HUT DAMAGED IN AUTUMN WIND
Poem by Du Fu

Collaborate & Compare

COMPARE THEMES

"Ode to the West Wind" and "Song of a Thatched Hut Damaged in Autumn Wind" share a topic—the effects of the wind in autumn. However, the two poems may express different **themes,** or messages about life or human nature.

Poets usually do not state their themes directly. It is up to readers to infer a theme based on a poem's imagery, figurative language, diction, and other elements. Some poems may have multiple themes.

To begin gathering details with which to make inferences about themes, complete the following chart.

	"ODE TO THE WEST WIND"	"SONG OF A THATCHED HUT DAMAGED IN AUTUMN WIND"
Form	*Sonnet, iambic pentameter, has rhyme and rhythm*	*Free verse, has repetition and alliteration*
Imagery	*Vivid images. Wind's power-blowing leaves and waves.*	*Scattered reeds and tattered cotton quilt are vulnerable*
Figurative Language	*Poet personifies the wind. Compares himself to a lyre.*	*Personifies wind as a strong force. "Wind howled angrily."*
Diction	*"Wild Spirit," "tameless, swift," "mighty harmonies"*	*Simple words used show the humility of the speaker.*
Other Elements	*The poem's sections focus on various traits of wind.*	*Appeals to reader's emotion by telling a compelling story.*

ANALYZE THE TEXTS

Discuss these questions in your group.

1. **Compare** With your group, review the imagery that you cited in your chart. How are the images in the two poems similar? How do they differ?

2. **Interpret** Both poems describe some of the ways we relate to nature. Discuss each poem's treatment of nature. Cite evidence in your discussion.

3. **Evaluate** In "Ode to the West Wind," Shelley uses elevated language and formal diction; however, in "Song of a Thatched Hut Damaged in Autumn Wind," Du Fu does the opposite. Which approach do you find most effective, and why?

4. **Draw Conclusions** According to the two poems, what insights about life or human nature can we gain by considering the wind and other elements of the natural world?

558 Unit 4

ENGLISH LEARNER SUPPORT

Perform Critical Analysis Use the following questions to help students analyze and compare the selections:

1. What are the central ideas in each poem? What key details are used to develop these ideas?

2. How do you think Shelley and Du Fu differ in their values? How might they be similar?

3. Are the poets' messages clear? Why or why not? **MODERATE/LIGHT**

RESPOND

COLLABORATE AND PRESENT

With your group, continue exploring the ideas in the poems by identifying and comparing their themes. Follow these steps:

1. **Make inferences about themes.** Review your charts as a group, considering details, imagery, figurative language, diction, and other elements from both poems. Then, work together to infer possible themes for each poem.

2. **Agree on a theme.** Determine a theme statement for each poem. You may use a chart like the one below to track the themes and supporting details your group identifies.

	THEME STATEMENT	SUPPORTING DETAILS
"Ode to the West Wind"	*After death, rebirth is inevitable.*	*The trumpet of a prophecy! O Wind, If Winter comes, can Spring be far behind?*
"Song of a Thatched Hut Damaged in Autumn Wind"	*Imagination can relieve us of suffering.*	*Oh, let this big house appear before my eyes and I will die of cold in my damaged hut, happy.*

3. **Present to the class.** Organize your ideas, and choose a spokesperson to present them to the class. Include clear statements of the theme for each poem, and explain similarities or differences in the two themes. Be sure to introduce your ideas, to include transitions from idea to idea in the body of your presentation, and to conclude your presentation effectively. You may add visuals or diagrams to help convey information to the class.

Go to the **Speaking and Listening Studio** for more on giving a presentation.

PRESENTATION TIPS
When giving a presentation, be sure to pace yourself and enunciate all of your words so your audience can understand you. Also, be sure to make eye contact and address one topic at a time so you don't lose your audience.

Collaborate & Compare 559

APPLY

COLLABORATE AND PRESENT

Reinforce the idea that poets may use their work as a means to describe nature's beauty or to revere its presence. On the surface, the poet may be describing nature, but a deeper analysis of the poem shows that the poet is describing something more subtle or abstract, as is the case in "Ode to the West Wind" and "Song of a Thatched Hut Damaged in Autumn Wind."

1. **Make inferences about Themes** Before students make inferences about the themes in the selections, ask them to define imagery, figurative language, diction, and any other terms they might consider in their analysis. Tell them that agreeing on these terms will ensure a smoother process as they look for evidence to support their ideas.

2. **Agree on a Theme** Encourage students to revisit the selections as much as they need before deciding on their themes. Remind them that sometimes it takes several close readings to understand the poet's intentions or message. It is not uncommon to miss key ideas the first time, but in subsequent readings, new ideas may rise to the surface.

3. **Present to the Class** Remind each group to choose a representative who can effectively convey their ideas. Tell students they can write down key ideas or notes on a note card to help them organize their thoughts before they present to the class. Remind them to speak clearly and use eye contact as a way to connect with the audience as they present.

WHEN STUDENTS STRUGGLE . . .

Summarize If students struggle with agreeing on a theme, encourage them to reread each selection and summarize each stanza or section as they read. Have students create a graphic organizer in which they can record the line numbers and their summaries. After they have completed their organizers, they can review their summaries to see if a theme or themes emerge.

 For additional support, go to the **Reading Studio** and assign the following Level Up tutorial: **Summarizing.**

Collaborate & Compare 559

PLAN

from SONGS OF INNOCENCE
Lyric Poetry by William Blake

from SONGS OF EXPERIENCE
Lyric Poetry by William Blake

GENRE ELEMENTS
LYRIC POETRY
Remind students that **lyric poetry** often has a musical quality, but its themes may not always be beautiful. At times, lyric poetry explores darker emotions and societal issues. In this lesson, students will analyze the symbols in lyric poetry and understand how historical background connects to the themes of poems.

LEARNING OBJECTIVES
- Analyze symbols and historical background.
- Conduct research about the historical background of William Blake's poetry.
- Write a problem-solution essay.
- Make a podcast.
- Compare poems.
- **Language** Debate contemporary social issues.

TEXT COMPLEXITY

Quantitative Measures	Songs of Innocence / Songs of Experience	Lexile: NA
Qualitative Measures	**Ideas Presented** Multiple levels, use of symbolism. Greater demand for inference.	
	Structures Used More complex, lyrical and poetic.	
	Language Used Implied meanings, allusive, figurative, and formal language. Complex sentence structures.	
	Knowledge Required Mostly familiar themes. Some knowledge of chimney sweepers needed.	

560A Unit 4

PLAN

Online

RESOURCES

- Unit 4 Response Log
- 🔊 Selection Audio
- 📖 Reading Studio: Notice & Note
- 📈 Level Up Tutorials: Theme, Using Context Clues
- 📝 Writing Studio: Writing Informative Texts
- 💬 Speaking and Listening Studio: Participating in Collaborative Discussions
- ✓ *Songs of Innocence* and *Songs of Experience* Selection Test

SUMMARIES

English

In "The Lamb," the speaker asks the lamb, "Who made thee?" and then explains that God made both him and the lamb. In "The Tyger," the speaker wonders "What immortal hand or eye" made the fierce tiger. In "The Chimney Sweeper," the speaker lost his mother and was sold to a chimney sweeper by his father. Tom, the young chimney sweeper, dreams that he and thousands of sweepers locked in coffins are set free by an angel— a thought that comforts him.

Spanish

En "El cordero", la voz narrativa le pregunta al cordero, "¿quién te creó?" y luego explica que Dios los creó a él y al cordero. En "El tigre", la voz narrativa se pregunta, ¿"qué mano u ojo inmortal" creó al feroz tigre? En "El limpiador de chimeneas", la voz narrativa pierde a su madre, y su padre lo vende a un limpiador de chimeneas. Tom, el joven limpiador de chimeneas, sueña que él y otros miles de limpiadores encerrados en ataúdes son liberado por un ángel. Ese pensamiento lo consuela.

SMALL-GROUP OPTIONS

Have students work in small groups and pairs to read and discuss the selections.

Think-Pair-Share

- After reading all the poems, pose this question: *How does William Blake view the world?*
- Have students think about the question individually and take notes.
- Then, have pairs listen, discuss, and formulate a shared response to the question. Direct them to include at least two reasons to support their inference.
- Finally, have pairs share their responses with the class.

Final Word

- Have students read the first poem.
- After reading, ask one student to describe his or her impressions of the poem.
- Have other students briefly give their impressions in turn.
- Go back to the original student and ask if he or she would like to revise his or her initial impression based on the responses of the group.
- Continue the activity with students until all have had an opportunity to revise their first impressions.
- Repeat the activity with the other poems.

Songs of Innocence / Songs of Experience **560B**

PLAN

Text X-Ray: English Learner Support
for *Songs of Innocence* and *Songs of Experience*

Use the Text X-Ray and the supports and scaffolds in the Teacher's Edition to help guide students at different proficiency levels through the selections.

INTRODUCE THE SELECTION
DISCUSS INNOCENCE AND EXPERIENCE

In this lesson, students will need to be able to discuss the difference between innocence and experience.

Provide the following explanation:

- Innocence is a lack of worldly experience; usually associated with being young.
- Experience is knowledge from observation and involvement in something over time; usually associated with being older.

Guide students to see how *innocence* and *experience* are antonyms. Then, have students discuss examples of innocence and experience.

Provide sentence frames, such as: *Childhood is a period of innocence because ____. One experience in life that is difficult is ____.*

CULTURAL REFERENCES

The following words or phrases may be unfamiliar to students:

- *dost* ("The Lamb," line 2): archaic form of *do*
- *thee* ("The Lamb," line 2): archaic form of *you*
- *bid thee feed* ("The Lamb," line 3): gave you an appetite to eat
- *o'er* ("The Lamb," line 4): contraction for *over*
- *mead* ("The Lamb," line 4): meadow
- *hush* ("The Chimney Sweeper," line 7): be quiet
- *burning bright* ("The Tyger," line 1): refers to a tiger's fiery orange fur and/or their fierce energy
- *thy* ("The Tyger," line 4): archaic form of *your*
- *deeps* ("The Tyger," line 5): oceans
- *thine* ("The Tyger," line 6): archaic form of *your*
- *woe* ("The Chimney Sweeper," line 8): sorrow; sadness

LISTENING

Identify Rhymes

Remind students that words that rhyme frequently share the same ending syllable. Have them listen for words that share the same vowel sound and ending consonant.

Use the following supports with students at varying proficiency levels:

- Read aloud the first stanza of "The Tyger." Emphasize the rhyming words *bright* and *night* and have students repeat them. Then, read aloud another stanza and have students tell you the rhymes they hear. Write pairs of rhyming words on the board, and have them identify letters and sounds that are the same. **SUBSTANTIAL**
- Have pairs read aloud stanzas from "The Tyger." Have one partner write down rhyming words they hear. Then, have them read aloud the list of rhymes and discuss shared letters or sounds and how spellings of the same sound may differ. **MODERATE**
- Have pairs read aloud stanzas from "The Tyger." Have one partner write down rhyming words they hear. Then, have them read aloud the list of words and discuss shared letters or sounds and how spellings of the same sound may differ. Have them repeat the activity for "The Lamb." **LIGHT**

560C Unit 4

PLAN

SPEAKING

Use Newly Acquired Vocabulary

Have students define new or unfamiliar words and discuss the poems using this newly acquired vocabulary.

Use the following supports with students at varying proficiency levels:

- Have students identify two or three newly acquired vocabulary words. Help students define them and then repeat the short definitions. **SUBSTANTIAL**
- Have students work with partners to identify five newly acquired vocabulary words. Have them discuss what each word means and then use them in sentences. **MODERATE**
- Have students work with partners to identify six newly acquired vocabulary words. Then, have students ask each other questions about the poems, using the new words. **LIGHT**

READING

Use Affixes

Remind students that they can look for prefixes and suffixes to help them decode longer words.

Use the following supports with students at varying proficiency levels:

- Write line 6 from "The Lamb" on the board: *"Softest clothing wooly bright."* Point out the endings *-est*, *-ing*, and *-y*. Underline the root words *soft*, *cloth*, and *wool*. Have students practice saying the words with and without the endings, noting changes in pronunciation when a suffix is added. **SUBSTANTIAL**
- Have students write a list of words with affixes as they reread "The Lamb." Have partners share and discuss their findings. **MODERATE**
- Have students write a list of words with affixes as they reread "The Lamb." Have partners share and discuss their findings. Then, have them repeat the activity for "The Tyger." **LIGHT**

WRITING

Write an Essay

Read the prompt on page 573. Help students write their problem-solution essay by exploring social issues.

Use the following supports with students at varying proficiency levels:

- Create a three-column chart with the heads *Issue*, *Problem*, and *Solution*. Show students images from online sources to help them name contemporary social issues. Have students draw, act out, or use their native languages to describe the problems and solutions suggested by the images and headlines. Use simple English to write their ideas in the chart. **SUBSTANTIAL**
- Have partners choose a contemporary social issue to write about. Provide sentence frames, such as: *One social issue that affects me is _____. A possible solution to the problem is _____. The solution you propose may not work because _____.* **MODERATE**
- Have small groups debate a contemporary social issue and use what they learn in their essays. **LIGHT**

TEACH

 Connect to the
ESSENTIAL QUESTION

Tell students that in *Songs of Innocence* and *Songs of Experience*, William Blake's outlook shifts dramatically and his perception of the world changes across the selections.

COMPARE POEMS

Ask students to predict key themes or ideas based on the titles of the poems and how Blake might convey the concept of innocence versus the concept of experience. Ask students to think about the word *experience*. Do they think Blake intends the notion of experience to be perceived as something positive, negative, or neutral, and why? Remind students to come back to these ideas as they read each of the selections and revise their responses to these questions as needed.

COLLABORATE & COMPARE

POEMS

from
SONGS OF INNOCENCE

by **William Blake**
pages 563–566

COMPARE POEMS

As you read, pay attention to the ways in which William Blake describes the two contrasting states of being—innocence and experience. How are the details in the poems similar or different, and how do they contribute to the themes described?

 **ESSENTIAL QUESTION:**

What shapes your outlook on life?

POEMS

from
SONGS OF EXPERIENCE

by **William Blake**
pages 568–570

560   Unit 4

 LEARNING MINDSET

Questioning Tell students that asking questions is an important skill that helps to develop comprehension as well as facilitates meaningful connections to a text. Let students know they can ask specific questions about what they are reading and learning. They can ask about what others think about a text or activity, which might help them better understand a work. If they don't know what questions to ask, they can listen to others' questions and build on their ideas. Encourage students to ask questions no matter how simple or complex they think their questions are and to speak up if they don't understand the concepts that are being taught.

560   Unit 4

QUICK START

What comes to mind when you think of innocence and experience? Write down a list of at least three ideas or images for each state.

INNOCENCE	EXPERIENCE
-babies -angels -puppies	-old people -professionals -wisdom

ANALYZE SYMBOLS

A **symbol** is a person, place, object, or action that has a concrete meaning in itself and also stands for something beyond itself, such as an idea or feeling. For example, a dove is widely known as a symbol of peace. In literature, symbols often take their meaning from the context in which they appear, and the symbolic meaning may be interpreted in different ways.

Symbols play an important role in Blake's poetry. Although at first glance the poems in *Songs of Innocence* and *Songs of Experience* seem simple and straightforward, Blake uses symbols to convey complex spiritual and social themes. As you read these poems, look for clues to help you interpret the symbols. Use this chart to jot down your interpretations.

PERSON, PLACE, OR OBJECT	CONCRETE MEANING	SYMBOLIC IDEA OR FEELING
lamb	small, soft, sweet animal	meek, mild, sweet, innocent
tiger	big, strong animal	fearful, power, strength
little child	a person with no experience	innocence, bright
immortal hand	the hand of something or someone who lives forever	God; something powerful

GET READY

GENRE ELEMENTS: LYRIC POETRY
- expresses personal thoughts or feelings
- written from a first-person perspective
- has a musical quality
- marked by imagination and evocative language

Songs of Innocence / Songs of Experience 561

TEACH

QUICK START

Encourage students to think not just of words that come to mind when they hear *innocence* and *experience*, but also images, ideas, characters, or even stories they have read or heard. Once students have compiled their lists, ask them to share in pairs or in small groups. Have each pair or small group come to a consensus about two or three ideas that represent each category. Ask them to share their finalized lists with the class.

ANALYZE SYMBOLS

Ask students what ideas come to mind when they hear the word *symbol*. Challenge them to provide examples they have heard or read about and to explain what these symbols represent. Remind students that a symbol can have multiple representations or interpretations—it may mean one thing in one context and another in a different one. Ask students to think of symbols that might have different interpretations. Provide an example to stimulate their thinking (e.g., snow might represent purity and beauty in one instance, but is also associated with winter, which is dreary and cold, and sometimes represents death). Encourage students to think of the different representations a symbol might have and how meaning might shift as a result of how it is used.

TEACH

UNDERSTAND HISTORICAL BACKGROUND

Challenge students to think about how social and political issues might impact the topics about which poets choose to write. Ask them to think about how or why poetry and other forms of literature serve as effective ways to engage the public to understand important issues. Let students know that other forms of art, including visual arts, dance, and song are all avenues for discussing difficult social or political issues. Then, ask students what contemporary works they have read or seen that address social or political ideologies. Ask students how they think writing or art can create a platform to discuss the topics.

ANNOTATION MODEL

Remind students they can use the graphic organizer on page 561 to organize their ideas about the symbols in the selections they read. Ask students to paraphrase Blake's ideas in the margins and note any symbols they think might have multiple meanings. Point out that they may follow this suggestion or use their own system for marking up the selection in their write-in text. They may want to color-code their annotations by using highlighters. Their notes in the margin may include questions about ideas that are unclear or topics they want to learn more about.

 **GET READY**

UNDERSTAND HISTORICAL BACKGROUND

Background information on historical, social, cultural, and economic issues may be important for understanding a poem's theme. William Blake sometimes used his poetry to comment on child labor, slavery, science, and other social and cultural issues. In *Songs of Innocence* and *Songs of Experience*, for example, Blake describes the plight of chimney sweepers, boys from poor families who were apprenticed to chimney sweeps and used to clean chimneys in London and other British cities.

During the Romantic period, most fireplaces in England burned coal for fuel, creating sticky soot that had to be brushed or scraped away. Children crawled up narrow chimneys to perform this work. Sometimes their masters would light fires underneath them to make sure they moved quickly. People who worked as sweepers rarely lived past middle age due to respiratory illnesses, cancer, and other diseases.

As early as 1788, legislation was enacted to prohibit children younger than eight from working as sweeps' apprentices. Subsequent legislation raised the minimum age again, but these laws were unenforced and ineffective. In 1834 Parliament passed the Chimney Sweeps Act; however, this too was largely ignored. It was not until 1875 that sweeps were required to be licensed and police were given the power to enforce legislation, bringing an end to the practice of child labor. As you read Blake's poems about chimney sweepers, make connections between this historical information and details of the poems.

ANNOTATION MODEL   NOTICE & NOTE

As you read, note clues to the meaning of symbols in Blake's poems. Also note any details about social conditions in Britain. This model shows one reader's notes about lines 1–6 of "The Lamb."

<u>Little Lamb, who made thee?</u>	The rhythm and sweet tone remind me of a nursery rhyme.
Dost thou know who made thee?	
Gave thee life & bid thee feed,	Details emphasize that the lamb is small and soft. This suggests it is a symbol of gentleness and innocence.
By the stream & o'er the mead;	
Gave thee clothing of delight,	
<u>Softest clothing wooly bright;</u>	

562   Unit 4

BACKGROUND

William Blake *(1757–1827) was born into a modest family in London. He learned to read and write at home, while studying the Bible and the works of John Milton. When he was 10, his father sent him to a drawing school. Blake began writing poetry when he was 12. However, the cost of the school was high, so four years later his parents apprenticed him to a master engraver.*

After setting up shop as an engraver, Blake developed a technique that allowed him to print pages of text and illustration from the same plate, which he then hand colored. Blake used this time-consuming process, called illuminated printing, to publish most of his works.

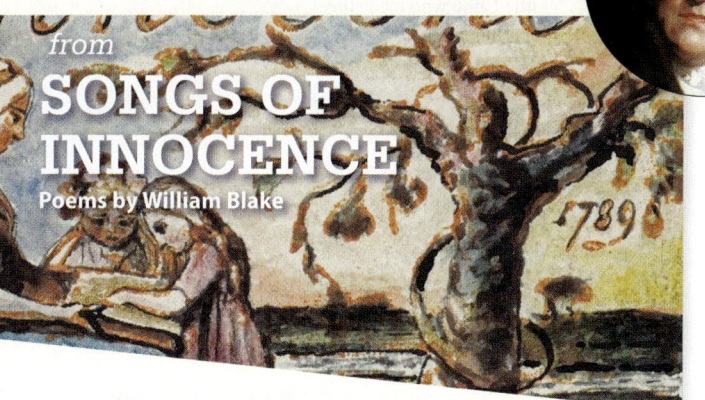

from SONGS OF INNOCENCE
Poems by William Blake

In 1782 Blake married Catherine Boucher. She was illiterate when they met, but Blake taught her how to read, write, and paint. She was an assistant in his work and became a skilled draftsperson.

In 1789 Blake completed his first illuminated book, Songs of Innocence, *featuring poems written for children that also depicted the innocent nature of childhood. Blake's later works were written on a grand scale, marked by prophetic and mythic visions. Imaginatively illustrated and difficult to understand, these complex works were largely ignored by his contemporaries. More than 100 years passed before people began to recognize Blake's stunning achievements as a poet and artist.*

In this selection, you will read two poems from Blake's first collection. The second collection, Songs of Experience, *which you will read next, includes poems that expand on similar themes, with contrasting perspectives. Two such poems, "The Lamb" and "The Tyger," are an example of companion poems that are in separate volumes.*

PREPARE TO COMPARE

As you read, think about how each poem expresses ideas about innocence or experience.

NOTICE & NOTE

Notice & Note
Use the side margins to notice and note signposts in the text.

TEACH

BACKGROUND
Some people believed that Blake wrote for "children and angels" because of the mystical concepts he addressed; he believed his writing was of national importance and that it could be understood by a majority of men. Because Blake lived in London at a time of great social and political change, the upheaval profoundly influenced his writing. He worked tirelessly to bring about a change both in people's minds and in the social order.

Ask students if they know any other authors whose works are influenced by social and political movements.

PREPARE TO COMPARE
Direct students to use the Prepare to Compare prompt to focus their reading.

IMPROVE READING FLUENCY

Repeated Reading Have students work with partners to read the poems in *Songs of Innocence*. First, use lines 1–10 of "The Lamb" on page 564 to model how to read with appropriate phrasing and emphasis. Have students follow along in their books as you read. Then, ask students to take turns reading with their partners. Encourage them to provide feedback and support when pronouncing new or unfamiliar words and to use reference books to define words they don't know. Remind students to pace their reading and emphasize important details and pauses so the person who is listening understands the speaker's tone.

TEACH

ANALYZE SYMBOLS

Discuss **symbolism** with students. Ask them why they think the word *Lamb* is capitalized. Have students reread the poem and identify details that refer to the Lamb's creator. (**Answer:** *In addition to representing gentleness, the lamb symbolizes Jesus Christ.*)

 For **reading support** for students at varying proficiency levels, see the **Text X-Ray** on page 560D.

ENGLISH LEARNER SUPPORT

Use Inductive Reasoning Explain that **inductive reasoning** is the process of logical reasoning from observations, examples, and details from the text to a general conclusion. Tell students that they will use inductive reasoning to arrive at a conclusion about the symbols in the poem or about the historical context by analyzing specific details. Provide students with sentence frames to guide their understanding of differences between inductive and deductive reasoning:

- *I know the poem was written during a time when _____ was happening because the poem states _____.*
- *By using symbols of _____, Blake suggests this poem addresses a social issue.*

Make sure students understand the fundamental differences between the two types of reasoning.
LIGHT

564 Unit 4

 **NOTICE & NOTE**

 The Lamb

    Little Lamb, who made thee?
    Dost thou know who made thee?
Gave thee life & bid thee feed,
By the stream & o'er the mead;
5 Gave thee clothing of delight,
Softest clothing wooly bright;
Gave thee such a tender voice,
Making all the vales rejoice!
    Little Lamb who made thee?
10   Dost thou know who made thee?

    Little Lamb I'll tell thee,
    Little Lamb I'll tell thee!
He is callèd by thy name,
For he calls himself a Lamb:
15 He is meek & he is mild,
He became a little child:
I a child & thou a lamb,
We are callèd by his name.
    Little Lamb God bless thee.
20   Little Lamb God bless thee.

4 mead: meadow.

8 vales: valleys.

ANALYZE SYMBOLS
Annotate: Mark references to the lamb's creator in lines 11–18.

Interpret: How does this passage develop the symbolic meaning of the lamb?

13–14 He . . . Lamb: In the New Testament, Jesus is sometimes called the Lamb of God.

564 Unit 4

ENGLISH LEARNER SUPPORT

Use Prereading Supports Model the process of using available features within a text, such as title, vocabulary, and art, to increase comprehension. Before students begin reading, ask them to observe the art on pages 563 and 564 to see what clues they can gather about the first poem, "The Lamb." Provide students with a graphic organizer that allows them to organize key ideas and supporting details. Model how to fill out the organizer by conducting a shared reading. Then, allow students to complete the graphic organizer with a partner.
ALL LEVELS

NOTICE & NOTE

CHECK YOUR UNDERSTANDING

Answer these questions about "The Lamb" before moving on to the next selection.

1. In "The Lamb," the speaker begins by asking —
   A whether the lamb is lost
   B how old the lamb is
   C who created the lamb
   D what is the lamb's name

2. Blake reveals that the poem's speaker is —
   F the lamb
   G a child
   H Jesus Christ
   J Blake himself

3. Which of God's characteristics does Blake emphasize in "The Lamb"?
   A Gentleness
   B Power
   C Beauty
   D Creativity

TEACH

CHECK YOUR UNDERSTANDING

Have students answer the questions independently.

Answers:
1. *C*
2. *G*
3. *A*

If they answer any questions incorrectly, have them reread the text to confirm their understanding. Then they may proceed to the next selection.

ENGLISH LEARNER SUPPORT

Oral Assessment Use the following questions to assess students' comprehension and speaking skills:

1. The speaker asks the lamb who _____. *(The speaker is asking who created the little lamb.)*

2. Is the speaker a child or an adult? *(The speaker is a child. In line 17, the speaker says, "I a child & thou a lamb. ...")*

3. Does the speaker call the lamb's creator meek and mild? *(yes)*
   SUBSTANTIAL/MODERATE

TEACH

UNDERSTAND HISTORICAL CONTEXT

Remind students that Blake was passionate about the social and political issues of this time and they influenced his writing significantly. Be sure students understand who chimney sweepers were. Ask them what kinds of things they can learn about chimney sweepers from the poem. (**Answer:** *Society didn't protect poor children from being exploited. They often worked as sweepers. The dangerous work conditions led to many deaths.*).

EL · ENGLISH LEARNER SUPPORT

Understand Nonstandard English Students may have trouble with Blake's use of ampersands (lines 4, 9, 11, 14, 17, 20, 22, 23), irregular apostrophes (lines 6, 12, 14, 23), and irregular capitalization (lines 13, 16, 19) in "The Chimney Sweeper." On the board, show the regularized punctuation, capitalization, and missing letters of the relevant words. Ask students to read some of the lines aloud to check their comprehension of the print cues. **ALL LEVELS**

EL · ENGLISH LEARNER SUPPORT

Read Linguistically Accommodated Content Provide students with adapted text and/or text that has summaries of difficult sections of "The Chimney Sweeper." As students improve their reading skills, have them practice fluency using texts at the appropriate level, gradually raising the level as their reading improves. Allow students to record their reading and listen to the results. Show them how to chart their fluency rates each time. **ALL LEVELS**

NOTICE & NOTE

The Chimney Sweeper

<u>When my mother died I was very young,</u>
<u>And my father sold me</u> while yet my tongue
Could scarcely cry "'weep! 'weep! 'weep! 'weep!"
<u>So your chimneys I sweep & in soot I sleep.</u>

5 There's little Tom Dacre, who cried when his head
That curl'd like a lamb's back, was shav'd, so I said,
"Hush, Tom! never mind it, for when your head's bare,
You know that the soot cannot spoil your white hair."

And so he was quiet, & that very night,
10 As Tom was a-sleeping he had such a sight!
<u>That thousands of sweepers, Dick, Joe, Ned, & Jack,</u>
<u>Were all of them lock'd up in coffins of black;</u>

And by came an Angel who had a bright key,
And he open'd the coffins & set them all free;
15 Then down a green plain, leaping, laughing they run,
And wash in a river and shine in the Sun.

Then naked & white, all their bags left behind,
They rise upon clouds, and sport in the wind.
And the Angel told Tom, if he'd be a good boy,
20 He'd have God for his father & never want joy.

And so Tom awoke; and we rose in the dark
And got with our bags & our brushes to work.
Tho' the morning was cold, Tom was happy & warm;
So if all do their duty, they need not fear harm.

3 'weep! 'weep!: the child's attempt to say "Sweep! Sweep!" — a chimney sweeper's street cry.

UNDERSTAND HISTORICAL CONTEXT
Annotate: Mark details in lines 1–14 that relate to the historical context of the poem.
Infer: What can you infer from these details about social conditions in late 18th century Britain?

18 sport: play or frolic.

20 want: lack.

WHEN STUDENTS STRUGGLE . . .

Understand Diction and Tone "The Chimney Sweeper" has challenging words and phrases. Give students time to work through Blake's word choices in the poem, using context clues and identifying the tone the words create. Have them use a graphic organizer like below.

Diction	Meaning	Tone It Creates
. . . yet my tongue / Could scarcely cry . . .	The speaker was still very young.	Empathy

 For additional support, go to the **Reading Studio** and assign the following Level Up tutorial: Using Context Clues.

NOTICE & NOTE

CHECK YOUR UNDERSTANDING

Answer these questions about "The Chimney Sweeper" before moving on to the next selection.

1. In "The Chimney Sweeper," the speaker knows Tom Dacre because —
   A they go to the same school
   B they are brothers
   C they work together
   D Tom appeared in a dream

2. Why does Tom cry in "The Chimney Sweeper"?
   F His hair is shaved off.
   G His hair becomes dirty.
   H His father sells him.
   J He sees boys in coffins.

3. Tom is "happy & warm" in the morning because he —
   A had a good night's sleep
   B worked over a warm fireplace
   C was allowed to miss work
   D dreamed of an angel comforting him

Songs of Innocence / Songs of Experience   567

TEACH

CHECK YOUR UNDERSTANDING

Have students answer the questions independently.

Answers:
1. C
2. F
3. D

If they answer any questions incorrectly, have them reread the text to confirm their understanding. Then they may proceed to the next selection.

ENGLISH LEARNER SUPPORT

Oral Assessment Use the following questions to assess students' comprehension and speaking skills.

1. Tom Dacre was a _____. *(young chimney sweeper)*
2. Tom cried because his head was _____. *(shaved)*
3. In Tom's dream an _____ sets children free. *(Angel)*

SUBSTANTIAL/MODERATE

Songs of Innocence / Songs of Experience   **567**

TEACH

BACKGROUND

Blake's later works were written on a grand scale, marked by prophetic and mythic visions. Imaginatively illustrated and difficult to understand, these complex works were almost totally ignored by his contemporaries. In his 60s, Blake at last found admirers among a group of young artists. During this period he created some of his best works, including illustrations for Dante's *Divine Comedy*. Blake died three months before his 70th birthday, "singing," a friend reported, "of the things he saw in heaven."

ANALYZE SYMBOLS

Remind students that they need to think about the context to determine what the tiger **symbolizes.** Ask students why they think the word *Tyger* is capitalized. Why might it be spelled differently from what they might be used to? (**Answer:** *The tiger seems to represent powerful and beautiful, yet also frightening, forces in nature.*)

 For **listening support** for students at varying proficiency levels, see the **Text X-Ray** on page 560C.

 **NOTICE & NOTE**

BACKGROUND

William Blake (1757–1827) published Songs of Experience in 1794 as a companion volume to Songs of Innocence. He said his purpose in putting them together was to show "the two contrary states of the human soul." The contrast between the collections lies in the perspectives of the speakers rather than the subjects of the poems. Much darker in mood and tone, Songs of Experience includes poems that link to poems in the earlier volume, including some with matching titles.

from SONGS OF EXPERIENCE
Poems by William Blake

The Tyger

Notice & Note
Use the side margins to notice and note signposts in the text.

4 symmetry (sĭm´ĭ-trē): balance or beauty of form.

7 he: the tiger's creator.

ANALYZE SYMBOLS
Annotate: Mark details in lines 1–12 that describe the tiger.
Analyze: What symbolic meaning is suggested by these details?

15 anvil (ăn´vĭl): iron block on which metal objects are hammered into shape.

Tyger! Tyger! burning bright
In the forests of the night,
What immortal hand or eye
Could frame thy fearful symmetry?

5   In what distant deeps or skies
Burnt the fire of thine eyes?
On what wings dare he aspire?
What the hand dare seize the fire?

And what shoulder, & what art,
10 Could twist the sinews of thy heart?
And when thy heart began to beat,
What dread hand? & what dread feet?

What the hammer? what the chain?
In what furnace was thy brain?
15 What the anvil? what dread grasp
Dare its deadly terrors clasp?

568   Unit 4

APPLYING ACADEMIC VOCABULARY

 **appreciate**   ☐ insight   **intensity**   ☐ invoke   **radical**

Write and Discuss Have students turn to a partner to discuss the following questions. Guide students to include the Academic Vocabulary words *appreciate, intensity,* and *radical* in their responses. Ask volunteers to share their responses with the class.

- What do you **appreciate** about William Blake's poetry?
- Why might the tiger's **intensity** in "The Tyger" frighten some people?
- Why do you think some people describe William Blake's work as **radical**?

568   Unit 4

When the stars threw down their spears
And watered heaven with their tears,
Did he smile his work to see?
20   Did he who made the Lamb make thee?

Tyger! Tyger! burning bright
In the forests of the night,
What immortal hand or eye
Dare frame thy fearful symmetry?

NOTICE & NOTE

TOUGH QUESTIONS

Notice & Note: Mark each question in the poem.

Draw Conclusions: Why does the poem consist of so many questions?

CHECK YOUR UNDERSTANDING

Answer these questions about "The Tyger" before moving on to the next selection.

1 What does the "immortal hand or eye" in "The Tyger" refer to?

 A God

 B Death

 C Mankind

 D Nature

2 Which aspect of nature does Blake associate with the tiger?

 F Wind

 G Air

 H Water

 J Fire

3 The lines "What the anvil? what dread grasp / Dare its deadly terrors clasp" express —

 A pity for the animals devoured by the tiger

 B fear that the tiger cannot be controlled

 C awe for the creator of such a terrifying creature

 D suspicion that the tiger is not real

Songs of Innocence / Songs of Experience   569

TEACH

TOUGH QUESTIONS

Sometimes writers include **rhetorical questions**—or questions that are not meant to be answered—in their works. Ask students to reread the poem, making sure to pay attention to the questions in the poem. (**Answer:** *Blake wants to engage the reader by asking questions that cause him or her to reflect on social conditions.*)

CHECK YOUR UNDERSTANDING

Have students answer the questions independently.

Answers:

1. A

2. J

3. C

If they answer any questions incorrectly, have them reread the text to confirm their understanding. Then they may proceed to the next selection.

ENGLISH LEARNER SUPPORT

Oral Assessment Use the following questions to assess students' comprehension and speaking skills:

1. Does the tiger make the speaker think of fire or wind? *(fire)*

2. Does the speaker think the tiger is ugly? *(no)*

3. Does the speaker think the tiger is scary? *(The tiger is described as beautiful and powerful, yet frightening because of how big and towering it can be.)* **SUBSTANTIAL/MODERATE**

Songs of Innocence / Songs of Experience   **569**

TEACH

✏️ UNDERSTAND HISTORICAL CONTEXT

Have students read the poem stanza by stanza, making sure they can provide a summary of each section before they move on. Ask students what stands out to them in this version of "The Chimney Sweeper." Ask how this second rendition of the poem is different from the version they read in *Songs of Innocence*. Once students understand the differences, guide them to identify language that hints at the tone of the piece. (**Answer:** *The tone is cynical, suggesting that the government and established religion of Britain encourage hypocrisy and fail to protect the vulnerable.*)

🔵 ENGLISH LEARNER SUPPORT

Demonstrate English Comprehension Provide students with a graphic organizer they can use to compare and contrast the main ideas and supporting details in "The Chimney Sweeper" from *Songs of Experience* and "The Chimney Sweeper" from *Songs of Innocence*. In each section of the organizer, provide examples from the poems and ask students to discuss, in pairs, how those details affect the overall poem. Ask students to complete the remainder of the graphic organizer with their own ideas from each poem.
MODERATE

✏️ NOTICE & NOTE

The Chimney Sweeper

A little black thing among the snow
Crying "'weep, 'weep," in notes of woe!
"Where are thy father & mother? say?"
"They are both gone up to the church to pray.

5 "Because I was happy upon the heath,
And smil'd among the winter's snow;
They clothed me in the clothes of death,
And taught me to sing the notes of woe.

"And because I am happy, & dance & sing,
10 They think they have done me no injury,
And are gone to praise God & his Priest & King,
Who make up a heaven of our misery."

2 'weep, 'weep: the child's attempt to say "Sweep, Sweep"—a chimney sweeper's street cry.

5 heath: a tract of open land that cannot be farmed.

UNDERSTAND HISTORICAL CONTEXT
Annotate: Mark details in lines 5–12 that help create the tone of "The Chimney Sweeper."

Infer: Identify the tone of this poem. What does it suggest about British society?

TO CHALLENGE STUDENTS . . .

Structure a Debate Ask students to pair up, and challenge them to structure a debate addressing which version of "The Chimney Sweeper" they think is more compelling and why. Each pair will choose the version of the poem they like best and then work together to identify pieces of evidence to support their ideas. Encourage students to use any notes or graphic organizers they have completed to guide their debates. Once pairs have structured an argument, give pairs an opportunity to debate with other pairs. Consider giving students an opportunity to provide each other feedback about their arguments.

NOTICE & NOTE

CHECK YOUR UNDERSTANDING

Answer these questions before moving on to the **Analyze the Text** section on the following page.

1. What is the "black thing" Blake refers to in "The Chimney Sweeper"?
   - A A child
   - B A piece of coal
   - C A chimney
   - D Soot-coated snow

2. Why don't the parents of the chimney sweeper see that he is being harmed by his work?
   - F He lies to them.
   - G He keeps up a cheerful appearance.
   - H He has run away from them.
   - J He praises God for his job.

3. In "The Chimney Sweeper," what does the phrase "make up a heaven of our misery" suggest?
   - A The church and the king profit from his sweeping.
   - B The priest and the king also suffer.
   - C His parents will be rewarded in heaven.
   - D His parents' religion glorifies suffering.

TEACH

CHECK YOUR UNDERSTANDING

Have students answer the questions independently.

Answers:
1. A
2. G
3. D

If they answer any questions incorrectly, have them reread the text to confirm their understanding. Then they may proceed to ANALYZE THE TEXTS on page 572.

ENGLISH LEARNER SUPPORT

Oral Assessment Use the following questions to assess students' comprehension and speaking skills

1. The "little black thing" in the poem is a _____. *(child)*
2. Does the speaker act happy? *(He smiles through it and keeps a positive attitude.)*
3. Do the speaker's parents know they are harming him? *(no)*

MODERATE

APPLY

ANALYZE THE TEXTS

Possible answers:

1. **DOK 2:** In "The Lamb," the repetition of words, such as *little* and *child,* helps create a gentle, sweet mood that reflects the child's innocent perspective.

2. **DOK 2:** Although this language suggests the frightening aspects of the tiger, the speaker doesn't criticize the creation of the tiger; instead he marvels at the power and daring required to create such an awesome animal.

3. **DOK 3:** Possible answer: Art isn't always pretty or gentle; it can also be disturbing or even frightening.

4. **DOK 4:** In the Songs of Innocence poem, Tom's hair and the boys' bodies are white, symbolizing their innocence. In the Songs of Experience poem, the child is described as black, which symbolizes his misery.

5. **DOK 4:** In the Songs of Innocence poem, a dream about an angel convinces Tom to accept his situation, and in the Songs of Experience poem, religion of that time allows the parents to subject their child to harsh labor without feeling guilty. Together, the poems suggest that Blake was critical of the church for reinforcing the use of child labor.

RESEARCH

Remind students that to identify the most credible and accurate informational sources online, they should go to sites that end in .gov or .edu. Consider having students pair up or work in small groups to brainstorm search terms before they begin their research.

Extend Students may have a difficult time coming up with names of poets to search. Consider providing them with a list of names to get started (e.g., Maya Angelou, Alice Walker, Robert Frost, C.S. Lewis, Adrienne Rich, Walt Whitman, and Langston Hughes). Remind students that they do not have to limit their search to a specific time period, which should give them many options from which to choose.

RESPOND

ANALYZE THE TEXT

Support your responses with evidence from the text.  **NOTEBOOK**

1. **Identify** Notice the words, phrases, and lines that Blake repeats in "The Lamb." What mood does this repetition help create?

2. **Interpret** In "The Tyger," the speaker describes the animal as "fearful" and "deadly." Do the negative connotations of this language suggest that the tiger should never have been created? Explain.

3. **Draw Conclusions** In "The Tyger," Blake uses words such as *art, hammer, furnace,* and *anvil* to describe the tiger's creation, as if the animal were a metal sculpture. What does this symbolic meaning of the tiger suggest about Blake's view of art?

4. **Analyze** Describe Blake's use of the colors white and black in "The Chimney Sweeper" poems. What do these colors symbolize?

5. **Notice & Note** In "The Chimney Sweeper" poems, the speakers have two sharply contrasting perspectives on religion. Considered together, what do both poems suggest about Blake's view of the religious establishment of his time? Explain.

RESEARCH

RESEARCH TIP
When researching social, historical, or political events, consider referring to an encyclopedia. Encyclopedias are useful because they tend to be organized according to a specific subject or domain. You may, for instance, refer to an encyclopedia of history.

As you've read, poets sometimes draw inspiration from social, historical, and political events. "The Chimney Sweeper" poems, for example, express social commentary on the use and abuse of young boys to clean chimneys before child labor laws were implemented. Research another William Blake poem that addresses a social, historical, or political issue or event. Use the graphic organizer below to explain the poem's social, historical, or political connection.

TITLE OF POEM	SOCIAL, HISTORICAL, OR POLITICAL CONNECTION
"London"	In "London," Blake describes the political corruption of the ruling class and the oppression imposed on the masses by the Church and State.

Extend Research another poet who writes about social, historical, or political events. What are some similarities and differences between this poet and William Blake? Consider organizing your findings in a Venn diagram.

 LEARNING MINDSET

Asking for Help Remind students that if they don't understand something, they should always ask for help. Tell students that they are resources for each other, so if you are not available to answer a question, they can offer support to each other. If students ask for help, you might say, "OK, so you didn't do as well as you wanted to. Let's look at this as an opportunity to learn," or "What learning strategies are you using? How about trying some different ones?" Help students understand that asking for help is an admirable quality, and it is an effective way to improve the quality of their work.

RESPOND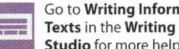

CREATE AND DISCUSS

Write an Essay Choose a social issue that is considered one of the compelling concerns of contemporary times. Write a short problem-solution essay to explore the issue and possible remedies.

- ❏ Focus on a problem that directly affects your community.
- ❏ If you are working actively to confront this social problem, share your firsthand knowledge.
- ❏ Ask yourself questions about the problem as a way to explore ways it might be solved. Your essay might include more than one approach.
- ❏ Identify a symbol that could meaningfully convey your message.

Make a Podcast Form a small group to plan a podcast. Identify the key ideas in your essay and organize them into discussion points. Then record a "talk" on these discussion points to create your podcast.

- ❏ Use your problem-solution essays as well as other research to support your views.
- ❏ Assign a host to keep the conversation flowing. Exchange ideas in a lively manner and try to avoid "talking-down" to your audience.
- ❏ Uphold the basic goal to leave your listeners motivated.

 Go to **Writing Informative Texts** in the **Writing Studio** for more help.

 Go to **Participating in Collaborative Discussions** in the **Speaking and Listening Studio** for help.

RESPOND TO THE ESSENTIAL QUESTION

 What shapes your outlook on life?

Gather Information Review your annotations and notes on poems from *Songs of Innocence* and *Songs of Experience*. Then, add relevant information to your Response Log. As you determine which information to include, think about:

- the experiences and characteristics of children and of adults—how they are similar and different
- how nature has influenced the way you think about life
- the tension between opposites, like innocence and experience, and how exploring such opposites helps us understand our world

ACADEMIC VOCABULARY

As you write and discuss what you learned from the poems, be sure to use the Academic Vocabulary words. Check off each of the words that you use.

- ❏ appreciate
- ❏ insight
- ❏ intensity
- ❏ invoke
- ❏ radical

APPLY

CREATE AND DISCUSS

Write an Essay Point out to the students that the list on page 573 can serve as a guideline for their problem-solution essays. Before students begin brainstorming their essays, consider facilitating a discussion about contemporary social and political topics they might have encountered and how those challenges have been addressed or are being addressed. Ask students to think about how they might address those issues differently or if there are solutions they think are already effective. If necessary, allow students to work in pairs to come up with ideas for their essays.

For **writing support** for students at varying proficiency levels, see the **Text X-Ray** on page 560D.

Make a Podcast Before students create their podcasts, give them time to create a plan of execution. Remind students to anticipate answers to questions they think their peers might have and include them in their podcasts. Encourage students to think about their goals for the podcast and how best to achieve those goals using the podcast. Encourage students to use the checklist on page 573 to guide their work.

RESPOND TO THE ESSENTIAL QUESTION

Allow time for students to add details from *Songs of Innocence / Songs of Experience* to their Unit 4 Response Logs.

APPLY

COMPARE POEMS

Before students complete the graphic organizer on page 574, ask them to reread the poems and underline or circle words that help them identify the tone or paint a picture in their minds. Have students use their notes to complete the graphic organizer. After students complete the graphic organizer, ask them to review their responses with a partner and agree on a tone for each poem.

ANALYZE THE TEXTS

Possible answers:

1. **DOK 3:** *In "The Lamb," the speaker says that God created the lamb. In "The Tyger," the speaker wonders if the same God who created the lamb could have created such a terrifying beast. These different responses reflect the feeling of security and comfort that comes with innocence and the greater understanding of complexity that comes with experience.*

2. **DOK 3:** *Possible answer: Blake's use of symbols is effective because it enables him to describe abstract concepts in a very concrete and accessible way.*

3. **DOK 2:** *They aren't the same because Blake focuses on two states of mind that affect how people perceive things in the world, rather than on the moral nature of the things that are perceived.*

4. **DOK 3:** *Possible answer: The poems do not value one over the other: both states of mind are necessary. The poems from Songs of Innocence suggests that innocence helps people see the goodness in the world, but the poems from Songs of Experience suggest that experience allows us to understand complexity and see through deception.*

 RESPOND

Collaborate & Compare

COMPARE POEMS

from
SONGS OF INNOCENCE
Poems by William Blake

from
SONGS OF EXPERIENCE
Poems by William Blake

Compare and contrast the perspectives of the poems from *Songs of Innocence* and *Songs of Experience*, using the following criteria:
- **Word choice:** Look for descriptive words and note how they are used to emphasize characteristics of a subject.
- **Ideas:** Identify common or contrasting ideas expressed in the poems.
- **Tone:** Notice the speaker's attitude toward the subject.

As you read, you may use a chart like this one to record similarities and differences between each linked pair of poems.

	"THE LAMB"	"THE TYGER"
Word Choice	*little, tender voice; wooly bright*	*burning bright; fire of thine eyes*
Ideas	*The lamb is meek and mild, and represents childlike innocence and purity.*	*The tiger is a powerful, yet beautiful creature that inspires fear.*
Tone	*Tenderness*	*Awe*

ANALYZE THE TEXTS

Discuss these questions in your group.

1. **Compare** "The Lamb" and "The Tyger" develop around questions posed at the beginning of each poem. How do the speakers' different responses to these questions reflect the contrast between innocence and experience?

2. **Critique** Does Blake use symbols effectively to help convey his themes? Why or why not?

3. **Interpret** Is Blake's view of innocence and experience essentially the same as the idea of good versus evil? Explain your response.

4. **Draw Conclusions** Do these poems suggest that innocence is better than experience? Explain your response.

 ENGLISH LEARNER SUPPORT

Perform Critical Analysis Use the questions below to help students analyze the selections:

1. Why do you think Blake wrote *Songs of Experience* after *Songs of Innocence* and not before? Why do you think he wrote about "The Lamb" in *Songs of Innocence* and about "The Tyger" in *Songs of Experience*? (*Possible answers: In our youth, we tend to be more innocent than in adulthood. The lamb is tame while the tiger is fierce.*)

2. Do you think Blake was effective in his approach to addressing the social conditions of this time? Why or why not? (*Possible answer: Yes, because he appeals to reader's emotion and uses specific details to explain social conditions.*) **MODERATE/LIGHT**

RESPOND

COLLABORATE AND PRESENT

With your group, continue exploring the ideas in the poems by identifying and comparing word choice, symbols, and themes. Follow these steps:

1. **Decide on the most important details with your group.** Review your chart to identify the most important details from each poem. What words or phrases stood out the most to you? Come to a consensus with your group.

2. **Come up with a message.** Determine a message for each poem based on the details, diction, ideas, and symbols. You may use a chart to keep track of the themes your group members come up with.

	DETAILS	MESSAGE
Songs of Innocence	Then down a green / plain, leaping, laughing / they run, / And wash in a river and / shine in the Sun.	Youth still have an untainted perspective of the world--they are eager, virtuous, and hopeful.
Songs of Experience	And what shoulder, & / what art, / Could twist the sinews of / thy heart? / And when thy heart / began to beat, / What dread hand? & / what dread feet?	Adulthood represents dark opposing forces because the human experience is tainted by oppression in society.

3. **Compare ideas.** Compare ideas with your group and discuss whether the messages are similar or different. Listen actively to the members of your group and ask them to clarify any points you do not understand.

4. **Present to the class.** Next, present your ideas to the class. Be sure to include clear statements on the theme for each poem. Discuss whether the messages are similar or different.

Go to **Participating in a Collaborative Discussion** in the **Speaking and Listening Studio** to support group discussion.

RESEARCH TIP
When discussing your ideas in a group, be sure to listen attentively. Give your peers an opportunity to share their ideas and respect their views. If you disagree with an idea, present evidence from the selections to support your ideas. Give all group members an opportunity to have a turn.

Collaborate & Compare 575

APPLY

COLLABORATE AND PRESENT

Reinforce the idea with the students that poets often use their work as a means to comment on social and political conditions. Rather than describing these issues explicitly, they may use symbols and other literary devices to engage readers or to create a vivid image for the audience. Remind students that as they continue to explore the ideas in the poems, they should compare word choice, symbols, and the themes.

1. **Decide on the most important details with your group.** Before students decide on the most important details in each poem, encourage them to brainstorm two or three ideas and then discuss each of their ideas and supporting evidence with their group members. From there, they can each choose one idea they think is the most important.

2. **Come up with a message.** Tell students that their collective message can be a combination of text and visuals, as long as they include the details they think are most important.

3. **Compare ideas.** Remind students that when they are in their groups, each person should have an opportunity to share while others listen. After each person shares his or her ideas, the others can ask questions and give the person an opportunity to integrate the feedback into their overall message.

4. **Present to the class.** Remind each group to choose a representative who can effectively convey their ideas. Let students know, that if necessary, they can write down key ideas or notes on a note card to help them organize their thoughts before they present them to the class. Remind students to speak clearly and use eye contact as a way to connect with the audience as they present.

WHEN STUDENTS STRUGGLE . . .

Craft a Coherent Message If students struggle to come up with a coherent message for each poem, provide them with a graphic organizer to help them synthesize their ideas.

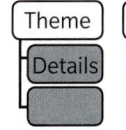

 For additional support, go to the **Reading Studio** and assign the following Level Up tutorial: **Theme.**

Collaborate & Compare 575

INDEPENDENT READING

READER'S CHOICE

Setting a Purpose Have students review their Unit 4 Response Logs and think about what they've already learned about the human relationship with the natural world. As they choose their Independent Reading selections, encourage them to consider what more they want to know.

NOTICE & NOTE

Explain that some selections may contain multiple signposts; others may contain only one. Moreover, the same type of signpost can occur many times in the same text.

LEARNING MINDSET

Persistence Tell students that making an effort and facing challenges is the key to growth and developing a learning mindset. Encourage students to approach challenges in learning with a positive attitude instead of quickly giving up. Model positive self-talk. For example, "I know I can do this if I keep at it."

INDEPENDENT READING

Reader's Choice

Select and Preview Select one or more of these options from your eBook to continue your exploration of the Essential Questions.

- Read the descriptions to see which text attracts your interest.
- Think about which genres you enjoy reading.

Notice & Note

In this unit, you practiced noticing and noting the signposts and asking big questions about nonfiction. As you read independently, these signposts and others will aid your understanding. Below are the key questions to ask when you read literature and nonfiction.

ESSENTIAL QUESTIONS

Review the four Essential Questions for this unit on page 491.

Reading Literature: Stories, Poems, and Plays	
Signpost	Key Question
Contrasts and Contradictions	Why did the character act that way?
Aha Moment	How might this change things?
Tough Questions	What does this make me wonder about?
Words of the Wiser	What's the lesson for the character?
Again and Again	Why might the author keep bringing this up?
Memory Moment	Why is this memory important?

Reading Nonfiction: Essays, Articles, and Arguments	
Signpost	Key Question(s)
Big Questions	What surprised me? What did the author think I already knew? What challenged, changed, or confirmed what I already knew?
Contrasts and Contradictions	What is the difference, and why does it matter?
Extreme or Absolute Language	Why did the author use this language?
Numbers and Stats	Why did the author use these numbers or amounts?
Quoted Words	Why was this person quoted or cited, and what did this citation add?
Word Gaps	Do I know this word from someplace else? Does it seem like technical talk for this topic? Do clues in the sentence help me understand the word?

576 Unit 4

ENGLISH LEARNER SUPPORT

Develop Fluency Select a passage from the text that matches students' reading abilities. Read it aloud while students follow along silently.

- Choral-read the passage with students. Then, have them reread the passage on their own. Have them sound out difficult words. Explain the meaning of the words as related to the passage. **SUBSTANTIAL**

- Give students time to practice reading the passage on their own. Have them underline any difficult words. Explain the pronunciation, meaning, and usage of these words. Have students fill out graphic organizers highlighting the main ideas of the passage. **MODERATE**

- Have students practice their reading in small groups. Encourage students to help each other with any difficult words. Have one student from each group share words they helped each other learn. **LIGHT**

INDEPENDENT READING

You can preview these texts in Unit 4 of your eBook.
Then check off the text or texts that you select to read on your own.

☐
EXPLANATORY ESSAY
William Blake: Visions and Verses
Rachel Galvin

Why was William Blake considered eccentric during his life but is now praised as a creative visionary?

☐
POEM
Frost at Midnight
Samuel Taylor Coleridge

How do the poet's memories of his childhood affect what he wants for his son?

☐
PERSONAL NARRATIVE
Walking with Wordsworth
Bruce Stutz

A naturalist describes continuity as well as change in the landscapes that Wordsworth held dear.

☐
EXPLANATORY ESSAY
from **A Defense of Poetry**
Percy Bysshe Shelley

Why does Shelley believe that poetry is the foundation of society as well as a source of beauty?

☐
POEM
The Skylark
John Clare

Clare contrasts young boys' fanciful view of flight with the skylark's awareness of nature's risks and dangers.

Collaborate and Share With a partner, discuss what you learned from at least one of your independent readings.
- Give a brief synopsis or summary of the text.
- Describe any signposts that you noticed in the text and explain what they revealed to you.
- Describe what you most enjoyed or found most challenging about the text. Give specific examples.
- Decide if you would recommend the text to others. Why or why not?

 Go to the **Reading Studio** for more resources on **Notice & Note.**

Independent Reading 577

INDEPENDENT READING

MATCHING STUDENTS TO TEXTS
Use the following information to guide students in choosing their texts.

William Blake: Visions and Verses **Lexile: 1130L**
Genre: explanatory essay
Overall Rating: Accessible

Frost at Midnight
Genre: poem
Overall Rating: Challenging

Walking with Wordsworth **Lexile: 1280L**
Genre: personal narrative
Overall Rating: Challenging

from **A Defence of Poetry** **Lexile: 1140L**
Genre: explanatory essay
Overall Rating: Challenging

The Skylark
Genre: poem
Overall Rating: Challenging

Collaborate and Share To assess how well students read the selections, walk around the room and listen to their conversations. Encourage students to focus and be specific in their comments.

 for Assessment

- Independent Reading Selection Tests

 Encourage students to visit the **Reading Studio** to download a handy bookmark of **NOTICE & NOTE** signposts.

WHEN STUDENTS STRUGGLE...

Keep Reading Logs As students read their selected texts, have them keep reading logs for each selection to note signposts and their thoughts about them. Use their logs to assess how well they are noticing and reflecting on elements of their texts.

Reading Log for (title)		
Location	**Signpost I Noticed**	**My Notes about It**

Independent Reading **577**

PLAN

UNIT 4 Tasks

- **WRITE AN EXPLANATORY ESSAY**

MENTOR TEXT

from
"FRANKENSTEIN: GIVING VOICE TO THE MONSTER"
Essay by Langdon Winner

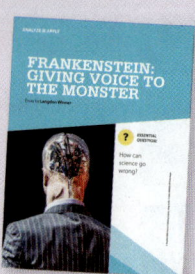

LEARNING OBJECTIVES

Writing Task

- Write an explanatory essay on human interactions with nature.
- Use word mapping, free writing, and group discussion to plan and organize an essay.
- Use the Mentor Text as a model for supporting key ideas with details.
- Develop a "big idea."
- Organize an essay into paragraphs that present key ideas.
- Use genre characteristics to write a first draft.
- Use a Revision Guide and peer review to revise a draft.
- Edit draft to engage readers, use sensory language, and provide smooth transitions between ideas.
- Use a rubric to evaluate writing.
- Publish writing to share with an audience.
- **Language** Use transition words to connect paragraphs.

Assign the Writing Task in **Ed**.

RESOURCES

- Unit 4 Response Log
- Writing Studio: Writing Informative Texts
- Grammar Studio: Module 3: Lesson 2: Adjective Phrases and Adverb Phrases

578A Unit 4

PLAN

Language X-Ray: English Learner Support

Use the instruction below and the supports and scaffolds in the Teacher's Edition to help you guide students of different proficiency levels.

INTRODUCE THE WRITING TASK

Remind students that an explanatory essay should contain facts but must still engage readers. An interesting title that arouses curiosity is a first step. Discuss other ways in which students can attract readers. For example, using descriptive words to paint pictures in readers' minds can also help them connect. Tell students that it's okay to leave out some details in order to stimulate the readers' imaginations.

Have students brainstorm questions they could use as titles. Provide sentence frames to help them discuss why or how an essay can hook readers, such as: *This is an intriguing question because it makes readers ____. This question would be more interesting if we add the descriptive word ____.*

WRITING

Use Transition Words

Remind students that paragraphs should flow smoothly so that readers can follow the writer's thoughts more easily.

Use the following supports with students at varying proficiency levels:

- Write a list of transition words and phrases that students can use to begin new paragraphs, such as: *Another example of this is ____. One more reason that supports this idea is ____.* Have students copy the transition language into their notebooks. **SUBSTANTIAL**
- Have pairs work together to identify transitional language in simple explanatory essays, and copy any words they find. Then, have them use the new words in revisions. **MODERATE**
- Have students exchange drafts of their essays and have them write ideas for improving transitions between paragraphs. **LIGHT**

SPEAKING

Use Sensory Language

Remind students that the five senses are sight, hearing, smell, taste, and touch.

Use the following supports with students at varying proficiency levels:

- Have students copy each sense on a separate index card. As you say and write sensory words, have them hold up each card for the sense it illustrates. **SUBSTANTIAL**
- Have partners discuss a classroom object. Have them include language that appeals to all five senses as they ask each other questions. For example: *How does the ____ smell?* **MODERATE**
- Have partners look for evocative images online or in print. Have them write down sensory language they read. Invite pairs to share words they find particularly evocative. **LIGHT**

Unit 4 Tasks   578B

WRITING

WRITE AN EXPLANATORY ESSAY

Introduce students to the Writing Task by reading the introductory paragraph with them. Remind students to refer to the notes they recorded in the Unit 4 Response Log as they plan and draft their essays. The Response Log should contain ideas about the relationships between humans and nature from a variety of perspectives. Drawing on these different perspectives will make their own writing more interesting and well informed.

 For **writing support** for students at varying proficiency levels, see the **Language X-Ray** on page 578B.

USE THE MENTOR TEXT

Point out that students' essays will be similar to the explanatory essay "Frankenstein: Giving Voice to the Monster" in that they will present facts and examples related to a topic. However, their essays may be shorter than the article and will present their own ideas, using their readings as sources on the topic of the human relationship with the natural world.

WRITING PROMPT

Review the prompt with students. Encourage them to ask questions about any part of the assignment that is unclear. Make sure they understand that the purpose of their essay is to answer the question using facts and examples from the texts they have read.

 **WRITING TASK**

Write an Explanatory Essay

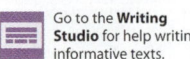 Go to the **Writing Studio** for help writing informative texts.

In this unit, you have read literature from the Romantic period. Many Romantic writers celebrated nature in their works. Others warned of the dangers of tampering with nature. For your next writing task, you will write an explanatory essay on the relationship between humans and nature, using your readings as sources to support your own ideas. The article "Frankenstein: Giving Voice to the Monster" is an explanatory essay that discusses the concept of the human creation of life using Mary Shelley's *Frankenstein* as a source. You will use this essay as a mentor text as you plan and draft your own essay.

As you write your explanatory essay, you can use the notes from your Response Log which you filled out after reading the texts in this unit.

Writing Prompt

Read the information in the box below.

> The human relationship with the natural world is a major topic of literature, including fiction, poetry, and literary essays.

This is the topic or context for your explanatory essay.

Think carefully about the following question.

> What can nature offer us?

How might this Essential Question relate to an explanatory essay?

Write an explanatory essay about how experiencing the natural world can alter a person's state of mind.

How might an experience of nature relate to an explanatory essay?

Be sure to—

Review these points as you write and again when you finish. Make any needed changes.

- ☐ have a "big idea" that your essay develops
- ☐ organize your essay into paragraphs that present a key idea, such as an opinion, an observation, or a claim
- ☐ support your key ideas with such evidence as facts, quotations from texts, expert opinions, or evidence
- ☐ write an opening that catches your reader's attention while introducing your topic
- ☐ write a conclusion that wraps up your ideas and leaves the reader with some "food for thought"

 LEARNING MINDSET

Belonging Remind students that they are all valuable members of the class and that each has something unique to offer. Emphasize that every student is important and can add to the learning environment through participation. Encourage students to participate in class discussions and to offer to help fellow students. Provide examples of appropriate times to offer to help a fellow student, such as when a student mentions that he or she doesn't understand a class assignment during a conversation.

WRITING

1 Plan

Before you begin planning your essay, go through your notes on the texts and look for anything you might use, such as something an author said about nature that you found particularly striking or true, or a thought you had in response. Think about your own experiences with the natural world and how they have affected you.

To generate more ideas for your essay, try these strategies:
- word mapping
- free writing
- group discussion

Review your notes and mark the ones that are most important. Then reflect and come up with your "big idea." You may need to do some more free writing. As E.M. Forster said, "How can I know what I think until I see what I say?"

Use a chart like the one below to plan your essay.

Explanatory Essay Planning Table	
Genre	Explanatory essay
Topic	Human relationship with nature
Details and ideas from texts	
Ideas from word mapping and/or free writing	
Ideas from group discussion	
Ideas from my personal experiences	
My "big idea"	

Background Reading Review the notes you have made in your Response Log that relate to the question "What can nature offer us?" Texts in this unit provide background reading that will help you formulate your "big idea" and your key ideas.

WRITING TASK

Go to **Writing Informative Texts: Developing a Topic** for help planning your explanatory essay.

Notice & Note
From Reading to Writing

As you plan your explanatory essay, apply what you've learned about signposts to your own writing. Remember that writers use common features called signposts to help convey their message to readers.

Think how you can incorporate **Quoted Words** into your essay.

Go to the **Reading Studio** for more resources on **Notice & Note**.

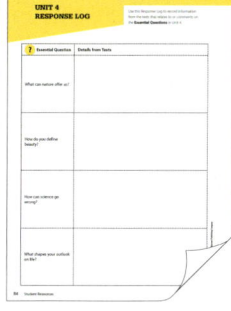

Use the notes from your Response Log as you plan your explanatory essay.

Write an Explanatory Essay 579

1 PLAN

Allow time for students to discuss the topic with partners or in small groups and then to complete the planning table independently.

■ English Learner Support

Understand Academic Language Make sure students understand such words and phrases used in the chart as *genre, topic, texts, word mapping, free writing,* and *personal experiences*. Explain the word meanings and concepts according to students' proficiency levels. Work with them to fill in the blank sections, providing text that they can copy into their charts as needed. **SUBSTANTIAL**

▶ NOTICE & NOTE

From Reading to Writing Remind students to incorporate Quoted Words into their writing. Quoted Words are used to include the opinions or conclusions of someone who is an expert on the topic. Students can also use Quoted Words to provide support for a point they are trying to make. Remind students to format direct quotations correctly and to give credit to the source.

Background Reading As students plan their essays, remind them to refer to the notes they took in the Response Log. They may also review the selections to find additional facts and examples to support ideas they want to include in their writing.

TO CHALLENGE STUDENTS . . .

Discuss in a Group Challenge students to think about ways humans have tried to alter nature and examples of times those ways have backfired, causing more harm than good. Have students break into small groups and discuss the topic, using examples from history or current events. Students may do additional research online or at the library to support the discussion. Encourage them to add points from their group discussion to their Response Log and think about how these might support their answer to the Essential Question.

Write an Explanatory Essay **579**

WRITING

Organize Your Ideas Tell students to use the ideas from their planning activities as they fill out the chart to organize the elements of their essays. Point out that each student's essay should include the following:

- a thought provoking introduction
- three supporting key ideas
- several supporting details for each key idea
- a final reflection or conclusion that provides "food for thought"

Students' essays should also clearly incorporate themes about the human relationship with the natural world. They should include relevant details and examples. Remind students that by thinking about their ideas and organizing their essay elements before beginning to write, they can best decide how to draft their essays and include all the essential elements.

② DEVELOP A DRAFT

Remind students to follow their charts as they draft their essays to include each element. Point out that they can still adjust their writing plan during this stage. For example, as they write they may find a detail doesn't support a key idea and choose a different one, or that a particular detail better supports a different key idea.

■ English Learner Support

Write a Group Essay Simplify the writing task and provide direct support by working together to write an explanatory paragraph that answers the Essential Question, with each student contributing according to his or her level of ability. **SUBSTANTIAL/MODERATE**

 **WRITING TASK**

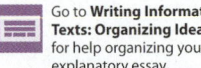 Go to **Writing Informative Texts: Organizing Ideas** for help organizing your explanatory essay.

Organize Your Ideas After you have gathered ideas from your planning activities, you need to organize them in a way that will help you draft your explanatory essay. You can use the chart below to help you organize the elements of your essay.

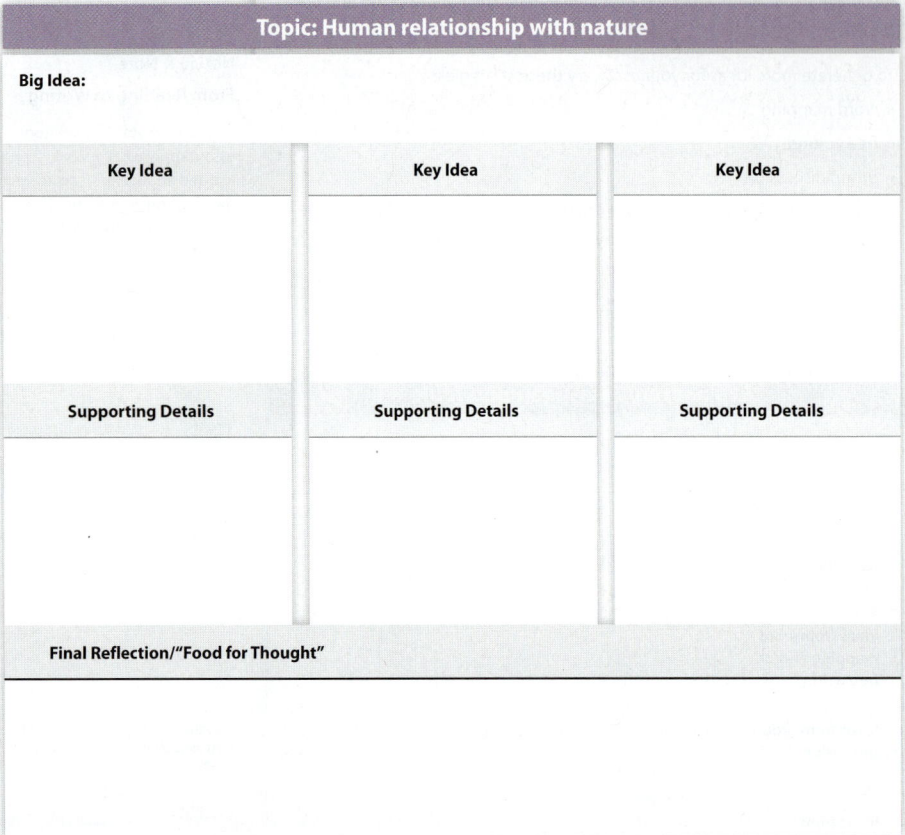

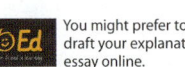 You might prefer to draft your explanatory essay online.

② Develop a Draft

Once you have completed your planning activities, you will be ready to begin drafting your explanatory essay. Refer to the elements of an explanatory essay and your organizing chart as well as any notes you took as you studied the texts in this unit. These will provide a kind of map for you to follow as you write. Using a word processor or online writing application makes it easier to make changes or move sentences around later when you are ready to revise your first draft.

580 Unit 4

WHEN STUDENTS STRUGGLE . . .

Draft the Essay Even when working from a chart to organize their essays' elements, students may struggle to get started on their drafts. For example, students may have difficulty knowing how to begin their essays. Encourage them to start with the key idea they feel most confident about and draft one of the body paragraphs that provides supporting details for that idea. Once they begin writing, they may find that their thoughts flow more freely, even for the more difficult sections. Remind students that a first draft does not have to be perfect. They will have time to revise and edit their writing later.

WRITING

WRITING TASK

Use the Mentor Text

Author's Craft
Your explanatory essay should include several key ideas supported by details. A key idea can be your opinion, an observation, or a claim; supporting details will include facts, quotes from background readings, or short anecdotes from your experiences or those of others. Each key idea and its supporting details should be organized together in a paragraph, but if a paragraph is very long, you should break it into two or more paragraphs.

> The possibility that artificial creatures, products of human hands, might achieve sentience and take on an active role in society is an age-old conception in world cultures. . . .
>
> In Greek mythology one finds the tale of Pygmalion who carves a statue named Galatea with whom he falls in love and who eventually comes to life. In Jewish folklore there are stories of the Golem, an artificial creature animated with surprising results.

The first sentence presents an observation.

These details are facts that support the observation.

Apply What You've Learned To develop a key idea, state an opinion, an observation, or a claim related to your big idea and then provide details that support it. Make sure all of the details you provide are relevant to this key idea.

Genre Characteristics
Bringing in background reading will enrich your essay. When you quote a text, make sure you introduce it by giving the author and the name of the text, as well as some information about the quote's relevance.

> In a live exchange on the internet, Microsoft cofounder Bill Gates offered similar views. "I am in the camp that is concerned about super intelligence," Gates wrote. "First the machines will do a lot of jobs for us and not be super intelligent. . . . A few decades after that though the intelligence is strong enough to be a concern."

Winner identifies where the quote came from, "live exchange on the internet," the author of the quote, Bill Gates, and states that Gates holds "similar views."

Apply What You've Learned Include quotes from your background readings to support your key ideas. For each quote, tell the reader where the quote is from and give some explanation of how it relates to one of your key ideas.

Write an Explanatory Essay **581**

WHY THIS MENTOR TEXT?
"Frankenstein: Giving Voice to the Monster" provides a good example of an explanatory essay. Use the instruction below to help students use the mentor text as a model for including several major ideas well supported by details.

USE THE MENTOR TEXT

Author's Craft Ask a volunteer to read aloud the first paragraph from "Frankenstein: Giving Voice to the Monster." Discuss the observation that is being made and how the observation relates to the overall theme of the article. Then, have a volunteer read aloud the second paragraph of the article. Discuss how the author supports the observation with specific historical facts. Talk about why these facts are relevant to the observation and the overall theme. Have students provide examples of possible supporting details that they could use to support opinions, observations, or claims in their essays.

Genre Characteristics Ask students to look for other quotes in the article "Frankenstein: Giving Voice to the Monster," such as the quote by Bill Gates in the third paragraph. Discuss how the author introduces the quote by identifying its source. Also discuss why the author chose to use this quote to enrich his essay. Engage students further in a discussion about how reading a variety of texts expands their ability to support their ideas and opinions. For example, Winner was likely already familiar with the texts he quoted to support his key ideas.

 ENGLISH LEARNER SUPPORT

Use the Mentor Text Use the following supports with students at varying proficiency levels after reading aloud the first paragraph of the mentor text:

- Have students draw pictures of imaginary creatures. Then, have students talk about the creatures they drew and why they aren't real. **SUBSTANTIAL**
- Ask students to underline any words or phrases that are difficult or unclear. Explain each of the words and phrases that students identify.

Ask students to rewrite in their own words the observation made by the author. **MODERATE**

- Remind students to look up any difficult words in the dictionary. Ask them to think about any mythical or imaginary creatures with which they are familiar. Have students write short paragraphs supporting the observation of the author, using the second paragraph as a model. **LIGHT**

Write an Explanatory Essay **581**

WRITING

3 REVISE

Have students answer each question in the chart to determine how they can use the revision tips and techniques to improve their drafts. Invite volunteers to model their revision techniques.

With a Partner Have students ask peer reviewers to evaluate their key ideas and supporting details by answering the following questions about their essays:

- Are key ideas clear? Why or why not?
- Which details do not provide support to key ideas? Why?
- What questions do you have about my main points or my big idea?

Students should use the reviewer's feedback to add relevant facts, details, examples, or quotations that further develop their key ideas and supporting details.

WRITING TASK

Go to **Writing Informative Texts: Precise Language and Vocabulary** for help revising your explanatory essay.

3 Revise

On Your Own Once you have written your draft, you'll want to go back and look for ways to improve your explanatory essay. As you reread and revise, think about whether you have achieved your purpose. The Revision Guide will help you focus on specific elements to make your writing stronger.

Revision Guide

Ask Yourself	Tips	Revision Techniques
1. Does my first paragraph engage the reader and introduce the topic and my big idea?	**Circle** the part that will grab the reader's interest and **underline** the sentences that introduce the topic and the big idea.	**Add** a surprising detail or vivid image. **Reword** or add a sentence to introduce the topic and big idea more clearly.
2. Do I present a few key ideas that support my big idea?	**Underline** the sentences that state your key ideas.	**Review** your planning notes and **look for** more key ideas to include.
3. Do I provide details that support my key ideas?	**Circle** the first word of each sentence that provides a supporting detail to see if each paragraph has more than one.	**Add** details from your notes or quotes from your background readings.
4. Do I provide smooth transitions between ideas and paragraphs?	**Underline** the transition words and phrases in your essay.	**Add** transition words and phrases to connect ideas.
5. Does my final reflection summarize my big idea?	**Underline** the sentence that summarizes your big idea.	**Look back** at your key ideas to see what conclusions you can draw from all of them.
6. Do I leave my reader with "food for thought"?	**Circle** your "food for thought" statement or question.	**Add** a sentence that invites the reader to consider a question not answered in your essay.

ACADEMIC VOCABULARY

As you conduct your **peer review**, be sure to use these words.

❏ appreciate
❏ insight
❏ intensity
❏ invoke
❏ radical

With a Partner Once you and your partner have worked through the Revision Guide on your own, exchange explanatory essays and evaluate each other's draft in a **peer review**. Focus on providing revision suggestions for at least three of the items mentioned in the chart. Explain why you think your partner's draft should be revised and what your specific suggestions are.

When receiving feedback from your partner, listen attentively and ask questions to make sure you fully understand the revision suggestions.

582   Unit 4

 ENGLISH LEARNER SUPPORT

Use Adjectives Review adjective usage, noting that in languages like Spanish, adjectives may follow the noun. Have students identify the adjectives in this passage from paragraph 10 of "Frankenstein: Giving Voice to the Monster":

> "His stern admonition to Victor is to recognize that the invention of something powerful, ingenious, even marvelous cannot be the end of the work at hand."
> (Adjectives: stern, powerful, ingenious, marvelous)

Encourage students to find opportunities to use adjectives to describe nouns in their essays.
MODERATE/LIGHT

WRITING TASK

④ Edit

Look closely at your essay to make sure you do not have fragments or run-on sentences, that you have used punctuation correctly, and that you have subject-verb agreement. Cut unnecessary words and break up long sentences.

Language Conventions

Sensory Language Sensory language includes descriptive words and phrases that appeal to the reader's senses. This language helps readers imagine they are seeing, hearing, tasting, touching, or smelling what the writer describes in the text.

Here is an example of text revised to make use of sensory language. Note the underlined sensory words and phrases in the revised text.

Original	Revised
The hiking trail near my house is nice in the springtime. There are a lot of wildflowers and pretty insects.	In the springtime, the hiking trail near my house turns <u>balmy</u> in the afternoon, when wildflowers release their <u>sweet scent</u> and the air <u>buzzes</u> with insects whose wings <u>flash with color</u>.

In this example, the writer has revised the text to use words and phrases that appeal to the senses. *Balmy* appeals to the sense of touch, *sweet scent* appeals to the sense of smell, *buzzes* appeals to the sense of hearing, and *flash with color* appeals to the sense of sight. Notice how the use of these words and phrases brings the writing to life for the reader and helps the reader to imagine the hiking trail in detail.

Look back at your writing to find places where you can add detail through sensory language. Try to incorporate all five senses.

⑤ Publish

Finalize your explanatory essay and choose a way to share it with your audience. Consider these options:

- Record your essay as a podcast.
- Compile the class's essays into an eBook.

WRITING

④ EDIT

Suggest that students read their drafts aloud to assess how clearly and smoothly they have presented their ideas, and to correct spelling and grammatical errors. Have students review their use of sensory language in their essays to make sure they are using descriptive words and phrases to appeal to the reader's senses.

LANGUAGE CONVENTIONS

Sensory Language Review the information about sensory language with students. Have students close their eyes and try to imagine themselves in the scene presented in the chart. First read aloud the original example. Then, read aloud the revised example. Discuss which one engaged their imaginations more and why the use of sensory language is important. To emphasize how students can apply this technique to their own writing, ask students to suggest ways to rewrite the following description using sensory language:

It was a cold rainy day. I was looking forward to going home and eating soup for lunch.

Be sure students add details to engage the senses. Ask such questions as "What did the sky look like? What did the rain sound and feel like? How did the soup smell and taste?"

■ English Learner Support

Use Sensory Words Give examples of words that relate to each of the five senses. Use gestures and movement to act them out as needed. Discuss how these words stimulate the reader's imagination. Have students provide their own examples of words according to their proficiency level. Encourage students to use these types of words to add detail to their essays. **SUBSTANTIAL/MODERATE**

⑤ PUBLISH

Students can present their essays compiled in an eBook available on a school website. Encourage others to read the essays and to write comments about them. The authors can then respond to the comments.

WHEN STUDENTS STRUGGLE . . .

Use Sensory Language Some students may have difficulty deciding how to use sensory words and phrases in their essays. Have students note a section of their essays into which they think they could incorporate sensory language. Then, have students break into small groups and work together to help each other to come up with ideas for each student's section. Students can decide how to use additional sensory language on their own when editing their essays. Encourage students to make a checklist of all five senses to see whether they can add many types of sensory language in their essays.

WRITING

USE THE SCORING GUIDE

Allow students time to read the scoring guide and to ask questions about any words, phrases, or ideas that are unclear. Then, have partners exchange final drafts of their explanatory essays. Ask them to score their partner's essay using the scoring guide. Each student should write a paragraph explaining the reasons for the score he or she awarded in each category.

WRITING TASK

Use the scoring guide to evaluate your essay.

Writing Task Scoring Guide: Explanatory Essay

	Organization/Progression	Development of Ideas	Use of Language and Conventions
4	• The introduction engages the reader and establishes the topic. • Every part of the paper supports the big idea. • Key ideas in the essay are organized in a logical manner. • There is a conclusion that summarizes the big idea and leaves the reader with "food for thought."	• Key ideas are presented in a way that clearly supports the big idea. • Details in each paragraph are relevant to the key idea.	• The writer's word choice and language are clear, concise, and appropriate to the expository writing task. • The writer shows consistent command of grammar with only minor errors in punctuation or spelling.
3	• The opening presents the topic but is only somewhat engaging to the reader. • The big idea of the essay is fairly clear but is presented in a formulaic manner. • Key ideas in the essay are mostly logical, although the organizational structure of the paper is weak at some points. • There is a conclusion but it does not fully summarize the big idea.	• Most key ideas are supported by details. • Details presented are mostly relevant to the key ideas, but some seem unnecessary or off topic.	• The writer's word choice and language are mostly clear and unambiguous, and the tone of the paper is appropriate. • The writer shows moderate command of grammar with occasional errors in spelling and grammar.
2	• The opening does not clearly introduce the topic and does not engage the reader. • The paper contains a big idea, but it is not clearly defined or focused. • The key ideas are not presented in a logical manner, and the organizational structure of the paper is often confused.	• Either the key ideas are not well supported by details, or the details given are irrelevant to the key idea. • Many details are irrelevant or off topic.	• The writing is formulaic and simple, and the tone is not appropriate to expository writing. • The writer makes many mistakes that 12th-grade students should not be making.
1	• The big idea of the paper is not clear at all, and the paper often wanders from the topic. • There is no organizational structure in the presentation of the key ideas.	• Either no details are given, or the details that are provided are irrelevant and do not support key ideas.	• The writing is vague and confusing. Sentences are simple and awkward. • The writer makes numerous errors in grammar and spelling.

Reflect on the Unit

By completing your explanatory essay, you have created a writing product that pulls together and expresses your thoughts about the reading you have done in this unit. Now is a good time to reflect on what you have learned.

Reflect on the Essential Questions

- Review the four Essential Questions on page 491. How have your answers to these questions changed in response to the texts you've read in this unit?

- What are some examples from the texts you've read that show human beings' relationship with the natural world?

Reflect on Your Reading

- Which selections were the most interesting or surprising to you?

- From which selection did you learn the most about human beings' relationship with the natural world?

Reflect on the Writing Task

- What difficulties did you encounter while working on your explanatory essay? How might you avoid them next time?

- Which parts of the essay were the easiest to write? The hardest to write? Why?

- What improvements did you make to your essay as you were revising?

UNIT 4 SELECTIONS
- "Lines Composed a Few Miles Above Tintern Abbey"
- "Composed upon Westminster Bridge, September 3, 1802"
- "I Wandered Lonely As a Cloud"
- "Ode on a Grecian Urn"
- from *Frankenstein*
- "Frankenstein: Giving Voice to the Monster"
- "Ode to the West Wind"
- "Song of a Thatched Hut Damaged in Autumn Wind"
- from *Songs of Innocence*
- from *Songs of Experience*

LEARNING MINDSET

Try Again Explain to students that learning from mistakes is an important part of developing a learning mindset. Remind them to expect to make mistakes because it is how we all learn. Mistakes can contribute to success when we learn from them and are willing to try again. It is important to focus not on the mistake, but on learning from it and trying again. Encourage students to share with the class mistakes they have made; what they learned from them; and how they eventually succeeded.

UNIT 5

Instructional Overview and Resources

		Instructional Focus	Online Ed Resources
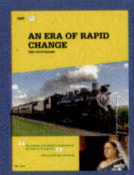	**Unit Introduction** **An Era of Rapid Change: The Victorians**	Unit 5 Essential Question Unit 5 Academic Vocabulary	Unit 5 Response Log

ANALYZE & APPLY

		Instructional Focus	Resources
	*from Jane Eyre* Novel by Charlotte Brontë Lexile 890L	**Reading** • Analyze First-Person Point of View • Analyze Setting **Writing:** Write a Comparison **Speaking and Listening:** Present Your Comparison **Vocabulary:** Foreign Words or Phrases **Language Conventions:** Gerunds and Gerund Phrases	Audio **Reading Studio:** Notice & Note **Writing Studio:** Writing Informative Texts **Speaking and Listening Studio:** Using Media in a Presentation **Vocabulary Studio:** Understanding Word Origins **Grammar Studio:** Gerunds and Gerund Phrases
	**"Factory Reform"** Documentary by Timelines.tv Lexile N/A	**Reading** • Evaluate Documentaries • Analyze the Media **Writing:** Write a Short Story **Speaking and Listening:** Present Your Story	Audio **Reading Studio:** Notice & Note **Writing Studio:** Writing Narratives **Speaking and Listening Studio:** Using Media in a Presentation; Giving a Presentation
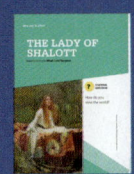	**"The Lady of Shalott"** Poem by Alfred, Lord Tennyson Lexile N/A	**Reading** • Analyze Allegory • Analyze Mood **Writing:** Illustrate a Narrative Poem **Speaking and Listening:** Recite a Poem	Audio **Reading Studio:** Notice & Note **Speaking and Listening Studio:** Giving a Presentation
	*from Great Expectations* Novel by Charles Dickens Lexile 880L	**Reading** • Analyze Plot • Analyze Characterization **Writing:** Write a Story **Speaking and Listening:** Discuss **Vocabulary:** Idioms **Language Conventions:** Imagery	Audio **Reading Studio:** Notice & Note **Writing Studio:** Writing Narratives **Speaking and Listening Studio:** Participating in Collaborative Discussions **Vocabulary Studio:** Using Context Clues
	**Mentor Text** **"The Victorians Had the Same Concerns about Technology As We Do"** Essay by Melissa Dickson Lexile 1240L	**Reading** • Analyze Compare and Contrast Essay • Evaluate Multimodal Texts **Writing:** Write an Op-Ed **Speaking and Listening:** Analyze and Discuss Your Ideas **Vocabulary:** Synonyms and Antonyms **Language Conventions:** Sentence Structure	Audio **Reading Studio:** Notice & Note **Writing Studio:** Writing Arguments **Speaking and Listening Studio:** Participating in Collaborative Discussions **Vocabulary Studio:** Synonyms and Antonyms **Grammar Studio:** Sentence Structure

SUGGESTED PACING: 30 DAYS

Unit Introduction: 1 | *from* Jane Eyre: 1 2 3 4 5 | Factory Reform: 6 7 8 | The Lady of Shalott: 9 10 11 | *from* Great Expectations: 12 13 14 15 16

PLAN

English Learner Support		Differentiated Instruction	Assessment
• Text X-Ray • Use Cognates • Respond to Questions • Make Connections • Develop Background Knowledge to Comprehend Language	• Acquire New Vocabulary • Participate in Shared Reading • Make Connections • Oral Assessment • Vocabulary Strategy • Language Conventions	**When Students Struggle** • Describe Characters • Synthesize Information • Reteaching: Analyze Setting **To Challenge Students** • Analyze Characters	**Selection Test**
• Text X-Ray • Use Prereading Supports to Enhance Comprehension		**When Students Struggle** • Analyze Documentaries	**Selection Test**
• Text X-Ray • Use Informal Language • Use Visual and Contextual Support • Recognize Symbolism • Oral Assessment		**When Students Struggle** • Understand Setting and Mood **To Challenge Students** • Allegory • Analyze Symbols	**Selection Test**
• Text X-Ray • Use Cognates • Learn Descriptive Words • Use Informal Language • Use Contextual Support	• Use Graphic Organizers to Enhance Comprehension • Monitor Understanding of Spoken Language • Oral Assessment • Learn Idioms • Language Conventions	**When Students Struggle** • Analyze Setting • Understand Characterization **To Challenge Students** • Conduct Research • Analyze Theme	**Selection Test**
• Text X-Ray • Use Cognates • Discuss Compare and Contrast • Internalize Academic Vocabulary	• Use Accessible Language • Use Visual and Contextual Support • Oral Assessment • Vocabulary Strategy • Use a Variety of Grammatical Structures	**When Students Struggle** • Use Graphic Aids • Reteaching: Evaluate Multimodal Texts	**Selection Test**

The Victorians Had the Same Concerns about Technology As We Do — 17, 18
Dover Beach / The Darkling Thrush — 19, 20, 21
My Last Duchess / Confession — 22, 23, 24, 25
Independent Reading — 26, 27
End of Unit — 28, 29, 30

An Era of Rapid Change: The Victorians 586B

PLAN

UNIT 5 Continued

	Instructional Focus	Resources (Online Ed)
COLLABORATE & COMPARE		
"Dover Beach" Poem by Matthew Arnold Lexile N/A **"The Darkling Thrush"** Poem by Thomas Hardy Lexile N/A	**Reading** • Analyze Extended Metaphors • Analyze Sound Devices **Writing:** Create a List **Speaking and Listening:** Discuss Your List	🔊 Audio **Close Read Screencast:** Modeled Discussion **Reading Studio:** Notice & Note **Speaking and Listening:** Participating in Collaborative Discussions; Giving a Presentation
Collaborate & Compare	**Reading:** Compare Themes	
"My Last Duchess" Poem by Robert Browning Lexile N/A **"Confession"** Poem by Linh Dinh Lexile N/A	**Reading** • Draw Conclusions About Speakers • Analyze Imagery **Writing:** Create an Oral Presentation **Speaking and Listening:** Present the Monologue	🔊 Audio **Reading Studio:** Notice & Note **Writing Studio:** Writing as a Process **Speaking and Listening Studio:** Giving a Presentation
Collaborate & Compare	**Reading:** Compare Themes	

INDEPENDENT READING

The Independent Reading selections are available only in the eBook.

Go to the Reading Studio for more information on **NOTICE & NOTE**.

"Sonnet 43"
Poem by Elizabeth Barrett Browning
Lexile N/A

"Remembrance"
Poem by Emily Brontë
Lexile N/A

END OF UNIT

Writing Task: Write a Research Report **Reflect on the Unit**	**Writing:** Write a Research Report **Language Conventions:** Combining Sentences	**Unit 5 Response Log** **Mentor Text:** "The Victorians Had the Same Concerns about Technology As We Do" **Writing Studio:** Writing Informative Texts **Speaking and Listening Studio:** Using Media in a Presentation **Grammar Studio:** Conjunctions and Interjections

586C Unit 5

PLAN

English Learner Support	Differentiated Instruction	Assessment
• Text X-Ray • Understand Meanings in English • Draw to Acquire Vocabulary • Oral Assessment • Use Support from Teacher to Read • Acquire Basic Vocabulary • Recognize the Elements of English Sound in Acquired Vocabulary	**When Students Struggle** • Sound Devices • Reteaching: Analyze Extended Metaphor • Analyze Theme	**Selection Test**
• Text X-Ray • Describe in Detail • Use Contextual Support • Demonstrate Comprehension • Oral Assessment • Ask Questions	**When Students Struggle** • Visualize Character • Identify Author's Purpose • Reteach: Analyze Imagery **To Challenge Students** • Make Additional Connections	**Selection Test**

"The Great Exhibition" Article by Lara Kriegel **Lexile 1120L**

"Christmas Storms and Sunshine" Short Story by Elizabeth Cleghorn Gaskell **Lexile 1050L**

"Evidence of Progress" Essay by Thomas Babington Macaulay **Lexile 1450L**

Selection Tests

• Language X-Ray • Internalize New Academic Language • Express Opinions • Combine Sentences Using Connecting Words • Use Visual Support	**When Students Struggle** • Draft the Report • Combine Sentences Using Conjunctions • Adapt the Report Using Images **To Challenge Students** • Understand Unintended Consequences	**Unit Test**

An Era of Rapid Change: The Victorians

TEACH

DISCUSS THE QUOTATION

Explain that this quotation is from an article that Macaulay wrote for *The Edinburgh Review* in 1835. Thomas Babington Macaulay, who later in life became Lord Macaulay, was a Whig politician, orator, essayist, and historian. He is most often remembered for his five-volume *History of England*. Macaulay's writings celebrated the importance of the English revolution and promoted the idea that English society was superior, a model of progress for less developed nations. His ideas were later criticized for the political and cultural bias that they illustrated.

Have students think about how Macaulay would have defined "progress," based on his statement and their knowledge of English history. Do they agree with his view of what constitutes progress? Why or why not?

■ **English Learner Support**

Learn New Language Ask students to listen carefully as you read Macaulay's quotation aloud. Make sure students understand that the word *emphatically*, as used in the quotation, means "definitely" or "absolutely."
ALL LEVELS

UNIT 5

AN ERA OF RAPID CHANGE
THE VICTORIANS

" The history of England is emphatically the history of progress. "

—Thomas Babington Macaulay

LEARNING MINDSET

Plan Explain to students that they are more likely to reach their goals if they plan ahead. When students receive an assignment, they should break down the assignment into the individual parts or steps to be completed. Then, they can create a plan for completing the steps in a timely manner. In the case of an assignment that will take a week, for example, the student might divide the assignment into four or five parts and plan to complete one part per day. For lengthier multi-week assignments, remind students that they can include some empty days in their plan as "padding," so that even if they run into unexpected issues that slow them down, they will still be able to complete the assignment on time.

UNIT 5

Discuss the **Essential Questions** with your whole class or in small groups. As you read An Era of Rapid Change, consider how the selections explore these questions.

? ESSENTIAL QUESTION:
What is a true benefactor?

In 19th-century Great Britain, there was a wide gap between the impoverished many and the wealthy few. Occasionally, well-to-do members of the middle and upper classes would become benefactors, providing financial or other material assistance to those who were less fortunate. How did benefactors determine who would receive their help? What made a person a good benefactor in Victorian Britain? Was the role ever abused? What role do benefactors play in modern society?

? ESSENTIAL QUESTION:
How do you view the world?

The 19th century was a time not only of changing technology, but also of changing ideas. As society evolved, so did people's thinking about such topics as religion, science, social structures, and their own place in the world. Some viewed progress with optimism for the future while others noted that progress brought its own set of challenges. When you look at the world around you today, what do you see?

? ESSENTIAL QUESTION:
What brings out cruelty in people?

Although the Victorian Era was a time of improvement in the quality of life for many, not all benefited equally. As is the case today, the daily life of some people was marked by needless cruelty. Who are the perpetrators and the victims of cruelty? What might motivate someone to treat another human or an animal cruelly? What roles do society and social structures play in promoting and/or preventing cruelty?

? ESSENTIAL QUESTION:
Which invention has had the greatest impact on your life?

The Victorian Era was a time of remarkable technological advancement. Great Britain led the Industrial Revolution, and the strength and influence of the British Empire ensured that British industry and inventions soon spread around the world. Many modern conveniences that we take for granted today were invented, or in the early stages of development, during that period. Which inventions do you use most in your everyday life? How would your life be different without them?

TEACH

Connect to the
ESSENTIAL QUESTIONS

Read aloud the Essential Questions and the paragraphs that follow them. Open the discussion of each idea by having students respond to the questions that conclude each paragraph.

? ESSENTIAL QUESTION:
What is a true benefactor?

Help students define *benefactor*. (*a person who provides a benefit, especially money*) Then, help students connect personally to the concept by asking them what type of benefactor they would be if they had unlimited resources. Who would they choose to help? How? Why?

? ESSENTIAL QUESTION:
How do you view the world?

Ask students to think about the factors that shape their personal views of the world. How have their views been shaped by their family background, culture, or education? Have their views about the world changed over time? If so, how?

? ESSENTIAL QUESTION:
What brings out cruelty in people?

Have students consider how cruelty sometimes intersects with such other concepts as social injustice, inequality, prejudice, positions of power, etc. Point out that cruelty can occur on both the personal and the societal level. Then, have students discuss what forces and conditions make widespread institutionalized forms of cruelty possible.

? ESSENTIAL QUESTION:
Which invention has had the greatest impact on your life?

Remind students that many of the inventions that might immediately come to mind could not exist without earlier inventions. Challenge students to identify the "small" underlying inventions that had to come before the "big" inventions that they are more familiar with.

TEACH

THE VICTORIANS

The following essay provides students with a historical context for the Unit 5 selections. It presents a brief overview of the Victorian Era, which dominated the greater part of the 19th century.

The New Monarchy Explain to students that *imperialism* refers to a nation expanding its size and/or area of influence by acquiring new territories or establishing economic and political dominance over other nations. Throughout Victoria's reign, the British Empire steadily expanded, starting with the annexation of New Zealand in 1840 and the acquisition of Hong Kong in 1842. India also came under direct administration by the British government during Victoria's reign.

While some British citizens and politicians opposed expansion, many were initially fascinated by the exploits of explorers and missionaries and saw imperialism as the key to Britain's prosperity and patriotic destiny. As the years passed, however, and conflicts involving the British colonies increased, support for imperialism waned.

Progress, Problems, and Reform Explain to students that one reason why reform happened so slowly was that the upper and middle classes had long believed that the poor were to blame for their own plight. It was only when that mindset began to change, and people in positions of power realized that poverty was not necessarily the fault of the poor, that they made changes in legislation. Encourage students to think about how the idea that poor people are responsible for their own problems might have shaped earlier events in British history, and how the idea persists in modern society.

COLLABORATIVE DISCUSSION

Ask groups to share their ideas with the class, providing evidence that supports their reasoning.

THE VICTORIANS

"The sun never sets on the British Empire," boasted the Victorians, and it was true: with holdings around the globe, from Africa to India, from New Zealand to Canada, it was always daytime in some part of the vast territory ruled by Great Britain. The phrase also captured the attitude of the era. During the reign of Queen Victoria, Britain was a nation in motion at the height of its power, both politically and economically. Abroad, Britain dominated world politics. At home, the Industrial Revolution was in full swing. For those with wealth and influence, Victoria's reign was a time not only of change but of prosperity. Yet, large segments of the population suffered greatly during this period, leading many writers to criticize the rapid pace and materialism of the age and the injustices that resulted.

The New Monarchy Queen Victoria, for whom the period is named, was just 18 years old when she came to the throne in 1837. She went on to rule for more than 60 years, longer than any English ruler before her. Victoria's devotion to hard work and duty, her insistence on proper behavior, and her support of British imperialism became the hallmarks of the Victorian period.

Victoria knew that previous monarchs had clashed with Parliament, and she realized that the role of royalty had to change. She accepted the concept of a constitutional monarchy in which she gave advice rather than orders, and yielded control of day-to-day governmental affairs to a series of very talented prime ministers. When the queen withdrew from politics and went into mourning in 1861, after the death of her beloved husband Prince Albert, the position of prime minister became even more important.

Progress, Problems, and Reform The Industrial Revolution had already transformed Britain into a modern industrial state by the time Victoria took the throne. By 1850 England boasted 18,000 cotton mills and produced half of the world's iron. Progress also brought new inventions, such as the telephone, light bulb, radio, and automobile, and advances in science and medicine, like the work of British surgeon Joseph Lister. Building on the ideas of Louis Pastuer, Lister developed standards for keeping hospitals clean and germ-free, vastly increasing the survival rates of his patients.

Some writers expressed enthusiasm for the material advantages afforded by the industrial age. Others were appalled by the materialism of the

COLLABORATIVE DISCUSSION
In a small group, review the timeline and discuss which events would have had the greatest effects on everyday life for people in Victorian Britain.

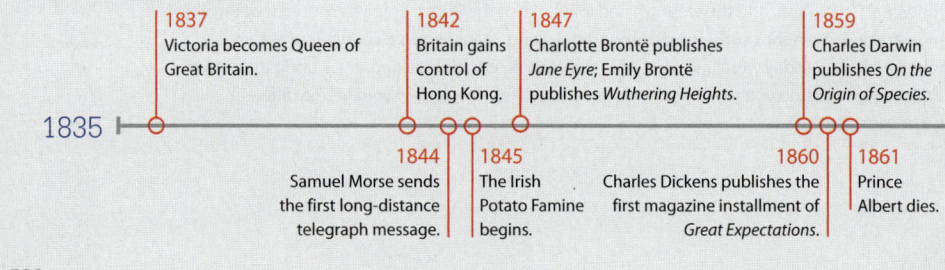

- 1835
- 1837 Victoria becomes Queen of Great Britain.
- 1842 Britain gains control of Hong Kong.
- 1844 Samuel Morse sends the first long-distance telegraph message.
- 1845 The Irish Potato Famine begins.
- 1847 Charlotte Brontë publishes *Jane Eyre*; Emily Brontë publishes *Wuthering Heights*.
- 1859 Charles Darwin publishes *On the Origin of Species*.
- 1860 Charles Dickens publishes the first magazine installment of *Great Expectations*.
- 1861 Prince Albert dies.

588 Unit 5

ENGLISH LEARNER SUPPORT

Build Background Knowledge To aid comprehension of the essay, provide students with the following definitions:

- *holdings:* property, such as land or territory
- *in full swing:* at the highest level or peak of activity
- *hallmark:* identifying feature or characteristic
- *squalid:* very dirty and unpleasant, often as a result of poverty
- *contemporary:* current
- *drawing room:* a formal room that was used for spending time with guests or relaxing
- *pretension:* desire to do something or claim to be something impressive or important **ALL LEVELS**

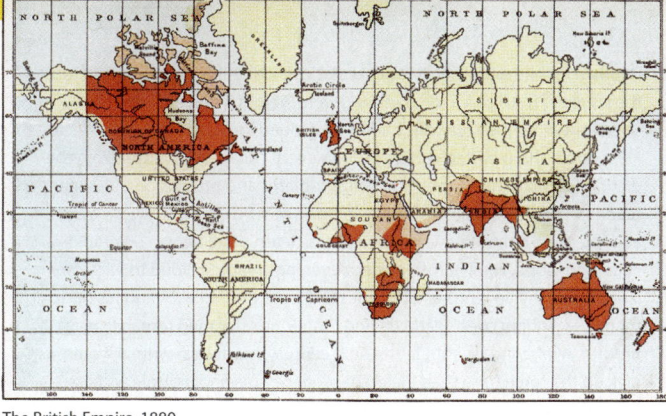

The British Empire, 1880

Victorian upper and middle classes—an attitude they considered tasteless, joyless, and destructive of community.

While the middle class grew more prosperous, conditions for the poor became intolerable. Factory workers, including many children, spent long hours toiling for low wages under harsh and dangerous conditions. In the 1840s, unemployment soared in England and the Great Famine devastated Ireland. Families without income and starving Irish immigrants crowded into England's already squalid slums.

Though Parliament enacted many important reforms during this period, change came slowly. The Great Reform Act of 1832 expanded suffrage, or the right to vote, to wealthy middle-class men. Before this law, only about 5 percent of Britain's population had the right to vote. In 1833 slavery was abolished in the British Empire, and the first laws restricting child labor were enacted. In decades that followed, laws were passed establishing public schools, improving sanitation and housing, legalizing trade unions, easing harsh factory conditions, and giving working-class men the right to vote.

Victorian Poetry Confronted with the harsh realities of the Victorian world, many poets followed the lead of the Romantics, focusing on idealized love and the awe-inspiring beauty of nature. But some poets, especially later in the century, addressed contemporary issues such as spiritual doubt and the loss of old customs, traditions, and values due to the pressures of industrialization and scientific discoveries.

RESEARCH
What about this historical period interests you? Choose a topic, event, or person to learn more about. Then, add your own entry to the timeline.

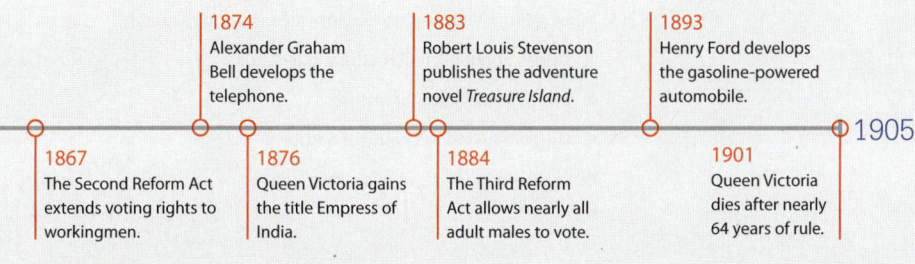

- **1867** The Second Reform Act extends voting rights to workingmen.
- **1874** Alexander Graham Bell develops the telephone.
- **1876** Queen Victoria gains the title Empress of India.
- **1883** Robert Louis Stevenson publishes the adventure novel *Treasure Island*.
- **1884** The Third Reform Act allows nearly all adult males to vote.
- **1893** Henry Ford develops the gasoline-powered automobile.
- **1901** Queen Victoria dies after nearly 64 years of rule.
- **1905**

An Era of Rapid Change 589

TEACH

Victorian Poetry Tell students that the status of poets and of poetry changed during the Victorian period. On the one hand, the Victorians revered their poets, seeing them as a higher order of human being—sensitive, intuitive, inspired—an image first popularized by the Romantics, particularly Byron. On the other hand, many readers, especially among the middle class, increasingly viewed poetry as irrelevant to their own lives. While poets continued to insist on "art for art's sake," the growing reading public turned to other forms of literature.

RESEARCH

To learn more about their chosen topic, encourage students to search for primary sources from the historical period. Have students choose excerpts from a source to present to the class.

WHEN STUDENTS STRUGGLE . . .

Vocabulary Support Model how to use context to build meaning for such complex terms as *Industrial Revolution*. Have students use context clues to help define these terms:

- *Parliament*: "British governing body made of elected officials"
- *constitutional monarchy*: "form of government in which the power of a king or queen is limited by a constitution"
- *materialism*: "emphasis on or desire for such material objects as money and possessions"

An Era of Rapid Change **589**

TEACH

Realism Tell students that many of the novels during this period were first published in serial form in magazines and newspapers; that is, in monthly installments of several chapters each. Readers might have to wait as long as two years to find out how a novel ended! Dickens is often considered the master of the serialized novel. Hordes of fans, not just in England but around the world, would rush to snatch up each new installment of his novels.

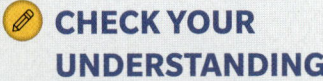

CHECK YOUR UNDERSTANDING

Have students answer the questions independently.

Answers:

1. C
2. G
3. D

If students answer any question incorrectly, have them reread the text to confirm their understanding.

Realism While many poets retreated from modern life, novelists embraced the issues of the age. Victorian novels were weighty affairs, quite literally—so weighty that they typically had to be divided into three volumes. Keen-eyed, sharp-witted writers probed every corner of society—from the drawing room to the slums, exposing problems and pretensions. Victorian readers craved this realism. They wanted to meet characters like themselves and the people they knew; they wanted to learn more about their rapidly changing world. Families often spent evenings reading aloud to each other, laughing at the adventures of Charles Dickens's Mr. Pickwick and his oddball friends or sighing over Heathcliff and Catherine's doomed romance in Emily Brontë's *Wuthering Heights*. In the next century, modernist writers would pick up the torch from their Victorian predecessors and grapple with issues the Victorians could not have imagined.

CHECK YOUR UNDERSTANDING

Choose the best answer to each question.

1. Which **best** describes the British government during the Victorian Era?
   A. Conflicts between Victoria and Parliament led to the weakening of the monarchy.
   B. Victoria and Parliament agreed to give primary authority to the prime minister.
   C. Victoria modified the role of the monarch and strengthened the position of the prime minster.
   D. Parliament took Victoria's retirement from politics as an opportunity to establish a constitutional monarchy.

2. The reforms enacted by Parliament primarily affected the lower classes by —
   F. increasing the oppression faced by factory workers
   G. slowly improving living and working conditions
   H. addressing the unemployment crisis that arose in the 1840s
   J. contributing to the development of slums

3. What topic in Victorian novels appealed most to readers?
   A. Stories about ancient myths and legends
   B. Celebrations of romantic love
   C. The awe-inspiring beauty of nature
   D. Realistic portrayals of everyday people

ACADEMIC VOCABULARY

Academic Vocabulary words are words you use when you discuss and write about texts. In this unit, you will learn the following five words:

 abandon   ☐ confine   ☐ conform   ☐ depress   ☐ reluctance

Study the Word Network to learn more about the word **abandon**.

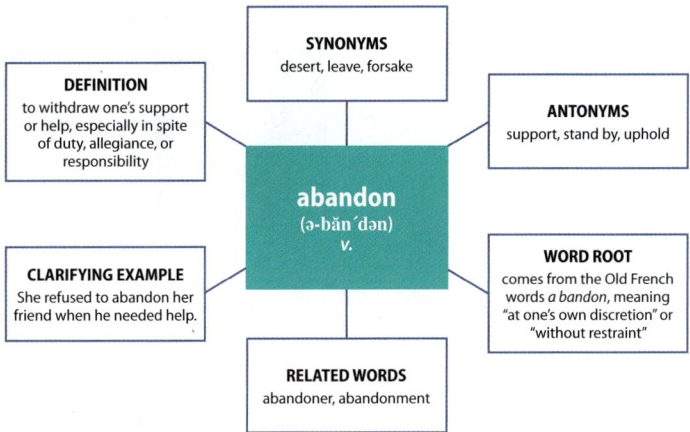

Write and Discuss Discuss your completed Word Network with a partner, making sure to talk through all of the boxes until you both understand the word, its synonyms, antonyms, and related forms. Then, fill out a Word Network for the remaining four words. Use a dictionary or online resource to help you complete the activity.

Go online to access the Word Networks.

RESPOND TO THE ESSENTIAL QUESTION

In this unit, you will explore four different **Essential Questions** about literature of the Victorian Era. As you read each selection, you will gather your ideas about one of these questions and write about it in a **Response Log**. At the end of the unit, you will have the opportunity to write a **research report** related to one of the essential questions. Filling out the Response Log after you read each text will help you prepare for this writing task.

You can also go online to access the Response Log.

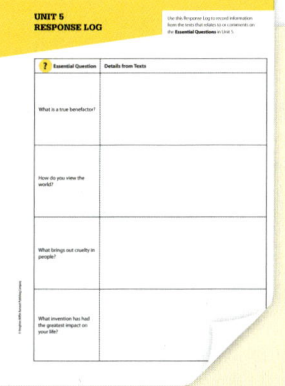

An Era of Rapid Change 591

TEACH

ACADEMIC VOCABULARY

Have students complete Word Networks for the remaining four vocabulary words. Encourage them to include all the categories shown in the completed network if possible, but point out that some words do not have clear synonyms or antonyms.

abandon (ə-băn′dən) *v.* To withdraw one's support or help from, especially in spite of duty, allegiance, or responsibility (Spanish cognate: *abandonar*)

confine (kən-fīn′) *v.* To keep within bounds; restrict (Spanish cognate: *confinar*)

conform (kən-fôrm′) *v.* To be similar to or match something or someone; to act or be in accord or agreement (Spanish cognate: *conformar*)

depress (dĭ-prĕs′) *v.* To cause to be sad or dejected (Spanish cognate: *deprimir*)

reluctance (rĭ-lŭk′təns) *n.* The state of being reluctant; unwillingness (Spanish cognate: *reluctancia*)

RESPOND TO THE ESSENTIAL QUESTION

Direct students to the Unit 5 Response Log. Explain that students will use it to record ideas and details from the selections that help answer one of the Essential Questions. When they work on the Writing Task at the end of the unit, their Response Logs will help them think about what they have read and make connections between texts.

An Era of Rapid Change **591**

PLAN

from JANE EYRE
Novel by Charlotte Brontë

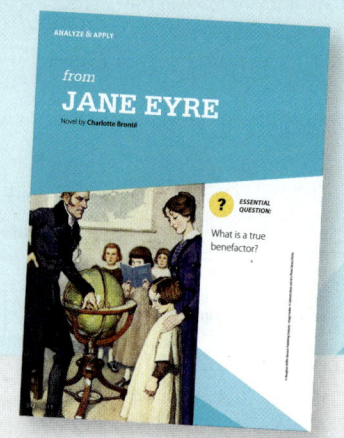

GENRE ELEMENTS
NOVEL

Tell students that a **novel** is a long work of fiction usually written from a first- or third-person point of view. Explain that novelists include details about **setting,** or the time and place where the action takes place, to create particular moods and to support the novel's themes. In this lesson, students will analyze how the setting of a novel contributes to its plot, characterization, and themes.

LEARNING OBJECTIVES

- Analyze first-person point of view and setting.
- Conduct research about ragged schools during the Victorian Era.
- Write a comparison between a novel and its film adaptation.
- Present a comparison.
- Identify foreign words and phrases.
- Use gerunds and gerund phrases.
- **Language** Ask questions about setting.

TEXT COMPLEXITY

Quantitative Measures	Jane Eyre	Lexile: 890L
Qualitative Measures	**Ideas Presented** Much is explicit, but moves to some implied meaning. Requires some inferential reasoning.	
	Structures Used Primarily explicit, excerpt structure with support from italicized summary. Largely chronological.	
	Language Used Archaic, formal, and figurative language. Complex sentence structures.	
	Knowledge Required Primarily familiar situations. Historical and cultural concepts may make heavier demands.	

PLAN

Online Ed

RESOURCES

- Unit 5 Response Log
- 🔊 Selection Audio
- 📖 Reading Studio: Notice & Note
- 📈 Level Up Tutorial: Character Traits; Synthesizing Information; Setting
- 📝 Writing Studio: Writing Informative Texts
- 💬 Speaking and Listening Studio: Using Media in a Presentation
- 🔤 Vocabulary Studio: Understanding Word Origins
- ❗ Grammar Studio: Module 3: Lesson 4: Gerunds and Gerund Phrases
- ✓ *Jane Eyre* Selection Test

SUMMARIES

English

In this excerpt, the narrator, Jane Eyre, has just arrived at Lowood Institution, a boarding school for orphans and poor girls. It doesn't take long for her to realize that the living conditions at Lowood are poor, but the kindness of a teacher and a chance meeting with another girl who also enjoys reading helps her cope.

Spanish

La narradora, Jane Eyre, acaba de llegar a Lowood, un internado para niñas huérfanas y pobres. No tarda en darse cuenta de las condiciones de miseria en que se vive en Lowood, pero la amabilidad de una profesora y el casual encuentro con otra niña, quien también disfruta leer, le sirven para enfrentar la situación.

SMALL-GROUP OPTIONS

Have students work in small groups and pairs to read and discuss the selection.

Reciprocal Teaching

- Have students read the text.
- After reading, ask students to write three to five questions about the text, using these frames: *How does the author use setting to _____? How does the author use dialogue to _____? How do the details about _____ affect _____? Why did Jane _____?*
- Form teams of three students.
- Have each student offer two questions for group discussion.
- Tell the group to reach a consensus on the answers and find supporting text evidence.

Think-Pair-Share

- After reading the text, pose this question: *What kind of place is Lowood?*
- Have students think about the question individually and take notes.
- Then, have pairs listen, discuss, and formulate a shared response to the question. Direct them to include at least two reasons to support their inference.
- Finally, have pairs share their response with the class.

Jane Eyre 592B

PLAN

Text X-Ray: English Learner Support
for *Jane Eyre*

Use the Text X-Ray and the supports and scaffolds in the Teacher's Edition to help guide students at different proficiency levels through the selection.

INTRODUCE THE SELECTION
DISCUSS BENEFACTORS AND CHARITY

In this lesson, students will need to be able to discuss charity and what makes a person a true benefactor.

Provide the following explanations:
- A *benefactor* is someone who provides financial or other support.
- *Charity* is help, usually in the form of money, food, clothing, or shelter, given out of kindness.

Have students ask questions and make statements about benefactors and charity. Provide sentence stems, such as: *One benefactor who helped me is ____. [Name of person] was my benefactor because ____. One thing I can donate to charity is ____.*

CULTURAL REFERENCES

The following words or phrases may be unfamiliar to students:
- *gathering my faculties* (paragraph 4): trying to make sense of things
- *drawing-room* (paragraph 5): a room in a large private house where guests are entertained
- *under-teacher* (paragraph 13): an assistant teacher, lower in rank than a regular teacher
- *Babel* (paragraph 33): refers to an ancient city in the Bible where people were confused by many different languages being spoken at once

LISTENING

Use New Expressions

Help students write a list of expressions they can use when responding to their classmates' ideas in the Quick Start activity on page 593. For example: *How did that make you feel? What did you find most challenging? That sounds hard; what did you do next?*

Use the following supports with students at varying proficiency levels:
- Slowly read aloud each new expression and have students repeat it. Then, have students practice saying the new expressions to partners. Partners should repeat what they heard, making corrections to pronunciation as needed. **SUBSTANTIAL**
- Have partners practice using the new expressions in appropriate places during the discussion. **MODERATE**
- Organize students into small groups. Have half of each small group use the new expressions to respond to each other's ideas. Have the other half of the group take notes about what they observe and hear. Have the note-takers share their notes with the whole group after the discussion. **LIGHT**

PLAN

SPEAKING

Ask Questions to Identify Setting Details

Remind students that setting is where and when a story takes place, and that novels may have multiple settings. Have students ask each other questions to identify details that describe the setting of *Jane Eyre*.

Use the following supports with students at varying proficiency levels:

- Read the first paragraph of the selection aloud. Have students repeat the words and phrases that indicate *when* the action in this paragraph takes place *(afternoon, dusk, twilight, night)* and *where* it takes places *(very far indeed from Gateshead; great grey hills; valley, dark with wood)* **SUBSTANTIAL**
- Have partners ask each other questions to identify words and phrases in paragraph 1 that describe the setting. For example: *What words describe* when *the scene takes place? (afternoon, dusk, twilight, night) What phrases describe* where *the scene takes place? (very far indeed from Gateshead; great grey hills; valley, dark with wood)* **MODERATE**
- Have partners conduct an interview between a reporter and Jane Eyre about her trip. Have them create a list of *where* and *when* questions. Then, have them give a brief oral summary of when and where Jane went. **LIGHT**

READING

Use Graphic Organizers

Tell students they can use graphic organizers to help them keep track of unfamiliar words as they read. After reading, they can use reference materials and classroom support to define the words, and then reread the text again.

Use the following supports with students at varying proficiency levels:

- Write the word *descended* (from paragraph 1) in the center of a word web. Help small groups use reference materials and peer support to fill in the web with related words and phrases. **SUBSTANTIAL**
- Have students reread the first two paragraphs and use a two-column chart to keep track of any unfamiliar words they encounter. Have them use reference materials to find definitions and then note if their comprehension of the content has changed. **MODERATE**
- Guide students to complete a Frayer Model about an unfamiliar word from the selection. Tell them to draw a square with four boxes labeled *Definition; Characteristics; Examples;* and *Non-examples* and write an unfamiliar word in a circle in the center. Then, direct them to complete the boxes to help them better understand the meaning of the word. **LIGHT**

WRITING

Use Gerund and Gerund Phrases

Review the difference between a verb and a noun. Remind students that adding an ending can change a word's part of speech.

Use the following supports with students at varying proficiency levels:

- Model how to turn the verbs *read* and *sleep* into nouns by adding the ending *-ing*. Write the verbs and nouns in sentences, and have students copy your work. **SUBSTANTIAL**
- Have partners work together to write sentences using the verbs *read* and *sleep*. Then, have them turn the verbs into nouns and write new sentences. **MODERATE**
- Have students do the previous activity. Then, have them exchange papers and revise for correct spelling, verb tense, and standard grammatical usage. **LIGHT**

TEACH

? Connect to the ESSENTIAL QUESTION

This excerpt from *Jane Eyre* provides insight into what makes a person a true benefactor, and demonstrates that not all people who are considered benefactors live up to the name. It also shows that people can become benefactors through words and actions even if they are not recognized as benefactors.

ANALYZE & APPLY

from JANE EYRE

Novel by **Charlotte Brontë**

? ESSENTIAL QUESTION:

What is a true benefactor?

GET READY

QUICK START

Think about a time of transition in your life, perhaps moving to a new neighborhood or changing schools. What were some of the obstacles you faced? What helped you adjust to your new circumstances? Discuss your experience with a partner.

ANALYZE FIRST-PERSON POINT OF VIEW

Stories are told from a narrative perspective, or **point of view.** In *Jane Eyre*, the story is narrated in the first-person point of view. The narrator is the character Jane, who uses the personal pronouns *I, me,* and *my.* Readers experience everything through her eyes. Jane's thoughts and commentary convey the intensity of her feelings about the Lowood boarding school and its occupants.

As you read, notice how Charlotte Brontë's use of the first-person point of view affects what you learn about the novel's characters, events, setting, and themes.

GENRE ELEMENTS: NOVEL

- is a long work of fiction
- is usually written in the first- or third-person point of view
- can develop characters and conflict more thoroughly than a short story
- often develops complex plot structures, including subplots

ANALYZE SETTING

The **setting** of a novel is the time and place in which the action occurs. This excerpt from *Jane Eyre* is set in a boarding school for girls. During the Victorian period, hundreds of charity schools were established in Britain to provide free education, clothing, lodging, and meals for orphans and poor children. They were funded by contributions from wealthy donors. Some of the people who ran these schools were very idealistic and treated students well. However, many schools were led by harsh disciplinarians and offered only the most basic education. Schools for the poorest children were called "ragged schools," a name inspired by the children's shabby clothing.

As you read, notice how the setting is connected to the novel's plot, characterization, and themes. Use a chart like this one to record details that reveal the historical, economic, and social context of the setting.

SETTING DETAILS	HISTORICAL, ECONOMIC, AND SOCIAL CONTEXT

Jane Eyre 593

TEACH

QUICK START

Have students read the Quick Start prompt, then organize them into pairs. Ask each pair to share their stories about times of transition, including the obstacles they faced and what they did to help themselves adjust to the new situations. Encourage pairs to share what they discussed with the rest of the class.

For **listening support** for students at varying proficiency levels, see the **Text X-Ray** on page 592C.

ANALYZE FIRST-PERSON POINT OF VIEW

Explain to students that the **point of view** of a story affects how a reader perceives what is happening in the story. Discuss the different points of view from which stories can be told, and explain that *Jane Eyre* is told from the main character's point of view, or in the first person. Discuss how a story might differ if told from another point of view, as well as the insights a reader might gain from hearing a story from the point of view of the person living it. Display this sentence from the selection:

> I was stiff with long sitting, and bewildered with the noise and motion of the coach: gathering my faculties, I looked about me.

Ask students to identify the words that indicate the point of view. (*I, my, me*) and then rewrite the sentence from a different point of view.

ANALYZE SETTING

Tell students that the **setting** of a story can be an imaginary place or a real place. The time can be the past, the present, or the future. In addition to time and place, setting can include the larger historical and cultural contexts that form the background for a narrative. Setting is one of the main elements in fiction and often plays an important role in what happens and why. Explain that understanding the context of this novel's **setting** will help them to better understand the story itself and why the characters behave and interact the way they do.

Explain that the setting of this novel showcases the historical, economic, and social contexts of the time period in which it takes place, and which directly affect the storyline and actions of the characters. Direct students to use the chart to record setting details as they come across them in the reading, to better understand the historical, economic, and social contexts in which the story takes place.

Jane Eyre **593**

TEACH

CRITICAL VOCABULARY

Encourage students to read both of the possible answers before deciding which word is used incorrectly. Remind them to look for context clues to help them make their choice.

Answers:

1. commenced
2. morose
3. ruddy

■ **English Learner Support**

Use Cognates Tell students that two of the Critical Vocabulary words have Spanish cognates: *morose/moroso, commence/comenzar.* **ALL LEVELS**

LANGUAGE CONVENTIONS

Gerunds and Gerund Phrases Review the information about **gerunds** and **gerund phrases.** Explain that gerunds are made by adding the suffix *-ing* to a verb, thereby transforming it into a noun. Explain that gerunds and gerund phrases can make writing more concise by helping to combine short sentences. Ask students to brainstorm examples of gerunds and gerund phrases, and then have them use these gerunds in sentences.

 ## ANNOTATION MODEL

Explain to students how to identify **setting** details. Remind them that these types of details help them better understand the context of the story. Point out that they may follow the suggested method for marking up the text or use their own system. They may want to color-code their annotations by using highlighters. Their notes in the margin may include questions about ideas that are unclear or observations they make about the setting and other details.

594   Unit 5

 **GET READY**

CRITICAL VOCABULARY

| ruddy | dismay | morose | vogue | commence | verandah |

To see how many Critical Vocabulary words you already know, identify which underlined word in each sentence is used incorrectly.

1. They <u>commenced</u> the meeting to the <u>verandah</u> after the office air conditioner broke down.
   a. commenced   b. verandah

2. Her <u>morose</u> face showed how much she appreciated the in-<u>vogue</u> garments presented at the fashion show.
   a. morose   b. vogue

3. She was quite <u>dismayed</u> at his <u>ruddy</u> complexion, and asked if he ever got outdoors to enjoy the sunshine.
   a. dismayed   b. ruddy

LANGUAGE CONVENTIONS

Gerunds and Gerund Phrases In this lesson, you will learn about gerunds and gerund phrases. A **gerund** is a verb ending in *-ing* that is used as a noun. You can add modifiers and complements to a gerund to make it a **gerund phrase.** Writers use gerunds and gerund phrases to effectively combine short sentences into one.

As you read the excerpt, notice the author's use of gerunds and gerund phrases.

ANNOTATION MODEL   NOTICE & NOTE

As you read, note the details that Brontë provides about the setting and how the narrator reacts to the treatment she receives from different people at the school. In the model, you can see one reader's notes about the excerpt from *Jane Eyre.*

| The refectory was a great, <u>low-ceiled, gloomy room</u>; on two long tables smoked basins of something hot, which, however, to my dismay, sent forth <u>an odor far from inviting</u>. I saw a <u>universal manifestation of discontent</u> when the <u>fumes of the repast met the nostrils of those destined to swallow it</u> . . . | *The room itself seems like it would make you lose your appetite. The narrator uses a formal, restrained tone to describe the food's awful smell, which suggests she's describing it when she's older.* |

594   Unit 5

BACKGROUND

Charlotte Brontë (1816–1855) grew up in a rural area of England, the daughter of a clergyman and a mother who died when she was five. She worked as a governess and teacher before beginning her writing career. Her first book was a collection of poetry that she wrote with two of her sisters, Emily and Anne. *Jane Eyre*, originally published under a pseudonym, was her first novel. It blended the suspense and moody atmosphere of a Gothic novel with a realistic portrayal of the moral, social, and economic pressures faced by a Victorian woman who lacked family support.

from JANE EYRE
Novel by Charlotte Brontë

SETTING A PURPOSE

As you read, pay attention to how Jane reacts to conditions at the school and to the people she meets there.

Orphaned as a young child, Jane Eyre has spent most of her childhood at Gateshead, the home of her wealthy yet heartless aunt, Mrs. Reed. At Gateshead, Jane is tormented by her cousins and repeatedly reminded of her low economic and social status. After a fight with one of her cousins, Jane's aunt decides to send her away to boarding school when she is 10 years old. As this excerpt begins, Jane has left Gateshead and is traveling by coach to the Lowood Institution, a boarding school for orphans and poor girls.

1 The afternoon came on wet and somewhat misty: as it waned into dusk, I began to feel that we were getting very far indeed from Gateshead: we ceased to pass through towns; the country changed; great grey hills heaved up round the horizon: as twilight deepened, we descended a valley, dark with wood, and long after night had overclouded the prospect, I heard a wild wind rushing amongst trees.

Notice & Note

Use the side margins to notice and note signposts in the text.

TEACH

BACKGROUND

After students read the Background note, explain that growing up without a mother, and with a father who had taken an oath of poverty, gave Brontë a unique perspective from which to write the novel. Explain that during Victorian times, taking care of other people's children as a governess or teacher was often the only option for women who lacked family money or a husband to provide for them. Point out that Brontë may have published *Jane Eyre* under a pseudonym (Currer Bell) because of the prejudice women writers faced during the Victorian period.

SETTING A PURPOSE

Direct students to use the Setting a Purpose prompt to focus their reading.

> For **speaking and reading support** for students at varying proficiency levels, see the **Text X-Ray** on page 592D.

TEACH

ANALYZE FIRST-PERSON POINT OF VIEW

Remind students that stories told in the first-person **point of view** allow the reader to see the narrator's surroundings through the narrator's own eyes. (**Answer:** *The description tells what happened to Jane, as well as what she saw, what she heard, and what she felt. These details can come only from the person experiencing it, so it is clear the story is told by Jane herself.*)

■ English Learner Support

Respond to Questions Place students into pairs or small groups, directing them to read paragraph 4 silently. Tell them to discuss the paragraph among themselves and find the answers to the following questions:

- What did Jane see?
- What did Jane hear?
- What did Jane feel?

Explain that the answers to these questions will help them understand that the story is being told from Jane's **point of view.** **MODERATE**

CRITICAL VOCABULARY

ruddy: Having a *ruddy* complexion, or a healthy reddish glow, often indicates that a person has spent time outdoors.

ASK STUDENTS to summarize how Jane describes Miss Miller. (*ordinary, ruddy in complexion, careworn countenance, hurried in gait*)

596   Unit 5

 **NOTICE & NOTE**

2   Lulled by the sound, I at last dropped asleep: I had not long slumbered when the sudden cessation of motion awoke me; the coach-door was open, and a person like a servant was standing at it: I saw her face and dress by the light of the lamps.

3   "Is there a little girl called Jane Eyre here?" she asked. I answered "Yes," and was then lifted out; my trunk was handed down, and the coach instantly drove away.

4   I was stiff with long sitting, and bewildered with the noise and motion of the coach: gathering my faculties, I looked about me. Rain, wind, and darkness filled the air; nevertheless, I dimly discerned a wall before me and a door open in it. Through this door I passed with my new guide: she shut and locked it behind her. There was now visible a house or houses—for the building spread far—with many windows, and lights burning in some; we went up a broad pebbly path, splashing wet, and were admitted at a door; then the servant led me through a passage into a room with a fire, where she left me alone.

5   I stood and warmed my numbed fingers over the blaze, then looked round; there was no candle, but the uncertain light from the hearth showed, by intervals, papered walls, carpet, curtains, shining mahogany furniture: it was a parlor, not so spacious or splendid as the drawing-room at Gateshead, but comfortable enough. I was puzzling to make out the subject of a picture on the wall, when the door opened, and an individual carrying a light entered; another followed close behind.

6   The first was a tall lady with dark hair, dark eyes, and a pale and large forehead; her figure was partly enveloped in a shawl, her countenance was grave, her bearing erect.

7   "The child is very young to be sent alone," said she, putting her candle down on the table. She considered me attentively for a minute or two, then further added—

8   "She had better be put to bed soon; she looks tired: are you tired?" she asked, placing her hand on my shoulder.

9   "A little, ma'am."

10 "And hungry too, no doubt: let her have some supper before she goes to bed, Miss Miller. Is this the first time you have left your parents to come to school, my little girl?"

11 I explained to her that I had no parents. She inquired how long they had been dead; then how old I was, what was my name, whether I could read, write, and sew a little: then she touched my cheek gently with her forefinger, and saying,

12 "She hoped I should be a good child," dismissed me along with Miss Miller.

13 The lady I had left might be about twenty-nine; the one who went with me appeared some years younger: the first impressed me by her voice, look, and air. Miss Miller was more ordinary; **ruddy** in complexion, though of a careworn countenance; hurried in gait and

ANALYZE FIRST-PERSON POINT OF VIEW
Annotate: In paragraph 4, mark details about what Jane sees after being lifted from the coach.

Analyze: How does this description give the impression that we see everything through Jane's eyes?

ruddy
(rŭd´ē) *adj.* having a healthy, reddish glow.

596   Unit 5

action, like one who had always a multiplicity of tasks on hand: she looked, indeed, what I afterwards found she really was, an under-teacher. Led by her, I passed from compartment to compartment, from passage to passage, of a large and irregular building; till, emerging from the total and somewhat dreary silence pervading that portion of the house we had traversed, we came upon the hum of many voices, and presently entered a wide, long room, with great deal tables, two at each end, on each of which burnt a pair of candles, and seated all round on benches, a congregation of girls of every age, from nine or ten to twenty. Seen by the dim light of the dips, their number to me appeared countless, though not in reality exceeding eighty; they were uniformly dressed in brown stuff frocks of quaint fashion, and long holland pinafores. It was the hour of study; they were engaged in conning[1] over their tomorrow's task, and the hum I had heard was the combined result of their whispered repetitions.

14   Miss Miller signed to me to sit on a bench near the door, then walking up to the top of the long room, she cried out—

15   "Monitors, collect the lesson-books and put them away!"

16   Four tall girls arose from different tables, and going round, gathered the books and removed them. Miss Miller again gave the word of command—

17   "Monitors, fetch the supper-trays!"

18   The tall girls went out and returned presently, each bearing a tray, with portions of something, I knew not what, arranged thereon, and a pitcher of water and mug in the middle of each tray. The portions were handed round; those who liked took a draught of the water, the mug being common to all. When it came to my turn, I drank, for I was thirsty, but did not touch the food, excitement and fatigue rendering me incapable of eating: I now saw, however, that it was a thin oaten cake, shared into fragments.

19   The meal over, prayers were read by Miss Miller, and the classes filed off, two and two, upstairs. Overpowered by this time with weariness, I scarcely noticed what sort of a place the bedroom was; except that, like the schoolroom, I saw it was very long. Tonight I was to be Miss Miller's bed-fellow; she helped me to undress: when laid down I glanced at the long rows of beds, each of which was quickly filled with two occupants; in ten minutes the single light was extinguished; amid silence and complete darkness, I fell asleep.

20   The night passed rapidly: I was too tired even to dream; I only once awoke to hear the wind rave in furious gusts, and the rain fall in torrents, and to be sensible that Miss Miller had taken her place by my side. When I again unclosed my eyes, a loud bell was ringing: the girls were up and dressing; day had not yet begun to dawn, and a rushlight or two burnt in the room. I too rose reluctantly; it was bitter

---

[1] **conning:** examining or studying.

ANALYZE SETTING

Annotate: Mark details in paragraph 18 about the girls' supper.

Draw Conclusions: What does this description suggest about living conditions at Lowood?

Jane Eyre   597

TEACH

ANALYZE SETTING

Remind students that the **setting** of a story may include details about how a place is run and what characters experience in that place. (**Answer:** *From the passage, readers can tell that Victorian charity schools relied on tight scheduling and that much of their instruction came from reading the Bible.*)

CRITICAL VOCABULARY

dismay: A situation that is upsetting will cause a person to feel dismay.

ASK STUDENTS why Jane felt *dismay* when she entered the refectory. (*She smelled an odor coming from the basins of food that she and the other students were supposed to eat.*)

morose: Rainy days can make a person feel *morose*, or gloomy.

ASK STUDENTS how Jane describes the teacher who yelled "Silence!" in the refectory. (*little and dark, smartly dressed, somewhat morose*)

598 Unit 5

 **NOTICE & NOTE**

cold, and I dressed as well as I could for shivering, and washed when there was a basin at liberty, which did not occur soon, as there was but one basin to six girls, on the stands down the middle of the room. Again the bell rang: all formed in file, two and two, and in that order descended the stairs and entered the cold and dimly-lit schoolroom: here prayers were read by Miss Miller; afterwards she called out—

21 "Form classes!"

22 A great tumult succeeded for some minutes, during which Miss Miller repeatedly exclaimed, "Silence!" and "Order!" When it subsided, I saw them all drawn up in four semi-circles, before four chairs, placed at the four tables; all held books in their hands, and a great book, like a Bible, lay on each table, before the vacant seat. A pause of some seconds succeeded, filled up by the low, vague hum of numbers; Miss Miller walked from class to class, hushing this indefinite sound.

23 A distant bell tinkled: immediately three ladies entered the room, each walked to a table and took her seat; Miss Miller assumed the fourth vacant chair, which was that nearest the door, and around which the smallest of the children were assembled: to this inferior class I was called, and placed at the bottom of it.

24 Business now began: the day's Collect was repeated, then certain texts of Scripture were said, and to these succeeded a protracted reading of chapters in the Bible, which lasted an hour. By the time that exercise was terminated, day had fully dawned. The indefatigable bell now sounded for the fourth time: the classes were marshalled and marched into another room to breakfast: how glad I was to behold a prospect of getting something to eat! I was now nearly sick from inanition, having taken so little the day before.

25 The refectory² was a great, low-ceiled, gloomy room; on two long tables smoked basins of something hot, which, however, to my **dismay**, sent forth an odor far from inviting. I saw a universal manifestation of discontent when the fumes of the repast met the nostrils of those destined to swallow it; from the van of the procession, the tall girls of the first class, rose the whispered words—

26 "Disgusting! The porridge is burnt again!"

27 "Silence!" ejaculated a voice; not that of Miss Miller, but one of the upper teachers, a little and dark personage, smartly dressed, but of somewhat **morose** aspect who installed herself at the top of one table, while a more buxom lady presided at the other. I looked in vain for her I had first seen the night before; she was not visible: Miss Miller occupied the foot of the table where I sat, and a strange, foreign looking, elderly lady, the French teacher, as I afterwards found, took the corresponding seat at the other board. A long grace was said and

ANALYZE SETTING
Annotate: Mark details about books and reading in paragraphs 22–25.
Analyze: What does this passage reveal about education at Victorian charity schools?

dismay
(dĭs-mā´) *v.* to upset or distress.

morose
(mə-rōs´, mô-) *adj.* sullen or gloomy.

---

² **refectory:** a room where meals are served in a school or institution.

598 Unit 5

 ENGLISH LEARNER SUPPORT

Develop Background Knowledge to Comprehend Language Direct students' attention to the phrase *marshalled and marched* in paragraph 24. Point out that this phrase is often used in reference to military groups, in which soldiers are marshalled, or arranged, and marched in formation to a destination. Explain that this phrase indicates that students at Lowood were expected to act with military-style discipline. **ALL LEVELS**

a hymn sung; then a servant brought in some tea for the teachers, and the meal began.

28   Ravenous, and now very faint, I devoured a spoonful or two of my portion without thinking of its taste; but the first edge of hunger blunted, I perceived I had got in hand a nauseous mess: burnt porridge is almost as bad as rotten potatoes; famine itself soon sickens over it. The spoons were moved slowly: I saw each girl taste her food and try to swallow it; but in most cases the effort was soon relinquished. <u>Breakfast was over, and none had breakfasted. Thanks being returned for what we had not got</u>, and a second hymn chanted, the refectory was evacuated for the schoolroom. I was one of the last to go out, and in passing the tables, I saw one teacher take a basin of the porridge and taste it; she looked at the others; all their countenances expressed displeasure, and one of them, the stout one, whispered—

29   "Abominable stuff! How shameful!"

30   A quarter of an hour passed before lessons again began, during which the schoolroom was in a glorious tumult; for that space of time, it seemed to be permitted to talk loud and more freely, and they used their privilege. The whole conversation ran on the breakfast, which one and all abused roundly. Poor things! it was the sole consolation they had. Miss Miller was now the only teacher in the room: a group of great girls standing about her, spoke with serious and sullen gestures. I heard the name of Mr. Brocklehurst pronounced by some lips; at which Miss Miller shook her head disapprovingly; but she made no great effort to check the general wrath: doubtless she shared in it.

31   A clock in the schoolroom struck nine; Miss Miller left her circle, and standing in the middle of the room, cried—

32   "Silence! To your seats!"

33   Discipline prevailed: in five minutes the confused throng was resolved into order, and comparative silence quelled the Babel clamour of tongues. The upper teachers now punctually resumed their posts: but still, all seemed to wait. Ranged on benches down the sides of the room, the eighty girls sat motionless and erect: a quaint assemblage they appeared, all with plain locks combed from their faces, not a curl visible; in brown dresses, made high and surrounded by a narrow tucker about the throat, with little pockets of holland (shaped something like a Highlander's purse) tied in front of their frocks, and designed to serve the purpose of a work-bag: all too wearing woollen stockings and country-made shoes, fastened with brass buckles. Above twenty of those clad in this costume were full-grown girls, or rather young women; it suited them ill, and gave an air of oddity even to the prettiest.

34   I was still looking at them, and also at intervals examining the teachers—none of whom precisely pleased me; for the stout one was

NOTICE & NOTE

CONTRASTS AND CONTRADICTIONS

Notice & Note: Mark two statements that express contradictory ideas in paragraph 28.

Infer: What do these statements suggest about how girls are treated at the school?

TEACH

CONTRASTS AND CONTRADICTIONS

Point out that contradictory statements help emphasize the difference between what is expected and what actually happens. (**Answer:** *The girls are expected to pray and give thanks for the meal they had received, even though the meal was inedible. This shows that the school is less concerned with the girls' welfare than with whether they are thankful for what is provided for them.*)

TO CHALLENGE STUDENTS...

Analyze Characters Invite groups of students to read paragraph 30 and assess Miss Miller's behavior when she is alone with the girls and dealing with the fallout from breakfast. Challenge them to compare her behavior at this point with how she must behave when other teachers are around. Ask them to consider the conflicts teachers might have felt while working at the school. Direct them to write a paragraph exploring this aspect of the story, and then invite volunteers to share their paragraphs with the class.

TEACH

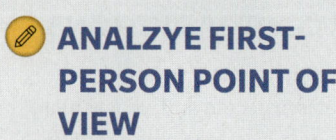

ANALZYE FIRST-PERSON POINT OF VIEW

Remind students that the first-person **point of view** allows readers to see what the narrator sees and gain insight into the narrator's perspective on it. (**Answer:** *When Jane discusses Miss Temple's hair, dress, and accessories, she knows the woman is wearing her hair and clothes in the current style. Jane would not have known this unless she had spent time in fashionable society.*)

■ English Learner Support

Respond to Questions Place students into pairs or small groups, directing them to read paragraph 37 silently. Tell them to discuss the paragraph among themselves and find the answers to the following questions:

1. What did Miss Temple look like?
2. How was her hair styled?
3. What was she wearing?

Direct students to answer in the first-person. (Example: "I see that Miss Temple wears stylish clothes."). Then, challenge partners to respond in the third-person. (Example: "The passage says Miss Temple wears stylish clothing."). Then, ask them to consider how these descriptions might have been different from another character's **point of view**.
MODERATE/LIGHT

600   Unit 5

NOTICE & NOTE

a little coarse, the dark one not a little fierce, the foreigner harsh and grotesque, and Miss Miller, poor thing! looked purple, weather-beaten, and over-worked—when, as my eye wandered from face to face, the whole school rose simultaneously, as if moved by a common spring.

35   What was the matter? I had heard no order given: I was puzzled. Ere I had gathered my wits, the classes were again seated: but as all eyes were now turned to one point, mine followed the general direction, and encountered the personage who had received me last night. She stood at the bottom of the long room, on the hearth; for there was a fire at each end: she surveyed the two rows of girls silently and gravely. Miss Miller approaching, seemed to ask her a question, and having received her answer, went back to her place, and said aloud—

36   "Monitor of the first class, fetch the globes!"

37   While the direction was being executed, the lady consulted moved slowly up the room. I suppose I have a considerable organ of Veneration, for I retain yet <u>the sense of admiring awe with which my eyes traced her steps</u>. Seen now, in broad daylight, <u>she looked tall, fair, and shapely</u>; brown eyes, with <u>a benignant light in their irids</u>,

ANALYZE FIRST-PERSON POINT OF VIEW
Annotate: Mark words and phrases in paragraph 37 that express Jane's admiration for Miss Temple.
Analyze: Which details reveal that Jane has spent time in fashionable society?

600   Unit 5

IMPROVE READING FLUENCY

Targeted Passage Conduct an echo reading of paragraphs 35 and 36 with the class. Explain that you will read a sentence with the correct pronunciation, intonation, and pace and that they should repeat the sentence, in unison, after you read. Direct them to continue to follow your example as you read each sentence. Point out the importance of intonation when reading questions and exclamations.

 Go to the **Reading Studio** for additional support in developing fluency.

and a fine penciling of long lashes round, relieved the whiteness of her large front; on each of her temples her hair, of a very dark brown, was clustered in round curls, according to the fashion of those times, when neither smooth bands nor long ringlets were in **vogue**; her dress, also in the mode of the day, was of purple cloth, relieved by a sort of Spanish trimming of black velvet; a gold watch (watches were not so common then as now) shone at her girdle. Let the reader add, to complete the picture, refined features; a complexion, if pale, clear; and a stately air and carriage, and he will have, at least, as clearly as words can give it, a correct idea of the exterior of Miss Temple—Maria Temple, as I afterwards saw the name written in a prayer-book entrusted to me to carry to church.

vogue
(vōg) *n.* the prevailing fashion, practice, or style.

38   The superintendent of Lowood (for such was this lady) having taken her seat before a pair of globes placed on one of the tables, summoned the first class round her, and **commenced** giving a lesson in geography; the lower classes were called by the teachers: repetitions in history, grammar, etc., went on for an hour; writing and arithmetic succeeded, and music lessons were given by Miss Temple to some of the elder girls. The duration of each lesson was measured by the clock, which at last struck twelve. The superintendent rose—

commence
(kə-měns´) *v.* to begin or start.

39   "I have a word to address to the pupils," said she.

40   The tumult of cessation from lessons was already breaking forth, but it sank at her voice. She went on—

41   "You had this morning a breakfast which you could not eat; you must be hungry—I have ordered that a lunch of bread and cheese shall be served to all."

42   The teachers looked at her with a sort of surprise.

43   "It is to be done on my responsibility," she added, in an explanatory tone to them, and immediately afterwards left the room.

44   The bread and cheese was presently brought in and distributed, to the high delight and refreshment of the whole school. The order was now given "To the garden!" Each put on a coarse straw bonnet, with strings of colored calico, and a cloak of grey frieze. I was similarly equipped, and, following the stream, I made my way into the open air.

45   The garden was a wide enclosure, surrounded with walls so high as to exclude every glimpse of prospect: a covered **verandah** ran down one side, and broad walks bordered a middle space divided into scores of little beds: these beds were assigned as gardens for the pupils to cultivate, and each bed had an owner. When full of flowers they would doubtless look pretty; but now, at the latter end of January, all was wintry blight and brown decay. I shuddered as I stood and looked round me: it was an inclement day for outdoor exercise; not positively rainy, but darkened by a drizzling yellow fog; all underfoot was still soaking wet with the floods of yesterday. The stronger among the girls ran about and engaged in active games, but sundry pale and thin

verandah
(və-răn´də) *n.* a porch or balcony.

ANALYZE SETTING
Annotate: Mark details in paragraph 45 showing how the girls feel about their exercise period.

Analyze: What does this description suggest about the school's attitude toward the girls' well-being?

Jane Eyre   601

ENGLISH LEARNER SUPPORT

Acquire New Vocabulary Help students improve their comprehension by providing definitions for the following words: *refined* (paragraph 37, "free from coarseness; well-bred"), *duration* (paragraph 38, "length of time"), *cessation* (paragraph 40, "ending"), *frieze* (paragraph 44, "a coarse, shaggy woolen cloth"), and *blight* (paragraph 45, "wilting of plants; decay"). **ALL LEVELS**

TEACH

ANALYZE SETTING

Explain to students that descriptions of how the girls spend their day, like those in paragraph 45, give the readers insights into the overall **setting** in which the girls live. (**Answer:** *The girls were sent out in drizzling fog to exercise in an area still rain-soaked from the day before. Many of the thin girls were too cold to participate, and some of them were sick and should have been kept inside. The school is clearly more focused on maintaining a rigid schedule than on the health and well-being of the students.*)

CRITICAL VOCABULARY

vogue: Fashions often come back into *vogue*, or in style, in 20-year cycles.

ASK STUDENTS which aspects of Miss Temple's appearance were in vogue. (*her round curls and her dress*)

commence: To *commence* something means to begin it.

ASK STUDENTS what lesson Miss Temple commenced after sitting in front of two globes. (*a lesson in geography*)

verandah: Large wrap-around porches are often called *verandahs*.

ASK STUDENTS why certain girls used the verandah during the exercise period. (*The pale and thin girls gathered on the verandah for shelter and warmth.*)

Jane Eyre   601

TEACH

LANGUAGE CONVENTIONS

Remind students that **gerunds** are verbs ending in *-ing* that are used as nouns. (**Answer:** *Jane is a contemplative person who tries to understand the situation she is in, as well as the people who are around her.*)

ENGLISH LEARNER SUPPORT

Participate in Shared Reading Organize students into pairs and ask each pair to read paragraphs 46–48. Students should take turns reading sentences from these paragraphs aloud. Have students read the paragraphs a second time, reading the sentences they didn't read the first time. Encourage students to provide support to each other as they read and to ask for help with pronunciation as needed. Remind students to listen closely to their partners as they read aloud, listening for correct pronunciation of new or difficult words. **MODERATE/LIGHT**

NOTICE & NOTE

LANGUAGE CONVENTIONS
Annotate: Mark the sentence that contains gerunds in paragraph 46.
Evaluate: What do these gerunds emphasize about Jane's character?

ones herded together for shelter and warmth in the verandah; and amongst these, as the dense mist penetrated to their shivering frames, I heard frequently the sound of a hollow cough.

46   As yet I had spoken to no one, nor did anybody seem to take notice of me; I stood lonely enough: but to that feeling of isolation I was accustomed; it did not oppress me much. I leant against a pillar of the verandah, drew my grey mantle close about me, and, trying to forget the cold which nipped me without, and the unsatisfied hunger which gnawed me within, delivered myself up to the employment of watching and thinking. My reflections were too undefined and fragmentary to merit record: I hardly yet knew where I was; Gateshead and my past life seemed floated away to an immeasurable distance; the present was vague and strange, and of the future I could form no conjecture. I looked round the convent-like garden, and then up at the house; a large building, half of which seemed grey and old, the other half quite new. The new part, containing the schoolroom and dormitory, was lit by mullioned and latticed windows, which gave it a church-like aspect; a stone tablet over the door, bore this inscription—

47   "Lowood Institution.—This portion was rebuilt A.D.—, by Naomi Brocklehurst, of Brocklehurst Hall, in this county."

48   "Let your light so shine before men that they may see your good works, and glorify your Father which is in heaven."— St. Matt. v. 16.

49   I read these words over and over again: I felt that an explanation belonged to them, and was unable fully to penetrate their import. I was still pondering the signification of "Institution," and endeavoring to make out a connection between the first words and the verse of Scripture, when the sound of a cough close behind me, made me turn my head. I saw a girl sitting on a stone bench near; she had bent over a book, on the perusal of which she seemed intent: from where I stood I could see the title—it was "Rasselas;" a name that struck me as strange, and consequently attractive. In turning a leaf she happened to look up, and I said to her directly—

50   "Is your book interesting?" I had already formed the intention of asking her to lend it to me some day.

51   "I like it," she answered, after a pause of a second or two, during which she examined me.

52   "What is it about?" I continued, I hardly know where I found the hardihood thus to open a conversation with a stranger; the step was contrary to my nature and habits: but I think her occupation touched a chord of sympathy somewhere; for I too liked reading, though of a frivolous and childish kind; I could not digest or comprehend the serious or substantial.

53   "You may look at it," replied the girl, offering me the book.

602   Unit 5

APPLYING ACADEMIC VOCABULARY

☑ **abandon**   ☐ **confine**   ☐ **conform**   ☑ **depress**   ☐ **reluctance**

Write and Discuss Have students turn to a partner to discuss the following questions. Guide students to include the Academic Vocabulary words *abandon* and *depress*, in their responses. Ask volunteers to share their responses with the class.

- Why might Jane have felt **abandoned** by her relatives at Gateshead?
- Why would Jane's first day at Lowood likely have **depressed** her?

602   Unit 5

54 I did so; a brief examination convinced me that the contents were less taking than the title: "Rasselas" looked dull to my trifling taste; I saw nothing about fairies, nothing about genii; no bright variety seemed spread over the closely-printed pages. I returned it to her; she received it quietly, and without saying anything she was about to relapse into her former studious mood: again I ventured to disturb her—

55 "Can you tell me what the writing on that stone over the door means? What is Lowood Institution?"

56 "This house where you are come to live."

57 "And why do they call it Institution? Is it in any way different from other schools?"

58 "It is partly a charity-school: you and I, and all the rest of us, are charity-children. I suppose you are an orphan: are not either your father or your mother dead?"

59 "Both died before I can remember."

60 "Well, all the girls here have lost either one or both parents, and this is called an institution for educating orphans."

61 "Do we pay no money? Do they keep us for nothing?"

62 "We pay, or our friends pay, fifteen pounds a year for each."

63 "Then why do they call us charity-children?"

64 "Because fifteen pounds is not enough for board and teaching, and the deficiency is supplied by subscription."

65 "Who subscribes?"

66 "Different benevolent-minded ladies and gentlemen in this neighborhood and in London."

67 "Who was Naomi Brocklehurst?"

68 "The lady who built the new part of this house as that tablet records, and whose son overlooks and directs everything here."

69 "Why?"

70 "Because he is treasurer and manager of the establishment."

71 "Then this house does not belong to that tall lady who wears a watch, and who said we were to have some bread and cheese."

72 "To Miss Temple? Oh, no! I wish it did: she has to answer to Mr. Brocklehurst for all she does. Mr. Brocklehurst buys all our food and all our clothes."

73 "Does he live here?"

74 "No—two miles off, at a large hall."

75 "Is he a good man?"

76 "He is a clergyman, and is said to do a great deal of good."

77 "Did you say that tall lady was called Miss Temple? "

78 "Yes."

79 "And what are the other teachers called?"

80 "The one with red cheeks is called Miss Smith; she attends to the work, and cuts out—for we make our own clothes, our frocks, and pelisses, and every thing; the little one with black hair is Miss

ANALYZE FIRST-PERSON POINT OF VIEW

Annotate: Mark paragraph 57.

Analyze: Why does Jane ask these questions? What do they indicate about the type of person she is?

Jane Eyre 603

TEACH

ANALYZE FIRST-PERSON POINT OF VIEW

Have students review how Jane described Miss Temple in paragraph 37. (**Answer:** *Jane admires Miss Temple for her appearance and style, and for the way she carries herself, while the girl admires her for being good, clever, and knowledgeable.*)

**NOTICE & NOTE**

Scatcherd; she teaches history and grammar, and hears the second class repetitions; and the one who wears a shawl, and has a pocket-handkerchief tied to her side with a yellow riband, is Madame Pierrot: she comes from Lisle, in France, and teaches French."

81 "Do you like the teachers?"

82 "Well enough."

83 "Do you like the little black one, and the Madame—?—I cannot pronounce her name as you do."

84 "Miss Scatcherd is hasty—you must take care not to offend her; Madame Pierrot is not a bad sort of person."

85 "But Miss Temple is the best—isn't she?"

86 "Miss Temple is very good, and very clever; she is above the rest, because she knows far more than they do."

87 "Have you been long here?"

88 "Two years."

89 "Are you an orphan?"

90 "My mother is dead."

91 "Are you happy here"?

92 "You ask rather too many questions. I have given you answers enough for the present: now I want to read."

93 But at that moment the summons sounded for dinner: all reentered the house. The odor which now filled the refectory was scarcely more appetizing than that which had regaled our nostrils at breakfast: the dinner was served in two huge tin-plated vessels, whence rose a strong steam redolent of rancid fat. I found the mess to consist of indifferent potatoes and strange shreds of rusty meat, mixed and cooked together. Of this preparation a tolerably abundant plateful was apportioned to each pupil. I ate what I could, and wondered within myself whether every day's fare would be like this.

94 After dinner, we immediately adjourned to the schoolroom: lessons recommenced, and were continued till five o'clock.

95 The only marked event of the afternoon was, that I saw the girl with whom I had conversed in the verandah, dismissed in disgrace, by Miss Scatcherd, from a history class, and sent to stand in the middle of the large schoolroom. The punishment seemed to me in a high degree ignominious, especially for so great a girl—she looked thirteen or upwards. I expected she would show signs of great distress and shame; but to my surprise she neither wept nor blushed: composed, though grave, she stood, the central mark of all eyes. "How can she bear it so quietly—so firmly?" I asked of myself. "Were I in her place, it seems to me I should wish the earth to open and swallow me up. She looks as if she were thinking of something beyond her punishment—beyond her situation: of something not round nor before her. I have heard of daydreams—is she in a daydream now? Her eyes are fixed on the floor, but I am sure they do not see it—her sight seems turned in, gone down into her heart:

ANALYZE FIRST-PERSON POINT OF VIEW
Annotate: Mark the girl's response to Jane's question about Miss Temple.

Compare: How does the girl's response contrast with Jane's reasons for admiring Miss Temple?

604 Unit 5

WHEN STUDENTS STRUGGLE...

Synthesize Information Direct students to refer back to the graphic organizer they created earlier to use the information from that chart to make a second chart showing actions between characters that benefit another character.

Character 1 (Giver)	Character 2 (Receiver)	Description of Benefaction

 For additional support, go to the **Reading Studio** and assign the following Level Up tutorial: Synthesizing Information.

she is looking at what she can remember, I believe; not at what is really present. I wonder what sort of a girl she is—whether good or naughty."

96   Soon after five P.M. we had another meal, consisting of a small mug of coffee and half a slice of brown bread. I devoured my bread and drank my coffee with relish; but I should have been glad of as much more—I was still hungry. Half an hour's recreation succeeded, then study; then the glass of water and the piece of oat-cake, prayers, and bed. Such was my first day at Lowood.

CHECK YOUR UNDERSTANDING

Answer these questions before moving on to the **Analyze the Text** section on the following page.

1 What is Miss Temple's reaction when she first meets Jane?
  A She is annoyed that Jane has arrived so late.
  B She expresses sympathy and concern for Jane.
  C She thinks Jane is too young for the school.
  D She fears that Jane will misbehave.

2 Why does Miss Temple order bread and cheese to be served on Jane's first day at Lowood?
  F She wants to celebrate Jane's arrival.
  G Mr. Brocklehurst is coming for a visit.
  H The students could not eat their breakfast.
  J The school has run out of other food.

3 Who makes the decisions about how Lowood is run?
  A Miss Temple
  B Miss Miller
  C Miss Scatcherd
  D Mr. Brocklehurst

NOTICE & NOTE

Jane Eyre   605

TEACH

CHECK YOUR UNDERSTANDING

Have students answer the questions independently.

Answers:
1. B
2. H
3. D

If they answer any questions incorrectly, have them reread the text to confirm their understanding. Then they may proceed to ANALYZE THE TEXT on page 606.

ENGLISH LEARNER SUPPORT

Oral Assessment Use the following questions to assess students' comprehension and speaking skills.

1. How does Miss Temple treat Jane when she first meets her? *(She shows concern and sympathy for her.)*

2. Why does Miss Temple give the students bread and cheese on Jane's first day? *(The students' breakfast was inedible.)*

3. Who is in charge of the Lowood school? *(Mr. Brocklehurst)*
   ALL LEVELS

Jane Eyre   **605**

APPLY

ANALYZE THE TEXT

Possible answers:

1. **DOK 2:** *Jane's experiences at Gateshead and Lowood are similar in that, at both places, only her basic needs are met. At neither place is she given love, support, or the freedom to become something more. At both places, she would have been constantly reminded of her social status and need of charity.*

2. **DOK 3:** *Lowood provides only the basic needs of its students—shelter, food and water, clothing, and a rudimentary education. It is clear these needs are only barely met, so the system does not seem to be functioning as well as it should to give the girls a real chance at a decent life.*

3. **DOK 3:** *It seems Mr. Brocklehurst may not really have the best interests of the Lowood students at heart, but may be managing the establishment because he wants people to say he does "a great deal of good." Although he buys all the food and clothes for the students, it appears he tries to spend as little as possible on them.*

4. **DOK 3:** *The first-person narration is effective. Reading the story from Jane's own point of view gives the reader an intimate look at what life was really like at Lowood. If it had been told in the third-person, the sense of intimacy felt between the reader and Jane might not exist, and much of the deeper meaning behind the text would be lost.*

5. **DOK 4:** *The girl behaves in a way that is different from how Jane expected her to behave and how Jane admits she herself would act if put into the same situation. This suggests Jane is proud and might not be able to hold her emotions in check as well as the older girl did.*

RESEARCH

Remind students they should confirm any information they find by checking multiple websites and assessing the credibility of each one.

Extend As students write their paragraphs, encourage them to consider what the details about education reveal about Brontë's opinion of ragged schools and other charitable education institutions of her time.

606 Unit 5

RESPOND

ANALYZE THE TEXT

Support your responses with evidence from the text. NOTEBOOK

1. **Compare** Reread the introductory note below Setting a Purpose on page 595. How does Jane's experience at Lowood compare with the life she led at Gateshead?

2. **Evaluate** England did not have government-funded schools in the period covered by the novel; because the children at Lowood are poor, they must rely on charity for their education. Based on Jane's descriptions of the setting, how well does this system serve the needs of students? Explain.

3. **Draw Conclusions** What does the excerpt hint about Mr. Brocklehurst's character?

4. **Critique** Is the first-person narration of *Jane Eyre* effective, or should Brontë have used the third-person point of view to tell the story? Give reasons for your opinion.

5. **Notice & Note** Jane is surprised that the older girl shows no emotion when Miss Scatcherd makes her stand in the middle of the room as punishment. What does this incident reveal about Jane's personality?

RESEARCH

Research "ragged schools" and other charitable education institutions in England during the Victorian era. Why did these schools exist? Who did they serve? What impact did they have on pupils? Use the following chart to record your findings.

RESEARCH TIP
When researching a specific part of a particular time period, it is best to use search strings that include all elements, starting with the most important. For example, for this research, the search string "ragged schools Victorian England" would be most likely to yield useful results.

PURPOSE	POPULATION SERVED	IMPACT ON POPULATION
Ragged schools were charity schools that provided a free education, and often lodging, food, and clothing to children.	*These schools served the poorest of society as well as children without parents (orphans).*	*Although conditions were very difficult for children who attended these schools, they were given education, food, clothing, and a place to stay - which was more than they would have had otherwise. It allowed them to have a chance at survival, no matter how small.*

Extend Use the information found in your research to explain how Charlotte Brontë utilized details about education in her writing. Write a brief paragraph analyzing the effectiveness of the author's use of such details.

606 Unit 5

WHEN STUDENTS STRUGGLE . . .

Reteaching: Analyze Setting Remind students that the setting of a story is more than just the location where the action takes place. Organize students into small groups, and ask them to consider all the aspects of setting that Brontë describes in this selection. Challenge them to explain how each of these details adds to the picture of Jane's situation and of the setting in which she finds herself. After small group discussion, ask each group to share one of its observations on how the setting unfolds throughout the story.

For additional support, go to the **Reading Studio** and assign the following **Level Up tutorial: Setting**.

CREATE AND PRESENT

Write a Comparison Obtain a filmed adaptation of *Jane Eyre* to view the scenes described in the novel excerpt. Focus on how effectively the film version captures the setting and overall atmosphere of the classic.

- ❏ Isolate a few striking descriptions of setting from the novel. Find and view similar scenes from film. Pause occasionally to examine shots.
- ❏ Make a chart, if you wish, to compare details from the novel and film.
- ❏ Consider how closely the filmed setting matches the novel. Think about any deliberate changes the director might have made.
- ❏ You may include other aspects for comparison, such as character portrayals. Cover how these elements are presented in both versions.

Present Your Comparison Now that you've written a comparison, present it to the group. If possible, play segments of the film version to illustrate your points.

- ❏ Read your comparison aloud or refer to it as you present your views.
- ❏ Encourage your listeners to react to your view and offer their own. Ask your listeners how well they followed your points, and if they can add ideas that might strengthen the comparison.

RESPOND TO THE ESSENTIAL QUESTION

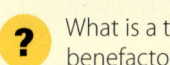 **What is a true benefactor?**

Gather Information Review your annotations and notes on the excerpt from *Jane Eyre*. Then, add relevant information to your Response Log. As you determine which information to include, think about:

- what a benefactor, or supporter, should provide to someone in need
- how a benefactor would act toward someone he or she was helping
- how a benefactor might try to help, but fail to provide the support a person truly needs

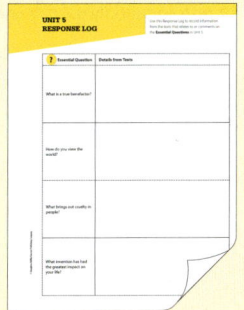

RESPOND

 Go to **Writing Informative Texts** in the **Writing Studio** to organize ideas for the comparison.

Go to **Using Media in a Presentation** in the **Speaking and Listening Studio** to learn more.

ACADEMIC VOCABULARY
As you write and discuss what you learned from *Jane Eyre*, be sure to use the Academic Vocabulary words. Check off each of the words that you use.

- ❏ abandon
- ❏ confine
- ❏ conform
- ❏ depress
- ❏ reluctance

APPLY

CREATE AND PRESENT

Write a Comparison Direct students to use their annotations to create a list of notes about **setting**. Encourage them to enter these notes in a graphic organizer, with space left to add notes from the film. Help students obtain a film version of *Jane Eyre* and then locate the portion of the film that corresponds with the text selection. Direct them to use the graphic organizer to take notes on the film, paying close attention to the ways the film version is similar to and different from the novel.

Present Your Comparison After students have viewed the film and taken notes, ask each of them to share one of the comparisons they made. After each student shares, poll the class to see who noted the same comparison. Ask those students to provide feedback, adding their own details to strengthen the comparison.

RESPOND TO THE ESSENTIAL QUESTION

Allow time for students to add details from *Jane Eyre* to their Unit 5 Response Logs.

APPLY

CRITICAL VOCABULARY

Answers:

1. outside
2. exposed to the sun
3. sad
4. beginning
5. unhappy
6. in style

VOCABULARY STRATEGY:
Foreign Words or Phrases

Practice and Apply

Answers:

1. café
2. genre
3. kindergarten
4. agenda

 **RESPOND**

WORD BANK
ruddy
dismay
morose
vogue
commence
verandah

CRITICAL VOCABULARY

Practice and Apply Choose the situation that best fits with the Critical Vocabulary word.

1. If you're drinking tea on the **verandah,** are you indoors or outside?
2. If your complexion is **ruddy,** have you been exposed to the sun or covered up?
3. If a movie were described as **morose,** would it be sad or funny?
4. If a class is **commencing,** is it beginning or ending?
5. If you are feeling **dismayed,** are you happy or unhappy?
6. If a woman's outfit is said to be in **vogue,** is it in style or out of style?

VOCABULARY STRATEGY:
Foreign Words or Phrases

Foreign words or phrases are often incorporated into English language usage. Typically, the meaning is similar to the way the word is used in the original language, but not always. Additionally, these words and phrases can be categorized based on use. For example, many German terms used in English refer to philosophy or sociology, while many Latin words deal with the law. French words, like the term *vogue* used in *Jane Eyre*, often refer to food or social class.

In the novel, Jane describes Miss Temple's appearance, including her physical form and how she presents herself through dress and style. The word *vogue* is not only descriptive of the woman's appearance but is also indicative of her social standing, indicating she is above those she is charged with teaching.

 Go to the **Vocabulary Studio** for more on understanding word origins.

WORD BANK
agenda
genre
café
kindergarten

Practice and Apply Read each of the clues to identify the foreign word or phrase commonly used in English.

DESCRIPTION	ORIGIN	WORD OR PHRASE
A restaurant serving coffee or other beverages along with baked goods or light meals	French	*café*
A category or type	French	*genre*
A program or class for those aged four to six	German	*kindergarten*
A program of things to be done or considered, or an unstated underlying motive	Latin	*agenda*

 ENGLISH LEARNER SUPPORT

Vocabulary Strategy Give students support in pronouncing words from the selection that may be difficult for them. For example, explain that the word *sundry* can be sounded out by separating each syllable: *sun – dry*. Explain that the second syllable *-dry* is not pronounced like the word *dry*. Rather, the *y* is pronounced like the long *e* in *heat*. Review the following words: *discerned, bewildered, tumult,* and *indefatigable*. **ALL LEVELS**

RESPOND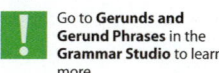

LANGUAGE CONVENTIONS:
Gerunds and Gerund Phrases

A **gerund** is a verb form ending in *-ing* that functions as a noun. **Gerund phrases** include the gerund plus its modifiers and complements. Gerunds and gerund phrases may perform any function that a noun performs and can appear in any part of a sentence where a noun could be used. Gerunds can add a sense of motion or action to a sentence.

PART OF THE SENTENCE	EXAMPLE
subject	**Having little food** was a way of life at Lowood.
direct object	The girls finished **gardening.**
indirect object	They gave **working** their full attention.
subject complement	Her best skill is **coping with hardship.**
object of the preposition	She came home weary from **working all day.**

Practice and Apply Write your own sentences with gerunds or gerund phrases using the sentences above as models.

Go to **Gerunds and Gerund Phrases** in the **Grammar Studio** to learn more.

Jane Eyre 609

APPLY

LANGUAGE CONVENTIONS:
Gerunds and Gerund Phrases

Review the information on **gerunds** and **gerund phrases.** Explain that gerunds, although derived from verbs, can be used like other nouns. Read the chart to students, examining how each gerund or gerund phrase is used as a different part of a sentence. Clarify any confusion about how the gerunds function as various parts of a sentence.

Practice and Apply Once students have written their own sentences, organize them into pairs. Direct students to share their sentences with their partners, and have their partners check for correct usage in each part of a sentence. After partners have reviewed each other's sentences, ask each pair to share one sentence with the class.

 ENGLISH LEARNER SUPPORT

Language Conventions Use the following supports with students at varying proficiency levels:

- Have students find other sentences in *Jane Eyre* that include **gerunds** or **gerund phrases,** and have them copy the sentences. Then, have them circle the gerunds and underline the gerund phrases. **SUBSTANTIAL**
- Have students work in pairs to choose sentences from the selection that could be rewritten using a gerund or gerund phrase. Have students rewrite the sentences, and then discuss how each sentence changes with the new wording. **MODERATE**
- Ask students to write two descriptive sentences about *Jane Eyre* using gerunds or gerund phrases. Have them share their sentences with partners, who should offer constructive suggestions to improve the way the gerunds are used. **LIGHT**

Jane Eyre **609**

PLAN

FACTORY REFORM
Documentary by Timelines.tv

GENRE ELEMENTS
DOCUMENTARY
Tell students that a **documentary** is a nonfiction film that covers a specific person, place, event, or idea. Explain that documentaries have structures, just like written texts. For example, documentary filmmakers may use a problem-solution structure or a cause-and-effect structure. They make claims and back them up with supporting statistics and other facts, and they enhance the narration with visuals and sound effects. In this lesson, students will evaluate how a historical documentary presents information about a problem and a solution.

LEARNING OBJECTIVES
- Evaluate documentaries.
- Conduct research about the history of conditions in American factories and the lives of American workers.
- Write a short story about a benefactor.
- Present a short story with illustrations.
- **Language** Rephrase key ideas from a film clip using the terms *subjective* and *objective*.

TEXT COMPLEXITY

Quantitative Measures	Factory Reform	Lexile: N/A
Qualitative Measures	**Ideas Presented** Literal, explicit, and direct. Purpose or stance clear.	
	Structure Used Primarily explicit, with support from drawings and video.	
	Language Used Familiar language with some idioms.	
	Knowledge Required Cultural and historical knowledge may make heavier demands.	

610A Unit 5

PLAN

RESOURCES
Online Ed

- Unit 5 Response Log
- Reading Studio: Notice & Note
- Level Up Tutorial: Summarizing
- Writing Studio: Writing Narratives
- Speaking and Listening Studio: Using Media in a Presentation; Giving a Presentation
- "Factory Reform" Selection Test

SUMMARIES

English
In this film clip, the narrator describes how people in Britain became increasingly aware of the suffering that was taking place beneath the prosperity brought about by the Industrial Revolution. The clip focuses on the actions of a philanthropic businessman, Titus Salt, and his creation of Saltaire, a humane living/working compound that allowed workers and employers to manufacture with dignity.

Spanish
En este clip de película, el narrador describe cómo la gente en Gran Bretaña se hizo cada vez más consciente del sufrimiento que estaba ocurriendo bajo la prosperidad que trajo la Revolución Industrial. El clip se enfoca en los actos de Titus Salt, un empresario filantrópico; y en su creación, Saltaire, un complejo de vivienda y trabajo humanitario que les permitía a los trabajadores y empleadores fabricar con dignidad.

 SMALL-GROUP OPTIONS

Have students work in small groups and pairs to read and discuss the selection.

Double-Entry Journal
- Have students use a notebook for recording their double-entry notes.
- Show students how to create a two-column format by drawing a line from top to bottom on each page. The left head should be *Quotes from the Film* and the right head should be *My Notes*.
- Encourage students to pause the film and copy important or confusing lines in the left column.
- Then, have students write their own questions, restatements, or interpretations in the right column next to the quoted material.
- Have partners exchange journals and respond to each other's notes.

Send a Problem
- After watching the first three minutes of the film, pose this question: *What do you notice about the structure of this film?*
- Call on a student to respond. Wait up to 11 seconds.
- If the student has no response, he or she must call on another student by name to answer the same question.
- Have students continue asking each other for assistance as needed. Monitor responses and ask more questions as appropriate.

Factory Reform **610B**

PLAN

Text X-Ray: English Learner Support
for "Factory Reform"

Use the Text X-Ray and the supports and scaffolds in the Teacher's Edition to help guide students at different proficiency levels through the selection.

INTRODUCE THE SELECTION

DISCUSS MANUFACTURING

In this lesson, students will need to be able to discuss how manufacturing can adversely affect people.

Remind students that a typical goal in manufacturing goods in factories is to produce things cheaply, quickly, and in mass quantities. Explain that this goal can at times be at odds with what is best for people working in or near the factories.

Ask students to discuss how factory owners can be more responsible and still achieve their production goals, and why this is important. Provide sentence frames, such as: *Manufacturers need to make sure their workers are _____. People who work in factories need _____.*

CULTURAL REFERENCES

The following words or phrases may be unfamiliar to students:

- *full steam:* something done with as much speed and power as possible
- *with a human face:* to make something easier to care about
- *heads held high:* feeling proud
- *pricking the conscience:* starting to think about what is right or wrong

LISTENING

Identify and Rephrase Key Ideas

Remind students that key ideas are the most important points. Guide them to use words from the film and their own words to rephrase key ideas.

Play the film clip and pause after every minute or so. Use the following supports with students at varying proficiency levels:

- Ask either/or questions about key ideas. For example: *Which is more important, that Titus Salt raised alpacas or that he knew children were dying? Is this idea subjective or/objective?* **SUBSTANTIAL**
- Ask general content questions to assess listening comprehension of key facts. For example: *What is an objective (or subjective) fact about Titus Salt?* **MODERATE**
- After re-watching the entire clip, have students use words from the clip and their own words to give an oral summary of the key ideas, utilizing the content terms. **LIGHT**

PLAN

SPEAKING

Describe Visuals

Have students pause the film at particularly interesting visuals and describe them in their own words.

Use the following supports with students at varying proficiency levels:
- Turn on the closed-caption subtitles and pause the film at a place where the subtitle features a noun shown in the visual. Point to the noun and its corresponding image as you read the word aloud. Have students repeat the nouns with you. **SUBSTANTIAL**
- Have partners take turns pausing the film and describing the visual with the subtitle feature off. Then, have them turn the subtitles on and use any words they see to describe the visual again. **MODERATE**
- Have partners take turns closing their eyes as the other partner describes the visual. Then, have partners open their eyes and look at the file and explain if what they are seeing is what their partner described. **LIGHT**

READING

Use Think Alouds to Improve Comprehension

Remind students that it is a good idea to pause as they read the subtitles to ask themselves questions about what they see on screen. Model how to use Think Alouds as you read the subtitles.

Use the following supports with students at varying proficiency levels:
- Read a subtitle and then have students repeat it. Model a Think Aloud: *I want to know what* boiler *means. The picture shows me black smoke. That is pollution. The next picture shows me machines. I think a boiler is a machine.* Ask yes/no questions to assess students' comprehension of the Think Aloud. **SUBSTANTIAL**
- Model the Think Aloud from the previous activity. Then, have partners take turns reading a subtitle and using clues from the visuals to recite their own brief Think Alouds. **MODERATE**
- Have partners each choose two places in the film clip to recite their own Think Alouds. Tell them to use complete sentences. **LIGHT**

WRITING

Write Dialogue

Tell students that each character in their story should have their own way of speaking based on their age and personality.

Use the following supports with students at varying proficiency levels:
- Write two or three descriptive sentences and have students copy them. For example: *My benefactor is a tall woman.* Ask: *Where in the sentence is the adjective located?* **SUBSTANTIAL**
- Create descriptive sentence frames for students. Circulate to correct usage of number and/or gender. For example: *I have kind_____ benefactors. _____ have _____ of money.* **MODERATE**
- Direct students to continue writing story drafts, paying attention to the use of possessive adjectives vs. definite articles. Give an example: *She broke her leg.* Instruct students to read aloud their descriptive stories with a partner. Have students copy down key adjectives and discuss whom these details belong to in the story. **LIGHT**

TEACH

Connect to the
ESSENTIAL QUESTION

The **documentary** tells the story of Titus Salt, a 19th-century industrial magnate who proved to be a true benefactor by investing a huge amount of money to make factories less harmful to workers. He also improved workers' quality of life by building places for the workers to live. The positive effects of his investment have lasted to the present day; the changes he made permanently improved industrial working conditions in Great Britain and elsewhere.

QUICK START

Have students work in pairs to discuss incidents in which they, someone they know, or a figure from history took a stand. What issues were involved? What were the results? Encourage students to incorporate these details into the paragraphs they write.

EVALUATE DOCUMENTARIES

Have students read the information about **documentaries** on page 610. Then, review the elements of documentaries described in the table. Ask students to discuss each element of historical documentaries, based on documentaries they may have seen in the past.

Encourage them to use these questions to analyze the elements in the film:

- What kind of **footage** was used in the film? How did the footage help convey information?
- What impression did the **illustrations** give of the time and place the film described? What did the illustrations show about Salt and Saltaire?
- What did the **sound effects** and **music** add to the film?
- Which parts of the film were **objective,** simply presenting facts? Which parts were **subjective,** reflecting the opinion of the filmmaker?

ANALYZE & APPLY

MEDIA

FACTORY REFORM

Documentary by Timelines.tv

ESSENTIAL QUESTION:

What is a true benefactor?

QUICK START

Write a paragraph about any incident in which an individual took a stand or made efforts on behalf of others. Share your paragraph with a partner.

EVALUATE DOCUMENTARIES

A **documentary** is a nonfiction film about social, political, or historical subject matter. A historical documentary usually focuses on a particular time period, person, or event and informs viewers by taking a detailed look at the subject. Documentary filmmakers often rely on visual and sound elements to immerse viewers in the subject and to convey certain viewpoints.

GENRE ELEMENTS: DOCUMENTARY

- informational
- covers a specific person, place, event, or idea
- should rely on facts, but may also express opinions
- uses visual and sound elements
- conveys information through a narrator (or voice-over narration)

Go to the **Speaking and Listening Studio: Using Media in a Presentation** to find out about visual and sound elements.

VISUAL AND SOUND ELEMENTS	• **Footage** is recorded material used to reveal information about a subject. It can include photos, film clips, even reenactments. • **Illustrations** can be used to help create a storyline by portraying important people and incidents. • **Music** and **sound effects** can be used to set a mood or to capture viewers' attention.
STRATEGIES FOR VIEWING	• Consider the viewpoint of the documentary. Is it **objective,** based strictly on the facts? Or does it make its points in a **subjective** way by sharing only certain views? • Note images used to help you connect ideas. • Think about what the creators emphasize and what impressions they might want to convey.

610 Unit 5

ENGLISH LEARNER SUPPORT

Use Prereading Supports to Enhance Comprehension Discuss the adjective *documentary* and the meaning of its the root word *document:* a record or report (noun); to report or record (verb). Documentaries are based on facts and real events or people. Explain that the suffix –ary means "connected to." Have students practice the root word as a noun and a verb by writing sentences. (Examples: I _____ the football game. The _____ revealed the winner of the football game.) **SUBSTANTIAL/MODERATE**

GET READY

BACKGROUND

"Factory Reform" is an excerpt from the documentary *History of Britain—Changing Lives* on the website Timelines.tv. It depicts manufacturer Titus Salt's advocacy for Britain's lower-class factory workers. In the Industrial Revolution, business owners became quite wealthy, while average citizens lived in poverty. Workers—men, women, and children—sometimes worked more than 14 hours per day and made very little money. Many were killed or severely injured; accidents ranging from falls to explosions were common in Victorian factories.

SETTING A PURPOSE

Pay attention to the visual and sound elements in the film. Listen for sounds and words in the narration that help to connect viewers to the conditions in Victorian factories. Also, note visual elements that may persuade you to take a certain viewpoint about the subject. ≡ NOTEBOOK .

For more online resources, log in to your dashboard and click on "**FACTORY REFORM**" from the selection menu.

As needed, pause the documentary to make notes about what impresses you or about ideas you might want to talk about later. Replay or rewind so you can clarify anything you do not understand.

Factory Reform 611

TEACH

BACKGROUND

After students have read the background paragraph on page 611, discuss the meaning of the word *reform* ("an improvement or change for the better"). Explain to students that what Salt did constituted a reform, or improvement, of working and living conditions for lower-class workers.

SETTING A PURPOSE

Direct students to use the Setting a Purpose prompt to focus their reading.

WHEN STUDENTS STRUGGLE . . .

Analyze Documentaries Discuss with students the changes Salt made in his factories and in Saltaire. Have them describe the workers' lives before Salt's reforms and after Salt's reforms, including working conditions, factory conditions, and living conditions.

Before Salt's Reforms	After Salt's Reforms

 For additional support, go to the **Reading Studio** and assign the following **Level Up tutorial: Summarizing**.

Factory Reform **611**

APPLY

ANALYZE THE MEDIA
Possible answers:

1. **DOK 2:** *The viewer can hear the sounds of machines running in the background. They give the viewer the feeling of being in the factory: the heat, the smell, the fatigue.*

2. **DOK 4:** *The footage portrays Saltaire as a well-constructed small city. It appears Salt invested much thought, time, and money to create it and to reflect values he thought would serve this community. Had this experiment failed, Salt risked losing everything he owned.*

3. **DOK 4:** *The presence of the narrator, set against the backdrop of a modern-day factory and the streets of Saltaire, helps to bring the actual setting to life while delivering details about Titus Salt and his efforts. In a sense, the narrator's presence helps viewers to vicariously "tour" the setting from his perspective. His voice-over, matched to the documentary's footage, introduces viewers to the Industrial Revolution, providing a historical context for Salt's time and the importance of his reforms.*

4. **DOK 3:** *The images of factories and workers were dark and often shadowed. Workers' faces looked sick and weak. The images of factory owners and the middle class were colorful. The people looked happy and healthy, with nice clothing and bright eyes.*

5. **DOK 2:** *Laws were passed, improving factories and reducing child labor. Workers also won the right to join unions. Men earned the right to vote.*

RESEARCH

As they watch the video, encourage students to take notes about key words they hear. Tell them that proper names would be significant, as would any terms that are repeated several times. When they do their research, they can refer back to their list of key words to help them locate relevant sources.

Connect Discuss the sounds and the images used in the video. Talk to students about how these sounds and images made them feel. Have students work in pairs to continue the discussion and then write a paragraph or create a storyboard to show how they would create the same feeling with images and sounds. Provide an example of a storyboard for students to look at, if possible.

RESPOND

ANALYZE MEDIA

Support your responses with evidence from the documentary.  NOTEBOOK

1. **Identify** At the start of the documentary, what sounds do you hear as the presenter gives background information? What mental images do these sounds conjure up?

2. **Analyze** How does footage of the community of Saltaire help to convey the risk Titus Salt took by moving his factory and investing in living quarters for his workers?

3. **Analyze** What does the appearance of a narrator, as well as the use of his voice-over, contribute to the documentary?

4. **Compare** "Factory Reform" repeatedly shows illustrations in a notebook that depict life in Victorian factories. How are workers depicted compared to images of the wealthy factory owners?

5. **Summarize** According to the documentary, how did Salt's factory influence future factory owners?

RESEARCH

"Factory Reform" portrays how Titus Salt demonstrated his social concerns, which led to great changes in factories and the lives of working families. The Industrial Revolution in Britain influenced an Industrial Revolution in America. Now that you're familiar with conditions in Victorian factories, research the history of conditions in American factories and the lives of American workers.

	VICTORIAN FACTORIES	AMERICAN FACTORIES
Conditions	Men in Bradford made less than fifty cents per day. Women and children earned half of that. Workers struggled with health and nutrition.	*Workers struggled for wages and better working conditions and lived in slums filled with disease.*
Child labor	Young children were used because of their low salaries. Boys were even fired once they reached adulthood.	*Child laborers were forced to work full-time to support their families.*
Risks	Factory workers were forced to work in dark coal mines and around dangerous machinery. Many lost their eyesight, limbs, and/or their lives while working.	*By 1900, industrial accidents killed 35,000 workers each year and maimed 500,000.*

Connect Recall the visual and sound elements in the documentary. If you were a director, how would you present examples of factory conditions? With a partner, write a description of visual and sound elements you would use to present the subject. You might choose to present your ideas in the form of a storyboard—a pictorial outline that shows a series of scenes.

RESEARCH TIP
When choosing sources for your research, look for keywords and synonyms from the class video or text. Use an online dictionary to define unfamiliar words, especially if they make it challenging for you to understand a source.

CREATE AND PRESENT

Write a Short Story Depict a time you received support from someone you might call a benefactor. The short story may be based on a real event or from your imagination.

- ❑ Determine where and when the story takes place.
- ❑ Create events in order to establish the conflict you faced and follow through to a clear resolution. To ensure a solid beginning, middle, and end, use a story map to plan the details of the plot.
- ❑ Use vivid language to paint clear pictures in readers' or listeners' minds.
- ❑ Reread and edit your narrative. Add more details as needed.

Present Your Story Read your short story aloud to a small group. Before you present:

- ❑ Create simple sketches to illustrate your narrative.
- ❑ Change your voice to match the changing events of your story. For example, let your tone convey curiosity, uncertainty, or excitement.

RESPOND

 Go to the **Writing Studio: Writing Narratives** for more help.

 Go to the **Speaking and Listening Studio: Giving a Presentation** to learn more.

RESPOND TO THE ESSENTIAL QUESTION

 What is a true benefactor?

Gather Information Review your notes on "Factory Reform." Then, add relevant information to your Response Log. As you determine which information to include, think about:

- the purpose of the documentary
- the use of visual and sound elements to influence viewers
- the conditions endured by Victorian factory workers
- the ways factory workers' lives were altered over time

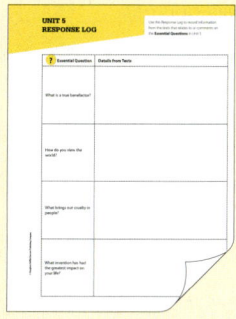

ACADEMIC VOCABULARY

As you write and discuss what you learned from the documentary, be sure to use the Academic Vocabulary words. Check off each of the words that you use.

- ❑ abandon
- ❑ confine
- ❑ conform
- ❑ depress
- ❑ reluctance

APPLY

CREATE AND PRESENT

Write a Short Story After students have finished writing drafts of their stories, have them read them aloud to a partner. Encourage their partners to provide feedback about anything that is unclear, as well as suggestions for additional details that might make the story easier to follow or more interesting.

For **writing support** for students at varying proficiency levels, see the **Text X-Ray** on page 610D.

Present Your Story Encourage students to create **illustrations** for their stories. Have them work with a partner to decide which scenes or events would be the most interesting to illustrate. Then, have them read their stories aloud to the class, showing their illustrations as they read. Remind them to read slowly enough so the class can follow the story and the illustrations.

RESPOND TO THE ESSENTIAL QUESTION

Allow time for students to add details from "Factory Reform" to their Unit 5 Response Logs.

PLAN

THE LADY OF SHALOTT

Narrative Poem by Alfred, Lord Tennyson

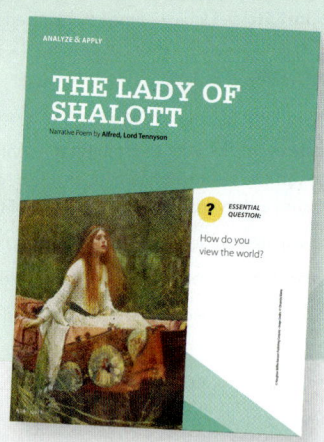

GENRE ELEMENTS
NARRATIVE POEM

Remind students that **narrative poems** have scenes with distinct **moods,** just like stories. Authors of narrative poetry can create mood by using precise words and sensory language to describe physical settings. The mood of a narrative poem is sometimes called its atmosphere because it creates an emotional setting that surrounds its readers. In this lesson, students will analyze the use of allegory and mood in a narrative poem.

LEARNING OBJECTIVES

- Analyze allegory and mood.
- Conduct research about the life of women in Victorian era England.
- Illustrate a narrative poem.
- Recite a poem.
- **Language** Use informal language to identify symbolism and allegory.

TEXT COMPLEXITY

Quantitative Measures	The Lady of Shalott	Lexile: N/A
Qualitative Measures	**Ideas Presented** Multiple levels, subtle, implied meanings and purpose. Use of symbolism.	
	Structures Used Primarily explicit. Support through sequential Parts with subheads.	
	Language Used Complex sentence structures with use of allusive, figurative, archaic, and formal language.	
	Knowledge Required Experiences less familiar to many. Cultural and historical knowledge may make heavier demands.	

614A Unit 5

PLAN

RESOURCES

Online  Ed

- Unit 5 Response Log
- 🔊 Selection Audio
- 📖 Reading Studio: Notice & Note
- 📊 Level Up Tutorial: Setting and Mood
- 💬 Speaking and Listening Studio: Giving a Presentation
- ✓ *The Lady of Shalott* Selection Test

SUMMARIES

English
In this narrative poem, the Lady of Shalott is cursed to view the world only in her mirror. When she sees Sir Lancelot in the mirror, however, she looks again with her own eyes. This activates the curse, and so she lies down in a small boat and dies as it floats to Camelot.

Spanish
En este poema narrativo, la dama de Shalottis está condenada a solo ver el mundo a través de su espejo. Sin embargo, cuando ve al caballero Lanzarote en el espejo, vuelve para mirarlo con sus propios ojos. Así se activa la maldición y luego ella se tumba en un pequeño bote y muere mientras flota hacia Camelot.

 SMALL-GROUP OPTIONS

Have students work in small groups and pairs to read and discuss the selection.

Activating Academic Vocabulary
- Provide a list of Academic Vocabulary words and phrases, such as *allegory, mood, scene, setting, sensory language, literal meaning, symbolic meaning, represents the idea,* and *rhyme.*
- After reading Part I of the poem, model how to use one or more Academic Vocabulary words and phrases to discuss the text.
- Encourage students to use the Academic Vocabulary words as they discuss and write about the text.

Silent Sustained Reading
- Set a timer for 15 minutes.
- Have students read the poem silently until the timer rings.
- Suggest that students keep a list of any unfamiliar words they want to look up after reading.
- Ask students to record the title, date, and number of pages read in a reading log.

The Lady of Shalott **614B**

PLAN

Text X-Ray: English Learner Support
for *The Lady of Shalott*

Use the Text X-Ray and the supports and scaffolds in the Teacher's Edition to help guide students at different proficiency levels through the selection.

INTRODUCE THE SELECTION
DISCUSS ISOLATION

In this lesson, students will need to be able to discuss the theme of isolation in a narrative poem.

Provide the following explanations:

- *Isolation* is separation from others, sometimes by being in a remote location.

Write and discuss how to use a list of words and phrases in the word family of *isolation: isolate, isolates, isolated, isolating, in isolation.*

Ask students to talk about times in their life when they felt isolated. Provide sentence frames, such as: *I felt isolated from my friends when ____. It felt like I was in isolation when ____. ____ can be very isolating because ____. ____ isolates us from others because ____.*

CULTURAL REFERENCES

The following words or phrases may be unfamiliar to students:

- *Camelot* (line 5): a fictional castle and court associated with the legendary King Arthur
- *hath* (line 24): archaic, third-person singular form of present tense "have"
- *the curse is come upon me* (line 116): an evil, magic spell has been activated on a person
- *they crossed themselves* (line 166): they made a religious sign asking for God's protection

LISTENING

Identify Rhymes

Remind students that not all rhyming sounds are spelled the same. Have students listen closely to identify the sounds that are being rhymed as they note the letters that correspond to each sound.

Use the following supports with students at varying proficiency levels:

- Have students listen as you read lines 1–4. Have them repeat the words that rhyme and name the vowel sound (*lie, rye, sky, by; long i*). Have them refer to the text to identify the letters that spell the long *i* sound in each word (*-ie, -ye, -y*). **SUBSTANTIAL**
- Have partners take turns reading aloud couplets to each other through line 9. Have them tell what sounds they hear being rhymed in each pair of end words. Direct them to identify the different spellings of each rhyming sound. **MODERATE**
- Have partners take turns reading aloud couplets to each other through Part I. Have them tell what sounds they hear being rhymed in each pair of end words and to note any different spellings of the same sound. **LIGHT**

PLAN

SPEAKING

Discuss Allegorical Meaning

Tell students that people can interpret the implied meaning of a poem in different ways. Help students fill in the chart related to allegorical meaning on the Get Ready page.

Use the following supports with students at varying proficiency levels:

- Say one possible meaning for each symbol in the chart. Have students say the symbolic element for that possible meaning. (*Example: This might be a symbol for being alone or lonely; island of Shalott*). **SUBSTANTIAL**
- Have partners ask each other questions about the allegorical meaning of each symbolic element in the chart. For example: *What is a possible meaning of the island of Shalott? What detail from the poem support my idea?* Students respond by completing these frames: *A possible meaning of the island of Shalott is ____. I think this because ____.* **MODERATE**
- Have pairs discuss the possible meanings and supportive details for each symbolic element. Then, have the pairs choose one allegorical meaning of the poem to support using their ideas: *This poem is an allegory for the life of an artist.* **LIGHT**

READING

Identify Rhythm

Remind students that rhythm sets the tone for a poem. Rhythm creates a pattern of language within and among its lines by using stressed and unstressed syllables in the words.

Use the following supports with students at varying proficiency levels:

- Lead students in echo-reading lines 1–4. Then read the lines aloud again, emphasizing the rhythm. Have students repeat each line after you until they have internalized the rhythm. **SUBSTANTIAL**
- Have pairs take turns reading aloud lines 1–18. Have them discuss the rhythm of the poem. Guide them to use the terms *stressed* and *unstressed syllable* in their discussion. **MODERATE**
- Have partners reread lines 1–9. Have them copy the lines and put a check mark over the stressed syllables. Then, have students compare the syllables they marked with a partner and take turns reading the lines using the agreed-upon stresses. **LIGHT**

WRITING

Illustrate a Narrative Poem

Explain to students that they can summarize the theme, symbolism, or a related detail of text through visual images they hear in a rhyme.

Use the following supports with students at varying proficiency levels:

- Help students write one aspect of the poem that they relate to. To prepare their presentation, have students complete this frame: *I illustrated ____ because ____.* **SUBSTANTIAL**
- Have students write two aspects of the poem that they relate to, then circle the one they will illustrate. To prepare their presentation, have students complete these frames: *The subject of my illustration is ____. I relate to this aspect of the poem because ____. My illustration shows this by ____.* **MODERATE**
- Have students write one aspect of the poem each related to the characters, setting, and events, then circle the one they will illustrate. **LIGHT**

The Lady of Shalott **614D**

TEACH

? Connect to the
ESSENTIAL QUESTION

This poem demonstrates the way two different individuals view the world—one through the veil of a mirror and one by looking at it straight on. Although *The Lady of Shalott* is cursed to look at the world as it passes by her back, most people can change the way they look at the world just by trying a different perspective.

ANALYZE & APPLY

THE LADY OF SHALOTT

Narrative Poem by **Alfred, Lord Tennyson**

? ESSENTIAL QUESTION:

How do you view the world?

LEARNING MINDSET

Grit Explain to students that our brains are muscles, and just like our bodies, the more we work them, the stronger they will become. Explain that one way to work your brain is to think in different ways, allowing your mindset to become as flexible as possible. Ask them to consider the most flexible people in their lives, and explain that those individuals are more likely to see opportunities where others see problems. It is important to encourage students' efforts and strategies, whether or not they reach the intended goals. This is the essence of grit—continuing forward no matter the obstacles that may be in front of you.

GET READY

QUICK START

Many legends and fairy tales depict a character who is confined to a place and shut off from the world. Imagine what it would be like to experience such isolation. How do you think it would affect you? What risks might you take to gain freedom and live among other people? Write a paragraph in response to these questions. Then, exchange paragraphs with a partner and discuss your thoughts.

ANALYZE ALLEGORY

An **allegory** is a story with two levels of meaning—a literal one and a symbolic one. In allegorical fiction and poetry, characters represent abstract qualities or ideas. Allegory is closely tied to symbolism. These forms of figurative language both use one thing to stand for another, and they allow writers to represent ideas in nontraditional ways. As in a fable or parable, the purpose of an allegory may be to convey truths about life, to teach religious or moral lessons, or to criticize social institutions.

Some critics of *The Lady of Shalott* argue that the poem is an allegory for the life of an artist, while others believe the poem represents the plight of women in Victorian society. As you read *The Lady of Shalott,* use a chart like this one to help you analyze symbolic elements that contribute to the poem's allegorical meaning.

GENRE ELEMENTS: NARRATIVE POETRY
- tells a story
- uses elements of fiction, such as character, setting, and plot
- is written in poetic form using lines and stanzas
- may be written with regular patterns of rhyme and meter, or in free verse without a regular structure

SYMBOLIC ELEMENT	POSSIBLE MEANING	SUPPORTING DETAILS
The island of Shalott		
Camelot		
The loom and the web		
The mirror		
Sir Lancelot		
The boat ride		

The Lady of Shalott 615

TEACH

QUICK START

Have students read the Quick Start prompt, and separate them into pairs or small groups. Ask each pair to answer the questions within their paragraphs. Direct students to share their writing with their partners or groups. Then, ask several students to share theirs with the whole group.

ANALYZE ALLEGORY

Explain to students that **allegories** are representations of abstract ideas. Most allegorical poems and stories are designed to express beliefs about life, offer examples toward teaching lessons, or condemn social policies and institutions. One way to look at this poem is that it represents the life of artists, or individuals who choose to look at life through the representations that they produce. Another way to look at the poem is that it shows how Victorian women were only given enough freedom to see their own small part of the world, while men were able to see the whole world from their own completely free perspectives.

Explain to students that symbols, imagery, and metaphors are frequently found in allegorical stories like this one. Remind students that symbols and metaphors are items that represent something else, and imagery includes vivid descriptions that paint a picture for readers, often clueing them in to deeper meanings within the story or poem. Challenge them to consider what the island, Camelot, loom, mirror, Sir Lancelot, and the boat ride represent, and how the story would be representative of a different idea if those objects were replaced.

 For **speaking support** for students at varying proficiency levels, see the **Text X-Ray** on page 614D.

The Lady of Shalott **615**

TEACH

ANALYZE MOOD

Explain to students how the **mood** of a poem can be seen in the feelings the piece elicits from readers. The mood can range across the entire spectrum of emotions, from the greatest joy to the deepest sorrow. Mood is created through the writer's use of language, like word choice and the flow of the words as they are said together. It is created through sound devices, like repetition and rhymes as seen in this poem. Explain that mood is additionally created through line structure, line length, and stanza structure.

Explain that, in *The Lady of Shalott*, Tennyson creates passages that have the same meter—four iambic feet with an unstressed syllable followed by a stressed one. Read the lines from the poem to students, using your fingers to show the meter count and ensuring you add emphasis to stressed syllables, so the students can hear the differences. Explain that this rhythm and meter combination creates the feeling of tranquility in the first part of the poem. Challenge students to consider how these elements work together to create the overall mood of Tennyson's poem.

ENGLISH LEARNER SUPPORT

Read Fluently Use the short excerpts on this page to build students' reading and speaking fluency. Choose one selection. Read it aloud slowly, then a second time more quickly. Model deliberate pausing and phrasing of each line. Have students first choral read the selection, then take turns reading it aloud with a partner. Provide supportive feedback, as needed. **SUBSTANTIAL**

 ## ANNOTATION MODEL

Explain to students how to pick out the images described in the poem and how to identify what mood is created by those images. Explain that these images are often symbolic, representing something more abstract than they might originally appear to do. Point out that they may follow this suggestion or use their own system for marking up the selection in their write-in text. They may want to color-code their annotations by using highlighters. Their notes in the margin may include questions about ideas that are unclear or topics they want to learn more about.

 **GET READY**

ANALYZE MOOD

Mood is the feeling or atmosphere that a writer creates for the reader. Some examples of words describing mood are *mysterious, somber,* and *joyful*. A poem's mood may change as a poem progresses. Elements that help create a poem's mood include diction, imagery, line length, stanza structure, and sound devices, such as repetition and rhyme.

Read these lines from the beginning of *The Lady of Shalott*:

> On either side the river lie
> Long field of barley and of rye,
> That clothe the wold and meet the sky;
> And through the field the road runs by
>   To many-towered Camelot;

Each line in this passage contains four iambic feet, consisting of an unstressed syllable followed by a stressed syllable. The strong, regular pattern of this meter, the rhyme scheme, and the imagery of King Arthur's mythical realm of Camelot contribute to a tranquil and orderly mood early in the poem. As you read, think about how these elements combine to create that mood or other moods that arise throughout Tennyson's poem.

ANNOTATION MODEL NOTICE & NOTE

As you read, note the use of vivid imagery and how this contributes to the overall mood of the poem. You can also mark up other places you find symbols or striking images. In the model you can see one reader's notes about *The Lady of Shalott*.

> Willows whiten, aspens quiver,
> Little breezes dusk and shiver
> Through the wave that runs forever
> By the island in the river
>   Flowing down to Camelot.
> Four gray walls, and four gray towers,
> Overlook a (space of flowers,)
> And the silent isle imbowers
>   The Lady of Shalott.

Word choices like whiten, quiver, dusk, and shiver give this stanza a mood of coldness and isolation.

The images of the trees and wind, a wave that runs forever, gray walls and towers, and a silent isle also contribute to the somber mood.

The phrase "space of flowers" adds a tiny element of hope.

BACKGROUND

Alfred, Lord Tennyson *(1809–1892) experienced misfortune early in life, but he became the most celebrated poet of his age. He left Cambridge University without completing his degree due to lack of funds, and soon afterward the death of his closest friend devastated him. Although he struggled financially and professionally for many years, his fortunes turned in 1850 when Queen Victoria named him poet laureate. Decades later, the rank of baron and title of "Lord" were bestowed upon him. The Lady of Shalott, an early work, was inspired by the legends of King Arthur.*

THE LADY OF SHALOTT

Narrative Poem by Alfred, Lord Tennyson

SETTING A PURPOSE

As you read, consider the situation in which the Lady of Shalott finds herself, and imagine what it would be like to see the world from her perspective.

Part I

On either side the river lie
Long fields of barley and of rye,
That clothe the wold and meet the sky;
And through the field the road runs by
    To many-towered Camelot;
And up and down the people go,
Gazing where the lilies blow
Round an island there below,
    The island of Shalott.

Notice & Note

Use the side margins to notice and note signposts in the text.

ANALYZE MOOD

Annotate: Mark the words or phrases that establish the moods of the first and second stanzas.

Analyze: How does the mood change from the first to the second stanza?

3 **wold:** rolling plain.

7 **blow:** bloom.

TEACH

ANALYZE ALLEGORY

Remind students that allegorical poems subtly represent deeper realities of life, often through descriptive imagery. (**Answer:** *Tennyson might have been trying to express how both women and artists are never appreciated enough while alive, but only after their deaths. Artists also work very diligently at pleasing their audiences, and women of this time were expected to work diligently toward pleasing society, their husbands, and their children. Additionally, the poet may be saying that artists see the world only through their own works, while women see the world through the eyes of their husbands and families.*)

ENGLISH LEARNER SUPPORT

Use Informal Language Read aloud lines 23–27, modeling appropriate intonation for each question. Then, have each student repeat these lines. Have students work in pairs to rewrite the questions using informal language. (*Examples: Has anyone seen her waving to us? Has anyone seen her standing at the window?*) Discuss what the author is implying to the reader by asking these questions. (*No one knows the Lady is there because they haven't seen her to wave to her, and they haven't seen her at her window.*)
SUBSTANTIAL/MODERATE

NOTICE & NOTE

10 Willows whiten, aspens quiver,
   Little breezes dusk and shiver
   Through the wave that runs forever
   By the island in the river
        Flowing down to Camelot.
15 Four gray walls, and four gray towers,
   Overlook a space of flowers,
   And the silent isle imbowers
        The Lady of Shalott.

   By the margin, willow-veiled,
20 Slide the heavy barges trailed
   By slow horses; and unhailed
   The shallop flitteth silken-sailed
        Skimming down to Camelot:
   But who hath seen her wave her hand?
25 Or at the casement seen her stand?
   Or is she known in all the land,
        The Lady of Shalott?

   Only reapers, reaping early
   In among the bearded barley,
30 Hear a song that echoes cheerly
   From the river winding clearly,
        Down to towered Camelot;
   And by the moon the reaper weary,
   Piling sheaves in uplands airy,
35 Listening, whispers "'Tis the fairy
        Lady of Shalott."

17 imbowers: encloses; surrounds.

ANALYZE ALLEGORY
Annotate: In lines 19–27, mark details that suggest the Lady of Shalott is invisible or unknown to the citizens of Camelot.
Interpret: How might these details relate to the allegorical meaning of the poem?

22 shallop (shăl´əp): a small open boat.

25 casement: a hinged window that opens outward.

Part II

   There she weaves by night and day
   A magic web with colors gay.
   She has heard a whisper say,
40 A curse is on her if she stay
        To look down to Camelot.
   She knows not what the curse may be,
   And so she weaveth steadily,
   And little other care hath she,
45   The Lady of Shalott.

618 Unit 5

TO CHALLENGE STUDENTS . . .

Allegory Remind students that an allegory is a story or poem that represents something more abstract, or difficult to explain. Provide them with this description: *The woman's scarf blew off in the bitter wind, chilling her to the bone. She shivered, knowing that tomorrow would bring drastic changes, and pulled her coat more tightly around her to ward off the cold.* Challenge students to examine the symbols in the example, and to consider what the cold might represent (*fear of change*). Challenge them to write a description of their own to represent something larger, and have other students guess the abstract concept they are representing with their descriptions.

And moving through a mirror clear
That hangs before her all the year,
Shadows of the world appear.
There she sees the highway near
50   Winding down to Camelot;
There the river eddy whirls,
And there the surly village churls,
And the red cloaks of market girls,
   Pass onward from Shalott.

55 Sometimes a troop of damsels glad,
An abbot on an ambling pad,
Sometimes a curly shepherd lad,
Or long-haired page in crimson clad,
   Goes by to towered Camelot;
60 And sometimes through the mirror blue
The knights come riding two and two:
She hath no loyal knight and true,
   The Lady of Shalott.

But in her web she still delights
65 To weave the mirror's magic sights,
For often through the silent nights
A funeral, with plumes and lights
   And music, went to Camelot;
Or when the moon was overhead,
70 Came two young lovers lately wed:
"I am half sick of shadows," said
   The Lady of Shalott.

Part III

A bowshot from her bower eaves,
He rode between the barley sheaves,
75 The sun came dazzling through the leaves,
And flamed upon the brazen greaves
   Of bold Sir Lancelot.
A red-cross knight forever kneeled
To a lady in his shield,
80 That sparkled on the yellow field,
   Beside remote Shalott.

NOTICE & NOTE

46–48 Weavers often used mirrors while working from the back of a tapestry to view the tapestry's appearance, but this one is used to view the outside world.

52 surly village churls: rude members of the lower class in a village.

55 damsels: young, unmarried women.

56 abbot . . . pad: the head monk in a monastery on a slow-moving horse.

58 page: a boy in training to be a knight.

ANALYZE ALLEGORY
Annotate: In lines 64–72, mark the words or phrases that represent the isolation experienced by the main character.

Infer: What does the Lady's statement in line 71 suggest about her character?

73 bowshot: the distance an arrow can be shot; **bower** (bou´ər) **eaves:** the part of the roof that extends above the Lady's private room.

76 brazen greaves: metal armor for protecting the legs below the knees.

78–79 A red cross . . . shield: His shield showed a knight wearing a red cross and kneeling to honor a lady. The red cross was a symbol worn by knights who had fought in the Crusades.

The Lady of Shalott   619

TEACH

ANALYZE ALLEGORY

Remind students that abstract ideas, like loneliness and freedom, are often represented in allegorical poetry. (**Answer:** *By saying, "I'm half sick of shadows," the Lady is expressing that she is tired of living life through the veil of the mirror and wishes she could live life more fully and love openly, like she sees others doing. This shows that she has a stronger will than her current life will allow, and that she wishes for the freedom to live life in the light.*)

WHEN STUDENTS STRUGGLE . . .

Understand Setting and Mood Direct students to develop a setting-and-mood chart to better understand the mood of each location in the poem. List the different settings, then direct students to describe the mood of that place through words of emotion or feeling.

| Setting/Location | Description | Mood |

 For additional support, go to the **Reading Studio** and assign the following Level Up tutorial: **Setting and Mood**.

The Lady of Shalott   **619**

TEACH

AGAIN AND AGAIN

Remind students that repetition is one of the techniques poets use to express mood. (**Answer:** The word *she* is repeated six times. The rest of the poem has been about the world around the Lady, and this stanza is all about her, so the reader can sense a shift from society to self with regard to the Lady of Shalott. From this, we understand that she is now making decisions that affect her life rather than letting life pass her by because of her fear of the curse.)

NOTICE & NOTE

82 gemmy: studded with gems.

87 blazoned (blā´zənd) **baldric:** a decorated leather belt worn across the chest to support a sword or, as in this case, a bugle.

The gemmy bridle glittered free,
Like to some branch of stars we see
Hung in the golden Galaxy.
85 The bridle bells rang merrily
    As he rode down to Camelot;
And from his blazoned baldric slung
A mighty silver bugle hung,
And as he rode his armor rung,
90   Beside remote Shalott.

All in the blue unclouded weather
Thick-jeweled shone the saddle leather,
The helmet and the helmet-feather
Burned like one burning flame together,
95   As he rode down to Camelot;
As often through the purple night,
Below the starry clusters bright,
Some bearded meteor, trailing light,
    Moves over still Shalott.

100 His broad clear brow in sunlight glowed;
On burnished hooves his war horse trode;
From underneath his helmet flowed
His coal-black curls as on he rode,
    As he rode down to Camelot.
105 From the bank and from the river
He flashed into the crystal mirror,
"Tirra lirra," by the river
    Sang Sir Lancelot.

AGAIN AND AGAIN

Notice & Note: In lines 109–113, mark the repeated words.

Infer: What effect does this repetition have on the stanza?

She left the web, she left the loom,
110 She made three paces through the room,
She saw the water lily bloom,
She saw the helmet and the plume,
    She looked down to Camelot.
Out flew the web and floated wide;
115 The mirror cracked from side to side;
"The curse is come upon me," cried
    The Lady of Shalott.

620   Unit 5

IMPROVE READING FLUENCY

Targeted Passage Using lines 91–99 as your base passage, conduct an echo reading activity with the students. Explain that you will read one sentence with the correct rate, flow, and prosody, and that they should, orally in unison, repeat the sentence after your reading. Direct them to follow your example when they parrot each sentence.

 Go to the **Reading Studio** for additional support in developing fluency.

Part IV

In the stormy east wind straining,
The pale yellow woods were waning,
120 The broad stream in his banks complaining,
　　Heavily the low sky raining
　　　　Over towered Camelot;
　　Down she came and found a boat
　　Beneath a willow left afloat,
125 And round about the prow she wrote
　　　　The Lady of Shalott.

　　And down the river's dim expanse
　　Like some bold seër in a trance,
　　Seeing all his own mischance—
130 With a glassy countenance
　　　　Did she look to Camelot.

NOTICE & NOTE

ANALYZE MOOD

Annotate: In lines 118–153, mark instances of imagery and sound devices.

Analyze: How do these images and sound devices help convey a tragic mood?

128 seër (sē´ər): someone who can see into the future; a prophet.

129 mischance: misfortune; bad luck.

The Lady of Shalott   621

TEACH

ANALYZE MOOD

Remind students that poets often create the moods of different passages through the use of strong images and sound devices like alliteration. (**Answer:** *The straining wind, the waning wood, the complaining stream, the low sky, the willow, the rain, the night, and the falling leaves all reinforce the approaching death of the Lady of Shalott, creating a mood of tragic finality. The repetition of soft l and s sounds reinforces the image of her sailing slowly down the river.*)

ENGLISH LEARNER SUPPORT

Use Visual and Contextual Support   Help students picture the scene described in the first two stanzas of Part IV of the poem. Slowly read each line one at a time. Pause after each line to allow students time to reflect on the imagery the author develops. Instruct students to sketch a picture of what they see as you continue reading. Place students in small groups to share and discuss their pictures. Help students use words from the poem to label their pictures.   **SUBSTANTIAL**

TO CHALLENGE STUDENTS . . .

Analyze Symbols   Place students in pairs or small groups. Direct them to identify all the major symbols within the poem. (*Examples: Camelot, the Island, the Lady, the Web, the Loom, the Mirror, Sir Lancelot*) From this list, each group should highlight words and phrases in the poem that describe those symbols. Then, direct students to use those notes to identify what each symbol represents from a more-abstract perspective. Challenge them to write a short description of how the words and phrases used by Tennyson clarify what each object represents, as well as how each of those symbols connect to form an overall allegorical picture.

TEACH

ANALYZE ALLEGORY

Explain to students that allegorical poems often express multiple meanings or represent multiple abstract ideas. (**Answer:** *The wording used to describe her death detailed the end as coming on slowly, taking a long time to finally put an end to her loneliness. The poet may have been expressing how women, when not given what they need, wither and die—and do so willingly so as to be free.*)

ENGLISH LEARNER SUPPORT

Recognize Symbolism Place students in pairs or small groups, directing them to reread lines 136–139 silently. Ask them to complete these thoughts: *When I think of the color white, I think of _____; A gentle breeze makes me think of _____; After the leaves fall off the trees, _____.* Then, ask students what these images might represent on a deeper, or more abstract, level by completing this sentence frame: *When the author wrote about _____, I think he really was talking about _____.* (Example: *When the author wrote about snowy white and falling leaves, I think he really was talking about the autumn and winter seasons, which is a time when everything dies.*) **MODERATE**

 **NOTICE & NOTE**

> And at the closing of the day
> She loosed the chain, and down she lay;
> The broad stream bore her far away,
> 135   The Lady of Shalott.
>
> Lying, robed in snowy white
> That loosely flew to left and right—
> The leaves upon her falling light—
> Through the noises of the night
> 140   She floated down to Camelot;
> And as the boat-head wound along
> The willowy hills and fields among,
> They heard her singing her last song,
>   The Lady of Shalott.
>
> 145 Heard a carol, mournful, holy,
> Chanted loudly, chanted lowly,
> Till her blood was frozen slowly,
> And her eyes were darkened wholly,
>   Turned to towered Camelot.
> 150 For ere she reached upon the tide
> The first house by the waterside,
> Singing in her song she died,
>   The Lady of Shalott.
>
> Under tower and balcony,
> 155 By garden wall and gallery,
> A gleaming shape she floated by,
> Dead-pale between the houses high,
>   Silent into Camelot.
> Out upon the wharfs they came,
> 160 Knight and burgher, lord and dame,
> And round the prow they read her name,
>   *The Lady of Shalott.*
>
> Who is this? and what is here?
> And in the lighted palace near
> 165 Died the sound of royal cheer;
> And they crossed themselves for fear,
>   All the knights at Camelot:
> But Lancelot mused a little space;
> He said, "She has a lovely face;
> 170 God in his mercy lend her grace,
>   The Lady of Shalott."

ANALYZE ALLEGORY
Annotate: Mark details about the Lady of Shalott's death in lines 145–153.
Interpret: What idea might be suggested by her death?

150 ere (âr): before.

160 burgher: a middle-class citizen of a town.

622   Unit 5

APPLYING ACADEMIC VOCABULARY

❑ abandon   confine   ❑ conform   ❑ depress    reluctance

Write and Discuss Have students turn to a partner to discuss the following questions. Guide students to include the Academic Vocabulary words *confine* and *reluctance* in their responses. Ask volunteers to share their responses with the class.

- Describe what the Lady's life must have been like locked away in her tower.
- Explain why the Lady might have waited so long to look at the world straight on.

NOTICE & NOTE

CHECK YOUR UNDERSTANDING

Answer these questions before moving on to the **Analyze the Text** section on the following page.

1. What will set off the Lady of Shalott's curse?
   A Viewing the world without looking through her mirror
   B Falling in love with a loyal knight
   C Asking forbidden questions
   D Taking a break from weaving her tapestry

2. Before Lancelot appears in her mirror, the Lady of Shalott —
   F feels tormented by her isolation
   G enjoys spending her time weaving
   H tries to undo the curse placed on her
   J yearns to live in Camelot

3. Lines 73–90 show that Lancelot's life is different from the Lady's by —
   A contrasting his boldness with her shyness
   B contrasting the way people react to him with the way they react to her
   C contrasting his freedom with her confinement
   D contrasting the appearance of his armor with the appearance of her gown

TEACH

CHECK YOUR UNDERSTANDING

Have students answer the questions independently.

Answers:
1. A
2. G
3. C

If they answer any questions incorrectly, have them reread the text to confirm their understanding. Then they may proceed to ANALYZE THE TEXT on page 624.

ENGLISH LEARNER SUPPORT

Oral Assessment Use the following questions to assess students' comprehension and speaking skills.

1. Explain the Lady's curse. *(If she looks at the world without her mirror, she dies.)*
2. How does the Lady usually spend her day? *(weaving)*
3. What does Lancelot have that the Lady doesn't? *(freedom)* **ALL LEVELS**

APPLY

ANALYZE THE TEXT

Possible answers:

1. **DOK 2:** *The Lady is tired of living a boring and unfulfilled life with no true contact with others—and only experiencing life through the reflection of a mirror. When she sees Lancelot, she becomes infatuated with him, and sees the possibility of another, less lonely kind of life.*

2. **DOK 2:** *Yes, it is likely. If she knew that breaking the curse would mean her death, she might choose to remain in her life as it is rather than die. OR No, it is not likely. Even if the curse means death, she is tired of living vicariously through others and wants to experience life out in the world with someone as fascinating as Lancelot.*

3. **DOK 3:** *The poem's rhyme scheme is AAAABCCCB. It gives the reader a long introduction (AAAA), followed by an idea (B), extended information about that idea (CCC), and a connection back to the idea (B). This rhyme scheme brings the reader around and through the experience of the poem just like a song would.*

4. **DOK 3:** *There are multiple images and symbols in the poem that speak directly to the experience of women in Victorian England. The island might be representative of how women were kept apart from much of society, through a lack of education and power. The mirror is also a representation of how women were kept separate—and were only allowed to look at the world through the filters of their husbands and families.*

5. **DOK 4:** *The word Camelot appears in the fifth line of each stanza; it rhymes with Shalott, which appears in the ninth line of each stanza. The repetition creates a refrain reminiscent of a ballad, giving the poem the mood of a bygone time. Additionally, the poem gives the impression that the Lady is meant to be part of Camelot, or at least part of the larger world, more so than she is while living under the curse.*

RESEARCH

Remind students that they should confirm any information they find by checking multiple websites and assessing the credibility of each one.

Extend Students may note that, during this period, women were kept to the roles of wife and mother, and their place in society was highly restricted. They were not allowed to vote, sue in a court of law, or own property. Women were considered the property of their fathers until they were married, then they became property of their husbands.

624   Unit 5

 **RESPOND**

ANALYZE THE TEXT

Support your responses with evidence from the text. 📓 **NOTEBOOK**

1. **Infer**   Why does the Lady of Shalott decide to look down upon Camelot?

2. **Draw Conclusions**   Is it likely that the Lady's actions would be different if she knew more about the curse? Why or why not?

3. **Analyze**   Identify the rhyme scheme of the poem. What effect does this rhyme scheme create?

4. **Interpret**   Which images, objects, or ideas in *The Lady of Shalott* can be seen as symbols that suggest the poem is an allegory for the experience of women in Victorian society?

5. **Notice & Note**   Consider the pattern of repetition of words in the fifth and ninth lines of each stanza. Also note that these lines are indented and usually shorter than the other lines in the stanza. How do these repeating patterns affect the mood of the poem?

RESEARCH

RESEARCH TIP
When researching the laws and rights of a group of people from history, it's best to use reliable sources that focus specifically on that time period. For this research, you should look for a resource that concentrates on the Victorian Era.

The Victorian Era was a difficult one for women. With a partner, research what life was like for women in England during this period (1832–1901).

QUESTION	ANSWER
How were women viewed during the Victorian Era?	*Many women were restricted to roles as wives and mothers. Wealthy women ran their homes, socialized, practiced decorative arts, and were educated. Middle class women kept house and may have helped in family businesses, but were not employed on their own. Upper working class women often served upper classes. Lower class women held the least-respected professions.*
What rights did women have during this time period?	*In this era, women had no more rights than children. They were not allowed to vote, sue in a court of law, or own property. Women were considered property of their fathers until they were married, then they became property of their husbands.*

Extend   If, as some critics say, this poem is an allegory for women's life in the Victorian Era, what kinds of allegories could represent what life is like for women in today's society? With a partner, discuss stories, poems, songs, or other forms of media that could be considered allegories for women's lives in today's world.

 LEARNING MINDSET

Questioning   Explain to students that asking questions means that they are open to new ideas and trying new things. Explain that to grow on a personal level, students need to develop themselves as learners, and asking questions contributes to that growth. It is essential for teachers to encourage students to feel comfortable asking questions. This is done by complimenting students' questions or thanking them for asking, as well as explaining how that mindset shows curiosity and leads to learning new things.

RESPOND

CREATE AND RECITE

Illustrate a Narrative Poem Create an illustration—such as a painting, drawing, or collage—to depict the characters, setting, and/or events of the story told in *The Lady of Shalott*.

- ❏ Decide what kind of illustration you will create.
- ❏ Reread the poem and form mental images of the characters, setting, and events in the poem.
- ❏ Choose the subject of your illustration by determining which aspect(s) of the story you relate to most strongly.
- ❏ Present your illustration to the class. Explain what inspired you or why you chose to focus on the subject of your illustration.

Recite a Poem With a group, recite part of *The Lady of Shalott* aloud for the class.

- ❏ Work with your group to select at least one stanza of the poem.
- ❏ Discuss how you will recite the section of the poem you've chosen. Will you recite it together as a choral reading? Will each member of your group speak a different part? Will you sing it like a song?
- ❏ Memorize your lines and rehearse them a few times with your group.
- ❏ Present the poem to the class, using appropriate volume, enunciation, and gestures.

Go to the **Speaking and Listening Studio** to find out more about giving a presentation.

RESPOND TO THE ESSENTIAL QUESTION

 How do you view the world?

Gather Information Review your annotations and notes on *The Lady of Shalott*. Then, add relevant information to your Response Log. As you determine which information to include, think about:

- how you view your world compared to how others might view your world
- how your mood can affect how you view the world around you
- how something such as an animal or the weather can represent something entirely unrelated

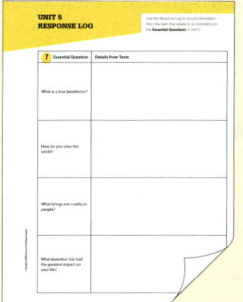

ACADEMIC VOCABULARY

As you write and discuss what you learned from the poem, be sure to use the Academic Vocabulary words. Check off each of the words that you use.

- ❏ abandon
- ❏ confine
- ❏ confirm
- ❏ depress
- ❏ reluctance

The Lady of Shalott 625

APPLY

CREATE AND RECITE

Illustrate a Narrative Poem Brainstorm with students possible objects or scenes they could illustrate from the poem. Direct them to select one item to draw, and to reread the sections of the poem corresponding to that image to help them form mental images. Challenge them to create visual representations of that image or scene, encouraging them to use various media to produce their illustrations. Select several volunteers to share their drawings, explaining why the object or scene was inspiring to them.

 For **writing support** for students at varying proficiency levels, see the **Text X-Ray** page 614D.

Recite a Poem Place students in pairs or small groups and assign each group one or more stanzas from the poem. Direct groups to discuss how they will recite their stanza for the group, and offer suggestions like individually, through choral reading, or through song. Allow them time to prepare, including memorizing lines, and rehearsing their presentations. Then, each group should recite assigned stanzas one at a time until the poem has been presented in its entirety.

RESPOND TO THE ESSENTIAL QUESTION

Allow time for students to add details from *The Lady of Shalott* to their Unit 5 Response Logs.

PLAN

from GREAT EXPECTATIONS
Novel by Charles Dickens

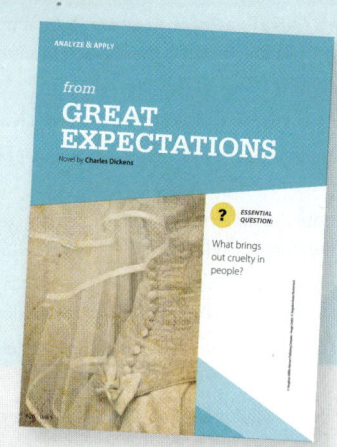

GENRE ELEMENTS
NOVEL

Tell students that a **novel** is a long work of fiction that often develops complex **plot** structures, including subplots. **Subplots** in novels connect with, and add interest to, the main plot. They are less important storylines but usually help to develop character and theme. Subplots can add complexity and tension, but there is a limit to how many subplots are effective. In this lesson, students will analyze the plot and **characterization** of a novel excerpt.

LEARNING OBJECTIVES
- Analyze plot and characterization.
- Conduct research about class structure in Victorian England.
- Write a short story about an unusual person.
- Participate in a discussion.
- Use context and knowledge to understanding idioms.
- Identify adjectives and verbs used to create imagery.
- **Language** Retell a story using indirect and direct objects.

TEXT COMPLEXITY

Quantitative Measures	**Great Expectations**	**Lexile: 880L**
Qualitative Measures	**Ideas Presented** Simple, single meaning. Much is explicit but moves to some implied meaning.	
	Structure Used Primarily explicit. Largely chronological.	
	Language Used Archaic and formal language. Complex sentence structures.	
	Knowledge Required Experiences may be less familiar to many. Historical and cultural references may make heavier demands.	

626A Unit 5

PLAN

Online

RESOURCES

- Unit 5 Response Log
- 🔊 Selection Audio
- 📖 Reading Studio: Notice & Note
- Level Up Tutorial: Setting and Mood; Character Traits
- Writing Studio: Writing Narratives
- Speaking and Listening Studio: Participating in Collaborative Discussions
- Vocabulary Studio: Using Context Clues
- ✓ *Great Expectations* Selection Test

SUMMARIES

English

In this excerpt, Pip, an orphan being raised by his sister, goes with his intimidating relative, Mr. Pumblechook, to the home of Miss Havisham. The dreary surroundings, a scornful girl, and the eccentric and creepy Miss Havisham make Pip anxious and uncomfortable. Worried that his sister might be angry if he doesn't cooperate, Pip manages to play cards with the girl to amuse Miss Havisham.

Spanish

En este pasaje, Pip, un huérfano criado por su hermana se va a la casa de la señorita Havishman con su intimidante pariente, el señor Pumblechook. Los lóbregos alrededores, una niña desdeñosa y la excéntrica y espeluznante señorita Havisham ponen a Pip ansioso e incómodo. Preocupado de que su hermana se moleste si no coopera, Pip se pone a jugar a las cartas con la niña para entretener a la señorita Havisham.

 SMALL-GROUP OPTIONS

Have students work in small groups and pairs to read and discuss the selection.

Reciprocal Teaching

- Have students read the text.
- After reading, ask students to write three to five 5 questions about the text, using these frames: *Why does Pip say ____? How does Pip describe ____? What does Pip think about ____? How do the details about ____ affect the ____? What does Pip do when ____?*
- Form teams of three students.
- Have students offer their three to five questions for group discussion.
- Encourage the group to reach consensus on the answers and find supporting text evidence.

Think-Pair-Share

- After reading the text, pose this question: *What kind of person is Pip?*
- Have students think about the question individually and make notes.
- Then, have pairs listen, discuss, and formulate a shared response to the question. Direct them to include at least two reasons to support their inference.
- Finally, have pairs share their responses with the class.

PLAN

Text X-Ray: English Learner Support
for *Great Expectations*

Use the Text X-Ray and the supports and scaffolds in the Teacher's Edition to help guide students at different proficiency levels through the selection.

INTRODUCE THE SELECTION
DISCUSS ATTITUDE AND BEHAVIOR

In this lesson, students will need to be able to discuss how a character's attitudes and behavior help reveal his or her personality.

Provide the following explanations:
- A character's *attitude* is his or her view or opinion about something.
- A character's *behavior* is the way he or she acts.

Explain to students that the way a character speaks and acts gives us clues about his or her personality.

Ask students to discuss examples of their own attitudes and behaviors. Provide sentence frames, such as: *I have a ____ attitude toward school ____ because ____. When I'm at school, my behavior is ____.*

CULTURAL REFERENCES

The following words or phrases may be unfamiliar to students:

- *be a credit unto them which brought you up by hand* (paragraph 10): honor the people who raised you
- *one-and-twenty* (paragraph 23): 21 years old
- *dressing-table* (paragraph 28): a table with a mirror and drawers for cosmetics, used while dressing and applying makeup
- *waxwork* (paragraph 31): a model, sometimes of a person, made out of wax
- *saving* (paragraph 81): except

LISTENING

Listen for Pronunciation

Remind students that they can ask for clarification if they do not understand how something is pronounced. For example: *Did you say m as in man or n as in no?*

Use the following supports with students at varying proficiency levels:

- Slowly read aloud the first sentence of paragraph 1, word by word, repeating as necessary. Then ask: *When did they have breakfast?* (eight o'clock) *What did the shopman eat?* (bread and butter) Assist students as they find and say the words from the text. **SUBSTANTIAL**
- Have pairs read sentence 1, paragraph 1, aloud to one another. Direct one speaker to slowly reread, one word at a time, while a listener copies what he or she hears. Direct listeners to ask for clarification as needed. Check their work with the text. Then, have them switch roles and repeat the activity for the second sentence. **MODERATE**
- Have partners do the previous activity. Then tell them to repeat the activity for the entire paragraph. **LIGHT**

626C Unit 5

PLAN

SPEAKING

Pronounce Long Vowel Sounds

Review with students the long vowel sound of /ē/ and /ā/. Use gestures and/or visuals to indicate where the sound occurs in the mouth.

Write the phonemes on the board for reference. Use the following supports with students at varying proficiency levels:

- Read the first sentence from paragraph 1 aloud to students, pausing to emphasize *tea* and *peas*. Instruct students to read along with you, repeating back the long vowel sound. **SUBSTANTIAL**
- Read the last sentence of paragraph 1 aloud. Ask students to identify and repeat words back to you with long /ē/ and /ā/ sounds. Ask: *Is there a pattern?* **MODERATE**
- Ask pairs to find 5 examples of each long vowel sound in the text. Instruct students to read the sentences aloud to one another, emphasizing the long vowel sound. **LIGHT**

READING

Decode Words

Remind students that paying attention to cognates, affixes, roots, and base words can help them sound out words as they read.

Use the following supports with students at varying proficiency levels:

- Provide students with a word bank of Spanish cognates: *conversation, combination, possessed*. Instruct students to copy the words, circle the base word, and underline the affixes. Have a choral reading of paragraph 1. **SUBSTANTIAL**
- Have students reread the first paragraph and note any cognates they recognize. Practice pronouncing nasal consonants /m/ and /n/ in the cognates, using gestures. **MODERATE**
- Have students repeat the previous activity in pairs, correcting each other's nasal consonant pronunciation as appropriate. **LIGHT**

WRITING

Describe Characters Using Imagery

Review the assignment on page 639 in the Student Edition. Remind students that there are many ways to describe characters, such as how they think and what they do.

Use the following supports with students at varying proficiency levels:

- Have students draw pictures of characters. Then, ask either/or questions to help students name character traits. For example: *Is your character happy or nervous?* Write student answers in complete sentences on the board and have students copy them. **SUBSTANTIAL**
- Create a Character Chart: Thoughts, Physical Traits, Speech, Actions. Instruct students to fill in their character's qualities. Provide sentence frames to begin paragraph draft: _____ (character) has/is _____ (quality). Ensure students use the verb forms correctly. **MODERATE**
- Have students draft a paragraph to describe their characters. Remind students that in English, adjectives usually come before the noun. **LIGHT**

Great Expectations **626D**

TEACH

? Connect to the ESSENTIAL QUESTION

One of the major themes in the works of Charles Dickens is that children and the poor were treated with cruelty in Victorian England. Ask students questions to stimulate conversation about the Essential Question. What is cruelty? What are some different ways that people can be cruel? What types of people might be cruel? Have students offer personal reflections of times they have experienced cruelty or been cruel. Ask students to share any lessons those experiences taught them.

ANALYZE & APPLY

from GREAT EXPECTATIONS

Novel by **Charles Dickens**

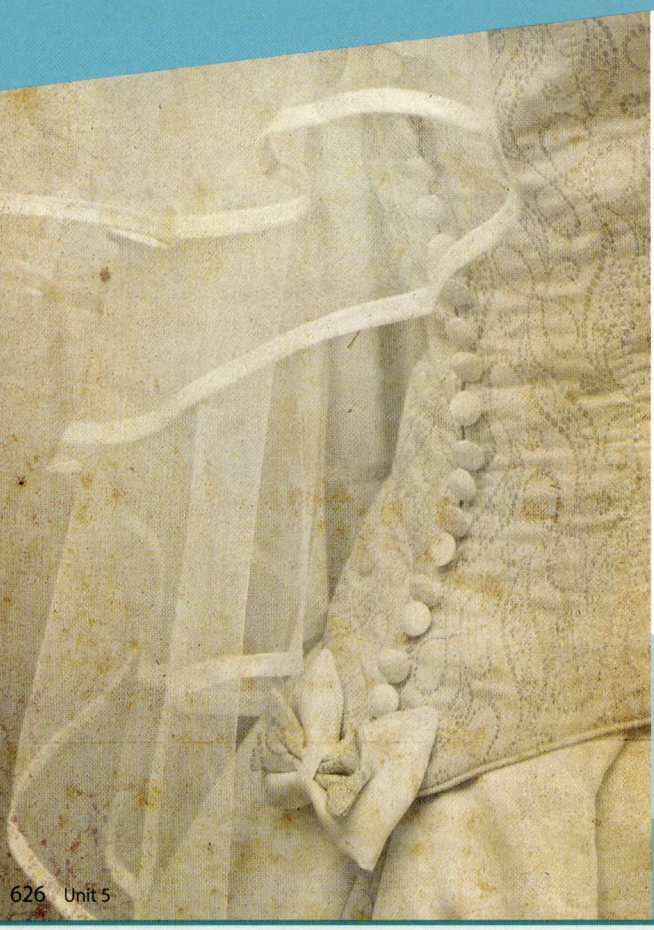

? ESSENTIAL QUESTION:

What brings out cruelty in people?

 LEARNING MINDSET

Grit Explain to students that the brain is similar to a muscle: the more you work it, the stronger it gets. Tell students that reading Charles Dickens is an opportunity to do some "heavy lifting." Encourage students to be flexible in their thinking patterns as they read because Dickensian prose will present some unfamiliar syntax and diction. Remind them that being flexible is important when working out, too. Praise students often for their effort and perseverance.

GET READY

QUICK START

Think about the strangest person you've ever met. What was this person like, and what made him or her unique? Use the chart to note interesting details about the person.

PERSON	CHARACTERISTICS

ANALYZE PLOT

Great Expectations is set in Victorian England following the Industrial Revolution. This social and historical context has an important influence on the **plot**—the series of events that occur in a literary work. During this time, class differences became more pronounced as the middle class grew wealthier while the poor sank deeper into poverty. In the excerpt you are about to read, the main character, Pip, visits the mansion of a wealthy old woman. He feels intimidated in her presence, especially when a girl who lives with her comments negatively about his lower-class background.

A **subplot** is an additional, or secondary, plot in a story. Subplots often concern the backstories of particular characters. The excerpt you will read has a subplot that relates to Miss Havisham, which is revealed in part by the old, yellowing wedding dress she wears. As you read, consider what this detail suggests about Miss Havisham's past and look for other ways the subplot is developed.

GENRE ELEMENTS: NOVEL

- is a long work of fiction
- is usually written in the first- or third-person point of view
- can develop characters and conflict more thoroughly than a short story
- often develops complex plot structures, including subplots

ANALYZE CHARACTERIZATION

Characterization is the way a writer creates and develops characters. There are four basic methods of characterization:

- The narrator may comment directly about a character, including discussion of the character's personality, social class, and economic status.
- The writer may describe the character's physical appearance.
- The writer may present the character's own thoughts, speech, and actions.
- The writer may develop the character through the thoughts, speech, and actions of other characters.

Characterization is often affected by the point of view from which a story is told, and it can have important relationships to the theme, setting, and plot. As you read the excerpt from *Great Expectations*, pay attention to the way Dickens portrays the characters in the selection. Also consider how these characterizations relate to the theme, setting, and plot of the story.

TEACH

QUICK START

Have students read the Quick Start prompt on page 627 and discuss with a partner. Encourage them to remain respectful while discussing the question. Then, have students focus on specific behaviors or traits that illustrate why they think their subject is strange.

ANALYZE PLOT

Help students understand that the **plot** is the sequence of actions and events in a literary work. Generally, plots are built around a **conflict,** or a problem or struggle between two or more opposing forces. Plots usually progress through four stages: exposition, rising action, climax, and falling action. The **exposition** provides background information and introduces the setting, characters, and conflict. During the **rising action,** the conflict becomes more intense and suspense builds as the main characters struggle to resolve their problem. The **climax** is the turning point in the plot when the outcome of the conflict becomes clear, usually resulting in a change in the characters or a solution to the conflict. The **falling action** shows the effects of the climax. The **resolution** often blends with the falling action and reveals the final outcome of the events.

Point out that a **subplot** contains all of the same elements as a plot, but is separate from, and secondary to, the main action of the story.

ANALYZE CHARACTERIZATION

Tell students that **characterization** is how the author presents and develops characters. Give students the following examples of characterization from the selection:

Direct comments by narrator: "the strangest lady I have ever seen, or shall ever see." (paragraph 29)

Character's physical appearance: "she had a long white veil dependent from her hair, and she had bridal flowers in her hair, but her hair was white." (paragraph 30)

Character's own thoughts, speech, and actions: "Broken! She uttered the word with an eager look, and with strong emphasis, and with a weird smile that had a kind of boast in it." (paragraphs 44–45)

Thoughts, speech, and actions of other characters: "Ah!" said the girl; "but you see she don't." (paragraph 9)

TEACH

CRITICAL VOCABULARY

Encourage students to read all the sentences before deciding which word best completes each one. Remind them to look for context clues that match the precise meaning of each word.

Answers:

1. *trinket*
2. *dogged*
3. *aversion*
4. *self-possessed*
5. *gilded*
6. *brooding*

■ **English Learner Support**

Use Cognates Tell students that one of the Critical Vocabulary words has Spanish cognates: aversion/aversión.
ALL LEVELS

LANGUAGE CONVENTIONS

Imagery Remind students that **imagery** is any language that is used by an author to help the reader better imagine the scene. The author's use of imagery creates vivid sensory experiences for the reader. To illustrate, give students example sentences with and without imagery, such as: "The dog ate from a garbage can," and "The scraggly hound chomped loudly on a bone it found in the stinking refuse." The imagery used by an author influences how the scene feels to the reader and highlights important details about the characters and setting.

ANNOTATION MODEL

Review with students the elements of **characterization** and **imagery.** Challenge them to mark adjectives that are used to describe characters as they read the selection. Point out that they may follow the suggested model or use their own system for marking up the selection in their write-in text. They may want to color-code their annotations by using highlighters. Their notes in the margin may include questions about ideas that are unclear or their own observations about the characters.

 **GET READY**

CRITICAL VOCABULARY

| self-possessed | trinket | aversion |
| gilded | dogged | brooding |

To see how many Critical Vocabulary words you already know, use them to complete the sentences.

1. Eva's favorite _____ was the necklace her grandmother gave her.
2. Overcome with _____ determination to complete the race, Andre made it to the finish line in record time.
3. After getting a bad stomach virus, Sarah developed a(n) _____ to strawberries.
4. Although Mary was very upset by the decision made, she was quite _____ at the meeting.
5. The featured exhibit at the museum was a collection of _____ sculptures.
6. When he heard the trip was canceled, he stormed off and sat _____ in the corner of the room.

LANGUAGE CONVENTIONS

Imagery To describe a scene or convey a mood, Dickens uses **imagery**—words and phrases that create vivid sensory experiences for the reader. Dickens frequently creates this imagery through effective use of precise adjectives and other descriptive words. As you read this selection from *Great Expectations*, pay attention to how these descriptions appeal to your senses and help you better understand the characters and setting of the story.

ANNOTATION MODEL   **NOTICE & NOTE**

As you read, mark adjectives that help to characterize Miss Havisham, Mr. Pumblechook, and others in the novel. The model shows one reader's notes about how Estella is characterized.

> She <u>seemed much older than I</u>, of course, being a girl, and <u>beautiful</u> and <u>self-possessed</u>; and she was as <u>scornful of me</u> as if she had been one-and-twenty, and a queen.

These descriptions characterize Estella as someone who is both self-assured and a bit snobby.

628 Unit 5

BACKGROUND

Charles Dickens (1812–1870) was born into a middle-class family in England. After his father went to prison, Dickens had to withdraw from school and work in a factory, an experience that deeply influenced his writing. *Great Expectations* is considered one of his finest works. The main character, Pip, is an orphan raised by his sister. In this excerpt, a relative named Mr. Pumblechook takes him to play at the house of Miss Havisham, a wealthy and eccentric old woman.

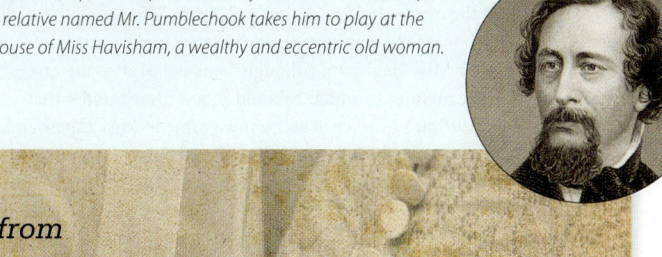

from GREAT EXPECTATIONS
Novel by Charles Dickens

SETTING A PURPOSE

As you read, allow yourself to visualize each of the scenes and characters as they are described. Consider how the author's characterization of the people in the story relates to the plot and theme of the selection.

1   Mr. Pumblechook and I breakfasted at eight o'clock in the parlor behind the shop, while the shopman took his mug of tea and hunch of bread-and-butter on a sack of peas in the front premises. I considered Mr. Pumblechook wretched company. Besides being possessed by my sister's idea that a mortifying and penitential character ought to be imparted to my diet—besides giving me as much crumb as possible in combination with as little butter, and putting such a quantity of warm water into my milk that it would have been more candid to have left the milk out altogether—his conversation consisted of nothing but arithmetic. On my politely bidding him Good morning, he said, pompously, "Seven times nine, boy?" And how should *I* be able to answer, dodged in that way, in a strange place, on an empty stomach! I was hungry, but before I had swallowed a morsel, he began a running sum that lasted all through the breakfast.

Notice & Note
Use the side margins to notice and note signposts in the text.

ANALYZE CHARACTERIZATION
Annotate: Mark details in paragraph 1 that reveal aspects of Mr. Pumblechook's character.

Analyze: Which methods of characterization does Dickens use to portray him?

Great Expectations 629

TEACH

✏️ LANGUAGE CONVENTIONS

Point out to students that the author is appealing to three different senses in paragraph 11: sight, hearing, and touch. (**Answer:** *The imagery creates a lonely and melancholy mood.*)

■ **English Learner Support**

Learn Descriptive Words Have students complete a graphic organizer like the one below to identify words from paragraph 11 that appeal to different senses.

Sight	Hearing	Touch
paved and clean	shrill	cold
empty and disused	howling	

MODERATE

✏️ **NOTICE & NOTE**

"Seven?" "And four?" "And eight?" "And six?" "And two?" "And ten?" And so on. And after each figure was disposed of, it was as much as I could do to get a bite or a sup, before the next came; while he sat at his ease guessing nothing, and eating bacon and hot roll, in (if I may be allowed the expression) a gorging and gormandising manner.

2   For such reasons I was very glad when ten o'clock came and we started for Miss Havisham's; though I was not at all at my ease regarding the manner in which I should acquit myself under that lady's roof. Within a quarter of an hour we came to Miss Havisham's house, which was of old brick, and dismal, and had a great many iron bars to it. Some of the windows had been walled up; of those that remained, all the lower were rustily barred. There was a courtyard in front, and that was barred; so, we had to wait, after ringing the bell, until some one should come to open it. While we waited at the gate, I peeped in (even then Mr. Pumblechook said, "And fourteen?" but I pretended not to hear him), and saw that at the side of the house there was a large brewery. No brewing was going on in it, and none seemed to have gone on for a long time.

3   A window was raised, and a clear voice demanded "What name?" To which my conductor replied, "Pumblechook." The voice returned, "Quite right," and the window was shut again, and a young lady came across the courtyard, with keys in her hand.

4   "This," said Mr. Pumblechook, "is Pip."

5   "This is Pip, is it?" returned the young lady, who was very pretty and seemed very proud; "come in, Pip."

6   Mr. Pumblechook was coming in also, when she stopped him with the gate.

7   "Oh!" she said. "Did you wish to see Miss Havisham?"

8   "If Miss Havisham wished to see me," returned Mr. Pumblechook, discomfited.

9   "Ah!" said the girl; "but you see she don't."

10   She said it so finally, and in such an undiscussible way, that Mr. Pumblechook, though in a condition of ruffled dignity, could not protest. But he eyed me severely—as if *I* had done anything to him!—and departed with the words reproachfully delivered: "Boy! Let your behavior here be a credit unto them which brought you up by hand!" I was not free from apprehension that he would come back to propound through the gate, "And sixteen?" But he didn't.

LANGUAGE CONVENTIONS
Annotate: Mark Dickens's use of imagery to describe the courtyard and buildings in paragraph 11.

Analyze: What mood does this imagery help create?

11   My young conductress locked the gate, and we went across the courtyard. It was paved and clean, but grass was growing in every crevice. The brewery buildings had a little lane of communication with it; and the wooden gates of that lane stood open, and all the brewery beyond stood open, away to the high enclosing wall; and all was empty and disused. The cold wind seemed to blow colder there, than outside the gate; and it made a shrill noise in howling in and out

630   Unit 5

🗨️ **ENGLISH LEARNER SUPPORT**

Use Informal Language Have students reread the first sentence in paragraph 2. Help them rephrase the sentence using informal language by providing this sentence frame: *"That's why I was glad _____, but I was not sure how _____."* (**Possible answer:** *That's why I was glad when we left for Miss Havisham's house, but I was not sure how I should behave there.*)

MODERATE

at the open sides of the brewery, like the noise of wind in the rigging of a ship at sea.

12 She saw me looking at it, and she said, "You could drink without hurt all the strong beer that's brewed there now, boy."

13 "I should think I could, miss," said I, in a shy way.

14 "Better not try to brew beer there now, or it would turn out sour, boy, don't you think so?"

15 "It looks like it, miss."

16 "Not that anybody means to try," she added, "for that's all done with, and the place will stand as idle as it is, till it falls. As to strong beer, there's enough of it in the cellars already, to drown the Manor House."

17 "Is that the name of this house, miss?"

18 "One of its names, boy."

19 "It has more than one, then, miss?"

20 "One more. Its other name was Satis; which is Greek, or Latin, or Hebrew, or all three—or all one to me—for enough."

21 "Enough House!" said I: "that's a curious name, miss."

22 "Yes," she replied; "but it meant more than it said. It meant, when it was given, that whoever had this house, could want nothing else. They must have been easily satisfied in those days, I should think. But don't loiter, boy."

23 Though she called me "boy" so often, and with a carelessness that was far from complimentary, she was of about my own age. She seemed much older than I, of course, being a girl, and beautiful and self-possessed; and she was as scornful of me as if she had been one-and-twenty, and a queen.

24 We went into the house by a side door—the great front entrance had two chains across it outside—and the first thing I noticed was, that the passages were all dark, and that she had left a candle burning there. She took it up, and we went through more passages and up a staircase, and still it was all dark, and only the candle lighted us.

25 At last we came to the door of a room, and she said, "Go in."

26 I answered, more in shyness than politeness, "After you, miss."

27 To this, she returned: "Don't be ridiculous, boy; I am not going in." And scornfully walked away, and—what was worse—took the candle with her.

28 This was very uncomfortable, and I was half afraid. However, the only thing to be done being to knock at the door, I knocked, and was told from within to enter. I entered, therefore, and found myself in a pretty large room, well lighted with wax candles. No glimpse of daylight was to be seen in it. It was a dressing-room, as I supposed from the furniture, though much of it was of forms and uses then quite unknown to me. But prominent in it was a draped table with a gilded looking-glass, and that I made out at first sight to be a fine lady's dressing-table.

NOTICE & NOTE

ANALYZE CHARACTERIZATION
Annotate: Mark details in paragraphs 12–23 that characterize the girl.

Draw Conclusions: What does this passage suggest about her personality?

self-possessed
(sĕlf´pə-zĕst´) adj. having calm and self-assured command of one's faculties, feelings, and behavior.

gilded
(gĭl´dĭd) adj. covered with or having the appearance of being covered with a thin layer of gold.

Great Expectations 631

WHEN STUDENTS STRUGGLE . . .

Analyze Setting Remind students that setting plays a major role in establishing mood in a scene. Have students reread paragraph 28 and help them identify elements that establish mood, such as the absence of daylight and the wax candles. Ask students what kind of mood these elements help to create. *(dark and mysterious)*

 For additional support, go to the **Reading Studio** and assign the following Level Up tutorial: Setting and Mood.

TEACH

ANALYZE CHARACTERIZATION

Point out to students that Estella repeatedly calls Pip "boy" and that Pip gives his direct impression of her in paragraph 23. Tell students to notice Estella's description of the house as well. (**Answer:** *Estella comes across as rude, arrogant, and snobby. She calls Pip "boy" in an insulting manner and speaks dismissively about Manor House.*)

CRITICAL VOCABULARY

self-possessed: The word *possessed* indicates control, so the word *self-possessed* means being in control of oneself or being sure of one's ability.

ASK STUDENTS what other words and phrases indicate that Estella is self-possessed. (*"She seemed much older than I," "a queen"*)

gilded: The word *gilded* looks like, and is related in meaning to, the word *gold*.

ASK STUDENTS what having a gilded looking-glass might indicate about Miss Havisham. (*She is or was a wealthy lady.*)

Great Expectations 631

TEACH

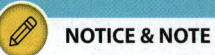

TO CHALLENGE STUDENTS...

Conduct Research It is a common misconception that white wedding gowns became popular in the Victorian era because they were symbols of bridal purity. Have students research the history of white wedding gowns in the Victorian era, and have them summarize what they learn about the cultural significance of these gowns. (White garments were actually considered status symbols for the wealthy during that period.) Ask students if their research adds to their understanding of Miss Havisham's character in any way.

29 Whether I should have made out this object so soon, if there had been no fine lady sitting at it, I cannot say. In an arm-chair, with an elbow resting on the table and her head leaning on that hand, sat the strangest lady I have ever seen, or shall ever see.

30 She was dressed in rich materials—satins, and lace, and silks—all of white. Her shoes were white. And she had a long white veil dependent from her hair, and she had bridal flowers in her hair, but her hair was white. Some bright jewels sparkled on her neck and on her hands, and some other jewels lay sparkling on the table. Dresses, less splendid than the dress she wore, and half-packed trunks, were scattered about. She had not quite finished dressing, for she had but one shoe on—the other was on the table near her hand—her veil was but half arranged, her watch and chain were not put on, and some lace for her bosom lay with those **trinkets**, and with her handkerchief, and gloves, and some flowers, and a Prayer-book, all confusedly heaped about the looking-glass.

31 It was not in the first few moments that I saw all these things, though I saw more of them in the first moments than might be supposed. But, I saw that everything within my view which ought to be white, had been white long ago, and had lost its luster and was faded and yellow. I saw that the bride within the bridal dress had withered like the dress, and like the flowers, and had no brightness left but the brightness of her sunken eyes. I saw that the dress had been put upon the rounded figure of a young woman, and that the figure upon which it now hung loose, had shrunk to skin and bone. Once, I had been taken to see some ghastly waxwork at the Fair, representing I know not what impossible personage lying in state. Once, I had been taken to one of our old marsh churches to see a skeleton in the ashes of a rich dress, that had been dug out of a vault under the church pavement. Now, waxwork and skeleton seemed to have dark eyes that moved and looked at me. I should have cried out, if I could.

32 "Who is it?" said the lady at the table.
33 "Pip, ma'am."
34 "Pip?"
35 "Mr. Pumblechook's boy, ma'am. Come—to play."
36 "Come nearer; let me look at you. Come close."
37 It was when I stood before her, avoiding her eyes, that I took note of the surrounding objects in detail, and saw that her watch had stopped at twenty minutes to nine, and that a clock in the room had stopped at twenty minutes to nine.
38 "Look at me," said Miss Havisham. " You are not afraid of a woman who has never seen the sun since you were born?"
39 I regret to state that I was not afraid of telling the enormous lie comprehended in the answer "No."

NOTICE & NOTE

ANALYZE CHARACTERIZATION

Annotate: In paragraphs 30 and 31, mark repeated words used to describe Miss Havisham and her dress.

Analyze: What does Dickens emphasize through the use of repetition in this description?

trinket
(trĭng´kĭt) *n.* a small ornament, such as a piece of jewelry.

Great Expectations 633

TEACH

ANALYZE CHARACTERIZATION

Point out to students that repetition can be used both to contrast elements and to highlight important details. (**Answer:** *He repeats the words* white, brightness, figure, waxwork, *and* skeleton. *This repetition emphasizes the contrast between the original appearance of Miss Havisham and her dress and their now-decayed appearance.*)

ENGLISH LEARNER SUPPORT

Use Contextual Support Point out to students the phrase "lying in state" in paragraph 31. In the consumable edition, have students underline the phrase "lying in state" in paragraph 31. Ask pairs to circle the context clues that help them derive meaning. As a class, discuss the meaning of the context clues such as *ghastly, skeleton,* and *vault.* Ask students what they think the phrase might mean based on these clues. Guide them to understand that the phrase means to be "placed on view before burial."

MODERATE/LIGHT

WHEN STUDENTS STRUGGLE...

Understand Characterization To help students keep track of the characters in the story so far, ask them to complete a graphic organizer like the one below, listing each character and descriptive words from the text.

Character	Description

 For additional support, go to the **Reading Studio** and assign the following **Level Up tutorial: Character Traits**.

CRITICAL VOCABULARY

trinket: The word *trinket* normally indicates that something is either small or of little value.

ASK STUDENTS which items on Miss Havisham's dressing table Pip would have considered trinkets. (*the jewels, watch and chain*)

Great Expectations **633**

TEACH

ANALYZE PLOT

Point out to students that Miss Havisham's mannerisms in paragraphs 40–45 are melodramatic and that she seems to want to draw attention to what she has been through. (**Answer:** *A man she was supposed to marry may have abandoned her.*)

■ **English Learner Support**

Use Graphic Organizers to Enhance Comprehension Remind students that adjectives and adverbs are words that modify other words. Provide students with a table that lists nouns and verbs from paragraph 45. Have students complete the table by writing the adjectives and adverbs that modify each word.

Noun	Verb	Adjective	Adverb
look		eager	
emphasis		strong	
smile		weird	
	took		slowly

MODERATE

CRITICAL VOCABULARY

dogged: The word *dogged* comes from the image of a dog's persistence when it tries to get or keep something it wants.

ASK STUDENTS what synonym for *dogged* is found in paragraph 50. *(obstinate)*

634 Unit 5

NOTICE & NOTE

40 "Do you know what I touch here?" she said, laying her hands, one upon the other, on her left side.
41 "Yes, ma'am." (It made me think of the young man.)
42 "What do I touch?"
43 "Your heart."
44 "Broken!"
45 She uttered the word with an <u>eager look</u>, and with <u>strong emphasis</u>, and with a <u>weird smile</u> that had a kind of <u>boast</u> in it. <u>Afterwards, she kept her hands there for a little while, and slowly took them away as if they were heavy.</u>

ANALYZE PLOT
Annotate: Mark details in paragraph 45 that describe how Miss Havisham delivers her remark about her heart.

Predict: Based on this remark and the way Miss Havisham is dressed, what do you predict the novel will reveal about her past?

46 "I am tired," said Miss Havisham. "I want diversion, and I have done with men and women. Play."
47 I think it will be conceded by my most disputatious reader, that she could hardly have directed an unfortunate boy to do anything in the wide world more difficult to be done under the circumstances.
48 "I sometimes have sick fancies," she went on, "and I have a sick fancy that I want to see some play. There, there!" with an impatient movement of the fingers of her right hand; "play, play, play!"
49 For a moment, with the fear of my sister's working me before my eyes, I had a desperate idea of starting round the room in the assumed character of Mr. Pumblechook's chaise-cart. But, I felt myself so unequal to the performance that I gave it up, and stood looking at Miss Havisham in what I suppose she took for a **dogged** manner, inasmuch as she said, when we had taken a good look at each other:

dogged
(dô´gĭd, dŏg´ĭd) *adj.* stubbornly persevering; tenacious.

50 "Are you sullen and obstinate?"
51 "No, ma'am, I am very sorry for you, and very sorry I can't play just now. If you complain of me I shall get into trouble with my sister, so I would do it if I could; but it's so new here, and so strange, and so fine—and melancholy—" I stopped, fearing I might say too much, or had already said it, and we took another look at each other.
52 Before she spoke again, she turned her eyes from me, and looked at the dress she wore, and at the dressing-table, and finally at herself in the looking-glass.
53 "So new to him," she muttered, "so old to me; so strange to him, so familiar to me; so melancholy to both of us! Call Estella."
54 As she was still looking at the reflection of herself, I thought she was still talking to herself, and kept quiet.
55 "Call Estella," she repeated, flashing a look at me. "You can do that. Call Estella. At the door."
56 To stand in the dark in a mysterious passage of an unknown house, bawling Estella to a scornful young lady neither visible nor responsive, and feeling it a dreadful liberty so to roar out her name, was almost as bad as playing to order. But, she answered at last, and her light came along the dark passage like a star.
57 Miss Havisham beckoned her to come close, and took up a jewel from the table, and tried its effect upon her fair young bosom and

634 Unit 5

IMPROVE READING FLUENCY

Targeted Passage Remind students that a comma is commonly used to indicate a pause. Have students read paragraphs 49–50 aloud, pausing at each comma. Point out that they should also pause at other punctuation marks, such as periods and colons. Make sure they use appropriate intonation when reading the question in paragraph 50.

 Go to the **Reading Studio** for additional support in developing fluency.

against her pretty brown hair. "Your own, one day, my dear, and you will use it well. Let me see you play cards with this boy."

58 "With this boy! Why, he is a common laboring-boy!"

59 I thought I overheard Miss Havisham answer—only it seemed so unlikely—"Well? You can break his heart."

60 "What do you play, boy?" asked Estella of myself, with the greatest disdain.

61 "Nothing but beggar my neighbor, Miss."

62 "Beggar him," said Miss Havisham to Estella. So we sat down to cards.

63 It was then I began to understand that everything in the room had stopped, like the watch and the clock, a long time ago. I noticed that Miss Havisham put down the jewel exactly on the spot from which she had taken it up. As Estella dealt the cards, I glanced at the dressing-table again, and saw that the shoe upon it, once white, now yellow, had never been worn. I glanced down at the foot from which the shoe was absent, and saw that the silk stocking on it, once white, now yellow, had been trodden ragged. Without this arrest of everything, this standing still of all the pale decayed objects, not even the withered bridal dress on the collapsed form could have looked so like grave-clothes, or the long veil so like a shroud.

64 So she sat, corpse-like, as we played at cards; the frillings and trimmings on her bridal dress, looking like earthy paper. I knew nothing then of the discoveries that are occasionally made of bodies buried in ancient times, which fall to powder in the moment of being distinctly seen; but, I have often thought since, that she must have looked as if the admission of the natural light of day would have struck her to dust.

65 "He calls the knaves, Jacks, this boy!" said Estella with disdain, before our first game was out. "And what coarse hands he has! And what thick boots!"

66 I had never thought of being ashamed of my hands before; but I began to consider them a very indifferent pair. Her contempt for me was so strong, that it became infectious, and I caught it.

67 She won the game, and I dealt. I misdealt, as was only natural, when I knew she was lying in wait for me to do wrong; and she denounced me for a stupid, clumsy laboring-boy.

68 "You say nothing of her," remarked Miss Havisham to me, as she looked on. "She says many hard things of you, yet you say nothing of her. What do you think of her?"

69 "I don't like to say," I stammered.

70 "Tell me in my ear," said Miss Havisham, bending down.

71 "I think she is very proud," I replied, in a whisper.

72 "Anything else?"

73 "I think she is very pretty."

74 "Anything else?"

AHA MOMENT

Notice & Note: Underline the sentence in paragraph 63 that expresses Pip's realization.

Draw Conclusions: What does this realization help us understand about the subplot involving Miss Havisham?

Great Expectations 635

APPLYING ACADEMIC VOCABULARY

 abandon   ✓ confine    conform    depress   ✓ reluctance

Write and Discuss Have students turn to a partner to discuss the following questions. Guide students to include the Academic Vocabulary words *confine* and *reluctance* in their responses. Ask volunteers to share their responses with the class.

- Why has Miss Havisham **confined** herself to her house for many years?
- What accounts for Pip's **reluctance** when Miss Havisham asks him to play?

TEACH

 ANALYZE PLOT

Ask students to consider what Miss Havisham might want to do with the information she gets from her line of questioning. Remind them of Miss Havisham's previous comment to Estella that Estella could break Pip's heart. **(Answer:** *She seems to enjoy Estella's disdainful treatment of him, and she may want to see Estella break his heart as hers was broken.)*

CRITICAL VOCABULARY

aversion: The root *vers-*, means "to turn," and the prefix *a-*, means "away," so *aversion* indicates a turning away from something.

ASK STUDENTS why Estella looked at Pip with extreme aversion. *(She thinks he is stupid and socially beneath her.)*

brooding: The word *brooding* originally meant sitting on eggs to hatch them, so it came to mean incubating something in one's mind.

ASK STUDENTS what Miss Havisham might have been brooding about. *(her wedding that never took place or her plans for Pip and Estella)*

636   Unit 5

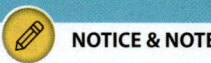 **NOTICE & NOTE**

aversion
(ə-vûr´zhən) *n.* a fixed, intense dislike; repugnance.

ANALYZE PLOT
Annotate: Reread paragraphs 68–80. Mark Miss Havisham's questions to Pip.

Infer: Why do you think Miss Havisham wants to know how Pip feels about Estella?

brooding
(broo´dĭng) *adj.* thinking about something moodily.

75 "I think she is very insulting." (She was looking at me then with a look of supreme **aversion**.)
76 "Anything else?"
77 "I think I should like to go home."
78 "And never see her again, though she is so pretty?"
79 "I am not sure that I shouldn't like to see her again, but I should like to go home now."
80 "You shall go soon," said Miss Havisham aloud. "Play the game out."
81 Saving for the one weird smile at first, I should have felt almost sure that Miss Havisham's face could not smile. It had dropped into a watchful and **brooding** expression—most likely when all the things about her had become transfixed— and it looked as if nothing could ever lift it up again. Her chest had dropped, so that she stooped; and her voice had dropped, so that she spoke low, and with a dead lull upon her; altogether, she had the appearance of having dropped, body and soul, within and without, under the weight of a crushing blow.
82 I played the game to an end with Estella, and she beggared me. She threw the cards down on the table when she had won them all, as if she despised them for having been won of me.
83 "When shall I have you here again?" said Miss Havisham. "Let me think."
84 I was beginning to remind her that today was Wednesday, when she checked me with her former impatient movement of the fingers of her right hand.
85 "There, there! I know nothing of days of the week; I know nothing of weeks of the year. Come again after six days. You hear?"
86 "Yes, ma'am."
87 "Estella, take him down. Let him have something to eat, and let him roam and look about him while he eats. Go, Pip."
88 I followed the candle down, as I had followed the candle up, and she stood it in the place where we had found it. Until she opened the side entrance, I had fancied, without thinking about it, that it must necessarily be nighttime. The rush of the daylight quite confounded me, and made me feel as if I had been in the candlelight of the strange room many hours.
89 "You are to wait here, you boy," said Estella; and disappeared and closed the door.

636   Unit 5

TO CHALLENGE STUDENTS...

Analyze Theme   One major theme that runs through many of Charles Dickens's works is *isolation*. Have students discuss in pairs or small groups how the theme of isolation applies to the three main characters in this selection. Have each group or pair focus on one of the characters. Suggest that students should consider how this theme affects the development of Dickens's characters and how it reflects Dickens' view of society. After groups have discussed the theme, have them report their conclusions to the class.

NOTICE & NOTE

CHECK YOUR UNDERSTANDING

Answer these questions before moving on to the **Analyze the Text** section on the following page.

1. What surprises Mr. Pumblechook when he arrives with Pip at Miss Havisham's house?

   A Pip shows poor manners when Estella greets them.

   B Estella doesn't want him to come inside the house.

   C Miss Havisham doesn't come down to say hello.

   D Estella is much prettier than he remembered.

2. What does Pip find most strange about Miss Havisham when he meets her?

   F She is very thin.

   G She is only wearing one shoe.

   H She is dressed in a wedding gown.

   J She doesn't seem to recognize him.

3. Why is Estella scornful toward Pip?

   A He is unable to play by himself.

   B He stares too much at Miss Havisham.

   C He is very shy and quiet.

   D He comes from a lower-class family.

Great Expectations 637

TEACH

CHECK YOUR UNDERSTANDING

Have students answer the questions independently.

Answers:

1. B
2. H
3. D

If they answer any questions incorrectly, have them reread the text to confirm their understanding. Then they may proceed to ANALYZE THE TEXT on page 638.

ENGLISH LEARNER SUPPORT

Oral Assessment Use the following questions to assess students' comprehension and speaking skills:

1. Does Estella let Mr. Pumblechook come inside? *(no)*

2. Miss Havisham is wearing _____. *(a wedding gown)*

3. Is Estella rude to Pip? *(yes)* **ALL LEVELS**

Great Expectations **637**

APPLY

ANALYZE THE TEXT

Possible answers:

1. **DOK 2:** *They may expect that Miss Havisham will reward Pip or provide some benefit to his family.*

2. **DOK 3:** *He relies on physical descriptions of her. Students might respond that this method is effective because it gives such a startling and memorable impression of her; others might feel that we learn too little of her thoughts and feelings.*

3. **DOK 3:** *Because she is so obsessed about her failed wedding plans and a man who broke her heart, she may encourage Estella to be cruel to Pip and break his heart.*

4. **DOK 2:** *Students may predict that Pip will fall in love with Estella.*

5. **DOK 4:** *He realizes that there are differences between the hands of upper- and lower-class people, and that his hands identify him as belonging to the lower class.*

RESEARCH

Tell students that every source has a potential bias. To detect bias, have students consider which facts authors choose to highlight, as well as the context in which the source was written.

Extend Inform students that they may already be familiar with some of Dickens' other works, such as *A Christmas Carol*. Ask students to look for another work by Dickens written from a first-person point of view. (Only one other major novel by Dickens, *David Copperfield*, is written from this point of view.)

RESPOND

ANALYZE THE TEXT

Support your responses with evidence from the text. NOTEBOOK

1. **Interpret** In paragraph 10, Mr. Pumblechook says to Pip, "Let your behavior here be a credit unto them which brought you up by hand!" What does this remark suggest about why Pip's family agreed to send him to visit Miss Havisham?

2. **Evaluate** What method of characterization does Dickens rely on most in his characterization of Miss Havisham? Is his use of this method effective? Explain why or why not.

3. **Draw Conclusions** Dickens introduces the subplot involving Miss Havisham's past through clues such as the yellowed wedding dress and her comment about her broken heart. How might this subplot relate to the events of this excerpt? Cite details in your response.

4. **Predict** Miss Havisham tells Pip to return in six days. What do you predict will happen on his future visits to her house?

5. **Notice & Note** In paragraph 66, Pip says that for the first time he feels ashamed of his hands. What has his experience in this wealthy household made him realize about himself?

RESEARCH

RESEARCH TIP
As you research, pay attention whenever you notice that sources disagree on certain points. Try to find out why they disagree and which source, if any, has the most accurate information.

Class differences are an important theme of *Great Expectations*. Conduct research on the class structure of Victorian England and note how this aligns with the excerpt you read from the novel. Use a chart like the one below to make your notes.

CLASS IN VICTORIAN ENGLAND	EXAMPLES FROM THE TEXT
It was common for children to be put to work in Victorian England.	*Pip's coarse hands and thick boots suggest that he has had to work hard even as a young boy.*

Extend Research some of Charles Dickens's other books, paying special attention to themes that are commonly explored in his writing. How might this information help you better understand the selection from *Great Expectations*?

 LEARNING MINDSET

Questioning Tell students that asking questions is one of the most important ways we learn new information. Asking questions means we are curious and open to new ideas. Help students get comfortable with asking questions by praising them each time they ask a question. When students get stuck, encourage them to ask questions to get "unstuck."

CREATE AND DISCUSS

Write a Story Write a short story about the most unusual person you've ever met. Use characterization to help your readers understand why this person is unusual.

- ❏ Describe what he or she looks like.
- ❏ Describe several of the person's most prominent personality traits.
- ❏ Use dialogue to bring the characters in your story to life.
- ❏ Include imagery to help your readers imagine the people, places, and events in the story.

Discuss People are often considered unusual when they behave in ways that fall outside of social norms or expectations. In a small group, discuss what kinds of behavior fall outside of the social norms of today's society. As you discuss, think about how Miss Havisham's behavior would be considered outside of the social norms of her day.

- ❏ Think about fashions that are accepted as normal in current society.
- ❏ Discuss what defines "normal" behavior. Make sure each member of your group has a chance to share his or her thoughts.
- ❏ Consider how the definition of "normal" changes over time, and discuss both the positive and negative results of living a life that others might believe to be strange or unique.

RESPOND TO THE ESSENTIAL QUESTION

 What brings out cruelty in people?

Gather Information Review your annotations and notes on *Great Expectations*. Then, add relevant information to your Response Log. As you determine which information to include, think about:

- a person's history and how this affects their decisions
- the times you have been or been tempted to be cruel and what motivated you
- the times when someone has been cruel to you and what might have motivated that person

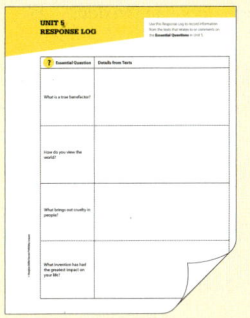

RESPOND

Go to **Writing Narratives** in the **Writing Studio** for more help writing a short story.

Go to **Participating in Collaborative Discussions** in the **Speaking and Listening Studio** for more help.

ACADEMIC VOCABULARY
As you write and discuss what you learned from *Jane Eyre*, be sure to use the Academic Vocabulary words. Check off each of the words that you use.

- ❏ abandon
- ❏ confine
- ❏ conform
- ❏ depress
- ❏ reluctance

Great Expectations 639

APPLY

CREATE AND DISCUSS

Write a Story Remind students of the elements of **plot** and have them incorporate these elements into their stories. Encourage them to refer to the four methods of **characterization** on page 627 and use some or all of these methods as they describe each character in their stories.

Discuss Encourage students to ask questions of other group members, but remind them to keep their questions constructive and respectful. Tell them to be aware that there may be differences in what other students consider "normal" behavior.

 For **writing** and **speaking support** for students at varying proficiency levels, see the **Text X-Ray** on page 626D.

RESPOND TO THE ESSENTIAL QUESTION

Allow time for students to add details from *Great Expectations* to their Unit 5 Response Logs.

APPLY

CRITICAL VOCABULARY

Answers:

1. a
2. b
3. b

VOCABULARY STRATEGY:
Idioms

Answers:

1. *like a dog with a bone*
2. *teach an old dog new tricks*
3. *dogfight*
4. *gone to the dogs*
5. *let sleeping dogs lie*

 **RESPOND**

WORD BANK
self-possessed
gilded
trinket
dogged
aversion
brooding

CRITICAL VOCABULARY

Practice and Apply Select the word that correctly finishes the sentence.

1. At Laura's church, the ceilings were _____.
   a. gilded
   b. dogged

2. James found a(n) _____ at the antique store.
   a. aversion
   b. trinket

3. When Janine met Eric, he was _____ over a book in the library.
   a. self-possessed
   b. brooding

VOCABULARY STRATEGY:
Idioms

 Go to the **Vocabulary Studio: Using Context Clues** for more on idioms.

An **idiom** is a common figure of speech whose meaning is different from the literal meaning of its words. For example, the phrase "raining cats and dogs" means that it is raining heavily, not that animals are falling from the sky. A **specialized dictionary** may list common idioms and explain their origins.

Practice and Apply Complete each sentence with the idiom in the diagram that makes the most sense. Use context and your knowledge of dog behavior to help you choose the correct idiom. When you are finished, try to explain the meaning of each idiom you used.

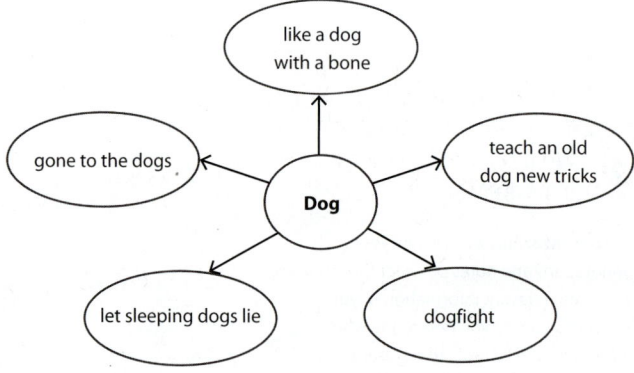

1. The possessive child clutched the toy _____.
2. I tried showing my grandfather a different way to fold his shirts, but you can't _____.
3. The combat flyer had a _____ with an enemy pilot.
4. The service wasn't great here last time, but now it has really _____.
5. Stop raking up the past; it's better to _____.

640 Unit 5

 ENGLISH LEARNER SUPPORT

Learn Idioms Help students complete the following idioms and their meanings:

1. To hit the *nail* or *ball* (circle one) on the head means to answer a question *correctly* or *incorrectly* (circle one).

2. To pull the *wool* or *wall* (circle one) over someone's eyes means to *trick* or *be honest with* (circle one) someone.

3. To be between a *rock* or *cloud* (circle one) and a hard place means to be between two *difficult* or *easy* (circle one) decisions. **ALL LEVELS**

LANGUAGE CONVENTIONS:
Imagery

Dickens carefully chose precise adjectives and other descriptive words and phrases to create vivid **imagery** in his stories. The majority of imagery in literature is visual, but imagery may also appeal to the readers' senses of smell, hearing, taste, and touch. In addition, images may re-create sensations of heat, movement, or bodily tension. Often the most effective imagery appeals to more than one sense simultaneously. The chart shows several kinds of imagery and provides examples.

KIND OF IMAGERY	SENSE TO WHICH IT APPEALS	EXAMPLE
Visual	Sight	faded, yellow clothes
Olfactory	Smell	a musty chamber
Auditory	Hearing	a shrill howling of the wind
Gustatory	Taste	sour milk
Tactile	Touch	coarse hands

Practice and Apply Read each of the following lines from *Great Expectations*. Identify the adjectives and verbs in each sentence that create imagery, and then write your own sentence using similar elements to appeal to the senses.

1. **It was paved and clean, but grass was growing in every crevice.** (paragraph 11)

2. **I entered, therefore, and found myself in a pretty large room, well lighted with wax candles.** (paragraph 28)

3. **I glanced down at the foot from which the shoe was absent, and saw that the silk stocking on it, once white, now yellow, had been trodden ragged.** (paragraph 63)

RESPOND

Go to **The Language of Narrative** in the **Writing Studio** for more on imagery.

Great Expectations 641

APPLY

LANGUAGE CONVENTIONS:
Imagery

Remind students that most descriptive language can be considered **imagery** if it relates to one of the senses: sight, hearing, smell, taste, and touch. Encourage them to study the chart on page 641 and then complete the Practice and Apply activity.

Practice and Apply Students' own sentences will vary.

Possible answers:

1. *verbs:* was, was growing; *adjectives:* paved, clean. *My sentence: It was long and wavy, but her hair fit nicely in a bun.*

2. *verbs:* entered, found; *adjectives:* large, well lighted. *My sentence: I left the room and saw her around the corner, deeply shadowed in the hall.*

3. *verbs:* glanced, saw, had been trodden; *adjectives:* absent, silk, white, yellow, ragged. *My sentence: I looked in the cluttered desk drawer and spotted my old blue pen, and I saw that the cap had been chewed to a twisted pulp.*

 ENGLISH LEARNER SUPPORT

Language Conventions Use the following supports with students at varying proficiency levels:

- Have students find other examples of **imagery** in *Great Expectations* paragraph 2. Discuss them aloud with the class. **SUBSTANTIAL**

- Direct students to describe a room in their house, using imagery that addresses all five senses. Have them work with partners to infer which room is being described. **MODERATE**

- Ask students to write several sentences describing a familiar place, using imagery to appeal to multiple senses. **LIGHT**

Great Expectations **641**

PLAN

MENTOR TEXT

THE VICTORIANS HAD THE SAME CONCERNS ABOUT TECHNOLOGY AS WE DO

Essay by Melissa Dickson

This essay serves as a **mentor text,** a model for students to follow when they come to the Unit 5 Writing Task: Write a Research Report.

GENRE ELEMENTS
ESSAY

Tell students that **essays** can be formal, informal, serious, or humorous. All essays include a thesis statement and usually focus on one topic. The author's purpose for writing an essay is revealed through the author's word choice and style. In this lesson, students will analyze the structure of a compare-and-contrast essay and evaluate the use of visuals in the text.

LEARNING OBJECTIVES

- Analyze a compare and contrast essay and evaluate multimodal texts.
- Conduct research about the effects of smartphones and social media on teenagers.
- Write an op-ed.
- Discuss and respond to op-eds.
- Use synonyms and antonyms.
- Use a variety of sentence structures.
- **Language** Use newly acquired vocabulary to describe images.

TEXT COMPLEXITY

Quantitative Measures	The Victorians Had the Same Concerns About Technology as We Do	Lexile: 1240L
Qualitative Measures	**Ideas Presented** Much is explicit but moves to some implied meaning.	
	Structures Used Complex, but mostly explicit. Exhibits traits of compare-and-contrast argument.	
	Language Used Increased academic, unfamiliar, and domain-specific words.	
	Knowledge Required Explores complex ideas.	

642A Unit 5

PLAN

Online Ed

RESOURCES

- Unit 5 Response Log
- Selection Audio
- Reading Studio: Notice & Note
- Level Up Tutorial: Reading Graphic Aids; Primary and Secondary Sources
- Writing Studio: Writing Arguments
- Speaking and Listening Studio: Participating in Collaborative Discussions
- Vocabulary Studio: Synonyms and Antonyms
- Grammar Studio: Module 4: Lesson 5: Sentence Structure
- "The Victorians Had the Same Concerns About Technology as We Do" Selection Test

SUMMARIES

English
In this essay, Melissa Dickson discusses the consequences of new technology on human interaction, and compares peoples' responses to changing technology through the ages.

Spanish
En este ensayo, Melissa Dickson discute las consecuencias de la nueva tecnología en las interacciones humanas y compara las respuestas de las personas con respecto a los cambios de la tecnología a través de los años.

SMALL-GROUP OPTIONS

Have students work in small groups and pairs to read and discuss the selection.

Jigsaw with Experts
- Divide the text into three parts, paragraphs 1–5; 6–9, and 10–14.
- Have students count off, or assign students a numbered section.
- After reading the text, have students form groups with other students who read the same section. Each expert group should discuss its section. Encourage them to use Academic Vocabulary.
- Then, have students form new groups with a representative from each section. These groups should discuss all the sections and the selection as a whole.

Pinwheel Discussion
- Arrange students in a group of eight with four students seated facing in and four students seated facing out.
- After reading two or three paragraphs of the selection, pose questions to students for discussion. For example: *Do you agree or disagree with the author's claim? Why?*
- Students in the inner circle remain stationary throughout the discussion. Students in the outer circle move to their right after discussing each question.

Victorians Had the Same Concerns About Technology as We Do **642B**

PLAN

 **Text X-Ray: English Learner Support**
for "The Victorians Had the Same Concerns About Technology as We Do"

Use the Text X-Ray and the supports and scaffolds in the Teacher's Edition to help guide students at different proficiency levels through the selection.

INTRODUCE THE SELECTION
DISCUSS HUMAN INTERACTION AND BEHAVIOR

In this lesson, students will need to discuss how new technological advances affect human interaction and behavior.

Remind students of the following word/term meanings:

- *Human interaction* refers to the ways people communicate and relate to each other.
- *Behavior* refers to the way people act or what they do.

Ask students to discuss various forms of technology, such as smartphones and computers, and how these devices affect their relationships to other people. Provide sentence frames, such as: *[Form of technology] affects how I interact with others because _____. [Form of technology] has changed my behavior by _____.*

CULTURAL REFERENCES

The following words or phrases may be unfamiliar to students:

- *hubbub* (paragraph 8): a loud noise, usually caused by a lot of people talking at once
- *adverts* (paragraph 9): advertisements
- *quacks* (paragraph 9): people who claim dishonestly to have special knowledge or skill in a particular field, typically medicine
- *take for granted* (paragraph 13): assume that something is true without questioning it
- *draw . . . a line of comparison* (paragraph 14): to separate two things to tell how they are alike

LISTENING

Identify Main Idea and Supporting Details

Tell students it is important to identify the main idea and supporting details. Answering questions will help them understand the main idea and supporting details.

Use the following supports with students at varying proficiency levels:

- Read the first paragraph twice aloud. Clarify any unfamiliar words or ideas. Then, ask students yes/no questions to ensure comprehension. For example: *Do we live in the Information Age?* (Yes.) *Do people have access to a lot of information?* (Yes.) **SUBSTANTIAL**
- Read the first two paragraphs aloud. Then, ask students questions to identify the main idea and supporting details. Provide sentence frames: *The main idea is ____.* (Technology has changed, but we still worry about the same things.) *One important detail is ____.* (We are overwhelmed with information.) **MODERATE**
- Read the first two paragraphs aloud. Ask students questions such as *What is the main idea? What is one supporting detail? How do people feel about technology?* **LIGHT**

PLAN

SPEAKING

Describe Visuals

Help students use their own words to describe the images used to support the text. Guide them to connect what they see to what they read in the text. Encourage students to use vocabulary about technology.

Use the following supports with students at varying proficiency levels:

- Say a noun and point to its corresponding image in one of the visuals. Have students repeat the nouns with you. Add adjectives to the nouns and repeat the activity. **SUBSTANTIAL**
- Have partners take turns describing one of the visuals in their own words. Then, have students review the text to find other words they can add to their descriptions. **MODERATE**
- Have one partner close his or her eyes as the other partner describes one of the visuals. Then have the student open his or her eyes and look at the image and explain if what is seen is what the partner described. Have partners discuss how the image supports the text. **LIGHT**

READING

Make Connections

Help students connect what they read in the text to personal experiences or other information they have read or heard.

Use the following supports with students at varying proficiency levels:

- Read one of the claims from the essay aloud, such as the first sentence in paragraph 13. Help students use words in the claim to connect it to their own experience. Provide a sentence frame, such as: [technology students use] _____ were once new. **SUBSTANTIAL**
- Have partners reread the first five paragraphs and identify a sentence that makes a claim. Have students rephrase the claim/opinion as a question they can ask their partner. For example: *Do you feel overwhelmed by technology? Why?* **MODERATE**
- Have students identify claims and opinions as they reread text. Guide them to use connecting words and phrases, such as *since, but,* and *on the other hand* as they discuss how the ideas in the text connect to their personal experience with technology. **LIGHT**

WRITING

Write an Op-Ed

Work with students to read the writing assignment on Student Edition page 651. Review what an op-ed is.

Use the following supports with students at varying proficiency levels:

- Work with students to make a list of the effects of social media and smart phones. Students can list effects in their home language and then use translation software to write the effects in English. **SUBSTANTIAL**
- Provide sentence frames to help students craft their op-eds: *I think smartphones _____ teenagers because _____. One reason I think this is _____. Another reason is _____.* **MODERATE**
- Have students work in pairs to draft a thesis statement and list reasons. Then, have students use this information to write their op-eds independently. Have pairs meet again for a peer review. **LIGHT**

TEACH

? Connect to the ESSENTIAL QUESTION

"The Victorians Had the Same Concerns About Technology as We Do" discusses how inventions have had impacts on our lives. Melissa Dickson relates our changing world to the changes society underwent during the Victorian age, and makes the reader consider not just the way technology impacts us today, but how it has impacted society for centuries.

MENTOR TEXT

At the end of the unit, students will be asked to write an informative essay. "The Victorians Had the Same Concerns About Technology as We Do" provides a model for how writers can develop their ideas in a research report.

ANALYZE & APPLY

THE VICTORIANS HAD THE SAME CONCERNS ABOUT TECHNOLOGY AS WE DO

Essay by **Melissa Dickson**

? ESSENTIAL QUESTION:

Which invention has had the greatest impact on your life?

GET READY

QUICK START

Think about and write down the number of times per day that you use technology (e.g., smartphone, social media, Internet, mobile apps, tablets). Imagine a day without these tools. How would you describe that day? List the descriptions in your notebook and share with a partner.

ANALYZE COMPARE AND CONTRAST ESSAY

A **thesis** is an expression of the main idea or purpose of an essay. In this essay, the thesis is articulated in the title. To convince readers to accept this thesis, Melissa Dickson structures her essay as a **point-by-point comparison** of the similarities between Victorian and contemporary concerns about technology. She compares both historical periods one point at a time, instead of discussing the Victorian period first and then the contemporary period. As you read, use a chart like the one below to keep track of the main points presented and Dickson's supporting details related to both the Victorian and current perspectives on this issue.

POINT #1	POINT #2
Victorian:	Victorian:
Current:	Current:

Evaluate the essay's organizational pattern and consider whether this structure effectively serves the author's intended purpose.

EVALUATE MULTIMODAL TEXTS

A **multimodal text** strategically employs two or more modes of communication—words and visuals, for instance—to help the reader construct meaning about the content. Graphic features—such as images, charts, and maps—can play an important role in communicating an author's meaning.

Melissa Dickson reproduces two Victorian Era images in her essay, commenting directly on one of them. As you read, think about how effectively Dickson uses these images to support her ideas.

GENRE ELEMENTS: ESSAY

- has an introduction that includes the broader subject as well as a specific topic, hooks the audience, and briefly describes how the topic will be developed
- contains a thesis statement that offers some original insight on the topic
- contains well-developed body paragraphs, each with a main idea related to the writer's thesis statement or position, and tangible evidence that supports those ideas
- has a conclusion that often neatly summarizes the topic and leaves the audience with something to think about

TEACH

QUICK START

After students have had a chance to brainstorm and discuss some phrases that describe a day when they couldn't use their technology, prompt them to think about some activities they might engage in instead of using technology. Could they read a new book, learn a foreign language, catch up with an old friend, or learn a new hobby? Ask students to think about the ways inventions, technology, and innovations might cause us harm or be a detriment to our development.

ANALYZE COMPARE AND CONTRAST ESSAY

Help students understand that the **thesis** in an essay expresses the claim the writer is trying to support. Prompt students to share their ideas about the thesis in "The Victorians Had the Same Concerns About Technology as We Do" based on the title of the article. Then, let students know that in the essay, author Dickson uses **point-by-point comparison** to shed light on the similarities and differences between the ways technology is used. Review the table and let students know they can use it to keep track of the writer's key points and comparisons.

EVALUATE MULTIMODAL TEXTS

Review the definition of a **multimodal text** with students and prompt them to identify some examples they've experienced in other texts. If students have a difficult time coming up with examples, offer some suggestions, such as comic strips, posters, or articles with graphs or timelines. Ask students how they think multimodal texts help an author to convey his or her message. What are some benefits of using multimodal texts? Are there any drawbacks? Encourage students to review the Victorian era images in Dickson's essay as they read, and to jot down notes about how the images impact the way they understand the text.

TEACH

CRITICAL VOCABULARY

Encourage students to read all the sentences before deciding which words best complete each one. Remind them to look for context clues that match the precise meaning of each word.

Answers:

1. *Luddite; immersion*
2. *cacophony; forebear*
3. *sea change; pervasive*
4. *posit; underpin*

■ English Learner Support

Use Cognates Tell students that three of the Critical Vocabulary words have Spanish cognates: *immersion/inmersión, cacophony/cacofonía, Luddite/luddite.*
ALL LEVELS

LANGUAGE CONVENTIONS

Sentence Structure Review the definitions of **simple sentence** and **complex sentence** with students. Prompt students to provide examples of each type of sentence. Consider writing simple sentences on the board and asking students to revise them to form complex sentences. Then, ask them how they think different sentence structures might impact the organization and overall tone of an essay.

ANNOTATION MODEL

Tell students it is important they understand how structure and organization contribute to the essay's thesis. Remind students to look for similarities and differences in the way Victorians and present-day people use and perceive technology. Let students know that as they read, they may underline similarities and circle differences. Point out that they may follow this suggestion or use their own system for marking up the selection in their write-in text. They can want to color-code their annotations by using highlighters. Their notes in the margin may include questions about ideas that are unclear or topics they want to learn more about.

 **GET READY**

CRITICAL VOCABULARY

| forebear | pervasive | sea change | immersion |
| underpin | cacophony | posit | Luddite |

To see how many Critical Vocabulary words you already know, use them to complete the sentences.

1. Mr. Keller's _____ position on the use of online platforms in the classroom conflicted with the school's plan to engage students by offering complete _____ in new technology.

2. Amid the _____ of fireworks and the cheering crowd, he thought of his _____ who had fought for his country's independence long ago.

3. Some researchers believe a(n) _____ is taking place in the minds of young people because they have allowed social media to have a(n) _____ influence on their ideas and behaviors.

4. Ample moisture and nutrients, the scientists _____, will _____ the bacteria's ability to multiply quickly.

LANGUAGE CONVENTIONS

Sentence Structure Writers use a variety of sentence structures to express ideas clearly. Simple sentences have one main clause, while other structures include more than one clause. These clauses are connected by commas and conjunctions or by semicolons. As you read, take note of the different kinds of sentences the author uses to convey her ideas.

ANNOTATION MODEL   **NOTICE & NOTE**

As you read, notice the parallels between the use of, and attitudes toward, technology in Victorian society and today's culture. Look for details that highlight similarities and differences between the two. In the model, you can see one reader's notes about the text.

> Many of us struggle with <u>the bombardment of information</u> we receive and experience anxiety as a result of new media, which we feel <u>threaten our relationships and "usual" modes of human interaction.</u>
>
> Though the technologies may change, these fears actually have a very long history: <u>more than a century ago our forebears had the same concerns.</u>

These details show that people in both Victorian society and today's culture are concerned with how distracting technology can be and the impact it has on relationships.

644   Unit 5

BACKGROUND

Melissa Dickson completed her PhD at King's College in London in 2013. In her doctoral thesis she wrote about the tales of the *Arabian Nights,* exploring how these Middle Eastern folktales influenced British drama, fiction, poetry, travel writing, and children's literature. "The Victorians Had the Same Concerns About Technology as We Do" grew out of her involvement in a project called "Diseases of Modern Life," which investigates 19th-century cultural, literary, and medical understandings of stress, overwork, and other disorders.

THE VICTORIANS HAD THE SAME CONCERNS ABOUT TECHNOLOGY AS WE DO

Essay by Melissa Dickson

SETTING A PURPOSE

As you read, make note of the author's thesis and the supporting details she uses to develop her main ideas.

1   We live, we are so often told, in an information age. It is an era obsessed with space, time and speed, in which social media inculcates[1] virtual lives that run parallel to our "real" lives and in which communications technologies collapse distances around the globe. Many of us struggle with the bombardment of information we receive and experience anxiety as a result of new media, which we feel threaten our relationships and "usual" modes of human interaction.

2   Though the technologies may change, these fears actually have a very long history: more than a century ago our **forebears** had the same concerns. Literary, medical and cultural responses in the Victorian age to the perceived problems of stress and overwork anticipate many of the preoccupations of our own era to an extent that is perhaps surprising.

---
[1] **inculcate:** to impress (something) upon the mind of another by frequent instruction or repetition; instill.

NOTICE & NOTE

Notice & Note
Use the side margins to notice and note signposts in the text.

ANALYZE COMPARE AND CONTRAST ESSAY

Annotate: Mark details in paragraph 2 about Victorian issues that also concern people today.

Connect: What are some recent complaints about the harmful effects of new technology that you have heard about?

forebear
(fôr´bâr) *n.* a person from whom one is descended; an ancestor.

TEACH

✏️ EVALUATE MULTIMODAL TEXTS

Remind students of the definition of a **multimodal text**. Ask them to think about why the article is considered a multimodal text. (**Answer:** *The cartoon demonstrates that like smartphones, telegraphs facilitated isolation, where people could be in one room and would rather use technology than speak to each other.*)

EL ENGLISH LEARNER SUPPORT

Internalize Academic Vocabulary Write the following words on the board: *multimodal text, confine, conform*. Review each term. Ask students to write about and discuss the selection using the terms.

- Provide students with sentence frames that require vocabulary words to complete. For example: *The article is a ____ because it uses texts and visuals to support its message. Teens ____ to the use of new technology*. Tell students to write the frames in their notebooks and complete them with a vocabulary word. Have them discuss their answers in groups.
  MODERATE

- Provide students with prompts that require them to use vocabulary words in their answers. For example: *Why do people conform to the use of technology?* Tell students to write their responses and then discuss them in pairs.
  LIGHT

CRITICAL VOCABULARY

underpin: The author uses *underpin* to support her notion that technology infringes upon human interaction.

ASK STUDENTS to explain a theme that underpins the essay. (*Even though times have changed, we continue to deal with the same challenges around technology.*)

pervasive: The author uses *pervasive* to describe the impact of the printing press during the Victorian era.

ASK STUDENTS to describe some pervasive ideas that might impact the ways teens behave towards their parents. (*Most parents expect their teens to obey their rules as long as they still live at home.*)

646   Unit 5

✏️ **NOTICE & NOTE**

3   This parallel is well illustrated by the following 1906 cartoon from *Punch*, a satirical British weekly magazine:

Worrying trends, 1906.

EVALUATE MULTIMODAL TEXTS

Annotate: Mark details in paragraphs 4 and 5 that support the idea presented in the cartoon.

Analyze: Which details in the cartoon support the author's thesis?

underpin
(ŭn-dər-pĭn´) *tr.v.* to give support or substance to.

4   The caption reads: "These two figures are not communicating with one another. The lady receives an amatory² message, and the gentleman some racing results." The development of the "wireless telegraph" is portrayed as an overwhelmingly isolating technology.

5   Replace these strange contraptions with smartphones, and we are reminded of numerous contemporary complaints regarding the stunted social and emotional development of young people, who no longer hang out in person, but in virtual environments, often at great physical distance. Different technology, same statement. And it's **underpinned** by the same anxiety that "real" human interaction is increasingly under threat from technological innovations that we have, consciously or unconsciously, assimilated into daily life. By using such devices, so the popular paranoia would have it, we are somehow damaging ourselves.

Cacophony of voices

6   The 19th century witnessed the rapid expansion of the printing industry. New techniques and mass publishing formats gave rise to a far more **pervasive** periodical press, reaching a wider readership

pervasive
(pər-vā´sĭv,-zĭv) *adj.* having the quality or tendency to pervade or permeate.

---
² **amatory:** of, relating to, or expressive of love, especially romantic love.

646   Unit 5

APPLYING ACADEMIC VOCABULARY

☐ abandon   ☑ **confine**   ☑ **conform**   ☐ depress   ☐ reluctance

Write and Discuss Have students turn to a partner to discuss the following questions. Guide students to include the Academic Vocabulary words *confine* and *conform* in their responses. Ask volunteers to share their responses with the class.

- How would you feel in a situation where you were **confined** to one location for the rest of your life?
- What kinds of social norms do you and your peers **conform** to?

than ever before. Many celebrated the possibility of instant news and greater communication. But concerns were raised about the overwhelmed middle-class reader who, it was thought, lacked the discernment to judge the new mass of information critically, and so read everything in a superficial, erratic manner.

7   The philosopher and essayist Thomas Carlyle, for example, lamented the new lack of direct contact with society and nature caused by the intervention of machinery in every aspect of life. <u>Print publications were fast becoming the principal medium of public debate and influence, and they were shaping and, in Carlyle's view, distorting human learning and communications.</u>

EVALUATE MULTIMODAL TEXTS

Annotate: Mark details in paragraphs 7 and 8 that are expressed visually in the illustration called *A London Street Scene*.

Analyze: What is the significance of this illustration?

John Orlando Parry, *A London Street Scene*, 1835. © Alfred Dunhill Collection

The Victorians Had the Same Concerns About Technology as We Do   647

TEACH

EVALUATE MULTIMODAL TEXTS

Encourage students to observe and dissect "A London Street Scene." Remind students that a picture can provide information that is not explicitly stated in the text. It also can complement details explicitly stated in a text. (**Answer:** *It shows the overwhelming amount of information and news people had to sort through.*)

ENGLISH LEARNER SUPPORT

Use Accessible Language Allow students to use words in their native language as they acquire and use new vocabulary. Ask students questions that connect their own experiences to the selection, then ask them to describe their own experiences with more detail.

- Provide students with sentence frames such as the following:

  In my life, I use technology to _____.

  The selection is interesting because _____.

  I agree/disagree with the selection because _____.

  Have students complete the sentences independently. Then, have them discuss their responses with a partner. **MODERATE**

- Provide students with the following prompts: *Can you relate to any of the examples in the selection? How are the details in the selection realistic? What did you learn from the selection?* Have students complete the sentences independently. Then, have them discuss their responses with a partner or in a small group. **LIGHT**

WHEN STUDENTS STRUGGLE . . .

Use Graphic Aids Ask students to use a graphic organizer to identify the main ideas in paragraphs 7 and 8. Then, ask them to work with a partner to identify details in the image that support the ideas they noted in their graphic organizers.

Key Ideas	In My Own Words	Clues from the Image

For additional support, go to the **Reading Studio** and assign the following **Level Up tutorial: Reading Graphic Aids**.

The Victorians Had the Same Concerns About Technology as We Do   **647**

TEACH

QUOTED WORDS

Remind students it's important to pay attention to quoted words in a text because they are often used for a specific purpose. (**Answer:** By including Mill's quote, the author shows that even well-respected historians agree with her point of view. The quote shows that throughout time, historians have professed similar views, and therefore, the reader is more likely to take Dickson's own words seriously.)

ANALYZE COMPARE AND CONTRAST ESSAY

Remind students to look for patterns or signal words that indicate a comparison between Victorian and current technologies, such as *too, also, both*. Then, ask them to read paragraphs 11–13 to determine similarities or differences between the impact of technology during the Victorian age and present day. (**Answer:** *Victorians once thought their new technologies were harming them. For example, they believed the telephone was causing deafness and that gases in their underground forms of transportation were choking people to death.*)

CRITICAL VOCABULARY

cacophony: The author uses *cacophony* to describe the sound of voices in the streets.

ASK STUDENTS how a teacher might react to the cacophony of sounds from a cell phone in class? (*The teacher might ask the student with the phone to step out.*)

sea change: The author uses *sea change* to explain the shifts in the way we read and think.

ASK STUDENTS what sea changes they have witnessed in the way we do things today? (*Most people own a cell phone instead of a house phone.*)

posit: The author uses *posit* to explain the ideas Nicolas Carr introduced.

ASK STUDENTS to posit their ideas about using essays as a platform to discuss social issues. (*It is an effective way to engage the masses.*)

immersion: The author uses *immersion* to explain that nowadays, people are less likely to spend time meaningfully engaged in a text because of technology.

ASK STUDENTS what other forms of *immersion* they have heard about. (*immersion in a hobby or a summer program, travel immersion, etc.*)

648   Unit 5

NOTICE & NOTE

cacophony
(kə-kŏf´ə-nē) *n.* jarring, discordant sound; dissonance.

QUOTED WORDS
Notice & Note: Mark the quoted words in paragraph 8.

Evaluate: The author could have paraphrased John Stuart Mill's ideas, or restated the ideas in her own words. What is the effect of including Mill's exact words?

ANALYZE COMPARE AND CONTRAST ESSAY
Annotate: Mark the concern expressed in paragraph 11 about how technology changes the way we read.

Connect: How does this concern relate to a Victorian concern about technology?

sea change
(sē chānj) *n.* a marked transformation.

posit
(pŏz´ĭt) *tr.v.* to assume or put forward, as for consideration or the basis of argument.

immersion
(ĭ-mûr´zhən, -shən) *n.* the act or instance of engaging in something wholly or deeply.

648   Unit 5

---

8   The philosopher and economist John Stuart Mill heartily agreed, expressing his fears in an essay entitled "Civilisation". He thought that the **cacophony** of voices supposedly overwhelming the general public was creating:

> A state of society where any voice, not pitched in an exaggerated key, is lost in the hubbub. Success in so crowded a field depends not upon what a person is, but upon what he seems: mere marketable qualities become the object instead of substantial ones, and a man's capital and labor are expended less in doing anything than in persuading other people that he has done it. Our own age has seen this evil brought to its consummation.

9   Individual authors and writers were becoming disempowered, lost in a glutted marketplace of ideas, opinions, adverts and quacks.

Old complaints

10   The parallels with the concerns of our own society are striking. Arguments along not at all dissimilar lines have been advanced against contemporary means of acquiring information, such as Twitter, Facebook, and our constant access to the internet in general.

11   In his 2008 article, "Is Google Making Us Stupid?", journalist Nicolas Carr speculated that "we may well be in the midst of a **sea change** in the way we read and think". Reading online, he **posits**, discourages long and thoughtful **immersion** in texts in favor of a form of skipping, scanning and digressing via hyperlinks that will ultimately diminish our capacity for concentration and contemplation.

12   Writers, too, have shared Carr's anxieties. Philip Roth and Will Self, for example, have both prophesied these trends as contributing to the death of the novel, arguing that people are increasingly unused to and ill-equipped to engage with its characteristically long, linear form.

13   Of course, all old technologies were once new. People were at one point genuinely concerned about things we take for granted as perfectly harmless now. In the later decades of the 19th century it was thought that the telephone would induce deafness and that sulphurous vapors were asphyxiating passengers on the London Underground. These then-new advancements were replacing older still technologies that had themselves occasioned similar anxieties on their introduction. Plato, as his oral culture began to transition to a literary one, was gravely worried that writing itself would erode the memory.

ENGLISH LEARNER SUPPORT

Use Visual and Contextual Support   Ask students to read the page and draw their attention to the quotation by John Stuart Mill at the top. Explain we can tell these are his exact words because they are indented and italicized. Define *indentation* and *italics*. Have students explain what these words mean in their own words or by drawing a diagram. Remind students they can also identify a quote when they see quotation marks.
ALL LEVELS

14   While we cannot draw too strict a line of comparison between 19th-century attitudes to such technologies as the telegraph, train, telephone, and newspaper and our own responses as a culture to the advent of the internet and the mobile phone, there are parallels that almost argue against the **Luddite** position. As dramatically as technology changes, we, at least in the way we regard it, remain surprisingly unchanged.

NOTICE & NOTE

LANGUAGE CONVENTIONS
Annotate: Mark how the clauses of sentences in paragraph 14 are joined.

Evaluate: How do these complex sentences contribute to the author's style and tone?

Luddite
(lŭd′ĭt) *n.* one who opposes technical or technological change.

CHECK YOUR UNDERSTANDING

Answer these questions before moving on to the **Analyze the Text** section on the following page.

1 The role of the graphic features in the essay is to —

  A Emphasize the ideas expressed by the author
  B Illustrate how distracted people can be
  C Show how pervasive technology is today
  D Suggest that technology has always been in the news

2 Based on the details in the essay, the 21st century is often referred to as the Information Age because people —

  F Always share information
  G Are continually distracted by new information
  H Have access to overwhelming amounts of information
  J Are unsure which information is accurate

3 The author refers to Plato in paragraph 13 to —

  A Suggest that he believed technology should be banned
  B Show that he had concerns about technology
  C Dismiss the opinions of those who fear technology
  D Contrast ancient ideas about technology with current ones

The Victorians Had the Same Concerns About Technology as We Do   649

ENGLISH LEARNER SUPPORT

Oral Assessment Use the following questions to assess students' comprehension and speaking skills.

1. Why are the visuals in the selection important? *(They emphasize the author's ideas.)*
2. Why is today known as the Information Age? *(People have access to a lot of information.)*
3. Was Plato worried about the spread of writing? *(yes)* **ALL LEVELS**

TEACH

LANGUAGE CONVENTIONS

Remind students of the different sentence structures and ask them to define a simple versus a complex sentence. Invite students to provide an example of each type of sentence from the selection. (**Answer:** *These complex sentences illustrate the author's serious tone and help to establish a formal mood. It's clear the author is educated on the topic.*)

CHECK YOUR UNDERSTANDING

Have students answer the questions independently.

Answers:

1. *A*
2. *H*
3. *B*

If they answer any questions incorrectly, have them reread the text to confirm their understanding. Then they may proceed to ANALYZE THE TEXT on page 650.

CRITICAL VOCABULARY

Luddite: The author uses *Luddite* to describe people who may take an anti-technology stance.

ASK STUDENTS how a *Luddite* might react to the use of social media in the classroom to complete assignments? *(He or she would likely be against this approach to classwork.)*

The Victorians Had the Same Concerns About Technology as We Do   **649**

APPLY

ANALYZE THE TEXT

Possible answers:

1. **DOK 2:** *She seems skeptical of their ideas. She states "all old technologies were once new. People were at one point genuinely concerned about things we take for granted as perfectly harmless now." This suggests she isn't too worried about the implications of technology.*

2. **DOK 4:** *Dickson's use of point-by-point comparison is effective because it makes it easier for the reader to draw parallels between Victorian and present-day beliefs toward technology use. It helps the reader understand that although the concerns may be similar, the experiences with today's digital tools are quite different, and people today are likely more overwhelmed by how much information they can access.*

3. **DOK 3:** *By integrating cartoons into the essay, the author is able to help the reader create a mental picture of the role technology has had on society throughout the centuries, and effectively conveys the idea that "as dramatically as technology changes, we, at least in the way we regard it, remain surprisingly unchanged."*

4. **DOK 4:** *While technology has some detriments, the concerns people have today are not new or foreign. The author appreciates the role of technology and seems to think that in some cases, people have overreacted to new technology. The author likely believes that a balance should be struck between human relationships and access to technology.*

5. **DOK 4:** *Nicholas Carr's quotation supports the author's idea that technology is constantly changing, and with every new innovation, there are new sets of problems to address.*

RESEARCH

Discuss with students the four main ways to conduct an online search for an editorial, and prompt them to think about which options make the most sense for this project. Before students begin, consider asking them to brainstorm search terms in groups.

Connect Before students begin their pros and cons lists, ask them to refer back to their notes on what life would be like without their favorite inventions or technology. What things would they be able to do? What wouldn't they be able to do? Prompt students to think about how adolescents or teenagers in other parts of the world may live with or without some of these forms of technology.

650 Unit 5

 **RESPOND**

ANALYZE THE TEXT

Support your responses with evidence from the text. 📓 NOTEBOOK

1. **Infer** Reread paragraph 1. Does Dickson agree with the contemporary concerns she summarizes here, or does she seem skeptical of them? Cite details from anywhere in the essay to support your response.

2. **Evaluate** Is point-by-point comparison an effective format for the essay, or should Dickson have discussed the Victorian elements first and then discussed contemporary elements? Explain your response.

3. **Evaluate** Do the images Dickson chose provide good support for her essay? Why or why not?

4. **Critique** Reread paragraph 14. Does Dickson's comparison of Victorian and contemporary fears offer a convincing reason not to worry about current technological changes? Explain your opinion.

5. **Notice and Note** How does the quotation from Nicholas Carr in paragraph 11 support the author's ideas?

RESEARCH

RESEARCH TIP
The four main ways to conduct an online search for an editorial or news article are searching by keywords, subject, title, and author. A keyword search retrieves the most results because it searches for the word(s) throughout the entire catalog or database. A subject search is more focused because it looks for the word in a specific field. If you know the name of an important author or the title of an article in your area of interest, you can search specifically for them.

Go online and find editorials and other arguments on the topic of how teenagers are affected by using smartphones and social media. Analyze how authors reach similar and different conclusions on this topic, and list your findings in the chart below.

AUTHOR'S NAME	TITLE OF WORK	AUTHOR'S POSITION
Suren Ramasubbu	"Influence of Social Media on Teenagers"; The Huffington Post	The lack in self-regulation and susceptibility to peer pressure makes adolescents vulnerable to social media threats such as depression and cyberbullying.

Connect Think about how social media and other digital tools impact your life. Create a list of pros and cons associated with your access to technology. Share your lists with a partner.

650 Unit 5

WHEN STUDENTS STRUGGLE . . .

Reteaching: Evaluate Multimodal Texts Encourage students to look for multimodal texts as they research articles on the impact of social media and smartphones on teenagers. Have them use the graphic organizer to guide them.

Title and Type of Visual	Primary or Secondary Source	What the Visual Shows	What It Means

 For additional support, go to the **Reading Studio** and assign the following 📖 Level Up tutorial: **Primary and Secondary Sources**.

RESPOND

CREATE AND DISCUSS

Write an Op-Ed Analyze the different authors' perspectives and ideas from the research you previously conducted. Then, write a brief opinion editorial that conveys your position on the topic of the impact social media and smartphones have on teenagers.

- ❏ Identify a clear thesis statement. What is your position on the topic?
- ❏ Who is your audience? Will your reader understand your argument?
- ❏ Is your argument organized in a way that effectively engages the reader?
- ❏ What evidence and details have you included to support your ideas?

Analyze and Discuss Your Ideas Find a partner and take turns reading your opinion editorials to each other. Analyze each other's conclusions and discuss whether or not you agree with each other's positions.

- ❏ Does your partner have a compelling argument?
- ❏ What evidence can you point to in your partner's writing that supports his or her thesis?
- ❏ Are your partner's introduction and conclusion clear and effective?

 Go to **Writing Arguments** in the **Writing Studio** for more help with writing an op-ed.

 Go to **Participating in Collaborative Discussions** in the **Speaking and Listening Studio** for more help.

RESPOND TO THE ESSENTIAL QUESTION

 Which invention has had the greatest impact on your life?

Gather Information Review your annotations and notes on the essay. Then, add relevant information to your Response Log. As you determine which information to include, think about:

- how technology has impacted your life
- how often you access social media or your smartphone
- how your life would be different if certain technological advances had not been made

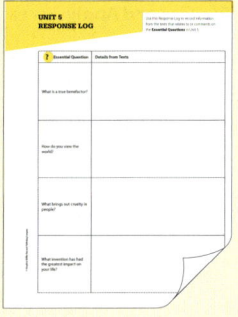

ACADEMIC VOCABULARY

As you write and discuss what you learned from the essay, be sure to use the Academic Vocabulary words. Check off each of the words that you use.

- ❏ abandon
- ❏ confine
- ❏ conform
- ❏ depress
- ❏ reluctance

APPLY

CRITICAL VOCABULARY

Answers:

1. cacophony
2. Luddite; forebear
3. underpin
4. posits; pervasive
5. sea change; immersion

VOCABULARY STRATEGY:
Synonyms and Antonyms

Practice and Apply

Answers:

1. forebear—noun; ancestor, forefather;
   My mother's forebears are from the Netherlands. My mother's ancestors are from the Netherlands.

2. underpin—verb; agree, support
   Luke's laziness underpins his poor test scores. Luke's laziness supports his poor test scores.

3. cacophony—noun; noise, racket, uproar
   The cacophony of bird noises woke up the baby. The uproar of bird noises woke up the baby.

4. sea change—noun; transformation, conversion
   By the late '90s there had been a sea change in the way people listened to music—from Walkmans® to CD players. By the late '90s there had been a transformation in the way people listened to music—from Walkmans to CD players.

5. posit—verb; hypothesize, assume
   My professor posited the bacteria would clean up the oil spill because this strain likes biofuels. My professor hypothesized the bacteria would clean up the oil spill because this strain likes biofuels.

6. immersion—noun; preoccupation, involvement, engagement
   My brother attended a Spanish-language immersion program in Barcelona. My brother attended a Spanish-language engagement program in Barcelona.

7. Luddite—noun; adversary, oppose
   My sister, the Luddite, never wants to watch films in 3D because she prefers classic back-and-white movies. My sister, the adversary, never wants to watch films in 3D because she prefers classic back-and-white movies.

652 Unit 5

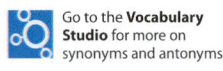 **RESPOND**

WORD BANK
forebear
underpin
pervasive
cacophony
sea change
posit
immersion
Luddite

Go to the **Vocabulary Studio** for more on synonyms and antonyms.

CRITICAL VOCABULARY

Practice and Apply Fill in the blanks with the correct words.

1. Micah's concentration was often interrupted by a(n) _____ of voices and laughter coming from downstairs.

2. Brenda considered her grandfather a(n) _____; her _____ always complained about technology.

3. Your lack of studying is likely to _____ poor scores in math class.

4. The author _____ that the _____ use of social media would ultimately cause people to feel less connected to others.

5. Some people believe video gaming will go through a(n) _____ because we will soon be able to create total _____ in virtual reality environments.

VOCABULARY STRATEGY:
Synonyms and Antonyms

Reference tools help writers understand the precise meaning of words so they can use them correctly. The thesaurus, for example, is used to find **synonyms,** or words with similar meaning, and **antonyms,** words that have opposite meaning. Take a look at this example of a thesaurus entry for the Critical Vocabulary word *pervasive.*

> **pervasive** adjective
> **synonyms:** prevalent, permeating, extensive, ubiquitous
> **antonyms:** limited, narrow, restricted

Practice and Apply For each Critical Vocabulary word, follow these steps:

1. Look up each word in a print or digital thesaurus, identify the synonyms appropriate to the meaning of each term as it is used in the selection.

2. Write a sample sentence using each word.

3. In each sentence, replace the vocabulary word with one of your synonyms. Make sure that the sentences make sense by having a partner check your work.

652 Unit 5

 ENGLISH LEARNER SUPPORT

Vocabulary Strategy Give students additional practice in determining synonyms and antonyms of Critical Vocabulary words. Have students work in pairs to look up antonyms for each word. Have them rewrite the sentences they wrote by using an antonym. Then, discuss with a partner how the antonym changes the meaning of the sentence.
ALL LEVELS

LANGUAGE CONVENTIONS:
Sentence Structure

Good writers use a variety of sentence structures to avoid monotony and to effectively articulate their ideas. The simplest structure has one **clause,** a group of words that contains a subject and a verb. More complex sentence structures include more than one clause. Study the examples in the chart.

SENTENCE STRUCTURE	EXAMPLE
A **simple sentence** has one independent clause and no subordinate clauses.	We live in the Information Age.
A **compound sentence** has two or more independent clauses joined by a comma and a coordinating conjunction, such as *and, or,* or *but.*	People love using social media, (but) some worry about how it will affect our relationships in the long run.
A **complex sentence** has an independent clause and one or more subordinate clauses. The subordinate clause begins with a subordinating conjunction, such as *when, as, after, because,* or *while.*	(After) comparing the concerns people had in the 19th century to those of people in the present day, the author concluded that humans will always be fearful of technology.
A **compound-complex sentence** has two or more independent clauses and at least one subordinate clause.	Teenagers are constantly bombarded by information, (but) they understand the need to think critically (when) it comes to online sources.

Notice how the conjunctions in the example sentences connect the ideas in the clauses. Without the conjunctions, each sentence would be a **run-on,** or multiple sentences written as if they were one. The writer's meaning would also be less clear without conjunctions.

Run-on example: Teenagers are constantly bombarded by information they understand the need to think critically it comes to online sources.

Practice and Apply Write a paragraph about an invention you believe you cannot live without. Then, go back and review the paragraph, making sure to scan for simple sentences and repeated subjects or verbs in different sentences. Combine these sentences to form complex sentences by compounding verbs and using subordinate clauses to show the relationships among your ideas.

RESPOND

Go to the **Grammar Studio** for more on sentence structure.

APPLY

LANGUAGE CONVENTIONS:
Sentence Structure

Tell students that the **sentence structure** in a text contributes to the overall tone and message, and helps the reader formulate his or her perception of the topic at hand. Review the definition of **clause** with students. Then, write varied sentences on the board and ask students to identify the clauses in each one. Walk students through the definitions of **simple, compound, complex,** and **compound-complex** sentences and make sure they understand the examples in the table.

Then, review **conjunctions** with students and have students identify them in the sentences. Prompt students to work in pairs to come up with their own examples, and then partner up with another pair to see if they agree on the sentence structures. Have students discuss how the use of conjunctions affects each sentence.

Finally, provide students with a series of **run-on** sentences. Ask them to work with a partner to underline the run-on, and then rewrite the sentence or combine the sentences to form compound, complex, or compound-complex sentences.

Practice and Apply After students have written their paragraphs, have them read their paragraphs to each other in pairs and discuss how they combined simple sentences or clauses to form more complex sentences. Encourage students to offer each other feedback on how they can revise run-ons or other sentences that can be written more effectively.

The Victorians Had the Same Concerns About Technology as We Do 653

ENGLISH LEARNER SUPPORT

Use a Variety of Grammatical Structures Use the following supports with students at varying proficiency levels:

- Provide students with a list of connecting words, such as *and, but,* and *because.* Have students repeat the words. Then, provide sentence frames, such as *I like technology _____ I can text my friends. I use my cell phone _____ tablet.* **SUBSTANTIAL**

- Provide students with a sentence frame related to the selection, such as *People often fear new technology _____ usually adapt to it.*

Ask students to complete it by using a connecting word. Then, have students work in pairs to write two sentences about technology using different connecting words. **MODERATE**

- Have students write compound and complex sentences about the selection. Then, pair students and have them discuss their sentences and why they chose the connecting words. **LIGHT**

PLAN

DOVER BEACH
Poem by Matthew Arnold

THE DARKLING THRUSH
Poem by Thomas Hardy

GENRE ELEMENTS
LYRIC POETRY

Explain to students that **lyric poetry** expresses strong feelings or thoughts about events like death, love, or loss. The two lyric poems they will read both use **extended metaphors** to express intense emotions. An extended metaphor is a longer comparison than a simple metaphor and is developed throughout a stanza or even an entire poem. In this lesson, students will analyze extended metaphors and sound devices used in lyric poetry of the Victorian era.

LEARNING OBJECTIVES

- Analyze extended metaphors and sound devices.
- Conduct research about historical developments during the Victorian era.
- Create a list of words and phrases describing an aspect of nature.
- Participate in a discussion and give a presentation.
- **Language** Identify sound devices.

TEXT COMPLEXITY

Quantitative Measures	Dover Beach/The Darkling Thrush	Lexile: NA
Qualitative Measures	**Ideas Presented** Multiple levels, use of symbolism. Greater demand for inference.	
	Structures Used More complex, lyrical and poetic.	
	Language Used Implied meanings, allusive, figurative, and formal language. Complex sentence structures.	
	Knowledge Required Mostly familiar themes, with some historical and geographical references.	

PLAN

Online

RESOURCES

- Unit 5 Response Log
- 🔊 Selection Audio
- Close Read Screencasts: Modeled Discussions
- Reading Studio: Notice & Note
- Level Up Tutorial: Figurative Language; Theme
- Speaking and Listening Studio: Participating in Collaborative Discussions; Giving a Presentation
- ✓ "Dover Beach" and "The Darkling Thrush" Selection Test

SUMMARIES

English

In "Dover Beach," the speaker looks out at the moonlit sea and calls his beloved to the window to breathe the sweet night air. Yet for him, the waves sound an "eternal note of sadness." Lamenting society's lack of faith as well as his own, the speaker beseeches his beloved to "be true."

In "The Darkling Thrush," the speaker is feeling dispirited on a gloomy winter day at the twilight of the 19th century. He hears the joyful singing of an old, frail thrush and wonders why the bird feels hopeful enough to sing so ecstatically when he himself feels so hopeless.

Spanish

En "Playa de Dover", la voz narrativa mira al mar alumbrado por la luna y llama a su amada a la ventana para que respire el dulce aire de la noche. Pero para él, las olas suenan como una "eterna nota de tristeza". La voz narrativa lamenta la falta de fe de la sociedad y la suya propia, y le ruega a su amada que "sea verdadera".

En "El tordo oscuro", el narrador se siente desanimado en un sombrío día de invierno durante el crepúsculo del siglo XIX. Escucha el alegre canto de un viejo y frágil tordo y se pregunta por qué el ave se siente tan esperanzado para cantar con tanto entusiasmo cuando él se siente tan desesperado.

👥 SMALL-GROUP OPTIONS

Have students work in small groups and pairs to read and discuss the selections.

Three-Minute Review

- After reading aloud "Dover Beach," set a timer for three minutes and have students work independently.
- During this time, ask students to reread the poem and write clarifying questions, observations, or unfamiliar words.
- After three minutes, have students share observations about the poem or any of the questions or notes they wrote.
- Briefly discuss students' observations and questions and clarify material as needed.

Final Word

- Have students reread "The Darkling Thrush."
- After reading, ask one student to describe his or her impressions of the poem.
- Have other students briefly give their impressions in turn.
- Go back to the original student and ask if he or she would like to revise any initial impressions based on the responses of the group.
- Continue the activity with students until everyone has had an opportunity to revise their first impressions.

Dover Beach / The Darkling Thrush **654B**

PLAN

Text X-Ray: English Learner Support
for "Dover Beach" and "The Darkling Thrush"

Use the Text X-Ray and the supports and scaffolds in the Teacher's Edition to help guide students at different proficiency levels through the selections.

INTRODUCE THE SELECTION
DISCUSS HISTORICAL DEVELOPMENTS

In this lesson, students will discuss how historical developments are conveyed through metaphors in poetry. Provide the following explanation:

A *historical development* is a change that affects many people during a particular period of time. Historical developments may be

- cultural (i.e., the desegregation of the U.S. during the civil rights era)
- religious (i.e., the Reformation brought change to Christianity)
- technological (i.e., the Industrial Revolution changed manufacturing)
- scientific (i.e., the development of antibiotics to aid in treating diseases)
- political (i.e., expanding voting rights to women and minorities)

Have students discuss historical developments and compare them with an aspect of nature. Use sentence frames, like: *One historical development that happened is _____. I can compare this to _____ to create a metaphor.*

CULTURAL REFERENCES

The following words or phrases may be unfamiliar to students:

- *ebb and flow* (Dover Beach, line 17): a rhythmic pattern of coming and going or decreasing and increasing
- *be true* (Dover Beach, line 29): be loyal
- *darkling* (Dover Beach, line 35): related to growing darkness
- *household fires* (The Darkling Thrush, line 8): fire lit in a home to keep warm or for cooking
- *evensong* (The Darkling Thrush, line 19): a service of evening prayers sung in a Christian church

LISTENING

Identify Sound Devices

Explain that poets use sound devices to make their poems sound more interesting and appealing. Review the meanings of common sound devices: alliteration, assonance, consonance, and onomatopoeia.

Use the following supports with students at varying proficiency levels:

- Read aloud lines 4–5 of "Dover Beach" and have students listen for alliteration. Elicit that the letter *g* is repeated in *gleams, gone,* and *glimmering*. Have students repeat the words, emphasizing the initial /g/. Repeat the activity for other alliteration in the poems. **SUBSTANTIAL**
- Have one partner read aloud lines 4–5 from "Dover Beach." Have the other partner tell what type of sound device he or she hears. Have them switch roles and repeat the activity for lines 21–23. **MODERATE**
- Have students work in pairs to take turns reading "Dover Beach" aloud. Have students pause when they hear a sound device. Students should identify the type of sound device. **LIGHT**

PLAN

SPEAKING

Analyze Extended Metaphor

Explain that analyzing an extended metaphor in poetry can help us see the imaginative ways poets use language to write about a subject.

Use the following supports with students at varying proficiency levels:

- Read aloud the first two lines of "Dover Beach." Then, ask questions about the extended metaphor of the poem: *Which is the main metaphor of the poem, the sea or the moon? (sea) What is another word related to "sea" in these lines? (tide)* **SUBSTANTIAL**
- Have partners read aloud lines 1–14 of "Dover Beach." Then, have them identify and say words and phrases related to the sea setting. **MODERATE**
- Have partners discuss the extended metaphors in both poems. Have them ask questions about each line of "Dover Beach" to determine if details in that line extend the metaphor. For example: *What has a tremulous cadence? How does this extend the metaphor?* **LIGHT**

READING

Create Dictionaries

Remind students that using a dictionary as they read can help them better understand the meaning of a poem.

Use the following supports with students at varying proficiency levels:

- Have students use drawings, peer support, and accessible language to make dictionaries for *straits, tranquil,* and *blanced*. Then echo read lines 1–9 of "Dover Beach." **SUBSTANTIAL**
- Have pairs work together to use drawings and accessible language to create a dictionary for 8–10 unfamiliar words in the poems. Then, have the pairs use the dictionaries while rereading the poems and discuss how the dictionary helped them better understand the poems. **MODERATE**
- Have students use drawings and accessible language to create dictionaries for 10–12 unfamiliar words in the poems. Have them also list synonyms for each word. Then have students reread the poems silently, using their dictionaries to review the words. **LIGHT**

WRITING

Use Connecting Words

Tell students that when they answer the questions in the chart for the Research activity on page 662, they can use connecting words and phrases such as *because, ever since,* and *as a result*.

Use the following supports with students at varying proficiency levels:

- Write two simple sentences on the board, such as *I feel happy. I am with my family.* Have students copy them using connecting words to join the sentences. Provide a word bank of connecting words. **SUBSTANTIAL**
- Have students use connecting words to complete these sentences: *Because I ____, I feel great. Ever since ____, I have been happy.* Have them use these models to answer the Research Activity questions. Then, have pairs exchange their work and underline connecting words. **MODERATE**
- Have students fill out the chart on page 662, using two different connecting words per answer. Have pairs exchange papers and underline connecting words. **LIGHT**

TEACH

 Connect to the
ESSENTIAL QUESTION

Remind students that literature often provides a window for readers to glimpse writers' reactions to cultural changes and historical events. In the next two poems, both Arnold and Hardy reflect on their feelings about the time period in which they lived. Ask students to think about the world in which they live and then discuss the Essential Question.

COMPARE THEMES

Point out that both poems use very specific word choice and poetic language to create vivid images, sounds, and moods that are important to the themes of these poems. Tell students to pay attention to how each writer uses nature as a backdrop to convey his message.

COLLABORATE & COMPARE

POEM
DOVER BEACH
by **Matthew Arnold**
pages 657–658

COMPARE THEMES
As you read, notice how the speakers in these poems use observations of nature as a springboard to discussing their feelings about the times they live in. Think about how the themes of these poems relate to each other. After you read both poems, you will collaborate with a small group on a final product.

 ESSENTIAL QUESTION:

How do you view the world?

POEM
THE DARKLING THRUSH
by **Thomas Hardy**
pages 660–661

654 Unit 5

GET READY

QUICK START

Our personal perspectives have a strong influence on how we react to things. Identify three important issues that affect your community, the country, or the world. Then, work with a partner to describe the different ways an optimist and a pessimist might view these issues. Use this chart to record your ideas.

OPTIMISTIC VIEW	PESSIMISTIC VIEW

ANALYZE EXTENDED METAPHORS

Like any metaphor, an **extended metaphor** is a comparison between two essentially unlike things that nevertheless have something in common. In an extended metaphor, however, the figurative comparison is made at length and in various ways throughout a stanza, a paragraph, or an entire literary work. An extended metaphor is similar to a metaphysical conceit, but the comparison is not as surprising.

Both of the poems you will read in this lesson contain extended metaphors. In "Dover Beach," for example, Matthew Arnold develops a metaphor comparing the sea to traditional religious faith. The poet first offers some specific observations about the sea, then connects these details to his ideas about faith.

As you read each poem, consider how the extended metaphor helps to convey a theme about the period when the poem was written.

GENRE ELEMENTS: LYRIC POETRY

- expresses strong feelings or thoughts
- has a musical quality
- deals with intense emotions surrounding events like death, love, or loss
- includes forms such as ode, elegy, and sonnet

TEACH

QUICK START

Show students a glass of water filled halfway. Ask them if the glass is half empty or half full. Tell them that the way they view the glass of water is based on their life experiences.

To assist students in choosing issues, have the class brainstorm important current issues, whether local, national, or global. To help them understand the activity, give this example:

Failing a Test	
Optimistic View	**Pessimistic View**
Learn from my mistake	Teacher's fault
My fault—didn't study	I never pass
Next time I will study	I never do well
Do homework	Why study?
Get study partner	Don't need to know this
Meet with teacher	
Review test	

ANALYZE EXTENDED METAPHORS

Tell students that just about anything can be compared to something else. When the comparison is figurative and is carried on many levels throughout an entire literary piece, the comparison becomes an **extended metaphor**.

For example, ask students to compare adolescence with the sea.

- Sometimes calm/quiet/contemplating/serene
- Sometimes rough/noisy/angry/struggling/raging
- Always moving/shifting/growing/reacting/changing
- Salty/weathered/experienced
- Supports life/relationships/nourishment/survival
- Complicated/changing/adjusting/modifying

Remind students that the extended metaphor in "Dover Beach" will exemplify a common theme found in the literature from the Victorian era.

TEACH

ANALYZE SOUND DEVICES

Tell students that reading a poem aloud will enable the reader to hear the sound devices used, especially subtle ones. Tell them that these sound devices are sometimes used over several lines or even a whole stanza. Give the following additional information about each type of sound device. After providing each example below, talk about the corresponding text-based example found on page 656.

Alliteration is a repetition of consonants. Ask students to think of some tongue twisters they learned growing up. *She sells seashells at the seashore.*

Assonance is a repetition of medial vowel sounds without a matching ending consonant. It is not to be confused with rhyming, in which there is typically a vowel and consonant sound at the end of a line that is matched to another line. *Maybe Sadie might stay the whole day.*

Consonance is a repetition of consonant sounds, either in the middle or at the end of a word, without repeating the same vowel sound. *"You talker, get back to picking!"*

Onomatopoeia is using words that imitate or imply the actual sound. *hissed, screeched, whizzed*

Provide time for students to practice reading the poems aloud to try to identify any sound devices.

ANNOTATION MODEL

Direct students to the annotation model on page 656, which suggests underlining words that appeal to the senses and images that develop mood and the **extended metaphor**. The model also circles words to identify **sound devices**. Point out that they may follow this suggestion or use their own system for marking up the selection in their write-in text. They may want to color-code their annotations by using highlighters. Their notes in the margin may include observations about the poem or questions about ideas that are unclear.

GET READY

ANALYZE SOUND DEVICES

The earliest poetry was composed to be sung in performance. Poets still use sound devices to create musical effects and to help unify lines and stanzas. The most common sound devices are rhyme and meter. Here are some other types of sound devices.

- **Alliteration**—the repetition of a consonant sound at the beginning of words (*His crypt the cloudy canopy*)
- **Assonance**—the repetition of a vowel sound in two or more stressed syllables that do not end with the same consonant (*The tide is full, the moon lies fair*)
- **Consonance**—the repetition of consonant sounds within and at the end of words (*Like strings of broken lyres*)
- **Onomatopoeia**—the use of words whose sounds echo their meanings (*grating*)

After you read these poems the first time, read them again aloud and notice how the sound devices appeal to your sense of hearing. Also, consider how sound devices support each poem's subject, mood, and theme.

ANNOTATION MODEL NOTICE & NOTE

As you read, notice how each poet uses nature imagery to appeal to the reader's senses and to develop an extended metaphor. Mark up examples of sound devices. In the model, you can see one reader's notes about the beginning of "Dover Beach."

> The sea is calm tonight.
>
> The tide is full, the moon lies fair
>
> Upon the straits – on the French coast the light
>
> Gleams and is gone; the cliffs of England stand,
>
> Glimmering and vast, out in the tranquil bay.
>
> Come to the window, sweet is the night air!

The imagery suggests nature's vastness and establishes a peaceful mood at the beginning. Alliteration of the "g" sound contributes to this mood.

The sixth line tells us the speaker is addressing someone in the same room.

BACKGROUND

Matthew Arnold *(1822–1888) was one of the leading poets and essayists of the Victorian era. In his youth, he struggled to live up to the expectations of his father, a famous headmaster of Rugby School. Arnold attended Rugby and then Oxford University; he later held teaching positions at both schools. While at Oxford, he began to gain recognition for his poetry. Arnold's poems are contemplative, often addressing serious themes of isolation and religious doubt.*

DOVER BEACH
Poem by Matthew Arnold

PREPARE TO COMPARE

As you read, note the imagery in the speaker's description of the natural world and the sound devices in his description. Consider the thoughts and feelings the speaker associates with the sea.

> The sea is calm tonight.
> The tide is full, the moon lies fair
> Upon the straits—on the French coast the light
> Gleams and is gone; the cliffs of England stand,
> 5 Glimmering and vast, out in the tranquil bay.
> Come to the window, sweet is the night air!
> Only, from the long line of spray
> Where the sea meets the moon-blanched land,
> Listen! you hear the grating roar
> 10 Of pebbles which the waves draw back, and fling,
> At their return, up the high strand,
> Begin, and cease, and then again begin,
> With tremulous cadence slow, and bring
> The eternal note of sadness in.

Notice & Note

Use the side margins to notice and note signposts in the text.

3 straits: the Strait of Dover, a narrow channel separating England and France, located at the northern end of the English Channel.

8 moon-blanched: shining palely in the moonlight.

13 tremulous cadence (trĕm´yə-ləs kād´ns): trembling rhythm.

Dover Beach / The Darkling Thrush 657

TEACH

BACKGROUND

Remind students that the Victorian age (1807–1901) followed the Romantic age and was characterized by advances in science and technology. The new innovations and knowledge challenged traditional belief systems, which led to religious doubt. Tell students that Matthew Arnold, who grew up in the academic world, became not only a poet but also a literary critic. He admired stylistic restraint and the ability of the poet to offer ethical or philosophical insight into the truths of life.

PREPARE TO COMPARE

Direct students to use the Prepare to Compare prompt to focus their reading.

EL ENGLISH LEARNER SUPPORT

Understand Meanings in English Before reading, have students pronounce each footnoted word or phrase in the side notes. Use visuals, gestures, or concrete examples to clarify word meanings. Instruct students to complete concept maps for the most challenging words to help them understand their meanings and connotations. **SUBSTANTIAL**

 For **listening and speaking support** for students at varying proficiency levels, see the **Text X-Ray** on pages 654C and 654D.

WHEN STUDENTS STRUGGLE . . .

Sound Devices Have students make a graphic organizer like below to identify **sound devices** in lines 1–14. Challenge them to find examples of each sound device.

Line	Words	Sound Device
2	tide, lies	assonance

 For additional support, go to the **Reading Studio** and assign the following **Level Up tutorial: Figurative Language**.

Dover Beach / The Darkling Thrush **657**

TEACH

ANALYZE SOUND DEVICES

Provide opportunities for students to read lines 29–37 aloud to a partner. Encourage discussion about the **sound devices** they identify. (**Answer:** *They help create an anxious or ominous mood.*)

ENGLISH LEARNER SUPPORT

Draw to Acquire Vocabulary Tell students that they can quickly draw pictures in response to an oral reading of the poem to help them understand how a poet uses words to create images. Read the poem aloud, pausing after each stanza to give students time to sketch a quick picture to capture the imagery. Then, have students share their drawings with partners, encouraging them to use words in the poem to explain their picture. Clarify any misinterpretations as needed. More advanced students can label their drawings with words.
MODERATE/LIGHT

 NOTICE & NOTE

15 Sophocles (sŏf´ə-klēz): an ancient Greek writer of tragic plays.

16 Aegean (ĭ-jē´ən): the Aegean Sea, the portion of the Mediterranean Sea between Greece and Turkey.

17 turbid: in a state of turmoil; muddled.

21 Sea of Faith: traditional religious beliefs about God and the world, long viewed as true and unshakable.

23 girdle: a belt or sash worn around the waist.

27 drear: dreary.

28 shingles: pebbly beaches.

ANALYZE SOUND DEVICES
Annotate: Read lines 29–37 aloud. Mark sound devices you notice.
Analyze: What mood do the sound devices help create?

---

15 Sophocles long ago
    Heard it on the Aegean, and it brought
    Into his mind the turbid ebb and flow
    Of human misery; we
    Find also in the sound a thought,
20 Hearing it by this distant northern sea.

    The Sea of Faith
    Was once, too, at the full, and round earth's shore
    Lay like the folds of a bright girdle furled.
    But now I only hear
25 Its melancholy, long, withdrawing roar,
    Retreating, to the breath
    Of the night wind, down the vast edges drear
    And naked shingles of the world.

    Ah, love, let us be true
    To one another! for the world, which seems
30 To lie before us like a land of dreams,
    So various, so beautiful, so new,
    Hath really neither joy, nor love, nor light,
    Nor certitude, nor peace, nor help for pain;
35 And we are here as on a darkling plain
    Swept with confused alarms of struggle and flight,
    Where ignorant armies clash by night.

CHECK YOUR UNDERSTANDING

Answer these questions about "Dover Beach" before moving on to the next selection.

1. In the poem, the speaker is —
   A looking out to sea from the English coast
   B sailing on a ship in the English Channel
   C swimming in the Aegean Sea
   D fighting in a war in France

2. What does the speaker compare to waves pulling back from the shore?
   F Armed conflict
   G Ships sailing into the channel
   H Loss of religious faith
   J Lovers parting

3. The speaker takes comfort in —
   A his spirituality
   B nature's beauty
   C social progress
   D personal relationships

Dover Beach / The Darkling Thrush 659

CHECK YOUR UNDERSTANDING

Have students answer the questions independently.

Answers:

1. A
2. H
3. D

If they answer any questions incorrectly, have them reread the text to confirm their understanding. Then they may proceed to the next selection on page 660.

ENGLISH LEARNER SUPPORT

Oral Assessment Use the following questions to assess students' comprehension and speaking skills.

1. In lines 1–6, the speaker is looking out _____. *(to sea from the English coast)*

2. Is faith important to the speaker? *(Yes.)*

3. Does the speaker's love for someone make him feel better? *(Yes.)*
   SUBSTANTIAL/MODERATE

Dover Beach / The Darkling Thrush **659**

TEACH

BACKGROUND

Thomas Hardy lived during a time of rapid change, fueled by increased scientific knowledge, technological innovations, and changes in moral conduct. Some of his novels, such as *Tess of the d'Urbervilles* and *Jude the Obscure*, were criticized as sympathizing with immoral behavior. In fact, *Jude the Obscure* was banned from bookstores, with one critic calling it "Jude the Obscene." Many critics labeled Hardy a pessimist because of the topics he wrote about. However, Hardy preferred to call himself a meliorist, someone who believes that human effort can make the world a better place. His writings explore the ironies of life and the indifference of nature and society to mankind's condition. He published 14 novels, three volumes of short stories, and over 1,000 poems, which earned him a burial place in the Poet's Corner at Westminster Abbey.

PREPARE TO COMPARE

Direct students to use the Prepare to Compare prompt to focus their reading.

ENGLISH LEARNER SUPPORT

Use Support from Teacher to Read Read the poem to students. Then, have students choral read the poem with you one stanza at a time. Stop after each stanza to have students identify words and phrases related to the scene, setting, and landscape. Make a master list of these words, clarifying their meanings as needed. Have students talk with a partner to discuss how the author's use of words helps develop the setting. **MODERATE**

 **NOTICE & NOTE**

BACKGROUND

Thomas Hardy (1840–1928) was born in a small village in southwestern England, the setting of many of his novels and poems. As a young man, he wrote poems and stories in his spare time while working as an architect. Hardy became famous for his novels, although their pessimism and controversial subject matter were often criticized. He published "The Darkling Thrush" just a few days before the end of the 19th century.

THE DARKLING THRUSH
Poem by Thomas Hardy

PREPARE TO COMPARE

As you read, notice the poet's word choices in describing a landscape.

I leant upon a coppice gate
    When Frost was specter-gray,
And Winter's dregs made desolate
    The weakening eye of day.
5 The tangled bine-stems scored the sky
    Like strings of broken lyres,
And all mankind that haunted nigh
    Had sought their household fires.

The land's sharp features seemed to be
10   The Century's corpse outleant,
His crypt the cloudy canopy,
    The wind his death-lament.
The ancient pulse of germ and birth
    Was shrunken hard and dry,
15 And every spirit upon earth
    Seem'd fervorless as I.

At once a voice arose among
    The bleak twigs overhead
In a full-hearted evensong

Notice & Note
Use the side margins to notice and note signposts in the text.

1 coppice (kŏp´ĭs) **gate:** a gate leading to a coppice, a small wood or thicket.

2 specter-gray: ghost-gray.

5 bine-stems scored: twining stems cut across.

6 lyres: harp-like musical instruments.

7 nigh: near.

10 outleant: outstretched.

13 germ: seed; bud.

19 evensong: evening song.

20   Of joy illimited;
     An aged thrush, frail, gaunt, and small,
        In blast-beruffled plume,
     Had chosen thus to fling his soul
        Upon the growing gloom.

25   So little cause for carollings
        Of such ecstatic sound
     Was written on terrestrial things
        Afar or nigh around,
     That I could think there trembled through
30   His happy good-night air
     Some blessed Hope, whereof he knew
        And I was unaware.

NOTICE & NOTE

20 illimited: unlimited.

22 blast-beruffled plume: wind-ruffled feathers.

ANALYZE EXTENDED METAPHORS

Annotate: Underline words that describe natural features in lines 9–16. Circle words that describe the century as it is compared to nature.

Analyze: What idea does this extended metaphor express?

CHECK YOUR UNDERSTANDING

Answer these questions before moving on to the **Analyze the Text** section on the following page.

1 What is the poem's setting?

   A Sunrise on a mountain slope

   B An open snowy field

   C A lake's frozen shore

   D The edge of the woods in winter

2 The lines "Had chosen thus to fling his soul / Upon the growing gloom" suggest that the thrush —

   F shares the speaker's sense of hopelessness

   G is defying the grimness of its surroundings

   H probably won't live much longer

   J has flown down from the tree branch

3 The speaker says in lines 29–32 that —

   A the thrush may have some unknown reason to be happy

   B he understands why the thrush sings joyfully

   C he mistook the thrush's singing as a sign of hope

   D the singing has plunged him even deeper into despair

Dover Beach / The Darkling Thrush   **661**

ENGLISH LEARNER SUPPORT

Oral Assessment Use the following questions to assess students' comprehension and speaking skills.

1. What is the poem's setting? *(the edge of the woods in winter)*

2. What is the thrush doing? *(refusing to accept the unpleasantness of what is around it)*

3. Does the speaker think the thrush has reason to be happy? *(Yes.)*
   SUBSTANTIAL/MODERATE

TEACH

ANALYZE EXTENDED METAPHORS

Remind students that this poem was written just a few days before the end of the 19th century and expresses how the poet felt about his changing world. Ask them to think about how they have felt when they experienced the coming of a new year. Ask them to imagine what it might feel like to leave one century and start a new one. As they make their annotations, encourage them to look at how Hardy uses elements of nature to make connections to the passing of the 19th century. (**Answer:** *The metaphor describes the 19th century as a corpse, suggesting that the speaker sees this period of time as lifeless and lacking all hope.*)

ENGLISH LEARNER SUPPORT

Acquire Basic Vocabulary Help students to understand the following time words: *second, minute, hour, day, week, month, year, decade, century, bicentennial, millennium, era*. Spell the words aloud and have pairs create flash cards. Then, have students work with their partner to put the time words (except for *era*) in order by length of time. **SUBSTANTIAL**

CHECK YOUR UNDERSTANDING

Have students answer the questions independently.

Answers:

1. D

2. G

3. A

If they answer any questions incorrectly, have them reread the text to confirm their understanding. Then they may proceed to ANALYZE THE TEXTS on page 662.

Dover Beach / The Darkling Thrush   **661**

APPLY

ANALYZE THE TEXT

Possible answers:

1. **DOK 4:** He compares the sea moving from high to low tide with the receding of religious faith from people's lives. He also compares the sound of the waves pushing pebbles to the shore with the sadness of this loss of faith.

2. **DOK 2:** Possible answer: People throughout history have thought about the sea and how it connects to their lives.

3. **DOK 2:** He describes the world as violent and joyless beneath its superficial beauty. By placing his faith in his relationship with his love, he hopes to make up for his loss of faith in the world.

4. **DOK 4:** The alliteration of the d sound in "dregs" and "desolate" and the assonance of the short e sound in "specter," "dregs," and "desolate" connect these words, emphasizing that the landscape is bleak and lifeless. This emphasis helps set up Hardy's theme about a general hopelessness at the end of the century.

5. **DOK 3:** The description of the bird is similar to the narrator's description of the desolate winter landscape at the end of the century. An expression of joy from such a bird is unexpected, just as the speaker is surprised to see any sign of hope at this time in the world.

RESEARCH

Remind students that they should use several sources to confirm information. Discuss why some websites are more credible than others.

Extend Provide these possible poem titles if students need assistance: Arnold poems: "East London," "A Wish"; Hardy poems: "The Ruined Maid," "The Voice."

 For **writing support** for students at varying proficiency levels, see the **Text X-Ray** on page 654D.

RESPOND

ANALYZE THE TEXT

Support your responses with evidence from the text.  **NOTEBOOK**

1. **Analyze** In "Dover Beach," how does Arnold use details about the sea to develop his extended metaphor about faith?

2. **Infer** Arnold refers to Sophocles in lines 15–20 of "Dover Beach." What idea does he suggest through this allusion to the ancient Greek playwright?

3. **Interpret** Reread lines 29–37 of "Dover Beach." How does the speaker's description of the world connect to his plea that he and his love "be true / To one another"?

4. **Analyze** How does Hardy's use of alliteration and assonance in lines 1–4 of "The Darkling Thrush" support the subject and theme of the poem?

5. **Draw Conclusions** In "The Darkling Thrush," why did Hardy choose to describe the bird as an "aged thrush, frail, gaunt, and small"?

RESEARCH TIP
When researching an aspect of a particular time period, it is easiest to find the answers you're looking for by using specific search strings. In this case, you might use strings like "Victorian + religion" or "how industrialization affected British rural life."

RESEARCH

Both of these poems reflect the poets' feelings about changes that occurred during their lifetimes. With a partner, research historical developments during the Victorian era. Use what you learn to answer the following questions.

QUESTION	ANSWER
What challenges to traditional religious beliefs occurred during the Victorian era?	Possible answers: New scientific ideologies Increase in the exchange of ideas because travel and communication became easier (steam engine, railway, telephone invented)
How did industrialization affect rural life in Britain during this period?	Possible answers: Exodus from rural communities to cities More opportunities for jobs, less clergy More leisure time

Extend Although the Victorian era is often characterized as a period of optimism and progress, some of its finest writers expressed a pessimistic outlook. Find other poems by Arnold and Hardy that address subjects such as loss and disillusionment. With a partner, discuss how they compare with the poems you read in this lesson.

WHEN STUDENTS STRUGGLE . . .

Reteaching: Extended Metaphor Give students the graphic organizer below and have them use it to compare the extended metaphors in "Dover Beach" and "The Darkling Thrush."

	Dover Beach	The Darkling Thrush
extended metaphor		

 For additional support, go to the **Reading Studio** and assign the following Level Up tutorial: Figurative Language.

RESPOND

CREATE AND DISCUSS

Create a List Select an aspect of nature, such as a season, a type of landscape, or a particular animal. Create a list of words and phrases that describe this aspect of nature, and then list thoughts or feelings that you associate with them. Include at least 20 words or phrases in your list. Review your analysis and interpretation of the two poems to see examples from Arnold and Hardy.

- Identify an aspect of nature that is representative of how you view the world.
- Review examples of how poets have used nature to represent ideas.
- Brainstorm and construct a list of words and phrases.

Discuss Your List People can react to the same sights and experiences in strikingly different ways. Share and discuss your list with a small group.

- Review each descriptive word or phrase with your group.
- Then, discuss the thoughts and feelings you associated with these details. Ask every group member to explain how their reactions compare with yours.
- Make sure to respect everyone's responses. If you are confused by a response, ask the student to clarify it.

RESPOND TO THE ESSENTIAL QUESTION

 How do you view the world?

Gather Information Review your annotations and notes on "Dover Beach" and "The Darkling Thrush." Then, add relevant details to your Response Log. As you determine which information to include, think about:

- how poets describe the natural world in different ways
- how you experience the world around you
- how similar elements can be used to express opposite ideas

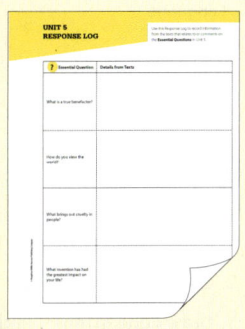

ACADEMIC VOCABULARY

As you write and discuss what you learned from the lyric poems, be sure to use the Academic Vocabulary words. Check off each of the words that you use.

- ❑ abandon
- ❑ confine
- ❑ conform
- ❑ depress
- ❑ reluctance

APPLY

CREATE AND DISCUSS

Create a List Encourage students to use their annotations to review how Arnold and Hardy described different aspects of nature. After selecting an aspect of nature to describe, students may find it helpful to organize their lists of words and phrases, and the associated thoughts and feelings, in a graphic organizer.

Discuss Your List Tell students that by sharing their lists, new ideas, additional words, and even another theme might emerge. Remind them to listen carefully to what others are saying so they can give appropriate feedback. Tell them to be sure to ask others for clarification and paraphrase to confirm understanding.

RESPOND TO THE ESSENTIAL QUESTION

Allow time for students to add details from "Dover Beach" and "The Darkling Thrush" to their Unit 5 Response Logs.

APPLY

COMPARE THEMES

Tell students that using a graphic organizer will assist them in making comparisons. Although the themes of the two poems are similar, the way those themes are developed is quite different. By using the graphic organizer on page 664, similarities and differences will be easier to identify.

Remind students that in order to infer, a reader must "read between the lines." Key statements, imagery, and figurative language must be analyzed to infer the themes of poems. The graphic organizer will help them identify specific details from which the themes can be inferred.

ANALYZE THE TEXTS

Possible answers:

1. **DOK 4:** *Arnold mostly describes the view through vivid imagery, such as "gleams and is gone" and "line of spray." Hardy uses precise language such as "coppice-gate," but he also relies on figurative language such as "specter-gray" and "like strings of broken lyres."*

2. **DOK 2:** *"Dover Beach" starts out with a calm mood that becomes more anxious as the poem develops, while the mood of "The Darkling Thrush" is consistently bleak.*

3. **DOK 3:** *Most students will say that "Dover Beach" is more hopeful because it stresses the importance of human relationships, while the speaker of "The Darkling Thrush" only speculates that the bird's singing may hint at an unknown reason for hope.*

4. **DOK 4:** *The extended metaphors connect abstract ideas with something tangible and commonplace, which makes it easier for readers to connect with the abstract ideas.*

664 Unit 5

 **RESPOND**

DOVER BEACH
Poem by Matthew Arnold

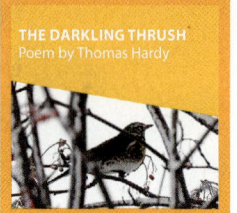
THE DARKLING THRUSH
Poem by Thomas Hardy

Collaborate & Compare

COMPARE THEMES

A poem's **theme** is the message the author conveys to the reader. Although even a short poem may express several ideas, the theme is the major idea that the poet communicates. Themes are developed through word choice, imagery, figurative language, and other elements.

In both "Dover Beach" and "The Darkling Thrush," the poets use their descriptions of nature to express themes about disillusionment and hopelessness.

Poets seldom directly state their themes, so you must infer them from a close reading of a poem. As you read to understand each poem's message, consider:

- **Key statements**—made by the speaker
- **Imagery**—details that appeal to the reader's senses
- **Figurative language**—phrases that communicate ideas beyond

With your group, complete the chart with details from both poems.

	"DOVER BEACH"	"THE DARKLING THRUSH"
Key Statements	Sea of Faith	Century Some blessed Hope
Imagery	turbid ebb and flow darkling plain	Frost was specter-gray tangled bine-stems
Figurative Language	Retreating, to the breath/ Of the night wind	strings of broken lyres corpse, crypt, death-lament

ANALYZE THE TEXTS

Discuss these questions in your group:

1. **Analyze** Both poems start out with descriptions of nature. What literary elements does each poet rely on to develop his description?
2. **Compare** How are these two poems similar or different in mood?
3. **Draw Conclusions** Which poem expresses a more hopeful view of the world? Explain.
4. **Analyze** Both poems include extended metaphors comparing something in nature with an abstract idea. How does this technique help the poets develop their poems?

664 Unit 5

WHEN STUDENTS STRUGGLE...

Analyze Theme Have students make a graphic organizer like below to list words and phrases from each poem that support the theme of hopelessness.

Dover Beach	Darkling Thrush
eternal note of sadness (line 14)	Winter's dregs made desolate (line 3)

 For additional support, go to the **Reading Studio** and assign the following Level Up tutorial: **Theme**.

RESPOND

COLLABORATE AND PRESENT

Now, with your group, continue exploring the ideas in the poems by identifying and comparing their themes. Follow these steps:

1. **Decide on the most important details** With your group, review your chart to identify the most important details from each poem. Identify points on which you agree, and resolve disagreements by identifying evidence from the poems that support your ideas.

2. **Determine a theme** Based on the word choices, figurative language, sound devices, and feelings evoked from each poem, determine a theme for each. You may use a chart to keep track of the themes your group members suggest.

	DETAILS	THEME
"DOVER BEACH"	Hath really neither joy, nor love, nor light, Nor certitude, nor peace, nor help for pain;	In a cruel and uncertain world, people can only place their trust in personal relationships.
"THE DARKLING THRUSH"	Had chosen… fling his soul Upon the growing gloom.	Even when life seems most desolate, there may be some cause for hope we are unaware of.

3. **Compare themes** Compare themes with your group and discuss whether the themes are similar or different. Listen actively to the members of your group and ask them to clarify any points you do not understand.

4. **Present to the class** Next, present your ideas to the class. Be sure to include clear statements on the theme for each poem. Discuss whether the themes are similar or different. You may add other visuals or diagrams to help convey information to the class.

Go to the **Speaking and Listening Studio** for more on giving a presentation.

Collaborate & Compare 665

APPLY

COLLABORATE AND PRESENT

Organize students into groups to complete this activity.

1. **Decide on the most important details** Remind students that there may be more than one theme in each of the poems. If there is disagreement about which details are the most important, point out that this may indicate that certain details support one theme while other details support a different theme.

2. **Determine a theme** Encourage students to use the graphic organizer on page 665 as they discuss the details and themes in each poem. Under DETAILS, tell them to list figurative language, **sound devices,** and other examples of word choice in each poem.

3. **Compare themes** If there are disagreements, remind students to ask each other to provide evidence to support their ideas. Encourage them to be open to new ideas that are backed by evidence.

4. **Present to the class** Group members should select a presenter or divide the presentation into parts so that each member can present one aspect. Remind them that visuals or diagrams can help them keep track of the ideas they want to present and also help their listeners follow their presentation more easily.

ENGLISH LEARNER SUPPORT

Recognize Sounds Vietnamese and Spanish speakers may have difficulty with the soft sound of *g*. Tell students that the English letter *g* can have two sounds. One is a hard *g* and sounds like the first *g* in *garage*. The other is a soft *g* and sounds like the last *g* in *garage*.

- Have students echo read the poems and raise their left hand for a hard *g* and their right hand for a soft *g*. **SUBSTANTIAL**
- Have students echo read the poems and circle words with a hard *g* and underline words with a soft *g*. Then, have them practice saying each word in pairs. **MODERATE**
- Have students read in pairs and make lists of hard *g* and soft *g* words. Have them discuss which *g* is more pleasing to the ear and why a poet might use each sound in a poem. **LIGHT**

PLAN

MY LAST DUCHESS
Poem by Robert Browning

CONFESSION
Poem by Linh Dinh

GENRE ELEMENTS
LYRIC POEM
Remind students that the **speaker** in a poem has a particular voice that reveals his/her attitude about the subject of the poem. For example, speakers might be cheerful, scornful, wistful, or angry. It is important to analyze the voice of the speaker in order to understand the speaker's character. In this lesson, students will draw conclusions about speakers in Victorian and contemporary poems.

LEARNING OBJECTIVES
- Draw conclusions about speakers and analyze imagery.
- Conduct research about how jealousy is addressed in different time periods and a variety of media.
- Create an oral presentation.
- Present a monologue.
- **Language** Write sentences using first-person point of view.

TEXT COMPLEXITY

	My Last Duchess/Confession	Lexile: NA
Quantitative Measures		
Qualitative Measures	**Ideas Presented** Multiple levels, subtle, implied meanings and purpose. Use of symbolism. Greater demand for inference.	
	Structures Used More complex, lyrical and poetic.	
	Language Used Implied meanings, allusive, figurative, and formal language. Complex sentence structures.	
	Knowledge Required Explores complex ideas. Refers to ideas that may be beyond students' experiences.	

666A Unit 5

PLAN

Online

RESOURCES

- Unit 5 Response Log
- Selection Audio
- Reading Studio: Notice & Note
- Level Up Tutorials: Character Traits, Author's Purpose; Imagery
- Speaking and Listening Studio: Giving a Presentation
- "My Last Duchess" and "Confession" Selections Test

SUMMARIES

English
In "My Last Duchess," the speaker gives a poetic monologue addressing the agent of a count about possible marriage to the count's daughter. He displays a portrait of his late wife, a life-loving woman, and implies that he killed her out of jealousy. In "Confession," the speaker is an artist who wants to make art that reveals the flaws which make human nature imperfect.

Spanish
En "Mi última duquesa", el narrador da un monologo poético al agente de un conde acerca del posible matrimonio con la hija de éste. Muestra un retrato de su difunta esposa, una mujer amante de la vida, e insinúa que la mató de celos. En "Confesión", el narrador es un artista que quiere crear arte que revele los defectos que hacen imperfecta a la naturaleza humana.

SMALL-GROUP OPTIONS

Have students work in small groups and pairs to read and discuss the selections.

Activating Academic Vocabulary

- Provide a list of Academic Vocabulary words and phrases, such as: *speaker, persona, attitude, voice, word choice, imagery, detail, convey, lyrical, compare, contrast, theme, line,* and *stanza*.
- After reading five lines, model how to use one or more Academic Vocabulary words and phrases to discuss the poems.
- Encourage students to use the Academic Vocabulary as they discuss and write about the poems.

Double-Entry Journal

- Have students use a notebook for recording their double-entry notes.
- Show students how to create a two-column format by drawing a line from top to bottom on each page. The left head is *Quotes from the Poem* and the right head is *My Notes*.
- Encourage students to copy important or confusing lines or verses in the left column.
- Students will write their own questions, restatements, or interpretations in the right column, next to the relevant lines or verses.

PLAN

Text X-Ray: English Learner Support
for "My Last Duchess" and "Confession"

Use the Text X-Ray and the supports and scaffolds in the Teacher's Edition to help guide students at different proficiency levels through the selections.

INTRODUCE THE SELECTION
DISCUSS *JEALOUSY* AND *CRUELTY*

In this lesson, students will need to be able to discuss the themes of jealousy and cruelty in poems.

Provide the following explanations:

- *Jealousy* is the feeling of being unhappy or angry when a person wants something someone else possesses.
- *Cruelty* is the desire to cause pain to others. A cruel person is unkind and harsh.

Guide students to use their personal experiences to discuss the effects of jealousy and cruelty.

Provide sentence frames, such as: *Some people are jealous of _____. An example of cruelty is _____. Jealousy can be harmful because _____. If someone is cruel at school, you can _____.*

CULTURAL REFERENCES

The following words or phrases may be unfamiliar to students:

- *'twas* (Duchess, line 13): archaic way of saying "it was"
- *a nine-hundred-years-old name* (Duchess, line 33): comes from many respected generations
- *e'en* (Duchess, line 42): archaic way of saying "even"
- *human condition* (Confession, line 14): the important events, situations, and characteristics that are essential to being human

LISTENING

Respond to Imagery

Review with students that imagery is an important literary device that allows readers to connect emotionally with a subject.

Use the following supports with students at varying proficiency levels:

- Slowly read aloud the phrase *"The jagged gaps of their stiff smiles"* from "Confession." Have students repeat the phrase and role play a stiff smile. Have students sketch an image to accompany the phrase. **SUBSTANTIAL**
- Direct one partner to read aloud an example of imagery from one of the poems. Have the other partner describe what image is seen in his or her mind. Have students switch roles to repeat the activity. **MODERATE**
- Have students listen and take notes about imagery as you read "Confession" aloud. Then, have partners describe the images in their own words. **LIGHT**

PLAN

SPEAKING

Respond to Speakers

Encourage students to think about the speakers of both poems and what it would be like to meet them.

Use the following supports with students at varying proficiency levels:

- Provide a list of descriptive words, such as: *kind, cruel, jealous, loving, boasting*. Slowly read aloud lines from the poems, and have students say the word that shows the speaker's attitude. **SUBSTANTIAL**
- Have partners read lines 21–24 from "The Last Duchess." Have them ask questions about the speaker's attitude, using sentence frames: *Is the speaker _____? Yes, the speaker is _____, because _____.* (No, the speaker is not being cruel. He is being jealous because he wants all her attention.) Repeat with lines 32–35 (*boasting*), lines 45–46 (*cruel*) and lines 54–56 (*boasting*). **MODERATE**
- Have partners discuss and compare the attitudes of the speakers of both poems. Direct them to ask each other clarifying questions as needed. **LIGHT**

READING

Make Inferences

Review inferences. Tell students to use what speakers say and what they know about people and the world to make assumptions about the speakers.

Use the following supports with students of varying proficiency levels:

- Read aloud lines of the poems and pause to have students echo-read after you. Ask either/or questions, such as: *The speaker says, "Perhaps I am a cruel artist." Does the speaker know he is cruel or does he want readers to decide?* (wants readers to decide) **SUBSTANTIAL**
- Have pairs independently read "Confession." Then, have them make inferences about the speaker's character, attitude and likes. Provide a sentence frame: *I can infer that the speaker _____ because _____.* **MODERATE**
- Have students independently reread both poems. Ask: *What do you think it would be like to meet the speakers of these poems? What would you expect them to be like?* Have small group members respond in turns, using text evidence to support their responses. **LIGHT**

WRITING

Write in First Person

Prepare students to write a script for the Create an Oral Presentation activity on page 675. Remind students that when authors write in the first-person point of view, they use the pronouns *I, me,* and *my*. The first-person speaker tells about his/her feelings, thoughts and experiences.

Use the following supports with students of varying proficiency levels:

- Have students write from the first-person point of view of the speaker of one of the two poems. Provide sentence starters, such as: *I am a _____. I like _____. Something important to me is _____. The Duchess was _____. I wish the Duchess _____.* **SUBSTANTIAL**
- Have students assume the persona of the speaker of one of the two poems. Direct students to write a paragraph describing the speaker's character traits (e.g., jealous, cruel, proud, inconsiderate) using the first-person point of view. **MODERATE**
- Have students write five sentences from the first-person point of view of the speaker of one of the two poems. Encourage students to use each pronoun at least once: *I, me, my*. Have partners exchange papers to check for pronoun agreement. **LIGHT**

TEACH

Connect to the ESSENTIAL QUESTION

Tell students that the speakers in the poems "My Last Duchess" and "Confession" display different kinds of cruelty towards others. Ask students to share with a partner a time when they experienced or witnessed a person acting cruelly. What do they think might have been the cause of the behavior?

COMPARE THEMES

Remind students that the **theme** is the message about life or human nature that the author wants to share. Point out that both poems address imperfections in human characters as seen in images. Tell students to take note of how the poets use imagery and word choices to develop their themes.

COLLABORATE & COMPARE

POEM

MY LAST DUCHESS

by **Robert Browning**
pages 669–670

COMPARE THEMES

As you read "My Last Duchess" and "Confession," take note of how each poem addresses the imperfections of human character. After you read both poems, you will collaborate with a small group to create a final presentation comparing their themes.

ESSENTIAL QUESTION:

What brings out cruelty in people?

POEM

CONFESSION

by **Linh Dinh**
page 672

QUICK START

You probably know someone who tends to magnify everyone else's flaws. What is the danger of being overly critical in your interactions with people? Discuss this question with a small group of classmates.

DRAW CONCLUSIONS ABOUT SPEAKERS

The **speaker** of a poem is the voice that talks to the reader. In many poems, the speaker expresses the poet's own thoughts and feelings. However, you should not assume that the speaker is the same as the poet, even if he or she uses the pronouns *I* and *me*.

Some poems have a fictional character, or **persona,** as the speaker. *Persona* is a Latin word meaning "actor's mask." A persona allows the poet to pretend to be someone with a different personality or situation. For example, in "Confession," Linh Dinh uses the persona of a painter to explore an idea about the visual arts.

A **dramatic monologue** is a type of persona poem in which the speaker addresses a silent or absent listener during an intense or emotionally complex moment. Dramatic monologues require readers to make inferences: the speakers reveal themselves by dropping clues that the reader must piece together. Browning's "My Last Duchess," a famous monologue, is set in 16th-century Italy. The speaker is a duke negotiating with an agent to marry a count's daughter. Notice how Browning begins the poem in the middle of their conversation:

> That's my last Duchess painted on the wall,
> Looking as if she were alive.

As you read, use a chart like the one below to gather evidence and draw conclusions about the character and circumstances of each poem's speaker.

GENRE ELEMENTS: LYRIC POETRY

- usually written in the first person
- expresses the feelings and thoughts of the speaker, who may be a fictional character
- uses sound devices, such as rhythm and repetition, to create a musical quality
- often deals with intense emotions surrounding events like death, love, or loss

	HOW SPEAKER VIEWS HIMSELF	HOW SPEAKER VIEWS OTHERS
"My Last Duchess"		
"Confession"		

My Last Duchess / Confession 667

TEACH

ANALYZE IMAGERY

Explain to students how a poet uses imagery to create vivid sensory experiences for the reader. Demonstrate for students how to create pictures in the mind based on the poet's **word choice.** Read aloud these lines from "Confession":

"I use my eyes and brushes to thread

The jagged gaps of their stiff smiles. I pamper

Each pimple, hump, massage each incrustation."

Point out words that help you visualize the artist's approach to painting portraits (*jagged gaps, pimple, hump, each incrustation*). Invite students to share the images they visualize from the poet's word choice.

■ English Learner Support

Describe in Detail Provide students with language frames they can use to evaluate the use of imagery in each of the selections. Consider using the following frames:

- The poet uses ____ to create visual imagery.
- The poet uses sensory images to express ____.
- The poem evokes feelings of ____ by ____.

Ask students to discuss their ideas in small groups.

ANNOTATION MODEL

Explain to students that one way to find imagery that helps express the theme is to underline important details. Point out that they may use a graphic organizer like the one suggested or their own system. They may want to color code their annotations. Their margin notes may include questions or ideas about what they want to learn more about.

GET READY

ANALYZE IMAGERY

Imagery refers to words and phrases that create vivid sensory experiences for the reader. Most imagery is visual, but imagery can also appeal to the senses of smell, hearing, taste, and touch. Imagery appears in all literary forms, but it is especially important in poetry for establishing a mood, expressing emotions, and conveying ideas.

The two poems in this lesson focus on a painting or the act of painting. Because of this subject, they are both rich in visual imagery. As you read, notice how each poet uses an image or group of images to support the poem's theme. Use a chart like this one to help you analyze ideas and feelings associated with the imagery.

EXAMPLE OF IMAGERY	IDEAS OR FEELINGS LINKED TO IMAGE

ANNOTATION MODEL   NOTICE & NOTE

As you read, draw conclusions about each poem's speaker. Also, note how the imagery in each poem helps create a mood or express a theme. In the model you can see one reader's notes about "My Last Duchess."

> That's my <u>last Duchess</u> painted on the wall,
> Looking as if she were alive. I call
> That piece a <u>wonder</u>, now: Frà Pandolf's hands
> Worked busily a day, and there she <u>stands</u>.
> <u>Will't please you sit and look at her?</u>

The Duke uses the term "last Duchess," which is a cold way to refer to his late wife.

He emphasizes how realistic the painting is, like he's describing a real person. The painting seems to have special importance to him.

ENGLISH LEARNER SUPPORT

Use Contextual Support Read aloud lines 7–8 from "Confessions." Invite students to ask for clarification of any unfamiliar words. Then, have students underline the word *cajole* and help them understand that the poet uses this word to emphasize the painter's attitude in working with people he paints. Ask students to circle context clues that give clues about the meaning of *cajole* and to write a definition of the word. Then, have pairs confirm their definitions by checking a dictionary. **MODERATE**

BACKGROUND

Robert Browning (1812–1889) showed intellectual brilliance at a young age. When his first book of poetry was harshly criticized for its personal content, he decided to write poems about people and characters other than himself. Browning married the poet Elizabeth Barrett in 1846; they lived happily together in Italy until her death 15 years later. After decades of obscurity, Browning began to gain recognition during the 1860s for his dramatic monologues. He is widely considered one of the most important poets of the Victorian Era.

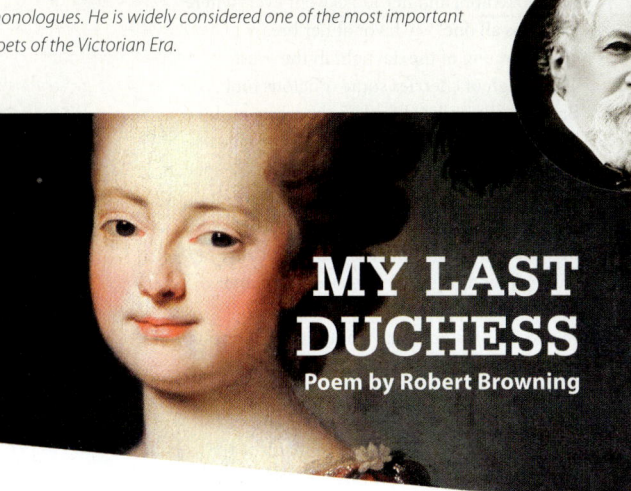

MY LAST DUCHESS
Poem by Robert Browning

PREPARE TO COMPARE

As you read, note what the speaker reveals about himself through the course of the poem. Pay close attention to his word choices and the imagery that helps describe his behaviors and feelings for his wife.

That's my last Duchess painted on the wall,
Looking as if she were alive. I call
That piece a wonder, now: Frà Pandolf's hands
Worked busily a day, and there she stands.
5 Will't please you sit and look at her? I said
"Frà Pandolf" by design, for never read
Strangers like you that pictured countenance,
The depth and passion of its earnest glance,
But to myself they turned (since none puts by
10 The curtain I have drawn for you, but I)
And seemed as they would ask me, if they durst,
How such a glance came there; so, not the first
Are you to turn and ask thus. Sir, 'twas not
Her husband's presence only, called that spot
15 Of joy into the Duchess' cheek: perhaps
Frà Pandolf chanced to say "Her mantle laps

NOTICE & NOTE

Notice & Note

Use the side margins to notice and note signposts in the text.

3 Frà Pandolf's: of Brother Pandolf, a fictitious friar-painter.

DRAW CONCLUSIONS ABOUT SPEAKERS
Annotate: Mark the phrases in lines 5–13 that hint at the character of the speaker.

Infer: What can you infer about the duke? What details support your inference?

11 durst: dared.

16 mantle: cloak.

My Last Duchess 669

TEACH

BACKGROUND

After reading the Background, tell students that the **dramatic monologue** form of poetry that Browning wrote so masterfully was originally a type of Old English poetry. Remind students that a **persona poem** is told by a character with a particular point of view. Explain to students how Browning's poem "My Last Duchess" reveals clues about the speaker, the duke of Ferrara, and his attitude toward his deceased wife. Have students make a short list of what they learn about the speaker throughout the poem.

PREPARE TO COMPARE

Direct students to use the Prepare to Compare prompt to focus their reading.

DRAW CONCLUSIONS ABOUT SPEAKERS

Remind students that in a **dramatic monologue**, the reader must make inferences to learn about the speaker. The poet's word choice provides clues about the speaker's attitude and circumstances. (**Possible answer:** *The duke is powerful—only he can show the painting. Others don't dare to ask about the expression on his wife's face. Since he is the only one that can show the painting, he is the only one that can explain the expression.*)

My Last Duchess / Confession 669

TEACH

ANALYZE IMAGERY

Point out to students that this section of the poem is part of a long quotation, which means it's the wanderer's words. The wanderer is telling the reader what happened. They can use these words to **infer,** or make an educated guess based on their prior knowledge and details in the text, what has happened. (**Answer:** *They seem to be totally opposite. The duchess is carefree, loves life, and finds happiness in little things. The duke seems angry and jealous and is obsessed with controlling the duchess. It bothers him that his wife finds happiness in things and people other than himself. He is arrogant because he feels she stoops to trifling, perhaps with common folk, even though he gave her social status—his 900-year-old name.*)

DRAW CONCLUSIONS ABOUT SPEAKERS

Remind students that the **persona poem** poet provides clues through word choice and imagery that allow the reader to draw conclusions about the speaker. Have students share their opinions of the duke based on their conclusions from the speaker's own words. (**Answer:** *The duke wanted the listener to communicate to his master how powerful he is, that his dowry demands will not be questioned and that the fair daughter and future wife should be aware of the Duke's expectations. He wished to frighten and bully the Count into positioning himself for the utmost gain. However, in doing so, he may have unintentionally revealed the possibility that he committed murder, which might result in his intended bride's family either telling authorities, or, at minimum, being fearful of him and walking away.*)

 For **speaking support** for students at varying proficiency levels, see the **Text X-Ray** on page 666D.

ENGLISH LEARNER SUPPORT

Demonstrate Comprehension Tell students the lines in the poem are the duke's words. Read aloud lines 43–47. Ask: *Does he expect an answer?* (No) *If the duke was speaking to you, how might you reply?* (I'll rise.) Point out other comments and let students give responses.

Explain the comments are unanswered in a dramatic monologue and readers have to imagine the listener's responses. Have pairs identify other comments and respond to them.
MODERATE/LIGHT

NOTICE & NOTE

ANALYZE IMAGERY
Annotate: Mark details in lines 22–34 that describe what the duchess was like.

Compare: How does her character differ from that of the duke?

27 officious: offering unwanted services; meddling.

35 trifling: actions of little importance.

41 forsooth: in truth; indeed.

49 munificence (myoo-nĭf´ĭ-səns): generosity.

50 just pretense: legitimate claim.

51 dowry (dou´rē): payment given to a groom by the bride's father.

54 Neptune: in Roman mythology, the god of the sea.

DRAW CONCLUSIONS ABOUT SPEAKERS
Annotate: Mark the words in lines 44–56 that reveal the duke's sense of his own authority and power.

Interpret: What is the duke's motivation for telling the listener the story of his late wife? Has he revealed more than he intended? Explain.

670 Unit 5

Over my lady's wrist too much," or "Paint
Must never hope to reproduce the faint
Half-flush that dies along her throat": such stuff
20 Was courtesy, she thought, and cause enough
For calling up that spot of joy. She had
A heart—how shall I say?—too soon made glad,
Too easily impressed; she liked whate'er
She looked on, and her looks went everywhere.
25 Sir, 'twas all one! My favor at her breast,
The dropping of the daylight in the West,
The bough of cherries some officious fool
Broke in the orchard for her, the white mule
She rode with round the terrace—all and each
30 Would draw from her alike the approving speech,
Or blush, at least. She thanked men—good! but thanked
Somehow—I know not how—as if she ranked
My gift of a nine-hundred-years-old name
With anybody's gift. Who'd stoop to blame
35 This sort of trifling? Even had you skill
In speech—(which I have not)—to make your will
Quite clear to such an one, and say, "Just this
Or that in you disgusts me; here you miss,
Or there exceed the mark"—and if she let
40 Herself be lessoned so, nor plainly set
Her wits to yours, forsooth, and made excuse
—E'en then would be some stooping; and I choose
Never to stoop. Oh sir, she smiled, no doubt,
Whene'er I passed her; but who passed without
45 Much the same smile? This grew; I gave commands;
Then all smiles stopped together. There she stands
As if alive. Will't please you rise? We'll meet
The company below, then. I repeat,
The Count your master's known munificence
50 Is ample warrant that no just pretense
Of mine for dowry will be disallowed;
Though his fair daughter's self, as I avowed
At starting, is my object. Nay, we'll go
Together down, sir. Notice Neptune, though,
55 Taming a sea horse, thought a rarity,
Which Claus of Innsbruck cast in bronze for me!

WHEN STUDENTS STRUGGLE . . .

Visualize Character Help students develop a mental picture of the duke's character by having them fill out a graphic organizer, such as a web diagram, with words and phrases that describe the duke (e.g., *arrogant, jealous, unkind, angry*). Instruct students to visualize him as if he were a person they know and to infer his traits and feelings from what he says about his last duchess.

 For additional support, go to the **Reading Studio** and assign the following **Level Up tutorial: Character Traits**.

670 Unit 5

CHECK YOUR UNDERSTANDING

Answer these questions about "My Last Duchess" before moving on to the next selection.

1 In the discussion of the duchess's portrait, the duke focuses on the —

   A value of the painting
   B style of the painter
   C duchess's beauty
   D expression on her face

2 The duke thinks that he should be admired because of his —

   F social status
   G intelligence
   H appearance
   J eloquence

3 Why didn't the duke tell his late wife that she was offending him?

   A He was worried she would leave him.
   B He was too proud to complain.
   C He wanted her to figure it out on her own.
   D He knew she would die soon.

CHECK YOUR UNDERSTANDING

Have students answer the questions independently.

Answers:

1. D
2. F
3. B

If they answer any questions incorrectly, have them reread the text to confirm their understanding. Then they may proceed to the next selection.

ENGLISH LEARNER SUPPORT

Oral Assessment Use the following questions to assess students' comprehension and speaking skills:

1. On the painting, the speaker focuses on her _____. *(face)*
2. Does the speaker think people should admire him? *(yes)*
3. Did the speaker complain to his wife about her behavior? *(no)*

SUBSTANTIAL/MODERATE

TEACH

BACKGROUND

Have students read the Background and tell them author Linh Dinh has written and published many works that have been translated into several languages. He writes about life in America, but also how it contrasts with his native Vietnam. Read this excerpt from his blog describing the alley culture in Vietnam:

"Up and down that alley, men relaxed at tiny cafes, under anchored umbrellas. Some read newspapers. A pair played elephant chess. Here and there, an old man sunned himself in front of his house. Food carts sold noodles, wontons or sticky rice. A man pushed a three-wheeled pedal wagon, laden with vegetables. Under a conical hat, a woman slowly drove her motorbike around, with a speaker that repeated, 'Hot bread here! Crusty, thick-bodied bread here!'"

Discuss the imagery Dinh uses to describe the activity in the alley. Ask students to share the ideas and feelings evoked by his words. Compare the author's use of imagery in the excerpt to the imagery in "Confession."

PREPARE TO COMPARE

Direct students to use the Prepare to Compare prompt to focus their reading.

ANALYZE IMAGERY

Discuss with students why poets might use contrasting images to evoke emotions in the reader. Point out the example of contrasting images in lines 1 and 2 of the poem with the words "cruel" and "lovingly." Ask students to explain the effect of this contrast on the reader. (**Answer:** *The contrast between "smooth, poreless skin" and skin with "rashes and eruptions" shows that the speaker acknowledges the imperfections in people and values both the flawless and the flawed, where the skin is a metaphor for the people themselves.*)

 For **listening** and **reading support** for students at varying proficiency levels, see the **Text X-Ray** on pages 666C and 666D.

672   Unit 5

 **NOTICE & NOTE**

BACKGROUND

Linh Dinh (1963–) *is a contemporary poet from Vietnam. He has authored two collections of stories, a novel, and several poetry collections. He is best known for* Postcards from the End of America, *a book of photographs and text documenting life in America. To create that work, he crisscrossed the country by bus, train, and foot, encountering people from all walks of life, including those living on the margins of society. His portrait of the nation underscores the strength it takes to overcome hardship.*

CONFESSION
Poem by Linh Dinh

PREPARE TO COMPARE

As you read this poem, note how the character of its speaker differs from that of the speaker in "My Last Duchess." Consider the ways that both poems express themes about the negative side of human nature.

Notice & Note

Use the side margins to notice and note signposts in the text.

Perhaps I'm a cruel artist. I always depict
In great details, lovingly, all the defects
On the faces and bodies of my models.
I use my eyes and brushes to thread
5 The jagged gaps of their stiff smiles. I pamper
Each pimple, hump, massage each incrustation.

I cajole my models into poses that are awkward,
Dangerous, unhygienic, sometimes mortifying.
I don't care to paint <u>smooth, poreless skin</u> but collect
10 All manners of <u>rashes and eruptions</u>. Inspired,
I've forced a hundred bodies—impossibly old,
Extremely young—onto appalling heaps,

Democratically naked, viscous with sweat, spit and etc.,
Just so I could render the human condition
15 Most accurately and movingly.

ANALYZE IMAGERY
Annotate: Mark contrasting images in lines 9–10.
Interpret: What idea does this contrast help convey?

672   Unit 5

WHEN STUDENTS STRUGGLE . . .

Identify Author's Purpose Remind students that authors have a purpose or reason for writing. Work with students to generate a list of words and phrases from the poem they believe cause the reader to think, feel, or act a certain way. Next to each word or phrase, have students describe the intended result.

Then, have students answer these questions about the text: *What does the poet want the reader to know, think, feel, or do? What words or phrases help reflect the purpose?*

 For additional support, go to the **Reading Studio** and assign the following **Level Up tutorial: Author's Purpose**.

NOTICE & NOTE

CHECK YOUR UNDERSTANDING

Answer these questions before moving on to the **Analyze the Texts** section on the following page.

1. What does the poem's use of the phrase *democratically naked* suggest?
   A The speaker's motivations are political.
   B Nakedness creates a natural equality among people.
   C The models never feel embarrassed when they are together.
   D People have voted to take off their clothes before posing.

2. Why does the speaker use such negative imagery to describe the models?
   F The speaker is trying to elicit disgust in a listener or reader.
   G The speaker wants to emphasize the unattractiveness of the models to a listener or reader.
   H The speaker wants a listener or reader to grasp how truly ugly human beings are.
   J The speaker wants a listener or reader to dwell on the flesh-and-bone reality of imperfect human bodies.

3. How would you characterize the artist's purpose in painting people?
   A To see beauty in everyone
   B To express anger by showing humans as ugly
   C To make a statement about society's ideals
   D To idealize human physical imperfections

Confession 673

TEACH

CHECK YOUR UNDERSTANDING

Have students answer the questions independently.

Answers:
1. B
2. J
3. C

If they answer any questions incorrectly, have them reread the text to confirm their understanding. Then they may proceed to ANALYZE THE TEXTS on page 674.

ENGLISH LEARNER SUPPORT

Oral Assessment Use the following questions to assess students' comprehension and speaking skills:

1. What does the phrase *"democratically naked"* mean? *(a democracy means equal for all and nakedness suggests all the flaws of individuals are out in the open)*

2. Why does the speaker use so much negative imagery? *(to call attention to the imperfections we all have)*

3. What was the artist's purpose in painting people the way he did? *(to make a statement about how society sees beauty and perfection)* **MODERATE**

My Last Duchess / Confession 673

APPLY

ANALYZE THE TEXT

Possible answers:

1. **DOK 4:** Browning has the duke repeatedly focus on the countenance of his former wife, in her portrait, which is examined side by side with her actions and behavior. The duke repeats her misdeeds, which shows he is a man who feels a need to prove he is in the right, when another is wrong and must shoulder the blame.

2. **DOK 3:** The statement of the speaker in lines 45–46 indicates that the duke has the capability to use his power to have his wife killed. This was left ambiguous by Browning, so that the reader could draw his own conclusions about whether he did or did not, creating an air of mystery and suspicion.

3. **DOK 2:** Browning may be illustrating the point "Art imitates life" to show how the truth is revealed in art. The duke maintains a focus on the portrait and control of the viewing of the portrait, which stays hidden behind a curtain. In this way, he can interpret it to his own liking and present the circumstances in his own favor. Likewise, the second piece of artwork is meant to impress the family of his new wife. The character of the duke as arrogant, jealous, and shallow is revealed through the art.

4. **DOK 4:** The descriptions of bodily imperfections and disease create a rather bold tone. The descriptions are graphic and may offend some. The speaker believes, however, that art should show the truth about people.

5. **DOK 3:** The speaker in "Confession" does not actually consider himself "cruel." Instead, he embraces the human condition in all its strength and imperfect conditions.

RESEARCH

To help students begin their research, have them share a movie, book, play, or song that deals with the topic of jealousy. Encourage them to summarize the plot in a few words and then to research others.

Extend If students have trouble coming up with the theme of a work, they may research themes around jealousy or literary themes to find one that best fits the storyline.

RESPOND

ANALYZE THE TEXTS

Support your responses with evidence from the text. NOTEBOOK

1. **Analyze** Which images does Browning use repeatedly in "My Last Duchess"? What does this repetition reveal about the speaker's personality?

2. **Draw Conclusions** In lines 45–46 of "My Last Duchess," the speaker says, "I gave commands; / Then all smiles stopped together." How do you interpret this statement? Why might Browning have chosen to have the duke describe his actions so ambiguously?

3. **Interpret** Browning devotes most of "My Last Duchess" to discussion of the portrait, and he ends with a description of another artwork. What theme about art and life does he develop in the poem?

4. **Analyze** What mood is created by the images of bodily imperfections and disease in "Confession"? How does this mood support the speaker's ideas about art?

5. **Draw Conclusions** Do you think the speaker of "Confession" really wants us to consider him cruel, or does he have a more idealistic reason for the way he paints? Explain your response.

RESEARCH

RESEARCH TIP
Use websites that give reviews of books, movies, and songs to discover likely titles.

Then, to gather information on years, media types, plots, and themes, search several additional websites.

Feelings of jealousy have been expressed by human beings throughout the ages and across societies. How often does our entertainment industry rely on tales of jealous behavior and its consequences? Research works, such as movies, books, plays, and songs, that address the topic of jealousy. Find several examples from different time periods in a variety of media. Use the graphic organizer below to help you organize and explain your findings.

TITLE	TYPE OF MEDIA	TIME FRAME	SYNOPSIS
Gone With the Wind	movie	1939	Scarlett is jealous of Melanie
Othello	play	1603	Jealousy between Iago and Othello
Bernadette	song	1967	Men are jealous of Bernadette's boyfriend

Extend Conduct a survey of your classmates to determine their top five favorite movies. Determine if any of the movies address the topic of jealous behavior, and discuss the themes, or messages about life or human nature, those movies express.

WHEN STUDENTS STRUGGLE . . .

Reteach: Analyze Imagery Read aloud lines 7–8 from "My Last Duchess." Explain to students the senses to which the images appeal and the feelings that the images evoke. Explain that the images appeal to sight. They evoke the idea of examining the portrait and the look on the duchess' face for her underlying emotion. Have students describe an image that a modern poet might use to capture the same feelings of despair and injustice.

For additional support, go to the **Reading Studio** and assign the following Level Up tutorial: **Imagery**.

RESPOND

CREATE AND PRESENT

Create an Oral Presentation "My Last Duchess" and "Confession" present contrasts in style, tone, and language. The speaker in "My Last Duchess" lived during the Renaissance, so he spoke very differently than the contemporary artist in "Confession." Develop an oral presentation in which you assume the persona of one of the two speakers and recite that poem as a monologue.

❏ Be sure you understand the emotions underlying specific words and phrases, as well as their purposes, and mark the text to indicate style of delivery.

❏ Plan appropriate gestures and movements along with effective intonation to guide emphasis.

❏ Remember to address your audience. Is the speaker talking to a listener or to himself?

Present the Monologue In a small group, present your monologue.

❏ Make sure your presentation helps others understand the poem.

❏ Be clear about the message you impart as the speaker of the poem.

❏ Analyze what you would do differently if you were to recite the second poem.

 Go to **Giving a Presentation** in the **Speaking and Listening Studio** for more about presenting to others.

RESPOND TO THE ESSENTIAL QUESTION

 What brings out cruelty in people?

Gather Information Review your annotations and notes on "My Last Duchess" and "Confession." Then, add relevant information to your Response Log. As you determine which information to include, think about:

- human nature and the human condition
- the difference between tolerance and acceptance
- ways that ego and self-obsession motivate behavior

ACADEMIC VOCABULARY
As you write and discuss what you learned from the poems, be sure to use the Academic Vocabulary words. Check off each of the words that you use.

❏ abandon
❏ confine
❏ confirm
❏ depress
❏ reluctance

APPLY

CREATE AND PRESENT

Create an Oral Presentation After students have selected their persona, encourage them to practice reciting their chosen poem aloud, remembering to stress emotions with their words and use gestures to emphasize points.

Present the Monologue Have students form peer groups to critique each other's monologues before presenting them to the class.

- Students should give concrete, specific ideas for how their peers might improve their monologue presentations.
- Students should review the suggestions and decide which ones to incorporate into their monologue.
- Pairs may then videotape their monologues for posting on the web.

RESPOND TO THE ESSENTIAL QUESTION

Allow time for students to add details from "My Last Duchess" and "Confession" to their Unit 5 Response Logs.

For **writing support** for students at varying proficiency levels, see the **Text X-Ray** on page 666D.

APPLY

COMPARE THEMES

Discuss with students the elements they will have to examine in order to determine the **themes** of the two poems. Remind students that themes are not usually directly stated. They must be inferred based on the details in the texts. Have students discuss details in the poems that reveal ideas about cruelty, the role of art, and human nature, then fill in the chart.

ANALYZE THE TEXTS

Possible answers:

1. **DOK 2:** The speaker's flaws in "My Last Duchess" are bravado, greed, conceit, and perhaps murder. The flaws of the painter in "Confession" are brutal honesty over human imperfections and a focus on the negative.

2. **DOK 2:** The speaker in "My Last Duchess" is shown to be self-absorbed through his disdainful description of the portrait of his late wife. He speaks of her too glad heart, her attention to men, his revered 900-year-old family name, his discussion of the dowry, and the idea that when he gave commands (perhaps orders) her smile stopped. In "Confession," the speaker first speaks of stiff smiles with jagged edges indicating that perhaps something is hidden, untruthful, and dangerous but then discusses awkward poses, rashes, and eruptions and makes one think of disease, death, and lack of humanity. Yet in the end, he is revealed to be a sensitive artist who understands human imperfection and wants to display it before the world.

3. **DOK 3:** Frá Pandolf and the painter in "Confession" are similar because both share a strong attention to detail, as Frá Pandolf captured the essence of the last duchess with her physical features that somewhat irritated the duke, and the painter takes note of very specific features and flaws in the subjects he paints. Frá Pandolf was directed by the duke, while the painter is free to capture what he sees in human nature to influence societal norms of beauty.

4. **DOK 4:** The duke may be a murderer, which would clearly pose a threat to society. In addition, his hunger for power over others could turn dangerous in many ways. The painter could threaten the societal norms with his unconventional attitude toward beauty, by highlighting imperfections and rejecting the 'perfect' image.

676 Unit 5

RESPOND

Collaborate & Compare

COMPARE THEMES

"My Last Duchess" and "Confession" both focus on art, and they also address cruelty. Still, the two poems express distinct ideas about human nature.

With your group, discuss each area of focus listed in the chart below and record what you notice under the appropriate poem.

MY LAST DUCHESS
Poem by Robert Browning

CONFESSION
Poem by Linh Dinh

	"MY LAST DUCHESS"	"CONFESSION"
Information from the title	the previous or deceased wife	the speaker will confess something
Identity of the speaker	a duke in Italy	a painter
Primary subject matter	a portrait of the duchess and a new wife	human imperfections
Use of imagery	through the portrait of the duchess	graphic descriptions of imperfections
Implied emotions	anger, fear, arrogance	humility, shock and disgust
The role of art	reflects and conceals emotions	equalizing, showing truth
View of human nature	cruelty of some towards others	tolerance of nature's cruelty

ANALYZE THE TEXTS

Discuss these questions in your group.

1. **Infer** What flaws of human nature are represented by the speakers in the two poems?

2. **Interpret** How does the imagery of the two poems help reveal the identity and character of each speaker? What conclusions about the speakers can you draw based on their word choices?

3. **Compare** What similarities do Frá Pandolf and the painter in "Confession" share? What differences distinguish the two?

4. **Evaluate** How might the duke and the painter in "Confession" pose a threat to their respective societies?

676 Unit 5

 ENGLISH LEARNER SUPPORT

Ask Questions Use the following questions to help students compare the selections:

1. How is the speaker in "My Last Duchess" different from the speaker in "Confession"? *(The duke in "My Last Duchess" is arrogant and brash as he expresses himself to the listener. The painter in "Confession" speaks boldly about the truth, but is compassionate toward others.)*

2. What do "My Last Duchess" and "Confession" help you learn about cruelty? *(Those who seek power can be cruel to others. Outward appearances show we all have imperfections.)*

MODERATE/LIGHT

RESPOND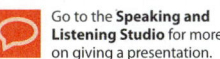

COLLABORATE AND PRESENT

In your group, continue exploring the ideas in the poems by identifying and comparing their themes. Follow these steps:

1. **Decide on the most important details.** As a group, review the information you gathered in the previous chart. Determine which points you agree on and resolve disagreements by identifying evidence from the poems that support your ideas.

2. **Determine themes.** Write theme statements, or statements that express each poem's message about life or human nature. Use the chart below to help you track your group's ideas and identify possible themes.

	NOTES	POSSIBLE THEMES
"My Last Duchess"	duke refuses to stoop	Arrogance stifles communication.
"Confession"	jagged, stiff smiles	Inner ugliness can't be hidden.

3. **Compare the themes.** Work together as a group to determine similarities and differences between the themes.

4. **Develop your ideas.** Organize your ideas around your points of comparison, and provide evidence and explanations for each.

5. **Present to the class.** Determine how you will present your comparison, who will present it, and if the use of any visuals or diagrams would help clarify your points. Consider using technology as a presentation tool.

Go to the **Speaking and Listening Studio** for more on giving a presentation.

APPLY

COLLABORATE AND PRESENT

Direct students in small groups as they work to identify the themes in the poems and fill out their charts. Remind students to carefully consider details and examples of imagery they have recorded in their notes to help them. Encourage students to share ideas before filling in their charts and preparing to present their ideas.

Decide on the most important details Before students decide the most important details in each of the poems, encourage them to each brainstorm two or three ideas and then discuss each of their ideas, with supporting evidence, with their group members. Direct students to look at their notes and mark the details they recorded that they think are the most important clues to the authors' purposes.

Determine themes Tell students that their collective message can be a combination of text and visuals, as long as they include the details they think are most important to answer the question of why the writer created the text.

Compare the themes Have students contribute all of their ideas to completing the group's chart. Remind them to think about what is the same and what is different about the writers' circumstances that influenced the development of the theme in each poem.

Develop your ideas Remind students when they prepare their presentations to think about their audience and make sure they include all of the necessary information and present their points in a way that is clear.

Present to the class Encourage students to speak clearly and use eye contact as a way to connect with the audience as they present.

TO CHALLENGE STUDENTS . . .

Make Additional Connections Have students choose either "My Last Duchess" or "Confession" and think of other poems they have read that have a similar style or a similar theme. Have students compare the poems based on their similarities and then write an original poem in the same manner. Have students recite their poems before the group.

INDEPENDENT READING

READER'S CHOICE

Setting a Purpose Have students review their Unit 5 Response Logs and think about what they've already learned about the Victorian era. As they choose their Independent Reading selections, encourage them to consider what more they want to know.

NOTICE & NOTE

Explain that some selections may contain multiple signposts; others may contain only one. Moreover, the same type of signpost can occur many times in the same text.

 LEARNING MINDSET

Seek Challenges Explain to students that to learn and grow, it is important to seek challenges. By choosing to take on a text that is difficult for them, they will build their reading skills and become more proficient. Struggling with a text does not mean that they are not smart or are not good readers, but they are doing the work of building their brain muscles and realizing their true potential.

 **INDEPENDENT READING**

Reader's Choice

Setting a Purpose Select one or more of these options from your eBook to continue your exploration of the Essential Questions.

- Read the descriptions to see which text grabs your interest.
- Think about which genres you enjoy reading.

ESSENTIAL QUESTIONS Review the four Essential Questions for this unit on page 587.

Notice & Note

In this unit, you practiced noticing and noting the signposts and asking big questions about nonfiction. As you read independently, these signposts and others will aid your understanding. Below are the anchor questions to ask when you read literature and nonfiction.

Reading Literature: Stories, Poems, and Plays	
Signpost	Key Question
Contrasts and Contradictions	Why did the character act that way?
Aha Moment	How might this change things?
Tough Questions	What does this make me wonder about?
Words of the Wiser	What's the lesson for the character?
Again and Again	Why might the author keep bringing this up?
Memory Moment	Why is this memory important?

Reading Nonfiction: Essays, Articles, and Arguments	
Signpost	Key Question(s)
Big Questions	What surprised me? What did the author think I already knew? What challenged, changed, or confirmed what I already knew?
Contrasts and Contradictions	What is the difference, and why does it matter?
Extreme or Absolute Language	Why did the author use this language?
Numbers and Stats	Why did the author use these numbers or amounts?
Quoted Words	Why was this person quoted or cited, and what did this add?
Word Gaps	Do I know this word from someplace else? Does it seem like technical talk for this topic? Do clues in the sentence help me understand the word?

678 Unit 5

 ENGLISH LEARNER SUPPORT

Develop Fluency Select a passage from the text that matches students' reading abilities. Read the passage aloud while students follow silently.

- Read each sentence aloud in chunks, pausing to have students echo back. Ask students to circle words they do not recognize and write them on the board. Provide the meaning and pronunciation of each word. **SUBSTANTIAL**
- Have student pairs read passages aloud to each other, alternating sentences and monitoring pronunciation. Check comprehension by asking questions about the text. **MODERATE**
- Display two or three comprehension questions, and challenge students to find the answers in a timed read. **LIGHT**

 Go to the **Reading Studio** for additional support in developing fluency.

678 Unit 5

INDEPENDENT READING

You can preview these texts in Unit 5 of your eBook.
Then check off the text or texts that you select to read on your own.

POEM
Sonnet 43
Elizabeth Barrett Browning

Is love an intense but simple feeling or a complex emotion with many dimensions?

POEM
Remembrance
Emily Brontë

Can love survive a loved one's death, or does it change as the survivor grows older?

ARTICLE
The Great Exhibition
Lara Kriegel

What looked like a giant greenhouse and brought visitors to London from all over the world?

SHORT STORY
Christmas Storms and Sunshine
Elizabeth Cleghorn Gaskell

Can two families divided by politics overcome their differences and discover the benefits of friendship?

ESSAY
Evidence of Progress
Thomas Babington Macaulay

During times of turmoil, how can you tell whether a nation is taking steps toward a better future?

Collaborate and Share Meet with a partner to discuss what you learned from at least one of your independent readings.

- Give a brief synopsis or summary of the text.
- Describe any signposts that you noticed in the text and explain what they revealed to you.
- Describe what you most enjoyed or found most challenging about the text. Give specific examples.
- Decide whether you would recommend the text to others. Why or why not?

 Go to the **Reading Studio** for more resources on **Notice & Note.**

INDEPENDENT READING

MATCHING STUDENTS TO TEXTS

Use the following information to guide students in choosing their texts.

Sonnet 43
Genre: poem
Overall Rating: Accessible

Remembrance
Genre: poem
Overall Rating: Accessible

The Great Exhibition — Lexile: 1120L
Genre: article
Overall Rating: Accessible

Christmas Storms and Sunshine — Lexile: 1050L
Genre: short story
Overall Rating: Challenging

Evidence of Progress — Lexile: 1450L
Genre: essay
Overall Rating: Challenging

Collaborate and Share To assess how well students read the selections, walk around the room and listen to their conversations. Encourage students to focus and be specific in their comments.

 for Assessment

- Independent Reading Selection Tests

 Encourage students to visit the **Reading Studio** to download a handy bookmark of **NOTICE & NOTE** signposts.

WHEN STUDENTS STRUGGLE . . .

Keep a Reading Log As students read their selected texts, have them keep a reading log for each selection to note signposts and their thoughts about them. Use their logs to assess how well they are noticing and reflecting on elements of their texts.

Reading Log for (title)		
Location	Signpost I Noticed	My Notes about It

PLAN

UNIT 5 Tasks

- **WRITE A RESEARCH REPORT**
- **GIVE A MULTIMODAL PRESENTATION**

MENTOR TEXT

THE VICTORIANS HAD THE SAME CONCERNS ABOUT TECHNOLOGY AS WE DO

Essay by Melissa Dickson

LEARNING OBJECTIVES

Writing Task

- Write a research report about how technology affects society in our time.
- Use strategies and organizers to plan a report.
- Use the Mentor Text as a model for writing a strong beginning "hook" and thesis statement.
- Use such genre characteristics as paraphrasing, summarizing, and using direct quotations.
- Write a first draft that includes relevant key ideas and supporting evidence.
- Use a Revision Guide and peer review to revise.
- Edit draft to combine sentences using conjunctions.
- Use a rubric to evaluate writing.
- Publish writing to share with an audience.
- **Language** Write with a variety of verbs.

Speaking Task

- Adapt a report as a multimodal presentation.
- Plan slides.
- Use graphics, images, and consistent design.
- Consider use of music, audio, or sound effects.
- Practice effective verbal and nonverbal techniques.
- Provide and consider advice for improvement.
- Deliver a presentation.
- **Language** Paraphrase a thesis and key ideas.

Assign the Writing Task in **Ed**.

RESOURCES

- Unit 5 Response Log
- Writing Studio: Writing Informative Texts
- Speaking and Listening Studio: Using Media in a Presentation
- Grammar Studio: Module 2: Lesson 7: Conjunctions and Interjections

PLAN

Language X-Ray: English Learner Support

Use the instruction below and the supports and scaffolds in the Teacher's Edition to help you guide students of different proficiency levels.

INTRODUCE THE WRITING TASK

Explain that writers of **research reports** organize their ideas carefully for maximum effect. Tell students to list all their key ideas in order of importance when planning research reports. They can judge the importance of each idea by how interesting, shocking, or impressive it will be to readers. Tell students also to write clear transitions between their key ideas. Discuss why it is important to start and end with the strongest key ideas. Have students brainstorm ideas for their reports, list them on the board, and rank them in order of importance. Then have them discuss what is surprising or impressive about each idea. Provide sentence frames such as: *The idea that _____ is more surprising/impressive than _____ because _____.*

WRITING

Vary Verbs

Remind students that verbs express action even if the action is mental rather than physical. Review a list of verbs related to thought and opinion, such as: *think, believe, state, claim, feel that, assert, have established, maintain, speculate, posit.*

Use the following supports with students at varying proficiency levels:

- Provide sentence frames for students to complete using the verbs provided at left: *I _____ that cell phones have improved people's lives. I _____ it would be hard to do my school work without a computer.* **SUBSTANTIAL**
- Have students use three to five verbs from the list to state claims in their drafts. Have pairs exchange papers and mark the verbs related to opinions and claims. **MODERATE**
- Have students write their drafts using at least five verbs from the list. Then, have students exchange drafts with a partner and suggest different verbs. **LIGHT**

SPEAKING

Paraphrase Ideas

Remind students that they can use their own words to restate their peers' ideas. Point out that when they paraphrase their peers, they can use more informal language, including contractions.

Use the following supports with students at varying proficiency levels:

- Use a Think-Aloud to paraphrase the claim "*Cell phone usage interferes with sleep.*" Say: *I know* interferes *means "stops." I don't want to stop my sleep. I can paraphrase this way: Cell phones are bad for sleep.* Have students repeat the claim and paraphrase. **SUBSTANTIAL**
- Have students write a list of contractions to use in paraphrasing key ideas. Then, have them use their notes and contractions to restate each other's ideas. **MODERATE**
- Have partners listen to each other's presentations and write the key ideas in their own words. Then, have them paraphrase each other's ideas orally. **LIGHT**

WRITING

WRITE A RESEARCH REPORT

Introduce students to the Writing Task by reading the introductory paragraph with them. Remind students to refer to the notes they recorded in their Unit 5 Response Logs as they plan and draft their reports. Their Response Logs should contain ideas about societal changes from a variety of perspectives. Drawing on these different perspectives will make their own writing more interesting and well informed.

 For **writing support** for students at varying proficiency levels, see the **Language X-Ray** on page 680B.

USE THE MENTOR TEXT

Point out that students' research reports will be similar to the essay "The Victorians Had the Same Concerns About Technology As We Do," in that they will use facts, examples, and quotes from outside sources to support their own analysis and present an original idea to the reader. Their reports, however, will focus on a specific modern invention.

WRITING PROMPT

Review the prompt with students. Encourage them to ask questions about any part of the assignment that is unclear. Make sure they understand that the purpose of their report is to answer the question using facts and ideas from the background readings and their research, along with their own analysis.

 **WRITING TASK**

Write a Research Report

 Go to the **Writing Studio** for help writing informative texts.

This unit focuses on the Victorian period, when rapid technological changes affected nearly every aspect of society, including government, transportation, communication, religious practice, and relations between classes. For this writing task, you will do some research and use outside sources to write about how technology has affected society in our own time. For an example of an essay that uses outside sources well, review the article "The Victorians Had the Same Concerns about Technology as We Do."

As you write your research report, you can use the notes from your Response Log that you filled out after reading the texts in this unit.

Writing Prompt

Read the information in the box below.

This is the topic or context for your research report.

> Both social science research and literature often explore the effects of technological developments on our lives.

Think carefully about the following question.

How might this Essential Question relate to your research report?

> Which invention has had the greatest impact on your life?

How does the research you will do relate to the topic of your report?

Write a research report about one modern invention that has changed the social order or the way people live their daily lives.

Be sure to —

Review these points as you write and again when you finish. Make any needed changes.

- ❑ develop research questions
- ❑ review many possible sources
- ❑ choose the best sources for your essay
- ❑ organize your report logically
- ❑ use evidence from your sources to support your own ideas
- ❑ cite each outside source in the text
- ❑ use quotations, paraphrasing, and summarizing; state most facts and ideas in your own words, using direct quotations when appropriate
- ❑ present a thesis statement
- ❑ include an introduction and conclusion

 LEARNING MINDSET

Try Again Explain to students that research is a process of finding the answer to a question. They may start out thinking they know the answer, but as they work, they may realize that their original ideas were incomplete or inaccurate. Point out that this finding is good news because it means they are learning from their research. Changing their answer to a question after doing some research simply shows that their research has increased their knowledge. Encourage students to talk to each other about how research has led them to revise their ideas.

1 Plan

Once you have thought about the writing prompt, it's time to plan your research and the writing of your report. First, identify an area of focus related to the topic. It can be helpful to think about background reading you have done or personal interests that you have. As part of your planning, you must also consider your purpose and audience. Follow the steps below to get started planning your research project.

Research Report Planning Table	
Identify research questions	What are some recent inventions? How do they affect my life?
Identify ideas from background reading	
Identify personal interests related to the topic	
Focus on one question/topic	
State your purpose	
Identify your audience	

Background Reading Review the notes you have taken in your Response Log that relate to the question, "Which invention has had the greatest impact on your life?" Texts in this unit provide background reading that will help you formulate and develop the topic for your research report.

WRITING TASK

Go to **Writing Informative Texts: Developing a Topic** for help planning your research report.

Notice & Note
From Reading to Writing

As you plan your research report, apply what you've learned about signposts to your own writing. Remember that writers use common features called signposts to help convey their message to readers.

Think how you can incorporate **Quoted Words** into your report.

Go to the **Reading Studio** for more resources on **Notice & Note**.

Use the notes from your Response Log as you plan your research report.

Write a Research Report **681**

WRITING

1 PLAN

Tell students that in this stage, they will start to make decisions about the topic they will research and write about. Encourage them to be open to new ideas and explore various options before deciding on the focus of their research.

■ English Learner Support

Understand Academic Language Clarify what is meant by inventions having an impact on society. Have students work in small mixed-level ability groups to list modern inventions and the way they have changed society and daily life. Then, brainstorm simple summaries of the effects of the inventions. An example of an invention is solar-powered cell phone chargers; their effect is that people can recharge cell phones at any time, anywhere. Another example is personal scent kits; their effect is to make it easier to find lost people with the help of tracking dogs. Next, have students work in pairs to decide on one invention they will research together. **ALL LEVELS**

▶ NOTICE & NOTE
From Reading to Writing

Remind students they can use **Quoted Words** in their writing, such as when they are including the opinions or ideas of someone who is an expert on the topic, or when they are using a text as evidence to support their analysis. Remind them to make sure they are punctuating quotations correctly and to identify their sources.

Background Reading As students plan their research reports, remind them to refer to the notes they took in their Response Logs. They may also review the selections to find additional facts and examples to support ideas they want to include in their writing.

TO CHALLENGE STUDENTS . . .

Understand Unintended Consequences Point out to students that some inventions changed society or daily life in surprising ways that people did not expect at all. For example, when home computers and printers became commonplace in the 1990s, people were expected to use much less paper, but they actually started using *more* paper because they were printing more files from their computers. Have students identify a modern invention that had a surprising or an unforeseen effect. Ask them to write an analysis of why the surprising effect happened or why it was unforeseen.

Write a Research Report **681**

WRITING

Organize Your Ideas Tell students that before they start writing, they should know what their thesis is and which key ideas they will use to support their thesis. They should also identify a "hook" to grab the reader's attention. Have students experiment with different kinds of hooks, such as:

- An interesting quote from their reading
- A surprising fact
- A very short anecdote
- A provocative question

Remind students that their introductory paragraph should give the reader some background and present the thesis. Their conclusion will remind the reader of their thesis, summarize the ideas they used to support it, and then leave the reader with more to think about.

Make sure students keep track of the sources they use in their reports so they can create their Works Cited page at the end. Point out that the Works Cited page should include only the sources they actually used in their papers, and not necessarily every source they consulted.

2 DEVELOP A DRAFT

Remind students each paragraph should have a key idea that supports their thesis statement. Make sure students understand they can use more than one source to support each key idea. Point out it is okay to change their writing plan if they decide that material from a certain source might provide better support for a different paragraph, or if they find they do not have enough notes or sources to support one of their ideas.

■ English Learner Support

Write Using Content-Based Vocabulary Help students get started on their drafts by having them first write a few sentences explaining why they think their chosen invention has been important to modern life. Provide the following sentence stems to help them start writing:

- I think <invention> is an important invention because _____.
- For example, in my life <invention> has _____.
- Without <invention>, people would/would not _____. **MODERATE**

682 Unit 5

 WRITING TASK

 Go to **Writing Informative Texts: Organizing Ideas** for help organizing your research report.

Organize Your Ideas After you have gathered ideas in your planning table, you need to organize them in a way that will help you draft your research report. You can use the chart below to help you organize your draft before you start writing.

Organize Your Research Report

Write a "hook." The opening sentence of your report should grab the reader's attention.	
Write a thesis statement. Use your planning table to write a thesis statement for your report.	
Outline the body of your report. List at least three key ideas that support your thesis statement.	
Write a conclusion. Restate your thesis statement, and summarize your key ideas.	
Keep a list of your sources. List all of the sources you plan to use along with the relevant publication information. You will use this list later to create your Works Cited page.	

 You might prefer to draft your research report online.

2 Develop a Draft

Once you have completed your planning, you will be ready to begin drafting your research report. Refer to your graphic organizers as well as any notes you took as you studied the texts in this unit. This material will provide ideas for you to develop as you write. Using a word processor or online writing application makes it easier to make changes or move sentences around later when you are ready to revise your first draft.

682 Unit 5

WHEN STUDENTS STRUGGLE . . .

Draft the Report Even when working from a chart to organize ideas and sources, students may struggle to get started on their drafts. Encourage students to write their research notes on index cards or strips of paper. Each card or strip should contain one idea, fact, or quotation from a background reading or their research. Have students lay the cards or strips on a table and move them around to experiment with organizing them. Tell students they do not need to use all their notes if some provide better support than others. Have them group the notes by the **key ideas** they support. Then, have them talk about what each set of notes has in common before writing a key idea sentence for each set.

WRITING TASK

Use the Mentor Text

Author's Craft
Your introduction should start with a "hook" to grab the reader's attention. It should also provide background on the topic. Near the end of your introduction, you should provide a thesis statement that tells the reader the main idea of your report. The thesis statement is a **claim**—something the reader might not already know or agree with. Note the introduction from "The Victorians Had the Same Concerns about Technology as We Do."

> Many of us struggle with the bombardment of information we receive and experience anxiety as a result of new media. . . .
>
> Though the technologies may change, these fears actually have a very long history. . . . Literary, medical, and cultural responses in the Victorian age to the perceived problems of stress and overwork anticipate many of the preoccupations of our own era. . . .

This is the background that introduces the topic.

This is the thesis statement. The reader should expect the author to present evidence supporting this statement.

Apply What You've Learned Review the notes from your research and the ideas in your planning table. Then, write a statement supported by your key ideas and evidence from your research. Remember that your thesis statement should present a claim that the reader may not already know or agree with.

Genre Characteristics
When writers use evidence from their sources, they introduce the idea or fact by identifying the source. Then, they present it by paraphrasing, summarizing, or using a direct quotation. Notice how the author of the article uses signal phrases to connect her sources with the ideas the sources support.

> Thomas Carlyle, for example, lamented the new lack of direct contact with society and nature. . . . Print publications were fast becoming the principal medium of public debate and influence. . . .

The author identifies the source and uses the signal phrase "for example" to show that the source supports the author's key idea.

Apply What You've Learned Introduce each source you use by giving the name of a person, organization, and/or the publication associated with the source. Use signal phrases to connect the source with the key idea it supports.

Write a Research Report   683

WRITING

WHY THIS MENTOR TEXT?
"The Victorians Had the Same Concerns About Technology As We Do" provides a good example of how to support a **claim** with evidence from research. Use the instruction below to help students use the mentor text as a model for using outside sources to support their own analyses.

USE THE MENTOR TEXT

Author's Craft Read aloud or have students read silently the explanation about what should be in their introduction. Then, read aloud the introduction from "The Victorians Had the Same Concerns About Technology As We Do." Have students explain what the reader can expect the essay to discuss, based on the introduction, and how this introduction makes the reader want to keep reading. Point out that the author starts with a background statement that draws on what the reader probably already knows, then the author proceeds to a thesis statement containing an idea that may be unfamiliar. The rest of the essay will explain and support that thesis statement.

Genre Characteristics Read aloud or have students read silently the explanation about using evidence from sources. Then, have a volunteer read the excerpt given as an example. Ask students to identify the name of the source and then summarize in their own words the idea that the author took from the source. (*As print became the main medium for public discussion and information, there was a new lack of direct contact with society and nature.*) Ask students to explain why the writer used this source. (*It provides an example that supports the author's key idea.*) Tell students they should use excerpts from sources as examples in their own writing.

 ENGLISH LEARNER SUPPORT

Internalize New Academic Language Support students in understanding and talking about the concepts in "Use the Mentor Text" by clarifying the words *claim, background, expect, source, support,* and *key idea*. Then, supply these sentence frames to practice using this vocabulary:

The background sentence assumes the reader already understands that ____. *(the bombardment of new media causes anxiety)*

The reader expects to learn about ____. *(how Victorians experienced the same anxiety)*

The author's source supports the key idea by ____. *(providing an example)* **MODERATE**

Write a Research Report   683

WRITING

3. REVISE

On Your Own Review with students the purpose of their research reports. Ask students to consider their reports from the perspective of a reader and decide whether they would find their reports interesting and informative. Have students answer each question in the chart to determine ways to improve their drafts. Have students choose two or three points to focus on in their revisions and explain why they have chosen those points.

With a Partner Have students ask peer reviewers to evaluate their reports by answering the following questions:

- Does the introduction make me want to keep reading?
- Does this report tell me something I didn't already know?
- Do the facts and ideas from outside sources support the key ideas?
- Is there anything that's unclear or that I need more information about?

After they have answered these questions about their partner's draft, direct students to give at least three recommendations for revisions.

 **WRITING TASK**

Go to **Writing Informative Texts: Precise Language and Vocabulary** for help revising your research report.

3. Revise

On Your Own Once you have written your draft, you'll want to go back and look for ways to improve your research report. As you reread and revise, think about whether you have achieved your purpose. The Revision Guide will help you focus on specific elements to make your writing stronger.

Revision Guide

Ask Yourself	Tips	Revision Techniques
1. Does the introduction engage the reader, provide background information, and clearly state the thesis?	**Circle** the engaging introduction, **underline** the background information, and **bracket** the thesis statement.	**Add** a quotation or interesting detail to hook readers. **Add** necessary background information. **Add** a thesis statement.
2. Does the body include only relevant key ideas and supporting evidence?	**Mark** the key ideas. **Number** supporting evidence for each key idea.	**Delete** irrelevant ideas and evidence. **Add** evidence to support ideas.
3. Are sources credited and citations punctuated correctly?	**Place check marks** next to material that requires citation.	**Add** parenthetical citations if necessary, and **correct** punctuation.
4. Does the conclusion restate the thesis?	**Bracket** the restatement of the thesis.	**Add** a sentence or two restating the thesis.
5. Is the Works Cited list complete and correctly formatted?	**Compare** parenthetical citations with the entries in your Works Cited list.	**Add** Works Cited entries if necessary and revise incorrectly formatted entries.

ACADEMIC VOCABULARY

As you conduct your **peer review,** be sure to use these words.

- ☐ abandon
- ☐ confine
- ☐ conform
- ☐ depress
- ☐ reluctance

With a Partner Once you and your partner have worked through the Revision Guide on your own, exchange research reports and evaluate each other's draft in a **peer review.** Focus on providing revision suggestions for at least three of the items mentioned in the chart. Explain why you think your partner's draft should be revised and what your specific suggestions are.

When receiving feedback from your partner, listen attentively and ask questions to make sure you fully understand the revision suggestions.

 ENGLISH LEARNER SUPPORT

Express Opinions Have students work in pairs and read their reports aloud to each other. Tell students to ask for clarification if any words are unfamiliar.

Have students retell what they learned from their partner's report. Then, supply these sentence stems to help them give feedback:

- I think this report is good because _____.
- To make this report better, you should _____. **MODERATE/LIGHT**

4 Edit

Once you have addressed the organization, use of supporting evidence, and logical flow of ideas in your paper, you can look to improve the finer points of your draft. Edit for effective sentence structure, smooth syntax, precise word choice, and Standard English grammar and punctuation.

Language Conventions

Combining Sentences Too many short sentences can result in a stiff style that doesn't clearly show the relationship between ideas. One way that writers connect ideas is by combining sentences using coordinating and subordinating conjunctions. In the examples below, the numbers [1] and [2] show the two ideas that are combined.

Go to the **Grammar Studio: Conjunctions and Interjections** to learn more about conjunctions.

Coordinating Conjunctions	Example
and, but, or, so, therefore	[1] Print publications were fast becoming the principal medium of public debate and influence, [2] **and** they were shaping and, in Carlyle's view, distorting human learning and communications.

Subordinating Conjunctions	Example
Time: when, as, before, after	**While** [1] we cannot draw too strict a line of comparison between 19th-century attitudes to such technologies as the telegraph, train, telephone, and newspaper and our own responses as a culture to the advent of the Internet and the mobile phone, [2] there are parallels that almost argue against the Luddite position.
Contrast: although, even though, even if, while	
Cause/effect: because, if, unless	

Note that when you use a subordinating conjunction, it can come at the beginning or in the middle of the sentence.

5 Publish

Finalize your research and choose a way to share it with your audience. Consider these options:
- Share it as an article on an open web platform.
- Ask your school librarian to make your work available in the library.

Write a Research Report 685

 **WRITING TASK**

4 EDIT

Ask students to read their drafts carefully to check for any grammatical errors or careless mistakes. Suggest students look for shorter sentences that could be combined. As they do this, students should check that they have made clear connections between ideas and that they have used correct punctuation when incorporating quotations.

LANGUAGE CONVENTIONS

Combining Sentences Explain to students that using connecting words and phrases helps the reader to follow their reasoning and understand how evidence from outside sources supports their key ideas. Ask for examples from volunteers for using the conjunctions given in the chart, and ask them to name other conjunctions not listed. Remind students to use a variety of sentence lengths.

Display these simple sentences and ask students for ideas about combining them with coordinating and subordinating conjunctions:
- Using outside sources makes an essay more interesting.
- It's important to support your ideas with evidence.
- Expert opinions are helpful.
- Authors should also present original ideas.

(*Possible answers:*
- *Although expert opinions are helpful, authors should also present original ideas.*
- *It's important to support your ideas with evidence, and using outside sources makes an essay more interesting.*)

■ English Learner Support

Combine Sentences Using Connecting Words Organize students into small groups. Have students write the sentences from the above activity and the conjunctions from the chart on strips of paper. Model how to make compound and complex sentences by moving around the sentence strips and conjunctions. Ask a volunteer from each group to write one or two sentences on the board, and invite members of other groups to say whether or not the sentences work. **MODERATE/LIGHT**

5 PUBLISH

Students should look for a web platform to upload their reports or have them held at the school library in print form or a database. Encourage students to share their reports with friends and family on social media or by email.

WHEN STUDENTS STRUGGLE...

Combine Sentences Using Conjunctions Display the sentences below. Ask students to choose the conjunction that best combines each pair.
- A research report includes facts and expert opinions. Authors should also include their own original ideas. (so/although/because) (*although*)
- It's important to grab the reader's attention in the first paragraph. The author should provide an interesting fact, quote, or question in the first few sentences. (after/unless/because) (*because*)

When students give their answer, ask them to explain the relationship the conjunction indicates.

Write a Research Report **685**

WRITING

USE THE SCORING GUIDE

Allow students time to read the scoring guide and to ask questions about any words, phrases, or ideas that are unclear. Then, have partners exchange final drafts of their research reports. Ask them to score their partner's research report using the scoring guide. Each student should write a paragraph explaining the reasons for the score he or she awarded in each category.

WRITING TASK

Use the scoring guide to evaluate your essay.

Writing Task Scoring Guide: Research Report

	Organization/Progression	Development of Ideas	Use of Language and Conventions
4	• The organization of the report is clear and appropriate to the purpose. • The writer has a clear thesis with all ideas strongly related to it, and the report is unified and coherent. • The writer's progression of ideas is logical, with meaningful transitions and sentence connections.	• Ideas are effectively developed; examples from outside sources are specific and well chosen. • The report is thoughtful and engaging. The writer uses material from outside sources to support personal thoughts and ideas. • The writer demonstrates a thorough understanding of research and writing.	• Word choice is purposeful and precise, maintains an appropriate tone, and contributes to the quality of the report. • The writer demonstrates a consistent command of spelling, capitalization, punctuation, grammar, and usage. • All sources cited are in correct format.
3	• The organization of the report is generally clear and appropriate to the purpose. • The writer has a clear thesis with most ideas related to it. • The paper is coherent, though it may lack unity in some places. • The writer's progression of ideas is generally logical and controlled, with smooth transitions and sentence connections.	• The development of ideas is sufficient; details and examples from outside sources are generally specific and appropriate. • The report reflects thoughtfulness. The writing is original rather than formulaic; evidence presented supports the writer's ideas. • The writer demonstrates a good understanding of research and writing.	• Word choice is mostly clear and specific, reflecting an awareness of purpose and tone, and contributing to the quality and clarity of the report. • The writer demonstrates adequate command of sentence boundaries, spelling, capitalization, punctuation, grammar, and usage. • Most sources cited are in correct format.
2	• The organizing structure of the report is evident but not always appropriate. • The report lacks clarity because the writer uses unsuitable organizational strategies. • Most ideas are related to the specified topic, but the writer's thesis is weak or unclear. • Transitions and sentence connections do not contribute to the progression of ideas.	• Ideas are only minimally developed. Examples are inappropriate or poorly presented. • The report reflects little thoughtfulness; it presents evidence from outside sources but not personal thoughts and ideas. • The writer demonstrates only a limited understanding of the task. • The writer's progression of ideas is not always logical and controlled.	• Word choice reflects only a basic awareness of the purpose of informative writing. It weakens the quality and clarity of the report. • The writer demonstrates only partial command of sentence boundaries, spelling, capitalization, punctuation, grammar, and usage. • Few sources cited are correctly formatted.
1	• The organizing structure of the report is inappropriate, and its weakness leads to a lack of clarity and direction in the report. • Most ideas are related to the specified topic, but the thesis lacks details or is unclear or illogical. • The writer fails to focus on the topic, includes extraneous information, or shifts abruptly from idea to idea.	• Ideas are poorly developed; the details and examples used are inappropriate, vague, or insufficient. • The writer's response to the prompt is vague or confused. • The report may be only weakly linked to the prompt, or developed in a manner that demonstrates a lack of understanding of the task. • The progression of ideas is weak.	• Word choice is vague or limited, reflecting little or no awareness of the purpose. It fails to establish an appropriate tone and detracts from the quality of the report. • The writer has little or no command of sentence boundaries, spelling, capitalization, punctuation, grammar, and usage. • Sources are not cited.

Give a Multimodal Presentation

You will now adapt your research report for a multimodal presentation to your classmates. You will also listen to their presentations, ask questions to better understand their ideas, and help them improve their work.

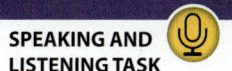

SPEAKING AND LISTENING TASK

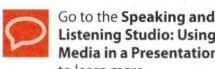

Go to the **Speaking and Listening Studio: Using Media in a Presentation** to learn more.

1 Adapt Your Report for a Multimodal Presentation

Review your research report. Use the chart below to guide you as you adapt your report to create slides and other presentation materials to convey your thesis, and present your key ideas in a clear and engaging way.

Presentation Planning Chart	
Plan Your Slides How will you present your introduction, thesis statement, key ideas and supporting evidence, and conclusion? What is the best way to convey this information on each slide?	
Use Graphics, Images, and a Consistent Design What design elements will make your slides visually appealing? How will these elements relate to the content of your report?	
Consider Adding Music, Animation, or Sound Effects Would including music, audio clips, or sound effects enhance the content of your presentation?	
Use Verbal Techniques Which sections of your report should be presented slowly? Which sections need emphasis?	
Use Nonverbal Techniques Which slides stand on their own and could be presented with little or no narration?	

Present Information 687

SPEAKING AND LISTENING

GIVE A MULTIMODAL PRESENTATION

Introduce students to the Speaking and Listening Task by having them discuss in small groups how watching a multimodal presentation is different from reading an article. Ask students to talk about what makes a presentation interesting for them and what they might include in a presentation that they did not include in their reports. Explain to students that they will probably want to do some additional research to find media they can use in their presentations. Point out that this task is an opportunity for them to be creative and to incorporate such original images as illustrations and diagrams.

1 ADAPT YOUR REPORT FOR A MULTIMODAL PRESENTATION

Have students read through the headings and questions in the chart and make quick notes about any ideas that occur to them. Emphasize to students that they should not simply present the text of their reports in slides; they should support their oral presentations with visual and audio elements. Point out that using such visual aids as diagrams and charts can help them explain concepts that may be difficult to explain using text alone.

 For **speaking support** for students at varying proficiency levels, see the **Language X-Ray** on page 680B.

WHEN STUDENTS STRUGGLE...

Adapt the Report Using Images Have students plan their presentations by gathering images that relate to their topics, and then practice explaining what they learned about that image from their research. Students may find it helpful to write key words, phrases, and facts on notecards to remind them of what they want to say about each image. Remind students that they are the class experts on their topics, so any information they provide will likely be interesting and helpful to the other students.

SPEAKING AND LISTENING

2 PRACTICE WITH A PARTNER OR GROUP

Review the information and tips with the class, ensuring that all the terms and ideas are clear. Remind students that the purpose of practicing their presentations is to gain useful feedback from their peers. Emphasize that speaking before a group makes most people feel nervous, so everyone should be as supportive and helpful as possible.

3 DELIVER YOUR PRESENTATION

Set aside time for all students to give their presentations. When everyone has finished, ask students to share their thoughts on how their classmates' feedback helped them improve their performance.

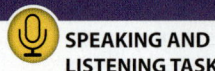 **SPEAKING AND LISTENING TASK**

As you work to improve your presentations, be sure to follow discussion rules:
- ❏ listen closely to each other
- ❏ don't interrupt
- ❏ stay on topic
- ❏ ask only helpful, relevant questions
- ❏ provide only clear, thoughtful, and direct answers

2 Practice with a Partner or Group

Once you've completed your draft, practice with a partner or group to improve both your presentation and your delivery.

Practice Effective Verbal Techniques
- ❏ **Enunciation** Replace words that you stumble over, and rearrange sentences so that your delivery is smooth.
- ❏ **Voice Modulation and Pitch** Use your voice to display enthusiasm and emphasis.
- ❏ **Speaking Rate** Speak slowly enough that listeners understand you. Pause now and then to let them consider important points.
- ❏ **Volume** Remember that listeners at the back of the room must be able to hear you.

Practice Effective Nonverbal Techniques
- ❏ **Eye Contact** Try to let your eyes rest on each member of the audience at least once.
- ❏ **Facial Expression** Smile, frown, or raise an eyebrow to show your feelings or to emphasize points.
- ❏ **Gestures** Stand tall and relaxed, and use natural gestures—shrugs, nods, or shakes of your head—to add meaning and interest to your presentation.

Provide and Consider Advice for Improvement

As a listener, pay close attention. Take notes about ways that presenters can improve their presentations and use verbal and nonverbal techniques more effectively. Paraphrase and summarize each presenter's thesis and key ideas to confirm your understanding, and ask questions to clarify any confusing expressions or ideas.

As a presenter, listen closely to questions and consider ways to revise your presentation to make sure your key ideas are clear and logically sequenced. Remember to ask for suggestions about how you might change onscreen text or images to make your presentation clearer and more interesting.

3 Deliver Your Presentation

Use the advice you received during practice to make final changes to your presentation. Then, using effective verbal and nonverbal techniques, present it to your classmates.

 ENGLISH LEARNER SUPPORT

Use Visual Support Ensure that students understand other students' presentations. Ask students to make a note about one or two images from each presentation and the content it relates to. Then, have them share what they noted with a partner and explain how the images helped them understand what the presenter was describing or explaining.
ALL LEVELS

Reflect on the Unit

By completing your research report, you have created a writing product that pulls together and expresses your thoughts about the reading you have done in this unit. Now is a good time to reflect on what you have learned.

Reflect on the Essential Questions

- Review the four Essential Questions on page 587. How have your answers to these questions changed in response to the texts you've read in this unit?

- What are some examples from the texts you've read that show how technology has altered the social order and the ways in which people live their daily lives?

Reflect on Your Reading

- Which selections were the most interesting or surprising to you?

- From which selection did you learn the most about how technology affects people's lives?

Reflect on the Writing Task

- What difficulties did you encounter while working on your research report? How might you avoid them next time?

- Which parts of the research report were the easiest to write? The hardest to write? Why?

- What improvements did you make to your research report as you were revising?

 REFLECT

UNIT 5 SELECTIONS
- from *Jane Eyre*
- "Factory Reform"
- "The Lady of Shalott"
- from *Great Expectations*
- "The Victorians Had the Same Concerns about Technology as We Do"
- "Dover Beach"
- "The Darkling Thrush"
- "My Last Duchess"
- "Confession"

LEARNING MINDSET

Questioning Remind students that asking questions is part of the learning process and that asking thoughtful questions demonstrates that they are engaging the material in a meaningful way. Encourage students to ask questions of their peers as well as their teachers. Direct them to write down questions in their notebooks and then review their notes from the unit to see whether they can find the answers for themselves. Have students share their questions, the answers that they found, and how they found their answers.

REFLECT

REFLECT ON THE UNIT

Have students reflect on the questions independently and write some notes in response to each one. Then, have students meet with partners or in small groups to discuss their reflections. Circulate during these discussions to identify the questions that are generating the liveliest conversations. Wrap up with a whole-class discussion focused on these questions.

UNIT 6

Instructional Overview and Resources

		Instructional Focus	Online Ed Resources
	**Unit Introduction** New Ideas, New Voices: Modern and Contemporary Literature	Unit 6 Essential Question Unit 6 Academic Vocabulary	**Stream to Start:** New Ideas, New Voices **Unit 6 Response Log**

ANALYZE & APPLY

	**"A Cup of Tea"** Short Story by Katherine Mansfield **Lexile 640L**	**Reading** • Analyze Third-Person Point of View • Evaluate a Character **Writing:** Write a Missing Scene from Another Point of View **Speaking and Listening:** Present a Scene **Vocabulary:** Denotation and Connotation **Language Conventions:** Precise Details	**Audio** **Reading Studio:** Notice & Note **Writing Studio:** Writing Narratives **Speaking and Listening Studio:** Giving a Presentation **Vocabulary Studio:** Denotation and Connotation **Grammar Studio:** Adjective Phrases and Adverb Phrases
	**"The Love Song of J. Alfred Prufrock"** Poem by T.S. Eliot **Lexile N/A**	**Reading** • Understand Modernist Poetry • Make Inferences • Analyze Stream of Consciousness **Writing:** Write a Poem **Speaking and Listening:** Present a Poem	**Audio** **Close Read Screencast:** Modeled Discussion **Reading Studio:** Notice & Note **Writing Studio:** Writing as a Process **Speaking and Listening Studio:** Giving a Presentation
	**"Shooting an Elephant"** Essay by George Orwell **Lexile 1070L**	**Reading** • Analyze Reflective Essay • Analyze Irony **Writing:** Write an Informational Essay **Speaking and Listening:** Discuss Your Essay **Vocabulary:** Etymology **Language Conventions:** Prepositional Phrases	**Audio** **Reading Studio:** Notice & Note **Writing Studio:** Writing Informative Texts **Speaking and Listening Studio:** Participating in Collaborative Discussions **Vocabulary Studio:** Understanding Word Origins **Grammar Studio:** Prepositional Phrases
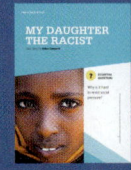	**"My Daughter the Racist"** Short Story by Helen Oyeyemi **Lexile 740L**	**Reading** • Analyze Setting • Make Predictions **Writing:** Write a Fictional Scene **Speaking and Listening:** Critique and Discuss **Vocabulary:** Idioms **Language Conventions:** Syntax	**Audio** **Reading Studio:** Notice & Note **Writing Studio:** Writing Narratives **Speaking and Listening Studio:** Participating in Collaborative Discussions **Vocabulary Studio:** Using Context Clues **Grammar Studio:** Sentence Structure

SUGGESTED PACING: 30 DAYS

Unit Introduction	A Cup of Tea	The Love Song of J. Alfred Prufrock	Shooting an Elephant	My Daughter the Racist
1	2 3 4	5 6 7 8	9 10 11 12	13 14 15 16 17

PLAN

English Learner Support	Differentiated Instruction	Assessment
• Background Knowledge	**When Students Struggle** • Identify Cause and Effect	
• Text X-Ray • Use Cognates • Use New Vocabulary • Narrate and Describe • Internalize New Language • Oral Assessment • Vocabulary Strategy • Language Conventions	**When Students Struggle** • Understand Point of View • Understand Character Motivation • Reteaching: Evaluate a Character **To Challenge Students** • Research Beauty and Fashion	**Selection Test**
• Text X-Ray • Learn New Vocabulary • Enhance Understanding • Oral Assessment	**When Students Struggle** • Make Inferences	**Selection Test**
• Text X-Ray • Use Cognates • Acquire New Vocabulary • Use Visual and Contextual Support • Express Opinions • Oral Assessment • Vocabulary Strategy • Language Conventions	**When Students Struggle** • Understand Situational Irony • Identify the Features of a Reflective Essay • Reteaching: Analyze a Reflective Essay **To Challenge Students** • Conduct Research	**Selection Test**
• Text X-Ray • Use Cognates • Use Prior Knowledge • Use Strategic Learning Techniques • Use Visual and Contextual Support • Express Ideas and Opinions • Ask and Give Information • Oral Assessment • Vocabulary Strategy • Language Conventions	**When Students Struggle** • Make Predictions about Characters • Evaluate Predictions • Reteaching: Analyze Setting **To Challenge Students** • Write and Perform Dialogue • Predict Character Behavior	**Selection Test**

The Second Coming / Symbols? I'm Sick of Symbols
18 19 20

Budget 2016: George Osborne's Speech / Will the Sugar Tax Stop Childhood Obesity?
21 22 23 24 25

Independent Reading
26 27

End of Unit
28 29 30

New Ideas, New Voices: Modern and Contemporary Literature

PLAN

UNIT 6 Continued

		Instructional Focus	Online Ed Resources
COLLABORATE & COMPARE			
	"The Second Coming" Poem by William Butler Yeats ••• "Symbols? I'm Sick of Symbols" Poem by Fernando Pessoa	**Reading** • Understand Symbolism • Analyze Rhythmic Patterns **Writing:** Write a Response to Literature **Speaking and Listening:** Give a Dramatic Reading	🔊 **Audio** **Reading Studio:** Notice & Note **Writing Studio:** Writing as a Process **Speaking and Listening Studio:** Giving a Presentation
	Collaborate & Compare	**Reading:** Compare Themes	
	MENTOR TEXTS "Budget 2016: George Osborne's Speech" Argument by George Osborne **Lexile 880L**	**Reading** • Evaluate Persuasive Techniques • Analyze Inductive Reasoning **Writing:** Develop a Persuasive Argument **Speaking and Listening:** Debate **Vocabulary:** Related Words **Language Conventions:** Relative Pronouns and Relative Clauses	🔊 **Audio** **Reading Studio:** Notice & Note **Writing Studio:** Writing Arguments **Speaking and Listening Studio:** Analyzing and Evaluating Presentations **Vocabulary Studio:** Analyzing Word Structure **Grammar Studio:** The Adjective Clause
	"Will the Sugar Tax Stop Childhood Obesity?" Argument by Chris Hall **Lexile 1260L**	**Reading** • Evaluate Arguments • Evaluate Counterarguments **Writing:** Evaluate an Argument **Speaking and Listening:** Discuss **Vocabulary:** The Greek Suffix -ize **Language Conventions:** Rhetorical Questions	🔊 **Audio** **Reading Studio:** Notice & Note **Writing Studio:** Evaluating Sources **Speaking and Listening Studio:** Participating in Collaborative Discussions **Vocabulary Studio:** Analyzing Word Structure
	Collaborate & Compare	**Reading:** Compare Arguments	

INDEPENDENT READING

The Independent Reading selections are available only in the eBook. Go to the Reading Studio for more information on Notice & Note.	 "Araby" Short Story by James Joyce **Lexile 930L**	 "Professions for Women" Essay by Virginia Woolf **Lexile 970L**

END OF UNIT

	Instructional Focus	Online Ed Resources
Writing Task: Write an Argument **Speaking and Listening Task:** Debate an Issue **Reflect on the Unit**	**Writing:** Write an Argument **Language Conventions:** Vary Syntax for Effect **Speaking:** Debate an Issue	**Unit 6 Response Log** **Mentor Texts:** "Budget 2016: George Osborne's Speech"/"Will the Sugar Tax Stop Childhood Obesity?" **Writing Studio:** Writing Arguments **Grammar Studio:** Sentence Structure

PLAN

English Learner Support	Differentiated Instruction	Online Ed Assessment
• Text X-Ray • Identify Affixes • Use Cognates • Use Visual and Contextual Support • Oral Assessment • Respond to Questions	**When Students Struggle** • Understand Symbolism	**Selection Test**
• Analyze Tone	**To Challenge Students** • Conduct Research	
• Text X-Ray • Use Cognates • Use Support from Peers to Develop Vocabulary • Oral Assessment • Vocabulary Strategy • Language Conventions	**When Students Struggle** • Reteaching: Evaluate Persuasive Techniques	**Selection Test**
• Text X-Ray • Use Cognates • Learn New Expressions • Oral Assessment • Vocabulary Strategy • Language Conventions	**When Students Struggle** • Reteaching: Analyze Arguments	**Selection Test**
• Express Ideas	**To Challenge Students** • Make a Speech	

"Do Not Go Gentle into that Good Night" Poem by Dylan Thomas

"Digging" Poem by Seamus Heaney

"Marriage Is a Private Affair" Short story by Chinua Achebe
Lexile 830L

Selection Tests

• Language X-Ray • Understand Academic Language • Write a Group Argument • Use the Mentor Text • Use Rhetorical Devices • Use Compound Sentences • Adapt the Debate	**When Students Struggle** • Draft the Argument • Use Complex Sentences • Provide Advice for Improvement **To Challenge Students** • Find an Interview	**Unit Test**

New Ideas, New Voices: Modern and Contemporary Literature

TEACH

DISCUSS THE QUOTATION

Tell students that this quotation is from an interview Walcott gave in 1985. Poet and playwright Derek Walcott was born on the British-ruled island of St. Lucia in 1930 and received a traditional British education. However, he never considered himself a British writer, identifying instead as a Caribbean writer. In his works, he explored such themes as colonialism and the complex intersections of race, culture, and language that had shaped St. Lucia, the Caribbean region, and his own identity. In 1992, Walcott was awarded the Nobel Prize for his poetry. He died in 2017.

Ask students how the view of the English language presented in the quote might represent a change from concepts of the English language that existed in past decades or centuries.

■ English Learner Support

Learn New Language Structures Explain that the word *itself* is a reflexive pronoun, a type of word that refers to something or someone already mentioned in the sentence. In the quote, it is used for emphasis and refers to "the English Language." **ALL LEVELS**

UNIT 6

NEW IDEAS, NEW VOICES

MODERN AND CONTEMPORARY LITERATURE

> " The English language is nobody's special property. It is the property of the imagination; it is the property of the language itself. "
>
> —Derek Walcott

LEARNING MINDSET

Growth Mindset As students prepare to embark on the final unit, ask them to think about where they were at the beginning of the course and how much progress they have made in their understanding of British literature thus far. Remind students that a growth mindset is one that focuses on making an effort to achieve learning goals and accepting mistakes as part of the learning process. Encourage students to think about which learning/studying methods have worked for them thus far and which have not. Challenge students to find ways to improve or replace the ones that have not.

UNIT 6

Discuss the Essential Questions with your whole class or in small groups. As you read New Ideas, New Voices, consider how the selections explore these questions.

? ESSENTIAL QUESTION:
What makes people feel insecure?

In the modern world, safety and security seem to be emphasized more than ever before in history. Yet people continue to experience insecurity in their daily lives, their relationships, and even their sense of self. How can insecurity affect a person from within? What types of insecurity come from the world around us? How much control do we have over the sources of insecurity in our lives?

? ESSENTIAL QUESTION:
Why is it hard to resist social pressure?

You have probably heard many times that the company you keep can influence your thoughts and actions for good or for bad. Peer pressure is certainly a powerful force, whether it is working on individuals or groups. Why do we feel the need to go along with the crowd? What are the benefits and the dangers of conforming to society's expectations? What happens when social pressure gets out of control?

? ESSENTIAL QUESTION:
What is the power of symbols?

At the most basic level, a symbol is anything that represents or stands for something else. We are surrounded by symbols every day. Written symbols appear on road signs and electronic devices. Symbols for individuals and concepts appear in books, music, movies, and TV shows. Why do we use symbols? Are symbols usually more or less effective than literal representations? How do differences in interpretation affect the power of symbols?

? ESSENTIAL QUESTION:
When should the government interfere in our decisions?

The question of how much influence a government should have over the lives of its citizens is an old one. Over the centuries, it has sparked debates, influenced the development of political parties, and even contributed to wars. Many people agree that some governmental authority is necessary to keep peace and order, but how much interference is too much? Conversely, when does it become necessary for individual rights to yield to government authority?

TEACH

Connect to the ESSENTIAL QUESTIONS

Read aloud the Essential Questions and the paragraphs that follow them. Open the discussion of each idea by having students respond to the questions that conclude each paragraph.

? ESSENTIAL QUESTION:
What makes people feel insecure?

Challenge students to identify the differences between external and internal sources of insecurity. Ask students to consider which one they think would be harder to overcome and why.

? ESSENTIAL QUESTION:
Why is it hard to resist social pressure?

Take an informal poll to see whether students feel that they more often encounter positive or negative social pressure. Then, have students write about times when they experienced social pressure. As time permits, ask students to share positive examples of times when they successfully resisted negative social pressure or benefitted from positive social pressure.

? ESSENTIAL QUESTION:
What is the power of symbols?

Emphasize the power of symbols by displaying the logos of several famous companies. Ask students what they associate with each logo. How do logos and other symbols get their power? How do they keep their power?

? ESSENTIAL QUESTION:
When should the government interfere in our decisions?

Have students in small group discussions identify both positive and negative examples of government interference. Encourage students to think of both contemporary and historical examples, from both their own state or country and from other countries.

TEACH

MODERN AND CONTEMPORARY LITERATURE

The following provides students with a historical context for the Unit 6 selections. It presents a brief overview of global conflicts and events of the 20th century and discusses how those events specifically influenced Great Britain and British literature.

World Wars Inform students that throughout the period of the world wars, an additional issue that Britain faced was the matter of independence for Ireland. The Irish had never accepted British rule and so were faced with a dilemma when Great Britain entered World War I: should they fight to defend an empire they hated? Many did fight for the empire, while others took the opportunity to revolt in a bid for independence known as the Easter Rising of 1916. The rebellion, which took place mainly in Dublin, did not initially have the full support of the Irish public. However, the extreme harshness of the British response to the rebellion whipped up support for the Irish nationalist cause. In 1921, after a long struggle, the British divided Ireland into two self-governing dominions: The Irish Free State and Northern Ireland. Independence for all but Northern Ireland was achieved in 1949; reunification of Ireland has never been achieved. In Northern Ireland, religious and political tensions related to British control have continued to the present day.

COLLABORATIVE DISCUSSION

Ask groups to share their ideas with the class.

MODERN AND CONTEMPORARY LITERATURE

At the turn of the 20th century, Great Britain was a nation at its peak. Under the reign of Victoria's successor, Edward VII, England was a land of prosperity, stability, and world dominance. However, vast changes were on the horizon. Over the course of the next hundred years, Britain would become embroiled in wars, experience economic depression, and face the end of its once-massive empire.

World Wars In 1914 a Serbian nationalist assassinated Archduke Franz Ferdinand, heir to the throne of Austria-Hungary. Austria declared war on Serbia, and like a line of dominoes, alliances fell into place: Austria and Germany on one side; Russia, France, and Britain on the other. Both sides became locked in bloody trench warfare. The Great War, as the conflict was then known, dragged on, devastating Europe, killing or wounding virtually an entire generation of young men, and bringing a profound sense of disillusionment to the people. In 1917 the United States entered the war, leading to Germany's capitulation the following year and an uneasy peace.

Britain had lost 750,000 men, and those who returned from World War I alive came home to unemployment and economic depression. France and Germany were hit even harder, while Russia was plunged into revolution and civil war. War-torn European nations turned to the United States for loans, but in 1929 the United States stock market crashed, causing a worldwide depression. In the economic and political chaos of the 1920s and early '30s, dictators seized power in Italy, Russia, and Germany. In 1939 German dictator Adolf Hitler made the decision to invade Poland, prompting Britain and France to declare war on Germany. Italy and Japan allied themselves with Germany, and World War II began.

Terrible as the Great War had been, for most British citizens it was a distant tragedy on foreign battlefields. World War II was different. After the fall of France in 1940, German planes began to attack Britain. Bombs rained down on London, and the entire population mobilized to defend the home front. Britain held out against Germany until the United States entered the war in 1941, and Hitler was finally defeated in 1945.

COLLABORATIVE DISCUSSION In a small group, review the timeline and discuss how outside events influenced British politics and literature.

692 Unit 6

ENGLISH LEARNER SUPPORT

Background Knowledge To aid comprehension of the essay, provide students with the following definitions:

- *successor*: a person who holds a job or position after someone else
- *virtually*: very nearly; almost entirely
- *disillusionment*: a sense or feeling that something is no longer good or true
- *mobilize*: to come together for action
- *ration*: to control the amount of something allowed to people
- *relinquish*: to give up something, especially power or control
- *upheaval*: a major change, usually causing conflict, confusion, or anxiety
- *alienation*: the feeling that one does not belong in a group or society

ALL LEVELS

The End of Empire After World War II, Britain was financially drained, burdened by debt and the need to rebuild its cities. Everything was rationed. Determined to provide at least the basic necessities, the government transformed Britain with a new national health care system and public education. Concerned with domestic issues, leaders had little desire to cling to colonies that were all too eager for self-rule. After World War I, Britain's grasp on its empire had already begun to loosen as the spirit of nationalism swept Europe and the colonial empires. Britain granted ever-greater degrees of self-determination to its colonies, eventually making some of these lands partners in the British Commonwealth of Nations rather than continuing to treat them as possessions. Soon after World War II, Britain gave India its independence. In the decades that followed, Britain yielded to nationalistic and economic pressures and relinquished control of most of its remaining colonies.

Literature in the 20th Century and Beyond After World War I, Europe was a place of uncertainty and upheaval. In England, the previously stable social order based on community and class distinctions was giving way to the anonymity of urban life. In the arts, modernism was a way of trying to make sense of this new, fragmented world. Visual artists, composers, and writers rejected traditional forms and experimented with new styles that better reflected the realities and values of modern life.

RESEARCH
What about this historical period interests you? Choose a topic, event, or person to learn more about. Then, add your own entry to the timeline.

1952 Elizabeth II ascends the throne.

1997 Great Britain returns Hong Kong to China after 155 years of colonial rule.

2007 British Indian author Salman Rushdie is awarded a knighthood from Queen Elizabeth II.

Present

1949 George Orwell publishes *1984*, a nightmarish vision of a totalitarian England.

1979 Margaret Thatcher becomes the first female prime minister.

2005 Bombs explode on the London Underground and a bus, killing 56.

New Ideas, New Voices 693

WHEN STUDENTS STRUGGLE . . .

Identify Cause and Effect Have students use cause-and-effect graphic organizers to trace the related events that occurred during the two world wars and the years in between. Help them see how these events ultimately ended Britain's role as the preeminent world power. Students may find it helpful to use more than one type of GO for the material. For example, a chain may be more useful for tracking the events of the world wars in the order that they occurred, while a table in which students can record events in the left column and the effect of the event in the right column may be more useful for identifying the effects of specific international events on British politics or society.

TEACH

The End of Empire Examples of members of the British Commonwealth of Nations include Canada, South Africa, Australia, and New Zealand, all of which became part of the Commonwealth in 1926.

The last trace of the British Empire did not disappear until 1997, when Hong Kong, which had been a British colony for 155 years, was returned to Chinese control.

Literature in the 20th Century and Beyond Explain that a number of new philosophies and the then-new field of psychology greatly influenced the development of new writing styles. During the 1920s, for example, the works of the psychoanalyst Sigmund Freud first appeared in English. Freud showed that character is not easily understood; people are complex, inconsistent, and unpredictable, driven by irrational urges that might be hidden even from themselves. Meanwhile, the French philosopher Henri Bergson argued that time is like a stream in which past, present, and future all flow together continuously. The combination of these ideas and others influenced the development of such techniques as stream-of-consciousness writing, in which the reader is inside the character's mind perceiving thoughts as they occur, not necessarily in order, rather than outside the character's mind, viewing events in chronological order.

RESEARCH

To learn more about their chosen topics, encourage students to search for primary sources from the historical period. Have students choose excerpts from sources to present to the class.

New Ideas, New Voices **693**

TEACH

✏️ CHECK YOUR UNDERSTANDING

Have students answer the questions independently.

Answers:

1. D
2. H
3. B

If students answer any question incorrectly, have them reread the text to confirm their understanding.

New narrative styles rejected traditional linear plot and character development, and instead placed the reader inside the character's mind. Many writers felt a sense of alienation from their own society after witnessing the horrors of war, and as a result explored themes of isolation, human relationships and vulnerabilities, and disillusionment.

The end of the British Empire also shaped and continues to shape literature. Writers from former colonies explore issues related to their countries' colonial past, while writers who have immigrated to England often address cultural tensions in their works. The multicultural perspective these writers bring has broadened the horizons of contemporary British literature.

CHECK YOUR UNDERSTANDING

Choose the best answer to each question.

1. Which most directly caused the outbreak of World War II?
   - **A** Italy's and Japan's alliance with Germany
   - **B** The crash of the United States stock market
   - **C** Hitler's seizure of power in Germany
   - **D** The invasion of Poland by Germany

2. British politicians after World War II —
   - **F** wanted to hold the British Empire together as long as possible
   - **G** believed that strengthening the colonies would help Britain recover from the war
   - **H** placed less emphasis on empire and focused more on domestic issues
   - **J** immediately granted independence to all former British colonies

3. Which was a primary aspect of modernism?
   - **A** Focus on nationalistic perspectives in the arts and literature
   - **B** Rejection of traditional forms in the arts and literature
   - **C** Focus on war recovery and domestic affairs in politics
   - **D** Rejection of colonialism and empire building in politics

ACADEMIC VOCABULARY

Academic Vocabulary words are words you use when you discuss and write about texts. In this unit, you will learn the following five words:

- ✓ arbitrary
- ☐ controversy
- ☐ convince
- ☐ denote
- ☐ undergo

Study the Word Network to learn more about the word **arbitrary**.

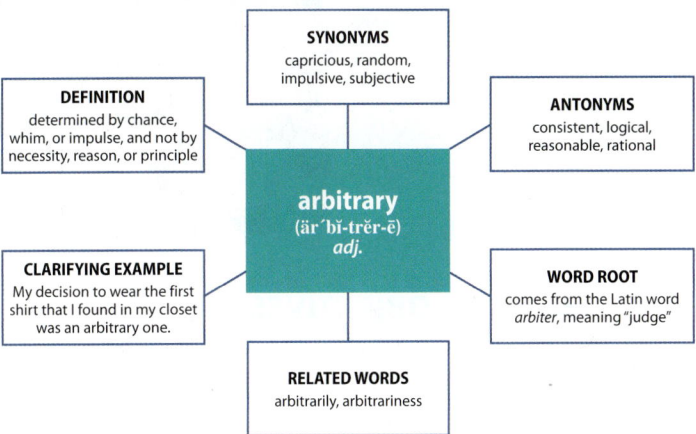

Write and Discuss Discuss your completed Word Network with a partner, making sure to talk through all of the boxes until you both understand the word, its synonyms, antonyms, and related forms. Then, fill out a Word Network for the remaining four words. Use a dictionary or online resource to help you complete the activity.

 Go online to access the Word Networks.

RESPOND TO THE ESSENTIAL QUESTIONS

In this unit, you will explore four different **Essential Questions** about New Ideas, New Voices. As you read each selection, you will gather your ideas about one of these questions and write about it in a **Response Log**. At the end of the unit, you will have the opportunity to write an **argument** related to one of the essential questions. Filling out the Response Log after you read each text will help you prepare for this writing task.

 You can also go online to access the Response Log.

New Ideas, New Voices **695**

TEACH

ACADEMIC VOCABULARY

Have students complete Word Networks for the remaining four vocabulary words. Encourage them to include all the categories shown in the completed network if possible, but point out that some words do not have clear synonyms or antonyms.

controversy (kŏn´trə-vûr´sē) *n.* Public disagreement, argument. (Spanish cognate: *controversia*)

convince (kən-vĭns´) *v.* Persuade or lead to agreement by means of argument. (Spanish cognate: *convencer*)

denote (dĭ-nōt´) *v.* To serve as a symbol for the meaning of; signify. (Spanish cognate: *denotar*)

undergo (ŭn´dər-gō´) *v.* To experience or be subjected to

RESPOND TO THE ESSENTIAL QUESTIONS

Direct students to their Unit 6 Response Logs. Explain that students will use them to record ideas and details from the selections that help answer one of the Essential Questions. When they work on the Writing Task at the end of the unit, their Response Logs will help them think about what they have read and make connections between the texts.

PLAN

A CUP OF TEA
Short Story by Katherine Mansfield

GENRE ELEMENTS
SHORT STORY
Tell students that a **short story** includes the basic elements of fiction but can be read in one sitting. Explain that it can be told from a **limited third-person point of view.** This point of view is similar to first person, as it focuses on the actions, thoughts, and feelings of the primary character. A limited third-person point of view is not quite as immediate as first person, however, and allows the reader to view the action at a slightly greater distance. In this lesson, students will analyze third-person point of view and evaluate a character.

LEARNING OBJECTIVES
- Analyze third-person point of view and evaluate a character.
- Conduct research about social changes for women in the 1920s.
- Write a missing scene from another point of view.
- Present a scene.
- Identify the denotation and connotation of words.
- Use precise details.
- **Language** Identify third-person point of view.

TEXT COMPLEXITY

Quantitative Measures	A Cup of Tea	Lexile: 640L
Qualitative Measures	**Ideas Presented** Much is explicit, but requires some inferential reasoning. Some use of irony.	
	Structures Used Clear, chronological, largely conventional.	
	Language Used Mostly explicit, some figurative language, dialect, and archaic language.	
	Knowledge Required Situations and subjects mostly familiar.	

696A Unit 6

PLAN

RESOURCES

- Unit 6 Response Log
- 🔊 Selection Audio
- 📖 Reading Studio: Notice & Note
- 📊 Level Up Tutorial: Point of View; Character Motivation; Making Inferences about Characters
- 💬 Writing Studio: Writing Narratives
- 🗨️ Speaking and Listening Studio: Giving a Presentation
- 🫧 Vocabulary Studio: Denotation and Connotation
- ❗ Grammar Studio: Module 3: Lesson 2: Adjective Phrases and Adverb Phrases
- ✅ "A Cup of Tea" Selection Test

SUMMARIES

English
Rosemary Fell, a very rich, though "not exactly beautiful," young woman, examines a costly trinket in a London shop. As she leaves, a poor young woman asks for money for a cup of tea. Rosemary takes the girl home with her, serves her tea, comforts her, and promises to help. When Rosemary's husband remarks that the girl is extremely pretty, Rosemary sends the girl away with a small sum of money.

Spanish
Rosemary Fell, una joven rica, pero "no exactamente hermosa", examina una chuchería costosa en una tienda de Londres. Al irse, una joven pobre le pide dinero para una taza de té. Rosemary se lleva a la joven a su casa, le sirve té, la consuela y promete ayudarla. Cuando su esposo comenta lo bonita que es la joven, Rosemary la despacha con una pequeña suma de dinero.

SMALL-GROUP OPTIONS

Have students work in small groups and pairs to read and discuss the selection.

Numbered Heads Together
- After students have read the selection, pose this question to the class: *Why might an author want two characters from different social classes to meet?*
- Have students form groups of four and number off 1-2-3-4 within the group.
- Ask students to discuss their responses to the question in their groups.
- Call a number from 1 to 4. The student with that number will then respond for the group.

Three-Minute Review
- After students read the selection, set a timer for three minutes.
- Have students work independently to write clarifying questions about what they read.
- After three minutes, ask volunteers to share their questions.
- Briefly discuss answers to each question.

PLAN

Text X-Ray: English Learner Support
for "A Cup of Tea"

Use the Text X-Ray and the supports and scaffolds in the Teacher's Edition to help guide students at different proficiency levels through the selection.

INTRODUCE THE SELECTION
DISCUSS INSECURITY AND SUPERIORITY

In this lesson, students will need to be able to discuss why people feel insecure or superior.

Provide the following explanations:
- When people feel *insecure*, they don't feel confident or safe.
- When people feel *superior*, they feel like they are better than others.

Explain that people may feel insecure around a person who acts in a superior way because they feel less valuable or respected.

Point out that *insecure* and *superior* are antonyms.

Ask students to discuss insecurity and superiority using sentence frames, such as: *When I feel insecure, I _____. _____ can make people feel superior to others.*

CULTURAL REFERENCES

The following words or phrases may be unfamiliar to students:

- *fairy godmother* (paragraph 21): a female character in fairy tales who has magical powers and brings good fortune to others
- *good heavens* (paragraph 33): informal expression of surprise or anger
- *touched beyond words* (paragraph 37): overcome by emotion; unable to speak
- *look after* (paragraph 39): take care of
- *as a matter of fact* (paragraph 52): actually; in addition to what has been said

LISTENING

Identify Point of View

As students listen to a rereading of the text, have them identify sentences written in the third-person point of view. Remind students that characters in a story told in the third person can still speak in the first person using pronouns *I*, *me*, *my*, and *mine*.

Use the following supports with students at varying proficiency levels:

- Read aloud this sentence from paragraph 2: "But if Rosemary wanted to shop she would go to Paris as you and I would go to Bond Street." Ask either/or questions to assess students' comprehension. For example: *Which words show third-person point of view,* Rosemary *and* she *or* you *and* I? *(Rosemary)* **SUBSTANTIAL**
- Have partners take turns reading aloud a sentence from the story that is written in third person. Direct the listener to identify which words show point of view using this sentence frame: *_____ tells me this story is written in third-person point of view.* **MODERATE**
- Read aloud one paragraph and have students identify third-person pronouns. **LIGHT**

696C Unit 6

PLAN

SPEAKING

Retell the Story

Have students retell the plot of the story using illustrations, such as simple drawings or selected images from print sources.

Use the following supports with students at varying proficiency levels:
- Have students choose one scene of the story to illustrate. Work with students to create a word bank of nouns and verbs that describe their images. Then, help them use the word bank to retell what happens in the scene using simple phrases. **SUBSTANTIAL**
- Have students choose one scene of the story. Ask partners to retell the plot events in their scene to each other. Provide sentence starters, such as: *This scene takes place in ____. The characters in this scene are ____.* **MODERATE**
- Have students choose several consecutive scenes of the story. Ask partners to retell the plot events in their chosen scenes. Remind them to use transition words as they go from one scene to the next. **LIGHT**

READING

Compare Characters

Remind students to pay close attention to what characters say, think, and do, in addition to how they look, as they compare and contrast Rosemary and the young girl.

Use the following supports with students at varying proficiency levels:
- Have students read paragraph 41 for words that describe the girl. **SUBSTANTIAL**
- Have partners create a two-column chart labeled *Rosemary* and *Girl* and have them list details about each character in the story. Then, have students use the details to compare the characters. Provide a sentence frame: *(Character) is ____, but (character) is ____.* **MODERATE**
- Have students silently reread paragraphs 10–42. As they read, direct them to create a two-column chart to list details about each character. Then, have partners use their charts to orally compare and contrast the two characters. **LIGHT**

WRITING

Use Connecting Words

Tell students that the use of connecting words will make their writing sound smoother and more like natural speech.

Use the following supports with students at varying proficiency levels:
- Provide a list of connecting words and phrases, such as *and, but, since, or, even if,* and *so that,* and have students copy it. Use each word or phrase in a short example sentence and have students copy it and underline the word or phrase. **SUBSTANTIAL**
- Have students copy the list from the previous activity. Provide sentence frames and have students use words from the list to complete them. For example: *Rosemary ____ the girl went upstairs, ____ only Rosemary sat down.* **MODERATE**
- Have small groups create a list of connecting words and phrases. After students write their missing scene (see page 709), have pairs exchange papers and suggest connecting words or phrases that could be used to make the writing flow more smoothly. **LIGHT**

TEACH

? Connect to the ESSENTIAL QUESTION

In Katherine Mansfield's short story "A Cup of Tea," the protagonist is a wealthy young woman whose behavior is often driven by her insecurity. As students read the story and analyze this character, they should think about the sources of her insecurity and how it shapes her thinking and actions.

ANALYZE & APPLY

A CUP OF TEA

Short Story by **Katherine Mansfield**

? ESSENTIAL QUESTION:

What makes people feel insecure?

QUICK START

How can social status affect a person's self-image? Discuss this question with a small group of students.

ANALYZE THIRD-PERSON POINT OF VIEW

When a writer uses the **third-person point of view,** the narrator is not a character in the story but an outside observer. Sometimes a third-person narrator is **omniscient** and can describe what all the characters are thinking and feeling. In modern fiction, authors more commonly use a **limited** third-person narrator, describing the thoughts, feelings, and observations of only one character. Readers may feel like they are looking over the shoulder of that character as the story's action unfolds. This technique often helps readers become more emotionally involved with the chosen character, but it can also lead to surprises because the narration is limited by the character's awareness and understanding of events.

In "A Cup of Tea," Katherine Mansfield's use of the third-person limited point of view influences the development of the characters. The narrator starts off describing the protagonist, Rosemary Fell, from a distance, as if discussing her with a friend. But soon the narrator focuses in on Rosemary, using slang and exaggeration to mimic Rosemary's speech and suggest how she perceives the world around her. As you read the story, notice how the narrator's conversational tone subtly reveals Rosemary's inner life.

EVALUATE A CHARACTER

Most complex characters are not entirely good or bad, and readers need to take various factors into account when evaluating them. A character's motivation may influence how you view his or her behavior; for example, a charitable donation may be motivated by compassion, vanity, or a combination of both. When evaluating a character, you should also consider the story's historical, social, and economic context. "A Cup of Tea" is set in London in the early 1900s, a time when rigid class distinctions would have made it seem improper for a wealthy woman to socialize with an impoverished one. This context influences the story's plot and theme, as well as Mansfield's characterization of the protagonist, Rosemary.

As you read "A Cup of Tea," use a chart like this one to help you evaluate Rosemary.

ACTION	MOTIVATION	OUTCOME

GENRE ELEMENTS: SHORT STORY

- includes the basic elements of fiction—setting, characters, plot, conflict, and theme
- centers on a particular moment or event or follows the life of one character
- can be read in one sitting
- may be told by a first-person narrator who is a character in the story or a third-person narrator outside the story

QUICK START

Have students read the Quick Start question. Make sure that students understand what *social status* means, and ask volunteers to suggest examples. Students should recognize that social status is often directly tied to wealth but can also depend on factors such as physical appearance and fame.

ANALYZE THIRD-PERSON POINT OF VIEW

Help students understand the idea of **limited third-person point of view** by having them imagine someone with a video camera walking alongside or just behind the main character. Explain that in addition to seeing the action of the story from that person's point of view, the narrator knows the thoughts and feelings of that character. Explain that the narrator is able to describe the character's internal world as well as the character's actions, but the narrator's perspective on other people and events is restricted by what the character can see and understand. Contrast this with **omniscient third-person point of view,** in which the narrator knows what all the characters are thinking and feeling.

EVALUATE A CHARACTER

Explain to students that one thing that makes good fiction memorable is complex characters who, like real people, are not all good or all bad but have a range of characteristics that may conflict with one another. An author portrays these various aspects of a character by having the character make decisions and react to events and experiences. When evaluating a character, readers should consider the social, historical, and economic context in which the story takes place, as these factors will impact the way that the author expects the reader to judge the character's actions. Remind students that many behaviors that would have been considered shocking or immoral 100 years ago are considered acceptable today.

TEACH

CRITICAL VOCABULARY

Explain to students that they should use the questions on page 698 to see how familiar they already are with vocabulary words that they will encounter in their reading. Read all of the Critical Vocabulary words aloud, and then encourage students to read all of the questions silently before deciding what the correct answers are.

Answers:

1. *vile*
2. *listless*
3. *presentable*
4. *engagement*
5. *tactfully*

■ **English Learner Support**

Use Cognates Point out that one of the meanings of the Spanish word *tacto* is the same as the English word *tact*. Although *tacto* has several meanings, the one that is the same as the English word *tact* is the idea of sensitivity or poise in delicate situations. Explain that the suffix *-ful* means "with," so to be *tactful* means showing or having tact. Tell students that the suffix *-ly* turns the adjective into an adverb and tells how something is done, so *tactfully* means to act in a way that shows sensitivity. Also point out that the adjective *presentable* has the same meaning in English as in Spanish.
ALL LEVELS

LANGUAGE CONVENTIONS

Help students understand the concept of **precise details** by asking them to imagine that they are looking at a picture and focusing very closely on one particular object. Explain that authors use precise details to make their stories more vivid and real for the reader, but the details can also convey something important about the characters or theme.

 ## ANNOTATION MODEL

Have students study the note-taking system illustrated in the Annotation Model on page 698. Explain that students can follow the same method to take notes as they read or use their own system for marking up their write-in text. They may want to color code their annotations. Their margin notes may include questions about the text or observations about characters and their motivations.

698 Unit 6

 **GET READY**

CRITICAL VOCABULARY

presentable   tactfully   listless   vile   engagement

To check your familiarity with the Critical Vocabulary words, answer the following questions.

1. What word would you use to describe something you strongly dislike?
2. Which word might describe someone who has fallen ill?
3. Which word describes how you try to look to meet someone's parents?
4. What's a word for when you have social plans?
5. Which word describes how you should handle a delicate situation?

LANGUAGE CONVENTIONS

Precise Details In both fiction and nonfiction, authors use precise details to shape and inform the perception of readers. Readers evaluate an author's use of details to analyze key ideas.

> For he took a pencil, leaned over the counter, and his <u>pale bloodless fingers</u> crept timidly towards those <u>rosy, flashing ones</u>, as he murmured gently: "If I may venture to point out to madam, the flowers on the little lady's bodice."

In this sentence, the detail of how Rosemary perceives her own fingers in comparison to the shopkeeper's gives us an insight into her character and her habit of comparing herself favorably to others. This is a key idea in the development of the story's theme.

ANNOTATION MODEL NOTICE & NOTE

As you read, notice how the third-person limited point of view shapes your impression of Rosemary. Pay attention to details and word choices that provide hints about Rosemary's character and motivation. In the model you can see one student's notes about the narrator's description of Rosemary in the opening paragraph.

Rosemary Fell was not exactly beautiful. No, you couldn't have called her beautiful. <u>Pretty? Well, if you took her to pieces</u> . . . But why be so cruel as to take anyone to pieces? <u>She was young, brilliant, extremely modern, exquisitely well dressed, amazingly well read</u> in the newest of the new books, and her parties were the most delicious mixture of the really important people and . . . artists—quaint creatures, <u>discoveries of hers, some of them too terrifying for words</u>, but others quite presentable and amusing.	The narrator describes the protagonist as if she is talking about a friend. The tone is conversational and intimate. The narrator is sympathetic towards Rosemary but also seems to mock her a little bit.

698 Unit 6

BACKGROUND

Katherine Mansfield (1888–1923) was born in New Zealand. She disliked her native country and was eager to leave home at 19 to settle in London, where she had attended school several years earlier. Mansfield struggled to earn a living in England and fell into some troubled romantic relationships. When she was 29 she contracted tuberculosis. In the last year of her life, Mansfield wrote some of her finest stories. By the end of her brief career, she gained recognition as a master of the modern short story, emphasizing psychological realism over dramatic action.

A CUP OF TEA
Short Story by Katherine Mansfield

SETTING A PURPOSE

As you read, pay attention to the author's use of third-person limited point of view and think about how the story might be different if it were told in omniscient point of view.

1   Rosemary Fell was not exactly beautiful. No, you couldn't have called her beautiful. Pretty? Well, if you took her to pieces . . . But why be so cruel as to take anyone to pieces? She was young, brilliant, extremely modern, exquisitely well dressed, amazingly well read in the newest of the new books, and her parties were the most delicious mixture of the really important people and . . . artists—quaint creatures, discoveries of hers, some of them too terrifying for words, but others quite **presentable** and amusing.

2   Rosemary had been married two years. She had a duck[1] of a boy. No, not Peter—Michael. And her husband absolutely adored her. They were rich, really rich, not just comfortably well off, which is odious and stuffy and sounds like one's grandparents. But if Rosemary wanted to shop she would go to Paris as you and I would go to Bond Street.[2] If she wanted to buy flowers, the car

---
[1] **duck:** a British expression for a darling person or thing.
[2] **Bond Street:** a London street famous for its fashionable shops.

Notice & Note

Use the side margins to notice and note signposts in the text.

LANGUAGE CONVENTIONS
Annotate: Mark words and phrases used to describe Rosemary in paragraph 1.

Draw Conclusions: What do these details suggest about how society views her?

presentable
(prĭ-zĕn´tə-bəl) *adj.* fit for introduction to others.

TEACH

BACKGROUND

Explain to students that Mansfield's short stories shaped the work of other modern short-story writers, thereby contributing to the development of the short story that we are familiar with today. Mansfield was inspired by the work of Russian playwright and short-story writer Anton Chekhov, who wrote stories with a simple plot structure that offered subtle observations about human behavior. Her stories explore the internal conflicts of complex characters who tend to be flawed yet sympathetic. Mansfield herself was no stranger to internal conflicts. She once married the musician G.C. Bowden, only to leave him the day after their wedding to return to her lover, violinist Garnet Trowell.

SETTING A PURPOSE

Direct students to use the Setting a Purpose prompt to focus their reading.

LANGUAGE CONVENTIONS

Direct students to look for adjectives and nouns that describe Rosemary. Have students describe in their own words what kind of person is likely to be described this way. (**Answer:** *She is seen as fashionable and a little daring in her tastes.*)

For **listening support** for students at varying proficiency levels, see the **Text X-Ray** on page 696C.

CRITICAL VOCABULARY

presentable: Rosemary invites a variety of people to her parties, some of whom dress and groom themselves nicely, so they are considered presentable.

ASK STUDENTS to explain how they prepare to go to an event where they need to be particularly presentable. (*Students may say that in order to be presentable, they put on a nice dress or suit and take extra care with their hair and makeup, or that they have to shave and wear a tie.*)

TEACH

 ANALYZE THIRD-PERSON POINT OF VIEW

Direct students to look for the exact language used to describe Rosemary's hands, and then point out the next sentence, which addresses the thoughts of the shopkeeper. Remind students that this story is in **limited third-person point of view**, which means that the narrator can only describe the thoughts of the main character and not those of other characters. (**Answer:** *The suggestion that the shopkeeper is admiring Rosemary's hands comes from her own thoughts rather than those of the shopkeeper. He may or may not be admiring her hands, but what is important is Rosemary's idea that he might be, as it reflects an aspect of her character that is important to the story.*)

🔵 ENGLISH LEARNER SUPPORT

Use New Vocabulary Pronounce and provide the definition for the word *admire* ("to look at and like something because it is beautiful"). Ask students to complete the sentences below, using correct forms of the verb *admire*.

- Rosemary _____ her hands. (*admires/has admired*)
- Rosemary thinks the shopkeeper _____ her hands. (*has admired/is admiring*)

Then, have students use these sentences to discuss what the narrator says about Rosemary's hands and the shopkeeper's thoughts. **SUBSTANTIAL/MODERATE**

 **NOTICE & NOTE**

pulled up at that perfect shop in Regent Street, and Rosemary inside the shop just gazed in her dazzled, rather exotic way, and said: "I want those and those and those. Give me four bunches of those. And that jar of roses. Yes, I'll have all the roses in the jar. No, no lilac. I hate lilac. It's got no shape." The attendant bowed and put the lilac out of sight, as though this was only too true; lilac was dreadfully shapeless. "Give me those stumpy little tulips. Those red and white ones." And she was followed to the car by a thin shopgirl staggering under an immense white paper armful that looked like a baby in long clothes. . . .

3   One winter afternoon she had been buying something in a little antique shop in Curzon Street. It was a shop she liked. For one thing, one usually had it to oneself. And then the man who kept it was ridiculously fond of serving her. He beamed whenever she came in. He clasped his hands; he was so gratified he could scarcely speak. Flattery, of course. All the same, there was something . . .

4   "You see, madam," he would explain in his low respectful tones, "I love my things. I would rather not part with them than sell them to someone who does not appreciate them, who has not that fine feeling which is so rare. . . ." And, breathing deeply, he unrolled a tiny square of blue velvet and pressed it on the glass counter with his pale fingertips.

5   Today it was a little box. He had been keeping it for her. He had shown it to nobody as yet. An exquisite little enamel box with a glaze so fine it looked as though it had been baked in cream. On the lid a minute creature stood under a flowery tree, and a more minute creature still had her arms around his neck. Her hat, really no bigger than a geranium petal, hung from a branch; it had green ribbons. And there was a pink cloud like a watchful cherub[3] floating above their heads. Rosemary took her hands out of her long gloves. She always took off her gloves to examine such things. Yes, she liked it very much. She loved it; it was a great duck. She must have it. And, turning the creamy box, opening and shutting it, she couldn't help noticing <u>how charming her hands were against the blue velvet. The shopman, in some dim cavern of his mind, may have dared to think so too</u>. For he took a pencil, leaned over the counter, and his pale bloodless fingers crept timidly towards those rosy, flashing ones, as he murmured gently: "If I may venture to point out to madam, the flowers on the little lady's bodice."[4]

6   "Charming!" Rosemary admired the flowers. But what was the price? For a moment the shopman did not seem to hear. Then a murmur reached her. "Twenty-eight guineas,[5] madam."

ANALYZE THIRD-PERSON POINT OF VIEW
Annotate: Mark the sentence in paragraph 5 that suggests what the shopkeeper may be thinking about Rosemary's hands.
Evaluate: Does this suggestion reflect his thoughts or Rosemary's. Explain.

---

[3] **cherub** (chĕr´əb): an angel depicted as a chubby child with wings.
[4] **bodice** (bŏd´ĭs): the part of a dress above the waist.
[5] **guineas** (gĭn´ēz): units of British money equal to one pound and one shilling, used mainly for pricing luxury items.

700   Unit 6

WHEN STUDENTS STRUGGLE . . .

Understand Point of View Help students understand **limited third-person point of view** by identifying specific places where the narrator says something that reflects Rosemary's thoughts, feelings, or personal perceptions. Use the chart below to guide students.

Quote from the Text	Rosemary's Thought, Feeling, or Perception	Why Not Objective?

 For additional support, go to the **Reading Studio** and assign the following 📘 **Level Up tutorial: Point of View**.

700   Unit 6

7   "Twenty-eight guineas." Rosemary gave no sign. She laid the little box down; she buttoned her gloves again. Twenty-eight guineas. Even if one is rich . . . She looked vague. She stared at a plump teakettle like a plump hen above the shopman's head, and her voice was dreamy as she answered: "Well, keep it for me—will you? I'll . . ."

8   But the shopman had already bowed as though keeping it for her was all any human being could ask. He would be willing, of course, to keep it for her forever.

9   The discreet door shut with a click. She was outside on the step, gazing at the winter afternoon. Rain was falling, and with the rain it seemed the dark came too, spinning down like ashes. There was a cold bitter taste in the air, and the new-lighted lamps looked sad. Sad were the lights in the houses opposite. Dimly they burned as if regretting something. And people hurried by, hidden under their hateful umbrellas. Rosemary felt a strange pang.[6] She pressed her muff to her breast; she wished she had the little box, too, to cling to. Of course, the car was there. She'd only to cross the pavement. But still she waited. There are moments, horrible moments in life, when one emerges from shelter and looks out, and it's awful. One oughtn't to give way to them. One ought to go home and have an extra-special tea. But at the very instant of thinking that, a young girl, thin, dark, shadowy—where had she come from?—was standing at Rosemary's elbow and a voice like a sigh, almost like a sob, breathed: "Madam, may I speak to you a moment?"

10 "Speak to me?" Rosemary turned. She saw a little battered creature with enormous eyes, someone quite young, no older than herself, who clutched at her coat-collar with reddened hands, and shivered as though she had just come out of the water.

11 "M-madam," stammered the voice. "Would you let me have the price of a cup of tea?"

12 "A cup of tea?" There was something simple, sincere in that voice; it wasn't in the least the voice of a beggar. "Then have you no money at all?" asked Rosemary.

13 "None, madam," came the answer.

14 "How extraordinary!" Rosemary peered through the dusk, and the girl gazed back at her. How more than extraordinary! And suddenly it seemed to Rosemary such an adventure. It was like something out of a novel by Dostoyevsky,[7] this meeting in the dusk. Supposing she took the girl home? Supposing she did do one of those things she was always reading about or seeing on the stage, what would happen? It would be thrilling. And she heard herself saying afterwards to the amazement of her friends: "I simply took her home

---

[6] **pang** (păng): a sudden sharp pain or feeling.
[7] **Dostoyevsky** (dŏs-tə-yĕf´skē): Feodor Dostoyevsky, a 19th-century Russian author who wrote a number of novels and stories dealing with the lives of the poor.

EVALUATE A CHARACTER
Annotate: Mark words and phrases in paragraph 14 that reveal Rosemary's thoughts about this encounter.

Evaluate: What is Rosemary's motivation for inviting the girl to her home?

TEACH

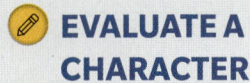

EVALUATE A CHARACTER

Remind students that the narrator follows Rosemary's point of view, so this point of view is limited to how she perceives the world around her and her own actions. Have them look for language that shows how Rosemary judges herself and how she expects the girl to judge her actions. Have students think about whether Rosemary's perception of her actions would be the same as the girl's or an outside observer's. Explain to students that understanding how Rosemary judges her own actions provides clues to her character. (**Answer:** *Rosemary's thoughts about her treatment of the girl suggest that she wants to be thought of as a kind and giving person, but in reality she tends to think of only herself.*)

 **NOTICE & NOTE**

with me," as she stepped forward and said to that dim person beside her: "Come home to tea with me."

15   The girl drew back startled. She even stopped shivering for a moment. Rosemary put out a hand and touched her arm. "I mean it," she said, smiling. And she felt how simple and kind her smile was. "Why won't you? Do. Come home with me now in my car and have tea."

16   "You—you don't mean it, madam," said the girl, and there was pain in her voice.

17   "But I do," cried Rosemary. "I want you to. To please me. Come along."

18   The girl put her fingers to her lips and her eyes devoured Rosemary. "You're—you're not taking me to the police station?" she stammered.

19   "The police station!" Rosemary laughed out. "Why should I be so cruel? No, I only want to make you warm and to hear—anything you care to tell me."

20   Hungry people are easily led. The footman[8] held the door of the car open, and a moment later they were skimming through the dusk.

21   "There!" said Rosemary. She had a feeling of triumph as she slipped her hand through the velvet strap. She could have said, "Now I've got you," as she gazed at the little captive she had netted. But of course <u>she meant it kindly</u>. Oh, <u>more than kindly</u>. She was going to prove to this girl that—<u>wonderful things did happen</u> in life, that—<u>fairy godmothers were</u> real, that—<u>rich people had hearts</u>, and that <u>women *were* sisters</u>. She turned impulsively, saying: "Don't be frightened. After all, why shouldn't you come back with me? We're both women. If I'm the more fortunate, you ought to expect . . ."

22   But happily at that moment, for she didn't know how the sentence was going to end, the car stopped. The bell was rung, the door opened, and with a <u>charming, protecting, almost embracing</u> movement, Rosemary drew the other into the hall. Warmth, softness, light, a sweet scent, all those things so familiar to her she never even thought about them, she watched that other receive. It was fascinating. She was like the little rich girl in her nursery with all the cupboards to open, all the boxes to unpack.

23   "Come, come upstairs," said Rosemary, longing to begin to be generous. "Come up to my room." And, besides, she wanted to spare this poor little thing from being stared at by the servants; she decided as they mounted the stairs she would not even ring for Jeanne, but take off her things by herself. The great thing was to be natural!

24   And "There!" cried Rosemary again, as they reached her beautiful big bedroom with the curtains drawn, the fire leaping on

---

[8] **footman:** a household servant, here functioning as Rosemary's chauffeur.

EVALUATE A CHARACTER
Annotate: Mark words and phrases in paragraphs 21–22 that describe how Rosemary views her treatment of the girl.
Evaluate: What do these thoughts suggest about her character?

TO CHALLENGE STUDENTS . . .

Research Beauty and Fashion The narrator says that Rosemary is well dressed but also hints that she might not be very pretty. Have students conduct research about the standards of beauty and fashion for women during this time period. Using their research, have students describe what Rosemary would wish to look like and what clothes she would want to wear.

her wonderful lacquer furniture, her gold cushions and the primrose and blue rugs.

25   The girl stood just inside the door; she seemed dazed. But Rosemary didn't mind that.

26   "Come and sit down," she cried, dragging her big chair up to the fire, "in this comfy chair. Come and get warm. You look so dreadfully cold."

27   "I daren't, madam," said the girl, and she edged backwards.

28   "Oh, please,"—Rosemary ran forward—"you mustn't be frightened, you mustn't, really. Sit down, and when I've taken off my things we shall go into the next room and have tea and be cozy. Why are you afraid?" And gently she half pushed the thin figure into its deep cradle.

29   But there was no answer. The girl stayed just as she had been put, with her hands by her sides and her mouth slightly open. To be quite sincere, she looked rather stupid. But Rosemary wouldn't acknowledge it. She leaned over her, saying: "Won't you take off your hat? Your pretty hair is all wet. And one is so much more comfortable without a hat, isn't one?"

30   There was a whisper that sounded like "Very good, madam," and the crushed hat was taken off.

31   "Let me help you off with your coat, too," said Rosemary.

32   The girl stood up. But she held on to the chair with one hand and let Rosemary pull. It was quite an effort. The other scarcely helped her at all. She seemed to stagger like a child, and the thought came and went through Rosemary's mind, that if people wanted helping they must respond a little, just a little, otherwise it became very difficult indeed. And what was she to do with the coat now? She left it on the floor, and the hat too. She was just going to take a cigarette off the mantelpiece when the girl said quickly, but so lightly and strangely: "I'm very sorry, madam, but I'm going to faint. I shall go off, madam, if I don't have something."

33   "Good heavens, how thoughtless I am!" Rosemary rushed to the bell.

34   "Tea! Tea at once! And some brandy immediately!"

35   The maid was gone again, but the girl almost cried out. "No, I don't want no brandy. I never drink brandy. It's a cup of tea I want, madam." And she burst into tears.

36   It was a terrible and fascinating moment. Rosemary knelt beside her chair.

37   "Don't cry, poor little thing," she said. "Don't cry." And she gave the other her lace handkerchief. She really was touched beyond words. She put her arm round those thin, birdlike shoulders.

38   Now at last the other forgot to be shy, forgot everything except that they were both women, and gasped out: "I can't go on no longer

ANALYZE THIRD-PERSON POINT OF VIEW

Annotate: In paragraph 32, underline Rosemary's thoughts about the girl's behavior and circle the girl's dialogue.

Analyze: How does the use of third-person limited point of view create irony here?

A Cup of Tea   703

IMPROVE READING FLUENCY

Targeted Passage Focus students' attention on paragraphs 15–20. Point out that this passage is a mixture of narration and dialogue and that the author uses punctuation to indicate questions and exclamations. Read the passage aloud, modeling proper intonation. Then, have students work in pairs to practice reading the passage aloud, conveying the emotion of each character and paying special attention to the punctuation.

Go to the **Reading Studio** for additional support in developing fluency.

TEACH

ANALYZE THIRD-PERSON POINT OF VIEW

Remind students that the narrator describes what Rosemary is thinking and her perceptions of other people and events, but that Rosemary does not always truly understand what is happening and often misunderstands what other people are thinking and feeling. Have students look for language that describes Rosemary's perception of the girl's behavior, as well as her own response to that behavior. Remind students that **irony** means that one or more characters does not know something that the reader knows. Have them compare what Rosemary thinks about the girl's behavior with what we find out through the dialogue. (**Answer:** *Because of the limited third-person point of view, the reader knows what Rosemary is thinking about the girl's behavior. When the girl speaks up to explain herself, it becomes clear that Rosemary has completely misunderstood the situation and why the girl is behaving the way she is. Rosemary thinks the girl is just lazy and doesn't realize that the girl is so hungry she can barely move.*)

For **reading support** for students at varying proficiency levels, see the **Text X-Ray** on page 696D.

A Cup of Tea   703

TEACH

ENGLISH LEARNER SUPPORT

Narrate and Describe Read paragraph 32 aloud. As you read, ask students to act out the action as Rosemary tries to get the girl's coat off. Have the student playing the girl read the dialogue at the end of the paragraph. Then, have students work in pairs to retell in their own words what happened in this scene.
ALL LEVELS

NOTICE & NOTE

like this. I can't bear it. I shall *do* away with myself. I can't bear no more."

39 "You shan't have to. I'll look after you. Don't cry anymore. Don't you see what a good thing it was that you met me? We'll have tea and you'll tell me everything. And I shall arrange something. I promise. *Do* stop crying. It's so exhausting. Please!"

40 The other did stop just in time for Rosemary to get up before the tea came. She had the table placed between them. She plied the poor little creature with everything, all the sandwiches, all the bread and butter, and every time her cup was empty she filled it with tea, cream and sugar. People always said sugar was so nourishing. As for herself she didn't eat; she smoked and looked away **tactfully** so that the other should not be shy.

41 And really the effect of that slight meal was marvelous. When the tea table was carried away a new being, a light, frail creature with tangled hair, dark lips, deep, lighted eyes, lay back in the big chair in a kind of sweet languor,[9] looking at the blaze. Rosemary lit a fresh cigarette; it was time to begin.

42 "And when did you have your last meal?" she asked softly.

43 But at that moment the door-handle turned.

44 "Rosemary, may I come in?" It was Philip.

45 "Of course."

46 He came in. "Oh, I'm so sorry," he said, and stopped and stared.

47 "It's quite all right," said Rosemary smiling. "This is my friend, Miss—"

48 "Smith, madam," said the languid figure, who was strangely still and unafraid.

49 "Smith," said Rosemary. "We are going to have a little talk."

50 "Oh, yes," said Philip. "Quite," and his eye caught sight of the coat and hat on the floor. He came over to the fire and turned his back to it. "It's a beastly[10] afternoon," he said curiously, still looking at that **listless** figure, looking at its hands and boots, and then at Rosemary again.

51 "Yes, isn't it?" said Rosemary enthusiastically. "**Vile**."

52 Philip smiled his charming smile. "As a matter of fact," said he, "I wanted you to come into the library for a moment. Would you? Will Miss Smith excuse us?"

53 The big eyes were raised to him, but Rosemary answered for her. "Of course she will." And they went out of the room together.

54 "I say," said Philip, when they were alone. "Explain. Who is she? What does it all mean?"

---

[9] **languor** (lăng´gər): a dreamy, lazy state.
[10] **beastly**: awful; unpleasant.

NOTICE & NOTE

tactfully
(tăkt´fəl-lē) *adv.* considerately and discreetly.

EVALUATE A CHARACTER
Annotate: Mark references to the girl's name in paragraphs 47–49.

Evaluate: What does it suggest about Rosemary that she hasn't asked for her name until now?

listless
(lĭst´lĭs) *adj.* lacking energy or disinclined to exert effort; lethargic.

vile
(vīl) *adj.* unpleasant or objectionable.

A Cup of Tea 705

APPLYING ACADEMIC VOCABULARY

 arbitrary  controversy ☑ convince  denote ☑ undergo

Write and Discuss Have students turn to a partner to discuss the following questions. Guide students to include the Academic Vocabulary words *undergo* and *convince* in their responses. Ask volunteers to share their responses with the class.

- What transformation does the girl **undergo** after taking her tea?
- How does Rosemary's husband use her insecurity to **convince** her to send the girl away?

TEACH

✏️ EVALUATE A CHARACTER

Point out to students that the author develops Rosemary's character through her internal thoughts and feelings, as well as through her actions and dialogue. Explain that the dialogue in paragraphs 47–49 is revealing because it shows something that Rosemary neglected to do. Ask students to think about whether Rosemary would behave this way with someone of her own class and why this matters. (**Answer:** *Rosemary has not thought to ask the girl's name up to now because she is not actually interested in her as a person and is not really trying to be her friend. The girl is an object for her to play with, and until she needed to explain the girl to her husband, the girl's name didn't matter to her.*)

CRITICAL VOCABULARY

tactfully: Rosemary wants the girl to be comfortable, so she tries to act tactfully, or considerately, while the girl is eating.

ASK STUDENTS what they do when they think someone is not acting tactfully. (*Students may say that they ignore the behavior or that they politely remind the person that their behavior is not tactful.*)

listless: Miss Smith is listless, or very tired, after eating so much food.

ASK STUDENTS if they often feel listless after a big meal. (*Students may say that they feel listless after a really big meal or if they eat a lot at the end of a hard day.*)

vile: Rosemary's husband comments on how beastly the weather is, and she responds by agreeing that it is vile.

ASK STUDENTS what they consider to be vile weather. (*Students may describe vile weather as weather that is very cold and wet or weather that is much too hot.*)

A Cup of Tea 705

TEACH

AHA MOMENT

An Aha Moment occurs in a story when a character realizes something they did not know or understand before. This realization may cause them to have an emotional reaction, make a decision, change their mind about something, or take action. Direct students to look for the language in paragraph 63 that describes Rosemary's emotional reaction. Ask students to explain Rosemary's reaction based on what they already know about her and then discuss how her reaction is related to her subsequent actions. (**Answer:** *The sentence "Her heart beat like a heavy bell" shows that Rosemary is upset. She is likely anxious because she is very insecure about her looks. She no longer wants to keep the girl around and would rather give her money to have her go away.*)

ENGLISH LEARNER SUPPORT

Internalize New Language Provide students with this list of emotions and character traits: *jealous, kind, patient, anxious, selfish, greedy, vain*. Have students look up the definitions for any of these words that are unfamiliar. Then, have them work in pairs to discuss how well each word describes Rosemary, using the following sentence frame: *Rosemary is very/a little/not at all _____.* **MODERATE**

CRITICAL VOCABULARY

engagement: Rosemary's husband jokingly suggests that the girl had an engagement, or an agreement to be somewhere else.

ASK STUDENTS how they feel when they have to cancel an engagement. (*Most students will say that they feel guilty about canceling engagements.*)

706   Unit 6

 **NOTICE & NOTE**

55 Rosemary, laughing, leaned against the door and said: "I picked her up in Curzon Street. Really. She's a real pick-up. She asked me for the price of a cup of tea, and I brought her home with me."

56 "But what on earth are you going to do with her?" cried Philip.

57 "Be nice to her," said Rosemary quickly. "Be frightfully nice to her. Look after her. I don't know how. We haven't talked yet. But show her—treat her—make her feel—"

58 "My darling girl," said Philip, "you're quite mad, you know. It simply can't be done."

59 "I knew you'd say that," retorted Rosemary. "Why not? I want to. Isn't that a reason? And besides, one's always reading about these things. I decided—"

60 "But," said Philip slowly, and he cut the end of a cigar, "she's so astonishingly pretty."

61 "Pretty?" Rosemary was so surprised that she blushed. "Do you think so? I—I hadn't thought about it."

62 "Good Lord!" Philip struck a match. "She's absolutely lovely. Look again, my child. I was bowled over when I came into your room just now. However . . . I think you're making a ghastly mistake. Sorry, darling, if I'm crude and all that. But let me know if Miss Smith is going to dine with us in time for me to look up *The Milliner's Gazette*."[11]

63 "You absurd creature!" said Rosemary, and she went out of the library, but not back to her bedroom. She went to her writing-room and sat down at her desk. Pretty! Absolutely lovely! Bowled over! Her heart beat like a heavy bell. Pretty! Lovely! She drew her checkbook towards her. But no, checks would be no use, of course. She opened a drawer and took out five pound notes, looked at them, put two back, and holding the three squeezed in her hand, she went back to her bedroom.

64 Half an hour later Philip was still in the library, when Rosemary

65 came in. "I only wanted to tell you," said she, and she leaned against the door again and looked at him with her dazzled exotic gaze, "Miss Smith won't dine with us tonight."

66 Philip put down the paper. "Oh, what's happened? Previous **engagement**?"

67 Rosemary came over and sat down on his knee. "She insisted on going," said she, "so I gave the poor little thing a present of money. I couldn't keep her against her will, could I?" she added softly.

68 Rosemary had just done her hair, darkened her eyes a little, and put on her pearls. She put up her hands and touched Philip's cheeks.

AHA MOMENT

Notice & Note: Mark the sentence in paragraph 63 that describes how Philip's comments have affected Rosemary.

Infer: Why is Rosemary rushing to give money to Miss Smith?

engagement
(ĕn-gāj´mənt) *n.* a promise or agreement to be at a particular place at a particular time.

---
[11] *The Milliner's Gazette*: an imaginary newsletter for working-class women. A milliner is a maker of women's hats.

706   Unit 6

WHEN STUDENTS STRUGGLE . . .

Understand Character Motivation Have students use the chart below to analyze the decision that Rosemary makes in paragraph 63. Ask why Rosemary changes her mind.

What Rosemary originally planned to do with the girl	What Rosemary expects to happen	What she decides to do instead

 For additional support, go to the **Reading Studio** and assign the following **Level Up tutorial: Character Motivation**.

69 "Do you like me?" said she, and her tone, sweet, husky, troubled him.
70 "I like you awfully," he said, and he held her tighter. "Kiss me."
71 There was a pause.
72 Then Rosemary said dreamily, "I saw a fascinating little box today. It cost twenty-eight guineas. May I have it?"
73 Philip jumped her on his knee. "You may, little wasteful one," said he.
74 But that was not really what Rosemary wanted to say.
75 "Philip," she whispered, and she pressed his head against her bosom, "am I *pretty?*"

NOTICE & NOTE

CHECK YOUR UNDERSTANDING

Answer these questions before moving on to the **Analyze the Text** section on the following page.

1 In paragraphs 3–5 what can you infer about the shopkeeper?

   A He has a secret crush on Rosemary.
   B He uses flattery to sell expensive things to rich people.
   C He isn't very interested in money.
   D He wishes he didn't have to sell his things.

2 In paragraphs 10–15, which sentence suggests Rosemary's motivation for taking Miss Smith home with her?

   F *"M-madam," stammered the voice. "Would you let me have the price of a cup of tea?"*
   G *There was something simple, sincere in that voice; it wasn't in the least the voice of a beggar.*
   H *It was like something out of a novel by Dostoyevsky, this meeting in the dusk.*
   J *And she heard herself saying afterwards to the amazement of her friends: "I simply took her home with me."*

3 How does Rosemary's husband convince her to send the girl away?

   A He plays on her insecurity about her looks.
   B He embarrasses her for not reading the paper.
   C He scolds her about money.
   D He flatters her need to feel superior.

A Cup of Tea 707

TEACH

CHECK YOUR UNDERSTANDING

Have students answer the questions independently.

Answers:

1. B
2. J
3. A

If they answer any questions incorrectly, have them reread the text to confirm their understanding. Then they may proceed to **ANALYZE THE TEXT** on page 708.

ENGLISH LEARNER SUPPORT

Oral Assessment Use the following questions to assess students' comprehension and speaking skills.

1. Does the shopkeeper want to sell Rosemary expensive things? *(yes)*
2. Rosemary invites the girl to her _____. *(home)*
3. Rosemary tells the girl to leave because her husband says the girl is _____. *(pretty)*

SUBSTANTIAL/MODERATE

APPLY

ANALYZE THE TEXT

Possible answers:

1. **DOK 4:** *Because we are only exposed to Rosemary's perspective, we take longer to understand how uncomfortable she is making Miss Smith, and we are surprised by Philip's comment about her beauty. If the story were told from an omniscient point of view, Rosemary would probably seem more insecure and selfish from the beginning.*

2. **DOK 3:** *He realizes how insecure she is about her looks and emphasizes Miss Smith's attractiveness to get Rosemary to change her mind.*

3. **DOK 4:** *Possible Answer: Mansfield conveys the theme that wealthy people are insecure and selfish because so much of their self-image is tied to their material possessions. Rosemary's motivation is related to this theme because she wants to help Miss Smith so she can resemble a character in a fashionable book, not because she really cares.*

4. **DOK 4:** *Students may respond that the context makes Rosemary more sympathetic because we understand how her social position isolates her from how most people live.*

5. **DOK 4:** *Possible Answer: She hasn't changed because she remains insecure about her appearance and she still seeks comfort in material possessions.*

RESEARCH

Remind students that they should look at multiple sources as they conduct their research and that their answers should synthesize and summarize what they learn from these sources.

Extend Based on their research, students will likely understand that women in the 1920s were becoming less dependent on men because they had opportunities to make money to support themselves. They were also more likely to form their own opinions and were expected to do so, rather than simply agreeing with their husbands or male relatives.

 **RESPOND**

ANALYZE THE TEXT

Support your responses with evidence from the text. NOTEBOOK

1. **Analyze** How does the third-person limited point of view affect your reaction to Rosemary and her plan to help Miss Smith? How might the story have been different if told by an omniscient narrator?

2. **Draw Conclusions** Reread paragraphs 60–62. Why does Philip speak so enthusiastically to his wife about Miss Smith's attractiveness? Explain.

3. **Analyze** What theme about wealthy people does Mansfield convey in "A Cup of Tea"? How do Rosemary's actions and motivation in trying to help Miss Smith relate to this theme?

4. **Connect** "A Cup of Tea" is set in a time when wealthy women did not have professions and were expected to appear fashionable. How does this context influence your evaluation of Rosemary's character?

5. **Notice & Note** Rosemary abandons her plan after Philip makes her aware of Miss Smith's beauty. Has this realization changed Rosemary? Why or why not?

RESEARCH TIP
When researching many aspects of a broad subject, look for websites run by organizations dedicated to that subject, and look through the website's menu for a "Resources" page. This is a good way to find helpful and credible sources.

RESEARCH

"A Cup of Tea" was written in 1922, at a time when British and American women's lives were undergoing radical change. Do some research to find out about some of the social changes of the 1920s, and complete the graphic organizer.

SOCIAL CHANGES FOR WOMEN IN THE 1920s	
Education	*More women went to college. Establishment of many all-girls colleges*
Political Power	*American women got the right to vote in 1920, Some British women could vote in 1918; all British women culd vote in 1928..*
Labor and Employment	*Many more women went to work outside the home as secretaries, teachers, and nurses.*
Fashion	*Stopped wearing corsets and long skirts and instead wore clothing conducive to physical activity. Wore makeup and cut their hair.*

Extend How did these changes affect women's relationships with men on an individual and societal level?

WHEN STUDENTS STRUGGLE . . .

Reteaching: Evaluate a Character Ask students to make a list of the characters in the story, what the reader knows about each character, and what Rosemary understands.

Character	What the Reader Knows	What Rosemary Understands

 For additional support, go to the **Reading Studio** and assign the following Level Up tutorial: Making Inferences about Characters.

CREATE AND DEBATE

Write a Missing Scene from Another Point of View We know that Rosemary goes back to her bedroom and gives Miss Smith some money before asking her to leave, but the scene is not in the story. Write this scene from Miss Smith's perspective using the third-person limited point of view.

- ❏ Remember that the third-person narrator is a voice outside of the story.
- ❏ The narrator should relate only Miss Smith's thoughts and feelings.

Present a Scene Read your scene to the group. Remember your presentational techniques as you convey your meaning.

- ❏ Practice reading your scene aloud.
- ❏ Determine the speed at which you will read, including where you will pause for effect.
- ❏ Select words and phrases you will emphasize.
- ❏ Determine where you might raise and lower your voice and when you will make eye contact with your audience.
- ❏ After your presentation, let the group comment or ask questions.

RESPOND TO THE ESSENTIAL QUESTION

What makes people feel insecure?

Gather Information Review your annotations and notes on "A Cup of Tea." Then, add relevant information to your Response Log. As you determine which information to include, think about:

- what we base our opinions of ourselves on
- how people can use our insecurities to manipulate us
- how comparing ourselves to others can affect our self-esteem

RESPOND

Go to **Writing Narratives** in the **Writing Studio** to find out more about writing fiction.

Go to the **Speaking and Listening Studio** to find out more about giving a presentation.

ACADEMIC VOCABULARY

As you write and discuss what you learned from the story, be sure to use the Academic Vocabulary words. Check off each of the words that you use.

- ❏ arbitrary
- ❏ controversy
- ❏ convince
- ❏ denote
- ❏ undergo

A Cup of Tea 709

APPLY

CREATE AND DEBATE

Write a Missing Scene from Another Point of View Explain to students that they are going to write a short fictional scene based on the characters and events in "A Cup of Tea" and that they should combine what they know from the story with their own imaginations. Have students first make notes of everything they know about Miss Smith. Then, ask them to think of questions to ask to help them imagine the scene. For example, will the girl be happy or unhappy? Why is she begging for money on the street? What does she need or want right now? What does she think of Rosemary? Remind them that although the scene will be from Miss Smith's perspective, the narrator will be a voice outside of the story, not Miss Smith herself.

For **writing support** for students at varying proficiency levels, see the **Text X-Ray** on page 696D.

Present a Scene Remind students that when they give a reading of their scene, they will want to capture their audience's attention by creating an experience that is different from just reading the scene on the page. Encourage them to bring the characters to life by varying their voice for each character and by using appropriate volume and intonation.

RESPOND TO THE ESSENTIAL QUESTION

Allow time for students to add details from "A Cup of Tea" to their Unit 6 Response Logs.

A Cup of Tea **709**

APPLY

CRITICAL VOCABULARY

Answers:

1. *listless*
2. *engagement*
3. *presentable*
4. *tactfully*
5. *vile*

VOCABULARY STRATEGY:
Denotation and Connotation

Answers:

1. *Denotation: very pleasant, delightful*
   Connotation: positive; fun; attractive; self-indulgent
2. *Denotation: to grasp and hold tightly*
   Connotation: somewhat negative; needy and uncomfortable
3. *Denotation: not feigned or affected, genuine*
   Connotation: lighthearted; confiding; slightly mocking and ironic

---

 **RESPOND**

WORD BANK
presentable
tactfully
listless
vile
engagement

CRITICAL VOCABULARY

Practice and Apply Complete the sentences with Critical Vocabulary words.

1. The baby is so pale and _____. She must be sick!
2. I'm sorry to cancel our plans, but I have another _____.
3. If I'd known I was having visitors I'd have tried to look _____ instead of wearing sweatpants.
4. I need to _____ remind her that she owes me money.
5. It's not pleasant to have dinner at your house because your mother's cooking is often _____.

VOCABULARY STRATEGY:
Denotation and Connotation

 Go to the **Vocabulary Studio** for more on denotation and connotation.

Connotation and denotation are ways of describing the meaning of words. **Denotation** is the literal definition of a word found in the dictionary. **Connotation** refers to the emotional associations of a word, which may be positive or negative. The way a word is used may influence its connotation.

> . . . her parties were the most delicious mixture of the really important people and . . . artists—quaint creatures, discoveries of hers, some of them too terrifying for words, but others quite <u>presentable</u> and amusing.

Here, the word *presentable* has a connotation of snobbery and privilege.

Practice and Apply In the sentences below from "A Cup of Tea," look up the underlined word in a dictionary and write its denotation. Then, make some notes about its connotation.

1. Her parties were the most <u>delicious</u> mixture of . . . people.

   Denotation:

   Connotation:

2. She saw a little battered creature with enormous eyes, . . . who <u>clutched</u> at her coat-collar with reddened hands.

   Denotation:

   Connotation:

3. The girl stayed just as she had been put, with her hands by her sides and her mouth slightly open. To be quite <u>sincere</u>, she looked rather stupid.

   Denotation:

   Connotation:

710 Unit 6

 ENGLISH LEARNER SUPPORT

Vocabulary Strategy Review the difference between **denotation** and **connotation**. Then, provide students with the following list of words from the selection, and have them write the denotation and connotation for each: *creatures* (paragraph 1): *denotation: living beings; connotation: indicating pity, scorn, or endearment*; *beamed* (paragraph 3): *denotation: smiled radiantly; connotation: indicating extreme happiness*; *clasped* (paragraph 3): *denotation: grasped firmly; connotation: indicating excitement or feigned excitement*; and *bloodless* (paragraph 6): *denotation: without blood, pale; connotation: unhealthy or lacking energy*.
ALL LEVELS

LANGUAGE CONVENTIONS:
Precise Details

In order to engage the reader, authors use precise details to illustrate or suggest key ideas. A good writer does not provide details arbitrarily, but rather makes very deliberate choices in using details to develop characters and themes.

> She had a feeling of triumph as she slipped her hand through the velvet strap.

In this sentence, the velvet strap reminds the reader that Rosemary lives a life of luxury and comfort.

> There was a whisper that sounded like "Very good, madam," and the crushed hat was taken off.

In this sentence, the "crushed hat" gives the reader a sense of the girl's poverty and misfortune.

Practice and Apply In the passages below from "A Cup of Tea," mark the precise details the author uses to develop the characters and theme.

> "Don't cry, poor little thing," she said. "Don't cry." And she gave the other her lace handkerchief. She really was touched beyond words. She put her arm round those thin, birdlike shoulders.

> When the tea table was carried away a new being, a light, frail creature with tangled hair, dark lips, deep, lighted eyes, lay back in the big chair in a kind of sweet languor, looking at the blaze.

How do these details contribute to the reader's understanding of the characters and the theme of the story?

RESPOND

APPLY

LANGUAGE CONVENTIONS:
Precise Details

Remind students that the term "**precise details**" refers to descriptions of objects, people, and surroundings that focus on something very specific and concrete. These details often appeal to the senses by describing colors, textures, shapes, smells, and sounds.

Practice and Apply Direct students to look for words and phrases that provide vivid descriptions of Rosemary and Miss Smith. Then, ask them to think about what they associate with these details and how those associations relate to the characters and theme of the story.

(**Answer:** *Rosemary's lace handkerchief reflects her material wealth. The girl's thin, birdlike shoulders reflect her poverty and frailness. The description of the girl after she's had tea shows that Rosemary sees her as pathetic and does not realize that her features are pretty. The reader sees these details again in a new light after Philip talks about how pretty the girl is.*)

 ENGLISH LEARNER SUPPORT

Language Conventions Help students talk about how details convey meaning using the following supports:

- Provide images or objects to illustrate the words *velvet, crushed, lace, tangled, strap,* and *handkerchief*. Ask students to write down each word and then think of other words that it reminds them of. For example, the word *velvet* might remind them of the words *soft* or *rich*.
  SUBSTANTIAL

- Have students work in small groups to create a word map for each of the following phrases to indicate other words or phrases they associate with it: *velvet strap, tangled hair, lace handkerchief*.
  MODERATE

PLAN

THE LOVE SONG OF J. ALFRED PRUFROCK
Poem by T. S. Eliot

GENRE ELEMENTS
MODERNIST POETRY

Tell students that **lyric poetry** expresses strong feelings or thoughts. Explain that the **modernist** poets wanted to break away from the flowery style of Romantic poetry. Modernist poetry reflected the growing unhappiness and alienation people felt after the Industrial Revolution. The disrupted syntax and experimental style of modernist poetry rejected traditional literary forms. In this lesson, students will analyze the techniques of modernist poetry.

LEARNING OBJECTIVES

- Understand modernist poetry, make inferences, and analyze stream of consciousness.
- Conduct research about stream-of-consciousness writing.
- Write a modernist poem.
- Present a poem.
- **Language** Share inferences about a poem's speaker using sentence frames.

TEXT COMPLEXITY

Quantitative Measures	The Love Song of J. Alfred Prufrock	**Lexile: N/A**
Qualitative Measures	**Ideas Presented** Subtle, implied meanings. Abstract ideas and use of metaphor and symbolism.	
	Structures Used Complex, modernist, stream of consciousness.	
	Language Used Allusive, figurative, archaic, and formal language. Complex sentence structures.	
	Knowledge Required Cultural and historical references make heavier demands.	

PLAN

RESOURCES
Online Ed

- Unit 6 Response Log
- Selection Audio
- Close Read Screencasts: Modeled Discussions
- Reading Studio: Notice & Note
- Level Up Tutorial: Making Inferences
- Writing Studio: Writing as a Process
- Speaking and Listening Studio: Giving a Presentation
- "The Love Song of J. Alfred Prufrock" Selection Test

SUMMARIES

English
In this poem, the title character is the speaker and protagonist. As he goes to an evening social gathering, Prufrock expresses his thoughts and feelings, and ponders whether to ask an "overwhelming question." Preoccupied with his appearance, his aging, and his feelings of insignificance and fear, he wonders whether his activities are worthwhile and what his life really means. He ends his monologue inconclusively, his question unasked and unanswered.

Spanish
En este poema, el personaje homónimo es el narrador y protagonista. Una noche, mientras va a una reunión social, Prufrock expresa sus pensamientos y sentimientos y reflexiona sobre si puede hacer una "pregunta abrumadora". Preocupado por su apariencia, su vejez y sus sentimientos de insignificancia y miedo, se pregunta si sus actividades valen la pena y cuál es el verdadero significado de su vida. Sin llegar a una conclusión, termina su monólogo, con su pregunta nunca hecha y nunca respondida.

SMALL-GROUP OPTIONS
Have students work in small groups and pairs to read and discuss the selection.

Reciprocal Teaching
- Have students read the poem.
- After reading, ask students to write three to five questions about the poem, using these stems: *What does the poet mean by _____? Why did the poet _____? How does the poet use _____ to _____? How does the _____ affect the _____?*
- Form teams of three students.
- Have each student offer two questions for group discussion.
- Encourage the group to reach a consensus on the answers and find supporting text evidence.

Think-Pair-Share
- After reading the poem, pose these questions: *If you made a film of this poem, what images would you use? Why?*
- Have students think about the questions individually and take notes.
- Then, have pairs listen, discuss, and formulate a shared response to the questions. Direct them to include at least two reasons to support their chosen images.
- Finally, have pairs share their responses with the class.

The Love Song of J. Alfred Prufrock

PLAN

Text X-Ray: English Learner Support
for "The Love Song of J. Alfred Prufrock"

Use the Text X-Ray and the supports and scaffolds in the Teacher's Edition to help guide students at different proficiency levels through the selection.

INTRODUCE THE SELECTION
DISCUSS STREAM OF CONSCIOUSNESS

In this lesson, students will need to be able to discuss how stream of consciousness is used in a poem. Provide the following explanation:

- *Stream of consciousness* refers to the continuous flow of ideas, thoughts, and feelings in a person's conscious mind.

Have students take a few minutes to let their mind wander. As they daydream, have them take notes or do a brief writing activity in which they describe what they think and feel. Then, have them share and discuss their experiences.

Ask questions, such as: *What did you think first? What did you think next? How were these two thoughts connected?*

CULTURAL REFERENCES

The following words or phrases may be unfamiliar to students:

- *sawdust restaurants with oyster-shells* (line 7): refers to restaurants where the floors are covered with sawdust and people can toss their oyster shells on the ground
- *Michelangelo* (line 14): famous Italian Renaissance sculptor, painter, architect, and poet
- *eternal Footman* (line 85): an imaginary butler serving people who are dead; a symbol of death

LISTENING

Take Dictation

Remind students that this poem is a dramatic monologue, but it is not written as prose. It has an experimental form and meter that uses a mix of rhyme and free verse.

Use the following supports with students at varying proficiency levels:

- Read the first nine lines of the poem aloud, emphasizing any rhyming words. Then, slowly reread each line. Have students write down the rhyming words they hear. After reading, write the rhyming words on the board and have students make corrections to their work, as needed. **SUBSTANTIAL**
- Have one partner slowly read lines 1–9 aloud as the other partner writes down rhyming words. Direct listeners to ask speakers to repeat words as needed. Then, have them switch roles and repeat the activity for lines 10–22. Have them check their work and make any necessary corrections. **MODERATE**
- Tell partners to repeat the previous activity for the entire poem. Have them point out the rhyming words they hear. **LIGHT**

712C Unit 6

PLAN

SPEAKING

Share Inferences

Remind students that they will enjoy a poem more if they look for clues to discover things about the speaker that are not directly stated. Direct them to use the question frame *Why do you think _____?* as they make inferences.

Use the following supports with students at varying proficiency levels:

- Have students read lines 1–4 aloud. Ask: *Where do you think they are going?* Have students use the sentence frame: *I think they are going to _____.* **SUBSTANTIAL**
- Have partners use the question frame as they take turns making inferences about the first 34 lines of the poem. **MODERATE**
- Have partners write other question frames they can use to ask each other about inferences. For example: *What can you infer from _____?* Then, have pairs use the frames to make inferences about the poem. **LIGHT**

READING

Adapt Text

Provide students with simplified versions of the poem that include summaries of each stanza.

Use the following supports with students at varying proficiency levels:

- Have students practice reading the simplified version of the poem. Have them circle and read aloud words they recognize. **SUBSTANTIAL**
- Have students complete the previous activity. Then, have them discuss how their fluency improved and why. **MODERATE**
- Have students record themselves reading the poem several times. Have them chart and discuss their fluency rates. **LIGHT**

WRITING

Vary Sentence Lengths

Introduce students to the writing assignment on Student Edition page 721. Explain that free verse often has a variety of sentence lengths. Have them review and compare the sentence lengths in Eliot's poem.

Use the following supports with students at varying proficiency levels:

- Provide a classroom object to describe. Write on the board two sentences of different lengths about the object. Have students copy them in their notebooks. For example: *The chair is brown. The chair is brown and clean.* **SUBSTANTIAL**
- Have partners use the sample sentences from the previous activity to help them write a free-verse stanza using a variety of sentence lengths. **MODERATE**
- Have students read their poem to a partner. Then, have them discuss the rhythm and flow of the writing. Guide them to give suggestions to each other for revising sentence lengths to make the writing sound more interesting. **LIGHT**

TEACH

? Connect to the ESSENTIAL QUESTION

People feel insecure, or unsure of themselves, for a variety of reasons. "The Love Song of J. Alfred Prufrock" delves into one man's experience of feeling outside of the world, too paralyzed by his fears and self-doubts to make the personal connections he so desperately craves.

ANALYZE & APPLY

THE LOVE SONG OF J. ALFRED PRUFROCK

Poem by **T. S. Eliot**

? ESSENTIAL QUESTION:

What makes people feel insecure?

LEARNING MINDSET

PLAN/PREDICT Explain to students that good planning is key to completing exemplary work efficiently. Planning often includes mapping out steps toward reaching a goal, and may include visualizing what needs to be done to best predict the order in which tasks should be accomplished. Explain that planning helps students learn to be disciplined, which will lead to reaching goals more easily in the future.

GET READY

QUICK START

Some people appear confident in any situation, while others are filled with doubts about themselves. What circumstances can diminish a person's confidence? Write a paragraph in response to this question. Then, discuss your ideas with a partner.

UNDERSTAND MODERNIST POETRY

Modernist poets such as T. S. Eliot abandoned traditional verse forms and experimented with literary techniques to better reflect the social and technological changes of their times. Eliot's poetry can be difficult to understand because he presents a patchwork of images, symbols, and allusions that readers must connect for themselves. Consider using the following strategies to help you interpret "The Love Song of J. Alfred Prufrock":

- Read the poem aloud, pausing between sections and lingering over striking images.
- Reread the poem more than once.
- Annotate the text by marking difficult lines and passages and paraphrasing or summarizing them.
- Consult the side notes for explanations of literary allusions.

MAKE INFERENCES

In his poetry, Eliot rarely expresses ideas in a straightforward manner. To understand and appreciate these poems, readers must make **inferences,** logical guesses based on clues found in the text. Making inferences is sometimes called "reading between the lines" because you come to an understanding of something that the author has not explicitly stated. For example, we can infer from the following lines that the speaker is going to a social gathering where he thinks he must hide his true personality or feelings from the other guests:

> There will be time, there will be time
> To prepare a face to meet the faces that you meet;

As you read "The Love Song of J. Alfred Prufrock," look for images that suggest thoughts and feelings. Use a chart like this one to record your inferences.

DETAILS FROM THE TEXT	MY INFERENCES

GENRE ELEMENTS: LYRIC POETRY

- expresses strong feelings or thoughts
- has a musical quality
- often deals with intense emotions surrounding events like death, love, or loss
- includes forms such as ode, elegy, and sonnet

TEACH

QUICK START

Have students read the Quick Start prompt, then consider possible circumstances that might make a person appear confident or unsure in a situation. Direct them to write their paragraphs and share them with their partners. Then ask several students to share their paragraphs with the whole group.

UNDERSTAND MODERNIST POETRY

Explain that Eliot, along with other modernist writers, experimented with traditional forms, changing them to better express the changes they were experiencing in the world and in themselves. Because of this, the collection of images, symbols, and allusions presented by Eliot in this poem can make it difficult to fully understand.

Describe several strategies students can use to help them more easily understand "The Love Song of J. Alfred Prufrock." These include reading the poem aloud multiple times, using the side notes to help explain certain phrases, and annotating the text so the students' own notes can provide insight into difficult parts.

MAKE INFERENCES

Explain that **inferences,** or logical guesses, are made by putting together clues from the reading. Explain that guessing at what the author is trying to convey takes careful study or "reading between the lines."

Read aloud the two lines from "The Love Song of J. Alfred Prufrock." Explain that the repeated phrase in the first line indicates there is more than enough time to act, and that the second line indicates what that action is: putting on one's "face," or the face worn to interact with others. Explain that social anxiety caused by insecurity, like Prufrock is experiencing, can make individuals feel like they have to don masks to blend in with others. Tell students that annotating the text or using a graphic organizer to record these observations will help students better understand the poem as a whole.

TEACH

ANALYZE STREAM OF CONSCIOUSNESS

Modernist writers broke with traditional writing forms, and one of the ways this happened was through the development of **stream-of-consciousness** writing. This writing depicts what really happens in people's minds: a constant stream of thoughts, emotions, memories, and associations.

Explain that a **dramatic monologue,** like this poem, is one speaker's collection of thoughts, put into words. Read the example aloud. Explain that to understand this jumble of thoughts, students should examine the emotions or ideas expressed in the writing rather than the literal meaning of each word.

 ANNOTATION MODEL

Explain to students how to make associations, or connections, between various elements of the poem. Explain that making these associations can help them better understand the meaning of the poem. Point out that they may follow the suggested annotation model or use their own system for marking up the selection in their write-in text. They may want to color-code their annotations by using highlighters. Their notes in the margin may include questions about ideas that are unclear or their own observations and associations.

 **GET READY**

ANALYZE STREAM OF CONSCIOUSNESS

One of the most radical breaks from convention in modernist literature was the development of **stream of consciousness.** This writing technique, used by both poets and fiction writers, presents the random flow of thoughts, emotions, memories, and associations running through the mind of a character or speaker. The goal is to re-create states of mind instead of describing them.

"The Love Song of J. Alfred Prufrock" is a dramatic monologue in which Prufrock addresses a silent listener with a tumble of thoughts, allusions, and figurative language, as in the following stanza:

> Shall I part my hair behind? Do I dare to eat a peach?
> I shall wear white flannel trousers, and walk upon the beach.
> I have heard the mermaids singing, each to each.

As you read the poem, try not to be put off by the seemingly nonsensical nature of the stream-of-consciousness verse, but be alert to any feelings or ideas that the images seem to suggest.

ANNOTATION MODEL NOTICE & NOTE

As you read, note down associations you can make between thoughts, images, and other elements in the poem. In the model, you can see one reader's notes about the opening lines of "The Love Song of J. Alfred Prufrock."

> Let us go then, you and I,
> When the evening is spread out against the sky
> Like a patient etherised upon a table;
> Let us go through certain half-deserted streets,
> The muttering retreats
> Of restless nights in one-night cheap hotels
> And sawdust restaurants with oyster-shells:

Prufrock addresses the listener—is that us?—with an invitation to walk with him through the city. What a strange simile he uses to describe the night sky!

He seems to be thinking about a tawdry side of town.

BACKGROUND

T. S. Eliot *(1888–1965) was one of the most influential poets and literary critics of the 20th century. He grew up in a cultured household in St. Louis, Missouri. While pursuing his graduate studies, he became involved with a circle of avant-garde writers and settled down in London. He published his first collection of poems,* Prufrock and Other Observations, *in 1917. The book baffled some reviewers but was hailed by modernists. Eliot followed it up in 1922 with* The Waste Land, *which made him internationally famous. The poem expresses the sense of alienation and spiritual loss felt by many in his generation.*

THE LOVE SONG OF J. ALFRED PRUFROCK

Poem by T. S. Eliot

SETTING A PURPOSE

As you read, consider why the speaker asks so many questions and whether or not those questions get answered.

> S'io credessi che mia risposta fosse
> a persona che mai tornasse al mondo,
> questa fiamma staria senza più scosse.
> Ma per ciò che giammai di questo fondo
> non tornò vivo alcun, s'i'odo il vero,
> senza tema d'infamia ti rispondo.

Let us go then, you and I,
When the evening is spread out against the sky
Like a patient etherised upon a table;
Let us go, through certain half-deserted streets,
5   The muttering retreats
Of restless nights in one-night cheap hotels
And sawdust restaurants with oyster-shells:
Streets that follow like a tedious argument
Of insidious intent
10 To lead you to an overwhelming question . . .

NOTICE & NOTE

Notice & Note

Use the side margins to notice and note signposts in the text.

S'io credessi . . . ti rispondo: These lines are from the *Inferno,* written in the early 14th century by Italian poet Dante Alighieri. As Dante visits hell, one of the damned agrees to speak of his torment only because he believes that Dante cannot return to the living world to repeat the tale.

3 etherised: given ether, a liquid used as an anesthetic.

9 insidious (ĭn-sĭd´ē-əs): more dangerous than it seems.

TEACH

✏️ ANALYZE STREAM OF CONSCIOUSNESS

Explain that to better understand **stream of consciousness,** and the interruptions in thought it often depicts, students should examine the emotions conveyed by these interruptions. (**Answer:** *His insecurity about his personal appearance makes it hard for him to "dare" to ask the overwhelming question.*)

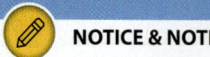

NOTICE & NOTE

Oh, do not ask, "What is it?"
Let us go and make our visit.

In the room the women come and go
Talking of Michelangelo.

15 The yellow fog that rubs its back upon the window-panes,
The yellow smoke that rubs its muzzle on the window-panes,
Licked its tongue into the corners of the evening,
Lingered upon the pools that stand in drains,
Let fall upon its back the soot that falls from chimneys,
20 Slipped by the terrace, made a sudden leap,
And seeing that it was a soft October night,
Curled once about the house, and fell asleep.

And indeed there will be time
For the yellow smoke that slides along the street
25 Rubbing its back upon the window-panes;
There will be time, there will be time
To prepare a face to meet the faces that you meet;
There will be time to murder and create,
And time for all the works and days of hands
30 That lift and drop a question on your plate;
Time for you and time for me,
And time yet for a hundred indecisions,
And for a hundred visions and revisions,
Before the taking of a toast and tea.

35 In the room the women come and go
Talking of Michelangelo.

ANALYZE STREAM OF CONSCIOUSNESS

Annotate: Mark interruptions in Prufrock's train of thought in lines 37–46.

Analyze: What connection can you make between Prufrock's thoughts about his appearance and the question he repeatedly asks in this passage?

And indeed there will be time
To wonder, "Do I dare?" and, "Do I dare?"
Time to turn back and descend the stair,
40 With a bald spot in the middle of my hair—
(They will say: "How his hair is growing thin!")
My morning coat, my collar mounting firmly to the chin,
My necktie rich and modest, but asserted by a simple pin—
(They will say: "But how his arms and legs are thin!")
45 Do I dare
Disturb the universe?
In a minute there is time
For decisions and revisions which a minute will reverse.

716 Unit 6

IMPROVE READING FLUENCY

Targeted Passage Conduct an echo reading activity with students using lines 23–34. Explain that you will read two or three lines with the correct pronunciation, intonation, and stress, and that they should repeat the lines after you, orally and in unison. Direct them to mimic you as closely as possible as you read through the stanza.

 Go to the **Reading Studio** for additional support in developing fluency.

For I have known them all already, known them all—
50 Have known the evenings, mornings, afternoons,
I have measured out my life with coffee spoons;
I know the voices dying with a dying fall
Beneath the music from a farther room.
   So how should I presume?

55 And I have known the eyes already, known them all—
The eyes that fix you in a formulated phrase,
And when I am formulated, sprawling on a pin,
When I am pinned and wriggling on the wall,
Then how should I begin
60 To spit out all the butt-ends of my days and ways?
   And how should I presume?

And I have known the arms already, known them all—
Arms that are braceleted and white and bare
(But in the lamplight, downed with light brown hair!)
65 Is it perfume from a dress
That makes me so digress?
Arms that lie along a table, or wrap about a shawl.
   And should I then presume?
   And how should I begin?
         . . . . .

70 Shall I say, I have gone at dusk through narrow streets
And watched the smoke that rises from the pipes
Of lonely men in shirt-sleeves, leaning out of windows? . . .

I should have been a pair of ragged claws
Scuttling across the floors of silent seas.
         . . . . .

75 And the afternoon, the evening, sleeps so peacefully!
   Smoothed by long fingers,
   Asleep . . . tired . . . or it malingers,
   Stretched on the floor, here beside you and me.
Should I, after tea and cakes and ices,
80 Have the strength to force the moment to its crisis?
But though I have wept and fasted, wept and prayed,
Though I have seen my head (grown slightly bald) brought in
         upon a platter,
I am no prophet—and here's no great matter;
I have seen the moment of my greatness flicker,
85 And I have seen the eternal Footman hold my coat, and snicker,
And in short, I was afraid.

54 presume: act overconfidently; dare.

55–58 And I have . . . on the wall: Prufrock recalls being scrutinized by women at other parties. He portrays himself as a live insect that has been classified, labeled, and mounted for display.

56 formulated: reduced to a formula.

MAKE INFERENCES
Annotate: Mark the metaphors in lines 55–61.

Infer: What do these metaphors suggest about how Prufrock feels among women at parties?

73–74 I should . . . silent seas: Here Prufrock presents an image of himself as a crayfish.

77 malingers (mə-lĭng′gərz): pretends illness in order to avoid duty or work.

81–83 But though . . . prophet: an allusion to the biblical story of John the Baptist, who is imprisoned by King Herod (Matthew 14; Mark 6). At the request of his wife, Herod had the Baptist's head cut off and brought to him on a platter.

The Love Song of J. Alfred Prufrock   717

TEACH

MAKE INFERENCES

Discuss the two metaphors in lines 55–61. (*Prufrock describes himself as an insect on display and his life as the butt-end of a cigarette.*) Ask students who Prufrock imagines will "pin" him to the wall. (*women*) Then, tell them to make an **inference** about his relationship with women at parties based on these images. (**Answer:** *He compares himself to an insect pinned alive into a display and his life to cigarette butts. The metaphors suggest he feels tormented and insignificant among the women.*)

ENGLISH LEARNER SUPPORT

Learn New Vocabulary Read line 77 aloud. Direct students to the side note for this line to help them understand the word *malinger*. Ask students to explain the differences between being asleep, being tired, and malingering. (*Asleep means you're actually sleeping; being tired means you would like to sleep; malingering means you're staying in bed to avoid tasks.*) **SUBSTANTIAL**

WHEN STUDENTS STRUGGLE . . .

Make Inferences Remind students that **inferences** are logical guesses based on clues found in the text. Challenge them to "read between the lines" as they read this poem. Provide them with a graphic organizer like the one below to use as they read the selection.

Phrase	Clues	Inference

 For additional support, go to the **Reading Studio** and assign the following **Level Up tutorial: Making Inferences.**

TEACH

UNDERSTAND MODERNIST POETRY

Remind students that literary **allusions** are indirect references to other literary works. Explain that such allusions are often used in **modernist poetry**. (*Answer: Comparing himself to Hamlet, Prufrock says he is not the hero of his story, but a minor character who avoids risks and is sometimes foolish.*)

ENGLISH LEARNER SUPPORT

Enhance Understanding Read lines 122–125 aloud, asking students to repeat the lines chorally. Direct them to the side note that explains what is meant by the "mermaids singing." Explain that this is a metaphor for how Prufrock is feeling. Ask them to consider why Prufrock does not believe the mermaids will sing to him. (*His insecurity is so strong that he feels like beautiful women—mermaids—would never be interested in him.*)

MODERATE/LIGHT

 **NOTICE & NOTE**

And would it have been worth it, after all,
After the cups, the marmalade, the tea,
Among the porcelain, among some talk of you and me,
90 Would it have been worth while,
To have bitten off the matter with a smile,
To have squeezed the universe into a ball
To roll it towards some overwhelming question,
To say: "I am Lazarus, come from the dead,
95 Come back to tell you all, I shall tell you all"—
If one, settling a pillow by her head,
    Should say: "That is not what I meant at all.
    That is not it, at all."

And would it have been worth it, after all,
100 Would it have been worth while,
After the sunsets and the dooryards and the sprinkled streets,
After the novels, after the teacups, after the skirts that trail along
    the floor—
And this, and so much more?—
It is impossible to say just what I mean!
105 But as if a magic lantern threw the nerves in patterns on a
    screen:
Would it have been worth while
If one, settling a pillow or throwing off a shawl,
And turning toward the window, should say:
    "That is not it at all,
110   That is not what I meant, at all."
    • • • • •
No! I am not Prince Hamlet, nor was meant to be;
Am an attendant lord, one that will do
To swell a progress, start a scene or two,
Advise the prince; no doubt, an easy tool,
115 Deferential, glad to be of use,
Politic, cautious, and meticulous;
Full of high sentence, but a bit obtuse;
At times, indeed, almost ridiculous—
Almost, at times, the Fool.

120 I grow old . . . I grow old . . .
I shall wear the bottoms of my trousers rolled.

Shall I part my hair behind? Do I dare to eat a peach?
I shall wear white flannel trousers, and walk upon the beach.
I have heard the mermaids singing, each to each.

125 I do not think that they will sing to me.

94 Lazarus: In the biblical story (John 11:17–44), Lazarus lay dead in his tomb for four days before Jesus brought him back to life.

105 magic lantern: a forerunner of the slide projector.

UNDERSTAND MODERNIST POETRY
Annotate: Mark the literary allusion in lines 111–119.
Summarize: Write a summary of this stanza.

115 deferential: yielding to someone else's opinion.
116 meticulous: extremely careful and precise about details.
117 obtuse: slow to understand; dull.

124–125 mermaids . . . to me: In mythology, mermaids attract mortal men by their beauty and their singing, sometimes allowing men to live with them in the sea.

718   Unit 6

APPLYING ACADEMIC VOCABULARY

☐ arbitrary   ☐ controversy   ☑ convince   ☑ denote   ☐ undergo

Write and Discuss Have students turn to a partner to discuss the following questions. Guide students to include the Academic Vocabulary words *convince* and *denote* in their responses. Ask volunteers to share their responses with the class.

- What does the allusion to the Fool in line 119 **denote**?
- What has Prufrock **convinced** himself about women in lines 124–125?

I have seen them riding seaward on the waves
Combing the white hair of the waves blown back
When the wind blows the water white and black.

We have lingered in the chambers of the sea
130 By sea-girls wreathed with seaweed red and brown
Till human voices wake us, and we drown.

NOTICE & NOTE

CHECK YOUR UNDERSTANDING

Answer these questions before moving on to the **Analyze the Text** section on the following page.

1. Which aspect of Prufrock's life is reflected in the simile comparing the evening to *a patient etherised upon a table*?
   A His fear of the evening
   B An illness he is recovering from
   C His profession as a doctor
   D His sense of paralysis

2. How does Prufrock feel about the guests at the party he is going to?
   F He feels alienated from them.
   G He feels hatred toward them.
   H He feels kindness from them.
   J He feels generosity toward them.

3. Lines 87–98 indicate that the woman Prufrock wants to talk to —
   A feels nervous in his presence
   B worries that he has gone insane
   C isn't interested in what he has to say
   D is trying to avoid him

The Love Song of J. Alfred Prufrock 719

TEACH

CHECK YOUR UNDERSTANDING

Have students answer the questions independently.

Answers:

1. D
2. F
3. C

If they answer any questions incorrectly, have them reread the text to confirm their understanding. Then they may proceed to ANALYZE THE TEXT on page 720.

ENGLISH LEARNER SUPPORT

Oral Assessment Use the following questions to assess students' comprehension and speaking skills.

1. By comparing the evening to "a patient etherized upon a table," what is Prufrock saying about himself? *(He feels paralyzed.)*

2. How does Prufrock feel about the people he will meet at the party? *(He feels alienated from them.)*

3. In lines 87–98, how does Prufrock imagine the woman will react to what he says? *(She won't be interested in what he has to say.)* **ALL LEVELS**

The Love Song of J. Alfred Prufrock **719**

APPLY

ANALYZE THE TEXT

Possible answers:

1. **DOK 4:** *Prufrock compares the fog to a stray cat. Just like a stray cat does not have a place where he feels he can belong, neither does Prufrock. He may feel like he is constantly wandering on the outskirts of life, rather than enjoying it from the inside like others do.*

2. **DOK 2:** *He most likely drinks coffee each morning, and counts each day as no more important than the spoon with which he stirs his coffee.*

3. **DOK 4:** *Both refer to instances where someone comes back from the dead to share stories. Prufrock feels like he is set apart from the world and the people in it, just like someone who is no longer part of this world because of death. Prufrock feels that if he could rid himself of his crippling fears, he could rise from the dead and share the story of his success with the world.*

4. **DOK 3:** *Not clarifying allows readers to use their own imaginations to guess what the question might have been. It also allows the question to be whatever readers want it to be—from their own similar experiences.*

5. **DOK 4:** *When new media and technologies come out, they can be overwhelming and cause feelings of confusion. Stream of consciousness reflects this feeling of being overwhelmed and confused, through its jumble of images and ideas.*

RESEARCH

Point students to the research tip to help them identify examples of **stream-of-consciousness** writing. Explain that they should be able to locate many of these works online.

Extend Ask several student volunteers to share their **stream-of-consciousness** writings with the whole group. Direct the other students to listen attentively to see if they can follow how the thoughts in the stream-of-consciousness writing relate to one another.

 **RESPOND**

ANALYZE THE TEXT

Support your responses with evidence from the text. 📓 NOTEBOOK

1. **Analyze** What does Prufrock compare the fog to in lines 15–22? How does this extended metaphor relate to his situation in the poem?

2. **Infer** What thought does Prufrock express in line 51 when he says, "I have measured out my life with coffee spoons"?

3. **Analyze** Read the side margin notes about the quotation from Dante's *Inferno* at the beginning of the poem and the allusion to Lazarus in line 94. What do the quotation and the allusion have in common? How are they connected to Prufrock's experience?

4. **Draw Conclusions** Why might Eliot have chosen not to clarify the nature of Prufrock's "overwhelming question" or what he wants to say to the woman at the party?

5. **Connect** Eliot wrote "The Love Song of J. Alfred Prufrock" at a time when new technology and media were rapidly changing society. How might Eliot's use of stream of consciousness reflect such changes?

RESEARCH

RESEARCH TIP
When researching writers from a specific era or who wrote in a specific style, focus your search on the "top" lists. Use search strings like "top modernist poets" or "best examples of stream-of-consciousness writing."

With a partner, find a work by each author listed in the chart that includes stream-of-consciousness writing. Choose a passage from each work and compare it to Eliot's use of this technique.

WRITER	NOTES ON STREAM OF CONSCIOUSNESS
James Joyce	*Possible passages: Ulysses*
Virginia Woolf	*Possible passages: The Waves*
William Faulkner	*Possible passages: The Sound and the Fury*

Extend For two minutes, write down every thought that goes through your mind. Do not worry about whether your writing is logical or coherent. Once you've finished, review your stream-of-consciousness writing and identify how your thoughts relate to one another.

 LEARNING MINDSET

Problem Solving Remind students that there are many different ways to approach—and solve—problems. Explain that while Person A might believe a certain method is the best way to solve a problem, that method may not be what works best for Person B, as everyone solves problems in their own unique ways. Remind students that problems will arise each time they try something new. Encourage them that solving each of these problems will help them learn and become smarter.

CREATE AND PRESENT

Write a Poem Modernist poetry often features confusing contradictions or contrasting imagery. Using this style as your base, write a poem that includes seemingly confusing contradictions or contrasting images. Reread examples from Eliot's poem to get ideas. Review your analysis and interpretation of Eliot's creative use of metaphors and analogies to gain a better understanding of how to do this.

- ❏ Study the examples in Eliot's poem.
- ❏ Brainstorm contradictions or incongruous images.
- ❏ Write a poem that includes these contradictions.
- ❏ Use a free-verse structure, and think about where you will break lines and why.

Present a Poem Now share your poem with the class. When you and your classmates read your poems aloud, provide thoughtful feedback to each other. Discuss your interpretations of the contradictory ideas or images in your poems.

- ❏ Practice reading your poem. Experiment with stressing different syllables to bring out the musical quality in the text.
- ❏ Practice making eye contact with your audience, and use facial expressions and natural gestures to convey the meaning of the poem.
- ❏ Finally, read your poem aloud to the class.

RESPOND TO THE ESSENTIAL QUESTION

 What makes people feel insecure?

Gather Information Review your annotations and notes on "The Love Song of J. Alfred Prufrock." Then, add relevant information to your Response Log. As you determine which information to include, think about:

- how you can feel insecure internally, but look confident externally
- what things might make you feel uncertain about yourself
- how important your self-talk is to how you feel about yourself

RESPOND

Go to **Giving a Presentation** in the **Speaking and Listening Studio** for more on presenting.

ACADEMIC VOCABULARY

As you write and discuss what you learned from the poem, be sure to use the Academic Vocabulary words. Check off each of the words that you use.

- ❏ arbitrary
- ❏ controversy
- ❏ convince
- ❏ denote
- ❏ undergo

The Love Song of J. Alfred Prufrock 721

APPLY

CREATE AND PRESENT

Write a Poem Direct students to find and present examples of contrasting or contradictory images in Eliot's poem. Ask them to explain how each is contradictory and what the poet intended by the contrast. Then, have students brainstorm ideas for contradictory or contrasting images they could use in their own poetry. Direct students to write a short, free-verse poem that includes these types of images.

 For **writing support** for students at varying proficiency levels, see the **Text X-Ray** on page 712D.

Present a Poem Allow students time to practice presenting their poems. Encourage them to experiment with diction, speed, and intonation, as well as using eye contact, facial expressions, and gestures to convey meaning. While each student presents, the other students should listen to identify the contradictions and contrasts, and the entire group should discuss these elements after the reading of each poem.

RESPOND TO THE ESSENTIAL QUESTION

Allow time for students to add details from "The Love Song of J. Alfred Prufrock" to their Unit 6 Response Logs.

PLAN

SHOOTING AN ELEPHANT
Essay by George Orwell

GENRE ELEMENTS
ESSAY
Tell students that an **essay** analyzes a topic or issue. A **reflective essay** makes a connection between a personal observation and a universal idea. Authors of reflective essays use common literary devices, such as figurative language and imagery, to make their reflections come alive. In this lesson, students will analyze a reflective essay and its situational irony.

LEARNING OBJECTIVES
- Analyze reflective essay and irony.
- Conduct research about the roles of military personnel around the world.
- Write an informational essay.
- Discuss and respond to essays.
- Use etymology.
- Use prepositional phrases.
- **Language** Describe the connection between visuals and text.

TEXT COMPLEXITY

Quantitative Measures	**Shooting an Elephant**	**Lexile: 1070L**
Qualitative Measures	**Ideas Presented** Much is explicit, but moves to some implied meaning. Requires some inferential reasoning.	
	Structures Used Largely chronological and conventional, anecdotal. Some use of backstory.	
	Language Used Complex sentence structures, idiomatic language.	
	Knowledge Required Less familiar scenarios, but familiar emotional situation.	

722A Unit 6

PLAN

Online

RESOURCES

- Unit 6 Response Log
- Selection Audio
- Reading Studio: Notice & Note
- Level Up Tutorial: Irony; Informational Text
- Writing Studio: Writing Informative Texts
- Speaking and Listening Studio: Participating in Collaborative Discussions
- Vocabulary Studio: Etymology
- Grammar Studio: Module 3 Lesson 1: Prepositional Phrases
- "Shooting an Elephant" Selection Test

SUMMARIES

English

In this essay, Orwell describes what happens when, as a young police officer in Burma, he is called upon to deal with an elephant on a rampage. When he discovers that the elephant has killed a man, Orwell sends for an elephant rifle. A huge crowd of excited Burmans follows him, expecting him to kill the elephant and hoping to get meat from the carcass. The elephant is calmly grazing and Orwell does not want to shoot it, but he feels he must show he is resolute. When he pulls the trigger, the elephant falls but continues to breathe. Orwell fires more shots before the elephant dies on its own. Afterward, Orwell says that he killed the elephant to avoid looking like a fool.

Spanish

En este ensayo, Orwell describe qué sucede cuando lo llaman para que se encargue de un elefante arrasador mientras era un joven oficial de policía en Birmania. Cuando descubre que el elefante mató a un hombre, Orwell pide un rifle para elefantes. Una multitud de birmanos emocionados lo sigue, esperando que mate al elefante para poder sacar la carne de su cuerpo. El elefante está pastando calmadamente y Orwell no quiere dispararle, pero siente que debe mostrar que es decidido. Cuando aprieta el gatillo, el elefante cae, pero continúa respirando. Orwell dispara más veces antes de que el elefante muera. Luego, Orwell dice que mató al elefante para no quedar como un tonto.

SMALL-GROUP OPTIONS

Have students work in small groups to read and discuss the selection.

Jigsaw with Experts
- Divide the text into three parts, paragraphs 1–2, 3–9, and 10–14.
- Have students count off.
- Have students form groups with other students who will read the same section. Each expert group should discuss its section. Encourage them to use the Academic Vocabulary.
- Then, have students form new groups with a member from each section. These groups should discuss all the sections.

Pinwheel Discussion
- Arrange students in groups of eight, with four students seated facing out and four students seated facing them.
- After reading two or three paragraphs of the selection, pose questions to students for discussion. For example: *How does the narrator feel? How do you know?*
- Students in the inner circle remain stationary, while students in the outer circle move to their right after discussing each question.

Shooting an Elephant **722B**

PLAN

Text X-Ray: English Learner Support
for "Shooting an Elephant"

Use the Text X-Ray and the supports and scaffolds in the Teacher's Edition to help guide students at different proficiency levels through the selection.

INTRODUCE THE SELECTION
DISCUSS SAVING FACE

In this lesson, students will need to be able to discuss how trying to save face can lead to making unfortunate choices.

Provide the following explanation:

- When you try to save face, you want to avoid humiliation and have others respect you.

Ask students to discuss situations in which someone tries to save face. Provide sentence frames, such as: *One example of saving face is when _____. Trying to save face can be a problem when _____.*

CULTURAL REFERENCES

The following words or phrases may be unfamiliar to students:

- *dirty work* (paragraph 2): activities that are dishonest
- *at close quarters* (paragraph 2): nearby or up close
- *lock-ups* (paragraph 2): jail
- *took to his heels* (paragraph 3): went on foot; ran
- *that would never do* (paragraph 9): that would be unacceptable

LISTENING

Seek Clarification

As partners discuss the Quick Start topic, guide them to ask for clarification as needed.

Use the following supports with students at varying proficiency levels:

- Provide student pairs with an index card that has a large question mark printed on it. Have students hold up the card if they need clarification or to have something repeated. Provide a question bank for students to refer to as they ask their questions, such as: *Can you repeat that? What did you mean by _____?* **SUBSTANTIAL**

- Have students raise their hands to indicate they need clarification. Tell the speaker to pause, and then have the student voice the question. Provide sentence starters, such as: *Why do you think that _____? I'm not sure what you mean by _____.* **MODERATE**

- As partners discuss, have them take notes about things that do not sound clear. Then, have them restate their notes as questions they can pose to each other. **LIGHT**

PLAN

SPEAKING

Connect Visuals to Text

Remind students that the essay's visuals add to and clarify the text.

Use the following supports with students at varying proficiency levels:

- Point to elements in the visuals and ask questions. For example: *Who is this? Where is he? What animal do you see?* **SUBSTANTIAL**
- Have partners ask each other *wh-* questions about the visuals. For example: *Who is in this picture? What is he doing? Where do you think he is going?* **MODERATE**
- Ask partners to take turns describing how each of the essay's visuals adds to or clarifies aspects of the text. **LIGHT**

READING

Use Pre-Reading Supports

Review how to use footnotes and the dictionary format of pre-taught vocabulary words to increase comprehension.

Use the following supports with students of varying proficiency levels:

- Point out the small number 1 after the location *Burma* in paragraph 1. Direct students to the corresponding footnote. Review how to use the pronunciation key and how to identify which part of the footnote tells where *Moulmein* is and which part tells what it is called now. **SUBSTANTIAL**
- Have students discuss the format of the definition of *imperialism* in the left column next to paragraph 2. Have partners use sentence frames to explain what each part of the definition tells them. For example: *The letter* n. *means that imperialism is a* ____. **MODERATE**
- Have students review the essay's footnotes and vocabulary definitions. Then, have them tell each other how their reading experience would change without the footnotes and definitions. **LIGHT**

WRITING

Write Hooks

Introduce students to the writing assignment on Student Edition page 735. Guide students to discuss and compare personal anecdotes about an exciting or interesting event.

Use the following supports with students of varying proficiency levels:

- Write sentences on the board, and ask questions to determine comprehension of successful "hooks." For example: *What is a more exciting hook, 'I saw a dog' or 'I saw a dog with no legs?'* Have students copy the hook that is more exciting. **SUBSTANTIAL**
- Have partners discuss exciting events they have experienced or seen. Then, have them write a sentence describing each event. Have pairs exchange sentences with other pairs and discuss whether each would make a good hook and why. **MODERATE**
- Have students write three possible hooks for their essays. Have partners number the hooks from least to most exciting. Then, have them explain their ranking. **LIGHT**

SHOOTING AN ELEPHANT

Essay by **George Orwell**

ESSENTIAL QUESTION:

Why is it hard to resist social pressure?

QUICK START

Think about how you behave with your peers. Then, think about how you behave in the presence of parents or other older adults. Compare and contrast your actions, then discuss with a partner why you may behave differently in these situations.

BEHAVIOR WITH PEERS	BEHAVIOR WITH PARENTS OR ADULTS

ANALYZE REFLECTIVE ESSAY

In a **reflective essay,** the author examines a personal experience and reveals what he or she learned from it. A good reflective essay offers insight into the author's personal growth and also connects a specific observation to some larger idea about life or society. For example, in "Shooting an Elephant," Orwell reflects on an incident he experienced as a young police officer in British-ruled Burma in the 1920s. By exploring this experience, Orwell allows readers to understand what he learned about the true nature of colonialism. As you read, pay attention to the thoughts and feelings that Orwell expresses as he describes the incident.

ANALYZE IRONY

Irony is a contrast between expectation and reality. This contrast often has the effect of surprising the reader or viewer. Irony may be subtle and easily overlooked or misunderstood. There are three main types of irony:

- **Situational irony** occurs when a character or the reader expects one thing to happen but something else actually happens.
- **Verbal irony** occurs when a character or the writer says one thing but means something quite different—often the opposite of what he or she has said.
- **Dramatic irony** occurs when the reader or viewer knows something that a character does not know.

In "Shooting an Elephant," Orwell relies on situational irony to drive home his insight about colonialism. As you read, notice how the young Orwell's expectations are overturned as he tries to carry out his responsibilities. Also pay attention to your own expectations about how he will behave in this situation.

GET READY

GENRE ELEMENTS: ESSAY
- a short piece of nonfiction
- offers an opinion on a subject
- formal essays have a serious and impersonal tone
- informal essays are loosely structured and have a conversational tone
- a reflective essay examines an experience in the author's life

TEACH

QUICK START

Have students read the Quick Start paragraph. Next, ask them to imagine attending a party that includes only their friends and then attending a party that includes both their peers and adults. Have students create two lists. One list should describe the activities that would most likely occur at a party with just their peers. The other list should describe the activities that would most likely occur at a party with both young people and adults. After they create both lists, have them share their lists with a partner to compare and contrast.

For **listening support** for students at varying proficiency levels, see the **Text X-Ray** on page 722C.

ANALYZE REFLECTIVE ESSAY

Explain to students that a **reflective essay** describes a personal experience in an author's life and relates it to a universal idea, which is a concept or message that could be meaningful to anyone. Discuss the features of a reflective essay. First, it is a **personal narrative.** Remind students that a narrative is written in the style of a story and can include dialogue and description. A personal narrative also includes the author's thoughts and feelings about what he or she experiences. An **anecdote** is another feature of this type of essay. Explain that this is a brief story that focuses on one event in a person's life. A **revelation** is a third feature of a reflective essay. This is a realization that leads the author to the universal idea, or main message, of his or her essay.

ANALYZE IRONY

Explain to students that **irony** is a contrast between what is expected and what actually occurs. There are different types of irony. The essay "Shooting an Elephant" primarily includes **situational irony.** Provide an example of this type of irony. (For example, suppose you are packing for a trip and are expecting days of sunshine based on a weather report. However, after you arrive you experience stormy weather instead, and the rain gear you usually pack was left behind at home.) Tell students that Orwell uses situational irony to convey meaning in his essay. Have them read paragraph 11 and then discuss why it is an example of situational irony. (The narrator thought the elephant would immediately collapse to the ground. Instead, it slowly fell to its knees.) Encourage students to watch for how the author uses situational irony to convey his ideas as they read the selection.

TEACH

CRITICAL VOCABULARY

Encourage students to read all the sentences before deciding which words best completes each one. Remind them to look for context clues that match the precise meaning of each word.

Answers:

1. *imperialism; supplant*
2. *prostrate; despotic*
3. *senility; labyrinth*
4. *cowed; garish*

■ English Learner Support

Use Cognates Tell students that some of the Critical Vocabulary words have Spanish cognates: *imperialism/imperialismo; supplant/suplantar; despotic/despótico; senility/senilidad.* **ALL LEVELS**

LANGUAGE CONVENTIONS

Review the definition of **prepositional phrase** with students. Explain that this type of phrase has two parts: a preposition and a noun or pronoun, which is the object of the proposition. It can contain modifiers that describe the noun or pronoun.

Provide this example sentence: *The maple syrup is in the wooden cupboard.* Tell students that "in the wooden cupboard" is the prepositional phrase in that sentence. It includes the preposition *in*, the object *cupboard*, and the modifier *wooden*. Tell students that prepositional phrases can add detail and clarity to writing. Then, have students create examples of prepositional phrases using five of the prepositions listed.

ANNOTATION MODEL

Remind students that taking notes can help them identify examples of **situational irony** or understand the author's main message as they read the selection. Tell students that circling words, making notes, and writing questions can help them determine how the author develops his ideas. Point out that they may follow the suggested method in the annotation model or use their own system for marking up the selection in their write-in text. They may want to color-code their annotations by using highlighters. Their notes in the margin may include questions about ideas that are unclear or their own observations.

724 Unit 6

 **GET READY**

CRITICAL VOCABULARY

| imperialism | supplant | despotic | garish |
| cowed | prostrate | labyrinth | senility |

To see how many Critical Vocabulary words you already know, use them to complete the sentences.

1. _____ in the United States led the president to _____ the rightful queen and annex Hawaii.

2. His words were muffled as he lay _____ on the rug before the _____ ruler.

3. His _____ sometimes made his speech a tangled _____ of half-expressed thoughts.

4. She was _____ by the bright lights and loud sounds of the _____ city.

LANGUAGE CONVENTIONS

In his essay, George Orwell uses **prepositional phrases** to add clarity to his descriptions of the village, the people, and the elephant. Prepositional phrases consist of a preposition, its object, and modifiers of the object.

Common prepositions include *above, at, before, below, by, down, for, from, in, into, near, of, on, out, over, through, to, up, with,* and *without.*

ANNOTATION MODEL NOTICE & NOTE

As you read the essay "Shooting an Elephant," practice taking notes, marking up the text and asking questions, to monitor your comprehension.

> In Moulmein, in Lower Burma, I was hated by large numbers of people—the only time in my life that I have been important enough for this to happen to me. I was subdivisional police officer of the town, and in an aimless, petty kind of way anti-European feeling was very bitter. No one had the guts to raise a riot, but if a European woman went through the bazaars alone somebody would probably spit betel juice over her dress. As a police officer I was an obvious target and was baited whenever it seemed safe to do so.

This statement seems ironic—I expect "important" people to be respected or admired.

Orwell's attitude toward the Burmese people must have been affected by this experience of being targeted.

724 Unit 6

BACKGROUND

George Orwell (1903–1950) was born in India. When he was 19, he joined the Indian Imperial police and left to serve in Burma, which at the time was ruled by Britain. Disillusioned with imperialism, he resigned in 1928 and decided to become a writer. In 1936 Orwell went to Spain to fight with antifascist forces in the Spanish Civil War, an experience that greatly influenced his political views. Throughout his life, Orwell spoke out against injustice. His most famous novels, *Animal Farm* and *1984*, reflect his dedication to political freedom.

SHOOTING AN ELEPHANT

Essay by George Orwell

SETTING A PURPOSE

Read George Orwell's essay to discover his ideas about imperialism and his role as an officer. How can you connect his turmoil with that of 21st-century officers?

1 In Moulmein, in Lower Burma,[1] I was hated by large numbers of people—the only time in my life that I have been important enough for this to happen to me. I was subdivisional police officer of the town, and in an aimless, petty kind of way anti-European feeling was very bitter. No one had the guts to raise a riot, but if a European woman went through the bazaars alone somebody would probably spit betel juice[2] over her dress. As a police officer I was an obvious target and was baited whenever it seemed safe to do so. When a nimble Burman tripped me up on the football[3] field and the referee (another Burman) looked the

Notice & Note
Use the side margins to notice and note signposts in the text.

LANGUAGE CONVENTIONS
Annotate: Mark the prepositional phrases in the first sentence of paragraph 1.

Evaluate: What do these prepositional phrases suggest about the importance of the experience Orwell is about to describe?

---
[1] **Moulmein** (mo͞ol-mān´), **in Lower Burma:** the main city of British-controlled Burma, now the independent Asian nation of Myanmar. Moulmein is now usually called Mawlamyine.
[2] **betel** (bēt´l) **juice:** the saliva created when chewing a mixture of betel palm nuts, betel palm leaves, and lime.
[3] **football:** soccer.

Shooting an Elephant 725

TEACH

BACKGROUND

After students read the Background, explain that many essayists use their work to discuss important topics or issues that affect society. Tell students that "Shooting an Elephant" describes the consequences of colonialism and imperialism. While Orwell was living and working in Burma, the Burmese people endured great poverty and a lack of freedom under British rule. His experiences there had a major impact on him: not only are they reflected in this essay, but they most likely affected his later work as a novelist. Social oppression and tyranny are two important themes in the books he wrote later in his life.

SETTING A PURPOSE

Direct students to use the Setting a Purpose prompt to focus their reading.

LANGUAGE CONVENTIONS

Remind students that **prepositional phrases** begin with a preposition and add detail and clarity to a text. They help describe where things are, when events take place, and so on. (**Answer:** *The prepositional phrases give a context and support how circumstances change, based on the setting.*)

> For **reading support** for students at varying proficiency levels, see the **Text X-Ray** on page 722D.

ENGLISH LEARNER SUPPORT

Acquire New Vocabulary Help students improve their comprehension by teaching the meaning of the following words in paragraph 1:

aimless—"without direction"

bazaar—"a market for buying food, cloth, and other goods, typically in a city or town in Asia"

nimble—"quick or graceful" **ALL LEVELS**

Shooting an Elephant 725

TEACH

 ## ANALYZE IRONY

Remind students that **situational irony** occurs when what is expected to happen in a situation is different from what actually occurs. Guide them to mark an example of situational irony in paragraph 2. (**Answer:** *Since Orwell has turned against imperialism we would expect him to sympathize with the Burmans but actually he hates them.*)

CRITICAL VOCABULARY

imperialism: During the 1800s, the *imperialism* of the British government led it to rule a number of other nations around the world.

ASK STUDENTS how the Burmese people seemed to feel about living under imperialism. (*The Burmans resented their British rulers and wanted to live freely.*)

cowed: Signs that a person may feel *cowed* can include hunched shoulders, a bowed head, or a frightened expression.

ASK STUDENTS which people Orwell describes as cowed. (*Orwell describes the long-term convicts as cowed.*)

supplant: When Britain took control of another country, the British *supplanted*, or replaced, leaders and officials from that nation with their own officials.

ASK STUDENTS what Orwell says will be supplanted in paragraph 2. (*He says the British Empire will be supplanted by younger empires.*)

prostrate: The author uses the term *prostrate* to help explain the condition of the Burmese people.

ASK STUDENTS how it might feel to be one of the "prostrate peoples." (*Possible answer: I think it would be very difficult and demoralizing to be subjected to the will of another person, group, or country.*)

despotic: The author uses the adjective *despotic* to describe a leader or government that is controlling and cruel.

ASK STUDENTS to identify characteristics of a despotic government. (*lack of freedom, tight control over citizens, no representation in government for the people*)

726   Unit 6

 **NOTICE & NOTE**

imperialism
(ĭm-pîr´ē-ə-lĭz əm): *n*. the extension of a nation's authority by territorial acquisition or by the establishment of economic and political dominance over other nations.

cowed
(koud): *adj*. frightened or subdued with threats or a show of force. cow *v*.

ANALYZE IRONY

Annotate: Mark evidence of situational irony in paragraph 2.

Analyze: Explain the situational irony in Orwell's feelings about British colonialism and about the Burmese people.

supplant
(sə-plănt´): *tr.v*. to take the place of or substitute for (another).

prostrate
(prŏs´trāt): *adj*. lying face down, as in submission or adoration.

despotic
(dĭ-spŏt´ĭk): *adj*. a person who wields power oppressively; a tyrant.

---

other way, the crowd yelled with hideous laughter. This happened more than once. In the end the sneering yellow faces of young men that met me everywhere, the insults hooted after me when I was at a safe distance, got badly on my nerves. The young Buddhist priests were the worst of all. There were several thousands of them in the town and none of them seemed to have anything to do except stand on street corners and jeer at Europeans.

2   All this was perplexing and upsetting. For at that time I had already made up my mind that **imperialism** was an evil thing and the sooner I chucked up[4] my job and got out of it the better. Theoretically—and secretly, of course—I was all for the Burmese and all against their oppressors, the British. As for the job I was doing, I hated it more bitterly than I can perhaps make clear. In a job like that you see the dirty work of Empire at close quarters. The wretched prisoners huddling in the stinking cages of the lock-ups, the gray, **cowed** faces of the long-term convicts, the scarred buttocks of the men who had been flogged with bamboos—all these oppressed me with an intolerable sense of guilt. But I could get nothing into perspective. I was young and ill-educated and I had had to think out my problems in the utter silence that is imposed on every Englishman in the East. I did not even know that the British Empire is dying, still less did I know that it is a great deal better than the younger empires that are going to **supplant** it. All I knew was that I was stuck between my hatred of the empire I served and my rage against the evil-spirited little beasts who tried to make my job impossible. With one part of my mind I thought of the British Raj[5] as an unbreakable tyranny, as something clamped down, *in saecula saeculorum*,[6] upon the will of **prostrate** peoples; with another part I thought that the greatest joy in the world would be to drive a bayonet into a Buddhist priest's guts. Feelings like these are the normal by-products of imperialism; ask any Anglo-Indian official, if you can catch him off duty.

3   One day something happened which in a roundabout way was enlightening. It was a tiny incident in itself, but it gave me a better glimpse than I had had before of the real nature of imperialism—the real motives for which **despotic** governments act. Early one morning the subinspector at a police station the other end of the town rang me up on the phone and said that an elephant was ravaging the bazaar. Would I please come and do something about it? I did not know what I could do, but I wanted to see what was happening and I got on to a pony and started out. I took my rifle, an old 44 Winchester and much too small to kill an elephant, but I thought the noise might be useful

---
[4] **chucked up:** threw off; gave up.
[5] **British Raj:** India and adjoining areas (such as Burma) controlled by Britain in the 19th and early 20th centuries. *Raj* is the word for "kingdom" or "rule" in Hindi, a chief language of India.
[6] ***in saecula saeculorum*** (ĭn sĕk´yə-lə sĕk-yə-lôr´əm) *Latin*: forever and ever.

726   Unit 6

WHEN STUDENTS STRUGGLE . . .

Understand Situational Irony   Have students use a graphic organizer like the one below to identify examples of **situational irony** from the selection. Challenge students to consider how they know that it is an example of irony.

Example from Selection	How Do You Know It Is Situational Irony?

 For additional support, go to the **Reading Studio** and assign the following **Level Up tutorial: Irony.**

in terrorem.[7] Various Burmans stopped me on the way and told me about the elephant's doings. It was not, of course, a wild elephant, but a tame one which had gone "must."[8] It had been chained up as tame elephants always are when their attack of "must" is due, but on the previous night it had broken its chain and escaped. Its mahout,[9] the only person who could manage it when it was in that state, had set out in pursuit, but had taken the wrong direction and was now twelve hours' journey away, and in the morning the elephant had suddenly reappeared in the town. The Burmese population had no weapons and were quite helpless against it. It had already destroyed somebody's bamboo hut, killed a cow and raided some fruit-stalls and devoured the stock; also it had met the municipal rubbish van, and, when the driver jumped out and took to his heels, had turned the van over and inflicted violences upon it.

4   The Burmese subinspector and some Indian constables[10] were waiting for me in the quarter where the elephant had been seen. It was a very poor quarter, a **labyrinth** of squalid bamboo huts, thatched with palm-leaf, winding all over a steep hillside. I remember that it was a cloudy stuffy morning at the beginning of the rains. We began questioning the people as to where the elephant had gone, and, as usual, failed to get any definite information. That is invariably the case in the East; a story always sounds clear enough at a distance, but the nearer you get to the scene of events the vaguer it becomes. Some of the people said that the elephant had gone in one direction, some said that he had gone in another, some professed not even to have heard of any elephant. I had almost made up my mind that the whole story was a pack of lies, when we heard yells a little distance away. There was a loud, scandalized cry of "Go away, child! Go away this instant!" and an old woman with a switch in her hand came round the corner of a hut, violently shooing away a crowd of naked children. Some more women followed, clicking their tongues and exclaiming; evidently there was something there that the children ought not to have seen. I rounded the hut and saw a man's dead body sprawling in the mud. He was an Indian, a black Dravidian coolie,[11] almost naked, and he could not have been dead many minutes. The people said that the elephant had come suddenly upon him round the corner of the hut, caught him with its trunk, put its foot on his back and ground him into the earth. This was the rainy season and the ground was soft, and his face had scored a trench a foot deep and

labyrinth
(lăb´ə-rĭnth): *n.* an intricate structure of interconnecting passages through which it is difficult to find one's way; a maze.

---

[7] *in terrorem* (ĭn tĕ-rôr´əm) *Latin:* for terror.
[8] **gone "must":** had an attack of must, a dangerous frenzy that periodically seizes male elephants.
[9] **mahout** (mə-hout´): an elephant keeper.
[10] **constables:** police officers.
[11] **Dravidian** (drə-vĭd´ē-ən) **coolie:** a dark-skinned menial laborer from the south of India.

TO CHALLENGE STUDENTS . . .

Conduct Research Have students research the history of British rule in Burma. Tell them to find out when it began and when it ended and why Britain decided to take control of this territory. Ask students to note any major events that took place under British rule. After they complete their research, have them write a paragraph to summarize their findings. When students have finished reading the selection, ask them to consider how their research affected their understanding of daily life in Burma at this time and the author's experiences there.

CRITICAL VOCABULARY

labyrinth: The term *labyrinth* is another word for maze and can be used to identify a complicated structure.

ASK STUDENTS to describe in their own words what a labyrinth of bamboo huts would look like. *(a group of huts that is arranged in a disorganized way and difficult to make your way through)*

TEACH

ANALYZE REFLECTIVE ESSAY

Remind students that a reflective essay offers insight into the author's personal growth by revealing specific observations on an event. (**Answer:** *The state of the corpse made him realize the seriousness of the situation.*)

NOTICE & NOTE

British troops patrolling a city in Burma

ANALYZE REFLECTIVE ESSAY

Annotate: Mark details Orwell uses to describe the corpse in paragraph 4.

Analyze: What do these details suggest about how this sight affected him?

a couple of yards long. He was lying on his belly with arms crucified and head sharply twisted to one side. His face was coated with mud, the eyes wide open, the teeth bared and grinning with an expression of unendurable agony. (Never tell me, by the way, that the dead look peaceful. Most of the corpses I have seen looked devilish.) The friction of the great beast's foot had stripped the skin from his back as neatly as one skins a rabbit. As soon as I saw the dead man I sent an orderly[12] to a friend's house nearby to borrow an elephant rifle. I had already sent back the pony, not wanting it to go mad with fright and throw me if it smelled the elephant.

5   The orderly came back in a few minutes with a rifle and five cartridges, and meanwhile some Burmans had arrived and told us that the elephant was in the paddy fields[13] below, only a few hundred yards away. As I started forward practically the whole population of

---
[12] **orderly:** a military aid.
[13] **paddy fields:** rice fields.

728   Unit 6

the quarter flocked out of the houses and followed me. They had seen the rifle and were all shouting excitedly that I was going to shoot the elephant. They had not shown much interest in the elephant when he was merely ravaging their homes, but it was different now that he was going to be shot. It was a bit of fun to them, as it would be to an English crowd; besides, they wanted the meat. It made me vaguely uneasy. I had no intention of shooting the elephant—I had merely sent for the rifle to defend myself if necessary—and it is always unnerving to have a crowd following you. I marched down the hill, looking and feeling a fool, with the rifle over my shoulder and an ever-growing army of people jostling at my heels. At the bottom, when you got away from the huts, there was a metalled road and beyond that a miry waste of paddy fields a thousand yards across, not yet ploughed but soggy from the first rains and dotted with coarse grass. The elephant was standing eighty yards from the road, his left side towards us. He took not the slightest notice of the crowd's

TEACH

AHA MOMENT

Guide students to consider what Orwell thinks should happen in paragraphs 8 and 9 of the text and how that differs from what is actually happening. Have them determine why this is an example of **situational irony**. (*Answer: He expected to be in charge of the Burmans and to control them, but in reality they are controlling him.*)

CRITICAL VOCABULARY

garish: The author describes the crowd's clothing as garish, or overly bright and gaudy.

ASK STUDENTS to describe in their own words what garish clothing might look like. (*Possible answers: brightly colored, different patterns, clashing, unattractive*)

730   Unit 6

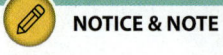

NOTICE & NOTE

approach. He was tearing up bunches of grass, beating them against his knees to clean them and stuffing them into his mouth.

6   I had halted on the road. As soon as I saw the elephant I knew with perfect certainty that I ought not to shoot him. It is a serious matter to shoot a working elephant—it is comparable to destroying a huge and costly piece of machinery—and obviously one ought not to do it if it can possibly be avoided. And at that distance, peacefully eating, the elephant looked no more dangerous than a cow. I thought then and I think now that his attack of "must" was already passing off; in which case he would merely wander harmlessly about until the mahout came back and caught him. Moreover, I did not in the least want to shoot him. I decided that I would watch him for a little while to make sure that he did not turn savage again, and then go home.

7   But at that moment I glanced round at the crowd that had followed me. It was an immense crowd, two thousand at the least and growing every minute. It blocked the road for a long distance on either side. I looked at the sea of yellow faces above the **garish** clothes—faces all happy and excited over this bit of fun, all certain that the elephant was going to be shot. They were watching me as they would watch a conjurer[14] about to perform a trick. <u>They did not like me, but with the magical rifle in my hands I was momentarily worth watching. And suddenly I realized that I should have to shoot the elephant after all. The people expected it of me and I had got to do it;</u> I could feel their two thousand wills pressing me forward, irresistibly. And it was at this moment, as I stood there with the rifle in my hands, that I first grasped the hollowness, the futility of the white man's dominion in the East. Here was I, the white man with his gun, standing in front of the unarmed native crowd—seemingly the leading actor of the piece; but in reality I was only an absurd puppet pushed to and fro by the will of those yellow faces behind. I perceived in this moment that when the white man turns tyrant it is his own freedom that he destroys. He becomes a sort of hollow, posing dummy, the conventionalized figure of a sahib.[15] For it is the condition of his rule that he shall spend his life in trying to impress the "natives," and so in every crisis he has got to do what the "natives" expect of him. He wears a mask, and his face grows to fit it. I had got to shoot the elephant. I had committed myself to doing it when I sent for the rifle. A sahib has got to act like a sahib; he has got to appear resolute, to know his own mind and do definite things. To come all that way, rifle in hand, with two thousand people marching at my heels, and then to trail feebly away, having done nothing—no, that was impossible. The crowd would laugh at me. And my whole

garish
(gâr´ĭsh, găr´): *adj.* overly bright or ornamented, especially in a vulgar or tasteless way; gaudy.

AHA MOMENT

Notice & Note: In paragraph 7, mark statements expressing Orwell's realization about his role as a colonial officer.

Analyze: How are these statements ironic?

---

[14] **conjurer** (kŏn´jər-ər): magician.
[15] **sahib** (sä´hĭb): a title of respect formerly used by native Indians to address a European gentleman.

730   Unit 6

APPLYING ACADEMIC VOCABULARY

☑ **arbitrary**   ☐ **controversy**   ☑ **convince**   ☐ **denote**   ☐ **undergo**

Write and Discuss Have students turn to a partner to discuss the questions below. Guide them to include the Academic Vocabulary words *arbitrary* and *convince* in their responses. Ask volunteers to share their responses with the class.

- Why does shooting the elephant at this point feel **arbitrary** to the narrator?
- Why does he finally **convince** himself to shoot the elephant?

life, every white man's life in the East, was one long struggle not to be laughed at.

8 But I did not want to shoot the elephant. I watched him beating his bunch of grass against his knees, with that preoccupied grandmotherly air that elephants have. It seemed to me that it would be murder to shoot him. At that age I was not squeamish about killing animals, but I had never shot an elephant and never wanted to. (Somehow it always seems worse to kill a *large* animal.) Besides, there was the beast's owner to be considered. Alive, the elephant was worth at least a hundred pounds; dead, he would only be worth the value of his tusks—five pounds, possibly. But I had got to act quickly. I turned to some experienced-looking Burmans who had been there when we arrived, and asked them how the elephant had been behaving. They all said the same thing: he took no notice of you if you left him alone, but he might charge if you went too close to him.

9 It was perfectly clear to me what I ought to do. I ought to walk up to within, say, twenty-five yards of the elephant and test his behavior. If he charged I could shoot, if he took no notice of me it would be safe to leave him until the mahout came back. But also I knew that I was going to do no such thing. I was a poor shot with a rifle and the ground was soft mud into which one would sink at every step. If the elephant charged and I missed him, I should have about as much chance as a toad under a steam-roller. But even then I was not thinking particularly of my own skin, only of the watchful yellow faces behind. For at that moment, with the crowd watching me, I was not afraid in the ordinary sense, as I would have been if I had been alone. A white man mustn't be frightened in front of "natives"; and so, in general, he isn't frightened. The sole thought in my mind was that if anything went wrong those two thousand Burmans would see me pursued, caught, trampled on and reduced to a grinning corpse like that Indian up the hill. And if that happened it was quite probable that some of them would laugh. That would never do. There was only one alternative. I shoved the cartridges into the magazine[16] and lay down on the road to get a better aim.

10 The crowd grew very still, and a deep, low, happy sigh, as of people who see the theater curtain go up at last, breathed from innumerable throats. They were going to have their bit of fun after all. The rifle was a beautiful German thing with cross-hair sights. I did not then know that in shooting an elephant one should shoot to cut an imaginary bar running from ear-hole to ear-hole. I ought, therefore, as the elephant was sideways on, to have aimed straight at his ear-hole; actually I aimed several inches in front of this, thinking the brain would be further forward.

---

[16] **magazine:** the compartment from which cartridges are fed into the rifle's firing chamber.

ANALYZE REFLECTIVE ESSAY

Annotate: In paragraph 9, mark Orwell's explanation of what he ought to have done in this situation.

Draw Conclusions: What idea does this paragraph convey about how imperialism affects the individuals who serve it?

TEACH

■ English Learner Support

Use Visual and Contextual Support Help students picture the scene described in paragraph 8 by asking them to visualize the elephant in the field, based on details in the text. Guide them to consider how the description of the elephant in this part of the selection differs from the dangerous animal described previously in the text. **MODERATE/LIGHT**

ANALYZE REFLECTIVE ESSAY

Remind students that a reflective essay includes a realization by the author that helps develop his or her main message. Then guide students to mark opinions in paragraph 14 about Orwell's choice to shoot the elephant. (**Answer:** *Orwell reveals that he only shot the elephant because he didn't want to look like a fool. The irony is his role as a British officer in India would appear to be about controlling the people, but instead he bends to their expectations of him.*)

IMPROVE READING FLUENCY

Targeted Passage Focus students' attention on paragraphs 8–10. Remind students that authors use punctuation to include additional details, ideas, and other information in a text. This punctuation indicates places where readers should pause as they read. Have students mark these forms of punctuation in the passage. Then, have pairs practice reading the text aloud, using the appropriate rate and paying special attention to the punctuation as they alternate reading paragraphs.

 Go to the **Reading Studio** for additional support in developing fluency.

TEACH

ENGLISH LEARNER SUPPORT

Express Opinions Point out to students that the narrator is conflicted about shooting the elephant. He kills the animal, even though he feels this is not the correct thing to do. Place students in same-level pairs to discuss the narrator's decision and to express their own opinions. **SUBSTANTIAL**

Have students work with a partner and use the following sentence frame to express an opinion: *I think the narrator (did/did not) _____ make the right choice.*

Have student pairs discuss their opinions about the narrator shooting the elephant. Guide them to provide a reason for their opinions and to cite details from the text as support. **MODERATE**

Have student pairs complete the previous activity. Then, have each student in the pair write a short paragraph to explain his or her point of view. Encourage pairs to work together and provide support to one another as they complete their paragraphs.
LIGHT

CRITICAL VOCABULARY

senility: The author describes the elephant as suffering from senility, or diminished cognitive function due to old age.

ASK STUDENTS to identify context clues in paragraph 11 that can help readers understand the meaning of *senility*. *(immensely old, paralyzed, sagged flabbily, slobbered, thousands of years old)*

NOTICE & NOTE

senility
(sĭ-nĭl´ĭ-tē): *n.* relating to or having diminished cognitive function, as when memory is impaired, because of old age.

11   When I pulled the trigger I did not hear the bang or feel the kick—one never does when a shot goes home—but I heard the devilish roar of glee that went up from the crowd. In that instant, in too short a time, one would have thought, even for the bullet to get there, a mysterious, terrible change had come over the elephant. He neither stirred nor fell, but every line of his body had altered. He looked suddenly stricken, shrunken, immensely old, as though the frightful impact of the bullet had paralyzed him without knocking him down. At last, after what seemed a long time—it might have been five seconds, I dare say—he sagged flabbily to his knees. His mouth slobbered. An enormous **senility** seemed to have settled upon him. One could have imagined him thousands of years old. I fired again into the same spot. At the second shot he did not collapse but climbed with desperate slowness to his feet and stood weakly upright, with legs sagging and head drooping. I fired a third time. That was the shot that did for him. You could see the agony of it jolt his whole body and knock the last remnant of strength from his legs. But in falling he seemed for a moment to rise, for as his hind legs collapsed beneath him he seemed to tower upwards like a huge rock toppling, his trunk reaching skyward like a tree. He trumpeted, for the first and only time. And then down he came, his belly towards me, with a crash that seemed to shake the ground even where I lay.

12   I got up. The Burmans were already racing past me across the mud. It was obvious that the elephant would never rise again, but he was not dead. He was breathing very rhythmically with long rattling gasps, his great mound of a side painfully rising and falling. His mouth was wide open—I could see far down into caverns of pale pink throat. I waited a long time for him to die, but his breathing did not weaken. Finally I fired my two remaining shots into the spot where I thought his heart must be. The thick blood welled out of him like red velvet, but still he did not die. His body did not even jerk when the shots hit him, the tortured breathing continued without a pause. He was dying, very slowly and in great agony, but in some world remote from me where not even a bullet could damage him further. I felt that I had got to put an end to that dreadful noise. It seemed dreadful to see the great beast lying there, powerless to move and yet powerless to die, and not even to be able to finish him. I sent back for my small rifle and poured shot after shot into his heart and down his throat. They seemed to make no impression. The tortured gasps continued as steadily as the ticking of a clock.

13   In the end I could not stand it any longer and went away. I heard later that it took him half an hour to die. Burmans were arriving with dahs[17] and baskets even before I left, and I was told they had stripped his body almost to the bones by the afternoon.

---
[17] **dahs:** large knives.

732   Unit 6

WHEN STUDENTS STRUGGLE...

Identify the Features of a Reflective Essay Have students use a graphic organizer like the one below to identify examples from the selection that indicate this is a **reflective essay.** Challenge students to think about how each feature contributes to the text as a whole.

Personal Narrative	Anecdote	Revelation

For additional support, go to the **Reading Studio** and assign the following **Level Up tutorial: Informational Text.**

14   Afterwards, of course, there were endless discussions about the shooting of the elephant. The owner was furious, but he was only an Indian and could do nothing. Besides, legally I had done the right thing, for a mad elephant has to be killed, like a mad dog, if its owner fails to control it. Among the Europeans opinion was divided. The older men said I was right, the younger men said it was a damn shame to shoot an elephant for killing a coolie, because an elephant was worth more than any damn Coringhee[18] coolie. And afterwards I was very glad that the coolie had been killed; it put me legally in the right and it gave me a sufficient pretext for shooting the elephant. I often wondered whether any of the others grasped that I had done it solely to avoid looking a fool.

---

[18] **Coringhee:** coming from a port in southeastern India.

NOTICE & NOTE

ANALYZE IRONY
Annotate: Mark the opinions of the Europeans in paragraph 14.
Analyze: What is ironic about Orwell's feeling glad that the coolie had been killed?

CHECK YOUR UNDERSTANDING

Answer these questions before moving on to the **Analyze the Text** section on the following page.

1 What annoyed the narrator?
   A The elephant's destruction of trees
   B How the Burmans mocked soldiers
   C The weather in Asia
   D His small gun

2 When Orwell finally sees the elephant, it is —
   F wild
   G ravenous
   H tame
   J gentle

3 The narrator had to shoot the elephant because —
   A so many people were watching
   B the elephant was charging toward him
   C his job was to protect the village people
   D the elephant was already injured

Shooting an Elephant   733

TEACH

 ANALYZE IRONY

Remind students that dramatic irony occurs when a reader knows something a character does not. In this case, the reader is aware of Orwell's secret thoughts while the wider public is not. (**Answer:** Orwell is glad that the coolie had been killed as it gave him a publicly acceptable reason to do what he did, although his actions were motivated by entirely different reasons.)

CHECK YOUR UNDERSTANDING

Have students answer the questions independently.
Answers:
1. B
2. H
3. A

If they answer any questions incorrectly, have them reread the text to confirm their understanding. Then they may proceed to ANALYZE THE TEXT on page 734.

 ENGLISH LEARNER SUPPORT

Oral Assessment Use the following questions to assess students' comprehension and speaking skills:

1. Did the Burmans mock Europeans? *(yes)*
2. In paragraph 6, the elephant was_____. *(peaceful, no more dangerous than a cow, harmless)*
3. Did the narrator shoot the elephant because people were watching? *(yes)* **SUBSTANTIAL/MODERATE**

Shooting an Elephant   733

APPLY

ANALYZE THE TEXT

Possible answers:

1. **DOK 2:** *He expects to find a dangerous animal, but the elephant appears calm and unthreatening.*

2. **DOK 3:** *The details of the description increase the reader's sympathy for the elephant and emphasize how cruel and senseless it was for Orwell to kill it.*

3. **DOK 3:** *He felt that if the Burmans lost respect for him and his fellow officers, they would lose control of the colony.*

4. **DOK 3:** *Possible answer: The facts that Orwell relates are probably true, but his portrayal of the Burmans is biased because he didn't know them as individuals and he only experiences their resentment toward him.*

5. **DOK 4:** *Because he had to play the role of the sahib, he couldn't think for himself or take actions that contradicted his assigned role.*

RESEARCH

Remind students that they should use a number of credible sources to gather their research and that their answers should combine and summarize what they uncover from these sources.

Extend Have students use various Internet resources to learn of Burma's history since independence and the struggles of the people there today.

RESPOND

ANALYZE THE TEXT

Support your responses with evidence from the text.  NOTEBOOK

1. **Analyze** Reread paragraphs 5 and 6. What is ironic about Orwell's first sighting of the elephant?

2. **Evaluate** Orwell describes the shooting and slow death of the elephant in excruciating detail. How does this description support his reflections in the essay?

3. **Draw Conclusions** At the end of the essay, Orwell wonders whether other Europeans realized that he shot the elephant "solely to avoid looking a fool." Why was it so important for him to keep up appearances before the Burmans?

4. **Critique** Do you think Orwell provides a reliable account of how the Burmans viewed him? Explain why or why not.

5. **Notice & Note** Orwell says that this experience taught him that "when the white man turns tyrant it is his own freedom that he destroys." In what ways did his role as a colonial policeman end his freedom?

RESEARCH

RESEARCH TIP
Place quotation marks around your search terms to get results that include the exact wording.

Burma (now called Myanmar) was one of many colonies that Britain ruled in the early 20th century. With a partner, research the history of British colonization of Burma. Use what you learn to answer the questions:

QUESTION	ANSWER
How did Britain gain control of Burma?	Burma shared a border with British-controlled India. Beginning in 1824, Britain and Burma fought a series of conflicts, with Britain gaining complete control of the country in 1885.
What issues fueled Burmese resentment of British rule?	British actions devastated Burma's social, political, and religious structure. British economic policies focused on exporting resources and did not benefit most Burmans.
What role did Buddhist monks play in opposition to colonialism?	The British tried to marginalize Buddhism in Burman society. Buddhist monks resisted, giving ethnic and religious identity to Burmans. This helped fuel Burman nationalism.
How did Burma gain independence?	After initially siding with Japan in WWII, the Burman army joined the British in 1945. Following the war, the British declared Burma independent in 1947.

Extend Conduct further research to learn about Burma's history following independence. Did Burmans enjoy greater freedom after the British left? What is life like in Myanmar today?

734 Unit 6

WHEN STUDENTS STRUGGLE . . .

Reteaching: Analyze Reflective Essay Guide students to draw a conclusion about Orwell's decision to shoot the elephant and how he feels about it. Discuss how this is an example of a revelation in a **reflective essay.** Remind students that a revelation is a realization the author makes. It relates to the main message or point of the essay.

 For additional support, go to the **Reading Studio** and assign the following Level Up tutorial: **Informational Text.**

734 Unit 6

CREATE AND DISCUSS

Write an Informational Essay Write about a social injustice occurring today. Describe the toll that this injustice takes on individuals. Use evidence from research or what you may have witnessed.

- Begin your essay with a hook—a stirring incident or anecdote.
- Create an effective transitional sentence to blend the hook with your informational writing.
- If you're truly concerned about an injustice, write about that. If a specific social or political wrong moves you, it will come through in the essay.
- Tease out any ironies you identify in the situation to help provoke deeper thought about the issue.
- Create a memorable theme or message to share an insight.

Discuss Your Essay Use your essay to generate discussion with your peers. Allow each participant time to share an experience as well as its possible outcomes.

- Read your essay to the members of your group.
- Ask each member of the group to give you brief feedback about your essay.
- Encourage the group to discuss ideas and questions raised in your essay.
- Listen and respond as other group members read their essays.

RESPOND TO THE ESSENTIAL QUESTION

? Why is it hard to resist social pressure?

Gather Information Review your annotations and notes on "Shooting an Elephant." Then, add relevant information to your Response Log. As you determine which information to include, think about:

- the strict roles assigned to men, women, and teens
- the consequences of being different
- social roles and responsibilities

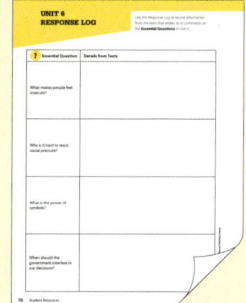

RESPOND

 Go to **Writing Informative Texts** in the **Writing Studio** to develop your essay.

Go to **Participating in Collaborative Discussions** in the **Speaking and Listening Studio** for more help.

ACADEMIC VOCABULARY

As you write and discuss what you learned from the essay, be sure to use the Academic Vocabulary words. Check off each of the words that you use.

- ❏ arbitrary
- ❏ controversy
- ❏ convince
- ❏ denote
- ❏ undergo

APPLY

CREATE AND DISCUSS

Write an Informational Essay Point out to students that the list on page 735 can serve as a guideline for their essays. Tell students that before they begin to write, they should brainstorm ideas that interest them. Have them consider social issues they have heard about recently and would like to learn more about. If students struggle to come up with ideas, provide them with some topics (equal rights, mass incarceration, health care, gun reform, and so on). Once they choose a topic, encourage them to identify a specific aspect they would like to address. Remind students to think about their audience, the message they want to convey, the tone they will use, and the best way to organize their essays.

For **writing support** for students at varying proficiency levels, see the **Text X-Ray** on page 722D.

Discuss Your Essay Remind students that speaking and listening are critical components of literacy. As they listen to each other's essays, they should write down any questions or comments to address at the end. Encourage students to note similarities and differences in their essays and to discuss why they chose their topics.

RESPOND TO THE ESSENTIAL QUESTION

Allow time for students to add details from "Shooting an Elephant" to their Unit 6 Response Logs.

APPLY

CRITICAL VOCABULARY

Answers:

1. imperialism; supplant
2. labyrinth; cowed
3. senility; garish
4. prostrate; despotic

VOCABULARY STRATEGY:
Etymology

Answers:

Student responses should reflect findings in a college-level dictionary and include a complete explanation of the etymology of each Critical Vocabulary term.

 **RESPOND**

CRITICAL VOCABULARY

WORD BANK
imperialism despotic
cowed labyrinth
supplant garish
prostrate senility

Practice and Apply Choose the word that best completes the sentence.

1. The economic interests of _____ led the British to seize control of local governments and _____ local officials.
2. As the elephant wove through the _____ of the village, the _____ residents sent word to the police of the event.
3. In his _____, he would dress in _____ costumes and relive the scene for any who would stop and listen.
4. As he gazed at the _____ form of the dead man, he felt the _____ expectation of the crowd pushing him toward an action he did not want to take.

Go to the **Vocabulary Studio** for more on understanding word origins.

VOCABULARY STRATEGY:
Etymology

Etymology is the history of a word. Most dictionary entries include etymologies that identify which language the word came from and what the original word meant. The etymology also traces the route by which a word passed into the English language.

The entry below gives the history of the Critical Vocabulary word *labyrinth*. It shows that *labyrinth* comes from the ancient Greek *laburinthos,* which refers to the Minotaur's maze in the Greek myth of Jason and the Argonauts.

> **lab·y·rinth** (lăb´ə-rĭnth): *n.* an intricate structure of interconnecting passages through which it is difficult to find one's way; a maze. [Middle English *laberinthe*, from Latin *labyrinthus*, from Greek *laburinthos*; possibly akin to *labrus*, double-headed axe used as a ritual weapon and a sign of authority in Minoan civilization, so that Greek *laburinthos* may originally have designated a Minoan palace as "the house of the double-headed axe"]

Practice and Apply Look up the remaining Critical Vocabulary words in a college-level dictionary and trace their etymology. Discuss with a partner how closely the original meaning resembles the usage of the word today.

736 Unit 6

 ENGLISH LEARNER SUPPORT

Vocabulary Strategy If students have difficulty tracing the etymology of Critical Vocabulary words, have them practice identifying and understanding root words instead. Help them identify the meaning of a Greek or Latin root in a familiar word, such as *empire*. Point out that this word contains the Latin root *imperium,* which means "rule or command." Then, ask students if they can discern the meaning of the vocabulary word *imperialism* as it appears in paragraph 2 of the selection, using context clues and the Latin root. Finally, guide them to write a definition for this term in their own words. **SUBSTANTIAL/MODERATE**

LANGUAGE CONVENTIONS:
Prepositional Phrases

A **prepositional phrase** begins with the preposition (such as *among* or *with*) and ends with its object. Prepositional phrases tell *where, when, how, what kind,* and other information that makes descriptions clearer and more vivid. Here is an example from the essay, "Shooting an Elephant."

> The orderly came back <u>in a few minutes</u> with a rifle and five cartridges, and meanwhile some Burmans had arrived and told us that the elephant was <u>in the paddy fields below</u>, only a few hundred yards away. As I started forward practically the whole population of the quarter flocked <u>out of the houses</u> and followed me.

Practice and Apply Identify the prepositional phrases in each sentence from "Shooting an Elephant." Then, write your own sentences, using prepositional phrases.

> Finally, I fired my two remaining shots into the spot where I thought his heart must be.

> Burmans were arriving with dahs and baskets even before I left, and I was told they had stripped his body almost to the bones by the afternoon.

> Among the Europeans opinion was divided.

RESPOND

Go to **Prepositional Phrases** in the **Grammar Studio** to learn more.

Shooting an Elephant 737

PLAN

MY DAUGHTER THE RACIST

Short Story by **Helen Oyeyemi**

GENRE ELEMENTS
SHORT STORY

Tell students that a **short story** has a single plot and **setting,** but the setting is not always named. Authors describe details about characters' surroundings to help readers get a picture in their minds about where and when the story takes place. In this lesson, students will analyze a setting and make predictions about characters and events.

LEARNING OBJECTIVES

- Analyze setting and make predictions.
- Conduct research about the role of women during wartime.
- Write an explanatory essay.
- Critique and discuss a story.
- Identify and use idioms.
- Use varied syntax.
- **Language** Discuss and confirm predictions using future tense verbs.

TEXT COMPLEXITY

Quantitative Measures	My Daughter the Racist	Lexile: 740L
Qualitative Measures	**Ideas Presented** Much is explicit, but requires some inferential reasoning.	
	Structures Used Clear, chronological, largely conventional. Some backstory.	
	Language Used Mostly explicit, some use of idioms.	
	Knowledge Required Situations may be beyond students' experience.	

PLAN

Online

RESOURCES

- Unit 6 Response Log
- 🔊 Selection Audio
- 📖 Reading Studio: Notice & Note
- 📈 Level Up Tutorial: Making Inferences About Characters; Making Predictions; Setting: Effect on Plot
- 📝 Writing Studio: Writing Narratives
- 💬 Speaking and Listening Studio: Participating in Collaborative Discussions
- 🔵 Vocabulary Studio: Using Context Clues
- ❗ Grammar Studio: Module 4: Lesson 5: Sentence Structure
- ✅ "My Daughter The Racist" Selection Test

SUMMARIES

English
A widow lives with her young daughter in a village in an unnamed country. The villagers are unhappy about the English-speaking soldiers patrolling their community, but after a chance confrontation, the widow and her daughter befriend one of the soldiers. The other villagers are suspicious of the friendship, and the widow is forced to make a difficult choice.

Spanish
Una viuda vive con su joven hija en una aldea en un país sin nombre. Los aldeanos están infelices con los soldados de habla inglesa que patrullan la comunidad, pero después de un enfrentamiento casual, la viuda y su hija se hacen amigas de uno de los soldados. Los otros aldeanos sospechan de su amistad y la viuda se ve obligada a tomar una decisión difícil.

SMALL-GROUP OPTIONS

Have students work in small groups and pairs to read and discuss the selection.

Think-Pair-Share
- After reading the essay, pose these questions: *If you made a short film of this short story, what scenes would you include? Why?*
- Have students think about these questions individually and make notes.
- Then, have pairs listen, discuss, and formulate a shared response to these questions. Direct them to include at least two reasons to support their chosen scenes.
- Finally, have pairs share their responses with the class.

Final Word
- Have students reread the first paragraph of the short story.
- After reading, ask one student to describe his or her impressions of the paragraph.
- Have other students briefly give their impressions in turn.
- Go back to the original student and ask if he or she would like to revise any initial impressions based on the responses of the group.
- Continue the activity with students until everyone has had an opportunity to revise their first impressions.

My Daughter the Racist **738B**

PLAN

Text X-Ray: English Learner Support
for "My Daughter the Racist"

Use the Text X-Ray and the supports and scaffolds in the Teacher's Edition to help guide students at different proficiency levels through the selection.

INTRODUCE THE SELECTION
DISCUSS RACISM

In this lesson, students will need to be able to discuss racism and why it exists.

Provide the following explanations:

- A *race* is a group of humans who share similar biological characteristics.
- *Racism* is the belief that one race is superior to others.
- A *racist* is a person who is prejudiced against people of other races.

Ask students to discuss racism using sentence frames, such as: *One example of a race is _____. One example of racism is _____. A racist person can cause problems when _____.*

CULTURAL REFERENCES

The following words or phrases may be unfamiliar to students:

- *somewhere about her person* (paragraph 1): in her pocket or attached to her
- *dying several thousand deaths* (paragraph 45): extremely embarrassed
- *dropped her* (paragraph 61): stopped being friends with her
- *come round* (paragraph 61): change one's mind to agree with something
- *talked back* (paragraph 66): replied defiantly or aggressively
- *fed up* (paragraph 66): annoyed or upset

LISTENING

Use New Expressions

Help students write a list of expressions for responding to their classmates' ideas in the Discussion activity on page 753. For example: *Would you please repeat that more slowly? Can you clarify that?*

Use the following supports with students at varying proficiency levels:

- Slowly read aloud each new expression and have students repeat it. Then, have students practice saying the new expressions to partners. Partners should repeat what they heard, making corrections to pronunciations as needed. **SUBSTANTIAL**
- Direct partners to practice using each of the new expressions in appropriate places during the discussion. **MODERATE**
- Have half of a small group use the new expressions to respond to each other's ideas. Have the other half take notes about what they observe and hear. Have note-takers share their notes with the whole group after the discussion. **LIGHT**

738C Unit 6

PLAN

SPEAKING

Discuss Predictions

Have students review language and useful expressions for making predictions. Help them practice common English phrases and use the simple future tense.

Use the following supports with students at varying proficiency levels:

- Write the following words and phrases on the board: *probably, likely, think, bet, will, be going to.* Have students repeat the words and phrases and then practice repeating them in simple sentences you provide, such as: *I bet the girl will like the soldier.* **SUBSTANTIAL**
- Have partners use words and phrases from the previous activity as they make predictions about the characters' actions in the story. **MODERATE**
- Direct one partner to state a few facts about a character's thoughts and feelings and the situation the character is in. Then, have them ask their partner's opinion about what the character will do next. **LIGHT**

READING

Question and Retell

Remind students to pause and ask themselves questions about what is happening as they read. Retelling or summarizing what they read can help them answer their questions.

Use the following supports with students at varying proficiency levels:

- Help students chorally read aloud paragraph 4. Model how to ask yourself a question, such as: *Why is the mother scared? Who is Noura?* Then model how to retell the plot in simpler language to answer your question: *The mother is scared the soldiers will shoot her daughter. Noura from next door does not think the soldiers will do it.* **SUBSTANTIAL**
- Have partners chorally read aloud paragraph 1. Have them hold up a finger when they want to pause to ask a question. After reading, have them summarize the text in simpler language and answer their questions. **MODERATE**
- Have students reread paragraphs 15–23. Tell them to pause to write questions as they read. After reading, have them write a brief summary of what they read. Then, have them discuss and answer their questions with a partner. **LIGHT**

WRITING

Use Transition Words

Remind students to use words that connect events and ideas when they write their fictional scenes, described on Student Edition page 753.

Use the following supports with students at varying proficiency levels:

- Write a list of transition words and phrases that students can use to begin new paragraphs, such as: *first, while, in the meantime, the next morning,* and *afterward.* Have students copy the transition words and phrases into their notebooks. **SUBSTANTIAL**
- Have small groups brainstorm transitional language and compile a list of words and phrases. Then, have them use the transitional language when revising their stories. **MODERATE**
- Have students exchange drafts of their stories. Tell them to write suggestions for how to improve the transition from one paragraph to the next. **LIGHT**

TEACH

? Connect to the ESSENTIAL QUESTION

Engage students in a discussion about the Essential Question. If students have a difficult time coming up with answers to the Essential Question, prompt them to think about a time when they have been pressured to do something that they did not want to do. What reasons convinced them to engage in the activity? Why didn't they say "no" even though they wanted to? What factors contributed to their decision making? Invite them to think about other situations where people end up doing something or thinking a certain way because of social pressure. Tell them that the main characters in "My Daughter the Racist" will face strong social pressure.

ANALYZE & APPLY

MY DAUGHTER THE RACIST

Short Story by **Helen Oyeyemi**

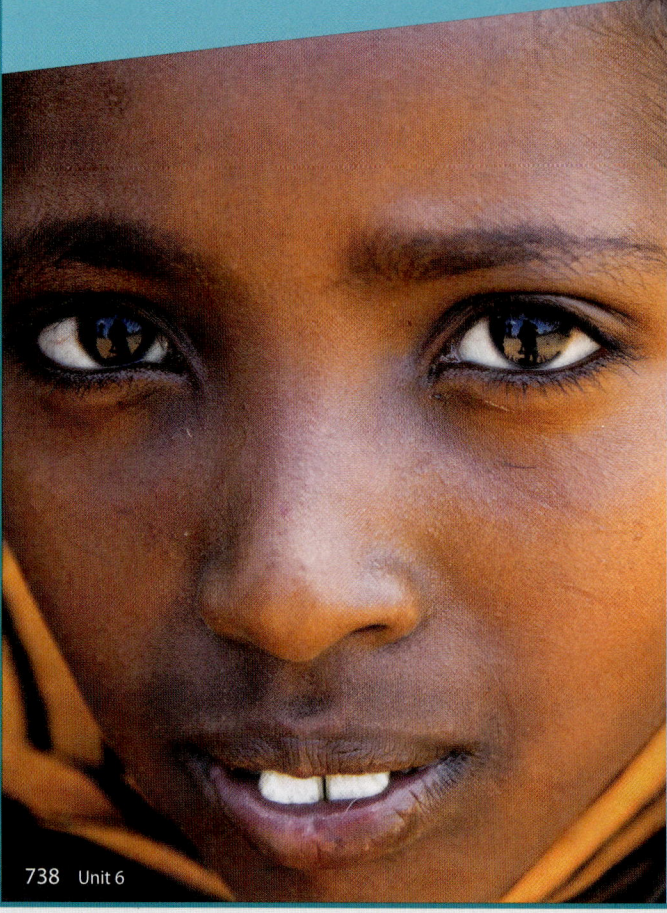

? ESSENTIAL QUESTION:

Why is it hard to resist social pressure?

GET READY

QUICK START

Think of a time when you stood up for something in which you believed. Freewrite about this event, making sure to explain any consequences or outcomes. Share your writing with a partner.

ANALYZE SETTING

Setting is the time and place of the action in a story. Setting also encompasses the culture and customs of the time and place. Religion, historical events, economic conditions, popular beliefs, and political climate are all part of a story's setting. "My Daughter the Racist" takes place in an unnamed country near a desert occupied by foreign troops.

As you read the story, notice how the historical and social context influence the characterization, plot, and theme of the story.

MAKE PREDICTIONS

You can use text clues to make **predictions** about what will happen next in a story. For example, near the beginning of "My Daughter the Racist," the narrator makes the following comment when discussing the tension between people in her village and foreign soldiers:

> And that girl of mine has really begun to stare at the soldiers, too, . . .

This remark hints that her daughter will somehow become involved in the tension between villagers and soldiers. As you read this story, try to anticipate what changes will occur in the lives of the main characters. Pay careful attention to the main characters' beliefs about themselves and their way of life, and consider how the events in the story might call these beliefs into question. Use a chart like this one to record your predictions.

GENRE ELEMENTS: SHORT STORY

- focuses on one incident and has a single plot and setting
- introduces a limited number of characters and covers a short period of time
- told from a first- or third-person point of view
- has one main conflict that the characters must resolve
- includes a theme, or message, about human nature or society

CLUE FROM TEXT	MY PREDICTION	WHAT HAPPENED
"She chopped all her hair off two months ago because she wanted to go around with the local boys . . ."	She is not a traditional girl and might get into some trouble.	She gets into a fight with local soldiers.

My Daughter the Racist 739

TEACH

QUICK START

Before students begin their freewriting, encourage them to think about why they decided to stand up for the thing they believed in. What would have happened if they had decided not to support this cause? After students have completed and shared their freewriting with a partner, prompt them to think about some of the causes people stand up for today. What factors drive people to support these causes? How are our lives or circumstances better, worse, or different as a result?

ANALYZE SETTING

Review the genre elements of a **short story** on page 739 with students, and point out that the **setting** is an important part of any story. After defining setting for students, explain that authors often use descriptions of landscape, scenery, seasons, weather, and other aspects of a physical location to provide a strong sense of setting. They may also describe more abstract elements (e.g., ideas, popular beliefs, or social conditions) that add to the setting. Emphasize that the setting can influence the characters, the plot, and the themes or messages in a story.

MAKE PREDICTIONS

Invite students to define the word **prediction.** If they struggle, explain that a prediction is a guess about what may happen in the future. Predictions may end up being true, or they can be proven false. Tell students that as they read they should use clues in the text to make predictions about how the story might unfold. Invite students to pay attention to descriptions of the **setting,** conversations between characters, and twists and turns in the plot to help them make predictions. Encourage them to use the table on page 739 to help them organize their ideas.

TEACH

CRITICAL VOCABULARY

Encourage students to read all the sentences before deciding which word best completes each one. Remind them to look for context clues that match the precise meaning of each word.

Answers:

1. *brazen*
2. *balmy*
3. *loftily*
4. *impeccably*

■ **English Learner Support**

Use Cognates Tell students that one of the Critical Vocabulary words has a Spanish cognate: *impeccable/impecablemente*. **ALL LEVELS**

LANGUAGE CONVENTIONS

Before reviewing the definition of **syntax** with students, ask them if they have ever heard the word. Tell students that syntax can describe both written and spoken language. Prompt them to think about how long sentences might affect the overall mood or tone of a story. Conversely, how might shorter sentences or even fragments affect the story? Ask students to think about why it is important for a writer to vary their syntax. Remind them to watch for how the syntax in "My Daughter the Racist" contributes to the story.

ANNOTATION MODEL

Remind students to pay attention to details about the **setting** as they read, as well as to details about the characters and the plot. Tell students that they may want to underline clues that help them predict what will happen next. Point out that they may follow the suggested annotation method on page 740 or use their own system for marking up the selection in their write-in text. They may want to color-code their annotations by using highlighters. Their notes in the margin may include questions about ideas that are unclear or their own observations about the setting or characters.

GET READY

CRITICAL VOCABULARY

| balmy | loftily | brazen | impeccably |

To see how many Critical Vocabulary words you already know, use them to complete the sentences.

1. Loy's _____ disregard of the rules landed him in the principal's office.
2. Cree wished she could trade in this snowy day for a sunny, _____ one.
3. Kaila _____ refused to play with the young boys, claiming she was so much older and more mature.
4. Because Eliot spoke French _____, the locals could not tell he was a foreigner.

LANGUAGE CONVENTIONS

Syntax refers to the way in which words are arranged in a sentence. To keep readers interested and to draw attention to particular ideas, writers vary their syntax. For example, they might use inverted word order, alternate long sentences with short ones, or even include sentence fragments. This selection uses a mixture of short and long sentences, as well as some fragments. As you read, notice how the syntax contributes to the overall mood and tone.

ANNOTATION MODEL   NOTICE & NOTE

As you read, notice details about the setting. Underline language that helps you predict what will happen next. In the model, you can see one reader's notes about the setting.

> They <u>fight</u> us and they try to tell us, in our own language, that they're freeing us. Maybe, maybe not. I look through the dusty window (I can never get it clean, <u>the desert is our neighbor</u>) and <u>I see soldiers every day</u>.

These details hint that the story takes place in a setting that is hot, near a desert. There is fighting taking place.

BACKGROUND

Helen Oyeyemi (1984–present) was born in Nigeria and raised in London. She has published novels, plays, and a collection of short stories. Oyeyemi wrote her first novel while still attending secondary school. Her story "My Daughter the Racist," which is set in an unnamed Middle Eastern or African country, was a finalist for the 2010 BBC National Short Story Award.

MY DAUGHTER THE RACIST

Short Story by Helen Oyeyemi

SETTING A PURPOSE

As you read, notice how the narrator's wish to support her daughter's independent spirit comes into conflict with the need to protect her.

1   One morning my daughter woke up and said all in a rush: "Mother, I swear before you and God that from today onwards I am racist." She's eight years old. She chopped all her hair off two months ago because she wanted to go around with the local boys and they wouldn't have her with her long hair. Now she looks like one of them; eyes dazed from looking directly at the sun, teeth shining white in her sunburnt face. She laughs a lot. She plays. "Look at her playing," my mother says. "Playing in the rubble of what used to be our great country." My mother exaggerates as often as she can. I'm sure she would like nothing more than to be part of a Greek tragedy. She wouldn't even want a large part, she'd be perfectly content with a chorus role, warning that fate is coming to make havoc of all things. My mother is a fine woman, all over wrinkles and she always has a clean handkerchief somewhere about her person, but I don't know what she's talking about with her rubble, rubble that—we live in a village, and it's not bad here. Not peaceful, but not bad. In

Notice & Note

Use the side margins to notice and note signposts in the text.

MAKE PREDICTIONS
Annotate: Mark details about the narrator's daughter in paragraph 1.

Predict: What expectations do you have about her personality based on these clues?

My Daughter the Racist   741

TEACH

ANALYZE SETTING

Remind students that the **setting** is more than just the physical location in which the story takes place—it is also the history, customs, traditions, beliefs, religious practices, and social and political conditions of the place. Prompt students to identify details that speak to these different aspects of a story's setting. (**Answer:** *The characters live in a very traditional village and follow strict customs. The villagers do not like the foreign soldiers. The soldiers and fighting will be an important part of the plot.*)

■ English Learner Support

Use Strategic Learning Techniques Use word webs to help students understand details related to the **setting** of the story.

- Provide students with a word web with "setting" at the center. Ask students to write specific words or details that relate to the setting of the story on the branches of the web. Ask them to share their webs in pairs or small groups. **SUBSTANTIAL**

- Ask students to create a word web for the setting of the story, as described above. Then, ask pairs or small groups to discuss what each of the details tells us about the story's setting. **MODERATE**

- Ask students to create a word web for the setting of the story, as described above. Then, explain that details about the setting fall into different categories, including *physical location*, *social or political conditions*, and *beliefs and traditions*. Explain the differences between these categories, and then ask students to group the details accordingly. Ask them to share their webs and groupings in pairs or small groups. **LIGHT**

For **reading support** for students at varying proficiency levels, see the **Text X-Ray** on page 738D.

 **NOTICE & NOTE**

ANALYZE SETTING

Annotate: Mark words and phrases in paragraph 2 that signal the social context. Mark the phrases in paragraph 3 that signal the historical context.

Infer: What do these details help you understand about the characters and plot?

---

cities it's worse. In the city center, where we used to live, a bomb took my husband and turned his face to blood. I was lucky, another widow told me, that there was something left so that I could know of his passing. But I was ungrateful. I spat at that widow. I spat at her in her sorrow. That's sin. I know that's sin. But half my life was gone, and it wasn't easy to look at what was left.

2   Anyway, the <u>village</u>. I live with my husband's mother, whom I now call my mother, because <u>I can't return to the one who gave birth to me. It isn't done. I belong with my husband's mother until someone else claims me</u>. And that will never happen, because I don't wish it.

3   The village is hushed. People observe the phases of the moon. In the city I felt the moon but hardly ever remembered to look for it. The only thing that disturbs us here in the village is the foreign soldiers. Soldiers, soldiers, soldiers, patrolling. They fight us and they try to tell us, in our own language, that they're freeing us. Maybe, maybe not. I look through the dusty window (I can never get it clean, the desert is our neighbor) and I see soldiers every day. They think someone dangerous is running secret messages through here; that's what I've heard. What worries me more is the young people of the village. They stand and watch the soldiers. And the soldiers don't like it, and the soldiers point their guns, especially at the young men. They won't bother with the women and girls, unless the woman or the girl has an especially wild look in her eyes. I think there are two reasons the soldiers don't like the young men watching them. The first reason is that the soldiers know they are ugly in their boots and fatigues, they are perfectly aware that their presence spoils everything around them. The second reason is the nature of the watching—the boys and the men around here watch with a very great hatred, so great that it feels as if action must follow. I feel that sometimes, just walking past them—when I block their view of the soldiers these boys quiver with impatience.

4   And that girl of mine has really begun to stare at the soldiers, too, even though I slap her hard when I catch her doing that. Who knows what's going to happen? These soldiers are scared. They might shoot someone. Noura next door says: "If they could be so evil as to shoot children then it's in God's hands. Anyway I don't believe that they could do it."

5   But I know that such things can be. My husband was a university professor. He spoke several languages, and he gave me books to read, and he read news from other countries and told me what's possible. He should've been afraid of the world, should've stayed inside with the doors locked and the blinds drawn, but he didn't do that, he went out. Our daughter is just like him. She is part of his immortality. I told him, when I was still carrying her, that that's what I want, that that's how I love him. I had always dreaded and feared pregnancy, for all the usual reasons that girls who daydream more than they live fear

NOTICE & NOTE

pregnancy. My body, with its pain and mess and hunger—if I could have bribed it to go away, I would have. Then I married my man, and I held fast to him. And my brain, the brain that had told me I would never bear a child for any man, no matter how nice he was, that brain began to tell me something else. Provided the world continues to exist, provided conditions remain favorable, or at least tolerable, our child will have a child and that child will have a child and so on, and with all those children of children come the inevitability that glimpses of my husband will resurface, in their features, in the way they use their bodies, a fearless swinging of the arms as they walk. Centuries from now some quality of a man's gaze, smile, voice, way of standing or sitting will please someone else in a way that they aren't completely aware of, will be loved very hard for just a moment, without inquiry into where it came from. I ignore the women who say that my daughter does things that a girl shouldn't do, and when I want to keep her near me, I let her go. But not too far, I don't let her go too far from me.

6   The soldiers remind me of boys from here sometimes. The way our boys used to be. Especially when you catch them with their helmets off, three or four of them sitting on a wall at lunchtime, trying to enjoy their sandwiches and the sun, but really too restless for both. Then you see the rifles beside their lunchboxes and you remember that they aren't our boys.

7   "Mother… did you hear me? I said that I am now a racist."

8   I was getting my daughter ready for school. She can't tie knots but she loves her shoelaces to make extravagant bows.

9   "Racist against whom, my daughter?"

10 "Racist against soldiers."

11 "Soldiers aren't a race."

12 "Soldiers aren't a race," she mimicked. "Soldiers aren't a race."

13 "What do you want me to say?"

14 She didn't have an answer, so she just went off in a big gang with her schoolfriends. And I worried, because my daughter has always seen soldiers—in her lifetime she hasn't known a time or place when the cedars stood against the blue sky without khaki canvas or crackling radio signals in the way.

15 An hour or so later Bilal came to visit. A great honor, I'm sure, a visit from that troublesome Bilal who had done nothing but pester me since the day I came to this village. He sat down with us and mother served him tea.

16 "Three times I have asked this daughter of yours to be my wife," Bilal said to my mother. He shook a finger at her. As for me, it was as if I wasn't there. "First wife," he continued. "Not even second or third—first wife."

MAKE PREDICTIONS
Annotate: Mark details in paragraphs 15–23 that describe Bilal's personality.

Predict: At this point in the story, what can you predict about Bilal's involvement in the story?

My Daughter the Racist   743

TEACH

MAKE PREDICTIONS

Remind students that it is important to keep track of new characters in the plot, as this can provide clues as to what will happen next. (**Possible answer:** *Because Bilal is described as "troublesome," and the narrator's daughter does not like him, one could guess that Bilal will likely be part of the conflict in the story.*)

WHEN STUDENTS STRUGGLE...

Make Predictions about Characters If students struggle with making **predictions** about Bilal's involvement in the story, provide them with a graphic organizer, like the one below, with keywords that they should focus on as they read.

Keywords	How Keyword Is Used	What It Tells Us About Bilal
tyrannical		

 For additional support, go to the **Reading Studio** and assign the following Level Up tutorial: Making Inferences About Characters.

My Daughter the Racist   743

TEACH

LANGUAGE CONVENTIONS

Remind students that an author might vary **syntax** by using inverted word order, by alternating long and short sentences, or by using sentence fragments. Explain that varying the syntax helps keep a story interesting and calls attention to certain details. (**Possible answer:** *The parallel structure ephasizes the danger that the girl was in.*)

> For **reading support** for students at varying proficiency levels, see the **Text X-Ray** on page 738D.

 **NOTICE & NOTE**

17 "Don't be angry, son," my mother murmured. "She's not ready. Only a shameless woman could be ready so soon after what happened."

18 "True, true," Bilal agreed. A fly landed just above my top lip and I let it walk.

19 "Rather than ask a fourth time I will kidnap her…"

20 "Ah, don't do that, son. Don't take the light of an old woman's eyes," my mother murmured, and she fed him honey cake. Bilal laughed from his belly, and the fly fled. "I was only joking."

21 The third time Bilal asked my mother for my hand in marriage I thought I was going to have to do it after all. But my daughter said I wasn't allowed. I asked her why. Because his face is fat and his eyes are tiny? Because he chews with his mouth open?

22 "He has a tyrannical mustache," my daughter said. "It would be impossible to live with." I'm proud of her vocabulary. But it's starting to look as if I think I'm too good for Bilal, who owns more cattle than any other man for miles around and could give my mother, daughter and I everything we might reasonably expect from this life.

23 Please, God. You know I don't seek worldly things. If you want me to marry again, so be it. But please—not Bilal. After the love that I have had…you don't believe me, but I would shatter.

24 My daughter came home for her lunch. After prayers we shared some cold karkedeh[1], two straws in a drinking glass, and she told me what she was learning, which wasn't much. My mother was there, too, rattling her prayer beads and listening indulgently. She made faces when she thought my daughter talked too much. Then we heard the soldiers coming past as usual, and we went and looked at them through the window. I thought we'd make fun of them a bit, as usual. But my daughter ran out of the front door and into the path of the army truck, yelling: "You! You bloody soldiers!" Luckily the truck's wheels crawled along the road, and the body of the truck itself was slumped on one side, resigned to a myriad of pot holes. Still, it was a very big truck, and my daughter is a very small girl.

25 I was out after her before I knew what I was doing, shouting her name. It's a good name—we chose a name that would grow with her, but she seemed determined not to make it to adulthood. I tried to trip her up, but she was too nimble for me. Everyone around was looking on from windows and the open gates of courtyards. The truck rolled to a stop. Someone inside it yelled: "Move, kid. We've got stuff to do."

26 I tried to pull my daughter out of the way, but she wasn't having any of it. My hands being empty, I wrung them. My daughter began to pelt the soldier's vehicle with stones from her pockets. Her pockets were very deep that afternoon, her arms lashed the air like whips.

LANGUAGE CONVENTIONS
Annotate: Parallel structure is the repetition of a grammatical form within a sentence. Mark an example of parallel structure in paragraph 24.

Analyze: What idea does this use of parallel structure emphasize?

---

[1] **karkedeh:** Egyptian drink made from dried hibiscus.

NOTICE & NOTE

Stone after stone bounced off metal and rattled glass, and I grabbed at her and she screamed: "This is my country! Get out of here!"

27 The people of the village began to applaud her. "Yes," they cried out, from their seats in the audience, and they clapped. I tried again to seize her arm and failed again. The truck's engine revved up and I opened my arms as wide as they would go, inviting everyone to witness. Now I was screaming too: "So you dare? You really dare?"

28 And there we were, mother and daughter, causing problems for the soldiers together.

29 Finally a scrawny soldier came out of the vehicle without his gun. He was the scrawniest fighting man I've ever seen—he was barely there, just a piece of wire, really. He walked towards my daughter, who had run out of stones. He stretched out a long arm, offering her chewing gum, and she swore at him, and I swore at her for swearing. He stopped about thirty centimeters away from us and said to my daughter: "You're brave."

30 My daughter put her hands on her hips and glared up at him.

31 "We're leaving tomorrow," the scrawny soldier told her.

32 Whispers and shouts: *the soldiers are leaving tomorrow!*

33 A soldier inside the truck yelled out: "Yeah, but more are coming to take our place," and everyone piped low. My daughter reached for a stone that hadn't fallen far. Who is this girl? Four feet tall and fighting something she knows nothing about. Even if I explained it to her she wouldn't get it. I don't get it myself.

34 "Can I shake your hand?" the scrawny soldier asked her, before her hand met the stone. I thought my girl would refuse, but she said yes. "You're okay," she told him. "You came out to face me."

35 "Her English is good," the coward from within the truck remarked.

36 "I speak to her in English every day," I called out. "So she can tell people like you what she thinks."

37 We stepped aside then, my daughter and I, and let them continue their patrol.

38 My mother didn't like what had happened. But didn't you see everyone clapping for us, my daughter asked. So what, my mother said. People clap at anything. Some people even clap when they're on an airplane and it lands. That was something my husband had told us from his travels—I hadn't thought she'd remember.

39 My daughter became a celebrity amongst the children, and from what I saw, she used it for good, bringing the shunned ones into the inner circle and laughing at all their jokes.

MAKE PREDICTIONS

Annotate: Mark details in paragraphs 33–37 that describe the girl's interaction with the soldier.

Predict: What do you think might happen if they meet again?

My Daughter the Racist 745

TEACH

ENGLISH LEARNER SUPPORT

Express Ideas and Opinions Tell students that it can be useful to share their ideas and opinions while they are reading. By doing so, they can learn from their peers and reevaluate their own ideas and opinions.

- Ask students to share their opinions about the narrator's daughter, as well as other characters in the story. Provide students with sentence frames they can use to express their opinions (e.g., I like/dislike _____ because _____). **SUBSTANTIAL**

- Ask partners to share what they like or don't like about the various characters in the story and then explain the reasons for their reactions. **MODERATE**

- Ask students to share what they dislike about one of the characters and then explain how they would change the description of the character to make the character more sympathetic. **LIGHT**

 ### ANALYZE SETTING

Invite students to share what they have learned about the social context in the story so far. How does this add to the tension in the story? (**Answer:** *At this point, the narrator and her family are at their home when the soldier visits. Because everyone is outside, the neighbors are able to see that the soldier is visiting the family, which contributes to the conflict between the narrator and Bilal.*)

CRITICAL VOCABULARY

balmy: The author uses *balmy* to describe mild and pleasant evenings in the village.

ASK STUDENTS whether the word *balmy* has a positive or negative connotation in paragraph 40. (*Positive; the narrator says that "such conversation on a balmy evening can be sweeter than sugar."*)

746 Unit 6

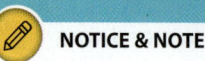 **NOTICE & NOTE**

balmy
(bä′mē) *adj.* mild and pleasant.

ANALYZE SETTING
Annotate: Mark details in paragraphs 40–51 that reveal more about the social context.

Analyze: How does the setting contribute to the plot at this point in the story?

40 The following week a foreigner dressed like one of our men knocked at my mother's door. It was late afternoon, turning to dusk. People sat looking out onto the street, talking about everything as they took their tea. Our people really know how to discuss a matter from head to toe; it is our gift, and such conversation on a **balmy** evening can be sweeter than sugar. Now they were talking about the foreigner who was at our door. I answered it myself. My daughter was at my side and we recognized the man at once; it was the scrawny soldier. He looked itchy and uncomfortable in his djellaba[2], and he wasn't wearing his keffiyeh[3] at all correctly—his hair was showing.

41 "What a clown," my daughter said, and from her seat on the cushioned floor my mother vowed that clown, or no clown, he couldn't enter her house.

42 "Welcome," I said to him. It was all I could think of to say. See a guest, bid him welcome. It's who we are. Or maybe it's just who I am.

43 "I'm not here to cause trouble," the scrawny soldier said. He was looking to the north, south, east, and west so quickly and repeatedly that for some seconds his head was just a blur. "I'm completely off duty. In fact, I've been on leave since last week. I'm just—I just thought I'd stick around for a little while. I thought I might have met a worthy adversary—this young lady here, I mean." He indicated my

---

[2] **djellaba** (jə-lä′bə): a long, loose, hooded garment with full sleeves, worn especially in Muslim countries.
[3] **keffiyeh** (kə-fē′ə): a square of cloth, often embroidered, traditionally worn as a headdress by Arab men, either by winding it around the head or by folding it into a triangle, draping it over the head, and securing it with an agal.

746 Unit 6

IMPROVE READING FLUENCY

Targeted Passage Have students work with partners to read page 746 together. Before they begin, model how to read the first few lines of paragraph 40. Have students follow along as you read with appropriate phrasing, emphasis, and intonation. Then, have partners take turns reading aloud each paragraph on this page. Encourage students to provide support to each other when pronouncing unfamiliar words. Remind students that when they are reading aloud for an audience, they should pace their reading so that the audience has time to follow the narrative and think about what is being described.

 Go to the **Reading Studio** for additional support in developing fluency.

daughter, who chewed her lip and couldn't stop herself from looking pleased.

44   "What is he saying?" my mother demanded.

45   "I'll just—go away, then," the soldier said. He seemed to be dying several thousand deaths at once.

46   "He'd like some tea…" my daughter told my mother. "We'll just have a quick cup or two," I added, and we took the tea out onto the verandah, and drank it under the eyes of God and the entire neighborhood. The neighborhood was annoyed. Very annoyed, and it listened closely to everything that was said. The soldier didn't seem to notice. He and my daughter were getting along famously. I didn't catch what exactly they were talking about, I just poured the tea and made sure my hand was steady. *I'm not doing anything wrong*, I told myself. *I'm not doing anything wrong.*

47   The scrawny soldier asked if I would tell him my name. "No," I said. "You have no right to use it." He told me his name, but I pretended he hadn't spoken. To cheer him up, my daughter told him her name, and he said: "That's great. A really, really good name. I might use it myself one day."

48   "You can't—it's a girl's name," my daughter replied, her nostrils flared with scorn.

49   "Ugh," said the soldier. "I meant for my daughter…"

50   He shouldn't have spoken about his unborn daughter out there in front of everyone, with his eyes and his voice full of hope and laughter. I can guarantee that some woman in the shadows was cursing the daughter he wanted to have. Even as he spoke someone was saying, May that girl be born withered for the grief people like you have caused us.

51   "Ugh," said my daughter. "I like that sound. Ugh, ugh, ugh."

52   I began to follow the conversation better. The scrawny soldier told my daughter that he understood why the boys lined the roads with anger. "Inside my head I call them the children of Hamelin[4]."

53   "The what?" my daughter asked.

54   "The who?" I asked.

55   "I guess all I mean is that they're paying the price for something they didn't do."

56   And then he told us the story of the Pied Piper of Hamelin[5] because we hadn't heard it before. We had nightmares that night, all three of us—my mother, my daughter and I. My mother hadn't even heard the story, so I don't know why she joined in. But somehow it was nice that she did.

---

[4] **Hamelin** (hăm´ə-lĭn): a city of northern Germany on the Weser River southwest of Hanover.

[5] **Pied Piper of Hamelin:** a tale of a piper who led children away from their homes using his music.

My Daughter the Racist   747

TEACH

✏️ MAKE PREDICTIONS

Invite students to think about the social dynamics described in the story. How might these dynamics influence how the characters treat each other? (**Possible answer:** *The villagers will understand that the narrator and her daughter were doing nothing wrong and will forgive them once the soldiers leave.*)

CRITICAL VOCABULARY

loftily: The narrator uses the word *loftily* to describe her daughter's haughty response.

ASK STUDENTS why the daughter responded loftily when her mother asked if she was still racist against soldiers. (**Possible answer:** *because she doesn't want to admit that she ever said that she was racist against soldiers*)

748   Unit 6

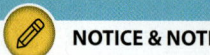 **NOTICE & NOTE**

57 On his second visit the scrawny soldier began to tell my daughter that there were foreign soldiers in his country, too, but that they were much more difficult to spot because they didn't wear uniforms and some of them didn't even seem foreign. They seemed like ordinary citizens, the sons and daughters of shopkeepers and dentists and restaurant owners and big businessmen. "That's the most dangerous kind of soldier. The longer those ones live amongst us, the more they hate us, and everything we do disgusts them…these are people we go to school with, ride the subway with—we watch the same movies and play the same video games. They'll never be with us, though. We've been judged, and they'll always be against us. Always."

58 He'd wasted his breath, because almost as soon as he began with all that I put my hands over my daughter's ears. She protested loudly, but I kept them there. "What you're talking about is a different matter," I said. "It doesn't explain or excuse your being here. Not to this child. And don't say 'always' to her. You have to think harder or just leave it alone and say sorry."

59 He didn't argue, but he didn't apologize. He felt he'd spoken the truth, so he didn't need to argue or apologize.

60 Later in the evening I asked my daughter if she was still racist against soldiers and she said **loftily**: "I'm afraid I don't know what you're referring to." When she's a bit older I'm going to ask her about that little outburst, what made her come out with such words in the first place. And I'm sure she'll make up something that makes her sound cleverer and more sensitive than she really was.

loftily
(lôf´tə-lē) *adv.* arrogantly; haughtily.

MAKE PREDICTIONS
Annotate: Mark details in paragraph 61 that tell how the villagers treated the narrator and her daughter.

Predict: Story plots are driven by conflict. Based on these details about conflict with their neighbors, what might happen to the narrator and her daughter as a result of their friendship with the soldier?

61 We were expecting our scrawny soldier again the following afternoon, my daughter and I. My daughter's friends had dropped her. Even the ones she had helped find favor with the other children forgot that their new position was due to her and urged the others to leave her out of everything. The women I knew snubbed me at market, but I didn't need them. My daughter and I told each other that everyone would come round once they understood that what we were doing was innocent. In fact we were confident that we could convince our soldier of his wrongdoing and send him back to his country to begin life anew as an architect. He'd confessed a love of our minarets.[5] He could take the image of our village home with him and make marvels of it.

---

[5] **minarets** (mĭn´ə-rĕt´): a tall slender tower attached to a mosque, having one or more projecting balconies from which a muezzin or a recording of a muezzin summons the people to prayer.

748   Unit 6

62   Noura waited until our mothers, mine and hers, were busy gossiping at her house, then she came to tell me that the men were discussing how best to deal with me. I was washing clothes in the bathtub and I almost fell in.

63   My crime was that I had insulted Bilal with my **brazen** pursuit of this soldier…

64   "Noura! This soldier—he's just a boy! He can hardly coax his beard to grow. How could you believe—"

65   "I'm not saying I believe it. I'm just saying you must stop this kind of socializing. And behave **impeccably** from now on. I mean—angelically."

66   Three months before I had come to the village, Noura told me, there had been a young widow who talked back all the time and looked haughtily at the men. A few of them got fed up, and they took her out to the desert and beat her severely. She survived, but once they'd finished with her she couldn't see out of her own eyes or talk out of her own lips. The women didn't like to mention such a matter, but Noura was mentioning it now, because she wanted me to be careful.

67   "I see," I said. "You're saying they can do this to me?"

68   "Don't smile; they can do it. You know they can do it! You know that with those soldiers here our men are twice as fiery. Six or seven of them will even gather to kick a stray dog for stealing food…"

69   "Yes, I saw that yesterday. Fiery, you call it. Did they bring this woman out of her home at night or in the morning, Noura? Did they drag her by her hair?"

70   Noura averted her eyes because I was asking her why she had let it happen and she didn't want to answer.

71   "You're not thinking clearly. Not only can they do this to you but they can take your daughter from you first, and put her somewhere she would never again see the light of day. Better that than have her grow up like her mother. Can't you see that that's how it would go? I'm telling you this as a friend, a true friend…my husband doesn't want me to talk to you anymore. He says your ideas are wicked and bizarre."

72   I didn't ask Noura what her husband could possibly know about my ideas. Instead I said: "You know me a little. Do you find my ideas wicked and bizarre?"

73   Noura hurried to the door. "Yes. I do. I think your husband spoilt you. He gave you illusions…you feel too free. We are not free."

74   I drew my nails down my palm, down then back up the other way, deep and hard. I thought about what Noura had told me. I didn't think for very long. I had no choice—I couldn't afford another visit

brazen
(brā´zən) *adj.* unrestrained by a sense of shame; rudely bold.

impeccably
(ĭm·pĕk´kə·blē) *adv.* in accordance with having no flaws; perfectly.

WORDS OF THE WISER

Notice & Note: Reread paragraphs 62–71. Mark the advice Noura gives to the narrator.

Draw Conclusions: Based on the information she tells the narrator, do you agree with Noura's advice? Explain why or why not.

My Daughter the Racist   749

APPLYING ACADEMIC VOCABULARY

 arbitrary  controversy  convince  denote   undergo

Write and Discuss Have students turn to a partner to discuss the following questions. Guide students to include the Academic Vocabulary words in their responses. Ask volunteers to share their responses with the class.

- Why does the narrator's friendship with the soldier create a **controversy**?
- What does Noura's story about the young widow **convince** the narrator to do?
- What change does the narrator's daughter **undergo** by the end of the story?

TEACH

WORDS OF THE WISER

Discuss with students that this signpost often alerts students to situations in which the central character may not be as fully aware of the implications of his or her actions as is evident to another character. (**Possible answer:** Students' answers will vary but should indicate an awareness of the cultural, social, and political environment described in the story.)

ENGLISH LEARNER SUPPORT

Ask and Give Information Have students work in pairs or small groups to ask each other questions about the story and then work together to decide on the answers. As students gain confidence, provide opportunities for them to ask questions of the whole class. Use the following questions as models for students: Why do you think the narrator didn't want to offend Bilal? Is Noura a good friend? Why or why not? Do you agree with the narrator's actions on pages 749 and 750? **ALL LEVELS**

CRITICAL VOCABULARY

brazen: The narrator describes her friendship with the soldier as brazen, or rudely bold.

ASK STUDENTS whether they think the narrator's behavior with the soldier was really brazen. *(Students will likely say that they do not consider her behavior brazen.)*

impeccably: The narrator realizes that in order to get her neighbors' attention off of her, she needs to behave impeccably, or perfectly.

ASK STUDENTS what word Noura uses as a synonym for *impeccably*. *(angelically)*

My Daughter the Racist   749

TEACH

✎ MAKE PREDICTIONS

Review with students how the story has unfolded up to this point. Ask students if they are surprised by how the narrator acted. (**Possible answer:** Students' answers will vary but should include an awareness of events leading up to this point and how they relate to this situation.)

 **NOTICE & NOTE**

MAKE PREDICTIONS

Annotate: Mark the sentences in paragraph 74 that explain how the narrator made sure the villagers no longer believed that she was friendly with the soldier.

Draw Conclusions: Were you expecting this outcome or did her actions surprise you? Explain.

from him. I wrote him a letter. I wonder if I'll ever get a chance to take back all that I wrote in that letter; it was hideous from beginning to end. Human beings shouldn't say such things to each other. I put the letter into an unsealed envelope and found a local boy who knew where the scrawny soldier lived. Doubtless Bilal read the letter before the soldier did, because by evening everyone but my daughter knew what I had done. My daughter waited for the soldier until it was fully dark, and I waited with her, pretending that I was still expecting our friend. There was a song she wanted to sing to him. I asked her to sing it to me instead, but she said I wouldn't appreciate it. When we went inside at last, my daughter asked me if the soldier could have gone home without telling us. He probably hated goodbyes.

75   "He said he would come…I hope he's alright…" my daughter fretted.
76   "He's gone home to build minarets."
77   "With matchsticks, probably."
78   And we were both very sad.

79   My daughter didn't smile for six days. On the seventh she said she couldn't go to school.
80   "You have to go to school," I told her. "How else will you get your friends back again?"
81   "What if I can't," she wailed. "What if I can't get them back again?"
82   "Do you really think you won't get them back again?"
83   "Oh, you don't even care that our friend is gone. Mothers have no feelings and are enemies of progress."
84   (I really wonder who my daughter has been talking to lately. Someone with a sense of humor very like her father's…)
85   I tickled the sole of her foot until she shouted.
86   "Let this enemy of progress tell you something," I said. "I'm never sad when a friend goes far away, because whichever city or country that friend goes to, they turn the place friendly. They turn a suspicious-looking name on the map into a place where a welcome can be found. Maybe the friend will talk about you sometimes, to other friends that live around him, and then that's almost as good as being there yourself. You're in several places at once! In fact, my daughter, I would even go so far as to say that the further away your friends are, and the more spread out they are, the better your chances of going safely through the world…"
87   "Ugh," my daughter said.

750 Unit 6

WHEN STUDENTS STRUGGLE...

Evaluate Predictions Provide students with an opportunity to review the **predictions** they made at the beginning of the story. Ask them to list each prediction they made in the first column of a two-column chart. Then, ask them to describe what actually happened in the second column. Have them compare the predictions with the actual outcomes. Were their predictions accurate, or were they surprised by the outcomes?

 For additional support, go to the **Reading Studio** and assign the following 📈 **Level Up tutorial: Making Predictions.**

NOTICE & NOTE

CHECK YOUR UNDERSTANDING

Answer these questions before moving on to the **Analyze the Text** section on the following page.

1 Why does the narrator's daughter cut her hair?
   A She wants to look pretty.
   B She wants the boys to notice her.
   C She wants to be able to play with the boys.
   D She wants to blend in with the soldiers.

2 Why is the narrator currently unmarried?
   F She is a widow.
   G She hasn't found a suitor.
   H She has to take care of her mother.
   J She isn't allowed to marry.

3 What can be inferred about the role of women in the society in which the story is set?
   A Women only work in the home.
   B Women are leaders in the community.
   C Women have a limited role in society.
   D Women are not allowed in public spaces.

My Daughter the Racist 751

TEACH

CHECK YOUR UNDERSTANDING

Have students answer the questions independently.

Answers:

1. C
2. F
3. C

If they answer any questions incorrectly, have them reread the text to confirm their understanding. Then they may proceed to ANALYZE THE TEXT on page 752.

ENGLISH LEARNER SUPPORT

Oral Assessment Use the following questions to assess students' comprehension and speaking skills.

1. The daughter cut her hair so she could play with _____. *(the boys)*
2. The narrator's husband was _____. *(killed)*
3. Are men and women in the village equal? *(no)*
   SUBSTANTIAL/MODERATE

My Daughter the Racist 751

APPLY

ANALYZE THE TEXT
Possible answers:

1. **DOK 2:** *Possible answer:* He is an idealistic person who admires the bravery of the narrator and her daughter. He feels a connection with them because he has experienced some sort of military occupation in his own country.

2. **DOK 3:** Noura is more conservative and practical minded than the narrator. Noura expresses her idealism in her commitment to her daughter and in her willingness to become friends with the soldier. But like the narrator, Noura can be caring and courageous; she takes a risk in warning the narrator about the men's plans for her.

3. **DOK 2:** *Possible answer:* Although it is important to test your boundaries so you can lead a fuller life, at some point you need to make practical concessions to keep you and your loved ones safe.

4. **DOK 4:** *Possible answer:* The narrator will regain acceptance in the village, although her neighbors will probably still feel some distrust toward her.

5. **DOK 4:** She understands that not all foreign soldiers are bad, and she has gained a better understanding of the world outside the village.

RESEARCH

Before students begin their research, review the importance of using specific search terms in order to find effective resources. Prompt students to brainstorm key terms they will search to find the information they need.

Connect Before students write about and share what they think it would be like to live in an occupied country, encourage them to review their notes about the characters and the **setting** in this story. How did the characters in this story react to foreign soldiers? How did the presence of the soldiers affect their daily lives? What insight does this provide into what it might feel like to be in a similar situation?

752   Unit 6

 **RESPOND**

ANALYZE THE TEXT
Support your responses with evidence from the text.   NOTEBOOK

1. **Infer** Why does the soldier come to visit the narrator and her daughter? Consider:
   - his initial encounter with the daughter
   - what he says about his home country

2. **Compare** In what ways is the narrator different from Noura? What do they have in common?

3. **Analyze** What is the theme of the story? How does this theme relate to the cultural and historical setting?

4. **Predict** How might relations between the villagers and the narrator change after the conclusion of the story? Explain the reasons for your prediction.

5. **Notice & Note** At the end of the story, the narrator tries to console her daughter with wise words about how absent friends enrich our lives, which the daughter undercuts with the comical exclamation "ugh." How has the daughter's life been enriched by her brief friendship with the foreign soldier?

RESEARCH

RESEARCH TIP
When researching historical information, make sure you access credible and reliable primary and secondary sources that provide relevant, accurate details and accounts. Avoid blogs or other personalized sites. Instead, consult major newspapers or sites that have *.edu* or *.gov* in their URL. These sites typically belong to the government or to educational institutions and therefore are more likely to have correct information.

Although Helen Oyeyemi chose not to name a specific country as the setting for her story, "My Daughter the Racist" seems to have been inspired by Western military operations in countries in the Middle East and Africa. Leaders of those operations say they want to help the people of those countries. However, the narrator reflects a common response to these claims when she says, "They fight us and they try to tell us, in our own language, that they're freeing us. Maybe, maybe not." With a partner, research involvement by Western nations in other countries and answer the following questions.

QUESTION	ANSWER
What set off the conflict?	
Why were Western troops sent to the country?	
How were ordinary citizens of the country affected by the fighting?	

Connect Think about how you would feel living in a country that has been occupied by foreign troops. How would you react? What would you do from day to day? Briefly describe what you think your experience would be like, and share your writing with a partner.

752   Unit 6

WHEN STUDENTS STRUGGLE . . .

Reteaching: Analyze Setting Prompt students to think about how the **setting** in the story affected the plot. Have students list the most important details about the setting, and then have them identify some of the key plot points in the story. Consider having them use a graphic organizer to show the connection between the two.

 For additional support, go to the **Reading Studio** and assign the following Level Up tutorial: Setting: Effect on Plot.

CREATE AND DISCUSS

Write a Fictional Scene In their last scene together, Noura and the narrator exchange harsh words after Noura warns the narrator to cut ties with the soldier. Write a new scene in which the two women get together after the narrator has followed Noura's advice. Will the women resume their former friendship, or does the conflict between them linger?

- Reread the scene between the narrator and Noura to refresh your memory of the disagreement between them.
- Freewrite some new dialogue between the women.
- Use the dialogue as the basis for your scene. Before you begin to write, decide whether you will stick with Oyeyemi's first-person narrator, write the scene with Nouri as the narrator, or use a third-person narrator.

Critique and Discuss In a small group, share your impressions of "My Daughter the Racist," informally critiquing the short story.

- Focus on the literary devices of setting and first-person point of view. Consider what the narrator relates about the political and social context, and how the setting drives the plot and affects characters.
- Evaluate the story in terms of originality. For example, why do you think writer Helen Oyeyemi never clearly identifies the setting? What aspects of the story seem provocative or thought provoking? How are genders represented? What might the writer be expressing through these representations?
- Find evidence of to support your views.

RESPOND TO THE ESSENTIAL QUESTION

Why is it hard to resist social pressure?

Gather Information Review your annotations and notes on "My Daughter the Racist." Then, add relevant information to your Response Log. As you determine which information to include, think about:

- the ways in which society impacts your own views and behavior
- a time you had to resist the influence of others
- the repercussions for standing up for what you believe in

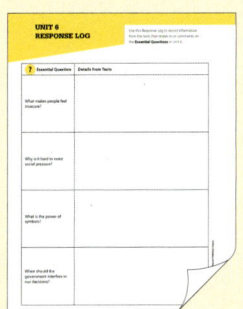

RESPOND

Go to **Writing Narratives** in the **Writing Studio** to learn more.

Go to **Participating in Collaborative Discussions** in the **Speaking and Listening Studio** to learn more.

ACADEMIC VOCABULARY

As you write and discuss what you learned from the short story, be sure to use the Academic Vocabulary words. Check off each of the words that you use.

- ❏ arbitrary
- ❏ controversy
- ❏ convince
- ❏ denote
- ❏ undergo

APPLY

CREATE AND DISCUSS

Write a Fictional Scene Explain to students that they are going to write a scene that is not included in "My Daughter the Racist," but that would ultimately occur were the story to continue: the encounter between the narrator and Noura that would bridge the conflict between them or allow it to continue. First have students make notes about what they know about the narrator and how she faced challenges in the past. For example, what actions did she take after her husband died? How does she handle the unwanted attentions of Bilal? How does she handle her sometimes rebellious daughter? Remind them that although the scene will be written in the first person, through the narrator's eyes, there will be two people in this encounter, so it may not goes as the narrator plans. Remind students that they should follow the guidelines on page 753 to help them as they write their scenes.

For **writing support** for students at varying proficiency levels, see the **Text X-Ray** on page 738D.

Critique and Discuss Remind students to use the checklist on page 753 to guide their discussions with their peers. Before students get into their small groups, give them some time to review the questions in the checklist and to come up with their own answers and evidence to support their ideas. Before students begin their discussions, remind them that it is OK to disagree with their peers, as long as they do so respectfully.

For **listening support** for students at varying proficiency levels, see the **Text X-Ray** on page 738C.

RESPOND TO THE ESSENTIAL QUESTION

Allow time for students to add details from "My Daughter the Racist" to their Unit 6 Response Logs.

APPLY

CRITICAL VOCABULARY

Answers:

1. Balmy *is used incorrectly; a person would not likely shiver in balmy, or hot and humid, weather.*

2. Loftily *is used incorrectly; a person who is passionate about a topic would not speak loftily, or arrogantly and condescendingly, about it.*

3. Brazen *is used incorrectly; speech that is brazen, or rude and bold, probably would not earn praise from teachers.*

4. Impeccably *is used correctly; impeccable, or flawless, behavior can get a child rewarded.*

VOCABULARY STRATEGY:
Idioms

Possible answers:

Idiom from the story:

- "These boys quiver with impatience" (The boys don't actually quiver; this phrase just means that they are so impatient that it's obvious in their body language.)

Common idioms:

- "Costs an arm and a leg"—is expensive
- To do something "at the drop of a hat"—to do something without warning

 **RESPOND**

WORD BANK
balmy
loftily
brazen
impeccably

 Go to the **Vocabulary Studio: Using Context Clues** for more on idioms.

CRITICAL VOCABULARY

Practice and Apply Explain whether or not the Critical Vocabulary words are used correctly in the following sentences.

1. When the weather turned **balmy,** Hillary began to shiver on the park bench.
2. Darryl spoke passionately and **loftily** when he told us about his time volunteering at the animal shelter.
3. Alice's **brazen** speech earned praise from teachers.
4. Whenever Sid's parents walk into a room, he behaves **impeccably** so he can get a reward.

VOCABULARY STRATEGY:
Idioms

An **idiom** is a common figure of speech whose meaning is different from the literal meaning of its words. Idioms are used in everyday speech and are often specific to a dialect. An example of an idiom in "My Daughter the Racist" appears in paragraph 24: "She made faces when she thought my daughter talked too much." *Made faces* does not mean she literally drew or crafted a face. This idiom means she tried to communicate with her granddaughter through facial expressions to prevent her from talking.

Practice and Apply Review the short story once again, this time identifying at least one additional idiom. Jot down each idiom you find and its possible meaning. Then, write a few idioms you know or use. Share your findings with a partner.

754 Unit 6

 ENGLISH LEARNER SUPPORT

Vocabulary Strategy Select four or five words from the story that students may have found challenging. Write the words on the board and model pronouncing them, slowly enunciating each syllable so that students can hear the sounds clearly. Ask students to repeat each word after you and then copy them in their notebooks. Then, have them pronounce the words for a native English-speaking partner and ask for feedback from the partner. Words students might have found challenging from this selection include *exaggerate, havoc, tragedy,* and *adversary.* **SUBSTANTIAL**

LANGUAGE CONVENTIONS:
Syntax

Syntax refers to the order of words or phrases in a sentence. The author of "My Daughter the Racist" varies the syntax throughout the story to create variety, to add emphasis, and to establish a conversational tone.

For example, in paragraph 4, the narrator uses a combination of short and long sentences to call attention to the soldiers:

> And that girl of mine has really begun to stare at the soldiers, too, even though I slap her hard when I catch her doing that. Who knows what's going to happen? These soldiers are scared. They might shoot someone. Noura next door says: "If they could be so evil as to shoot children then it's in God's hands. Anyway I don't believe that they could do it."

The varied structure of the sentences places emphasis on the girl's boldness and suggests that something could happen between the daughter and the soldiers. By posing the question, "Who knows what's going to happen?" readers are drawn in and begin to anticipate how the plot will unfold.

In paragraph 58, the narrator uses a sentence fragment in saying:

> "It doesn't explain or excuse your being here. Not to this child. And don't say 'always' to her. . . ."

The sentence fragment—following a longer, complete sentence—emphasizes the narrator's protectiveness toward her child and stresses how she wants the soldier to behave. The fragment in this dialogue also mirrors the way people naturally speak. The effect is realistic-sounding dialogue.

Practice and Apply Write a brief paragraph in which you react to the plot in "My Daughter the Racist." Be sure to vary the syntax of your sentences to keep readers engaged and to emphasize certain ideas.

RESPOND

Go to **Sentence Structure** in the **Grammar Studio** to learn more.

APPLY

LANGUAGE CONVENTIONS:
Syntax

Review the definition of **syntax** and the examples on page 755, and then ask students to provide their own examples of varied syntax from "My Daughter the Racist." For each example they provide, ask them whether the syntax adds emphasis, creates a realistic impression, or simply creates variety. Then, prompt students to think about how the story would have been different if the author had used less variety in her syntax.

- **Practice and Apply** After students have written their paragraphs reacting to the plot in "My Daughter the Racist," invite them to share their paragraphs with a partner. After partners have read each other's paragraphs, prompt them to provide feedback to each other about the **syntax** in the paragraphs. Did they vary the syntax enough to keep readers engaged? Did the syntax help them emphasize certain ideas? Could they vary the syntax even more?

ENGLISH LEARNER SUPPORT

Language Conventions Use the following supports with students at varying proficiency levels:

- Review the definitions of *inverted syntax* and *sentence fragment* with students. Then, have students identify one sentence from "My Daughter the Racist" that is a sentence fragment and another sentence that uses inverted syntax. **SUBSTANTIAL**

- Have students identify at least one sentence fragment and one example of inverted syntax in the story. Then, have them rewrite these examples as complete sentences with regular syntax and compare how different the new sentences sound. **MODERATE**

- Have students write two of their own sentences about "My Daughter the Racist" that demonstrate inverted syntax and sentence fragments. Then, have them share their sentences with a partner, and ask the partner to identify which type of varied syntax each sentence demonstrates. **LIGHT**

PLAN

THE SECOND COMING
Poem by William Butler Yeats

SYMBOLS? I'M SICK OF SYMBOLS
Poem by Fernando Pessoa

GENRE ELEMENTS
POETRY

Remind students that poetry is written in lines and stanzas and can convey emotions in very few words. Explain that authors use **symbols** in their poems to represent ideas or feelings. Colors, objects, seasons, people, and situations can all be used as symbols in a poem. In this lesson, students will learn more about symbolism and analyze rhythmic patterns in poems.

LEARNING OBJECTIVES

- Understand symbolism and analyze rhythmic patterns.
- Conduct research about the history of symbols.
- Write a response to the use of symbols in poetry.
- Give a dramatic reading.
- **Language** Interpret symbols in poems read aloud.

TEXT COMPLEXITY

	The Second Coming / Symbols? I'm Sick of Symbols	Lexile: NA
Quantitative Measures		
Qualitative Measures	**Ideas Presented** Multiple levels, subtle, implied meanings and purpose. Use of symbolism and irony. Greater demand for inference.	
	Structures Used More complex. Use of rhythm and free verse.	
	Language Used Implied meanings, allusive, figurative, and formal language. Complex sentence structures.	
	Knowledge Required Explores complex ideas. Refers to historical context and ideas that may be beyond students' experiences.	

PLAN

Online

RESOURCES

- Unit 6 Response Log
- Selection Audio
- Reading Studio: Notice & Note
- Level Up Tutorial: Symbols and Allegories
- Writing Studio: Writing as a Process
- Speaking and Listening Studio: Giving a Presentation
- "The Second Coming" and "Symbols? I'm Sick of Symbols" Selection Test

SUMMARIES

English

"The Second Coming" presents a vision of the chaos and destruction that the speaker believes will precede a new cycle of human existence.

The speaker in "Symbols? I'm Sick of Symbols" uses a playful, ironic voice to make fun of symbols and remind us that real meaning comes from what happens to people in their daily lives.

Spanish

"La segunda llegada" presenta una visión del caos y la destrucción que el narrador cree que precederá al nuevo ciclo de la existencia humana. En "¿Símbolos? Estoy harto de los símbolos", el narrador usa una voz irónica y pícara para burlarse de los símbolos y recordarnos que el significado real viene de lo que nos pasa a las personas día a día.

SMALL-GROUP OPTIONS

Have students work in small groups and pairs to read and discuss the selections.

Activating Academic Vocabulary

- Provide a list of academic vocabulary words and phrases, such as: *speaker, symbol, symbolism, word choice, imagery, detail, convey, irony, conversational tone, formal language, theme, line,* and *stanza*.
- After reading five lines, model how to use one or more academic vocabulary words and phrases to discuss the poems.
- Encourage students to use the academic vocabulary as they discuss and write about the poems.

Double-Entry Journal

- Have students use a notebook for recording their double-entry notes.
- Show students how to create a two-column format by drawing a line from top to bottom on each page. The left head should be *Quotes from the Poem,* and the right head should be *My Notes*.
- Encourage students to copy important or confusing lines in the left column.
- Then, have students write their own questions, restatements, or interpretations in the right column next to the quoted material.
- Have students exchange journals and help answer each other's questions.

PLAN

Text X-Ray: English Learner Support
for "The Second Coming" and "Symbols? I'm Sick of Symbols"

Use the Text X-Ray and the supports and scaffolds in the Teacher's Edition to help guide students at different proficiency levels through the selections.

INTRODUCE THE SELECTION
DISCUSS SYMBOLS

In this lesson, students will need to be able to discuss the use of symbols and symbolism in poetry.

Provide the following explanations as you point out the difference between the two terms:

- A *symbol* is something that represents something else. For example, a physical object can stand for an emotion or idea.
- *Symbolism* is the use of symbols to create symbolic meaning.

Guide students to discuss familiar symbols.

Provide sentence frames, such as: *A common symbol used in/on traffic/politics/specific holiday is ____. The symbol ____ means ____.*

CULTURAL REFERENCES

The following words or phrases may be unfamiliar to students:

- *twenty centuries* (The Second Coming, line 19): 2,000 years, the length of time since the birth of Jesus Christ
- *come round* (The Second Coming, line 21): happening
- *Bethlehem* (The Second Coming, line 22): birthplace of Jesus Christ
- *left her* (Symbols? I'm Sick of Symbols, line 24): ended a romantic relationship
- *go back to* (Symbols? I'm Sick of Symbols, line 27): resume a romantic relationship with

LISTENING

React to Symbolism

Review with students that symbolism is an important literary device that allows readers to connect more emotionally with an idea or concept.

Use the following supports with students at varying proficiency levels:

- Slowly read aloud the first two lines of "The Second Coming." Say: *The gyre stands for chaos or spinning out of control. The falcon stands for people or society. The falconer stands for control, reason, and order.* Have students repeat what you say. **SUBSTANTIAL**
- Direct one partner to read aloud an example of symbolism from one of the poems. Have the other partner say what they think the symbol represents. Have students switch roles to repeat the activity. **MODERATE**
- Direct one partner to read aloud an example of symbolism from one of the poems. Have the other partner explain what the symbol represents and why they think it is or isn't effective. Have students switch roles to repeat the activity. **LIGHT**

PLAN

SPEAKING

Use Punctuation and Phrasing

Remind students that punctuation and line breaks give clues to how poems should be phrased when read aloud.

Use the following supports with students at varying proficiency levels:

- Read aloud the first three lines of "Symbols? I'm Sick of Symbols." Point out the question mark, ellipses, and periods, and model how each type of punctuation influences the inflection and phrasing. Have students practice reading the lines aloud to a partner. **SUBSTANTIAL**
- Have pairs practice reading the poems to each other. Have them correct each other's phrasing as needed. Model how to give feedback: *The semi-colon tells you to pause.* **MODERATE**
- Have partners explain to each other how the punctuation marks and line breaks of the poems give clues about how to use inflection, expression, and phrasing in their dramatic reading. **LIGHT**

READING

Make Inferences

Remind students that they can make inferences about what speakers are like from what the speakers say and what they already know.

Use the following supports with students at varying proficiency levels:

- Read aloud lines of the poems and ask either/or questions. For example: *"Things fall apart." Is the speaker calm or worried?* (worried) **SUBSTANTIAL**
- Have pairs read "Symbols? I'm Sick of Symbols" silently. Then, have them state inferences about the speaker. Provide a sentence frame: *I can infer that the speaker is ____ because ____.* **MODERATE**
- Have students reread both poems silently. Have partners take turns making inferences about the speakers. Have them include evidence from the poem in their inference. **LIGHT**

WRITING

Use Pre-Taught Vocabulary

Provide students with a word bank of pre-taught content-based and academic vocabulary that they can refer to as they do their freewriting.

Use the following supports with students at varying proficiency levels:

- Have students copy the list of pre-taught vocabulary in their notebooks. Ask yes/no questions to determine comprehension of word meanings. **SUBSTANTIAL**
- Have students exchange freewriting to check each other's use of pre-taught vocabulary. Direct them to write corrections as needed. **MODERATE**
- After freewriting, have students add to the word bank with words from their writing and define unfamiliar words for peers. Have them use the new words in the next freewrite. **LIGHT**

TEACH

 Connect to the ESSENTIAL QUESTION

Explain to students that **symbolism** is a type of figurative language in which something stands for something else. Have them share with a partner an example of symbolism in a familiar book or movie. How did the symbolism help convey the message of the book or movie? As they read "The Second Coming" and "Symbols? I'm Sick of Symbols," remind students to note the symbols in the poems.

COMPARE THEME

Remind students that a **theme** is a message about life or human nature that an author wants to share. Point out that the theme in both poems can be understood, in part, by studying the **symbolism** in the poems. Tell students to note how the poets use symbols, imagery, and word choice to develop their themes. Then, look for similarities and differences in the themes of the two poems.

COLLABORATE & COMPARE

POEM

THE SECOND COMING

by **William Butler Yeats**
pages 759–760

COMPARE THEME

The poems you are about to read make use of symbols—a type of figurative language. As you read, look for people, places, or objects that seem likely to have a symbolic meaning, and consider how these might be related to the themes of the poems. Also make note of the similarities and differences between the two poems. After reading, you will collaborate with a small group on a final project.

 ESSENTIAL QUESTION:

What is the power of symbols?

POEM

SYMBOLS? I'M SICK OF SYMBOLS

by **Fernando Pessoa**
pages 762–763

756 Unit 6

 LEARNING MINDSET

Persistence Emphasize the importance of continuing to try even when things are challenging. Tell students that persistence means not giving up when things become difficult, because challenges are a part of learning. Having a learning mindset of persistence helps us meet and overcome these challenges. Model positive self-talk for students, such as "I know I can do this, if I keep at it." Ask students to come up with their own positive self-talk statements and share them with the class.

QUICK START

Think about the last time you were expecting something big to happen—something you might be dreading or something you were looking forward to. What was it like to wait, anticipating a big change? How did you feel? Discuss with a partner or a small group.

UNDERSTAND SYMBOLISM

A **symbol** is a person, place, or object that has a concrete meaning in itself and also represents something beyond itself, such as an idea or feeling. This chart provides some examples of common symbols.

SYMBOL	WHAT IT REPRESENTS
dove	peace
fox	cleverness
rose	romantic love
water	purification or cleansing
winter	death

Symbolism is the practice of using symbols, and it is also the name of a literary movement that began in France in the late 19th century. The Symbolists emphasized the use of symbols to suggest states of mind and ideas that cannot be expressed directly. Like many modernist writers, Yeats was strongly influenced by this literary movement. His poems often feature complex symbols drawn from a wide variety of sources, including the Bible, Irish folklore, and occult practices.

Fernando Pessoa was also influenced by symbolism, but nothing about this Portuguese poet's work is easy to pin down. Pessoa wrote his poems through multiple personas, which he called "heteronyms." Each heteronym is a well-defined character who has his own approach to the art of poetry. The poem "Symbols? I'm Sick of Symbols" was written under the heteronym Álvaro de Campos, a naval engineer who lives in London. While some of Pessoa's heteronyms fully embrace symbolism, in this poem Campos playfully criticizes the movement.

As you read, consider which people, places, and objects could be symbolic of ideas or feelings. Also, think about how the poets develop the moods and themes of their poems through the use of symbols.

GENRE ELEMENTS: LYRIC POETRY

- expresses the thoughts and feelings of the speaker
- uses sound devices such as rhyme and rhythm to create a musical quality
- often deals with intense emotions surrounding events such as love, death, or loss

The Second Coming / Symbols? I'm Sick of Symbols 757

TEACH

QUICK START

Ask students to read the Quick Start and discuss the questions with a partner. Have students share an example of a time when they were expecting something big to happen, either good or bad. If students struggle to come up with ideas, provide them with examples to stimulate their thinking (planning a trip or vacation; an important exam; participating in a big sporting event or performance). Discuss the possible feelings they may have had in anticipation of either a positive or a challenging experience.

UNDERSTAND SYMBOLISM

Have students read the definition of **symbol.** Point out that an author may use a person, place, or object as a symbol. Explain that the term **symbolism** is used to describe both the use of symbols and a literary movement in the late 19th century that strongly influenced Yeats. Tell students that Pessoa was also influenced by this movement, even though his poem "Symbols? I'm Sick of Symbols" is a criticism of it. Explain that through the use of symbolism, a poet can convey important ideas and strong feelings and emotions. Have students review the symbols and their meanings in the chart on page 757. What other common symbols can they think of that convey a specific meaning?

The Second Coming / Symbols? I'm Sick of Symbols 757

TEACH

ANALYZE RHYTHMIC PATTERNS

Tell students that some poetry follows specific patterns of stressed and unstressed syllables called **meter.** Explain that the stressed and unstressed syllables help to create rhythm in poetry. Have students refer to the chart on page 758 to help them understand the various meters, focusing on **iambic pentameter.** Explain that the word *pentameter* indicates that there are five **feet** and that *iambic* indicates that the feet consist of one unstressed syllable followed by one stressed syllable. Then, read aloud lines 1-4 from "The Second Coming":

Turning and turning in the widening gyre

The falcon cannot hear the falconer;

Things fall apart; the center cannot hold;

Mere anarchy is loosed upon the world,

Ask students to identify the use of iambic pentameter in these lines.

ENGLISH LEARNER SUPPORT

Identify Affixes Explain to students that many English words have prefixes derived from Greek or Latin. Read aloud the terms in the chart on page 758. Have students identify the prefixes that indicate the number of **feet,** and explain that these prefixes are derived from Greek. Have students use dictionaries to fill in the chart below with other words that use each prefix.

Prefix	Number	Words
mono-	one	[monogamy]
di-	two	[dioxide]
tri-	three	[tricycle]
tetra-	four	[tetrahedron]
penta-	five	[pentathalon]
hexa-	six	[hexagon]

ANNOTATION MODEL

Explain that one way to annotate a poem is to underline important words or phrases that might be **symbols.** Point out that students may use an annotation method like the one illustrated on page 758 or their own system for marking up their text. They may want to color-code their annotations. Their margin notes may include questions they have or their ideas about what certain words or phrases might symbolize.

758 Unit 6

 **GET READY**

ANALYZE RHYTHMIC PATTERNS

In poetry, **meter** is a pattern of stressed and unstressed syllables. Each unit of meter, known as a **foot,** consists of a combination of stressed and unstressed syllables. These patterns create rhythm, which brings out the musical quality of language and often serves to unify a work of literature.

An **iamb** is a foot that contains one unstressed syllable (˘) followed by one stressed syllable (´). For example, the word *apart* is an iamb. A **trochee** is a foot that contains one stressed syllable followed by one unstressed syllable, as in the word *falcon*. The chart shows the most common types of feet. It also shows terms that describe the number of feet in a line.

RHYTHMIC PATTERNS	
TYPE OF FOOT	iamb (˘ ´) trochee (´ ˘) anapest (˘ ˘ ´) dactyl (´ ˘ ˘)
NUMBER OF FEET	monometer—one dimeter—two trimeter—three tetrameter—four pentameter—five hexameter—six

Many forms of poetry are written in **iambic pentameter,** with five iambic feet in each line. In "The Second Coming," Yeats primarily uses irregular rhythms, but several of the lines are written in perfect iambic pentameter. When he uses regular metrical lines among lines with irregular meter, he creates a dramatic rhythm that helps support his theme.

Pessoa's poem, on the other hand, is written in **free verse,** which is poetry that does not follow any regular patterns of rhyme or meter. Pessoa creates a unique, irregular rhythm by using conversational language and alternating between long and short lines.

ANNOTATION MODEL

 NOTICE & NOTE

As you read, mark any people, places, or objects that could be symbolic and make note of what you think they could symbolize. In the model, you can see one reader's notes about "The Second Coming."

Turning and turning in the widening gyre,	The poem starts off dramatically with two dactyl feet. The falcon that cannot hear the falconer may symbolize loss of control.
The falcon cannot hear the falconer;	
Things fall apart; the center cannot hold;	

758 Unit 6

BACKGROUND

William Butler Yeats (1865–1939) is widely considered the finest English language poet of the 20th century. He was born in a suburb of Dublin, Ireland, but he spent much of his childhood with his grandparents in the countryside, where he learned about Irish history and mythology—subjects that would heavily influence his writing. In addition to his poetry, Yeats was a dramatist who helped found Dublin's prestigious Abbey Theatre. In 1923 he was awarded the Nobel Prize for Literature. Yeats wrote "The Second Coming" in 1919, shortly after the Russian Revolution and the end of World War I—events that traumatized Europe.

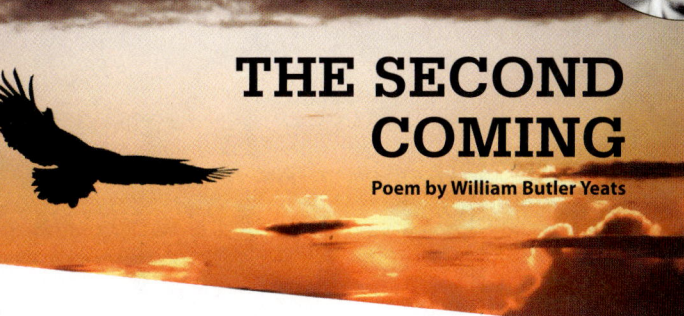

THE SECOND COMING
Poem by William Butler Yeats

PREPARE TO COMPARE

As you read, look for places and objects in the poem that could be symbols and consider what they might represent.

Turning and turning in the widening gyre
The falcon cannot hear the falconer;
Things fall apart; the center cannot hold;
Mere anarchy is loosed upon the world,
5 The blood-dimmed tide is loosed, and everywhere
The ceremony of innocence is drowned;
The best lack all conviction, while the worst
Are full of passionate intensity.

Surely some revelation is at hand;
10 Surely the Second Coming is at hand.
The Second Coming! Hardly are those words out

NOTICE & NOTE

Notice & Note

Use the side margins to notice and note signposts in the text.

1 gyre (jīr): spiral.

6 ceremony of innocence: the rituals (such as the rites of baptism and marriage) that give order to life.

10 Second Coming: Christ's return to Earth predicted in the New Testament to be an event preceded by a time of terror and chaos.

ANALYZE RHYTHMIC PATTERNS

Annotate: Mark the meter in lines 7–10.

Analyze: Where does Yeats vary the rhythm from iambic pentameter? What effect does this have?

The Second Coming / Symbols? I'm Sick of Symbols 759

TEACH

BACKGROUND

Throughout his life, Yeats had an intense interest in mysticism and the supernatural. This fascination grew stronger after his marriage in 1917 to Georgie Hyde-Lees, a spiritualist medium. In fact, Yeats created an entire system based on the metaphors and **symbols** revealed during his wife's séances. Many of his best works—including "Sailing to Byzantium" and "The Second Coming"—were produced in the following decade and reflect Yeats's new beliefs.

Explain to students that Yeats's poem also reflects a time of chaos in the world after the end of World War I. Explain that the war, which took a toll on many countries, and the political unrest in Yeats's home country of Ireland, serve as the backdrop for "The Second Coming."

PREPARE TO COMPARE

Direct students to use the Prepare to Compare prompt to focus their reading.

ANALYZE RHYTHMIC PATTERNS

Remind students that **iambic pentameter** is a pattern of five **feet**, each consisting of one unstressed syllable followed by one stressed syllable. The poet's use of this **meter** creates a rhythmic quality that helps set the tone of the poem. (**Possible answer:** *Yeats varies the rhythm in lines 9 and 10, perhaps as a way of illustrating the advance of chaos in the world. It contributes to the foreboding tone of the poem.*)

For **listening support** for students at varying proficiency levels, see the **Text X-Ray** on page 756C.

WHEN STUDENTS STRUGGLE . . .

Understand Symbolism Read aloud lines 5–6 from "The Second Coming." Tell students that these lines include an example of the **symbolism** found in the poem. Have them find references to water in these lines. (*the tide; is drowned*). Read the note that explains the phrase "ceremony of innocence." Then, discuss with the students what the references to water likely symbolize. (*death*)

 For additional support, go to the **Reading Studio** and assign the following **Level Up tutorial: Symbols and Allegories.**

The Second Coming / Symbols? I'm Sick of Symbols 759

TEACH

ENGLISH LEARNER SUPPORT

Use Cognates Tell students that several words in the poem have Spanish cognates: *gyre/giro, ceremony/ceremonia, innocence/inocencia, conviction/convicción, intensity/intensidad, revelation/revelación.*
ALL LEVELS

Read aloud lines 18–22 of "The Second Coming." Tell students that in order to understand the **symbols** an author uses, we often need to rely on the surrounding context to interpret the meaning and the tone. Have students annotate the text as instructed, and then ask them to share which words helped them to determine the symbol's meaning. *(twenty centuries, Bethlehem)* (**Answer:** *the birth of Christ*)

 NOTICE & NOTE

12 *Spiritus Mundi* (spîr´ĭ-tōōs mōōn´dē) *Latin:* Spirit of the World. Yeats used this term to refer to the collective unconscious, a supposed source of images and memories that all human beings share.

14 This image suggests the Great Sphinx in Egypt, built more than 40 centuries ago.

UNDERSTAND SYMBOLISM
Annotate: Mark the symbol in line 20.
Analyze: What might this object symbolize?

When a vast image out of *Spiritus Mundi*
Troubles my sight: somewhere in sands of the desert
A shape with lion body and the head of a man,
15   A gaze blank and pitiless as the sun,
Is moving its slow thighs, while all about it
Reel shadows of the indignant desert birds.
The darkness drops again; but now I know
That twenty centuries of stony sleep
20   Were vexed to nightmare by a rocking cradle,
And what rough beast, its hour come round at last,
Slouches towards Bethlehem to be born?

 ENGLISH LEARNER SUPPORT

Use Visual and Contextual Support Read lines 14–17 aloud. Invite students to ask for clarification of any words that are unfamiliar. Then, have students underline the word *indignant* and find the definition in a dictionary *(feeling strong displeasure)*. Ask students to visualize the scene in these lines to determine why the desert birds might be described as *indignant*. (**Possible answer:** *The sphinx-like beast is described in the previous line as "moving its slow thighs," which would disturb the birds that were sitting on it.*) **MODERATE**

NOTICE & NOTE

CHECK YOUR UNDERSTANDING

Answer these questions about "The Second Coming" before moving on to the next selection.

1. What situation is suggested by the phrase the center cannot hold in line 3?
   - A Repressive government
   - B Political disagreement
   - C Artistic freedom
   - D Descent into chaos

2. Why does the speaker say in line 10 that the Second Coming is at hand?
   - F Religious leaders have announced it.
   - G The world is full of turmoil.
   - H He had a vision of Christ's rebirth.
   - J He feels hopeful about the future.

3. Which of the following phrases is ironic in the context of the poem?
   - A *mere anarchy* (line 4)
   - B *passionate intensity* (line 8)
   - C *stony sleep* (line 19)
   - D *rough beast* (line 21)

TEACH

CHECK YOUR UNDERSTANDING

Have students answer the questions independently.

Answers:

1. B
2. F
3. D

If they answer any questions incorrectly, have them reread the text to confirm their understanding. Then, they may proceed to the next selection on page 762.

 ENGLISH LEARNER SUPPORT

Oral Assessment Use the following questions to assess students' comprehension and speaking skills.

1. What do the words "the center cannot hold" mean? *(People will disagree or be divided.)*

2. Why does the speaker expect the Second Coming to happen? *(The future seems frightening, and events seem out of control.)*

3. What phrase is surprising, based on what people usually associate with the Second Coming? *(rough beast)* **MODERATE/LIGHT**

TEACH

BACKGROUND

Tell students that Fernando Pessoa was not a well-known author in his lifetime, but he is now considered one of the greatest Portuguese poets. Although born in Portugal, he was raised in South Africa, but later returned to Portugal. Much of his work was written in English, including three books of poetry in English, although he also wrote in Portuguese and French. What made Pessoa's work particularly innovative was his use of over 70 different personas, or assumed names, under which he published his poems and literary criticism.

PREPARE TO COMPARE

Direct students to use the Prepare to Compare prompt to focus their reading.

 UNDERSTAND SYMBOLISM

Remind students that a **symbol** is a person, object, or idea that stands for something beyond itself, such as an idea or feeling. (**Possible answer:** *His elaboration suggests that the beauty of these objects lies in their specific details, not in the ideas they represent.*)

 For **speaking support** for students at varying proficiency levels, see the **Text X-Ray** on page 756D.

 **NOTICE & NOTE**

BACKGROUND

Fernando Pessoa (1888–1935) was born in Lisbon, Portugal, but spent part of his childhood in South Africa where he attended an English school. After studying briefly at the University of Lisbon, he worked as a commercial translator while publishing literary criticism, poetry, and prose. Pessoa wrote in English as well as Portuguese. His work was not well known in his lifetime. After he died, thousands of unpublished manuscript pages were discovered, revealing the full extent of his achievement. Today Pessoa is considered one of the masters of modernist poetry.

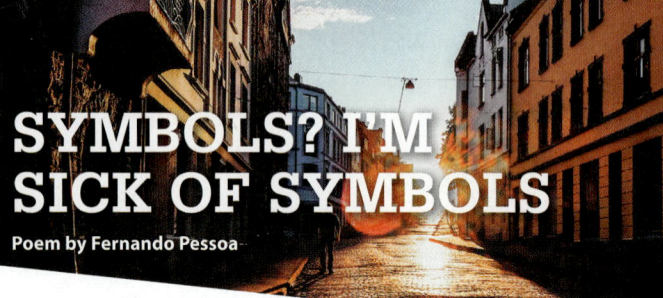

SYMBOLS? I'M SICK OF SYMBOLS

Poem by Fernando Pessoa

PREPARE TO COMPARE

As you read, pay attention to how Pessoa uses symbols and imagery to convey ideas in the poem.

Notice & Note

Use the side margins to notice and note signposts in the text.

Symbols? I'm sick of symbols . . .
Some people tell me that everything is symbols.
They're telling me nothing.

What symbols? Dreams . . .
5 Let the sun be a symbol, fine . . .
Let the moon be a symbol, fine . . .
Let the earth be a symbol, fine . . .
But who notices the sun except when the rain stops
And it breaks through the clouds and points behind its back
10 To the blue of the sky?
And who notices the moon except to admire
Not it but the beautiful light it radiates?
And who notices the very earth we tread?
We say earth and think of fields, trees and hills,
15 Unwittingly diminishing it,
For the sea is also earth.
Okay, let all of this be symbols.
But what's the symbol—not the sun, not the moon, not the earth—
In this premature sunset amid the fading blue

UNDERSTAND SYMBOLISM

Annotate: Mark the symbols mentioned in lines 5–7.

Analyze: What idea does the speaker express in his elaboration of these symbols in lines 8–16?

762 Unit 6

WHEN STUDENTS STRUGGLE . . .

Understand Symbolism Have students list the three symbols addressed by the speaker in lines 5–7. Tell students to draw an image of each of these symbols, and then label each image with a word or two that explains what it might be used to symbolize.

Then, have students read lines 18–24. Explain that the speaker's intent is to show that there is often more to life than a symbol can express.

 For additional support, go to the **Reading Studio** and assign the following **Level Up tutorial: Symbols and Allegories.**

762 Unit 6

20 With the sun caught in expiring tatters of clouds
    And the moon already mystically present at the other end of the sky
    As the last remnant of daylight
    Gilds the head of the seamstress who hesitates at the corner
    Where she used to linger (she lives nearby) with the boyfriend who
       left her?
25 Symbols? I don't want symbols.
    All I want—poor frail and forlorn creature! —
    Is for the boyfriend to go back to the seamstress.

NOTICE & NOTE

CHECK YOUR UNDERSTANDING

Answer these questions before moving on to the **Analyze the Text** section on the following page.

1 In lines 8–10, the speaker describes —

  A the abstract idea of the sun

  B the sun as a symbol of hope

  C how the sun appears after a rainfall

  D the beauty of a sunset

2 What idea does the speaker convey in line 16 when he says <u>the sea is also earth</u>?

  F Symbolic language is often too vague.

  G The sea and the earth are both symbols.

  H Seawater is often mixed with earth.

  J Rising seas are diminishing the earth.

3 Why does the seamstress hesitate at the corner?

  A She is waiting for the boyfriend to join her.

  B She used to spend time there with her boyfriend.

  C She doesn't want to walk home in the dark.

  D She doesn't want to walk back to work.

The Second Coming / Symbols? I'm Sick of Symbols 763

TEACH

CHECK YOUR UNDERSTANDING

Have students answer the questions independently.

Answers:

1. C

2. H

3. B

If they answer any questions incorrectly, have them reread the text to confirm their understanding. Then, they may proceed to ANALYZE THE TEXTS on page 764.

 ENGLISH LEARNER SUPPORT

Oral Assessment Use the following questions to assess students' comprehension and speaking skills.

1. What does the speaker describe in lines 8–10? *(the sun after the rain stops)*

2. Why does the speaker say that "the sea is also earth"? *(Seawater is often mixed with earth.)*

3. The seamstress hesitates because she is thinking about _____. *(her boyfriend)*
   SUBSTANTIAL/MODERATE

The Second Coming / Symbols? I'm Sick of Symbols **763**

APPLY

ANALYZE THE TEXT

Possible answers:

1. **DOK 2:** *Because the best people lack determination, bad people who are full of anger and hatred take power.*

2. **DOK 4:** *The Second Coming is supposed to be a time when good will triumph over evil, but the image that the speaker sees is frightening and pitiless.*

3. **DOK 3:** *The figure of the sphinx represents the unknown and frightening aftermath of the breakdown of society. The Russian Revolution and World War I both damaged the social and political systems that had kept order in Europe.*

4. **DOK 4:** *He uses short, choppy sentences to discuss the symbols, and longer, more flowing sentences to discuss detailed experiences.*

5. **DOK 3:** *The symbols he mentions are vague, while the image of the seamstress is very detailed and suggests a story that he finds emotionally engaging.*

RESEARCH

Review the Research Tip on page 764 with students. Note the differences in the requirements for citations of online and print sources. Remind students that they should confirm any information they find online by checking multiple websites and assessing the credibility of each one.

Extend Encourage students to consider differences between Yeats's ideas about the Sphinx or the Second Coming and other common ideas about these symbols. Then, ask them to discuss whether they think most people agree on the meanings of the symbols in the chart.

RESPOND

ANALYZE THE TEXT

Support your responses with evidence from the text. 📓 NOTEBOOK

1. **Interpret** In lines 7–8 of "The Second Coming," what does the speaker mean when he says, "The best lack all conviction, while the worst / Are full of passionate intensity"?

2. **Analyze** What is ironic about the image that comes to the speaker's mind after he declares, "Surely the Second Coming is at hand"?

3. **Connect** What does the sphinx-like image in lines 13–22 of "The Second Coming" symbolize? How might this symbol be related to historical events around the time Yeats wrote this poem, such as the Russian Revolution or World War I?

4. **Analyze** Reread lines 5–7 and 8–16 of "Symbols? I'm Sick of Symbols." How does Pessoa change the poem's rhythm when he goes from mentioning common symbols to describing more detailed experiences?

5. **Draw Conclusions** In "Symbols? I'm Sick of Symbols," what does the speaker value in the image of the seamstress that he doesn't find in symbols such as the sun, the moon, and the earth?

RESEARCH TIP
Remember that when you do research, you need to keep track of where you find information. For print sources, make a note of the title, author, publisher, publication date, and page number. For online sources, make a note of the website, URL, article title, author, and access date.

RESEARCH

Objects and images gain symbolic meaning over time. With a small group, research the history behind these familiar symbols.

SYMBOL	HISTORY
the Statue of Liberty	*The Statue of Liberty was given to the United States by France, as a symbol of freedom.*
the skull and crossbones symbol	*The skull and crossbones is a symbol of death, used to mark tombstones in the Middle Ages. Later, it became associated with pirate ships. It has been used to mark toxic materials.*
the Bluetooth symbol	*The Bluetooth symbol was inspired by a tenth-century Danish king, Harald Blatand. The symbol shows his initials in Danish runes.*

Extend With your group, discuss the difference between familiar symbols, such as the ones in the chart, and the symbols in "The Second Coming," which take on meaning from their context in the poem.

764 Unit 6

LEARNING MINDSET

Problem Solving Tell students that there are many different ways to solve a problem. Remind them that everyone solves problems in their own unique way and there is no one right way. Explain that they should try several strategies when they are faced with problems, including being patient, persevering, and asking for help. Remind students that everyone runs into problems when learning something new and that every problem solved will make them smarter.

RESPOND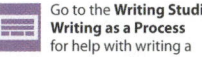

CREATE AND PRESENT

Write a Response to Literature How do the poems connect to your own experiences and thoughts about symbolism? Capture your thoughts and feelings by freewriting about the use of symbols in poems. Then, use ideas from your writing to decide what feelings and emotions you want to convey in a dramatic reading of one of the poems.

- ❏ Set a time limit of 10–15 minutes for your writing.
- ❏ Write without stopping to check spelling or grammar.
- ❏ At the end of your time limit, read what you wrote and underline all the ideas you would like to convey in a dramatic poetry reading.
- ❏ If your freewriting doesn't yield any useful ideas, try another session.

Give a Dramatic Reading Work with a partner to create a dramatic reading of one of the poems.

- ❏ Begin by discussing the impact of the poet's word choices.
- ❏ Practice reading each line of your chosen poem in a way that conveys your personal connection to the poem's meaning.
- ❏ Consider how you will accompany the words with movements or gestures.
- ❏ Take turns rehearsing with a partner, giving and receiving feedback.
- ❏ Present your dramatic reading to the class, using appropriate volume, phrasing, and expression.

 Go to the **Writing Studio: Writing as a Process** for help with writing a response to literature.

 Go to the **Speaking and Listening Studio: Giving a Presentation** for help with reciting a poem.

RESPOND TO THE ESSENTIAL QUESTION

 What is the power of symbols?

Gather Information Review your annotations and notes on "The Second Coming" and "Symbols? I'm Sick of Symbols." Then, add relevant details to your Response Log. As you determine which information to include, think about:

- how you've used symbols to express yourself
- how symbols help you understand difficult concepts
- how symbols can express double meanings

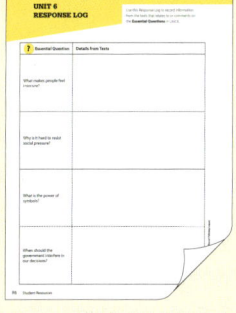

ACADEMIC VOCABULARY

As you write and discuss what you learned from the poems, be sure to use the Academic Vocabulary words. Check off each of the words that you use.

- ❏ arbitrary
- ❏ controversy
- ❏ convince
- ❏ denote
- ❏ undergo

The Second Coming / Symbols? I'm Sick of Symbols 765

APPLY

CREATE AND PRESENT

Write a Response to Literature Have students follow the checklist on page 765 to guide them as they freewrite about the use of symbols in poems. After students have finished their freewriting, have them read through what they have written and look for ideas that might help them as they plan their dramatic reading.

Give a Dramatic Reading Have students work in pairs to critique each other's dramatic readings before presenting them to the class.

- Encourage students to give specific suggestions about how their partners might improve their readings.
- Tell students to review their partner's suggestions and decide which ones to incorporate into their reading.

Students may consider videotaping their readings for posting on the internet.

For **writing** and **reading support** for students at varying proficiency levels, see the **Text X-Ray** on page 756D.

RESPOND TO THE ESSENTIAL QUESTION

Allow time for students to add details from "The Second Coming" and "Symbols? I'm Sick of Symbols" to their Unit 6 Response Logs.

APPLY

COMPARE THEMES

Discuss with students the effect **symbolism** has on the **themes** of the two poems. Tell students that although the two poems deal with **symbols** differently, their themes share a similarity because they both express discomfort or dissatisfaction with something. Have students discuss some of the key symbols in each poem and how they contribute to the themes of the poems.

ANALYZE THE TEXTS

Possible answers:

1. **DOK 2:** *Yeats creates powerful and complex symbols to express a vision of a turning point in history. Pessoa uses imagery to create precise descriptions of ordinary experiences, which he contrasts with the vagueness of symbols.*

2. **DOK 4:** *The tone of Yeats's poem is one of dread or alarm, which reflects the topic of an ominous future. The tone of Pessoa's poem is informal and annoyed. This tone helps convey a more lively look at something that bothers him.*

3. **DOK 4:** *Pessoa offers clearer statements of ideas. This clarity reflects his speaker's idea that symbols are too vague.*

4. **DOK 4:** *Answers will vary. Some students may respond that Yeats's poem speaks to the turmoil in the world today. Others may respond that most readers today are less receptive to prophetic visions and would relate more to the personal view of life offered in Pessoa's poem.*

 **RESPOND**

THE SECOND COMING
Poem by William Butler Yeats

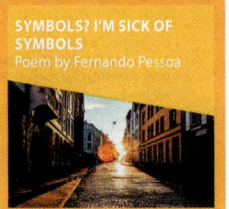

SYMBOLS? I'M SICK OF SYMBOLS
Poem by Fernando Pessoa

Collaborate & Compare

COMPARE THEMES

Symbols play an important role in both "The Second Coming" and "Symbols? I'm Sick of Symbols." However, the poems are quite different from each other. Yeats uses symbols to express a grand vision, while Pessoa works on a much more modest scale to make a point about symbolism. Compare how the two authors develop their themes. As you consider the themes of the poems, think about:

- key statements made by the speaker or any characters in the poem
- central images that play important symbolic roles or evoke the theme
- tone, or the overall mood or feeling of the poem

In a small group, identify similarities and differences between the two poems. Record your thoughts in the chart.

	"THE SECOND COMING"	"SYMBOLS? I'M SICK OF SYMBOLS"
Key Statements	*Surely some revelation is at hand;*	*Some people tell me that everything is symbols. / They're telling me nothing.*
Central Images, Symbols	*The image of the Sphinx-like beast*	*The seamstress standing on the corner at sunset*
Tone	*A tone of dread and darkness*	*a conversational, annoyed, ironic tone*

ANALYZE THE TEXTS

Discuss these questions in your group.

1. **Compare** What similarities and differences do you see in how the two poets use imagery and symbols?

2. **Analyze** What is the overall tone of each poem? How does the tone reflect the poem's topic?

3. **Evaluate** Which poet expresses ideas more clearly? How might this relate to their different approaches to symbolism?

4. **Critique** Yeats's speaker expresses a prophetic view of history, while Pessoa's speaker gets emotional about something he observes on a street corner. Which poem is more likely to appeal to readers today? Explain.

 ENGLISH LEARNER SUPPORT

Analyze Tone Remind students that an author's tone is his or her attitude toward a topic. Provide them with a list of words describing different tones to use in a small-group discussion.

1. Which words describe the tone of Yeats's poem? What evidence supports this tone?
   (Possible answers: uneasy, somber, ominous; "blood-dimmed," "pitiless," "rough beast")

2. Which words describe the tone of Pessoa's poem? What evidence supports this tone?
   (Possible answers: reflective, critical; "Okay, let all of this be symbols. But what's the symbol...")

MODERATE/LIGHT

RESPOND

RESEARCH AND SHARE

Now your group can continue exploring the ideas in these texts by identifying and comparing their themes. Follow these steps:

1. **Decide on the most important details.** With your group, review the chart you created to identify the most important details, including symbols, from each poem. Identify points you agree on, and resolve disagreements through discussion, basing your decisions on evidence from the texts.

2. **Create theme statements.** State a theme for each poem, using complete sentences. Remember, it is up to you and your group to infer the themes based on details. You can use a chart like the one shown here to determine the theme of each poem.

DETAIL	DETAIL	DETAIL
contrast between the words "everything" and "nothing" in the first stanza	tone of annoyance	the seamstress and her boyfriend as a representation of human relationships

↓ ↓ ↓

THEME
The theme of "Symbols, I'm Sick of Symbols" is related to the author's frustration about the overuse of symbolism in literature.

3. **Compare and contrast themes.** With your group, discuss similarities and differences in the themes of the poems. Listen actively to the members of your group, take notes, and ask the group to clarify any points you do not understand. Identify points of agreement or disagreement before you present your ideas.

4. **Present your ideas to the class.** Now it is time to present your ideas. State your conclusions about the themes of the poems. Cite text evidence from the poems to support your ideas. Discuss points of similarity and difference in the themes. You may adapt the charts you created or use other visuals to help convey your ideas to the class.

Go to **Giving a Presentation** in the **Speaking & Listening Studio** for more help.

APPLY

RESEARCH AND SHARE

Direct students to work in small groups to identify the most important details in the poems and to fill out the chart.

1. **Decide on the most important details.** Before students decide together on the most important details in each of the poems, encourage students to brainstorm, individually, two or three ideas. Then, have them present each of their ideas, with supporting evidence, to their group members.

2. **Create theme statements.** After students have reached consensus on the most important details in each poem, have them use these details to write a **theme** statement for each poem.

3. **Compare and contrast themes.** Tell students that the themes of the poems are quite different, but they also share some similarities. Have students think about what is the same and what is different about the themes of each poem.

4. **Present your ideas to the class.** Remind students that as they prepare their presentations, they should think about their audience and make sure they are presenting their points in a way that is clear and engaging. Encourage them to speak clearly and to use eye contact to connect with the audience as they present.

TO CHALLENGE STUDENTS...

Conduct Research Challenge students to think further about the topic of **symbols.** They might start by thinking of a familiar symbol they see every day. Encourage them to conduct research on the origin of the symbol, its meaning, and how it is used to evoke emotion or influence people. If students cannot think of a symbol, have them search online for examples. Encourage them to add details from their research to the Response Log and to think about how these details support their answer to the Essential Question.

PLAN

MENTOR TEXT

BUDGET 2016: GEORGE OSBORNE'S SPEECH

Speech by George Osborne

> This speech serves as a **mentor text**, a model for students to follow when they come to the Unit 6 Writing Task: Write an Argument.

GENRE ELEMENTS
SPEECH

Remind students that some **speeches** and other types of **persuasive texts** are based on **logical fallacies**. These common errors in reasoning will undermine the logic of an argument, either because they are irrelevant points or they lack evidence to support a claim. For example, generalizations based on insufficient or biased evidence can lead to rushed conclusions. In this lesson, students will evaluate the validity of arguments and counterarguments.

LEARNING OBJECTIVES

- Evaluate arguments and counterarguments.
- Conduct research about the purposes of taxes.
- Develop a persuasive argument.
- Participate in a debate.
- Use synonyms and antonyms.
- Use relative pronouns and relative clauses.
- **Language** Justify responses to arguments.

TEXT COMPLEXITY

Quantitative Measures	Budget 2016: George Osborne's Speech	Lexile: 880L
Qualitative Measures	**Ideas Presented** Simple, single meaning. Literal, explicit, and direct. Purpose and stance clear.	
	Structures Used Persuasive. Use of appeals and evidence to support claim.	
	Language Used Complex and varied sentence structure.	
	Knowledge Required Requires knowledge of governmental tax system.	

768A Unit 6

PLAN

Online Ed

RESOURCES

- Unit 6 Response Log
- Selection Audio
- Reading Studio: Notice & Note
- Level Up Tutorial: Persuasive Techniques
- Writing Studio: Writing Arguments
- Speaking and Listening Studio: Analyzing and Evaluating Presentations
- Vocabulary Studio: Analyzing Word Structure
- Grammar Studio: Module 4 Lesson 2: The Adjective Clause
- "Budget 2016: George Osborne's Speech" Selection Test

SUMMARIES

English

In this speech, George Osborne, the chief financial minister of Britain from 2010-2016, claims that sugary drinks lead to childhood obesity. He announces a new tax on sugar in soft drinks in order to combat this health crisis.

Spanish

George Osborne, el ministro de finanzas de Gran Bretaña de 2010 a 2016, afirma que las bebidas azucaradas conllevan a la obesidad infantil y anuncia un nuevo impuesto al azúcar en los refrescos para combatir esta crisis sanitaria.

SMALL-GROUP OPTIONS

Have students work in small groups and pairs to read and discuss the selection.

Reciprocal Teaching

- Have students read the speech.
- After reading, ask students to write 3–5 questions about the section, using these stems: *Why does Osborne say _____? What does Osborne believe about _____? What example does Osborne use to _____?*
- Form groups of three students.
- Each student offers two questions for group discussion.
- Group reaches consensus on the answers and finds supporting text evidence.

Think-Pair-Share

- After reading the speech, pose these questions: *What facts or phrases from the text would you include in a public service announcement? What visuals would you use?*
- Have students think about the questions individually and take notes.
- Then, have pairs listen, discuss, and formulate a shared response to the questions.
- Finally, have pairs share their responses with the class.

PLAN

Text X-Ray: English Learner Support
for Budget 2016: George Osborne's Speech

Use the Text X-Ray and the supports and scaffolds in the Teacher's Edition to help guide students at different proficiency levels through the selection.

INTRODUCE THE SELECTION
DISCUSS LOGICAL, ETHICAL, AND EMOTIONAL APPEALS

In this lesson, students will need to be able to discuss the differences among logical, ethical, and emotional appeals in arguments.

Remind students that logical appeals are based on reasons, ethical appeals are based on values, and emotional appeals are based on feelings.

Have students use prior knowledge to discuss various appeals to persuade students not to cheat on tests. Provide sentence frames, such as: _____ will appeal to the audience's logic. The idea that _____ will appeal to the audience's ethics. _____ will appeal to the audience's emotions.

CULTURAL REFERENCES

The following words or phrases may be unfamiliar to students:

- *Mr. Deputy Speaker* (paragraph 1): an elected official who helps run debates in governmental meetings
- *give credit where credit is due* (paragraph 4): give praise when it is deserved, even if you don't want to give it
- *ducked* (paragraph 5): avoided; hid from

LISTENING

Respond to Arguments

Help students listen for key words and phrases in arguments and restate them in their counterarguments.

Use the following supports with students at varying proficiency levels:

- State an argument, such as: *Sugar is bad for you.* State a counterargument: *Sugar is not bad for you if you only eat a little.* Ask: *What words did I repeat?* (sugar is; bad for you) **SUBSTANTIAL**
- Have one student state an argument related to a school rule. Have another student repeat words from the argument as he or she states a counterargument. **MODERATE**
- Have a student state an argument about a school rule. Have a partner use words from the argument to give a counterargument. Have them keep debating with other counterarguments. **LIGHT**

PLAN

SPEAKING

Use of Informal and Formal Language

Remind students to pay attention to their use of formal and informal language when making logical, ethical, and emotional appeals.

Use the following supports with students at varying proficiency levels:

- Model a formal and informal emotional appeal and have students repeat each one. *Formal: We are responsible for our children's health. Informal: Do you want to see a bunch of sick kids?* **SUBSTANTIAL**
- Have students write formal and informal emotional appeals about issues that are important to them. Then, have them orally share the two versions with a partners. Have listeners identify the language they hear. **MODERATE**
- Have students write paragraphs for emotional appeals in both formal and informal language. Have them share their appeals. Have listeners raise their hands when they hear a switch in language. **LIGHT**

READING

Identify Appeals

Help students identify persuasive techniques in Osborne's speech and explain how they know an appeal is logical, ethical, or emotional.

Use the following supports with students at varying proficiency levels:

- Tell the students that *generation* means all of the people born and living in the same time period. Read aloud the second bullet point in paragraph 1 and have students echo-read, following along with their fingers. Have them underline phrases that show an appeal to logic, such as *experts predict; half of all boys; 70% of girls*. **SUBSTANTIAL**
- Have pairs take turns reading aloud appeals from the text. Have listeners identify if it is logical, ethical, or emotional. **MODERATE**
- Have pairs take turns reading aloud appeals from the text. Have listeners identify if each is logical, ethical, or emotional. Then, have listeners explain their responses. **LIGHT**

WRITING

Justify Responses

Provide students with language they can use to justify their responses in the debate outlined on Student Edition page 775.

Use the following supports with students at varying proficiency levels:

- Write sentence stems on the board and have students copy them. For example: *I agree that _____. I disagree with this statement _____*(have them copy from the article). **SUBSTANTIAL**
- Write sentence stems on the board and have students copy them. For example: *I agree that _____. I disagree with this statement _____*(have them copy from the article). Then, have them write more stems they can use in their debate. **MODERATE**
- Have students write paragraphs explaining how to respectfully justify their responses to arguments in a debate. Guide them to include examples of phrases they can use. **LIGHT**

TEACH

 Connect to the ESSENTIAL QUESTION

Tell students that the United States is considered by many to be a beacon of freedom and individual rights. Throughout our history, struggles between individuals' rights and society's needs have challenged the role of the government. Ask students to read and discuss the essential question with a partner or within a group.

MENTOR TEXT

At the end of this unit, students will be asked to write an argument. "Budget 2016: George Osborne's Speech" provides a model for how a writer can use persuasive techniques and inductive reasoning to support an argument.

COMPARE ARGUMENTS

Tell students that a person can use several techniques to convince another person to adopt a point of view. Ask students to think about the techniques they used in the past when they have written a persuasive essay. Have them consider what other techniques might be used when giving a speech or writing an editorial. Tell students to pay close attention to how the persuasive techniques are used in the following selections.

COLLABORATE & COMPARE

SPEECH

BUDGET 2016: GEORGE OSBORNE'S SPEECH

by **George Osborne**
pages 771–772

COMPARE ARGUMENTS

As you read George Osborne's speech, pay attention to the techniques he uses to influence his audience. Also pay attention to the way he uses evidence to build the case for the plan he puts forward. Notice how the information in the speech is presented, and ask whether it appeals to logic or emotion. After you read both selections, you will collaborate with a group on a final project.

 ESSENTIAL QUESTION:

When should the government interfere in our decisions?

EDITORIAL

WILL THE SUGAR TAX STOP CHILDHOOD OBESITY?

by **Chris Hall**
pages 781–783

Budget 2016: George Osborne's Speech

QUICK START

Think about a time when you had to convince someone to give you permission to do or buy something. Jot down techniques you used to get what you wanted. Share with a classmate how successful you were.

EVALUATE PERSUASIVE TECHNIQUES

George Osborne delivered the speech you are about to read to members of Britain's Parliament, but it was also broadcast on television to all British citizens. His goal was to persuade both of these audiences about the merits of his government's taxing and spending policies, including a tax on sugar. **Persuasive techniques** are the methods used to influence others. Writers use these techniques to enhance their arguments and communicate more effectively with an **audience,** or the specific people to whom an argument is addressed. As you read, evaluate how well Osborne uses the following kinds of appeals:

- **Logical appeals** are arguments that use facts and evidence to support a position, appealing to an audience's reasoning or intellect.
- **Ethical appeals** invoke shared values and principles. They call upon the audience's sense of right and wrong.
- **Emotional appeals** are intended to arouse strong feelings in an audience, such as pity or fear.

ANALYZE INDUCTIVE REASONING

Inductive reasoning is a method of argument in which a writer presents evidence about an issue or problem and then draws a conclusion from the evidence. This conclusion presents the writer's belief about how to resolve the issue or problem. When you analyze an inductive argument, it is important to think critically because writers sometimes introduce **logical fallacies,** or errors in logic or reasoning.

As you read and analyze the argument put forth in Osborne's speech, focus on answering these questions:

Is the evidence provided thorough?	Determine whether Osborne has provided sufficient evidence to support his conclusion.
Is the evidence valid and relevant?	Determine whether Osborne presents facts that can be verified with reputable sources.
Does the conclusion follow logically from the evidence?	Determine whether the facts and evidence provided by Osborne lead logically to the conclusion he has presented.

GENRE ELEMENTS: SPEECH

- is a talk or public address presented to an audience
- may have one or more purposes, such as to entertain, to explain, or to persuade
- may conclude with a call to action
- may be recorded or transcribed for later reading and analysis

TEACH

CRITICAL VOCABULARY

Put the vocabulary words on the board. Read them aloud to students one at a time. Have students volunteer possible meanings to each word. Have them complete the activity on page 770 of the Student Edition.

Answers:

1. *compulsory*
2. *levy*
3. *incentive*
4. *implementation*

■ **English Learner Support**

Use Cognates Tell students that the following word has Spanish, Italian, and French cognates: *incentive/incentivo/incoraggiante/motivation*. **ALL LEVELS**

LANGUAGE CONVENTIONS

Relative Pronouns and Relative Clauses Remind students that the term *relative* can mean something that has a necessary dependence on another thing. This will help them to identify **relative clauses** in sentences because they are dependent on the noun in the sentence. The **relative pronouns** *that, which, where, when, who,* and *whom* begin **relative clauses** and describe the nouns in the complex sentences they complete. The relative pronoun is determined by the type of noun it is modifying.

ANNOTATION MODEL

Remind students of the annotation model on page 770, which suggests underlining phrases that identify the different kinds of appeals used by the writer. Point out that they may follow this suggestion or use their own system for marking up the selection in their write-in text. They may want to color-code their annotations by using highlighters. Their notes in the margin may include questions about ideas that are unclear or topics they want to learn more about.

GET READY

CRITICAL VOCABULARY

incentive   levy   implementation   compulsory

To see how many Critical Vocabulary words you already know, use them to complete the sentences.

1. It is a requirement that you attend school until a certain age. This is called _____ education.

2. The government can increase its revenue with a new _____ on services that are not currently being taxed.

3. Many times the government will provide a(n) _____, such as a tax rebate, so companies will invest in the production of energy-saving products.

4. New laws voted on by the Congress may take several years for the _____ to be fully realized.

LANGUAGE CONVENTIONS

Relative Pronouns and Relative Clauses Relative pronouns connect relative, or adjective, clauses to the words they modify in a sentence. Relative pronouns include *that, which, who, whom,* and *whose*. The noun or pronoun that a relative clause modifies is the antecedent of the relative pronoun.

> George Osborne, who served as Chancellor of Exchequer, delivered a speech about a new tax on sugary drinks.

In this sentence, *who* is the relative pronoun and *who served as Chancellor of Exchequer* is the relative clause. *George Osborne* is the antecedent of the relative pronoun.

ANNOTATION MODEL   NOTICE & NOTE

As you read, make note of how the author uses facts, statistics, and other kinds of evidence to support his argument. The model shows how one reader annotated the beginning of the speech.

> Mr. Deputy Speaker, you cannot have a long-term plan for the country unless you have a long-term plan for our children's healthcare. Here are the facts we know.
>
> - Five-year-old children are consuming their body weight in sugar every year.
>
> - Experts predict that within a generation, over half of all boys and 70% of girls will be overweight or obese.

This is a logical appeal: children's health issues affect the nation's future.

These surprising facts all relate to children's health.

BACKGROUND

George Osborne (b. 1971) served as chief financial minister of the United Kingdom as Chancellor of Exchequer from 2010 to 2016. His responsibilities included controlling public spending and raising money through taxation or borrowing. He delivered a speech about the government's budget plan to the House of Commons on March 1, 2016. In this speech, he announced that a new tax on sugar in soft drinks would take effect in 2018.

BUDGET 2016: GEORGE OSBORNE'S SPEECH

Speech by George Osborne

PREPARE TO COMPARE

As you read Osborne's speech, think about the methods he uses to persuade his audience. Paying attention to how Osborne presents his message will allow you to compare his argument to that of Chris Hall, the author of the next selection.

1   Mr Deputy Speaker, you cannot have a long term plan for the country unless you have a long term plan for our children's health care. Here are the facts we know.
   - Five-year-old children are consuming their body weight in sugar every year.
   - Experts predict that within a generation, over half of all boys and 70% of girls could be overweight or obese.

2   Here's another fact that we all know. Obesity drives disease. It increases the risk of cancer, diabetes and heart disease—and it costs our economy £27 billion a year; that's more than half the entire NHS[1] paybill.

3   And here's another truth we all know. One of the biggest contributors to childhood obesity is sugary drinks. A can of cola typically has nine teaspoons of sugar in it. Some popular

---
[1] **NHS:** National Health Service (United Kingdom)

NOTICE & NOTE

Notice & Note

Use the side margins to notice and note signposts in the text.

NUMBERS AND STATS

Notice & Note: Mark the statistics Osborne includes in paragraph 1.

Evaluate: How effective are these statistics as a way to introduce the topic?

TEACH

BACKGROUND

George Osborne was the Chancellor of Exchequer of the United Kingdom from 2010–2016. This position is one of the most senior members of the Cabinet and can be equated to the Chairman of the Federal Reserve in the United States. As a conservative, he pursued austerity policies reducing Britain's national debt. He was criticized for reducing funding for services and not reducing taxes. When Theresa May became Prime Minister in 2016, she fired Osborne. No longer a Member of Parliament, he currently is Editor of the *Evening Standard*.

PREPARE TO COMPARE

Direct students to use the Prepare to Compare prompt to focus their reading.

For **reading support** for students at varying proficiency levels, see the **Text X-Ray** on page 768D.

NUMBERS AND STATS

Remind students that sometimes numbers are written in word form, usually any number ten or less. Numbers and statistics are important details that support an argument in a logical appeal. (**Answer:** *The statistics are effective at capturing the attention of the audience because they are surprising and alarming. They also suggest that something needs to be done to address the issue of childhood obesity. It should be noted that Osborne did not cite any sources for the statistical facts he presented.*)

ENGLISH LEARNER SUPPORT

Use Support from Peers to Develop Vocabulary Match students with partners of varying language skills so they can discuss, using the term **logical appeal,** how George Osborne used numbers and statistics in paragraphs 1 and 2 to convince Congress to levy a sugar tax. **MODERATE/LIGHT**

TEACH

✏️ EVALUATE PERSUASIVE TECHNIQUES

Tell students that an ethical appeal is helpful because if people think that an action is "doing the right thing," they are more likely to do it. (**Answer:** *Osborne verifies the companies' credibility by admitting they are lowering sugar content. Osborne's validity is established when he seemingly argues the issue from both sides. It is therefore more likely the audience will think he is a credible speaker and agree with him.*)

✏️ LANGUAGE CONVENTIONS

Tell students that sentences are more varied when relative clauses are used. (**Answer:** *"Which means they can reduce the sugar content on their products" is the relative clause. It gives more details about the levy on sugary drinks.*)

✏️ ANALYZE INDUCTIVE REASONING

Have students look for the specific reasons Osborne uses to support his solution to child obesity. He uses **inductive reasoning** in his speech because he begins with details to support a generalization. (**Answer:** *The tax is to meant to lower consumption, so the projected tax revenues may be exaggerated. There are also other causes of obesity, so taxing soft drink companies won't end childhood obesity.*)

CRITICAL VOCABULARY

incentive: The speech uses this term to describe how a tax will encourage people not to drink sugary drinks.

ASK STUDENTS what *incentives* they have to do well in school. (*good grades, respect from peers, parents, college*)

levy: The speech uses this term to place a tax on a group.

ASK STUDENTS if they can name the type of taxes that have been *levied* in their country. (*sales tax, tourist tax*)

implementation: The speech uses this term to describe how the tax will be put into action.

ASK STUDENTS who would control *implementation* of the sugar tax. (*The Parliament would be in charge.*)

compulsory: The speech uses this term to explain that students will have to participate in sports activities.

ASK STUDENTS to name something that is *compulsory*. (*School attendance*)

772   Unit 6

✏️ NOTICE & NOTE

EVALUATE PERSUASIVE TECHNIQUES

Annotate: Mark phrases in paragraph 4 that suggest Osborne is making an ethical appeal.

Analyze: How does mentioning the steps the soft drink industry is taking strengthen Osborne's argument?

incentive
(ĭn-sĕn´tĭv) *n.* something, such as the fear of punishment or the expectation of reward, that induces action or motivates effort.

levy
(lĕv´ē) *n.* a tax or fine imposed on a person or business.

implementation
(ĭm-plə-mən-tā´shən) *n.* the process of putting into practical effect; carry out.

LANGUAGE CONVENTIONS

Annotate: Mark the relative clause in paragraph 7.

Analyze: What is the antecedent of the relative clause?

ANALYZE INDUCTIVE REASONING

Annotate: Mark sentences in paragraphs 8 and 9 that summarize the actions that Parliament wants to take to make children healthier and the results they expect to see.

Analyze: Can you find any logical fallacies in Osborne's argument for his plan to fight childhood obesity?

compulsory
(kəm-pŭl´sə-rē) *adj.* obligatory; required.

772   Unit 6

---

drinks have as many as 13. That can be more than double a child's recommended added sugar intake.

4   Let me give credit where credit is due. Many in the soft drinks industry recognize there's a problem and have started to reformulate their products. . . . So industry can act, and with the right **incentives** I'm sure it will.

5   Mr Deputy Speaker, I am not prepared to look back at my time here in this Parliament, doing this job and say to my children's generation: I'm sorry. We knew there was a problem with sugary drinks. We knew it caused disease. But we ducked the difficult decisions and we did nothing.

6   So today I can announce that we will introduce a new sugar **levy** on the soft drinks industry. Let me explain how it will work. It will be levied on the companies. It will be introduced in two years' time to give companies plenty of space to change their product mix. It will be assessed on the volume of the sugar-sweetened drinks they produce or import. There will be two bands—one for total sugar content above 5 grams per 100 millilitres; a second, higher band for the most sugary drinks with more than 8 grams per 100 millilitres. Pure fruit juices and milk-based drinks will be excluded, and we'll ensure the smallest producers are kept out of scope. We will of course consult with Parliament on **implementation**.

7   We're introducing the levy on the industry which means they can reduce the sugar content of their products—as many already do. It means they can promote low sugar or no sugar brands—as many already are. They can take these perfectly reasonable steps to help with children's health. Of course, some may choose to pass the price onto consumers and that will be their decision, and this would have an impact on consumption too. We understand that tax affects behavior. So let's tax the things we want to reduce, not the things we want to encourage.

8   The OBR[2] estimate that this levy will raise £520 million. And this is tied directly to the second thing we're going to do today to help children's health and wellbeing. We're going to use the money from this new levy to double the amount of funding we dedicate to sport in every primary school. And for secondary schools we're going to fund longer school days for those that want to offer their pupils a wider range of activities, including extra sport. It will be voluntary for schools. **Compulsory** for the pupils. There will be enough resources for a quarter of secondary schools to take part—but that's just a start. . . .

9   A determination to improve the health of our children. A new levy on excessive sugar in soft drinks. The money used to double sport in our schools. A Britain fit for the future. We're not afraid to put the next generation first.

---
[2] **OBR:** Office for Budget Responsibility (United Kingdom).

NOTICE & NOTE

CHECK YOUR UNDERSTANDING

Answer these questions before moving on to the **Analyze the Text** section on the following page.

1. Read this sentence from the speech.

   We're going to use the money from this new levy to double the amount of funding we dedicate to sport in every primary school.

   Which persuasive technique is used in the sentence?

   A A logical appeal

   B A legislative appeal

   C An ethical appeal

   D An emotional appeal

2. At the beginning of paragraphs 1, 2, and 3, the author most likely repeats the phrases <u>facts we know</u> and <u>truth we know</u> in order to make —

   F himself appear trustworthy to the audience

   G logical connections between the evidence he presents

   H an emotional appeal

   J a bandwagon appeal

3. Which one of the questions below should be asked *first* to effectively analyze Osborne's reasoning that a tax on sugary drinks will make children healthier?

   A How true are the three facts that he states are already known?

   B How many schools want to implement programs that promote sports?

   C What are the other causes of childhood obesity?

   D How much will people pay for sugary drinks?

Budget 2016: George Osborne's Speech 773

TEACH

CHECK YOUR UNDERSTANDING

Have students answer the questions independently.

Answers:

1. D
2. G
3. C

If they answer any questions incorrectly, have them reread the text to confirm their understanding. Then they may proceed to ANALYZE THE TEXT on page 774.

ENGLISH LEARNER SUPPORT

Oral Assessment Use the following questions to assess students' comprehension and speaking skills.

1. Osborne says that the money from the tax will help increase funding for sports in schools. What kind of appeal is this? *(This is an appeal to emotion.)*

2. In paragraphs 1–3, why does the author repeat the words "facts we know" and "truth we know"? *(to make connections between the evidence he provides)*

3. What additional facts would help show whether the tax would make children healthier? *(facts about other causes of childhood obesity)* **LIGHT**

APPLY

ANALYZE THE TEXT

Possible answers:

1. **DOK 4:** *Osborne effectively appeals to logic by presenting facts and details (five-year-old, nine and 13 teaspoons of sugar, over half of boys and 70% of girls). He appeals to emotion by mentioning how obesity was linked to cancer, diabetes, and heart disease. He appeals to ethics by indicating it was the Parliament's responsibility to address the problems of sugary drinks.*

2. **DOK 1:** *that a levy on sugary drinks can help solve the problem of childhood obesity*

3. **DOK 3:** *Osborne provides much support but there are several fallacies in his argument. He fails to address all causes of childhood obesity, including diet. It remains to be seen the effect the tax will have on the reduction of sugar intake, or the revenue it will generate. Not all children will participate since participation by schools is voluntary.*

4. **DOK 4:** *He is mostly successful, because he provides facts and statistics that show childhood obesity is on the rise, and presents a logical solution—a tax—that will discourage consumption of sugary drinks and raise money for programs to improve children's health. However, his argument is based on assumptions about the causes of childhood obesity (sugary drinks) and the willingness of Britons to participate in his solution to the problem.*

5. **DOK 4:** *Factual information provides details. The details presented indicate how the tax will be levied. Facts can give the illusion that something is well thought out.*

RESEARCH

Tell students there are many kinds of taxes. Most have heard of the national income tax, but there are obscure taxes that are built into prices such as those found in the price of gasoline. This tax can vary from one location to another.

See chart on page 774 for possible answers.

Extend Remind students that in order to analyze their beliefs about taxation, they need to consider their beliefs about the purpose of government. For example, a person should analyze who is responsible for reducing childhood obesity, the government or the parent, before he or she determines if the sugar tax is necessary.

774   Unit 6

RESPOND

ANALYZE THE TEXT

Support your responses with evidence from the text.   NOTEBOOK

1. **Analyze** In what ways does Osborne effectively use persuasive techniques?
2. **Identify** What conclusion does Osborne draw based on the evidence he presents?
3. **Critique** Does Osborne provide adequate support for his argument?
4. **Evaluate** Osborne's speech has two audiences—the Parliament and the British people. How successful is he in addressing both of them?
5. **Notice & Note** In paragraph 6, what is the effect of providing the numbers to explain the two bands of sugar content in sweetened drinks?

RESEARCH

RESEARCH TIP
Start your research by accessing your state government's website. Then, expand your search by going to your county website. Sites that end in *.gov* are websites that are managed by a government agency. However, *.com* websites may also be helpful.

The national government, states, and counties levy taxes on goods and services to generate money. Research to discover the purpose of the following taxes and at which level of government they are collected. Use the empty rows in the chart to add additional taxes that you might find in your research.

TAX	PURPOSE	LEVEL (NATION/STATE/COUNTY)
Income Tax	*Levied on income earned*	*National*
State Tax	*Levied on income earned*	*43 states*
Property Tax	*Levied on owned property*	*State/county*
Gasoline Tax	*Levied on gasoline*	*National/state/county*
Capital Gains Tax	*profit from sale of property or investment*	*National*
Inheritance Tax	*Levied on property that is inherited*	*National/state*
Sales Tax	*tax on sale of goods*	*State/county*
Business Profit Tax	*income earned by companies*	*National*

Extend Many people believe they are taxed too much. Others think we need more taxes so the government can fund more programs to help keep people safe and healthy. Consider the taxes above and what you learned from your research to determine which taxes you think are the most important and which ones are the least important.

774   Unit 6

WHEN STUDENTS STRUGGLE . . .

Reteaching: Evaluate Persuasive Techniques Use the graphic organizer below to help students collect examples of the techniques used by Osborne.

Logical	Ethical	Emotional
Percentages of obesity	Right thing to do	Give more money to schools
Cost of obesity	Protect children	Put the next generation first

 For additional support, go to the **Reading Studio** and assign the following Level Up tutorial: **Persuasive Techniques.**

RESPOND

CREATE AND DEBATE

Develop a Persuasive Argument With a small group, decide on a tax you want to support or eliminate. Divide the group into two teams, each taking a *For* or *Against* stance. Both sides should take the following steps:

- Determine the facts that can be used to support your stance. This will be the basis for your logical appeal.
- Determine how the tax benefits the community or has had negative consequences. Choose words that illicit strong emotions to develop your emotional appeal.
- Develop your ethical appeal by explaining how the tax is the "right thing to do" or how the tax is "unfair and imbalanced."
- Write down your argument statements that you will use to persuade others to agree with your argument. Organize them in order so you can present a cohesive presentation.
- Be sure to anticipate the other side's argument so you can make counterarguments.

Debate Set up a time to meet in front of the class to hold a debate. Each person on the team should take part in presenting a statement using at least one kind of persuasive technique.

- Set up debate rules to define how both sides will present their arguments.
- Both sides should have the opportunity to make counterarguments.

 Go to the **Writing Studio** to find out more about writing arguments.

 Go to the **Speaking and Listening Studio: Analyzing and Evaluating Presentations** to learn more.

RESPOND TO THE ESSENTIAL QUESTION

 When should the government interfere with our decisions?

Gather Information Review your annotations and notes on "Budget 2016: George Osborne's Speech." Then, add relevant details to your Response Log. As you determine which information to include, think about:

- the types of persuasive techniques that the author uses
- whether his reasoning is valid, logical, and stands on a firm premise
- what you have learned from your research and discussions

ACADEMIC VOCABULARY

As you write and discuss what you learned from the speech, be sure to use the Academic Vocabulary words. Check off each of the words that you use.

- ☐ arbitrary
- ☐ controversy
- ☐ convince
- ☐ denote
- ☐ undergo

APPLY

CREATE AND DEBATE

Develop a Persuasive Argument Refer students to the research charts they completed to provide a list of types of taxes. If necessary, brainstorm additional taxes that students might be interested in researching. Suggest that using a graphic organizer will organize the advantages and disadvantages of the tax. Groups should be made up of at least six people. After choosing the tax to debate, suggest that the three pairs of students in each group select a type of appeal they want to present. All three appeal types should be represented. The partnership should determine who wants to support the tax and who wants to argue against it. Tell students to use the check boxes on page 775 to guide them in the process.

For **writing support** for students at varying proficiency levels, see the **Text X-Ray** on page 768D.

Debate Assist students in developing procedural rules that include how long each person may speak and how much time can be made for rebuttal statements. Suggest that students research common debate procedures before they make their decisions.

RESPOND TO THE ESSENTIAL QUESTION

Allow time for students to add details from Budget 2016: George Osborne's Speech to their Unit 6 Response Logs.

APPLY

CRITICAL VOCABULARY

Answers:

1. incentive
2. compulsory
3. levy
4. implementation

VOCABULARY STRATEGY:
Related Words

Explain that words that have the same root or base word make up a word family, or words that have related meanings. When students come across an unfamiliar word, they should look for the root or base word to see if they know the meaning of that word. Then, they can look at the prefixes or suffixes and use what they know about these word parts to determine the meaning of the unfamiliar word. For example, the Greek root *chron* means "time." Words with the same root that are related are *chronology* and *chronic*.

Possible Answers:

1. lack of discretion
2. something that impedes; an obstruction
3. the act or process of consuming; taking in food; eating or drinking
4. the act of believing or supposing in advance
5. acting or practicing exclusion; preventing from being included

776   Unit 6

RESPOND

WORD BANK
incentive
levy
implementation
compulsory

 Go to the **Vocabulary Studio** for more on analyzing word structure.

CRITICAL VOCABULARY

Practice and Apply Write the Critical Vocabulary word that has the same or similar meaning as the given word.

1. reward
2. mandatory
3. tax
4. enactment

VOCABULARY STRATEGY:
Related Words

Often you can use related words to figure out the meaning of an unfamiliar word. For example, you might not know the meaning of *compulsory*. However, if you are familiar with the related word *compel*, which means "to force or require," you could guess that *compulsory* describes something that is required.

Practice and Apply Use the related word in parentheses to help you determine the meaning of each boldface word. Check your work by consulting a dictionary.

1. (discreet) Some people may consider calling children overweight to be an **indiscretion.**
2. (impede) Members of Parliament who disagree with Osborne might be an **impediment** to passing a sugar tax.
3. (consume) Obesity in children has been blamed on **consumption** of sugary drinks.
4. (suppose) Osborne's **presupposition** for his proposal is that sugary drinks are the main cause of childhood obesity.
5. (exclude) Osborne's proposal has **exclusionary** measures for milk and fruit juices.

776   Unit 6

ENGLISH LEARNER SUPPORT

Vocabulary Strategy Show students how to use a thesaurus to find related words to complete word webs using the vocabulary words. Use the diagram below as an example.

Students should use each word in a sentence to show the relationship to the circled word.

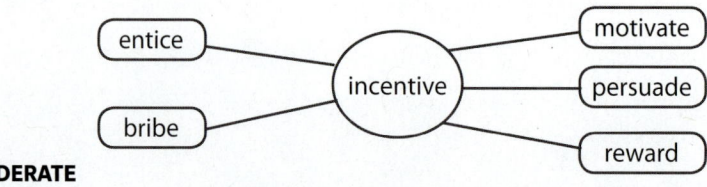

MODERATE

RESPOND

LANGUAGE CONVENTIONS:
Relative Pronouns and Relative Clauses

Good writers look for opportunities to combine short, choppy sentences into longer ones. This helps to connect ideas and vary sentence structure. One way to combine sentences is to use relative pronouns and relative clauses. **Relative pronouns** are used to help identify or provide more information about the person or thing that is being discussed. The noun or pronoun that a relative clause modifies is the **antecedent** of the relative pronoun. The chart shows the relative pronouns and explains how to use them.

RELATIVE PRONOUN(S)	USED TO MODIFY
who, whom	people
which	things
that, whose	people or things

> Go to **The Adjective Clause** in the **Grammar Studio** for more on relative pronouns and clauses.

Read these sentences:

> The tax is intended to help reduce the amount of sugar in popular drinks.
>
> The tax will be implemented two years from now.

Now read the sentence below, which combines the first two sentences into one by using a relative pronoun.

> The tax, (which) will be implemented two years from now, is intended to help reduce the amount of sugar in popular drinks.

In the sentence above, *which* is used because the antecedent of the relative pronoun is a thing. The relative pronoun *which* begins a **relative clause** that describes the tax. This clause can also be called an adjective clause.

Practice and Apply Complete the table below. First, identify the antecedent. Then, use a relative clause to combine each pair of sentences. Circle the relative pronoun and underline the relative clause in your combined sentence.

SENTENCES	COMBINED SENTENCE
1. The speaker gave a speech about sugar tax. 2. The speaker answered questions that followed.	The speaker, (who) gave a speech about the sugar tax, answered questions that followed.
1. The soft drink companies were aware of the problem. 2. The soft drink companies began to reduce the amount of sugar in their products.	The soft drink companies, (which) were aware of the problem, began to reduce the amount of sugar in their products.
1. The schools sought extra funding from the government. 2. The schools agreed to lengthen school days.	The schools, (whose) athletic programs sought funding from the government, agreed to lengthen school days.

Budget 2016: George Osborne's Speech 777

ENGLISH LEARNER SUPPORT

Language Conventions Have students find the **relative pronouns** in each sentence. Advanced students can separate the sentence into two sentences and discuss the advantages of combining them.

1. Our favorite sandwich shop, *where* we eat lunch every day, is closing.
2. The runner, *who* usually runs short distances, ran a marathon.
3. This seminar, *which* I attend every year, is about social media.
   MODERATE/LIGHT

APPLY

LANGUAGE CONVENTIONS:
Relative Pronouns and Relative Clauses

Tell students that relative pronouns are very helpful in combining sentences in varied patterns. Using different sentence structures helps develop the writer's voice and keeps the reader or listener engaged.

Review page 777 with students. Provide the following additional practice in combining two sentences into one using a **relative pronoun** and a **relative clause.**

- Money from the tax will help students.
- The money will be used to increase physical activity in schools.

Combined sentence:

- The money *that* comes from the sugar tax will be used to increase physical activity in schools.

Practice and Apply Direct students to use relative pronouns and relative clauses as they combine the sentences on page 777.

Possible Answers: *See completed chart on page 777.*

PLAN

MENTOR TEXT

WILL THE SUGAR TAX STOP CHILDHOOD OBESITY?

Editorial by Chris Hall

> This editorial serves as a **mentor text,** a model for students to follow when they come to the Unit 6 Writing Task: Write an Argument.

GENRE ELEMENTS
EDITORIAL

Remind students that **editorial** writers need to establish **credibility** so audiences will take their opinions seriously. Editorial writers might directly state their qualifications as experts in a field, or they may describe personal experiences with the issues at stake. In this lesson, students will evaluate the arguments and counterarguments in an editorial.

LEARNING OBJECTIVES

- Evaluate arguments and counterarguments.
- Conduct research about taxes in the United Kingdom.
- Write an opinion essay about an argument.
- Participate in a discussion.
- Use the Greek suffix -ize.
- Use rhetorical questions.
- **Language** Ask rhetorical questions using conditional verbs.

TEXT COMPLEXITY

Quantitative Measures	Will the Sugar Tax Stop Childhood Obesity?	Lexile: 1260L
Qualitative Measures	**Ideas Presented** Simple, single meaning. Literal, explicit, and direct. Purpose and stance clear.	
	Structures Used Persuasive. Use of appeals and evidence to support claim.	
	Language Used Complex and varied sentence structure.	
	Knowledge Required Requires some specialized knowledge of nutrition and governmental tax system.	

PLAN

Online Ed

RESOURCES

- Unit 6 Response Log
- 🔊 Selection Audio
- 📖 Reading Studio: Notice & Note
- 📊 Level Up Tutorial: Analyzing Arguments
- 📄 Writing Studio: Evaluating Sources
- 💬 Speaking and Listening Studio: Participating in Collaborative Discussions
- 🔵 Vocabulary Studio: Analyzing Word Structure
- ✓ "Will the Sugar Tax Stop Childhood Obesity?" Selection Test

SUMMARIES

English

In this editorial, British personal trainer Chris Hall claims that the tax on sugar is not enough to reduce or eliminate childhood obesity. He argues that people should be more concerned with children reducing food consumption, especially unhealthy foods, and getting sufficient exercise.

Spanish

En este editorial, el entrenador personal británico, Chris Hall, afirma que el impuesto al azúcar no es suficiente para reducir o eliminar la obesidad infantil. Alega que los padres deben ocuparse más de que sus hijos reduzcan el consumo de alimentos, especialmente de alimentos poco saludables, y de que hagan suficiente ejercicio.

SMALL-GROUP OPTIONS

Have students work in small groups and pairs to read and discuss the selection.

Silent Sustained Reading

- Set a timer for fifteen minutes.
- Have students read the editorial silently until the timer rings.
- Suggest that students keep lists of any unfamiliar words they want to look up after reading.
- Ask students to record the title, date, and number of pages read in reading logs.

Pinwheel Discussion

- Arrange students in groups of eight with four students seated facing in and four students seated facing out.
- After reading a paragraph of the selection, pose a question to students for discussion. For example: *Why is the writer of this editorial a credible source?*
- Students in the inner circle remain stationary throughout the discussion. Students in the outer circle move to their right after discussing each question.

Will the Sugar Tax Stop Childhood Obesity? **778B**

PLAN

Text X-Ray: English Learner Support
for "Will the Sugar Tax Stop Childhood Obesity?"

Use the Text X-Ray and the supports and scaffolds in the Teacher's Edition to help guide students at different proficiency levels through the selection.

INTRODUCE THE SELECTION
DISCUSS CONSUMPTION AND OBESITY

In this lesson, students will need to be able to discuss how consumption of food and drink is related to obesity.

Provide the following explanations:
- *Consumption* is the act of eating or drinking.
- *Obesity* refers to the state of being very overweight.

Have students use prior knowledge to discuss how consumption habits can lead to obesity. Provide sentence frames, such as: *The consumption of ____ can lead to obesity. Obesity can be caused by the consumption of too much ____.*

CULTURAL REFERENCES

The following words or phrases may be unfamiliar to students:

- *the million-dollar question* (paragraph 1): idiom used to signal that a particular question is important and hard to answer
- *drive down* (paragraph 3): *lower*
- *to point the finger* (paragraph 5): *to accuse*
- *stand a fighting chance* (paragraph 11): *to have the possibility of success if a great effort is made*

LISTENING

Understand Main Ideas

Tell students that they can ask themselves *who, what, where, when,* and *why* questions in order to understand what an editorial will be about.

Use the following supports with students at varying proficiency levels:

- Read aloud the first paragraph and ask questions. Accept one-word answers or have students point to the words in the text that answer the questions. For example: *Who made the sugar tax? (United Kingdom government) What will the tax help stop? (obesity crisis)* **SUBSTANTIAL**
- Have partners take turns reading aloud the first four paragraphs to each other. Then, have them ask each other *wh-* questions about what they just heard. **MODERATE**
- Have partners take turns reading aloud the first four paragraphs to each other. Then, have them ask each other *wh-* questions about what they just heard. Have them read the rest of the article and have them state the main idea of each paragraph. **LIGHT**

SPEAKING

Ask Rhetorical Questions

Remind students that rhetorical questions are questions that are either so obvious they don't need to be answered, or the answer is something to think about. Help students ask rhetorical questions.

Use the following supports with students at varying proficiency levels:

- Model simple rhetorical questions and have students practice asking them. For example: *Did you know that sodas can be bad for your health? Will a tax keep people from buying sugary drinks?* **SUBSTANTIAL**
- Point out the conditional verbs from the Beginning activity. Then, have partners use conditional verbs like *can, could, will, would, may,* and *might* to ask each other rhetorical questions that have obvious answers about familiar topics. **MODERATE**
- Have partners choose familiar topics and use three conditional verbs to ask each other rhetorical questions that have obvious answers. Then, have them use the verbs to ask rhetorical questions that need time to consider before answering. **LIGHT**

READING

Use Graphic Organizers

Tell students that they can use graphic organizers to help them keep track of unfamiliar words as they read. After reading, they can use reference materials and classroom support to define the words, then reread the text again.

Use the following supports with students of varying proficiency levels:

- Reread the first paragraph with students. Have them use a word web with the word *halt* written in the center. Show students how to use a thesaurus. Help small groups use peer support to fill in the web with related words and phrases. **SUBSTANTIAL**
- Have students reread the first two paragraphs and use two-column charts for any unfamiliar words. Guide them to use reference materials to help them write definitions in their charts. Then, have them reread the paragraphs, noting if their understanding has changed. **MODERATE**
- Show students how to draw and use a Frayer Model. Guide them to draw squares of four boxes and write *obesity* in circles in the center. Have them label the other four boxes: Definition; Characteristics; Examples; Non-examples. Tell pairs to discuss their completed Frayer Models. **LIGHT**

WRITING

Use Vocabulary

Provide a word bank of basic and content vocabulary students can use when writing their essays, such as: *In my opinion, the author claims that, sugar tax, obesity, consumption, logical, convincing,* and *poorly supports the idea.*

Use the following supports with students of varying proficiency levels:

- Have students practice writing the vocabulary terms. Have them sound out the letters as they write them. **SUBSTANTIAL**
- Have students write each word or phrase from the word bank in a sentence. **MODERATE**
- Have students write paragraphs using all the terms from the word bank. Tell them they can use similar words, such as *convinced* or *supported*. Pairs can exchange paragraphs and revise for correct spelling and verb tense. **LIGHT**

TEACH

? Connect to the ESSENTIAL QUESTION

Remind students that the role of the government is to protect its citizens. Tell them to consider when government responsibility ends and individual responsibility begins. Ask students to think about this as they respond to the essential question.

MENTOR TEXT

At the end of the unit, students will be asked to write arguments about a social or political issues in their community, such as recycling or homelessness. "Will the Sugar Tax Stop Childhood Obesity?" provides a model for how a writer can present an argument in a cohesive way, using evidence, rhetorical questions, and several kinds of persuasive appeals.

COMPARE ACROSS GENRES

Tell students that to think critically, they must be aware of the persuasive techniques used by others. Students should always seek knowledge, but maintain a skeptical attitude to be sure that they recognize not only persuasive appeals, but logical fallacies, misinformation, or exaggerated statistics.

COLLABORATE & COMPARE

EDITORIAL

WILL THE SUGAR TAX STOP CHILDHOOD OBESITY?

by **Chris Hall**
pages 781–783

COMPARE ARGUMENTS

Now that you've read "Budget 2016: George Osborne's Speech," read an argument that takes a position opposing the one set forth in the speech. As you read, note the primary argument made by the writer and how he develops his argument with evidence and reasoning. Also notice whether the evidence ever causes you to question your own opinion on this matter. After you read both selections, you will collaborate with a small group on a final project.

 ESSENTIAL QUESTION:

When should the government interfere in our decisions?

SPEECH

BUDGET 2016: GEORGE OSBORNE'S SPEECH

by **George Osborne**
pages 771–772

Will the Sugar Tax Stop Childhood Obesity?

QUICK START

Think about a problem or issue in your school or community. What was one proposed solution? Did the solution effectively solve the problem or issue? What solution would you have proposed? Discuss your ideas with a partner.

EVALUATE ARGUMENTS

A strong argument clearly states a **claim,** or position on an issue, and has key ideas to back up that claim. It also provides sufficient evidence to support the claim and key ideas. **Evidence** may include facts, examples, statistics, and expert opinions.

In his editorial, Chris Hall makes an argument about the effectiveness of using a sugar tax on certain beverages to combat childhood obesity. As you read, use the questions below to help you evaluate the strength of his argument.

- **Claim:** Is Hall's claim about sugary drinks and the effectiveness of taxation credible and supported by sound reasons and evidence?
- **Reasoning:** Is Hall's argument based on logic? Does he introduce any logical fallacies or errors in presenting his conclusions? For example, does he make any generalizations that are too broad?
- **Evidence:** Are the facts, examples, and other details included in the article valid, authoritative, relevant, and sufficient?

EVALUATE COUNTERARGUMENTS

An effective argument anticipates opposing viewpoints and provides counterarguments to challenge or disprove them. A **counterargument** is an argument made to oppose another argument. In structuring a counterargument, a writer often acknowledges an opposing viewpoint or claim and then states or implies the counterargument which refutes that viewpoint, supporting it with facts and evidence.

OPPOSING VIEW	HALL'S COUNTERARGUMENT	HALL'S FACTS AND EVIDENCE
Increased consumption of sugar-sweetened beverages is impacting rising rates of obesity and type 2 diabetes.	Sugar-sweetened beverage consumption is rising, but it is not the root of the obesity and type 2 diabetes problem.	Less than 2% of weight gain is caused by sugary drinks.

As you read the editorial, note the counterarguments Hall presents, paying attention to the quality of the facts and evidence that support them.

GENRE ELEMENTS: EDITORIAL

- states an opinion rather than being objective
- appears in a dedicated editorial/opinion section of a newspaper or broadcast
- presents the ideas of the news staff or is submitted by an independent writer
- may note opposing viewpoints and provide counterarguments to disprove them

TEACH

CRITICAL VOCABULARY

Write the vocabulary words on the board. Read them aloud to students one at a time. Have students choose words and discuss possible meanings with partners. Permit volunteers to share possible meanings and provide sentences using the words. Have them complete the activity on page 780 of the student edition.

Answers:

1. *demonize*
2. *consumption*
3. *attribute*
4. *theorize*

■ English Learner Support

Use Cognates Tell students that the following words have Spanish, Portuguese, Italian and French cognates: *attribute/atributo; consumption/consumo/consumo/consommation.* **ALL LEVELS**

LANGUAGE CONVENTIONS

Rhetorical Questions Explain to students that writers can use rhetorical questions to capture the attention of their audience. Rhetorical questions are not meant to be answered, but are used to get the audience thinking about something important, involve them emotionally, or simply prepare them for what will be coming next.

ANNOTATION MODEL

Remind students of the annotation model on page 780, which suggests underlining phrases that indicate how the writer develops the argument. Point out that they may follow this suggestion or use their own system for marking up the selection in their write-in text. They may want to color-code their annotations by using highlighters. Their notes in the margin may include questions about ideas that are unclear or topics they want to learn more about.

780 Unit 6

 **GET READY**

CRITICAL VOCABULARY

| theorize | attribute | demonize | consumption |

To preview the Critical Vocabulary words, use context clues and your knowledge of word roots and suffixes to fill in the correct word for each sentence.

1. I know you do not agree with them, but there is no need to _____ them at every opportunity.
2. My _____ of fresh fruit increases in the summer when my favorite kinds of fruit are in season.
3. I _____ my success in school to my good teachers and study habits.
4. Historians can _____, but nobody knows for sure what Shakespeare was doing during his "lost years."

LANGUAGE CONVENTIONS

Rhetorical Questions In this lesson, you will learn how writers use **rhetorical questions** to enhance arguments and effectively convey ideas. As you read "Will the Sugar Tax Stop Childhood Obesity?" watch for questions that the author uses to get the reader to think critically about and get emotionally involved in the topic of discussion.

ANNOTATION MODEL  **NOTICE & NOTE**

As you read, note how the author develops his argument. In the model, you can see one reader's notes about how the author introduces his argument.

> With the release of the United Kingdom's 2016 budget, it seems everyone is talking about the sugar tax. Over the last few days I've read several opinions on whether this is a good idea and ultimately, whether it will help to halt the obesity crisis—the million dollar question!

The writer sets himself up as an authority on the topic, but he has gotten his knowledge from reading opinions. Is his argument based on solid facts, or on the opinions of others?

The writer prepares the reader for an argument against the sugar tax by questioning whether it is a "good idea" and pointing out the high stakes involved: public health and large amounts of money.

780 Unit 6

BACKGROUND

Chris Hall is a personal trainer based in Oxford, England. As part of his stated mission, Hall feels compelled to keep up to date with the latest research on health, nutrition, and exercise. He writes articles about health-related issues for a fitness blog and for major news websites.

WILL THE SUGAR TAX STOP CHILDHOOD OBESITY?

Editorial by Chris Hall

PREPARE TO COMPARE

As you read, pay attention to the argument that the author is making. Note any details that support his argument or errors in logic that undermine his argument. Paying attention to how he presents his message and employs reasoning will allow you to compare his argument to that of George Osborne, the author of the first selection.

1   With the release of the United Kingdom's 2016 budget, it seems everyone is talking about the sugar tax. Over the last few days I've read several opinions on whether this is a good idea and ultimately, whether it will help to halt the obesity crisis—the million dollar question!

2   The Government's new tax on sugary drinks will be split into two bands: the first for total sugar above 5g per 100ml, and the second for when total sugar exceeds 8g per 100ml. To give you some context, a typical cola contains 10.6g of sugar per 100ml, while typical orange juice has 8g.

3   The tax won't be placed on pure fruit juices or milk based drinks. But in an effort to drive down childhood obesity, is this the right approach?

4   There's no denying it: our consumption of sugar-sweetened beverages (SSBs) has risen in recent decades, and there is

NOTICE & NOTE

Notice & Note

Use the side margins to notice and note signposts in the text.

LANGUAGE CONVENTIONS
Annotate: Mark the rhetorical question in paragraph 3.
Analyze: How does the author use this rhetorical question to develop his argument?

Will the Sugar Tax Stop Childhood Obesity?   781

ENGLISH LEARNER SUPPORT

Learn New Expressions Tell students that the term "million-dollar question" is an idiom. An idiom is a phrase that has a different meaning than the literal interpretation of the words within a phrase. This term does not mean that the question cost a million dollars or that the person who answers it will earn a million dollars. It means that it is a very important question. Discuss with students how the author uses this term in paragraph 1.
MODERATE/LIGHT

TEACH

BACKGROUND

Chris Hall is the founder and executive trainer of Hall Personal Training in Oxford, England. He published his editorial in the *Huffington Post* in March of 2016. He specializes in nutrition, weight loss, endurance, and strength training as they relate to overall health.

PREPARE TO COMPARE

Direct students to use the Prepare to Compare prompt to focus their reading.

LANGUAGE CONVENTIONS

Tell students that rhetorical questions are often used to prepare audience members to open their minds to a new idea or solution as well hearing about the author's position. (**Answer:** *The question is used to introduce the author's argument against the sugar tax. By asking if the tax is the "right approach," he makes it clear that he does not agree with the tax even though he has not stated his opinion yet.*)

For **listening** and **reading support** for students at varying proficiency levels, see the **Text X-Ray** on pages 778C and 778D.

Will the Sugar Tax Stop Childhood Obesity?   **781**

TEACH

✏ EVALUATE COUNTERARGUMENTS

Tell students that in paragraph 8, Hall uses an effective technique by appearing to agree with his opponents as he begins his counterargument. (**Answer:** *The author's counterargument is that even though the government is correct to acknowledge and take action against the obesity crisis, the government's actions will not be effective.*)

✏ EVALUATE ARGUMENTS

Tell students as they read to look for the different solutions that Hall proposes. (**Answer:** *Hall supports the recommendation to address overeating and overconsumption of fatty foods to combat obesity with sound evidence. He presents information about the increase in calorie intake in paragraph 6 and gives comparative statistics about calories that come from other types of food in paragraph 7. Although the decline in physical activity is mentioned, Hall fails to provide statistical evidence to support that exercise is more effective than reduction in sugary drink intake at combating obesity.*)

CRITICAL VOCABULARY

theorize: The editorial uses this term to discuss a premise that sugary drinks create obesity.

ASK STUDENTS how they would theorize the cause of childhood obesity. (*I would theorize that a lack of exercise and a diet rich in fat causes childhood obesity.*)

attribute: The editorial uses this term to discuss the causes of obesity.

ASK STUDENTS what behaviors they would attribute *to* a healthy lifestyle. (*A healthy lifestyle can be attributed to a healthy diet, rest, exercise, and lack of stress.*)

demonize: The editorial uses this term to overemphasize the effect of sugar on obesity.

ASK STUDENTS for examples of ideas, activities, or objects that have become demonized. (*Students might mention senior trips, violent video games, or cell phones.*)

consumption: The editorial uses this word to discuss the amount of sugar ingested.

ASK STUDENTS what they think their daily consumption of sugar might be. (*Answers will vary.*)

782   Unit 6

✏ NOTICE & NOTE

theorize
(thē´ə-rīz, thîr´īz) *v.* to formulate theories or a theory; speculate.

attribute
(ə-trĭb´yōōt) *v.* to regard as arising from a particular cause or source; ascribe.

demonize
(dē´mə-nīz) *v.* to represent as evil or diabolic.

consumption
(kən-sŭmp´shən) *n.* an amount consumed.

EVALUATE COUNTERARGUMENTS
Annotate: Mark evidence in paragraphs 8–9 that contradicts the opposing view that increased prices will force people to drink healthier beverages.

Analyze: What counterargument does Hall make to refute the government's view?

EVALUATE ARGUMENTS
Annotate: In paragraphs 10–11, mark the author's recommendations for combating the obesity crisis.

Evaluate: Which claim or recommendation is best supported by the evidence the author presents? Cite examples from the article to support your answer.

782   Unit 6

---

evidence to suggest that this increase is having an impact on obesity and the rising number of cases of type 2 diabetes. But sugary drinks alone are not the root of the problem.

5   The number of articles, statements and scientific studies linking sugary drinks to weight gain makes it easy to point the finger, and come to the conclusion that sugary drinks should be eliminated. In theory, this makes a lot of sense, but when you compare the theoretical data with the observed data, you can see that the actual weight gain associated with sugary drinks is in fact ten times less than was originally **theorized**, and actually, less than 2% of weight gain can be **attributed** to drinking sugary drinks!

6   It's only in the last ten years or so that sugar has been **demonized** for our increasing waistlines. Interestingly, our total **consumption** of sugar in the UK has actually fallen by 20 per cent in the last 30 years! In fact, it is our eating patterns as a whole that are to blame. If you look at the most recent data on calorie consumption, we are both eating more (approximately 445 calories more) but also moving less than we were 40 years ago.

7   Interestingly out of the 445 extra calories we're now consuming, less than 10 percent are from sweeteners/sugar; that's only 45 calories! The remaining calories can be blamed on our increased consumption of refined grains such as french fries, potatoes, crisps[1] and baked goods, along with fats and oils.

8   Now, placing a tax on sugary drinks does indicate that the Government is realizing the extent of the obesity crisis and starting to do something about it. But let's be honest, the price isn't going to increase so dramatically that it will force those who buy them to find a healthier alternative. In fact, a lot of the 'healthier' alternatives are probably going to have just the same impact (if not worse!) than if you were to choose a sugary drink.

9   Milkshakes, flavored waters and off-the-shelf cold coffees can contain nearly as much sugar, if not more, than your average can of soda and they tend to be higher in calories! In fact, if you compare a standard 471ml bottle of chocolate milkshake to a can of cola you'll find the milkshake has an extra 203 calories. Yet these drinks are exempt from the tax!

10   If we are serious about tackling childhood obesity, then we must not be naive enough as to think that pushing up the cost of fizzy drinks is going to have a noticeable impact. It is more important to focus on the issue of over-eating in general, and reducing our consumption of delicious but unhealthy foods such as refined grains and fatty foods.

11   It's also crucially important that we remain active and encourage our children to put the digital tablet down, get up off the sofa and out into the fresh air. Only then do I believe we'll stand a fighting chance of tackling the obesity crisis. . . .

---
[1] **crisps:** a British term for potato chips.

APPLYING ACADEMIC VOCABULARY

☐ arbitrary   ☐ controversy   ☐ convince   ☑ denote   ☑ undergo

Write and Discuss Have students turn to partners to discuss the following questions. Guide students to include the academic vocabulary words *denote* and *undergo* in their responses. Ask volunteers to share their responses with the class.

- What does the tax on sugary drinks **denote** about the government's priorities?
- What kind of changes might people need to **undergo** to enable them to lose weight?

12 Any move to tackle the obesity crisis must be praised, but the issue is much more deeply rooted in our lifestyles than what we drink. Any serious attempt to tackle the crisis must face up to this fact, and make real efforts to encourage change.

CHECK YOUR UNDERSTANDING

Answer these questions before moving on to the **Analyze the Text** section on the following page.

1. Which sentence best describes the author's opinion of the sugar tax?
   A The sugar tax is not a useful response to the obesity crisis.
   B The sugar tax will cause a substantial decrease in purchases of sugar-sweetened beverages.
   C The sugar tax will motivate British people to be more active.
   D The sugar tax does not address the main causes of increased obesity rates in Britain.

2. Which of the following would the author of the article most likely support?
   F A sugar tax that is higher than the one proposed
   G A public health campaign to educate citizens on nutritious food choices
   H A tax on all beverages with sugar, including milkshakes and fruit juice
   J A public health campaign to educate citizens on how sugar consumption causes weight gain

3. Read this sentence from the speech.

   It's only in the last ten years or so that sugar has been demonized for our increasing waistlines.

   This sentence shows that the author believes —
   A the size of the average person's waistline has increased during the past ten years because of sugar consumption
   B overconsumption of sugar for the past ten years is primarily responsible for the country's current obesity crisis
   C scientists have found solid evidence linking obesity to sugar consumption during the past ten years
   D people have put too much emphasis on the role of sugar in the obesity crisis during the past ten years

APPLY

ANALYZE THE TEXT

Possible answers:

1. **DOK 2:** *The author argues that the sugar tax will be ineffective in reducing childhood obesity because it will not raise sugary drink prices enough to reduce consumption. The sugar tax does not address the main causes of increased rates of obesity; therefore, it does not promote decreasing caloric consumption, increasing physical activity, or changing diets to healthier choices.*

2. **DOK 4:** *The author most likely chooses to use counterarguments because his editorial is a direct response to Osborne's speech. Because the opposing claims had already been presented in the speech, the author directly addresses them to provide context and establish his credibility.*

3. **DOK 2:** *He believes that they are not good for people, but also that they are not any worse than other beverages. He doesn't see them as a threat to public health on their own.*

4. **DOK 3:** *The author of the argument makes suitable claims but does not always follow them up with solid evidence. He does not cite sources of facts and statistics. He links ideas that are not directly related. In paragraph 8, he claims the sugar tax will not raise the price enough to force people to buy healthier beverages. Instead of providing evidence of how the tax will impact prices, he proposes that "healthier" substitutes may even provide worse consequences. The link between the first claim and the second claim is not logical.*

5. **DOK 4:** *The author could strengthen his argument by backing unsupported claims with citations. He claims that people are moving less than they did 40 years ago. He also claims that the tax will not raise prices significantly enough to affect consumer behavior. Neither claim is substantiated with facts, data, or resources.*

RESEARCH

Tell students that BBC News, part of the British Broadcasting Company, might provide some information for this activity. Remind them to use other sources, maybe one from the United States. Remind them to look at the dates of articles to get the most recent information.

 **RESPOND**

ANALYZE THE TEXT

Support your responses with evidence from the text. **NOTEBOOK**

1. **Summarize** In your own words, describe the argument the author makes about the sugar tax. Explain why he feels the tax will or will not be effective.

2. **Analyze** Consider the most likely source of the opposing viewpoints that the author addresses with his counterarguments—George Osborne's speech. Why does the author most likely choose to structure parts of his editorial using counterarguments?

3. **Infer** How does the author of the article view sugar-sweetened beverages?

4. **Evaluate** How well does the author develop his argument? Does it contain any errors in logic that undermine the argument?

5. **Critique** Identify an aspect of the author's argument that is weak or lacks support. How could the author strengthen that part of the argument?

RESEARCH

RESEARCH TIP
When you are looking for credible and up-to-date information on a recent or developing news story, be sure to evaluate the type of sources you find. Although opinion pieces, editorials, and blog posts can contain valuable information and give the reader insight into multiple sides of a topic, they may not always cite the most accurate or up-to-date information, and may only present information that supports the author's point of view or argument.

When Hall wrote the editorial "Will the Sugar Tax Stop Childhood Obesity?" the tax had not yet been implemented. Conduct research to locate the most recent information about how the tax works and what effects it may have had in the United Kingdom. Use the chart to record the results of your research.

IMPLEMENTATION DATE	*projected to go into effect April 2018*
AMOUNT OF THE TAX	*projected 2017: 18p/liter for drinks greater than 5 g per 100 mL; 24p/liter for drinks greater than 8 g per 100 mL*
HEALTH EFFECTS OF THE TAX	*decreases in childhood tooth decay, type 2 diabetes, and possible 3.7 million cases of obesity prevented over the first decade of the tax*
TOTAL EARNINGS FROM THE TAX	*earnings of 520 million pounds for first year of tax, possibly lower if drink companies reformulate drinks to contain less sugar and avoid the tax*

WHEN STUDENTS STRUGGLE . . .

Reteaching: Analyze Arguments Tell students that recognizing supporting details is a key strategy to analyzing an argument. Let students work in pairs to find supporting details.

Claim Statement	Supporting details
Sugary drinks are not the problem.	Sugar consumption down 20% in 30 years
Eating patterns are to blame.	Potatoes, chips, fries baked good, fats, and oils

 For additional support, go to the **Reading Studio** and assign the following **Level Up tutorial: Analyzing Arguments.**

RESPOND

CREATE AND DISCUSS

Evaluate an Argument Write a three-paragraph opinion essay in which you evaluate the author's argument and use of counterarguments in "Will the Sugar Tax Stop Childhood Obesity?" Consider reviewing your notes and annotations in the text before you begin.

- ❏ Introduce your essay by identifying the author's primary argument and indicating your evaluation of the argument.
- ❏ Then, explain your evaluation of the author's argument. Include details about how the author develops specific lines of reasoning and counterarguments.
- ❏ In your final paragraph, sum up your evaluation of the author's argument and offer praise or constructive criticism as necessary.

Discuss In a small group, discuss your opinions about the author's arguments in "Will the Sugar Tax Stop Childhood Obesity?" Are they logical, convincing, and well supported, or illogical, unconvincing, and poorly supported? Are all parts of the argument developed equally?

- ❏ Review the editorial with your group to identify the main arguments and counterarguments the author uses.
- ❏ Then, discuss your individual evaluations of those arguments and counterarguments. As you discuss, listen closely and ask each other questions to help clarify when ideas are unclear.
- ❏ Finally, end the discussion by identifying similarities, differences, and/or common themes in the evaluations of each member of your group.

Go to the **Writing Studio** to find out more about evaluating sources.

Go to the **Speaking and Listening Studio: Participating in Collaborative Discussions** for more.

RESPOND TO THE ESSENTIAL QUESTION

 When should the government interfere in our decisions?

Gather Information Review your annotations and notes on "Will the Sugar Tax Stop Childhood Obesity?" Then, add relevant details to your Response Log. As you determine which information to include, think about:

- the role government influence plays in everyday life
- what kinds of decisions should always be left in the hands of individuals
- who gets to determine what is the "common good"

ACADEMIC VOCABULARY

As you write and discuss what you learned from the editorial, be sure to use the Academic Vocabulary words. Check off each of the words that you use.

- ❏ arbitrary
- ❏ controversy
- ❏ convince
- ❏ denote
- ❏ undergo

APPLY

CREATE AND DISCUSS

Evaluate an Argument Remind students to use their annotation notes to help them develop their arguments.

The first paragraph should include the author's claim and the students' reactions to that claim. The second paragraph is where students need to provide evidence for their reactions. This paragraph should be detailed, providing specific examples that support the students' evaluations.

The third paragraph should include constructive criticism. Remind students that even if they agree with Hall, they should provide examples or suggestions on how the editorial could be improved.

 For **writing support** for students at varying proficiency levels, see the **Text X-Ray** on page 778D.

Discuss Remind students they should develop ground rules for their discussion. Some processes they should consider include who is going to talk first, how feedback will be provided, and how disagreements will be handled. Remind students that clarifying questions should be asked of others to be sure there is understanding. Each group member should record similarities, differences, and common themes found in the evaluations.

RESPOND TO THE ESSENTIAL QUESTION

Allow time for students to add details from "Will the Sugar Tax Stop Childhood Obesity?" to their Unit 6 Response Logs.

APPLY

CRITICAL VOCABULARY

Answers:

1. attribute; When you attribute something to someone or something, you are either blaming them for it or giving them credit for it.

2. theorize; Both hypotheses and theories are types of guesses.

3. consumption; Consumption is a measurement of how much is used or eaten.

4. demonize; To demonize something is to make it appear evil or in a negative light.

VOCABULARY STRATEGY:
The Greek Suffix *-ize*

Tell students when they take a noun and add the suffix *-ize* the word becomes a verb.

Review the meanings of the suffix *-ize* as found on Student Edition page 786.

Provide additional examples:

- *Summary* is a noun meaning a brief synopsis of something.
- To *summarize* means you are engaging in making a brief synopsis of something.
- *Critic* is a noun meaning someone who analyzes.
- To *criticize* could mean to become like a critic or to engage in analyzing.

Practice and Apply

Possible answers:

1. Here *-ize* means to perform, engage in, or produce. To agonize is to produce or engage in agony about something.

2. Here *-ize* means to cause to be or become. To colonize something is to cause it to be or make it into a colony.

3. Here *-ize* means to cause to be or become. To familiarize is to become familiar with something or to make someone familiar with something.

4. Here *-ize* means to treat as. To satirize is to treat something in a satirical way.

5. Here *-ize* means to conform to or resemble. To standardize something is to make it conform to a standard.

 **RESPOND**

WORD BANK
theorize
attribute
demonize
consumption

 Go to the **Vocabulary Studio: Analyzing Word Structure** for more on Greek suffixes.

CRITICAL VOCABULARY

Practice and Apply With a partner, discuss and then write down an answer to each of the following questions. Then, work together to write a sentence for each vocabulary word.

1. Which vocabulary word goes with *blame* and *credit*? Why?
2. Which vocabulary word goes with *hypothesis*? Why?
3. Which vocabulary word goes with *use*? Why?
4. Which vocabulary word goes with *negative*? Why?

VOCABULARY STRATEGY:
The Greek Suffix *-ize*

The Greek suffix *-ize* has several related meanings. A few of its meanings are listed below:

- to cause to be or become
- to cause to conform to or resemble
- to treat as
- to perform, engage in, or produce

Understanding the different meanings of the suffix *-ize* can help you determine the meaning of a word when you encounter it. Take a look at an example from "Will the Sugar Tax Stop Childhood Obesity?" below.

> It's only in the last ten years or so that sugar has been <u>demonized</u> for our increasing waistlines.

In the word *demonize*, the suffix *-ize* means "to treat as." Hall suggests that opponents of sugar are representing it as something evil or diabolic.

Practice and Apply Determine which meaning of the Greek suffix *-ize* helps you best understand the meaning of these words. Write your own definition of the word, incorporating the meaning of the Greek suffix.

1. agonize
2. colonize
3. familiarize
4. satirize
5. standardize

 ENGLISH LEARNER SUPPORT

Vocabulary Strategy Tell students **attribute** is used to say that one thing is the result of another. In the editorial, "Weight gain can be attributed to sugary drinks." means sugary drinks cause weight gain. Ask students what this example means: "Weight gain can be attributed to lack of exercise." *(Lack of exercise causes weight gain.)* Have them answer the questions below:

What causes good English? *(Good English is attributed to daily practice.)*

What can be attributed to success? *(Success is attributed to hard work.)* **LIGHT**

RESPOND

LANGUAGE CONVENTIONS:
Rhetorical Questions

A **rhetorical question** is a question to which no answer is expected. Rhetorical questions are often used to emphasize meaning and evoke an emotional or thoughtful response in the reader. Writers and speakers also use them to suggest that their claims are so obvious everyone should agree with them. Employed appropriately, rhetorical questions can enhance an argument.

In "Will the Sugar Tax Stop Childhood Obesity?" Hall uses a rhetorical question in the third paragraph:

> The tax won't be placed on pure fruit juices or milk based drinks. But in an effort to drive down childhood obesity, is this the right approach?

Hall does not expect his readers to have a ready answer for the question. Rather, he uses the question to make readers think critically about both the claim of those who promote the sugar tax and about his own claim that the tax will not have the desired effect.

By starting the question with the word *but*, he first signals to the reader he is going to introduce a new idea that is at odds with what he just described. Then, he uses the strong phrase *drive down* to emphasize the idea that firm action and struggle will be necessary to combat childhood obesity. Finally, he uses the emotionally charged word *right*, which encourages the reader to consider the question in ethical terms of right and wrong.

Practice and Apply Reread your evaluation of Hall's argument, looking for places where you could use rhetorical questions to strengthen your position. Rewrite one of your paragraphs so it includes a rhetorical question.

Will the Sugar Tax Stop Childhood Obesity? 787

APPLY

LANGUAGE CONVENTIONS:
Rhetorical Questions

Explain to students that **rhetorical questions** are questions asked without the intention of receiving answers. They are often used by writers for many reasons:

- to emphasize meaning.
- to evoke an emotional response.
- to stimulate thinking.
- to suggest the answer is so obvious that agreement is assumed.

After reviewing the sample of the **rhetorical question** in the editorial on Student Edition page 787, explain to students Hall utilizes other persuasive techniques within his **rhetorical question.** He has carefully chosen the words in his rhetorical question to provide added emphasis. He appeals to the readers' emotions by using the phrase *drive down,* indicating urgency. The phrase *right approach* implies that ethical readers should agree with his approach.

Practice and Apply Remind students rhetorical questions are very effective if used properly. Although there are several places rhetorical questions could have been asked, overuse of them would be ineffective and possibly condescending.

> For **speaking support** for students at varying proficiency levels, see the **Text X-Ray** on page 778D.

 ENGLISH LEARNER SUPPORT

Language Conventions To help students understand rhetorical questions, give the following examples of rhetorical questions and when they might be used.

Are you kidding me? *(Implies something is unbelievable.)*

Can birds fly? *(Implies the answer is obvious. Often asked after a statement that can't be refuted.)*
LIGHT

Will the Sugar Tax Stop Childhood Obesity? **787**

APPLY

COMPARE ARGUMENTS

Compare and Synthesize Tell students that the word *synthesis* means the combination of ideas. When "*ize*" is added to *synthesis*, it means to engage in the combining of ideas. Tell students that in this activity, they will use their annotation notes to revisit the conclusions of both authors and then synthesize the information they provided, to form their own opinions.

ANALYZE THE TEXTS

Possible answers:

1. **DOK 4:** *Osborne and Hall give seemingly contradictory information about the health impact of sugary drinks. Osborne gives statistics to prove how dangerous they are, while Hall gives statistics to show that they do not have as large an impact as was thought. Readers of both arguments must carefully evaluate which source of information is more reliable and may need to do more research to clarify understanding.*

2. **DOK 3:** *Osborne believes in financial means of motivation. He believes that taxation can be used to reduce negative behaviors and funnel money into things that encourage good behaviors. Hall seems to believe that behavioral changes will grow out of greater awareness of the issues at stake and that financial motivators will not be effective.*

3. **DOK 4:** *Hall would most likely support Osborne's initiatives to increase physical education in schools. In paragraph 11, he specifically mentions that children need to be getting outside and staying more active.*

4. **DOK 4:** *Osborne's argument is more effective because it is more focused and logical. He has one main area of focus, the sugar tax and the evidence supporting its creation, and he sticks to proving his point. Hall introduces many interesting ideas, but some of them are not developed fully and lack support. His article skips around more, so that the logic he is using is not always clear, which undermines his argument.*

 RESPOND

Collaborate & Compare

COMPARE ARGUMENTS

Compare and Synthesize When you read just one argument, you primarily learn about only one point of view on a topic, even though the opposing point of view is usually acknowledged. Reading at least two arguments provides a more well-rounded and thorough understanding of the topic. When you compare two opposing arguments on the same topic, you can synthesize the information, taking into account all of the evidence provided by both arguments, as you evaluate each author's claim and determine your own opinion.

In a small group, complete the graphic organizer. Use the information you gather to decide whether you believe that a sugar tax will help reduce obesity in children.

BUDGET 2016: GEORGE OSBORNE'S SPEECH
Speech by George Osborne

WILL THE SUGAR TAX STOP CHILDHOOD OBESITY?
Editorial by Chris Hall

OSBORNE'S CONCLUSION	HALL'S CONCLUSION
Taxing sugary drinks will stop childhood obesity.	Focus on not over-eating, reduce high caloric foods, such as refined grains and fatty foods, put down electronic devices, and exercise.

MY CONCLUSION
Answers will vary

ANALYZE THE TEXTS

Discuss these questions in your group.

1. **Analyze** Which elements of the arguments offered by each author are most in conflict? How might the conflict affect readers?
2. **Compare** Both authors believe that people's behaviors need to change. How do their views on the best way to change behavior differ?
3. **Synthesize** Which part of Osborne's plan would Hall be most likely to support?
4. **Evaluate** Which author's argument do you find more effective and why?

788   Unit 6

 ENGLISH LEARNER SUPPORT

Express Ideas Provide students with sentence frames they can use to compare and evaluate the authors' arguments.

1. George Osborne concludes that taxing sugary drinks will _____. However, Chris Hall concludes that a sugar tax will _____.

2. I believe that _____'s argument is more effective because _____. He supports his claim by _____.   **MODERATE/LIGHT**

RESPOND

RESEARCH AND SHARE

Now your group can continue exploring the ideas in these texts by collaborating on research to present a public policy proposal for reducing obesity. Follow these steps:

1. **Develop Questions** In your group, brainstorm questions that you will need to research answers for in order to create your public policy proposal. Determine the most important questions and reach agreement on which group member will research each question. If you have more questions than group members, combine related questions before making research assignments.

2. **Gather Information** As you begin to research your question(s), make sure that the sources you consult are relevant, reliable, and credible. Although some overlap may be unavoidable, try to research only your own question(s) and not those of other group members so that each person has a meaningful share in the research process.

3. **Share Research** Once each group member has completed his or her research, discuss your findings as a group and take notes about the answer to each research question. You can use a table like the one below to track your group's research.

RESEARCH QUESTION	ANSWER
How much weekly exercise should children have?	Answers will vary
What are the health benefits of participating in team sports?	Answers will vary
Should children particpate in exercise classes?	Answers will vary
What is the recommended caloric intake for children?	Answers will vary

4. **Collaborate and Create** Now that your group has researched questions related to reducing obesity, it is time to develop your public policy. Discuss the findings as a group, and try to reach an agreement on a public policy addressing obesity that is supported by facts and evidence from your research. Working together and using your notes, draft a paragraph that details your public policy proposal. Be sure to explain your reasoning and back up your ideas with evidence.

Go to **Participating in Collaborative Discussions** in the **Speaking and Listening Studio** to learn more.

Collaborate & Compare 789

APPLY

RESEARCH AND SHARE

Ask students to consider the issue of rapid increase of obesity and the health problems associated with it. Tell them they will work in groups to write public policy statements.

1. **Develop Questions** Tell students that during the brainstorming process all questions should be written down. During the decision process is when questions can be revised, combined, or discarded. *(See annotations on page 789 for sample questions.)*

2. **Gather Information** Tell students if they come across information that one of their group members can use, give that person the resource so that it may help his or her efforts.

3. **Share Research** Students should use the graphic organizer provided to record everyone's research. Members should check to be sure the answers are answered completely.

4. **Collaborate and Create** If students have trouble choosing a specific policy, have them choose a policy that meets one of the following criteria:
   - the one that has the most direct and immediate impact on obesity.
   - the one that is easiest to implement.
   - the one that will most likely have the most buy-in from a community.

TO CHALLENGE STUDENTS...

Make a Speech Have students turn one of the policy statements into a political speech. Have them practice eye contact, intonation, pausing, and emphasis. If possible, visuals should be developed to illustrate statistics or facts. After the speech, students should ask for feedback from the audience on ways to improve the message and/or the delivery.

INDEPENDENT READING

READER'S CHOICE

Setting a Purpose Have students review their Unit 6 Response Log and think about what they've already learned about the role of government and the responsibilities they have to individuals and communities. As they choose their Independent Reading selections, encourage them to consider what more they want to know.

NOTICE & NOTE

Explain that some selections may contain multiple signposts; others may contain only one. Moreover, the same type of signpost can occur many times in the same text.

LEARNING MINDSET

Grit Tell students that hard work is an important part of developing a learning mindset. Remind them that our brains are like muscles; the more students exercise them, the stronger they become. Encourage students to look for opportunities to emerge from problems. Praise students for their effort, not just for successes.

INDEPENDENT READING

Reader's Choice

Setting a Purpose Select one or more of these options from your eBook to continue your exploration of the Essential Questions.

- Read the descriptions to see which text grabs your interest.
- Think about which genres you enjoy reading.

ESSENTIAL QUESTIONS Review the four Essential Questions for this unit on page 691.

Notice & Note

In this unit, you practiced noticing and noting the signposts and asking big questions about nonfiction. As you read independently, these signposts and others will aid your understanding. Below are the anchor questions to ask when you read literature and nonfiction.

Reading Literature: Stories, Poems, and Plays	
Signpost	Key Question
Contrasts and Contradictions	Why did the character act that way?
Aha Moment	How might this change things?
Tough Questions	What does this make me wonder about?
Words of the Wiser	What's the lesson for the character?
Again and Again	Why might the author keep bringing this up?
Memory Moment	Why is this memory important?

Reading Nonfiction: Essays, Articles, and Arguments	
Signpost	Key Question(s)
Big Questions	What surprised me? What did the author think I already knew? What challenged, changed, or confirmed what I already knew?
Contrasts and Contradictions	What is the difference, and why does it matter?
Extreme or Absolute Language	Why did the author use this language?
Numbers and Stats	Why did the author use these numbers or amounts?
Quoted Words	Why was this person quoted or cited, and what did this add?
Word Gaps	Do I know this word from someplace else? Does it seem like technical talk for this topic? Do clues in the sentence help me understand the word?

ENGLISH LEARNER SUPPORT

Develop Fluency Select a passage from the text that matches students' reading abilities. Read the passage aloud while students follow along silently.

- Have students echo-read a simple sentence, repeating the words as they are read aloud. Explain any words or concepts students don't understand using native language, gestures, or pictures. **SUBSTANTIAL**
- Have students echo-read a few simple sentences, and have them reread the passage silently. Then, ask students a simple content question. Use sentence frames to help students respond to the question. **MODERATE**
- Have students read and reread a few paragraphs of a passage silently. Ask students a few questions to check their comprehension. **LIGHT**

 Go to the **Reading Studio** for additional support in developing fluency.

INDEPENDENT READING

You can preview these texts in Unit 6 of your eBook.

Then, check off the text or texts that you select to read on your own.

SHORT STORY

Araby
James Joyce

Can a poor schoolboy hope to impress a girl with a small gift?

SPEECH

Professions for Women
Virginia Woolf

Woolf relates two strategies she has used to confront obstacles which all women face.

POEM

Do Not Go Gentle into That Good Night
Dylan Thomas

A son pleads with his dying father to resist death and hold on to life for as long as possible.

POEM

Digging
Seamus Heaney

Can a son fulfill his own life's purpose while taking a completely different path from his father?

SHORT STORY

Marriage Is a Private Affair
Chinua Achebe

Nnaemeka married for love, offending his father. Can he bridge the rift he created by choosing his own path?

Collaborate and Share Get with a partner to discuss what you learned from at least one of your independent readings.

- Give a brief synopsis or summary of the text.
- Describe any signposts that you noticed in the text and explain what they revealed to you.
- Describe what you most enjoyed or found most challenging about the text. Give specific examples.
- Decide if you would recommend the text to others. Why or why not?

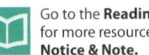 Go to the **Reading Studio** for more resources on **Notice & Note.**

Independent Reading 791

INDEPENDENT READING

MATCHING STUDENTS TO TEXTS

Use the following information to guide students in choosing their texts.

Araby Lexile: 930L
  Genre: short story
  Overall Rating: Challenging

Professions for Women Lexile: 970L
  Genre: essay
  Overall Rating: Challenging

Do Not Go Gentle into That Good Night
  Genre: poem
  Overall Rating: Challenging

Digging
  Genre: poem
  Overall Rating: Challenging

Marriage Is a Private Affair Lexile: 830L
  Genre: short story
  Overall Rating: Challenging

Collaborate and Share To assess how well students read the selections, walk around the room and listen to their conversations. Encourage students to be focused and specific in their comments.

 for Assessment

- Independent Reading Selection Tests

 Encourage students to visit the **Reading Studio** to download a handy bookmark of **NOTICE & NOTE** signposts.

WHEN STUDENTS STRUGGLE...

Keep a Reading Log As students read their selected texts, have them keep a reading log for each selection to note signposts and their thoughts about them. Use their logs to assess how well they are noticing and reflecting on elements of their texts.

Reading Log for (title)		
Location	Signpost I Noticed	My Notes about It

PLAN

UNIT 6 Tasks

- **WRITE AN ARGUMENT**
- **DEBATE AN ISSUE**

MENTOR TEXT

BUDGET 2016: GEORGE OSBORNE'S SPEECH
Speech by George Osborne

WILL THE SUGAR TAX STOP CHILDHOOD OBESITY?
Editorial by Chris Hall

LEARNING OBJECTIVES

Writing Task

- Write an argument about a social or political issue.
- Plan and organize an argument.
- Use the Mentor Text as a model for using facts and statistics related to claims.
- Use genre characteristics such as counterarguments and transitions.
- Use a Revision Guide and peer review to revise a draft.
- Edit draft to vary syntax for effect.
- Use a rubric to evaluate writing.
- Publish writing to share with an audience.
- **Language** Write with a variety of sentence structures and lengths.

Speaking Task

  Adapt an argument for a debate.
- Use a graphic organizer to plan the debate.
- Prepare briefs and rebuttals.
- Use effective language and organization.
- Work with a team to improve the presentation.
- Practice effective verbal and nonverbal techniques with others.
- Consider ways to revise and clarify the presentation.
- Hold a debate.
- **Language** Respond to counterarguments using a respectful, formal tone.

Assign the Writing Task in **Ed**.

RESOURCES

- Unit 6 Response Log
- Writing Studio: Building Effective Support
- Listening and Speaking Studio: Delivering Your Presentation
- Grammar Studio: Module 1 Lesson 1: Sentence Fragments and Run-on Sentences

PLAN

Language X-Ray: English Learner Support

Use the instruction below and the supports and scaffolds in the Teacher's Edition to help you guide students of different proficiency levels.

INTRODUCE THE WRITING TASK

Explain that writers of arguments must be careful that the reasoning behind their ideas makes sense. Tell students that logical fallacies are errors in reasoning that undermine the soundness of an argument. Drawing hasty conclusions, using false cause-and-effect reasoning, oversimplifying a claim, or restating an argument without actually proving it are all examples of logical fallacies. Remind students to address all opposing arguments rather than avoid them, and to not divert attention by changing the subject.

Discuss why it is important to research and support the reasoning underlying all the claims in an argument. Provide such sentence frames as: *When you draw a hasty conclusion, you _____ . One event may follow another, but it doesn't always mean _____ .*

WRITING

Vary Sentences

Remind students that even informational writing needs to have a pleasing rhythm to keep readers interested. Tell them to mix short declarative sentences with longer and more explanatory or descriptive sentences.

Use the following supports with students at varying proficiency levels:

- Provide sentence frames to help students vary sentence lengths. Have students copy the frames and help them complete them. **SUBSTANTIAL**
- Have students write two short related sentences and give them to a partner to rewrite into a compound or complex sentence. For example: *Obesity drives disease. Cancer is a disease. Obesity drives such diseases as cancer.* **MODERATE**
- Have partners exchange arguments and review each paragraph for variety of sentence length. Have them mark places where a shorter or longer sentence would work better. **LIGHT**

SPEAKING

Use Formal Tone

Provide a bank of phrases to use in formal arguments: *hasty conclusion, cause-and-effect reasoning, unrelated chronological events, insufficient evidence, oversimplified claim, restated the argument without proving it, diverted attention by changing the subject.*

Use the following supports with students at varying proficiency levels:

- Use phrases from the bank in oral sentences and have students repeat them. **SUBSTANTIAL**
- Have partners take turns using phrases from the bank in simple sentences. Provide a sentence frame: *I don't agree with ____ because ____.* **MODERATE**
- Have partners take turns using phrases from the bank in formal sentences. For example: *I appreciate your point, but I think you've drawn a hasty conclusion.* **LIGHT**

Unit 6 Tasks **792B**

WRITING

WRITE AN ARGUMENT

Introduce students to the Writing Task by reading the introductory paragraph with them. Remind students to refer to the notes they recorded in the Unit 6 Response Log as they plan and draft their arguments. The Response Log should contain ideas about social or political issues students face in their communities from a variety of perspectives. Drawing on these different perspectives will make their own writing more interesting and well informed.

 For **writing support** for students at varying proficiency levels, see the **Language X-Ray** on page 800B.

USE THE MENTOR TEXT

Students should use both mentor texts, George Osborne's speech given to the House of Commons and Chris Hall's editorial, as models. Point out that their arguments may be similar in that they will present facts and examples related to a topic. They will, however, write an original argument using their own ideas about social or political issues they face in their communities.

WRITING PROMPT

Review the prompt with students. Encourage them to ask questions about any part of the assignment that is unclear. Make sure they understand that the purpose of their argument is to answer the question by writing about a social or political issue they face in their own community and the role of the government toward individuals and communities.

 **WRITING TASK**

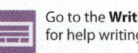 Go to the **Writing Studio** for help writing arguments.

Write an Argument

This unit focuses on modern and contemporary literature. Responding to the devastation of two world wars and the loss of the once-powerful British Empire, British writers struggled to carve out a role for themselves in their new and different world. For this writing task, you will write an argument about a social or political issue in your community, such as school choice or homelessness. You can use both George Osborne's speech given to the House of Commons and Chris Hall's editorial as mentor texts to write your own argument.

As you write your argument, you can use the notes from your Response Log, which you filled out after reading the texts in this unit.

Writing Prompt

Read the information in the box below.

> Think about various issues facing your own community—such as conservation efforts, homelessness, taxes, or unemployment. Consider the role of the government and what responsibilities they have to individuals and communities.

This is the topic or context for your argument

Think carefully about the following Essential Question.

> When should the government interfere in our decisions?

How might this Essential Question relate to your argument?

Write an argument about a social or political issue facing your community and the government's role in helping to solve this issue.

Choose an issue that you care about or that means something to you.

Be sure to—

- ❏ clearly state a claim, or thesis statement, about the issue you chose
- ❏ develop your argument with key ideas, supported by relevant evidence
- ❏ address opposing claims with legitimate counterarguments
- ❏ establish logical relationships between all of the elements of your argument
- ❏ use specific rhetorical devices to support your claim and counterarguments
- ❏ write a conclusion that summarizes your argument
- ❏ maintain a formal tone through the use of Standard English

Review these points as you write and again when you finish. Make any needed changes.

 LEARNING MINDSET

Asking for Help Remind students of the importance of asking for help in order to develop a learning mindset. Explain that seeking help from a variety of such sources as teachers, parents, and other students can contribute to success when students struggle. Encourage students not to think of asking for help as failure but rather as a path to eventual success.

1 Plan

Before you begin to write, plan your argument using the chart below. Think of two or three political or social issues that interest you—homelessness, school choice, conservation—then, choose one about which you will make a claim. Think about the government's role, as opposed to the responsibility of individual citizens on this issue. Make a list of key questions about your topic to help focus your research. Then, gather facts and evidence from reliable sources online, and talk to informed members of your community. Consider both sides of the argument carefully and use any background reading or class discussions to generate key ideas to help develop your claim, or thesis statement.

Argument Planning Chart	
Topic	Argument
Questions to consider	When should the government interfere in our decisions?
Ideas from background reading	
Ideas from class discussions	
Claim	

Background Reading Review the notes you have taken in your Response Log that relate to the question, "When should the government interfere in our decisions?" Texts in this unit provide background reading that will help you formulate your argument.

WRITING TASK

Go to **Writing Arguments: What is a Claim?** for help planning your argument.

Notice & Note
From Reading to Writing

As you plan your argument, apply what you've learned about signposts to your own writing. Remember that writers use common features, called signposts, to help convey their message to readers.

Think how you can incorporate **Numbers and Stats** into your argument.

 Go to the **Reading Studio** for more resources on **Notice & Note**.

Use the notes from your Response Log as you plan your argument.

TO CHALLENGE STUDENTS...

Find an Interview Challenge students to incorporate facts and ideas in their arguments from an interview with a community or government leader about a social or political issue in their community. They might find interviews with community or government leaders written in newspapers or magazines as well as recorded on television or online. Encourage students to add details from an interview to the Response Log and think about how these details support their answer to the Essential Question.

WRITING

1 PLAN

Allow time for students to discuss the topic with partners or in small groups and then to complete the planning table independently.

■ English Learner Support

Understand Academic Language Make sure students understand such words and phrases used in the Graphic Organizer as *topic, background reading, class discussion, claim.* Use examples, pictures, and native language as needed. Work with students to fill the blank sections of the Graphic Organizer with their own ideas. Provide text that they can copy if needed. **SUBSTANTIAL**

▶ NOTICE & NOTE
From Reading to Writing

Remind students to incorporate **Numbers and Stats** into their writing. Numbers and Stats can be used to support points made in their argument. These also provide precision and help in making comparisons. Remind students to use only relevant and accurate Numbers and Stats directly related to and supportive of the point being made.

Background Reading As students plan their arguments, remind them to refer to the notes they took in the Response Log. They may also review the selections to find additional facts and examples to support ideas they want to include in their writing.

WRITING

Organize Your Ideas Tell students to use the ideas from their planning activities as they fill out the chart to organize key ideas in support of their claims. Students should also use the Graphic Organizer to show opposing arguments they can anticipate and to develop counterarguments. Point out that each student's argument should include the following elements:

- A claim
- Key ideas to support their claim
- Opposing arguments
- Counterarguments

Students' arguments should also clearly answer the Essential Question and relate to the theme about social or political issues they face in their communities. They should include rhetorical devices to support their claims and to help develop their counterarguments. Remind students that by thinking about and organizing their ideas before they begin to write, they can best decide how to draft their arguments.

2 DEVELOP A DRAFT

Remind students to follow their charts as they draft their arguments to include all the elements. Point out that they can still make changes to their writing plan during this stage. As they write, they may discover that they need a different key idea to support their claim or another counterargument for an opposing argument.

■ English Learner Support

Write a Group Argument Simplify the writing task for students by having them work together to create a group argument. Help the students decide on a claim as a group. Have them work together to develop one key idea that supports the claim, an opposing argument, and a counterargument. Provide language support as needed. **MODERATE/LIGHT**

 **WRITING TASK**

 Go to **Writing Arguments: Building Effective Support** for help organizing your ideas.

Organize Your Ideas After completing the planning chart, you should have a claim on which to base your argument. Use this chart to organize key ideas in support of your claim. Anticipate any opposing arguments and develop counterarguments. Think about how you might use rhetorical devices in supporting your claim and developing counterarguments.

Claim: *The government should provide basic shelter for the homeless.*

Key ideas	Opposing arguments	Counterarguments

2 Develop a Draft

Once you have completed your planning activities, you will be ready to begin drafting your argument. Refer to your planning and organizational charts, as well as any notes you took as you studied the texts in this unit. These will provide a plan for you to follow as you write. Using a laptop or computer makes it easier to make changes or move sentences around later when you are ready to revise your first draft.

You may prefer to draft your argument online.

WHEN STUDENTS STRUGGLE . . .

Draft the Argument Students may struggle even when working from Graphic Organizer charts to get started on their drafts. For example, students may have difficulty knowing where to begin. Suggest to these students to start writing a section that they feel the most confident about. They can start with a few sentences or a paragraph explaining their claim, a key idea, or even a counterargument. Once they begin writing, they may find it easier to continue with other sections. Remind students they will revise and edit their drafts later, so they don't need to worry about making mistakes at this point.

WRITING

WRITING TASK

Use the Mentor Text

Author's Craft
In supporting your claim, it's important to use strong, reliable, and relevant evidence. Specific details such as facts, examples, statistics, and quotations from experts contribute to a logical and effective argument. Note how George Osborne uses clear, reliable facts and statistics that are directly related to his claim and that will likely catch his listeners' attention.

> Children are consuming their body weight in sugar every year.
>
> Experts predict that within a generation over half of all boys, and 70% of girls could be overweight or obese.
>
> . . . Obesity drives disease. . . . cancer, diabetes and heart disease . . . One of the biggest contributors to childhood obesity is sugary drinks.
>
> A can of cola typically has nine teaspoons of sugar in it.

Osborne's serious and surprising details draw his listeners in and help them to understand his point of view. His use of statistics helps give weight to his argument that excessive sugar is harmful to children's health.

Apply What You've Learned As you search for evidence to support your claim, look for interesting facts, statistics, and examples that might surprise your reader. Be sure to use enough detail to make a convincing argument.

Genre Characteristics
An effective counterargument acknowledges the opposition with a respectful tone. In his editorial, Chris Hall recognizes the validity of the opposing view before presenting specific evidence to refute the tax on sugary drinks.

> There's no denying it: our consumption of sugar sweetened beverages (SSBs) has risen in recent decades, and there is evidence to suggest that this increase is having an impact on obesity and the rising number of cases of type 2 diabetes. But sugary drinks alone are not the root of the problem.

Hall agrees that there is a problem with sugar consumption and then acknowledges the valid evidence offered by the opposing view. Note the transition sentence at the end of the paragraph. This shows he will present a counterclaim.

Apply What You've Learned Maintain a formal tone when you are making a counterargument. Begin by respectfully presenting the opposition view of a particular point. Then, transition smoothly into your counterargument.

Write an Argument 795

WHY THIS MENTOR TEXT?
George Osborne's speech and Chris Hall's editorial provide good examples of an argument. Use the instruction below to help students use the mentor texts as models for integrating clear, reliable facts and statistics into their writing, as well as presenting effective and respectful counterarguments.

USE THE MENTOR TEXT

Author's Craft Ask a volunteer to read aloud the author's claim. Then, have a volunteer read each of the selected statistics. Discuss why each statistic is important to supporting key points of his claim. Discuss why the author likely chose these particular statistics. Ask students to think about how the statistics help listeners better understand his point of view and add weight to his argument. Remind students to find relevant and reliable statistics, facts, examples, or quotations from experts to contribute to their arguments and further convince their readers. Have students provide ideas about where they might find these to use in their own writing.

Genre Characteristics Ask a volunteer to read the counterargument selection from Chris Hall's editorial. Ask students how Hall recognizes the validity of the opposing view. Discuss how he uses this acknowledgment along with a transition to effectively and smoothly introduce his counterclaim. Remind students to maintain a formal and respectful tone in their arguments. Have students provide examples. Discuss how and why a respectful tone contributes to a stronger argument. Also remind students to make transitions smoothly and effectively when providing counterarguments to opposing arguments.

 ENGLISH LEARNER SUPPORT

Use the Mentor Text Use the following supports with students at varying proficiency levels:

- Explain the concept of a statistic using pictures. Select a simple statistic from the text, such as "half of all boys and 70% of girls" and draw a representation of boys and girls to illustrate. **SUBSTANTIAL**

- Reinforce the concept of a statistic. Have students find a statistic from the text and underline it. Then, have them draw a representation to illustrate what the statistic means. Be sure students understand what the statistic represents, and explain any difficult words. **MODERATE**

- Encourage use of statistics. Have students find a statistic in the text and underline it. Have them write a sentence explaining why the statistic is important. Remind students to look up any unfamiliar words they come across. **LIGHT**

Write an Argument 795

WRITING

3 REVISE

Have students answer each question in the chart to determine how they can improve their drafts. Invite volunteers to model their revision techniques.

With a Partner Have students ask peer reviewers to evaluate their key ideas, facts, and evidence by answering the following questions:

- Is my claim well supported by key ideas? Why or why not?
- Are my key ideas supported by clear, relevant facts and evidence? Why or why not?
- Are my opposing claims addressed by well-supported counterarguments? Why or why not?
- Did I use rhetorical devices effectively? Why or why not?
- What questions do you have about my main points?

Students should use the reviewer's feedback to add relevant facts, details, examples, or quotations that further develop their main points.

WRITING TASK

Go to **Writing Arguments: Formal Style** for help revising your argument.

3 Revise

On Your Own Once you have written your draft, you'll want to go back and look for ways to improve your argument. As you reread and revise, think about whether you have achieved your purpose. The Revision Chart will help you focus on specific elements to make your writing stronger.

Revision Guide

Ask Yourself	Tips	Revision Techniques
1. Did I make a claim that states my position clearly?	**Highlight** your thesis statement.	If necessary, **add** a sentence or two to clarify your claim. **Add** an interesting example or related quotation to hook your reader.
2. Did I back up my claim with key ideas, supported by facts and evidence?	**Highlight** your key ideas and **underline** supporting facts and evidence.	**Read** your thesis statement aloud, followed by your key ideas. Does your argument make sense so far? **Add** more support if you can.
3. Are opposing claims addressed with well-supported counterarguments?	**Ask** a classmate to challenge your claim.	**Elaborate** by adding opposing claims and counterarguments to refute them, as needed.
4. Did I transition smoothly between ideas, paragraphs, and sentences?	**Underline** transitional words and phrases.	**Clarify** the relationship between the claim and key ideas and evidence by adding transitions.
5. Did I use rhetorical devices effectively?	**Highlight** any rhetorical devices.	**Add** appropriate rhetorical devices, such as repetition or rhetorical questions, to support and emphasize your claim and counterarguments.
6. Does my conclusion effectively restate my claim?	**Underline** your conclusion.	**Add** a statement that summarizes your claim.

ACADEMIC VOCABULARY

As you conduct your **peer review**, be sure to use these words.

- ☐ arbitrary
- ☐ controversy
- ☐ convince
- ☐ denote
- ☐ undergo

With a Partner Once you and your partner have worked through the Revision Guide on your own, exchange arguments and evaluate each other's draft in a **peer review**. Focus on providing revision suggestions for at least three of the items mentioned in the chart. Explain why you think your partner's draft should be revised and what your specific suggestions are. When receiving feedback from your partner, listen attentively and ask questions to make sure you fully understand the revision suggestions.

796 Unit 6

 ENGLISH LEARNER SUPPORT

Use Rhetorical Devices Explain that writers often use rhetorical devices for emphasis. Have students identify the rhetorical device used in this passage from Chris Hall's editorial (paragraph 3):

But in an effort to drive down childhood obesity, is this the right approach? (*rhetorical question, a question that a person is not expected to answer*)

Discuss and provide examples of other rhetorical devices such as repetition. Encourage students to find opportunities to use rhetorical devices in their writing.   **LIGHT**

4 Edit

Now that you've revised the content of your argument, it's time to improve the finer points of your draft. Edit for the proper use of Standard English conventions and make sure to correct any misspellings or grammatical errors.

Language Conventions

Vary Syntax for Effect Vary the **syntax,** or word order, of your sentences for more effective writing. When you use the same sentence patterns repeatedly, your writing becomes boring and your readers tend to lose interest. As you edit your argument, try the following strategies:

- To create a smooth flow, **vary sentence structure** by combining shorter sentences into compound or complex sentences.
- **Vary sentence lengths** within paragraphs to emphasize certain ideas.

The chart includes specific examples of the authors' uses of both strategies.

Strategy	Osborne	Hall
Vary sentence structure by combining shorter sentences into compound or complex sentences.	Pure fruit juices and milk-based drinks will be excluded, and we'll ensure the smallest producers are kept out of scope.	In theory, this makes a lot of sense, but when you compare the theoretical data with the observed data, you can see that the actual weight gain associated with sugary drinks is in fact ten times less than was originally theorized . . .
Vary sentence lengths within paragraphs. (Osborne: short—long) (Hall: long—short)	Obesity drives disease. It increases the risk of cancer, diabetes and heart disease—and it costs our economy £27 billion a year; that's more than half the entire NHS paybill.	Milkshakes, flavored waters and off-the-shelf cold coffees can contain nearly as much sugar as, if not more than, your average can of soda, and they tend to be higher in calories! . . . Yet these drinks are exempt from the tax!

WRITING TASK

! Go to **Sentence Structure** in the **Grammar Studio** to learn more.

5 Publish

Finalize your argument and choose a way to share it with your audience. Consider these options:

- Submit your argument as a letter to the editor of your local newspaper.
- Post your argument on an online news forum.

Write an Argument 797

WHEN STUDENTS STRUGGLE . . .

Use Complex Sentences Some students may have difficulty deciding how to incorporate complex sentences in their writing. Ask students to find a complex sentence in one of the mentor texts. Remind them that complex sentences are made up of an independent clause and at least one dependent clause. An independent clause can stand alone as a sentence but a dependent clause cannot. Have them identify these clauses in their selected sentence. Encourage students to review their arguments and provide at least one complex sentence to add depth to their writing.

WRITING

4 EDIT

Suggest that students read their drafts aloud to assess how clearly and smoothly they have presented their ideas and to correct spelling and grammatical errors. Have students review their use of variety in their syntax.

LANGUAGE CONVENTIONS

Vary Syntax for Effect Review the information about varying syntax for effect in writing. Then, discuss the example sentences taken from the mentor texts in the chart, asking students to identify how each of the writers varied sentence structure and length. To emphasize how variety in syntax can improve writing, have students rewrite the following sentence to combine the two short sentences into a compound or complex sentence:

- Drug use among teens in our city has increased. A 30% increase in drug-related crimes by minors was reported last year. (*Connecting words can be used to combine the sentences to make a compound sentence. One sentence can also be changed into a dependent clause and added with a conjunction to an independent clause.*)

Emphasize how variety in sentence length adds interest to writing. Select a section of one of the mentor texts and have students mark each sentence, using different colors for sentences of different lengths to highlight the variety.

■ English Learner Support

Use Compound Sentences Discuss how to form compound sentences by using connecting words. Provide examples of two short sentences combined with a connecting word. Encourage students to use these words to connect shorter sentences to add variety in their writing as they edit their arguments. **MODERATE/LIGHT**

5 PUBLISH

Students can present their arguments compiled in an eBook available on a school website. Encourage others to read the arguments and write comments about them. The authors can then respond to the comments.

Write an Argument 797

WRITING

USE THE SCORING GUIDE

Allow students time to read the scoring guide and to ask questions about any words, phrases, or ideas that are unclear. Then, have partners exchange final drafts of their arguments. Ask them to score their partner's argument using the scoring guide. Each student should write a paragraph explaining the reasons for the score he or she awarded in each category.

 **WRITING TASK**

Use the scoring guide to evaluate your argument.

Writing Task Scoring Guide: Argument

	Organization/Progression	Development of Ideas and Evidence	Use of Language and Conventions
4	• Organization is appropriate to the purpose. • Claim is stated clearly, with all ideas strongly related to the claim. • Key ideas and evidence are organized consistently and logically with meaningful transitions.	• Introduction is memorable and persuasive; the claim states a position on a substantive topic. • Key ideas support the claim. • Opposing views are anticipated and addressed effectively. • Argument is supported by a variety of rhetorical devices. • Conclusion summarizes the claim.	• Writing reflects purposeful, precise word choice and maintains formal, respectful tone. • Sentences are varied. • Writing shows a consistent command of spelling, capitalization, punctuation, grammar, and usage conventions.
3	• For the most part, structure is appropriate and effective. • Claim is stated clearly, with most ideas related to the claim. Minor lapses in focus. • Organization of key ideas and evidence is confusing in a few places, and a few more transitions are needed.	• Introduction needs more to hook the reader; the claim states a position on an issue. • Key ideas support the claim but could be more convincing. • Counterarguments need further development. • Rhetorical devices do not directly support the argument. • Conclusion restates the claim.	• For the most part, writing reflects specific word choice. Style is informal in a few places and the tone defensive at times. • Sentences are reasonably varied. • Writing shows adequate command of spelling, capitalization, punctuation, grammar, and usage conventions, with few errors.
2	• Organization is evident but not always appropriate. • Irrelevant information is included or many ideas are not strongly connected to the claim. • Progression is not always logical; weak transitions, wordiness, or repetition affect the flow.	• The introduction is ordinary; the claim lacks clarity. • Key ideas are not always relevant. • Opposing views are anticipated but not addressed logically. • No clear relationship between rhetorical devices and argument. • The conclusion includes an incomplete summary of claim.	• Writing uses general or imprecise word choice, with little awareness of appropriate tone. • Sentences are often awkward, with little variation. • Writing shows only a partial command of spelling, capitalization, punctuation, grammar, and usage conventions, with some distracting errors.
1	• Organization is inappropriate to the purpose or no pattern is followed. • Claim is missing, unclear, or illogical; writing may include extraneous information or abrupt shifts between ideas. • Progression is weak; repetition, wordiness, and lack of transitions result in random or illogical presentation.	• The introduction is missing. • Significant support and evidence are missing. • Counterclaims are neither anticipated nor addressed. • Rhetorical devices are not included. • The conclusion is missing.	• Writing is vague, with limited word choice and a disrespectful tone. • Awkward sentences, fragments, and run-on sentences make the writing hard to follow. • Writing shows little or no command of spelling, capitalization, punctuation, grammar, and usage, with serious and persistent errors.

Debate an Issue

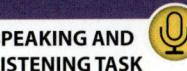

SPEAKING AND LISTENING TASK

You will now adapt your argument for a debate with your classmates. You also will listen to other debate teams and prepare to critique their presentations.

Go to the **Speaking and Listening Studio: Analyzing and Evaluating a Presentation** to learn more.

❶ Adapt Your Argument for a Debate

Review your written argument, and use the chart below to guide you as you adapt it and plan for a debate. Note that one team will argue for your claim, and the other will argue against it.

Plan the Debate		
Identify two debate teams with two or three members each. Team 1: _____ _____ Team 2: _____ _____	Appoint a moderator to introduce the debate and the speakers and to keep everyone on task. Moderator: _____	Assign debate roles to each member: 1. Introduce team's argument: _____ 2. Refute opposing team: _____ 3. Present summary and closing statement: _____
Prepare Briefs	**Prepare Rebuttals**	
Identify your claim: List key ideas and evidence that support your claim: Summarize your argument in a closing statement:	Identify the opposing claim: Identify weaknesses in the opposing claim and possible counterarguments:	

Debate an Issue 799

SPEAKING AND LISTENING

DEBATE AN ISSUE

Introduce students to the Speaking and Listening Task by discussing what makes reading an argument different from hearing someone speak about the topic. Point out that people read at different rates, and a reader can stop and reread a passage if they don't understand it. Have students consider how a speaker can debate the issue presented in their argument in a way that listeners can best follow and understand. Remind students that their pace, volume, and tone can also make them sound more convincing, interesting, and engaging.

❶ ADAPT YOUR ARGUMENT FOR A DEBATE

Have students review the chart to adapt and plan their argument for a debate. Explain how they can take key points, supporting facts, opposing arguments, and counterarguments from their arguments to prepare briefs and rebuttals. Assist students in finding classmates to fill the designated roles. Then work with the class to discuss some general principles for debating a topic orally (Examples: Use concise, clear sentences. Repeat key ideas. Emphasize supporting facts by speaking more slowly. Use respectful and formal language).

 For **speaking support** for students at varying proficiency levels, see the **Language X-Ray** on page 792B.

 ENGLISH LEARNER SUPPORT

Adapt the Debate Use the following supports with students at varying proficiency levels:

- Assist students in translating their ideas and words into English as they work together to fill out the chart. **SUBSTANTIAL**
- Review the chart with students to ensure students' understanding of the vocabulary. Have students work as a group to discuss how they could fill out the chart. Then have students fill out the chart providing assistance as needed. **MODERATE**
- Review the chart with students. Remind students to look up unfamiliar words. Then have students work together to fill out the chart and present their debate. **LIGHT**

SPEAKING AND LISTENING

2 PRACTICE WITH A PARTNER OR GROUP

Review the information and tips with the class, ensuring that all the terms and ideas are clear. Remind students that the purpose of practicing their presentations is to gain useful feedback from their peers. Emphasize that speaking before a group makes most people feel nervous, so everyone should be as supportive and helpful as possible.

3 HOLD THE DEBATE

Set aside time for all students to stage their debate. When everyone has finished, ask students to share their thoughts on how their classmates' feedback helped them improve their performance.

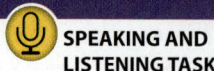 **SPEAKING AND LISTENING TASK**

As you work to improve your presentations, be sure to follow discussion rules:
- ❏ listen closely to each other
- ❏ don't interrupt
- ❏ stay on topic
- ❏ ask helpful, relevant questions
- ❏ provide clear, thoughtful, and direct answers

2 Practice with Your Team

Once you've prepared your materials, work with your team to improve the presentation of your claim, key ideas, and evidence. Also practice rebuttals. Practice listening and responding respectfully.

Practice Effective Verbal and Nonverbal Techniques

- ❏ **Voice** Enunciate your words clearly and speak slowly and loudly enough so that everyone can hear you. Use your voice to show enthusiasm and emphasis.
- ❏ **Eye Contact** Try to let your eyes rest on each member of the audience at least once.
- ❏ **Facial Expression** Smile, frown, or raise an eyebrow to show your feelings or to emphasize points.
- ❏ **Gestures** Use natural gestures to add meaning and interest to your presentation.

Provide and Consider Advice for Improvement

As you and your team practice, take notes and provide helpful advice to each other. Consider ways to revise your presentation to make sure your points are clear and logically sequenced.

3 Hold the Debate

Set up the classroom for a formal debate, with the team members facing the audience. Follow the format below:

- ❏ **Pro Speaker 1:** Present claim and supporting evidence for the "pro," or supportive, side of the argument. —5 minutes
- ❏ **Con Speaker 2:** Ask probing questions that will prompt the other team to address flaws in the argument. —3 minutes
- ❏ **Pro Speaker 2:** Respond to the questions posed by the opposing team and provide counterarguments. —3 minutes
- ❏ **Con Speaker 1:** Present the claim and supporting evidence for the "con," or opposed, side of the argument. —5 minutes
- ❏ **Pro Speaker 2:** Ask probing questions that will prompt the other team to address flaws in the argument. —3 minutes
- ❏ **Con Speaker 2:** Respond to the questions posed by the opposing team and provide counterarguments. —3 minutes
- ❏ **Pro Speaker 3:** Summarize the claim and evidence for the "pro" side and explain why your claim is more valid. —3 minutes
- ❏ **Con Speaker 3:** Summarize the claim and evidence for the "con" side and explain why your claim is more valid. —3 minutes

---

WHEN STUDENTS STRUGGLE...

Provide Advice for Improvement Some students may find it difficult to listen, observe, and take notes to offer advice about the debate content, as well as verbal and nonverbal presentation techniques for their fellow students as they practice. Divide the tasks among the group of students. Have one student take note of presentation content, one of voice quality, one of eye contact, one of facial expressions, and one of gestures. Students can also make a checklist of important points to evaluate their classmates' debating and presentation skills.

Reflect on the Unit

By completing your argument, you have created a writing product that pulls together and expresses your thoughts about the reading you have done in this unit. Now is a good time to reflect on what you have learned.

Reflect on the Essential Questions

- Review the four Essential Questions on page 691. How have your answers to these questions changed in response to the texts you've read in this unit?

- What are some examples from the texts you've read that show how people relate to society?

Reflect on Your Reading

- Which selections were the most interesting or surprising to you?

- From which selection did you learn the most about how people relate to society?

Reflect on the Writing Task

- What difficulties did you encounter while working on your argument? How might you avoid them next time?

- What part of the argument was the easiest to write? The hardest to write? Why?

- What improvements did you make to your argument as you were revising?

UNIT 6 SELECTIONS
- "A Cup of Tea"
- "The Love Song of J. Alfred Prufrock"
- "Shooting an Elephant"
- "My Daughter The Racist"
- "The Second Coming"
- "Symbols? I'm Sick of Symbols"
- "Budget 2016: George Osborne's Speech"
- "Will the Sugar Tax Stop Childhood Obesity?"

LEARNING MINDSET

Self-Reflection Remind students that an important part of developing a learning mindset is understanding their own strengths and weaknesses through self-reflection. Tell them that reflection on successes, struggles, and failures will help them grow as learners. As students reflect on the unit, encourage them to think about what they learned about their strengths and weaknesses.

REFLECT ON THE UNIT

Have students reflect on the questions independently and write some notes in response to each one. Then have students meet with partners or in small groups to discuss their reflections. Circulate during these discussions to identify the questions that are generating the liveliest conversations. Wrap up with a whole-class discussion focused on these questions.

Student Resources

Response Logs	R1
Using a Glossary	R7
Pronunciation Key	R7
Glossary of Academic Vocabulary	R8
Glossary of Critical Vocabulary	R9
Index of Skills	R14
Index of Titles and Authors	R21
Acknowledgments	R22

HMH *Into Literature* Studios
For more instruction and practice, visit the HMH *Into Literature* Studios.

 Reading Studio

 Writing Studio

 Speaking & Listening Studio

 Grammar Studio

 Vocabulary Studio

UNIT 1 RESPONSE LOG

Use this Response Log to record information from the texts that relates to or comments on the **Essential Questions** in Unit 1.

? Essential Question	Details from Texts
What makes someone a hero?	
What is true chivalry?	
Can we control our fate?	
What happens when a society unravels?	

UNIT 2 RESPONSE LOG

Use this Response Log to record information from the texts that relates to or comments on the **Essential Questions** in Unit 2.

? Essential Question	Details from Texts
What can drive someone to seek revenge?	
How does time affect our feelings?	
What's the difference between love and passion?	
How do you defy expectations?	

UNIT 3 RESPONSE LOG

Use this Response Log to record information from the texts that relates to or comments on the **Essential Questions** in Unit 3.

? Essential Question	Details from Texts
How can satire change people's behavior?	
What is your most memorable experience?	
What keeps women from achieving equality with men?	
Why are plagues so horrifying?	

UNIT 4 RESPONSE LOG

Use this Response Log to record information from the texts that relates to or comments on the **Essential Questions** in Unit 4.

? Essential Question	Details from Texts
What can nature offer us?	
How do you define beauty?	
How can science go wrong?	
What shapes your outlook on life?	

R4 Student Resources

UNIT 5 RESPONSE LOG

Use this Response Log to record information from the texts that relates to or comments on the **Essential Questions** in Unit 5.

? Essential Question	Details from Texts
What is a true benefactor?	
How do you view the world?	
What brings out cruelty in people?	
What invention has had the greatest impact on your life?	

UNIT 6
RESPONSE LOG

Use this Response Log to record information from the texts that relates to or comments on the **Essential Questions** in Unit 6.

? Essential Question	Details from Texts
What makes people feel insecure?	
Why is it hard to resist social pressure?	
What is the power of symbols?	
When should the government interfere in our decisions?	

Using a Glossary

A glossary is an alphabetical list of vocabulary words. Use a glossary just as you would a dictionary—to determine the meanings, parts of speech, pronunciation, and syllabification of words. (Some technical, foreign, and more obscure words in this book are defined for you in the footnotes that accompany many of the selections.)

Many words in the English language have more than one meaning. This glossary gives the meanings that apply to the words as they are used in the selections in this book.

The following abbreviations are used to identify parts of speech of words:

adj. adjective   *adv.* adverb   *n.* noun   *v.* verb

Each word's pronunciation is given in parentheses. A guide to the pronunciation symbols appears in the Pronunciation Key below. The stress marks in the Pronunciation Key are used to indicate the force given to each syllable in a word. They can also help you determine where words are divided into syllables.

For more information about the words in this glossary or for information about words not listed here, consult a dictionary.

Pronunciation Key

Symbol	Examples	Symbol	Examples	Symbol	Examples
ă	pat	m	mum	ûr	urge, term, firm, word, heard
ā	pay	n	no, sudden* (sud´n)	v	valve
ä	father	ng	thing	w	with
âr	care	ŏ	pot	y	yes
b	bib	ō	toe	z	zebra, xylem
ch	church	ô	caught, paw	zh	vision, pleasure, garage
d	deed, milled	oi	noise	ə	about, item, edible, gallop, circus
ĕ	pet	ŏŏ	took	ər	butter
ē	bee	ōō	boot		
f	fife, phase, rough	ŏŏr	lure		
g	gag	ôr	core		
h	hat	ou	out		
hw	which	p	pop		**Sounds in Foreign Words**
ĭ	pit	r	roar	KH	German ich, ach; Scottish loch
ī	pie, by	s	sauce	N	French, bon (bôn)
îr	pier	sh	ship, dish	œ	French feu, œuf; German schön
j	judge	t	tight, stopped	ü	French tu; German über
k	kick, cat, pique	th	thin		
l	lid, needle* (nēd´l)	*th*	this		
		ŭ	cut		

*In English the consonants *l* and *n* often constitute complete syllables by themselves.

Stress Marks

The relative emphasis with which the syllables of a word or phrase are spoken, called stress, is indicated in three different ways. The strongest, or primary, stress is marked with a bold mark (´). An intermediate, or secondary, level of stress is marked with a similar but lighter mark (´). The weakest stress is unmarked. Words of one syllable show no stress mark.

GLOSSARY OF ACADEMIC VOCABULARY

abandon (ə-băn′dən) *v.* to withdraw one's support or help, especially in spite of duty, allegiance, or responsibility.

ambiguous (ăm-bĭg′yo͞o-əs) *adj.* open to more than one interpretation.

anticipate (ăn-tĭs′ə-pāt) *v.* to see as a probable occurrence; expect.

appreciate (ə-prē′shē-āt) *v. tr.* to recognize the quality, significance, or magnitude of.

arbitrary (är′bĭ-trĕr-ē) *adj.* determined by chance, whim, or impulse, and not by necessity, reason, or principle.

collapse (kə-lăps′) *v.* to break down or fall apart suddenly and cease to function.

conceive (kən-sēv′) *v.* to understand or form in the mind; to devise.

confine (kən-fīn′) *v.* to keep within bounds; restrict.

conform (kən-fôrm′) *v.* to be similar to or match something or someone; to act or be in accord or agreement.

controversy (kŏn′trə-vûr-sē) *n.* public disagreement, argument.

convince (kən-vĭns′) *v.* persuade or lead to agreement by means of argument.

denote (dĭ-nōt′) *v.* to serve as a symbol for the meaning of; signify.

depress (dĭ-prĕs′) *v.* to cause to be sad or dejected.

displace (dĭs-plās′) *v.* to move, shift, or force from the usual place or position.

drama (drä′mə) *n.* a prose or verse composition intended to be acted out.

encounter (ĕn-koun′tər) *n.* to confront in battle or competition.

exploit (ĭk-sploit′) *v.* to take advantage of; to use for selfish or unethical purposes.

insight (ĭn′sīt) *n.* the ability to discern the true nature of a situation.

integrity (ĭn-tĕg′rĭ-tē) *n.* the quality of being ethically or morally upright.

intensity (ĭn-tĕn′sĭ-tē) *n.* a high degree of concentration, power, or force.

invoke (ĭn-vōk′) *v.* to call on for assistance, support, or inspiration.

military (mĭl′ĭ-tĕr-ē) *n.* the armed forces of a nation considered collectively; *adj.* of, related to, or characteristic of members of the armed forces.

persist (pər-sĭst′) *v.* to hold firmly to a purpose or task in spite of obstacles.

radical (răd′ĭ-kəl) *adj.* departing markedly from the usual or customary; extreme or drastic.

reluctance (rĭ-lŭk′təns) *n.* the state of being reluctant; unwillingness.

subordinate (sə-bôr′dn-ĭt) *adj.* subject to the authority or control of another.

undergo (ŭn-dər-gō′) *v.* to experience or be subjected to.

violate (vī′ə-lāt) *tr. v.* to disregard or act in a manner that does not conform to (a law or promise, for example).

visual (vĭzh′o͞o-əl) *adj.* seen or able to be seen by the eye; visible

widespread (wīd′sprĕd′) *adj.* occurring or accepted widely.

GLOSSARY OF CRITICAL VOCABULARY

abate (ə-bāt′) *v.* to reduce in amount, degree, or intensity; lessen.

abrogate (ăb′rə-gāt) *v.* to revoke or nullify.

abyss (ə-bĭs′) *n.* an immeasurably deep chasm, depth, or void.

accolade (ăk′ə-lād, -lād) *n.* a special acknowledgement; an award.

affairs (ə-fârz′) *n.* personal business.

affliction (ə-flĭk′shən) *n.* something that causes suffering or pain.

aghast (ə-găst′) *adj.* struck by shock, terror, or amazement.

algorithm (ăl′gə-rĭth-əm) *n.* a finite set of unambiguous instructions that, given some set of initial conditions, can be performed in a prescribed sequence to achieve a certain goal and that has a recognizable set of end conditions.

anecdote (ăn′ĭk-dōt) *n.* a short account of an interesting or humorous incident.

appraise (ə-prāz′) *tr. v.* 1. to estimate the price or value of: appraise a diamond; appraise real estate. 2. to make a considered judgment about.

ardor (är′dər) *n.* intensity of emotion, especially strong desire, enthusiasm, or devotion.

artifice (är′tə-fĭs) *n.* cleverness or ingenuity in making or doing something.

attribute (ə-trĭb′yo͞ot) *v.* to regard as arising from a particular cause or source; ascribe.

aversion (ə-vûr′zhən) *n.* a fixed, intense dislike; repugnance.

autonomy (ô-tŏn′ə-mē) *n.* the condition or quality of being autonomous; independence.

bailiff (bā′lĭf) *n.* an overseer of an estate; a steward.

baleful (bāl′fəl) *adj.* harmful or malignant in intent or effect.

balmy (bä′mē) *adj.* mild and pleasant.

bequeath (bĭ-kwēth′, -kwēth′) *tr. v.* to pass (something) on to another; hand down.

bereft (bĭ-rĕft′) *adj.* 1. deprived of something. 2. lacking something needed or expected.

brazen (brā′zən) *adj.* unrestrained by a sense of shame; rudely bold.

brooding (bro͞o′dĭng) *adj.* thinking about something moodily.

cacophony (kə-kŏf′ə-nē) *n.* jarring, discordant sound; dissonance.

calamity (kə-lăm′ĭ-tē) *n.* an event that brings terrible loss, lasting distress, or severe affliction; a disaster.

chafe (chāf) *v. intr.* to cause irritation by rubbing or friction: The high collar chafed against my neck.

chow (chou) *n.* food; victuals.

collateral (kə-lăt′ər-əl) *adj.* concomitant or accompanying.

commence (kə-mĕns′) *v.* to begin or start.

commend (kə-mĕnd′) *tr. v.* to commit to the care of another; entrust.

compulsory (kəm-pŭl′sə-rē) *adj.* obligatory; required.

condone (kən-dōn′) *v.* to overlook, forgive, or disregard (an offense) without protest or censure.

congenial (kən-jēn′yəl) *adj.* agreeable, sympathetic.

consumption (kən-sŭmp′shən) *n.* an amount consumed.

cowed (koud) *tr. v.* to frighten or subdue with threats or a show of force.

GLOSSARY OF CRITICAL VOCABULARY

curate (kyoor´āt) *tr. v.* to gather and present to the public.

demonize (dē´mə-nīz) *v.* to represent as evil or diabolic.

deprivation (dĕp-rə-vā´shən) *n.* the condition of being deprived; lacking the basic necessities or comforts of life.

despotic (dĭ-spŏt´ĭk) *adj.* of or relating to a person who wields power oppressively, or a tyrant.

discourse (dĭs´kôrs) *n.* verbal exchange or conversation.

dismay (dĭs-mā´) *v.* to upset or distress.

dissimulation (dĭ-sĭm´yə-lā-shən) *n.* deceit or pretense.

dogged (dô´gĭd, dŏg´ĭd) *adj.* stubbornly perservering; tenacious.

domain (dō-mān´) *n.* a sphere of activity, influence, or knowledge.

dominion (də-mĭn´yən) *n.* rule or power to rule; mastery.

double entendre (dûb´əl än-tän´drə) *n.* an expression having a double meaning.

emulation (ĕm´yə-lā-shən) *n.* competitive imitation.

encumbrance (ĕn-kŭm´brəns) *n.* a burden or impediment.

engagement (ĕn-gāj´mənt) *n.* a promise or agreement to be at a particular place at a particular time.

entail (ĕn-tāl´) *v.* involve as a consequence.

ersatz (ĕr´zäts, ĕr-zäts´) *adj.* being an usually inferior imitation or substitute; artificial.

eschew (ĕ-shoō´, ĕs-choō´) *tr. v.* to avoid using, accepting, participating in, or partaking of.

esprit de corps (ĕ-sprē´ də kôr´) *n.* a spirit of devotion and loyalty among group members.

evanescent (ĕv-ə-nĕs´ənt) *adj.* vanishing or likely to vanish like vapor.

exorbitant (ĭg-zôr´bĭ-tənt) *adj.* beyond what is reasonable or customary, especially in cost or price.

expound (ĭk-spound´) *v.* to explain in detail; elucidate.

extract (ĭk-străkt´) *v.* to draw or pull out, often with great force or effort.

extremist (ĭk-strē´mĭst) *adj.* advocating or resorting to measures beyond the norm, especially in politics.

feeble (fē´bəl) *adj.* lacking strength.

finite (fī´nīt) *adj.* having bounds; limited.

flotsam (flŏt´səm) *n.* discarded or unimportant things.

forebear (fôr´bâr) *n.* a person from whom one is descended; an ancestor.

forge (fôrj) *v.* to form (metal, for example) by heating in a forge and beating or hammering into shape.

garish (gâr´ĭsh, găr´-) *adj.* overly bright or ornamented, especially in a vulgar or tasteless way; gaudy.

genre (zhän´rə) *n.* a category within an art form, based on style or subject.

gilded (gĭl´dĭd) *adj.* covered with or having the appearance of being covered with a thin layer of gold.

guile (gīl) *n.* clever trickery; deceit.

hierarchy (hī´ə-rär-kē) *n.* a ranking of status within a group.

huddle (hŭd´l) *v.* to crowd together, as from cold or fear.

ignoble (ĭg-nō´bəl) *adj.* not noble in quality, character, or purpose; base or dishonorable.

immersion (ĭ-mûr´zhən, -shən) *n.* the act or instance of engaging in something wholly or deeply.

impeccably (ĭm-pĕk´ə-blē) *adv.* in accordance with having no flaws; perfectly.

imperialism (ĭm-pîr´ē-ə-lĭz-əm) *n.* the extension of a nation's authority by territorial acquisition or by the establishment of economic and political dominance over other nations.

implementation (ĭm-plə-mən-tā´shən) *n.* the process of putting into practical effect; carry out.

inanimate (ĭn-ăn´ə-mĭt) *adj.* not having the qualities associated with active, living organisms.

GLOSSARY OF CRITICAL VOCABULARY

inarticulate (ĭn-är-tĭk´yə-lĭt) *adj.* uttered without the use of normal words or syllables; incomprehensible as speech or language.

incentive (ĭn-sĕn´tĭv) *n.* something, such as the fear of punishment or the expectation of reward, that induces action or motivates effort.

inculcate (ĭn-kŭl´kāt, ĭn´kŭl-) *v.* to impress (something) upon the mind of another by frequent instruction or repetition; instill.

incumbent (ĭn-kŭm´bənt) *adj.* required as a duty or an obligation.

inducement (ĭn-do͞os´mənt, -dyo͞os´-) *n.* an incentive.

infantry (ĭn´fən-trē) *n.* the branch of an army made up of units trained to fight on foot.

infuse (ĭn-fyo͞oz´) *v.* to fill or cause to be filled with something.

inoculate (ĭ-nŏk´yə-lāt) *v.* to safeguard as if by inoculation; to protect.

labyrinth (lăb´ə-rĭnth) *n.* an intricate structure of interconnecting passages through which it is difficult to find one's way; a maze.

levy (lĕv´ē) *v.* to impose (a tax or fine, for example) on someone.

listless (lĭst´lĭs) *adj.* lacking energy or disinclined to exert effort; lethargic: felt tired and listless.

loathsome (lōth´səm) *adj.* causing loathing; abhorrent.

loftily (lôft´ĭ-ly) *adv.* arrogantly; haughtily.

luddite (lŭd´īt) *n.* one who opposes technical or technological change.

malady (măl´ə-dē) *n.* a disease, disorder, or ailment.

manacle (măn´ə-kəl) *v.* to restrain the action or progress of something or someone.

mandatory (măn´də-tôr-ē) *adj.* required or commanded by authority; obligatory.

meme (mēm) *n.* a unit of cultural information, such as a cultural practice or idea, that is transmitted verbally or by repeated action from one mind to another.

mire (mīr) *v.* to hinder, entrap, or entangle.

misdeed (mĭs-dēd´) *n.* a wrong or illegal deed; a wrongdoing.

misogyny (mĭ-sŏj´ə-nē) *n.* hatred or mistrust of women.

monetize (mŏn´ĭ-tīz, mŭn´-) *tr. v.* to convert into a source of income.

morose (mə-rōs´, mô-) *adj.* sullen or gloomy.

odious (ō´dē-əs) *adj.* extremely unpleasant; repulsive.

ominous (ŏm´ə-nəs) *adj.* menacing; threatening.

pension (pĕn´shən) *n.* a sum of money paid regularly as a retirement benefit.

pervasive (pər-vā´sĭv,-zĭv) *adj.* having the quality or tendency to pervade or permeate.

plateau (plă-tō´) *intr. v.* to reach a stable level; level off.

plight (plīt) *n.* a situation, especially a bad or unfortunate one.

posit (pŏz´ĭt) *tr. v.* to assume or put forward, as for consideration or the basis of argument.

preamble (prē´ăm-bəl, prē-ăm´-) *n.* a preliminary statement.

precipice (prĕs´ə-pĭs) *n.* an overhanging or extremely steep mass of rock; the brink of a dangerous or disastrous situation.

prerogative (prĭ-rŏg´ə-tĭv) *n.* an exclusive right or privilege held by a person or group, especially a hereditary or official right.

prescient (prĕsh´ənt) *adj.* of or relating to prescience—which means knowledge of actions or events before they occur.

presentable (prĭ-zĕn´tə-bəl) *adj.* fit for introduction to others.

prodigious (prə-dĭj´əs) *adj.* enormous.

prognosis (prŏg-nō´sĭs) *n.* a prediction of the probable course and outcome of a disease.

promiscuously (prə-mĭs´kyo͞o-əs-lə) *adv.* lacking standards of selection; acting without careful judgment; indiscriminate.

GLOSSARY OF CRITICAL VOCABULARY

prostrate (prŏs´trāt) *adj.* lying face down, as in submission or adoration.

pyrrhic victory (pĭr´ĭk vĭk´tə-rē) *n.* a victory that is offset by staggering losses.

quell (kwĕl) *tr. v.* to pacify; quiet.

ransack (răn´săk) *tr. v.* to go through (a place) stealing valuables and causing disarray.

realm (rĕlm) *n.* kingdom.

rebuke (rĭ-byōōk´) *tr. v.* to criticize (someone) sharply; reprimand.

recoil (rĭ-koil´) *v.* to shrink back, as in fear or repugnance.

redress (rĭ-drĕs´) *n.* repayment for a wrong or an injury.

repine (rĭ-pīn´) *v.* to be discontented; complain or fret.

rotation (rō-tā´shən) *n.* regular and uniform variation in a sequence or series.

ruddy (rŭd´ē) *adj.* having a healthy reddish glow.

rudiment (rōō´də-mənt) *n.* fundamental element, principle, or skill.

salutation (săl-yə-tā´shən) *n.* a polite expression of greeting or goodwill.

satire (săt´īr) *n.* a literary work in which human foolishness or vice is attacked through irony, derision, or wit.

scorn (skôrn) *n.* contempt or disdain.

scrounge (skrounj) *v. intr.* to obtain by salvaging or foraging; round up.

scrupulous (skrōō´pyə-ləs) *adj.* conscientious and exact; having scruples.

sea change (sē chānj) *n.* a marked transformation.

self-possessed (sĕlf-pə-zĕst´) *adj.* having calm and self-assured command of one's faculties, feelings, and behavior.

senility (sĭ-nĭl´ĭ-tē) *n.* relating to or having diminished cognitive function, as when memory is impaired, because of old age.

sentient (sĕn´shənt) *adj.* having sense perception; conscious.

smart (smärt) *v.* to suffer acutely, as from mental distress, wounded feelings, or remorse.

sovereignty (sŏv´ər-ĭn-tē, sŏv´rĭn-) *n.* complete independence and self-government.

spoof (spōōf) *n.* a satirical imitation; a parody or send-up.

succinct (sək-sĭngkt´) *adj.* characterized by clear, precise expression in few words; concise and terse.

summon (sŭm´ən) *v.* to bring into existence or readiness.

superficial (sōō-pər-fĭsh´əl) *adj.* apparent rather than actual or substantial; shallow.

supplant (sə-plănt´) *tr. v.* to take the place of or substitute for (another).

sustenance (sŭs´tə-nəns) *n.* something, especially food, that sustains life or health.

tactfully (tăkt´fəl-lə) *adv.* considerately and discreetly.

theorize (thē´ə-rīz, thîr´īz) *v.* to formulate theories or a theory; speculate.

treachery (trĕch´ə-rē) *n.* an act of betrayal.

trinket (trĭng´kĭt) *n.* a small ornament, such as a piece of jewelry.

tumult (tōō´mŭlt) *n.* a state of agitation of the mind or emotions.

undaunted (ŭn-dôn´tĭd, -dän´-) *adj.* not discouraged or disheartened; resolutely courageous.

underpin (ŭn-dər-pĭn´) *tr. v.* to give support or substance to.

usurp (yōō-sûrp´) *v.* to seize unlawfully by force.

Utopian (yōō-tō´pē-ən) *adj.* excellent or ideal but impracticable; visionary.

valor (văl´ər) *n.* courage, bravery.

veracity (və-răs´ĭ-tē) *n.* conformity to fact or truth; accuracy.

verandah (və-răn´də) *n.* a porch or balcony.

GLOSSARY OF CRITICAL VOCABULARY

vexation (vĕk-sā´shən) *n.* a source of irritation or annoyance.

vigilance (vĭj´ə-ləns) *n.* alert watchfulness.

vile (vīl) *adj.* unpleasant or objectionable.

vindication (vĭn-dĭ-kā´shən) *n.* justification.

virtue (vûr´cho͞o) *n. Archaic* chastity, especially in a woman.

visitation (vĭz-ĭ-tā´shən) *n.* a gathering of people in remembrance of a deceased person.

vogue (vōg) *adj.* the prevailing fashion, practice, or style.

wail (wāl) *v.* to make a long, loud, high-pitched cry, as in grief, sorrow, or fear.

writ (rĭt) *n.* a written order issued by a court, commanding the party to whom it is addressed to perform or cease performing a specified act.

Index of Skills

Key
Teacher's Edition subject entries and page references are printed in **boldface** type. Subject entries and page references that apply to both the Student Edition and the Teacher's Edition appear in lightface type.

A

academic citations, 684
Academic Vocabulary, 5, 21, 41, 61, 79, 93, 105, 123, 132, 143, 273, 279, 291, 303, 311, 321, 331, 345, 356, 365, 377, 393, 403, 417, 431, 443, 459, 473, 484, 495, 511, 519, 531, 543, 557, 573, 582, 591, 607, 613, 625, 639, 651, 663, 675, 684, 695, 709, 721, 735, 753, 765, 775, 785, 796
active voice, 133, 380, 395
adjective, 405
Again and Again (Notice & Note), 454, 620
Aha Moment (Notice & Note), 50, 528, 620, 706, 730
allegory, 615, 618, 619, 622
alliteration, 7, 23, 656
analogy, 325
analyze
   allegory, 615, 618, 619, 622
   Analyze Media, 612
   Analyze the Text, 20, 40, 60, 78, 92, 104, 108, 122, 124, 176, 198, 226, 248, 272, 290, 302, 310, 320, 322, 330, 344, 348, 376, 392, 402, 416, 430, 442, 446, 458, 472, 476, 510, 518, 530, 542, 556, 558, 572, 574, 606, 623, 638, 650, 662, 664, 674, 676, 708, 720, 734, 752, 764, 766, 774, 784, 788
   apostrophe (figure of speech), 514, 516
   arguments, 281, 284, 286, 287
   author's perspective, 463, 466, 469, 470
   author's purpose, 382, 383, 384, 390
   characterization, 65, 67, 70, 71, 627, 629, 631, 633
   compare and contrast essay, 643, 645, 648
   conflict, 45, 48, 49, 51, 52, 56, 58, 147, 182, 185, 212, 238, 257
   counterarguments, 421, 424
   diction, 548, 551, 554
   documentaries, 610
   dramatic plot, 147, 153, 156, 167, 171, 179, 188, 197, 220, 231, 241, 255, 268
   epic poem, characteristics of, 7, 10, 12, 15, 17
   extended metaphors, 655, 661
   fantasy, 65, 68, 73, 74, 76, 77
   first-person point of view, 593, 596, 600, 603, 604

   form (poetry), 547, 549, 552, 555
   graphic features, 435, 438, 440
   heroic couplets, 367, 370
   historical setting, 449, 451, 454, 455, 456
   idea development, 397, 400
   imagery, 498, 501, 503, 508, 668, 670, 672
   inductive reasoning, 769, 772
   irony, 723, 726, 732
   key ideas, 281, 286, 288
   metaphysical conceits, 305, 308
   mock epic, 368, 371, 375
   mood, 616, 617, 621
   motivation, 521, 524, 525, 526
   narrator, 25, 30, 31, 34, 35, 38, 449, 452, 455
   Old English poetry, 7, 11, 16, 18
   plot, 627, 634, 636
   primary sources, 83, 86, 91
   reflective essay, 723, 730
   rhetorical devices, 325, 328
   rhyme scheme, 513, 516
   rhythmic patterns, 758, 759
   romantic poetry, 497, 500, 504, 506
   satire, 367, 372, 373
   satirical devices, 379, 385, 387, 390
   science fiction, 521, 523, 527
   setting, 593, 597, 598, 601, 739, 742, 747
   soliloquy, 148, 159, 195, 200, 218, 232
   sonnets, 295, 298, 300
   sound devices, 656, 658
   speaker, 314, 318
   stanza structure, 513, 516
   stream of consciousness, 714, 716
   structure, 25, 28, 39
   symbols, 561, 564, 568
   text features, 335, 339
   third-person point of view, 697, 700, 704
   tone, 111, 113, 116, 119, 397, 401
anapest, 757
annotate. See also Annotation Model
Annotation Model, 8, 26, 46, 66, 84, 98, 112, 148, 282, 296, 306, 314, 326, 336, 368, 380, 398, 408, 422, 436, 450, 464, 498, 514, 522, 536, 548, 562, 594, 616, 628, 644, 656, 668, 698, 714, 724, 740, 758, 770, 780
antecedent, 95, 777
antithesis, 325

antonym, 404, 532
apostrophe (figure of speech)
   analyze, 514, 516
   write poem using, 519
appeals
   emotional, 769
   ethical, 769
   logical, 769
Applying Academic Vocabulary, 14, 30, 35, 50, 54, 70, 89, 102, 171, 180, 205, 229, 245, 264, 284, 303, 308, 315, 328, 341, 372, 384, 388, 412, 425, 437, 456, 467, 504, 526, 538, 568, 602, 622, 635, 646, 705, 718, 730, 749, 782
appositive phrases, 66, 69, 81
appositives, 66, 69, 81
argument, writing an, 792–798
   author's craft, 795
   background reading, 793
   develop a draft, 794
   edit, 797
   genre characteristics, 795
   mentor text use, 795
   organize ideas, 794
   plan, 793
   publish, 797
   revise, 796
   Scoring Guide, 798
   writing prompt, 792
argumentative essay, 291
arguments
   adapt for debate, 799
   analyze, 281, 284
   appeals, 769
   call to action, 325, 769
   claim, 281, 421, 779
   compare, 768, 788–789
   counterarguments, 421, 424, 779, 782
   Create and Discuss, 291, 431, 785
   evaluate, 421, 425, 428, 779, 782, 785
   evidence, 281, 421, 779
   fallacies, 421, 769
   genre elements, 421
   persuasive, 776
   reasoning, 769, 779
   reasons, 281, 421
article, genre elements, 335
aside, 145
assonance, 656
audience, 97

   author's purpose and, 108
   persuasive techniques and, 769
author's craft
   argument, 795
   explanatory essay, 581
   literary analysis, 355
   personnal narrative, 485
   research report, 683
   short story, 131
author's perspective, 463, 470
   analyze, 463, 466, 469
author's purpose, 108
   analyze, 382, 383, 384, 390
   Collaborate and Present, 109
   evaluate, 97, 100, 102
   understand, 379

B

background, historical. See historical context
background reading
   argument, 793
   explanatory essay, 579
   literary analysis, 353
   personal narrative, 481
   research report, 681
   short story, 129
bias, 82, 83, 92, 104, 248, 290, 349
blank verse, 145
brainstorm, 345, 349, 444, 477, 483, 511, 663, 721, 789

C

caesura, 7
casting, 276
cause/effect, Analyze the Text, 92, 248, 348
central ideas, Collaborate and Present, 447
character motivations. See motivation
characterization, 65, 627
cite evidence, Analyze the Text, 330, 348
claim, 281, 421, 779
classical allusions, 274, 474
clauses, relative, 770, 772, 777
climax, 147
Close Read Screencast, 10, 164, 186, 219, 234, 269, 381
coherence, 686, 720
Collaborate & Compare, 108–109, 124–125, 348–349, 446–447, 476–477, 558–559, 574–575,

R14 Student Resources

664–665, 676–677, 766–767, 788–789
collaborative discussion, 2, 140, 362, 492, 588, 692
combining sentences, 293, 685
comedy, 144
compare
　across genres, 82, 324, 334, 348, 420, 434, 446, 448, 462, 476, 778
　Analyze Media, 612
　Analyze the Text, 108, 124, 198, 248, 272, 302, 322, 348, 442, 472, 558, 574, 606, 664, 676, 752, 766, 788
　arguments, 768, 788–789
　author's purpose, 109
　collaborate and. See Collaborate & Compare
　poems, 560, 574
　prepare to, 85, 99, 113, 118, 315, 318, 327, 337, 423, 437, 451, 465, 549, 554, 563, 657, 660, 669, 672, 759, 762, 771, 781
　primary sources, 96, 108
　themes, 110, 124–125, 312, 322–323, 546, 558–559, 654, 664–665, 666, 676–677, 766–767
compare and contrast essay
　analyze, 643, 645, 648
　Create and Discuss, 105
comparison
　Create and Present, 176, 607
　point-by-point, 643
complex sentence, 653
compose. See develop draft
compound sentence, 653
compound-complex sentence, 653
comprehension, monitor, 538
conclusions, draw. See draw conclusions
concrete noun, 405
conflict, 147
　analyze, 45, 48, 49, 51, 52, 56, 58, 147, 182, 185, 212, 238, 257
conjunctions
　coordinating, 282, 293, 422, 433, 685
　subordinating, 422, 433, 685
connect, 97
　Analyze the Text, 104, 310, 330, 416, 518, 556, 708, 720, 764
　research, 20, 60, 612, 650, 752
　connect to history, 325, 327, 407, 409, 412
connotation, 63, 405, 460, 710
consonance, 656
content, author's purpose and, 108
context
　author's purpose and, 108
　historical, 325, 407, 562, 566, 570
context clues, 62, 80, 332, 394, 404, 418

contradiction, 379. See also Contrasts and Contradictions (Notice & Note)
contrast, Analyze the Text, 446, 476
Contrasts and Contradictions (Notice & Note), 29, 75, 99, 207, 342, 388, 414, 467, 599
coordinating conjunctions, 282, 293, 422, 433, 685
counterarguments, analyze, 421, 424, 779, 782
Create and Adapt, analysis, 443
Create and Debate
　debate notes, 345
　missing scene, 709
　persuasive argument, 775
Create and Discuss
　argument, 291, 785
　character motivation, 198
　compare-and-contrast essay, 105
　diary entry, 417
　essay, 573
　eulogy, 273
　fictional scene, 753
　imagery board, 123
　informational essay, 735
　letter, 321
　list, 663
　op-ed, 651
　problem–solution essay, 459
　reflective essay, 543
　science fiction story, 531
　script, 273
　short story, 613, 639
　summary, 511
Create and Dramatize
　fantasy, 79
Create and Present
　argument, 431
　comparison, 176, 607
　epic, 21
　hero, 61
　journal entry, 248
　movie trailer, 279
　narrative, 279
　news briefing, 248
　poem, 21, 721
　poem using apostrophe, 519
　reflective essay, 311
　response to literature, 765
　scene, 61, 93, 226
　short story, 41
　sonnet, 303
　speech, 331
　visual representation, 557
Create and Recite
　illustration for narrative poem, 625
Create and Research
　informal notes, 473
　informational poster, 473

Critical Vocabulary, 8, 22, 26, 42, 46, 62, 66, 80, 84, 94, 98, 106, 282, 292, 326, 332, 336, 346, 380, 394, 398, 404, 408, 418, 422, 432, 444, 450, 460, 464, 474, 522, 532, 536, 544, 594, 608, 628, 640, 644, 652, 698, 710, 724, 736, 740, 754, 770, 776, 780, 786
critique
　Analyze the Text, 40, 108, 272, 430, 442, 530, 542, 574, 606, 650, 734, 766, 774, 784
　fictional scene, 753

D

dactyl, 757
dash, 336, 347
debate an issue, 799–800. See also Create and Debate
　adapt argument for, 799
　hold debate, 800
　practice with team, 800
denotation, 460, 710
details, precise, 698, 699, 711
develop a draft
　argument, 794
　explanatory essay, 580
　literary analysis, 354
　personal narrative, 482
　research report, 682
　short story, 130
dialogue, 145
diary
　entry, Create and Discuss, 417
　genre elements, 97, 407
diction, 63, 368
　analyze, 548, 551, 552
dictionary, specialized, 640
direct quotation, 436, 445, 485
direct statements, 25
discussion. See collaborative discussion; Create and Discuss; group discussion; small group discussion
documentary, 610
domain-specific words, 292
double entendre, 284
draft writing. See develop a draft
dramatic irony, 145, 723
dramatic monologue, 667
dramatic plot, analyze, 147, 153, 156, 167, 171, 179, 188, 197, 220, 231, 241, 268
dramatic reading, 765
draw conclusions
　about speakers, 667, 669
　Analyze the Text, 20, 40, 60, 78, 92, 176, 198, 248, 320, 376, 416, 458, 472, 510, 518, 530, 558, 572, 574, 606, 624, 638, 662, 664, 674, 708, 720, 764

E

edit draft
　argument, 797
　explanatory essay, 583
　literary analysis, 357
　personal narrative, 485
　research report, 685
　short story, 133
editorial, genre elements, 397, 779
effective words, 398, 405
em dash, 336, 347
emotional appeals, 769
en dash, 336
end rhyme, 513
English Learner Support, 1, 2, 10, 12, 14, 16, 19, 22, 23, 26, 27, 28, 29, 30, 32, 34, 36, 39, 42, 43, 46, 48, 51, 52, 54, 56, 58, 59, 62, 63, 66, 68, 69, 71, 72, 74, 75, 76, 77, 80, 81, 84, 85, 87, 89, 90, 91, 94, 95, 98, 101, 103, 106, 107, 108, 112, 113, 115, 117, 119, 120, 121, 124, 126, 129, 130, 131, 133, 135, 138, 140, 153, 156, 158, 160, 162, 167, 171, 175, 180, 182, 183, 185, 186, 189, 190, 196, 197, 198, 200, 203, 208, 209, 211, 215, 221, 223, 225, 228, 231, 232, 233, 235, 236, 239, 241, 244, 246, 247, 250, 252, 254, 258, 259, 262, 265, 267, 269, 270, 271, 274, 275, 276, 278, 282, 283, 284, 285, 287, 289, 292, 293, 295, 297, 299, 300, 301, 307, 308, 309, 314, 315, 317, 319, 322, 325, 329, 331, 332, 333, 336, 337, 338, 339, 341, 342, 343, 346, 347, 348, 350, 353, 354, 355, 356, 357, 360, 362, 370, 371, 373, 374, 375, 380, 382, 384, 385, 386, 387, 390, 391, 394, 395, 398, 401, 404, 405, 408, 410, 411, 412, 413, 414, 415, 418, 419, 422, 425, 427, 429, 432, 433, 436, 438, 441, 444, 445, 446, 450, 451, 452, 453, 454, 457, 460, 461, 464, 465, 466, 467, 469, 470, 471, 474, 475, 476, 478, 481, 482, 483, 484, 485, 487, 490, 492, 498, 500, 501, 502, 503, 505, 507, 508, 509, 514, 516, 517, 522, 524, 525, 526, 528, 529, 532, 533, 536, 538, 540, 541, 544, 545, 548, 549, 551, 553, 555, 558, 564, 565, 566, 567, 569, 570, 571, 574, 576, 579, 580, 581, 582, 583, 586, 588, 594, 596, 597, 598, 600, 601, 602, 603, 605, 608, 609, 610, 616, 618, 621, 622, 623, 628, 630, 633, 634, 635, 637, 640, 641, 644, 645, 646, 647, 648, 649, 652, 653, 657, 658, 659, 660, 661, 665, 668, 670, 671, 673,

Index of Skills　R15

676, 678, 681, 682, 683, 684, 685, 688, 690, 692, 698, 700, 704, 706, 707, 710, 711, 717, 718, 719, 724, 725, 731, 732, 733, 736, 737, 740, 741, 742, 745, 746, 749, 751, 754, 755, 758, 760, 761, 763, 766, 770, 771, 773, 776, 777, 780, 781, 783, 786, 787, 788, 790, 793, 794, 795, 796, 797, 799
enunciation, 688, 800
epic, Create and Present, 21
epic poem
   analyze characteristics of, 7, 10, 12, 15, 17
   genre elements, 7
essay
   argumentative, 291
   compare-and-contrast, 105
   evaluate, 535, 537, 539
   formal, 535
   genre elements, 535, 643, 723
   informal, 535
   informational, 735
   reflective, 543, 723, 730
   write, 573
Essential Question, 1, 6, 21, 24, 41, 44, 61, 64, 79, 82, 93, 96, 105, 110, 123, 126, 137, 139, 146, 273, 276, 279, 280, 291, 294, 303, 304, 311, 312, 321, 324, 331, 334, 345, 350, 359, 361, 366, 377, 378, 393, 396, 406, 417, 420, 431, 434, 443, 448, 459, 462, 473, 478, 489, 491, 496, 512, 520, 534, 543, 576, 578, 587, 592, 610, 614, 626, 642, 654, 666, 678, 680, 691, 696, 712, 722, 738, 756, 768, 778, 790, 792
   reflect on, 137, 359, 489, 585, 689, 801
   respond to, 21, 41, 61, 79, 93, 105, 123, 143, 273, 279, 291, 303, 311, 321, 331, 345, 377, 393, 403, 417, 431, 443, 459, 473, 495, 511, 519, 531, 546, 557, 573, 591, 607, 613, 625, 639, 651, 663, 675, 695, 709, 721, 735, 753, 765, 775, 785
establish a purpose. *See* Setting a Purpose
ethical appeals, 769
etymology, 736
eulogy, 273
evaluate
   Analyze the Text, 20, 60, 78, 104, 108, 124, 176, 198, 226, 248, 272, 322, 330, 344, 376, 416, 431, 458, 542, 556, 558, 606, 638, 650, 676, 734, 766, 774, 784, 788
   arguments, 421, 425, 428, 779, 782
   author's purpose, 97, 100, 102
   characters, 697, 701, 703, 705
   counterarguments, 779, 782, 785

essay, 535, 537, 539
   multimodal texts, 643, 646, 647
   persuasive techniques, 769, 772
evaluative questions, 535
evidence, 281, 779. *See also* cite evidence
exaggeration, 379
explanatory essay, writing an, 578–584
   author's craft, 581
   background reading, 579
   develop a draft, 580
   edit draft, 583
   genre characteristics, 581
   mentor text use, 581
   organize ideas, 580
   plan for writing, 579
   publish, 583
   revise draft, 582
   Scoring Guide, 584
   writing prompt, 578
exposition, 147
extended metaphors, 655, 661
external conflict, 45
Extreme or Absolute Language (Notice & Note), 88, 428

F

fallacies, logical, 421, 769
   false cause-and-effect, 421
   hasty generalization, 421
   oversimplification, 421
   red herring, 421
falling action, 147
fantasy, 65
   analyze, 65, 68, 73, 74, 76, 77
fictional scene, 753
figurative language, 306, 313, 316, 664
film, genre elements, 276
film clip, 277, 610
first-person point of view, analyze, 593, 596, 600, 603, 604
foil, 147
foot, in poetry, 757
foreign words or phrases, 608
foreshadowing, 60
form (poetry), analyze, 547, 548, 552, 555
formal essay, 535
formal language, 98, 103, 107, 326, 333
frame story, 25
free verse, 547, 757
From Reading to Writing (Notice & Note), 129, 353, 481, 579, 681, 793

G

gather information, 21, 41, 61, 79, 93, 105, 123, 272, 279, 291, 303, 311, 321, 331, 345, 337, 393, 403, 417, 431, 443, 459, 473, 477, 511, 519, 531, 543, 557, 573, 607, 613, 625,

639, 651, 663, 675, 709, 721, 735, 753, 765, 775, 785, 789
generate questions, 112
genre, 82, 283, 324, 334, 348, 420, 434, 446, 448, 462, 476, 778
genre characteristics
   argument, 795
   explanatory essay, 581
   literary analysis, 355
   personnal narrative, 485
   research report, 683
   short story, 131
Genre Elements
   argument, 421
   article, 335
   diary, 97
   documentary, 610, 627
   editorial, 397, 779
   epic poetry, 7
   essay, 535, 643, 723
   film, 276
   letters, 83
   literary criticism, 281
   lyric poetry, 111, 305, 313, 497, 547, 561, 655, 667, 713, 757
   memoir, 463
   narrative poetry, 25, 615
   novel, 449, 521, 593
   ode, 513
   romance, 45
   satire, 367, 379
   short story, 65, 697, 739
   sonnet, 295
   speech, 325, 769
   tragic drama, 147
gerund, 594, 602, 609
gerund phrase, 594, 602, 609
Glossary of Academic Vocabulary, R8
Glossary of Critical Vocabulary, R9–13
graphic features, analyze, 435, 438, 440
Greek suffix *-ize*, 786
group discussion, 123, 579

H

heroic couplet, 368
   analyze, 367, 370
historical background. *See* historical context
historical context, 325, 407, 562, 566, 570
historical setting, analyze, 449, 451, 453, 454, 455, 456
history, connect to, 325, 327, 407, 409, 412
homophones, 22
Horatian satire, 367
hyperbole, 313, 379
hyphen, 336, 347

I

iamb, 757
iambic, 295
iambic pentameter, 145, 295, 367, 513, 757
ideas
   analyze and discuss, 651
   development of, analyze, 397, 400
   identify, 574
   present, 665
identify
   Analyze Media, 612
   Analyze the Text, 40, 344, 542, 572, 774
identity patterns, Analyze the Text, 302, 518
idiom, 640, 754
illustration
   documentary, 610
   narrative poem, 625
imagery, 23, 497, 628, 630, 641, 664, 668
   analyze, 497, 501, 503, 508, 668, 670, 672
imagery board, 123
Improve Reading Fluency, 13, 32, 51, 72, 87, 152, 159, 188, 201, 210, 240, 243, 256, 267, 286, 316, 340, 374, 386, 414, 426, 440, 453, 468, 502, 516, 527, 537, 550, 563, 600, 620, 634, 703, 716, 731, 746
independent clause, 464
Independent Reading, 126–127, 350–351, 478–479, 576–577, 678–679, 790–791
indirect quotation, 436, 445, 485
inductive reasoning, analyze, 769, 772
infer, Analyze the Text, 40, 78, 92, 104, 122, 176, 416, 446, 458, 476, 556, 588, 624, 650, 662, 676, 720, 752, 784
inferential questions, 535
informal essay, 535
informal language, 98, 103, 107
informal notes, 473
information gathering. *See* gather information
informational essay, 735
informational poster, 473
Instructional Overview and Resources, 1A–1F, 138A–138F, 360A–360F, 490A–490D, 586A–586D, 690A–690D
intensive pronoun, 408, 410, 419, 425
internal conflict, 45
interpret
   Analyze the Text, 92, 123, 124, 198, 248, 310, 320, 330, 376, 430, 446, 472, 510, 518, 530, 558, 572, 574, 624, 638, 662, 674, 676, 764
   figurative language, 313, 316
   ideas in poetry, 306

interpretations of drama, analyze, 276
inverted sentences, 26, 33, 43
inverted syntax, 548
irony, 306, 723, 726, 732

J
journal entry, 248
Juvenalian satire, 367

K
kennings, 7
key ideas, analyze, 281
key statements, in poem, 664

L
language
  formal, 98, 107, 326, 333
  informal, 98, 107
  sensory, 522, 583
Language Conventions
  active and passive voice, 380, 382, 395
  appositives and appositive phrases, 66, 69, 81
  combining sentences, 285, 293, 685
  coordinating conjunctions, 282, 285, 422, 425, 433
  dashes and hyphenation, 336, 339, 347
  direct and indirect quotations, 436, 438, 445
  effective words, 398, 399, 405
  formal and informal language, 98, 103, 107
  formal language, 326, 333
  gerunds and gerund phrases, 594, 602, 609
  imagery, 628, 630, 641
  intensive pronouns, 408, 419
  inverted sentences, 26, 33, 43
  mood, 8, 13, 23
  paradox, 148, 223, 275
  parallel structure, 536, 539, 545, 744
  participles, 450, 454, 461
  precise details, 698, 699, 711
  prepositional phrases, 724, 725, 737
  quotations, 357
  reflexive pronouns, 408, 410, 419
  relative clauses, 770, 772, 777
  relative pronouns, 770, 777
  rhetorical questions, 780, 781, 787
  sensory language, 522, 525, 533, 583
  sentence structure, 644, 649, 653
  subject-verb agreement, 84, 87, 95
  subordinate clauses, 464, 474
  subordinating conjunctions, 422, 425, 433
  syntax, 740, 744, 755, 797
  tone, 46, 59, 63
  use active and passive voice appropriately, 133

Language X-Ray: English Learner Support, 128B, 352B, 480B, 578B, 680B, 792B
Latin roots, 106, 544
Learning Mindset, 1, 6, 20, 24, 40, 126, 128, 137, 138, 149, 176, 227, 248, 350, 352, 359, 360, 378, 392, 420, 430, 478, 480, 489, 490, 496, 510, 560, 572, 576, 578, 585, 586, 614, 624, 626, 638, 678, 680, 689, 690, 712, 720, 756, 764, 790, 792, 801
letter
  Create and Discuss, 321
  genre elements, 83
lighting, 276
limited third-person narrator, 697
list, Create and Discuss, 663
literal questions, 535
literary allusions, 432
literary analysis, writing a, 352–358
  author's craft, 355
  background reading, 353
  develop draft, 354
  edit draft, 357
  genre characteristics, 355
  language conventions, 357
  mentor text use, 355
  organize ideas, 354
  plan for writing, 353
  publish, 357
  revise draft, 356
  Scoring Guide, 358
  writing prompt, 352
literary criticism, genre elements, 281
literature
  reading, 126
  signposts/anchor questions for reading, 126, 350, 478, 576, 678, 790
  write response to, 765
living for the moment, Collaborate and Present, 323
logical appeals, 769
logical fallacies, 769
lyric poetry, genre elements, 111, 305, 313, 497, 547, 561, 655, 667, 713

M
make connections. *See* connect
make inferences, 83, 90, 407, 410, 559, 713, 717. *See also* infer
make predictions, 45, 53, 55, 435, 437, 440, 739, 741, 745, 748, 750. *See also* predict
media, analyze, 612
memoir, 463
  connect to, 463, 468
  genre elements, 463
Memory Moment (Notice & Note), 14

Mentor Text, 64A, 64, 128, 131, 280A, 280, 352, 355, 462A, 462, 480, 483, 534A, 534, 578, 581, 642A, 642, 680, 683, 768A, 768, 778A, 778, 792, 795
mentor text use, for writing
  argument, 795
  explanatory essay, 581
  literary analysis, 355
  personal narrative, 483
  research report, 683
  short story, 131
message, 97
metaphor, 313
  extended, 655, 661
metaphysical conceit, 304, 308
meter (poetry), 145, 757
mock epic, 368
  analyze, 368, 371, 375
modernist poetry, understand, 713, 718
modulation, voice, 688
monitor comprehension, 112, 114, 115, 118, 120, 535, 538
monologue
  dramatic, 667
  present, 675
mood, 8, 22, 616. *See also* tone
  analyze, 616, 617, 621
  language conventions, 8, 13, 23
moral dilemma, 521
motivation, 521
  analyze, 521, 524, 525, 526
movie trailer, 279
multimodal presentation
  adapt report for, 687
  deliver, 688
  practice for, 688
multimodal text, 435
  evaluate, 643, 646, 647
multiple meaning words, 62, 332
music, in documentary, 610

N
narrative
  Create and Present, 279
  presenting a, 487–488
narrative poetry
  genre elements, 25
  illustrate, 625
narrator, 25
  analyze, 25, 30, 31, 34, 35, 38, 449, 452, 455
  limited third-person, 697
news briefing, 248
nonfiction, signposts/anchor questions for reading, 126, 350, 478, 576, 678, 790
nonrestrictive appositive, 81
nonverbal techniques, 688, 800
notes, informal, 472

Notice & Note
  Again and Again, 620
  Aha Moment, 50, 528, 620, 706, 730
  Contrasts and Contradictions, 29, 75, 99, 207, 342, 388, 414, 467, 599
  Extreme or Absolute Language, 88, 428
  From Reading to Writing, 129, 353, 481, 579, 681, 793
  Memory Moment, 14
  Numbers and Stats, 771
  Quoted Words, 540, 648
  Tough Questions, 38, 569
  Words of the Wiser, 164, 749
novel, genre elements, 449, 521, 593, 627
Numbers and Stats (Notice & Note), 771

O
objective viewpoint, 610
ode, 547
  genre elements, 513
Old English poetry, analyze, 7, 11, 16, 18
onomatopoeia, 656
op-ed, 651
oral presentation, 675. *See also* Create and Present; present; presentation
organize ideas
  argument, 794
  explanatory essay, 580
  literary analysis, 354
  personal narrative, 482
  research report, 682
  short story, 130
overstatement, 379
oxymoron, 275

P
paradox, 148, 223, 275, 306, 379
parallel structure, 536, 539, 545, 744. *See also* parallelism
parallelism, 325. *See also* parallel structure
paraphrase, 112, 335
participial phrase, 461
participle, 461, 450
passive voice, 133, 380, 382, 395
peer review, 132, 484, 356, 582, 684, 796
pentameter, 295
persona, 667
personal narrative, writing a, 480–486
  author's craft, 483
  background reading, 481
  develop draft, 482
  edit draft, 485
  genre characteristics, 483
  language conventions, 485
  mentor text use, 483
  organize ideas, 482
  plan for writing, 481
  publish, 485

Index of Skills R17

revise draft, 484
Scoring Guide, 486
writing prompt, 480
persuasive argument, develop, 775
persuasive techniques, evaluate, 769, 772
phrases
  foreign, 608
  gerund, 594, 602, 609
  prepositional, 724, 725, 737
pitch, voice, 688
plan for writing
  argument, 793
  explanatory essay, 579
  literary analysis, 353
  personal narrative, 481
  research report, 681
  short story, 129
plot, analyze, 147, 627, 634, 636. *See also* dramatic plot.
plural, 84
podcast, 135–136, 573
poems/poetry
  compare, 560
  Create and Present, 21, 519, 721
  genre elements, 757
  interpret ideas in, 306
  lyric, 497, 655, 667, 713
  modernist, 713
  narrative, 625
  present, 519
  present as monologue, 675
  romantic, 497, 500, 504, 506
  summarize, 296, 300
  Victorian, 589
  write, using apostrophe, 519
point of view
  first-person, 593, 596, 600, 603, 604
  objective/subjective, in documentary, 610
  third-person, 697, 700, 704
point-by-point comparison, 643
Practice and Apply
  critical vocabulary, 22, 42, 62, 80, 94, 106, 292, 332, 346, 394, 404, 418, 432, 444, 460, 474, 532, 544, 608, 640, 652, 710, 736, 754, 776, 786
  language conventions, 23, 43, 63, 81, 95, 107, 275, 293, 333, 347, 405, 433, 445, 461, 475, 533, 545, 609, 641, 653, 711, 737, 755, 777, 787
  vocabulary strategy, 22, 42, 62, 80, 94, 106, 274, 292, 332, 346, 394, 404, 418, 432, 444, 460, 474, 532, 544, 608, 640, 652, 710, 736, 754, 776, 786
precise details, 698, 699, 711
predict, Analyze the Text, 60, 176, 638, 752
predictions. *See* make predictions
prepositional phrases, 724, 725, 737

present. *See also* Create and Present; presentation
  author's purpose, 109
  comparison, 176, 607, 677
  epic, 21
  essay, 311
  graphic, 443
  ideas, 575, 665
  living for the moment, 323
  monologue, 675
  persuasive speech, 431
  poem, 519, 721
  scene, 79, 709
  short story, 41, 613
  sonnet, 303
  speech, 331
  theme, 125
  visual representation, 557
presentation
  multimodal, 687–688
  oral, 675
primary sources, 83
  analyze, 83, 86, 91
  compare, 96, 108–109
problem–solution essay, 459
pronouns, relative, 770, 777
publish
  argument, 797
  explanatory essay, 583
  literary analysis, 357
  personal narrative, 485
  research report, 685
  short story, 133
pull quote, 435
purpose. *See* author's purpose; Setting a Purpose

Q

question, Analyze the Text, 542
questions
  evaluative, 535
  inferential, 535
  literal, 535
  rhetorical, 780, 781, 787
quotations, 357
Quoted Words (Notice & Note), 540, 648

R

realism, Victorian novels, 590
reasoning, 779
  inductive, 769, 772
reasons, 281, 421
recite, poetry, 625
Reflect on the Unit, 137, 359, 489, 585, 689, 801
reflective essay
  analyze, 723, 730
  Create and Present, 311
  write, 543

reflexive pronoun, 408, 410, 419, 425
related words, 776
relative clauses, 464, 475, 770, 772, 777
relative pronouns, 464, 770, 777
repetition, 325
report, research. *See* research report
reread confusing passages, 112
research, 3, 20, 40, 60, 78, 92, 104, 122, 141, 272, 278, 290, 302, 310, 320, 330, 344, 363, 376, 392, 402, 416, 430, 442, 458, 472, 493, 510, 518, 530, 542, 556, 572, 589, 606, 612, 624, 638, 650, 662, 674, 693, 708, 720, 734, 752, 764, 774, 784, 789
research report, multimodal presentation of, 687–688
research report, writing a, 680–686
  author's craft, 683
  background reading, 681
  develop a draft, 682
  edit, 685
  genre characteristics, 683
  mentor text use, 683
  organize ideas, 682
  plan, 681
  publish, 685
  revise, 684
  Scoring Guide, 686
  writing prompt, 680
Research and Share, 349, 477, 767, 789
resolution, 147, 295
response to literature, Create and Present, 765
Response Logs, 5, 143, 365, 495, 591, 695, R1–R6
restrictive appositive, 81
revise draft
  argument, 796
  explanatory essay, 582
  literary analysis, 356
  personal narrative, 484
  research report, 684
  short story, 132
rhetorical devices, 325, 328. *See also* entries for specific devices
rhetorical questions, 325, 780, 781, 787
rhyme scheme, 513, 516
rhythm, 7
rhythmic patterns, analyze, 757
rising action, 147
romance, genre elements, 45
romantic poetry, 497, 500, 504, 506
romanticism, 497
roots,
  Greek, 444
  Latin, 106, 544
run-on sentence, 653

S

satire, 367
  analyze, 367, 372, 373
  genre elements, 367, 379
satirical devices, analyze, 379
scatter plot graph, 435
scene, 145
  Create and Present, 61, 93, 226
  write missing, 709
science fiction, 521
  analyze, 521, 523, 527
  write, 531
Scoring Guide
  argument, 798
  explanatory essay, 584
  literary analysis, 358
  narrative essay, 486
  research report, 686
  short story, 134
script, Create and Discuss, 273
senses, 94
sensory language, 522, 583
sentence length, vary, 797
sentence structure, 644, 653, 797
sentences
  combining, 293, 685
  length, 797
  types, 653
set design, 276
setting, analyze, 593, 597, 598, 601, 739, 742, 747
Setting a Purpose, 10, 28, 47, 67, 150, 177, 199, 227, 249, 277, 283, 297, 307, 369, 382, 399, 409, 500, 515, 523, 537, 595, 611, 617, 629, 645, 699, 715, 725, 741, 790
Shakespearean drama
  conventions of drama, 145
  Elizabethan staging, 144
  Globe Theatre, 144
  Renaissance drama, 144
  Shakespearean language, 145
  Shakespearean tragedy, 144
short story
  Create and Discuss, 639
  Create and Present, 41, 613
  genre elements, 65, 697, 739
short story, writing a, 128–134
  author's craft, 131
  background reading, 129
  develop draft, 130
  edit draft, 133
  genre characteristics, 131
  language conventions, 133
  mentor text use, 131
  organize ideas, 130
  plan for writing, 129
  publish, 133

revise draft, 132
Scoring Guide, 134
writing prompt, 128
simile, 313
simple sentence, 653
singular, 84
situational irony, 723
small group discussion, 198, 459
soliloquy, 145, 148
   analyze, 148, 159, 195, 200, 218, 232
sonnet, 295, 547
   analyze, 295, 298, 300
   Create and Present, 303
   genre elements, 295
sound devices, analyze, 656, 658
sound effects, 610
speaker, 314, 667
   analyze, 314, 318
   draw conclusions about, 667, 669
specialized dictionary, 640
speech
   Create and Present, 331
   genre elements, 325, 769
stage direction, 145
Standard English, 107. *See also* formal language
stanza structure, analyze, 513, 516
stream of consciousness, analyze, 714, 716
structure
   analyze, 25, 28, 39
   sentence, 644, 649, 653
   stanza, 513, 516
subject, 25
subject-verb agreement, 84, 87, 95
subjective viewpoint, 610
subordinate clause, 464
subordinating conjunctions, 422, 433, 475, 685
subplot, 147, 627
subtitle, 435
summarize, 335, 338, 341
   Analyze the Text, 302, 320, 344, 442, 784
   poetry, 296, 300
summary, Create and Discuss, 511
symbolism, 757, 760, 762
symbols, 561, 757
   analyze, 561, 564, 568
synonym, 418
syntax, 368, 548, 740, 744, 755
   inverted, 548
   vary, for effect, 797
synthesize
   Analyze Media, 612
   Analyze the Text, 226, 322, 348, 416, 446, 476, 510, 788
   arguments, 788

T

text. *See also* Analyze the Text
   paraphrase, 335, 338, 341
   summarize, 335, 338, 341
Text Complexity, 6A, 24A, 44A, 64A, 82A, 96A, 110A, 144A, 276A, 280A, 294A, 304A, 312A, 324A, 334A, 366A, 378A, 396A, 406A, 420A, 434A, 448A, 462A, 496A, 512A, 520A, 534A, 546A, 560A, 592A, 610A, 614A, 626A, 642A, 654A, 666A, 696A, 712A, 722A, 738A, 756A, 768A, 778A
text features, 335, 435
   analyze, 335, 339
Text X-Ray: English Learner Support, 6C–6D, 24C–24D, 44C–44D, 64C–64D, 82C–82D, 96C–96D, 110C–110D, 144C–144D, 276C–276D, 280C–280D, 294C–294D, 304C–304D, 312C–312D, 324C–324D, 334C–334D, 366C–366D, 378C–378D, 396C–396D, 406C–406D, 420C–420D, 434C–434D, 448C–448D, 462C–462D, 496C–496D, 512C–512D, 520C–520D, 534C–534D, 546C–546D, 560C–560D, 592C–592D, 610C–610D, 614C–614D, 626C–626D, 642C–642D, 654C–654D, 666C–666D, 696C–696D, 712C–712D, 722C–722D, 738C–738D, 756C–756D, 768C–768D, 778C–778D
thematic map, 435
theme, 25, 558
   Collaborate and Present, 125
   compare, 110, 124, 546, 558–559, 654, 664–665, 666, 676–677, 766–767
   poem, 664
thesis, 643
third-person point of view, analyze, 697, 700, 704
title, 435
To Challenge Students, 12, 15, 31, 49, 53, 58, 71, 90, 99, 123, 129, 145, 151, 166, 177, 193, 199, 216, 218, 231, 241, 253, 259, 261, 287, 311, 318, 342, 353, 369, 370, 385, 409, 410, 427, 438, 455, 470, 481, 501, 508, 528, 540, 552, 554, 570, 579, 599, 618, 621, 632, 636, 677, 681, 702, 727, 745, 747, 767, 789, 793
tone, 25, 46, 63, 111, 574
   analyze, 111, 113, 116, 119
   language conventions, 46, 63
Tough Questions (Notice & Note), 38, 569
tragedy, 144
tragic drama, genre elements, 147
tragic hero, 144
trochee, 757
turn (sonnet), 295

U

understand historical context, 562, 566, 570
understand modernist poetry, 713, 718
understand symbolism, 757, 760, 762
understatement, 379
usage, 42

V

verbal irony, 379, 723
verbal techniques, 688, 800
verisimilitude, 449
verse drama, 145
visual representation, create, 557
visualize, 112
vocabulary
   Academic Vocabulary, 5, 21, 41, 61, 79, 93, 105, 123, 132, 143, 273, 279, 291, 303, 311, 321, 331, 345, 356, 365, 377, 393, 403, 417, 431, 443, 459, 473, 484, 495, 511, 519, 531, 543, 557, 573, 582, 591, 607, 613, 625, 639, 651, 663, 675, 684, 695, 709, 721, 735, 753, 765, 775, 785, 796
   Critical Vocabulary, 8, 22, 26, 42, 46, 62, 66, 80, 84, 94, 98, 106, 282, 292, 326, 336, 380, 394, 398, 404, 408, 418, 422, 432, 436, 444, 450, 460, 464, 474, 522, 532, 536, 544, 594, 608, 628, 640, 644, 652, 698, 710, 724, 736, 740, 754, 770, 776, 780, 786
Vocabulary Strategy
   antonyms, 404, 532, 652
   classical allusions, 274, 474
   connotation, 460, 710
   consult a dictionary, 94
   context clues, 80, 394
   denotation, 460, 710
   domain-specific words and phrases, 292
   etymology, 736
   foreign words and phrases, 346, 608
   Greek roots and prefixes, 444
   Greek suffix *-ize*, 786
   homophones, 22
   idiom, 754, 640
   Latin roots, 106, 544
   literary allusions, 432
   multiple meaning words, 62, 332
   related words, 776
   synonyms, 418, 652
   usage, 42
voice modulation, 688, 800
voice pitch, 688
volta, 295
volume, voice, 688

W

When Students Struggle, 3, 11, 27, 29, 47, 55, 57, 60, 69, 73, 75, 78, 86, 88, 92, 101, 104, 109, 114, 115, 118, 122, 125, 127, 130, 133, 136, 141, 144, 150, 153, 160, 169, 174, 179, 181, 184, 191, 194, 202, 206, 212, 217, 220, 228, 233, 235, 237, 242, 246, 252, 255, 258, 260, 265, 270, 277, 281, 288, 290, 296, 298, 300, 302, 306, 307, 310, 313, 320, 323, 327, 330, 338, 344, 349, 351, 354, 357, 363, 367, 371, 376, 383, 389, 399, 400, 402, 406, 411, 413, 416, 428, 439, 442, 447, 449, 469, 472, 477, 479, 482, 485, 488, 493, 506, 515, 518, 525, 530, 539, 542, 551, 556, 559, 566, 575, 577, 580, 583, 589, 597, 604, 606, 611, 619, 631, 633, 647, 650, 657, 662, 664, 670, 672, 674, 679, 682, 685, 687, 693, 700, 706, 708, 717, 726, 732, 734, 743, 750, 752, 759, 762, 774, 784, 791, 794, 797, 800
word choice, 23, 574. *See also* diction
Word Network, 5, 143, 365, 495, 591, 695
words
   foreign, 608
   multiple meaning, 62, 332
   related, 776
Words of the Wiser (Notice & Note), 164, 749
writing activities
   argument, 291, 431, 775, 792–798
   character sketch, 61
   comparison, 105, 176, 607
   editorial, 651
   essay, 311, 393, 443, 543, 573, 735
   eulogy, 273
   explanatory essay, 578–584
   journal entry, 248, 417
   letter, 321
   literary analysis, 352–358
   notes, 345, 459, 473
   personal narrative, 480–487
   poem, 21, 303, 377, 519, 721

research report, 680–686
satire, 403
scene, 79, 93, 709, 753
short story, 41, 128–134 279, 531, 613, 639
speech, 331

summary, 511
writing process
  develop draft, 130, 354, 482, 580, 682, 794
  edit draft, 133, 357, 485, 583, 685, 797

plan for writing, 129, 353, 481, 681, 579, 793
publish, 133, 357, 485, 583, 685, 797
revise draft, 132, 356, 484, 582, 683, 796
writing prompt

argument, 792
explanatory essay, 578
literary analysis, 352
personal narrative, 480
research report, 680
short story, 128

INDEX OF TITLES AND AUTHORS

A
Alfred, Lord Tennyson, 617
Anonymous, 113
Arnold, Matthew, 657

B
Beowulf (excerpt), 9
Beowulf Poet, 9
Blake, William, 563
Brontë, Charlotte, 595
Browning, Robert, 669
Budget 2016: George Osborne's Speech, 772
Burney, Fanny, 409

C
Canterbury Tales, The (excerpt), 27
Chaucer, Geoffrey, 27
Chimney Sweeper, The, (from *Songs of Experience*) 570
Chimney Sweeper, The, (from *Songs of Innocence*) 566
Chivalry, 67
Composed upon Westminster Bridge, September 3, 1802, 506
Confession, 672
Cup of Tea, A, 699

D
Darkling Thrush, The, 660
Defoe, Daniel, 451
Dickens, Charles, 629
Dickson, Melissa, 645
Dinh, Linh, 672
Donne, John, 307
Dover Beach, 657
Du Fu, 554

E
Education Protects Women from Abuse, 437
Elizabeth I (Queen), 327
Elliot, T. S., 715
Encounter with King George III, An, 409

F
Factory Reform, 611
For Army Infantry's First Women, Heavy Packs and the Weight of History, 337
Frankenstein (excerpt), 523
Frankenstein: Giving Voice to the Monster, 537

G
Gaiman, Neil, 67

Girard, René, 283
Great Expectations (excerpt), 629

H
Hall, Chris, 778
Hamlet (film version), 277
Hamlet's Dull Revenge, 283
Hardy, Thomas, 660
Hatch, Steven, M.D., 465
Howe, Fanny, 118

I
Inferno: A Doctor's Ebola Story (excerpt), 465
I Wandered Lonely As a Cloud, 508

J
Jane Eyre (excerpt), 595
Journal and Letters of Fanny Burney, The (excerpt), 409
Journal of the Plague Year, A (excerpt), 451

K
Keats, John, 515
Khazan, Olga, 437

L
Lady of Shalott, The, 617
Lamb, The, 564
Lines Composed a Few Miles Above Tintern Abbey, 500
Loneliness, 118
Lovesong of J. Alfred Prufrock, The, 715

M
Mahdawi, Arwa, 399
Malory, Thomas (Sir), 47
Mansfield, Katherine, 699
Marah, 99
Marvell, Andrew, 315
Modest Proposal, A, 381
Morte D'Arthur, Le (excerpt), 47
My Daughter the Racist, 741
My Last Duchess, 669
My Syrian Diary (excerpt), 99

O
Ode on a Grecian Urn, 515
Ode to the West Wind, 549
Orwell, George, 725
Osborne, George, 772
Oyeyemi, Helen, 741

P
Paston Family, 85
Paston Letters, The (excerpt), 85
Pessoa, Fernando, 762
Philipps, Dave, 337
Pope, Alexander, 369

R
Rape of the Lock, The (excerpt), 369
Rich, Adrienne, 318

S
Satire Is Dying Because the Internet Is Killing It, 399
Second Coming, The, 759
Shakespeare, William, 149
Shelley, Mary, 523
Shelley, Percy Bysshe, 549
Shooting an Elephant, 725
Song of a Thatched Hut Damaged in Autumn Wind, 554
Sonnet 30, 298
Sonnet 75, 300
Speech Before the Spanish Armada Invasion, 327
Spenser, Edmund, 297
Swift, Jonathan, 381
Symbols? I'm Sick of Symbols, 762

T
To His Coy Mistress, 315
Tragedy of Hamlet, The, 149
Twenty-One Love Poems (Poem III), 318
Tyger, The, 568

V
Valediction: Forbidding Mourning, A, 307
Victorians Had the Same Concerns about Technology as We Do, The, 645
Vindication of the Rights of Woman, A (excerpt), 423

W
Wanderer, The, 113
Wife of Bath's Tale, The, 27
Will the Sugar Tax End Childhood Obesity?, 778
Winner, Langdon, 537
Wollstonecraft, Mary, 423
Wordsworth, William, 499

Y
Yeats, William Butler, 759

ACKNOWLEDGMENTS

Excerpts from *Beowulf* translated by Seamus Heaney. Translation copyright © 2000 by Seamus Heaney. Reprinted by permission of W. W. Norton & Company, Inc. and Faber & Faber Ltd.

Excerpt from "Budget 2016: George Osborne's Speech" by George Osborne from www.gov.uk. Contains Parliamentary information licensed under the Open Parliament License v3.0.

"Chivalry" from *Smoke and Mirrors* by Neil Gaiman. Text copyright © 1998 by Neil Gaiman. Reprinted by permission of Writers House, LLC.

"Confession" from *Borderless Bodies* by Linh Dinh. Text copyright © 2005 by Linh Dinh. Reprinted by permission of Linh Dinh.

"A Cup of Tea" from *The Short Stories of Katherine Mansfield* by Katherine Mansfield. Text copyright © 1923 by Penguin Random House LLC, renewed by J. Middleton Murry. Reprinted by permission of Alfred A. Knopf, an imprint of the Knopf Doubleday Publishing Group, a division of Penguin Random House LLC. All rights reserved. Any third-party use of this material, outside of this publication, is prohibited. Interested parties must apply directly to Penguin Random House LLC for permission.

"Education Protects Women from Abuse" by Olga Khazan as first published in *The Atlantic Magazine*, May 14, 2014. Text copyright © 2014 by The Atlantic Media Co. Reprinted by permission of Tribune Content Agency, LLC. All rights reserved. Distributed by Tribune Content Agency, LLC.

"For Army Infantry's 1st Women, Heavy Packs and the Weight of History" by Dave Phillips from *The New York Times*, May 27, 2017. Text copyright © 2017 by The New York Times. Reprinted by permission of PARS International Corps on behalf of The New York Times. All rights reserved. Protected by the Copyright Laws of the United States. Any printing, copying, redistribution, or retransmission of this Content without express written permission is prohibited. www.nytimes.com

Excerpt from "Frankenstein: Giving Voice to the Monster" by Langdon Winner from www.langdonwinner.com, July 7, 2017. Text copyright © 2017 by Langdon Winner. Reprinted by permission of Langdon Winner.

Excerpt from "Hamlet's Dull Revenge" by René Girard from *Stanford Literature Review 1*, Fall 1984. Text copyright © 1984 by René Girard. Reprinted by permission of Martha Girard.

Excerpt from *Inferno: A Doctor's Ebola Story* by Steven Hatch. Text copyright © 2017 by Steven Hatch. Reprinted by permission of St. Martin's Press.

Excerpt from *Le Morte D'Arthur* by Sir Thomas Malory, retold by Keith Baines. Text copyright © 1962 by Keith Baines. Reprinted by permission of Penguin Random House LLC. All rights reserved. Any third-party use of this material, outside of this publication, is prohibited. Interested parties must apply directly to Penguin Random House LLC for permission.

"Loneliness" from *Second Childhood* by Fanny Howe. Text copyright © 2014 by Fanny Howe. Reprinted by permission of The Permissions Company, Inc., on behalf of Graywolf Press. www.graywolfpress.org

"The Love Song of J. Alfred Prufrock" from *Collected Poems 1909-1962* by T.S. Eliot. Text copyright © 1930, 1940, 1941, 1942, 1943, 1958, 1962, 1963 by T.S. Eliot, renewed 1970 by Esme Valerie Eliot. Reprinted by permission of Faber and Faber Ltd.

"My Daughter the Racist" from *Mr. Fox* by Helen Oyeyemi. Text copyright © 2011 by Helen Oyeyemi. Reprinted by permission of Riverhead, an imprint of Penguin Publishing Group, a division of Penguin Random House LLC, Penguin Canada, a division of Penguin Random House Canada Limited, and the Wylie Agency, Inc. on behalf of the author. All rights reserved. Any third-party use of this material, outside this publication, is prohibited. Interested parties must apply directly to Penguin Random House LLC for permission.

"My Syrian Diary: Parts 1-3" by Marah from www.NewsDeeply.com. Text copyright © 2014 by Syria Deeply. Reprinted by permission of News Deeply, Inc.

Excerpt from *The Pastons: A Family in the War of the Roses* edited by Richard Barber. Text copyright © 1981 by Richard Barber. Reprinted by permission of Boydell & Brewer Ltd.

Quote from *A Dance with Dragons* by George R. R. Martin. Text copyright © 2011 by George R. R. Martin. Reprinted by permission of Bantam Books, an imprint of Random House, a division of Penguin Random House LLC. All rights reserved. Any third-party use of this material, outside of this publication, is prohibited. Interested parties must apply directly to Penguin Random House LLC for permission.

Quote by Derek Walcott from "Derek Walcott, the Art of Poetry No. 37" by Edward Hirsch from *The Paris Review*, Winter 1986. Text copyright © 1986 by The Paris Review. Reprinted by permission of The Paris Review.

"Satire is dying - the internet is killing it" by Arwa Mahdawi from www.theguardian.com, August 19, 2014. Text copyright © 2014 by The Guardian News & Media Ltd. Reprinted by permission of The Guardian News & Media Ltd.

"The Second Coming" from *The Collected Works of W. B. Yeats, Volume I: The Poems, Revised* by W. B. Yeats, edited by Richard J. Finneran. Text copyright 1924 by The Macmillan Company, renewed 1952 by Bertha Georgie Yeats. Reprinted by permission of Scribner, a division of Simon & Schuster, Inc. All rights reserved.

"Shooting an Elephant" from *Shooting an Elephant and Other Essays* by George Orwell. Text copyright 1950 by Sonig Brownell, renewed © 1978 by Sonig, Pitt-Rivers. Reprinted by permission of Houghton Mifflin Harcourt Publishing Company and A.M. Heath & Co. Ltd.

ACKNOWLEDGMENTS

"Song of a Thatched Hut Damaged in Autumn Wind" by Du Fu, translated by Tony Barnstone and Chou Ping from *The Anchor Book of Chinese Poetry: From Ancient to Contemporary, the Full 3000-Year Tradition* edited by Tony Barnstone and Chou Ping. Text copyright © 2005 by Tony Barnstone and Chou Ping. Reprinted by permission of Penguin Random House LLC. All rights reserved. Any third-party use of this material, outside of this publication, is prohibited. Interested parties must apply directly to Penguin Random House LLC for permission.

"Symbols? I'm Sick of Symbols" by Fernando Pessoa from *Fernando Pessoa & Co.: Selected Poems*, edited and translated by Richard Zenith. Translation copyright © 1998 by Richard Zenith. Reprinted by permission of Grove Atlantic, Inc.

"III" from *Twenty-One Love Poems* by Adrienne Rich. Text copyright © 1978 by W. W. Norton & Company, Inc. Reprinted by permission of W. W. Norton & Company, Inc.

"The Victorians Had the Same Concerns About Technology as We Do" by Melissa Dickson from www.theconversation.com, June 21, 2016. Text copyright © 2016 by Melissa Dickson. Reprinted by permission of Melissa Dickson.

"The Wanderer" from *Poems and Prose from the Old English* translated by Burton Raffel. Text copyright © 1997 by Yale University Press. Reprinted by permission of Yale University Press.

Excerpt from "The Wife of Bath's Tale" from *The Canterbury Tales* by Geoffrey Chaucer, translated by Nevill Coghill. Translation copyright 1951, renewed © 1958, 1960, 1975, 1977 by Nevill Coghill. Reprinted by permission of Penguin Books Ltd. and Curtis Brown Group Ltd.

Excerpt from "Will the Sugar Tax Stop Childhood Obesity?" by Chris Hall from the HuffPost blog, March 22, 2016. Text copyright © 2016 by Chris Hall. Reprinted by permission of Chris Hall.